BUS

ACPL ITEM
DISCARDED

THE CRB COMMODITY YEARBOOK
2004

 Commodity Research Bureau

WILEY

John Wiley & Sons, Inc.

Publisher
Davidson C. Lowdon

Editor in Chief
Christopher J. Lown

Contributing Author
Richard W. Asplund

Commodity Research Bureau
330 South Wells Street, Suite 1112
Chicago, Illinois 60606-7104 USA
800.621.5271 or 312.554.8456
Fax: 312.939.4135
Website: www.crbtrader.com
Email: info@crbtrader.com

TABLE OF CONTENTS

CRB Futures Market Service

Fundamental Market Research

Commonly known as the Blue Sheet, this weekly publication from CRB is the industry's *oldest* and *most respected* fundamental newsletter.

A wealth of fundamental research and commentary not found anywhere else, this eight-page market letter covers **over 35 major markets**. Includes specific instructions on what to look for in each market, when to buy or go short, where to place stops, initial objectives, and much more to help make you a *more profitable trader*.

Also featured is "Outlook on Futures," a penetrating front-page analysis of the week's most active commodity or general futures-related economic condition.

Technical indicators, trends, patterns, and changes in the markets are identified and interpreted by experienced market analysts. When you combine fundamental and technical analysis you have *the most complete picture of market activity* possible.

FMS is available as a weekly mailed, emailed, or online publication, and also as a daily download from the CRB DataCenter. Online and Email subscribers can view and download the weekly editions back to 1998!

For more information, visit www.crbtrader.com, or call 800-621-5271

Commodity Research Bureau • 330 South Wells Street, Suite 1112 • Chicago IL, 60606 USA
Phone: 312.554.8456 or 800.621.5271 • Fax: 312.939.4135 • info@crbtrader.com • www.crbtrader.com

ACKNOWLEDGEMENTS

The editors wish to thank the following for source material:

Agricultural Marketing Service (AMS)
Agricultural Research Service (ARS)
American Bureau of Metal Statistics, Inc. (ABMS)
American Forest & Paper Association (AF & PA)
The American Gas Association (AGA)
American Iron and Steel Institute (AISI)
American Metal Market (AMM)
Bureau of the Census
Bureau of Economic Analysis (BEA)
Bureau of Labor Statistics (BLS)
Chicago Board of Trade (CBT)
Chicago Mercantile Exchange (CME / IMM / IOM)
Coffee, Sugar & Cocoa Exchange (CSCE)
Commodity Credit Corporation (CCC)
Commodity Futures Trading Commision (CFTC)
The Conference Board
Economic Research Service (ERS)
Edison Electric Institute (EEI)
E D & F Man Cocoa Ltd
Farm Service Agency (FSA)
Federal Reserve Bank of St. Louis
Fiber Economics Bureau, Inc.
Florida Department of Citrus
Food and Agriculture Organization of
    the United Nations (FAO)

Foreign Agricultural Service (FAS)
Futures Industry Association (FIA)
International Cotton Advisory Committee (ICAC)
International Rubber Study Group (IRSG)
Johnson Matthey
Kansas City Board of Trade (KCBT)
Leather Industries of America
MidAmerica Commodity Exchange (MidAm)
Minneapolis Grain Exchange (MGE)
National Agricultural Statistics Service (NASS)
National Coffee Association of U.S.A., Inc. (NCA)
New York Cotton Exchange (NYCE / NYFE / FINEX)
New York Mercantile Exchange (NYMEX)
    Commodity Exchange, Inc. (COMEX)
Oil World
The Organisation for Economic Co-Operation
    and Development (OECD)
Random Lengths
The Silver Institute
The Society of the Plastics Industry, Inc. (SPI)
United Nations (UN)
United States Department of Agriculture (USDA)
United States Geological Survey (USGS)
Wall Street Journal (WSJ)
Winnipeg Commodity Exchange (WCE)

THE COMMODITY PRICE TREND

The Reuters-Commodity Research Bureau Futures Index in 2003 closed the year at 255.29, up +8.86% from the 2002 close of 234.52. The rally in the Reuters-CRB Futures Index in 2003 produced the second consecutive yearly gain, adding to the +23.04% rally seen in 2002. In the recession year of 2001, the Reuters-CRB Futures Index fell −16.34%.

Four of the six Reuters-CRB Futures Price Sub-indices posted gains in 2003: Industrials (+45.31%), Precious Metals (+25.94%), Grains (+19.93%), and Energy (+11.87%). Two of the six Sub-indices posted declines: Softs (-17.53%) and Livestock (-5.26%). The decline in two of the Sum-indices in 2003 contrasted with 2002 when all six Sub-indices posted gains.

The Reuters-CRB Futures Index showed weakness in early 2003 due to the war with Iraq because it produced uncertainty and a weak US economy. However, the Index recovered after the war and stabilized through July of 2003. In late-July, the Index entered a 5-month-long bull market that continued into December. That bull market was driven by (1) the sharp recovery in the US economy in the latter half of 2003 which boosted demand for industrial goods, and (2) the severe weakness in the dollar. Because the dollar index in 2003 plunged by 15%, the cost of real goods was driven higher when priced in terms of the lower US dollar.

Energy
The Reuters-CRB Energy Sub-index, which is comprised of Crude Oil, Heating Oil, and Natural Gas, accounts for 18% of the overall Index. The Energy Sub-index in 2003 closed +11.87%, extending the gain of +56.52 seen in 2002. Crude oil, heating oil, and natural gas all showed strong gains during the year, boosted by the recovery in the global economy in the second half of the year and by supply concerns as OPEC kept its production tight and as Iraq production lagged.

Grains
The Reuters-CRB Grains and Oilseeds Sub-index, which is comprised of Corn, Soybeans, and Wheat, accounts for 18% of the overall Index. The Grains and Oilseeds Sub-index in 2003 closed +19.93%, adding to the +18.35% gain seen in 2002. Corn prices closed the year moderately higher at $2.53 per bushel because of the hot and dry growing season in the US which resulted in lower than expected yields. Soybeans posted a 6-year high of $8.02 per bushel late in the year because of a tight supply situation and large Chinese purchases of soybeans from the US. China in 2003 had to import more than half of the soybeans that it consumed. Wheat posted a new 1-1/4 year high of $4.09 per bushel in November due to the hot and dry weather over the summer and tight supplies.

Industrials
The Reuters-CRB Industrials Sub-index, which is comprised of Copper and Cotton, accounts for 12% of the overall Index. The Industrials Sub-index showed a sharp gain of +45.31% in 2003, adding to the +24.51% gain seen in 2002. Copper staged a very sharp rally during the year because of the recovery in the US economy and then closed the year at a 6-year high of 104.30 cents per pound. Cotton rallied sharply during the year due in part to strong export demand to China, which saw a 14% decline in its own domestic cotton crop.

Livestock
The Reuters-CRB Livestock Sub-index, which is comprised of Live Cattle and Live Hogs, accounts for 12% of the overall Index. The Livestock Sub-index closed −5.26% in 2003, posting another weak year after showing a +1.44% increase in 2002 and a −2.43% decline in 2001. Live cattle rallied sharply in the July-November 2003 period but then plunged by about 20% in December after the first case of mad cow disease was found in the US. Live hogs closed the year slightly higher with the rally late in the year due to hopes for improved pork demand given the concerns about beef.

Precious Metals
The Reuters-CRB Precious Metals Sub-index, which is comprised of Gold, Platinum, and Silver, accounts for 17% of the overall Index. The Precious Metals Sub-index rallied sharply by +25.94% in 2003, adding to the +17.13% gain seen in 2002. Gold, silver, and platinum all staged sharp rallies during the year and hit new highs in the last week of 2003 due to improved consumer demand and the weakness in the dollar.

Softs
The Reuters-CRB Softs Sub-index, which is comprised of Cocoa, Coffee, Orange Juice, and Sugar #11, accounts for 23% of the overall Index. The Softs Sub-index in 2003 closed sharply lower by −17.63%, nearly reversing the +20.13% gain seen in 2002. Cocoa closed the year -25% lower as the political situation stabilized in the Ivory Coast, the world's largest producer of cocoa. Coffee closed the year at the top of its 55-70 cent trading range on tight supplies caused by a poor harvest in Brazil. Orange juice closed sharply lower on the year due to falling demand by calorie-conscious consumers and a 25% increase in Florida's crop production. Sugar plunged during the year due to the 11th consecutive year of worldwide production surpluses.

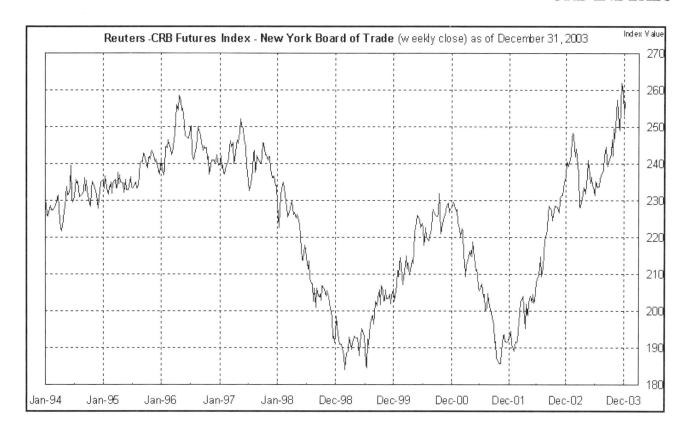

Reuters -CRB Futures Index - New York Board of Trade (weekly close) as of December 31, 2003

Monthly Reuters-CRB Futures Index High, Low and Close (1967=100)

Year		Jan.	Feb.	Mar.	Apr.	May	June	July	Aug.	Sept.	Oct.	Nov.	Dec.	Range
1994	High	229.80	229.20	231.00	227.80	239.20	239.70	234.70	235.40	234.40	235.20	234.70	237.18	239.70
	Low	226.20	225.70	227.40	227.80	225.20	235.90	230.40	228.00	228.60	227.00	228.80	226.97	225.20
	Close	225.60	227.60	227.70	225.00	235.50	230.40	233.70	231.90	229.90	233.30	229.20	236.64	----
1995	High	237.96	236.16	236.89	237.70	237.12	238.00	235.90	240.27	245.81	242.67	244.49	246.47	246.47
	Low	232.58	230.97	231.07	233.16	229.55	232.18	229.31	231.71	239.38	238.32	240.85	240.93	229.31
	Close	232.78	234.25	232.94	235.30	232.72	233.38	233.23	239.97	241.73	242.22	241.84	243.18	----
1996	High	247.56	251.21	253.50	263.79	261.24	252.92	251.90	252.04	250.35	249.59	247.08	246.85	263.79
	Low	238.63	245.62	242.72	250.19	251.79	246.64	240.09	242.83	243.10	237.78	235.99	238.12	235.99
	Close	247.53	248.77	251.40	256.09	254.07	248.67	241.99	249.46	245.63	237.83	243.36	239.61	----
1997	High	244.30	243.91	248.01	249.00	254.79	249.98	243.38	245.30	244.50	247.62	243.52	238.39	254.79
	Low	238.93	236.14	241.64	237.64	245.54	238.52	232.01	236.69	240.03	238.34	235.27	228.84	228.84
	Close	238.99	242.41	245.17	248.29	250.96	239.42	242.75	241.98	243.06	240.04	235.92	229.14	----
1998	High	235.36	236.08	231.74	229.09	226.67	216.75	216.75	207.48	205.03	206.57	206.73	197.29	236.08
	Low	221.56	223.97	223.04	223.42	214.03	208.42	205.99	195.18	196.31	201.34	195.18	187.89	187.89
	Close	234.28	227.65	228.88	223.99	215.90	214.63	206.00	195.68	203.30	203.28	195.42	191.22	----
1999	High	198.96	191.45	193.28	192.89	193.99	193.43	192.91	199.59	209.41	209.91	207.54	206.20	209.91
	Low	187.18	182.76	183.38	187.14	185.05	185.07	182.67	190.14	199.03	199.66	202.23	200.74	182.67
	Close	189.74	182.95	191.83	192.39	186.72	191.54	190.36	199.35	205.19	201.52	204.07	205.14	----
2000	High	213.70	215.29	217.88	214.15	226.12	227.29	225.69	228.02	232.20	234.38	231.46	233.37	234.38
	Low	201.43	206.74	209.61	207.61	211.86	222.23	217.42	217.76	224.74	218.38	220.93	225.46	201.43
	Close	210.46	208.78	214.37	211.03	222.27	223.93	218.61	227.41	226.57	219.28	229.79	227.83	----
2001	High	232.58	228.34	225.75	216.39	219.29	212.39	209.27	202.90	202.34	191.09	192.74	193.94	232.58
	Low	223.02	219.68	210.24	208.87	208.43	203.86	201.84	197.02	188.24	182.83	181.83	187.73	181.83
	Close	224.12	221.78	210.26	214.50	209.00	205.56	202.70	199.63	190.49	185.66	192.66	190.61	----
2002	High	195.97	193.53	205.45	208.39	205.33	209.33	215.10	219.24	229.62	231.67	231.83	238.39	238.39
	Low	186.38	187.19	192.26	195.21	197.42	199.56	207.24	208.46	217.60	223.82	223.29	230.17	186.38
	Close	187.29	192.33	204.92	201.16	204.20	209.29	210.97	219.20	226.53	228.91	230.64	234.52	----
2003	High	248.92	251.59	247.23	236.62	242.16	238.25	237.20	243.74	246.07	250.67	257.54	263.60	263.60
	Low	234.58	245.39	228.10	228.77	231.26	231.39	230.36	233.96	236.79	241.68	244.79	249.60	228.10
	Close	248.45	247.25	232.15	232.53	235.55	233.78	234.21	243.70	243.66	247.58	248.44	255.29	----

Source: Reuters

CRB INDEXES

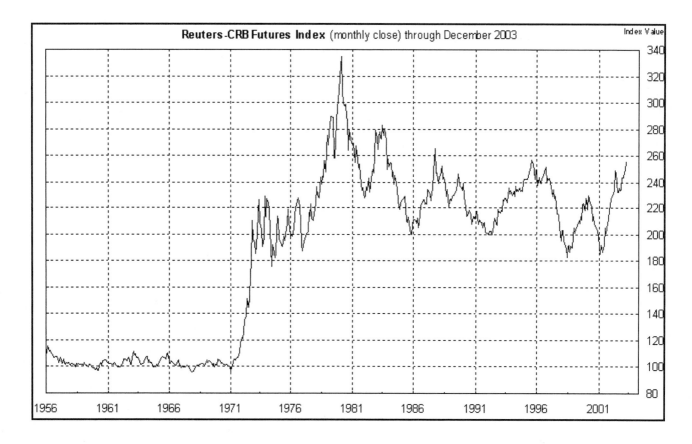

Reuters-CRB Futures Index (monthly close) through December 2003

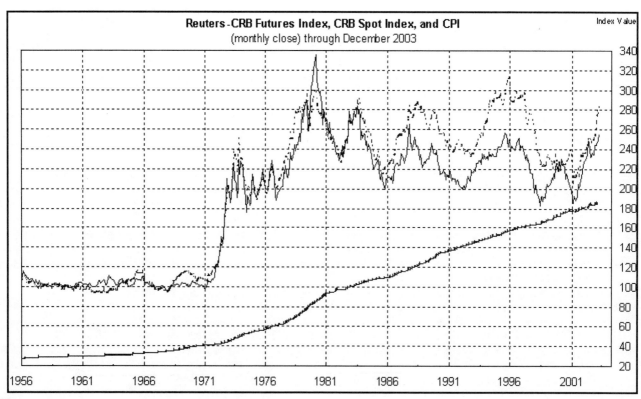

Reuters-CRB Futures Index, CRB Spot Index, and CPI
(monthly close) through December 2003

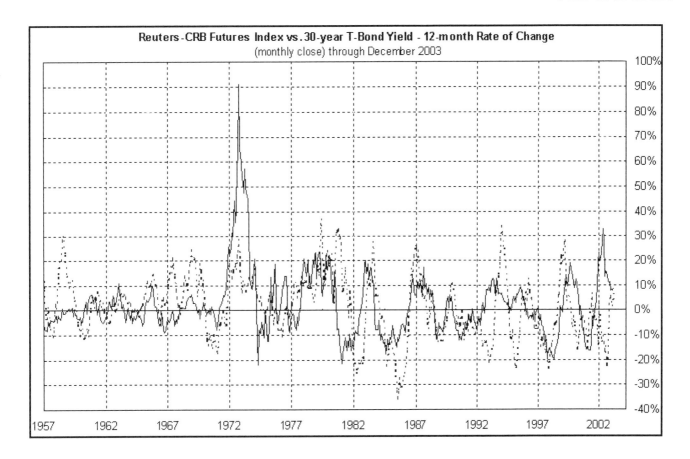

Reuters-CRB Futures Index vs. 30-year T-Bond Yield - 12-month Rate of Change
(monthly close) through December 2003

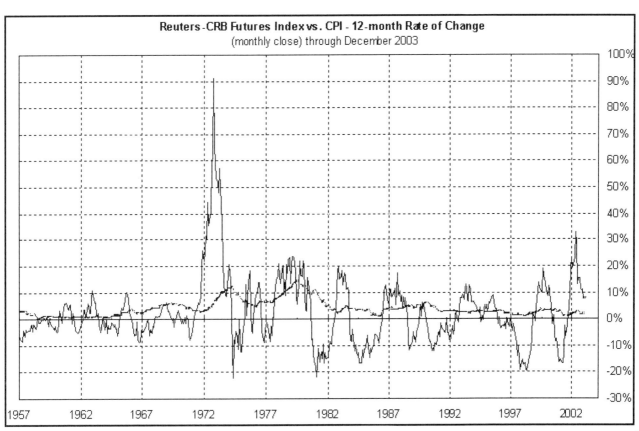

Reuters-CRB Futures Index vs. CPI - 12-month Rate of Change
(monthly close) through December 2003

CRB INDEXES

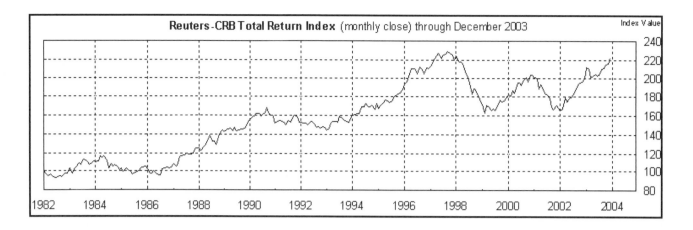

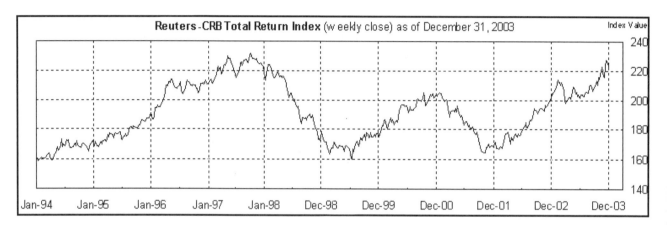

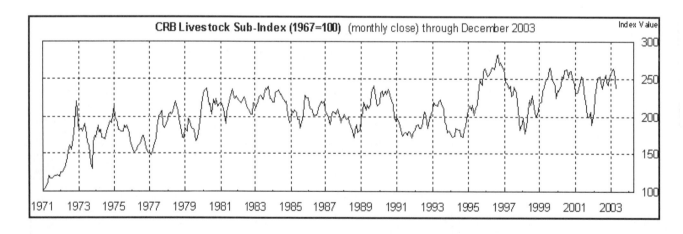

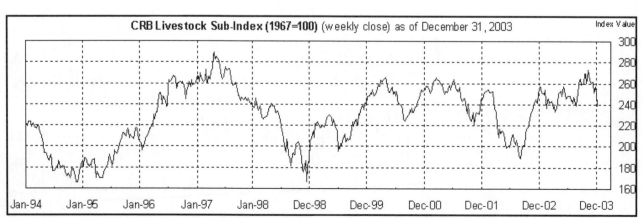

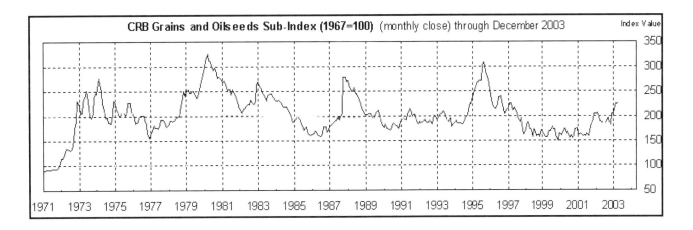

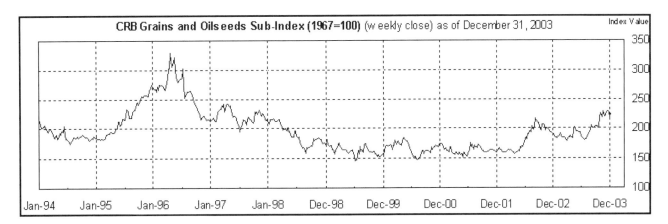

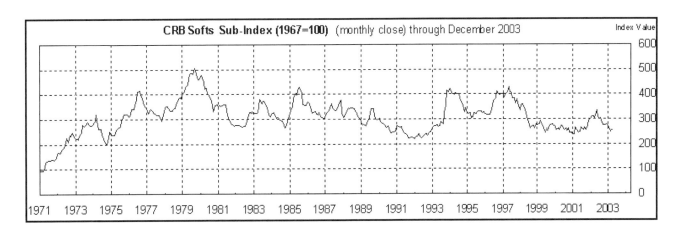

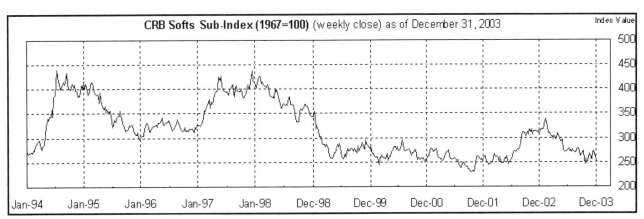

CRB INDEXES

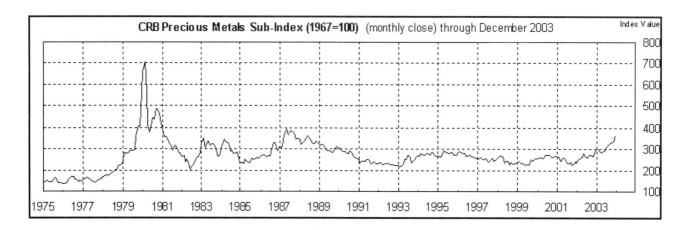

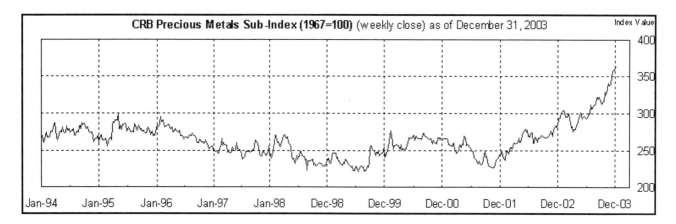

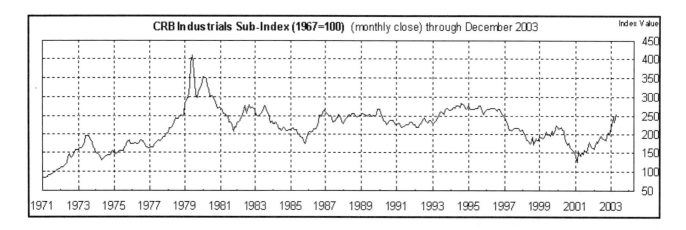

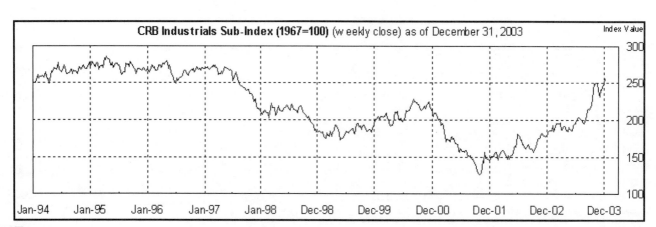

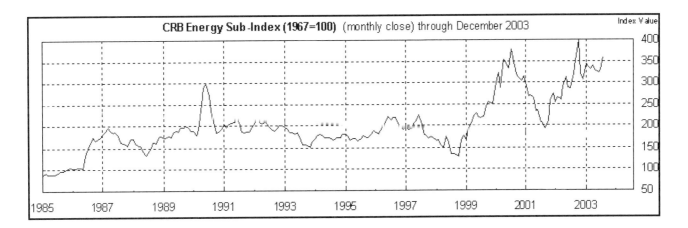

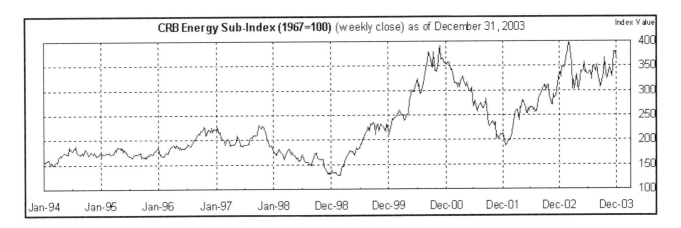

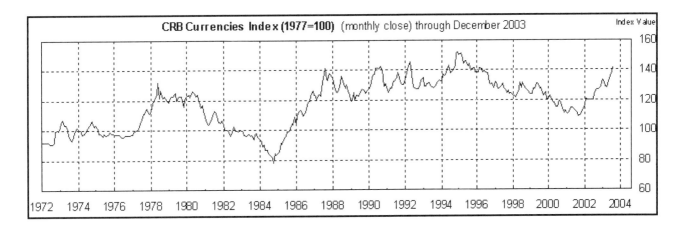

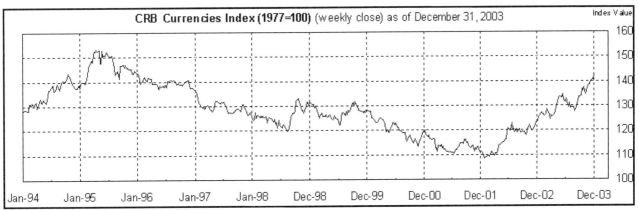

CRB INDEXES

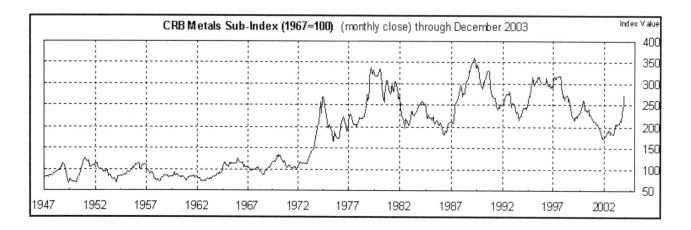

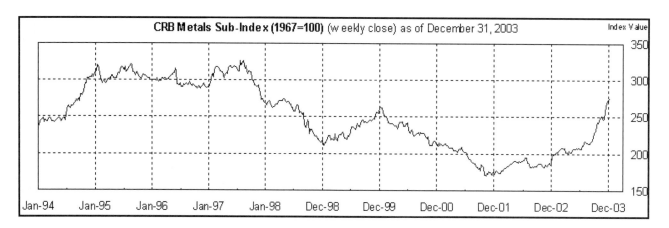

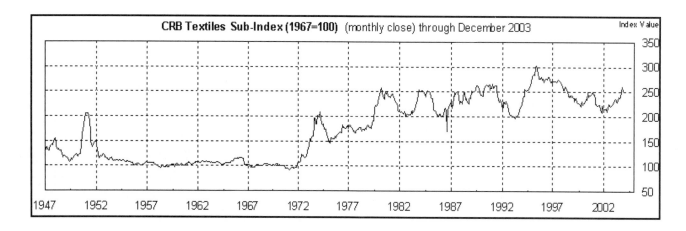

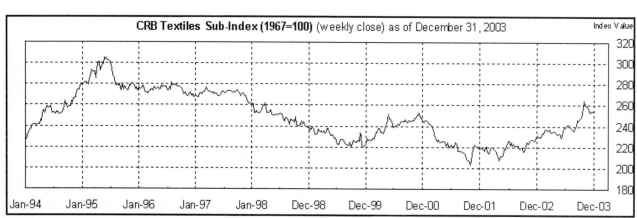

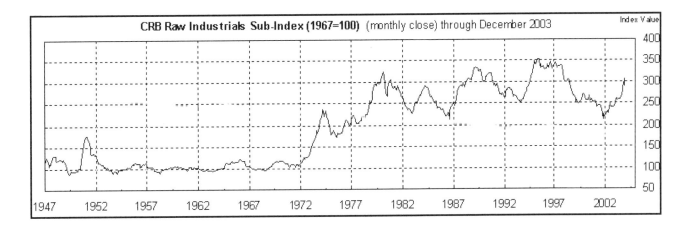

CRB Raw Industrials Sub-Index (1967=100) (monthly close) through December 2003

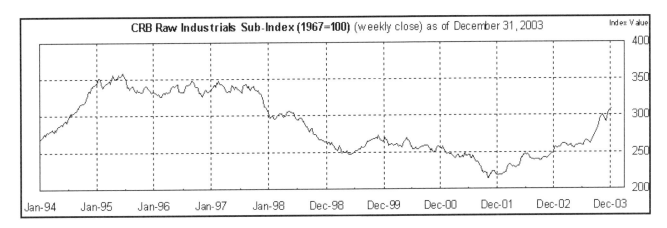

CRB Raw Industrials Sub-Index (1967=100) (weekly close) as of December 31, 2003

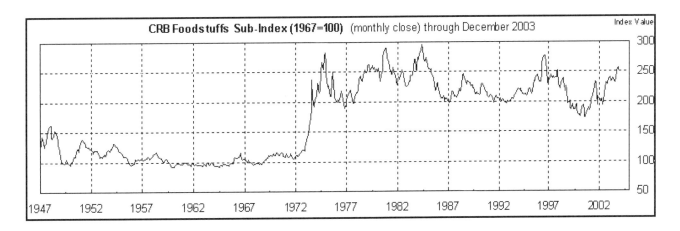

CRB Foodstuffs Sub-Index (1967=100) (monthly close) through December 2003

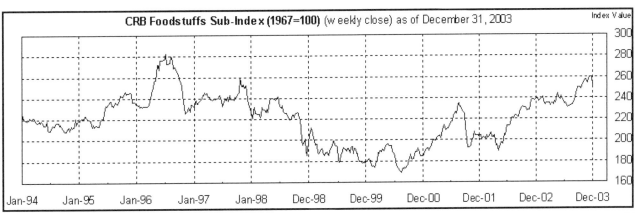

CRB Foodstuffs Sub-Index (1967=100) (weekly close) as of December 31, 2003

CRB INDEXES

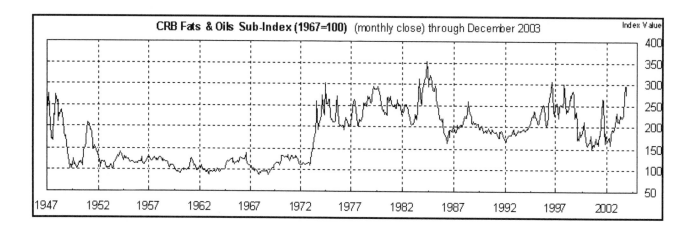

CRB Fats & Oils Sub-Index (1967=100) (monthly close) through December 2003

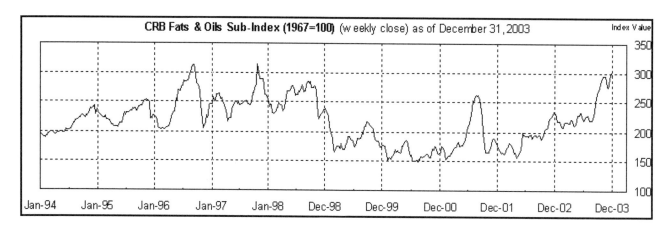

CRB Fats & Oils Sub-Index (1967=100) (weekly close) as of December 31, 2003

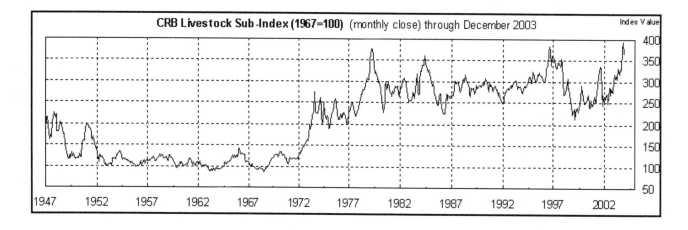

CRB Livestock Sub-Index (1967=100) (monthly close) through December 2003

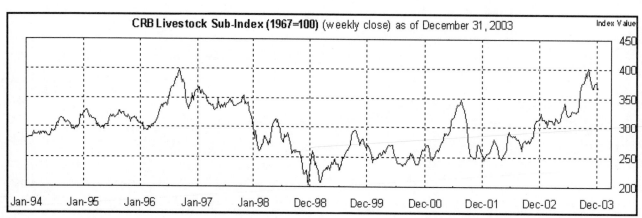

CRB Livestock Sub-Index (1967=100) (weekly close) as of December 31, 2003

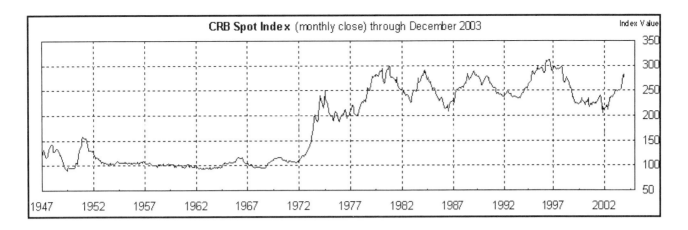

CRB Spot Index (monthly close) through December 2003

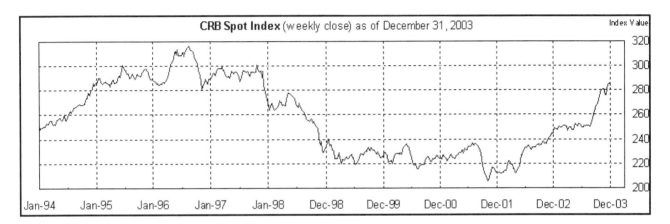

CRB Spot Index (weekly close) as of December 31, 2003

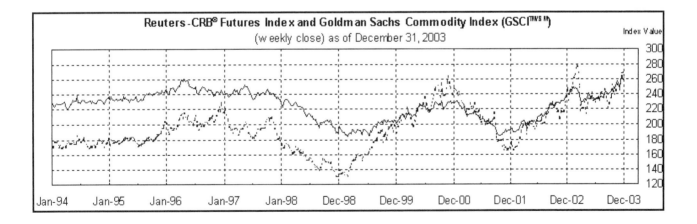

Reuters-CRB® Futures Index and Goldman Sachs Commodity Index (GSCI™SM)
(weekly close) as of December 31, 2003

Reuters-CRB® Futures Index and CRB Spot Index
(weekly close) as of December 31, 2003

MAJOR COMMODITY BULL MARKET EMERGES IN 2003

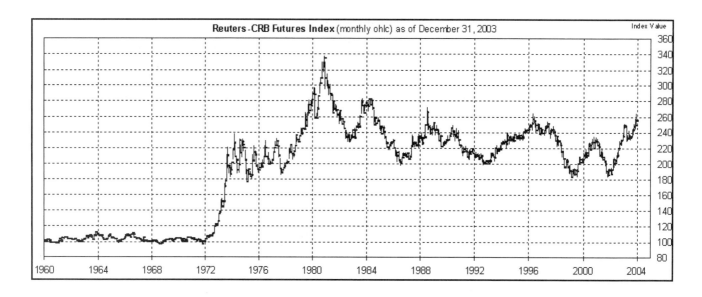

Reuters-CRB Futures Index (monthly ohlc) as of December 31, 2003

The rally in commodity prices that began in 2001 is taking on major proportions and is now ranked as the third largest commodity rally seen in the past 4 decades. This report analyzes the reasons behind the rally and investigates the question of whether the rally will continue.

The current bull market in commodity prices began in October 2001 when the Reuters-CRB Futures index posted a 4-1/2 year low of 182.83. That low was just marginally above the 7-year low of 182.67 posted in July 1999 and represented a double bottom for chart pattern followers. From the October 2001 low, the Reuters-CRB index rallied by a total of 44.2% to the 7-3/4 year high of 236.60 posted in December 2003.

The current 2001-2003 rally of 44.2% is the third largest rally in percentage terms seen in the past four decades, falling behind only the 146.7% rally seen in 1971-1974 and the 82.8% rally seen in 1977-1980. The rally in commodity prices in the 1971-1980 period could actually be seen as a single rally if the consolidation period in 1974-1977 is seen as merely a pause before the rally continued in the 1977-1980 period. If the 1971-1980 rally in commodity prices is seen as a single rally, then the total percentage gain was 250% from the low of 96.40 in October 1971 to the high of 337.60 in November 1980. Then the current rally would be the second, rather than the third, largest rally seen in the past 4 decades.

The bull market seen in commodities in the 1970s was primarily a monetary phenomenon driven by a stimulative monetary policy and a surge in inflation. The CPI in the 1970s surged to 12% in late 1974, fell back through 1977, but then surged to a peak of 14.8% in March 1980. The surge in inflation was finally stopped by Paul Volcker who took over as Federal Reserve Chairman in 1979 and implemented a strict monetarist policy of controlling the money supply. That effort was successful in cracking the back of inflation, and the CPI fell back to hit a low of +1.1% in December 1986. Since the inflation debacle of the 1970s, the Federal Reserve has been very successful in containing inflation and has since kept the CPI mostly below 4%. In fact the CPI has averaged only +3.1% since 1983.

The Fed's success in containing inflation led to comparatively stable commodity prices in the last two decades. There have been two significant commodity rallies, but both were less than 40%. The rally in 1986-1988 totaled +38.8% and the rally in 1992-1996 totaled +33.1%. Both those rallies were less than the rally seen so far in the 2001-2003 period.

The big question going forward is whether the current commodity rally will blossom into even larger dimensions. The duration of the current rally is only 26 months so far, which makes it the second shortest rally of the five largest rallies seen since 1960. That suggests that the current rally could easily last longer. The longest rally was the 1977-80 rally, which lasted more than 3 years (39 months) and was 13 months longer than the current rally.

It is easy to argue that the current commodity bull market could last at least through 2004 and perhaps beyond. The driving force for the rally is the surge in world economic growth that started in mid-2003 and should continue at least through 2004. That surge in economic growth has boosted demand for basic commodities at a time when many suppliers were caught off-guard with their produc-

Commodity Bull Markets Ranked by Percentage Gain (1960-2003)

	---------------------- Low ----------------------		--------------------- High ---------------------		Percent Rally	Rally Duration (months)	Correlation (Reuters-CRB - CPI)	Avg CPI (yr-yr%)
1971-74	October 1971	96.40	February 1974	237.80	146.7%	28	0.97	4.9%
1977-80	August 1977	184.70	November 1980	337.60	82.8%	39	0.96	10.2%
2001-03	October 2001	182.83	December 2003	263.60	44.2%	26	0.95	1.9%
1986-88	July 1986	196.16	June 1988	272.19	38.8%	23	0.89	3.2%
1992-96	August 1992	198.17	April 1996	263.79	33.1%	44	0.96	2.8%

Source: Commodity Research Bureau

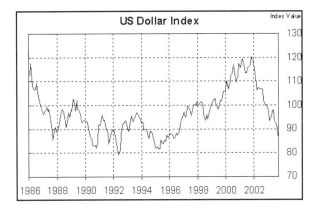

US Dollar Index

tion levels at relatively low levels. It will take months if not years for producers to ramp supply back up to meet demand.

The rally in commodity prices is also being driven by the severe weakness in the dollar against the world's major currencies. The nearby chart shows that the dollar index, which shows the value of the dollar against a basket of foreign currencies, has plunged by more than 25% in the past 2 years. Weakness in the dollar boosts the prices of commodities because commodities have a real, intrinsic value and when the value of the dollar falls, the price of those commodities appreciates when expressed in terms of weaker dollars. The price of commodities as expressed in dollars is important because the bulk of international trade in commodities is carried out between buyers and sellers in terms of prices set in US dollars.

The weak dollar is being driven primarily by the Fed's extraordinarily easy monetary policy whereby the Fed is targeting the federal funds rate at a 4-decade low of 1.00% and is aggressively pumping reserves and dollars into the US banking system. The market is only expecting the Fed to raise its funds rate target by one-half percentage point in 2004, which would still leave the funds rate target at an extraordinarily low 1.50%. That means that the Fed's monetary policy through 2004 is likely to remain very easy, thus contributing to ongoing dollar weakness and commodity price strength. The weak dollar is also being driven by the massive US current account deficit, which is largely the result of structural problems such as the low US savings rate and the huge US demand for imported energy, factors that are unlikely to be resolved anytime in the foreseeable future.

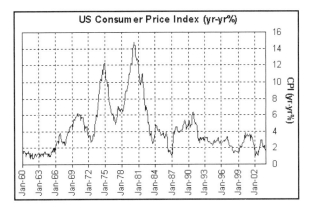

US Consumer Price Index (yr-yr%)

But while the commodity rally may continue in coming months, the rally is unlikely to turn into anything approaching the size of the rally seen in the 1970s when commodity prices rallied by 250% over the course of the decade. The main reason is because the Fed still has inflation firmly under control and will quickly step in with a tighter monetary policy if inflation starts to get out of hand, in contrast to the 1970s when the Fed completely lost control of the situation.

During the current commodity bull market, inflation has averaged only +1.9%, which is the lowest of any of the other five bull markets in the past 4 decades (see the table at the beginning of this report). The core CPI, excluding food and energy, is currently in even better shape and fell to a 4-decade low of +1.1% in December 2003. By contrast, inflation (CPI growth) averaged +4.9% during the 1971-1974 rally and +10.2% during the 1977-1980 rally. The current low inflation rate is the key factor allowing the Fed to maintain its 1.00% funds rate target. If the inflation rate does begin to creep higher, the Fed will undoubtedly respond by slowly raising interest rates to curb economic demand and raw commodity demand. It is unthinkable that the Fed would allow inflation to approach even 6%, let alone double-digit levels, because the Federal Reserve, and indeed the entire political class in Washington, learned their lesson about the severe economic damage that flows from high inflation rates. That suggests that there is an eventual limit to the size of the current commodity bull market.

But why hasn't the surge in raw commodity prices shown up in the prices of the services and finished goods that the CPI measures? The answer is that most companies have been absorbing the higher commodity prices as a higher cost of doing business and haven't yet raised their prices. For example, French tire-maker Michelin SA said in late February 2004 that the 41% jump in its natural-rubber costs in 2003 was the main reason its 2003 net income declined by 45%.

Companies need to keep their prices down because competition is very keen in virtually all industries, and businesses want to maintain their sales and market shares. Most businesses can afford to hold down their prices for the time being because profits have improved sharply in the past year and because the surge in labor productivity since the mid-1990s means companies have lower per-unit labor costs, giving them some room to absorb higher raw commodity input prices. However, companies will not be able to absorb commodity price gains forever, and will eventually be forced to raise prices to maintain profit margins that are acceptable to their shareholders, thus leading to upward pressure on finished goods prices and the CPI index. That is why the CPI is likely to creep higher as 2004 wears on. In fact, the pricing of the Treasury's inflation-indexed T-note currently suggests inflation expectations of +2.3%, which is 0.4 percentage points higher than the December CPI rate of +1.9% y/y.

The strong correlation between the Reuters-CRB Futures Index and the CPI during bull markets supports the thesis that the CPI will move higher in 2004. The correlation between the Reuters-CRB Futures Index and the CPI index over a rolling, or backward-looking, 24-month period has averaged 0.69 since 1960, although it fluctuates widely and even turns negative fairly often. However, during bull markets, there is a very high correlation between the Reuters-CRB Futures Index and the CPI, as seen in the table at the beginning of this report. The correlation during the current 2001-2003 rally is 0.95, just slightly below the 0.96 and 0.97 correlations seen during the two rallies in the 1970s. Looking within the current 2001-2002 commodity bull market, the correlation during 2002 was negative for most of the year, but in 2003 the Reuters-CRB Futures Index and the CPI index became closely synchronized and showed an increasingly strong correlation through the end of 2003. That high correlation supports the thesis that the CPI will be moving higher in 2004 as higher commodity prices have a greater effect on the CPI.

Looking at the components of the commodity price rally provides important information on the reasons behind the commodity rally and whether it will continue. Four of the six Reuters/CRB Futures Price sub-indices posted gains in 2003: Industrials (+45.31%), Precious Metals (+25.94%), Grains (+19.93%), and Energy (+11.87%). Two of the six sub-indices posted declines: Softs (-17.53%) and Livestock (-5.26%). There were different reasons behind the price movement in each sector.

The fact that all the sectors didn't rise together supports the theory that the commodity bull market is not being driven by monetary policy but rather by specific circumstances in each market. Energy rallied because of increased world demand for oil combined with restrictive OPEC production. Softs (coffee, cocoa, sugar, orange juice) were weak mainly because of weaker demand and/or supply factors in each particular market. Meats closed lower because of the mad cow disease found in December. The bulk of the rally in the grain sub-index was caused by Chinese buying of soybeans and by weather problems during the summer of 2003 in the US. The rally in the industrials sub-index (which includes copper) and the precious metals sub-index was caused by the generalized factors behind the commodity rally as a whole, i.e., increased US economic growth, the weak dollar, and Chinese demand.

Chinese demand, in fact, is a key reason behind the current rally in the commodity indexes. China's economy grew at a 9.1% GDP growth rate in 2003 and sucked in a huge amount of raw materials to fuel its growth. Chinese demand has been a key factor behind the rallies in such commodities as copper, nickel, steel, lumber, and many other raw materials for the manufacturing and construction sectors. For example, in the copper market, JP Morgan estimates that China now accounts for 19.6% of global copper demand versus only 14.7% for the US, which is a radical shift from just several years ago when the US consumed roughly 50% more copper than China. Chinese demand has helped drive copper prices to a new 8-year high in February 2004, which represents more than a doubling of copper prices since the low in 2001. Nickel prices have nearly doubled since mid-2003 and are at 14-year highs. Hot-rolled steel prices have rallied by roughly 80% in the past year. Platinum is at an all-time high. Lumber prices have nearly doubled in the past year. In the scrap steel markets, US steel consumers, who are being squeezed by sharply higher steel prices, are pressuring Washington for export restrictions on scrap steel because so much is being shipped out to the Far East to meet Chinese demand for steel.

The fact that the third largest commodity bull market in four decades is in progress suggests that we are in the midst of fundamental global changes. The rally is due in part to business-cycle factors such as a US economic recovery and a weak dollar. However, there are fundamental structural factors behind the rally, primarily the globalization of commodity demand and the surge in emerging countries. Socialist economics has been relegated to the dustbin of history and it is now clear that the only way forward is through market-driven capitalism. The yoke of economic oppression is being thrown off by literally billions of people. Countries such as China and India, with more than a billion people each, are having a greater impact on the global economy every year.

With the massive pent-up demand for basic consumer and industrial products in those countries, there will be a substantial and long-term increase in the demand for raw commodities to produce those goods. It seems a foregone conclusion that there will be substantial demand for raw commodities in the coming years, and that producers will be unable to respond quickly with higher supply. It also seems a sure bet that the Fed will not act quickly to curb the commodity price rally because the rally is not producing a generalized breakout in the CPI (inflation) and because the Fed is trying to promote healing in the US labor market. That suggests that as long as there are no major global external shocks (e.g., financial collapses or wars), the commodity rally will continue and perhaps reach even larger proportions.

Richard W. Asplund, CRB Chief Economist, February 2004.

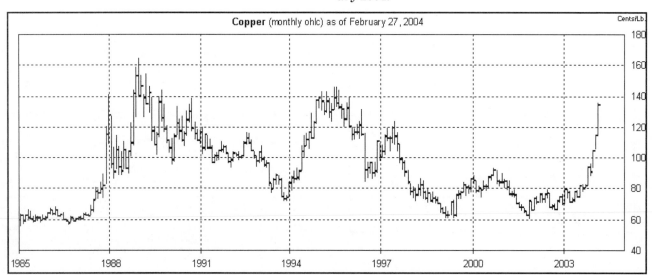

US ECONOMIC SURGE DRIVES GLOBAL ECONOMIC RECOVERY

World economic growth improved to +3.2% in 2003, up from +3.0% in 2002 and the 11-year low of +2.4% seen in 2001, according to statistics from the IMF. Stronger world economic growth in 2003 was mainly due to the sharp upward rebound in the US economy, which helped pull the rest of the world out of the 2000-2003 slump. However, there were independent sources of strength as well, such as the +9.1% growth rate in China and the +3.2% GDP growth rate in Japan. Japan finally appears to be turning around after the dismal +1.4% average annual GDP growth rate seen since 1990. The UK was also a source of strength with a 2003 GDP growth rate of +5.3% through Q3. However, the Euro-Zone lagged behind with a growth rate of only +0.6% in 2003 and expectations for meager growth of +1.8% in 2004. The German economy in 2003 in fact showed a decline of –0.1% and is expected to see a poor growth rate of +1.7% in 2004. The French economy showed a decline of –0.4% in Q2 and –0.3% in Q3 (year-on-year).

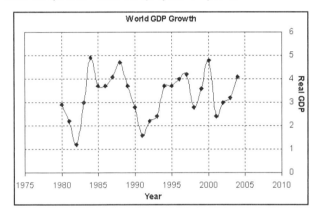

On balance, world economic growth is expected to improve significantly in 2004. The IMF is forecasting world growth at +4.1%, which would be a 4-year high. World growth in 2004 will benefit from expansionary monetary policies throughout the world and pent-up demand after the 2000-03 slowdown. There are factors that will likely limit world economic growth in 2004, such as high energy prices and the weak dollar which is depressing exports outside the US. However, the world economy is expected to shake off these negative factors to put in the best GDP performance in 4 years.

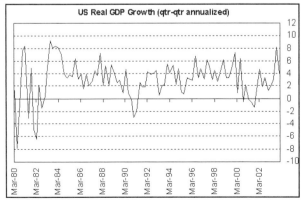

US economic optimism grows – Optimism on the US economy prevailed as 2003 ended. The US economy rebounded sharply higher in the second half of 2003 after the war with Iraq concluded in April. The US economy finally began firing on all cylinders after the shocks from the technology and stock market bust in 2000 and the 9/11 terrorist attack of September 11, 2001. The US economy was temporarily on the mend in 2002 but then the impending war with Iraq in 2003 delayed the recovery. But as 2003 ended, all signs were pointing upward with US economic growth surging, with the US labor market slowly improving, with commodity prices rising, and with world economic growth also on the mend.

US GDP Overview – The US economy weakened in late 2002 because of the impending war with Iraq with GDP growth in Q4-2002 at a 2-year low of +1.3%. However, the US economy then began to improve in Q1-2003 to +2.0% and then to +3.1% after the war with Iraq ended in April. The US economy then soared by +8.2% in Q3, which was the strongest quarterly growth rate since 1984. The US economy remained strong at +4.1% in Q4.

The upward rebound in the US economy seen in the second half of 2003 marked the end of the economic bust that started in mid-2000 when the US stock market bubble burst. The US economy was in an official recession in the March-November 2001 period, according to the National Bureau of Economic Research, the official arbiter for dating US recessions. That 8-month recession was slightly shorter than the average recession seen since World War II. Despite the recession, US GDP in 2001 was still positive at +0.5%, but down sharply from +3.7% in 2000 and +4.5% in 1999. In 2002, the economy recovered to a modest growth rate of +2.2% and then improved further to +3.1% in 2003. Looking ahead, market participants are generally looking for the US economy to grow in the +4.0 to +4.5% area in 2004, which would be moderately above the +3.7% average growth rate seen in the 1992-2000 expansion period.

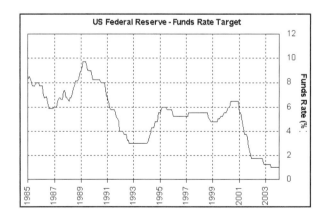

Fed policy – The Fed's extremely accommodative monetary policy was a key factor behind the upward rebound in the US economy in 2003. The Fed came into 2003 with an extremely low federal funds target of 1.25% and then the Fed cut the rate by another 25 basis points to 1.00% on June 25, 2003. The funds rate target then stayed at that level through the remainder of 2003, which was the lowest level for the funds rate target in 40 years.

The Fed implemented such an accommodative monetary policy because it was concerned about the US economy and the possibility of deflation. The Fed was clearly aware of the damage that deflation did to the Japanese economy throughout the 1990's. The Fed was basically willing to do whatever it took to get the US economy back on track to healthy growth. There was even talk early in the year that the Fed might have to take extraordinary measures such as massive bond purchases to stimulate the economy since the funds rate was already near zero at 1%. However, by the end of 2003 with the economy rebounding, the Fed was moving toward a more neutral monetary policy. At the last FOMC meeting of 2003, the Fed kept its language that rates would remain low for a "considerable period" but the Fed adopted a nearly symmetrical view towards inflation which was viewed at the time as the Fed's first step toward a tighter policy bias. As 2003 ended, the marketplace was expecting the Fed to raise the funds rate target by 25 basis points by summer 2004 and by another 25 basis points by autumn 2004.

Fiscal Policy – Another key factor behind the surge in the US economy in the latter half of 2003 was the Bush tax cuts, which created a very stimulative fiscal policy. During the 2003 fiscal year (which ended September 30, 2003), the Bush tax cuts put an extra $117 billion of cash into taxpayers' pockets, according to the Congressional Budget Office. The tax cut stimulus will continue into 2004 with some $120 billion in tax cuts in fiscal 2004. Although consumers typically spend only about one-third of their tax cuts (with the rest going to savings and debt payoffs), the tax cuts nevertheless represented an important shot in the arm for the economy in 2003.

Labor market – There was a great deal of talk during 2003 about a "jobless recovery" since the economy showed positive GDP growth during every quarter in 2003 and yet the US labor market worsened in early 2003 and only began to show a mild recovery in the latter half of the year. The US unemployment rate peaked in June 2003 at a 10-year high of 6.4%. The unemployment rate then slowly tailed off through the end of 2003 and fell to 5.7% by December 2003. Still, that showed a much worse unemployment situation than the remarkable 34-year low of 3.8% posted just several years ago in April 2000.

The payroll data also displayed the dismal US labor market seen during 2003. The US economy lost a net 53,000 jobs in 2003, following a loss of 563,000 jobs in 2002 and 1.782 million jobs in 2001. For the entire labor market recession, which began in earnest in April 2001, the US economy lost a net 2.464 million jobs through December

2003 based on the establishment survey payroll data.

The dismal US labor market seen in the 2000-2003 period undercut the overall economy by slashing personal income and by dampening consumer spirits. Businesses during the 2000-2003 period cut their labor forces as far as they could in order to minimize their expenses, repair their profit margins, and keep their risks down in the event of another external shock to the economy such as the 9/11 terrorist attack. Still, as 2003 ended, the US labor market was showing some signs of life. Payroll jobs rose in the last four months of the year and businesses were under pressure to hire more workers due to the sharp upturn in the US economy.

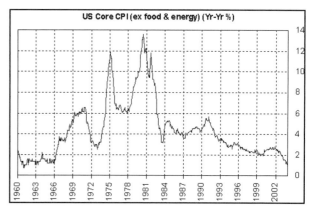

Inflation – The US consumer price index (CPI) peaked in early 2003 at a 2-1/4 year high of +3.0%, but then eased to a 14-month low of +1.8% by November 2003. That was only 0.7 points above the cyclical trough of +1.1% posted in 2002, which was the lowest CPI growth rate since 1965. The CPI was pushed higher in 2003 by strong energy prices, which surged in early 2003 in the run-up to the US-Iraq war and then rallied further later in 2003 as OPEC kept production levels tight and as the world economy started to recover.

Excluding the impact of strong energy prices, the "core" CPI statistics (i.e., excluding the volatile energy and food categories) illustrated the trends toward disinflation. The core CPI fell steadily through 2002 and 2003 from the 8-year high of 2.8% seen in December 2001 to the 40-year low of +1.1% seen in November and December 2003, the lowest level for core US inflation since 1963.

The low US inflation rate was due to a combination of factors, including tepid economic demand, aggressive competition from overseas producers, downward pressure on US wages with the weak labor market, and a general psychology among US businesses of trying to hold the line on price hikes to boost sales. While the core PPI was still pointing downward as 2003 ended, the general consensus is that US inflation was close to hitting bottom and would likely turn slightly higher in 2004 in response to the stronger US and global economy.

Productivity – The US economy in 2003 continued to show extraordinary levels of productivity. Non-farm productivity in Q3-2003 hit a 2-year high of 9.5%, which was only 0.2 points below the 20-year high of +9.7% posted in Q1-2002. The 12-quarter moving average for productivity in Q3-2003 rose to a 30-year high of +4.2%, going all the way back to 1973 when economists generally agree that US productivity showed a permanent downward shift. But since 1995, US productivity has shown a permanent upward shift,

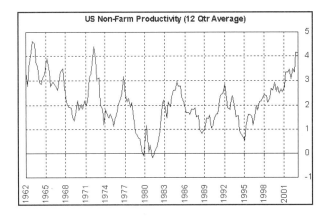

US Non-Farm Productivity (12 Qtr Average)

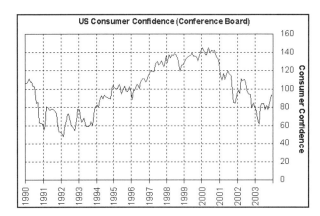

US Consumer Confidence (Conference Board)

which is thought to be the result of major technological improvements in information, communication and transportation systems.

The permanent upward shift in US productivity means that more output is being produced for a given hour of employee labor. That has very favorable consequences for the US economy, including higher wages for employees, higher profits for businesses, and a firewall against inflation for the Fed. The high level of productivity also means that the Fed can allow a higher US GDP growth rate without worrying about the US economy overheating and producing an inflation surge.

US Sector Analysis – Through the 2000-2003 economic slump, the US consumer was the hero that helped support the overall US economy and prevent a more serious recession from developing. The US housing sector was also a major contributor to economic growth during the 2000-2003 economic slump as low mortgage rates helped fuel a housing boom. The consumer and housing sectors were able to offset the sharp decline in business spending seen in 2000-2003 and weak overseas demand for US exports. But as 2003 ended, all the US economic sectors were looking strong and the US economy was firing on all cylinders.

Consumer Spending – US consumer spending is critical to the US economy since it accounts for about two-thirds of the economy. US personal consumption came into 2003 on a weak note at +2.5% in Q1-2003 but then soared to a 13-year high of +6.9% by Q3, which was the strongest level since 1986. US consumer spending was driven by pent-up demand following the war with Iraq and by improved consumer confidence due to the stronger economy in the latter half of 2003 and the improvement in the US labor market.

US consumer spending in 2003 was boosted by two key factors: (1) the ongoing mortgage refinancing boom into early 2003, and (2) by the Bush tax cuts. The refinancing boom of 2002 and early 2003 allowed consumers to cut their mortgage costs, thus putting more dollars to spend into their pocketbooks. Likewise, the Bush tax cuts in fiscal 2003 gave consumers an additional $117 billion of cash to either spend or save, thus providing another powerful stimulant to consumer spending.

As 2003 ended, the Conference Board's US consumer confidence index was at 91.7 in December, just mildly below the 15-month high of 92.5 seen in November. That was sharply higher than the 10-year trough of 61.4 seen during March at the height of the US-Iraq war. Still, US consumer confidence in 2004 has a long way to go before recovering to the 120-140 range seen in the late 1990s. US consumer confidence at the end of 2003 continued to be undercut by

the poor US labor market and concerns about job security.

Housing – The US housing sector provided strong support for the overall US economy during the 2000-2003 US economic slump. The US housing sector was driven primarily by low mortgage rates. The 30-year fixed mortgage rate fell to a 4-decade low of 5.21% in June 2003. Even though mortgage rates rose during the latter half of 2003, the 30-year mortgage rate closed 2003 at 5.81%, which was lower than the rates seen at any time during the 1970s through 1990s. The low level of mortgage rates provided a powerful inducement to consumers to either buy a home for the first time or to trade up to a more expensive home.

Existing and new home sales both hit record highs in late 2003. Existing home sales ended 2003 moderately below the record high of 6.68 million units posted in September. New home sales ended 2003 moderately below the record high of 1.200 million posted in June 2003. Housing starts in December posted a 19-year high of 2.088 million units.

The boom in the US housing sector had significant carry-over implications for the rest of the US economy since there is a strong multiplier effect as home purchasers stock their homes with new appliances and furnishings and renovate older homes. Although the US housing sector is likely to cool somewhat in 2004 if interest rates rise as expected, mortgage rates are still likely to be historically low and the US housing sector is still likely to be a major contributor to the US economy in 2004.

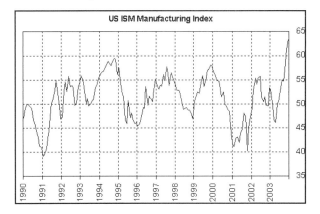

US ISM Manufacturing Index

Manufacturing – The US manufacturing sector finally came alive by the end of 2003 after a long period of weakness from late 2000 to early 2003. Although the service sector increasingly dominates the US economy, the US goods manufacturing sector is still a critical sector that accounts for about one-seventh of the US economy. The sharp upward rebound in the US manufacturing sector towards the end of 2003 was best seen by the rally in the Institute of Supply Management (ISM) manufacturing index in December to a 20-year high of 63.4. The 17.2 point rally in the ISM index to the December 20-year high from the 2-year trough of 46.2 seen in April 2003 illustrated the much-improved fortunes for the US manufacturing sector. In November, US industrial production improved to +2.3% year-on-year, which was a 3-year high.

The improvement in US industry production was partially the result of a very tight inventory situation. That meant that once demand emerged, businesses had to order new products quickly because their inventory buffers were already very low. The business inventories-to-sales ratio in December was at a record low of 1.34 months.

Despite the improvement in output from the US manufacturing sector, the job situation in the US manufacturing sector remained dismal through the end of 2003. Payrolls through December 2003 fell for 41 straight months, going back to the last increase which was seen in July 2000. Over that time frame, a total of 3.014 million jobs were lost in the US manufacturing sector. There were cyclical factors behind those job losses, but in fact there were also permanent, structural factors during that period as US companies shifted production offshore and as the US imported cheaper manufactured products from overseas. The majority of those 3 million jobs will never come back to the US manufacturing sector. Still, the job situation in the US manufacturing sector should slowly improve in 2004 as the US manufacturing sector slowly regains some of its health.

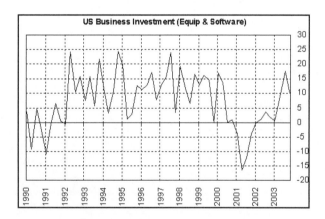

Business Investment – US business investment fell off a cliff in late 2000 and early 2001 after the stock market bubble burst in mid-2000. US businesses slashed new investment spending in order to conserve cash and to hunker down for the recession that officially started in 2001. But business investment spending hit bottom in 2001, and has been on a steady upward recovery track ever since. In fact by Q3-2003, business investment in equipment and software recovered sharply to a 3-year high of +17.6% from the trough of –16.4% seen in Q2-2001. That helped worked off excess capacities that plagued the high-tech sector following the stock market bubble.

The outlook for US business investment looks fairly strong given that many businesses have cut production capacity to the bone and now need to ramp up production in order to meet demand. However, US businesses will remain cautious in 2004 and are not likely to boost production capacity much past a 3-6 month forecast horizon since

there is still concern about the possibility of another external shock and since there is still some reluctance to believe that the economic surge will last.

US Trade – Global demand for US exports slowly improved in 2003, finishing the year at a 3-year high of +7.1% y/y. That was a dramatic improvement from the trough of –15.7% export growth seen in late 2001. The stronger demand for US exports provided a strong boost to the overall US economy. At the same time, US import growth was even stronger than export growth since the US economy was stronger than those of its overseas trading partners during 2003. Import demand during 2003 ranged from +18% early in 2003 to +10% late in the year.

The cyclical imbalance caused by the strength of imports relative to exports produced a record high US trade deficit of $489 billion for 2003, or an average deficit of $40.8 billion per month. However, the US trade deficit was also due to the fundamental long-term factors of massive US demand for imported energy and by the weak US savings rate which creates the need to import foreign capital (which is the flip-side of the US trade and current account deficits).

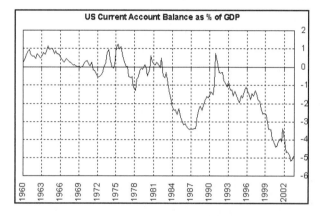

The US current account deficit in 2003 hit record highs, leading to an overall deficit for the year near $550 billion. The fact that the US current account amounts to a record 5% of US GDP presents a severe macroeconomic problem for the US. The US must import about $1.5 billion in foreign capital every calendar day in order to support the US current account imbalance. To the extent that foreigners are reluctant to invest that much capital in dollar-denominated assets, the dollar must fall in order to make those investments cheaper and more attractive to foreign investors. As 2003 ended, the US dollar remained under severe downward pressure and there continued to be talk about the remote possibility of a run on US assets. The OECD in its November 2003 Economic Outlook projected that the US current account deficit would remain very high in 2004 at 5.1% of GDP, posing a continued challenge for the US dollar and for US macroeconomic policy.

Richard W. Asplund, CRB Chief Economist, February 2004.

CHINA BREAKS OUT AS MAJOR PLAYER IN GLOBAL COMMODITY AND FINANCIAL MARKETS

It is difficult for Americans, with our relatively stable and comfortable political economy, to comprehend the scale of the changes occurring in China. China is on a remarkable growth path after its leaders in the late 1970s decided to throw off the burden of socialist economics and adopt an aggressive market-driven and export-driven growth model. This has led to a massive scale of economic growth in China, to the extent where two Goldman Sachs economists have predicted that the Chinese economy in 25 years will surpass that of the US. In fact, China is currently creating much of the ongoing rally in commodity prices and has become an increasingly important player in the global financial markets as well. This report will investigate the extent of China's growing influence in the global commodity and financial markets.

China's demand potential is massive

China has 1.287 billion people, according to the latest CIA World Factbook data, a population that is roughly 1 billion more than the US population of 290 million. China's population, combined with its strong economic growth since the late 1970s, has pushed its $1.24 trillion economy into position as the sixth largest in the world, but still it is only 12% of the size of the US economy.

However, these figures are understated because they ignore the fact that China has a severely undervalued currency, which makes the simple conversion of the size of its economy into dollars at the fixed currency rate deceptive. The more accurate way to convert the size of the Chinese economy into dollars is to use "purchasing-power parity", which uses a currency rate based on equalized product prices rather than the fixed currency rate to convert the Chinese economy into dollar terms.

When one uses the purchasing-power parity method of comparing China's economy to the rest of the world, China's economy is the second largest economy in the world next to the US. The CIA World Factbook, using purchasing-power parity, places the size of China's GDP output in 2002 at $5.989 trillion, well ahead of Japan's $3.651 trillion economy and Germany's $2.16 trillion economy. Based on this method, China's economy is 57% of the US GDP, which is $10.45 trillion.

Despite the large size of China's overall economy, however, its per-capita GDP was only $5,000 in 2003, as reported in the CIA World Factbook using purchasing-power parity. That is less than one-seventh of the US's per capita GDP of $37,600. The $32,600 per-capita difference between Chinese and US GDP adds up to a total of nearly $42 trillion when multiplied by China's population. That means that it would take an additional $42 trillion of GDP output for the average Chinese citizen to catch up to the living standard of the average US citizen. That is roughly four times the size of yearly US GDP output.

But whatever numbers are used, there is a massive amount of economic demand in China that is waiting to be tapped. To repeat, it would take $42 trillion worth of GDP output (or four times the US economy) just to bring China up to current American living standards, and that does not include future population growth or any attempt to exceed current US living standards. That demand includes all types of housing and personal property, such as cars, appliances, clothes, electronics etc, that Chinese consumers would undoubtedly like to acquire.

Much of this demand will eventually come from the rural poor who are now moving into China's cities in massive numbers. Chinese President and Communist party leader Hu Jintao, the successor in 2003 to former President Jiang Zemin, announced a "people first" program that includes bettering the lives of some 800 million rural residents. Part of the government's plan is to transfer between 300 million and 500 million rural residents into cities by 2020. If the government's goal is taken at face value of moving 300 million people into cities in the next 16 years, the lower end of its target range, that would involve nearly 19 million people per year. That is the equivalent of building more than two cities the size of metropolitan New York City every year. That is the source of the huge domestic demand for China's construction industry and for the raw commodities that feed the construction industry such as lumber, concrete, steel, copper, plastic, etc.

But the source of China's economic growth is not coming from just internal domestic demand. In fact, much of China's growth is coming from exports because China consciously adopted the export-driven method of economic development that has proven to be so successful in countries such as Japan and the Asian Tigers. China is aggressively developing its export industries in order to employ its citizens and pull its overall economy up by its bootstraps. As a result, China's demand for raw commodities is due to domestic demand but also to its export industries.

Chinese Economy Expected to Maintain Strong Growth

The Chinese economy in 2003 grew by +9.1%, well above its average growth rate of +7.5% seen in the 1998-2002 period. The Chinese government expects GDP growth of more than +7% in 2004. The Chinese GDP growth rate in 2003 of +9.1% far outstripped that of any of the G7 countries of +5.6% in the UK, +4.3% in the US, +2.1% in Canada, +0.9% in Japan, and +0.6% in the Euro-Zone.

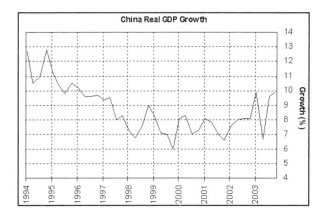

Remarkably, China has been able to sustain its average GDP growth rate over the last six years without significant inflation. China's inflation rate averaged near zero in the 6 years through mid-2003, but then started climbing in late 2003 to reach a 6-1/2 year high of +3.2% year-on-year in January 2004.

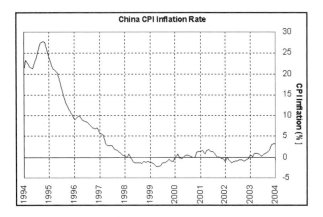

The strong Chinese GDP growth rate of +9.1% in 2003, combined with the rise in the CPI to the 6-1/2 year high of +3.2%, has led to fears that the Chinese economy is overheating. The money supply is growing at a torrid rate of +18% due in part to China's effort to suppress the value of the yuan by aggressively buying dollars and pumping yuan into China's banking system. Chinese authorities in late 2003 and early 2004 took some action to try to cool their economy by announcing that banks should limit lending growth to just +16% rather than the +21% growth seen in 2003. In addition, the government started refusing permits for new production facilities in some industries such as aluminum and cellular phones, and restricting lending in certain industries such as property and construction. But it is not clear whether this will be successful in curbing lending.

Chinese authorities are very reluctant to raise interest rates to cool credit growth and thus slow the economy because that would put additional upward pressure on the yuan and hurt its export industries. Chinese authorities have so far put off an interest rate hike, but it appears likely that an interest rate hike will have to come in 2004 along with additional restrictions on lending.

In short, Chinese authorities are doing a high-wire act as they try to foster strong economic growth in their country and boost employment without causing a bubble that will eventually collapse into a recession. The country is already seeing not only macroeconomic imbalances, but is also experiencing shortages in raw materials such as coal, oil, and steel. In addition, there has been a surge in industrial accidents and there are serious environmental problems. Nevertheless, China is expected to muddle through its various economic and social problems and maintain a strong GDP growth rate through 2004.

Chinese trade surges

As China pursues its export-led development model, its foreign trade has surged. As seen in the nearby chart, exports have quintupled in the past decade. Foreign trade now accounts for more than one-half of China's GDP, compared with only about 23% of GDP in the US and 21% in

Japan. In fact, in 2003 China eclipsed Japan to become the third largest trading nation in the world behind only the US and Germany.

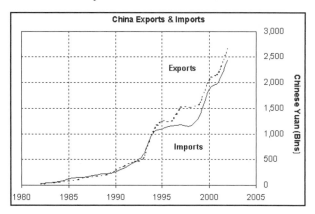

China became a full member of the world's trading system in December 2001 when it became a full member of the World Trade Organization (WTO). That gave China preferential trading status with the world's key economies but also obligated China to cut its trade and tariff barriers.

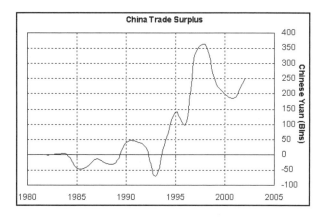

With the surge in exports, China's trade surplus has also grown in the past decade, as seen in the nearby chart. However, the Chinese trade surplus reached a peak in 1998 and has been more moderate since then. The reason behind the decline in the trade surplus was a surge in import growth, which has actually exceeded export growth. In 2003, Chinese exports grew about +33% while imports grew even faster by +39%. Thus while China is often excoriated by US politicians for its emphasis on exports, the data shows that China is also a huge importer as well.

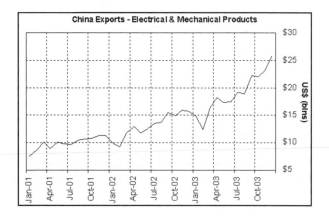

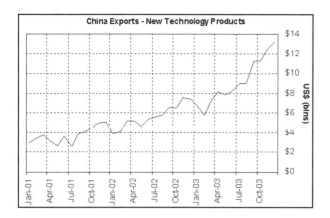

China Exports - New Technology Products

China is heavily dependent on raw material imports to feed its domestic economy and its export industries. However, China also has many assembly plants that import parts and partially finished goods and then use cheap labor to assemble and export the final product. These assembly parts are in such industries as textiles, electronics, and machinery. As seen in the nearby charts, China's exports of electrical and mechanical products, and new technology products, have grown rapidly in the past two years to record highs.

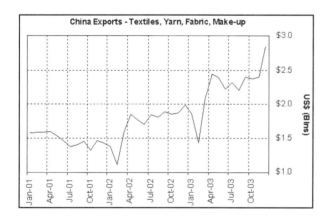

China Exports - Textiles, Yarn, Fabric, Make-up

China has also become a major exporter of textile products, which has turned China into a major importer of cotton, prices for which rallied 47% in 2003. Chinese buying of cotton is expected to be especially heavy in 2004 since the US Department of Agriculture is forecasting that China's domestic cotton crop will drop by 14% in 2004.

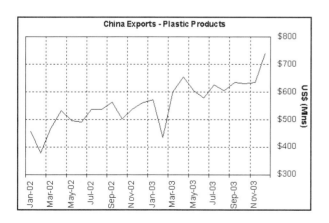

China Exports - Plastic Products

China has also become a major exporter of plastic products, as seen in the nearby chart. This has led to China becoming a major importer of raw plastic and also of petroleum to be used as a source of domestically produced raw plastic.

US trade deficit with China has grown but so have exports to China

The US trade deficit with China has been steadily growing in the past decade, as seen in the nearby chart. This is due to the fact that US imports from China have been growing much faster than US exports to China in terms of absolute dollar amounts. US imports from China increased by $27 billion (a 22% increase) to $152 billion in 2003 from $125 billion in 2002. Meanwhile, US exports to China rose by $6 billion (+28%) to $28 billion in 2003 from $22 billion in 2002. The fact that US imports rose faster than exports in absolute dollar terms pushed the US trade deficit with China up by 20% in 2003 to $124 billion from $103 billion in 2002.

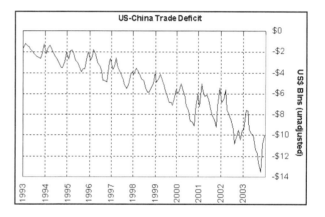

US-China Trade Deficit

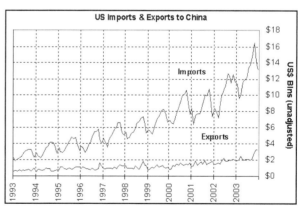

US Imports & Exports to China

The growth in the US trade deficit with China has made China the new bogeyman for Washington's politicians, much like Japan was back in the 1980s. Populist US politicians are claiming that China is using unfair trade practices and a cheap currency to steal both jobs and export opportunities from the US. However, US consumers are in fact benefiting from this trade with China since they are able to buyer cheaper goods and thus save money to buy other goods.

Also lost in the political rhetoric about the threat posed by Chinese imports is the fact that US exports to China have more than tripled over the past decade. China is now the US's fastest growing export destination, with US exports to China rising 28% in 2003 from 2002. China is a particularly aggressive buyer of some US farm products like soybeans and, in fact, the US in 2003 actually ran a trade surplus with China in agriculture goods. China is also a key source of demand for goods exported from its trading partners in Asia. China accounts for more than one-third of the increase in total exports by countries such as Japan, South Korea, Australia and Taiwan.

In order to curb the US trade deficit with China, the Bush Administration has been putting pressure on China to revalue its currency higher. This is because of complaints by US exporters that China is artificially depressing the value of its currency in order to keep its export prices cheap. The Chinese government has kept the yuan pegged at 8.28 yuan per dollar since 1995.

In fact, the Chinese currency is severely undervalued as measured by the *Economist* magazine's "Big Mac Index." In a light-hearted, but surprisingly effective way, the *Economist* uses McDonald's Big Mac as a benchmark product to apply the purchasing-power parity (PPP) theory to see whether currencies are over or under valued. The basic idea of purchasing-power parity is that goods should be similarly priced in different nations if their currencies are fairly aligned. The January issue of the *Economist* found that the cheapest comparable hamburger in China is $1.23, compared with the average price of $2.80 for a Big Mac in the US. The *Economist* says that suggests the Chinese yuan is undervalued against the dollar by a whopping 56%.

Chinese authorities have been doing everything they can to resist an upward revaluation in the yuan because that might dent Chinese exports and also might cause problems within the Chinese banking system. However, there is little doubt that Chinese authorities will have to make at least a small upward adjustment in the yuan in coming quarters.

Chinese demand for raw commodities is surging

Chinese demand for raw commodities has been a key factor driving the sharp rally seen in commodity prices in the 2001-2003 period. China cannot produce all the raw commodities it needs to feed both its domestic and export industries, and thus Chinese imports of raw materials have surged in recent years. This has put sharp upward pressure on the global prices of those commodities. Several examples of how Chinese demand has pushed up commodity prices follow.

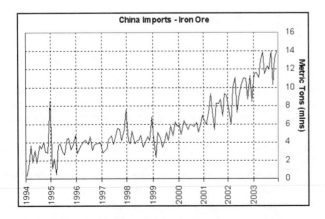

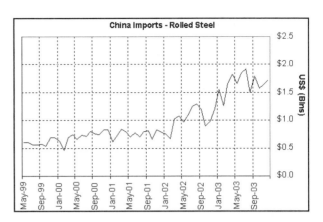

Steel – China is the world's largest steel consumer. China's National Bureau of Statistics reported that China's steel consumption in 2003 was 260 million tons, which accounts for 36% of the world's total consumption of 720 million tons. China has been unable to produce all that steel domestically and as a result its imports of iron ore and rolled steel have risen dramatically. Specifically, Chinese imports of iron ore, which is the main ingredient in steel, has grown by more than 60% in the past two years. Chinese imports of rolled steel have tripled in the past two years.

Chinese steel consumption stems in large part from its fast-growing construction and auto industries. The number of Chinese-built autos and trucks is expected to soar to 6 million vehicles in 2005, up 33% from 2000. In response to the Chinese demand and the increased world demand, steel prices spiked upward in February 2004 by 30-50% from just a month earlier.

In fact, US steel companies that use scrap steel as their raw material have been feeling severe pain as scrap steel prices soar. The price of scrap steel has more than doubled to $350 per ton from the $100-150 per ton a year earlier. US exports of steel scrap in 2003 rose 21% from 2002 to 12 million metric tons, according to the US Geological Survey. China has been buying up US scrap steel for use in its steel making plants, thus creating shortages and putting an upward squeeze on steel prices.

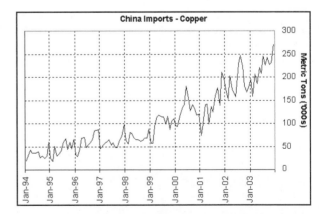

Copper – Copper provides an excellent proxy for industrial commodity demand in general, because it is a key metal used in the construction, electrical, manufacturing, and auto industries. For example, the average US single-family home contains about 400 pounds of copper in wiring and pipes, and an auto has about 50 pounds of copper, according to the Copper Development Association. As a result, with China's fast-growing construction and auto industries, among others, copper is in heavy demand in China.

Copper consumption in China soared by an estimated 20% in 2003 and China consumed about 20% of the world's copper in 2003. Chinese copper imports, as the nearby chart shows, have risen by 250% in the past three years. Chile is a major copper producer and its central bank reports that copper exports to China in January 2004 rose 37% year-on-year while exports to the US fell 54%, providing dramatic evidence of how copper exports from Chile are being diverted from the US to China. China's aggressive buying has been a key reason behind the fact that copper prices have nearly doubled in the past year to hit a new 8-year high.

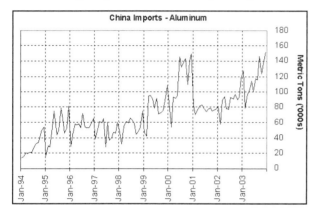

Aluminum - Another key raw material for the construction and auto industries is aluminum. The nearby chart shows how Chinese aluminum imports have roughly doubled in the past two years. Aluminum prices in the past year have rallied to current levels near $1,700 per metric ton from about $1,400 per metric ton a year earlier, representing a rally of about 20%.

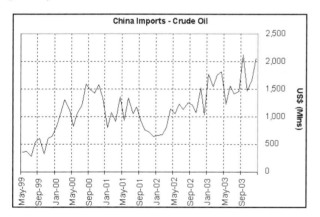

Energy – With its booming economy, China surpassed Japan in 2003 as the world's second largest oil consumer. China's consumption of 5.4 million barrels per day falls behind only the US's consumption of 20.2 million barrels per day. To meet its needs, China's oil imports in 2003 rose roughly 30% from the previous year to 2 million barrels per day. Chinese oil imports now account for more than a third of its total consumption. Moreover, China's oil imports will double to 4 million barrels per day by 2010 and grow to 85% of its total consumption by 2030, according to the International Energy Agency (IEA). According to Cambridge Energy Associates, China's share of total world oil consumption will grow to 9% by 2010 from the current level of 7%,

thus crowding out other world oil consumers.

The source of the increasing demand for crude oil in China is for auto and truck gasoline, factories, raw material for the petrochemical and plastics industries, and electricity production. In the auto sector, for example, the number of autos in China is expected to quintuple to 100 million within the next decade, according to the Development Research Center, a Chinese research group, which would be about half of the autos in the US. Chinese demand for gasoline is likely to quintuple as well within the next decade.

China's heavy consumption of crude oil, combined with its own lackluster domestic production, has forced China out into the world oil markets to try to find new supplies. China has been trying to secure oil fields for its national oil companies, but has mostly been buying crude oil on the world oil markets, thus driving up prices. In fact, Chinese demand was a key factor keeping oil prices high through 2003.

Coal is another key commodity in China because China relies on coal for 70% of its electricity production. China consumed about 1.5 billion tons of coal in 2003, accounting for more than 30% of world consumption. China has been experiencing serious electricity shortages in many parts of the country and its demand for coal for electricity production will grow in coming years.

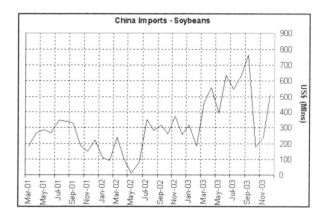

Soybeans – China is also a major player in the agricultural markets with its need to feed 1.3 billion people. China grows only about one-half the soybeans it needs and must therefore import more than half of its soybean consumption from overseas. China is expected to import a record 808 million bushels of soybeans in 2004, which would be more than double its 2003 imports, according to a recent estimate from the US Department of Agriculture. Chinese buying was a major factor pushing soybean prices higher in 2003 as China imported $5.4 billion worth of soybeans according to Chinese government statistics.

Commodity Exchanges – A key sign of China's growing importance in the world commodities markets is the growing trading volume on China's commodity futures exchanges. China had about 60 futures exchanges in the early 1990s but Chinese regulators became concerned about rampant speculation and forced the merger or closure of most of its commodity exchanges into the current three exchanges. Volume at China's three futures exchanges hit a record high of $1.3 trillion in 2003, which compares favorably to the $2 trillion volume at the London Metals Exchange in 2003.

The Shanghai Futures Exchange currently trades copper and plans to roll out a contract for fuel oil in the near future. The Dalian commodity exchange trades soybeans and plans to roll out a corn contract. The Zhengzhou commodity exchange trades cotton and plans to roll out a low-quality wheat contract. The Chinese futures exchanges are also planning to roll out futures contracts for sugar, rice, crude oil, and stock indices once the China Securities Regulatory Commission grants its permission.

The Chinese government has moved very slowly in allowing the futures market to develop. Chinese nationals are not allowed to trade on foreign futures markets without a special hedging permit, and foreigners are generally not allowed to trade on Chinese exchanges.

The Chicago Board of Trade (CBOT) and Dalian commodity exchange on November 15, 2003, signed an information-sharing agreement with a view toward developing products together. Both exchanges currently have soybean contracts. The CBOT entered the agreement with the Dalian as a means to gain a foothold in China when regulators start to ease up on trading restrictions. With China's massive trade in raw commodities, the local futures markets are likely to grow quickly for both hedging and speculative purposes, once regulators can ensure controlled growth and fair markets.

Chinese Stocks Offer Opportunities and Risks

The Chinese stock market is a tale of two markets — stocks traded outside China and stocks traded inside China. There are about 1,200 Chinese stocks listed on China's two mainland stock exchanges, the Shanghai Stock Exchange and the Shenzhen Stock Exchange. Stocks traded *inside* China are represented in the nearby chart by the Shanghai Composite Index, which is comprised of A and B shares of Chinese companies listed on the Shanghai Stock Exchange. Stocks traded *outside* China are represented in the same chart by the Hang Seng China Enterprises Index, which is comprised by 32 mainland state-owned Chinese companies (H-Shares) listed on the Hong Kong Stock Exchange. The indices are plotted with a common percentage index scale with January 1995 set at 100.

Stocks that trade inside China did well during the late 1990s and into early 2001 as seen by the rally in the Shang-

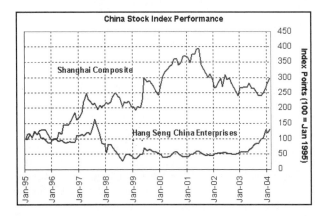

hai Composite Index. However, their performance since then has been poor, with a 21% loss in 2001 and an 18% loss in 2002. The losses in 2001 and 2002 have yet to be overcome by the 10% rally in 2003 and the 12% rally in January/February 2004.

By contrast, the Hang Seng China Enterprises index, representing stocks listed outside mainland China, fared

poorly in the late 1990s, traded sideways through 2002, but then rallied sharply by 152% in 2003. The index by early 2004 had more than doubled from the level seen at the beginning of 2003. The recent strong performance of the Hang Seng China Enterprises Index is representative of other Chinese stock benchmarks that trade outside China, such as US mutual funds that invest in Chinese stocks and the American Depository Receipts (ADRs) of Chinese companies that trade on the New York Stock Exchange.

The domestic Chinese stock market has been hurt by a number of factors. The key factor is overhang from the fact that the Chinese government owns about two-thirds of the total stock in listed shares, representing about $300 billion in non-tradable shares. The markets are fearful of a bloodbath if the government starts to try to sell its shares into the marketplace. In addition, stocks listed inside China are not subject to strict rules on accounting, transparency, disclosure, and corporate governance, thus increasing the risks of those stocks. Moreover, there are concerns about spillover effects into the stock market from the poor health of China's largest banks and brokerage firms. China also has yet to develop an educated investor class of individuals who have the money to invest in stocks.

The Chinese government has taken some steps to try to attract foreign investment into China's stock market in order to support prices. Prior to 2002, foreign investors were only allowed to buy B-shares in Chinese companies. A-shares, which generally trade at a higher premium, were reserved for Chinese investors. However, the Chinese government started a program in late 2002 called the Qualified Financial Institutional Investor (QFII) program that allowed 10 large global investment banks to buy A-shares and then resell those shares to global institutional investors. This program has brought some $800 million of new investment into China's domestic stock market in the past year, about one-half of the authorized amount. However, the domestic Chinese stock market still suffers from difficult problems that will only be solved with dramatic reform measures from the government.

Despite the problems on China's domestic stock exchanges, global investors are eager to invest in China's future with its huge population and strong economic growth. The solution for most investors has been to invest in Chinese companies that are listed on exchanges in Hong Kong or New York or to invest in China-focused mutual funds. Investors poured $475 million in new investment into China-focused mutual funds in 2003, funds that produced an average return for the year of +63%, according to mutual fund tracker Lipper Inc. Another way to play China is to buy the stocks of global companies that are benefiting with their trade with China or to invest in Asia-Pacific or Emerging Growth mutual funds that have large exposure to China.

The sharp rally in Chinese stocks seen in the past year has led to concerns that the rally has overreached and that valuations have become much too high. Valuations on A-share stocks in China are very high at 30 times trailing earnings. Speculative excess can also be seen by the fact that the closed-end investment company, The China Fund Inc., which trades on the New York Stock Exchange with the symbol of CHN and invests in small and mid-sized Chinese stocks, traded with a share price of 25% to 50% more than the value of its underlying portfolio in early 2004, showing that investors are bidding the closed-end fund up higher than its intrinsic value.

While there are questions about whether now is the time to invest in Chinese stocks, there is little doubt that some Chinese companies and other global companies selling into China will be big winners in coming years as they take advantage of the huge demand that is emerging in China.

Chinese influence in debt markets grows with huge foreign exchange reserves

China's foreign exchange reserves have nearly tripled in the past several years to recent levels over $400 billion, giving China some serious clout in the US Treasury security market. There are concerns in the US that China can threaten to stop purchasing Treasury securities, or threaten to sell the Treasury securities it already owns, thus pushing up the key US government's financing costs and a key US benchmark interest rate.

How did China acquire these reserves? China is running a trade surplus of about 250 billion yuan or US$30

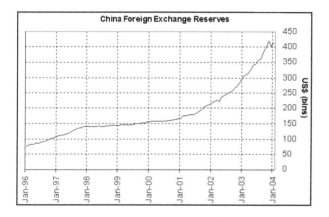

billion. Because China has a non-convertible currency, the government requires exporters to turn their dollars and other foreign currencies over to the central bank to be converted into yuan at the fixed rate of 8.277 yuan per dollar.

Thus, by virtue of its trade surplus and its non-convertible currency, the Chinese central bank accumulates US dollars and other foreign currency reserves denominated in euros, yen, and other global currencies. Most of the Chinese central bank's reserves are in dollars, however, because that is the preferred unit of trade for global commerce. The Chinese central bank wants to earn interest on those dollars and the safest and most liquid place to place those dollars is in US Treasury securities. The Chinese central bank has therefore become a huge buyer of US Treasury securities, with purchases in 2003 running more than $60 billion.

As the nearby chart shows, China's foreign exchange reserves have grown dramatically and totaled $403.3 billion as of January 2004. China's reserves grew by $160 billion just in 2003. China now has the second highest foreign exchange reserves of any nation in Asia, falling behind

only Japan, which has $673.5 billion. If fact, Asia as a whole now holds $1.94 trillion of the world's reserves of just over $3 trillion. This has prompted Asian central banks to purchase about two-thirds of the US government debt issued over the past 2 years. The nearby chart shows how foreign entities, primarily foreign central banks, have bought nearly $1 trillion in US Treasury T-bonds and T-notes just since January 1995 and how those purchases picked up sharply in 2002 and 2003 as the US budget deficit soared and Treasury debt sales increased.

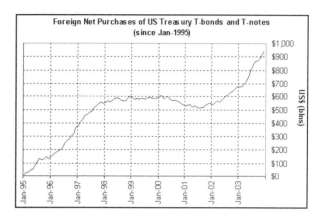

China's rapid accumulation of reserves is causing a major macroeconomic problem for the nation because the Chinese central bank typically prints new yuan in order to buy the dollars from exporters. This has led to 18% growth in the Chinese money supply. Although Chinese inflation is currently only about 3%, there are concerns that the rapid growth in the money supply will overheat the economy and cause some serious inflation problems down the road. In fact, the Chinese central bank has been trying to cut back on money supply growth and credit creation by "sterilizing" its dollar purchases with offsetting T-bill sales to banks, and by encouraging banks to restrict credit to certain industries. However, the central bank has only achieved modest success in curbing credit and China's macroeconomic imbalances are in fact growing.

The rapid growth of its foreign exchange reserves and the inflationary implications of absorbing those reserves are putting serious pressure on the Chinese central bank to revalue the yuan higher. There is speculation that the Chinese central bank in 2004 will revalue the yuan higher by up to 5% and perhaps even move to a crawling peg against a basket of currencies in 2005 in order to protect itself from dollar weakness. Revaluing the yen will eventually bring some relief to the nation's macroeconomic imbalances. But in the meantime, China will continue to be a major buyer in the US Treasury market and will wield influence in Washington as a significant financier of the US budget deficit.

Richard W. Asplund, CRB Chief Economist, February 2004.

FREE-TRADE TALKS PRODUCE SOME SUCCESS BUT MOVE FROM GLOBAL TO REGIONAL

Summary – Free trade is one of the cornerstones of the global market economy. Yet the current round of global trade talks, the Doha Round, is at a standstill due to the intractable problem of agriculture subsidies. The US, frustrated by an attack on its agriculture subsidies and by the difficulty of negotiating in the WTO multilateral platform, has instead turned its attention to negotiating a series of regional and bilateral trade agreements. The breakdown of the Doha Round in November 2003 was a big disappointment for those hoping for an extra boost to global GDP in coming years from a successful global trade agreement. Yet all is not lost, and the pressure on the US and EU to curb their agriculture subsidies may yet produce progress in coming years and a better free trade round if and when it finally concludes.

Benefits of free trade

Economic doctrine teaches that free trade benefits all parties involved by allowing the most efficient producers to produce goods and services that they are best in producing, thus boosting overall GDP output and allowing global consumers to benefit from low prices and good quality for the goods and services that they purchase. Imposing barriers to trade at the borders of nations results in inefficiencies and distortions, thus lowering output and raising prices.

In fact, the benefits of free trade can be substantial. The World Trade Organization (WTO), for example, estimates that the 1994 Uruguay Round trade deal boosted world income by somewhere between $109 billion and $510 billion, depending on different assumptions. The WTO also cites economists as estimating that a one-third cut in current barriers to trade in agriculture, manufacturing, and services would boost the world economy by $613 billion, which is equivalent to adding an economy the size of Canada to the world economy.

The costs of protectionism

The cost of trade barriers can be substantial to consumers in the form of higher prices. The WTO estimates, for example, that European agricultural protectionism results in the average European family of four paying $1,500 per year more in food costs. US consumers may not notice that their sugar is over-priced, but US consumers pay an extra $3 billion per year for sugar, according to the WTO, because of US government policies in protecting the US sugar industry from global competition. Sugar prices in the US are near 20 cents per pound versus 7 cents elsewhere in the world. High US sugar prices decimated the US candy industry, a big consumer of sugar, and resulted in the loss of 7,500-10,000 jobs in the US, according to the Sugar Users Association. In another example, trade restrictions in the textile industry cost UK consumers an estimated 500 million pounds-sterling more for their clothing and about CD$780 million more for Canadian consumers, according to the WTO.

Despite theoretical agreement on the overall benefits of free trade, there are concerns about the local dislocations that occur as production moves to more efficient locales,

since that usually results in lost jobs. Lost jobs are a much more visible manifestation of free trade than the diffused benefits of higher overall GDP output and lower prices for consumers. Concerns about lost jobs often lead to calls for protectionism, which some politicians are only too happy to accommodate. Protectionist rhetoric sometimes wins more votes that promoting the benefits of free trade.

Yet, protectionism causes insidious damage to an economy by raising prices and undercutting exports. The most notorious example of a disastrous protectionist policy was the Smoot-Hawley Tariff of 1930 passed by the US Congress, which caused US trade to plunge and is widely blamed as a key factor that worsened the impact of the Great Depression. The Smoot-Hawley debacle traced its roots to promises by Herbert Hoover during the 1928 presidential election to help farmers who had seen tough times in the 1920s. That mistake provides an important and enduring lesson about the costs of bowing to agricultural protectionism.

Federal Reserve Chairman Greenspan, in testimony before Congress in March 2004, warned Congress not to succumb to recent signs that "creeping protectionism" was taking hold in Washington. Mr. Greenspan noted that capitalism involves the process of "creative destruction," a term coined by famed economist Joseph A. Schumpeter. Mr. Greenspan admitted that global competition can be "disruptive" but he said that on balance the US has greatly prospered by being open and flexible. Mr. Greenspan testified, "Time and again through our history, we have discovered that attempting to merely preserve the comfortable features of the present, rather than reaching for new levels of prosperity, is a sure path to stagnation."

The current mishmash we call the world trading system reflects the conflicted views on the benefits of free trade. Many nations want free trade to boost their exports, but not when it comes to protecting themselves from imports. These countries want to protect their favored local industries, which provide jobs for their people and political support for their politicians, even if those industries are highly inefficient and consumers in their country could buy the same or better quality products from overseas at a lower cost. The governments in those countries keep protecting these favored local industries even though their consumers pay higher prices, and even though other industries in their country might benefit if they entered free trade agreements that gave their other industries better access to foreign markets.

Adopting free trade requires political leadership and faith in the ability of a nation to adapt. The movement to global free trade only moves forward in fits and starts, with each major step forward only coming after long and difficult negotiations and compromises. Yet, there does continue to be progress toward a freer global trading system.

Bush administration plays the reluctant free trader

The Bush Administration has aggressively pursued free trade talks on a multitude of fronts, including within the WTO, within the Americas, and with a number of different countries in bilateral talks. The Bush Administration has had a number of successes, including the Central American Free Trade Agreement, and bilateral agreements with Australia and other nations. Nevertheless, the Bush Administration has been criticized for playing politics with trade and for coddling selected US industries such as steel, sugar, cotton, and others.

The Bush Administration soon after coming into office succumbed to pressure from the steel industry for tariff protection from foreign competitors. In an ill-conceived bow to protectionist political pressures, the Bush Administration and Congress in 2002 approved steel tariffs ranging from 8% to 30%, covering roughly 80% of steel products produced in the US. However, the Bush Administration was finally forced to lift the steel tariffs in December 2003 when the WTO ruled that the tariffs were illegal and authorized Europe and Asian nations to impose retaliatory tariffs against the US.

Rather than challenge the authority of the WTO and take a hit on retaliatory tariffs on other US exporting industries, the Bush Administration backed down and repealed the steel tariffs. The timing was fortuitous because just two months later, steel consumers (as opposed to steel producers) were in Washington screaming about high steel prices, something the Bush steel tariffs actually promoted in the previous year. The steel tariff debacle provided another lesson highlighting the harmful overall effect of tariffs and reinforcing the benefits of letting the marketplace do its job by allowing buyers and sellers of products and services to mediate supply, demand and prices without undue interference from the government.

In another protectionist move, the Bush Administration in November 2003 placed limits of the imports of Chinese-made knit fabric, dressing gowns, and bras, by invoking the highly questionable tactic of using a safeguard clause in WTO regulations to protect against a sudden surge in imports. The Bush Administration was roundly criticized by free trade observers for that unilateral action against China, which is at odds with the spirit of WTO rules.

The Bush Administration has also engaged in other trade spats with China. Most recently, the Bush Administration in mid-March 2004 said that the US would file the first formal trade case against China at the WTO charging that China imposes an discriminatory tax on imported semiconductors. If the Bush Administration goes ahead with its plans, that would be the first formal trade case against China since China joined the WTO in 2001.

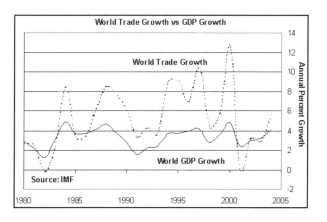

World Trade Growth vs GDP Growth

Growth in global trade outpaces GDP growth

Despite difficult free talks and various trade spats, world trade on the whole has moved forward at an impressive rate. In the past 50 years, world trade has grown by an average of +6% per year, faster than GDP growth. The chart above shows how world trade has grown faster than GDP growth on average since 1980. Increased world trade has been sparked by lower trade barriers and technological improvements in global commerce in transportation, communications, information, and finance.

The chart above also shows that world trade is highly dependent on the business cycle, rising in good economic times and falling in bad times. During the global economic slump in late 2000 to early 2003, world trade growth fell sharply. However, the IMF estimates that world trade in 2004 will improve to +5.5%, faster than projected world GDP growth of +4.1%.

Development of the world trading system

The current world trading system was built after World War II with the development of the General Agreement on Tariffs and Trade (GATT). GATT provided the fundamental rules and negotiating platform to promote free trade. The GATT Uruguay Round in 1986-94 then succeeded in creating the World Trade Organization (WTO) in 1995, which has now taken over responsibility for world trade. Membership in WTO is voluntary, but upon joining, a nation agrees to abide by WTO trading rules.

The WTO has nearly 150 member nations and accounts for 97% of world trade. The WTO key functions are as follows (see www.wto.org):

- Administering trade agreements
- Acting as a forum for trade negotiations
- Settling trade disputes
- Reviewing national trade policies
- Technical assistance and training for developing nations
- Cooperating with other international organizations

Being a member of the WTO carries benefits such as lower-cost access to the markets of other members. But being a member also carries responsibilities such as lowering tariffs and other trade barriers. The most visible recent member was China who joined the WTO in 2001. China's trade has soared in the past several years, in part because of its WTO membership and its full integration into the world trading system.

Prospects for the Doha Round

The Doha Round is the current round of global trade talks that began in November 2001 at the fourth WTO Ministerial Conference in Doha, Qatar. The stated deadline for the Doha Round is January 1, 2005. The Doha Round is focused on lowering trade barriers in agriculture, textiles, and services. The World Bank has estimated that a successful Doha Round could raise global GDP by more than $500 billion per year by 2015 and that 60% of that gain would go to poor countries.

The Doha Round is currently at a standstill and the prospects look bleak for an agreement before the deadline in less than 10 months. The Doha Round broke down at the

WTO ministerial meeting in Cancun, Mexico in September 2003 after an impasse between the poor nations and the rich nations.

The trouble started when the proposal by the EU and the US on cutting agricultural support was far less than other key parties expected when the Doha Round began. The EU, for example, planned to keep in place its agricultural export subsidies, one of the worst types of trade protection. Support by developed nations to their farmers has been estimated to be running at $300 billion per year for the past 15 years. The protection of farmers in the developed countries means that there is excess production dumped on the world markets, thus depressing the world prices of agricultural products and forcing farmers in developing countries out of business.

US support of the cotton industry is particularly egregious with the US government providing some $4 billion of subsidies to the cotton industry each year. The government subsidies have caused overproduction of cotton in the US, which is in turn dumped on world markets and depresses cotton prices. Weak cotton prices through early 2002 decimated cotton farmers in developing nations and infuriated African nations that depend on cotton exports as one of their primary sources of exports and foreign exchange. Cotton is only one example of how US taxpayer dollars are used to support the US agricultural industry and cause collateral damage outside the US. The US government spends an estimated $19 billion per year in total on farm subsidies.

Agricultural subsidies in Europe are even larger than in the US. Under the EU's common agricultural policy (CAP), the EU props up local agricultural prices to keep inefficient farmers in business and the excess production is then dumped on the world markets, driving even efficient producers overseas out of business because of artificially low world prices. The EU also imposes tariffs on agricultural imports to keep lower priced agricultural products out of the EU.

In response to the paltry offer by the EU and the US on agriculture in the Doha Round talks, an alliance formed of emerging countries called the G21, led by Brazil, China, and India. The G21 group, which represents half the world's population and two-thirds of the world's farmers, demanded much more aggressive action by the EU and US on cutting agricultural protection. Yet the G21 offered little in exchange for big cuts in US and EU agricultural subsidies and most of the G21 countries wanted to keep intact their own agricultural trade protections. The EU and US responded to the G21 challenge by playing hardball on agriculture and other issues, and the Cancun ministerial meeting then quickly broke down in acrimony.

In an effort to get the ball rolling again, US Trade Representative Robert Zoellick in January 2004 sent letters to all the member nations of the WTO expressing his desire to restart global trade talks and convene another ministerial meeting later in 2004. The US made clear that it would put more pressure on the EU to reform its CAP agricultural support policies. Yet progress on restarting the global trade talks will be difficult.

Following up on its attack on US and EU agricultural subsidies, Brazil brought a legal challenge against the US at the WTO for its cotton subsidies. A decision is expected by spring. WTO members are now free to bring legal action at the WTO on farm issues now that the so-called peace period has ended whereby nations involved in the Uruguay Round agreed not to bring trade actions on agriculture until after 2003. Some nations such as Brazil believe that they are better off trying to have the WTO declare US and EU agriculture subsidies illegal, rather than trying to twist arms at the bargaining table.

The breakdown of the Doha ministerial talks in Cancun in September raised larger questions about whether a global trade agreement can ever be reached under the WTO negotiating platform. A global trade agreement at the WTO must be reached by consensus and any single nation, or groups of nations, can basically torpedo the entire process. There are a few smaller nations that are more interested in grandstanding for their local political constituents than in seriously negotiating toward another world trade agreement. US Trade Representative Robert Zoellick has referred to several "won't do" nations who he says are good at making demands but are poor at creating compromises.

US strategy switches to bilateral and regional trade agreements

After the Cancun debacle, the US moved toward a policy of focusing on bilateral and regional trade agreements, rather than a global agreement through the WTO. These agreements are easier for the US to negotiate and difficult issues such as agriculture can simply be left out of the agreement. In addition, if the US can negotiate enough bilateral and regional agreements, then eventually these trade blocs might be cobbled together into a global agreement. This is a clearly inferior approach to an all-encompassing world trade agreement, but at least nations are still making progress at lowering trade barriers, making compromise easier when it comes time to negotiate a grand global agreement.

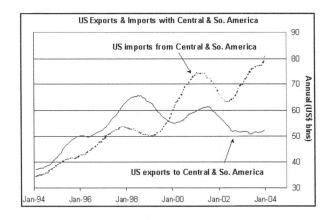

Free trade talks in the Americas reach impasse

Soon after the WTO talks broke down in September, the Bush Administration turned its attention to the "Free Trade Area of the Americas" (FTAA) trade negotiations ahead of the ministerial meeting that took place in late November 2003 in Miami. The FTAA initiative was formally launched nine years ago and seeks to combine 34 countries in the western hemisphere (North, Central and South America) into a free trade zone encompassing 800 million people.

However, the same problems that torpedoed the WTO talks in Cancun quickly threatened the FTAA talks. In particular, Brazil made the same demands for the US to slash its agricultural subsidies in return for considering extending free trade into services and protections for intellectual property. Brazil is a large agricultural producer and wants freer access to US markets. At present, for example, Brazil can't sell raw beef to the US because of presumptive health reasons and Brazil's sugar exports face quotas and tariffs as high as 200%.

For its part, the US refused to negotiate in FTAA on agriculture except within the context of global negotiations also involving Europe and Japan. The US didn't want to make concessions on agriculture in the FTAA without extracting concessions from the EU, Japan and other nations on agriculture as well.

In order to avoid another embarrassing collapse at the Miami talks, the FTAA group agreed to water down the FTAA framework by adopting a two-tiered approach whereby members could agree to core requirements but opt out of more controversial free-trade issues. This has been referred to "FTAA-lite" or an "a la carte" approach to an FTAA trade agreement.

FTAA negotiators held high-level talks in early February to discuss what should be in the core requirements. While the talks are progressing, any FTAA-lite agreement would clearly be much less than members had earlier hoped and there is no assurance that even an FTAA-lite can be finished by the deadline in early 2005.

Central American Free Trade Agreement (Cafta) is reached in December

After the FTAA meeting in Miami, the US turned its attention to regional and bilateral trade talks within the Americas. On December 17, 2003, the US announced the "Central American Free Trade Agreement," or Cafta, involving El Salvador, Guatemala, Honduras, and Nicaragua. The Cafta group was later expanded to include Costa Rico in late January and the Dominican Republican in mid-March 2004. The Cafta region includes about $30 billion worth of two-way trade with the US, i.e., $16.03 billion worth of US imports from the region and $14.09 billion of US exports to the region.

President Bush has signaled that he will sign Cafta, allowing Congress to vote on the pact by the August recess. However, passage may be difficult given that 2004 is an election year when free trade and job losses are political hot potatoes.

Aside from the framework of FTAA and Cafta, the US and Chile in 2003 completed a trade agreement that went into effect on January 1, 2004. The US is also pursuing a separate bilateral trade agreement with Panama.

As the US was wrapping up Cafta, Brazil made its own moves within South America, seeking to band together with other South American countries to boost their bargaining position with the US in the FTAA talks. South America already has its own free trade zone called Mercosur, which includes Brazil, Argentina, Uruguay, and Paraguay. Associate members include Chile and Bolivia. Brazil is now seeking to bring Peru and Venezuela into Mercosur.

Maneuvering between the US and Brazil will be a key to the success of the FTAA talks and indeed to the Doha Round. The marketplace will therefore be carefully watching how US and Brazilian trade relations play out in coming months.

NAFTA reaches 10ᵗʰ birthday

Cafta is being viewed as an extension of the North American Free Trade Agreement (NAFTA), the 10-year-old free trade agreement among the US, Canada, and Mexico. NAFTA has generally been considered a success, although it has not lived up to some of the highest expectations when it was signed.

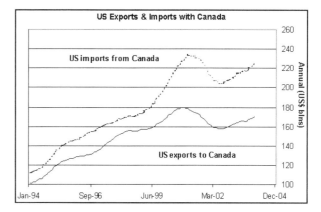

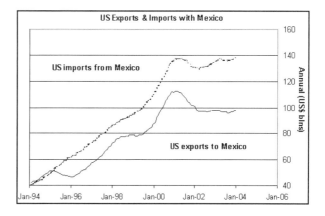

Trade among the US, Canada, and Mexico has grown dramatically in the past 10 years, driven in part by the NAFTA free trade zone. US exports to Canada over the past 10 years have grown by 70% and US exports to Mexico have grown by nearly 250%. At the same time, Canadian exports to the US have nearly doubled, and Mexican exports to the US have more than tripled. The US trade deficits with Canada and Mexico have also grown sharply over the past decade, but that has been the case with US trade with all major trading partners.

NAFTA has had a "miniscule" net effect on jobs in the US, according to a report by Carnegie Endowment for International Peace, negating the fears fostered by H. Ross Perot in the 1992 presidential election who said NAFTA would cause "a giant sucking sound" of US jobs moving to Mexico. For the US, the benefits from NAFTA mainly come from US consumers being able to purchase goods more cheaply and from increasing US export business to Mexico and Canada. Also, US-based companies can operate more efficiently within North America by having access to tariff-free movement of goods and services through the Mexican and Canadian borders.

There is controversy about how well Mexico has fared under NAFTA, but there is general agreement that Mexico is better off with NAFTA than without. Mexico has deep-seated problems and a free trade agreement by itself has not been enough to pull Mexico out of poverty. In addition, Mexico is now losing ground to China in the competition for low-wage jobs. Yet, Mexico is not turning against trade. On the contrary, Mexico and Japan in early March 2004 agreed on the framework of a free trade agreement.

US reaches bilateral agreements with Australia and Morocco

The US has been pursuing bilateral trade agreements with a variety of countries outside the big trading blocs. Congress in 2003 approved bilateral trade agreements with Chile and Singapore. US trade negotiators in March 2004 completed a free-trade agreement with Morocco, which now goes to Congress. US negotiators are currently pursuing bilateral trade agreements with Thailand, Bahrain, and four countries in southern Africa. The US already has bilateral free trade pacts in place with Jordan and Israel.

The US and Australia in February 2004 reached a free trade agreement. While Australia only has 20 million people, Australia is America's ninth largest trading partner with $28 billion in two-way trade. The agreement was note-

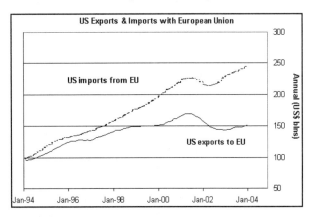

worthy since Australia is only the second industrialized nation next to Canada to open its markets to the US and the US expects to significantly boost the export of manufactured goods to Australia. However, the US-Australian trade agreement left in place US protection of sugar and Australian subsidies of pharmaceuticals.

European Union expansion means larger free trade zone

The European Union is by definition a free-trade zone, and it is growing in size. The European Union, with its

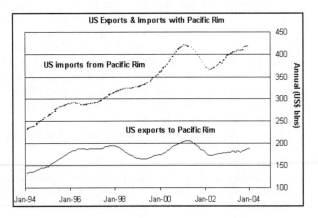

economic and political integration, was established with the ratification of the Maastricht Treaty in 1993. The EU currently consists of 15 nations and will expand to 25 nations in May 2004. A sub-set of the EU, the Euro-Zone nations, have gone further than free trade and have adopted a common currency, the euro. This is an even greater stimulus to free trade because it eliminates the uncertainties and inefficiencies associated with currency fluctuations.

Asia negotiates its own free trade agreements

Asian nations are also making a push for regional and bilateral trade agreements. As mentioned earlier, Japan in early 2004 reached a free trade agreement with Mexico, which it views as a foot-hold into the US and Canada. Japan also has a trade agreement with Singapore and is pushing for trade agreements with other nations.

The nations of southeastern Asia, or ASEAN, entered into a free trade agreement back in 1992 that remains in progress and is due to be fully implemented by 2020. The nations in the ASEAN Free Trade Agreement include Brunei, Cambodia, Indonesia, Laos, Malaysia, Myanmar, Philippines, Singapore, Thailand, and Vietnam. The ASEAN region has a population of about 500 million, combined GDP of $737 billion, and total trade of $720 billion.

China is aggressively seeking free trade talks on a variety of fronts. China and ASEAN have agreed to negotiate a free trade agreement. A free trade agreement between China and ASEAN would include 1.7 billion people and $1.2 trillion in two-way trade. China is currently in talks with Australia about the feasibility of negotiating a free trade agreement.

On the Indian subcontinent, seven nations in January 2004 entered into the South Asian Free Trade Agreement (Safta). Under Safta, the nations agreed to cut their inter-regional tariffs beginning on January 1, 2006, to between 0% and 5% over the next decade. The nations in Safta include erstwhile enemies India and Pakistan, along with Bangladesh, Bhutan, the Maldives, Nepal, and Sri Lanka. The seven nations in the group, which is called the South Asia Association of Regional Cooperation, account for some 1.5 billion people, many of whom live in poverty.

Looking forward

There will undoubtedly be further progress on free trade through the remainder of 2004. The US will be pushing for progress in the Doha Round and on the FTAA talks. There will also likely be progress on additional regional and bilateral trade agreements. Progress in 2004 may be slowed, however, by the fact that 2004 is an election year in the US and that free trade and job exports are hot political issues. Nevertheless, world trade negotiators will continue plugging along with the knowledge that free trade is a way to boost world GDP and improve the quality of life for millions of people.

Richard W. Asplund, CRB Chief Economist, March 2004

MAD COW DISEASE ARRIVES IN NORTH AMERICA IN 2003 AND ROILS THE MARKETS

Summary – Mad cow disease, long a problem in Britain, arrived in Canada in March 2003 and in the US in December 2003. Although only one mad cow has been confirmed in the US so far, the fact that mad cow disease has breeched the US border means that the US can no longer consider itself immune from the mad cow problem. The discovery of the mad cow in Washington state resulted in a plunge in cattle prices and the shutdown of US beef exports to more than 50 countries, causing serious disruptions and financial losses in the US beef industry. The US government has so far responded to the problem by trying to reassure the public about the safety of US beef and taking some limited regulatory measures. At this point, however, the US government is not sure how widespread any mad cow problem may be in the US, and it would not be surprising if the government finds additional cases of mad cow with its more aggressive testing program.

What is mad cow disease?

Bovine spongiform encephalopathy (BSE) is commonly known as "mad cow" disease because the disease affects the central nervous system and eats away a cow's brain, causing the cow to act erratically before finally dying. BSE is caused by misfolded proteins called prions, which become infectious and accumulate in neural tissues, thus causing a fatal, degenerative, neurological disease. The disease is usually spread to other cattle by eating contaminated tissues. Tests have shown that the misfolded prions can survive all usual sterilization measures including boiling, cooking, radiation, and the high-pressure steam used on surgical instruments.

BSE was first diagnosed in 1986 in Great Britain. The exact origins of BSE are still not known, but it is thought to have started when cattle were given feed that was contaminated with scrapie-infected sheep meat-and-bone meal. Scrapie is a prion disease in sheep that is similar to BSE in cattle.

The first cases of transmission of mad cow disease to humans emerged in 1995 when two teenagers in the UK were diagnosed with a variant of the rare disorder known as Cruetzfeldt-Jacob disease (CJD). CJD is known to occur spontaneously in elderly humans, but the type of CJD found in patients that develop the disease from eating BSE-contaminated meat is a variant of spontaneous CJD and is referred to as vCJD.

Mad cow disease arrives in Canada in May 2003

In May 2003, veterinary officials in Alberta confirmed that an 8-year-old cow tested positive for BSE. After the animal displayed typical signs of BSE at the slaughter house, the meat from that cow was declared unfit for human consumption and was kept from other meat bound for packing plants and stores, and the rendered byproduct was not mixed with byproduct from other cows. Nevertheless, the US, Japan, South Korea, Australia, and other countries temporarily banned imports of Canadian beef. Three months later in August 2003, the US eased a ban on most types of processed Canadian beef, accounting for about 40%

of the total value of Canadian beef and cattle sales to the US, but still banned live cattle imports.

The single case of mad cow disease cost the Canadian beef industry dearly. It is estimated that Canada's beef industry lost $2.5 billion in the six months after its mad cow case was discovered and the Canadian cattle market is likely to stay depressed for the next several years. A surplus of milk currently exists in Canada because dairy cows cannot be exported due to the US ban on Canadian live cattle, thus putting downward pressure on Canadian milk prices and harming Canadian dairy farmers.

The US Department of Agriculture (USDA) is currently considering whether to allow certain classes of live Canadian cattle and other ruminants to be imported into the US for the first time since May 20, 2003. A decision is expected sometime in April. Because of this, Canadian ranchers are holding onto more of their cattle, awaiting the removal of the ban, instead of sending them to processing plants. If the Canadian live cattle ban is lifted, it could add to the already-large US surplus of beef.

It is perhaps surprising to note that Canada's first brush with mad cow disease actually occurred more than a decade ago. In December 1993, a cow imported from Britain in 1987 was found to have BSE. Canada's agriculture department (Agriculture Canada) decided to destroy the animal carcass and its 5 herd mates and additional measures were taken immediately to deal with any risk that Canadian cattle might have been affected. Although the disease is not contagious within a herd, other members of the herd may also contract the disease since they eat the same feed. Moreover, if the neural tissues, such as brain and spinal cord, of previously infected cows make it into the feed chain, then other cows could contract the disease. Despite the 1993 case of mad cow disease, Canadian officials did not impose a ban on the use of rendered cattle material in cattle feed until 1997.

After the 1993 incident, the Canadian government destroyed any cow imported from Britain between 1982 and 1990 to reduce the risk of further cases. In total, 363 animals were destroyed, including any offspring of the cattle, and their owners compensated.

Mad cow disease strikes the US

Mad cow disease struck the US on December 22, 2003, when US officials announced that a four-year-old Holstein cow from a diary farm in Mabton, Washington, tested positive for bovine spongiform encephalopathy (BSE). The cow was considered a "downer" because it was unable to walk, and the Moses Lake plant, following federally mandated procedures, removed the brain and spinal cord for further testing and kept it apart from the meat.

The Holstein was slaughtered along with 20 other head of cattle at a Moses Lake, Washington, meatpacking plant and quickly turned into hamburger that was distributed to retailers in eight states and one territory: Alaska, California, Guam, Hawaii, Idaho, Montana, Nevada, Oregon, and Washington state. A day after the confirmation of BSE, the USDA ordered a recall of all of the 10,410 pounds of meat made at the plant on the day the infected cow was slaughtered. Unfortunately, by then much of the meat had already been consumed by humans.

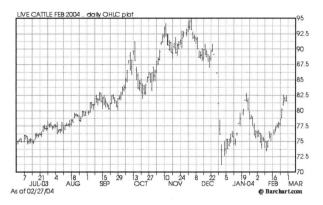

LIVE CATTLE FEB 2004 .. daily OHLC plot
As of 02/27/04   @ Barchart.com

Cattle prices initially plunge

Cattle prices quickly plunged once the news emerged that mad cow disease was found in the cow in Washington state. More than 50 countries, including Japan, South Korea, and Mexico, all top US beef importers, banned imports of US beef following the December 2003 announcement, threatening an export trade valued at up to $3.8 billion per year. In the matter of a week, February live cattle futures prices plunged by nearly 20 cents per pound or more than 20%. The cattle futures markets were locked limit down for several consecutive sessions.

The BSE announcement had collateral effects in markets other than cattle and beef prices. Corn, a staple in the cattle diet, dropped due to fears that a large-scale slaughter of US cattle might be necessary, thus reducing the need for corn feed. At the same time, soybean prices were boosted by expectations that further restrictions on the use of cattle byproducts in the feed for other animals would boost the need for soybeans to add protein to animal feed. Prices were supported for beef-alternatives such as pork and poultry.

The shares of publicly traded companies that process beef or own restaurants with beef as a mainstay, such as McDonald's Corp., dropped as well. Companies and manufacturers of large farm equipment also saw stock prices fall. Companies that process alternatives to beef or sell diagnostic tests to detect BSE saw a gain in their stocks. Meat processing and packaging plants, such as Tyson Foods (with 49% of its business in beef), Cargill Inc., and Swift foods, began laying off workers and reducing the hours and shifts of thousands of workers. Up to 50,000 jobs in various related industries are in jeopardy if the import bans remain in place.

LIVE CATTLE NEAREST FUTURES .. weekly OHLC plot
As of 03/15/04   @ Barchart.com

Despite the initial panic, cattle prices by March 2004 were able recover more than one-third of their initial losses, as seen in the nearby nearest-futures chart of live cattle. The partial recovery in prices was due mainly to the fact that US consumers, who buy about 90% of the beef produced in the US, have maintained their strong consumption demand for US beef. With USDA assurances that US beef is safe to eat and promises for more extensive testing at processing plants this year, consumers are showing confidence in the government's ability to police the food supply and are continuing to buy beef, thus preventing a melt-down in the US beef industry.

Most of the 2.6 billion pounds of US beef that was marked for export will remain here, but the supply glut of beef hasn't necessarily translated into substantially lower retail beef prices in stores and restaurants. Last year's record prices for US beef were largely offset by grocers and restaurants that didn't fully pass along their higher beef costs to consumers and therefore may not be inclined to pass along their savings this year.

The US beef industry in 2003 enjoyed a sharp rally in cattle prices, thus providing a price buffer once mad cow disease hit. One of the main reasons for the rally in US cattle prices in 2003 was the discovery of mad cow disease in Alberta, Canada, in May 2003, which prompted the US to ban all imports of Canadian cattle, shrinking US supplies of beef. The US was a big importer of Canadian beef, importing some 1.7 million Canadian cattle in 2002, most of which ended up at meatpackers. Cattle prices in 2003 were also boosted by drought in some areas of the Midwest and Great Plains, which forced US ranchers to shrink the size of their herds due to thinning pastures and underweight cattle. Moreover, consumer demand increased in 2003 for beef due to low-carb, high protein diet trends.

How can the US recover from its first mad cow episode?

Efforts to recover from mad cow disease in the US fall into several categories. Progress in these areas may eventually convince Japan and other countries to drop their import ban on US cattle, and for US consumers to be fully confident in the safety of the beef supply. So far, only Mexico has eased its ban on US beef, allowing in certain types of processed beef.

Tracking system – US investigators determined that the mad cow found Washington state was born in Alberta, Canada, in April 1997, where it most likely ate contaminated feed before being sold 2 years later to a US dairy farm along with a group of 80 other dairy cattle. US federal officials were able to locate and identify only 27 of the 80 cows from the group due to the lack of a national cattle-identification system, as is used in Canada. The USDA has been dragging its feed on considering the possibility of a national cattle-identification system due to the price tag and opposition from the cattle industry. Yet a tracking system would allow quick identification of any future mad cows, the likely source of their infection, and their herd mates.

Slaughter-house rules – Since the mad cow discovery, the USDA has decided to ban cattle that are unable to walk from the food supply. The USDA has also banned for human food the most infectious parts of cattle by requiring the removal of brains, spinal cords, and intestines from older cows at slaughter. This will provide at least a first line of defense that the sickest cows won't make it into the US food chain.

Feed restrictions – Immediately after the discovery of mad cow in December 2003, the US Food and Drug Administration (FDA), which has responsibility for regulating animal feed and pet food, banned the use of cow blood as a milk-supplement for calves. This was due to the fact that studies have suggested that blood may also be infectious. The FDA is currently leaning toward banning the use of ruminant blood and blood products, as well as poultry litter, which could contain currently banned cattle proteins, and human "plate waste," which consists of food discarded after human use in restaurants. *Ruminants* are animals such as cows and sheep whose stomachs include four chambers. In 1997, the FDA banned the use of ruminant proteins in feed for other ruminants. The US government has not adopted a blanket ban on the use of cattle or ruminant by-products in the feed for all livestock and pets. Through BSE-contaminated pet food, cats have proven to be susceptible to a feline-version of BSE.

There are clearly risks in BSE-type diseases jumping from animal to animal and to humans, and for the diseases to mutate in the process. As mentioned earlier, BSE is thought to have developed when cattle were fed feed contaminated with scrapie-infected sheep remains, meaning scrapie may have transmutated into BSE. Because of the possibility of transmutations, the safest course of action would be to simply have a total ban on the use of cattle by-products in the feed for any type of animal. So far, the FDA has stated that they want a better handle on the BSE risk situation before it considers any further feed restrictions.

Testing – Prior to the outbreak of mad cow disease in the US, the US government was testing 20,000 cows out of the 35 million cows slaughtered each year (i.e., 1 out of every 1,700, or 0.06 of one percent). Immediately after the mad cow discovery, the USDA boosted its target testing number to 40,000 cows displaying the basic symptoms of BSE at slaughterhouses. Recently, the USDA announced a new, one-time plan to test more than 221,000 cattle beginning on June 1, 2004 and lasting 12 to 18 months. The tests will target the cattle that exhibit coordination problems, have died for unknown reasons, or show symptoms of nervous system disorders. The USDA estimates that this group totals 446,000, or 1.3% of the US cattle slaughtered each year. In addition, 40,000 cattle over 30 months old that appear healthy at the time of slaughter will also be tested. This one-time testing program is not designed to ensure that US beef is BSE-free, but to simply determine the statistical prevalence of the disease in the US.

This is far short of Japan's demands that testing be done on all US cattle. Japan requires BSE testing for every cow slaughtered in its country, but that is easier for Japan since Japan slaughters only 1.3 million cattle per year versus 35 million in the US. Since the US is not likely to expand testing to all cattle anytime soon, Japan has indicated that it may settle for allowing the import of cattle that have been tested for BSE.

To help with the magnitude of new tests, the USDA plans to certify a network of state and university laboratories to handle mad cow testing. However, the USDA continues to ban testing by outside private laboratories. The USDA has expressed concern that any false positives might cause cattle prices to crash, upset overseas customers, and cause additional US consumer concern about beef safety. How-

ever, critics charge that the USDA is simply trying to preserve its bureaucratic turf and is moving too slowly. Several US companies have expressed their desire to test every cow that goes through their meat-packing plants, but the USDA has gone as far as to warn that anyone testing without its approval could face criminal charges.

Consumer awareness – Although danger to the public of contracting variant Creutzfeldt-Jacob disease through mad cow disease is low, consumers can decrease their risks even further by avoiding any material that comes from the head as well as any meat that is taken from close to the spinal column or that contains bone that is part of the spinal cord (e.g., like T-bone). Experts also note that there may be risks in pizza toppings, taco fillings, hot dogs, salami, bologna and other products that contain ground beef and beef from machinery that squeezes out bits of meat that cling to the spinal column and other bones. The FDA also reminds the public that cooking meat will not kill mad cow disease if the meat is infected.

UK experience with mad cow

The UK is ground zero for the mad cow problem, meaning the UK provides important lessons for the US on what to expect from the disease. The UK outbreak occurred because calves in the UK were fed BSE-contaminated cattle meat-and-bone meal as a source of protein. The UK mad cow epidemic peaked in 1993, and in a decade's time, caused the eventual destruction of 3.7 million British cattle. Before the infected herds were slaughtered and the outbreak was curbed, approximately 750,000 infected British cows entered the human food chain as hamburgers, sausages, and other meat products.

In 1996, Great Britain banned the most infective portions of a cow, brain and spinal cord material, from the human food supply in order to prevent further animal-to-human transmission of mad cow disease. It also banned the use of meat-and-bone meal in animal feed. Britain is still in the final stages of its multiyear BSE epidemic, with 147 animals confirmed infected with mad cow disease in 2003.

To date, a total of 139 Britons have died of variant Creutzfeldt-Jacob disease. The disease seems to have peaked and is possibly on the decline with 28 deaths reported in 2000, 17 deaths in 2002, and 18 deaths in 2003. The number of British vCJD cases could increase once again in the future because it is not clear whether the disease incubates in some people longer than in others. Recently, it was reported that a British man died from vCJD after receiving a blood transfusion from an infected donor who also died of vCJD. On the brighter side, the loss of human life was much less than early predictions that up to 500,000 deaths could occur.

The British beef industry sustained billions of dollars of losses as countries around the world banned imports of all British beef and beef products. The US banned British beef in 1989 and has not yet lifted its ban. However, the UK beef industry is slowly recovering. UK consumers are becoming more confident about beef safety and Britain's McDonald's franchises, Burger Kings, and steakhouses are back to doing brisk business. In July 2003, Great Britain's Food Standards Agency recommended that the government lift a ban preventing cattle older than 30 months from entering the food chain. The ban had been ordered because BSE tends to show in older cows and the incubation period is believed to be 2 to 8 years. As a precaution, the agency has recommended that all older cows must first test negative for BSE before they can be sold as beef, a practice currently followed by other European countries.

Mad cow disease may emerge again in the US

Although only one mad cow has so far been found in the US, the scope of any mad cow problem in the US is presently unknown because so few cows are tested for BSE in the US. The mad cow that was found in Washington State was found more by accident than by any statistically accurate testing program since the US at that time only tested 0.06 of one percent of cows slaughtered in a year. The new testing program will be an improvement but it will take up to a year to determine the scope of any mad cow problem in the US. The markets need to be on guard that the stepped-up testing program may find additional cases of mad cow disease in the US.

Richard W. Asplund, CRB Chief Economist, March 2004

Volume U.S.

U.S. Futures Volume Highlights
2003 in Comparison with 2002

2003 Rank	Top 50 Contracts Traded in 2003	2003 Contracts	%	2002 Contracts	%	2002 Rank
1	Eurodollars (3-month), CME	208,771,164	33.38%	202,080,832	32.31%	1
2	E-Mini S&P 500 Index, CME	161,176,639	25.77%	115,741,691	18.51%	2
3	T-Notes (10-year), CBT	146,745,281	23.46%	95,786,299	15.32%	3
4	T-Notes (5-year), CBT	73,746,445	11.79%	50,512,085	8.08%	6
5	E-Mini NASDAQ 100, CME	67,888,938	10.86%	54,491,180	8.71%	5
6	T-Bonds (30-year), CBT	63,521,507	10.16%	56,082,284	8.97%	4
7	Crude Oil, NYMEX	45,436,931	7.27%	45,679,468	7.30%	7
8	S&P 500 Index, CME	20,175,462	3.23%	23,699,667	3.79%	9
9	Corn, CBT	19,118,715	3.06%	18,132,447	2.90%	10
10	Natural Gas, NYMEX	19,037,118	3.04%	24,357,792	3.89%	8
11	Soybeans, CBT	17,545,714	2.81%	14,475,100	2.31%	11
12	Gold (100 oz.), COMEX Div. of NYMEX	12,235,689	1.96%	9,018,183	1.44%	14
13	Heating Oil #2, NYMEX	11,581,670	1.85%	10,695,202	1.71%	13
14	Euro FX, CME	11,193,922	1.79%	6,986,600	1.12%	16
15	Unleaded Regular Gas, NYMEX	11,172,050	1.79%	10,979,736	1.76%	12
16	Mini ($5) Dow Jones Industrial Index, CBT	10,859,690	1.74%	2,224,757	0.36%	36
17	Federal Funds (30-day), CBT	8,271,726	1.32%	6,285,789	1.01%	20
18	Soybean Meal, CBT	8,158,445	1.30%	7,174,507	1.15%	15
19	TRAKRS Commodity, CME	7,424,763	1.19%			
20	Soybean Oil, CBT	7,417,340	1.19%	6,816,483	1.09%	18
21	Sugar #11, NYBOT	7,140,724	1.14%	6,173,756	0.99%	21
22	Wheat, CBT	6,967,416	1.11%	6,872,891	1.10%	17
23	Japanese Yen, CME	6,085,209	0.97%	4,394,982	0.70%	24
24	TRAKRS Gold, CME	6,065,013	0.97%			
25	Live Cattle, CME	4,436,089	0.71%	3,851,736	0.62%	25
26	NASDAQ 100, CME	4,421,221	0.71%	4,903,287	0.78%	22
27	Dow Jones Industrial Index, CBOT	4,416,302	0.71%	6,485,501	1.04%	19
28	T-Notes (2-year), CBT	4,415,906	0.71%	3,203,855	0.51%	26
29	Canadian Dollar, CME	4,219,618	0.67%	3,134,963	0.50%	28
30	Silver (5,000 oz), COMEX Div. of NYMEX	4,111,190	0.66%	3,135,564	0.50%	27
31	E-Mini Russell 2000 Index, CME	3,878,935	0.62%	859,885	0.14%	45
32	Swiss Franc, CME	3,596,658	0.58%	2,830,738	0.45%	29
33	Coffee C, NYBOT	3,211,031	0.51%	2,718,508	0.43%	32
34	High Grade Copper, COMEX Div. of NYMEX	3,089,270	0.49%	2,807,286	0.45%	30
35	Cotton #2, NYBOT	3,035,992	0.49%	2,327,960	0.37%	35
36	Wheat, KCBT	2,632,033	0.42%	2,738,536	0.44%	31
37	British Pound, CME	2,595,155	0.41%	2,166,469	0.35%	37
38	TRAKRS Select 50 Index, CME	2,436,699	0.39%	4,614,721	0.74%	23
39	Henry Hub Swap, NYMEX	2,356,600	0.38%			
40	Lean Hogs, CME	2,164,155	0.35%	1,931,260	0.31%	39
41	Cocoa, NYBOT	2,128,206	0.34%	2,079,980	0.33%	38
42	Mexican Peso, CME	2,123,623	0.34%	1,354,256	0.22%	40
43	LMC TRAKRS Index, CME	1,803,316	0.29%	2,697,494	0.43%	33
44	Australian Dollar, CME	1,609,289	0.26%	1,049,220	0.17%	43
45	E-Mini S&P 400 Index, CME	1,417,513	0.23%			
46	TRAKRS Euro Currency Index, CME	1,196,525	0.19%			
47	LIBOR (1-month), CME	1,138,358	0.18%	1,110,934	0.18%	42
48	Wheat, MGE	1,066,489	0.17%	1,199,149	0.19%	41
49	Interest Rate Swap (10-year), CBT	1,038,777	0.17%	661,527	0.11%	48
50	TRAKRS Index, CME	994,756	0.16%	2,469,467	0.39%	34
	Top 50 Contracts	1,027,270,647		838,994,027*		
	Contracts Below the Top 50	15,698,017	1.51%	12,316,360	1.45%	
	TOTAL	**1,042,968,664**	**100.00%**	**851,310,387**	**100.00%**	

* For 2002 Top 50 contracts totaled 842,704,977 including 5 contracts that are not among 2003's Top 50.

U.S. Futures Volume Highlights
2003 in Comparison with 2002

2003 RANK	EXCHANGE	2003 CONTRACTS	%	2002 CONTRACTS	%	2002 RANK
1	Chicago Mercantile Exchange (CME)	530,989,007	50.91%	444,537,987	52.22%	1
2	Chicago Board of Trade (CBT)	373,669,290	35.83%	276,316,047	32.46%	2
3	New York Mercantile Exchange (NYMEX)**	111,789,658	10.72%	107,359,719	12.61%	3
4	New York Board of Trade (NYBOT)*	18,822,048	1.80%	16,272,144	1.91%	4
5	Kansas City Board of Trade (KCBT)	2,634,424	0.25%	2,755,949	0.32%	5
6	OneChicago	1,619,194	0.16%	184,081	0.02%	9
7	BrokerTec Futures Exchange	1,356,825	0.13%	2,109,670	0.25%	6
8	Minneapolis Grain Exchange (MGE)	1,087,020	0.10%	1,201,543	0.14%	7
9	NASDAQ LIFFE Markets	858,900	0.08%	90,091	0.01%	10
10	MidAmerica Commodity Exchange	142,298	0.01%	483,156	0.06%	8
	TOTAL	**1,042,968,664**	**100.00%**	**851,310,387**	**100.00%**	

** Includes Comex Division.

* Includes the New York Futures Exchange, New York Cotton Exchange and Coffee, Sugar and Cocoa Exchange.

BrokerTec Futures Exchange (BTEX)

FUTURE	CONTRACT UNIT	2003	2002	2001	2000	1999
30-Year T-Bonds	100,000 USD	374,115	870,832	36,293		
10-Year T-Notes	100,000 USD	654,800	764,667	35,342		
5-Year T-Notes	100,000 USD	327,910	474,171	17,836		
Total		**1,356,825**	**2,109,670**	**89,471**		

Chicago Board of Trade (CBT)

FUTURE	CONTRACT UNIT	2003	2002	2001	2000	1999
Wheat	5,000 bu	6,967,416	6,872,891	6,801,541	6,407,531	6,570,025
Mini Wheat	1,000 bu	22,288				
Corn	5,000 bu	19,118,715	18,132,447	16,728,748	17,185,442	15,724,845
Mini Corn	1,000 bu	53,404				
Oats	5,000 bu	318,898	415,140	440,854	402,190	371,406
Soybeans	5,000 bu	17,545,714	14,475,100	12,150,369	12,627,950	12,481,947
Mini Soybeans	1,000 bu	250,447				
Soybean Oil	60,000 lbs	7,417,340	6,816,483	6,034,325	5,369,903	5,663,895
Soybean Meal	100 tons	8,158,445	7,174,507	6,743,772	6,317,988	6,326,897
Rice	200,000 lbs	265,234	193,723	121,661	169,133	139,592
Mini Silver	1,000 oz	34,804	7,723	1,087		
Mini Gold	33.2 troy oz	145,173	9,024	717		
T-Bonds (30-year)	100,000 USD	63,521,507	56,082,284	58,579,290	62,750,843	90,042,282
Mini T-Bonds (30-year)	50,000 USD	15,707	10,009	4,383		
T-Notes (10-year)	100,000 USD	146,745,281	95,786,299	57,585,828	46,700,538	34,045,758
Mini T-Notes (10-year)	50,000 USD	49	96	213		
T-Notes (5-year)	100,000 USD	73,746,445	50,512,085	31,122,401	23,331,981	16,983,812
T-Notes (2-year)	200,000 USD	4,415,906	3,203,855	2,389,165	1,477,253	1,047,348
Agency Debt (10-year)	100,000 USD	89,342	486,300	1,189,389	1,334,340	
Agency Debt (5-year)	100,000 USD	2,000				
Mini Eurodollars	500,000 USD	543	1,541	483		
Interest Rate Swap (10-year)	100,000 USD	1,038,777	661,527	58,884		
Interest Rate Swap (5-year)	100,000 USD	110,275	53,030			
Municipal Note Index (10-year)	100,000 USD	94,541	8,678			
30-Day Federal Funds	5,000,000 USD	8,271,726	6,285,789	4,686,695	1,443,665	1,023,716
Dow Jones Industrial Index	10 USD x Index	4,416,302	6,485,501	4,901,949	3,572,428	3,896,086
Mini ($5) Dow Jones Industrial Index	5 USD x Index	10,859,690	2,224,757			
Dow Jones AIGCI Index	100 x Index	43,321	14,782	4,292		
Total		**373,669,290**	**276,316,119**	**209,988,002**	**189,662,407**	**195,147,279**

Chicago Mercantile Exchange (CME)

Future	Contract Unit	2003	2002	2001	2000	1999
Lean Hogs	40,000 lbs	2,164,155	1,931,260	2,018,339	2,111,807	2,358,096
Pork Bellies, Frozen	40,000 lbs	161,329	152,054	196,359	309,576	368,309
Butter	40,000 lbs	8,544	5,897	1,374	5,366	3,354
Nonfat Dry Milk	44,000 lbs	230	12	48		
Class III Milk	200,000 lbs	191,351	103,375			
Class IV Milk	200,000 lbs	137	4,714	6,513	4,868	
Live Cattle	40,000 lbs	4,436,089	3,851,736	4,279,273	3,681,512	3,839,548
Feeder Cattle	44,000 lbs	704,852	585,517	616,988	582,279	650,071

VOLUME U.S.

Chicago Mercantile Exchange (CME) (Continued)

Future	Contract Unit	2003	2002	2001	2000	1999
Random Lumber	80,000 bd ft	223,891	164,423	206,840	221,168	287,856
T-Bills (90-day)	1,000,000 USD	3,974	4,619	31,113	16,763	41,260
Eurodollar (3-month)	1,000,000 USD	208,771,164	202,080,832	184,015,496	108,114,998	93,418,498
Euroyen	1,000,000,000 JPY	179,573	231,723	494,519	1,079,074	945,419
EuroYen LIBOR	100,000,000 JPY	1,650	2,302	17,474	7,924	3,869
2-Year SWAP		6,640	5,671			
5-Year SWAP		43,616	13,301			
10-Year SWAP		40,030	7,234			
28-Day Mexican TIIE	1,200,000 MXN	3,506				
One Month LIBOR	3,000,000 USD	1,138,358	110,934	1,315,593	896,269	843,054
British Pound	62,500	2,595,155	2,166,469	2,078,834	2,029,542	2,738,600
Brazilian Real	100,000	277	4	3,937	2,067	59,104
Canadian Dollar	100,000	4,219,618	3,134,963	2,961,680	2,460,134	2,573,762
CME $ Index	1,000 USD x Index	457				
Euro FX	125,000	11,193,922	6,986,600	5,898,429	4,267,408	3,002,453
E-Mini Euro FX	62,500	16,860	7,252	13,244	29,942	1,775
Japanese Yen	12,500,000	6,085,209	4,394,982	4,552,599	3,965,377	5,935,843
E-Mini Japanese Yen	6,250,000	2,740	2,557	2,023	6,166	1,072
Mexican Peso	500,000	2,123,623	1,354,256	1,069,327	1,117,304	1,143,641
New Zealand Dollar	100,000	120,235	54,148	21,766	32,862	42,646
Norwegian Krone	227,000	388	303			
Russian Ruble		4,420				
South African Rand	500,000	73,542	55,275	65,327	40,701	51,762
Swedish Krona	193,600	4	1			
Swiss Franc	125,000	3,596,658	2,830,738	2,901,939	3,241,207	4,114,824
Australian Dollar	100,000	1,609,289	1,049,220	832,707	749,555	861,023
Australian Dollar / Canadian Dollar	200,000 AUD	220	16			
Australian Dollar / Japanese Yen	200,000 AUD	94	16			
British Pound / Japanese Yen	125,000 GBP	894	519			
British Pound / Swiss Franc	125,000 GBP	103	263			
Canadian Dollar / Japanese Yen		102				
Swiss Franc / Japanese Yen	250,000 CHF	247	54			
Euro / Australian Dollar	125,000 EUR	554	306			
Euro / Canadian Dollar	125,000 EUR	247	5			
Euro / British Pound	125,000 EUR	65,696	7,166	127	973	3,332
Euro / Japanese Yen	125,000 EUR	161,600	58,768	98,970	4,289	2,018
Euro / Swiss Franc	125,000 EUR	1,794	949	182	2	398
Nikkei 225	5 USD x Index	765,463	571,241	476,274	455,298	513,848
S&P 500 Index	500 USD x Index	20,175,462	23,699,667	22,478,152	22,467,859	27,003,387
E-Mini S&P	50 USD x Index	161,176,639	115,741,691	39,434,843	19,211,355	10,953,551
S&P 500 Barra Growth Index	500 USD x Index	5,119	7,756	12,408	16,733	11,015
S&P 500 Barra Value Index	500 USD x Index	14,131	17,238	24,319	31,121	26,698
S&P Financial Sector Index	125 USD x Index	4,093	5,052			
S&P Technology-Telecomm Sector Index	125 USD x Index	60	1,410			
S&P MidCap 400 Index	500 USD x Index	302,817	387,800	378,526	332,438	326,117
S&P SmallCap 600 Index	200 USD x Index	1,635	191			
E-mini S&P SmallCap 600 Index	100 USD x Index	1,417,513	343,087			
Fortune E-50 Index	20 USD x Index	32	392	3,694	19,838	
NASDAQ 100 Index	500 USD x Index	4,421,221	4,903,287	5,586,750	5,094,042	2,360,938
E-Mini NASDAQ 100 Index	20 USD x Index	67,888,938	54,491,180	32,550,233	10,817,277	682,059
E-Mini NASDAQ Composite Index	20 USD x Index	6,444				
Russell 2000 Index	500 USD x Index	655,778	843,479	714,259	508,726	363,041
E-Mini Russell 2000 Index	100 USD x Index	3,878,935	859,885	26,012		
Russell 1000 Index	100 USD x Index	14,941				
TRAKRS Select 50 Index	1 USD x Index	2,436,069	4,614,721			
LMC TRAKRS Index	1 USD x Index	1,803,316	2,697,494			
TRAKRS Commodity	1 USD x Index	7,424,763				
TRAKRS Euro Currency	1 USD x Index	1,196,525				
TRAKRS Gold	1 USD x Index	6,065,013				
TRAKRS Index	1 USD x Index	994,756	2,469,467			
HDD Weather	100 x HDD	6,058	2,334	131	67	336
HDD Seasonal Weather	100 x HDD	225				
CDD Weather	100 x CDD	8,176	1,831		20	
Euro HDD Seasonal Weather	100 x EHDD	375				
Goldman Sachs Commodity Index	250 USD x Index	371,473	518,323	479,646	1,002,673	926,933
Total		**530,989,007**	**443,537,987**	**315,971,885**	**195,106,470**	**168,013,693**

Kansas City Board of Trade (KCBT)

FUTURE	CONTRACT UNIT	2003	2002	2001	2000	1999
Wheat	5,000 bu	2,632,033	2,738,536	2,357,004	2,427,950	2,321,059
Value Line Index	100 USD x Index	2,391	17,370	17,773	9,954	1,264
Total		**2,634,424**	**2,755,949**	**2,375,133**	**2,446,607**	**2,375,271**

MidAmerica Commodity Exchange (MidAm)

FUTURE	CONTRACT UNIT	2003	2002	2001	2000	1999
Wheat	1,000 bu	5,580	74,454	52,285	77,477	132,392
Corn	1,000 bu	39,555	107,388	118,574	270,890	291,186
Soybeans	1,000 bu	97,163	299,694	281,451	572,672	651,268
Total		**142,298**	**483,156**	**582,872**	**1,649,549**	**2,433,894**

Minneapolis Grain Exchange (MGE)

FUTURE	CONTRACT UNIT	2003	2002	2001	2000	1999
Wheat	5,000 bu	1,066,489	1,199,149	967,666	955,659	1,119,812
Hard Winter Wheat Index	5,000 bu	16,535				
National Corn Index	5,000 bu	3,996	2,253			
Total		**1,087,020**	**1,201,543**	**968,699**	**958,420**	**1,134,945**

New York Board of Trade (NYBOT)*

FUTURE	CONTRACT UNIT	2003	2002	2001	2000	1999
Coffee 'C'	37,500 lbs	3,211,031	2,718,508	2,199,371	2,134,961	2,659,233
Mini Coffee	12,500 lbs	332	784			
Sugar #11	112,000 lbs	7,140,724	6,173,756	5,150,329	5,933,850	5,911,299
Sugar #14	112,000 lbs	133,811	141,017	116,733	122,976	138,661
Cocoa	10 metric tons	2,128,206	2,079,980	2,005,817	2,110,048	1,868,036
Cotton #2	50,000 lbs	3,035,992	2,327,960	2,259,665	2,597,757	2,448,087
Orange Juice Frozen Concentrate	15,000 lbs	652,715	577,757	577,496	712,204	793,882
US Dollar / Canadian Dollar	200,000 USD	2,458	2,581	1,854	2,825	3,406
US Dollar / Swedish Krona	200,000 USD	12,377	2,983	2,564	2,423	
US Dollar / Norwegian Krone	200,000 USD	11,350	1,178	746	58	
US Dollar / Swiss Franc	200,000 USD	26,119	11,159	10,737	16,671	25,523
US Dollar / Japanese Yen	200,000 USD	43,351	58,583	16,338	30,353	41,632
US Dollar / British Pound	125,000 GBP	40,467	31,956	17,379	14,202	16,571
US Dollar / Czech Koruna		527				
US Dollar / Hungarian Forint		1,120				
US Dollar / South African Rand	100,000 USD	31,272	11,081	4,793	9,984	10,859
Canadian Dollar / Japanese Yen	200,000 CAD	16,440	8,593	18,865	5,380	
Australian Dollar / US Dollar	100,000 AUD	6,061	8,043	2,640	44,307	40,711
Australian Dollar / Canadian Dollar	200,000 AUD	15,104	5,181	17,886	2,064	
Australian Dolar / New Zealand Dollar	200,000 AUD	16,357	9,525	12,673	15,333	26,088
New Zealand Dollar / US Dollar	100,000 NZD	26,395	13,289	24,426	23,866	70,717
Australian Dollar / Japanese Yen	200,000 AUD	41,468	21,870	31,250	32,390	18,538
British Pound / Swiss franc	125,000 GBP	20,503	13,204	21,379	11,061	28,789
British Pound / Japanese Yen	125,000 GBP	52,145	30,925	42,651	85,530	69,207
Swiss Franc / Japanese Yen	200,000 CHF	22,193	9,038	15,196	13,662	20,988
Euro		60,926	81,998	64,431	97,032	85,211
Euro / US Dollar, Small		5,365	2,560	2,299	6,508	2,337
Euro / Australian Dollar	100,000 EUR	30,466	14,635	17,006	7,674	
Euro / Canadian Dollar	100,000 EUR	49,890	17,731	11,712	8,396	
Euro / Czech Koruna		2,774				
Euro / Hungarian Forint		24				
Euro / Japanese Yen	100,000 EUR	346,751	337,756	294,733	278,119	192,987
Euro / Swedish Krona	100,000 EUR	49,977	45,757	30,354	54,076	101,605
Euro / British Pound	100,000 EUR	117,989	124,485	112,727	159,862	200,560
Euro / Norwegian	100,000 EUR	29,815	17,670	4,488	2,461	10,452
Euro / Swiss Franc	100,000 EUR	133,218	69,057	44,162	69,538	147,650
US Dollar Index	1,000 USD x Index	563,032	411,571	342,948	297,745	356,544
NYSE Composite Index	500 USD x Index	34,021	216,479	217,772	130,984	334,222
Revised NYSE Composite Index	50 USD x Index	7,143				
Russell 1000 Index	500 USD x Index	677,626	646,455	313,318	94,736	161,114
Russell 1000 Growth Index		836				
Russell 1000 Value Index		415				
Russell 2000 Index		10				
Russell 3000 Index		96				
Reuters-CRB Futures Index	500 USD x Index	23,156	14,283	16,878	63,494	88,696
Total*		**18,822,048**	**16,272,144**	**14,034,168**	**15,214,853**	**15,958,237**

NASDAQ LIFFE Markets (NQLX)

FUTURE	CONTRACT UNIT	2003	2002	2001	2000	1999
Single Stock Futures		576,765	72,897			
Exchange Traded Funds		282,135	17,194			
Total		**858,900**	**90,091**			

VOLUME U.S.

New York Mercantile Exchange (NYMEX)

COMEX Division

FUTURE	CONTRACT UNIT	2003	2002	2001	2000	1999
Gold	100 oz	12,235,689	9,018,183	6,785,340	6,643,464	9,575,788
Silver	5,000 oz	4,111,190	3,135,564	2,569,198	3,117,017	4,157,500
High Grade Copper	25,000 lbs	3,089,270	2,807,286	2,856,641	2,778,124	2,852,962
Aluminum	44,000 lbs	107,490	74,000	43,089	46,099	27,978
Total		**19,543,639**	**15,035,033**	**12,258,659**	**12,626,367**	**16,645,688**

NYMEX Division

FUTURE	CONTRACT UNIT	2003	2002	2001	2000	1999
Palladium	100 oz	95,613	41,053	25,925	50,766	75,394
Platinum	50 oz	268,305	219,771	205,969	320,924	567,268
No. 2 Heating Oil, NY	1,000 bbl	11,581,670	10,695,202	9,264,472	9,631,376	9,200,703
Unleaded Gasoline, NY	1,000 bbl	11,172,050	10,979,736	9,223,510	8,645,182	8,701,216
Crude Oil	1,000 bbl	45,436,931	45,679,468	37,530,568	36,882,692	37,860,064
E-Mini Crude Oil	400 bbl	277,411	210,228			
Brent Crude Oil	1,000 bbl	30	1,516	49,565		
Propane	42,000 gal	14,710	12,826	10,566	26,075	37,544
Natural Gas	10,000 MMBTU	19,037,118	24,357,792	16,468,355	17,875,013	19,165,096
E-Mini Natural Gas	4,000 MMBTU	115,502	67,981			
Central Appalachian Coal (CAPP)	1,500 tons	1,586	4,124	2,209		
PJM Monthly		142,859				
Henry Hub Swap		2,356,600				
WTI Crude Oil Calendar Swap		33,785				
NYISO A		88,826	1,268			
NYISO G		52,996	4,848			
NYISO J		10,245	758			
PJM Daily		30,221				
PJM Weekly		3,963				
Coal		3,649				
Columbia Gulf Onshore Basis		3,526				
TETCO ELA Basis		4,872				
ANR - Oklahoma Basis		8,235	856			
Dominion Trans - Appalachian Basis		95,595	1,898			
MichCon Basis		81,074	856			
WAHA Basis		134,632				
NGPL Louisiana Basis		2,260				
NGPL Mid-Continent		32,580	1,666			
NGPL TEX/OK Basis		13,418	2,072			
Northern Natural Gas Ventura Basis		65,843	5,525			
Northern Natural Gas Demarcation Basis		35,901	4,950			
Permian Basis		211,397	1,340			
PG&E Citygate Basis		110,812	186			
PG&E Malin Basis		241,769	11,564			
Sumas Basis		172,313	5,890			
TCO Basis		103,343	3,610			
Texas Eastern Zone M-3 Basis		178,591	7,702			
TETCO STX Basis		13,132				
Transco Zone 3 Basis Swap		2,750				
NY Harbor Heating Oil Calendar Swap		2,355				
Gasoline vs. Heating Oil Swap		150				
CIG Rockies		7,026				
NY Harbor Resid Fuel 1.0% Sulfur Swap		375				
Total		**92,246,019**	**92,324,686**	**72,781,325**	**73,461,273**	**75,769,318**
Total**		**111,789,658**	**107,359,719**	**85,039,984**	**86,087,640**	**92,415,006**

ONECHICAGO

FUTURE	CONTRACT UNIT	2003	2002	2001	2000	1999
Single Stock Futures		1,488,573	151,878			
Exchange Traded Funds		127,424	32,203			
Dow Jones MicroSector Index		3,197				
Total		**1,619,194**	**184,081**			

Total US Futures Volume

		2003	2002	2001	2000	1999
TOTAL FUTURES		1,042,968,664	851,310,387	629,212,715	491,451,073	477,919,308
PERCENT CHANGE		22.51%	35.30%	28.03%	2.83%	-5.02%

* Includes the New York Futures Exchange, New York Cotton Exchange and Coffee, Sugar and Cocoa Exchange.

** Includes Commodity Exchange, Inc.

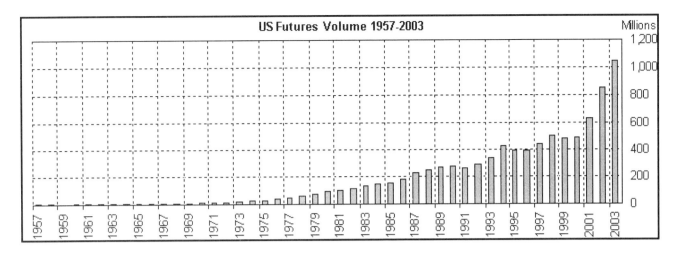

Options Traded on U.S. Securities Exchanges Volume Highlights
2003 in Comparison with 2002

2003 RANK	EXCHANGE	2003 CONTRACTS	%	2002 CONTRACTS	%	2002 RANK
1	Chicago Board of Options Exchange	283,946,495	31.28%	267,616,496	34.29%	1
2	International Stock Exchange	244,968,190	26.98%	152,399,279	19.53%	3
3	American Stock Exchange	180,074,778	19.84%	186,039,445	23.84%	2
4	Philadelphia Stock Exchange	112,705,597	12.41%	88,955,247	11.40%	4
5	Pacific Stock Exchange	86,152,637	9.49%	85,426,649	10.95%	5
	TOTAL	907,847,697	100.00%	780,437,116	100.00%	

Options Traded on U.S. Futures Exchanges Volume Highlights
2003 in Comparison with 2002

2003 RANK	EXCHANGE	2003 CONTRACTS	%	2002 CONTRACTS	%	2002 RANK
1	Chicago Mercantile Exchange (CME)	109,220,627	49.27%	113,909,833	53.44%	2
2	Chicago Board of Trade (CBT)	80,521,459	36.32%	67,566,482	31.70%	1
3	New York Mercantile Exchange (NYMEX)	25,435,781	11.47%	26,384,716	12.38%	3
4	New York Board of Trade (NYBOT)	6,010,110	2.71%	4,656,335	2.18%	4
5	Kansas City Board of Trade (KCBT)	465,381	0.21%	570,887	0.27%	5
6	Minneapolis Grain Exchange (MGE)	46,711	0.02%	61,226	0.03%	6
7	MidAmerica Commodity Exchange (MidAm)	0	0.00%	97	0.00%	7
	TOTAL	221,700,069	100.00%	213,149,576	100.00%	

** Includes Commodity Exchange, Inc.

* Includes the New York Futures Exchange, New York Cotton Exchange and Coffee, Sugar and Cocoa Exchange.

Options Volume on U.S. Futures Exchange 1999-2003
Chicago Board of Trade (CBT)

Option	Contract Unit	2003	2002	2001	2000	1999
Wheat	5,000 bu	1,788,500	1,773,559	1,714,041	1,563,557	1,516,037
Corn	5,000 bu	4,515,240	5,397,748	4,864,294	5,135,111	4,205,325
Oats	5,000 bu	36,163	90,780	70,218	52,760	56,418
Soybeans	5,000 bu	4,885,399	4,227,445	3,829,236	3,890,510	4,792,245
Soybean Oil	60,000 lbs	665,532	659,302	672,284	490,666	801,367
Soybean Meal	100 tons	546,267	404,351	606,187	657,709	709,194
Rice	200,000 lbs	34,978	35,272	23,233	32,955	48,515
T-Bonds	100,000 USD	15,180,025	15,324,548	13,478,771	17,267,458	34,680,068
T-Notes (10-year)	100,000 USD	41,165,629	31,741,521	19,983,876	10,629,021	9,738,808
T-Notes (5-year)	100,000 USD	9,697,455	7,533,556	4,681,604	3,733,542	2,537,044
T-Notes (2-year)	200,000 USD	11,874	32,468	44,185	3,824	1,780
Interest Rate Swap (10-year)	100,000 USD	1,787	8,453			
Interest Rate Swap (5-year)	100,000 USD	100				
30-Day Federal Funds	5,000,000 USD	1,614,319				
Flexible US T-Bonds		57,442	38,456	38,160	18,781	54,454
Flexible T-Notes (10-year)		56,920	60,577	45,700	24,670	6,150
Flexible T-Notes (5-year)		200	4,225	2,200	12,160	2,593
Dow Jones Industrial Index	10 USD x Index	263,629	234,219	288,364	200,379	229,560
Total		80,521,459	67,566,482	50,345,068	43,866,151	59,413,936

VOLUME U.S.

Chicago Mercantile Exchange (CME)

Option	Contract Unit	2003	2002	2001	2000	1999
Lean Hogs	40,000 lbs	129,227	156,699	171,472	161,931	231,273
Pork Bellies, Frozen	40,000 lbs	7,991	5,595	6,901	29,712	16,780
Butter	50,000 lbs	800	259	38	385	752
Mini BFP Milk	100,000 lbs	1,269	2,107	2,836	263	387
Class III Milk	200,000 lbs	79,901	23,852			
Class IV Milk	200,000 lbs	41	543	1,448	656	
Live Cattle	40,000 lbs	664,291	476,467	688,149	622,590	545,709
Feeder Cattle	44,000 lbs	179,347	121,226	186,247	132,086	130,410
Random Lumber	80,000 bd ft	18,139	14,665	25,752	19,413	24,745
Euroyen	100,000,000 JPY	53	318	2,225	9,756	41,073
Eurodollar (3-month)	1,000,000 USD	100,823,779	105,580,961	88,174,799	28,590,428	24,884,494
One Month LIBOR	3,000,000 USD	4,191	395	2,106	2,236	1,916
British Pound	62,500	156,569	121,443	147,205	174,928	208,921
Canadian Dollar	100,000	206,862	153,329	109,908	75,934	121,933
Japanese Yen	12,500,000	489,123	849,646	839,069	567,896	1,100,130
Mexican Peso	500,000	5,050	5,688	5,331	5,741	8,133
Swiss Franc	125,000	53,766	82,285	119,051	125,360	178,433
Australian Dollar	100,000	42,495	18,098	30,050	10,337	9,509
CME $ Index	1,000 USD x Index	1,000				
Euro FX	125,000 EUR	1,187,819	929,518	655,991	371,737	167,078
Nikkei 225	5 USD x Index	8,564	4,197	3,339	4,270	6,007
S&P 500 Index	500 USD x Index	4,986,456	5,235,388	4,381,924	4,352,249	4,603,946
E-Mini S&P	50 USD x S&P Index	112,864	46,355	21,777	18,814	54,480
S&P MidCap 400 Index	500 USD x Index	780	2,573	4,007	2,911	3,841
NASDAQ 100 Index	500 USD x Index	50,439	71,991	121,895	699,264	225,981
Russell 2000	500 USD x Index	4,048	4,602	10,941	8,047	1,230
CDD Weather	100 x CDD	230	32			
HDD Weather	100 x HDD	501	281			
HDD Seasonal Weather	100 x HDDSW	3,390				
CDD Seasonal Weather	100 x CDDSW	150				
Goldman Sachs Commodity Index	250 USD x Index	1,492	1,318	3,343	3,281	2,573
Total		**109,220,627**	**113,909,833**	**95,740,352**	**36,007,913**	**32,723,766**

New York Board of Trade (NYBOT)**

Option	Contract Unit	2003	2002	2001	2000	1999
Coffee 'C'	37,500 lbs	1,328,081	1,063,090	799,506	909,251	1,369,021
Sugar #11	112,000 lbs	1,690,190	1,380,300	1,305,470	2,027,581	2,275,704
Cocoa	10 metric tons	497,188	743,237	436,295	495,221	364,450
Cotton #2	50,000 lbs	2,157,441	1,171,843	1,025,578	1,027,002	706,589
Orange Juice Frozen Concentrate	15,000 lbs	195,541	175,794	170,756	237,673	351,763
US Dollar Index	500 USD x Index	29,532	28,694	15,365	14,650	11,654
Large Euro / US Dollar		578	69	932	676	7,137
Australian Dollar / Canadian Dollar	200,000 AUD	3	1			
Australian Dollar / Japanese Yen	200,000 AUD	3	2			
Australian Dollar / New Zealand Dollar	200,000 AUD	1				
Australian Dollar / US Dollar	200,000 AUD	10				
Euro / Swedish Krona	100,000 EUR	2	2			
Euro / British Pound	100,000 EUR	253	14	936	1,232	2,228
Euro / Japanese Yen	100,000 EUR	776	104	685	1,492	5,200
British Pound / Japanese Yen	125,000 GBP	209	156	16	0	291
New Zealand Dollar / US Dollar	200,000 NZD	13	3			
US Dollar / Canadian Dollar	200,000 USD	60	140			
US Dollar / South African Rand	100,000 USD	1	600			
US Dollar / Japanese Yen	12,500,000 JPY	112	70	867	0	2,431
US Dollar / Norwegian Krone	200,000 USD	3				
US Dollar / British Pound	125,000 GBP	31				
US Dollar / Swedish Krona	200,000 USD	3	1			
NYSE Composite Index	500 USD x Index	25,320	89,791	78,053	93,912	112,052
Revised NYSE Composite Index	50 USD x Index	18,912				
Russell 1000 Growth Index	500 USD x Index	358				
Russell 1000 Value Index	500 USD x Index	1,578				
Russell 1000 Index	500 USD x Index	61,264	1,449	9,905	48,245	69,990
Russell 2000 Index	500 USD x Index	734				
Reuters-CRB Futures Index	500 USD x Index	1,913	974	891	3,306	8,868
Total**		**6,010,110**	**4,656,335**	**3,857,721**	**4,922,626**	**5,519,619**

Kansas City Board of Trade (KCBT)

Option	Contract Unit	2003	2002	2001	2000	1999
Wheat	5,000 bu	465,381	570,823	24,311	218,052	143,974
Total		465,381	570,887	24,356	218,062	146,105

Minneapolis Grain Exchange (MGEX)

Option	Contract Unit	2003	2002	2001	2000	1999
American Spring Wheat	5,000 bu	39,764	61,086	29,112	41,441	53,246
Hard Winter Wheat Index	5,000 bu	5,773				
National Corn Index	5,000 bu	1,174	140			
Total		46,711	61,226	29,830	42,658	53,870

New York Mercantile Exchange (NYMEX)*

COMEX Division

Option	Contract Unit	2003	2002	2001	2000	1999
Gold	100 oz	4,310,318	1,948,564	1,975,019	2,083,414	2,815,831
Silver	5,000 oz	560,018	530,831	483,386	579,085	725,885
High Grade Copper	25,000 lbs	47,326	37,315	50,826	65,043	160,857
Aluminum	44,000 lbs	2,679				642
Total		4,920,341	2,516,710	2,509,231	2,727,542	3,703,215

NYMEX Division

Option	Contract Unit	2003	2002	2001	2000	1999
Platinum	50 oz	633	456	1,813	7,065	11,146
Heating Oil	42,000 gal	668,859	602,170	704,972	1,385,968	695,558
Heating Oil 1-month CSO		2,430	747			
Heating Oil 2-month CSO		100	275			
Unleaded Gasoline	1,000 bbl	616,245	721,932	1,040,030	1,012,460	600,009
Unleaded Gasoline 1-month CSO		3,465	1,087			
Unleaded Gasoline 2-month CSO		25				
Crude Oil	1,000 bbl	10,237,121	11,460,857	7,726,076	7,460,052	8,161,976
Crude Oil 1-month CSO		164,928	92,603			
Crude Oil 6-month CSO		300	250			
Crude Oil 12-month CSO		825	2,905			
Crude Oil APO		131				
Natural Gas	10,000 MMBTU	8,742,277	10,966,023	5,974,240	5,335,800	3,749,454
Natural Gas 1-month CSO		13,557	4,636			
Gas-Crude Oil Spread	1,000 bbl	35,797	6,521	14,992	16,348	46,281
Heating Oil-Crude Oil Spread	1,000 bbl	28,747	6,364	13,014	42,363	46,482
Total		20,515,440	23,868,006	15,475,878	15,260,056	13,320,610
Total*		25,435,781	26,384,716	17,985,109	17,987,598	17,023,825

Total US Options Volume

	2003	2002	2001	2000	1999
TOTAL OPTIONS	221,700,069	213,149,576	168,211,323	103,065,376	115,000,090
PERCENT CHANGE	4.01%	26.72%	63.21%	-10.38%	-9.79%

* Includes the New York Futures Exchange, New York Cotton Exchange and Coffee, Sugar and Cocoa Exchange.

** Includes Commodity Exchange, Inc.

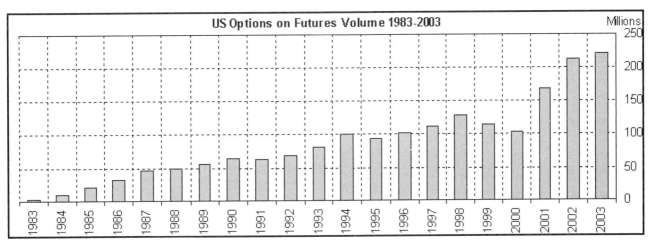

Volume Worldwide

Australian Stock Exchange (ASX), Australia

	2003	2002	2001	2000	1999
S&P/ASX Index	67,769				
All Futures on Individual Equities	267,630				
Total Futures	**335,399**				
S&P / ASX Index	630,900				
All Options on Individual Equities	15,988,740				
Total Options	**16,619,640**				

Bolsa de Mercadorias & Futuros (BM&F), Brazil

	2003	2002	2001	2000	1999
Arabica Coffee	478,544	446,115	475,034	390,513	317,722
Robusta Conillon Coffee	405	475			
Live Cattle	113,473	152,939	92,365	149,795	123,442
Feeder Cattle	9,475	1,295			
Sugar Crystal	40,257	48,326	93,904	52,552	33,764
Cotton	172	75	15	306	5,115
Corn	43,902	16,616	4,588	8,084	10,432
Soybean Futures	2,917	624	83	2,257	13,424
Gold Forward	483	4,425	484	1,520	25
Gold Spot	98,386	65,892	42,971	95,494	155,947
Anhydrous Fuel Alcohol	49,158	62,896	67,527	53,963	
Bovespa Stock Index Futures	6,630,407	5,231,780	5,151,572	7,000,335	5,551,918
INrX-50	85				
Bovespa Mini Index	1,158,155	592,342	110,943		
IGP-M	780	64,868			
Interest Rate	57,641,625	48,568,401	46,241,111	37,626,151	22,235,992
Interest Rate Swap	888,957	474,713	964,419	6,656,112	8,224,534
Interest Rate x Exchange Rate Swap	3,520,170	3,185,443	3,645,863	2,216,247	2,440,318
Interest Rate x Reference Rate Swap	5,052	1,628	27,953	33,753	80,140
Interest Rate x Price Index Swap (formerly Inflation)	666,988	183,647	99,900	67,468	17,163
Interest Rate x Ibovespa Index Swap	435	224	1,392	33	42
Exchange Rate Swap	9,778	1			
Price Index	13,200				
ID x US Dollar Spread Futures	731,544	586,143	1,375,846	5,059,141	2,126,164
FRA on ID x US Dollar Spread	22,823,905	18,571,494	16,524,996		
ID x US Dollar Spread Swap	234,958	981,454			
ID x US Dollar MIni Swap with reset	1,057,259				
ID x IGP-M Spread Futures	760				
ID Forward with Reset	50	8,986	602,431	370,747	
Global 2040	160				
C-Bond	35,903	13,696	2,605	983	646
US Dollar	16,784,939	16,132,798	18,636,578	20,208,454	11,420,923
Mini US Dollar	625,382	182,673	10,845	0	110
US Dollar forward points	227,097	116,199			
Euro	300	125	170		
Total Futures	**113,895,061**	**95,912,579**	**94,175,252**	**80,073,865**	**52,797,466**
Gold on Actuals	173,142	213,130	156,447	119,512	283,221
Gold Exercise	82,728	102,904	58,316	34,114	35,634
US $ Denominated Arabica Coffee	37,423	34,689	12,818	8,137	42,918
US $ Denominated Arabica Coffee Exercise	1,143	2,720	1,130	1,041	4,856
Live Cattle	764		1,204	1,533	
Live Cattle Exercise	42				
Interest Rate	182,183				
Interest Rate (IDI)	1,772,583	2,539,353	1,129,060	661,218	0
Interest Rate (IDI) Exercise	155,263	15,910	89,013	58,100	22,461
Interest Rate (volatility)	9,810				
IDI Index (volatility)	1,185				
Fexible Bovespa Stock Index	1,216,418	578,467	273,888	116,976	257,870
US Dollar on Actuals	2,148,440	947,759	1,211,601	1,328,215	694,483
US Dollar Exercise	130,187	152,174	139,057	75,685	50,741
US Dollar Volatility	30,030				
Flexible Currency	949,200	1,098,543	570,739	458,631	807,153
Total Options	**6,890,541**	**5,703,209**	**3,696,233**	**3,455,810**	**3,133,632**

BOVESPA, Brazil

	2003	2002	2001	2000	1999
Ibovespa Index	1,600,261	1,144,628			
IbrX-50 Index	200				
All Options on Individual Equities	175,622,679	89,740,269			
Total Options	**177,223,140**	**90,884,897**			

Budapest Commodity Exchange (BCE), Hungary

	2003	2002	2001	2000	1999
Corn	12,513	9,450	15,733	41,956	48,918
Feed Wheat	711	1,316	2,403	726	48
Feed Barley	354	118	433	1,369	2,518
Wheat	6,883	9,271	14,987	21,345	65,823
Black Seed	1,031	392	1,101	845	7,351
Rapeseed	24				
Ammonium Nitrate	3	2	17	67	
US Dollar	1,153,307	389,001	425,125	486,860	470,550
Japanese Yen	197,763	179,650	226,639	232,844	101,884
EUR	1,602,075	698,888	1,840,127	1,306,688	596,258
British Pound	62,270	4,410	15,426	42,380	17,103
Czech Koruna	3,370	8,720			
Polish Zloty	3,565	1,330			
Swiss Franc	188,786	32,780	63,010	38,901	72,500
EURCHF	111				
EURUSD	937				
EURJPY	373				
EURPLN	433				
GBPCHF	27				
GBPUSD	68				
USDCHF	86				
USDJPY	139				
USDPLN	719				
3-Month BUBOR	1,540	3,400	7,585		
Total Futures	**3,237,088**	**1,338,846**	**2,612,788**	**2,174,480**	**1,588,047**
Corn	888	305	511	697	1,665
Wheat	242	150	164	19	3,464
US Dollar	21,650	24,250			
EUR	414,095	260,850	11,000		
EUR/USD	15				
Total Options	**436,890**	**285,555**	**11,675**	**859**	**5,649**

Budapest Stock Exchange (BSE), Hungary

	2003	2002	2001	2000	1999
Budapest Stock Index (BUX) Futures	400,003	292,128	1,236,405	839,978	1,555,939
3-Month BUBOR	150				
EUR/HUF	178,460	74,800	41,722	22,536	33,527
JPY/HUF	67,390	3,761	3,084		
CHF/HUF	326,090	75,150	7,064	7,064	120
CZK/HUF	3,770				
EUR/HUF	514,451				
GBP/HUF	1,000	1,600	1,000	1,000	150
PLN/HUF	1,800				
USD/HUF	36,586	125,689	116,176	74,790	25,106
GBP/USD	72,350	3,100			
GBP/CHF	33,000				
GBP/JPY	4,800				
GBP/SEK	23,300				
EUR/CHF	43,575				
EUR/GBP	25,100				
EUR/NOK	23,900				
EUR/JPY	8,200				
EUR/PLN	24,200				
EUR/SEK	2,039,000				
EUR/USD	249,750	41,800			
USD/CHF	16,440				
USD/JPY	146,525	1,700			
USD/NOK	5,000				
USD/SEK	300				
CHF/JPY	200	200			
All Futures on Individual Equities	694,553	452,638	879,049	456,510	181,031
Total Futures	**4,939,893**	**1,072,566**	**2,286,300**	**1,402,378**	**1,814,078**

Dalian Commodity Exchange (DCE), China

	2003	2002	2001	2000	1999
Soybeans	19,287	31,313,335			
No 1 Soybeans	60,000,808	12,689,935			
Soybean Meal	14,953,398	4,404,134			
Total Futures	**74,973,493**	**48,407,404**			

VOLUME WORLDWIDE

EUREX, Frankfurt, Germany

(formerly DTB and SOFFEX)	2003	2002	2001	2000	1999
DAX	27,181,218	19,996,503	14,686,359	11,524,330	12,876,982
HEX 25	32,589	44,524			
NEMAX 50	750,125	4,704,283	5,409,482	702,873	
TecDAX	181,954				
DJ Global Titans 50	2,017	965	871		
DJ Euro STOXX 50	116,035,326	86,354,731	37,828,500	14,315,518	5,341,864
DJ Euro STOXX Automobiles	152,714	83,677			
DJ Euro STOXX Banks	483,451	560,757	113,478		
DJ Euro STOXX Basic Resources	10,185				
DJ Euro STOXX Chemicals	54				
DJ Euro STOXX Construction	481				
DJ Euro STOXX Cyclical Goods and Services	40				
DJ Euro STOXX Energy	105,614	77,762			
DJ Euro STOXX Financial Services	995	110			
DJ Euro STOXX Food and Beverage	8,538				
DJ Euro STOXX Healthcare	3,281	9,037	2,399		
DJ Euro STOXX Industry Goods and Services	230				
DJ Euro STOXX Insurance	323,207	151,250			
DJ Euro STOXX Media	8,339	698			
DJ Euro STOXX Non-Cyclical Goods and Services	444				
DJ Euro STOXX Media	42				
DJ Euro STOXX Technology	281,967	303,315	82,321		
DJ Euro STOXX Telecom	192,907	279,535	47,967		
DJ Euro STOXX Utilities	16,927	1,304			
DJ STOXX 50	970,107	690,719	452,830	355,801	326,136
DJ STOXX 600 Banks	8,595	25,376	11,259		
DJ STOXX 600 Healthcare	41,394	100,674	11,968		
DJ STOXX 600 Insurance	170				
DJ STOXX 600 Technology	8,331	13,306	5,152		
DJ STOXX 600 Telecom	20,537	20,403	6,900		
DJ STOXX 600 Utilities	9,651				
Swiss Market Index (SMI)	8,969,235	7,019,626	5,099,537	4,586,219	6,515,036
Exchange Traded Funds	187,996	56,126			
Swiss Government Bond (CONF)	284,809	275,392	416,883	479,350	577,030
Euro-BUND	244,414,274	191,263,413	178,011,304	151,326,295	121,311,878
Euro-BOBL	150,087,139	114,678,996	99,578,068	62,502,582	45,481,843
3-Month Euribor	503,951	527,815	663,980	1,224,877	3,031,138
Euro-BUXL	666				
Euro-SCHATZ	117,370,528	108,760,955	92,637,630	42,822,290	17,748,784
Total Futures	**668,650,028**	**536,013,920**	**435,141,707**	**289,952,183**	**244,754,731**
DAX	41,521,920	44,027,830	44,102,502	31,941,562	32,613,783
HEX 25	7,128	14			
NEMAX 50	48,969	634,195	1,726,251	473,297	
TecDAX	13,477				
DJ Global Titans 50	48	40	104		
DJ Euro STOXX 50	61,794,673	39,477,430	19,046,893	8,197,999	3,791,738
DJ Euro STOXX Automobile	50,673	35,303			
DJ Euro STOXX Banks	413,834	898,989	20,434		
DJ Euro STOXX Chemicals	2				
DJ Euro STOXX Energy	63,427	64,012			
DJ Euro STOXX Financial Services	307	146			
DJ Euro STOXX Healthcare	19	2,456	96		
DJ Euro STOXX Insurnce	269,736	114,021			
DJ Euro STOXX Technology	86,830	382,141	19,031		
DJ Euro STOXX Telecom	110,664	314,976	9,677		
DJ STOXX 50	55,417	39,594	44,400	61,530	80,254
DJ STOXX 600 Healthcare	11,270	45,040			
DJ STOXX 600 Technology	4				
DJ STOXX 600 Telecom	2				
DJ STOXX 600 Utilities	1,633				
Swiss Market Index (SMI)	3,983,918	4,230,082	3,179,143	3,474,369	3,669,386
Euro-BUND	27,316,536	18,125,981	22,054,064	26,291,123	24,940,113
Euro-SCHATZ	11,723,090	8,954,263	10,075,031	1,954,183	450,836
Euro-BOBL	10,498,534	4,529,387	6,188,962	2,436,491	1,787,840
All Options on Individual SMI Component Equities	46,302,221	34,496,338	35,239,133	35,648,521	28,570,528
All Options on Nordic Equities	13,265,471	20,601,113	16,165,675	4,536,186	111,332
All Options on Dutch Equities	6,862,703	2,708,256	835,418		
All Options on Exchange Traded Funds	70,350	6,069			
All Options on French Equities	1,487,428	246,562			
All Options on German Equities	120,211,761	85,111,674	276,825	9,905	
All Options on Italian Equities	80,041	16,675			
All Options on US Equities	30,198	123,966	38,196		
Total Options	**346,282,284**	**265,186,953**	**239,052,063**	**164,119,313**	**134,392,178**

EURONEXT, Amsterdam

(Formerly EOE, AFM and AEX, Netherlands)	2003	2002	2001	2000	1999
Live Hogs (AVC)	1,257	4,959	32,437	32,020	43,051
Potatoes (APC)	40,265	39,285	61,184	63,184	67,663
AEX Stock Index (FTI)	5,215,465	4,231,053	3,317,913	2,674,824	2,925,385
Light AEX Stock Index (FTIL)	6,639	12,401	8,211	20,700	12,445
FTSE Eurotop 100 Index (FETI)	313	1,073	253	2,112	292
Euro/US Dollar (FED)	1,405	568	2,346	989	167
US Dollar/Euro (FDE)	1,088	1,077	2,234	3,656	1,241
All Futures on Individual Equities	32,429	37,042	8,387	773	
Total Futures	**5,298,861**	**4,328,952**	**3,437,501**	**2,801,241**	**3,053,182**
Euro / US Dollar (EDX)	74,279	21,692	29,760	30,835	17,398
US Dollar / Euro	64,045	40,677	39,790	63,560	87,249
EOE Stock Index	14,120,099	9,133,875	6,569,129	4,953,037	5,527,137
Light AEX Stock Index (AEXL)	131,209	86,403	50,241	37,782	38,872
FTSE Eurotop 100 Index (ETI)	1,560	5,919	5,210	9,940	11,017
All Options on Individual Equities	59,754,703	64,076,106	56,348,323	50,345,697	40,653,520
Total Options	**74,145,895**	**73,368,051**	**63,065,039**	**55,488,681**	**46,500,810**

EURONEXT, United Kingdom

(LCE merged with LIFFE in 1996)	2003	2002	2001	2000	1999
3-Month Short Sterling	42,323,094	34,307,727	34,945,053	22,606,948	27,272,559
3-Month Euroswiss	5,009,460	4,976,206	4,694,391	4,621,559	5,956,797
1-Month Eonia	58,341				
3-Month Euribor	137,692,190	105,756,584	91,083,198	58,016,852	35,657,690
Long Gilt	10,150,267	7,789,011	6,710,557	5,350,705	8,421,533
Schatz	2,543	228,125			
2-Year Swapnote EUR	580,516	977,127	686,450		
5-Year Swapnote EUR	1,022,358	1,437,955	1,502,104		
10-Year Swapnote EUR	1,031,016	1,613,672	1,967,221		
2-Year Swapnote USD	1,120	8,191			
5-Year Swapnote USD	17,660	13,399			
10-Year Swapnote USD	28,595	50,102			
Japanese Government Bond	44,613	37,723	72,182	379,541	465,727
FTSE 100 Index	20,252,114	17,238,726	12,698,908	10,142,828	8,704,574
FTSE Eurotop 100 Index	109,846	129,414	130,824	153,792	139,552
FTSE Eurotop 300 Index	344,100				
FTSEurofirst 80 Index	210,171				
MSCI Euro Index	107,207	114,576	124,202	77,140	41,746
MSCI Pan-Euro Index	563,944	552,460	373,259	166,135	22,172
FTSE Mid 250 Index	5,422	804	559	8,706	47,663
Barley	1,058	2,708	5,614	3,567	6,526
Cocoa #7	2,328,609	1,802,142	1,514,384	1,636,322	1,862,119
Robusta Coffee	2,320,831	1,905,319	1,547,838	1,470,980	1,565,708
Wheat	91,387	80,784	95,676	87,387	100,127
White Sugar	1,062,494	1,044,806	898,261	907,399	990,595
All Futures on Individual Equities	6,349,198	3,935,121	2,325,744		
Total Futures	**231,708,154**	**184,026,644**	**161,522,775**	**105,712,717**	**97,689,714**
3-Month Short Sterling	14,162,149	7,364,057	7,692,455	4,167,648	6,451,680
3-Month Sterling Mid-curve	967,384	346,001	427,975	127,080	112,735
3-Month Euroswiss	65,925	81,467	82,145	68,922	89,777
3-Month Euribor	57,733,239	33,481,758	21,643,698	7,900,121	4,819,366
3-Month Euribor Mid Curve	4,907,879	1,419,271	963,417	432,445	3,200
2-Year Swapnote	15,904	8,816	450		
5-Year Swapnote	2,452	5,992	1,730		
10-Year Swapnote	7,888	2,730	2,429		
FTSE 100 Index (ESX)	14,619,893	13,263,116	11,848,155	6,285,819	4,858,373
FTSE 100 Index (SEI)	55,215	110,800	320,461	531,389	843,100
FTSEurofirst 80 Index	1,841				
FTSEurofirst 100 Index	1,166				
FTSE 100 Index FLEX	1,066,997	595,486	229,152	71,898	58,878
Cocoa	188,822	194,682	94,505	7,119	22,758
US Dollar Coffee	143,148	139,394	80,197	119,200	186,155
Wheat	3,262	8,092	12,693	15,610	41,436
White Sugar	66,561	43,900	70,526	121,671	105,932
All Options on Individual Equities	10,108,068	12,889,422	10,725,183	5,484,873	3,601,383
Total Options	**104,117,793**	**69,954,984**	**54,225,252**	**25,342,092**	**22,350,317**

VOLUME WORLDWIDE

EURONEXT, Brussels

(Formerly BELFOX)	2003	2002	2001	2000	1999
Bel 20 Index	328,673	507,229	543,501	780,301	823,244
Total Futures	**328,673**	**2,653,399**	**3,438,621**	**30,299,351**	**5,711,482**
Bel 20 Index	320,540	747,161	727,853	911,275	1,151,862
All Options on Individual Equities	319,850	450,734	404,559	589,218	530,389
Total Options	**640,390**	**1,197,895**	**1,132,412**	**1,503,453**	**1,700,728**

EURONEXT, Lisbon

	2003	2002	2001	2000	1999
PSI-20 Index	214,415	346,134			
All Futures on Individual Equities	560,224	2,928,883			
Total Futures	**774,639**	**3,275,017**			
All Options on Individual Equities	74,664	5,228			
Total Options	**74,664**	**6,755**			

EURONEXT, Paris

(Formerly MATIF and MONEP, France)	2003	2002	2001	2000	1999
3-Month Euribor	51	5,910	2,965	195,169	2,968,774
Wheat #2	114,758	107,602	57,159	33,038	43,193
Corn	90,973	98,654	57,664	27,677	7,158
Rapeseed	174,538	165,462	135,655	115,840	137,244
CAC 40 Stock Index 10 Euro	29,319,624	26,411,321	22,923,597	18,249,903	20,973,911
DJ Euro STOXX(SM) 50	11,866	187,623	887,447	999,596	437,447
DJ STOXX 50	6	1,896	2,330	23,603	103,160
Total Futures	29,711,816	26,991,450	42,042,673	62,968,563	35,630,883
Rapeseed	7,003	9,834	7,554	5,313	3,332
Wheat	7,643	1,679			
CAC 40 Index (Long Term)	73,668,131	84,342,670	107,251,388	84,036,775	75,652,724
All Options on Individual Equities*	174,487,319	246,165,884	178,330,328	89,434,383	68,095,743
Total Options	**248,170,096**	**330,520,413**	**285,592,240**	**173,531,463**	**152,453,289**

Helsinki Exchanges (HEX), Finland

(formerly the Finnish Options Market Exchange)	2003	2002	2001	2000	1999
STOX Stock Future	1,648,009	2,157,347	988,503	853,872	820,574
HEXTech Index	79	282	41		
Total Futures	**1,648,088**	**2,157,629**	**988,544**	**874,862**	**1,101,616**
All Options on Individual Equities (STOX)	320,255	486,581	152,052	324,526	1,263,363
Total Options	**320,255**	**486,729**	**155,092**	**332,154**	**1,533,496**

Copenhagen Stock Exchange / The FUTOP Market, Denmark

	2002	2001	2000	1999	1998
KFX Stock Index	610,908	434,163	459,007	995,934	1,093,917
Total Futures	**610,908**	**434,163**	**459,007**	**1,029,369**	**1,135,288**
KFX Stock Index	8,440	7,722	5,529	10,277	18,128
All Options on Individual Equities	142,702	94,911	26,041	3,838	2,656
Total Options	**151,142**	**102,633**	**31,570**	**16,503**	**27,920**

International Petroleum Exchange (IPE), United Kingdom

	2003	2002	2001	2000	1999
Crude Oil	24,012,969	21,493,486	18,396,069	17,297,974	15,982,355
Gasoil	8,429,981	8,156,358	7,230,408	7,115,435	6,150,912
Natural Gas - Seasons	600	450	1,005	50	
Natural Gas - Quarters	1,590	4,155	3,900	1,465	
Natural Gas BOM	1,455	90	2,570	2,555	4,270
Natural Gas Daily (NBP)	74,180	180	1,540	5,440	12,000
Natural Gas Monthly (NBP)	737,610	578,925	462,665	515,305	290,750
Total Futures	**33,258,385**	**30,233,664**	**26,098,207**	**24,938,224**	**22,442,222**
Crude Oil	49,520	146,809	252,217	452,284	495,798
Gasoil	33,339	61,001	60,240	100,631	104,813
Total Options	**82,859**	**207,810**	**312,457**	**552,915**	**600,611**

Italian Derivatives Market of the Italian Stock Exchange, Italy

	2003	2002	2001	2000	1999
MIB 30 Index	4,263,886	4,877,464	4,634,329	4,260,085	5,094,312
Mini FIB 30 Index	2,570,238	2,132,937	1,400,135	358,439	
MIDEX	358	774	743	2,044	5,144
All Futures on Individual Equities	468,083	59,853			
Total Futures	**7,302,565**	**7,071,028**	**6,035,207**	**4,620,568**	**5,099,456**
MIB 30 Index	2,505,351	2,588,402	2,716,271	2,843,986	2,236,241
All Options on Individual Equities	7,924,078	7,587,199	8,329,533	5,875,138	1,947,931
Total Options	**10,429,429**	**10,175,601**	**11,045,804**	**8,719,124**	**4,184,172**

Korea Futures Exchange (KFE), Korea

	2003	2002	2001	2000	1999
Korea Treasury Bonds	10,290,042	12,777,991	9,323,430	1,538,507	295,833
5-Year Treasury Bond	171,538				
Monetary Stabilization Bond	207,209	1,688			
KOSDAQ 50 Index	652,712	380,491	466,479		
Gold	56,998		608	62,936	40,509
US Dollar	15,606,123	1,434,591	1,676,979	1,355,730	259,249
Total Futures	**26,984,622**	**14,596,861**	**11,468,906**	**2,959,974**	**945,403**
Korea Treasury Bond	1,229	24,790			
KOSDAQ 50 Index	3	44	85		
Total Options	**1,232**	**26,434**	**85**	**16,705**	**61,398**

Korea Stock Exchange (KSE), Korea

	2003	2002	2001	2000	1999
KOPSI 200	62,204,783	42,868,164	31,502,184	19,666,518	17,200,349
Total Futures	**62,204,783**	**42,868,164**	**31,502,184**	**19,666,518**	**17,200,349**
KOPSI 200 Index	2,837,724,953	1,889,823,786	823,289,608	193,829,070	79,936,658
All Options on Individual Equities	8,159	57,918			
Total Options	**2,837,733,112**	**1,889,881,704**	**823,289,608**	**193,829,070**	**79,936,658**

London Metal Exchange (LME), United Kingdom

	2003	2002	2001	2000	1999
High Grade Primary Aluminum	26,953,102	22,330,491	23,767,595	25,443,980	22,211,729
Aluminum Alloy	703,356	895,726	819,206	643,659	740,955
North American Special Aluminum Alloy	833,022	173,127			
Copper - Grade A	19,437,740	16,579,090	17,797,929	17,565,260	16,789,674
Standard Lead	4,504,246	3,411,156	3,096,929	3,222,766	3,310,109
Primary Nickel	4,220,434	3,187,275	3,194,758	5,126,919	5,396,342
Special High Grade Zinc	10,470,171	8,100,114	6,113,484	7,549,121	7,341,620
Tin	1,448,083	1,625,470	1,432,814	1,846,413	1,770,807
Total Futures	**68,570,154**	**56,303,779**	**56,224,495**	**61,413,076**	**57,563,009**
High Grade Primary Aluminum	1,618,895	877,429	1,547,829	2,437,147	1,502,276
Aluminum Alloy	541	379	5,787	3,101	1,037
North American Special Aluminum Alloy	50	22			
Copper - Grade A	1,239,523	888,068	1,053,373	1,172,551	1,156,929
Standard Lead	95,967	50,413	86,098	76,256	114,498
Primary Nickel	144,489	67,781	133,039	415,373	250,823
Special High Grade Zinc	386,652	300,347	188,147	555,127	520,942
Tin	8,070	14,671	27,150	71,845	147,615
Primary Aluminum TAPOS	137,598	74,943	80,244	251,846	299,167
Copper Grade A TAPOS	90,381	32,939	39,472	46,498	41,261
Lead TAPOS	1,551	1,697	1,512	329	
Nickel TAPOS	4,950	6,642	10,937		
NASAA TAPOS	768				
Special High Grade Zinc TAPOS	8,738	14,884	14,807	1,948	
Total Options	**3,738,173**	**2,330,225**	**3,188,755**	**5,032,171**	**4,034,548**

Malaysia Derivatives Exchange, Malaysia

(formerly the KLCE and KLOFFE)	2003	2002	2001	2000	1999
Crude Palm Oil	1,434,713	911,015	479,799	308,622	388,105
3-Month KLIBOR	126,289	61,369	54,914	44,812	28,670
3-Year Malaysian Gov't Securities (FMG3)	781				
5-Year Malaysian Gov't Securities (FMG5)	116,221	72,959			
10-Year Malaysian Gov't Securities (FMG10)	11				
KLSE Composite Index (FKLI)	331,445	231,444	287,528	366,942	436,678
Total Futures	**2,009,460**	**1,276,787**	**822,241**	**720,376**	**853,453**

VOLUME WORLDWIDE

MEFF Renta Fija (RF), Spain

	2003	2002	2001	2000	1999
10-Year Notional Bond	1,382	46,771	290,608	1,094,548	3,614,750
Total Futures	**1,382**	**46,771**	**290,608**	**1,094,922**	**3,639,648**

MEFF Renta Variable (RV), Spain

	2003	2002	2001	2000	1999
IBEX 35 Plus Index	3,545,942	3,896,643	4,305,035	4,183,028	5,101,588
Mini IBEX 35 Index	1,070,853	724,424	22,423		
All Futures on Individual Equities	12,492,568	12,645,186	8,766,165		
Total Futures	**17,109,363**	**17,267,294**	**13,108,293**	**4,183,028**	**5,101,588**
IBEX 35 Plus Index	2,981,593	2,693,086	557,306	766,078	861,255
All Options on Individual Equities	11,378,992	18,701,248	22,628,132	16,580,519	8,091,728
Total Options	**14,360,585**	**24,068,192**	**23,628,446**	**17,346,597**	**8,952,983**

Mercado a Termino de Rosario (ROFEX), Argentina

	2003	2002	2001	2000	1999
Wheat	859	1,913	11,632		
Corn	4	14	222		
Rosafe Soybean Index (ISR)	11,912	11,811	145,655		
Rosafe Corn Index (IMR)	615	555	1,107		
US Dollar (DLR)	2,694,348	385,139			
Euro (EC)	575				
Total Futures	**2,708,313**	**399,432**	**159,935**		
Wheat	128	2	7,596		
Rosafe Soybean Index (ISR)	1,134	4,636	55,304		
Rosafe Corn Index (IMR)	50	443	998		
US Dollar (DLR)	132,871	3,957			
Total Options	**134,183**	**9,038**	**63,898**		

Mexican Derivatives Exchange (MEXDER), Mexico

	2002	2002	2001	2000	1999
US Dollar	81,395	52,108			
IPC Stock Index	220,731	49,243			
CETE 91	11,398,544	3,568,951			
TIIE 28	162,077,312	80,595,463			
M3 Bond	4,683	9,214			
M10 Bond	38,279				
Total Futures	**173,820,944**	**84,274,979**			

Montreal Exchange (ME), Canada

	2003	2002	2001	2000	1999
3 Month Bankers Acceptance (BAX)	6,578,451	4,789,319	4,234,236	4,992,957	6,047,542
30-Day Overnight Repo Rate (ONX)	6,055	6,817			
Canadian Government Bonds (OBA)	3,754				
10 Year Canadian Gov't Bond (CGB)	2,397,119	1,803,420	1,835,229	1,501,264	1,598,463
S&P Canada 60 Index (SXF)	1,681,994	1,450,860	1,174,328	1,272,244	262,058
Gold Index (SXA)	1,454	739			
Banking Index (SXB)	110	187			
Information Technology Index (SXH)	6,890	7,071			
Energy Index (SXY)	452	85			
Total Futures	**10,676,279**	**8,058,498**	**7,260,999**	**7,766,687**	**7,931,831**
3-Month Bankers Acceptance (OBX)	341,245	57,950	89,339	249,976	168,903
10-Year Canadian Gov't Bond (OBK,OBV,OBZ)	744	3,774	20,369	8,877	9,190
S&P Canada 60 Index (SXF)	38,221	47,749	35,585	88,923	40,650
i60 Index (XIU)	130,508	237,325	127,731	120,556	
Barclays iUnits S&P/TSX Capped Gold Index Fund	18,199				
Barclays iUnits S&P/TSX Capped Financials Index	101,914				
Barclays iUnits S&P/TSX Capped IT Index Fund	9,721				
Barclays iUnits S&P/TSX Capped Energy Index Fund	10,917				
All Options on Individual Equities	6,355,251	6,086,675	5,099,894	4,753,495	1,439,476
Total Options	**7,006,720**	**6,433,473**	**5,372,930**	**5,221,827**	**1,660,886**

National Stock Exchange of India

	2003	2002	2001	2000	1999
Interest Rate	10,781				
S&P CNX Nifty Index	10,557,024	1,641,779	750,956		
All Futures on Individual Equities	25,573,756	8,557,332	435,701		
Total Futures	**36,141,561**	**10,199,111**	**1,186,657**		
S&P CNX Nifty Index	1,332,417	314,478	7,596		
All Options on Individual Equities	5,607,990	2,773,524	55,304		
Total Options	**6,940,407**	**3,088,002**	**62,900**	**3,156,181**	**2,439,089**

New Zealand Futures Exchange (NZFOE), New Zealand

	2003	2002	2001	2000	1999
3-Year Government Stock	1,101	5,279	62,521	3,867	2,356
10-Year Government Stock	735	2,000	32,319	8,024	2,853
90-Day Bank Bill	484,263	607,453	915,225	781,074	816,931
NZSE-10 Captial Share Price Index	21	99	637	1,087	1,842
Total Futures	**486,120**	**614,831**	**1,010,852**	**794,502**	**825,546**
90-Day Bank Bill	7,130	8,909	18,320	22,906	11,600
Total Options	**7,130**	**12,187**	**34,932**	**88,296**	**36,221**

OM Stockholm (OMS), Sweden

	2003	2002	2001	2000	1999
Interest Rate	6,674,408	5,586,173	7,033,675	5,371,720	8,002,707
OMX Index	14,567,900	13,331,795	14,906,505	11,477,162	11,931,352
All Futures on Individual Equities	1,424,890	1,290,181	1,468,018	2,144,767	1,129,453
Total Futures	**22,667,198**	**20,208,149**	**23,408,198**	**18,993,709**	**21,063,746**
OMX Index	6,371,381	4,916,726	4,587,544	4,167,448	5,733,106
All Options on Individual Equities	43,098,768	35,795,942	34,729,075	30,691,587	26,824,117
Total Options	**49,470,149**	**40,712,668**	**39,327,619**	**34,874,575**	**32,558,877**

Oslo Stock Exchange (OSE), Norway

	2003	2002	2001	2000	1999
Forwards	436,943	191,374	302,497	260,521	170,950
OBX	764,376	689,904	521,314	750,264	675,240
Total Futures	**1,201,319**	**881,278**	**837,341**	**1,024,266**	**875,530**
OBX	543,090	700,313	662,394	1,025,027	978,014
All Options on Individual Equities	2,079,405	1,594,138	2,346,339	2,062,350	2,580,178
Total Options	**2,622,495**	**2,294,451**	**3,008,733**	**3,087,377**	**3,558,192**

Shanghai Metal Exchange, China

	2003	2002	2001	2000	1999
Copper	11,166,288	5,796,300	4,088,943	2,674,016	2,559,687
Aluminum	2,155,498	2,355,796	1,448,192	455,206	256,485
Rubber	26,757,964	4,020,987	73,200	1,000,299	318,096
Total Futures	**40,079,750**	**12,173,083**	**5,610,335**	**4,129,521**	**3,134,268**

Singapore Exchange (SGX), Singapore

	2003	2002	2001	2000	1999
Eurodollar	18,802,104	19,504,044	17,684,054	10,083,633	8,999,879
Singapore Dollar Interest Rate	58,353	128,034	111,210	61,300	18,725
Nikkei 225 Index	7,098,920	4,857,565	4,573,348	4,484,978	5,429,843
Straits Times Index	6,601	7,329	20,023	47,106	
MSCI Singapore Index	1,046,326	711,687	488,489	479,486	291,527
MSCI Taiwan Index	5,455,812	4,628,247	3,902,738	3,390,153	2,362,385
Middle East Crude Oil	2,590	1,282			
Euroyen TIBOR	2,015,211	1,812,175	2,711,826	7,149,469	6,777,548
Euroyen LIBOR	110,529	255,256	452,559	326,849	374,198
5-Year Singapore Gov't Bond	14,598	68,327	79,246		
10-Year Japanese Gov't Bond	92	360			
Mini Japanese Gov't Bond	745,091	630,761	545,189	718,353	168,829
All Futures on Individual Equities	549	13,690	6,575		
Total Futures	**35,356,776**	**32,623,190**	**30,606,546**	**26,804,964**	**24,480,004**
Euroyen TIBOR	13	14,855	47,127	57,095	234,630
Japanese Government Bond	2,074	247	228	299	1,962
MSCI Taiwan Index	40,274	47,897	42,899	1,107	8,828
Nikkei 225 Index	249,087	201,206	291,052	708,498	1,137,716
Total Options	**291,448**	**264,205**	**383,316**	**766,999**	**1,383,136**

Taiwan Futures Exchange, Taiwan

	2003	2002	2001	2000	1999
TAIEX	6,514,691	4,132,040	2,844,707	1,339,908	971,578
Mini TAIEX	1,316,712	1,044,058	413,343		
Taiwan Stock Exchange Electronic Sector Index	990,752	834,920	635,661	409,706	87,156
Taiwan Stock Exchange Bank & Insurance Sector Index	1,126,895	366,790	452,541	177,175	18,938
Taiwan 50 Index	4,068				
Total Futures	**9,953,118**	**6,377,808**	**4,346,252**	**1,926,789**	**1,077,672**
TAIEX	21,720,083	15,664,464	5,137		
All Options on Individual Equities	201,733				
Total Options	**21,921,816**	**15,664,464**	**5,137**		

VOLUME WORLDWIDE

South African Futures Exchange (SAFEX), Africa

	2003	2002	2001	2000	1999
White Maize (WMAZ)	1,160,919	918,764	563,510	245,396	
Yellow Maize (YMAZ)	249,691	290,921	77,933	57,666	
WEAT	186,942	86,057	23,992	9,279	
SUNS	61,055	60,271	25,249	5,751	
SOYA	536	464			
All Share Index	8,521,365	6,975,380	8,044,557	5,817,231	6,037,573
Industrial Index	79,270	480,497	2,304,176	3,303,760	2,838,168
Gold Mining Index (GLDX)	1,072	6,505			1,260
Financial Index (FINI)	41,198	146,945	10,585	25,788	80,497
Government Bond Index (GOVI)	344	668			
JBAR	2				
RESI	12,053	35,249	2,933	460	14,120
Kruger Rand (KGRD)	36,323				
R 150	1,794	1,640	2,055	1,600	1,723
R 153	5,844	4,065	1,788	1,063	1,026
R 157	1,340	846			
R 194	1,856				
All Futures on Individual Equities	4,585,919	2,224,684	811,156	29,991	82,901
Total Futures	**14,947,523**	**11,233,002**	**11,868,242**	**9,505,060**	**9,064,389**
White Maize (WMAZ)	535,408	443,624	269,887	116,714	
Yellow Maize (YMAZ)	82,062	120,599	27,785	12,117	
WEAT	22,306	41,192	8,694	3,429	
SUNS	7,224	7,207	5,775	1,904	
SOYA	80	170			
All Share Index	10,501,861	10,916,338	17,926,295	12,137,585	8,511,293
Industrial Index	4,108	44,100	337,289	898,320	973,633
Financial Index (FINI)	2,132	32,180	15,804	12,894	123,585
R 150	590	1,500	780	0	955
R 153	16,785	19,119	9,449	3,099	2,720
R 157	2,430	3,567			
R 194	1,980	1,800			
All Options on Individual Equities	6,877,254	8,102,185	5,705,719	1,992,579	82,576
Total Options	**18,054,220**	**19,733,581**	**24,307,477**	**15,178,641**	**9,701,962**

Sydney Futures Exchange (SFE), Australia

	2003	2002	2001	2000	1999
SPI 200 & SPI	4,288,848	3,761,904	3,881,745	3,824,860	3,819,800
Australian Dollar	25,566	29,076	40,654		
30-Day Interbank Cash Rate	53,141				
90-Day Bank Bills	11,435,471	8,486,560	9,108,108	7,700,381	7,184,423
3-Year Treasury Bonds	19,246,934	16,459,043	15,718,248	12,359,076	10,787,444
3-Year Interest Rate Swaps	401	300			
10-Year Treasury Bonds	6,705,904	5,200,290	5,296,233	4,981,880	5,345,640
10-Year Interest Rate Swaps	200	1,300			
d-cypha NSW Base Load Electricity	2,730	160			
d-cypha VIC Base Load Electricity	2,766	100			
d-cypha QLD Base Load Electricity	1,335	80			
d-cypha SA Base Load Electricity	1,420				
d-cypha NSW Peak Period Electricity	1,927	310			
d-cypha VIC Peak Period Electricity	1,762	160			
d-cypha QLD Peak Period Electricity	660	230			
d-cypha SA Peak Period Electricity	235	45			
Fine Wool	2,467	1,755	2,385	3,063	4,106
Broad Wool	2,003	2,756	944	417	699
Greasy Wool	9,095	14,180	8,621	11,126	16,108
MLA/SFE Cattle	1,175	175			
All Futures on Individual Equities	47,822	29,286	12,545	8,817	8,658
Total Futures	**41,831,862**	**33,987,967**	**34,075,508**	**28,901,368**	**27,183,166**
SPI 200 & SPI	585,620	414,598	516,432	1,098,919	1,237,294
90-Day Bank Bills	250,876	227,208	267,808	326,638	453,048
3-Year Treasury Bond	220,382	237,509	301,782	319,383	289,196
Overnight 3-Year Treasury Bond	1,151,097	1,048,753	618,011	477,192	217,959
3-Year Bonds Intra-Day	583,719	277,905			
10-Year Treasury Bonds	38,972	24,037	36,341	104,948	242,732
10-Year Bonds Intra-Day	6,307	1,880			
Overnight 10-Year Treasury Bond	86,313	22,629	29,671	47,373	169,347
d-cypha SA Peak Period Electricity	10				
d-cypha VIC Peak Period Electricity	5				
Greasy Wool	177	1,038	20	3	30
Total Options	**2,923,478**	**2,255,557**	**1,770,371**	**2,375,579**	**2,610,167**

Tel-Aviv Stock Exchange (TASE), Israel

	2003	2002	2001	2000	1999
TA-25 Index	10,210	32,214	53,198		
Shekel-Dollar Rate	85	67			
Total Futures	**10,295**	**32,281**	**53,198**		
TA-25 Index	29,352,985	29,425,456	26,871,775		
TA-Banks Index	610	3,453	35,940		
Shekel-Dollar Rate	8,343,368	11,542,803	6,049,954		
Shekel-Euro Rate	391,221	415,712	23,940		
Total Options	**38,088,184**	**41,387,424**	**32,981,609**		

Wiener Borse - Derivatives Market of Vienna, Austria

(formerly the AFOE)	2003	2002	2001	2000	1999
ATX Index	49,441	99,397	271,741	431,048	598,981
CeCe (5 Eastern European Indices)	63,439	68,542	164,278	227,829	203,421
Total Futures	**112,880**	**167,939**	**436,019**	**658,877**	**802,582**
ATX Index	27,608	68,903	123,757	205,286	395,323
All Options on Individual Equities	1,252,041	1,090,225	1,239,969	0	802,924
Total Options	**1,279,649**	**1,159,145**	**1,365,633**	**218,099**	**1,230,375**

Winnipeg Commodity Exchange (WCE), Canada

	2003	2002	2001	2000	1999
Wheat	59,194	89,136	166,932	164,981	106,378
Flaxseed	4,438	25,586	72,476	101,216	78,433
Canola (Rapeseed)	1,547,283	1,828,122	2,424,973	1,858,773	1,685,756
Western Barley	200,701	212,019	237,574	266,077	211,377
Total Futures	**1,811,616**	**2,155,796**	**2,903,826**	**2,391,565**	**2,086,909**
Wheat	4	101	243	210	115
Flaxseed	10	97	2,300	6,437	3,295
Western Barley	2,778	1,819	5,728	6,656	1,648
Canola	28,368	35,470	125,236	63,641	61,476
Total Options	**31,160**	**37,487**	**133,507**	**76,944**	**66,534**

Hong Kong Futures Exchange (HKFE), Hong Kong

	2003	2002	2001	2000	1999
Hang Seng Index	6,800,360	4,802,422	4,400,071	4,023,138	5,132,332
Mini Hang Seng Index	1,248,295	1,107,964	769,886	120,165	
H-Shares Index	47,941				
MSCI China Free Index	190	1,869	3,141		
Dow Jones Industrial Average	9,091	6,773			
1-Month HIBOR	310	970	14,315	12,075	9,726
3-Month HIBOR	47,799	280,257	629,491	325,155	308,646
3-Year Exchange Fund Note	2,012	3,673	1,175		
All Futures on Individual Equities	18,654	21,056	7,756	3,322	5,696
Total Futures	**8,174,652**	**6,228,037**	**5,830,672**	**4,521,926**	**5,563,358**
Hang Seng Index	2,118,792	1,070,431	716,114	544,047	714,309
Mini Hang Seng Index	32,131	6,176			
All Options on Individual Equities	4,220,638	3,724,760	4,002,655	4,188,702	2,197,972
Total Options	**6,371,561**	**4,801,367**	**4,718,880**	**4,738,644**	**2,966,014**

Fukuoka Futures Exchange (FFE), Japan

(Formerly KCE)	2003	2002	2001	2000	1999
Red Beans	40,675	42,650	54,845	37,689	92,622
Imported Soybeans	28,938	30,108	122,429	307,676	498,795
Non-GMO Soybeans	499,526	824,629	1,478,070	1,284,179	
Refined Sugar	1,421	1,432	1,437	1,443	1,421
Corn	1,881,771	1,331,933	2,016,968	2,357,240	2,897,402
Broiler	44,376	754,626	2,693,858	2,443,593	1,203,656
Soybean Meal	242,676	185,608			
Total Futures	**2,739,383**	**3,170,986**	**6,367,607**	**6,431,820**	**4,693,896**

Tokyo International Financial Futures Exchange (TIFFE), Japan

	2003	2002	2001	2000	1999
3-Month Euroyen TIBOR	4,155,800	4,470,763	7,624,711	17,077,791	14,572,255
3-Month Euroyen LIBOR	3,000		2,904	8,255	57,479
5-Year Yen Swapnote	205,092				
10-Year Yen Swapnote	408,025				
Total Futures	**4,771,917**	**4,470,763**	**7,628,909**	**17,089,946**	**14,658,415**

VOLUME WORLDWIDE

Kansai Agricultural Commodities Exchange (KANEX), Japan

(Formerly OGE, OSE and KGE)	2003	2002	2001	2000	1999
Red Beans	12,080	45,786	30,069	47,563	177,039
Imported Soybeans	41,126	161,244	465,057	872,373	1,245,358
Non-GMO Soybeans	622,337	767,206	971,980	856,623	
Refined Sugar	2,842	2,864	2,874	2,886	2,842
Raw Sugar	18,956	42,736	94,961	231,550	462,427
Raw Silk (formerly at Kobe Raw Silk Exchange)	8,009	69,609	269,199	188,091	178,114
Frozen Shrimp	1,144,264	1,937,842			
Corn 75 Index	317,561	499,912	263,520		
Coffee Index	1,274,190	961,715	371,272		
Total Futures	**3,441,365**	**4,488,914**	**2,901,551**	**2,447,652**	**2,442,440**
Raw Sugar	2,931	3,040	6,097	12,388	30,363
Total Options	**2,931**	**3,040**	**6,097**	**12,388**	**30,363**

Central Japan Commodity Exchange (CJCE), Japan

(formerly NGSE, NTE, and TDCE)	2003	2002	2001	2000	1999
Red Beans	30,100	71,057	29,614	45,297	147,511
Imported Soybeans	409	20,273	60,759	372,475	348,567
Non-GMO Soybeans	418,476	18,419	22,471	65,642	
Hen Egg	399,167	338,291	596,415	590,274	390,475
Gasoline	16,705,638	15,212,512	14,392,478	11,048,071	
Kerosene	13,984,740	14,338,356	12,346,595	8,714,440	
Total Futures	**31,538,530**	**30,011,863**	**27,846,712**	**21,328,867**	**1,327,024**

Osaka Securities Exchange(OSE), Japan

	2003	2002	2001	2000	1999
Nikkei 225 Index	13,058,425	10,841,300	9,516,875	7,426,478	9,067,883
Nikkei 300 Index	172,862	293,438	961,566	1,281,029	1,470,954
Total Futures	**13,231,287**	**11,134,754**	**10,478,441**	**8,707,853**	**10,540,224**
Nikkei 225 Index	14,958,100	9,428,235	6,953,222	5,715,856	5,753,760
Nikkei 300 Index	234	568	609	674	652
All Options on Individual Equities	45,412	21,415	38,077	103,556	683,778
Total Options	**15,003,746**	**9,450,218**	**6,991,908**	**5,820,086**	**6,438,191**

Osaka Mercantile Exchange (OME), Japan

(formerly KRE and OTE)	2003	2002	2001	2000	1999
Cotton Yarn (20S)	11,681	34,055	113,074	183,568	189,240
Cotton Yarn (40S)	7,687	45,650	90,591	83,508	34,378
Rubber (RSS3)	1,550,423	1,300,492	710,872	1,404,451	1,546,297
Rubber (TSR20)	1,985,225	587,641	66,268	213,758	
Rubber Index	1,423,491	1,885,262	967,915	1,561,707	1,355,731
Aluminum	963,464	1,285,419	1,438,450	1,695,737	2,218,159
Nickel	220,618	69,133			
Total Futures	**6,162,589**	**5,207,652**	**3,387,170**	**5,142,913**	**5,352,572**

Tokyo Commodity Exchange (TOCOM), Japan

	2003	2002	2001	2000	1999
Gold	26,637,897	20,506,652	9,791,711	7,841,692	16,011,962
Silver	1,160,565	930,886	660,864	558,770	966,838
Platinum	14,211,824	14,436,155	16,244,583	13,577,201	13,277,043
Palladium	275,322	87,883	117,098	1,007,307	5,832,649
Aluminum	329,565	513,892	735,366	543,015	710,782
Gasoline	25,677,079	20,866,237	16,441,056	14,370,266	3,973,668
Kerosene	13,208,350	10,482,433	8,301,559	6,741,173	1,441,163
Crude Oil	1,809,711	2,037,215	911,597		
Gas Oil	372,977				
Rubber	3,568,929	5,551,837	3,334,411	6,195,440	6,193,292
Total Futures	**87,252,219**	**75,413,190**	**56,538,245**	**50,851,882**	**48,442,161**

Tokyo Stock Exchange (TSE), Japan

	2003	2002	2001	2000	1999
10-Year Government Yen Bond	6,465,073	6,356,612	7,377,641	9,909,127	9,727,855
TOPIX Stock Index	9,359,047	7,131,178	5,071,946	4,148,776	3,157,441
Electric Appliance Index	724	466	350	2,610	182
Bank Index	140,331	141,751	13,298	50,545	25,719
Total Futures	**15,965,175**	**13,630,046**	**12,465,433**	**14,254,348**	**13,023,411**
TOPIX	98,137	93,249	7,623	2,630	2,030
10-Year Government Yen Bond	972,518	1,036,395	1,062,235	1,271,887	1,137,319
Total Options	**1,070,655**	**1,129,644**	**1,069,858**	**1,274,517**	**1,139,349**

Tokyo Grain Exchange (TGE), Japan

	2003	2002	2001	2000	1999
American Soybeans	1,745,697	1,001,747	1,740,613	2,355,163	3,279,175
Non-GMO Soybeans	6,735,421	3,416,660	3,342,542	2,875,667	
Soybean Meal	52,039	210,829	268,513		
Arabic Coffee	5,019,572	4,844,715	4,465,044	4,231,369	3,508,798
Red Beans	555,190	593,087	1,093,922	680,751	1,378,169
Corn	5,984,743	7,431,128	10,341,897	8,341,227	8,107,879
Refined Sugar	2,842	2,864	2,874	2,886	2,842
Robusta Coffee	617,327	460,507	420,873	729,618	699,153
Raw Sugar	371,896	709,394	1,031,530	1,561,657	1,042,427
Total Futures	**21,084,727**	**18,670,931**	**22,707,808**	**20,778,338**	**18,018,443**
American Soybean	17,548	21,515	19,040	84,819	79,955
Corn	12,214	16,511	52,012	113,888	141,578
Raw Sugar	5,979	19,309	37,544	85,957	153,285
Total Options	**35,741**	**57,335**	**108,596**	**284,664**	**374,818**

Yokohama Commodity Exchange (YCE), Japan

(formerly Maebashi Dried Cocoon & Yokohama Raw Silk Ex.)	2003	2002	2001	2000	1999
Raw Silk	919,049	698,321	602,727	789,795	704,657
Internaional Raw Silk	11,581	40,935	241,004	387,081	
Dried Cocoon	27,368	29,385	69,789	208,119	191,048
Potato	894,160	738,569	399,351		
Total Futures	**1,852,158**	**1,507,210**	**1,312,871**	**1,384,995**	**895,705**
Total Futures	**1,927,472,371**	**1,473,598,607**	**1,173,022,823**	**952,905,056**	**781,797,938**
Percent Change	**30.80%**	**25.62%**	**23.10%**	**21.89%**	**-2.04%**
Total Options	**4,012,673,793**	**2,898,783,708**	**1,630,793,276**	**722,899,112**	**523,145,631**
Percent Change	**38.43%**	**77.75%**	**125.59%**	**38.18%**	**51.70%**
Total Futures and Options	**5,940,146,164**	**4,372,382,315**	**2,803,816,099**	**1,675,804,168**	**1,304,943,569**
Percent Change	**35.86%**	**55.94%**	**67.31%**	**28.42%**	**14.17%**

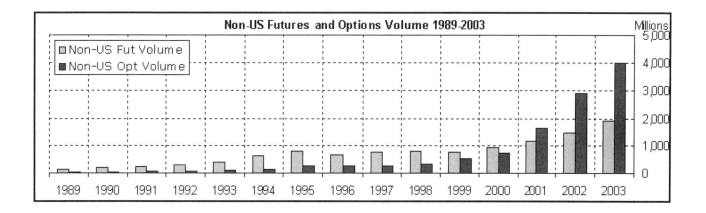

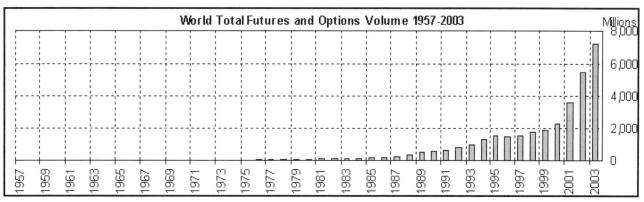

Conversion Factors

Commonly Used Agricultural Weights and Measurements

Bushel Weights:
wheat and soybeans = 60 lbs.
corn, sorghum and rye = 56 lbs.
barley grain = 48 lbs.
barley malt = 34 lbs.
oats = 32 lbs.

Bushels to tonnes:
wheat and soybeans = bushels X 0.027216
barley grain = bushels X 0.021772
corn, sorghum and rye = bushels X 0.0254
oats = bushels X 0.014515

1 tonne (metric ton) equals:
2204.622 lbs.
1,000 kilograms
22.046 hundredweight
10 quintals

1 tonne (metric ton) equals:
36.7437 bushels of wheat or soybeans
39.3679 bushels of corn, sorghum or rye
45.9296 bushels of barley grain
68.8944 bushels of oats
4.5929 cotton bales (the statistical bale used by the USDA and ICAC contains a net weight of 480 pounds of lint)

Area Measurements:
1 acre = 43,560 square feet = 0.040694 hectare
1 hectare = 2.4710 acres = 10,000 square meters
640 acres = 1 square mile = 259 hectares

Yields:
wheat: bushels per acre X 0.6725 = quintals per hectare
rye, corn: bushels per acre X 0.6277 = quintals per hectare
barley grain: bushels per acre X 0.538 = quintals per hectare
oats: bushels per acre X 0.3587 = quintals per hectare

Commonly Used Weights

The troy, avoirdupois and apothecaries' grains are identical in U.S. and British weight systems, equal to 0.0648 gram in the metric system. One avoirdupois ounce equals 437.5 grains. The troy and apothecaries' ounces equal 480 grains, and their pounds contain 12 ounces.

Troy weights and conversions: 100 kilograms = 1 quintal
24 grains = 1 pennyweight
20 pennyweights = 1 ounce
12 ounces = 1 pound
1 troy ounce = 31.103 grams
1 troy ounce = 0.0311033 kilogram
1 troy pound = 0.37224 kilogram
1 kilogram = 32.1507 troy ounces
1 tonne = 32,151 troy ounces

Avoirdupois weights and conversions:
27 11/32 grains = 1 dram
16 drams = 1 ounce
16 ounces = 1 lb.
1 lb. = 7,000 grains
14 lbs. = 1 stone (British)
100 lbs. = 1 hundredweight (U.S.)
112 lbs. = 8 stone = 1 hundredweight (British)
2,000 lbs. = 1 short ton (U.S. ton)
2,240 lbs. = 1 long ton (British ton)
160 stone = 1 long ton
20 hundredweight = 1 ton
1 lb. = 0.4536 kilogram
1 hundredweight (cwt.) = 45.359 kilograms
1 short ton = 907.18 kilograms
1 long ton = 1,016.05 kilograms

Metric weights and conversions:
1,000 grams = 1 kilogram

1 tonne = 1,000 kilograms = 10 quintals
1 kilogram = 2.204622 lbs.
1 quintal = 220.462 lbs.
1 tonne = 2204.6 lbs.
1 tonne = 1.102 short tons
1 tonne = 0.9842 long ton

U.S. dry volumes and conversions:
1 pint = 33.6 cubic inches = 0.5506 liter
2 pints = 1 quart = 1.1012 liters
8 quarts = 1 peck = 8.8098 liters
4 pecks = 1 bushel = 35.2391 liters
1 cubic foot = 28.3169 liters

U.S. liquid volumes and conversions:
1 ounce = 1.8047 cubic inches = 29.6 milliliters
1 cup = 8 ounces = 0.24 liter = 237 milliliters
1 pint = 16 ounces = 0.48 liter = 473 milliliters
1 quart = 2 pints = 0.946 liter = 946 milliliters
1 gallon = 4 quarts = 231 cubic inches = 3.785 liters
1 milliliter = 0.033815 fluid ounce
1 liter = 1.0567 quarts = 1,000 milliliters
1 liter = 33.815 fluid ounces
1 imperial gallon = 277.42 cubic inches = 1.2 U.S. gallons = 4.546 liters

ENERGY CONVERSION FACTORS

U.S. Crude Oil (average gravity)
1 U.S. barrel = 42 U.S. gallons
1 short ton = 6.65 barrels
1 tonne = 7.33 barrels

Barrels per tonne for various origins

Abu Dhabi	7.624
Algeria	7.661
Angola	7.206
Australia	7.775
Bahrain	7.335
Brunei	7.334
Canada	7.428
Dubai	7.295
Ecuador	7.58
Gabon	7.245
Indonesia	7.348
Iran	7.37
Iraq	7.453
Kuwait	7.261
Libya	7.615
Mexico	7.104
Neutral Zone	6.825
Nigeria	7.41
Norway	7.444
Oman	7.39
Qatar	7.573
Romania	7.453
Saudi Arabia	7.338
Trinidad	6.989
Tunisia	7.709
United Arab Emirates	7.522
United Kingdom	7.279
United States	7.418
Former Soviet Union	7.35
Venezuela	7.005
Zaire	7.206

Barrels per tonne of refined products:

aviation gasoline	8.9
motor gasoline	8.5
kerosene	7.75
jet fuel	8
distillate, including diesel	7.46

(continued above)

residual fuel oil	6.45
lubricating oil	7
grease	6.3
white spirits	8.5
paraffin oil	7.14
paraffin wax	7.87
petrolatum	7.87
asphalt and road oil	6.06
petroleum coke	5.5
bitumen	6.06
LPG	11.6

Approximate heat content of refined products:
(Million Btu per barrel, 1 British thermal unit is the amount of heat required to raise the temperature of 1 pound of water 1 degree F.)

Petroleum Product	Heat Content
asphalt	6.636
aviation gasoline	5.048
butane	4.326
distillate fuel oil	5.825
ethane	3.082
isobutane	3.974
jet fuel, kerosene	5.67
jet fuel, naptha	5.355
kerosene	5.67
lubricants	6.065
motor gasoline	5.253
natural gasoline	4.62
pentanes plus	4.62

Petrochemical feedstocks:

naptha less than 401*F	5.248
other oils equal to or greater than 401*F	5.825
still gas	6
petroleum coke	6.024
plant condensate	5.418
propane	3.836
residual fuel oil	6.287
special napthas	5.248
unfinished oils	5.825
unfractionated steam	5.418
waxes	5.537

Source: U.S. Department of Energy

Natural Gas Conversions

Although there are approximately 1,031 Btu in a cubic foot of gas, for most applications, the following conversions are sufficient:

Cubic Feet			MMBtu		
1,000	(one thousand cubic feet)	=	1 Mcf	=	1
1,000,000	(one million cubic feet)	=	1 MMcf	=	1,000
10,000,000	(ten million cubic feet)	=	10 MMcf	=	10,000
1,000,000,000	(one billion cubic feet)	=	1 Bcf	=	1,000,000
1,000,000,000,000	(one trillion cubic feet)	=	1 Tcf	=	1,000,000,000

Aluminum

Aluminum, symbol Al, is a silvery, lightweight metal that is the most abundant metallic element in the earth's crust. Aluminum was first isolated in 1825 by a Danish chemist, Hans Christian Oersted, using a chemical process involving a potassium amalgam. A German chemist, Friedrich Woehler, improved Oersted's process by using metallic potassium in 1827. He was the first to show aluminum's lightness. In France, Henri Sainte-Claire Deville isolated the metal by reducing aluminum chloride with sodium and established a large-scale experimental plant in 1854. He displayed pure aluminum at the Paris Exposition of 1855.

In 1886, Charles Martin Hall in the US and Paul L.T. Heroult in France simultaneously discovered the first practical method for producing aluminum through electrolytic reduction. The low-cost Hall-Heroult process is still the major method used for the commercial production of aluminum today.

By volume, aluminum weighs less than one-third as much as steel. This high strength-to-weight ratio makes aluminum a good choice for construction of aircraft, railroad cars, and automobiles. Aluminum is used in cooking utensils and the pistons of internal-combustion engines because of its high heat conductivity. Aluminum foil, siding, and storm windows make excellent insulators. Because it absorbs relatively few neutrons, aluminum is used in low-temperature nuclear reactors. Aluminum is also useful in boat hulls and various marine devices due to its resistance to corrosion in salt water. There were 23 primary aluminum reduction plants in the US as of 2001, operated by 12 different companies.

Aluminum futures and options are traded on the New York Mercantile Exchange (NYMEX) and the London Metal Exchange. Aluminum futures are traded on the Tokyo Commodity Exchange (TOCOM), the Osaka Mercantile Exchange (OME), and the Shanghai Futures Exchange (SHFE). The NYMEX aluminum futures contract calls for the delivery of 44,000 pounds of aluminum and the contract is priced in terms of cents per pound.

Prices – NYMEX aluminum prices in 2003 staged a very sharp rally in the latter half of 2003 due to the sharp upward rebound in US economic activity and to the weak dollar. Aluminum futures closed 2003 at 74.6 cents per pound, up 16.6% from the 2002 close of 63.95 cents. The 2003 close of 74.6 cents was only mildly below the contract high of 76.95 cents posted in September 2000 before the 2000-03 economic slump began in earnest.

Supply – World production of aluminum rose 6.6% in 2002, the latest reporting year for the data series, to a record high of 25.900 million metric tons, up from 24.300 million in 2001. The world's largest producers of aluminum are China with 16.6% of world production, Russia (12.9%), US (10.5%), Canada (10.5%), and Australia (7.1%). US production of aluminum in 2003 was on track to rise slightly to 2.7 million metric tons, up from 2.707 million in 2002 but still well below the high near 4 million seen in the early 1990s. The US produced 2.930 million metric tons of aluminum from scrap in 2002, more than the 2.707 million metric tons produced from mined ore.

Demand – US consumption of aluminum in 2002 rose to 6.310 million metric tons from 6.230 million in 2001, although the 2001-2002 levels were depressed from the previous several years due to weak US economic growth.

Trade – US imports of aluminum in 2002 rose to 4.060 million metric tons from 3.740 million in 2001. US imports in 2002 rose slightly to 1.320 million metric tons from 1.300 million in 2001.

World Production of Primary Aluminum   In Thousands of Metric Tons

Year	Australia	Brazil	Canada	China	France	Germany	Norway	Russia	Spain	United Kingdom	United States	Vene-zuela	World Total
1994	1,317	1,185	2,255	1,450	437	505	857	2,670	338	231	3,299	585	19,211
1995	1,297	1,188	2,172	1,680	372	575	847	2,724	361	238	3,375	630	19,668
1996	1,372	1,195	2,283	1,770	380	576	863	2,874	362	240	3,577	629	20,800
1997	1,495	1,200	2,327	1,960	399	572	919	2,906	360	248	3,603	634	21,700
1998	1,627	1,208	2,374	2,340	424	612	996	3,005	362	258	3,713	585	22,600
1999	1,718	1,250	2,390	2,530	455	634	1,020	3,146	364	272	3,779	570	23,600
2000	1,769	1,271	2,373	2,800	441	644	1,026	3,245	366	305	3,668	569	24,400
2001[1]	1,798	1,131	2,583	3,250	462	652	1,068	3,300	376	341	2,637	571	24,300
2002[2]	1,836	1,318	2,709	4,300	450	650	1,096	3,347	380	340	2,707	570	25,900

[1] Preliminary.   [2] Estimate.   *Source: U.S. Geological Survey (USGS)*

Production of Primary Aluminum (Domestic and Foreign Ores) in the U.S.   In Thousands of Metric Tons

Year	Jan.	Feb.	Mar.	Apr.	May	June	July	Aug.	Sept.	Oct.	Nov.	Dec.	Total
1994	293	261	286	269	277	268	275	274	267	277	270	280	3,299
1995	281	253	280	272	285	277	288	286	280	289	285	299	3,375
1996	301	283	303	293	303	293	301	302	292	304	295	305	3,577
1997	305	277	307	295	304	296	305	304	294	307	298	310	3,603
1998	309	280	312	305	316	307	319	318	309	315	307	317	3,713
1999	315	287	320	309	319	310	319	324	310	323	316	328	3,779
2000	329	308	327	316	327	299	296	296	291	300	289	291	3,668
2001	256	220	232	225	229	215	214	212	206	214	208	205	2,637
2002	210	197	220	216	228	225	238	237	227	235	232	241	2,707
2003[1]	242	220	238	225	228	221	226	225	217	224	215		2,707

[1] Preliminary.   *Source: U.S. Geological Survey (USGS)*

ALUMINUM

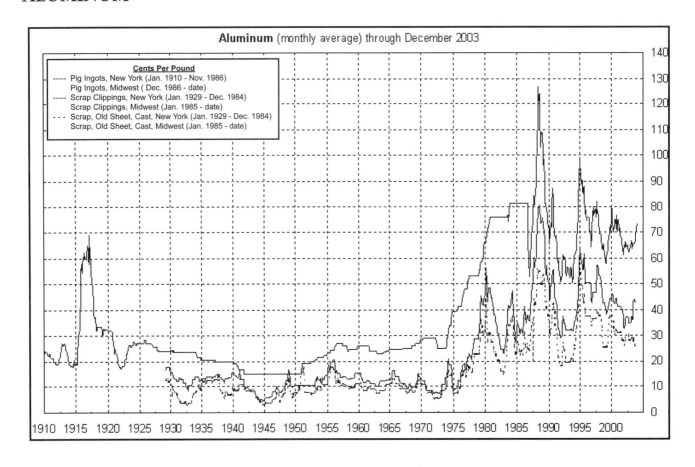

Aluminum (monthly average) through December 2003

Cents Per Pound
----- Pig Ingots, New York (Jan. 1910 - Nov. 1986)
Pig Ingots, Midwest (Dec. 1986 - date)
----- Scrap Clippings, New York (Jan. 1929 - Dec. 1984)
Scrap Clippings, Midwest (Jan. 1985 - date)
- - - Scrap, Old Sheet, Cast, New York (Jan. 1929 - Dec. 1984)
Scrap, Old Sheet, Cast, Midwest (Jan. 1985 - date)

Salient Statistics of Aluminum in the United States   In Thousands of Metric Tons

Year	Net Import Reliance as a % of Apparent Consumption	Production Primary	Production Second-ary	Primary Ship-ments	Recovery from Scrap OLd	Recovery from Scrap New	Apparent Con-sumption	Wrought Products Plate, Sheet, Foil	Wrought Products Rolled Structural Shapes[3]	Wrought Products Ex-truded Shapes[4]	Wrought Products All	Castings Perma-nent Mold	Castings Die	Castings Sand	Castings All	Total All Net Ship-ments
1993	19	3,695	2,944	7,326	1,630	1,312	6,612	4,030	297	1,300	5,770	225	645	103	994	6,770
1994	30	3,299	3,086	8,169	1,500	1,583	6,879	4,810	296	1,420	6,690	247	551	208	1,050	7,740
1995	23	3,375	3,189	8,258	1,510	1,684	6,295	4,900	526	1,540	7,130	442	627	207	1,440	8,580
1996	22	3,577	3,310	8,330	1,570	1,730	6,610	4,430	350	1,540	6,480	473	612	180	1,390	7,860
1997	23	3,603	3,550	8,880	1,530	2,020	6,720	4,710	315	1,610	6,800	468	670	153	1,410	8,210
1998	25	3,713	3,440	9,260	1,500	1,950	7,090	4,760	551	1,560	7,040	511	584	134	1,350	8,390
1999	30	3,779	3,700	9,840	1,570	2,120	7,770	5,000	549	1,640	7,360	484	1,020	158	1,790	9,150
2000	33	3,668	3,450	9,830	1,370	2,080	7,530	4,840	592	1,640	7,240	549	991	152	1,850	9,080
2001	35	2,637	2,970	9,310	1,210	1,760	6,230	4,380	354	1,460	6,330	489	871	124	1,650	7,980
2002[1]	39	2,707	2,930	9,640	1,170	1,750	6,310	4,510	369	1,450	6,470	NA	NA	NA	NA	NA

[1] Preliminary.   [2] To domestic industry.   [3] Also rod, bar & wire.   [4] Also rod, bar, tube, blooms & tubing.   [5] Consists of total shipments less shipments to other mills for further fabrication.   NA = Not available.   E = Net exporter.   *Source: U.S. Geological Survey (USGS)*

Supply and Distribution of Aluminum in the United States   In Thousands of Metric Tons

Year	Apparent Consump-tion	Production Primary	Production From Old Scrap	Imports	Exports	Inventories December 31 Private	Inventories December 31 Govern-ment[2]	Year	Apparent Consump-tion	Production Primary	Production From Old Scrap	Imports	Exports	Inventories December 31 Private	Inventories December 31 Govern-ment[2]
1991	5,043	4,121	1,317	1,490	1,762	1,945	2	1997	6,720	3,603	1,530	3,080	1,570	1,860	[4]
1992	5,715	4,042	1,612	1,725	1,453	2,156	57	1998	7,090	3,713	1,500	3,550	1,590	1,930	----
1993	6,612	3,695	1,632	2,545	1,207	2,209	57	1999	7,770	3,779	1,570	4,000	1,650	1,870	----
1994	6,879	3,299	1,503	3,382	1,365	2,149	57	2000	7,530	3,668	1,370	3,910	1,760	1,550	----
1995	6,295	3,375	1,505	2,975	1,610	2,099	57	2001[1]	6,230	2,637	1,210	3,740	1,590	1,300	----
1996	6,610	3,577	1,570	2,810	1,500	1,860	57	2002[2]	6,310	2,707	1,170	4,060	1,590	1,320	----

[1] Preliminary.   [2] Estimate.   [3] National Defense Stockpile.   [4] Less than 1/2 unit.   Source: U.S. Geological Survey (USGS)

Aluminum Products Distribution of End-Use Shipments in the United States   In Thousands of Metric Tons

Year	Building & Construction	Consumer Durables	Containers & Packaging	Electrical	Exports	Machinery & Equipment	Trans-portaion	Other	Total
1993	1,240	563	2,180	609	1,090	477	1,970	259	8,390
1994	1,400	647	2,270	682	1,200	572	2,310	276	9,360
1995	1,220	621	2,310	657	1,310	570	2,610	279	9,570
1996	1,330	655	2,180	671	1,290	569	2,640	291	9,610
1997	1,320	694	2,220	708	1,360	626	2,990	318	10,200
1998	1,390	725	2,270	714	1,260	629	3,250	273	10,500
1999	1,470	760	2,320	739	1,330	661	3,600	293	11,200
2000	1,450	767	2,260	771	1,280	679	3,600	293	11,100
2001	1,500	681	2,250	686	902	641	3,190	367	10,200
2002[1]	1,560	722	2,260	677	1,070	616	3,410	390	10,700

[1] Preliminary.   *Source: U.S. Geological Survey (USGS)*

World Consumption of Primary Aluminum   In Thousands of Metric Tons

Year	Brazil	Canada	China	France	Germany	India	Italy	Japan	Rep. of Korea	Russia	United Kingdom	United States	World Total
1992	377.1	420.4	1,253.8	730.5	1,457.1	414.3	660.0	2,271.6	397.0	1,242.0	550.0	4,616.9	18,529.5
1993	378.9	492.5	1,339.9	667.2	1,150.7	475.3	554.0	2,138.3	524.8	657.0	540.0	4,877.1	18,122.6
1994	414.1	559.0	1,500.1	736.3	1,370.3	475.0	660.0	2,344.8	603.9	470.0	570.0	5,407.1	19,670.8
1995	500.6	611.9	1,941.6	743.8	1,491.3	581.0	665.4	2,335.6	675.4	476.0	620.0	5,054.8	20,480.9
1996	497.0	619.9	2,135.3	671.7	1,355.4	584.8	585.1	2,392.6	674.3	443.8	571.0	5,348.0	20,596.4
1997	478.6	628.2	2,260.3	724.2	1,558.4	553.4	671.0	2,434.3	666.3	469.2	583.0	5,390.0	21,721.8
1998	521.4	720.6	2,425.4	733.8	1,519.0	566.5	675.4	2,082.0	505.7	489.2	579.0	5,813.6	21,797.2
1999	463.1	777.2	2,925.9	774.2	1,438.6	569.5	735.3	2,112.3	814.0	562.8	496.8	6,203.3	23,323.0
2000	513.8	798.7	3,499.1	780.4	1,490.3	602.4	780.3	2,224.9	822.6	748.4	575.5	6,079.5	24,811.4
2001[1]	550.8	759.6	3,545.4	772.9	1,590.9	558.0	770.4	2,014.0	849.6	786.2	433.3	5,117.0	23,612.8

[1] Preliminary.   *Source: American Metal Market (AMM)*

Salient Statistics of Recycling Aluminum in the United States

Year	Percent Recycled	New Scrap[1]	Old Scrap[2]	Recycled Metal[3]	Apparent Supply	New Scrap[1]	Old Scrap[2]	Recycled Metal[3]	Apparent Supply
		In Thousands of Metric Tons				Value in Millions of Dollars			
1992	40	1,140	1,610	2,760	6,870	1,450	2,040	3,500	8,710
1993	37	1,310	1,630	2,940	7,920	1,540	1,920	3,460	9,300
1994	36	1,580	1,500	3,090	8,460	2,480	2,360	4,840	13,300
1995	40	1,680	1,510	3,190	7,980	3,190	2,850	6,040	15,100
1996	40	1,730	1,570	3,310	8,340	2,730	2,480	5,200	13,100
1997	41	2,020	1,530	3,550	8,740	3,430	2,590	6,020	14,800
1998	38	1,950	1,500	3,440	9,040	2,810	2,160	4,970	13,100
1999	37	2,120	1,570	3,700	9,890	3,070	2,280	5,350	14,300
2000	36	2,080	1,370	3,450	9,610	3,420	2,260	5,670	15,800
2001	37	1,770	1,210	2,980	8,000	2,680	1,840	4,530	12,100

[1] Scrap that results from the manufacturing process.   [2] Scrap that results from consumer products.   [3] Metal recovered from new plus old scrap.
Source: U.S. Geological Survey (USGS)

Producer Prices for Aluminum Used Beverage Can Scrap   In Cents Per Pound

Year	Jan.	Feb.	Mar.	Apr.	May	June	July	Aug.	Sept.	Oct.	Nov.	Dec.	Average
1994	38.45	43.08	42.50	46.60	45.50	48.98	56.40	56.00	56.00	62.64	70.40	71.00	53.13
1995	74.85	72.24	65.00	65.00	65.00	65.00	65.00	67.98	64.80	58.45	57.00	58.50	64.91
1996	57.73	56.00	56.24	58.90	59.00	49.70	47.50	49.25	50.20	48.50	49.03	53.50	52.96
1997	56.98	59.00	59.00	58.27	58.05	58.05	58.32	59.60	59.50	59.13	59.00	57.12	58.50
1998	54.53	57.00	57.00	52.95	49.85	47.09	45.50	44.50	46.21	44.50	44.50	46.14	49.15
1999	44.50	44.50	44.20	45.68	47.45	46.50	48.40	49.00	49.00	53.79	55.50	57.64	48.84
2000	58.58	62.90	61.50	56.85	54.50	54.50	56.50	57.00	57.00	56.20	53.50	53.50	56.88
2001	54.26	55.50	55.45	54.50	54.23	50.79	46.93	45.50	45.50	44.63	44.50	44.50	49.71
2002	44.50	44.66	47.21	49.41	48.68	48.50	46.89	45.06	46.36	47.07	49.76	50.29	47.37
2003	50.50	52.30	52.45	49.43	50.17	49.75	49.22	49.83	47.43	50.17	52.00	53.73	50.58

Source: American Metal Market (AMM)

ALUMINUM

Average Price of Cast Aluminum Scrap (Crank Cases) in Chicago   In Cents Per Pound

Year	Jan.	Feb.	Mar.	Apr.	May	June	July	Aug.	Sept.	Oct.	Nov.	Dec.	Average
1994	20.00	25.79	28.33	32.50	32.50	33.18	35.90	36.50	41.07	44.45	50.50	53.50	36.19
1995	53.53	54.08	49.02	48.50	44.41	42.50	43.76	45.80	45.05	39.27	37.50	37.50	45.08
1996	37.50	37.50	37.50	37.50	37.50	37.50	37.50	36.50	35.40	33.80	33.50	33.50	36.27
1997	36.09	36.50	36.50	36.50	36.50	36.50	36.50	39.36	38.60	38.50	38.50	38.07	37.34
1998	37.50	37.50	37.50	35.95	35.50	31.59	25.50	25.50	25.50	25.50	25.50	25.50	30.71
1999	25.50	25.50	25.50	25.50	26.45	29.23	36.83	37.50	37.50	37.50	37.50	37.50	31.87
2000	37.50	37.50	37.50	35.55	31.09	30.32	30.30	32.00	32.00	31.09	31.00	31.00	33.04
2001	31.00	31.00	31.00	31.00	31.00	31.00	28.29	28.00	28.00	28.00	26.40	26.00	29.25
2002	26.00	27.47	28.95	30.00	30.00	30.00	30.00	29.64	28.00	28.00	28.00	28.00	28.67
2003	28.10	30.00	30.00	29.00	29.00	27.90	26.68	26.00	26.00	26.00	26.00	26.00	27.56

Source: American Metal Market (AMM)

Aluminum Exports of Crude Metal and Alloys from the United States   In Thousands of Metric Tons

Year	Jan.	Feb.	Mar.	Apr.	May	June	July	Aug.	Sept.	Oct.	Nov.	Dec.	Total
1994	22.1	18.3	28.3	17.9	37.5	30.5	30.6	38.3	40.3	24.8	26.1	24.1	338.9
1995	26.1	32.7	25.4	31.1	31.4	20.7	26.6	39.2	38.9	33.0	30.4	33.6	369.1
1996	23.1	27.9	31.2	34.3	46.2	54.3	36.3	33.7	30.2	40.3	33.2	26.2	416.9
1997	31.0	25.5	22.5	33.0	24.1	34.9	23.9	33.2	34.4	26.5	33.0	30.0	352.0
1998	21.2	21.4	21.8	17.4	22.6	21.8	20.9	21.5	28.0	23.9	20.4	24.7	265.6
1999	18.6	26.7	23.9	22.7	25.2	27.7	23.7	27.5	26.1	31.4	30.3	34.8	318.6
2000	18.7	27.2	30.2	21.9	24.4	22.4	20.5	24.2	20.5	20.7	20.7	21.6	273.0
2001	19.6	16.1	18.9	14.7	16.8	15.6	12.4	14.5	12.6	18.9	16.7	15.1	191.9
2002	17.1	15.2	15.6	16.4	19.4	18.3	15.0	15.5	17.5	19.8	19.4	16.4	205.6
2003[1]	14.3	14.8	14.5	16.9	17.0	17.8	16.5	20.4	18.7	22.9			208.6

[1] Preliminary.   Source: U.S. Geological Survey (USGS)

Aluminum General Imports of Crude Metal and Alloys into the United States   In Thousands of Metric Tons

Year	Jan.	Feb.	Mar.	Apr.	May	June	July	Aug.	Sept.	Oct.	Nov.	Dec.	Total
1994	200.2	157.8	282.0	206.9	251.9	179.3	202.8	198.3	160.0	183.4	240.1	222.2	2,484.9
1995	214.0	168.0	204.0	195.0	184.0	172.0	136.0	134.0	117.0	137.0	139.0	133.0	1,933.0
1996	158.0	150.0	148.0	188.0	176.0	169.0	139.0	149.0	136.0	170.0	147.0	180.0	1,910.0
1997	145.0	147.0	209.0	196.0	198.0	167.0	157.0	152.0	150.0	175.0	146.0	222.0	2,060.0
1998	220.0	204.0	202.0	200.0	189.0	243.0	170.0	204.0	198.0	198.0	189.0	177.0	2,394.0
1999	191.0	200.0	240.0	311.0	281.0	258.0	213.0	219.0	178.0	202.0	178.0	180.0	2,651.0
2000	246.0	213.0	206.0	211.0	233.0	234.0	250.0	206.0	189.0	186.0	181.0	137.0	2,490.0
2001	193.0	200.0	237.0	197.0	209.0	179.0	201.0	198.0	252.0	220.0	248.0	227.0	2,561.0
2002	272.0	205.0	223.0	221.0	221.0	263.0	228.0	279.0	235.0	196.0	264.0	186.0	2,793.0
2003[1]	215.0	246.0	350.0	202.0	265.0	261.0	233.0	194.0	215.0	210.0			2,869.2

[1] Preliminary.   Source: U.S. Geological Survey (USGS)

Average Open Interest of Aluminum Futures in New York   In Contracts

Year	Jan.	Feb.	Mar.	Apr.	May	June	July	Aug.	Sept.	Oct.	Nov.	Dec.
1999	----	----	----	----	1,032	1,461	1,875	1,984	1,767	1,244	625	615
2000	794	580	254	326	965	2,035	3,938	4,803	4,580	4,598	3,587	2,046
2001	2,446	3,173	3,450	3,529	3,269	3,724	3,891	3,459	2,753	3,728	3,644	3,276
2002	3,277	2,744	2,738	2,250	2,397	2,902	3,903	4,618	4,643	5,139	8,057	10,479
2003	9,573	9,163	6,960	7,190	7,686	8,529	8,402	8,445	7,655	7,283	8,434	9,471

Source: New York Mercantile Exchange (NYMEX), COMEX Division

Volume of Trading of Aluminum Futures in New York   In Contracts

Year	Jan.	Feb.	Mar.	Apr.	May	June	July	Aug.	Sept.	Oct.	Nov.	Dec.	Total
1999	----	----	----	----	6,179	5,875	5,275	3,373	3,114	2,801	639	722	27,978
2000	1,224	2,394	1,664	1,901	3,859	3,566	6,295	3,767	5,993	6,365	5,055	4,016	46,099
2001	7,361	1,694	4,410	2,822	2,853	4,634	4,404	3,794	1,428	2,887	4,251	2,551	43,089
2002	2,774	4,635	4,924	2,593	5,388	5,389	8,953	4,194	2,571	7,328	16,185	9,066	74,000
2003	12,565	9,625	8,163	5,440	10,567	8,463	11,797	9,451	5,119	6,222	8,536	11,542	107,490

Source: New York Mercantile Exchange (NYMEX), COMEX Division

Antimony

Antimony is a lustrous, extremely brittle and hard crystalline semi-mental that is silvery white in its most common allotropic form. Antimony is a poor conductor of heat and electricity. In nature, antimony has a strong affinity for sulfur and for such metals as lead, silver, and copper. Antimony is primarily a byproduct of the mining, smelting and refining of lead, silver, and copper ores. There is no longer any mine production of antimony in the US.

The most common use of antimony is in antimony trioxide, a chemical that is used as a flame retardant in textiles, plastics, adhesives and building materials. Antimony trioxide is also used in battery components, ceramics, bearings, chemicals, glass, and ammunition.

Prices – Antimony prices in 2003 rallied sharply to an average of 110.89 cents per pound. That was a 7-year high and was up sharply by 17% from the 2002 level of 94.83 cents. Bullish factors were the same as for other key metals in 2003—the weak dollar and much stronger US economic growth in the second half of the year.

Supply – World mine production of antimony in 2002 fell –14.2% to 143,000 metric tons from the record high production level of 167,000 metric tons in 2001. China accounted for 91% of world antimony production in 2002, with only South Africa (4.1% of world production) and Bolivia (1.5%), showing world production shares above 1%. The 14.2% drop in antimony production in 2002 was mainly due to the -13.3% drop in Chinese production to 130,000 metric tons from a record 150,000 tons in 2001. US secondary production of antimony in 2002 fell slightly to 5,350 metric tons from 5,380 metric tons in 2001.

Demand – US industrial consumption of antimony in 2002 fell to 12,900 metric tons from 13,100 in 2001. Of that consumption in 2002, 57% was for flame-retardants at 7,420 metric tons, down from 7,570 metric tons in 2001.

Trade – US imports in 2002 of antimony ore fell to 1,320 metric tons from 2,610 in 2001, with the antimony content falling to 1,310 metric tons from 2,290 in 2001. Imports of antimony oxide in 2002 rose to 27,900 from 27,700 in 2001. US exports of antimony oxide fell to 3,260 metric tons from 5,880 metric tons in 2001.

World Mine Production of Antimony (Content of Ore)   In Metric Tons

Year	Australia	Bolivia	Canada	China[2]	Guatemala	Kyrgyzstan	Mexico[3]	Peru[4]	Russia	South Africa	Thailand	Turkey	World Total
1999	1,679	2,790	357	89,600	----	100	126	255	4,000	5,278	59	180	107,000
2000	1,511	1,907	364	110,000	----	150	39	461	4,500	4,104	84	360	125,000
2001[1]	1,380	2,264	234	150,000	----	150	----	274	4,500	4,827	18	370	167,000
2002[2]	1,200	2,200	143	130,000	----	150	----	300	----	5,800	24	370	143,000

[1] Preliminary.   [2] Estimate.   [3] Includes antimony content of miscellaneous smelter products.   [4] Recoverable.
Source: U.S. Geological Survey (USGS)

Salient Statistics of Antimony in the United States   In Metric Tons

Year	Avg. Price cents/lb. CIF U.S. Ports	Production[3] Primary[2] Mine	Production[3] Primary[2] Smelter	Production[3] Secondary (Alloys)[2]	Imports for Consumption Ore Gross Weight	Imports for Consumption Ore Antimony Content	Imports for Consumption Oxide (Gross Weight)	Exports (Oxide)	Industry Stocks, December 31[3] Metallic	Industry Stocks, December 31[3] Oxide	Industry Stocks, December 31[3] Sulfide	Industry Stocks, December 31[3] Other	Industry Stocks, December 31[3] Total[4]
1999	62.7	450	15,300	8,220	3,590	2,870	23,100	3,190	2,430	5,780	W	2,720	10,900
2000	65.5	W	13,300	7,700	4,630	3,690	28,500	6,040	2,540	3,970	W	270	6,780
2001[1]	64.7	----	9,080	5,380	2,610	2,290	27,700	5,880	645	4,090	W	256	4,990
2002[2]	88.4	----	W	5,350	1,320	1,310	27,900	3,260	729	4,510	W	253	5,490

[1] Preliminary.   [2] Estimate.   [3] Antimony content.   [4] Including primary antimony residues & slag.   W = Withheld proprietary data.
Source: U.S. Geological Survey (USGS)

Industrial Consumption of Primary Antimony in the United States   In Metric Tons (Antimony Content)

Year	Metal Products Ammunition	Metal Products Antimonial Lead	Metal Products Sheet & Pipe	Metal Products Bearing Metal & Bearings	Metal Products Solder	Metal Products Total All Metal Products	Non-Metal Products Retardents Plastics	Non-Metal Products Retardents Total	Non-Metal Products Ceramics & Glass	Non-Metal Products Pigments	Non-Metal Products Plastics	Non-Metal Products Total	Grand Total
1999	W	1,110	W	29	136	2,440	6,370	7,140	1,120	1,020	1,580	3,940	13,500
2000	W	1,040	W	42	135	2,980	8,940	9,910	1,020	620	1,330	3,490	16,400
2001	W	1,060	W	52	78	2,800	6,210	7,570	518	653	1,050	2,760	13,100
2002[1]	W	887	W	42	89	2,760	6,060	7,420	505	565	1,090	2,710	12,900

[1] Preliminary.   [2] Estimated coverage based on 77% of the industry.   W=Withheld proprietary data.   *Source: U.S. Geological Survey (USGS)*

Average Price of Antimony[1] in the United States   In Cents Per Pound

Year	Jan.	Feb.	Mar.	Apr.	May	June	July	Aug.	Sept.	Oct.	Nov.	Dec.	Average
2000	66.50	66.50	66.50	66.50	66.50	66.50	68.38	69.00	84.40	91.00	91.00	91.00	74.48
2001	84.90	75.00	75.00	75.00	75.00	75.00	75.00	75.00	73.26	69.50	69.50	69.50	74.31
2002	69.50	69.50	69.50	69.50	64.22	65.13	73.09	86.97	113.24	149.59	141.91	135.25	94.83
2003	121.53	109.15	118.48	119.49	119.77	119.07	107.86	105.01	105.01	105.01	102.76	97.52	110.89

[1] Prices are for antimony metal (99.65%) merchants, minimum 18-ton containers, c.i.f. U.S. Ports.   *Source: American Metal Market (AMM)*

Apples

The apple tree is the common name of trees from the rose family, Rosaceae, and the fruit that comes from them. The apple tree is a deciduous plant and grows mainly in the temperate areas of the world. The apple tree probably originated in the Caspian and Black Sea area. Apples were the favorite fruit of the ancient Greeks and Romans. The early settlers brought apple seeds with them and introduced them to America. John Champman, also known as Johnny Appleseed, was responsible for extensive planting of apple trees in the Midwestern United States.

Supply – US production of apples in 2003 was forecast at 220.633 million bushels (42-pound units), up 8% from the poor crop level seen in 2002. Despite the 8% increase,

the 2003 crop size was the second lowest since 1988 and fell behind the 5-year average of 242.120 million bushels. The rise in US apple production in 2003 was mainly due to a sharp 63% increase in apple production in the US Midwest. Production in the eastern US rose 27%, but production in the key western US fell by 5%. Production of red and golden delicious apples in 2003 continued to fall and accounted for only 41% of total US apple production versus 50% in 2000.

Demand – The utilization breakdown of the 2002 apple crop showed that 63% of apples were for fresh consumption, 18% for juice and cider, 13% for canning, 3% for dried apples, and 2% for frozen apples.

World Production of Apples[3], Fresh (Dessert & Cooking)   In Thousands of Metric Tons

Year	Argen-tina	Canada	France	Germany	Hungary	Italy	Japan	Nether-lands	South Africa	Spain	Turkey	United States	World Total
1998-9	1,316	523	1,794	1,980	482	2,243	879	507	675	722	2,450	5,283	46,734
1999-00	847	582	2,166	1,936	420	2,196	928	575	581	887	2,500	4,822	47,575
2000-1	1,331	532	2,300	2,631	700	2,267	800	500	668	699	2,400	4,801	47,935
2001-2	900	467	2,055	1,522	605	2,220	931	500	584	962	2,450	4,277	45,467
2002-3[1]	1,000	402	2,060	1,563	540	2,210	926	370	600	683	2,200	3,881	43,625
2003-4[2]	----	440	2,080	1,407	480	1,989	892	385	----	818	2,500	4,242	38,510

[1] Preliminary.   [2] Estimate.   [3] Commercial crop.   *Source: Foreign Agricultural Service, U.S. Department of Agriculture (FAS-USDA)*

Salient Statistics of Apples[2] in the United States

	Production		Growers Prices		Utilization of Quantities Sold							Avg. Farm Price cents	Farm Value Million	Foreign Trade[4] Domestic			Fresh Per Capita Con-sump-tion
				Pro-cessing $/ton			Processed[5]							Exports Fresh	Imports Fresh		
	Total	Utilized	Fresh cents/lb.		Fresh	Canned	Dried	Frozen	Juice & Cider	Other[3]					Dried[5] & Dried[5]	
Year					Millions of Pounds						/lb.	$	Metric Tons			Lbs.
1997	10,324	10,254	22.1	130.0	5,815	1,499	267	349	2,145	180	15.4	1,575.4	539.1	18.0	173.6	18.4
1998	11,646	10,763	17.3	94.6	6,413	1,174	330	266	2,485	95	12.2	1,316.2	660.3	15.7	171.8	19.4
1999	10,631	10,447	21.3	128.0	5,995	1,319	263	271	2,473	126	15.0	1,563.6	571.9	21.5	195.3	19.0
2000	10,584	10,322	17.8	101.0	6,267	1,184	248	196	2,335	93	12.8	1,320.8	743.6	33.3	180.6	17.9
2001	9,429	9,214	22.9	108.0	5,470	1,258	221	249	1,946	71	15.8	1,453.1	592.4	21.4	193.9	
2002[1]	9,525	8,375	25.6	126.0	5,366	1,064	229	157	1,538	50	18.8	1,572.2	691.9		157.1	

[1] Preliminary.   [2] Commercial crop.   [3] Mostly crushed for vinegar, jam, etc.   [4] Year beginning July.   [5] Fresh weight basis.
Source: Economic Research Service, U.S. Department of Agriculture (ERS-USDA)

Price of Apples Received by Growers (for Fresh Use) in the United States   In Cents Per Pound

Year	Jan.	Feb.	Mar.	Apr.	May	June	July	Aug.	Sept.	Oct.	Nov.	Dec.	Average
1998	21.9	20.8	20.5	19.4	17.8	16.3	12.7	13.8	22.6	22.1	17.5	14.9	18.4
1999	15.8	15.0	15.3	14.1	13.3	12.7	16.3	22.7	21.6	24.3	22.9	23.2	18.1
2000	21.8	20.3	19.8	19.3	17.8	16.1	16.2	19.5	23.3	21.8	18.5	18.1	19.4
2001	15.8	15.2	14.6	15.7	15.2	14.9	15.2	17.3	21.2	24.8	23.5	23.1	18.0
2002	22.1	21.6	22.0	21.8	21.5	22.0	20.6	24.5	30.0	30.1	26.8	26.3	24.1
2003[1]	25.8	24.6	22.6	23.4	21.8	22.4	20.0	25.8	25.1	27.3	27.4	28.5	24.6

[1] Preliminary.   Source: Economic Research Service, U.S. Department of Agriculture (ERS-USDA)

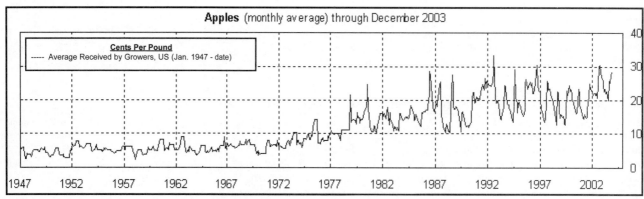

Apples (monthly average) through December 2003

Arsenic

Arsenic, symbol As, is a silver-gray, extremely poisonous, semi-metallic element. Arsenic, which is odorless and flavorless, has been known since ancient times, but it wasn't until the Middle Ages that its poisonous characteristics first become known. Metallic arsenic was first produced in the 17th century by heating arsenic with potash and soap. Arsenic is rarely found in nature in its elemental form and is generally recovered as a by-product of ore processing.

The U.S. Geological Survey reported that no arsenic was removed from domestic ores in the United States. All arsenic metals and compounds used in the U.S. are imported. More than 95 percent of the arsenic consumed is in compound form, mostly as arsenic trioxide, which in turn is converted into arsenic acid. Production of chromated copper arsenate, a wood preservative, accounts for over 90 percent of the domestic consumption of arsenic trioxide. Three companies in the US manufacture chromate copper arsenate. Another company used arsenic acid to produce an arsenical herbicide. Arsenic metal is used to produce nonferrous alloys, primarily for lead-acid batteries.

One area where there is increased consumption of arsenic is in the semiconductor industry. Very high-purity arsenic is used in the production of gallium arsenide. High speed and high frequency integrated circuits that use gallium arsenide have better signal reception and lower power consumption. It is estimated that 30 metric tons per year of high-purity arsenic is used in the production of semiconductor materials.

The largest domestic market for arsenic in the U.S. is in the production of arsenical wood preservatives. That is expected to continue, although there are increasing environmental concerns that could limit its use in the future. Demand for arsenic and arsenic compounds, therefore, derives from new home construction and from renovation and wooden deck construction. Arsenic and arsenic compounds are very toxic and increased scrutiny of products using arsenic is expected to result in more environmental regulations in the future, thus reducing future demand for arsenic.

Recently, small doses of arsenic have been found to put some forms of cancer into remission. It can also help thin blood. Homoeopathists have successfully used undetectable amounts of arsenic to cure stomach cramps. Traditionally used as a nonferrous alloy for enhancing properties such as hardening of lead and resistance to corrosion. Arsenic is also used in the manufacture of glass and in the making of CCA pressure-treated wood.

Supply – US supply of arsenic in 2002 fell to 19,700 metric tons from 25,000 metric tons in 2001. World production of white arsenic (arsenic trioxide) in 2002 was unchanged from 2001 at a 22-year low of 35,000 metric tons. The world's largest producer by far is China with 46% of world production, followed by Chile with 23% of world production.

Demand – Demand for arsenic fell to 19,600 metric tons in 2002 from 24,900 metric tons in 2001. Of that demand, 17,300 metric tons was for wood preservatives, 700 metric tons for glass, 650 metric tons for non-ferrous alloys and electric usage, and 200 for other uses.

Trade – US imports of trioxide arsenic in 2002 fell to 24,700 metric tons from 31,500 metric tons in 2001. US exports were negligible at 100 metric tons, up from 57 metric tons in 2001.

World Production of White Arsenic (Arsenic Trioxide)   In Metric Tons

Year	Belgium	Bolivia	Canada[4]	Chile	China	France	Germany	Mexico	Namibia[3]	Peru	Phillippines	Russia[5]	World Total
1993	2,000	663	250	6,200	14,000	3,000	300	4,447	2,290	391	2,000	2,000	42,100
1994	2,000	341	250	4,050	18,000	6,000	300	4,400	3,047	286	----	1,500	46,800
1995	2,000	362	250	4,076	21,000	5,000	250	3,620	1,661	285	----	1,500	47,000
1996	2,000	255	250	8,000	15,000	3,000	250	2,942	1,559	111	----	1,500	42,900
1997	2,000	282	250	8,350	15,000	2,500	250	2,999	1,297	637	----	1,500	42,000
1998	1,500	284	250	8,400	15,500	2,000	200	2,573	175	624	----	1,500	40,300
1999	1,500	437	250	8,000	16,000	1,000	200	2,419	----	1,611	----	1,500	41,800
2000	1,500	318	250	8,000	16,000	1,000	200	2,522	----	2,495	----	1,500	38,800
2001[1]	1,000	846	250	8,000	16,000	1,000	100	2,381	----	1,958	----	1,500	35,000
2002[2]	1,000	850	250	8,000	16,000	1,000	100	2,300	----	2,000	----	1,500	35,000

[1] Preliminary.   [2] Estimate.   [3] Output of Tsumeb Corp. Ltd. only.   [4] Includes low-grade dusts that were exported to the U.S. for further refining.   [5] Formerly part of the U.S.S.R.; not reported separately until 1992.   *Source: U.S. Geological Survey (USGS)*

Salient Statistics of Arsenic in the United States   In Metric Tons (Arsenic Content)

	---------------- Supply ----------------				-- Distribution --		------------------ Estimated Demand Pattern ------------------						-- Average Price --			
	---- Imports ----		Industry			Industry	Agricul-			Wood	Non-Ferrous Alloys &			Trioxide Mexican	Metal Chinese		
Year	Metal	Compounds	Stocks Jan. 1	Total	Apparent Demand	Stocks Dec.31	tural Chemicals	Glass	Preservatives	Electric	Other	Total		-- Cents/Pound --		Imports Trioxide[3]	Exports
1993	767	20,900	----	21,667	21,300	----	3,000	900	16,200	800	400	21,300	33	44	27,500	364
1994	1,330	20,300	----	21,630	21,500	----	1,200	700	18,000	1,300	300	21,500	32	40	26,800	79
1995	557	22,100	----	22,700	22,300	----	1,000	700	19,600	600	400	22,300	33	66	29,000	430
1996	252	21,200	----	21,400	21,400	----	950	700	19,200	250	300	21,400	33	40	28,000	36
1997	909	22,800	----	23,700	23,700	----	1,400	700	20,000	900	300	23,700	31	32	30,000	61
1998	997	29,300	----	30,300	30,100	----	1,500	900	26,500	1,200	300	30,100	30	40	38,600	177
1999	1,300	22,100	----	23,400	22,000	----	1,100	600	19,500	850	200	22,000	----	----	29,100	1,350
2000	830	23,600	----	24,500	24,400	----	----	700	21,800	700	250	24,400	----	----	31,100	41
2001[1]	1,030	23,900	----	25,000	24,900	----	----	750	21,900	1,000	250	24,900	----	----	31,500	57
2002[2]	879	18,800	----	19,700	19,600	----	----	700	17,300	650	200	19,600	----	----	24,700	100

[1] Preliminary.   [2] Estimate.   [3] For Consumption.   Source: U.S. Geological Survey (USGS)

Barley

Barley is the common name for any of a genus of cereal grass and is native to Asia and Ethiopia. Barley is an ancient crop and was grown by the Egyptians, Greek, Romans and Chinese. Barley is now the world's fourth largest grain crop, after wheat, rice, and corn. Barley is planted in the spring in most of Europe, Canada and the United States. The U.S. barley crop year begins June 1. It is planted in the autumn in parts of California, Arizona and along the Mediterranean Sea. Barley is hardy and drought resistant and can be grown on marginal cropland. Salt-resistant strains are being developed for use in coastal regions. Barley grain, along with hay, straw, and several by-products are used for animal feed. Barley is used for malt beverages and in cooking. Barley, like other cereals, contains a large proportion of carbohydrate (67%) and protein (12.8%). Barley futures are traded on the Winnipeg Commodity Exchange (WCE), the London International Financial Futures and Options Exchange (LIFFE) and the Budapest Commodity Exchange.

Prices – Barley prices on the Winnipeg nearest futures chart started out 2003 in the CD$180 per metric ton area, fell sharply by about 38% to the year's low of CD$112 in July, and then recovered slightly to close the year at CD$135 per metric ton.

Supply – World barley production in 2002/3 fell to 132.791 million metric tons, down from 141.788 million in 2001/2. World production is expected to recover in 2003/4 to 139.652 million metric tons. The EU is by far the world's largest producer of barley with 48.023 million metric tons in 2002/3, accounting for 36% of world production, followed by Russia at 18.700 million (14%), and the Ukraine at 10.350 million (8%). US production in 2002/3 fell to a record low of 4.933 million metric tons (only 3.7% of world production) from 5.430 million in 2001/2 but is expected to expand sharply to 6.011 million in 2003/4 (USDA). US planted acreage for barley has shown a steady contraction, averaging around 5 million acres in recent years versus 7 million in the mid-1990s. North Dakota and Montana are the largest producing states.

Demand – U.S. total barley use in 2003/4 is expected to increase to 283.0 million bushels from the post-war record low of 269.0 million in 2002/3. Seed use has run at about 8.0 million bushels in the past several years, feed & residual use is expected to rise to 85.0 million in 2003/4 from 65.0 million in 2002/3, and demand for use in food and alcohol beverages remains steady at 164.0 million bushels.

Trade – World trade in barley fell to 16.663 million metric tons from 17.231 million in 2001/2 and is expected to remain lower at 15.625 million in 2003/4. The European Union is the largest exporter with at least a third of the total, with Russia, the Ukraine, and Australia exporting much of the balance. Importing countries are many, with Saudi Arabia being the largest importer.

World Barley Supply and Demand   In Thousands of Metric Tons

| | | | | Exports | | | Imports | | | | Utilization | | | Ending Stocks | | |
Year	Aus-tralia	Can-ada	EC-15	Total Non-US	U.S.	Total Exports	Saudi Arabia	Unac-ounted	Total Imports	Russia	U.S.	Total Util-ization	Canada	U.S.	Total Stocks
1994-5	1,356	2,551	5,061	18,451	1,355	19,806	4,235	99	19,167	24,087	8,726	165,712	1,820	2,451	28,570
1995-6	3,375	2,596	2,480	18,347	1,182	19,529	3,876	214	19,172	17,566	7,635	150,965	1,749	2,168	19,700
1996-7	3,967	3,442	6,183	21,798	1,214	23,012	5,887	737	22,342	16,435	8,459	149,480	2,919	2,383	23,761
1997-8	2,838	1,897	2,990	11,755	1,071	12,826	4,026	483	12,826	16,494	6,879	146,037	2,459	2,596	32,137
1998-9	4,241	1,185	8,894	17,235	550	17,785	5,814	809	17,785	12,900	7,207	138,916	2,737	3,084	28,850
1999-00	2,870	1,806	10,443	17,927	853	18,780	5,900	110	18,780	11,441	6,752	132,559	2,838	2,424	24,026
2000-1	3,922	1,956	6,159	15,840	1,068	16,908	5,100	535	16,908	12,700	6,427	134,508	2,516	2,314	22,775
2001-2	4,150	1,126	3,082	16,714	517	17,231	6,000	121	17,231	14,250	5,669	136,258	2,047	2,021	28,305
2002-3[1]	2,200	304	6,000	16,131	551	16,682	7,300	125	16,682	15,500	5,187	135,036	1,441	1,510	26,061
2003-4[2]	4,300	2,000	3,000	14,900	625	15,525	5,500	755	15,525	17,500	5,618	144,131	2,191	2,012	19,182

[1] Preliminary.   [2] Estimate.   *Source: Foreign Agricultural Service, U.S. Department of Agriculture (FAS-USDA)*

World Production of Barley   In Thousands of Metric Tons

Year	Aus-tralia	Canada	China	Den-mark	France	Ger-many	India	Russia	Spain	Tur-key	United Kingdom	United States	World Total
1994-5	2,913	11,690	4,411	3,446	7,646	10,902	1,310	27,000	7,596	6,500	5,945	8,162	161,046
1995-6	5,823	13,035	4,089	3,864	7,739	11,891	1,730	15,800	5,200	6,900	6,833	7,824	142,095
1996-7	6,696	15,562	4,000	3,953	9,540	12,074	1,510	15,900	9,600	7,200	7,780	8,544	143,541
1997-8	6,482	13,527	4,000	3,887	10,181	13,399	1,462	20,800	8,600	7,300	7,828	7,835	154,491
1998-9	5,987	12,709	2,656	3,565	10,591	12,512	1,680	9,800	10,902	7,500	6,630	7,667	135,586
1999-00	5,032	13,196	2,970	3,680	9,540	13,300	1,470	10,600	7,430	6,600	6,580	6,103	127,735
2000-1	6,743	13,172	2,646	3,980	9,950	12,110	1,447	14,100	11,280	7,400	6,490	6,939	133,257
2001-2	8,423	10,846	2,893	3,980	9,800	13,500	1,432	19,500	6,250	6,900	6,700	5,430	141,788
2002-3[1]	3,713	7,489	2,470	4,150	11,000	11,000	1,500	18,700	8,200	7,400	6,000	4,933	132,792
2003-4[2]	8,000	12,300	2,200					15,500		7,000		6,011	137,252

[1] Preliminary.   [2] Estimate.   *Source: Foreign Agricultural Service, U.S. Department of Agriculture (FAS-USDA)*

Barley Acreage and Prices in the United States

Year Beginning June 1	Acreage ----- 1,000 Acres ----- Planted	Harvested for Grain	Yield Per Harvested Acre -- Bushels --	Received by Farmers[3] All	Feed[4]	Malting[4]	Portland No. 2 Western	National Average Loan Rate	Target Price	Put Under Support (mil. Bu.)	% of Pro-duction
1996-7	7,094	6,707	58.5	2.70	2.32	2.86	3.07	1.55	NA	28.7	7.3
1997-8	6,706	6,198	58.1	2.33	1.86	2.69	2.49	1.57	NA	33.3	9.3
1998-9	6,337	5,864	60.0	1.95	1.55	2.33	1.96	1.56	NA	25.9	7.4
1999-00	5,194	4,734	59.2	2.10	1.65	2.50	2.11	1.59	NA	13.6	4.9
2000-1	5,864	5,213	61.1	2.12	1.74	2.36	2.25	1.62	NA	16.0	5.0
2001-2	4,967	4,289	58.2	2.18	1.74	2.58		1.62	NA	NA	NA
2002-3[1]	5,071	4,129	54.9	2.69	2.16	2.97					
2003-4[2]	5,299	4,688	58.9	2.85	2.31	3.12					

Seasonal Prices / Government Price Support Operations (Dollars per Bushel)

[1] Preliminary. [2] Estimate. [3] Excludes support payments. [4] Duluth through May 1998. *Source: Economic Research Service, U.S. Department of Agriculture (ERS-USDA)*

Salient Statistics of Barley in the United States   In Millions of Bushels

Year Beginning June 1	Beginning Stocks	Produc-tion	Imports	Total Supply	Food & Acohol Beverages	Seed	Feed & Residual	Total	Exports	Total Disap-pearance	Gov't Owned	Privately Owned[3]	Total Stocks
1996-7	99.6	392.4	36.8	528.8	160.9	11.1	216.5	388.5	30.8	419.3	0	109.5	109.5
1997-8	109.5	360.0	40.3	509.6	161.6	10.4	144.0	316.0	74.4	390.3	0	119.2	119.2
1998-9	119.2	359.9	29.8	501.2	161.4	8.6	161.1	331.1	28.5	359.5	0.3	141.4	141.7
1999-00	141.7	352.1	25.0	448.5	162.5	9.5	136.0	308.0	30.0	338.0	0	111.0	111.0
2000-1	111.0	318.7	29.0	459.0	164.0	8.0	123.0	295.0	58.0	353.0	0	106.0	106.0
2001-2	106.0	249.4	24.0	380.0	164.0	8.0	88.0	260.0	26.0	287.0	0	93.0	93.0
2002-3[1]	93.0	226.6	18.0	338.0	164.0	8.0	65.0	237.0	30.0	269.0	0	69.0	69.0
2003-4[2]	69.0	276.1	25.0	370.0			75.0		25.0	273.0	0	97.0	97.0

[1] Preliminary. [2] Estimate. [3] Uncommitted inventory. [4] Includes quantity under loan & farmer-owned reserve. *Source: Economic Research Service, U.S. Department of Agriculture (ERS-USDA)*

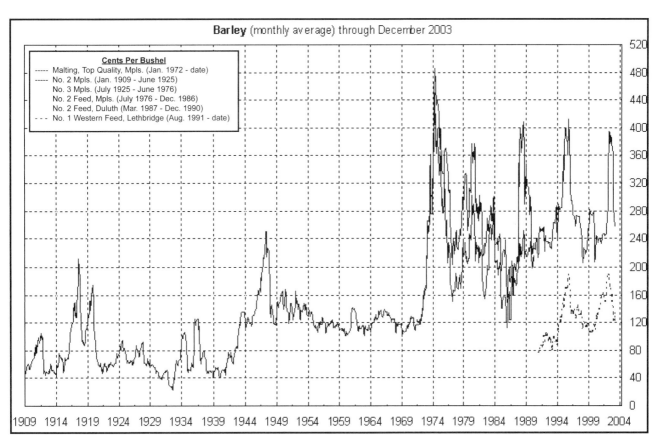

BARLEY

Average Price Received by Farmers for All Barley in the United States   In Dollars Per Bushel

Year	June	July	Aug.	Sept.	Oct.	Nov.	Dec.	Jan.	Feb.	Mar.	Apr.	May	Average
1996-7	3.55	3.18	2.99	2.78	2.69	2.65	2.67	2.52	2.45	2.37	2.29	2.31	2.70
1997-8	2.26	2.27	2.35	2.38	2.44	2.61	2.43	2.42	2.40	2.13	2.16	2.13	2.33
1998-9	1.93	2.01	2.07	2.01	1.91	2.05	2.03	1.89	1.90	2.00	1.78	1.82	1.95
1999-00	1.70	2.04	2.37	2.03	1.96	2.14	2.25	2.04	2.13	2.23	2.09	2.19	2.10
2000-1	2.04	2.70	2.23	1.81	1.97	2.15	2.22	2.00	2.10	2.07	2.05	2.12	2.12
2001-2	1.98	2.00	2.41	2.24	2.29	2.30	2.21	2.09	2.17	2.17	2.09	2.24	2.18
2002-3	2.09	2.14	2.68	2.64	2.64	2.79	2.91	2.85	2.87	2.83	2.87	2.91	2.69
2003-4[1]	3.01	2.74	2.91	2.88	2.77	2.86	2.94	2.70					2.85

[1] Preliminary.   *Source: Economic Research Service, U.S. Department of Agriculture (ERS-USDA)*

Average Price Received by Farmers for Feed Barley in the United States   In Dollars Per Bushel

Year	June	July	Aug.	Sept.	Oct.	Nov.	Dec.	Jan.	Feb.	Mar.	Apr.	May	Average
1996-7	3.22	2.79	2.60	2.34	2.10	1.90	1.96	1.95	2.01	2.22	2.33	2.45	2.32
1997-8	2.31	2.04	2.10	2.29	2.05	1.98	1.66	1.58	1.56	1.51	1.42	NQ	1.86
1998-9	1.82	1.62	1.49	1.40	1.46	1.47	1.55	1.58	1.60	1.49	1.54	1.62	1.55
1999-00	1.55	1.48	1.50	1.64	1.61	1.66	1.64	1.63	1.68	1.78	1.68	1.94	1.65
2000-1	1.73	1.71	1.50	1.54	1.71	1.87	1.90	1.80	1.77	1.76	1.73	1.91	1.74
2001-2	1.77	1.63	1.54	1.71	1.86	1.79	1.77	1.67	1.69	1.75	1.79	1.89	1.74
2002-3	1.83	1.88	2.05	2.23	2.26	2.32	2.14	2.17	2.20	2.30	2.22	2.33	2.16
2003-4[1]	2.35	2.23	2.40	2.30	2.25	2.44	2.30	2.20					2.31

[1] Preliminary.   *Source: National Agricultural Statistical Service, U.S. Department of Agriculture (NASS-USDA)*

Average Open Interest of Western Feed Barley Futures in Winnipeg   In Contracts

Year	Jan.	Feb.	Mar.	Apr.	May	June	July	Aug.	Sept.	Oct.	Nov.	Dec.
1996	13,803	12,979	15,746	18,022	19,045	18,502	15,504	14,190	16,647	20,143	21,233	24,590
1997	22,718	19,290	15,080	14,620	14,385	12,291	10,023	13,641	12,909	13,147	14,473	13,576
1998	15,789	17,337	18,039	14,706	12,666	10,847	9,915	10,384	11,420	11,460	11,338	8,622
1999	8,231	10,635	10,579	9,713	8,333	8,993	10,348	11,959	13,206	15,014	15,662	15,031
2000	16,709	20,500	21,100	22,501	20,299	17,402	15,128	15,095	15,885	14,921	17,192	19,605
2001	19,453	20,515	19,163	19,458	16,020	15,778	16,475	17,202	16,926	13,577	11,407	10,480
2002	9,771	10,653	11,255	11,113	11,141	11,068	11,271	13,046	13,845	12,172	9,000	8,027
2003	8,559	8,203	8,546	9,028	9,631	10,290	10,676	9,580	8,409	7,154	7,524	5,346

Source: Winnipeg Commodity Exchange (WCE)

Volume of Trading of Western Barley Futures in Winnipeg   In Contracts

Year	Jan.	Feb.	Mar.	Apr.	May	June	July	Aug.	Sept.	Oct.	Nov.	Dec.	Total
1996	24,789	14,762	22,492	29,326	25,659	22,968	33,908	24,878	25,456	50,745	33,702	26,124	334,809
1997	30,608	30,298	25,910	23,511	17,228	18,912	15,615	21,993	23,291	29,418	31,629	16,201	284,614
1998	23,954	23,472	23,904	23,553	17,395	20,273	21,011	18,101	16,097	21,330	21,589	8,315	238,994
1999	15,463	17,539	13,853	17,179	8,911	16,294	17,936	15,837	29,141	16,662	26,445	16,117	211,377
2000	23,371	22,598	21,563	23,631	19,816	24,298	15,230	11,981	23,105	23,447	42,529	14,508	266,077
2001	26,836	18,732	16,962	24,993	26,361	20,465	20,849	20,137	19,735	21,276	14,926	6,302	237,574
2002	14,268	16,370	15,924	17,663	21,440	18,349	19,860	23,436	22,431	14,471	17,035	10,772	212,019
2003	10,555	18,933	13,069	18,879	13,900	15,153	13,293	29,799	19,438	18,937	17,768	10,977	200,701

Source: Winnipeg Commodity Exchange (WCE)

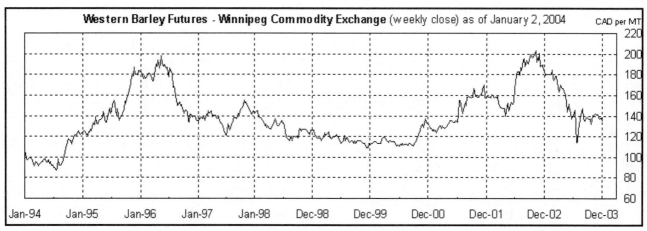

Western Barley Futures - Winnipeg Commodity Exchange (weekly close) as of January 2, 2004   CAD per MT

Bauxite

Bauxite is a naturally occurring, heterogeneous material comprised of one or more aluminum hydroxide minerals plus various mixtures of silica, iron oxide, titanium, alumina-silicates, and other impurities in trace amounts. Bauxite is an important ore of aluminum and forms by the rapid weathering of granite rocks in warm, humid climates. It is easily purified and can be converted directly into either alum or metallic aluminum. It is a soft mineral with hardness varying from 1 to 3, and specific gravity from 2 to 2.55. Bauxite is dull in appearance and may vary in color from white to brown. It usually occurs in aggregates in pea-sized lumps.

Bauxite is the only raw material used in the production of alumina on a commercial scale in the United States. Bauxite is classified according to the intended commercial application, such as abrasive, cement, chemical, metallurgical, and refractory. Of all the bauxite mined, about 95 percent is converted to alumina for the production of aluminum metal with some smaller amounts going to nonmetal uses as various forms of specialty alumina. Small amounts are used in non-metallurgical bauxite applications. Quantities of bauxite are also used to produce aluminum chemicals and in the steel industries. Australia, Guinea, and Jamaica are large miners of bauxite.

Supply – World production of bauxite in 2002 rose 5.1%

to a record high 144 million metric tons from 137 million metric tons in 2001. The world's largest producer of bauxite is Australia with 38% of world production in 2002. Other key producers are Guinea (10.9%), Brazil (9.7%), Jamaica (9.1%), and China (8.3%). Chinese production rose sharply by 22% to 12.0 million metric tons in 2002 from 2001, and production has quadrupled in the past 10 years. India's bauxite production is also rising rapidly and showed an 18% annual gain in 2002 to 9.274 million metric tons, more than triple the amount seen 15 years ago.

Demand – US consumption of bauxite in 2002 rose slightly to 9.970 million metric tons from 9.770 million in 2001. The alumina industry took 93% of bauxite production in 2002, or 9.290 million metric tons. The refractory industry took 1.2% of US bauxite supply in 2002 (115,000 metric tons), the abrasive industry took 0.5% (52,000 metric tons), and the chemical industry took the remainder.

Trade – The US relies on imports for virtually 100% of its consumption needs. Domestic ore, which is less than 1 percent of the US requirement for bauxite, was mined by one company from surface mines in the states of Alabama and Georgia. US imports of bauxite fell to 7.577 million metric tons in 2002 from 8.542 million metric tons in 2001. US exports of bauxite were negligible at 42,000 metric tons, down from 81,000 metric tons in 2001.

World Production of Bauxite — In Thousands of Metric Tons

Year	Australia	Brazil	China	Greece	Guinea	Guyana[2]	Hungary	India	Jamaica[3]	Russia[3]	Sierra Leone	Suriname	World Total
1993	41,320	10,001	3,500	2,205	15,300	2,125	1,561	5,277	11,307	4,260	1,165	3,421	110,000
1994	41,733	8,673	3,700	2,196	13,300	1,732	836	4,809	11,564	3,000	735	3,772	106,000
1995	42,655	10,214	5,000	2,200	15,800	2,028	1,015	5,240	10,857	3,100	----	3,530	112,000
1996	43,063	10,998	6,200	2,452	15,600	2,475	1,044	5,757	11,863	3,300	----	3,695	117,000
1997	44,465	11,671	8,000	1,877	16,359	2,467	743	6,019	11,987	3,350	----	3,877	122,000
1998	44,553	11,961	8,200	1,823	15,570	2,267	1,138	6,102	12,646	3,450	----	3,931	123,000
1999	48,416	14,372	8,500	1,883	15,590	2,359	935	6,712	11,688	3,750	----	3,714	129,000
2000	53,802	14,290	9,000	1,991	15,700	2,471	1,047	7,562	11,127	4,200	----	3,610	136,000
2001[1]	53,285	13,178	9,800	2,052	15,700	1,985	1,000	7,864	12,370	4,000	----	4,512	137,000
2002[2]	54,024	13,900	12,000	2,492	15,700	2,000	1,000	9,274	13,119	3,800	----	4,500	144,000

[1] Preliminary. [2] Estimate. [3] Dry Bauxite equivalent of ore processed. *Source: U.S. Geological Survey (USGS)*

Salient Statistics of Bauxite in the United States — In Thousands of Metric Tons

Year	Net Import Reliance as a % of Apparent Consumption	Average Price FOB Mine $ per Ton	Consumption by Industry — Total	Alumina	Abrasive	Chemical	Refractory	Dry Equivalent — Imports[3] (for Consumption)	Exports[3]	Consumption	Stocks, December 31 — Producers & Consumers	Government	Total
1993	100	15-24	11,917	11,002	203	225	429	11,838	90	12,200	1,590	16,938	18,500
1994	99	15-24	11,200	10,400	197	192	350	11,349	129	11,200	1,560	17,200	18,800
1995	99	15-18	10,900	10,100	133	201	394	10,582	108	10,900	1,730	16,300	18,100
1996	100	15-18	11,000	10,300	117	W	380	10,552	132	11,000	1,930	15,700	17,600
1997	100	15-18	11,500	10,700	98	W	466	11,069	85	11,500	2,260	14,300	16,500
1998	100	----	12,700	12,000	135	W	332	11,393	99	12,700	1,860	11,000	12,800
1999	100	----	11,700	11,100	113	W	251	10,189	149	11,700	1,440	6,800	8,250
2000	100	----	10,800	10,100	111	W	160	8,860	142	10,800	1,300	5,710	7,000
2001[1]	100	----	9,770	9,010	61	W	175	8,542	81	9,770	1,740	2,070	3,810
2002[2]	100	----	9,970	9,290	52	W	115	7,577	42	9,970	1,260	1,770	3,030

[1] Preliminary. [2] Estimate. [3] Including concentrates. W = Withheld to avoid disclosing company proprietary data.
Source: U.S. Geological Survey (USGS)

11

Bismuth

Bismuth is a rare metallic element with a pinkish tinge. Bismuth has been known since ancient times, but it was confused with lead, tin, and zinc until the middle of the 18th century. Among the elements in the earth's crust, bismuth is ranked about 73rd in natural abundance. This makes bismuth about as rare as silver. Most industrial bismuth is obtained as a by-product of ore extraction.

Bismuth is useful for castings because of the unusual way it expands on solidifying. Some of bismuth's alloys have unusually low melting points. Bismuth is one of the most difficult of all substances to magnetize. It tends to turn at right angles to a magnetic field. Because of this property, it is used in instruments for measuring the strength of magnetic fields.

Bismuth finds a wide variety of uses such as pharmaceutical compounds, ceramic glazes, crystal ware, and chemicals and pigments. Bismuth is found in household pharmaceuticals and is used to treat stomach ulcers. Bismuth is opaque to X rays and can be used in fluoroscopy. Bismuth has also found new use as a nontoxic substitute for lead in various applications such as brass plumbing fixtures, crystal ware, lubricating greases, pigments, and solders. There has been environmental interest in the use of bismuth as a replacement for lead used in shot for waterfowl hunting and in fishing sinkers. Another use has been in galvanizing to improve drainage characteristics of galva-

nizing alloys. Zinc-bismuth alloys have the same drainage properties as zinc-lead without being as hazardous.

Prices – The dealer price of bismuth in 2002 fell to a 9-year low of $3.14 per pound from $3.74 in 2001. The weak price was due to the weak global economy in 2002, but prices were set to recover in 2003 along with most other basic commodities.

Supply – World mine production of bismuth in 2002 fell to 4,070 metric tons from 4,270 metric tons in 2001. The world's largest producer in 2002 was China with 32% of world production, followed by Mexico (30%), Peru (25%), and Canada (5%). As for refined metal, China had 24% of production, Mexico had 23%, Belgium had 19%, and Peru had 13% in 2002. There is no domestic refinery production of bismuth in the US currently.

Demand – US consumption of bismuth in 2002 rose to 2,320 metric tons from 2,200 metric tons in 2001. Of that, 46% went for fusible alloys, 35% to chemicals, 17% to metallurgical additives, and 2% to other alloys and uses.

Trade – US imports of bismuth fell to 1,930 metric tons in 2002 from 2,220 metric tons in 2001. Of US imports, 38% came from Belgium, 27% came from Mexico, and 1% came from Peru in 2002. Exports of bismuth and alloys was negligible in 2002 at 131 metric tons, down from 541 metric tons in 2001.

World Production of Bismuth   In Metric Tons (Mine Output=Metal Content)

	Mine Output, Metal Content						Refined Metal						
Year	Canada	China	Japan	Mexico	Peru	Total	Belgium	China	Kazak- hastan	Japan	Mexico	Peru	Total
1995	187	740	177	995	900	3,430	800	800	33	591	924	581	3,840
1996	150	610	169	1,070	1,000	3,600	800	750	50	562	957	939	4,180
1997	196	550	30	1,642	1,000	4,360	800	760	50	550	990	774	4,070
1998	186	240	24	1,204	1,000	3,980	700	820	50	479	1,030	832	4,330
1999	264	2,680	24	548	1,000	5,490	700	860	55	481	412	705	3,610
2000	202	1,120	26	1,112	1,000	3,800	700	770	55	518	1,083	744	4,220
2001[1]	258	1,250	28	1,390	1,000	4,270	700	1,230	130	550	1,390	640	5,050
2002[2]	189	1,300	28	1,200	1,000	4,070	1,000	1,250	130	560	1,200	650	5,190

[1] Preliminary.   [2] Estimate.   *Source U.S. Geological Survey (USGS)*

Salient Statistics of Bismuth in the United States   In Metric Tons

	Bismuth Consumed, By Uses							Imports from				Dealer Price $ Per Pound
	Metal- lurgical	Other Alloys	Fusible	Chem-	Total Con-	Consumer Stocks	Exports of Metal	Metallic Bismuth from				
Year	Additives	& Uses	Alloys	icals[3]	sumption	Dec. 31	& Alloys	Belgium	Mexico	Peru	Total	
1995	257	27	544	1,320	2,150	390	261	636.0	444.0	10.9	1,450	3.85
1996	231	35	401	855	1,520	122	151	584.0	453.0	19.5	1,490	3.65
1997	252	31	593	655	1,530	213	206	691.0	601.0	163.0	2,170	3.50
1998	335	32	741	884	1,990	175	245	739.0	807.0	68.8	2,720	3.60
1999	340	31	823	855	2,050	130	257	742.0	277.0	6.8	2,110	3.85
2000	346	34	889	861	2,130	118	491	832.0	516.0	20.4	2,410	3.70
2001[1]	369	45	981	805	2,200	95	541	728.0	605.0	----	2,220	3.74
2002[2]	388	50	1,070	813	2,320	111	131	724.0	518.0	19.5	1,930	3.14

[1] Preliminary.   [2] Estimate.   [3] Includes pharmaceuticals.   *Source: U.S. Geological Survey (USGS)*

Average Price of Bismuth (99.99%) in the United States   In Dollars Per Pound

Year	Jan.	Feb.	Mar.	Apr.	May	June	July	Aug.	Sept.	Oct.	Nov.	Dec.	Average
2000	----	----	3.93	----	----	3.53	----	----	3.38	----	----	4.00	3.71
2001	----	----	4.15	----	----	3.73	----	----	3.58	----	----	3.43	3.72
2002	----	3.20	3.20	3.10	3.05	3.05	2.94	2.90	2.90	2.90	2.90	2.90	3.00
2003	2.90	2.90	2.90	2.92	2.98	2.98	2.98	2.98	2.98	2.98	2.98	2.98	2.96

Source: American Metal Market (AMM)

Broilers

Broiler chickens are raised for meat rather than for eggs. The broiler industry was started in the late 1950's when chickens were selectively bred for meat production. Broiler chickens are housed in massive flocks mainly between 20,000 and 50,000 birds, with some flocks reaching over 100,000 birds. Broiler chicken farmers usually rear five or six batches of chickens per year.

After just six or seven weeks, broiler chickens are slaughtered (a chicken's natural lifespan is around seven years). Chickens marketed as pouissons, or spring chickens, are slaughtered after four weeks. A few are kept longer than seven weeks to be sold as the larger roasting chickens.

Prices – The average price received by farmers for broilers (live weight) rose to an average 35.3 cents per pound in 2003. That was slightly below the 10-year average of 36 cents but represented a recovery from 2002 when the average price of 30.4 cents was the lowest level seen in more

than 10 years. Average wholesale broiler prices (ready-to-cook) were on track to rise to about 61 cents per pound in 2003, up from the 10-year low of 55.54 cents seen in 2002.

Supply – Total production of broilers in 2003 rose slightly by +0.9% to 32.533 billion pounds, up from 32.240 billion in 2002. The number of broilers raised for commercial production rose 2.6% to 8.732 billion in 2003, up from 8.511 billion in 2002. Furthermore, in addition to a larger number of broilers, the average weight per bird rose by 1.6% to 5.20 pounds, up from 5.12 pounds in 2002.

Demand – US per capita consumption of broilers in 2003 was unchanged from 2002 at a record 80.5 pounds (ready-to-cook) per person per year. US consumption of chicken has nearly doubled in the past two decades, up from as little as 47.0 pounds in 1980, as consumers have switched to the leaner and healthier meat of chicken versus beef.

Broiler Supply and Prices in the United States

Year & Quarters	Number (Millions)	Federally Inspected Slaughter			Total Production RTC[3] (Mil. Lbs.)	Per Capita Consumption RTC Basis (Mil. Lbs.)	Prices	
		Average Weight (Pounds)	Liveweight Pounds (Mil. Lbs.)	Certified RTC Weight (Mil. Lbs.)			Farm	Geogia Dock[4]
							Cents per Pound	
1998	7,825	4.86	38,016	27,832	27,863	72.6	39.81	59.81
1999	8,112	4.99	40,444	29,741	29,741	77.0	36.89	58.75
2000	8,239	5.00	38,417	30,397	30,495	77.4	35.20	58.14
2001	8,387	5.04	42,337	31,257	31,266	76.6	39.58	62.08
2002[1]	8,511	5.12	43,529	32,190	32,240	80.5	30.42	61.65
2003[2]	8,509	5.19	44,185	32,666	32,637	81.4	35.33	64.80
I	2,039	5.17	10,537	7,770	7,770	19.6	34.00	61.93
II	2,145	5.20	11,152	8,238	8,238	20.6	33.67	63.35
III	2,215	5.15	11,408	8,454	8,454	21.3	36.33	66.61
IV	2,114	5.25	11,102	8,200	8,175	19.9	37.33	67.32

[1] Preliminary. [2] Estimate. [3] Total production equals federal inspected slaughter plus other slaughter minus cut-up & further processing condemnation. [4] Ready-to-cook basis. *Source: Economic Research Service, U.S. Department of Agriculture (ERS-USDA)*

Salient Statistics of Broilers in the United States

Year	Commercial Production		Average		Value of Production (Mil. $)	Total Chickens[3] Supply and Distribution						Consumption	
						Production			Storage Stocks		Broiler		
	Number (Mil. Lbs.)	Liveweight (Mil. Lbs.)	Liveweight Per Bird (Pounds)	Average Price (Cents/Lb.)		Federally Inspected	Other Chickens	Total	January 1	Exports	Feed Ratio (Pounds)	Total (Mil. Lbs.)	Per Capita[4] (Pounds)
						In Millions of Pounds							
1996	7,597	36,479	4.80	38.1	13,903	26,124	491	26,615	567	4,685	4.7	21,854	70.40
1997	7,764	37,541	4.84	37.7	14,159	27,041	510	27,570	647	5,048	6.3	22,541	71.90
1998	7,934	38,554	4.86	39.3	15,145	27,612	525	28,137	614	5,099	7.2	22,942	72.60
1999	8,146	40,830	5.01	37.1	15,129	29,468	554	30,022	717	5,312	6.7	24,631	77.00
2000	8,263	41,516	5.02	33.6	13,953	30,209	531	31,740	804	5,612	7.8	25,132	77.40
2001[1]	8,389	42,446	5.06	39.3	16,694	30,816	614	31,330	807	6,357	5.5	25,075	76.90
2002[2]	8,590	44,050	5.13	30.5	13,435	31,583	500	32,083	717	6,530	5.4	25,571	80.80

[1] Preliminary. [2] Estimate. [3] Ready-to-cook. [4] Retail weight basis. *Source: Economic Research Service, U.S. Department of Agriculture (ERS-USDA)*

Average Wholesale Broiler[1] Prices RTC (Ready-to-Cook) (In Cents Per Pound)

Year	Jan.	Feb.	Mar.	Apr.	May	June	July	Aug.	Sept.	Oct.	Nov.	Dec.	Average
1997	61.99	59.53	58.41	59.77	58.53	59.05	63.04	63.25	59.86	55.39	54.62	52.25	58.81
1998	54.66	56.40	58.10	58.52	60.08	64.26	68.53	72.13	70.53	68.04	64.13	60.45	62.99
1999	59.33	58.23	56.79	55.08	60.02	60.33	59.46	57.65	57.15	54.87	59.52	58.42	58.07
2000	55.43	53.84	54.48	55.39	55.71	56.01	56.61	55.47	58.35	57.22	58.22	57.23	56.16
2001	56.87	57.47	58.95	58.46	59.40	59.88	60.43	60.90	61.93	60.17	58.89	55.98	59.11
2002	56.86	55.91	55.17	53.47	56.42	58.44	57.47	55.72	55.88	52.97	53.42	54.74	55.54
2003[2]	60.46	60.49	60.02	57.78	59.44	61.56	62.80	63.20	64.08	63.59	64.45	65.71	61.97

[1] 12-city composite wholesale price. [2] Preliminary. *Source: Economic Research Service, U.S. Department of Agriculture (ERS-USDA)*

Butter

Butter is a dairy product produced by churning the fat from milk, usually cow's milk, until it solidifies. In some parts of the world, butter is also made from the milk of goats, sheep, and even horses. Butter has been in use since 2,000 BC. Today butter is used principally as a food item, but in ancient times it was used more as an ointment, medicine, or illuminating oil. Butter was first churned in skin pouches thrown back and forth or swung over the backs of trotting horses.

It takes about 10 quarts of milk to produce 1 pound of butter. The manufacture of butter is the third largest use of milk in the US. California is generally the largest producing state, followed closely by Wisconsin, with Washington as a distant third. Commercially finished butter is comprised of milk fat (80% to 85%), water (12% to 16%), and salt (about 2%). Although the price of butter is highly correlated with the price of milk, it also has its own supply and demand dynamics.

The consumption of butter has dropped in recent decades because pure butter has a high level of animal fat and cholesterol that has been linked to obesity and heart disease. Per capita consumption of butter in the US in 2000, the latest reporting year, was 4.6 pounds, little changed from 1980 but sharply lower than 7.5 pounds in 1960 and 17.3 pounds in 1930. The primary substitute for butter is margarine, which is produced from vegetable oil rather than milk fat. US per capita consumption of margarine has risen from 2.6 pounds in 1930 to recent levels near 8.3 pounds, much higher than US butter consumption.

Futures on butter are traded at the Chicago Mercantile Exchange (CME). The CME's butter futures contract calls for the delivery of 40,000 pounds of Grade AA butter and is priced in cents per pound.

Prices – Butter futures traded in a relatively narrow range early in the year, generally between $1.15 to $1.20 per pound. Butter then staged a sharp rally late in the year to post a new 2-year high and closed the year at $1.36, up 14% from the 2002 close of $1.19. Butter rallied late in 2003 and early in 2004 on concerns about mad cow disease and whether that would result in the slaughter of a large number of cows thereby cutting milk production. Butter also benefited from the general rally in commodity prices seen in late 2003 due to the weak dollar and stronger US economic growth.

Supply – US production of butter in 2003 fell to 1.253 billion pounds, down from 1.360 billion in 2002. World production of butter in 2002 rose to 6.121 million metric tons, up from 5.737 million metric tons in 2001. India is by far the world's largest producer of butter with 42.5% of the world's production in 2002. After India, the world's largest butter producers are the US with 9.5% of world production, France with 7.4%, New Zealand with 5.6%, and Russia with 4.7%.

Demand – US usage of butter in 2003 fell to 1.192 billion pounds from 1.293 billion pounds in 2002.

Trade – US imports of butter in 2003 fell to 31.73 million pounds from 34.80 million pounds in 2002, accounting for a meager 2% of US usage.

Supply and Distribution of Butter in the United States   In Millions of Pounds

| | Supply | | | | Distribution | | | | | | | 93 Score | |
| | | | | | Domestic Disappearance | | Department of Agriculture | | | | | AA Wholesale Price | |
Year	Pro-duction	Cold Storage Stocks[3] Jan. 1[5]	Imports	Total Supply	Total	Per Capita (Pounds)	Exports	Jan. 1 Stocks[4]	Dec. 31 Stocks[4]	Removed by USDA Programs	Total Use	California ----- $ per Pound -----	Chicago
1994	1,296	244	2.745	1,543	1,255	4.8	203	229	68	204.3	1,463	.9581	.7068
1995	1,264	80	1.537	1,348	1,186	4.5	100	68	3	77.8	1,329	----	.8188
1996	1,174	19	10.545	1,204	1,148	4.3	83	3	0	0.1	1,190	----	1.0824
1997	1,151	14	24.154	1,177	1,115	4.1	46	0	0	38.4	1,156	----	1.1625
1998	1,082	21	70.369	1,243	1,220	4.4	33	0	0	12.6	1,229	----	1.7685
1999	1,167	26	39.813	1,337	1,307	4.7	20	0	0	3.7	1,314	----	1.2396
2000	1,274	25	32.400	1,331	1,329	4.6	7	0	0	8.8	1,307	----	1.1768
2001[1]	1,237	24	75.000	1,336	1,268			0	0			----	1.6630
2002[2]	1,355	56	34.800	1,445	1,293			0	1			----	1.1059

[1] Preliminary.   [2] Estimates.   [3] Includes butter-equivalent.   [4] Includes butteroil.   [5] Includes stocks held by USDA.
Source: Economic Research Service, U.S. Department of Agriculture (ERS-USDA)

Commercial Disappearance of Creamery Butter in the United States   In Millions of Pounds

Year	First Quarter	Second Quarter	Third Quarter	Fourth Quarter	Total	Year	First Quarter	Second Quarter	Third Quarter	Fourth Quarter	Total
1992	214.6	216.6	236.8	276.2	944.3	1998	289.0	276.3	255.3	308.6	1,137.0
1993	224.6	231.5	271.9	312.7	1,040.6	1999	299.3	316.4	318.3	374.8	1,308.8
1994	261.7	254.9	285.0	298.3	1,097.3	2000	300.8	286.9	332.3	380.6	1,300.6
1995	335.7	269.0	261.2	304.9	1,186.0	2001	290.9	278.4	316.1	397.0	1,282.4
1996	325.6	301.8	237.5	310.3	1,180.0	2002	313.5	263.5	317.4	393.4	1,287.8
1997	302.7	250.7	265.8	287.6	1,109.0	2003[1]	304.2	275.0	315.7	406.5	1,301.4

[1] Preliminary.   Source: Economic Research Service, U.S. Department of Agriculture (ERS-USDA)

World (Total) Butter[3] Production   In Thousands of Metric Tons

Year	Aus-tralia	France	Ger-many	India	Ireland	Nether-lands	New Zealand	Poland	Russia	Uk-raine	United Kingdom	United States	World Total
1996	153	462	480	1,400	150	122	309	160	290	163	129	533	5,136
1997	147	466	442	1,470	145	134	307	178	280	109	139	522	5,171
1998	154	463	426	1,600	145	149	343	183	270	113	137	530	5,336
1999	176	448	427	1,750	143	140	316	168	260	108	143	579	5,513
2000	180	453	426	1,950	144	126	344	169	265	135	132	570	5,688
2001	160	450	425	2,250	131	128	352	181	270	156	130	559	6,015
2002[1]	164	450	420	2,400	132	120	370	180	280	125	132	615	6,296
2003[2]	150	----	----	2,500	----	----	390	185	270	120	----	610	6,349

[1] Preliminary.   [2] Forecast.   [3] Factory (including creameries and dairies) & farm.   *Source: Foreign Agricultural Service, U.S. Department of Agriculture (FAS-USDA)*

Production of Creamery Butter in Factories in the United States   In Millions of Pounds

Year	Jan.	Feb.	Mar.	Apr.	May	June	July	Aug.	Sept.	Oct.	Nov.	Dec.	Total
1996	132.4	114.7	111.9	109.3	100.9	72.7	75.2	73.2	80.7	96.6	95.3	111.3	1,174.5
1997	127.6	108.6	105.4	118.3	102.7	82.0	80.0	68.8	79.3	83.3	89.1	106.0	1,151.3
1998	117.8	105.7	106.7	107.1	92.6	69.9	63.8	64.3	68.2	88.5	91.1	106.3	1,081.9
1999	123.3	111.5	113.7	106.4	104.7	86.0	75.8	66.1	78.8	93.0	90.4	117.2	1,166.8
2000	139.9	128.2	121.0	111.7	108.9	89.1	85.4	83.7	89.9	103.9	100.4	111.6	1,273.6
2001	127.4	111.8	111.4	109.0	111.0	86.8	84.2	75.6	86.7	109.9	100.1	123.0	1,236.8
2002[1]	140.1	124.2	127.7	131.6	125.5	95.8	94.4	88.9	92.8	102.6	103.9	127.6	1,355.1
2003[2]	141.4	128.4	126.3	122.7	114.7	83.8	79.5	70.1	73.1	97.0	88.0	114.4	1,239.5

[1] Preliminary.   [2] Estimate.   *Source: Economic Research Service, U.S. Department of Agriculture (ERS-USDA)*

Cold Storage Holdings of Creamery Butter on First of Month in the United States   In Millions of Pounds

Year	Jan.	Feb.	Mar.	Apr.	May	June	July	Aug.	Sept.	Oct.	Nov.	Dec.
1996	18.6	25.5	33.7	48.7	39.8	34.0	29.7	31.7	27.3	21.4	20.5	17.6
1997	13.7	23.2	36.0	50.3	86.8	104.2	93.7	85.6	69.5	43.9	26.6	15.4
1998	20.8	34.2	44.2	55.9	67.4	72.7	60.6	51.0	41.1	34.1	31.2	28.7
1999	25.9	60.8	95.0	108.4	125.5	136.6	120.6	123.6	90.7	71.5	64.2	30.2
2000	25.1	82.4	107.8	114.0	126.9	138.2	145.8	136.9	101.3	85.0	58.3	27.3
2001	24.1	68.4	86.1	96.2	112.3	138.0	153.5	151.1	118.0	110.9	100.8	57.9
2002	55.9	99.2	130.1	145.2	196.6	226.8	243.0	245.3	229.5	209.1	164.6	135.6
2003[1]	157.8	202.7	238.2	248.6	266.4	289.8	292.0	283.9	253.9	207.2	170.2	122.5

[1] Preliminary.   *Source: Agricultural Statistics Board, U.S. Department of Agriculture (ASB-USDA)*

Average Price of Butter at Chicago Mercantile Exchange[1]   In Cents Per Pound

Year	Jan.	Feb.	Mar.	Apr.	May	June	July	Aug.	Sept.	Oct.	Nov.	Dec.	Average
1996	75.4	66.4	65.5	69.0	87.8	129.3	145.3	145.5	145.5	128.6	74.1	71.9	100.4
1997	81.9	98.4	106.3	95.6	86.1	105.5	102.7	102.5	101.6	135.3	148.8	120.1	116.2
1998	109.2	139.8	134.1	136.4	153.2	186.7	203.1	216.6	273.1	242.3	187.9	140.8	177.6
1999	144.4	133.1	130.3	103.9	111.0	147.7	134.7	141.4	135.8	113.8	109.6	94.2	125.0
2000	91.6	92.9	99.7	108.7	122.2	128.6	120.3	120.3	119.1	116.9	151.7	150.0	118.5
2001	122.3	138.1	154.9	174.7	190.4	197.4	192.4	204.5	219.7	151.9	135.2	130.2	167.6
2002	134.5	124.3	124.7	117.1	105.9	104.3	103.0	97.5	96.4	103.2	104.3	112.0	110.6
2003	108.2	104.1	109.2	109.1	109.2	111.4	119.9	117.1	117.3	118.5	120.6	129.7	114.5

[1] Data from June 1998 through December 2001 are for Wholesale Price of 92 Score Creamery (Grade A) Butter, Central States; prior to June 1998 are for Grade AA in Chicago.   *Source: Economic Research Service, U.S. Department of Agriculture (ERS-USDA)*

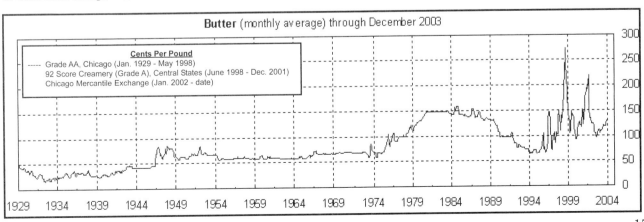

Cadmium

Cadmium is a soft, bluish-white, metallic element that can easily be shaped and cut with a knife. The atomic symbol is Cd, and the atomic number is 48. Cadmium melts at 321 degrees Celsius and boils at 765 degrees Celsius. Cadmium burns brightly in air when heated, forming the oxide CdO. In 1871, the German chemist Friedrich Stromeyer discovered cadmium in incrustations in zinc furnaces.

Rare greenockite is the only mineral bearing cadmium. Cadmium occurs most often in small quantities associated with zinc ores, such as sphalerite. Electrolysis or fractional distillation is used to separate the cadmium and zinc. It is estimated that at least 80% of world cadmium output is as a by-product from zinc refining. The remaining 20% comes from secondary sources and recycling of cadmium products. Cadmium recycling has been practical only from nickel-cadmium batteries and from some alloys and dust from electric-arc furnaces.

Cadmium is used primarily for metal plating and coating operations in transportation equipment, machinery, baking enamels, photography, and television phosphors. It is also used in pigments and lasers, and in nickel-cadmium and solar batteries.

Prices – Cadmium prices in the past 6 years have been at severely depressed levels, reflecting the decreased demand for the substance. Cadmium prices in 2003 rose 26% to 29 cents per pound from 23 cents in 2002. The 2003 price of 29 cents was an improvement from the record low of 14 cents in 1999 but it was still far below the 20-year average price of $1.59 per pound.

Supply – World cadmium production in 2002 fell to a 27-year low of 15,800 metric tons. China and Japan were the largest producers of cadmium in 2002, each producing 2,500 metric tons, representing 15.8% of world production. US production of cadmium in 2002 rose +3% to 700 metric tons from the record low of 680 metric tons in 2001. The US production level in 2002 was less than half the level seen just two years earlier. The US in 2002 accounted for just 4.4% of world production.

Demand – Consumption of cadmium has been declining fairly steeply in the last few years due to environmental concerns. Of the total apparent consumption, some 75 percent was for batteries. Another 12 percent went into pigments while coatings and plating used 8 percent. Stabilizers for plastics took 4 percent while nonferrous alloys and other uses took 1 percent.

Trade – The US in 2002 relied on imports for virtually none of its cadmium usage, down from 38% as recently as 1998. US imports of cadmium have plunged in recent years and in 2002 fell to a negligible 25 metric tons from 107 metric tons in 2001 and 425 metric tons in 2000. US exports of cadmium fell to 194 metric tons in 2002 from 272 metric tons in 2001.

World Refinery Production of Cadmium   In Metric Tons

Year	Australia	Belgium	Canada	China	Finland	Germany	Italy	Japan	Kazak-hstan	Mexico	United Kingdom	United States[3]	World Total
1995	838	1,710	2,349	1,450	539	1,150	308	2,652	794	689	549	1,270	20,100
1996	639	1,579	2,537	1,570	648	1,150	296	2,344	800	784	541	1,530	18,900
1997	632	1,420	2,260	1,980	650	1,145	287	2,473	745	1,223	455	2,060	20,300
1998	585	1,318	2,090	2,130	520	1,020	328	2,337	1,622	1,218	440	1,240	20,200
1999	462	1,235	1,911	2,150	700	1,145	360	2,567	1,246	1,275	547	1,185	20,200
2000	552	1,148	2,024	2,370	683	1,130	284	2,472	257	1,268	503	1,890	20,100
2001[1]	378	1,236	1,429	2,510	604	540	312	2,486	170	1,241	485	680	18,000
2002[2]	350	117	896	2,500	----	422	300	2,500	600	1,200	450	700	15,800

[1] Preliminary.   [2] Estimate.   [3] Primary and secondary metal.   *Source: U.S. Geological Survey (USGS)*

Salient Statistics of Cadmium in the United States   In Metric Tons of Contained Cadmium

Year	Net Import Reliance as a % of Apparent Consumption	Production (Metal)	Producer Shipments	Cadmium Sulfide Production	Production Other Compounds	Imports of Cadmium Metal[3]	Exports[4]	Apparent Consumption	Industry Stocks Dec. 31[5]	New York Dealer Price $ per Pound
1995	E	1,270	1,280	105	936	848	1,050	1,160	990	1.84
1996	32	1,530	1,310	119	720	843	201	2,250	1,140	1.24
1997	19	2,060	1,370	113	607	790	554	2,510	1,090	.51
1998	38	1,240	1,570	125	638	514	180	2,100	729	.28
1999	9	1,190	1,020	64	604	294	20	1,850	893	.14
2000	6	1,890	1,580	42	417	425	314	2,010	1,200	.16
2001[1]	3	680	954	31	----	107	272	659	1,110	.23
2002[2]	0	700	776	33	----	25	194	2,250	63	.29

[1] Preliminary.   [2] Estimate.   [3] For consumption.   [4] Cadmium metal, alloys, dross, flue dust.   [5] Metallic, Compounds, Distributors.
[6] Sticks & Balls in 1 to 5 short ton lots.   E = Net exporter.   *Source: U.S. Geological Survey (USGS)*

Average Price of Cadmium (99.95%) in the United States   In Dollars Per Pound

Year	Jan.	Feb.	Mar.	Apr.	May	June	July	Aug.	Sept.	Oct.	Nov.	Dec.	Average
2002	----	30.50	30.07	27.50	27.50	27.50	27.59	29.50	31.15	43.15	56.58	64.52	35.96
2003	58.33	55.00	55.00	55.00	59.29	67.50	67.50	67.50	67.50	63.15	57.50	57.50	60.90

Source: American Metal Market (AMM)

Canola (Rapeseed)

Canola is a genetic variation of rapeseed that was developed by Canadian plant breeders specifically for its nutritional qualities and its low level of saturated fat. The term *Canola* is a contraction of "Canadian oil." The history of canola oil begins with the rapeseed plant, a member of the mustard family. The rape plant is grown both as feed for livestock and birdfeed. For 4,000 years, the oil from the rapeseed was used in China and India for cooking and as lamp oil. During World War II, rapeseed oil was used as a marine and industrial lubricant. After the war, the market for rapeseed oil plummeted. Rapeseed growers needed other uses for their crop, and that stimulated the research that led to the development of canola. In 1974, Canadian plant breeders from the University of Manitoba produced canola by genetically altering rapeseed. Each canola plant produces yellow flowers, which then produce pods. The tiny round seeds within each pod are crushed to produce canola oil. Each canola seed contains approximately 40% oil. The rest of the seed is processed into canola meal, which is used as high protein livestock feed.

The climate in Canada is especially suitable for canola plant growth. Today, over 13 million acres of Canadian soil are dedicated to canola production. Canola oil is Canada's leading vegetable oil. Due to strong demand from the US for canola oil, approximately 70% of Canada's canola oil is exported to the US. Canola oil is used as a salad oil, cooking oil, and for margarine as well as in the manufacture of inks, biodegradable greases, pharmaceuticals, fuel, soap, and cosmetics.

Canola futures and options are traded at the Winnipeg Exchange. The futures contract calls for the delivery of 20 metric tons of canola and 5 contracts are together called a "1 board lot." The contract is priced in Canadian dollars per metric ton.

Prices – Canola prices on the Winnipeg nearest-futures chart generally range-traded during 2003 between CD$330 and $390 per metric ton. Canola futures ended 2003 at CD$365, which was below the year's high of $388.90 that was posted in late October 2003. Canola prices were pushed lower during the year due to a bumper crop, although demand rose to absorb almost all of that higher supply. As the year ended, prices were on the rise as stocks were being drawn down.

Supply – World rapeseed production in 2003/4 was forecast by the USDA at 38.00 million metric tons, up sharply by 17% from 32.50 million in 2002/3. China is the world's largest producer of rapeseed (canola) with 32% of world production (2003/4), followed by the European Union (25%), Canada (18%), and India (15%). China's production in 2003/4 rose sharply by 10% to a forecasted 11.60 million metric tons from 10.55 million in 2002/3. Canada's production soared by 60% to 6.67 million in 2003/4 from 4.18 million in 2002/3. EU production collectively rose slightly by 1.3% to 9.45 in 2003/4 from 9.33 in 2002/3. US production only accounted for 1.8% of world production and fell slightly by 1.4% to 700,000 metric tons in 2003/4 from 710,000 in 2002/3. Ending stocks of rapeseed in 2003/4 were forecast by the USDA at 1.85 million metric tons, down sharply by 32% from 2.71 million in 2002/3. Canola oil is the world's third largest source of vegetable oil accounting for 13% of world vegetable oils, following soybean oil at 32%, and palm oil at 28%. Canola oil production in 2003/4 rose sharply by 12% to 13.25 million metric tons in 2003/4 from 11.78 million in 2002/3.

Demand – Crush demand was strong in 2003/4 with a forecasted 35.29 million metric ton demand for canola for crushing into oil and meal, up by 13% from 31.11 million in 2002/3. The crush demand of 35.29 million accounted for 92% of world production in 2003/4. Consumption of rapeseed oil in 2003/4 rose by 11% to 13.21 million metric tons from 11.85 million in 2002/3. Consumption of rapeseed meal in 2003/4 rose by 12% to 21.09 million metric tons from 18.78 million in 2002/3.

Trade – World exports of rapeseed rose by 16% to 5.43 million metric tons in 2003/4, up from 4.69 million. World exports in 2003/4 accounted for 14% of world production. The US is a net importer of rapeseed products. US imports of rapeseed oil in fiscal year 2003 fell to 445,000 metric tons from 503,000 in FY-2002/3. US imports of rapeseed meal in FY-2003 fell to 919,000 from 836,000 in 2002.

World Production of Canola (Rapeseed)   In Thousands of Metric Tons

Year	Austrlia	Canada	China	Czecho-slovakia	France	Germany	India	Pakistan	Poland	Sweden	United Kingdom	Former USSR	World Total
1992-3	179	3,872	7,653	375	1,810	2,617	4,872	243	758	247	1,150	329	25,285
1993-4	305	5,480	6,940	377	1,550	2,848	5,390	225	594	313	1,136	211	26,735
1994-5	309	7,233	7,492	452	1,800	2,837	5,884	225	756	214	1,298	244	30,310
1995-6	557	6,436	9,777	662	2,700	3,127	6,000	255	1,377	215	1,330	252	34,435
1996-7	624	5,062	9,200	521	2,870	2,150	6,942	255	449	139	1,410	226	31,531
1997-8	856	6,392	9,578	575	3,496	2,867	4,935	286	595	132	1,527	221	33,108
1998-9	1,690	7,643	8,300	680	3,734	3,388	4,900	292	1,099	129	1,566	339	35,885
1999-00	2,460	8,798	10,132	931	4,392	4,285	5,110	279	1,132	154	1,737	505	42,525
2000-1	1,905	7,205	11,381	844	3,481	3,286	3,725	297	958	112	1,157	522	37,559
2001-2[1]	1,797	4,926	11,331	973	2,874	4,160	4,500	231	1,064	112	1,157	440	35,995
2002-3[2]	841	4,178	10,552	710	3,317	3,870	3,600	221	995	165	1,468	493	32,453
2003-4[3]	1,400	6,670	11,600	400	----	----	5,800	241	750	----	----	----	37,990

[1] Preliminary.   [2] Estimate.   [3] Forecast.   *Source: Economic Research Service, U.S. Department of Agriculture (ERS-USDA); The Oil World*

CANOLA

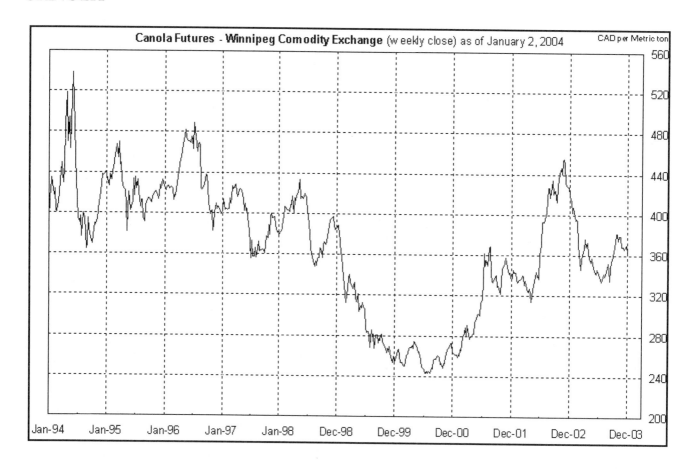

Volume of Trading of Canola Futures in Winnipeg   In Contracts

Year	Jan.	Feb.	Mar.	Apr.	May	June	July	Aug.	Sept.	Oct.	Nov.	Dec.	Total
1994	119,691	103,517	85,125	100,923	111,962	79,307	83,903	95,712	54,893	87,350	101,727	96,797	1,120,907
1995	75,068	87,113	86,340	67,937	95,447	85,126	94,576	70,904	94,794	126,210	84,991	107,177	1,075,683
1996	99,542	95,034	76,704	128,169	148,189	103,892	135,652	87,896	108,490	161,894	90,105	110,453	1,346,020
1997	121,433	133,056	131,473	148,647	117,219	116,117	80,867	72,602	93,967	150,065	97,984	124,245	1,387,675
1998	100,926	144,309	110,708	140,789	130,551	121,829	107,816	89,457	121,573	181,002	127,120	181,278	1,557,358
1999	129,758	59,772	132,732	143,282	102,838	134,179	94,256	113,913	130,505	184,973	157,428	179,798	1,563,434
2000	137,528	182,744	163,038	169,807	168,164	152,358	79,071	91,762	146,890	208,639	154,727	204,045	1,858,773
2001	196,137	292,226	286,463	247,744	205,798	188,175	163,901	155,531	143,220	205,016	174,910	165,852	2,424,973
2002	164,945	179,753	166,889	159,981	133,202	139,256	132,524	174,527	131,034	170,873	105,661	169,477	1,828,122
2003	129,903	152,738	108,991	153,528	120,178	152,979	90,909	66,768	109,760	217,310	90,950	153,269	1,547,283

Source: Winnipeg Commodity Exchange (WCE)

Average Open Interest of Canola Futures in Winnipeg   In Contracts

Year	Jan.	Feb.	Mar.	Apr.	May	June	July	Aug.	Sept.	Oct.	Nov.	Dec.
1994	50,335	55,280	54,899	58,012	60,567	55,434	54,733	57,044	57,049	54,375	55,045	49,475
1995	47,579	43,662	36,530	32,580	38,361	42,961	43,607	42,828	51,067	57,638	46,640	45,444
1996	42,646	43,808	45,126	47,989	54,228	52,176	49,387	40,619	42,242	52,273	53,121	54,323
1997	48,681	48,281	50,815	50,025	49,212	43,941	35,496	30,039	25,255	36,674	38,702	42,510
1998	35,864	46,678	49,161	48,683	56,163	60,285	57,627	51,462	53,919	56,651	51,426	60,663
1999	57,958	64,014	57,851	57,351	51,808	53,039	49,273	41,819	53,425	67,244	63,780	64,286
2000	59,057	65,545	65,296	66,253	65,855	59,673	46,813	51,367	59,342	72,618	64,862	65,170
2001	57,537	73,539	88,111	78,143	77,425	84,315	72,430	70,137	67,275	71,651	65,580	66,884
2002	57,821	56,443	53,321	56,830	50,924	38,901	48,329	54,286	53,630	50,379	56,896	57,983
2003	52,818	54,749	55,369	53,480	50,549	49,930	47,479	45,314	44,510	49,008	45,423	48,655

Source: Winnipeg Commodity Exchange (WCE)

World Supply and Distribution of Canola and Products   In Thousands of Metric Tons

	Canola					Canola Meal					Canola Oil				
Year	Pro- duction	Exports	Imports	Crush	Ending Stocks	Pro- duction	Exports	Imports	Con- sumption	Ending Stocks	Pro- duction	Exports	Imports	Con- sumption	Ending Stocks
1996-7	31,531	5,673	5,967	28,853	2,047	17,531	4,361	4,023	17,265	510	10,525	2,625	2,547	10,507	390
1997-8	33,108	6,902	6,757	31,204	1,081	18,838	4,581	4,417	18,742	442	11,425	3,024	2,685	11,030	446
1998-9	35,885	6,836	6,990	31,952	2,241	19,173	2,052	2,167	19,365	365	11,847	1,844	1,625	11,586	488
1999-00	42,525	8,912	8,988	37,346	4,116	22,451	2,719	2,652	22,400	349	13,728	1,798	1,522	13,381	559
2000-1	37,559	7,852	7,402	35,189	2,666	21,171	2,212	2,173	21,151	330	13,032	1,183	1,229	12,949	688
2001-2[1]	35,995	5,844	5,648	33,201	2,712	20,057	1,883	1,834	20,076	262	12,677	1,186	1,085	12,723	541
2002-3[2]	32,453	4,687	4,511	31,211	1,842	18,850	1,938	1,927	18,830	271	11,781	1,042	1,096	11,927	449
2003-4[3]	37,990	5,413	5,204	35,393	1,750	21,449	2,404	2,227	21,295	248	13,291	1,226	1,211	13,293	432

[1] Preliminary.   [2] Estimate.   [3] Forecast.   *Source: Economic Research Service, U.S. Department of Agriculture (ERS-USDA); The Oil World*

Salient Statistics of Canola and Canola Oil in the United States   In Thousands of Metric Tons

	Canola							Canola Oil						
	Supply				Disappearance			Supply				Disappearance		
Year	Stocks June 1	Pro- duction	Imports	Total	Crush	Exports	Total[3]	Stocks June 1	Pro- duction	Imports	Total	Domestic	Exports	Total
1996-7	40	219	259	518	395	79	474	35	155	502	692	529	133	662
1997-8	36	355	355	746	589	126	715	30	205	504	739	529	158	687
1998-9	19	710	310	1,039	698	246	944	52	250	503	805	603	123	726
1999-00	77	621	242	940	722	136	858	79	281	534	894	669	129	798
2000-1	50	909	217	1,176	773	220	993	96	292	545	933	797	85	882
2001-2	39	908	125	1,072	757	218	975	51	266	503	820	680	116	796
2002-3[1]	68	706	197	971	587	284	871	24	246	445	715	604	73	677
2003-4[2]	72	686	290	1,048	764	195	959	38	299	600	937	837	75	912

[1] Preliminary.   [2] Forecast.   [3] Includes planting seed and residual.   *Source: Economic Research Service, U.S. Department of Agriculture*

Wholesale Price of Canola Oil in Midwest[2]   In Cents Per Pound

Year	Jan.	Feb.	Mar.	Apr.	May	June	July	Aug.	Sept.	Oct.	Nov.	Dec.	Average
1996	50.75	50.75	50.75	50.75	50.75	50.75	50.75	50.75	50.75	60.56	90.00	90.00	58.11
1997	90.00	90.00	90.00	90.00	90.00	90.00	90.00	90.00	90.00	82.00	82.00	82.00	88.00
1998	28.00	29.00	30.30	30.58	31.13	28.45	28.44	26.85	29.75	28.20	27.19	26.10	28.67
1999	25.31	21.44	20.69	21.50	20.38	20.58	19.33	19.75	19.25	18.44	18.19	17.95	20.23
2000	17.31	16.50	17.25	18.69	17.75	16.45	15.50	15.69	15.60	15.00	15.31	15.50	16.38
2001	14.81	15.19	16.69	16.69	18.00	19.25	22.50	21.80	19.94	19.00	20.56	21.88	18.86
2002	20.81	21.31	27.44	21.94	21.95	23.19	25.06	28.45	29.81	30.75	34.19	41.19	27.17
2003[1]	24.30	28.88	27.63	27.44	28.13	27.13	26.56	26.30	28.44				27.20

[1] Preliminary.   [2] Data prior to 1998 are for Refined (Denatured), in Tanks in New York
Source: Economic Research Service, U.S. Department of Agriculture (ERS-USDA)

Average Price of Canola in Vancouver   In Canadian Dollars Per Tonne

Year	Jan.	Feb.	Mar.	Apr.	May	June	July	Aug.	Sept.	Oct.	Nov.	Dec.	Average
1996	424.07	422.60	417.55	443.94	473.04	469.28	470.38	453.86	453.53	444.01	432.30	439.79	445.36
1997	441.96	441.68	457.95	448.09	446.00	428.47	395.58	400.68	390.38	398.81	419.12	410.21	423.24
1998	416.48	428.88	434.68	441.44	450.56	443.11	404.86	387.05	389.34	400.40	412.17	417.41	418.87
1999	402.74	368.17	363.24	362.16	353.21	356.53	317.36	305.73	302.93	302.68	297.76	287.62	335.01
2000	286.09	277.92	280.97	287.34	284.59	274.12	265.32	262.24	269.17	265.32	267.75	278.59	274.95
2001	279.07	285.05	302.04	299.59	310.00	320.79	356.98	368.33	351.01	332.16	328.99	334.53	322.38
2002	329.23	328.38	329.39	316.74	318.67	330.21	369.42	401.78	408.43	413.64	436.25	418.74	366.74
2003	396.78	380.81	351.97	362.89	344.59	333.48	322.64	319.37	324.07	338.93	343.65	338.57	346.48

Source: Winnipeg Commodity Exchange (WCE)

Average Wholesale Price of Canola Meal, 36% Pacific Northwest   In Dollars Per Short Ton

Crop Year	Oct.	Nov.	Dec.	Jan.	Feb.	Mar.	Apr.	May	June	July	Aug.	Sept.	Average
1996-7	----	----	----	----	----	----	----	----	----	----	----	----	192.02
1997-8	----	----	----	----	----	----	----	----	----	----	----	----	131.15
1998-9	----	----	----	----	----	----	----	----	----	----	----	----	112.28
1999-00	----	----	----	----	----	----	----	----	----	----	----	----	117.07
2000-1	122.58	132.30	142.34	140.53	132.90	132.01	140.25	144.00	149.30	154.29	142.60	137.27	139.20
2001-2	142.85	142.44	129.48	135.34	137.33	150.15	146.60	141.90	142.10	153.40	149.10	149.30	143.33
2002-3	131.50	134.70	142.17	154.10	155.80	147.55	145.60	148.50	146.95	137.10	135.50	149.20	144.06
2003-4[1]	169.65	187.19	181.35	201.07									184.82

[1] Preliminary.   *Source: Economic Research Service, U.S. Department of Agriculture (ERS-USDA)*

Cassava

Cassava is a perennial woody shrub with an edible root. Cassava, which is also called manioc, mandioca, or yucca, grows in tropical and subtropical areas of the world. Cassava has been known since the 1500s and originates from Latin America. The cassava's starchy roots are a major source of dietary energy for more than 500 million people. Cassava is the highest producer of carbohydrates among staple crops, and it ranks fourth in food crops in developing countries. The leaves of the cassava plant are also edible and are relatively rich in protein and vitamins A and B.

Cassava is drought-tolerant and needs less soil preparation and weeding than other crops. Because cassava can be stored in the ground for up to 3 years, it also serves as a reserve food when other crops fail. The cassava is propagated by cuttings of the woody stem, thereby resulting in a low multiplication rate compared to crops propagated by true seeds.

One problem with cassava is the poisonous cyanides, which need to be destroyed before consumption. The cyanide content differs with each variety of cassava, but higher cyanide is usually correlated to high yields. The cyanide content can be destroyed through heat and various processing methods such as grating, sun drying, and fermenting.

Cassava is the primary source of tapioca. Cassava is also eaten raw or boiled, and is processed into livestock feed, starch and glucose, flour, and pharmaceuticals. One species of cassava has been successfully grown for its rubber.

Prices – The prices of tapioca (hard pellets, FOB Rotterdam) rose in the first quarter of 2003 to $94 per metric ton from $90 in 2002 and the recent trough of $82 in 2001. Still, tapioca prices are far below the 10-year average of $118 per metric ton.

Supply – World production of cassava in 2000, the latest full reporting year for the series, rose by +2.2% to 172.737 million metric tons from 169.026 million in 1999. The world's largest producers of cassava in 2000 were Nigeria (with 18.9% of world production), Brazil (13.3%), Thailand (10.7%), and Indonesia (9.5%).

Trade – World exports of tapioca in 2002 fell to 3.560 million metric tons from 5.140 million in 2001. Thailand accounted for 86% of world exports in 2002, followed by Vietnam with 9% of world exports and Indonesia with 4%. The world's two main importers of tapioca in 2002 were China with 49% of world imports and the European Union with 44% of world imports.

World Cassava Production   In Thousands of Metric Tons

Year	Brazil	China	Ghana	India	Indo-nesia	Mozam-bique	Nigeria	Para-guay	Tan-zania	Thailand	Uganda	Congo	World Total
1995	25,423	3,501	6,612	5,929	15,442	4,178	31,404	3,054	5,969	17,388	2,224	17,500	165,436
1996	24,584	3,601	7,111	5,443	17,002	4,734	31,418	2,648	5,992	17,388	2,245	18,000	164,711
1997	24,305	3,651	7,000	5,868	15,134	5,337	30,409	3,155	5,700	18,084	2,291	16,973	164,373
1998	19,503	3,701	7,227	6,000	14,696	5,639	32,695	3,300	6,128	15,591	3,204	17,060	162,856
1999	20,864	3,751	7,845	6,700	16,438	5,353	32,697	3,694	7,182	16,507	4,875	16,500	171,918
2000	23,336	3,801	8,107	6,800	16,089	5,362	32,010	2,719	7,120	19,064	4,966	15,959	178,567
2001	22,479	3,851	8,966	6,900	17,055	5,400	32,586	3,568	6,884	18,396	5,265	15,436	183,289
2002[1]	23,108	3,851	9,731	6,900	16,723	5,400	34,476	4,142	6,888	16,870	5,300	14,929	184,853

[1] Estimate.   *Source: Food and Agriculture Organization of the United Nations (FAO-UN)*

Prices of Tapioca, Hard Pellets, F.O.B. Rotterdam   U.S. Dollars Per Tonne

Year	Jan.	Feb.	Mar.	Apr.	May	June	July	Aug.	Sept.	Oct.	Nov.	Dec.	Average
1995	164	170	180	178	174	176	183	176	178	184	182	178	177
1996	167	160	155	158	163	154	149	154	146	139	140	133	152
1997	133	118	112	108	114	110	100	97	100	102	102	100	108
1998	96	100	98	104	106	104	105	106	112	122	124	109	107
1999	104	102	101	102	108	104	99	102	100	99	100	97	102
2000	94	90	88	92	85	88	88	81	78	74	76	79	84
2001	83	80	77	78	80	82	84	84	87	83	84	84	82
2002	86	82	82	84	87	91	96	97	95	93	93	89	90
2003	91	92	95	96									94

Source: The Oil World

World Trade in Tapioca   In Thousands of Metric Tons

Year	China	Indonesia	Thailand	Viet Nam	Total World Exports	China	EC-12[2]	Japan	Rep. of Korea	United States	Former USSR	Total World Imports
		Exports						**Imports**				
1995	10	481	3,297	1	3,860	362	2,924	16	140	----	----	3,590
1996	11	389	3,607	1	4,052	75	3,321	22	554	----	----	4,174
1997	11	247	4,155	68	4,519	242	3,413	15	585	----	----	4,605
1998	10	221	3,199	87	3,555	250	2,620	19	463	----	----	3,536
1999	10	340	4,341	117	4,857	381	3,781	18	212	----	----	4,501
2000	10	151	3,915	215	4,334	170	3,765	19	292	----	----	4,555
2001	10	177	4,494	409	5,140	1,950	2,728	20	445	----	----	5,288
2002[1]	----	130	3,067	308	3,560	1,760	1,576	14	157	----	----	3,601

[1] Estimate.   [2] Intra-EU trade is excluded.   *Source: The Oil World*

Castor Beans

Castor bean plants are native to the Ethiopian region of tropical east Africa. The seeds of the castor bean are used to produce castor oil. The average castor bean seed contains 35% to 55% oil. The oil is removed from the bean seeds by either pressing or solvent extraction. Castor oil is used in many products. In the US, the paint and varnish industry is the largest single market for castor oil. It is also used for coating fabrics, insulation, cosmetics, skin emollients, hair oils, inks, nylon plastics, greases, and hydraulic fluids.

Ricin is one of the most deadly, naturally occurring poisons known. It received attention when it was used in a subway attack in Japan in 1995 and again recently when it was sent to a Congressional office in an envelope in February 2004. Ricin is found in all parts of the castor bean plant, but the most concentrated amounts are found in the cake by-product after oil extraction. One non-deadly use for ricin is for medical research where it is being studied for use as a potential treatment for cancer.

Supply – World production of castor-seed beans in 2002/3 fell to 989,000 metric tons from 1.033 million metric tons in 2001/2. The world's largest producer of castor-seed beans by far is India with 59% of world production in 2002 at 580,000 metric tons. The second and third largest producers are China with 27% of world production (265,000 metric tons) and Brazil with 7% of world production (72,000 metric tons).

Demand – US consumption of castor oil in 2002/3 fell sharply to 20.971 million pounds from 34.099 million pounds in 2001/2. US consumption of castor oil has fallen by more than half in the past three years.

World Production of Castorseed Beans   In Thousands of Metric Tons

Crop Year	Brazil	China	Ecuador	India	Mexico	Paraguay	Pakistan	Philip-pines	Sudan	Tanzania	Thailand	Former U.S.S.R.	World Total
1996-7	41	222	4	770	1	15	5	4	1	2	15	3	1,116
1997-8	97	180	4	829	2	16	5	4	1	3	11	2	1,189
1998-9	17	230	4	840	1	19	6	4	1	3	7	2	1,168
1999-00	33	250	4	910	1	8	3	4	1	3	7	2	1,261
2000-1[1]	116	300	4	867	1	11	1	4	1	3	9	2	1,353
2001-2[2]	100	260	4	600	1	13	2	4	1	3	9	2	1,033
2002-3[3]	72	265	4	580	1	12	2	4	1	3	9	2	989

[1] Preliminary.   [2] Estimate.   [3] Forecast.   *Sources: Foreign Agricultural Service, U.S.Department of Agriculture (FAS-USDA); The Oil World*

Castor Oil Consumption[2] in the United States   In Thousands of Pounds

Year	Oct.	Nov.	Dec.	Jan.	Feb.	Mar.	Apr.	May	June	July	Aug.	Sept.	Total
1997-8	3,276	4,353	4,367	4,409	3,035	4,389	4,218	3,645	4,651	4,350	3,489	4,210	48,392
1998-9	2,348	3,579	3,740	3,323	4,197	5,004	5,218	4,639	4,396	4,471	4,465	4,494	49,874
1999-00	4,281	3,917	4,682	3,819	4,328	5,346	4,135	3,341	4,268	3,884	4,257	4,573	50,831
2000-1	2,694	4,601	2,386	3,975	2,896	3,209	3,159	3,840	3,112	3,050	4,686	2,257	39,865
2001-2	4,127	2,346	1,650	3,012	3,703	3,129	3,062	3,096	1,243	2,992	2,872	2,867	34,099
2002-3	3,281	1,887	1,528	1,641	1,642	1,629	1,123	1,315	1,518	1,839	1,449	2,119	20,971
2003-4[1]	2,072	1,836	1,779										22,748

[1] Preliminary.   [2] In inedible products (Resins, Plastics, etc.).   *Source: Bureau of the Census, U.S. Department of Commerce*

Castor Oil Stocks in the United States, on First of Month   In Thousands of Pounds

Year	Oct.	Nov.	Dec.	Jan.	Feb.	Mar.	Apr.	May	June	July	Aug.	Sept.
1997-8	25,098	24,188	25,425	17,543	12,736	7,138	2,804	18,897	15,386	24,682	16,586	29,862
1998-9	40,018	46,809	36,881	35,668	31,961	22,252	13,771	11,950	5,568	13,952	34,956	25,944
1999-00	44,427	34,180	31,191	44,315	36,632	26,885	25,486	27,605	39,038	38,118	42,934	31,015
2000-1	32,585	35,858	30,058	24,728	32,566	35,186	24,808	51,808	57,910	48,415	40,279	59,461
2001-2	53,083	45,933	23,973	38,459	31,058	36,743	39,591	39,528	43,227	50,814	49,283	53,075
2002-3	41,322	37,282	33,195	32,983	25,926	20,551	22,460	15,337	23,212	24,138	32,110	27,827
2003-4[1]	26,463	17,753	16,630	18,582								

[1] Preliminary.   *Source: Bureau of the Census, U.S. Department of Commerce*

Average Wholesale Price of Castor Oil No. 1, Brazilian Tanks in New York   In Cents Per Pound

Year	Jan.	Feb.	Mar.	Apr.	May	June	July	Aug.	Sept.	Oct.	Nov.	Dec.	Average
1997	41.50	41.50	41.50	41.50	41.50	41.50	41.50	41.50	41.50	41.50	41.50	41.50	41.50
1998	41.50	41.50	41.50	41.50	41.50	48.00	48.00	48.00	48.00	48.00	48.00	48.00	45.29
1999	48.00	48.00	48.00	48.00	48.00	48.00	48.00	48.00	48.00	48.00	48.00	48.00	48.00
2000	47.00	47.00	47.00	47.00	47.00	47.00	47.00	48.00	48.00	48.00	48.00	48.00	47.42
2001	48.00	48.00	48.00	48.00	48.00	48.00	48.00	48.00	48.00	48.00	47.50	47.50	47.92
2002	47.50	47.50	47.50	47.50	47.50	47.50	47.00	47.00	47.00	47.00	47.00	47.00	47.25
2003	47.00	47.00	47.00	47.00	47.00	47.00	47.00	47.00	47.00				47.00

Source: Foreign Agricultural Service, U.S. Department of Agriculture (FAS-USDA)

Cattle and Calves

The cattle and beef industry begins with the cow-calf operation, which breeds the new calves. Most ranchers breed their herds of cows in summer, thus producing the new crop of calves in spring (the gestation period is about nine months). This allows the calves to be born during the milder weather of spring thus having ample forage available through the summer and early autumn. The calves are weaned from the mother after 6-8 months and most are then moved into the "stocker" operation. The calves usually spend the next 6-10 months in the stocker operation, growing to near full-sized by foraging for summer grass or winter wheat. When the cattle reach 600-800 pounds, they are typically sent to a feedlot and become "feeder cattle". In the feedlot, the cattle are fed a special food mix to encourage rapid weight gain. The mix includes grain (corn, milo, or wheat), a protein supplement (soybean, cottonseed, or linseed meal), and roughage (alfalfa, silage, prairie hay, or an agricultural by-product such as sugar beet pulp). The animal is considered "finished" when it reaches full weight and is ready for slaughter, typically at around 1,200 pounds, which produces a dressed carcass of around 745 pounds. After reaching full weight, the cattle are sold for slaughter to a meat packing plant. The beef industry as a whole is estimated at $175 billion. Futures on live cattle and feeder cattle are traded at the Chicago Mercantile Exchange.

Prices – Cattle prices rallied sharply through most of 2003, but then plunged in late December after a cow from a Washington state dairy farm was found to have mad cow disease. On the nearest futures chart, live cattle prices started 2003 at around 80 cents per pound, traded sideways in a choppy range between about 71-82 cents through July, and then rallied very sharply to an all-time record high of 104.25 cents/pound in November. Prices then plunged in late December by about 20% on the mad cow scare, finally closing the year mildly lower near 74 cents.

Cattle prices rallied in the July-December period on a combination of events including (1) the fact that mad cow disease was found in a cow in Alberta, Canada in May, thus leading to increased demand for US cattle exports after most nations banned Canadian beef, (2) drought and poor grain-growing conditions in some parts of the US which reduced cattle weights and herd sizes, (3) higher demand for choice cuts of beef with the increasing popularity of the high-protein Atkins and South Beach diets, and (4) low inventories as ranchers rushed their cattle to market to take advantage of high prices.

But when mad cow disease hit the US on December 23, cattle prices gave back all their gains of the year, and then some. As of the end of 2003, 43 nations had banned the import of US beef. However, US consumer demand for beef did not show much of a dent from the mad cow scare as government officials insisted there was no risk from eating US beef. As 2003 ended, US officials in January were scrambling to determine what type of inspection and rules would assure US consumers of beef's safety and convince foreign countries to lift their ban on US beef.

Supply – The US is the world's largest producer of beef and veal with an estimated 12.226 million metric tons of production, accounting for about 25% of world production, which totaled 49.789 million metric tons in 2003 (USDA). The other key producers in 2003 were Brazil (7.530 million metric tons), European Union (7.360 million metric tons), and China (6.020 million metric tons).

Demand – The US is by far the largest consumer of beef at 12.422 million metric tons in 2003, down slightly from 12.738 million in 2002. The USDA is forecasting US consumption to fall to 11.962 million metric tons in 2004 due in part to the mad cow disease scare. The other key consumers of beef are the European Union (7.598 million metric tons in 2003), Brazil (6.460 million metric tons), and China (6.007 million tons).

Trade – Despite the fact that the US is the world's largest producer of beef, the US is a net importer of beef. The beef the US exports is typically grain-fed, high-quality choice cut meat, whereas imports are typically lower-quality grass-fed beef that is destined for processing into items such as ground beef. The key countries to which the US exports its beef are Japan, South Korea, Mexico, and Canada. The key countries from which the US imports beef are Australia, Canada, New Zealand, Argentina, and Brazil. US beef exports in 2003 were approximately 1.2 million tons (USDA), accounting for about 10% of production.

World Cattle and Buffalo Numbers as of January 1   In Thousands of Head

Year	Argen-tina	Aust-ralia	Brazil	China	Colom-bia	France	Ger-many	India	Mexico	Russia	Ukraine	United States	World Total (Mil. Head)
1995	54,207	25,736	149,315	123,317	17,556	20,524	15,962	293,922	30,191	43,296	19,624	102,785	1,073
1996	53,569	26,500	149,228	104,000	18,478	20,662	15,890	296,462	28,140	39,700	17,558	103,548	1,048
1997	51,696	26,780	146,110	110,318	19,038	20,557	15,760	299,802	26,822	35,800	15,313	101,656	1,043
1998	49,238	26,710	144,670	121,757	19,507	20,154	15,227	303,030	25,628	31,500	12,579	99,744	1,043
1999	49,437	26,688	143,893	124,354	20,621	20,097	14,942	306,967	24,859	28,600	11,722	99,115	1,041
2000	49,832	27,588	146,272	126,983	21,700	20,197	14,657	312,572	23,715	27,000	10,627	98,198	1,045
2001	50,167	27,720	150,382	128,663	22,676	20,518	14,557	313,774	22,551	25,500	9,424	97,277	1,040
2002	50,369	27,870	156,314	128,242	23,757			317,000	21,296	24,510	9,433	96,704	1,047
2003[1]	50,869	26,900	161,463	130,848				323,000	20,519	23,500	9,108	96,106	1,014
2004[2]	51,119	26,500	165,491	133,023				327,250	19,524	22,345	8,700	95,133	1,019

[1] Preliminary.   [2] Forecast.   *Source: Foreign Agricultural Service, U.S. Department of Agriculture (FAS-USDA)*

CATTLE AND CALVES

Cattle Supply and Distribution in the United States   In Thousands of Head

Year	Cattle & Calves on Farms January 1	Imports	Calves Born	Total Supply	Federally Inspected	Other[3]	All Commercial	Farm	Total Slaughter	Deaths on Farms	Exports	Total Disappearance
					Commercial							
1994	100,974	2,083	40,105	143,799	34,719	745	35,464	227	35,691	4,254	231	40,176
1995	102,755	2,786	40,264	145,805	36,272	798	37,069	225	37,294	4,382	95	41,771
1996	103,548	1,965	39,823	145,336	37,435	917	38,351	224	38,575	4,572	174	43,321
1997	101,656	2,046	38,961	142,663	37,101	792	37,893	218	38,111	4,676	282	43,069
1998	99,744	2,034	38,812	140,590	36,209	714	36,923	215	37,138	4,210	285	41,633
1999	99,115	1,945	38,796	139,856	36,737	695	37,432	210	37,642	4,114	329	42,085
2000	98,198	2,187	38,631	139,016	36,720	658	37,378	210	37,588	4,097	481	42,166
2001	97,277	2,437	38,280	137,994	35,752	625	36,377	200	36,577	4,211	678	41,466
2002[1]	96,704	2,503	38,193	137,400	36,140	641	36,780	190	36,970		243	
2003[2]	96,106	1,730	38,000	135,836	35,840	616	36,455				100	

[1] Preliminary.   [2] Estimate.   [3] Wholesale and retail.   *Source: Economic Research Service, U.S. Department of Agriculture (ERS-USDA)*

Beef Supply and Utilization in the United States

Year/ Quarter	Beginning Stocks	Commercial	Total	Imports	Total Supply	Exports	Ending Stocks	Total Disappearance	Carcass Weight	Retail Weight
		Production			Million Pounds				Per Capita Disappearance — Pounds	
1999	296	26,386	27,579	2,874	30,453	2,329	302			69.1
I	296	6,399	6,695	628	7,323	564	309			16.7
II	309	6,627	6,936	812	7,748	557	293			17.7
III	293	6,838	7,131	742	7,873	593	294			17.2
IV	294	6,522	6,816	692	7,508	615	302			15.8
2000	314	26,777	28,244	3,031	31,259	2,468	402			69.5
I	314	6,653	6,967	720	7,687	540	369			17.2
II	367	6,699	7,066	820	7,886	565	374			17.5
III	380	6,914	7,294	775	8,069	625	378			18.0
IV	406	6,511	6,917	700	7,617	620	412			16.7
2001		26,107	26,107	3,164	29,268	2,269				66.2
I		6,182	6,182	785	6,967	569				16.1
II		6,502	6,502	839	7,341	509				16.8
III		6,723	6,723	848	7,571	583				17.0
IV		6,700	6,700	689	7,389	610				16.3
2002[1]		27,090	27,090	3,218	30,308	2,447				67.6
I		6,377	6,377	737	7,114	572				16.2
II		6,833	6,833	934	7,767	601				17.5
III		7,097	7,097	839	7,936	662				17.3
IV		6,783	6,783	708	7,491	612				16.6
2003[2]		26,772	26,772	2,860	29,632	2,604				65.6
I		6,287	6,287	810	7,097	585				16.2
II		6,907	6,907	741	7,648	678				16.9
III		7,078	7,078	619	7,697	681				16.8
IV		6,500	6,500	690	7,190	660				15.7

[1] Preliminary.   [2] Forecast.   *Source: Economic Research Service, U.S. Department of Agriculture (ERS-USDA)*

United States Cattle on Feed in 13 States   In Thousands of Head

Year/ Quarter	Number on Feed[3]	Placed on Feed	Marketings	Other Disappearance	Year/ Quarter	Number on Feed[3]	Placed on Feed	Marketings	Other Disappearance
2000	11,475	25,348	24,100	925	2002[1]	11,565	23,513	23,639	846
I	11,475	6,107	6,150	250	I	11,565	5,942	5,709	221
II	11,182	5,656	6,187	262	II	11,577	5,364	6,243	211
III	10,389	7,043	6,269	147	III	10,487	6,246	6,176	141
IV	11,016	6,542	5,494	266	IV	10,416	5,961	5,511	273
2001	11,798	24,092	23,401	924	2003[2]	10,593	24,944	23,507	868
I	11,798	5,685	5,703	257	I	10,593	5,790	5,558	208
II	11,523	5,888	6,133	267	II	10,703	5,849	6,440	189
III	11,011	6,331	6,058	159	III	9,923	6,850	6,377	183
IV	11,125	6,188	5,507	241	IV	10,213	6,455	5,132	288

[1] Preliminary.   [2] Estimate.   [3] Beginning of period.   *Source: Economic Research Service, U.S. Department of Agriculture (ERS-USDA)*

CATTLE AND CALVES

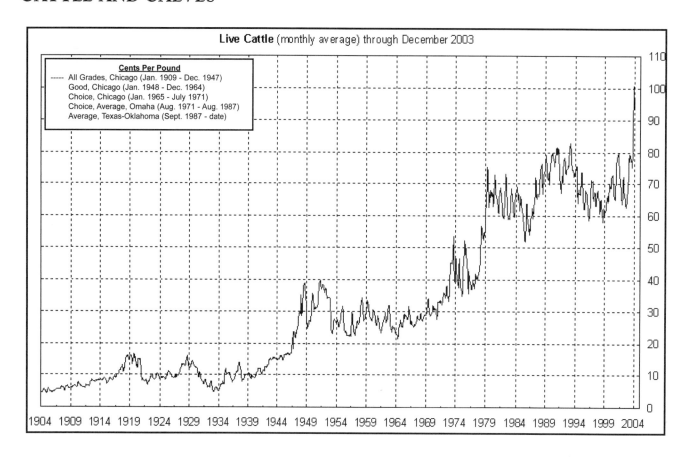

Live Cattle (monthly average) through December 2003

Cents Per Pound
- ----- All Grades, Chicago (Jan. 1909 - Dec. 1947)
  Good, Chicago (Jan. 1948 - Dec. 1964)
  Choice, Chicago (Jan. 1965 - July 1971)
  Choice, Average, Omaha (Aug. 1971 - Aug. 1987)
  Average, Texas-Oklahoma (Sept. 1987 - date)

United States Cattle on Feed, 1000+ Capacity Feedlots[2], on First of Month In Thousands of Head

Year	Jan.	Feb.	Mar.	Apr.	May	June	July	Aug.	Sept.	Oct.	Nov.	Dec.
1994	8,256	8,139	7,981	7,960	7,772	7,511	6,910	6,841	6,949	7,295	7,988	8,198
1995	8,031	8,119	8,227	8,328	8,233	8,182	7,734	7,391	7,189	7,722	8,420	8,685
1996	8,667	8,304	8,152	8,286	7,758	7,253	6,578	6,337	6,612	7,486	8,534	9,003
1997	8,943	8,813	8,769	8,904	8,484	8,231	7,679	7,536	7,850	8,558	9,390	9,718
1998	9,455	9,180	8,835	8,607	8,295	8,289	7,825	7,706	7,750	8,376	9,190	9,404
1999	9,021	8,917	8,878	8,899	8,583	8,547	8,183	7,889	8,185	8,793	9,789	10,020
2000	9,752	9,885	9,695	9,593	9,391	9,411	8,959	8,812	8,972	9,502	10,192	10,213
2001	11,798	11,941	11,695	11,523	11,170	11,245	11,011	10,891	10,855	11,125	11,863	11,891
2002	11,565	11,572	11,518	11,577	10,951	10,970	10,487	10,089	10,129	10,416	10,742	10,898
2003[1]	10,593	10,660	10,526	10,703	10,530	10,534	9,923	9,590	9,834	10,213	11,038	11,330

[1] Preliminary. [2] 7 States through 2000. *Source: Economic Research Service, U.S. Department of Agriculture (ERS-USDA)*

United States Cattle Placed on Feed, 1000+ Capacity Feedlots[2] In Thousands of Head

Year	Jan.	Feb.	Mar.	Apr.	May	June	July	Aug.	Sept.	Oct.	Nov.	Dec.	Total
1994	1,416	1,256	1,518	1,310	1,359	1,113	1,520	1,761	1,915	2,244	1,642	1,345	18,399
1995	1,631	1,532	1,681	1,403	1,673	1,356	1,404	1,653	2,173	2,278	1,804	1,446	20,034
1996	1,312	1,441	1,666	1,150	1,242	1,068	1,483	1,965	2,267	2,536	1,953	1,423	19,506
1997	1,663	1,552	1,694	1,296	1,612	1,224	1,751	2,111	2,278	2,454	1,826	1,304	20,765
1998	1,492	1,290	1,421	1,358	1,740	1,314	1,677	1,773	2,254	2,396	1,732	1,250	19,697
1999	1,681	1,563	1,741	1,443	1,733	1,515	1,565	2,085	2,345	2,629	1,823	1,408	21,531
2000	1,931	1,606	1,736	1,470	1,998	1,413	1,674	2,091	2,286	2,387	1,678	1,440	21,710
2001	2,263	1,580	1,842	1,551	2,372	1,965	1,986	2,204	2,141	2,702	1,908	1,578	24,092
2002	2,179	1,810	1,953	1,453	2,267	1,644	1,840	2,218	2,188	2,389	1,977	1,595	23,513
2003[1]	2,101	1,652	2,037	1,875	2,302	1,672	1,997	2,379	2,474	2,781	1,926	1,748	24,944

[1] Preliminary. [2] 7 States through 2000. *Source: Economic Research Service, U.S. Department of Agriculture (ERS-USDA)*

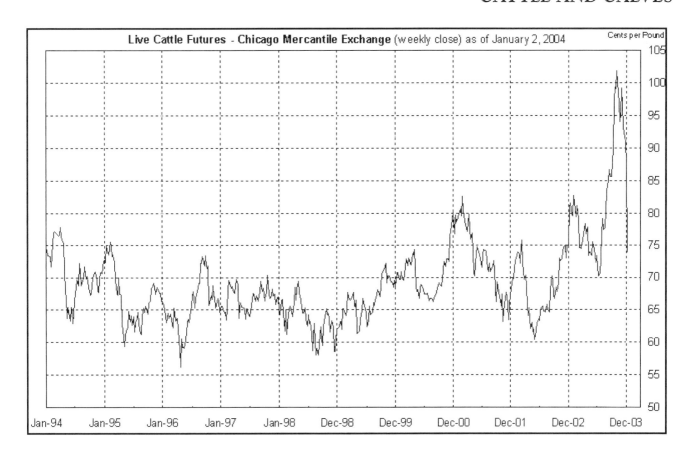

Live Cattle Futures - Chicago Mercantile Exchange (weekly close) as of January 2, 2004

United States Cattle Marketings, 1000+ Capacity Feedlots[2]   In Thousands of Head

Year	Jan.	Feb.	Mar.	Apr.	May	June	July	Aug.	Sept.	Oct.	Nov.	Dec.	Total
1994	1,481	1,357	1,467	1,430	1,542	1,632	1,550	1,602	1,525	1,504	1,370	1,432	17,892
1995	1,484	1,372	1,513	1,437	1,667	1,754	1,698	1,815	1,594	1,529	1,478	1,412	18,753
1996	1,626	1,541	1,476	1,613	1,747	1,696	1,678	1,653	1,342	1,431	1,418	1,415	18,636
1997	1,728	1,554	1,497	1,648	1,785	1,732	1,852	1,755	1,528	1,545	1,429	1,499	19,552
1998	1,689	1,579	1,580	1,609	1,681	1,727	1,755	1,687	1,577	1,537	1,455	1,564	19,440
1999	1,738	1,560	1,668	1,681	1,696	1,835	1,816	1,747	1,682	1,570	1,530	1,601	20,124
2000	1,747	1,749	1,764	1,601	1,863	1,828	1,784	1,895	1,708	1,647	1,568	1,500	20,654
2001	2,042	1,745	1,916	1,815	2,196	2,122	2,047	2,186	1,825	1,896	1,800	1,811	23,401
2002	2,083	1,801	1,825	1,996	2,171	2,076	2,193	2,135	1,848	1,979	1,731	1,801	23,639
2003[1]	1,959	1,715	1,798	1,985	2,233	2,222	2,270	2,075	2,032	1,855	1,537	1,740	23,421

[1] Preliminary.   [2] 7 States through 2000.   *Source: Economic Research Service, U.S. Department of Agriculture (ERS-USDA)*

Quarterly Trade of Live Cattle in the United States   In Head

	Imports					Exports				
Year	First Quarter	Second Quarter	Third Quarter	Fourth Quarter	Annual	First Quarter	Second Quarter	Third Quarter	Fourth Quarter	Annual
1994	569,466	540,845	386,596	585,597	2,082,504	51,803	43,115	62,729	73,144	230,791
1995	868,694	804,686	488,515	624,350	2,786,245	26,597	18,441	19,794	29,716	94,548
1996	605,648	467,059	391,633	501,108	1,965,448	33,906	42,796	42,757	54,848	174,307
1997	494,637	500,052	423,838	627,825	2,046,352	63,217	58,153	81,095	79,879	282,344
1998	538,018	503,547	373,451	618,993	2,034,009	69,824	63,459	53,145	98,781	285,209
1999	549,847	424,182	313,211	657,836	1,945,076	51,830	59,195	47,049	171,245	329,319
2000	580,174	537,009	346,087	724,016	2,187,286	117,889	67,895	72,028	223,430	481,242
2001	700,239	612,645	444,637	679,194	2,436,715	111,549	75,152	297,069	194,683	678,453
2002	785,559	398,072	474,128	845,214	2,502,973	73,401	62,140	49,930	57,472	242,943
2003[1]	630,303	408,833	142,780	548,112	1,730,028	38,246	34,145	10,953	16,571	99,915

[1] Preliminary.   *Source: Economic Research Service, U.S. Department of Agriculture (ERS-USDA)*

CATTLE AND CALVES

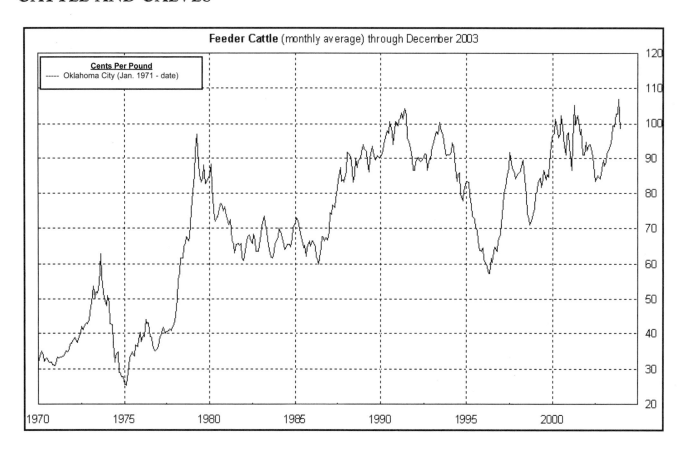

Average Slaughter Steer Price, Choice 2-4, Texas, 1100-1300 Lb.   In Dollars Per 100 Pounds

Year	Jan.	Feb.	Mar.	Apr.	May	June	July	Aug.	Sept.	Oct.	Nov.	Dec.	Average
1997	65.07	65.35	67.44	67.66	67.36	63.53	63.80	65.19	66.04	66.93	67.66	65.91	66.00
1998	64.57	60.77	64.52	65.00	64.52	63.85	60.28	60.00	57.93	61.54	62.23	59.97	62.10
1999	61.46	63.17	64.75	65.34	65.00	66.15	64.51	65.29	66.05	69.63	70.28	69.01	65.89
2000	69.07	68.88	71.74	73.13	71.28	69.41	67.22	65.02	65.43	68.51	72.19	76.41	69.86
2001	78.79	79.40	79.44	76.50	74.93	72.64	70.71	69.07	68.75	66.30	63.60	63.62	71.98
2002	64.00	71.24	71.97	67.63	65.49	63.85	63.57	63.41	65.63	65.64	70.21	73.11	67.15
2003	78.24	80.39	77.34	78.98	78.90	76.49	75.61	79.77	87.37	97.63	100.31	91.11	83.51

Source: Economic Research Service, U.S. Department of Agriculture (ERS-USDA)

Average Price of Steers (Feeder) in Oklahoma City   In Dollars Per 100 Pounds

Year	Jan.	Feb.	Mar.	Apr.	May	June	July	Aug.	Sept.	Oct.	Nov.	Dec.	Average
1997	71.52	76.77	79.66	81.60	85.43	87.04	91.67	88.69	87.23	85.66	84.37	85.25	83.74
1998	85.58	86.53	87.87	89.46	86.84	79.54	74.13	72.72	71.13	71.85	74.24	75.71	79.63
1999	79.49	80.92	83.21	84.44	81.80	84.37	86.80	83.84	85.24	84.75	89.13	95.92	84.99
2000	96.49	97.21	101.16	99.01	95.88	97.01	102.11	99.05	93.41	90.84	96.19	97.40	97.15
2001	93.08	86.63	94.17	105.06	99.71	102.16	100.39	96.74	98.31	91.06	90.83	94.51	96.05
2002	92.43	93.66	94.06	91.76	90.78	85.68	83.29	85.19	84.71	84.23	85.69	89.43	88.41
2003	87.76	88.84	91.31	92.94	93.58	96.04	99.28	99.15	102.68	102.63	106.87	104.66	97.15

Source: Economic Research Service, U.S. Department of Agriculture (ERS-USDA)

Federally Inspected Slaughter of Cattle in the United States   In Thousands of Head

Year	Jan.	Feb.	Mar.	Apr.	May	June	July	Aug.	Sept.	Oct.	Nov.	Dec.	Total
1997	3,169	2,726	2,795	2,998	3,125	3,003	3,127	3,050	2,909	3,156	2,698	2,811	35,567
1998	2,977	2,691	2,838	2,872	2,906	3,050	2,987	2,987	2,938	2,991	2,717	2,834	34,787
1999	2,904	2,665	2,990	2,916	2,947	3,154	3,037	3,099	3,045	3,033	2,882	2,814	35,486
2000	2,878	2,883	3,078	2,735	3,128	3,191	2,918	3,211	2,984	3,082	2,879	2,665	35,631
2001	2,947	2,533	2,867	2,667	3,152	3,075	2,898	3,193	2,758	3,103	2,854	2,726	34,771
2002	2,999	2,564	2,688	2,899	3,098	3,017	3,141	3,163	2,816	3,205	2,812	2,719	35,120
2003[1]	2,950	2,519	2,725	2,918	3,201	3,205	3,240	3,088	3,074	2,946	2,380	2,618	34,863

[1] Preliminary.   *Source: National Agricultural Statistics Board, U.S. Department of Agriculture (NASS-USDA)*

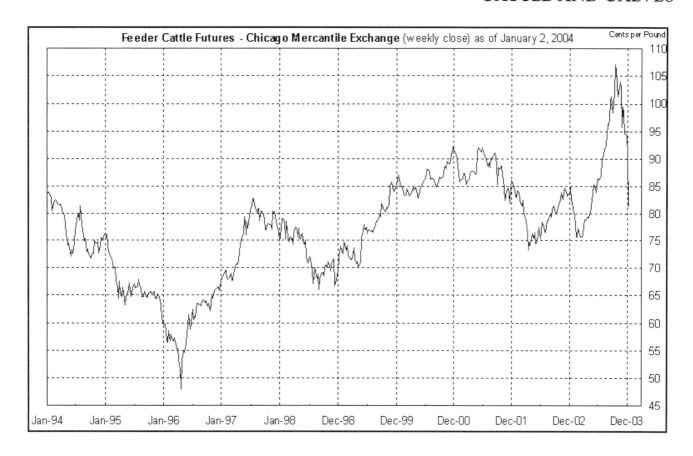

Feeder Cattle Futures - Chicago Mercantile Exchange (weekly close) as of January 2, 2004

Average Open Interest of Live Cattle Futures in Chicago   In Contracts

Year	Jan.	Feb.	Mar.	Apr.	May	June	July	Aug.	Sept.	Oct.	Nov.	Dec.
1994	87,923	87,578	83,949	70,287	72,851	75,470	76,663	72,988	73,391	67,924	74,152	68,600
1995	80,306	78,793	76,821	64,763	61,460	56,783	58,077	55,511	58,319	62,222	69,495	69,065
1996	72,870	83,064	91,348	97,315	97,911	96,320	96,547	93,557	92,804	88,467	88,062	87,305
1997	97,014	103,437	108,157	98,354	99,640	96,279	99,042	98,590	94,137	93,579	100,368	102,741
1998	105,559	102,036	101,264	88,257	88,167	87,493	86,776	86,874	95,013	102,636	108,263	106,156
1999	115,254	115,283	115,410	104,482	103,290	101,078	96,843	101,858	121,305	123,466	126,040	120,204
2000	128,918	123,980	123,925	122,596	117,834	106,196	116,266	120,526	123,945	123,517	131,773	132,239
2001	132,298	132,866	131,312	123,075	112,180	114,970	116,162	105,252	114,214	109,677	108,574	95,182
2002	93,589	91,566	98,176	98,343	98,846	91,129	93,541	92,966	109,651	111,338	121,671	116,588
2003	111,874	105,882	98,943	96,875	107,193	111,397	113,324	115,417	130,836	124,525	113,224	106,522

Source: Chicago Mercantile Exchange (CME)

Volume of Trading of Live Cattle Futures Chicago   In Thousands of Contracts

Year	Jan.	Feb.	Mar.	Apr.	May	June	July	Aug.	Sept.	Oct.	Nov.	Dec.	Total
1994	280,820	291,834	262,399	264,242	372,913	363,935	318,198	317,127	270,048	308,879	275,875	254,626	3,580,896
1995	289,710	259,210	391,721	287,194	285,686	290,224	245,250	266,793	233,402	220,130	246,655	241,130	3,257,105
1996	312,018	275,399	333,200	457,536	385,875	303,091	319,815	299,498	278,083	339,419	312,577	309,681	3,926,192
1997	361,620	352,173	312,113	331,948	285,885	303,369	387,526	324,943	316,822	374,632	238,003	330,608	3,919,642
1998	355,728	400,210	327,169	400,584	296,651	321,370	334,424	369,604	370,282	373,207	318,152	349,125	4,216,506
1999	298,814	342,572	338,076	320,457	296,512	342,854	287,557	266,544	371,735	345,269	375,960	253,198	3,839,548
2000	347,290	323,524	356,258	236,494	302,001	244,755	248,377	293,450	277,913	293,972	397,879	359,599	3,681,512
2001	511,050	357,474	385,581	302,829	348,294	289,093	318,564	324,614	340,969	403,101	403,009	294,695	4,279,273
2002	331,026	275,699	387,115	448,508	304,900	247,940	286,248	288,525	314,927	352,487	315,658	298,703	3,851,736
2003	378,862	343,931	334,007	306,713	391,477	311,239	449,966	319,677	473,218	469,405	324,732	332,862	4,436,089

Source: Chicago Mercantile Exchange (CME)

CATTLE AND CALVES

Beef Steer-Corn Price Ratio in the United States

Year	Jan.	Feb.	Mar.	Apr.	May	June	July	Aug.	Sept.	Oct.	Nov.	Dec.	Average
1996	20.3	18.1	17.2	15.1	13.9	14.2	14.0	15.0	19.1	23.6	25.8	24.9	18.4
1997	24.2	24.6	24.3	24.3	25.4	25.4	27.0	26.6	26.6	26.5	27.1	26.5	25.7
1998	25.8	24.8	25.2	27.5	28.3	28.3	27.9	31.6	32.2	32.1	32.3	30.0	28.8
1999	30.2	31.0	31.8	32.4	32.8	33.9	37.5	37.8	38.3	41.5	41.7	38.9	35.7
2000	37.5	35.9	36.2	37.0	34.7	37.4	42.9	44.7	42.6	40.5	39.7	39.0	39.0
2001	40.1	40.2	41.1	42.1	42.5	43.6	40.1	38.7	37.7	38.1	36.6	34.6	39.6
2002	36.1	38.1	38.2	37.0	35.3	34.0	31.2	28.3	27.4	29.3	31.5	32.3	33.2
2003[2]	33.4	33.4	32.9	33.7	33.4	33.6	36.3	38.8	40.6	46.1	45.5	41.3	37.4

[1] Bushels of corn equal in value to 100 pounds of steers and heifers.   [2] Preliminary.   *Source: Economic Research Service, U.S. Department of Agriculture*

Farm Value, Income and Wholesale Prices of Cattle and Calves in the United States

Year	January 1 Per Head Dollars	January 1 Total Million $	Gross Income From C & C[2] Million $	At Ohama[3] Steers[3] Choice	At Ohama[3] Steers[3] Select	At Ohama[3] Heifers Select	At Ohama[3] Heifers Choice	Feeder Heifers at Oklahoma City[5]	Cows, Boning Utility Sioux Falls[6]	Cows, Commercial Sioux Falls	Wholesale Prices, Central U.S. Choice 700-850 lb.	Wholesale Prices, Central U.S. Select 700-850 lb.	Wholesale Prices, Central U.S. Cow[6], Canner[7]
							Dollars per 100 Pounds						
1996	503	52,056	31,251	74.50	61.83	61.22	64.18	57.21	30.45	33.70	102.01	95.70	58.16
1997	525	53,383	36,322	65.92	63.85	63.36	65.66	72.04	34.27	36.14	102.56	95.92	64.30
1998	603	60,193	33,720	60.07	56.17	55.17	59.23	67.89	36.19	38.93	98.42	92.20	61.49
1999	594	58,834	36,861	65.64			65.68	71.90	38.40	40.61	110.91	103.07	66.51
2000	683	67,099	41,078	69.52			69.55	82.23	41.71	44.45	117.45	108.83	72.57
2001	725	70,495	40,803	67.68			67.81	84.19	44.39	46.65	122.17	114.42	55.32
2002[1]	747	72,284		66.39			67.39	76.70	40.47	39.63	113.59	107.66	

[1] Preliminary.   [2] Excludes interfarm sales & Gov't. payments. Cash receipts from farm marketings + value of farm home consumption.   [3] 1,000 to 1,100 lb.   [4] 1,000 to 1,200 lb.   [5] 1992 to date are 700 to 750 lb., 1987 thru 1991 are 600 to 700 lb.   [6] All weights.   [7] & Cutter.
Source: Economic Research Service, U.S. Department of Agriculture (NASS-USDA)

Average Price Received by Farmers for Beef Cattle in the United States — In Dollars Per 100 Pounds

Year	Jan.	Feb.	Mar.	Apr.	May	June	July	Aug.	Sept.	Oct.	Nov.	Dec.	Average
1996	59.10	57.90	56.80	54.90	54.70	56.40	59.10	61.30	63.80	63.30	63.40	61.00	59.30
1997	61.40	61.90	64.80	64.80	65.10	62.30	62.80	63.90	63.60	63.30	63.30	62.90	63.30
1998	62.50	60.40	61.30	63.00	63.00	61.80	58.40	57.40	56.10	58.00	58.10	56.80	59.70
1999	59.00	60.60	62.40	62.70	62.10	63.70	62.60	63.50	63.80	66.20	66.20	66.60	63.28
2000	67.80	67.60	69.80	71.30	69.40	68.50	67.50	65.50	65.30	66.70	69.10	71.90	68.37
2001	74.80	74.70	76.00	75.40	73.60	73.60	71.80	70.60	69.00	66.50	64.00	64.80	71.23
2002	67.10	70.00	70.60	67.30	65.10	64.00	63.70	64.40	64.50	64.60	67.30	70.40	66.58
2003[1]	73.20	74.00	72.70	74.60	75.50	74.90	75.80	79.90	85.10	92.00	93.70	90.50	80.16

[1] Preliminary.   *Source: National Agricultural Statistics Service, U.S. Department of Agriculture (NASS-USDA)*

Average Price Received by Farmers for Calves in the United States — In Dollars Per 100 Pounds

Year	Jan.	Feb.	Mar.	Apr.	May	June	July	Aug.	Sept.	Oct.	Nov.	Dec.	Average
1996	61.80	60.20	59.40	55.10	54.40	55.10	56.80	59.30	61.00	60.10	61.20	61.80	58.90
1997	68.10	74.90	80.00	82.20	84.30	85.40	86.90	88.00	86.90	84.30	82.90	83.30	82.30
1998	86.60	88.70	89.80	90.80	88.90	81.70	76.60	76.90	74.10	75.70	77.50	80.20	82.30
1999	83.20	86.90	87.30	88.20	87.60	89.00	89.20	89.60	90.90	91.90	93.00	98.60	89.62
2000	103.00	105.00	109.00	111.00	107.00	104.00	106.00	106.00	103.00	102.00	106.00	106.00	105.67
2001	108.00	109.00	112.00	112.00	111.00	110.00	108.00	106.00	107.00	99.70	96.70	101.00	106.70
2002	102.00	105.00	105.00	101.00	99.50	96.50	92.40	94.90	92.40	92.00	91.90	95.30	97.33
2003[1]	96.80	97.30	97.00	99.10	100.00	107.00	103.00	107.00	109.00	113.00	112.00	112.00	104.43

[1] Preliminary.   *Source: National Agricultural Statistics Board, U.S. Department of Agriculture (NASS-USDA)*

Federally Inspected Slaughter of Calves and Vealers in the United States — In Thousands of Head

Year	Jan.	Feb.	Mar.	Apr.	May	June	July	Aug.	Sept.	Oct.	Nov.	Dec.	Total
1996	140	140	141	128	133	131	156	153	146	159	139	149	1,715
1997	143	122	128	126	114	115	131	123	133	137	121	142	1,534
1998	125	111	125	107	99	115	131	122	132	121	109	127	1,422
1999	103	98	115	95	87	102	109	115	117	102	100	110	1,252
2000	91	92	97	75	86	91	92	98	91	95	91	90	1,088
2001	89	77	82	72	77	75	81	92	77	91	85	82	981
2002	86	71	76	80	76	74	94	94	87	98	88	96	1,019
2003[1]	92	81	83	77	74	72	83	78	80	85	76	95	976

[1] Preliminary.   *Source: Crop Reporting Board, U.S. Department of Agriculture (CRB-USDA)*

Cement

Cements are made in a wide variety of compositions and are used in many different ways The best-known cement is Portland cement, which is bound with sand and gravel to create *concrete*. Concrete is used to unite the surfaces of various materials and to coat surfaces to protect them from various chemicals. Portland cement is almost universally used for structural concrete. It is manufactured from lime-bearing materials, usually limestone, together with clays, blast-furnace slag containing alumina and silica or shale in a combination of approximately 60 percent lime, 19 percent silica, 8 percent alumina, 5 percent iron, 5 percent magnesia, and 3 percent sulfur trioxide. To slow the hardening process, gypsum is often added. In 1924, the name "Portland cement" was coined by Joseph Aspdin, a British cement maker, because of the resemblance between concrete made from his cement and Portland stone. The United States did not start producing Portland cement in any great quantity until the 20th century. Hydraulic cements are those that set and harden in water. Clinker cement is an intermediate product in cement manufacture. The production and consumption of cement is directly related to the level of activity in the construction industry.

Prices – The average value (F.O.B. mill) of Portland cement in 2002 was $76.00 per ton, down from $76.50 in 2001. That was well above the 10-year average price of $71.50.

Supply – World production of hydraulic cement in 2002, the latest reporting year, reached a record high of 1.80 billion metric tons. The world's largest hydraulic cement producer is China with 39% of world production, followed by India with 5.6%, the US with 5.1%, and Japan with 4.0%. Other large producers include South Korea, Germany, and Brazil. US mills produced approximately 90.78 million metric tons of Portland cement in 2003, which was a record high and up from 86.97 million in 2002 and 88.12 million in 2001.

Demand – US consumption of cement in 2002 fell to 110.02 million tons from 112.81 million in 2001.

Trade – US exports of hydraulic and clinker cement rose to 834 million tons in 2002 from 746 million in 2001. The major suppliers of cement to the US are Canada, Thailand, China, Venezuela, and Greece. The US exports only a very small portion of cement, less than 1% of production.

World Production of Hydraulic Cement   In Thousands of Short Tons

Year	Brazil	China	France	Germany	India	Italy	Japan	Rep. of Korea	Russia	Spain	Turkey	United States	World Total
1995	28,256	475,910	19,692	33,302	62,000	33,715	90,474	55,130	36,500	26,423	33,153	76,906	1,445,000
1996	34,597	491,190	19,514	31,533	75,000	33,327	94,492	58,434	27,800	25,157	35,214	80,818	1,493,000
1997	38,096	511,730	19,780	35,945	80,000	33,721	91,938	60,317	26,700	27,632	36,035	84,255	1,540,000
1998	39,942	536,000	19,500	36,610	85,000	35,512	81,328	46,091	26,000	33,080	38,200	85,522	1,540,000
1999	40,270	573,000	20,219	35,912	90,000	37,299	80,120	48,157	28,400	35,782	34,258	87,777	1,600,000
2000	39,208	597,000	20,137	34,727	95,000	38,925	81,097	51,255	32,400	38,115	35,825	89,510	1,650,000
2001[1]	38,927	661,040	19,839	30,989	100,000	39,804	76,550	52,046	35,300	40,512	30,125	90,450	1,730,000
2002[2]	39,500	704,720	20,000	30,000	100,000	40,000	71,800	55,514	37,700	42,500	32,577	91,266	1,800,000

[1] Preliminary.   [2] Estimate.   *Source: U.S. Geological Survey (USGS)*

Salient Statistics of Cement in the United States

Year	Net Import Reliance as a % of Apparent Consumption	Production Portland	Production Others[3]	Production Total	Capacity Used at Mills (Portland Mills) %	Shipments From Mills Total Mil. Tons	Shipments From Mills Value[4] Mil. $	Average Value (F.O.B. Mill) $ per ton	Stocks at Mills Dec. 31	Exports	Apparent Consumption	Imports for Consumption[5] by Country Canada	Japan	Mexico	Spain	Total
		Thousand Tons							Million Tons			Thousands of Short Tons				
1995	11	73,303	3,603	76,906	81.2	78,518	5,329	67.87	5,814	759	86,003	4,886	[6]	850	1,501	13,848
1996	12	75,797	3,469	79,266	83.4	83,963	5,952	70.89	5,488	803	90,355	5,351	[6]	1,272	1,595	14,154
1997	14	78,948	3,634	82,582	84.7	90,359	6,637	73.46	5,784	791	96,018	5,350		995	1,845	17,596
1998	19	79,942	3,989	83,931	84.9	96,857	7,404	76.45	5,393	743	103,460	5,957		1,280	2,204	24,086
1999	23	81,577	4,375	85,952	83.6	103,271	8,083	78.27	6,367	694	108,862	5,511		1,286	1,900	29,351
2000	20	83,514	4,332	87,846	80.7	105,557	8,293	78.56	7,566	738	110,470	4,948		1,409	1,177	28,683
2001[1]	21	84,450	4,450	88,900	79.1	112,510	8,600	76.50	6,600	746	112,810	5,110		1,645	651	25,861
2002[2]	19	85,283	4,449	89,732	78.7	108,500	8,250	76.00	7,680	834	110,020	5,181		1,228	327	24,169

[1] Preliminary.   [2] Estimate.   [3] Masonry, natural & pozzolan (slag-line).   [4] Value received F.O.B. mill, excluding cost of containers.   [5] Hydraulic & clinker cement for consumption.   [6] Less than 1/2 unit.   *Source: U.S. Geological Survey (USGS)*

Shipments of Finished Portland Cement from Mills in the United States   In Thousands of Metric Tons

Year	Jan.	Feb.	Mar.	Apr.	May	June	July	Aug.	Sept.	Oct.	Nov.	Dec.	Total
1997	4,111.3	4,487.1	5,739.1	7,009.5	7,489.3	7,733.7	8,132.4	7,909.2	8,186.1	8,678.9	6,108.6	5,471.9	81,064.3
1998	4,552.0	4,559.7	5,867.4	7,009.7	7,420.2	8,095.1	8,295.6	7,963.3	8,089.5	8,404.6	6,640.5	6,059.4	82,956.8
1999	4,487.3	5,132.9	6,380.5	7,112.2	7,406.9	8,096.9	7,782.2	8,173.2	7,652.7	8,204.2	7,453.4	5,959.1	83,841.5
2000	4,765.5	5,343.1	7,196.9	6,930.2	8,448.2	8,391.5	7,843.8	8,982.3	7,860.8	8,474.2	6,587.0	4,865.5	84,980.3
2001	5,107.6	5,088.8	6,684.5	7,799.4	8,507.9	8,385.8	8,333.2	8,851.2	7,512.2	8,953.3	7,353.3	5,548.0	88,124.9
2002	5,554.3	5,369.3	6,133.9	7,859.7	8,291.4	8,135.6	8,466.9	8,676.2	7,909.7	8,326.1	6,956.3	5,293.4	86,972.9
2003[1]	5,489.6	4,559.9	6,511.6	8,009.0	8,290.4	8,521.9	9,078.5	8,837.0	8,758.7	9,777.7	6,983.4		92,528.3

[1] Preliminary.   *Source: U.S. Geological Survey (USGS)*

Cheese

Since prehistoric times, humans have been making and eating cheese. Dating back as far as 6,000 BC, archaeologists have discovered that cheese had been made from cow and goat milk and stored in tall jars. The Romans turned cheese making into a culinary art, mixing sheep and goat milk and adding herbs and spices for flavoring. By 300 AD, cheese was being exported regularly to countries along the Mediterranean coast.

Cheese is made from the milk of cows and other mammals such as sheep, goats, buffalo, reindeer, camels, yaks, and mares. More than 400 varieties of cheese exist. There are three basic steps common to all cheese making. First, proteins in milk are transformed into curds, or solid lumps. Second, the curds are separated from the milky liquid (or whey) and shaped or pressed into molds. Finally, the shaped curds are ripened according to a variety of aging and curing techniques. Cheeses are usually grouped according to their moisture content into fresh, soft, semi-soft, hard, and very hard cheeses, with many classifications overlapping due to texture changes with aging.

Cheese is a multi-billion dollar a year industry in the US. Cheddar cheese is the most common natural cheese produced in the US, accounting for 35% of US production. Cheeses originating in America include Colby, cream cheese,

and Monterey Jack. Varieties other than American cheeses, mostly Italian, now have had a combined level of production that easily exceeds American cheeses. Annual cheese consumption in the US totals about 29 pounds per person.

Prices – Cheese prices in 2003 rallied to an average of 131.0 cents per pound from 118.2 cents in 2002. The average price of cheese in 2003 was mildly below the 10-year average price of about 135.0 cents. Cheese prices in 2003 recovered from the very weak years seen in 2000 (116.1 cents) and 2002 (118.2 cents), which were the lowest prices seen since 1975.

Supply – US production of cheese in 2003 was on track to fall slightly to 8.595 billion pounds, down from 8.599 billion in 2002. The 2002 production level of 8.599 billion was an all-time record high for the US cheese industry. World production of cheese in 2002 rose to 12.680 million metric tons from 12.421 million in 2001. The US is the world's largest producer of cheese with 29.9% of world production in 2002, followed by France (13.7%), and Germany (9.0%).

Trade – US imports of cheese in 2002 rose to 475 million pounds from 445 million in 2001. US exports of cheese in rose to 119 million pounds in 2002 from 115 million pounds in 2001.

World Production of Cheese   In Thousands of Metric Tons

Year	Argentina	Australia	Brazil	Canada	Denmark	France	Germany	Italy	Netherlands	New Zealand	United Kingdom	United States	World Total
1994	385	234	330	282	286	1,541	855	913	648	192	326	3,054	11,194
1995	370	241	360	277	311	1,579	875	942	680	197	354	3,138	11,345
1996	390	268	385	289	298	1,594	947	950	688	230	364	3,274	11,059
1997	415	285	405	329	290	1,645	990	985	693	240	368	3,325	11,388
1998	407	305	421	330	289	1,648	1,008	1,003	638	266	358	3,398	11,378
1999	446	320	434	329	293	1,658	1,006	969	655	245	361	3,581	11,750
2000	445	373	445	328	305	1,720	1,098	958	683	297	332	3,746	12,223
2001	440	374	460	329	312	1,740	1,125	972	650	281	365	3,747	12,313
2002[1]	370	413	470	335	317	1,740	1,145	980	640	312	365	3,900	12,649
2003[2]	340	371	480	330						272		3,975	12,647

[1] Preliminary.   [2] Estimate.   Source: Foreign Agricultural Service, U.S. Department of Agriculture (FAS-USDA)

Supply and Distribution of All Cheese in the United States   In Millions of Pounds

	Supply					Cheese 40-lb. Blocks Wisconsin Assembly Points cents/lb.	Distribution						
	Production		January 1 Commercial Stocks						American Cheese Removed by USDA Programs		Domestic Disappearance		
Year	Whole Milk[2]	All Cheese[3]		Imports[4]	Total Supply		Exports & Shipments[5]	Gov't - Dec. 31 Stocks		Total Disappearance	American Cheese Donated	Total	Per Capita
1993	2,957	6,528	470	321	7,303	131.50	38	2.2	8.3	6,853	0	6,766	26.24
1994	2,974	6,735	466	335	7,536	131.50	49	.9	6.9	7,094	0	6,994	26.82
1995	3,131	6,917	437	340	7,695	132.80	65	.4	6.1	7,279		7,174	26.90
1996	3,281	7,218	412	338	7,968	146.80	72	.3	4.6	7,478		7,364	27.30
1997	3,286	7,330	487	312	8,130	132.40	83	.5	11.3	7,647		7,511	27.50
1998	3,315	7,492	481	371	8,344	158.10	81	.6	8.2	7,799		7,662	27.70
1999	3,533	7,894	518	436	8,847	142.28	85	1.0	4.6	8,219		8,086	29.00
2000	3,642	8,258	621	416	9,295	116.14	105	2.3	28.0	8,555		8,409	29.80
2001	3,544	8,261	706	445	9,412	144.93	115	4.0	3.9	8,741		8,426	29.60
2002[1]	3,709	8,599	659	475	9,733	118.22	119	2.7	15.1	8,983			

[1] Preliminary.   [2] Whole milk American cheddar.   [3] All types of cheese except cottage, pot and baker's cheese.   [4] Imports for consumption.
[5] Commercial.   Source: Economic Research Service, U.S. Department of Agriculture (ERS-USDA)

Production of Cheese in the United States   In Millions of Pounds

Year	American — Whole Milk	American — Part Skim	American — Total	Swiss, Including Block	Munster	Brick	Lim-burger	Cream & Neufchatel Cheese	Italian Varieties	Blue Mond	All Other Varieties	Total of All Cheese[2]	Cottage Cheese — Lowfat	Cottage Cheese — Curd[3]	Cottage Cheese — Creamed[4]
1993	2,957	3.7	2,961	231.4	117.5	12.5	.9	539.9	2,494.5	33.3	137.2	6,528	317.0	471.4	430.5
1994	2,974	24.7	2,999	221.2	113.6	12.2	.8	573.4	2,625.7	36.5	152.1	6,735	321.1	463.3	410.0
1995	3,131	24.0	3,155	221.7	109.1	10.4	.9	543.8	2,674.4	36.6	164.6	6,917	325.9	458.9	384.9
1996	3,281	NA	3,281	219.0	106.8	10.6	.7	574.7	2,812.4	38.3	106.7	7,218	329.9	448.3	360.4
1997	3,286	NA	3,286	207.6	100.2	8.5	.7	614.9	2,881.4	42.8	119.8	7,330	346.7	458.5	359.5
1998	3,315	NA	3,315	206.4	94.6	7.6	.9	621.3	3,004.7	[5]	166.0	7,492	361.2	465.8	366.8
1999	3,533	NA	3,533	221.0	80.3	8.1	.7	639.3	3,144.7	[5]	181.0	7,894	359.3	464.8	360.6
2000	3,642	NA	3,642	229.3	85.5	8.6	.6	687.4	3,288.9	[5]	219.7	8,258	363.7	461.0	371.5
2001	3,544	NA	3,544	245.5	82.2	8.7	.7	645.1	3,425.9	[5]	199.6	8,261	370.2	453.2	371.6
2002[1]	3,709	NA	3,709	254.1	80.4	9.3	.7	709.6	3,506.5	[5]	208.3	8,599	374.3	437.9	372.4

[1] Preliminary.   [2] Excludes full-skim cheddar and cottage cheese.   [3] Includes cottage, pot, and baker's cheese with a butterfat content of less than 4%.   [4] Includes cheese with a butterfat content of 4 to 19 %.   [5] Included in All Other Varieties.   *Source: Economic Research Service, U.S. Department of Agriculture ERS-USDA)*

Average Price of Cheese, 40-lb. Blocks, Chicago Mercantile Exchange[2]   In Cents Per Pound

Year	Jan.	Feb.	Mar.	Apr.	May	June	July	Aug.	Sept.	Oct.	Nov.	Dec.	Average
1994	132.2	134.2	140.0	143.3	125.7	120.2	129.1	132.2	135.6	135.4	127.9	121.3	131.5
1995	124.5	130.4	131.1	122.8	122.1	126.9	126.7	132.2	141.3	145.0	145.8	144.6	132.8
1996	139.3	139.3	140.9	145.1	151.8	151.5	158.2	167.6	145.5	162.3	133.9	126.0	146.8
1997	127.9	132.3	134.0	125.6	116.5	117.9	123.3	137.6	141.4	142.4	143.8	146.1	132.4
1998	144.5	144.7	138.8	129.7	123.0	151.3	162.6	166.9	171.0	183.5	188.7	192.5	158.1
1999	162.4	131.5	134.0	133.6	124.8	138.1	159.7	189.0	167.3	134.0	117.3	115.7	142.3
2000	114.6	111.6	112.2	110.7	110.6	120.0	125.2	125.5	133.4	109.4	107.5	113.0	116.1
2001	110.3	120.0	131.9	140.5	160.3	166.8	168.5	171.8	173.9	139.7	126.4	129.1	144.9
2002	132.4	120.8	121.3	124.5	120.1	113.0	108.9	115.8	120.4	119.5	108.9	113.1	118.2
2003[1]	109.3	109.2	108.2	112.3	114.2	118.6	151.2	160.0	160.0	158.8	139.3	133.8	131.2

[1] Preliminary.   [2] Data through December 2001 are for Wholesale Price of Cheese, 40-lb. Blocks, Wisconsin Assembly Points.
Source: Economic Research Service, U.S. Department of Agriculture (ERS-USDA)

Production[2] of Cheese in the United States   In Millions of Pounds

Year	Jan.	Feb.	Mar.	Apr.	May	June	July	Aug.	Sept.	Oct.	Nov.	Dec.	Total
1994	538.3	505.8	591.8	554.3	590.4	558.7	550.7	562.4	565.5	574.5	559.3	578.3	6,730
1995	559.3	523.3	596.0	559.6	595.3	579.2	556.5	550.8	571.3	588.6	584.7	618.4	6,883
1996	590.0	576.0	625.4	606.0	636.5	595.8	582.2	589.5	584.5	612.2	595.5	623.9	7,218
1997	598.1	577.1	638.0	598.5	642.0	623.4	613.2	596.5	604.3	615.5	594.5	627.9	7,329
1998	617.2	574.3	646.7	636.9	650.4	639.9	607.9	596.4	583.8	633.2	637.8	667.4	7,492
1999	631.6	591.7	698.2	663.8	668.9	664.4	641.3	642.6	637.6	666.5	683.4	704.2	7,894
2000	692.9	649.5	714.8	694.0	730.4	695.7	687.6	683.8	653.8	688.5	675.0	688.4	8,255
2001	680.3	625.3	713.7	670.2	706.8	678.5	676.0	660.0	641.8	682.1	691.2	703.1	8,129
2002	717.5	667.9	742.8	719.2	748.3	708.3	692.2	714.3	683.9	732.2	725.4	747.2	8,599
2003[1]	717.8	653.5	735.4	721.4	742.2	714.5	717.2	709.0	712.1	741.4	710.4	753.1	8,628

[1] Preliminary.   [2] Excludes cottage cheese.   *Source: National Agricultural Statistics Service, U.S. Department of Agriculture (NASS-USDA)*

Cold Storage Holdings of All Varieties of Cheese in the United States, on First of Month Millions of Pounds

Year	Jan.	Feb.	Mar.	Apr.	May	June	July	Aug.	Sept.	Oct.	Nov.	Dec.
1994	465.2	495.2	473.6	473.3	487.9	513.4	521.4	506.3	474.7	453.0	448.3	434.2
1995	436.9	449.7	448.7	458.8	466.1	465.8	473.6	482.4	458.1	428.5	418.7	393.6
1996	412.1	441.3	466.4	490.9	525.5	541.8	542.8	536.6	506.9	495.8	494.6	480.2
1997	487.0	501.5	494.6	517.0	555.4	584.3	604.8	604.9	582.3	543.7	505.0	474.4
1998	480.4	509.3	521.5	533.1	557.6	568.5	583.7	595.8	576.8	553.0	522.7	494.5
1999	517.2	622.4	635.9	645.1	688.7	741.3	728.4	748.7	694.7	651.3	622.0	591.7
2000	621.3	728.1	757.2	765.1	794.0	811.4	828.1	870.3	839.9	780.9	732.0	696.0
2001	707.8	709.9	723.9	711.6	711.8	712.1	739.2	752.6	721.2	708.7	672.2	631.3
2002	660.0	693.6	720.3	731.7	765.6	789.0	797.6	833.6	801.5	753.9	720.4	697.1
2003[1]	730.1	759.5	768.5	770.5	777.4	791.0	799.7	809.0	794.2	771.6	722.4	695.5

Quantities are given in net weight.   [1] Preliminary.   *Source: National Agricultural Statistics Service, U.S. Department of Agriculture (NASS-USDA)*

Chromium

Chromium is a steel-gray, hard, and brittle, metallic element that can take on a high polish. Its symbol is Cr and atomic number is 24. Chromium and its compounds are toxic. Discovered in 1797 by Louis Vauquelin, chromium is named after the Greek word for color, khroma. Vauquelin also discovered that an emerald's green color is due to the presence of chromium, and many precious stones owe their color to the presence of chromium compounds.

Chromium is primarily found in chromite ore. The primary use of chromium is to form alloys with iron, nickel, or cobalt. Chromium improves hardness and resistance to corrosion and oxidation in iron, steel, and nonferrous alloys. It is a critical alloying ingredient in the production of stainless steel, making up 10% or more of the final composition. More than half of chromium production is used in metallic products, and about one-third is used in refractories. Chromium is also used as a lustrous decorative plating agent, in pigments, leather processing, plating of metals, and catalysts.

Supply – World production of chromium in 2002 rose +7.4% to 13.000 million metric tons from the 6-year low of 12.100 million metric tons in 2001. The world's largest producers of chromium are South Africa with about 45% of world production, Kazakhstan with 17%, India with 14%, and Zim-babwe with 6%. India has emerged as a major producer of chromium in the past two decades. India's 2002 production level of 1.900 million metric tons was 5 times the level of 360,000 metric tons seen 20 years earlier. South Africa's production in the late-1990s roughly doubled from the levels seen in the 1980s, but has flattened out in the past 8 years to an average year 6 metric tons per year. Kazakhstan's production in 2002 of 2.300 million was slightly above its 10-year average production level of 2.14 million metric tons. Zimbabwe's production in 2002 posted a new 25-year high of 780,000 metric tons.

Demand – Based on the most recently available data, the metallurgical and chemical industry accounts for 94% of chromium usage in the US, with the remaining 6% used by the refractory industry.

Trade – The US relied on imports for a record low 63% of its chromium consumption in 2002, down from 78% in 2000 and 2001 and 80% in 1998 and 1999. US chromium imports in 2002 fell to a record low 174,000 metric tons from 239,000 in 2001, and was less than half of the 453,000 metric ton import level in 2000. US exports of chromium are negligible and fell to 10,000 metric tons in 2002 from 38,000 in 2001.

World Mine Production of Chromite   In Thousands of Metric Tons (Gross Weight)

Year	Albania	Brazil	Cuba	Finland	India	Iran	Kazak-hstan	Mada-gascar	Philip-pines	South Africa	Turkey	Zim-babwe	World Total
1993	115	308	18	511	1,000	124	2,900	144	62	2,840	767	252	9,300
1994	118	360	29	573	909	354	2,100	90	76	3,640	1,270	517	10,400
1995	160	448	31	598	1,540	371	2,420	106	111	5,090	2,080	707	14,000
1996	144	408	37	582	1,363	130	1,190	137	107	5,078	1,279	697	11,600
1997	106	301	44	589	1,363	169	1,796	140	88	6,162	1,703	640	13,600
1998	102	537	46	498	1,311	212	1,603	104	54	6,480	1,404	605	13,700
1999	71	488	52	597	1,473	255	2,406	----	20	6,817	770	653	14,300
2000	63	603	56	628	1,947	153	2,607	119	26	6,622	546	668	14,700
2001[1]	130	409	50	575	1,678	105	2,046	52	27	5,502	390	780	12,200
2002[2]	135	280	46	566	1,900	80	2,369	11	24	6,436	314	749	13,500

[1] Preliminary.   [2] Estimate.   *Source: U.S. Geological Survey (USGS)*

Salient Statistics of Chromite in the United States   In Thousands of Metric Tons (Gross Weight)

Year	Net Import Reliance as a % of Apparent Consumption	Production of Ferro-chromium	Exports	Imports for Consumption	Reexports	Consumption by - Primary Conumer Groups - Total	Metal-lurgical & Chemical	Refractory	Government[5] Stocks, Dec. 31-- Metal-lurgical & Chemical	Refractory	Total Stocks	$ per Metric Ton - South Africa[3]	Turkish[4]
1993	81	63	18	329	2	337	314	23	259	16	275	60	110
1994	75	67	31	272		322	302	20	250	17	266	60	110
1995	80	73	24	415		W	W	W	194	11	205	80	230
1996	79	37	47	361		W	W	W	165	8	173	80	230
1997	75	61	27	349		W	W	W	167	8	175	75	150
1998	80	W	55	383		W	W	W	W	W	159	68	145
1999	80	W	53	475		W	W	W	W	W	130	63	145
2000	78	W	86	453		W	W	W	396	241	637	60-65	140-150
2001[1]	78	W	38	239		W	W	W	396	241	637	NA	NA
2002[2]	63	W	10	174		W	W	W	78	126	204	NA	NA

[1] Preliminary.   [2] Estimate.   [3] Cr_2O_3, 44% (Transvaal).   [4] 48% Cr_2O_3.   [5] Data through 1999 are for Consumer.   W = Withheld.
Source: U.S. Geological Survey (USGS)

Coal

Coal is a sedimentary rock composed primarily of carbon, hydrogen, and oxygen. Coal is a fossil fuel formed from ancient plants buried deep in the Earth's crust over 300 million years ago. Historians believe coal was first used commercially in China for smelting copper and for casting coins around 1,000 BC. Almost 92% of all coal consumed in the US is burned by electric power plants, and coal accounts for about 55% of total electricity output. Coal is also used in the manufacture of steel. The steel industry first converts coal into coke, then combines the coke with iron ore and limestone, and finally heats the mixture to produce iron. Other industries use coal to make fertilizers, solvents, medicine, pesticides, and synthetic fuels.

There are four types of mined coal: anthracite (used in high-grade steel production), bituminous (used for electricity generation and for making coke), sub-bituminous, and lignite (both used primarily for electricity generation).

Coal futures trade at the New York Mercantile Exchange (NYMEX). The contract trades in units of 1,550 tons and is priced in terms of dollars and cents per ton.

Supply – US production of bituminous coal in 2003 fell slightly to 1.07 billion tons from 1.09 billion tons in 2002. Wyoming is the largest producer of coal in the US with 34% of the total, followed by West Virginia (14%), and Kentucky (11%).

Demand – US consumption of coal in 2002 rose slightly to 1.07 billion tons.

Trade – US exports of coal in 2002 totaled 39.6 million tons, accounting for about 4% of US production. The key exporting destinations for the US are Canada and Europe.

World Production[3] of Coal (Monthly Average)   In Thousands of Metric Tons

Year	Australia	Canada	China	Czech-Rep.	Germany	India	Indonesia	Kazakhstan	Poland	Russia	Ukraine	United Kingdom	United States
1994	14,721	3,054	103,325	1,448	4,802	20,974	2,603	8,298	11,094	14,730	7,608	4,149	78,131
1995	15,921	3,216	113,394	1,431	4,905	22,785	3,460	6,626	11,349	14,743	6,796	4,420	78,091
1996	16,120	3,336	116,417	1,378	4,428	23,840	3,945	6,086	11,425	13,875	6,178	4,183	80,426
1997	17,235	3,435	114,402	1,339	4,267	24,764	4,340	6,268	11,427	13,317	6,293	4,041	82,398
1998	18,247	3,190	94,806	1,343	3,776	24,356	5,027	5,672	9,644	12,779	6,431	3,431	84,484
1999	18,751	3,043	80,200	1,193	3,657	25,004	5,892	4,644	9,301	13,799	6,804	3,090	83,191
2000	25,292	2,817	70,782	1,238	3,111	25,802	6,402	6,239	8,598	14,292	6,749	2,600	81,164
2001	27,409	2,845	80,040	1,261	2,406	26,563	7,554	6,355	8,658	15,507	6,908	2,677	84,771
2002[1]	21,739	2,537	92,339	1,206	2,197	27,938	8,588	5,884	8,676	15,198	6,838	2,482	81,139
2003[2]			104,686	1,133	2,095	28,297	7,641	6,248	8,541	16,068	6,491	2,482	81,139

[1] Preliminary.   [2] Estimate.   [3] All grades of anthracite and bituminous coal, but excludes recovered slurries, lignite and brown coal..
NA = Not avaliable.   *Source: United Nations*

Production of Bituminous & Lignite Coal in the United States   In Thousands of Short Tons

Year	Alabama	Colorado	Illinois	Indiana	Kentucky	Montana	Ohio	Pennsylvania	Texas	Virginia	West Virginia	Wyoming	Total
1994	23,266	25,304	52,797	30,927	161,642	41,640	29,897	62,237	52,346	37,129	161,776	237,092	1,033,504
1995	24,640	25,710	48,180	26,007	153,739	39,451	26,118	61,576	52,684	34,099	162,997	263,822	1,032,974
1996	24,637	24,886	46,656	29,670	152,425	37,891	28,572	67,942	55,164	35,590	170,433	278,440	1,063,856
1997	24,468	27,449	41,159	35,497	155,853	41,005	29,154	76,198	53,328	35,837	173,743	281,881	1,089,932
1998	23,224	30,825	38,182	36,297	145,609	42,092	28,600	76,519	53,578	34,059	175,794	313,983	1,109,768
1999	19,504	29,989	40,417	34,004	139,626	41,102	22,480	76,368	53,071	32,181	157,919	337,119	1,095,474
2000	19,324	29,137	33,444	27,965	130,688	38,352	22,269	74,619	49,498	32,834	158,257	338,900	1,073,612
2001	19,513	33,372	33,783	36,738	134,298	39,143	25,400	74,784	45,042	33,060	162,631	368,749	1,125,749
2002[1]	19,062	35,103	33,358	35,513	124,388	37,386	21,157	67,104	45,247	30,126	150,222	373,161	1,092,916
2003[2]	19,680	35,818	31,700	35,241	112,966	36,111	21,592	65,541	47,260	31,126	142,294	376,517	1,074,630

[1] Preliminary.   [2] Estimate.   *Source: Energy Information Administration, U.S. Department of Energy (EIA-DOE)*

Production[2] of Bituminous Coal in the United States   In Thousands of Short Tons

Year	Jan.	Feb.	Mar.	Apr.	May	June	July	Aug.	Sept.	Oct.	Nov.	Dec.	Total
1994	76,578	81,569	95,969	87,534	82,105	86,223	77,421	93,881	88,346	85,085	86,317	87,856	1,028,884
1995	88,351	83,893	93,020	80,092	83,291	84,210	79,511	88,035	89,052	90,573	86,779	81,292	1,032,974
1996	83,013	83,671	90,392	88,158	88,562	83,824	88,331	94,664	87,388	94,195	86,400	86,493	1,059,104
1997	92,425	88,028	92,265	87,909	94,296	86,382	88,666	89,319	92,298	94,562	83,344	94,913	1,085,254
1998	97,012	86,167	95,091	91,735	90,397	92,099	90,497	91,212	95,442	96,723	90,544	94,567	1,106,128
1999	90,928	92,015	98,672	88,630	84,436	89,734	87,759	92,600	92,248	89,146	90,885	92,450	1,089,503
2000	87,222	86,846	99,045	81,793	88,715	90,583	84,442	96,361	88,848	92,542	94,035	87,272	1,077,704
2001	96,721	86,802	99,176	89,954	94,840	92,657	89,037	99,048	88,985	99,529	93,736	88,234	1,118,719
2002	101,939	90,208	90,108	90,039	91,673	85,555	86,190	92,054	92,212	94,033	87,836	91,058	1,092,905
2003[1]	92,649	82,130	88,994	88,819	90,055	87,982	88,231	89,285	90,131	96,148	86,052	94,154	1,074,630

[1] Preliminary.   [2] Includes small amount of lignite.   *Source: Energy Information Administration, U.S. Department of Energy (EIA-DOE)*

COAL

Production[2] of Pennsylvania Anthracite Coal   In Thousands of Short Tons

Year	Jan.	Feb.	Mar.	Apr.	May	June	July	Aug.	Sept.	Oct.	Nov.	Dec.	Total
1994	318	335	415	380	375	379	346	457	412	453	452	395	4,717
1995	304	304	372	332	335	353	307	396	428	445	388	347	4,682
1996	302	349	367	371	361	335	367	418	385	557	505	434	4,751
1997	351	366	492	374	351	390	407	423	415	448	384	415	4,678
1998	306	305	309	405	384	388	525	454	452	533	167	167	4,612
1999	355	369	389	354	459	402	343	436	479	414	407	406	4,808
2000	271	283	382	342	375	383	366	430	412	417	402	366	4,432
2001	302	275	323	283	300	297	328	358	318	375	349	173	3,681
2002	131	117	116	121	122	240	116	126	119	130	120	126	1,584
2003[1]	108	98	98	115	114	107	97	95	100	139	119	124	1,314

[1] Preliminary.   [2] Represents production in Pennsylvania only.   *Source: Energy Information Administration, U.S. Department of Energy (EIA-DOE)*

Salient Statistics of Coal in the United States   In Thousands of Short Tons

Year	Production	Imports	Consumption	Exports Brazil	Canada	Europe	Asia	Total	Total Ending Stocks[2]	Losses & Unaccounted For[3]
1993	945,424	7,309	944,081	5,197	8,889	37,575	19,500	74,519	120,458	-13,924
1994	1,033,504	7,584	951,461	5,482	9,193	35,825	17,957	71,359	169,358	-2,743
1995	1,032,974	7,201	962,039	6,351	9,427	48,620	19,095	88,547	169,083	-7,863
1996	1,063,856	7,126	1,005,573	6,540	12,029	47,193	17,980	90,473	151,627	-7,366
1997	1,089,932	7,487	1,030,453	7,455	14,975	41,331	14,498	83,545	140,374	-4,418
1998	1,117,535	8,724	1,038,972	6,475	19,901	33,773	12,311	77,295	164,602	-13,118
1999	1,100,431	9,089	1,044,536	4,442	19,826	22,508	9,157	58,476	183,523	-6,525
2000	1,073,612	12,513	1,080,894	4,536	18,769	24,969	6,702	58,489	140,020	-12,956
2001	1,127,689	19,787	1,060,789	4,574	17,633	20,821	3,246	48,666	181,926	-3,885
2002[1]	1,093,806	16,875	1,071,862	3,538	16,686	15,574	1,735	39,601	181,885	-741

[1] Preliminary.   [2] Producer & distributor and consumer stocks, excludes stocks held by retail dealers for consumption by the residential and commercial sector.   [3] Equals production plus imports minus the change in producer & distributor and consumer stocks minus consumption minus exports.
Source: Energy Information Administraion, U.S. Department of Energy (EIA-DOE)

Consumption and Stocks of Coal in the United States   In Thousands of Short Tons

Year	Electric Utilities Anthracite	Bituminous	Lignite	Total	Industrial Coke Plants	Other Industrial[2]	Residential and Commercial	Total	Stocks, Dec. 31[3] Consumer Electric Utilities	Coke Plants	Other Industrials	Producers and Distributors
1993	951	732,736	79,821	831,645	31,323	74,892	6,221	944,081	111,341	2,401	6,716	25,284
1994	1,123	737,102	79,045	838,354	31,740	75,179	6,013	951,286	126,897	2,657	6,585	33,219
1995	978	749,951	78,078	850,230	33,011	73,055	5,807	962,104	126,304	2,632	5,702	34,444
1996	1,009	795,252	78,421	896,921	31,706	71,689	6,006	1,006,321	114,623	2,667	5,688	28,648
1997	1,014	821,823	77,524	921,364	30,203	71,515	6,463	1,029,544	98,826	1,978	5,597	33,973
1998	867	832,094	77,906	936,619	28,189	67,439	4,856	1,037,103	120,501	2,026	5,545	36,530
1999	686	815,909	77,525	940,922	28,108	64,738	4,879	1,038,647	141,604	1,943	5,569	39,475
2000	NA	781,821	75,794	985,821	28,939	65,208	4,127	1,084,095	102,296	1,494	4,587	31,905
2001	NA	NA	NA	964,489	26,075	65,268	4,369	1,060,202	138,496	1,510	6,006	35,900
2002[1]	NA	NA	NA	975,858	22,537	63,077	4,369	1,065,842	142,026	1,163	5,792	31,968

[1] Preliminary.   [2] Including transportation.   [3] Excludes stocks held at retail dealers for consumption by the residential and commercial sector.
Source: Energy Information Administration, U.S. Department of Energy (EIA-DOE)

Average Prices of Coal in the United States   In Dollars Per Short Ton

Year	End-Use-Sector Electric Utilities	Coke Plants	Other Industrial[3]	Imports[4]	Exports Steam	Metallurgical	Total Average[4]	Year	End-Use-Sector Electric Utilities	Coke Plants	Other Industrial[3]	Imports[4]	Exports Steam	Metallurgical	Total Average[4]
1993	28.58	47.44	32.23	29.89	36.03	44.11	41.41	1998	25.64	46.06	32.30	32.18	30.27	44.53	38.89
1994	28.03	46.56	32.55	30.21	34.34	42.77	39.93	1999	24.72	45.85	31.59	30.77	29.91	41.91	36.50
1995	27.01	47.34	32.42	34.13	34.51	44.30	40.27	2000	24.28	44.38	31.46	30.10	29.67	38.99	34.90
1996	26.45	47.33	32.32	33.78	34.09	45.49	40.76	2001	24.68	46.42	32.26	34.00	31.88	41.63	36.97
1997	26.16	47.36	32.41	34.32	32.45	45.47	40.55	2002[1]	24.74	50.67	35.49	35.51	34.51	45.41	40.44

[1] Preliminary.   [2] Estimate.   [3] Manufacturing plants only.   [4] Based on the free alongside ship (F.A.S.) value.   NA = Not available.
Source: Energy Information Administration, U.S. Department of Energy (EIA-DOE)

Trends in Bituminous Coal, Lignite and Pennsylvania Anthracite in the U.S.   In Thousands of Short Tons

| | ----------------------------- Bituminous Coal and Lignite ----------------------------- | | | | ----------- Labor Productivity ----------- | | | ----------------- Pennsylvania Anthracite ----------------- | | | | | All Mines |
| | --------------------- Production --------------------- | | | | Under- | Surface | Average | Under- | | | | Labor Product. | Labor Product. |
Year	Under-gound	Surface	Total	Miners[1] Employed	ground	Surface	Average	Under-ground	Surface	Total	Miners[1] Employed	Short Tons Miner/Hr.	Short Tons Miner/Hr.
					- Short Tons Per Miner Per Hour -								
1993	350,637	590,482	941,119	101,322	2.95	7.23	4.70	416	3,889	4,306	1,124	1.85	4.70
1994	399,103	634,401	1,033,504	97,500	3.19	7.67	4.98	343	4,278	4,621	1,183	1.93	4.98
1995	396,249	636,725	1,032,974	90,252	3.39	8.48	5.38	428	4,254	4,682	1,069	2.08	5.38
1996	409,849	654,007	1,063,856	83,462	3.57	9.05	5.69	391	4,360	4,751	1,171	1.92	5.69
1997	420,657	669,274	1,089,932	81,516	3.83	9.46	6.04	419	4,259	4,678	1,287	1.76	6.04
1998	417,728	699,807	1,117,535	85,418	3.90	9.58	6.20	408	4,823	5,231	1,281	2.04	6.20
1999	391,790	708,642	1,100,431	78,723	3.99	10.39	6.61	377	4,376	4,753	1,326	1.76	6.61
2000	373,659	699,953	1,073,612	72,748	4.15	11.01	6.99	301	4,271	4,572	1,272	1.89	6.99
2001	380,627	745,308	1,127,689	77,088	4.02	10.60	6.82	341	1,143	1,484	955	.81	6.82
2002	357,385	735,910	1,094,283	75,466	3.98	10.38	6.80	305	1,189	1,494	872	.78	6.80

[1] Excludes miners employed at mines producing less than 10,000 tons.   *Source: Energy Information Administration, U.S. Department of Energy (EIA-DOE)*

Average Mine Prices of Coal in the United States   In Dollars Per Short Ton

| | ----- Average Mine Price by Method ----- | | | -------------- Average Mine Prices by Rank -------------- | | | | Bituminous & Lignite FOB Mines[2] | Anthracite FOB Mines[2] | All Coal CIF[3] Electric Utility Plants |
Year	Under-ground	Surface	Total	Lignite	Sub-bituminous	Bituminous	Anthracite[1]			
1993	26.92	15.67	19.85	11.11	9.33	26.15	32.94	20.56	37.80	28.58
1994	26.39	15.02	19.41	10.77	8.37	25.68	36.07	25.68	36.07	28.03
1995	26.18	14.25	18.83	10.83	8.10	25.56	39.78	25.56	39.78	27.01
1996	25.96	13.82	18.50	10.92	7.87	25.17	36.78	25.17	36.78	26.45
1997	25.68	13.39	18.14	10.91	7.42	24.64	35.12	24.64	35.12	26.16
1998	25.64	12.92	17.67	10.80	6.96	24.87	42.91	24.87	42.91	25.64
1999	24.33	12.37	16.63	11.04	6.87	23.92	35.13	23.92	35.13	24.72
2000	23.84	12.26	16.44	11.41	7.12	24.15	40.90	24.15	40.90	24.28
2001	25.37	13.18	17.38	11.52	6.67	25.36	47.67	25.36	47.67	24.68
2002	26.68	13.65	17.98	11.07	7.34	26.57	47.78	26.57	47.78	24.74

[1] Produced in Pennsylvania.   [2] FOB = free on board.   [3] CIF = cost, insurance and freight.   W = Withheld data.

Source: Energy Information Adminstration, U.S. Department of Energy (EIA-DOE)

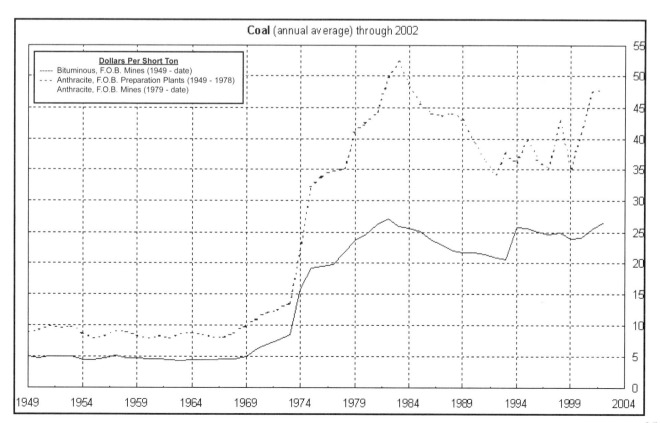

Coal (annual average) through 2002

Dollars Per Short Ton
----- Bituminous, F.O.B. Mines (1949 - date)
- - - Anthracite, F.O.B. Preparation Plants (1949 - 1978)
       Anthracite, F.O.B. Mines (1979 - date)

Cobalt

Cobalt is a lustrous, silvery-white, magnetic, metallic element used chiefly for making alloys. Cobalt was known in ancient times and used by the Persians in 2250 BC to color glass. The name cobalt comes from the German word *kobalt* or *kobold*, meaning evil spirit. Miners gave cobalt its name because it was poisonous and troublesome since it polluted and degraded other mined elements, like nickel. In the 1730s, George Brandt first isolated metallic cobalt and was able to show that cobalt was the source of the blue color in glasses. In 1780, it was recognized as an element. Generally found in the form of ores, cobalt is not found as a free metal. It tends to be produced as a by-product of nickel and copper mining.

Cobalt is used in high temperature steel alloys, fasteners in gas turbine engines, magnets and magnetic recording media, drying agents for paints, pigments, and in steel-belted radial tires. Cobalt-60, an important radioactive tracer and cancer-treatment agent, is an artificially produced radioactive isotope of cobalt.

Prices – The price of cobalt plunged in 2002 to $6.90 per pound from $10.55 in 2001. The 2002 price was down by a dramatic 76% from the record high of $29.21 per pound posted in 1995.

Supply – World mine production of cobalt in 2002 rose slightly by +0.5% to a 12-year high of 36,900 metric tons from 36,700 metric tons in 2001. Zambia was the world's largest mine producer of cobalt in 2002 with 7,600 metric tons of production, followed by Australia with 6,600 metric tons, Canada with 5,300 metric tons, and Russia with 4,600 metric tons. Russian production is on the upswing and rose by 21% in 2002 from 2001. Australian production rose 6.5% in 2002 to 6,600 metric tons, and tripled its output from 10 years earlier. When factoring in countries that are big refiners of cobalt, versus miners, Finland takes the world production record with 10,000 metric tons of production in 2001 and Norway had production of 4,500 metric tons.

The United States does not mine or refine cobalt although some cobalt is produced as a by-product of mining operations. The US cobalt supply was made up of imports, stock releases, and secondary materials. Secondary production included extraction from super-alloy scrap, cemented carbide scrap and spent catalysts. In the US there were two domestic producers of extra-fine cobalt powder. One produced the powder from imported primary metal and the other from recycled materials. There were seven companies that produced cobalt compounds. US secondary production of cobalt in 2002 fell to 2,700 metric tons from 2,740 metric tons in 2001.

Demand – US consumption of cobalt in 2002 fell to 10,800 metric tons from 11,800 metric tons in 2001. The largest use by far was for super-alloys with 4,850 metric tons of consumption.

Trade – US imports of cobalt in 2002 fell slightly to 9,400 metric tons, but that was only mildly below the record high of 9,410 metric tons seen in 2001. The US relies on imports for 75% of its cobalt consumption.

World Mine Production of Cobalt   In Metric Tons (Cobalt Content)

Year	Australia	Bots-wana	Canada	Cuba	Finland (Refinery)	France (Refinery)	Japan (Refinery)	New Caledonia	Norway (Refinery)	Russia	Congo³	Zambia	World Total
1993	1,900	205	5,108	1,061	2,200	144	191	800	2,414	3,500	2,459	4,840	21,900
1994	2,300	225	4,265	972	3,000	146	161	1,000	2,823	3,000	826	3,600	18,000
1995	2,500	271	5,339	1,591	3,610	161	227	1,100	2,804	3,500	1,647	5,908	24,500
1996	2,800	408	5,714	2,011	4,160	174	258	1,100	3,098	3,300	2,000	6,959	26,200
1997	3,000	334	5,709	2,358	5,000	159	264	1,000	3,417	3,300	3,500	6,037	27,400
1998	3,300	335	5,861	2,665	10,600	300	480	1,000	4,500	3,600	5,000	11,900	35,300
1999	4,100	331	5,323	2,537	10,000	300	480	1,100	4,500	3,900	6,000	5,640	31,600
2000	5,600	308	5,298	2,943	10,000	300	480	1,200	4,500	4,000	10,000	4,600	37,200
2001¹	6,200	325	5,326	3,411	10,000	300	480	1,400	4,500	4,600	13,000	8,000	45,800
2002²	6,700	269	5,093	3,400	10,000	300	480	1,400	4,500	4,600	12,500	10,000	47,600

¹ Preliminary.   ² Estimate.   ³ Formerly Zaire.   *Source: U.S. Geological Survey (USGS)*

Salient Statistics of Cobalt in the United States   In Metric Tons (Cobalt Content)

Year	Net Import Reliance as a % of Apparent Consumption	Cobalt Secondary Production	Processors and Consumer Stocks Dec. 31	Imports for Consumption	Ground Coat Frit	Stainless & Heat Resisting	Catalysts	Super-alloys	Tool Steel	Magnetic Alloys	Pigments	Drier in Paints, etc.³	Cutting & Wear-Resistant Material	Welding Materials	Total Apparent Uses	Price $ Per Pound⁴
1993	79	1,566	819	5,950	W	41	935	2,530	59	569	193	732	569	171	7,350	13.79
1994	81	1,570	914	6,780	W	41	871	2,810	84	698	198	809	723	312	8,730	24.66
1995	79	1,860	818	6,440	196	38	732	2,940	146	757	172	770	748	287	8,970	29.21
1996	76	2,280	770	6,710	391	38	652	3,360	95	719	191	733	722	347	9,380	25.50
1997	76	2,750	763	8,430	490	38	734	4,170	112	879	201	556	789	342	11,200	23.34
1998	73	3,080	750	7,670	W	38	W	4,060	96	771	W	W	844	421	11,500	21.43
1999	73	2,720	738	8,150	W	W	W	3,830	W	794	W	W	755	291	10,700	17.02
2000	74	2,550	820	8,770	W	W	W	4,070	W	625	W	W	760	867	11,600	15.16
2001¹	78	2,740	852	9,410	W	W	W	4,850	W	472	W	W	720	661	11,800	10.55
2002²	75	2,700	917	8,450	W	W	W	3,700	W	416	W	W	617	634	9,860	6.91

¹ Preliminary.   ² Estimate.   ³ Or related usage.   ⁴ Annual spot for cathodes.   W = Withheld proprietary data.
Source: U.S. Geological Survey (USGS)

Cocoa

Cocoa is the common name for a powder derived from the fruit seeds of the cacao tree. The Spanish called cocoa "the food of the gods" when they came upon it in South America 500 years ago. Today, it remains a precious commodity. Dating back to the time of the Aztecs, cocoa was mainly used as a beverage. The processing of the cacao seeds, also known as cocoa beans, begins when the harvested fruit is fermented or cured into a pulpy state for three to nine days. The cocoa beans are then dried in the sun and cleaned in special machines before they are roasted to bring out the chocolate flavor. After roasting, they are put into a crushing machine and ground into cocoa powder. Cocoa has a high food value because it contains as much as 20 percent protein, 40 percent carbohydrate, and 40 percent fat. It is also mildly stimulating because of the presence of theobromine, an alkaloid that is closely related to caffeine. Roughly two-thirds of cocoa bean production is used to make chocolate and one-third to make cocoa powder.

The four major West African cocoa producers are the Ivory Coast, Ghana, Nigeria and Cameroon, that together account for about two-thirds of world production. The Ivory Coast produces about 43 percent of the world's cocoa. The next largest producer is Ghana with about 14 percent of the world's output. Nigeria produces about 6 percent of the world's cocoa. Outside of West Africa, the major producers of cocoa are Indonesia, Brazil, Malaysia, Ecuador, and the Dominican Republic. Cocoa producers like Ghana and Indonesia have been making efforts to increase cocoa production while producers like Malaysia have been switching to other crops. Ghana has had an ongoing problem with black pod disease and with smuggling of the crop into neighboring Ivory Coast. Brazil was once one of the largest producers but has had problems with witches' broom disease. In West Africa, the main crop harvest starts in the September-October period and can be extended into the January-March period. Cocoa trees reach maturity in 5-6 years but can live to be 50 years old or more. During the course of a growing season, the cocoa tree will produce thousands of flowers but only a few will develop into cocoa pods.

Cocoa futures and options are traded at the CSCE Division of the New York Board of Trade (NYBOT) and on the London International Financial Futures and Options Exchange (LIFFE). The futures contracts call for the delivery of 10 metric tons of cocoa and the contract is priced in US dollars per metric ton.

Prices – Cocoa prices on the CSCE nearest-futures chart posted a new 20-year high of $2,420 per metric ton in early 2003 and then fell sharply early in the year, spending the latter half of the year consolidating in the range mainly between $1400-1800. However, that was still well above the all-time contract low of $674 posted as recently as December 2000. Cash cocoa in late 2000 hit lows not seen since the early 1970s. Prices were boosted in 2002 and early 2003 by tighter supplies and by unrest in the Ivory Coast. The cocoa market is very sensitive to developments in West Africa and particularly in the Ivory Coast where most of the world's cocoa is produced. Developments there that would in any way hinder the harvesting and movement of cocoa to the market are seen as very bullish and result in higher prices. Prices in early 2003 fell back as the cocoa market moved into a surplus situation in 2002/3 versus the deficit seen in 2001/2. Production was strong in West Africa as producers responded to high prices by maximizing output, thus putting downward pressure on prices.

Supply – The International Cocoa Organization (ICCO) estimates that global cocoa production in the 2002/3 (Oct/Sep) season was 3.102 million metric tons, up 8.4% from 2.861 million in 2001/2. Cocoa beans are processed or ground to produce the ingredients that are used in making chocolate and chocolate products. Those ingredients are mainly cocoa powder and cocoa butter. The trend among cocoa processors has been to grind beans to produce cocoa powder rather than butter because the demand for cocoa butter has been weaker since there are less expensive substitutes for making chocolate. World grindings are forecast in 2002/3 at 2.996 million metric tons, up 4.1% from 2.877 million in 2001/2. West Africa is expected to produce the most significant contribution to the rise in global output where production is forecast to increase by close to 9 percent (up 167,000 metric tons to 2.109 million metric tons), followed by the Americas (up 33,000 metric tons or 9 percent), while production in the Asia and Oceania regions is likely to remain the same.

End-of-season stocks are forecast in 2002/3 at 1.191 million metric tons, up 6.7% from 1.116 million in 2001/2. The ICCO forecasts that the cocoa market in 2002/3 was in a surplus state of 75,000 metric tons, which is a bearish factor and a switch from a 45,000 metric ton deficit in 2001/2.

World Supply and Demand Cocoa   In Thousands of Metric Tons

Crop Year Beginning October	Stocks Oct. 1	Net World Production	Total Availability	Seasonal Grindings	Closing Stocks	Stock Change	Crop Year Beginning October	Stocks Oct. 1	Net World Production	Total Availability	Seasonal Grindings	Closing Stocks	Stock Change
1988-9	959	2,460	3,419	2,118	1,283	323	1996-7	1,636	2,712	4,348	2,730	1,598	-39
1989-90	1,283	2,425	3,708	2,212	1,477	194	1997-8	1,598	2,635	4,233	2,773	1,440	-158
1990-1	1,477	2,510	3,987	2,351	1,616	139	1998-9	1,440	2,808	4,248	2,756	1,470	31
1991-2	1,616	2,269	3,885	2,284	1,584	-32	1999-00	1,470	3,036	4,506	2,988	1,495	25
1992-3	1,581	2,360	3,941	2,395	1,532	-53	2000-1	1,495	2,803	4,298	3,067	1,210	-285
1993-4	1,532	2,472	4,004	2,465	1,520	-12	2001-2[1]	1,210	2,773	3,983	2,865	1,097	-113
1994-5	1,520	2,353	3,873	2,483	1,372	-148	2002-3[2]	1,097	3,045	4,142	2,954	1,166	68
1995-6	1,372	2,941	4,313	2,655	1,636	264	2003-4[3]	1,166	3,068	4,234	3,042	1,168	3

[1] Preliminary.   [2] Estimate.   [3] Forecast.   [4] Obtained by adjusting the Gross World Crop for one percent loss in weight.
Source: ED&F Man Cocoa Ltd.

COCOA

World Production of Cocoa Beans   In Thousands of Metric Tons

Crop Year Beginning October	Brazil	Came-roon	Colom-bia	Domin-ican Republic	Ecuador	Ghana	Indo-nesia	Ivory Coast	Mal-aysia	Mexico	Nigeria	Papua New Guinea	World Total
1994-5	215	109	48	57	83	310	238	862	120	43	145	29	2,353
1995-6	222	117	45	55	103	404	284	1,265	116	30	165	35	2,941
1996-7	183	121	39	47	101	323	327	1,130	102	35	160	28	2,712
1997-8	173	114	38	60	28	409	331	1,090	57	30	165	26	2,635
1998-9	138	123	39	22	72	398	396	1,175	79	25	200	35	2,808
1999-00	124	115	37	28	92	435	415	1,404	37	31	175	46	3,036
2000-1	163	131	42	37	81	395	393	1,185	29	33	177	39	2,803
2001-2[1]	124	126	42	44	72	340	443	1,240	10	31	167	38	2,773
2002-3[2]	162	140	43	45	78	490	425	1,315	15	32	150	40	3,045
2003-4[3]	170	130	42	45	95	475	465	1,300	20	30	160	40	3,068

[1] Preliminary.   [2] Estimate.   [3] Forecast.   Source: ED&F Man Cocoa Ltd

World Consumption of Cocoa[4]   In Thousands of Metric Tons

Year	Belgium	Brazil	Cote d'Ivoire	France	Germany	Italy	Malaysia	Nether-lands	Singa-pore	United Kingdom	United States	Former U.S.S.R.	World Total
1993-4	50	210	110	95	310	65	103	331	59	170	317	75	2,465
1994-5	53	174	108	108	280	69	101	350	59	154	331	75	2,483
1995-6	54	183	130	111	270	73	96	385	63	191	345	75	2,655
1996-7	55	180	145	106	255	71	103	402	61	172	394	74	2,730
1997-8	55	188	195	107	240	72	94	425	68	174	399	50	2,773
1998-9	55	191	210	124	197	72	109	415	63	166	406	48	2,756
1999-00	55	202	230	142	215	73	117	437	60	167	439	62	2,988
2000-1[1]	55	195	285	148	225	73	121	440	59	159	445	67	3,067
2001-2[2]	NA	173	276	NA	NA	NA	93	NA	62	NA	393	70	2,865
2002-3[3]	NA	189	275	NA	NA	NA	123	NA	74	NA	402	60	2,954

[1] Preliminary.   [2] Estimate.   [3] Forecast.   [4] Figures represent the grindings of cocoa beans in each country.   NA = Not available.
Source: ED&F Man Cocoa Ltd

Raw Cocoa Grindings in Selected Countries   In Metric Tons

Year	Total	First Quarter	Second Quarter	Third Quarter	Fourth Quarter	Total	First Quarter	Second Quarter	Third Quarter	Fourth Quarter
			Germany[2]					Netherlands		
1990	281,855	69,125	64,613	70,994	77,123	247,590	62,243	58,817	58,702	67,828
1991	290,703	73,172	72,396	70,934	73,661	274,741	64,299	71,643	63,973	74,826
1992	319,251	78,661	73,797	80,111	86,682	293,157	77,954	71,537	69,871	73,795
1993	298,681	74,119	69,805	74,010	80,747	320,060	78,338	75,548	81,183	84,991
1994	296,219	80,242	68,033	67,706	80,238	334,384	83,963	78,055	84,249	88,117
1995	258,817	69,441	56,478	61,523	71,375	355,492	91,314	85,248	85,311	93,619
1996	251,070	69,520	59,471	65,824	56,255	388,412	100,866	90,724	99,549	97,273
1997	245,244	61,379	57,402	65,233	61,230	407,340	102,338	100,132	101,817	103,053
1998	217,442	62,154	47,565	55,267	52,456	427,393	104,936	108,101	108,580	105,776
1999[1]	195,732	48,486	48,605	47,321	51,320	415,250	107,189	102,933	98,828	106,300
			United Kingdom					United States[3]		
1990	124,791	32,116	29,322	29,419	33,934	216,740	51,559	51,683	58,278	55,220
1991	148,191	32,902	36,016	41,863	37,410	255,781	51,191	64,365	66,544	73,681
1992	159,284	39,831	37,903	37,120	44,430	313,921	70,335	74,515	84,109	84,962
1993	171,343	44,575	41,975	37,496	47,297	321,905	78,968	77,720	84,593	80,624
1994	163,170	44,131	39,063	39,591	40,385	322,629	71,398	78,805	86,247	86,179
1995	159,877	43,410	35,348	34,431	46,688	338,401	78,835	78,886	87,360	93,320
1996	189,037	50,500	44,535	48,855	45,147	351,042	79,044	82,713	93,933	95,352
1997	173,522	44,059	42,702	41,180	45,581	397,895	95,435	97,223	105,984	99,253
1998	171,773	45,787	42,338	40,047	43,601	397,389	99,189	96,341	104,359	97,500
1999[1]	167,556	42,557	39,758	40,238	45,003	418,996	98,218	102,488	107,568	110,722

[1] Preliminary.   [2] Beginning October 1990, includes former East Germany.   [3] Data incomplete January 1984-March 1991, excludes one major processor.   Source: Foreign Agricultural Service, U.S. Department of Agriculture (FAS-USDA)

Imports of Cocoa Butter in Selected Countries   In Metric Tons

Year	Australia	Austria	Belgium	Canada	France	Germany	Italy	Japan	Nether-Lands	Sweden	Switzer-land	United Kingdom	United States
1992	10,697	5,249	31,836	10,706	28,560	44,906	8,431	15,835	29,999	5,885	17,422	26,300	99,509
1993	13,129	5,417	28,989	10,225	30,611	37,269	9,851	16,422	51,559	6,390	16,711	25,941	85,400
1994	13,030	5,410	34,061	11,551	36,698	59,170	9,173	15,937	43,192	7,079	17,242	35,453	54,550
1995	12,150	7,425	26,185	11,146	40,245	69,928	12,027	12,898	38,300	7,078	17,835	30,654	57,210
1996	14,316	7,124	23,771	12,166	47,349	69,298	11,178	16,096	39,193	5,698	18,690	32,781	68,761
1997	14,896	6,922	34,222	16,782	46,516	71,094	9,706	16,609	29,023	6,937	19,058	37,021	87,687
1998	16,305	5,984	25,722	16,941	43,610	76,057	8,957	15,363	28,523	7,403	19,857	32,951	65,306
1999	22,573	5,363	42,278	17,323	49,722	70,323	8,281	17,824	35,602	6,884	21,278	39,648	80,475
2000	20,591	4,425	52,917	22,005	48,033	71,985	11,106	21,696	27,253	5,986	19,923	36,360	94,649
2001[1]	20,632	NA	51,576	23,307	51,101	80,278	10,935	21,665	NA	NA	20,604	40,668	80,806

[1] Preliminary.   NA = Not available.   *Source: ED&F Man Cocoa Ltd*

Imports of Cocoa Liquor and Cocoa Powder in Selected Countries   In Metric Tons

| | ---------- Cocoa Liqour ---------- | | | | | | ---------- Cocoa Powder ---------- | | | | | | |
Year	France	Germany	Nether-lands	Japan	United Kingdom	United States	Denmark	France	Germany	Italy	Japan	Nether-lands	United States
1992	45,056	2,540	7,130	2,246	3,611	24,255	3,291	14,896	27,745	14,469	6,067	9,412	56,089
1993	41,999	1,694	15,543	2,468	1,490	31,641	3,402	16,773	25,732	13,221	5,771	5,626	66,533
1994	42,392	2,682	14,913	2,312	4,443	26,846	3,625	19,215	28,806	12,884	6,461	10,078	67,207
1995	46,570	5,083	6,822	1,832	5,030	19,192	3,229	17,081	32,247	15,265	6,310	10,048	66,075
1996	62,938	7,437	9,926	2,133	5,069	15,357	3,711	18,398	36,211	15,006	13,069	6,678	68,658
1997	61,148	10,299	8,401	1,393	5,860	17,850	4,189	19,555	35,069	15,872	8,941	4,424	71,024
1998	70,883	9,121	12,534	1,144	3,813	21,894	3,865	19,533	32,479	17,122	8,779	3,746	84,211
1999	74,721	13,833	25,639	1,421	4,396	12,823	3,676	19,342	33,404	16,464	9,779	8,405	84,975
2000	67,812	14,295	33,815	1,618	8,529	10,902	3,348	21,932	34,601	18,261	11,245	22,492	86,908
2001[1]	67,590	17,548	NA	1,613	10,290	17,937	4,014	18,987	29,775	NA	11,424	NA	83,169

[1] Preliminary.   NA = Not available.   *Source: ED&F Man Cocoa Ltd*

Imports of Cocoa and Products in the United States   In Thousands of Metric Tons

Year	Jan.	Feb.	Mar.	Apr.	May	June	July	Aug.	Sept.	Oct.	Nov.	Dec.	Total
1994	67	68	56	61	49	51	49	58	58	61	45	48	672
1995	68	54	44	48	47	48	48	51	53	49	54	79	643
1996	90	87	90	80	55	49	62	53	53	60	60	86	821
1997	80	47	77	71	64	54	59	47	64	61	56	88	768
1998	86	105	90	71	55	65	65	62	72	63	54	77	865
1999	100	79	81	93	51	60	77	62	68	67	82	102	922
2000	111	128	101	91	70	67	70	70	86	76	59	69	999
2001	108	97	77	47	68	61	80	78	76	86	92	118	989
2002	86	73	72	61	76	71	86	97	61	65	89	72	909
2003[1]	114	73	91	70	67	73	93	78	78	94	84	115	1,031

[1] Preliminary.   *Source: Foreign Agricultural Service, U.S. Department of Agriculture (FAS-USDA)*

Visible Stocks of Cocoa in Port of Hampton Road Warehouses[1], at End of Month   In Thousands of Bags

Year	Jan.	Feb.	Mar.	Apr.	May	June	July	Aug.	Sept.	Oct.	Nov.	Dec.
1994	2,329.6	2,441.1	2,443.9	2,522.9	2,533.1	2,460.2	2,445.4	2,335.0	2,308.4	2,360.2	2,306.9	2,253.7
1995	2,152.7	2,098.6	2,195.7	2,212.3	2,120.2	2,016.0	1,919.8	1,786.6	1,713.1	1,598.2	1,463.9	1,470.3
1996	1,439.8	1,492.8	1,458.0	1,549.6	1,561.7	1,493.9	1,412.3	1,315.4	1,239.6	1,338.9	1,108.1	1,116.2
1997	1,128.3	1,132.1	1,133.0	1,094.0	1,010.5	970.2	872.4	840.1	727.3	763.9	695.7	704.8
1998	726.5	693.4	841.9	842.5	811.6	764.7	714.3	712.3	795.4	801.9	705.9	673.0
1999	661.6	693.2	642.5	579.7	536.9	500.7	489.0	472.7	473.4	451.8	438.9	421.2
2000	469.7	448.4	571.7	583.4	711.1	672.4	720.3	925.2	921.4	839.7	762.9	816.0
2001	741.9	657.4	632.0	607.7	577.3	518.8	498.2	487.5	475.2	506.8	509.0	511.4
2002	504.7	462.8	436.7	424.0	383.8	353.4	327.4	273.3	255.4	194.8	181.5	169.9
2003	149.9	121.7	103.1	102.3	80.5	71.9	69.2	67.7	56.9	53.0	49.6	49.3

[1] Licensed and unlicensed warehouses approved by the CSCE.   *Source: New York Board of Trade (NYBOT)*

COCOA

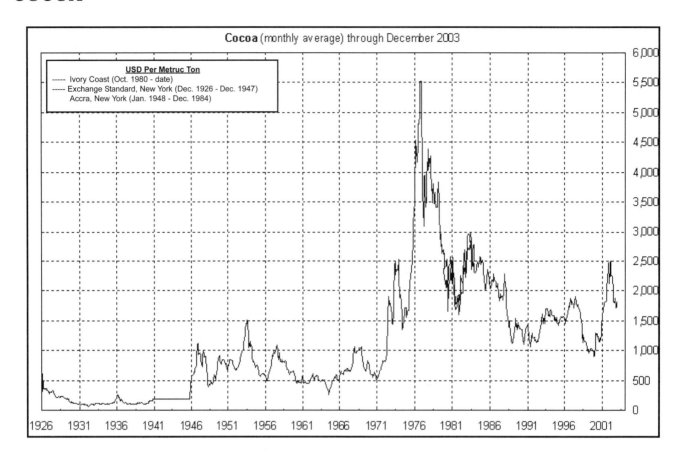

Cocoa (monthly average) through December 2003

USD Per Metruc Ton
----- Ivory Coast (Oct. 1980 - date)
----- Exchange Standard, New York (Dec. 1926 - Dec. 1947)
Accra, New York (Jan. 1948 - Dec. 1984)

Visible Stocks of Cocoa in Philadelphia (Del. River) Warehouses[1], at End of Month   In Thousands of Bags

Year	Jan.	Feb.	Mar.	Apr.	May	June	July	Aug.	Sept.	Oct.	Nov.	Dec.
1994	831.5	937.7	1,004.2	1,010.9	1,055.4	1,095.2	1,076.0	1,029.8	968.5	857.1	843.9	818.9
1995	807.5	1,034.3	1,038.9	1,020.2	963.7	924.3	860.7	759.2	852.2	727.0	666.0	735.6
1996	960.2	1,005.2	1,205.6	1,658.8	1,871.3	1,851.7	1,969.1	1,816.2	1,851.1	1,705.1	1,671.7	1,696.5
1997	1,753.0	1,634.4	1,579.6	1,641.0	1,578.7	1,625.9	1,696.2	1,637.6	1,530.9	1,491.8	1,414.2	1,394.0
1998	1,420.3	1,435.7	1,592.6	1,555.3	1,398.5	1,287.8	1,279.8	1,376.9	1,373.7	1,260.6	1,406.7	1,637.1
1999	1,763.0	1,832.8	1,982.7	2,217.8	2,019.4	1,999.6	2,084.6	2,133.4	2,144.1	2,015.5	1,774.4	1,608.5
2000	1,619.0	1,801.7	2,466.4	2,582.0	2,581.6	2,363.7	2,168.3	2,101.6	2,105.1	2,039.1	1,697.4	1,589.4
2001	1,844.0	2,082.3	2,173.3	1,960.0	1,785.9	1,610.4	1,391.6	1,543.0	1,391.3	1,131.4	1,303.2	1,682.1
2002	1,701.5	1,876.7	1,849.3	1,708.0	1,746.4	1,689.5	1,793.1	1,832.7	1,750.9	1,334.5	1,162.7	1,250.6
2003	1,347.2	1,422.0	1,327.9	1,326.5	1,217.2	1,202.3	1,229.2	1,123.7	930.6	798.9	723.7	806.0

[1] Licensed and unlicensed warehouses approved by the CSCE.   *Source: New York Board of Trade (NYBOT)*

Visible Stocks of Cocoa in New York Warehouses[1], at End of Month   In Thousands of Bags

Year	Jan.	Feb.	Mar.	Apr.	May	June	July	Aug.	Sept.	Oct.	Nov.	Dec.
1994	271.0	275.0	280.8	296.6	358.6	394.1	447.5	447.5	467.3	427.3	407.2	556.1
1995	560.5	634.5	559.2	539.4	510.4	561.1	579.3	595.4	459.9	598.7	679.7	598.7
1996	667.6	646.1	632.7	627.2	656.1	633.5	1,191.7	1,154.2	1,121.4	973.2	950.1	919.0
1997	984.7	981.3	945.0	1,250.0	1,574.4	1,524.7	1,512.8	1,348.0	1,217.3	1,073.7	1,020.0	980.4
1998	973.9	1,342.7	1,271.3	1,675.7	1,552.3	1,516.7	1,404.6	1,293.1	1,300.1	1,126.4	989.2	1,031.6
1999	1,085.0	1,089.3	1,083.1	1,134.1	1,139.4	1,114.3	1,093.5	974.5	941.9	821.7	847.5	1,573.1
2000	1,633.7	1,689.5	1,926.9	2,049.8	1,926.7	1,789.6	1,632.2	1,383.7	1,323.7	1,234.8	1,100.0	1,019.4
2001	1,005.6	1,173.8	1,119.6	1,024.9	967.5	906.6	776.2	758.5	657.6	687.4	750.8	1,196.2
2002	1,088.9	870.8	892.0	816.1	739.1	736.0	640.9	553.6	670.1	525.7	473.1	554.8
2003	614.6	625.4	593.7	612.9	515.1	476.1	423.6	388.2	483.4	301.9	391.3	342.9

[1] Licensed and unlicensed warehouses approved by the CSCE.   *Source: New York Board of Trade (NYBOT)*

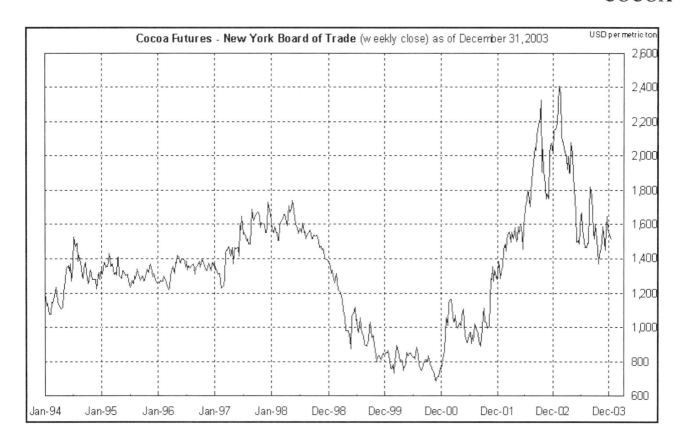

Average Open Interest of Cocoa Futures in New York   In Contracts

Year	Jan.	Feb.	Mar.	Apr.	May	June	July	Aug.	Sept.	Oct.	Nov.	Dec.
1994	89,174	87,349	91,715	82,500	82,970	72,288	72,249	69,614	73,436	74,163	72,232	75,995
1995	78,873	80,786	82,299	78,435	80,547	75,496	74,975	65,794	68,547	72,758	76,680	79,844
1996	90,478	93,533	98,049	95,390	96,346	88,232	80,873	77,134	77,942	79,572	77,139	78,592
1997	86,960	90,589	96,771	96,956	94,651	97,385	101,815	101,138	106,487	108,263	99,544	97,009
1998	90,574	82,205	78,022	73,237	79,294	74,347	74,295	73,975	71,978	74,139	74,127	73,480
1999	77,067	72,324	69,221	65,856	71,990	75,195	70,787	69,939	74,572	79,770	89,035	92,609
2000	100,540	110,316	106,056	102,382	113,239	111,948	112,864	117,260	123,463	138,523	139,141	138,266
2001	132,711	119,459	114,036	102,275	107,008	111,224	104,473	99,280	92,235	96,204	93,088	92,326
2002	97,563	98,169	96,336	98,851	103,746	100,701	107,080	102,441	107,294	107,880	82,236	82,844
2003	96,375	91,944	83,625	83,230	95,307	96,813	89,846	78,197	76,468	86,392	99,038	94,185

Source: New York Board of Trade (NYBOT)

Volume of Trading of Cocoa Futures in New York   In Contracts

Year	Jan.	Feb.	Mar.	Apr.	May	June	July	Aug.	Sept.	Oct.	Nov.	Dec.	Total
1994	178,303	190,804	205,623	188,004	267,188	251,300	193,883	241,340	142,589	183,975	210,635	164,917	2,417,006
1995	197,032	183,784	191,328	208,707	169,061	199,211	140,789	205,169	120,433	149,810	211,171	113,603	2,090,098
1996	177,720	226,701	213,189	242,988	164,749	183,544	159,070	164,719	107,634	167,227	185,226	128,809	2,121,576
1997	180,669	172,510	219,896	235,020	130,041	251,471	186,280	200,707	168,981	204,394	180,805	143,735	2,274,509
1998	175,844	145,311	171,333	192,120	143,602	183,719	131,642	156,737	115,066	125,320	155,280	114,606	1,810,580
1999	136,109	155,090	141,090	180,837	130,019	230,925	125,360	144,290	147,124	143,335	209,608	124,249	1,868,036
2000	156,812	231,562	232,803	186,837	147,072	267,470	124,906	191,849	111,740	174,216	186,515	98,266	2,110,048
2001	311,900	168,587	164,131	136,021	154,397	201,299	108,189	207,569	118,428	124,884	202,847	107,565	2,005,817
2002	155,699	187,550	129,833	217,590	160,364	220,289	176,450	209,249	138,394	207,310	162,982	114,270	2,079,980
2003	172,845	215,240	136,564	179,956	176,969	207,255	143,888	206,428	146,113	197,316	209,775	135,857	2,128,206

Source: New York Board of Trade (NYBOT)

Coconut Oil and Copra

Coconut oil and copra come from the fruit of the coconut palm tree, which originated in Southeast Asia. Coconut oil has been used for thousands of years as cooking oil, and is still a staple in the diets of many people living in tropical areas. Until shortages of imported oil developed during WWII, Americans also used coconut oil for cooking.

Copra is the meaty inner lining of the coconut. It is an oil-rich pulp with a light, slightly sweet, nutty flavor. Copra is used mainly as a source of coconut oil and is also used shredded for baking. High-quality copra contains about 65% to 72% oil, and oil made from the copra is called crude coconut oil. Crude coconut oil is processed from copra by expeller press and solvent extraction. It is not considered fit for human consumption until it has been refined, which consists of neutralizing, bleaching and deodorizing it at high heat with a vacuum. The remaining oil cake obtained as a by-product is used for livestock feed.

Premium grade coconut oil, also called virgin coconut oil, is oil made from the first pressing with out the addition of any chemicals. Premium grade coconut oil is more expensive than refined or crude oil because the producers use only selected raw materials and there is a lower production yield due to only one pressing.

Coconut oil accounts for approximately 20% of all vegetable oils used worldwide. Coconut oil is used in margarines, vegetable shortening, salad oils, confections, and in sports drinks to boost energy and enhance athletic performance. It is also used in the manufacture of soaps, detergents, shampoos, cosmetics, candles, glycerin and synthetic rubber. Coconut oil is very healthy, unless it is hydrogenated, and is easily digested.

Prices – The price of coconut oil (crude) in December 2003 was 21.00 cents per pound, little changed from the 2002 average of 21.01 cents. The 2003 price was a 13-year low going back to 20.66 in 1990. Coconut prices in 2003 were down by more than 50% from the peak of 42.42 cents seen in 1996.

Supply – World production of copra in 2003/4 was forecast at 5.38 million metric tons, up 5.3% from 5.11 million in 2002/3. Ending stocks were unchanged in 2003/4 from 2002/3 at 20,000 metric tons. World production of coconut oil in 2003/4 was forecast at 3.33 million metric tons, up 5.0% from 3.17 million 2002/3. The world's largest producer of copra in 2003 by far was the Philippines with 41% of world production, followed by Indonesia with 26%.

Demand – Virtually all of world production of copra in 2003/4 went for crushing into coconut meal and oil (98.7%). World consumption of coconut oil in 2003/4 rose 2.2% to 3.32 million metric tons.

Trade – Copra is generally crushed in the country of origin, so exports of copra account for less than 4% of world production. However, exports of coconut oil in 2003/4 rose 7.3% to 1.91 million metric tons, accounting for 57% of world production.

World Production of Copra   In Thousands of Metric Tons

Year	India	Indonesia	Ivory Coast	Malaysia	Mexico	Mozambique	New Guinea	Philippines	Sri Lanka	Thailand	Vanuatu	Vietnam	World Total
1994	592	1,270	65	60	216	74	104	1,930	104	100	27	210	5,072
1995	655	1,080	72	66	217	74	125	2,500	113	103	30	208	5,544
1996	720	1,155	75	60	204	75	178	1,725	75	61	33	210	4,880
1997	720	1,300	45	60	217	76	159	2,210	67	61	34	96	5,363
1998	735	965	43	50	237	76	143	2,270	71	61	43	68	5,077
1999	718	860	36	48	199	73	146	1,250	68	65	30	72	3,874
2000	700	1,330	45	49	202	75	152	2,140	98	69	27	45	5,248
2001[1]	710	1,180	45	49	198	75	70	2,790	95	69	24	50	5,668
2002[2]	720	1,240	45	58	165	75	81	2,065	70	69	27	52	4,982
2003[3]	690	1,270	45	60	172	75	85	2,020	75	70	28	53	4,960

[1] Preliminary.   [2] Estimate.   [3] Forecast.   *Source: The Oil World*

World Supply and Distribution of Coconut Oil   In Thousands of Metric Tons

	Production							Consumption						Ending Stocks		
Year	India	Indonesia	Malaysia	Philippines	Total	Exports	Imports	European Union	India	Indonesia	Philippines	United States	Total	Philippines	United States	Total
1993-4	343	704	32	1,242	3,009	1,361	1,437	547	346	337	294	483	2,962	181	74	457
1994-5	383	638	36	1,564	3,312	1,775	1,760	660	384	492	309	491	3,325	99	74	430
1995-6	397	612	35	1,206	2,912	1,374	1,405	606	396	373	306	427	3,005	100	38	368
1996-7	424	756	35	1,257	3,150	1,726	1,658	688	432	213	339	504	3,067	92	68	384
1997-8	442	652	39	1,628	3,411	2,125	2,111	771	440	211	302	540	3,184	32	178	598
1998-9	431	458	51	783	2,369	1,040	1,136	578	446	110	295	461	2,744	58	69	319
1999-00	421	787	54	1,198	3,100	1,805	1,725	754	435	110	299	420	2,927	112	62	412
2000-1[1]	431	700	49	1,731	3,517	2,182	2,179	729	448	280	348	437	3,357	60	118	570
2001-2[2]	421	746	49	1,441	3,213	1,828	1,878	693	448	304	372	516	3,346	60	103	486
2002-3[3]	435	756	55	1,292	3,085	1,782	1,784	634	458	245	362	463	3,187	55	67	387

[1] Preliminary.   [2] Estimate.   [3] Forecast.   *Source: The Oil World*

Supply and Distribution of Coconut Oil in the United States   In Millions of Pounds

	----- Rotterdam -----						---------- Disappearance ----------			------- Production of Coconut Oil (Refined) -------				
	Copra	Coconut	Imports				Total	Edible	Inedible		Oct.-	Jan.-	April-	July-
	Tonne	Oil, CIF	For Con-	Stocks	Total		Total	Products	Products	Total	Dec.	Mar.	June	Sept.
Year	-------- $ U.S. --------		sumption	Oct. 1	Supply	Exports	Domestic							
1993-4	388	564	999	251	1,250	20	1,067	234	716	536.2	155.6	129.0	131.8	119.8
1994-5	432	656	1,100	163	1,263	18	1,082	247	694	546.8	137.5	142.7	144.3	122.3
1995-6	487	746	873	163	1,036	11	941	221	453	445.0	127.5	118.4	132.8	66.4
1996-7	452	693	1,188	83	1,271	11	1,111	120	471	324.2	77.0	61.5	101.5	84.2
1997-8	391	625	1,440	149	1,589	7	1,190	141	472	397.8	113.4	103.6	100.4	80.4
1998-9	468	748	791	392	1,183	11	1,021	144	380	363.2	89.6	82.9	99.3	91.4
1999-00	357	539	926	152	1,078	14	927	221	371	442.3	69.1	117.0	129.6	126.7
2000-1	208	323	1,100	136	1,236	8	968	237	297	534.9	135.7	128.3	146.9	124.0
2001-2[1]	245	388	1,150	260	1,410	11	1,100	294	302	501.8	139.5	126.1	115.4	120.8
2002-3[2]	293	458	1,150	301	1,451	10	1,201	305	310	546.7	128.8	137.0	155.6	125.2

[1] Preliminary.   [2] Estimate.   *Source: Bureau of Census, U.S. Department of Commerce*

Consumption of Coconut Oil in End Products (Edible and Inedible) in the U.S.   In Millions of Pounds

Year	Jan.	Feb.	Mar.	Apr.	May	June	July	Aug.	Sept.	Oct.	Nov.	Dec.	Total
1994	74.4	77.4	77.5	80.4	86.6	88.8	76.0	88.4	65.1	74.6	85.1	95.0	969.3
1995	78.2	79.5	86.5	81.0	79.7	82.0	76.5	71.4	61.6	62.1	59.8	59.9	878.0
1996	47.0	54.3	60.1	60.2	68.6	54.6	55.1	47.9	44.9	49.6	50.3	47.9	640.7
1997	44.1	44.8	52.8	46.1	41.9	49.4	49.9	48.3	66.9	53.4	43.9	48.0	589.5
1998	51.5	48.1	59.4	54.3	54.5	47.0	49.3	50.3	53.7	49.4	50.0	42.1	609.6
1999	39.9	44.7	50.8	43.0	41.4	45.4	36.9	33.3	46.2	41.5	43.6	38.8	505.5
2000	49.4	44.0	52.7	54.6	51.4	56.6	49.1	56.2	54.7	44.1	44.3	43.0	600.0
2001	49.3	40.6	45.5	42.5	48.3	43.3	46.5	45.6	48.4	50.3	44.4	45.5	550.2
2002	55.4	41.3	50.8	59.3	53.9	46.4	50.7	51.8	45.9	54.3	56.1	49.4	615.4
2003[1]	51.2	49.3	56.8	50.6	52.3	46.7	48.9	49.6	50.3	47.8	41.8	38.5	583.7

[1] Preliminary.   *Source: Bureau of Census, U.S. Department of Commerce*

Stocks of Coconut Oil (Crude and Refined) in the U.S., on First of Month   In Millions of Pounds

Year	Jan.	Feb.	Mar.	Apr.	May	June	July	Aug.	Sept.	Oct.	Nov.	Dec.
1994	291.7	316.5	284.5	251.5	237.6	199.9	151.4	163.7	156.0	164.1	166.2	152.9
1995	155.6	173.6	168.1	163.7	148.5	183.5	163.8	136.9	124.1	162.9	199.7	187.7
1996	164.7	229.1	200.4	217.7	173.6	175.9	171.5	116.7	113.8	84.0	78.6	65.0
1997	125.9	147.4	141.1	204.5	174.5	161.3	143.8	143.4	154.3	149.6	162.1	194.2
1998	274.2	332.4	344.5	337.4	318.8	300.6	366.3	424.6	434.4	392.6	431.8	447.3
1999	401.7	446.5	387.5	366.3	309.8	240.5	134.7	197.5	191.8	152.0	106.4	142.2
2000	93.6	123.6	100.1	99.6	102.3	104.0	137.7	163.6	161.4	136.4	178.1	161.6
2001	245.4	280.3	357.8	276.5	286.9	194.3	254.4	260.9	246.4	259.7	234.1	231.3
2002	245.9	238.8	249.6	251.3	233.5	231.6	303.3	301.6	245.8	226.5	273.8	264.1
2003[1]	195.2	194.0	214.3	224.9	223.7	187.8	162.2	202.9	195.6	218.9	184.6	186.1

[1] Preliminary.   NA = Not available.   *Source: Bureau of Census, U.S. Department of Commerce*

Average Price of Coconut Oil (Crude) Tank Cars in New York   In Cents Per Pound

Year	Jan.	Feb.	Mar.	Apr.	May	June	July	Aug.	Sept.	Oct.	Nov.	Dec.	Average
1994	30.30	29.69	27.31	28.19	29.45	30.25	29.56	30.35	30.63	30.60	34.19	33.69	30.35
1995	32.50	32.00	31.13	31.00	30.50	35.00	37.90	35.63	35.00	36.00	37.88	33.69	34.02
1996	35.80	36.63	36.75	38.75	39.50	42.25	41.80	42.80	47.20	48.00	49.50	50.00	42.42
1997	44.20	44.00	42.88	42.50	42.50	35.00	36.50	36.50	37.00	37.25	37.25	37.25	39.40
1998	37.25	37.25	37.25	37.25	37.25	37.00	36.50	35.50	36.50	39.00	37.50	38.50	37.23
1999	35.38	35.00	34.00	34.06	38.25	42.13	39.83	36.08	46.00	46.00	46.00	46.00	39.89
2000	40.88	32.94	28.81	26.63	24.25	21.90	19.63	18.58	16.40	16.81	17.50	15.70	23.34
2001	26.00	24.00	22.75	22.50	21.00	21.00	24.00	26.50	26.50	26.50	24.50	24.50	24.15
2002	16.38	17.38	17.25	18.75	20.05	21.13	21.06	21.35	28.50	28.25	27.13	26.00	21.94
2003[1]	26.00	26.00	24.60	24.50	24.50	25.00	25.00	25.00	25.00	21.00	21.00	21.00	24.05

[1] Preliminary.   *Source: Economic Research Service, U.S. Department of Agriculture (ERS-USDA)*

Coffee

Coffee is one of the world's most important cash commodities and is second in value only to crude oil. Coffee is the common name for any type of tree in the genus madder family. It is actually a tropical evergreen shrub that has the potential to grow 100 feet tall. The coffee tree grows in tropical regions between the Tropics of Cancer and Capricorn in areas with abundant rainfall, year-round warm temperatures averaging about 70 degrees Fahrenheit, and with no frost. The coffee plant will produce its first full crop of beans at about 5 years old and then be productive for about 15 years. The average coffee tree produces enough beans to make about 1 to 1 ½ pounds of roasted coffee per year. It takes approximately 4,000 handpicked green coffee beans to make a pound of coffee. Actually, wine was the first drink made from the coffee tree using the coffee cherries, honey, and water. In the 17th century, the first coffee house, also known as a "penny university" because of the price per cup, opened in London. The London Stock Exchange grew from one of these first coffee houses.

Coffee is generally classified into two types of beans – arabica and robusta. The most widely produced coffee is arabica, which makes up about 70 percent of total production. It grows mostly at high altitudes of 600 to 2,000 meters, with Brazil and Colombia being the largest producers. Arabic coffee is traded on the New York Board of Trade. The stronger of the two types is robusta. It is grown at lower altitudes with the largest producers being Indonesia, West Africa, Brazil, and Vietnam. Robusta coffee is traded on the LIFFE exchange.

Ninety percent of the world coffee trade is in green (unroasted) coffee beans. Seasonal factors have a significant influence on the price of coffee. There is no extreme peak in world production at any one time of the year, although coffee consumption declines by 12 percent or more below the year's average in the warm summer months. Therefore, coffee imports and roasts both tend to decline in spring and summer and pick up again in fall and winter.

Coffee futures are traded on the Bolsa de Mercadorias & Futuros (BM&F), the Tokyo Grain Exchange (TGE), the London International Financial Futures and Options Exchange (LIFFE), and the CSCE Division of the New York Board of Trade (NYBOT). Options are traded on the BM&F, the LIFFE and the CSCE.

Prices – Coffee prices in 2003 on the CSCE nearest-futures chart remained in a relatively narrow 25-cent trading range between about 50 cents and 75 cents per pound. Coffee prices in the past 3 years have been trading in a narrow and depressed price range with the all-time contract low of 41.50 cents posted in December 2001. Some grades of cash coffee prices in late 2001 hit lows not seen since the 1960s. As 2004 began, however, coffee prices were perking up and posted new 3-1/2 year highs. The main bullish factor was tighter world supplies of coffee due to a small 2003/4 harvest by Brazil that was completed in September 2003. Brazil is the world's leading producer of coffee, and its harvest was hurt by the biennial production cycle and dry weather. Coffee prices in 2003 were also boosted by the weak dollar.

The very low prices for coffee seen in the past several years have created serious problems for coffee producers. When prices fall below the costs of production, there is little or no economic incentive to produce coffee. The result is that coffee trees are neglected or completely abandoned. When prices are low, producers cannot afford to hire the labor needed to maintain the trees and pick the crop at harvest. The result is that trees yield less due to reduced use of fertilizer and fewer employed coffee workers. One effect is a decline in the quality of the coffee that is produced. Higher quality Arabica coffee is often produced at higher altitudes, which entails higher costs. It is this coffee that is often abandoned. Although the pressure on producers is severe, the market should eventually come back into balance as supply falls to meet demand, thus boosting prices. In fact, Brazil's 2003/4 crop was sharply lower, in part, because of poor yields caused by the neglect of groves during the long period of weak prices.

Supply – World coffee production in 2003/4 (July-June) was forecast by the USDA at 105.3 million bags (60 kilograms or about 132.3 pounds), down sharply by 15% from the 2002/3 season. The main reason for the decline in world production in 2003/4 was a poor crop in Brazil, the world's leading producer of coffee with roughly 40% of world production. Being in the Southern Hemisphere, the Brazilian coffee crop is harvested starting in May and extending for several weeks into what are the winter months. Brazil is subject to frosts and freezes and a major freeze occurs about every five years. These events occur most often in June, July and August. Brazilian production in 2003/4 is forecast at 32.0 million bags, down 5% from forecasts back in June 2003. Brazilian production spiked up to 51.60 million bags in 2002/3, depressing world coffee prices, but then production in 2003/4 plunged to the lowest yearly level in 4 years (since 30.80 million in 1999/00). Other key coffee-producing countries are Columbia (with 9% of world production), Vietnam (8%), and Indonesia (5%). In the US, the only areas that produce any significant amount of coffee are Puerto Rico and Hawaii. World stocks of coffee at the end of the 2003/4 season are forecast to plunge by 24% to 21.4 million bags from 28.2 million bags at the beginning of the marketing year.

Demand – World coffee consumption in 2002/3 was estimated by the USDA at 114.0 million bags, up less than 1% from the 2001/02 level. The U.S. is the largest consumer of coffee with consumption of 18.9 million bags in 2002, down from 19.3 million in 2001.

Trade – World coffee exports in 2003/4 are forecasted by the USDA to fall to a 3-year low of 85.87 million bags, down 5% from 90.86 million in 2002/3. The main reason for the decline in exports was simply the lower overall production of coffee in 2003/4. Brazil's exports in 2003/4 fell sharply by 17% to 24.5 million bags as a result of the poor harvest. The US imports virtually all of its coffee consumption.

World Supply and Distribution of Coffee   In Thousands of 60 Kilogram Bags (132.276 Lbs. Per Bag)

Crop Year	Beginning Stocks	Pro- duction	Imports	Supply	Total Exports	Bean Exports	Rst/Grn Exports	Soluble Exports	Domestic Use	Ending Stocks
1994-5	34,301	97,042	1,070	132,413	68,672	64,432	230	4,010	22,526	41,215
1995-6	41,215	88,946	1,079	131,240	74,103	69,021	231	4,851	24,049	33,088
1996-7	33,088	103,786	1,091	137,965	84,509	79,918	196	4,395	24,361	29,095
1997-8	29,095	97,687	1,220	128,002	77,939	73,249	193	4,497	25,180	24,883
1998-9	24,883	108,453	1,435	134,771	84,759	80,491	259	4,009	25,613	24,399
1999-00	24,399	113,433	1,274	139,106	92,400	87,250	275	4,875	25,444	21,262
2000-1	21,262	116,896	1,484	139,642	90,663	84,598	268	5,797	26,091	22,888
2001-2[1]	22,888	110,756	1,617	135,261	87,388	80,846	324	6,218	27,452	20,421
2002-3[2]	20,421	124,179	1,566	146,166	90,860	84,070	328	6,462	27,087	28,219
2003-4[3]	28,219	105,262	1,444	134,925	85,873	79,199	361	6,313	27,673	21,379

[1] Preliminary.   [2] Estimate.   [3] Forecast.   *Source: Foreign Agricultural Service, U.S. Department of Agriculture (FAS-USDA)*

World Production of Green Coffee   In Thousands of 60 Kilogram Bags (132.276 Lbs. Per Bag)

Crop Year	Brazil	Colombia	Costa Rica	El Salvador	Ethiopia	Guate- mala	India	Indo- nesia	Ivory Coast	Mexico	Uganda	Vietnam	World Total
1994-5	28,000	13,000	2,492	2,314	3,800	3,500	3,060	6,400	3,733	4,030	3,100	3,500	97,024
1995-6	16,800	12,939	2,595	2,325	3,800	3,827	3,717	5,800	2,900	5,400	4,200	3,917	88,946
1996-7	28,000	10,779	2,376	2,498	3,800	4,141	3,417	7,900	5,333	5,300	4,297	5,750	103,788
1997-8	23,500	12,043	2,455	2,040	3,833	4,200	3,805	7,000	4,080	4,950	3,032	7,000	97,652
1998-9	35,600	10,868	2,459	1,860	3,867	4,300	4,415	6,950	2,217	5,010	3,640	7,500	108,453
1999-00	30,800	9,512	2,688	2,612	3,833	4,364	4,870	6,660	5,700	6,193	3,097	11,010	113,433
2000-1	34,100	10,500	2,502	1,624	3,683	4,564	5,020	6,495	4,333	4,800	3,205	15,333	116,896
2001-2[1]	35,100	11,950	2,338	1,610	3,756	3,530	5,010	6,160	3,033	4,200	3,166	12,833	110,756
2002-3[2]	51,600	11,712	2,188	1,302	3,750	3,802	4,588	6,140	1,817	4,350	2,800	11,167	124,179
2003-4[3]	32,000	11,800	2,220	1,300	3,250	3,802	4,587	5,700	1,300	4,650	3,200	11,833	105,262

[1] Preliminary.   [2] Estimate.   [3] Forecast.   *Source: Foreign Agricultural Service, U.S. Department of Agriculture (FAS-USDA)*

World Exportable[4] Production of Green Coffee   In Thousands of 60 Kilogram Bags (132.276 Lbs. Per Bag)

Crop Year	Brazil	Colombia	Costa Rica	El Salvador	Ethiopia	Guate- mala	Indonesia	Ivory Coast	Kenya	Mexico	Uganda	Vietnam	World Total
1994-5	18,300	11,564	2,252	2,079	2,300	3,220	4,440	3,687	1,562	3,030	3,040	----	74,957
1995-6	6,300	11,439	2,360	2,055	2,300	3,527	3,750	2,852	1,789	4,340	4,140	3,700	65,393
1996-7	17,000	9,279	2,130	2,268	2,300	3,856	5,820	5,282	1,115	4,450	4,217	5,463	79,817
1997-8	12,000	10,483	2,150	1,805	2,250	3,850	5,360	4,025	1,005	3,955	2,952	6,717	72,986
1998-9	23,100	9,418	2,154	1,633	2,234	3,900	5,350	2,159	1,125	4,050	3,580	7,200	83,162
1999-00	18,000	7,982	2,347	2,445	2,200	3,964	5,305	5,640	1,662	5,138	3,017	10,660	88,121
2000-1	21,000	8,970	2,157	1,473	2,016	4,139	5,160	4,271	841	3,822	3,124	14,916	90,965
2001-2[1]	21,400	10,360	1,988	1,466	1,906	3,110	4,695	2,969	846	3,200	3,086	12,333	83,528
2002-3[2]	38,100	10,222	1,883	1,164	1,900	3,382	4,660	1,752	897	3,400	2,720	10,667	97,371
2003-4[3]	18,000	10,295	1,895	1,162	1,400	3,382	4,205	1,300	1,029	3,700	3,120	11,300	77,882

[1] Preliminary.   [2] Estimate.   [3] Forecast.   [4] Marketing year begins in October in some countries and April or July in others. Exportable production represents total harvested production minus estimated domestic consumption.   *Source: Foreign Agricultural Service, U.S. Department of Agriculture*

Green Coffee Imports in the United States   In Thousands of 60 Kilogram Bags (132.276 Lbs. Per Bag)

Year	Brazil	Colombia	Costa Rica	Dominican Republic	Ecuador	El Salvador	Ethiopia	Guate- mala	Indonesia	Mexico	Peru	Vene- zuela	Grand Total
1991	5,335	3,048	603	343	785	868	31	1,489	536	2,993	610	108	18,849
1992	4,253	4,852	662	254	753	1,344	23	1,812	581	3,042	526	104	21,673
1993	3,376	2,957	437	213	671	1,274	192	1,815	542	2,947	158	444	18,023
1994	2,850	2,372	325	207	969	376	215	1,403	558	2,516	249	295	14,913
1995	2,302	2,485	388	266	745	284	109	1,637	513	2,887	621	89	15,886
1996	1,852	3,011	482	255	665	401	137	1,748	1,246	3,734	441	445	17,947
1997	2,331	3,179	608	150	431	500	308	1,921	1,325	2,935	652	65	18,848
1998	2,688	3,410	771	164	347	501	183	1,563	1,273	2,471	771	146	18,998
1999	4,659	3,359	684	35	419	550	77	2,148	724	3,182	762	372	20,559
2000[1]	2,569	3,147	705	28	164	1,209	91	2,377	692	3,610	857	32	21,625

[1] Preliminary.   *Source: Bureau of Census, U.S. Department of Commerce*

COFFEE

Monthly Green Coffee Imports in the United States   In Thousands of 60 Kilogram Bags[2]

Year	Jan.	Feb.	Mar.	Apr.	May	June	July	Aug.	Sept.	Oct.	Nov.	Dec.	Total
1994	1,538	1,152	1,409	1,077	1,082	1,151	1,195	1,560	1,266	1,127	1,103	1,213	14,872
1995	1,469	1,253	1,702	1,221	1,190	1,240	1,117	1,094	1,220	1,326	1,492	1,563	15,886
1996	1,824	1,657	1,753	1,395	1,444	1,236	1,329	1,341	1,364	1,279	1,485	1,828	17,936
1997	1,582	1,837	1,966	1,792	1,738	1,583	1,783	1,391	1,147	1,215	1,184	1,629	18,848
1998	1,747	1,893	1,827	1,587	1,540	1,412	1,386	1,478	1,369	1,499	1,423	1,837	18,998
1999	1,742	1,866	2,243	1,787	1,602	1,691	1,488	1,639	1,491	1,470	1,639	1,903	20,561
2000	2,094	2,012	2,317	1,922	2,079	1,858	1,793	1,699	1,496	1,480	1,431	1,445	21,625
2001	1,654	1,602	1,811	1,717	1,723	1,599	1,767	1,521	1,335	1,378	1,465	1,722	19,294
2002	1,554	1,290	1,497	1,600	1,574	1,460	1,686	1,687	1,741	1,765	1,698	1,833	19,384
2003[1]	1,882	1,679	1,883	1,797	1,605	1,592	1,895	1,623	1,615	1,625	1,407	1,725	20,329

[1] Preliminary.   [2] 132.276 pounds per bag.   *Source: Bureau of the Census, U.S. Department of Commerce*

Average Price of Brazilian[1] Coffee in New York   In Cents Per Pound

Year	Jan.	Feb.	Mar.	Apr.	May	June	July	Aug.	Sept.	Oct.	Nov.	Dec.	Average
1994	71.42	80.14	84.72	87.14	118.37	136.43	211.81	192.38	212.73	191.21	172.83	159.73	143.24
1995	162.81	161.07	171.48	166.54	161.72	145.22	139.68	149.54	130.26	127.23	125.33	110.46	145.95
1996	127.54	144.05	140.99	132.92	134.76	125.44	106.93	108.28	103.10	105.77	103.76	103.71	119.77
1997	127.28	160.21	179.75	183.73	209.62	184.21	158.52	158.25	167.77	152.12	149.07	171.12	166.80
1998	179.83	177.78	154.84	141.11	124.89	104.09	96.04	101.92	92.76	91.32	96.67	100.28	121.81
1999	99.43	91.72	88.90	86.14	96.29	91.69	78.13	76.67	70.43	78.74	98.41	109.47	88.84
2000	97.68	91.51	89.93	86.46	87.23	78.32	79.89	70.57	71.14	72.28	68.95	64.39	79.86
2001	62.38	62.50	60.35	55.11	57.19	51.86	46.43	46.49	42.42	38.63	42.28	41.60	50.60
2002	42.56	42.79	48.79	49.90	45.19	42.96	43.58	40.55	44.46	45.28	48.37	46.70	45.09
2003	49.14	48.54	43.77	48.71	51.06	47.11	49.64	52.88	55.19	53.51	54.15	56.92	50.89

[1] And other Arabicas.   *Source: Coffee Publications, Inc.*

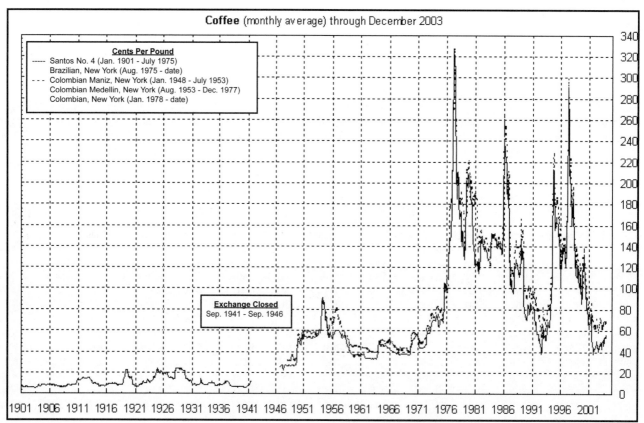

Average Monthly Retail [1] Price of Coffee in the United States   In Cents Per Pound

Year	Jan.	Feb.	Mar.	Apr.	May	June	July	Aug.	Sept.	Oct.	Nov.	Dec.	Average
1996	357.7	359.0	355.0	352.7	344.4	343.8	338.0	339.0	333.3	334.4	328.3	330.7	343.0
1997	330.0	331.6	351.2	389.4	410.9	442.8	462.8	466.9	461.7	439.2	430.3	416.1	411.1
1998	402.5	397.3	403.3	395.9	387.8	378.6	377.1	370.4	362.0	350.3	348.2	344.6	376.5
1999	343.5	342.8	347.6	346.6	349.5	342.1	342.0	342.8	339.3	348.2	333.7	334.7	342.7
2000	365.4	367.7	363.3	358.4	353.1	343.1	344.6	344.4	333.9	331.7	324.3	321.2	345.9
2001	322.4	321.7	320.5	312.8	309.7	315.6	309.7	304.6	302.5	301.5	298.8	291.3	309.3
2002	293.6	294.6	285.9	297.6	301.1	293.8	297.7	292.9	292.1	287.2	288.2	283.8	292.1
2003	299.9	292.4	293.3	300.8	293.7	293.1	294.4	292.1	291.9	282.5	227.9	NA	287.5

[1] Roasted in 13.1 to 20 ounce cans.   Source: Coffee Publications, Inc.

Average Price of Colombian Mild Arabicas[1] in the United States   In Cents Per Pound

Year	Jan.	Feb.	Mar.	Apr.	May	June	July	Aug.	Sept.	Oct.	Nov.	Dec.	Average
1996	119.08	134.94	160.60	134.31	142.56	133.25	135.39	137.68	123.30	127.77	129.41	126.41	133.73
1997	146.18	188.62	212.96	199.22	318.50	227.15	190.57	193.46	196.29	169.40	161.38	183.32	198.92
1998	184.21	190.59	166.07	158.17	146.33	135.83	125.03	129.45	117.56	115.01	121.74	123.96	142.83
1999	123.07	116.92	117.05	114.02	123.95	121.45	107.05	105.28	97.77	103.69	126.76	140.35	116.45
2000	130.13	124.73	119.51	112.67	110.31	100.30	101.67	91.87	89.98	90.25	84.01	75.81	102.60
2001	75.33	76.70	76.94	78.25	80.92	74.38	69.70	73.50	68.80	62.88	65.72	62.57	72.14
2002	63.46	65.64	71.16	70.17	63.44	60.86	59.60	58.98	62.49	66.54	72.83	67.92	65.26
2003	69.68	69.60	61.82	66.12	67.56	65.01	67.84	68.65	68.37	66.59	67.04	69.38	67.31

[1] ICO monthly and composite indicator prices on the New York Market, 1979 ICA Agreement basis.   Source: Coffee Publications, Inc.

Average Price of Other Mild Arabicas[1] in the United States   In Cents Per Pound

Year	Jan.	Feb.	Mar.	Apr.	May	June	July	Aug.	Sept.	Oct.	Nov.	Dec.	Average
1996	109.38	122.71	119.05	122.01	128.56	124.46	120.47	122.49	114.05	120.62	119.90	115.01	119.89
1997	131.83	167.20	193.82	204.43	264.50	212.55	186.52	185.17	184.38	161.45	154.15	174.25	185.02
1998	175.04	175.87	154.82	147.08	134.35	121.56	113.86	119.89	108.07	107.07	113.84	115.54	132.25
1999	110.99	103.24	103.23	99.69	109.10	104.21	90.85	87.64	81.06	92.22	112.74	123.56	101.54
2000	109.17	101.17	98.26	92.76	91.76	84.10	85.20	74.52	73.83	75.43	70.47	64.81	85.12
2001	64.98	67.00	65.88	65.68	68.94	63.79	58.47	59.68	57.71	56.23	58.96	55.63	61.91
2002	57.34	60.51	66.38	65.78	58.45	55.12	53.07	52.02	57.58	64.05	70.15	64.75	60.43
2003	65.22	67.60	61.66	65.35	66.47	61.34	62.32	63.60	65.50	62.58	62.36	65.01	64.08

[1] ICO monthly and composite indicator prices on the New York Market, 1979 ICA Agreement basis.   Source: Coffee Publications, Inc.

Average Price of Robustas 1976[1] in the United States   In Cents Per Pound

Year	Jan.	Feb.	Mar.	Apr.	May	June	July	Aug.	Sept.	Oct.	Nov.	Dec.	Average
1996	91.99	98.99	91.99	91.45	92.10	86.46	78.14	80.16	74.83	72.97	70.51	63.08	82.72
1997	67.66	76.65	81.31	78.48	95.74	91.94	82.52	76.92	77.43	76.90	78.20	84.65	80.70
1998	86.03	85.79	84.67	90.60	92.64	84.55	78.40	79.98	80.88	80.36	80.40	82.82	83.93
1999	81.65	77.68	72.70	68.89	68.28	66.20	62.28	63.80	60.44	59.25	64.10	66.40	67.64
2000	53.62	49.41	47.26	45.21	45.19	43.72	41.93	38.94	39.47	36.55	33.34	30.78	42.12
2001	31.00	31.96	30.96	28.59	29.71	29.33	27.59	25.86	23.79	21.26	22.03	23.57	27.14
2002	22.88	24.46	29.77	30.35	29.43	29.26	29.31	28.74	33.31	34.44	39.38	38.68	30.83
2003	42.75	42.35	38.26	38.68	38.90	35.33	36.71	37.92	38.76	37.32	36.05	37.59	38.39

[1] ICO monthly and composite indicator prices on the New York Market, 1979 ICA Agreement basis.   Source: Coffee Publications, Inc.

Average Price of Composite 1979[1] in the United States   In Cents Per Pound

Year	Jan.	Feb.	Mar.	Apr.	May	June	July	Aug.	Sept.	Oct.	Nov.	Dec.	Average
1996	100.33	110.50	105.89	107.09	110.24	105.79	99.97	102.73	96.52	98.56	97.14	90.04	102.07
1997	100.03	121.89	137.47	142.20	180.44	155.38	135.04	132.63	132.51	121.09	118.16	130.02	133.91
1998	130.61	130.78	119.93	119.66	114.23	103.84	97.32	101.25	95.82	95.01	98.26	100.73	108.95
1999	97.63	92.36	89.41	85.72	89.51	85.41	78.21	77.22	71.94	76.36	88.22	95.63	85.64
2000	82.15	76.15	73.49	69.53	69.23	64.56	64.09	57.59	57.31	56.40	52.18	48.27	64.25
2001	49.19	49.39	48.52	47.31	49.38	46.54	43.07	42.77	41.17	42.21	44.24	43.36	45.60
2002	43.46	44.30	49.49	50.19	47.30	45.56	44.70	42.79	47.96	50.79	54.69	51.68	47.74
2003	54.04	54.07	49.61	51.87	53.19	48.90	50.89	52.22	54.10	51.72	49.81	52.44	51.91

[1] ICO monthly and composite indicator prices on the New York Market, 1979 ICA Agreement basis.   Source: Coffee Publications, Inc.

COFFEE

Average Open Interest of Coffee 'C' Futures in New York   In Contracts

Year	Jan.	Feb.	Mar.	Apr.	May	June	July	Aug.	Sept.	Oct.	Nov.	Dec.
1994	54,796	50,230	53,713	57,226	58,574	54,589	43,056	35,052	35,800	34,258	31,046	31,134
1995	34,455	35,391	36,925	34,387	34,615	34,462	30,156	27,448	27,800	28,408	24,505	26,412
1996	28,430	28,224	28,127	28,793	28,394	25,096	26,188	25,799	23,929	26,202	27,599	27,201
1997	38,516	42,888	39,092	32,644	30,324	22,552	21,497	19,818	22,788	25,109	23,636	28,577
1998	30,042	30,539	30,211	32,617	36,345	36,651	37,531	30,074	30,429	32,940	31,677	32,816
1999	36,194	36,693	41,294	43,846	45,947	45,675	45,411	46,725	46,255	47,956	46,271	46,764
2000	47,829	50,620	50,565	53,662	49,692	50,293	45,513	40,177	40,133	42,906	43,187	45,086
2001	48,914	53,050	58,111	57,722	53,481	58,311	57,888	57,243	55,674	58,345	55,317	53,953
2002	57,897	66,825	66,798	66,207	66,289	68,994	69,197	69,635	70,079	73,753	73,431	69,343
2003	69,508	71,682	76,934	77,954	72,716	72,155	72,110	68,259	73,809	79,038	81,253	76,628

Source: New York Board of Trade (NYBOT)

Volume of Trading of Coffee 'C' Futures in New York   In Contracts

Year	Jan.	Feb.	Mar.	Apr.	May	June	July	Aug.	Sept.	Oct.	Nov.	Dec.	Total
1994	188,508	219,455	208,113	284,734	380,119	304,542	210,479	196,685	159,574	177,424	184,172	142,713	2,658,073
1995	169,250	191,352	213,326	156,191	163,248	186,550	162,562	161,076	165,337	152,959	157,240	123,923	2,003,014
1996	203,369	186,526	152,797	197,442	137,454	158,929	171,800	196,991	136,054	196,696	135,305	166,213	2,039,576
1997	242,719	280,014	267,369	223,330	219,214	186,227	135,664	136,807	142,610	151,171	145,610	163,446	2,294,181
1998	155,774	194,435	186,712	194,732	157,935	189,768	165,868	189,047	156,556	172,956	197,776	133,471	2,095,030
1999	216,810	201,670	252,841	243,630	237,968	243,164	187,019	232,817	151,724	270,013	244,258	177,309	2,659,223
2000	158,962	232,174	166,970	224,266	177,753	218,467	198,975	175,868	119,304	163,399	187,230	111,593	2,134,961
2001	189,977	221,775	167,466	236,757	182,621	220,708	134,809	250,151	100,443	153,739	229,495	111,430	2,199,371
2002	201,327	279,966	229,764	295,701	159,670	225,177	174,567	254,563	232,255	250,483	236,307	178,728	2,718,508
2003	205,420	283,317	169,611	334,188	255,935	270,424	237,210	278,746	332,473	309,930	314,182	219,595	3,211,031

Source: New York Board of Trade (NYBOT)

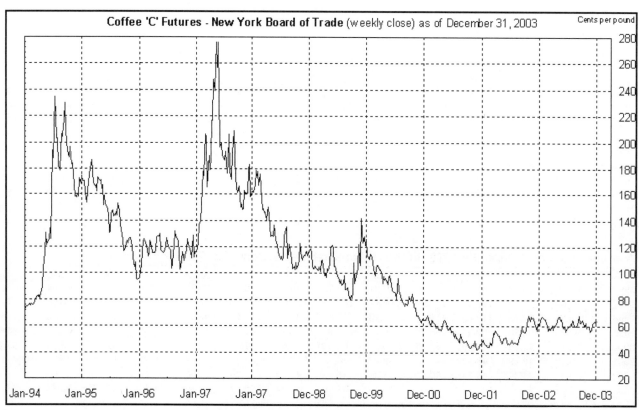

Coke

Coke is the hard and porous residue left after certain types of bituminous coals are heated to high temperatures (up to 2,000 degrees Fahrenheit) for about 17 hours. It is blackish-gray and has a metallic luster. The residue is mostly carbon. Coke is used as a reducing agent in the smelting of pig iron and the production of steel. Petroleum coke is made from the heavy tar-like residue of the petroleum refining process. It is used primarily to generate electricity.

Supply – Coke production in the US rose to 285.686 million barrels in 2002 from 298.261 million in 2001. That was well below the production record of 369.305 million barrels posted in 1957. US stocks at coke plants (Dec 31) fell to 606,000 tons in 2002 from 981,000 tons in 2001.

Trade – US exports fell sharply to 594,000 tons from 1.069 million tons in 2001. Most of those exports were to Canada. US imports rose to 3.096 million tons in 2002 from 2.340 million tons in 2001. About one-half of the imports were from Japan.

Salient Statistics of Coke in the United States   In Thousands of Short Tons

| | Coke and Breeze Production at Coke Plants | | | | | | | Producer and Distributor | Exports | | Imports | |
| | By Census Division | | | | | | | | | | | |
Year	Middle Atlantic	East North Central	East South Central	Other	Total	Coke Total	Breeze Total	Consumption[2]	Stocks Dec. 31	Canada	Total	Japan	Total
1997	8,994	8,882	3,393	2,080	23,349	22,116	1,233	24,017	1,294	498	832	1,018	1,565
1998	6,371	9,224	2,922	2,766	21,283	20,041	1,242	23,108	933	830	1,129	2,062	3,834
1999	5,869	10,115	2,821	2,448	21,253	20,016	1,237	22,423	852	686	898	2,012	3,224
2000	6,095	10,835	2,558	2,608	22,096	20,808	1,289	23,242	1,054	795	1,146	1,884	3,781
2001	W	10,272	1,979	7,893	20,144	18,949	1,195	20,293	981	793	1,069	1,508	2,340
2002[1]	W	7,952	1,925	7,332	17,209	16,099	1,109	18,977	606	493	594	1,508	3,096

[1] Preliminary.   [2] Equal to production plus imports minus the change in producer and distributor stocks minus exports.
Source: Energy Information Administration, U.S. Department of Energy (EIA-DOE)

Production of Petroleum Coke in the United States   In Thousands of Barrels

Year	Jan.	Feb.	Mar.	Apr.	May	June	July	Aug.	Sept.	Oct.	Nov.	Dec.	Total
1997	19,798	17,594	20,603	21,274	22,210	21,052	21,619	22,229	21,630	21,782	20,313	21,827	251,931
1998	20,929	18,968	21,998	21,834	21,790	20,856	21,790	22,469	21,526	21,234	20,837	22,258	256,489
1999	22,312	20,084	22,148	21,444	21,410	20,943	21,741	22,180	21,249	22,166	21,695	22,866	260,238
2000	21,502	20,017	21,654	21,161	21,785	22,095	23,321	22,835	22,455	22,121	22,628	24,262	265,836
2001	23,970	21,112	23,299	23,713	42,465	23,345	23,838	23,339	22,321	23,306	23,350	24,203	298,261
2002	24,543	22,849	23,529	23,850	24,713	23,305	24,556	23,939	23,465	22,527	23,497	24,913	285,686
2003[1]	23,420	20,030	23,810	23,768	24,831	24,054	26,080	25,746	24,072	24,588			288,479

[1] Preliminary.   *Source: Energy Information Administration, U.S. Department of Energy (EIA-DOE)*

Coal Receipts and Average Prices at Coke Plants in the United States

| | Coal Receipts at Coke Plants | | | | | Average Price of Coal Receipts at Coke Plants | | | | |
| | By Census Division, In Thousands of Short Tons | | | | | By Census Division, In Dollars per Short Ton | | | | |
Year	Middle Atlantic	East North Central	East South Central	Other	Total	Middle Atlantic	East North Central	East South Central	Other	Total
1997	11,555	10,825	4,290	2,880	29,550	47.05	49.12	47.72	W	47.61
1998	8,430	12,442	3,777	3,705	28,354	44.16	48.39	46.43	W	46.06
1999	7,784	13,524	3,571	3,276	28,155	44.33	47.74	45.28	W	45.85
2000	7,971	14,020	3,209	3,520	28,720	42.89	45.62	44.74	W	44.38
2001	W	13,084	2,678	10,622	26,384	W	47.53	47.69	W	46.42
2002[1]	W	10,657	2,335	9,244	22,236	W	52.88	50.03	W	51.27

[1] Preliminary.   W = Withheld proprietary data.   *Source: Energy Information Administration, U.S. Department of Energy (EIA-DOE)*

Coal Carbonized and Coke and Breeze Stocks at Coke Plants in the U.S.   In Thousands of Short Tons

| | Coal Carbonized at Coke Plants | | | | | Stocks at Coke Plants, Dec. 31 | | | | | | |
| | By Census Division | | | | | By Census Division | | | | | | |
Year	Middle Atlantic	East North Central	East South Central	Other	Total	Middle Atlantic	East North Central	East South Central	Other	Total	Coke Total	Breeze Total
1997	11,655	11,366	4,299	2,883	30,203	297	509	159	465	1,430	1,294	135
1998	8,401	12,311	3,736	3,741	28,189	160	526	176	215	1,077	933	144
1999	7,799	13,404	3,584	3,321	28,108	69	500	157	277	1,003	852	150
2000	8,129	13,971	3,290	3,549	28,939	148	628	166	255	1,197	1,054	143
2001	W	12,981	2,608	10,486	26,075	W	637	266	607	1,510	981	88
2002[1]	W	10,703	2,319	9,515	22,537	W	492	288	383	1,163	606	141

[1] Preliminary.   W = Withheld proprietary data.   *Source: Energy Information Administration, U.S. Department of Energy (EIA-DOE)*

Copper

The word copper comes from name of the Mediterranean island Cyprus that was a primary source of the metal. Dating back more than 10,000 years, copper is man's oldest metal. From the Pyramid of Cheops in Egypt, archeologists have recovered a portion of a water plumbing system whose copper tubing was found in serviceable condition after more than 5,000 years.

Copper is one of the most widely used industrial metals because it is an excellent conductor of electricity, has strong corrosion-resistance properties, and is very ductile. It is also used to produce the two alloys of brass (a copper-zinc alloy) and bronze (a copper-tin alloy), both of which are far harder and stronger than the pure metal. Electrical uses of copper account for about 75% of total copper usage and building construction is the single largest market. Copper is biostatic, meaning that bacteria will not grow on its surface, and is therefore used in air-conditioning systems, food processing surfaces, and doorknobs to prevent the spread of disease. Today the copper content of US coins is 2.6% for the penny, 75% for the nickel, and 91.67% for the dime, quarter, and half dollar. Known worldwide resources of copper are estimated at nearly 5.8 trillion pounds, of which only about 0.7 trillion (12%) have been mined.

Copper futures and options are traded on the London Metal Exchange (LME) and the COMEX Division of the New York Mercantile Exchange (NYMEX). Copper futures are traded on the Shanghai Futures Exchange. The Comex copper futures contract calls for the delivery of 25,000 pounds of Grade 1 electrolyte copper and is priced in terms of cents per pound.

Prices – Comex copper futures prices traded sideways in the first half of 2003 but then staged an impressive rally late in 2003 as the US economy surged. Demand for copper has a strong correlation with US economic growth and with the US building industry. Copper prices were also boosted by the weakness in the dollar. Copper prices closed 2003 at a 6-1/2 year high of $1.04 per pound. That is, however, still well below the 13-year high on the copper nearest-futures chart of $1.46 posted in July 1995 and the record high of $1.65 posted in December 1988.

Supply – World production of copper in 2001, the latest reporting year, rose by 3.8% to 13.700 million metric tons from 13.200 million in 2000. The world's largest producer of copper is Chile with 34.6% of world production, followed by the US with 9.8%, Indonesia with 7.7%, and Australia with 6.3%. US production of refined copper in 2003 was on track to fall to 1.3 million tons from 1.508 million in 2002.

Demand – US consumption of copper in 2001 fell to 2.620 million metric tons from 3.030 million in 2000. The primary consumer of copper in the US is wire rod mills with 74% of usage, followed by brass mills with 24% of usage.

Trade – US exports of copper in 2003 were set to rebound sharply higher from the depressed levels of 22,500 metric tons in 2001 and 26,600 metric tons in 2002. US imports of copper in 2003 were set to fall slightly from 927,000 metric tons in 2002.

World Mine Production of Copper (Content of Ore) — In Thousands of Metric Tons

Year	Australia	Canada[3]	Chile	China	Indonesia	Mexico	Peru	Poland	Russia[4]	South Africa	United States[3]	Zambia	World Total
1992	378.0	768.6	1,932.7	334	280.8	279.0	345.6	331.9	699	176.1	1,760	429.5	9,470
1993	402.0	732.6	2,055.4	345	298.6	301.2	355.0	382.6	584	166.3	1,800	396.2	9,430
1994	415.6	616.8	2,219.9	396	322.2	294.7	395.9	378.0	573	160.1	1,820	373.2	9,490
1995	397.8	726.3	2,488.6	445	443.6	333.6	409.7	384.2	525	161.6	1,850	316.0	10,000
1996	547.3	688.4	3,115.8	439	507.5	340.7	484.2	421.9	523	152.6	1,920	334.0	11,000
1997	558.0	659.5	3,392.0	511	529.1	390.5	506.5	414.8	505	153.1	1,940	352.9	11,500
1998	607.0	705.8	3,686.8	504	780.8	384.6	483.3	436.2	500	166.0	1,860	315.0	12,100
1999	739.0	620.1	4,391.2	533	766.0	381.2	536.4	464.0	530	144.3	1,600	270.0	12,700
2000[1]	829.0	633.9	4,602.4	613	1,012.1	364.6	553.9	456.2	570	137.1	1,440	241.2	13,200
2001[2]	869.0	632.8	4,739.0	588	1,050.0	367.4	722.0	474.0	620	141.9	1,340	299.3	13,700

[1] Preliminary.   [2] Estimate.   [3] Recoverable.   [4] Formerly part of the U.S.S.R.; data not reported separately until 1992.
Source: U.S. Geological Survey (USGS)

Commodity Exchange Inc. Warehouse Stocks of Copper, on First of Month — In Thousands of Short Tons

Year	Jan.	Feb.	Mar.	Apr.	May	June	July	Aug.	Sept.	Oct.	Nov.	Dec.
1994	74.0	56.7	49.8	37.2	31.6	30.4	36.0	37.4	28.5	17.9	20.3	21.5
1995	27.0	18.7	17.7	9.0	11.5	7.0	13.1	16.7	16.5	11.2	6.1	5.4
1996	24.0	12.1	12.8	13.9	20.7	13.2	7.4	17.3	22.1	21.7	30.8	38.5
1997	29.5	19.0	24.8	43.6	49.5	43.0	46.3	30.0	46.5	61.5	67.8	79.8
1998	91.5	100.7	112.3	112.6	107.6	84.8	63.5	55.7	56.6	67.7	69.4	74.7
1999	93.9	101.8	112.3	123.1	132.6	131.7	133.7	120.2	108.8	97.5	90.9	90.9
2000	91.6	95.6	95.6	95.9	865.2	75.0	73.6	73.2	62.8	62.3	63.4	64.9
2001	64.7	79.3	90.0	105.1	126.5	150.9	165.1	176.1	186.8	199.6	211.0	236.2
2002	269.2	284.8	304.0	314.1	326.0	337.4	355.7	374.6	375.9	380.3	381.6	382.8
2003	399.3	395.2	373.7	362.7	351.2	NA	320.5	310.6	303.9	299.0	294.4	288.1

Source: New York Mercantile Exchange (NYMEX), COMEX division

Salient Statistics of Copper in the United States   In Thousands of Metric Tons

	New Copper Produced					Imports[3]			Exports			Stocks, Dec 31		Blister &	Apparent Consumption	
	From Domestic Ores													Material	Refined	Primary
			Refin-	Foreign	Total	Secon-dary Re-	Unmanu-		Ore, Concen-			Primary Producers	in	Copper	& Old
Year	Mines	Smelters	eries	Ores[3]	New	covered[4]	factured	Refined	trate[6]	Refined[7]	COMEX	(Refined)	Solution	(Reported)	Copper[8]
1992	1,760	1,180	1,110	96	1,710	555	593	289	266	177	96	205	166	2,178	2,311
1993	1,800	1,270	1,210	89	1,790	543	607	313	227	217	67	153	146	2,360	2,510
1994	1,850	1,310	1,280	64	1,840	500	763	470	261	157	24	119	167	2,680	2,690
1995	1,850	1,250	1,300	91	1,930	443	825	429	239	217	22	163	171	2,530	2,540
1996	1,920	1,300	1,290	147	2,010	428	961	543	195	169	27	146	173	2,610	2,830
1997	1,940	1,440	1,370	113	2,070	498	999	632	127	93	83	314	180	2,790	2,940
1998	1,860	1,490	1,290	238	2,140	466	1,190	683	37	86	85	532	160	2,890	3,030
1999	1,600	1,090	1,110	196	1,890	381	1,280	837	63	25	83	565	138	2,980	3,130
2000[1]	1,450	W	865	163	1,590	357	1,350	1,060	107	94	59	334	122	3,030	3,130
2001[2]	1,340	W	808	192	1,630	316	1,400	991	45	23	244	952	98	2,620	2,500

[1] Preliminary.   [2] Estimate.   [3] Also from matte, etc., refinery reports.   [4] From old scrap only.   [5] For consumption.   [6] Blister (copper content).   [7] Ingots, bars, etc.   [8] Old scrap only.   *Source: U.S. Geological Survey (USGS)*

Consumption of Refined Copper[3] in the United States   In Thousands of Metric Tons

| | By-Products | | | | | | By Class of Consumer | | | | | | Total |
| | | Wire | Ingots & | Cakes | | | Wire Rod | Brass | Chemiacl | Ingot | | Miscel- | Con- |
Year	Cathodes	Bars	Ingot Bars	& Slabs	Billets	Other[4]	Mills	Mills	Plants	Makers	Foundries	laneous[5]	sumption
1992	1,974.9	W	20.0	43.7	W	139.6	1,675.0	458.5	0.9	3.0	15.0	25.8	2,178.2
1993	2,130.0	W	37.7	55.5	W	136.0	1,819.1	503.0	0.9	2.2	10.2	27.6	2,360.0
1994	2,410.0	W	37.3	73.2	W	164.0	2,060.0	568.0	1.1	4.5	11.1	30.4	2,680.0
1995	2,250.0	W	31.3	75.9	W	181.0	1,950.0	533.0	1.1	7.7	15.6	31.4	2,530.0
1996	2,320.0	W	26.8	80.8	W	181.0	1,980.0	588.0	1.1	3.6	15.8	28.6	2,610.0
1997	2,490.0	W	29.4	81.1	W	194.0	2,140.0	597.0	1.0	4.2	16.6	29.9	2,790.0
1998	2,600.0	W	30.7	76.2	W	184.0	2,170.0	659.0	1.1	5.4	19.2	31.8	2,890.0
1999	2,710.0	W	24.4	79.3	W	166.0	2,230.0	691.0	1.2	4.5	21.2	29.8	2,980.0
2000[1]	2,730.0	W	23.8	101.0	W	175.0	2,240.0	723.0	1.2	4.6	24.3	32.5	3,030.0
2001[2]	2,360.0	W	24.0	95.9	W	143.0	1,940.0	623.0	1.2	4.6	22.8	30.9	2,620.0

[1] Preliminary.   [2] Estimate.   [3] Primary & secondary.   [4] 1991 to date include Wirebars and Billets.   [5] Includes iron and steel plants, primary smelters producing alloys other than copper, consumers of copper powder and copper shot, and other manufacturers.   W - Withheld proprietary data. *Source: U.S. Geological Survey (USGS)*

London Metals Exchange Warehouse Stocks of Copper, at End of Month   In Thousands of Metric Tons

Year	Jan.	Feb.	Mar.	Apr.	May	June	July	Aug.	Sept.	Oct.	Nov.	Dec.
1994	597.6	554.5	504.3	446.4	379.0	350.9	338.9	367.8	359.3	333.1	318.4	302.2
1995	309.9	280.9	239.9	204.9	197.9	166.5	151.5	163.1	178.2	193.6	222.2	364.8
1996	355.1	348.4	322.3	303.9	309.7	263.0	227.6	275.5	240.7	122.1	96.1	119.6
1997	194.2	216.2	177.2	145.8	133.0	128.3	234.9	278.7	332.8	344.6	338.8	337.8
1998	365.7	376.0	339.5	262.3	261.8	249.3	260.9	307.7	414.2	460.6	511.9	590.1
1999	646.9	695.9	722.2	748.2	776.6	754.8	769.6	789.0	774.0	793.8	779.7	790.5
2000	807.3	824.1	755.4	697.8	605.7	553.4	487.8	449.2	401.5	380.9	349.4	357.4
2001	349.9	327.9	400.5	445.2	431.3	464.7	651.9	661.2	729.0	737.2	780.4	799.5
2002	855.5	910.9	950.9	973.8	958.3	892.1	893.6	896.6	870.6	863.2	862.8	855.9
2003[1]	833.8	825.9	813.2	768.2	740.8	665.8	612.6	620.3	580.4	516.5	467.0	

[1] Preliminary.   *Source: American Bureau of Metal Statistics (ABMS)*

Copper Refined from Scrap in the United States   In Thousands of Metric Tons

Year	Jan.	Feb.	Mar.	Apr.	May	June	July	Aug.	Sept.	Oct.	Nov.	Dec.	Total
1994	33.3	28.3	37.9	30.7	37.1	28.7	26.9	33.0	38.7	27.0	34.3	37.3	391.7
1995	30.9	30.6	36.0	32.7	33.7	28.2	18.7	25.1	25.4	25.0	26.2	24.4	319.0
1996	25.0	23.7	25.5	22.5	26.8	30.9	24.4	25.0	26.8	30.6	25.9	26.3	333.0
1997	35.9	30.0	36.4	32.6	35.4	30.8	26.4	28.4	34.3	36.5	24.6	29.3	383.0
1998	25.9	28.6	23.7	31.0	17.8	21.4	24.2	23.9	23.8	31.8	23.2	26.3	336.0
1999	20.1	21.8	23.7	17.6	16.2	17.5	21.2	18.2	21.3	21.0	17.7	20.0	230.0
2000	19.4	18.6	25.8	22.5	22.1	15.4	11.7	19.7	14.1	14.3	19.7	15.6	208.0
2001	15.4	14.2	15.2	13.4	12.8	13.2	13.9	13.5	12.3	10.2	6.4	5.7	154.0
2002	7.1	6.2	7.2	7.6	8.2	7.8	7.0	7.6	7.1	6.3	5.1	3.9	81.1
2003[1]	5.8	3.9	5.7	3.9	4.1	4.9	4.9	3.9	4.2	4.5	4.4		54.7

[1] Preliminary.   *Source: U.S. Geological Survey (USGS)*

COPPER

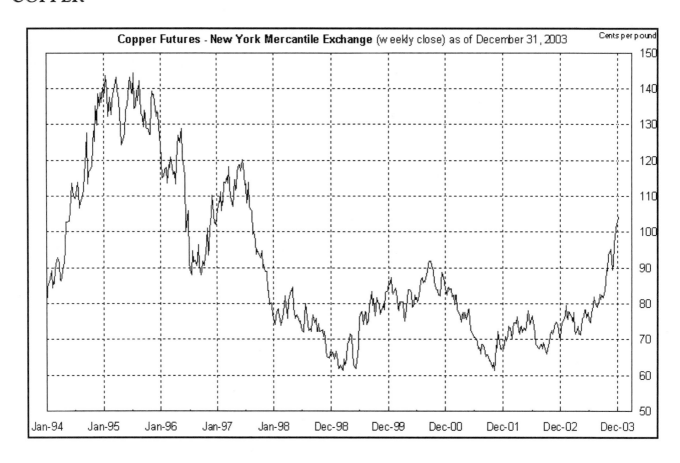

Average Open Interest of Copper Futures in New York   In Contracts

Year	Jan.	Feb.	Mar.	Apr.	May	June	July	Aug.	Sept.	Oct.	Nov.	Dec.
1994	65,518	65,446	66,177	59,346	63,825	60,383	51,616	46,855	56,344	59,060	59,158	51,078
1995	52,632	50,770	47,267	47,793	50,089	48,200	40,968	37,744	33,709	36,476	38,475	35,996
1996	47,771	45,706	42,732	46,771	47,284	52,558	56,564	56,549	55,408	58,124	61,031	55,807
1997	54,468	56,022	58,205	50,574	56,740	56,774	47,767	44,632	49,612	54,912	67,026	67,502
1998	69,607	72,302	67,154	68,670	65,033	66,002	63,271	61,116	60,520	62,944	67,984	76,846
1999	76,861	73,109	75,318	70,534	76,341	70,842	75,640	70,084	80,188	72,240	69,179	69,819
2000	82,289	73,778	68,026	75,520	69,531	63,786	71,389	79,565	83,546	73,609	74,161	70,349
2001	77,952	76,721	78,034	83,647	72,970	85,495	83,690	88,782	87,004	88,166	85,809	68,981
2002	72,823	79,806	79,156	75,229	74,350	80,981	82,661	102,056	99,225	99,470	89,213	79,218
2003	81,820	81,499	72,484	85,485	77,704	81,509	82,868	94,517	92,768	106,924	103,218	90,310

Source: New York Mercantile Exchange (NYMEX), COMEX division

Volume of Trading of Copper Futures in New York   In Contracts

Year	Jan.	Feb.	Mar.	Apr.	May	June	July	Aug.	Sept.	Oct.	Nov.	Dec.	Total
1994	197,959	233,016	231,239	207,963	247,143	297,393	188,644	242,393	219,788	208,957	290,585	178,887	2,737,967
1995	242,760	267,883	232,229	242,302	195,554	274,587	167,836	213,110	169,689	181,945	185,141	146,378	2,519,414
1996	184,431	173,689	157,553	210,836	200,469	255,172	150,445	174,351	166,537	250,420	227,800	160,216	2,311,919
1997	193,543	221,504	190,000	218,607	164,728	238,918	191,609	198,156	197,746	202,615	203,376	135,368	2,356,170
1998	172,133	223,117	197,652	264,061	175,956	217,316	202,596	213,541	196,355	195,255	250,986	174,642	2,483,610
1999	159,147	288,394	230,716	296,162	224,221	319,157	244,567	267,325	220,958	193,628	231,399	177,288	2,852,962
2000	220,488	276,374	195,668	261,971	232,971	241,854	187,453	283,328	171,080	243,342	266,051	197,544	2,778,124
2001	240,588	246,052	247,722	279,348	260,697	317,001	159,394	298,639	129,622	190,469	337,589	149,520	2,856,641
2002	217,598	233,704	164,747	254,259	218,091	267,201	263,395	303,642	195,637	232,731	276,492	179,789	2,807,286
2003	232,921	269,806	249,306	274,079	221,364	301,709	252,713	324,175	196,481	230,413	363,865	172,438	3,089,270

Source: New York Mercantile Exchange (NYMEX), COMEX division

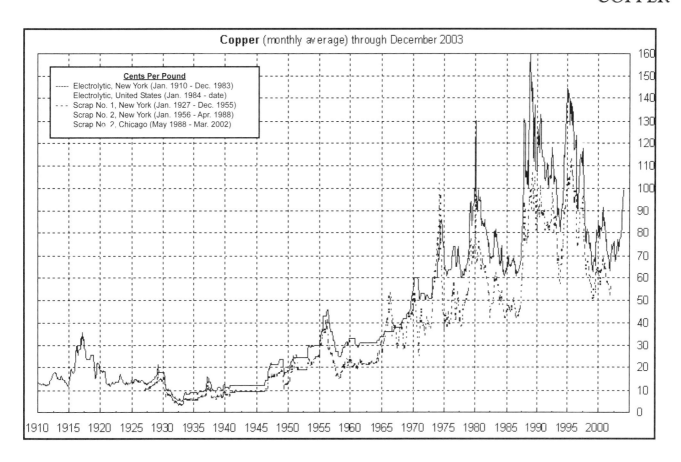

Producers' Price of Electrolytic (Wirebar) Copper, Delivered to U.S. Destinations In Cents Per Pound

Year	Jan.	Feb.	Mar.	Apr.	May	June	July	Aug.	Sept.	Oct.	Nov.	Dec.	Average
1994	95.65	99.13	101.76	99.87	112.30	120.58	123.68	121.38	132.53	130.91	141.92	148.86	119.05
1995	151.91	146.00	151.14	146.00	139.80	149.51	150.00	149.77	144.14	140.00	148.48	143.78	146.74
1996	130.09	128.75	130.20	131.29	135.33	116.55	103.63	104.14	102.51	101.80	112.58	114.78	117.86
1997	120.29	121.02	126.50	121.70	127.25	129.57	121.94	114.11	107.14	105.08	99.53	91.39	115.55
1998	88.88	87.52	91.69	93.54	90.02	86.90	87.37	85.30	87.62	84.26	83.51	78.30	87.09
1999	77.07	75.96	74.50	78.79	81.07	77.23	88.02	87.88	92.89	91.26	91.10	93.35	84.09
2000	96.83	94.41	91.63	89.32	94.80	92.74	95.81	98.67	103.49	99.63	95.25	98.92	95.96
2001	95.70	94.01	92.07	88.27	88.85	84.58	81.44	79.34	77.41	75.21	78.13	79.83	84.57
2002	81.79	84.23	86.60	85.11	85.22	88.23	84.44	79.82	79.71	80.16	84.57	75.56	82.62
2003	78.62	80.21	78.87	75.60	78.56	80.44	81.55	83.51	85.34	91.50	96.47	103.72	84.53

Source: American Metal Market (AMM)

Dealers' Buying Price of No. 2 Heavy Copper Scrap in Chicago[1] In Cents Per Pound

Year	Jan.	Feb.	Mar.	Apr.	May	June	July	Aug.	Sept.	Oct.	Nov.	Dec.	Average
1994	50.80	56.11	59.61	62.00	64.86	72.32	76.40	74.30	75.69	76.45	78.10	82.95	69.13
1995	89.48	90.79	89.39	91.75	85.91	88.73	92.32	92.65	92.70	90.64	92.00	92.00	90.70
1996	87.17	82.90	83.24	83.29	82.95	71.48	61.43	62.00	62.00	63.00	64.84	66.00	72.53
1997	68.73	71.63	77.50	79.18	77.33	78.19	72.64	70.24	65.67	63.74	61.31	58.43	70.38
1998	53.26	52.58	53.09	54.00	52.60	49.64	48.00	47.71	46.00	44.00	40.00	40.00	48.41
1999	36.32	36.00	36.00	36.00	39.60	41.77	41.00	45.09	46.19	48.00	48.00	48.67	41.90
2000	50.00	50.00	50.00	49.15	49.00	49.00	49.30	52.65	54.60	55.00	52.65	51.00	51.04
2001	51.62	49.16	49.00	49.81	50.00	50.00	49.14	44.00	44.00	43.48	41.45	41.47	46.93
2002	41.00	41.00	41.00	41.00	41.00	41.00	41.00	41.00	41.00	41.00	41.00	41.00	41.00
2003	41.00	41.00	41.00	41.00	41.00	41.00	41.00	41.00	41.00	48.17	56.00	56.00	44.10

Source: American Metal Market (AMM)

COPPER

Imports of Refined Copper into the United States — In Thousands of Metric Tons

Year	Jan.	Feb.	Mar.	Apr.	May	June	July	Aug.	Sept.	Oct.	Nov.	Dec.	Total
1994	28.7	33.6	49.8	36.8	36.1	46.8	35.6	34.4	34.7	62.4	35.9	36.2	470.0
1995	34.9	30.0	37.1	36.9	36.5	37.9	31.5	31.8	28.7	38.7	44.4	40.3	429.0
1996	43.1	41.2	48.2	49.6	56.8	44.6	53.8	64.8	62.3	46.1	61.8	47.2	543.0
1997	55.4	48.0	43.6	43.6	61.0	42.0	53.1	73.3	53.8	55.0	53.4	42.0	632.0
1998	62.8	49.6	59.9	64.7	57.6	52.8	45.0	51.7	71.1	52.7	62.0	63.4	683.0
1999	64.7	53.2	68.1	59.9	62.3	63.8	73.0	84.5	90.3	81.0	59.0	77.5	837.0
2000	84.9	67.8	85.5	92.1	83.6	84.5	89.4	83.0	98.6	112.0	100.0	73.7	1,060.0
2001	105.0	91.6	90.1	94.4	70.3	72.7	61.7	66.3	83.5	71.0	110.0	74.4	991.0
2002	82.5	87.8	53.0	92.6	59.9	76.2	80.3	90.5	69.9	79.0	82.0	73.0	927.0
2003[1]	60.7	87.8	69.9	78.5	72.7	62.3	74.0	78.1	81.7	82.0			897.2

[1] Preliminary.   *Source: U.S. Geological Survey (USGS)*

Exports of Refined Copper from the United States — In Thousands of Metric Tons

Year	Jan.	Feb.	Mar.	Apr.	May	June	July	Aug.	Sept.	Oct.	Nov.	Dec.	Total
1994	13.0	10.2	10.7	6.8	14.8	9.1	15.6	10.9	15.4	15.9	13.1	21.1	157.0
1995	11.1	24.0	25.6	18.2	23.4	38.9	16.3	16.6	12.1	9.0	12.5	9.5	217.0
1996	13.7	16.5	12.7	12.3	10.8	10.7	15.7	17.7	14.5	16.4	12.8	16.0	170.0
1997	11.1	9.8	6.5	6.5	71.9	8.2	6.9	7.5	6.3	7.4	8.2	8.5	93.3
1998	6.2	12.1	12.2	7.5	7.8	6.4	7.5	6.4	5.8	5.0	3.6	6.2	86.2
1999	2.4	1.1	1.8	1.3	1.6	4.2	1.6	1.5	1.2	1.4	3.7	3.3	25.2
2000	1.6	5.3	22.0	12.2	18.1	12.8	6.7	4.4	2.9	4.3	1.2	2.1	93.6
2001	1.2	.9	.8	1.9	1.0	.8	1.7	2.6	1.2	4.6	5.3	.6	22.5
2002	.4	.7	3.2	.7	.8	6.8	7.7	2.6	1.3	.6	.5	1.5	26.6
2003[1]	2.5	.8	1.5	.6	15.9	23.0	5.1	4.1	4.3	4.6			74.9

[1] Preliminary.   *Source: U.S. Geological Survey (USGS)*

Stocks of Refined Copper in the United States, on First of Month — In Thousands of Short Tons

Year	Jan.	Feb.	Mar.	Apr.	May	June	July	Aug.	Sept.	Oct.	Nov.	Dec.
1994	103.0	87.7	83.6	72.8	70.7	70.4	73.3	81.1	74.6	66.5	52.7	53.6
1995[2]	55.8	39.6	37.0	22.6	33.1	30.8	27.0	50.0	60.6	71.1	69.4	73.4
1996	120.0	131.4	125.5	123.1	126.3	107.9	102.8	106.2	104.7	68.0	76.0	77.5
1997	88.2	98.8	104.4	116.0	117.9	121.7	122.9	148.8	177.1	197.9	227.6	253.3
1998	281.5	282.2	312.7	315.7	304.5	308.6	306.2	319.0	334.1	367.4	407.2	444.6
1999	562.6	593.1	614.6	653.5	676.6	687.8	668.4	657.2	639.7	611.2	626.5	608.2
2000	619.2	620.8	619.5	582.9	537.0	508.8	467.8	418.0	397.7	394.3	379.1	344.2
2001	383.8	408.4	416.2	481.9	552.6	585.7	626.7	733.1	767.4	895.6	916.6	985.7
2002	1,045.1	1,096.2	1,132.4	1,155.3	1,175.0	1,158.8	1,126.7	1,132.2	1,123.0	1,123.7	1,110.5	1,109.0
2003[1]	1,119.8	109.7	1,038.8	1,042.1	998.3	959.8	891.8	848.9	855.6	825.2	760.9	

Recoverable copper content.   [1] Preliminary.   [2] New reporting method beginning January 1995, includes Comex, London Metal Exchange, and Refiners. Beginning January 1999, includes Consumers.   *Source: American Bureau of Metal Statistics (ABMS)*

Stocks of Refined Copper Outside the United States, on First of Month — In Thousands of Short Tons

Year	Jan.	Feb.	Mar.	Apr.	May	June	July	Aug.	Sept.	Oct.	Nov.	Dec.
1994	1,075.0	1,095.5	1,046.8	984.9	913.7	859.5	843.7	839.7	874.6	870.7	835.1	818.4
1995[2]	611.6	655.8	622.2	577.9	537.0	525.6	494.9	464.7	465.7	467.7	481.4	503.5
1996	560.2	566.0	552.5	517.5	498.7	563.9	507.9	476.6	544.4	499.5	391.8	362.0
1997	405.4	469.5	476.3	445.7	413.5	402.4	408.3	489.6	550.9	607.7	574.5	553.3
1998	580.8	512.4	487.3	438.1	371.1	368.0	335.7	324.0	387.2	468.0	506.9	509.0
1999	922.6	944.3	960.3	963.0	990.5	1,008.3	993.3	990.0	1,017.0	996.9	1,001.5	992.0
2000	983.8	1,034.9	1,040.7	1,011.4	988.6	880.9	866.0	857.3	837.0	826.7	784.1	764.8
2001	795.0	999.5	986.4	971.2	995.7	969.4	1,000.8	1,091.0	1,108.7	1,083.3	1,021.0	1,104.5
2002	1,241.3	1,273.5	1,291.5	1,370.4	1,391.1	1,399.4	1,289.0	1,342.6	1,369.1	1,321.1	1,219.7	1,224.5
2003[1]	1,238.8	2,147.6	1,188.0	1,216.3	1,147.4	1,109.8	1,129.2	1,139.9	1,150.9	1,140.5	1,164.5	

Recoverable copper content.   [1] Preliminary.   [2] New reporting method beginning January 1995, includes London Metal Exchange and Refiners. Beginning January 1999, also includes Shanghai Metal Exchange, Consumers and Other.   *Source: American Bureau of Metal Statistics (ABMS)*

Production of Refined Copper in the United States   In Thousands of Short Tons

Year	Jan.	Feb.	Mar.	Apr.	May	June	July	Aug.	Sept.	Oct.	Nov.	Dec.	Total
1994	160.9	150.1	167.8	157.2	165.5	160.4	148.9	165.6	162.1	157.3	153.3	159.8	2,360
1995	202.7	185.5	204.8	194.6	210.0	198.3	193.8	208.8	199.0	206.5	211.3	208.1	2,423
1996	210.8	197.6	209.7	212.4	213.5	193.4	206.1	199.5	198.8	223.1	199.3	212.0	2,476
1997	206.0	192.0	204.0	202.0	198.0	179.0	207.0	203.0	213.0	222.0	205.0	212.0	2,470
1998	214.0	204.0	216.0	209.0	197.0	188.0	197.0	203.0	201.0	217.0	207.0	217.0	2,490
1999	185.0	178.0	220.0	198.0	186.0	175.0	163.0	161.0	172.0	172.0	157.0	162.0	2,130
2000	157.0	149.0	173.0	144.0	161.0	146.0	134.0	149.0	141.0	140.0	147.0	154.0	1,800
2001	155.0	144.0	156.0	145.0	155.0	157.0	146.0	143.0	148.0	149.0	152.0	150.0	1,800
2002	134.0	117.0	124.0	129.0	134.0	128.0	130.0	124.0	120.0	129.0	120.0	119.0	1,508
2003[1]	124.0	110.0	118.0	100.0	101.0	107.0	111.0	110.0	112.0	110.0	104.0		1,317

Recoverable copper content.   [1] Preliminary.   *Source: U.S. Geological Survey (USGS)*

Stocks of Refined Copper in the United States, on First of Month   In Thousands of Short Tons

Year	Jan.	Feb.	Mar.	Apr.	May	June	July	Aug.	Sept.	Oct.	Nov.	Dec.
1992	75.3	76.3	67.2	69.7	75.9	65.0	62.2	71.2	87.1	99.5	110.3	107.1
1993	135.4	152.7	144.3	132.3	146.0	153.6	137.1	151.0	128.4	117.2	124.6	107.1
1994	103.0	87.7	83.6	72.8	70.7	70.4	73.3	81.1	74.6	66.5	52.7	53.6
1995[2]	55.8	39.6	37.0	22.6	33.1	30.8	27.0	50.0	60.6	71.1	69.4	73.4
1996	120.0	131.4	125.5	123.1	126.3	107.9	102.8	106.2	104.7	68.0	76.0	77.5
1997	88.2	98.8	104.4	116.0	117.9	121.7	122.9	148.8	177.1	197.9	227.6	253.3
1998	281.5	282.2	312.7	315.7	304.5	308.6	306.2	319.0	334.1	367.4	407.2	444.6
1999	562.6	593.1	614.6	653.5	676.6	687.8	668.4	657.2	639.7	611.2	626.5	608.2
2000	619.2	620.8	619.5	582.9	537.0	508.8	467.8	418.0	397.7	394.3	379.1	344.2
2001[1]	383.8	408.4	416.2	481.9	552.6	585.7	626.7	733.1	767.4	895.6		

Recoverable copper content.   [1] Preliminary.   [2] New reporting method beginning January 1995, includes Comex, London Metal Exchange, and Refiners.
Beginning January 1999, includes Consumers.   *Source: American Bureau of Metal Statistics (ABMS)*

Deliveries of Refined Copper to Fabricators in the United States   In Thousands of Short Tons

Year	Jan.	Feb.	Mar.	Apr.	May	June	July	Aug.	Sept.	Oct.	Nov.	Dec.	Total
1994	193.3	168.6	204.6	178.3	187.8	171.9	154.3	194.6	188.2	188.7	167.5	175.1	2,173
1995[2]	233.8	209.2	239.1	200.9	230.0	210.5	187.1	208.8	202.9	224.7	222.4	175.5	2,545
1996	221.6	227.2	240.0	242.2	270.7	222.1	233.8	246.8	277.5	239.7	240.6	231.9	2,896
1997	246.3	234.5	240.6	247.4	254.9	228.1	241.1	258.2	252.3	259.2	256.0	236.6	2,959
1998	284.5	248.4	288.1	289.2	278.7	258.0	252.4	242.1	260.7	232.0	251.9	220.0	3,106
1999	199.6	202.8	235.0	221.4	206.3	201.9	188.0	186.8	193.7	182.3	182.4	175.2	2,375
2000	166.8	161.3	176.3	157.0	173.7	161.3	145.2	149.7	150.6	154.8	149.8	162.7	1,909
2001	166.1	150.8	167.4	148.4	167.6	165.2	162.7	154.0	151.6	160.7	154.7	147.5	1,897
2002	152.1	126.0	140.7	149.3	148.6	136.2	147.9	141.1	129.5	141.6	124.5	129.7	1,667
2003[1]	136.4	123.4	124.6	106.6	107.7	117.0	127.1	120.6	125.8	125.9	112.4		1,448

Recoverable copper content.   [1] Preliminary.   [2] New reporting method beginning January 1995, includes crude copper deliveries.
Source: American Bureau of Metal Statistics (ABMS)

Deliveries of Refined Copper to Fabricators Outside the United States   In Thousands of Short Tons

Year	Jan.	Feb.	Mar.	Apr.	May	June	July	Aug.	Sept.	Oct.	Nov.	Dec.	Total
1990	419.9	466.3	436.7	392.9	408.3	466.7	303.7	373.5	370.8	448.9	469.1	420.7	4,972
1991	405.0	404.4	391.5	361.2	406.3	433.5	368.5	323.4	420.7	499.1	391.4	483.4	4,807
1992	453.7	408.9	441.8	416.4	413.4	432.4	410.4	364.7	432.6	403.5	406.1	461.3	5,045
1993	427.9	392.9	452.3	361.7	422.2	442.6	384.4	347.9	387.5	414.8	463.4	458.5	4,956
1994	399.8	429.5	481.2	466.5	468.9	428.1	387.9	369.2	423.5	448.9	457.1	436.0	5,197
1995[2]	758.5	810.1	892.8	882.2	853.0	867.3	863.7	814.1	803.4	835.1	796.6	726.2	9,903
1996	875.2	859.4	934.3	907.2	816.7	950.7	908.3	817.4	911.5	1,056.0	922.7	918.3	10,878
1997	862.2	889.7	977.9	1,007.1	991.1	982.7	897.8	873.9	886.2	1,009.0	980.4	966.6	11,349
1998	1,091.7	973.8	1,062.0	1,055.5	995.7	1,014.8	986.8	924.8	913.3	987.9	982.1	1,023.0	12,011
1999[1]	314.5	745.5											6,360

Recoverable copper content.   [1] Preliminary.   [2] New reporting method beginning January 1995, includes crude copper deliveries.
Source: American Bureau of Metal Statistics (ABMS)

Corn

Corn is a member of the grass family of plants and is a native grain of the American continents. Fossils of corn pollen that are over 80,000 years old have been found in the lake sediment under Mexico City. Archaeological discoveries show that cultivated corn existed in the southwestern US for at least 3,000 years, indicating that the indigenous people of the region cultivated corn as a food crop long before the Europeans reached the New World. Corn is a hardy plant that grows in many different areas of the world. It can grow at altitudes as low as sea level and as high as 12,000 feet in the South American Andes Mountains. Corn can also grow in tropical climates that receive up to 400 inches of rainfall per year or in areas that receive only 12 inches of rainfall per year. Corn is used primarily as livestock feed in both the United States and the rest of the world. Other uses for corn are alcohol additives for gasoline, adhesives, corn oil for cooking and margarine, sweeteners, and as a food for humans. Corn is the largest crop in the US, both in terms of the value of the crop and of the acres planted.

The largest futures market for corn is at the Chicago Board of Trade. Corn futures also trade at the Bolsa de Mercadorias & Futuros (BM&F) in Brazil, the Budapest Commodity Exchange, the Marche a Terme International de France (MATIF), the Mercado a Termino de Buenos Aires in Argentina, the Kanmon Commodity Exchange (KCE) in Korea, and the Tokyo Grain Exchange (TGE). The CBOT futures contract calls for the delivery of 5000 bushels of No. 2 yellow corn at par contract price, No. 1 yellow at 1-1/2 cents per bushel over the contract price, or No. 3 yellow at 1-1/2 cents per bushel below the contract price.

Prices – Corn prices in 2003 on the nearest futures chart fluctuated in a range between about $2.05 and $2.60 per bushel, with the year's low of $2.04 being seen in late July. Prices then staged a rally in the latter half of 2003 and closed the year at $2.53, only mildly below the 1-1/2 year high of $2.62 posted in May. Prices fell during the summer due to a bumper crop of corn in the US. However, corn prices then firmed up during the latter half of the year as stronger export demand emerged. In 2004 US exports are expected to post a 5-year high because of a poor crop in Argentina (which may have the smallest crop in 8 years in its 2004 growing year) and because of lower exports from China, which in the latter part of 2003 restricted its corn exports due to tight domestic supplies.

Supply – World production of corn in 2002/03 was 603.465 million metric tons, up slightly by 0.7% from 599.349 million in 2001/2 (USDA). World production is forecasted to rise by 0.6% to 607.118 million in 2003/04 (USDA). The US is the world's largest producer of corn with 228.805 million metric tons in 2002/03, accounting for 38% of world production. The second largest producer is China with 121.300 million metric tons (20%), then Brazil with 45.000 million (7.5%), and then the EU with 40.089 million (6.6%). World ending-stocks in 2002/03 year period rose to 630.803

million metric tons from 621.830 million in 2001/02 and are expected to rise further to 641.930 million in 2003/04 (USDA). The crop year goes from September to August, but the international trade year goes from October to September. US farmers planted 79.054 million acres of corn (up from 75.752 million acres in 2001/02) and a slight increase to 79.066 million acres was forecast in 2003/4. Yields in 2002/03 fell sharply to 130.0 bushels per acre from 138.2 bushels in 2002/01, but are expected to recover to 143.2 bushels in 2003/4. US production in 2003/4, according to preliminary figures, was 10.278 billion bushels (11-1-03 USDA estimate), up by a hefty 14.1% from 9.008 billion bushels in 2002/3. The largest corn producing states in the US in 2003 were Iowa (18.7%), Illinois (17.0%), Nebraska (10.5%), Minnesota (9.9%), and Indiana (8.0%).

Demand – World consumption of corn rose to 630.803 million metric tons in 2002/3 from 621.830 million in 2001/2 and is expected to rise further to 641.930 million in 2003/4. The US was the world's largest consumer of corn in 2002/3 with 201.669 million metric tons (32% of world total), followed by China at 126.500 million (20%), Brazil at 36.500 million (5.8%), and Mexico at 24.700 million (3.9%). Corn is the leading U.S. feed grain with sorghums a distant second. Animal feed usage in 2001/02 of 5.80 billion bushels compares with 5.89 billion in 2000/01. Corn used to make ethanol in 2003/4 was 1.10 billion bushels, up 15% from 953 million in 2002/3, accounting for a hefty 45% of overall corn usage. Demand for corn as a sweetener (high fructose corn syrup or HFCS) was 530.0 million bushels in 2003/4, accounting for 22% of overall corn demand. Corn demand in 2003/4 for glucose/dextrose was 220.0 million bushels (9% of total consumption) and for starch was 260.0 million bushels (11%).

Trade – World trade in corn was forecast at 77.520 million metric tons in 2003/4, slightly lower than the 77.924 million in 2002/3 and the 78.067 million in 2001/2. The US was the world's largest exporter in 2002/3 at 41.177 million metric tons, accounting for 53% of total world exports. After the US, the world's largest exporters in 2002/3 were China at 15.244 million (20%), Argentina at 12.349 million (16%), and Brazil a distant fourth at 3.181 million (4%). Argentine corn exports are volatile and are expected to be about 9.000 million metric tons in 2003/4, down from the record 12.349 million in 2002/3 but above 8.581 million in 2001/2. US exports in 2003/4 are forecasted to rise sharply to 50.000 million, more than recovering from the decline to 41.177 million seen in 2002/3 from 47.271 million in 2001/02. Importers of corn are spread among a variety of countries with the leaders in 2002/3 being Japan at 16.868 million metric tons (22%), South Korea with 8.786 million (11%), Mexico with 5.284 million (6.8%), and Taiwan at 4.758 million (6.1%). The US is a very small importer of corn at 374,000 metric tons (2002/3), accounting for only 0.5% of world imports.

World Production of Corn or Maize   In Thousands of Metric Tons

Crop Year	Argentina	Brazil	Canada	China	France	India	Italy	Mexico	Romania	South Africa	United States	Yugo-slavia	World Total
1994-5	11,360	37,440	7,043	99,280	12,640	8,884	7,320	17,005	8,500	4,866	255,295	7,415	560,288
1995-6	11,100	32,480	7,271	112,000	12,394	9,530	8,454	17,780	9,923	10,171	187,970	8,537	517,352
1996-7	15,500	35,700	7,542	127,470	14,432	10,612	9,547	18,922	9,610	10,136	234,518	8,293	592,172
1997-8	19,360	30,100	7,180	104,309	16,754	10,852	10,005	17,368	12,680	7,693	233,864	9,564	575,363
1998-9	13,500	32,393	8,952	132,954	15,204	10,680	8,600	17,789	8,000	7,946	247,882	8,386	605,631
1999-00	17,200	31,641	9,161	128,086	15,643	11,470	10,020	19,240	10,500	11,455	239,549	10,500	607,258
2000-1	15,400	41,536	6,827	106,000	16,070	12,068	10,140	17,917	4,800	8,040	251,854	2,940	588,035
2001-2[1]	14,700	35,501	8,389	114,088	16,410	13,510	10,550	20,400	7,000	10,050	241,485	6,200	598,799
2002-3[2]	15,500	45,000	8,975	121,300	16,440	11,100	10,550	19,280	7,300	9,675	228,805	5,400	602,969
2003-4[3]	12,500	40,000	9,600	114,000	11,450	14,000	8,200	19,000	6,000	8,000	256,911		609,063

[1] Preliminary.   [2] Estimate.   [3] Forecast.   *Source: Foreign Agricultural Service, U.S. Department of Agriculture (FAS-USDA)*

World Supply and Demand of Course Grains   In Millions of Metric Tons/Hectares

Crop Year Beginning Oct.1	Area Harvested	Yield	Pro-duction	World Trade	Total Con-sumption	Ending Stocks	Stocks as % of Con-sumption[3]
1994-5	323.6	2.69	869.6	98.5	857.9	192.1	22.4
1995-6	314.0	2.55	801.2	88.1	840.4	152.9	18.2
1996-7	322.8	2.81	907.8	94.3	874.0	186.7	21.4
1997-8	311.0	2.84	882.4	85.8	871.8	197.4	22.6
1998-9	307.9	2.89	890.7	96.7	870.9	217.2	24.9
1999-00	299.7	2.93	877.4	104.8	883.7	210.8	23.9
2000-1	296.0	2.90	859.0	104.4	881.6	188.2	21.3
2001-2	300.4	2.97	891.3	102.2	904.0	175.5	19.4
2002-3[1]	292.6	2.98	871.5	104.4	902.0	145.0	16.1
2003-4[2]	300.1	2.95	884.1	103.0	929.3	99.8	10.7

[1] Preliminary.   [2] Estimate.   [3] Represents the ratio of marketing year ending stocks to total consumption.   *Source: Foreign Agricultural Service, U.S. Department of Agriculture (FAS-USDA)*

Acreage and Supply of Corn in the United States   In Millions of Bushels

Crop Year Beginning Sept. 1[3]	Planted	Harvested For Grain	Harvested For Silage	Yield Per Harvested Acre Bushels	Carry-over, Sept. 1 On Farms	Carry-over, Sept. 1 Off Farms	Supply Beginning Stocks	Supply Pro-duction	Supply Imports	Supply Total Supply
		In Thousands of Acres		Bushels						
1994-5	79,175	72,887	5,601	138.6	395.4	454.7	850	10,051	10	10,910
1995-6	71,245	64,995	5,295	113.5	740.9	816.9	1,558	7,400	16	8,974
1996-7	79,229	72,644	5,607	127.1	196.6	229.3	426	9,233	13	9,672
1997-8	79,537	72,671	6,054	126.7	475.0	408.2	883	9,207	9	10,099
1998-9	80,165	72,589	5,913	134.4	640.0	667.8	1,308	9,759	19	11,088
1999-00	77,386	70,487	6,037	133.8	797.0	990.0	1,787	9,431	15	11,239
2000-1	79,551	72,440	6,082	136.9	793.0	924.5	1,718	9,915	7	11,693
2001-2	75,752	68,808	6,148	138.2	753.2	1,146.0	1,899	9,507	10	11,416
2002-3[1]	79,054	69,313	7,490	130.0	586.8	1,009.6	1,596	9,008	14	10,619
2003-4[2]	78,736	71,139	6,528	142.2	484.9	601.8	1,087	10,114	10	11,211

[1] Preliminary.   [2] Estimate.   *Source: Economic Research Service, U.S. Department of Agriculture (ERS-USDA)*

Production of Corn (For Grain) in the United States, by State   In Million of Bushels

Year	Illinois	Indiana	Iowa	Kansas	Mich-igan	Minn-esota	Missouri	Nebraska	Ohio	South Dakota	Texas	Wis-consin	Total
1994	1,786.2	858.2	1,930.4	304.6	260.9	915.9	273.7	1,153.7	486.5	367.2	238.7	437.1	10,102.7
1995	1,130.0	598.9	1,402.2	244.3	249.6	731.9	149.9	854.7	375.1	193.6	216.6	347.7	7,373.9
1996	1,468.8	670.4	1,711.2	357.2	211.5	868.8	340.4	1,179.8	310.8	365.0	198.2	333.0	9,232.6
1997	1,425.5	701.5	1,642.2	371.8	255.1	851.4	299.0	1,135.2	475.7	326.4	241.5	402.6	9,206.8
1998	1,473.5	760.4	1,769.0	419.0	227.6	1,032.8	285.0	1,239.8	470.9	429.6	185.0	404.2	9,758.7
1999	1,491.0	748.4	1,758.2	420.2	253.5	990.0	247.4	1,153.7	403.2	367.3	228.3	407.6	9,437.3
2000	1,668.6	815.9	1,740.0	416.0	244.3	957.0	396.1	1,014.3	485.1	431.2	235.6	363.0	9,968.4
2001	1,649.2	884.5	1,664.4	387.4	199.5	806.0	345.8	1,139.3	437.5	370.6	167.6	330.2	9,506.8
2002	1,496.0	631.6	1,963.5	290.0	232.3	1,051.9	283.5	940.8	252.6	304.0	205.7	391.5	9,007.7
2003[1]	1,812.2	786.9	1,884.0	300.0	263.3	970.9	302.4	1,124.2	478.9	427.4	194.7	367.7	10,113.9

[1] Preliminary.   *Source: National Agricultural Statistics Service, U.S. Department of Agriculture (NASS-USDA)*

CORN

Supply and Disappearance of Corn in the United States   In Millions of Bushels

Crop Year Beginning Sept. 1	Supply Beginning Stocks	Supply Pro-duction	Supply Imports	Total Supply	Domestic Use Food, Alcohol & Industrial	Domestic Use Seed	Domestic Use Feed & Residual	Total	Exports	Total Disap-pearance	Ending Inventory Gov't Owned[3]	Ending Inventory Privately Owned[4]	Total
1999-00	1,787	9,431	15.0	11,232	1,913	19.9	5,664	7,597	1,937	9,515	15.0	1,744	1,718
Sept.-Nov.	1,787	9,431	3.5	11,221	459	0	2,189	2,648	534	3,182	19.3	8,005	8,039
Dec.-Feb.	8,039	----	3.0	8,043	447	0	1,526	1,973	468	2,441	15.1	5,590	5,602
Mar.-May	5,602	----	6.0	5,607	512	0	1,059	1,571	451	2,021			3,586
June-Aug.	3,586	----	2.0	3,588	496	0	890	1,386	485	1,871			1,718
2000-1	1,718	9,968	7.0	11,693	1,967		5,842	7,809	1,941	9,740			1,899
Sept.-Nov.	1,718	9,968	1.0	11,687	466		2,131	2,597	507	3,104			8,530
Dec.-Feb.	8,522	----	1.0	8,523	465		1,607	2,072	415	2,488			6,043
Mar.-May	6,043	----	3.0	6,046	524		1,153	1,677	455	2,122			3,924
June-Aug.	3,924	----	1.0	3,925	512		951	1,463	564	2,026			1,899
2001-2	1,899	9,507	10.0	11,416	2,054		5,861	7,915	1,905	9,820			1,596
Sept.-Nov.	1,899	9,507	2.0	11,408	489		2,207	2,696	448	3,144			8,265
Dec.-Feb.	8,265	----	2.0	8,266	480		1,542	2,022	448	2,471			5,795
Mar.-May	5,795	----	4.0	5,799	544		1,161	1,705	497	2,203			3,597
June-Aug.	3,597	----	2.0	3,599	540		950	1,490	512	2,002			1,596
2002-3[1]	1,596	9,008	14.0	10,619	2,346		5,593	7,939	1,592	9,532			1,087
Sept.-Nov.	1,596	9,008	3.0	10,608	552		2,024	2,576	393	2,970			7,638
Dec.-Feb.	7,638	----	4.0	7,642	564		1,547	2,111	400	2,510			5,132
Mar.-May	5,132	----	5.0	5,137	619		1,140	1,759	393	2,152			2,985
June-Aug.	2,985	----	2.0	2,987	612		882	1,494	406	1,900			1,087
2003-4[2]	1,087	10,114	10.0	11,211	2,510		5,800	8,310	2,000	10,310			901
Sept.-Nov.	1,087	10,114	2.0	11,203	598		2,187	2,785	473	3,259			7,945

[1] Preliminary.   [2] Estimate.   [3] Uncommitted inventory.   [4] Includes quantity under loan and farmer-owned reserve.

Source: Economic Research Service, U.S. Department of Agriculture (ERS-USDA)

Corn Production Estimates and Cash Price in the United States

Year	Corn for Grain Production Estimates Aug. 1	Sept. 1	Oct. 1	Nov. 1	Final	St. Louis No. 2 Yellow	Omaha No. 2 Yellow	Gulf Ports No. 2 Yellow	Kansas City No. 2 White	Chicago No. 2 Yellow	Average Farm Price[2]	Value of Pro-duction (Million Dollars)
	In Thousands of Bushels					Dollars Per Bushel						
1995-6	8,121,520	7,832,140	7,541,400	7,373,700	7,373,876	4.06	3.87	4.30	4.14	3.97	3.24	24,118
1996-7	8,694,628	8,803,928	9,012,148	9,265,288	9,232,557	2.90	2.70	3.07	3.09	2.84	2.71	25,149
1997-8	9,275,870	9,267,655	9,311,705	9,359,485	9,206,832	2.60	2.36	2.78	2.93	2.56	2.43	22,352
1998-9	9,592,089	9,737,949	9,743,399	9,836,069	9,758,685	1.99	1.88	2.35	2.51	2.06	1.94	18,922
1999-00	9,560,919	9,380,947	9,466,977	9,537,137	9,437,337	2.02	1.80	2.23	1.98	1.97	1.84	17,104
2000-1	10,369,369	10,362,374	10,191,817	10,053,942	9,968,358	2.01	1.82	2.26	2.06	1.99	1.86	18,499
2001-2	9,266,397	9,238,356	9,429,543	9,545,513	9,506,840	2.15	1.95	2.35	2.20	2.13	1.98	18,888
2002-3	8,886,009	8,848,529	8,969,836	9,003,364	9,007,659	2.24	2.24	2.71	3.03	2.40	2.32	20,975
2003-4[1]	10,064,452	9,944,418	10,207,141	10,277,932	10,113,887			2.72			2.26	24,804

[1] Preliminary.   [2] Season-average price based on monthly prices weighted by monthly marketings.   *Source: Economic Research Service, U..S. Department of Agriculture (ERS-USDA)*

Distribution of Corn in the United States   In Millions of Bushels

Crop Year Beginning Sept. 1	HFCS	Glucose & Dextrose	Starch	Alcohol Fuel	Alcohol Beve-rage[3]	Seed	Cereal & Other Products	Total	Livestock Feed[4]	Exports (Including Grain Equiv. of Products)	Domestic Disap-pearance	Total Utilization
1995-6	482	237	219	396	125	20.2	133	1,592	4,693	2,227.8	6,301	8,528
1996-7	504	246	229	429	130	20.3	135	1,672	5,277	1,797.4	6,991	8,789
1997-8	513	229	246	481	133	20.4	182	1,784	5,482	1,504.4	7,287	8,791
1998-9	531	219	240	526	127	19.8	184	1,826	5,468	1,984.2	7,314	9,298
1999-00	540	222	251	566	130	20.3	185	1,893	5,665	1,936.6	7,578	9,515
2000-1	530	218	247	628	130	19.3	185	1,938	5,842	1,941.3	7,799	9,740
2001-2	541	217	246	706	131	20.1	186	2,026	5,877	1,888.9	7,931	9,820
2002-3[1]	532	225	256	996	131	20.1	187	2,326	5,650	1,675.0	7,935	9,610
2003-4[2]	535	225	260	1,150	132		188	2,490				

[1] Preliminary.   [2] Estimate.   [3] Also includes nonfuel industrial alcohol.   [4] Feed and waste (residual, mostly feed).   *Source: Economic Research Service, U.S. Department of Agriculture (ERS-USDA)*

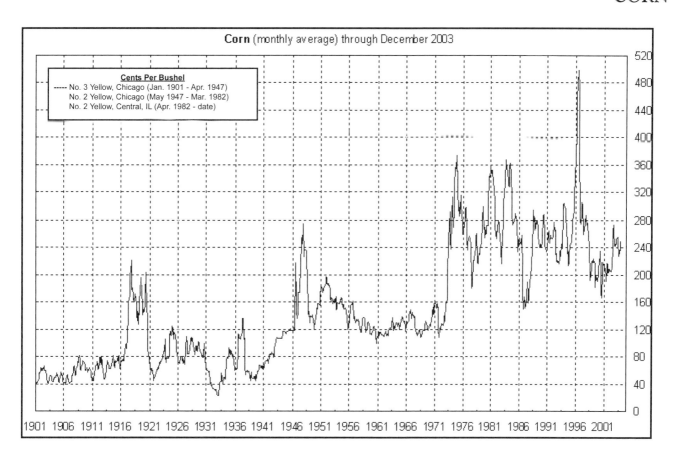

Average Cash Price of Corn, No. 2 Yellow in Central Illinois   In Dollars Per Bushel

Year	Sept.	Oct.	Nov.	Dec.	Jan.	Feb.	Mar.	Apr.	May	June	July	Aug.	Average
1994-5	2.08	1.92	2.03	2.16	2.22	2.27	2.36	2.41	2.50	2.65	2.79	2.68	2.34
1995-6	2.83	3.12	3.22	3.36	3.53	3.71	3.92	4.47	4.86	4.74	4.70	4.48	3.91
1996-7	3.39	2.81	2.63	2.62	2.62	2.71	2.90	2.87	2.74	2.59	2.44	2.60	2.74
1997-8	2.61	2.66	2.70	2.60	2.60	2.58	2.59	2.41	2.37	2.29	2.16	1.86	2.45
1998-9	1.78	1.94	2.09	2.08	2.07	2.05	2.09	2.05	2.03	1.99	1.67	1.84	1.97
1999-00	1.81	1.72	1.82	1.84	1.95	2.03	2.08	2.09	2.15	1.83	1.53	1.49	1.86
2000-1	1.58	1.81	1.96	2.01	1.99	1.95	1.92	1.87	1.78	1.76	1.92	2.00	1.88
2001-2	1.94	1.84	1.90	1.97	1.95	1.92	1.92	1.89	1.96	2.04	2.22	2.50	2.00
2002-3	2.57	2.41	2.36	2.32	2.29	2.33	2.31	2.36	2.40	2.37	2.13	2.26	2.34
2003-4[1]	2.25	2.11	2.26	2.38									2.25

[1] Preliminary.   *Source: Economic Research Service, U.S. Department of Agriculture (ERS-USDA)*

Average Cash Price of Corn, No. 2 Yellow at Gulf Ports[2]   In Dollars Per Bushel

Year	Sept.	Oct.	Nov.	Dec.	Jan.	Feb.	Mar.	Apr.	May	June	July	Aug.	Average
1994-5	2.48	2.44	2.43	2.61	2.72	2.72	2.79	2.79	2.84	3.04	3.23	3.21	2.78
1995-6	3.32	3.57	3.63	3.76	4.00	4.18	4.34	4.80	5.17	4.99	5.07	4.73	4.30
1996-7	3.69	3.27	2.97	2.97	3.02	3.08	3.25	3.17	3.01	2.86	2.69	2.86	3.07
1997-8	2.88	3.05	2.98	2.89	2.90	2.88	2.89	2.71	2.69	2.64	2.55	2.24	2.78
1998-9	2.18	2.43	2.47	2.42	2.48	2.40	2.45	2.39	2.35	2.36	2.12	2.20	2.35
1999-00	2.21	2.17	2.17	2.21	2.36	2.42	2.42	2.43	2.43	2.13	1.91	1.91	2.23
2000-1	2.03	2.15	2.26	2.45	2.40	2.35	2.32	2.22	2.14	2.11	2.30	2.36	2.26
2001-2	2.27	2.19	2.28	2.35	2.34	2.30	2.28	2.21	2.29	2.37	2.53	2.79	2.35
2002-3	2.89	2.79	2.77	2.71	2.69	2.69	2.67	2.67	2.74	2.72	2.72	2.44	2.71
2003-4[1]	2.63	2.65	2.75	2.84									2.72

[1] Preliminary.   [2] Barge delivered to Louisiana Gulf.   *Source: Economic Research Service, U.S. Department of Agriculture (ERS-USDA)*

CORN

Weekly Outstanding Export Sales and Cumulative Exports of U.S. Corn — In Thousands of Metric Tons

Marketing Year 2001/02 Week Ending		2001/02 Out-standing Sales	Cumu-lative Exports	Marketing Year 2002/03 Week Ending		2002/03 Out-standing Sales	Cumu-lative Exports	Marketing Year 2003/04 Week Ending		2003/04 Out-standing Sales	Cumu-lative Exports
Sept.	6 2001	7,090	567	Sept.	5 2002	6,206	439	Sept.	4 2003	7,626	461
	13	6,692	1,660		12	6,418	1,276		11	7,683	1,319
	20	6,553	2,992		19	6,352	2,080		18	8,252	2,127
	27	7,018	3,780		26	6,852	2,536		25	8,274	3,021
Oct.	4	6,862	4,552	Oct.	3	7,024	3,034	Oct.	2	8,451	3,800
	11	6,944	5,287		10	6,890	3,836		9	9,229	4,661
	18	7,074	6,059		17	6,584	4,659		16	9,062	5,581
	25	6,788	6,909		24	6,973	5,299		23	9,634	6,490
Nov.	1	7,028	7,569		31	7,629	5,729		30	10,207	7,346
	8	6,838	8,566	Nov.	7	7,986	6,521	Nov.	6	10,239	8,062
	15	6,824	9,261		14	8,119	7,322		13	10,243	8,975
	22	6,603	10,131		21	8,308	8,285		20	10,601	10,219
	29	7,635	10,618		28	7,922	9,345		27	10,313	11,356
Dec.	6	7,541	11,595	Dec.	5	7,415	10,399	Dec.	4	10,342	12,366
	13	7,399	12,339		12	7,081	11,444		11	10,319	13,312
	20	7,596	13,051		19	6,635	12,568		18	9,847	14,737
	27	7,347	13,825		26	6,561	13,013		25	9,763	15,579
Jan.	3 2002	6,830	14,456	Jan.	2 2003	5,860	13,998	Jan.	1 2004	9,150	16,608
	10	7,110	15,092		9	5,635	14,839		8	8,986	17,611
	17	7,432	16,075		16	5,596	15,551		15	9,113	18,483
	24	7,415	16,834		23	5,219	16,241		22	8,944	19,427
	31	7,944	17,637		30	5,267	16,938		29	9,043	20,310
Feb.	7	8,339	18,278	Feb.	6	5,029	17,793	Feb.	5	9,441	21,064
	14	8,530	19,260		13	4,827	18,462		12	9,522	21,936
	21	8,410	20,187		20	4,775	19,183		19		
	28	7,285	21,710		27	5,465	19,904		26		
Mar.	7	7,338	22,704	Mar.	6	5,631	20,444	Mar.	4		
	14	7,283	23,849		13	6,013	21,231		11		
	21	7,090	24,831		20	6,066	21,880		18		
	28	6,788	26,090		27	5,571	22,732		25		
Apr.	4	6,302	27,020	Apr.	3	5,458	23,706	Apr.	1		
	11	6,315	27,893		10	5,380	24,469		8		
	18	6,281	28,841		17	5,152	25,283		15		
	25	6,522	29,726		24	5,379	25,955		22		
May	2	6,405	30,601	May	1	5,431	26,483		29		
	9	6,836	31,637		8	5,879	27,099	May	6		
	16	6,814	32,618		15	5,804	27,923		13		
	23	6,582	33,979		22	5,640	28,723		20		
	30	6,219	34,761		29	5,289	29,608		27		
June	6	6,469	35,819	June	5	5,302	30,325	June	3		
	13	6,414	36,917		12	5,178	31,191		10		
	20	6,335	37,922		19	5,264	31,918		17		
	27	6,623	38,618		26	5,117	32,834		24		
July	4	5,933	39,667	July	3	5,075	33,596	July	1		
	11	5,717	40,599		10	4,839	34,309		8		
	18	5,402	41,687		17	4,532	35,086		15		
	25	5,026	42,732		24	4,238	35,928		22		
Aug.	1	4,596	43,489		31	3,851	36,739		29		
	8	4,271	44,621	Aug.	7	3,684	37,238	Aug.	5		
	15	3,592	45,706		14	3,180	38,006		12		
	22	2,848	46,634		21	2,653	38,728		19		
	29	2,082	47,460		28	1,900	39,646		26		

Source: Foreign Agricultural Service, U.S. Department of Agriculture (FAS-USDA)

Average Price Received by Farmers for Corn in the United States   In Dollars Per Bushel

Year	Sept.	Oct.	Nov.	Dec.	Jan.	Feb.	Mar.	Apr.	May	June	July	Aug.	Average
1994-5	2.19	2.06	1.99	2.13	2.19	2.23	2.30	2.36	2.41	2.51	2.63	2.63	2.26
1995-6	2.69	2.79	2.87	3.07	3.09	3.37	3.51	3.85	4.14	4.20	4.43	4.30	3.53
1996-7	3.55	2.89	2.66	2.63	2.69	2.65	2.79	2.80	2.69	2.56	2.42	2.50	2.74
1997-8	2.52	2.54	2.51	2.52	2.56	2.55	2.54	2.41	2.34	2.28	2.19	1.89	2.40
1998-9	1.83	1.91	1.93	2.00	2.06	2.05	2.06	2.04	1.99	1.97	1.74	1.75	1.94
1999-00	1.75	1.69	1.70	1.82	1.91	1.98	2.03	2.03	2.11	1.91	1.64	1.52	1.84
2000-1	1.61	1.74	1.86	1.97	1.98	1.96	1.96	1.89	1.82	1.76	1.87	1.90	1.86
2001-2	1.91	1.84	1.85	1.98	1.97	1.93	1.94	1.91	1.93	1.97	2.13	2.38	1.98
2002-3	2.47	2.34	2.28	2.32	2.33	2.34	2.33	2.34	2.38	2.34	2.17	2.15	2.32
2003-4[1]	2.20	2.12	2.20	2.32	2.46								2.26

[1] Preliminary.   Source: Economic Research Service, U.S. Department of Agriculture (ERS-USDA)

Corn Price Support Data in the United States

Crop Year Beginning Sept. 1	National Average Loan Rate[3] --- Dollars Per Bushel ---	Target Price	Placed Under Loan	% of Pro-duction	Acquired by CCC	Owned by CCC Aug. 31	CCC Inventory As of Dec. 31 CCC Owned	CCC Inventory As of Dec. 31 Under CCC Loan	Quantity Pledged (Thousands of Bushels)	Face Amount (Thousands of Dollars)
1993-4	1.72	2.75	618	9.7	0	45	54	812	13,697	26,052
1994-5	1.89	2.75	2,002	19.8	0		44	1,598	26,318	53,474
1995-6	1.89	2.75	970	9.2	0		42	579	677,115	1,232,669
1996-7	1.89	NA	561		0		30	756	970,590	1,764,291
1997-8	1.89	NA	1,132		19		2	81	1,129,915	2,062,308
1998-9	1.89	NA	823		0		15		1,129,915	2,062,308
1999-00	1.89	NA					26		1,420,878	2,590,443
2000-1	1.89	NA					36		1,393,947	2,562,172
2001-2[1]	1.89	NA					24			
2002-3[2]	1.98	2.60								

[1] Preliminary.   [2] Estimate.   [3] Findley or announced loan rate.   Source: National Agricultural Statistics Service, U.S. Department of Agriculture (NASS-USDA)

U.S. Exports[1] of Corn (Including Seed), By Country of Destination   In Thousands of Metric Tons

Year Beginning Oct. 1	Algeria	Canada	Egypt	Irael	Japan	Mexico	Rep. of Korea	Russia	Saudi Arabia	Spain	Taiwan	Vene-zuela	Total
1993-4	1,095	574	1,402	268	11,923	1,678	631	2,259	851	1,102	5,015	751	33,015
1994-5	798	1,108	2,342	658	16,030	3,165	8,866	9	864	2,337	6,150	886	58,596
1995-6	507	736	1,854	625	14,900	6,268	7,333	50	844	1,156	5,600	479	52,660
1996-7	862	879	2,364	556	15,425	3,141	5,404	88	1,025	1,080	5,609	730	46,638
1997-8	829	1,404	1,951	141	13,957	4,423	3,364	1	883	141	3,488	645	37,755
1998-9	947	898	2,954	395	15,375	5,576	6,659	405	1,175	92	4,538	1,329	51,949
1999-00	1,099	1,080	3,542	748	14,939	4,910	2,822	491	1,197	16	4,989	1,146	49,378
2000-1	1,180	2,797	4,116	621	14,091	5,928	3,109	26	1,003	0	4,894	1,152	48,192
2001-2	1,343	3,979	4,283	847	14,817	4,025	1,085	86	670	5	4,599	502	47,058
2002-3[2]	1,009	3,814	2,920	313	14,511	5,235	272		222		4,219	651	41,037

[1] Excludes exports of corn by-products.   [2] Preliminary.   Source: Economic Research Service, U.S. Department of Agriculture (ERS-USDA)

Stocks of Corn (Shelled and Ear) in the United States   In Millions of Bushels

Year	On Farms Mar. 1	On Farms June 1	On Farms Sept. 1	On Farms Dec. 1	Off Farms Mar. 1	Off Farms June 1	Off Farms Sept. 1	Off Farms Dec. 1	Total Stocks Mar. 1	Total Stocks June 1	Total Stocks Sept. 1	Total Stocks Dec. 1
1994	2,210.2	1,203.0	395.4	5,417.5	1,785.5	1,156.9	454.7	2,663.0	3,995.7	2,359.9	850.1	8,080.5
1995	3,502.0	2,072.0	740.9	3,960.0	2,089.7	1,342.9	816.9	2,145.8	5,591.7	3,414.9	1,557.8	6,105.8
1996	2,000.2	780.1	196.6	4,800.0	1,799.3	937.8	229.3	2,103.0	3,799.5	1,717.9	425.9	6,903.0
1997	2,870.0	1,501.0	475.0	4,822.0	1,624.1	995.6	408.2	2,424.8	4,494.1	2,496.6	883.2	7,246.8
1998	2,975.0	1,830.0	640.0	5,320.0	1,964.9	1,209.8	667.8	2,731.8	4,939.9	3,039.8	1,307.8	8,051.8
1999	3,570.0	2,257.0	797.0	5,195.0	2,128.4	1,359.2	990.0	2,844.4	5,698.4	3,616.2	1,787.0	8,039.4
2000	3,300.0	2,029.8	793.0	5,550.0	2,301.9	1,556.1	924.5	2,972.2	5,601.9	3,585.9	1,717.5	8,522.2
2001	3,600.0	2,230.8	753.2	5,275.0	2,443.0	1,693.2	1,146.0	2,989.7	6,043.0	3,924.0	1,899.1	8,264.7
2002	3,355.0	2,020.6	586.8	4,800.0	2,440.3	1,576.3	1,009.6	2,838.0	5,795.3	3,596.9	1,596.4	7,638.0
2003[1]	2,940.0	1,620.2	484.9	5,286.0	2,191.9	1,364.7	601.8	2,658.8	5,131.9	2,984.9	1,086.7	7,944.8

[1] Preliminary.   Source: National Agricultural Statistics Service, U.S. Department of Agriculture (NASS-USDA)

CORN

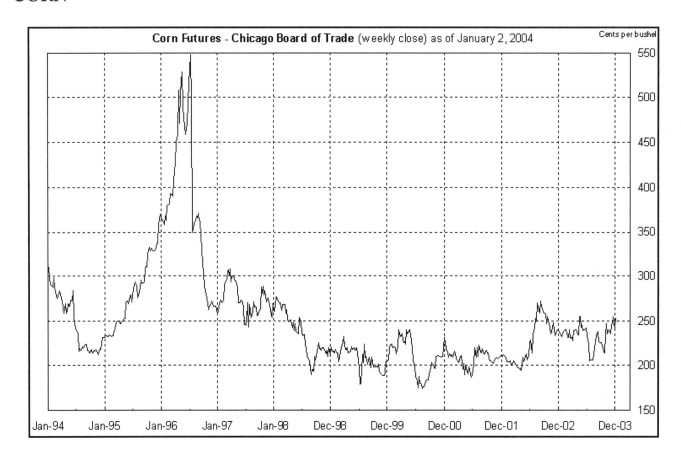

Corn Futures - Chicago Board of Trade (weekly close) as of January 2, 2004   Cents per bushel

Volume of Trading of Corn Futures in Chicago   In Thousands of Contracts

Year	Jan.	Feb.	Mar.	Apr.	May	June	July	Aug.	Sept.	Oct.	Nov.	Dec.	Total
1994	1,251.4	1,035.6	1,045.6	1,108.8	1,079.2	1,455.0	747.6	601.8	615.0	703.0	1,025.4	861.4	11,529.8
1995	787.2	832.4	973.7	987.7	1,213.7	1,759.5	1,293.7	1,318.6	1,220.2	1,613.2	1,743.1	1,356.0	15,105.1
1996	1,992.2	1,819.6	1,607.6	2,655.2	2,085.2	1,545.1	1,590.5	1,144.6	1,183.4	1,435.7	1,514.7	1,046.3	19,620.2
1997	1,160.6	1,483.0	1,693.3	1,780.1	1,291.7	1,347.5	1,527.7	1,318.3	1,060.2	1,700.2	1,434.4	1,188.0	16,985.0
1998	1,250.2	1,276.5	1,432.8	1,620.3	1,148.5	1,771.0	1,415.3	1,231.4	1,126.3	1,319.3	1,217.2	986.6	15,795.5
1999	955.1	1,374.2	1,440.1	1,420.6	975.1	1,597.4	1,708.0	1,669.8	1,131.9	1,096.2	1,500.9	855.6	15,724.8
2000	1,502.2	1,580.9	1,713.1	1,386.3	1,789.7	1,830.7	1,178.3	1,291.8	1,057.4	1,256.1	1,612.8	986.1	17,185.4
2001	1,397.2	1,197.4	1,329.5	1,518.7	1,173.2	1,612.1	2,023.5	1,549.0	1,072.3	1,223.3	1,741.2	891.4	16,728.7
2002	996.3	1,449.6	944.7	1,498.0	1,434.5	1,851.5	1,958.4	2,158.7	1,635.4	1,523.3	1,801.4	880.5	18,132.4
2003	1,204.0	1,559.1	1,156.9	1,633.1	1,657.0	1,951.2	1,499.3	1,830.6	1,389.7	2,057.7	1,815.9	1,364.3	19,118.7

Source: Chicago Board of Trade (CBT)

Average Open Interest of Corn Futures in Chicago   In Contracts

Year	Jan.	Feb.	Mar.	Apr.	May	June	July	Aug.	Sept.	Oct.	Nov.	Dec.
1994	346,077	336,342	327,539	305,722	262,621	246,308	215,081	208,990	212,983	243,678	262,849	250,646
1995	292,090	311,372	336,433	355,443	368,381	427,744	413,839	418,450	439,170	473,698	490,970	487,977
1996	500,837	508,496	469,697	453,707	403,118	350,066	304,265	298,894	302,170	326,373	332,809	306,256
1997	305,779	347,392	382,261	351,852	290,649	274,760	267,531	281,194	307,415	378,453	379,045	331,386
1998	328,020	341,444	358,221	366,657	337,703	327,237	297,894	318,162	321,992	332,337	342,868	322,157
1999	357,682	363,153	357,126	343,624	338,467	323,658	329,460	315,858	316,247	410,955	461,037	389,187
2000	445,999	478,892	482,080	487,758	476,891	445,018	391,967	387,289	356,583	397,966	454,920	414,851
2001	454,326	469,027	440,548	455,718	424,386	423,840	389,898	387,710	370,315	419,447	462,930	416,593
2002	459,314	464,368	431,923	430,712	411,346	430,856	458,081	509,069	501,523	485,859	496,998	450,016
2003	455,967	469,611	445,343	411,983	406,987	385,775	384,561	383,590	356,181	420,680	470,165	447,455

Source: Chicago Board of Trade (CBT)

Corn Oil

Corn oil is a bland, odorless oil produced by refining the crude corn oil that is mechanically extracted from the germ of the plant seed. High-oil corn, the most common type of corn used to make corn oil, typically has oil content of 7% or higher compared to about 4% of normal corn. Corn oil is widely used as a cooking oil, for making margarine and mayonnaise, as well as for making soap, paints, inks, varnishes, and cosmetics. For humans, studies have shown that that no vegetable oil is more effective than corn oil in lowering blood cholesterol levels.

Prices –The average corn oil price for 2002/3 of 28.17 cents was sharply higher than the range of 17-19 cents seen in 1999/2000 through 2001/02. Seasonally, prices tend to be highest around March/April and lowest late in the calen-

dar year.

Supply – Corn oil production in 2002/3 rose by 4.7% to a record high 2.575 billion pounds from 2.459 billion in 2001/2. Seasonally, production tends to peak around December and March and reaches a low in July. Stocks on October 1 at the end of the 2002/3 marketing year were tight at 104 million pounds, down from 117 million in 2001/2 and 267 million in 2000/1.

Demand – US usage was 1.400 billion pounds in 2002/3, up from 1.342 billion in 2001/2.

Exports – Corn oil exports in 2002/3 accounted for nearly half of US production at 46%. US corn oil exports in 2002/3 rose to 1.200 billion pounds from 1.190 billion pounds in 2001/2.

Supply and Disappearance of Corn Oil in the United States   In Millions of Pounds

Crop Year Beginning Oct. 1	Stocks Oct. 1	Pro- duction	Imports	Total Supply	Baking and Frying Fats	Salad and Cooking Oil	Marg- arine	Total Edible Products	Domestic Disap- pearance	Exports	Total Disap- pearance
1997-8	129	2,335	28.1	2,492	W	375	W	492	1,272	1,118	2,390
1998-9	102	2,374	42.4	2,518	W	384	W	496	1,394	989	2,383
1999-00	135	2,501	17.5	2,654	W	800	W	953	1,417	970	2,387
2000-1	267	2,403	27.3	2,698	W	956	W	1,298	1,630	951	2,581
2001-2	117	2,461	61.0	2,639	W	W	W	950	1,363	1,172	2,535
2002-3[1]	104	2,453	65.0	2,622					1,618	890	2,508
2003-4[2]	114	2,650	65.0	2,829					1,804	900	2,704

[1] Preliminary.   [2] Estimate.   W = Withheld proprietary data.   *Source: Economic Research Service, U.S. Department of Agriculture (ERS-USDA)*

Production[2] of Crude Corn Oil in the United States   In Millions of Pounds

Year	Oct.	Nov.	Dec.	Jan.	Feb.	Mar.	Apr.	May	June	July	Aug.	Sept.	Total
1997-8	199.2	207.5	202.0	171.4	162.7	201.0	203.9	201.2	201.4	192.8	202.8	188.9	2,335
1998-9	209.2	199.4	189.2	182.9	177.0	201.0	201.1	205.3	205.7	194.8	212.5	196.3	2,374
1999-00	204.3	212.3	218.6	214.8	199.0	214.9	210.5	213.6	204.3	226.4	225.3	201.9	2,546
2000-1	208.6	192.7	190.4	198.9	180.5	201.6	200.7	206.2	204.0	205.7	211.1	203.2	2,404
2001-2	196.0	203.3	206.5	200.1	183.8	187.1	189.4	219.8	227.3	220.2	217.0	211.0	2,462
2002-3	218.6	195.0	212.3	206.8	181.7	206.0	199.7	203.6	207.1	216.5	202.5	203.2	2,453
2003-4[1]	209.1	196.5	193.2										2,395

[1] Preliminary.   [2] Not seasonally adjusted.   *Source: Bureau of the Census, U.S. Department of Commerce*

Consumption Corn Oil, in Refining, in the United States   In Millions of Pounds

Year	Oct.	Nov.	Dec.	Jan.	Feb.	Mar.	Apr.	May	June	July	Aug.	Sept.	Total
1997-8	87.5	83.8	100.6	83.0	89.2	100.5	92.5	100.5	104.2	90.6	101.7	94.6	1,129
1998-9	106.6	104.4	105.0	82.0	W	102.0	94.6	101.7	104.3	90.1	97.0	103.5	1,190
1999-00	96.2	97.1	114.7	94.9	89.2	W	W	W	W	W	134.2	129.6	1,296
2000-1	136.2	112.2	129.3	106.7	122.6	118.7	111.9	140.4	W	W	W	W	1,467
2001-2	W	W	W	W	W	W	W	W	W	W	W	W	W
2002-3	W	W	W	W	W	W	W	W	W	W	W	W	W
2003-4[1]	W	W	W	W									

[1] Preliminary.   W = Withheld proprietary data.   *Source: Bureau of Census, U.S. Department of Commerce*

Average Corn Oil Price, Wet Mill in Chicago   In Cents Per Pound

Year	Oct.	Nov.	Dec.	Jan.	Feb.	Mar.	Apr.	May	June	July	Aug.	Sept.	Average
1997-8	25.20	26.25	26.28	26.04	27.31	28.50	30.93	33.20	32.82	31.52	29.93	29.25	28.94
1998-9	29.46	29.65	29.88	29.15	26.58	23.01	23.08	22.96	22.95	22.43	22.41	22.08	25.30
1999-00	21.97	21.96	21.68	20.81	20.06	19.28	18.32	16.63	14.57	13.55	13.03	11.85	17.81
2000-1	10.52	10.37	10.54	10.25	11.06	11.91	13.76	14.84	15.94	17.28	18.73	17.30	13.54
2001-2	17.18	18.30	22.45	20.54	18.35	18.37	17.70	17.00	17.60	19.10	21.72	21.40	19.14
2002-3	22.45	26.90	28.25	29.30	28.90	27.20	27.55	29.10	30.15	29.90	30.68	27.71	28.17
2003-4[1]	26.99	27.56	28.73	29.26									28.14

[1] Preliminary.   *Source: Economic Research Service,U.S. Department of Agriculture (ERS-USDA)*

Cotton

Cotton is a natural vegetable fiber that comes from small trees and shrubs of a genus belonging to the mallow family, one of which is the common American Upland cotton plant. Cotton has been used in India for at least the last 5,000 years and probably much longer, and was also used by the ancient Chinese, Egyptians, and North and South Americans. Cotton was one of the earliest crops grown by European settlers in the US.

Cotton requires a long growing season, plenty of sunshine and water during the growing season, and then dry weather for harvesting. In the United States, the Cotton Belt stretches from northern Florida to North Carolina and westward to California. In the US, planting time varies from the beginning of February in Southern Texas to the beginning of June in the northern sections of the Cotton Belt. The flower bud of the plant blossoms and develops into an oval boll that splits open at maturity. At maturity, cotton is most vulnerable to damage from wind and rain. Approximately 95% of the cotton in the US is now harvested mechanically with spindle-type pickers or strippers and then sent off to cotton gins for processing. There it is dried, cleaned, separated, and packed into bales.

Cotton is used in a wide range of products from clothing to home furnishings to medical products. The value of cotton is determined according to the staple, grade, and character of each bale. Staple refers to short, medium, long, or extra-long fiber length, with medium staple accounting for about 70% of all US cotton. Grade refers to the color, brightness, and amount of foreign matter and is established by the US Department of Agriculture. Character refers to the fiber's diameter, strength, body, maturity (ratio of mature to immature fibers), uniformity, and smoothness. Cotton is the fifth leading cash crop of the US and is one of the nation's principal agricultural exports.

Cotton futures and options are traded on the New York Cotton Exchange, a division of the New York Board of Trade. Cotton futures are also traded on the Bolsa de Mercadorias & Futuros (BM&F). Cotton yarn futures are traded on the Central Japan Commodity Exchange (CCOM) and the Osaka Mercantile Exchange (OME). The New York Cotton Exchange's futures contract calls for the delivery of 50,000 pounds net weight (approximately 100 bales) of No. 2 cotton with quality of Strict Low Middling and a staple length of 1-and-2/32 inch. Delivery points include Texas (Galveston and Houston), New Orleans, Memphis, and Greenville/ Spartanburg in South Carolina.

Prices – Cotton prices on the New York Board of Trade nearest futures chart started 2003 near 50 cents/pound and then showed a fairly steady rally during the year to post an 8-year high of 85 cents in October, finally closing the year near 75 cents. Bullish factors during 2003 included very tight stocks, aggressive Chinese import buying, the upward rebound in the US economy, and the weak US dollar.

Supply – World cotton production in 2003/4 was forecast at 92.195 million bales (480 pounds per bale), up 4.5% from 88.184 million in 2002/3 (USDA as of Jan-2004). World ending stocks for 2003/4 are forecasted at 32.358 million bales, down 12.5% from 36.971 million in 2002/3. The world's largest cotton producers are China with 30.200 million bales of production in 2003/4 (representing 24% of world production), the US with 18.224 million bales (20%), India with 12.7 million bales (14%), and Pakistan with 7.600 million bales (8%).

US cotton production for 2003/4 was forecast at 18.224 million bales, up 5.9% from 17.209 million in 2002/3. US ending stocks for 2003/4 are forecasted at 4.250 million bales, down 21.1% from 5.385 million in 2002/3. US farmers planted 13.631 million acres of cotton in 2003/4, down from 13.958 million in 2002/3, and harvested acres were also lower at 12.107 million versus 12.427 million in 2002/3. However, yields were higher in 2003/4 at 722 pounds/acre versus 675 pounds in 2002/3, thus leading to the 6% increase in production in 2003/4. The leading states with US cotton production in 2002/3 were Texas (with 9.7% of US production), Georgia (5.0%), Mississippi (4.9%), Arkansas (4.1%), and California (3.5%). Texas saw a big 17% decline in production in 2002/3, but there were large increases in South Carolina (+152%), Alabama (+44%), Louisiana (+38%), Georgia (+36%) and North Carolina (+36%).

US production of cotton cloth has fallen sharply in the past three years to below 4 billion square yards to 3.524 million in the latest full reporting year of 2002. That illustrates the movement of the textile industry out of the US to low-wage foreign countries.

Demand – World consumption of cotton for 2003/4 was forecast at 97.111 million bales, down slightly by –0.8% from 97.923 million in 2002/3. That consumption of 97.111 million in 2003/4 far outstripped the production level of 92.195 million, a bullish factor for prices. That was the second consecutive year in which consumption was higher than production, thus leading to the sharp drawdown in stocks. Consumption of cotton continues to move toward countries with low wages, which are becoming the main producers of cotton products. The largest consumers of cotton are China (31%), India (14%), and Pakistan (10%). US consumption was forecast at 6.200 million bales in 2003/4, down -14.7% from 7.269 million in 2002/3. US consumption of 6.200 million in 2003/4 was far below US production of 18.224 million, allowing the US to be the number one world exporter of cotton by far.

Trade – World trade in cotton in 2003/4 is forecasted to rise about 5% to 32 million bales from the previous year. The world's largest exporters of cotton in 2003/4 are forecasted to be the US with 13.200 million bales (41% of world exports), Uzbekistan (9%), and Brazil (5%). Brazil in 2003/4 is projected to show a sharp 237% increase in cotton exports. A decline in exports of -38% is projected for Australia for 2003/4, -14% for Uzbekistan, and a -15% decline for Greece. US cotton exports in 2003/4 are projected to rise 11% to 13.200 million bales from 11.900 million in 2002/3, largely due to increased Chinese demand. The main destinations for US exports in 2003/4 were forecasted to be China (16%), Mexico (16%), Indonesia (7%), Taiwan (5%), and Thailand (5%).

The world's largest importers in 2003/4 are forecasted to be China with 7.000 million bales (22% of world imports) and Indonesia (7%). China's imports in 2003/4 rose sharply by 124% from the previous year, clearly a major driving factor for world cotton demand and prices.

Supply and Distribution of All Cotton in the United States   In Thousands of 480-Pound Bales

Crop Year Beginning Aug. 1	Acre Planted (1,000 Acres)	Acre Harvested (1,000 Acres)	Acre Yield Lbs./acre	Supply Beginning Stocks[3]	Supply Pro-duction[4]	Supply Imports	Supply Total	Disappearance Mill Use	Disappearance Exports	Disappearance Total	Disappearance Unac-counted	Disappearance Ending Stocks	Farm Price[5] Cents per Lb.	"A" Index Price[6] Cents per Lb.	Value of Pro-duction Million $
1994-5	13,720	13,322	708	3,530	19,662	20	23,212	11,198	9,402	20,600	38	2,650	72.0	92.66	6,796.7
1995-6	16,931	16,007	537	2,650	17,900	408	20,958	10,604	7,675	18,322	-27	2,609	76.5	85.61	6,574.6
1996-7	14,653	12,888	705	2,609	18,942	403	21,954	11,126	6,865	17,991	8	3,971	70.5	78.66	6,408.1
1997-8	13,898	13,406	673	3,971	18,793	13	22,777	11,349	7,500	18,849	-41	3,887	66.2	72.11	5,975.6
1998-9	13,393	10,684	625	3,887	13,918	443	18,248	10,401	4,344	14,699	394	3,939	61.7	58.97	4,119.9
1999-00	14,874	13,425	607	3,939	16,968	97	21,004	10,240	6,750	16,944	145	3,915	46.8	52.85	3,809.6
2000-1	15,517	13,053	632	3,915	17,188	16	21,119	8,862	6,740	15,602	483	6,000	51.6	57.25	4,260.4
2001-2	15,769	13,828	705	6,000	20,303	21	26,324	7,696	11,000	18,696	-180	7,448	32.0	41.88	3,121.8
2002-3[1]	13,958	12,427	665	7,448	17,209	67	24,724	7,269	11,900	19,169	-170	5,385	45.7	55.81	3,777.1
2003-4[2]	13,483	12,058	725	5,385	18,224	50	23,650	6,200	13,200	19,400		4,250	63.8		5,581.6

[1] Preliminary.   [2] Estimate.   [3] Excludes preseason ginnings (adjusted to 480-lb. bale net weight basis).   [4] Includes preseason ginnings.
[5] Marketing year average price.   [6] Average of 5 cheapest types of SLM 1 3/32 staple length cotton *offered on the European market.*
Source: Economic Research Service, U.S. Department of Agriculture (ERS-USDA)

World Production of All Cotton   In Thousands of 480-Pound Bales

Crop Year Beginning Aug. 1	Argen-tina	Brazil	China	Egypt	India	Iran	Mexico	Pakistan	Sudan	Turkey	United States	Uzbek-istan	World Total
1994-5	1,608	2,526	19,900	1,170	11,148	762	460	6,250	400	2,886	19,662	5,778	85,857
1995-6	1,929	1,791	21,900	1,088	13,250	800	974	8,200	490	3,911	17,900	5,740	93,063
1996-7	1,493	1,286	19,300	1,568	13,918	825	1,078	7,323	460	3,600	18,942	4,813	89,589
1997-8	1,406	1,745	21,100	1,532	12,337	600	984	7,175	400	3,651	18,793	5,228	91,570
1998-9	920	2,100	20,700	1,050	12,883	638	1,039	6,300	250	3,860	13,918	4,600	84,879
1999-00	615	3,100	17,600	1,050	12,180	650	669	8,600	240	3,634	16,968	5,180	87,242
2000-1	735	4,100	20,300	920	10,900	735	363	8,200	340	3,600	17,188	4,400	88,526
2001-2	300	3,518	24,400	1,441	12,300	575	432	8,300	275	3,975	20,303	4,900	98,349
2002-3[1]	290	3,890	22,600	1,310	10,600	460	194	7,800	375	4,134	17,209	4,600	87,989
2003-4[2]	475	4,400	25,500	1,000	12,500	380	300	8,350	500	4,200	17,559	4,300	94,495

[1] Preliminary.   [2] Estimate.   *Source: Foreign Agricultural Service, U.S. Department of Agriculture (FAS-USDA)*

World Stocks and Trade of Cotton   In Thousands of 480-Pound Bales

Crop Year Beginning Aug. 1	Beginning Stocks United States	Beginning Stocks Uzbek-istan	Beginning Stocks China	Beginning Stocks World Total	Imports Indo-nesia	Imports Mexico	Imports Russia	Imports Turkey	Imports World Total	Exports United States	Exports Uzbek-istan	Exports China	Exports World Total
1994-5	3,530	1,006	5,251	26,758	2,075	580	2,159	1,060	30,618	9,402	5,006	183	28,452
1995-6	4,028	956	8,828	29,884	2,139	695	1,100	574	27,529	7,675	4,524	21	27,359
1996-7	2,609	1,304	14,052	36,614	2,147	900	1,000	1,150	28,763	6,865	4,550	10	26,494
1997-8	3,971	822	16,655	40,059	1,923	1,600	1,225	1,450	26,488	7,500	4,570	34	26,590
1998-9	3,887	635	19,955	43,684	2,329	1,488	850	1,139	25,248	4,344	3,812	681	23,649
1999-00	3,939	603	21,133	44,885	2,076	1,813	1,600	2,400	28,276	6,750	4,100	1,700	27,226
2000-1	3,922	838	14,958	41,672	2,650	1,865	1,650	1,750	26,479	6,763	3,400	446	26,464
2001-2	6,001	743	14,351	42,452	2,356	1,900	1,850	2,868	29,408	11,000	3,400	342	29,023
2002-3[1]	7,448	1,043	12,858	47,190	2,250	2,300	1,700	2,100	30,460	11,900	3,550	751	30,629
2003-4[2]	5,385	843	8,934	37,308	2,250	1,750	1,650	2,350	30,735	12,000	3,150	150	33,732

[1] Preliminary.   [2] Estimate.   *Source: Foreign Agricultural Service, U.S. Department of Agriculture (FAS-USDA)*

World Consumption of All Cottons in Specified Countries   In Thousands of 480-Pound Bales

Year	Brazil	China	Egypt	France	Ger-many	India	Italy	Japan	Mexico	Pakistan	United States	Uzbek-istan	World Total
1994-5	3,996	20,200	1,140	532	660	10,545	1,539	1,754	890	6,750	11,198	827	84,758
1995-6	3,904	19,700	1,010	484	606	11,977	1,539	1,529	1,100	7,200	10,647	873	86,040
1996-7	3,900	20,300	919	536	640	13,120	1,562	1,401	1,600	7,000	11,126	750	88,021
1997-8	3,400	19,600	1,033	505	650	12,675	1,612	1,400	1,950	7,187	11,349	850	87,157
1998-9	3,900	19,200	950	495	575	12,620	1,400	1,250	2,150	7,000	10,401	825	85,350
1999-00	4,100	22,200	850	500	650	13,500	1,300	1,280	2,400	7,650	10,241	850	91,812
2000-1	4,350	23,500	750	425	600	13,550	1,330	1,150	2,100	8,100	8,882	1,100	91,954
2001-2	3,950	26,000	600	425	525	13,275	1,300	1,050	2,100	8,500	7,721	1,200	94,511
2002-3[1]	3,450	28,900	900	350	500	13,300	1,200	1,000	2,200	9,200	7,269	1,300	97,452
2003-4[2]	3,650	30,400	900	320	475	13,500	1,100	950	2,200	9,400	6,400	1,300	98,452

[1] Preliminary.   [2] Estimate.   *Source: Foreign Agricultural Service, U.S. Department of Agriculture (FAS-USDA)*

COTTON

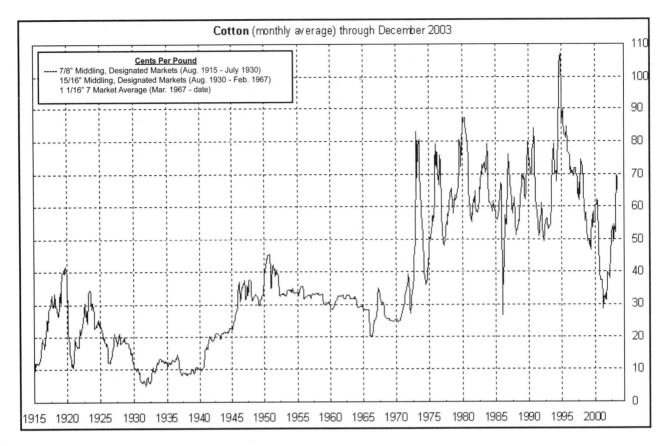

Cotton (monthly average) through December 2003

Cents Per Pound
----- 7/8" Middling, Designated Markets (Aug. 1915 - July 1930)
15/16" Middling, Designated Markets (Aug. 1930 - Feb. 1967)
1 1/16" 7 Market Average (Mar. 1967 - date)

Average Spot Cotton Prices[2], C.I.F. Northern Europe   In U.S. Cents Per Pound

Crop Year Beginning Aug. 1	Argentina "C"[3] 1 1/16"	Australia M 1 3/32"	Cotlook Index A	Cotlook Index B	Egypt Giza[4] 81	Greece M 1 3/32"	Mexico[5] M 1 3/32"	Pakistan Sind/ Punjab[6]	Tanzania AR[7] Type 3	Turkey Izmir[8] 1 3/32"	U.S. Calif. ACALA SJV[9]	U.S. Memphis Terr.[10] M 1 3/32"	U.S. Orleans/ Texas[11] M 1 1/32"
1990-1	77.06	85.58	82.90	77.80	177.43	84.24	84.46	77.19	89.62	81.32	92.84	88.13	80.35
1991-2	55.08	65.97	63.05	58.50	128.10	65.90	68.19	58.14	68.90	74.66	74.47	66.35	63.41
1992-3	64.31	64.01	57.70	53.70	99.24	56.92	----	52.66	62.24	----	68.37	63.08	58.89
1993-4	80.20	72.81	70.60	67.30	88.35	58.81	----	54.42	69.83	59.80	77.55	72.80	69.78
1994-5	101.88	81.05	92.75	92.40	93.70	88.64	82.65	73.75	----	----	106.40	98.67	95.70
1995-6	82.98	93.75	85.61	81.06	----	84.95	94.94	81.86	96.20	90.38	103.49	94.71	90.37
1996-7	79.71	83.24	78.59	74.80	----	75.85	79.60	73.37	79.22	----	89.55	82.81	79.77
1997-8	69.96	77.49	72.19	70.69	----	72.03	81.70	72.93	84.04	----	85.11	78.12	74.74
1998-9	57.19	66.48	58.91	54.26	----	58.66	65.78	----	72.70	----	78.57	73.65	70.95
1999-00[1]	----	61.97	52.80	49.55	----	51.71	56.43	----	55.67	----	68.76	60.22	55.67

[1] Preliminary.   [2] Generally for prompt shipment.   [3] 1 1/32 prior to January 20, 1984; 1 1/16 since.   [4] Dendera until 1969/70; Giza 67 1969/70 until December 1983; Giza 69/75/81 until November 1990; Giza 81 since.   [5] S. Brazil Type 5, 1 1/32 prior to 1968-69; 1 1/16 until 1987/88; Brazilian Type 5/6, 1 1/16 since.   [6] Punjab until 1979/80; Sind SG until June 1984; Sind/Punjab SG until January 1985; Afzal 1 until January 1986; Afzal 1 1/32 since.   [7] No. 1 until 1978/79; No. 1/2 until February 1986; AR' Mwanza No. 3 until January 1992; AR' Type 3 since.   [8] Izmir ST 1 White 1 1/16 RG prior to 1981/82; 1 3/32 from 1981/82 until January 1987; Izmir/Antalya ST 1 White -3/32 RG since.   [9] SM 1 3/32 prior to 1975/76; SM 1 1/8 since.   [10] SM 1 1/16 prior to 1981/82; Middling 1 3/32 since.   [11] Middling 1 prior to 1988/89; Middling 1 1/32 since.   *Source: International Cotton Advisory Committee*

Average Producer Price Index of Gray Cotton Broadwovens   Index 1982 = 100

Year	Jan.	Feb.	Mar.	Apr.	May	June	July	Aug.	Sept.	Oct.	Nov.	Dec.	Average
1994	109.9	110.8	115.4	115.7	114.9	114.9	115.0	117.5	117.6	118.9	117.2	118.0	116.2
1995	117.8	120.2	120.7	121.6	123.4	123.6	124.1	125.4	125.3	123.7	123.7	123.8	122.6
1996	123.6	123.7	122.0	122.0	121.1	120.7	120.7	119.9	119.7	120.4	120.0	120.4	121.2
1997	120.3	120.8	120.7	120.8	121.2	120.6	121.4	121.6	121.4	120.8	121.6	121.2	121.0
1998	122.8	122.0	122.1	121.5	121.8	120.8	120.0	119.1	118.8	118.1	117.3	117.8	120.2
1999	117.1	117.3	118.8	116.5	116.4	116.1	116.5	112.9	112.9	113.1	112.6	108.6	114.9
2000	112.1	111.1	106.9	108.2	108.6	107.7	108.3	108.8	110.1	110.2	112.3	112.3	109.7
2001	112.8	113.1	113.1	112.7	112.8	112.9	113.2	112.9	112.9	112.0	111.2	111.1	112.6
2002	110.7	109.9	110.1	108.1	107.3	108.0	106.9	107.0	106.9	105.9	105.7	106.2	107.7
2003[1]	105.7	105.2	105.0	105.9	106.0	106.7	107.2	109.1	109.6	110.5	110.5	108.7	107.5

[1] Preliminary.   *Source: Bureau of Labor Statistics (0337-01), U.S. Department of Commerce*

Average Price of Strict Low Midd. 11/16,Cotton at Designated U.S. Mkts   In Cents Per Pound (Net Weight)

Year	Aug.	Sept.	Oct.	Nov.	Dec.	Jan.	Feb.	Mar.	Apr.	May	June	July	Average
1994-5	70.32	71.10	67.58	72.00	81.92	88.11	91.89	104.20	104.94	105.38	106.96	93.26	88.14
1995-6	85.90	90.00	84.65	84.16	82.18	81.81	81.56	81.13	84.69	83.22	80.23	76.84	83.03
1996-7	76.15	75.24	72.21	70.12	71.98	70.53	70.53	71.12	69.09	69.30	71.03	71.83	71.59
1997-8	71.61	70.75	69.46	68.90	64.57	62.75	63.66	67.04	61.88	65.21	73.50	74.18	67.79
1998-9	71.87	71.75	67.61	64.95	59.88	56.20	55.46	58.17	57.01	55.54	53.74	49.23	60.12
1999-00	49.72	48.39	49.46	48.12	46.65	51.92	54.29	57.67	53.76	58.31	54.97	55.13	52.36
2000-1	59.33	60.62	60.54	62.16	61.04	56.66	54.10	47.22	42.19	40.02	37.38	37.48	51.56
2001-2	36.05	33.22	28.42	31.23	32.21	32.13	31.60	33.23	31.86	31.14	36.36	39.78	33.10
2002-3	39.20	37.91	39.62	44.98	46.38	48.60	51.35	53.82	53.38	48.94	50.92	54.45	47.46
2003-4[1]	51.94	58.02	69.38	68.88	65.09	68.21							63.59

[1] Preliminary.   [2] Grade 41, leaf 4, staple 34, mike 35-36 and 43-49 , strength 23.5-26.4.   *Source: Agricultural Marketing Service, U.S. Department of Agriculture (AMS-USDA)*

Average Spot Cotton, 1 3/32 , Price (SLM) at Designated U.S. Markets   In Cents Per Pound (Net Weight)

Year	Aug.	Sept.	Oct.	Nov.	Dec.	Jan.	Feb.	Mar.	Apr.	May	June	July	Average
1994-5	71.46	72.42	68.82	73.38	83.41	89.92	94.25	106.66	107.50	107.93	109.52	96.31	90.13
1995-6	88.31	92.71	87.06	86.43	84.25	84.32	84.04	83.65	87.25	85.90	82.71	78.86	85.46
1996-7	77.97	76.92	73.90	71.74	75.75	72.53	72.86	73.60	71.23	71.38	73.25	74.04	73.76
1997-8	73.69	72.64	71.13	70.35	66.30	64.55	65.78	69.25	64.31	67.66	76.02	76.63	69.86
1998-9	73.93	73.75	69.90	67.18	62.18	58.56	58.27	61.34	60.33	58.89	56.85	52.61	62.82
1999-00	52.90	51.27	52.43	51.51	49.73	55.02	57.38	61.02	57.52	63.09	59.28	58.80	55.83
2000-1	62.60	63.62	63.13	65.08	64.73	60.18	57.18	50.08	44.94	42.54	39.88	39.96	54.49
2001-2	38.88	36.11	31.55	34.03	34.82	34.55	34.08	36.04	34.84	34.03	39.31	42.86	35.93
2002-3	42.31	41.07	43.08	48.78	50.70	52.87	55.34	57.88	57.54	52.96	55.09	58.46	51.34
2003-4[2]	55.87	61.76	73.27	72.63	68.90								45.19

[1] Preliminary.   *Source: Agricultural Marketing Service, U.S. Department of Agriculture (AMS-USDA)*

Average Spot Prices of U.S. Cotton[1], Base Quality (SLM) at Designated Markets   In Cents Per Pound

Crop Year Beginning Aug. 1	Dallas (East Tex.-Okl.)	Fresno (San Joaquin Valley)	Greenville (South-east)	Greenwood (South Delta)	Lubbock (West Texas)	Memphis (North Delta)	Phoenix Desert (South-west)	Average
1993-4[2]	66.22	65.04	67.46	67.04	65.92	67.04	64.16	66.13
1994-5	86.96	93.73	87.17	87.25	86.66	87.25	87.96	88.14
1995-6	80.89	87.40	83.86	83.76	80.64	83.76	80.90	83.03
1996-7	70.29	74.47	72.33	72.11	69.89	72.11	69.88	71.58
1997-8	65.93	71.79	68.60	68.36	65.88	68.36	65.63	67.79
1998-9	57.66	63.78	62.06	61.82	57.76	61.82	55.92	60.12
1999-00	50.49	56.67	53.81	53.34	50.12	53.34	48.79	52.36
2000-1	51.03	52.45	52.63	52.32	50.71	52.32	49.47	51.56
2001-2	32.59	34.64	33.02	33.24	32.39	33.24	32.60	33.10
2002-3[3]	46.76	47.52	48.28	48.46	46.51	48.47	46.27	47.46

[1] Prices are for mixed lots, net weight, uncompressed in warehouse.   [2] 1993 prices are for mixed lots, net weight, compressed, FOB car/truck.
[3] Preliminary.   *Source: Agricultural Marketing Service, U.S. Department of Agriculture (AMS-USDA)*

Average Price[1] Received by Farmers for Upland Cotton in the United States   In Cents Per Pound

Year	Aug.	Sept.	Oct.	Nov.	Dec.	Jan.	Feb.	Mar.	Apr.	May	June	July	Average
1994-5	66.8	65.9	66.2	68.5	73.3	78.7	80.2	82.6	77.6	76.2	86.5	80.1	72.0
1995-6	72.2	74.8	74.2	75.0	75.7	76.4	75.7	76.8	78.9	76.7	76.9	73.6	75.4
1996-7	71.9	71.6	71.5	69.7	69.3	67.9	68.1	69.3	67.6	68.3	67.1	67.5	69.3
1997-8	67.0	69.6	69.4	67.9	63.8	61.1	62.5	63.9	63.6	63.5	69.7	68.0	65.2
1998-9	66.0	66.2	65.9	64.6	60.6	58.1	55.6	55.1	55.6	55.0	54.6	53.8	60.2
1999-00	52.7	45.3	46.3	44.3	42.8	43.1	46.8	47.7	45.4	47.6	45.1	48.8	45.0
2000-1	51.4	50.6	55.5	58.0	57.8	52.1	48.5	41.1	42.6	40.9	39.2	38.9	49.8
2001-2	37.3	36.5	30.7	27.8	30.8	27.3	28.0	28.4	27.2	26.7	33.7	35.3	29.8
2002-3	33.0	35.2	39.4	43.0	44.3	45.5	45.2	47.3	45.0	45.6	45.3	46.9	43.0
2003-4[2]	46.3	55.7	68.0	63.4	64.1	63.8							60.2

[1] Weighted average by sales.   [2] Preliminary.   *Source: Agricultural Marketing Service, U.S. Department of Agriculture (AMS-USDA)*

COTTON

Purchases Reported by Exchanges in Designated U.S. Spot Markets[1]   In Running Bales

Crop Year Beginning Aug. 1	Aug.	Sept.	Oct.	Nov.	Dec.	Jan.	Feb.	Mar.	Apr.	May	June	July	Market Total
1994-5	92,401	98,251	426,371	1,075,829	1,491,429	608,701	233,159	149,762	49,192	44,228	43,821	13,244	4,326,388
1995-6	60,442	38,855	73,857	209,279	381,943	765,502	153,758	241,197	225,797	73,459	59,042	31,324	2,314,455
1996-7	62,884	73,925	148,337	477,331	613,430	696,494	412,095	242,606	72,234	130,163	201,557	93,205	3,224,261
1997-8	48,504	106,503	323,400	367,010	617,470	655,432	482,625	396,946	92,072	210,906	105,139	39,647	3,445,654
1998-9	27,193	52,066	114,998	229,743	498,082	414,832	191,872	236,762	71,993	63,335	62,192	64,092	2,027,160
1999-00	83,564	95,241	195,370	320,434	517,579	744,400	294,843	189,460	89,473	129,879	49,012	33,942	2,743,197
2000-1	63,607	69,083	143,938	323,891	288,242	217,755	215,318	191,667	274,185	193,774	152,905	167,647	2,302,012
2001-2	118,000	94,697	214,785	644,860	225,869	289,778	180,362	278,853	84,259	155,391	143,422	93,489	2,523,765
2002-3	43,047	49,671	194,020	204,564	369,838	481,730	432,055	169,064	170,951	213,679	149,780	86,830	2,565,229
2003-4	125,240	245,295	273,028	167,285	321,083	417,090							3,098,042

[1] seven markets.   Source: Agricultural Marketing Service, U.S. Department of Agriculture (AMS-USDA)

Production of Cotton (Upland and American-Pima) in the U.S.   In Thousands of 480-Pound Bales

Year	Ala-bama	Arizona	Arkan-sas	California	Georgia	Louis-iana	Missis-sippi	Missouri	North Carolina	South Carolina	Ten-nessee	Texas	Total American-Pima
1994	726	862	1,772	2,902	1,537	1,512	2,132	615	829	393	885	4,968	337.7
1995	492	793	1,468	2,312	1,941	1,375	1,841	513	798	376	724	4,460	367.6
1996	789	778	1,636	2,390	2,079	1,286	1,876	591	1,002	455	675	4,345	528.5
1997	550	847	1,683	2,191	1,919	986	1,821	565	930	410	662	5,140	548.0
1998	553	608	1,209	1,146	1,542	641	1,444	350	1,026	350	546	3,600	442.3
1999	625	716	1,428	1,580	1,567	901	1,731	472	816	281	595	5,050	674.3
2000	543	791	1,425	2,210	1,663	911	1,711	540	1,429	379	710	3,940	389.1
2001	920	690	1,833	1,770	2,220	1,034	2,396	695	1,673	423	978	4,260	700.4
2002[1]	570	613	1,669	1,460	1,578	739	1,935	610	806	131	818	5,040	678.3
2003[2]	820	560	1,780	1,500	2,150	1,020	2,100	690	1,100	330	860	4,200	429.0

[1] Preliminary.   [2] Forecasted.   Source: Agricultural Statistics Board, U.S. Department of Agriculture (ASB-USDA)

Cotton Production and Yield Estimates

Year	Forecast of Production (1,000 Bales of 480 Lbs.[1]) Aug. 1	Sept. 1	Oct. 1	Nov. 1	Dec. 1	Jan. 1	Actual Crop	Forecasts of Yield (Lbs. Per Harvested Acre) Aug. 1	Sept. 1	Oct. 1	Nov. 1	Dec. 1	Jan. 1	Actual Crop
1994	19,195	19,025	19,303	19,453	19,573	19,728	19,662	690	690	690	695	699	710	708
1995	21,811	20,266	18,771	18,838	18,236	17,971	17,900	663	615	574	567	551	540	537
1996	18,577	17,900	18,189	18,594	18,738	18,951	18,942	686	661	673	698	704	709	705
1997	17,783	18,418	18,410	18,848	18,819	18,977	18,793	637	658	665	673	672	686	673
1998	14,263	13,563	13,288	13,231	13,452	----	13,918	640	614	616	612	621	----	625
1999	18,304	17,535	16,430	16,531	16,875	----	16,968	649	621	588	592	604	----	607
2000	19,159	18,315	17,485	17,510	17,399	----	17,220	648	622	620	622	619	----	631
2001	20,003	19,992	20,072	20,175	20,064	----	20,084	670	679	681	685	691	----	698
2002	18,439	18,134	18,070	17,815	17,375	----	17,209	675	675	674	665	648	----	665
2003	17,104	16,939	17,559	18,215	18,215	----	18,224	667	667	696	722	722	----	725

[1] Net weight bales.   Source: Agricultural Statistics Board, U.S. Department of Agriculture (ASB-USDA)

Supply and Distribution of Upland Cotton in the United States   In Thousands of 480-Pound Bales

Crop Year Beginning Aug. 1	Area Planted (1,000 Acres)	Harvested (1,000 Acres)	Yield Lbs./Acre	Beginning Stocks[3]	Supply Pro-duction[4]	Imports	Total	Disappearance Mill Use	Exports	Total	Ending Stocks	Farm Price[5] Cents/Lb.
1994-5	13,552	13,156	705	3,303	19,324	18	22,645	11,109	8,978	20,087	2,588	72.0
1995-6	16,717	15,796	533	2,588	17,532	400	20,520	10,538	7,375	17,913	2,543	75.4
1996-7	14,376	12,612	701	2,543	18,413	403	21,359	11,020	6,399	17,419	3,920	69.3
1997-8	13,648	13,157	666	3,920	18,245	13	22,178	11,234	7,060	18,294	3,822	65.2
1998-9	13,064	10,449	619	3,822	13,476	431	17,729	10,254	4,056	14,264	3,836	60.2
1999-00	14,584	13,138	595	3,836	16,294	53	20,183	10,055	6,303	16,358	3,665	45.0
2000-1	15,347	12,884	626	3,665	16,799	8	20,472	8,738	6,303	15,041	5,879	49.8
2001-2	15,499	13,560	694	5,879	19,603	5	25,487	7,592	10,603	18,195	7,120	29.8
2002-3[1]	13,714	12,184	651	7,120	16,530	8	23,659	7,166	11,266	18,432	5,140	44.5
2003-4[2]	13,304	11,880	719	5,140	17,795	20	22,933	6,110	12,675	18,785	4,148	

[1] Preliminary.   [2] Estimate.   [3] Excludes preseason ginnings (adjusted to 480-lb. bale net weight basis).   [4] Includes preseason ginnings.   [5] Marketing year average price.   [6] Average of 5 cheapest types of SLM 1 3/32 staple length cotton offered on the European market.   Source: Economic Research Service, U.S. Department of Agriculture (ERS-USDA)

68

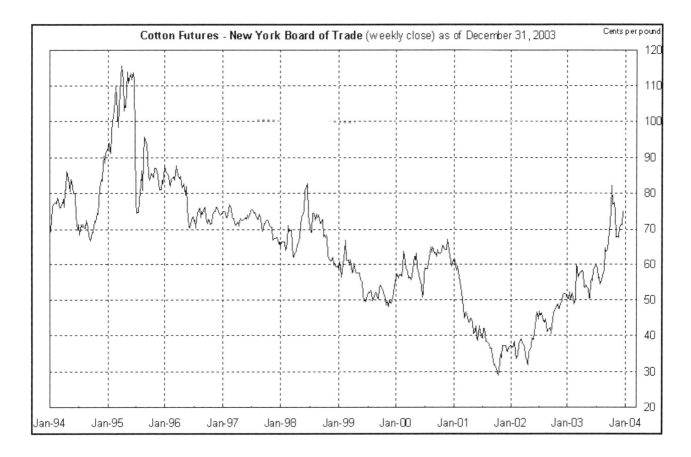

Average Open Interest of #2 Cotton Futures in New York   In Contracts

Year	Jan.	Feb.	Mar.	Apr.	May	June	July	Aug.	Sept.	Oct.	Nov.	Dec.
1994	54,424	55,558	53,724	54,670	52,830	51,001	52,357	50,597	50,955	51,561	53,563	59,065
1995	71,353	75,100	79,090	71,488	71,714	68,159	65,656	69,653	69,528	65,768	38,475	35,996
1996	58,001	60,231	57,542	61,795	64,555	62,342	61,921	60,182	58,168	58,415	57,397	47,652
1997	59,909	65,392	72,130	76,779	73,464	70,296	73,893	79,309	87,134	92,430	89,150	87,120
1998	89,358	86,739	81,236	85,505	84,562	90,178	81,652	78,571	85,378	88,970	88,917	77,873
1999	79,598	75,794	62,857	60,384	61,470	66,789	68,975	65,690	63,976	60,369	63,746	61,474
2000	63,987	67,720	69,788	56,038	54,058	48,024	53,621	63,069	73,735	67,767	65,017	62,931
2001	71,849	73,383	71,389	70,407	66,680	64,032	61,183	65,257	65,496	59,777	56,896	58,156
2002	64,096	64,572	63,451	63,827	67,601	65,848	74,892	72,612	69,554	71,526	82,802	74,685
2003	83,775	89,852	91,336	78,658	73,146	69,137	62,565	62,781	80,348	108,981	97,809	79,437

Source: New York Board of Trade (NYBOT)

Volume of Trading of #2 Cotton Futures in New York   In Contracts

Year	Jan.	Feb.	Mar.	Apr.	May	June	July	Aug.	Sept.	Oct.	Nov.	Dec.	Total
1994	210,011	207,421	210,363	252,614	179,591	208,945	161,688	128,879	140,574	179,604	205,936	203,021	2,289,998
1995	223,073	290,600	286,098	219,187	214,052	185,276	183,171	199,050	191,534	196,676	195,601	141,116	2,525,434
1996	215,882	196,225	147,393	251,786	236,684	264,047	131,183	177,430	166,629	229,305	229,281	128,010	2,373,855
1997	201,610	253,475	302,609	258,851	175,227	314,406	234,718	202,008	212,966	216,771	266,800	197,839	2,837,280
1998	221,308	289,222	310,075	362,688	218,595	407,922	226,138	230,752	195,690	303,849	272,775	161,816	3,200,830
1999	179,049	244,300	209,127	250,622	157,552	260,649	187,631	178,236	175,282	193,552	298,531	120,120	2,454,651
2000	270,792	279,566	248,017	220,222	232,947	272,023	147,878	175,707	154,735	172,875	242,013	180,982	2,597,757
2001	267,930	270,876	237,356	215,903	175,808	214,513	132,065	118,685	98,947	152,702	258,847	116,033	2,259,665
2002	156,834	248,299	162,781	237,861	188,340	234,442	170,893	128,185	145,946	199,779	296,859	157,741	2,327,960
2003	202,615	267,234	217,791	325,627	249,314	271,822	164,027	127,080	283,988	422,132	356,052	148,310	3,035,992

Source: New York Board of Trade (NYBOT)

COTTON

Daily Rate of Upland Cotton Mill Consumption[2] on Cotton-System Spinning Spindles in the U.S.
In Thousands of Running Bales

Crop Year Beginning Aug. 1	Aug.	Sept.	Oct.	Nov.	Dec.	Jan.	Feb.	Mar.	Apr.	May	June	July	Average
1994-5	41.0	41.4	41.1	41.8	41.7	42.6	42.1	42.4	41.1	40.2	39.2	37.2	41.0
1995-6	38.8	39.4	37.6	38.1	37.9	37.5	38.1	39.5	39.4	39.6	40.5	39.8	38.9
1996-7	40.5	40.7	40.5	41.5	41.1	41.3	40.4	39.4	41.0	41.0	40.9	42.5	40.9
1997-8	40.7	42.4	42.0	42.4	43.9	41.8	41.7	41.1	40.5	40.8	40.0	41.5	41.6
1998-9	39.3	38.7	39.9	37.4	37.5	38.6	38.2	37.9	37.8	37.5	37.7	36.8	38.1
1999-00	36.1	36.4	37.3	37.2	37.6	36.8	37.5	37.6	37.5	37.0	38.1	36.5	37.1
2000-1	36.4	35.6	34.5	33.0	34.4	33.5	31.9	31.8	30.6	29.7	27.6	28.6	32.3
2001-2	28.8	28.1	27.5	26.3	27.1	27.1	27.5	27.9	27.4	28.1	29.0	31.9	28.1
2002-3	27.1	27.8	27.3	27.7	28.5	26.8	26.7	26.4	25.7	24.6	24.2	25.7	26.5
2003-4[1]	22.7	22.5	22.5	24.0	24.2								23.2

[1] Preliminary. [2] Not seasonally adjusted. *Source: Bureau of the Census: U.S. Department of Commerce*

Consumption of American and Foreign Cotton in the United States In Thousands of Running Bales

Year	Aug.	Sept.	Oct.	Nov.	Dec.	Jan.	Feb.	Mar.	Apr.	May	June	July	Total
1994-5	870	1,070	873	838	897	858	878	1,097	847	842	999	681	10,750
1995-6	829	1,020	798	761	801	744	787	1,029	810	824	1,040	731	10,216
1996-7	847	1,028	829	816	858	810	819	1,014	834	840	1,044	781	10,519
1997-8	868	1,100	872	855	951	848	861	1,068	839	854	1,017	770	10,902
1998-9	835	1,013	834	758	796	979	795	983	777	793	970	678	10,210
1999-00	762	949	793	757	801	736	769	966	772	771	990	670	9,735
2000-1	766	929	741	663	749	661	657	837	641	628	727	510	8,510
2001-2	616	751	600	521	563	541	580	759	575	594	754	571	7,425
2002-3	574	733	585	545	598	671	556	708	541	523	616	456	7,106
2003-4[1]	476	599	482	468	508								6,078

[1] Preliminary. *Source: Bureau of the Census, U.S. Department of Commerce*

Exports of All Cotton[2] from the United States In Thousands of Running Bales

Year	Aug.	Sept.	Oct.	Nov.	Dec.	Jan.	Feb.	Mar.	Apr.	May	June	July	Total
1994-5	531	333	341	710	1,098	1,115	1,383	1,392	1,104	684	410	300	9,402
1995-6	315	245	452	733	1,230	1,262	1,295	777	576	343	263	183	7,675
1996-7	257	171	277	573	899	666	728	848	711	631	604	501	6,866
1997-8	458	299	400	581	774	734	777	888	669	477	574	571	7,202
1998-9	402	280	265	795	1,027	156	182	221	169	256	260	330	4,344
1999-00	254	146	167	455	654	658	736	978	708	659	508	479	6,402
2000-1	430	336	382	435	541	564	614	720	568	692	784	648	6,715
2001-2	612	824	678	649	927	964	1,042	1,225	999	842	1,067	679	10,505
2002-3	472	653	373	626	935	1,206	873	1,597	1,174	1,150	1,273	1,231	11,561
2003-4[1]	810	555	446	758	1,116								8,845

[1] Preliminary. *Source: Foreign Agricultural Service, U.S. Department of Agriculture (FAS-USDA)*

U.S. Exports of American Cotton to Countries of Destination In Thousands of 480-Pound Bales

Crop Year Beginning Aug. 1	Canada	China	Hong Kong	Indo-nesia	Italy	Japan	Rep. of Korea	Mexico	Philip-pines	Taiwan	Thai-land	United Kingdom	Total
1993-4	165	1,183	314	653	96	790	976	653	168	277	356	65	6,847
1994-5	253	2,257	347	925	83	1,061	951	558	173	441	352	89	9,401
1995-6	294	1,845	223	794	115	940	769	618	144	331	255	85	7,674
1996-7	253	1,756	129	594	46	630	568	733	84	197	255	66	6,862
1997-8	288	737	151	464	85	637	712	1,447	53	220	376	13	7,202
1998-9	281	71	245	229	29	406	381	1,359	59	82	249	6	4,298
1999-00	245	147	316	573	61	424	307	1,500	71	257	476	4	6,401
2000-1	322	124	287	558	52	355	489	1,760	42	237	367	1	6,740
2001-2[1]	235	306	407	947	58	385	577	1,516	126	693	693	0	10,397
2002-3[2]	303	1,800	364	842	79	355	390	1,784	103	576	546	4	11,235

[1] Preliminary. [2] Estimate. *Source: Foreign Agricultural Service, U.S. Department of Agriculture (FAS-USDA)*

Cotton[1] Government Loan Program in the United States

Crop Year Beginning Aug. 1	Support Price -- Cents Per Lb. --	Target Price	Put Under Support Ths Bales	% of Pro-duction	Acquired ----- Ths. Bales -----	Owned July 31	Crop Year Beginning Aug. 1	Support Price -- Cents Per Lb. --	Target Price	Put Under Support Ths Bales	% of Pro-duction	Acquired ----- Ths. Bales -----	Owned July 31
1993-4	52.35	72.9	7,721	49.0	3	14	1998-9	51.92	NA	4,724	36.8	31	3
1994-5	50.00	72.9	4,716	24.4	3	3	1999-00	51.92	NA	8,721	54.9	2	1
1995-6	51.92	72.9	3,478	19.8	0	0	2000-1	51.92	NA	8,837	52.6	6	5
1996-7	51.92	NA	3,340	18.1	0	0	2001-2[2]	51.92	NA	13,655	69.7	2	2
1997-8	51.92	NA	4,281	23.5	0	0	2002-3[2]	52.00	74.2				

[1] Upland.   [2] Preliminary.   [3] Less than 500 bales.   NA = Not applicable.   *Source: Economic Research Service, U.S. Department of Agriculture (ERS-USDA)*

Production of Cotton Cloth[1] in the United States — In Millions of Square Yards

Year	First Quarter	Second Quarter	Third Quarter	Fourth Quarter	Total Year	Year	First Quarter	Second Quarter	Third Quarter	Fourth Quarter	Total Year
1994	1,073	1,125	1,131	1,143	4,473	1999	1,170	1,164	1,078	1,039	4,451
1995	1,169	1,137	1,090	1,093	4,488	2000	1,075	1,129	1,111	1,079	4,395
1996	1,182	1,230	1,198	1,187	4,796	2001	1,047	976	873	811	3,706
1997	1,211	1,276	1,283	1,309	5,078	2002	893	912	894	825	3,524
1998	1,226	1,167	1,218	1,142	4,753	2003[2]	841	781	664		3,048

[1] Cotton broadwoven goods over 12 inches in width.   [2] Preliminary.   *Source: Bureau of Census, U.S. Department of Commerce*

Cotton Ginnings[1] in the United States To: In Thousands of Running Bales

Crop Year	Aug. 1	Sept. 1	Sept. 15	Oct. 1	Oct. 15	Nov. 1	Nov. 15	Dec. 1	Dec. 15	Jan. 1	Jan. 15	Feb. 1	Total Crop
1994-5	113	680	943	2,324	5,002	8,878	12,479	15,587	17,465	18,438	18,842	19,028	19,127
1995-6	17	433	898	2,455	4,795	8,430	11,262	14,199	16,101	17,011	17,292	17,416	17,469
1996-7	48	342	637	2,146	4,780	8,876	11,906	14,623	16,528	17,681	18,101	18,308	18,439
1997-8	2	359	683	1,210	3,752	7,930	11,601	14,735	16,662	17,613	18,013	18,170	18,301
1998-9	146	523	739	2,056	4,265	7,359	9,366	11,310	12,558	13,160	13,376	13,458	13,534
1999-00	81	561	1,018	2,690	4,885	8,263	11,006	13,379	14,992	15,965	16,322	16,468	16,528
2000-1	245	842	1,454	3,264	5,930	9,221	11,546	13,657	15,364	16,097	16,518	16,648	16,742
2001-2	99	609	802	2,007	4,562	8,748	12,522	15,498	17,727	18,672	19,242	19,587	19,771
2002-3	56	537	898	1,648	3,523	6,685	9,294	12,367	14,395	15,689	16,337	16,589	17,206
2003-4[2]	29	567	958	2,004	3,827	7,396	10,527	13,477	15,686	16,914	17,426	17,620	

[1] Excluding linters.   [2] Preliminary.   *Source: National Agricultural Statistics Service, U.S. Department of Agriculture (NASS-USDA)*

Fiber Prices in the United States   In Cents Per Pound

Year	Cotton[1] Actual	Cotton[1] Raw[5] Equivalent	Rayon[2] Actual	Rayon[2] Raw[5] Equivalent	Polyester[3] Actual	Polyester[3] Raw[5] Equivalent	Price Ratios[4] in Percent Cotton/Rayon	Price Ratios[4] in Percent Cotton/Polyester
1995	100.76	111.95	118.67	123.61	88.83	92.53	.91	1.21
1996	86.24	95.83	118.00	122.92	81.10	84.48	.78	1.14
1997	76.29	84.77	115.00	119.79	69.50	72.40	.71	1.17
1998	74.21	82.45	110.25	114.84	62.50	65.11	.72	1.29
1999	61.45	68.28	98.92	103.04	51.67	53.82	.66	1.27
2000	64.06	71.17	97.58	101.65	57.08	59.46	.70	1.19
2001	47.08	52.32	98.50	102.61	60.42	62.93	.52	.83
2002	45.56	50.63	97.83	101.91	61.17	63.72	.50	.79
2003[6]	62.54	69.49	90.25	94.01	60.67	63.20	.74	1.11
Jan.	54.39	60.43	94.00	97.92	61.00	63.54	.62	.95
Feb.	56.13	62.37	93.00	96.88	61.00	63.54	.64	.98
Mar.	60.16	66.84	93.00	96.88	62.00	64.58	.69	1.04
Apr.	59.84	66.49	92.00	95.83	63.00	65.63	.69	1.04
May	56.09	62.32	92.00	95.83	63.00	65.63	.65	1.01
June	57.12	63.47	90.00	93.75	62.00	64.58	.68	.98
July	60.97	67.74	88.00	91.67	60.00	62.50	.74	1.08
Aug.	58.44	64.93	88.00	91.67	59.00	61.46	.71	1.06
Sept.	64.75	71.94	88.00	91.67	59.00	61.46	.79	1.17
Oct.	75.14	83.49	88.00	91.67	59.00	61.46	.91	1.36
Nov.	77.01	85.57	88.00	91.67	59.00	61.46	.93	1.39
Dec.	70.48	78.31	89.00	92.71	60.00	62.50	.85	1.25

[1] SLM-1 1/16 at group B Mill points, net weight.   [2] 1.5 and 3.0 denier, regular rayon staples.   [3] Reported average market price for 1.5 denier polyester staple for cotton blending.   [4] Raw fiber equivalent.   [5] Actual prices converted to estimated raw fiber equivalent as follows: cotton, divided by 0.90, rayon and polyester, divided by 0.96.   [6] Preliminary.   *Source: Economic Research Service, U.S. Department of Agriculture (ERS-USDA)*

Cottonseed and Products

Cottonseed is crushed to produce both oil and meal. Oil is typically used for cooking oil and the meal is fed to livestock. Before the cottonseed is crushed for oil and meal, it is delinted of its linters. Linters are used for padding in furniture, absorbent cotton swabs, and for manufacture of many cellulose products. The sediment left by cottonseed oil refining, called foots, provides fatty acids for industrial products. The value of cottonseeds represents a hefty 18% of a cotton producer's income.

Prices – The price of cottonseed oil in 2003 rose sharply by 59% to 37.00 cents/pound from 23.34 cents in 2002, and more than double the dismal 2001 price of 15.41. The price of cottonseed meal in 2003 rose to an average $149 per short ton, up from $141.37 in 2002. Cottonseed oil and meal prices were boosted throughout 2003 by the sharp 50% rally seen in cotton prices.

Supply – World production of cottonseed was forecast at 34.83 million metric tons, up from 32.84 million in 2002/3. World ending stocks in 2003/4 are forecasted at 360,000 metric tons, down from 380,000 in 2002/3. World production of cottonseed oil was forecast to rise to 3.74 million metric tons in 2003/4 from 3.49 million in 2002/3. World production of cottonseed meal in 2003/4 was forecast to rise to 11.90 million metric tons from 11.17 million in 2002/3.

US production of cottonseed in 2003/4 rose to 6.689 million short tons from 6.184 million in 2002/3. US stocks fell to 347,000 tons from 400,000 tons in 2002/3. A total of 2.750 million tons of cottonseed were forecasted to be crushed in 2003/4, up from 2.495 million tons in 2002/3.

Trade – World trade in cottonseed was forecast at 1.07 million metric tons in 2003/4, a little higher than 1.06 million in 2002/3. That accounts for only 3% of world production, showing that most countries use the cottonseed domestically.

World Production of Cottonseed   In Thousands of Metric Ton

Crop Year	Argentina	Australia	Brazil	China	Egypt	Greece	India	Mexico	Pakistan	Turkey	United States	Former USSR	World Total
1994-5	638	474	980	7,727	411	574	4,709	187	2,959	930	6,898	3,380	33,129
1995-6	748	595	690	8,487	384	725	5,339	344	3,604	1,288	6,213	3,150	35,290
1996-7	564	859	568	7,481	560	540	5,890	421	3,189	1,220	6,480	2,707	34,557
1997-8	542	941	763	8,193	564	590	5,150	348	3,124	1,193	6,291	2,692	34,522
1998-9	337	1,012	961	8,012	379	665	5,420	369	2,990	1,282	4,867	2,580	32,868
1999-00	223	1,047	1,310	6,817	375	730	5,300	237	3,824	1,315	5,764	2,832	33,695
2000-1	257	1,062	1,720	7,868	340	720	4,800	128	3,651	1,289	5,838	2,530	34,021
2001-2[1]	102	968	1,407	9,470	518	700	5,370	154	3,610	1,240	6,761	2,716	37,055
2002-3[2]	85	371	1,520	8,758	475	650	4,700	68	3,400	1,370	5,823	2,581	33,568

[1] Preliminary.   [2] Estimate.   Source: The Oil World

Salient Statistics of Cottonseed in the United States   In Thousands of Short Tons

Crop Year Beginning Aug. 1	Stocks	Production	Total Supply	Crush	Exports	Other	Total Disappearance	Farm Price $/Ton	Value of Production Mil. $	Oil Million Lbs.	Meal Thousand Sh. Tons
1995-6	551	6,849	7,399	3,882	114	2,886	6,882	106	731.0	1,229	1,748
1996-7	517	7,144	7,681	3,860	116	3,182	7,158	126	914.6	1,310	1,807
1997-8	523	6,935	7,553	3,885	149	2,957	6,990	121	835.4	1,224	1,769
1998-9	563	5,365	6,135	2,719	68	2,955	5,742	129	687.2	832	1,232
1999-00	393	6,354	7,055	3,079	198	3,505	6,781	89	565.5	939	1,390
2000-1	274	6,436	7,084	2,753	235	3,669	6,657	105	675.7	847	1,338
2001-2	427	7,452	8,206	2,791	274	4,742	7,807	91	667.3	876	1,294
2002-3[1]	400	6,184	6,688	2,495	371	3,475	6,341	101	616.4	725	1,114
2003-4[2]	347	6,694	7,266	2,700	300	3,931	6,931	117	784.2	850	1,215

[1] Preliminary.   [2] Estimate.   Source: Economic Research Service, U.S. Department of Agriculture (ERS-USDA)

Average Wholesale Price of Cottonseed Meal (41% Solvent)[2] in Memphis   In Dollars Per Short Ton

Year	Jan.	Feb.	Mar.	Apr.	May	June	July	Aug.	Sept.	Oct.	Nov.	Dec.	Average
1995	106.75	97.50	100.30	98.10	92.75	108.75	116.90	116.50	137.60	153.25	165.00	185.80	123.27
1996	208.80	202.80	195.60	220.00	191.25	192.20	201.56	193.10	193.10	183.25	196.60	224.50	200.23
1997	207.20	183.75	189.10	189.10	193.75	190.30	170.75	176.25	192.00	189.10	189.10	190.50	188.41
1998	153.10	139.10	128.70	116.25	105.00	129.40	146.65	130.30	115.60	106.50	107.90	119.75	124.85
1999	110.60	101.25	106.90	110.90	108.75	114.50	115.00	100.65	111.92	111.83	112.00	124.20	110.71
2000	126.88	130.50	129.38	125.00	123.25	130.63	131.88	130.50	153.12	150.00	141.88	160.83	136.15
2001	184.00	148.75	138.13	140.00	137.50	126.88	129.69	130.63	131.25	131.25	128.13	134.17	138.37
2002	133.13	125.00	131.88	124.30	120.88	137.50	151.50	159.75	156.38	150.10	150.00	156.00	141.37
2003[1]	157.38	143.60	142.40	142.40	131.75	131.50	143.00	151.70	153.20	163.50	182.50	185.00	152.33

[1] Preliminary.   Source: Economic Research Service, U.S. Department of Agriculture (ERS-USDA)

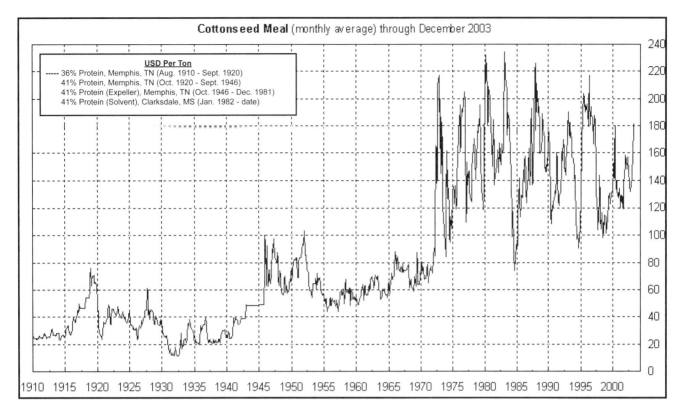

Cottonseed Meal (monthly average) through December 2003

USD Per Ton
----- 36% Protein, Memphis, TN (Aug. 1910 - Sept. 1920)
41% Protein, Memphis, TN (Oct. 1920 - Sept. 1946)
41% Protein (Expeller), Memphis, TN (Oct. 1946 - Dec. 1981)
41% Protein (Solvent), Clarksdale, MS (Jan. 1982 - date)

Supply and Distribution of Cottonseed Oil in the United States   In Millions of Pounds

Crop Year Beginning Oct. 1	Supply				Disappearance			Per Capita Cunsump. of Salad & Cook Oils - In Lbs. -	Utilization			Prices	
									Food Uses			$/Met. Ton	
	Stocks	Pro-duction	Imports	Total Supply	Domestic	Exports	Total		Short-ening	Salad & Cooking Oils	Total	U.S.[3] (Crude)	Rott[4] (Cif)
1997-8	66	1,224	.1	1,291	1,004	208	1,212	29	208	184	414	663	693
1998-9	79	832	48.2	958	772	111	882	28	170	262	457	633	632
1999-00	76	939	8.1	1,023	833	141	974	29	183	320	554	474	496
2000-1	49	847	----	896	673	131	804	35	178	205	426	352	428
2001-2	93	876	----	969	779	150	930		200	317	539	396	441
2002-3[1]	40	725	21.0	786	639	111	750		172	W	427	832	982
2003-4[2]	36	850	----	886	731	115	846					723	

[1] Preliminary.   [2] Estimate.   [3] Valley Points FOB; Tank Cars.   [4] Rotterdam; US, PBSY, fob gulf.   W = Withheld proprietary data.

Source: Economic Research Service, U.S. Department of Agriculture (ERS-USDA)

Consumption of Crude Cottonseed Oil in Refining in the United States   In Millions of Pounds

Year	Oct.	Nov.	Dec.	Jan.	Feb.	Mar.	Apr.	May	June	July	Aug.	Sept.	Total
1997-8	73.1	73.1	77.2	85.0	75.7	70.2	72.1	57.1	51.9	54.9	57.5	30.1	778.1
1998-9	52.9	49.6	50.2	46.6	48.9	50.7	36.4	28.3	28.4	30.5	46.2	43.5	512.3
1999-00	51.9	57.3	61.5	60.0	58.1	67.8	62.0	52.7	43.2	22.7	45.8	37.2	620.1
2000-1	56.9	53.7	56.7	67.4	61.6	59.5	38.1	46.0	51.4	42.8	49.6	29.8	613.6
2001-2	48.5	63.9	61.6	65.2	58.3	58.9	56.6	56.9	45.2	37.1	53.0	47.5	652.7
2002-3	48.5	59.5	56.0	66.8	55.8	57.1	59.2	49.7	42.4	31.9	38.7	34.9	600.5
2003-4[1]	60.1	63.5	61.5										740.1

[1] Preliminary.   *Source: U.S. Bureau of Census, U.S. Department of Commerce*

Exports of Cottonseed Oil (Crude and Refined) from the United States   In Thousands of Pounds

Year	Jan.	Feb.	Mar.	Apr.	May	June	July	Aug.	Sept.	Oct.	Nov.	Dec.	Total
1997	25,722	26,835	22,647	22,230	30,319	9,535	25,207	24,717	8,919	15,351	24,217	8,164	243,863
1998	24,003	15,077	16,150	22,874	20,791	22,994	15,348	14,392	8,818	11,056	7,610	11,447	190,560
1999	11,541	10,235	7,780	11,387	6,328	7,161	8,725	8,111	9,275	11,060	12,313	23,025	126,941
2000	10,627	9,447	13,181	8,258	7,402	7,550	11,546	10,642	16,467	13,263	11,652	8,898	128,934
2001	14,684	6,638	7,237	10,595	12,722	7,525	10,325	20,809	6,439	19,891	5,662	19,831	142,358
2002	12,905	17,550	12,137	8,319	21,013	9,444	7,863	8,727	6,831	12,698	11,105	10,761	139,353
2003[1]	7,012	8,483	10,413	8,262	9,706	8,134	6,620	8,613	8,764	8,689	9,349	8,127	102,172

[1] Preliminary.   *Source: Economic Research Service, U.S. Department of Agriculture (ERS-USDA)*

COTTONSEED AND PRODUCTS

Cottonseed Crushed (Consumption) in the United States   In Thousands of Short Tons

Year	Aug.	Sept.	Oct.	Nov.	Dec.	Jan.	Feb.	Mar.	Apr.	May	June	July	Total
1995-6	264.4	245.5	337.1	386.7	362.4	402.3	373.5	381.4	349.6	325.2	223.7	209.2	3,861
1996-7	229.2	225.0	331.7	355.1	352.6	381.0	362.8	362.2	334.4	351.3	280.8	294.0	3,860
1997-8	244.4	178.6	329.7	374.5	371.3	428.4	352.3	370.8	359.1	309.1	278.8	277.6	3,875
1998-9	246.0	174.9	272.7	254.3	262.7	282.2	259.5	280.2	205.5	172.0	159.9	149.2	2,719
1999-00	166.8	230.7	281.6	302.5	296.4	300.2	299.4	297.7	263.5	250.3	221.3	153.5	3,064
2000-1	170.8	141.1	265.9	252.3	241.5	295.2	268.7	261.9	186.0	228.3	241.9	199.2	2,753
2001-2	186.8	147.6	267.5	287.0	273.1	281.3	253.2	251.8	243.0	233.3	200.3	166.3	2,791
2002-3	195.1	131.4	207.8	242.5	236.6	274.5	224.5	230.4	241.5	203.6	179.4	127.4	2,495
2003-4[1]	138.7	98.9	251.6	254.8	252.0								2,390

[1] Preliminary.   Source: Economic Research Service, U.S. Department of Agriculture (ERS-USDA)

Production of Cottonseed Cake and Meal in the United States   In Thousands of Short Tons

Year	Aug.	Sept.	Oct.	Nov.	Dec.	Jan.	Feb.	Mar.	Apr.	May	June	July	Total
1995-6	120.1	113.6	159.9	178.2	161.0	183.8	169.8	168.3	158.7	147.1	102.4	102.7	1,766
1996-7	100.9	99.1	146.1	161.5	158.2	174.5	164.6	162.1	152.2	160.7	128.6	123.2	1,732
1997-8	128.2	92.1	147.8	168.7	178.2	194.4	158.5	170.4	162.3	141.8	128.8	124.0	1,795
1998-9	114.7	77.1	118.7	115.9	122.5	130.2	114.8	127.2	90.6	75.6	75.6	71.0	1,234
1999-00	82.1	107.5	132.1	140.8	138.3	135.3	137.7	140.2	120.0	109.4	109.3	79.5	1,432
2000-1	74.1	79.3	134.1	121.4	117.1	136.0	118.9	120.3	83.4	101.0	114.3	89.7	1,290
2001-2	83.9	70.8	118.5	126.5	118.2	129.0	112.5	115.0	109.2	107.9	96.3	73.7	1,261
2002-3	92.4	79.3	95.5	112.6	108.0	123.0	100.3	96.7	108.9	89.8	81.4	63.0	1,151
2003-4[1]	74.9	59.5	112.3	111.0	112.5								1,129

[1] Preliminary.   Source: Bureau of Census, U.S. Department of Commerce

Production of Crude Cottonseed Oil[2] in the United States   In Millions of Pounds

Year	Aug.	Sept.	Oct.	Nov.	Dec.	Jan.	Feb.	Mar.	Apr.	May	June	July	Total
1995-6	87.8	84.3	105.2	121.6	111.6	130.9	121.4	125.6	110.4	101.9	73.3	76.7	1,251
1996-7	70.3	69.4	98.9	114.8	115.9	123.9	114.8	114.7	103.7	109.8	86.9	85.9	1,209
1997-8	80.6	66.0	97.8	120.3	119.6	136.4	111.1	115.5	112.7	96.1	87.3	88.8	1,232
1998-9	77.8	59.6	78.3	80.0	80.6	84.0	80.2	86.7	64.4	53.4	52.4	45.9	843
1999-00	56.1	69.6	88.3	95.4	94.2	93.4	93.2	93.8	82.6	75.7	70.2	49.2	962
2000-1	55.1	52.1	84.3	76.8	73.5	85.9	78.4	76.4	53.9	66.8	66.6	55.7	826
2001-2	57.5	42.2	79.4	86.2	81.7	87.5	78.3	78.2	74.6	74.5	61.8	50.6	853
2002-3	60.2	53.7	62.8	72.1	67.9	80.8	65.6	66.7	71.0	59.9	52.8	39.9	753
2003-4[1]	45.0	40.7	77.5	78.2	79.0								769

[1] Preliminary.   [2] Not seasonally adjusted.   Source: Bureau of Census, U.S. Department of Commerce

Production of Refined Cottonseed Oil in the United States   In Millions of Pounds

Year	Aug.	Sept.	Oct.	Nov.	Dec.	Jan.	Feb.	Mar.	Apr.	May	June	July	Total
1995-6	80.5	69.0	74.0	89.5	86.9	91.7	84.6	89.8	81.7	75.0	53.8	54.5	931
1996-7	62.4	53.0	64.9	82.8	82.2	85.9	80.7	78.1	75.2	76.9	56.4	53.6	852
1997-8	57.4	38.1	48.3	71.0	74.8	82.2	73.1	68.2	69.8	55.2	50.3	53.0	741
1998-9	55.8	29.1	51.1	47.9	48.5	45.4	47.3	49.0	35.2	27.4	27.5	29.7	494
1999-00	44.8	42.4	50.4	55.6	59.5	58.3	56.7	65.8	60.0	51.0	41.9	22.0	608
2000-1	44.4	36.2	55.1	52.2	54.9	65.7	59.8	57.8	36.9	44.8	50.0	41.5	599
2001-2	49.4	29.6	48.2	63.6	61.3	64.9	58.0	58.5	56.2	56.7	45.2	36.8	628
2002-3	52.7	47.1	48.3	59.2	55.7	66.5	55.6	56.8	58.9	49.4	42.4	31.7	624
2003-4[1]	38.5	34.6	59.8	63.5	61.5								619

[1] Preliminary.   Source: Bureau of the Census, U.S. Department of Commerce

Stocks of Cottonseed Oil (Crude and Refined) in the U.S., at End of Month   In Millions of Pounds

Year	Aug.	Sept.	Oct.	Nov.	Dec.	Jan.	Feb.	Mar.	Apr.	May	June	July
1995-6	87.8	82.1	82.6	89.3	94.8	118.2	147.2	151.2	155.6	143.3	128.1	125.4
1996-7	101.2	94.1	97.5	102.5	106.0	120.9	133.7	137.5	131.7	116.1	103.4	85.9
1997-8	78.0	66.4	68.6	86.4	105.3	133.8	141.2	140.7	159.8	150.4	130.9	118.8
1998-9	97.3	78.6	89.1	110.0	85.5	109.5	113.3	125.3	126.0	112.0	100.7	83.7
1999-00	107.8	76.0	81.1	88.7	85.1	84.5	79.6	115.2	127.4	127.5	103.0	81.3
2000-1	59.9	49.0	66.5	75.2	95.0	109.5	134.4	139.9	133.5	123.5	126.8	114.0
2001-2	97.7	91.8	113.8	112.9	109.8	124.9	120.3	106.9	110.3	97.3	82.7	61.8
2002-3	46.1	39.7	32.8	40.2	38.0	46.1	58.8	72.2	83.3	84.2	91.4	64.0
2003-4[1]	50.5	36.0	51.9	56.1	68.2							

[1] Preliminary.   Source: Bureau of Census, U.S. Department of Commerce

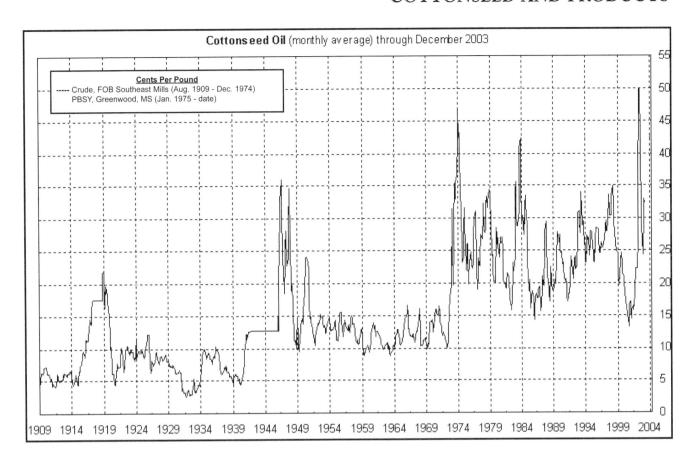

Average Price of Crude Cottonseed Oil, PBSY, Greenwood, MS.[1] in Tank Cars   In Cents Per Pound

Year	Jan.	Feb.	Mar.	Apr.	May	June	July	Aug.	Sept.	Oct.	Nov.	Dec.	Average
1994	33.16	29.96	29.60	29.06	29.66	27.55	24.20	23.71	24.51	23.64	24.85	25.50	27.12
1995	28.70	29.95	27.14	27.61	27.51	30.04	30.63	30.26	28.61	27.61	26.27	26.10	26.36
1996	24.45	24.35	24.25	26.77	28.46	27.94	28.25	27.81	26.13	24.55	24.28	24.29	25.96
1997	25.21	25.44	26.18	25.10	25.19	25.01	26.53	27.11	28.03	28.47	29.11	26.78	26.51
1998	27.69	29.37	30.46	32.47	33.13	30.22	29.40	30.11	33.26	33.99	34.16	33.40	31.47
1999	31.72	28.21	26.27	24.39	24.25	25.19	24.70	21.39	20.22	20.15	19.69	21.25	23.95
2000	21.98	22.65	23.70	24.57	22.97	21.54	21.03	20.17	18.52	18.16	17.83	17.25	20.86
2001	16.24	15.20	15.53	14.03	14.53	13.27	16.78	17.18	15.78	14.44	15.91	16.07	15.41
2002	16.38	15.89	16.77	16.98	17.95	19.48	21.30	22.32	22.32	26.84	36.90	46.89	23.34
2003	49.82	49.90	47.52	44.57	42.33	28.69	24.38	25.51	29.64	32.93	32.24	33.26	36.73

[1] Data prior to 1995 are F.O.B. Valley Points, Southeastern mills.   *Source: Economic Research Service, U.S. Department of Agriculture (ERS-USDA)*

Exports of Cottonseed Oil to Important Countries from the United States   In Thousands of Metric Tons

Year	Canada	Dominican Republic	Egypt	Guate- mala	Japan	Mexico	Nether- lands	El Salvador	South Korea	Turkey	Vene- zuela	Total
1994	10.8	.0	7.5	12.3	29.8	10.3	1.9	26.1	16.9		4.4	135.6
1995	12.0		10.3	1.9	17.9	5.7	1.4	37.8	19.2		2.8	137.7
1996	23.2	.0		1.7	15.8	3.3		20.6	7.2		.0	96.0
1997	28.0	.0		.4	11.3	2.5	4.2	25.3	1.9	2.5		110.6
1998	37.6	.1			6.0	6.1		16.1	2.1		.0	86.9
1999	37.5				4.2	5.4	.5	.8	.0			57.0
2000	40.2	.0			7.6	7.9	.4		.1			58.5
2001	26.0	.0		.5	6.5	8.6	3.1	4.8	2.5			64.6
2002	36.4		3.0		5.4	6.9		1.8	4.7	.3		63.2
2003[1]	33.8				3.5	7.2		.0	.7			46.3

[1] Preliminary.   *Source: Foreign Agricultural Service, U.S. Department of Agriculture (FAS-USDA)*

Reuters-CRB Futures Index

The Reuters Commodity Research Bureau Futures Price Index was first calculated by Commodity Research Bureau, Inc. in 1957 and made its inaugural appearance in the 1958 CRB Commodity Year Book.

The Index originally consisted of two cash markets and 26 futures markets which were traded on exchanges in the U.S. and Canada. It included barley and flaxseed from the Winnipeg exchange; cocoa, coffee "B", copper, cotton, cottonseed oil, grease wool, hides, lead, potatoes, rubber, sugar #4, sugar #6, wool tops and zinc from New York exchanges; and corn, oats, wheat, rye, soybeans, soybean oil, soybean meal, lard, onions, and eggs from Chicago exchanges. In addition to those 26, the Index also included the spot New Orleans cotton and Minneapolis wheat markets.

Like the Bureau of Labor Statistics spot index, the Reuters-CRB Futures Price Index is calculated to produce an unweighted geometric mean of the individual commodity price relatives. In other words, a ratio of the current price to the base year average price. Currently, 1967 is the base year the Index is calculated against (1967 = 100).

The formula considers all future delivery contracts that expire on or before the end of the sixth calendar month from the current date, using up to a maximum of five contracts per commodity. However, a minimum of two contracts must be used to calculate the current price, even if the second contract is outside the six-month window. Contracts are excluded when in their delivery period.

The 2003 closing value of 255.29 was 8.86 percent higher than the 2002 close of 234.52. 14 of the 17 component commodities finished higher for the year.

Futures Markets

Futures and options on the Reuters-CRB Futures Price Index are traded on the New York Board of Trade (NYBOT).

Reuters-CRB Futures Index Component Commodities by Group

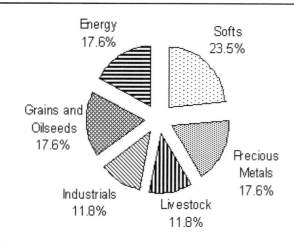

Groups:	Components
Energy:	Crude Oil, Heating Oil, Natural Gas
Grains and Oilseeds:	Corn, Soybeans, Wheat
Industrials:	Copper, Cotton
Livestock:	Live Cattle, Live Hogs
Precious Metals:	Gold, Platinum, Silver
Softs:	Cocoa, Coffee, Orange Juice, Sugar #11

The Reuters-CRB Futures Index is computed using a three-step process:

1) Each of the Index's 17 component commodities is arithmetically averaged using the prices for all of the designated contract months which expire on or before the end of the sixth calendar month from the current date, except that: a) no contract shall be included in the calculation while in delivery; b) there shall be a minimum of two contract months for each component commodity (adding contracts beyond the six month window if necessary); c) there shall be a maximum of five contract months for each commodity (dropping the most deferred contracts to remain at five, if necessary). The result is that the Index extends six to seven months into the future depending on where one is in the current month. For example, live cattle's average price on October 30, 1995 would be computed as follows:

$$\text{Cattle Average} = \frac{\text{Dec. '96} + \text{Feb. '97}}{2}$$

2) These 17 component averages are then geometrically averaged by multiplying all of the numbers together and taking the 17th root.

$$\text{Geometric Average} = \sqrt[17]{\text{Crude Avg.} * \text{Heating Oil Avg.} * \text{Sugar Avg.} \ldots}$$

3) The resulting average is divided by 30.7766, the 1967 base-year average for these 17 commodities. That result is then multiplied by an adjustment factor of .8486. This adjustment factor is necessitated by the nine revisions to the Index since its inception in 1957. Finally, that result is multiplied by 100 in order to convert the Index into percentage terms:

$$\text{Reuters-CRB Futures Index} = \frac{\text{Current Geometric Average}}{\text{1967 Geometric Avg. (30.7766)}} * .8486 * 100$$

REUTERS-CRB FUTURES INDEX

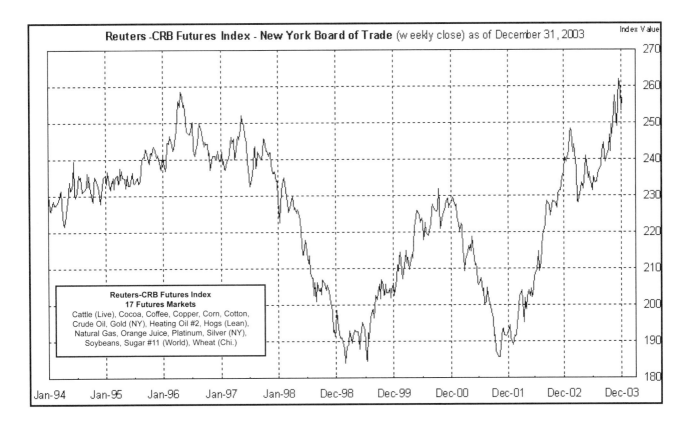

Average Open Interest of Reuters-CRB Futures Index in New York   In Contracts

Year	Jan.	Feb.	Mar.	Apr.	May	June	July	Aug.	Sept.	Oct.	Nov.	Dec.
1994	2,607	3,146	2,680	2,691	2,339	2,698	3,838	5,146	4,562	4,942	4,535	2,800
1995	2,144	2,164	2,147	2,370	2,016	2,144	2,053	2,070	2,062	1,942	2,003	1,640
1996	1,934	1,826	1,753	2,355	1,881	1,890	1,562	1,345	1,596	1,853	1,861	1,866
1997	1,944	2,128	2,090	2,245	2,192	1,817	1,957	1,741	1,656	1,843	1,789	1,752
1998	1,679	1,557	1,626	1,509	1,641	1,895	1,832	1,719	1,839	2,162	2,639	2,787
1999	2,863	3,027	3,153	3,041	3,785	3,388	3,300	3,443	4,231	4,851	4,579	4,087
2000	3,487	3,525	3,271	3,117	3,155	2,737	2,104	1,640	1,551	1,632	1,544	1,438
2001	1,280	1,063	1,032	1,036	969	1,006	1,058	1,048	993	559	354	404
2002	422	514	458	384	400	412	489	399	583	646	684	710
2003	748	877	835	849	939	905	858	917	1,078	1,029	1,013	757

Source: New York Board of Trade (NYBOT)

Volume of Trading of Reuters-CRB Futures Index in New York   In Contracts

Year	Jan.	Feb.	Mar.	Apr.	May	June	July	Aug.	Sept.	Oct.	Nov.	Dec.	Total
1994	6,956	7,473	10,085	10,274	11,298	14,652	10,560	8,967	7,445	6,575	10,186	5,515	109,986
1995	6,151	5,545	5,763	7,955	7,877	7,573	6,875	10,094	7,376	5,030	5,865	5,309	81,413
1996	7,490	6,041	6,428	10,784	9,526	5,543	7,476	5,816	6,311	6,527	5,990	3,181	81,113
1997	6,645	4,942	5,245	8,600	8,156	7,776	6,248	7,685	4,537	4,588	3,468	3,592	71,482
1998	7,659	4,623	3,953	3,890	2,933	5,634	3,394	4,578	5,101	4,013	8,814	4,401	58,993
1999	7,606	7,766	7,556	7,808	4,986	8,404	4,378	12,053	6,660	8,063	9,497	3,932	88,709
2000	14,975	6,760	3,941	7,582	7,402	8,924	2,023	3,973	1,333	2,122	3,254	1,205	63,494
2001	2,428	1,823	1,310	2,062	930	1,965	880	2,021	625	1,263	843	728	16,878
2002	1,251	1,231	896	1,472	785	1,191	1,217	915	1,100	1,654	1,430	1,141	14,283
2003	2,289	2,154	1,826	1,634	1,514	2,106	1,632	1,350	1,712	2,123	2,502	2,314	23,156

Source: New York Board of Trade (NYBOT)

Currencies

A currency rate involves the price of the base currency (e.g., the dollar) quoted in terms of another currency (e.g., the yen) or in terms of a basket of currencies (e.g., the dollar index). The world's major currencies have traded in a floating-rate exchange rate regime ever since the Bretton-Woods international payments system broke down in 1971 when President Nixon broke the dollar's peg to gold. The key factor affecting a currency's value is central bank monetary policy. An easy monetary policy (low interest rates) is bearish for a currency because the central bank is aggressively pumping new currency reserves into the marketplace and because foreign investors are not attracted to the low interest rate returns available in the country. By contrast, a tight monetary policy (high interest rates) is bullish for a currency because of the tight supply of new currency reserves and attractive interest rate returns for foreign investors.

Currency values are also affected by economic growth and investment opportunities in the country. A country with a strong economy and lucrative investment opportunities will typically have a strong currency because global companies and investors want to buy into that country's investment opportunities.

Another key factor driving currency values is the nation's current account balance. A current account *surplus* is bullish for a currency due to the net inflow of the currency, while a current account *deficit* is bearish for a currency due to the net outflow of the currency. Futures on major currencies and on cross-currency rates are traded at the Chicago Mercantile Exchange and the FINEX exchange.

Dollar – The sharp sell-off in the dollar that began in early 2002 continued into 2003. The dollar index temporarily rebounded upward during summer of 2003 as the US economic rebound started, but then the dollar showed weakness again during autumn and the dollar index in December 2003 posted a new 7-year low. There were two major bearish factors for the dollar during 2003: (1) the Fed's expansionary monetary policy, and (2) the massive US current account deficit. With its 1% federal funds target, the Fed aggressively pumped dollar reserves into the banking system, keeping interest rates low but also creating an oversupply of dollars that depressed the dollar's value against other currencies as well as against real commodities.

At the same time, the US in 2003 ran a record US current account deficit near $550 billion, which is roughly equal to 5% of US GDP. That meant that the US had to import more than $1.5 billion of capital every calendar day in order to cover its trade and services deficit. Cyclical factors such as weak overseas demand for US exports were partly to blame for the US current account deficit. However, structural issues were the main cause of the current account deficit. Those issues were the heavy US demand for imported energy, the need for the US to import capital to cover the burgeoning US federal budget deficit, and the perennially weak US household savings rate. The OECD expects the massive US current account deficit to continue near 5.1% in 2004, meaning the dollar will remain under a cloud.

Euro – The euro rallied fairly steadily against the dollar starting in Q2-2002 and on through 2003. The euro in December 2003 posted a record high against the dollar of 1.1978 euros/USD. The euro's rally was mainly driven by the fact that the European Central Bank (ECB) held to a tighter monetary policy than the US Fed by keeping its refinancing rate pegged at 2% through the second half of 2003, a full percentage point higher than the Fed's 1.00% funds rate target. Higher European interest rates encouraged European investors to keep their investment capital at home in higher-yielding debt instruments. Still, Europe had its share of problems during 2003 with very weak economic growth, ongoing structural problems related to heavy business regulation, a sclerotic labor market, and fiscal problems where Germany and France couldn't keep their budget deficits below the 3% Euro-zone ceiling in 2003.

Yen – The dollar/yen traded mostly sideways in early 2003 but then dropped sharply in late 2003 to post a new 3-year low of 107.50 yen/$. The Bank of Japan spent much of 2003 intervening in support of the dollar/yen because Japanese government policy was to prevent a significant appreciation in the yen so that the Japanese economy could benefit from increased exports. In spite of that effort, the dollar dropped against the yen due to the dollar's weak fundamentals.

British Pound – The British pound rallied sharply against the dollar beginning in early 2002 and lasted through 2003. The British pound in December 2003 posted a 5-year high of $1.72, which was only about 1 cent below the 11-year high of $1.7325 posted in October 1998. The British pound was supported by the relative economic strength seen in Britain and by the fact that the Bank of England was the first of the major G7 central banks to raise interest rates, pushing the base rate up 0.25 percentage points to 3.75% on November 6, 2003.

Reuters-CRB Currencies Index   1977 = 100

Year	Jan.	Feb.	Mar.	Apr.	May	June	July	Aug.	Sept.	Oct.	Nov.	Dec.	Average
1994	128.54	129.57	130.89	130.57	132.23	134.18	137.60	137.51	139.78	141.94	140.29	137.85	135.08
1995	139.31	140.54	147.85	152.52	150.20	150.85	150.58	145.41	143.89	146.33	145.21	143.83	146.38
1996	141.69	141.01	141.12	139.61	138.11	138.37	139.53	140.52	139.51	138.74	139.92	137.47	139.63
1997	134.61	130.30	129.56	128.71	130.83	131.75	130.14	126.84	128.02	129.07	129.58	126.93	129.70
1998	125.06	126.10	125.65	124.96	124.33	122.86	121.89	120.65	126.18	130.98	128.86	130.69	125.68
1999	130.97	128.48	126.37	125.74	125.32	124.63	124.08	126.89	128.89	130.66	128.24	127.71	127.33
2000	127.65	124.37	124.01	123.43	119.42	122.54	121.59	119.04	117.11	115.99	114.89	117.55	120.63
2001	118.42	116.58	114.25	113.01	112.24	110.92	111.29	114.02	115.20	114.04	112.69	112.01	113.72
2002	110.20	109.38	110.40	111.33	114.54	117.39	121.30	119.68	119.54	119.02	120.77	121.97	116.29
2003	125.37	126.36	126.61	126.42	132.07	133.04	130.30	128.77	130.93	135.96	136.23	140.44	131.04

Average.   *Source: Reuters*

U.S. Dollars per British Pound

Year	Jan.	Feb.	Mar.	Apr.	May	June	July	Aug.	Sept.	Oct.	Nov.	Dec.	Average
1994	1.4933	1.4787	1.4921	1.4832	1.5038	1.5261	1.5446	1.5421	1.5647	1.6073	1.5864	1.5582	1.5317
1995	1.5742	1.5727	1.6004	1.6087	1.5886	1.5960	1.5955	1.5668	1.5595	1.5782	1.5612	1.5411	1.5786
1996	1.5289	1.5376	1.5278	1.5159	1.5154	1.5417	1.5538	1.5501	1.5595	1.5863	1.6629	1.6660	1.5622
1997	1.6590	1.6258	1.6095	1.6285	1.6325	1.6457	1.6717	1.6044	1.6020	1.6331	1.6887	1.6606	1.6385
1998	1.6347	1.6402	1.6615	1.6720	1.6370	1.6509	1.6429	1.6355	1.6814	1.6933	1.6613	1.6713	1.6568
1999	1.6495	1.6269	1.6213	1.6085	1.6147	1.5957	1.5754	1.6051	1.6237	1.6570	1.6206	1.6131	1.6176
2000	1.6395	1.6007	1.5810	1.5807	1.5084	1.5102	1.5082	1.4885	1.4341	1.4509	1.4252	1.4657	1.5161
2001	1.4767	1.4522	1.4438	1.4350	1.4268	1.4025	1.4149	1.4376	1.4646	1.4520	1.4358	1.4422	1.4403
2002	1.4314	1.4233	1.4233	1.4434	1.4601	1.4849	1.5566	1.5375	1.5562	1.5576	1.5718	1.5882	1.5029
2003	1.6184	1.6077	1.5832	1.5751	1.6230	1.6606	1.6242	1.5942	1.6141	1.6778	1.6899	1.7536	1.6352

Average.   *Source: FOREX*

Volume of Trading of British Pound Futures in Chicago   In Contracts

Year	Jan.	Feb.	Mar.	Apr.	May	June	July	Aug.	Sept.	Oct.	Nov.	Dec.	Total
1994	278,825	359,264	367,818	311,269	241,414	348,188	259,710	261,557	308,111	274,492	294,803	329,995	3,635,446
1995	295,416	263,900	351,089	124,103	195,292	264,635	133,691	219,644	271,815	129,859	191,694	334,952	2,776,090
1996	239,698	270,247	350,969	287,349	316,413	341,492	216,712	181,815	332,895	209,828	183,558	326,369	3,257,345
1997	240,280	168,714	289,352	185,273	236,648	279,338	265,125	194,612	234,092	202,058	144,975	286,099	2,726,566
1998	174,345	126,907	231,941	175,668	217,110	322,996	211,706	277,322	291,374	201,960	146,837	255,545	2,633,711
1999	182,398	151,829	350,218	205,348	285,044	332,107	250,328	178,203	275,899	177,921	163,232	181,470	2,733,997
2000	199,577	179,811	270,898	138,872	133,307	225,758	136,227	155,884	245,069	100,723	100,684	152,465	2,039,275
2001	125,643	126,230	198,749	126,975	166,262	248,926	164,219	183,572	197,117	178,944	161,367	187,388	2,065,392
2002	182,013	168,158	230,355	168,201	174,050	239,757	133,306	138,290	185,291	177,535	160,887	198,017	2,155,860
2003	158,326	161,822	217,383	158,137	164,674	288,625	214,871	163,548	284,467	212,596	206,163	364,543	2,595,155

Source: International Monetary Market (IMM), division of the Chicago Mercantile Exchange (CME)

Average Open Interest of British Pound Futures in Chicago   In Contracts

Year	Jan.	Feb.	Mar.	Apr.	May	June	July	Aug.	Sept.	Oct.	Nov.	Dec.
1994	39,223	43,878	35,554	44,725	46,577	41,801	37,633	34,988	40,751	42,648	49,684	65,834
1995	47,740	44,935	36,805	23,161	26,571	28,402	22,662	34,932	38,900	34,485	43,634	49,804
1996	40,315	50,106	52,349	54,954	52,573	61,461	55,080	50,862	53,868	51,934	62,128	47,652
1997	40,479	38,370	43,742	37,701	40,956	48,890	60,592	50,829	41,801	35,752	56,825	44,667
1998	33,616	31,282	38,712	41,256	47,303	55,511	39,156	49,645	63,756	53,458	54,004	53,578
1999	51,519	59,705	66,913	64,937	58,744	60,414	65,206	54,373	50,949	65,038	49,468	34,191
2000	37,192	45,329	51,645	41,488	51,965	43,009	30,766	36,320	42,781	30,978	34,627	32,913
2001	28,776	30,555	36,532	34,713	39,836	48,310	33,273	40,935	50,083	38,579	40,461	35,424
2002	26,450	31,023	30,474	39,952	46,178	47,355	38,138	31,320	31,513	29,599	40,901	36,671
2003	36,892	33,066	27,042	25,274	36,171	50,118	41,702	46,979	40,183	55,884	66,660	70,197

Source: International Monetary Market (IMM), division of the Chicago Mercantile Exchange (CME)

CURRENCIES

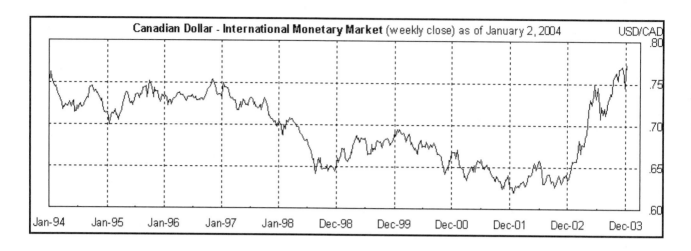

Canadian Dollars per U.S. Dollar

Year	Jan.	Feb.	Mar.	Apr.	May	June	July	Aug.	Sept.	Oct.	Nov.	Dec.	Average
1994	1.3175	1.3419	1.3645	1.3821	1.3805	1.3831	1.3818	1.3777	1.3536	1.3495	1.3649	1.3896	1.3656
1995	1.4120	1.3995	1.4065	1.3749	1.3607	1.3772	1.3609	1.3550	1.3495	1.3449	1.3525	1.3685	1.3718
1996	1.3664	1.3753	1.3651	1.3591	1.3690	1.3649	1.3687	1.3717	1.3691	1.3501	1.3382	1.3621	1.3633
1997	1.3484	1.3555	1.3727	1.3947	1.3793	1.3844	1.3769	1.3894	1.3865	1.3863	1.4127	1.4272	1.3845
1998	1.4407	1.4335	1.4159	1.4294	1.4449	1.4647	1.4865	1.5344	1.5212	1.5430	1.5400	1.5429	1.4831
1999	1.5189	1.4971	1.5174	1.4868	1.4614	1.4691	1.4877	1.4921	1.4772	1.4767	1.4671	1.4713	1.4852
2000	1.4480	1.4499	1.4600	1.4681	1.4944	1.4762	1.4778	1.4819	1.4841	1.5119	1.5425	1.5219	1.4847
2001	1.5021	1.5227	1.5579	1.5581	1.5403	1.5238	1.5294	1.5384	1.5665	1.5708	1.5934	1.5793	1.5486
2002	1.5996	1.5961	1.5872	1.5814	1.5491	1.5312	1.5447	1.5685	1.5747	1.5783	1.5715	1.5588	1.5701
2003	1.5395	1.5119	1.4752	1.4567	1.3819	1.3520	1.3801	1.3948	1.3638	1.3226	1.3128	1.3121	1.4003

Average.　*Source: FOREX*

Volume of Trading of Canadian Dollar Futures in Chicago　In Contracts

Year	Jan.	Feb.	Mar.	Apr.	May	June	July	Aug.	Sept.	Oct.	Nov.	Dec.	Total
1994	114,908	124,120	188,569	108,066	97,771	237,920	103,086	172,988	191,563	105,815	128,899	209,631	1,783,336
1995	126,828	138,251	188,703	91,458	119,567	148,314	128,002	131,981	261,402	213,286	97,156	174,511	1,819,459
1996	124,219	124,654	186,534	129,105	149,127	179,150	123,604	138,816	194,077	179,652	194,001	263,924	1,986,863
1997	189,879	127,310	295,170	151,141	230,733	276,764	146,870	187,149	262,260	268,428	130,528	322,879	2,589,111
1998	172,027	202,027	277,089	142,616	143,170	291,488	153,415	214,046	288,749	148,714	148,906	209,962	2,392,209
1999	170,975	173,034	279,945	203,427	164,352	309,740	216,066	186,031	263,380	167,703	165,587	277,211	2,577,451
2000	184,171	182,462	280,898	155,044	162,780	295,480	165,972	188,459	241,197	161,625	150,275	265,763	2,434,126
2001	194,738	201,075	317,860	188,203	228,359	350,967	221,558	235,883	265,096	214,085	218,108	287,335	2,923,267
2002	222,878	191,493	338,303	249,581	222,156	358,727	278,828	204,168	279,134	245,261	207,379	324,380	3,122,288
2003	270,811	256,672	475,496	289,192	353,096	494,150	331,345	266,189	393,329	285,682	294,352	509,304	4,219,618

Source: International Monetary Market (IMM), division of the Chicago Mercantile Exchange (CME)

Average Open Interest of Canadian Dollar Futures in Chicago　In Contracts

Year	Jan.	Feb.	Mar.	Apr.	May	June	July	Aug.	Sept.	Oct.	Nov.	Dec.
1994	28,277	38,157	48,411	42,730	44,363	42,845	35,370	39,582	49,312	40,706	42,353	59,763
1995	55,863	44,677	33,706	45,394	47,832	36,677	44,930	42,629	49,526	43,032	40,047	40,592
1996	31,028	37,674	38,551	41,411	46,470	37,141	37,522	42,063	44,014	68,674	82,817	72,586
1997	55,949	56,600	72,803	82,732	73,747	57,243	43,937	59,112	56,387	59,265	75,027	74,221
1998	63,300	67,862	61,528	58,938	64,859	74,027	71,313	75,193	60,863	51,967	61,318	50,271
1999	50,061	71,819	63,782	73,773	84,885	71,923	65,877	71,458	61,994	58,749	59,941	51,967
2000	66,374	64,528	58,621	60,389	76,444	69,033	67,198	65,370	65,779	81,995	77,746	65,452
2001	54,369	58,660	72,051	64,550	65,407	62,489	54,742	54,580	73,647	71,610	82,083	67,578
2002	68,927	72,132	70,484	68,120	81,574	86,250	74,347	63,116	63,605	57,031	60,648	71,852
2003	82,870	105,051	107,507	97,515	96,689	85,665	68,741	63,518	70,261	79,754	82,366	74,271

Source: International Monetary Market (IMM), division of the Chicago Mercantile Exchange (CME)

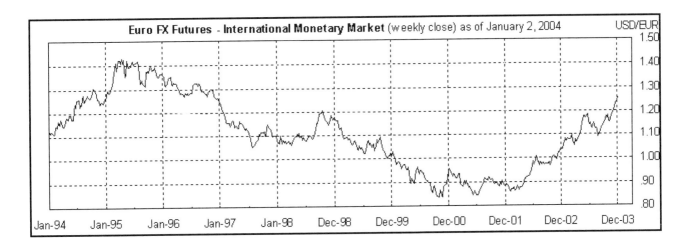

Euro[1] per U.S. Dollar

Year	Jan.	Feb.	Mar.	Apr.	May	June	July	Aug.	Sept.	Oct.	Nov.	Dec.	Average
1994	1.1138	1.1183	1.1412	1.1390	1.1636	1.1819	1.2167	1.2182	1.2314	1.2559	1.2357	1.2129	1.1857
1995	1.2380	1.2536	1.3030	1.3292	1.3085	1.3196	1.3340	1.2939	1.2782	1.2987	1.2947	1.2757	1.2939
1996	1.2629	1.2543	1.2544	1.2430	1.2278	1.2386	1.2554	1.2686	1.2587	1.2532	1.2695	1.2416	1.2523
1997	1.2088	1.1592	1.1460	1.1396	1.1441	1.1309	1.0999	1.0694	1.0976	1.1190	1.1418	1.1114	1.1306
1998	1.0859	1.0896	1.0854	1.0931	1.1099	1.1015	1.0991	1.1041	1.1566	1.2015	1.1680	1.1746	1.1224
1999	1.1584	1.1202	1.0882	1.0700	1.0622	1.0385	1.0366	1.0603	1.0501	1.0705	1.0327	1.0117	1.0666
2000	1.0135	.9842	.9644	.9450	.9080	.9496	.9394	.9042	.8706	.8533	.8554	.9004	.9240
2001	.9380	.9208	.9085	.8931	.8747	.8536	.8616	.9023	.9123	.9062	.8882	.8913	.8959
2002	.8828	.8706	.8767	.8866	.9179	.9567	.9924	.9781	.9810	.9818	1.0020	1.0210	.9456
2003	1.0636	1.0778	1.0795	1.0875	1.1580	1.1670	1.1374	1.1154	1.1260	1.1701	1.1714	1.2314	1.1321

Average. [1] Data through December 1998 are theoretical based on DEM * 1.95583.   *Source: FOREX*

Volume of Trading of Euro FX Futures in Chicago   In Contracts

Year	Jan.	Feb.	Mar.	Apr.	May	June	July	Aug.	Sept.	Oct.	Nov.	Dec.	Total
1998	----	----	----	----	3	0	0	0	0	0	0	3	36
1999	68,961	96,573	288,397	157,601	183,729	276,410	259,735	258,072	422,761	302,526	303,117	382,954	3,000,836
2000	404,903	334,967	452,393	289,398	318,313	382,162	234,921	303,320	486,283	287,741	297,038	466,719	4,258,158
2001	453,510	373,233	556,379	368,320	407,698	585,288	425,070	494,717	533,909	533,609	545,042	781,066	6,057,841
2002	567,785	582,292	783,331	650,169	611,387	917,661	821,580	525,538	675,268	525,230	426,665	625,372	7,712,278
2003	610,612	749,195	977,919	785,534	902,748	1,103,826	866,150	824,466	1,112,408	1,069,590	958,905	1,232,569	11,193,922

Source: International Monetary Market (IMM), division of the Chicago Mercantile Exchange (CME)

Average Open Interest of Euro FX Futures in Chicago   In Contracts

Year	Jan.	Feb.	Mar.	Apr.	May	June	July	Aug.	Sept.	Oct.	Nov.	Dec.
1998	----	----	----	----	1	1	1	1	1	1	0	7	7
1999	8,261	30,546	37,837	37,881	46,446	50,615	46,777	55,858	49,352	57,380	79,577	92,730
2000	63,124	68,413	61,180	59,110	67,644	63,361	57,723	69,561	77,617	73,314	58,846	65,346
2001	89,049	91,130	90,127	78,762	89,390	94,160	84,637	104,437	112,797	108,445	108,999	104,323
2002	100,258	108,955	113,075	112,413	136,660	135,364	112,462	101,992	99,365	85,462	103,156	108,602
2003	105,762	106,905	100,759	85,604	108,619	111,651	96,338	98,671	95,553	102,568	113,601	131,560

Source: International Monetary Market (IMM), division of the Chicago Mercantile Exchange (CME)

CURRENCIES

Japanese Yen per U.S. Dollar

Year	Jan.	Feb.	Mar.	Apr.	May	June	July	Aug.	Sept.	Oct.	Nov.	Dec.	Average
1994	111.33	106.22	105.00	103.36	103.76	102.37	98.65	99.88	98.78	98.36	98.08	100.08	102.16
1995	99.67	98.14	90.40	83.59	84.96	84.55	87.22	94.72	100.49	100.76	101.93	101.84	94.02
1996	105.66	105.57	105.90	107.23	106.42	108.91	109.21	107.84	109.87	112.40	112.35	114.01	108.78
1997	117.93	122.90	122.72	125.66	118.93	114.25	115.30	117.90	120.85	121.06	125.35	129.62	121.04
1998	129.39	125.71	129.04	131.79	135.01	140.40	140.75	144.51	134.45	120.49	120.41	117.01	130.75
1999	113.23	116.62	119.49	119.73	121.88	120.69	119.38	113.16	107.00	105.94	104.62	102.64	113.70
2000	105.29	109.49	106.34	105.65	108.19	106.15	108.03	108.06	106.79	108.39	108.94	112.18	107.79
2001	116.83	116.17	121.44	123.64	121.66	122.38	124.45	121.29	118.64	121.35	122.39	127.72	121.50
2002	132.77	133.50	131.11	130.75	126.29	123.25	118.02	119.04	120.88	123.92	121.50	121.83	125.24
2003	118.76	119.39	118.76	119.81	117.37	118.31	118.64	118.61	114.94	109.51	109.17	107.70	115.91

Average.   *Source: FOREX*

Volume of Trading of Japanese Yen Futures in Chicago   In Contracts

Year	Jan.	Feb.	Mar.	Apr.	May	June	July	Aug.	Sept.	Oct.	Nov.	Dec.	Total
1994	585,097	590,993	620,463	444,750	504,329	748,201	596,535	570,601	537,083	486,731	492,217	554,317	6,731,317
1995	604,876	499,587	839,134	450,204	451,565	465,660	305,499	499,051	662,417	363,440	407,842	370,287	5,919,562
1996	431,105	412,270	473,070	415,810	438,466	566,723	461,813	328,638	549,694	343,145	388,033	482,170	5,290,937
1997	411,601	457,171	564,776	402,703	604,616	564,155	424,281	528,237	611,843	529,557	425,817	644,814	6,169,571
1998	557,789	500,854	636,600	480,331	453,351	1,017,003	515,927	590,808	895,764	551,920	386,306	467,196	7,053,849
1999	418,110	524,625	672,674	400,434	473,385	687,098	476,937	422,277	679,114	310,526	390,508	469,118	5,924,806
2000	433,899	299,111	569,748	250,482	265,785	427,445	248,759	285,889	367,085	213,903	222,692	405,187	3,989,985
2001	258,575	223,715	598,374	295,424	351,158	459,419	307,350	369,357	518,622	286,191	350,088	595,855	4,614,128
2002	415,702	417,497	630,832	391,668	318,478	461,712	301,232	234,168	499,210	349,451	255,356	535,807	4,811,113
2003	423,901	388,298	634,434	453,373	495,643	621,041	518,764	426,979	730,977	396,636	353,359	641,804	6,085,209

Source: International Monetary Market (IMM), division of the Chicago Mercantile Exchange (CME)

Average Open Interest of Japanese Yen Futures in Chicago   In Contracts

Year	Jan.	Feb.	Mar.	Apr.	May	June	July	Aug.	Sept.	Oct.	Nov.	Dec.
1994	101,792	94,470	73,286	57,281	65,835	70,759	73,734	72,798	63,419	63,091	80,053	92,834
1995	86,569	86,852	77,649	63,379	67,644	56,285	48,680	63,463	73,830	67,336	73,335	70,268
1996	80,645	78,915	71,643	76,655	73,832	85,398	77,941	73,535	86,723	76,620	72,130	67,301
1997	73,391	82,542	78,466	81,117	85,984	73,322	62,488	82,369	96,468	90,080	130,606	121,001
1998	95,338	101,448	97,183	97,389	106,139	132,732	113,084	145,241	108,808	88,991	89,108	79,262
1999	78,767	81,859	96,271	87,829	118,819	120,681	118,329	136,826	115,884	82,657	87,869	87,595
2000	93,785	125,318	95,034	75,631	80,840	68,359	60,966	79,195	64,845	64,648	68,719	100,713
2001	89,680	90,652	109,536	96,244	89,377	82,838	93,430	107,588	102,710	75,096	97,368	137,756
2002	129,917	123,735	95,535	72,358	88,905	88,324	77,168	71,683	79,980	80,104	74,584	99,643
2003	116,574	107,929	101,809	81,168	107,090	102,507	107,450	125,884	149,978	152,368	138,799	147,255

Source: International Monetary Market (IMM), division of the Chicago Mercantile Exchange (CME)

Swiss Franc Futures - International Monetary Market (weekly close) as of January 2, 2004   USD/CHF

Swiss Francs per U.S. Dollar

Year	Jan.	Feb.	Mar.	Apr.	May	June	July	Aug.	Sept.	Oct.	Nov.	Dec.	Average
1994	1.4707	1.4558	1.4295	1.4363	1.4120	1.3723	1.3256	1.3176	1.2895	1.2636	1.2974	1.3275	1.3665
1995	1.2865	1.2694	1.1691	1.1362	1.1678	1.1564	1.1542	1.1958	1.1868	1.1444	1.1440	1.1624	1.1811
1996	1.1810	1.1942	1.1945	1.2194	1.2546	1.2574	1.2324	1.2022	1.2333	1.2583	1.2757	1.3296	1.2361
1997	1.3925	1.4543	1.4622	1.4614	1.4298	1.4419	1.4810	1.5123	1.4702	1.4507	1.4057	1.4393	1.4501
1998	1.4756	1.4616	1.4896	1.5050	1.4782	1.4951	1.5126	1.4927	1.4002	1.3376	1.3856	1.3600	1.4495
1999	1.3856	1.4273	1.4656	1.4972	1.5078	1.5359	1.5472	1.5092	1.5251	1.4891	1.5541	1.5827	1.5022
2000	1.5888	1.6326	1.6624	1.6638	1.7151	1.6422	1.6503	1.7146	1.7564	1.7727	1.7772	1.6778	1.6878
2001	1.6296	1.6681	1.6903	1.7115	1.7525	1.7842	1.7564	1.6791	1.6338	1.6337	1.6501	1.6569	1.6872
2002	1.6710	1.6972	1.6741	1.6527	1.5868	1.5389	1.4731	1.4968	1.4929	1.4922	1.4647	1.4360	1.5564
2003	1.3748	1.3609	1.3617	1.3770	1.3091	1.3196	1.3597	1.3813	1.3741	1.3234	1.3314	1.2627	1.3446

Average.   Source: FOREX

Volume of Trading of Swiss Franc Futures in Chicago   In Contracts

Year	Jan.	Feb.	Mar.	Apr.	May	June	July	Aug.	Sept.	Oct.	Nov.	Dec.	Total
1994	467,930	498,186	534,057	394,814	350,355	521,986	423,700	414,561	492,822	397,617	426,432	368,155	5,290,615
1995	441,183	439,121	579,510	321,736	402,216	374,352	249,013	353,817	417,160	328,248	311,200	289,039	4,506,595
1996	321,668	301,971	317,936	314,692	329,676	349,509	345,546	247,502	393,374	333,207	339,849	451,999	4,046,929
1997	360,482	316,346	436,807	343,582	432,533	389,458	316,105	305,189	394,103	429,683	220,959	344,886	4,290,133
1998	308,046	256,815	448,008	318,515	319,210	367,417	310,745	360,394	438,052	300,715	251,266	290,785	3,969,968
1999	294,598	262,128	416,987	284,021	323,252	384,664	351,105	311,835	482,425	407,570	287,172	304,493	4,110,250
2000	326,213	313,127	385,297	252,122	247,653	301,236	214,594	216,576	344,515	176,202	185,388	267,322	3,230,245
2001	193,487	203,006	280,280	168,700	191,601	325,961	257,565	229,380	261,837	227,481	238,232	297,281	2,874,811
2002	195,322	183,156	281,307	211,505	208,078	297,010	187,191	218,533	323,067	237,559	207,825	271,584	2,822,137
2003	236,109	289,893	412,709	256,871	277,835	384,893	314,997	252,056	349,889	237,163	283,751	300,492	3,596,658

Source: International Monetary Market (IMM), division of the Chicago Mercantile Exchange (CME)

Average Open Interest of Swiss Franc Futures in Chicago   In Contracts

Year	Jan.	Feb.	Mar.	Apr.	May	June	July	Aug.	Sept.	Oct.	Nov.	Dec.
1994	41,914	46,280	44,134	37,450	42,071	49,162	45,223	43,746	44,495	39,587	51,539	55,424
1995	39,726	44,364	39,358	30,270	30,586	26,766	23,121	30,267	34,228	34,889	38,033	44,741
1996	42,280	42,902	36,924	39,233	46,810	44,848	38,300	40,298	43,695	47,613	53,581	59,405
1997	51,652	54,114	51,121	45,725	48,651	42,530	55,279	58,098	49,296	43,585	51,822	48,560
1998	57,740	46,160	67,722	67,303	63,477	77,564	85,984	70,569	81,465	57,413	44,810	43,436
1999	39,434	58,279	66,250	66,530	73,322	75,322	66,603	71,060	60,214	65,020	67,936	64,507
2000	55,660	69,983	57,703	41,732	46,159	41,727	36,894	50,595	57,439	47,313	48,870	55,982
2001	50,121	44,405	46,470	41,641	53,265	60,943	53,687	60,986	61,689	48,962	53,445	46,771
2002	35,116	44,388	45,434	38,248	55,039	54,573	42,060	38,102	37,675	35,796	48,951	50,107
2003	56,268	57,099	50,008	37,451	53,642	49,688	41,489	50,677	52,641	54,259	62,584	60,475

Source: International Monetary Market (IMM), division of the Chicago Mercantile Exchange (CME)

CURRENCIES

United States Merchandise Trade Balance   In Millions of Dollars

Year	Jan.	Feb.	Mar.	Apr.	May	June	July	Aug.	Sept.	Oct.	Nov.	Dec.	Total
1994	-11,999	-13,573	-11,477	-13,405	-14,079	-14,009	-15,831	-14,232	-14,566	-14,926	-15,292	-13,272	-166,192
1995	-15,746	-14,221	-14,487	-16,051	-16,010	-15,862	-15,887	-13,415	-13,243	-13,108	-12,324	-12,600	-173,729
1996	-15,623	-12,911	-14,574	-15,897	-16,826	-14,839	-17,757	-16,759	-17,976	-15,320	-15,176	-17,695	-191,270
1997	-18,167	-16,780	-14,896	-16,505	-16,982	-15,610	-15,864	-16,909	-16,524	-16,270	-16,605	-16,962	-196,652
1998	-17,187	-18,331	-20,615	-20,860	-22,236	-20,404	-21,066	-22,291	-21,611	-20,990	-21,539	-21,059	-246,853
1999	-23,409	-25,233	-25,741	-25,851	-27,753	-30,381	-31,227	-30,518	-30,573	-31,576	-32,401	-32,255	-345,434
2000	-34,116	-34,708	-37,215	-36,934	-36,910	-37,827	-38,091	-36,839	-39,682	-40,205	-38,955	-39,360	-452,423
2001	-39,161	-34,648	-38,815	-37,270	-34,690	-35,760	-35,633	-34,458	-35,660	-35,034	-34,095	-31,534	-427,215
2002	-33,467	-36,412	-36,663	-39,773	-41,698	-40,830	-39,304	-42,070	-41,938	-40,647	-44,147	-47,447	-482,872
2003[2]	-44,859	-43,654	-47,507	-46,359	-46,654	-45,076	-45,032	-44,721	-46,574	-47,113	-43,605		-546,713

[1] Not seasonally adjusted.   [2] Preliminary.   *Source: Bureau of Economic Analysis, U.S. Department of Commerce (BEA)*

Index of Real Trade-Weighted Dollar Exchange Rates for Total Agriculture[2]   2000 = 100

Year		Jan.	Feb.	Mar.	Apr.	May	June	July	Aug.	Sept.	Oct.	Nov.	Dec.
1996	U.S. Markets	81.6	81.0	81.3	81.4	82.1	82.4	81.8	81.3	82.1	83.0	82.7	83.4
	U.S. Competitors	66.1	65.6	66.1	67.2	68.0	67.7	66.7	66.3	67.4	68.0	67.5	68.8
1997	U.S. Markets	84.8	85.6	86.6	86.9	84.8	84.7	86.3	87.6	87.5	88.1	90.5	94.1
	U.S. Competitors	70.8	73.3	74.3	74.9	73.6	74.2	76.6	78.8	77.5	76.9	77.1	80.3
1998	U.S. Markets	95.3	94.5	93.8	93.4	95.3	96.9	96.7	98.7	96.6	91.6	92.5	91.0
	U.S. Competitors	82.7	81.7	81.8	81.1	81.1	82.7	82.7	83.4	79.8	76.1	78.0	77.1
1999	U.S. Markets	92.1	94.1	94.9	94.6	95.8	95.8	95.5	94.5	94.5	93.5	93.8	93.9
	U.S. Competitors	78.6	81.8	84.0	85.2	86.2	87.7	87.6	86.5	87.4	86.0	88.5	89.4
2000	U.S. Markets	95.0	96.7	97.2	98.2	100.3	99.2	99.4	100.4	102.1	104.0	104.2	103.2
	U.S. Competitors	88.5	91.6	94.2	96.7	101.6	97.1	98.0	102.2	107.0	110.3	110.0	103.4
2001	U.S. Markets	103.0	104.8	107.0	107.4	107.8	109.0	108.9	107.0	107.5	106.6	107.9	108.6
	U.S. Competitors	99.2	102.7	104.9	106.9	109.1	112.3	110.8	105.7	105.8	106.1	106.6	105.2
2002	U.S. Markets	109.7	111.1	110.1	109.7	107.6	106.3	104.7	105.9	107.0	107.3	106.1	104.9
	U.S. Competitors	106.8	109.9	109.3	109.2	105.6	101.0	98.0	100.2	100.2	100.3	97.9	94.7
2003[1]	U.S. Markets	103.6	104.3	103.8	102.3	99.0	99.0	100.4	101.2	99.7	97.3	96.7	95.7
	U.S. Competitors	90.3	89.5	89.7	87.6	80.9	80.2	82.7	84.9	83.4	79.5	78.8	76.8

[1] Preliminary.   [2] Real indexes adjust nominal exchange rates for differences in rates of inflation, to avoid the distortion caused by high-inflation countries. A higher value means the dollar has appreciated. Federal Reserve Board Index of trade-weighted value of the U.S. dollar against 10 major currencies. Weights are based on relative importance in world financial markets.   *Source: Economic Research Service, U.S. Department of Agriculture*

United States Balance on Current Account[1]   In Millions of Dollars

Year	First Quarter	Second Quarter	Third Quarter	Fourth Quarter	Annual
1994	-16,427	-26,893	-38,521	-36,403	-118,244
1995	-20,975	-30,122	-33,230	-21,496	-105,823
1996	-15,904	-28,569	-44,161	-29,187	-117,821
1997	-23,367	-26,380	-40,586	-38,039	-128,372
1998	-31,519	-49,176	-67,690	-55,442	-203,827
1999	-51,124	-70,268	-89,564	-81,900	-292,856
2000	-84,780	-97,915	-116,015	-111,631	-410,341
2001	-104,004	-99,964	-103,636	-86,140	-393,744
2002	-106,728	-122,827	-122,724	-128,586	-480,865
2003[2]	-138,707	-139,394	-135,041		-550,856

[1] Not seasonally adjusted.   [2] Preliminary.   *Source: Bureau of Economic Analysis, U.S. Department of Commerce (BEA)*

Merchandise Trade and Current Account Balances   In Billions of Dollars

Year	Merchandise Trade Balance					Current Account Balance				
	Canada	Germany	Japan	Switzerland	U.K.	Canada	Germany	Japan	Switzerland	U.K.
1994	14.8	50.9	144.1	1.6	-17.0	-13.0	-24.3	130.3	17.5	-10.3
1995	25.8	65.1	132.1	.9	-19.0	-4.4	-20.7	111.2	21.4	-14.3
1996	31.1	70.6	83.7	.9	-21.4	3.4	-7.9	65.8	21.9	-13.5
1997	18.6	71.3	101.6	-.3	-20.2	-8.2	-3.1	94.3	25.5	-2.9
1998	15.3	77.8	122.5	-1.6	-36.2	-8.3	-6.7	121.0	26.0	-8.0
1999	25.9	70.9	123.2	-.2	-44.6	1.2	-19.1	107.0	28.4	-31.0
2000	39.9	58.6	116.6	-2.5	-45.4	18.1	-20.4	116.8	31.0	-25.6
2001	39.8	89.5	70.3	-2.1	-47.6	18.9	2.1	91.1	24.6	-25.1
2002[1]	33.9	104.0	88.7	1.4	-50.2	13.1	26.8	124.1	26.3	-29.1
2003[2]	36.6	109.3	112.2	1.8	-50.0	14.6	30.2	159.9	28.1	-32.4

[1] Estimate.   [2] Projection.   *Source: Organization for Economic Cooperation and Development (OECD)*

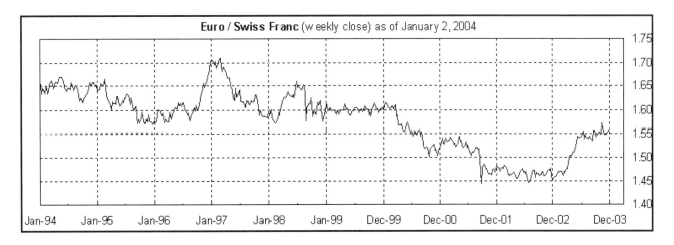

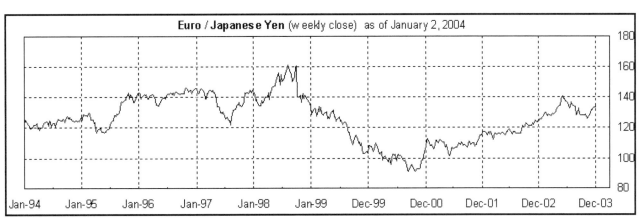

Diamonds

The diamond, which is the mineral form of carbon, is the hardest, strongest natural material known on earth. The word *diamond* is derived from *adamas*, the ancient Greek term meaning "invincible." Diamonds form deep within the Earth and are typically billions of years old. Diamonds have also have been found in and near meteorites and their craters. Diamonds are considered precious gemstones but lower grade diamonds are used for industrial applications such as drilling, cutting, grinding and polishing. The South African De Beers cartel controls the largest portion of the world's natural diamond production.

Supply – World production of natural gem diamonds in 2001, the latest reporting year, rose sharply to 68.500 million carats from 62.0 million in 2000. The world's largest producers of natural gem diamonds in 2001 were Botswana (representing 29% of world production), Russia at 17%, and Australia at 16%. World production of industrial diamonds fell to 48.0 million carats in 2001 (the latest reporting year) from 55.7 million in 2000. The world's largest producers of industrial diamonds are Australia (27%), Russia (24%), Congo (19%), South Africa (14%), and Botswana (11%).

Trade – The US relied on net imports for 89% of its consumption of natural diamonds, which totaled 1.8 million carats in 2002.

World Production of Natural Gem Diamonds In Thousands of Carats

Year	Angola	Aust- ralia	Bots- wana	Brazil	Central African Republic	China	Congo[3]	Ghana	Namibia	Russia	Sierra Leone	South Africa	World Total
1997	1,110	18,100	15,111	100	400	230	3,300	664	1,350	11,200	300	4,500	57,200
1998	2,400	18,400	14,800	100	330	230	5,080	658	1,350	11,500	200	4,280	60,400
1999	3,360	13,400	17,200	900	311	230	4,120	546	1,630	11,500	450	4,010	61,100
2000	3,914	12,000	18,500	1,000	346	230	3,500	792	1,450	11,600	450	4,320	61,600
2001[1]	4,653	10,700	19,800	1,000	360	235	9,100	936	1,487	11,600	450	4,470	69,500
2002[2]	5,400	15,100	21,300	700	375	235	9,100	770	1,350	11,500	450	4,350	76,500

[1] Preliminary. [2] Estimate. [3] Formerly Zaire. *Source: U.S. Geological Survey (USGS)*

World Production of Natural Industrial Diamonds[4] In Thousands of Carats

Year	Angola	Aust- ralia	Bots- wana	Brazil	Central African Republic	China	Congo[3]	Ghana	Russia	Sierra Leone	South Africa	Vene- zuela	World Total
1997	124	22,100	5,000	----	100	900	18,677	166	11,200	100	5,540	85	64,500
1998	364	22,500	5,000	----	200	900	21,000	165	11,600	50	6,420	17	68,700
1999	373	16,381	5,730	----	120	920	16,000	136	11,500	150	6,010	36	57,800
2000	435	14,700	6,160	----	115	920	14,200	198	11,600	150	6,470	80	55,500
2001[1]	517	13,100	6,600	----	120	950	9,100	234	11,600	150	6,700	38	49,500
2002[2]	600	18,500	7,100	----	125	955	9,100	193	11,500	150	6,530	40	55,200

[1] Preliminary. [2] Estimate. [3] Formerly Zaire. *Source: U.S. Geological Survey (USGS)*

World Production of Synthetic Diamonds In Thousands of Carats

Year	Belarus	China	Czech Republic	France	Greece	Ireland	Japan	Russia	South Africa	Sweden	Ukraine	United States	World Total
1997	25,000	16,000	5,000	3,000	750	60,000	32,000	80,000	60,000	25,000	8,000	125,000	450,000
1998	25,000	16,500	5,000	3,000	750	60,000	32,000	80,000	60,000	25,000	8,000	140,000	463,000
1999	25,000	16,500	3,000	3,000	750	60,000	32,000	80,000	----	25,000	8,000	161,000	420,000
2000	25,000	16,800	----	3,000	750	60,000	33,000	80,000	----	20,000	8,000	182,000	429,000
2001[1]	25,000	17,000	----	3,000	----	60,000	33,000	80,000	60,000	20,000	8,000	202,000	508,000
2002[2]	25,000	17,000	----	3,000	----	60,000	34,000	80,000	60,000	20,000	8,000	222,000	529,000

[1] Preliminary. [2] Estimate. *Source: U.S. Geological Survey (USGS)*

Salient Statistics of Industrial Diamonds in the United States In Millions of Carats

	Bort, Grit & Powder & Dust									Stones (Natural)					
	Production														
Year	Manu- factured Diamond	Secondary	Imports for Con- sumption	Exports & Reexports	In Manu- factured Products	Gov't Sales	Apparent Con- sumption	Price Value of Imports $ Per Carat	Secon- dary Pro- duction	Imports for Con- sumption	Exports & Reexports	Gov't Sales	Apparent Con- sumption	Price Value of Imports $ Per Carat	Net Import Reliance % of Con- sumption
1997	125.0	10.0	254.0	126.0	----	.7	264.0	.43	.5	2.8	.6	1.2	3.9	7.69	87
1998	140.0	10.0	221.0	104.0	----	[3]	267.0	.44	.5	4.7	.8	.8	5.2	3.92	90
1999	208.0	10.0	208.0	98.0	----	[3]	328.0	.44	.4	3.1	.7	.6	3.4	4.61	88
2000	248.0	10.0	291.0	98.0	----	----	451.0	.39	[3]	2.5	1.6	1.0	2.2	5.31	86
2001[1]	308.0	10.0	281.0	88.0	----	----	511.0	.31	[3]	2.5	1.0	.5	2.2	3.54	83
2002[2]	310.0	8.4	195.0	81.0	----	----	432.0	.34	[3]	2.2	1.0	.4	1.8	5.43	89

[1] Preliminary. [2] Estimate. [3] Less than 1/2 unit. *Source: U.S. Geological Survey (USGS)*

Eggs

Eggs are a low-priced protein source that are consumed worldwide. Each commercial chicken lays between 265-280 eggs per year. In the United States, the grade and size of eggs are regulated under the federal Egg Products Inspection Act (1970). The grades of eggs are AA, A, and B, and must have sound, whole shells and must be clean. The difference among the grades of eggs is internal and mostly reflects the freshness of the egg. Table eggs vary in color and can be determined by the color of the chicken's earlobe—white earlobes lay white eggs, reddish-brown earlobes lay brown eggs, etc. In the US, egg size is determined by the weight of a dozen eggs, not individual eggs, and range from Peewee to Jumbo. Store-bought eggs in the shell stay fresh for 3 to 5 weeks in a home refrigerator, according to the USDA.

Eggs are primarily used as a source of food, although eggs are also widely used for medical purposes. Fertile eggs, as a source of purified proteins, are used to produce many vaccines. Flu vaccines are produced by growing single strains of the flu virus in eggs, which are then extracted to make the vaccine. Eggs are also used in biotechnology to create new drugs. The hen's genetic make-up can be altered so the whites of the eggs are rich in tailored proteins that will form the basis of medicines to fight cancer and other diseases. The US biotech company Viragen and the Roslin Institute in Edinburgh have produced eggs with 100 mg or more of the easily-extracted proteins used in new drugs to treat various illnesses including ovarian and breast cancers.

Prices – The average wholesale price of shell eggs (large) recovered to 79.66 cents per dozen in 2003 from the 15-year low of 57.17 cents seen in 2002.

Supply – US egg production in 2003 was on track to fall 0.4% to 86.345 billion eggs from the record high of 86.659 billion in 2002. World production of eggs in 2002, the last full reporting year, rose +2.1% to a record high of 795.711 billion eggs. China produced 49% of the world's eggs in 2002, with production in 2003 rising +3.1% from 2002 to 389.000 billion eggs, and more than tripling since 1986. US egg production, which accounts for 10.7% of world production, has risen by about 23% over that same time frame. Russia is the world's third largest producer of eggs with 4.3% of world production. Mexico, the world's fourth largest producer of eggs, is an emerging force in the egg market with 4.2% of world production and has nearly doubled its production in the past 15 years.

Demand – US consumption of eggs in 2003 fell slightly by 0.4% to 6.160 billion dozen eggs from the record high of 6.184 billion in 2002. The forecast is for consumption to rise to a new record high of 6.205 billion in 2004. US consumption of eggs has increased due to the focus on a low-carbohydrate diet since eggs are high in protein.

Trade – US imports of eggs fell sharply by 42% to 8.0 million dozen eggs in 2003, returning to more normal levels after the 14-year high spike of 13.8 million seen in 2002. US exports of eggs in 2003 fell –7.9% to 168.0 million dozen from 182.5 million in 2002. US exports represent only about 2% of overall US production, showing that most US-produced eggs are consumed domestically.

World Production of Eggs   In Millions of Eggs

Year	Brazil	China	France	Germany	Italy	Japan	Mexico	Russia	Spain	Ukraine	United Kingdom	United States	World Total[3]
1993	12,700	235,960	15,355	13,678	11,502	43,252	21,471	40,300	8,454	11,766	10,645	72,072	593,734
1994	13,460	281,010	16,370	13,960	11,599	43,047	25,896	37,400	9,670	10,145	10,620	74,136	643,045
1995	16,065	301,860	16,911	13,838	12,017	42,167	25,760	33,720	9,983	9,404	10,644	74,592	670,211
1996	15,932	253,680	16,500	13,922	11,923	42,786	26,045	31,500	8,952	8,763	10,668	76,536	631,846
1997	12,596	282,350	16,084	14,025	12,298	42,588	28,170	31,900	9,450	8,242	10,752	77,676	666,748
1998	13,636	307,760	16,900	14,164	12,433	42,117	29,898	33,000	9,084	8,269	10,812	79,896	695,281
1999	14,768	365,300	17,550	14,341	12,660	41,975	32,428	33,000	9,216	8,740	10,293	82,944	762,077
2000[1]	15,654	377,420	17,500	14,350	12,400	41,800	33,310	33,500	8,900	8,000	10,000	84,420	778,995
2001[2]	16,435	389,000	17,450	14,350	12,400	42,000	33,640	34,200	9,000	7,700	9,800	85,020	795,711

[1] Preliminary.   [2] Forecast.   [3] Selected countries.   *Source: Foreign Agricultural Service, U.S. Department of Agriculture (FAS-USDA)*

Salient Statistics of Eggs in the United States

	-- Hens & Pullets --		Rate of Lay	--------- Eggs ---------						----- Consumption -----		
	On Farm Dec. 1[3]	Average Number During Year	Per Layer During Year[4]	Total Produced	Price in Cents Per Dozen	Value of Production[5] Million Dollars	Total Egg Production	Imports[6]	Exports[6]	Used for Hatching	Total	Per Capita Eggs[6]
Year	----- Thousands -----		(Number)	------- Millions -------			-------------------------- Million Dozen --------------------------					(Number)
1995	298,753	293,854	253	74,591	62.4	3,880	6,216	4.1	208.9	847.2	5,167	235.7
1996	303,754	297,958	256	76,281	74.9	4,762	6,367	5.4	253.1	863.8	5,242	234.6
1997	312,137	304,230	255	77,532	70.3	4,540	6,489	6.9	227.8	894.7	5,359	235.8
1998	321,718	312,035	255	79,754	66.8	4,439	6,671	5.8	218.8	921.8	5,522	240.1
1999	329,320	322,354	257	82,715	62.2	4,287	6,928	7.4	161.9	941.7	5,817	250.0
2000	332,410	327,985	257	84,386	61.8	4,345	7,050	8.4	171.1	940.2	5,927	251.8
2001	338,628	335,012	256	85,745	62.2	4,446	7,172	8.9	190.0	953.0	6,019	252.6
2002[1]	339,827	339,024	257	87,179	59.0	4,263	7,240	13.8	182.5	959.8	6,086	252.6
2003[2]	339,989	337,262	259	87,196			7,260	8.0	168.0	975.0	6,105	251.0

[1] Preliminary.   [2] Forecast.   [3] All layers of laying age.   [4] Number of eggs produced during the year divided by the average number of all layers of laying age on hand during the year.   [5] Value of sales plus value of eggs consumed in households of producers.   [6] Shell-egg equivalent of eggs and egg products.   *Source: National Agricultural Statistics Service, U.S. Department of Agriculture (NASS-USDA)*

EGGS

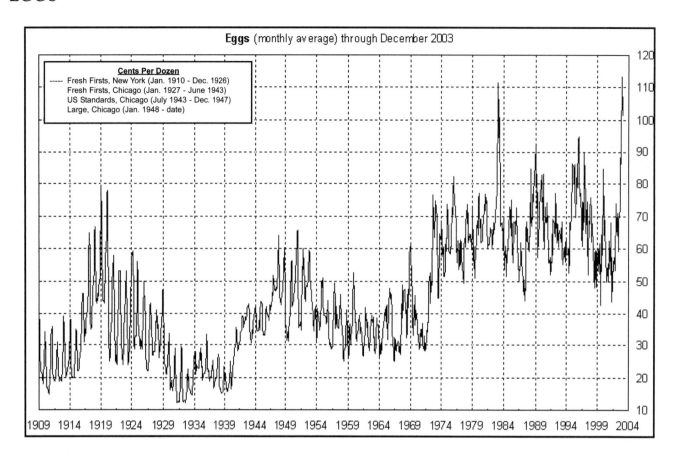

Eggs (monthly average) through December 2003

Cents Per Dozen
----- Fresh Firsts, New York (Jan. 1910 - Dec. 1926)
Fresh Firsts, Chicago (Jan. 1927 - June 1943)
US Standards, Chicago (July 1943 - Dec. 1947)
Large, Chicago (Jan. 1948 - date)

Average Price Received by Farmers for All Eggs in the United States   In Cents Per Dozen

Year	Jan.	Feb.	Mar.	Apr.	May	June	July	Aug.	Sept.	Oct.	Nov.	Dec.	Average
1994	62.3	64.0	65.7	61.3	58.7	57.7	58.4	60.3	60.8	57.7	61.7	62.0	60.9
1995	61.1	60.7	60.4	60.8	55.5	57.3	60.9	62.9	66.4	66.3	75.7	79.0	63.9
1996	78.2	75.7	79.1	75.8	69.3	70.7	69.8	73.7	75.8	73.5	82.0	87.9	76.0
1997	76.5	76.1	72.3	66.0	64.2	59.4	65.6	63.1	69.6	65.9	80.8	78.7	69.9
1998	74.3	64.9	69.9	63.7	54.9	59.6	58.2	65.0	63.3	66.3	72.8	75.5	65.7
1999	72.5	66.1	68.6	60.3	54.9	56.2	58.8	59.7	57.5	52.0	64.1	60.3	60.9
2000	57.8	67.8	56.9	64.7	52.0	61.8	56.5	66.4	59.2	66.8	72.0	80.7	63.6
2001	67.2	68.2	69.1	65.0	55.2	55.0	54.0	56.6	55.5	59.9	64.1	59.0	60.7
2002	62.3	55.9	68.5	52.2	50.5	62.1	60.8	66.4	57.1	56.0	70.7	62.8	60.4
2003¹	63.6	59.3	68.7	69.0	58.7	78.8	72.6	81.5	78.3	84.1	105.0	86.8	75.5

Source: Economic Research Service, U.S. Department of Agriculture (NASS-USDA)

Average Wholesale Price of Shell Eggs (Large) Delivered, Chicago   In Cents Per Dozen

Year	Jan.	Feb.	Mar.	Apr.	May	June	July	Aug.	Sept.	Oct.	Nov.	Dec.	Average
1994	62.07	64.89	68.28	58.34	55.12	55.05	58.75	60.63	59.21	55.93	61.50	62.88	60.22
1995	58.55	58.24	60.22	59.87	52.50	56.84	68.10	65.93	71.10	71.34	83.93	86.35	66.08
1996	85.25	80.00	86.12	78.88	69.77	73.00	74.73	80.59	83.80	79.13	93.68	94.60	81.63
1997	79.77	75.18	77.25	68.55	64.40	61.02	74.66	66.07	74.26	68.39	89.87	82.68	73.51
1998	75.20	64.92	74.68	63.64	51.91	61.86	65.00	68.76	67.76	71.45	75.85	75.27	68.03
1999	72.34	62.13	67.85	52.74	51.35	47.86	58.40	59.30	52.86	48.38	59.26	56.38	57.40
2000	54.97	59.65	52.93	61.71	42.59	55.18	52.80	64.39	58.08	66.45	74.26	84.90	60.66
2001	68.52	64.45	69.00	66.12	50.61	49.81	52.83	55.46	50.21	57.41	62.50	58.05	58.75
2002	60.43	52.00	68.00	47.23	43.73	56.40	53.02	57.16	53.20	54.43	74.00	66.38	57.17
2003	69.57	65.39	71.05	68.83	59.10	68.76	72.39	88.26	86.21	92.07	113.16	101.09	79.66

Source: National Agricultural Statistics Service, U.S. Department of Agriculture (NASS-USDA)

Total Egg Production in the United States   In Millions of Eggs

Year	Jan.	Feb.	Mar.	Apr.	May	June	July	Aug.	Sept.	Oct.	Nov.	Dec.	Total
1994	6,186	5,598	6,320	6,073	6,189	5,992	6,205	6,272	6,125	6,377	6,265	6,516	74,121
1995	6,369	5,714	6,448	6,177	6,251	6,010	6,145	6,146	5,990	6,260	6,232	6,523	74,265
1996	6,398	5,954	6,495	6,243	6,340	6,169	6,440	6,447	6,235	6,495	6,409	6,696	76,321
1997	6,577	5,909	6,625	6,355	6,519	6,292	6,457	6,500	6,366	6,664	6,572	6,841	77,677
1998	6,766	6,109	6,869	6,603	6,665	6,456	6,720	6,694	6,480	6,791	6,723	7,047	79,923
1999	6,979	6,281	7,052	6,784	6,941	6,742	6,903	6,971	6,860	7,131	7,018	7,279	82,939
2000	7,157	6,648	7,234	7,013	7,104	6,801	7,061	7,104	6,854	7,130	7,027	7,287	84,420
2001	7,226	6,524	7,336	7,099	7,240	6,992	7,195	7,221	7,044	7,347	7,191	7,420	85,835
2002[1]	7,264	6,581	7,417	7,105	7,297	7,126	7,347	7,356	7,147	7,412	7,226	7,451	86,729
2003[2]	7,390	6,665	7,424	7,187	7,327	7,105	7,403	7,367	7,112	7,439	7,326	7,520	87,265

[1] Preliminary.   [2] Estimate.   Source: National Agricultural Statistics Service, U.S. Department of Agriculture (NASS-USDA)

Per Capita Disappearance of Eggs[4] in the United States   In Number of Eggs

Year	First Quarter	Second Quarter	Third Quarter	Fourth Quarter	Total	Total Consumption (Million Dozen)	Year	First Quarter	Second Quarter	Third Quarter	Fourth Quarter	Total	Total Consumption (Million Dozen)
1993	46.1	44.0	43.8	46.0	179.7	3,825	1999	62.7	62.8	63.8	66.2	255.7	4,070
1994	45.0	43.0	43.9	46.0	177.9	3,864	2000	64.5	64.0	64.2	65.6	258.2	4,124
1995	44.0	43.1	42.7	45.0	174.9	3,834	2001	64.5	64.2	64.7	66.6	252.7	6,077
1996	44.5	42.1	43.4	45.0	175.0	3,893	2002[1]	62.4	62.6	64.0	64.6	255.5	6,184
1997	59.0	59.3	59.7	62.1	240.1	3,894	2003[2]	62.5	62.9	63.6	65.1	254.1	6,160
1998	60.5	60.5	61.1	63.2	244.9	3,993	2004[3]	62.8	62.7	63.8	65.0	254.4	6,205

[1] Preliminary.   [2] Estimate.   [3] Forecast   Source: Economic Research Service, U.S. Department of Agriculture (ERS-USDA)

Egg-Feed Ratio[1] in the United States

Year	Jan.	Feb.	Mar.	Apr.	May	June	July	Aug.	Sept.	Oct.	Nov.	Dec.	Average
1994	7.9	8.0	8.4	7.7	7.2	7.0	8.0	9.0	9.2	8.9	10.3	9.9	8.5
1995	9.4	9.3	9.0	8.9	7.5	7.6	8.0	8.5	8.9	8.6	10.1	10.0	8.8
1996	9.8	8.7	9.1	7.9	6.5	6.7	6.3	6.9	8.1	9.3	11.3	12.5	8.6
1997	10.1	9.9	8.6	7.4	7.1	6.6	8.2	7.8	9.3	8.7	11.4	11.0	8.8
1998	10.1	8.3	9.4	8.5	6.7	8.0	7.9	10.8	10.7	11.3	12.6	12.8	9.7
1999	11.7	10.6	11.3	9.2	7.8	8.2	9.9	10.1	9.3	8.0	11.9	10.1	9.8
2000	8.9	11.3	8.0	9.9	6.4	9.5	9.2	12.9	10.3	12.2	13.1	15.0	10.6
2001	10.9	11.4	11.6	11.3	8.6	8.5	7.9	8.4	8.5	10.3	11.5	9.3	9.9
2002	10.2	8.4	11.6	7.4	6.7	9.5	7.5	7.9	7.1	6.6	10.5	8.9	8.5
2003[2]	9.0	8.6	9.5	9.4	6.9	8.8	9.8	12.8	11.6	12.6	15.7	12.1	10.6

[1] Pounds of laying feed equivalent in value to one dozen eggs.   [2] Preliminary.   Source: Economic Research Service, U.S. Department of Agriculture (ERS-USDA)

Hens and Pullets of Laying Age (Layers) in the United States, on First of Month   In Thousands

Year	Jan.	Feb.	Mar.	Apr.	May	June	July	Aug.	Sept.	Oct.	Nov.	Dec.
1994	290,413	289,625	290,416	290,979	289,125	288,398	287,454	288,484	292,116	294,576	295,719	298,509
1995	300,331	298,202	297,689	296,290	294,697	290,806	289,018	286,519	289,595	290,889	294,486	298,293
1996	299,261	298,320	298,348	298,029	295,123	293,740	294,044	296,612	296,911	298,433	299,910	303,754
1997	305,011	303,449	304,276	303,997	302,766	300,692	299,007	298,844	300,138	305,664	307,146	312,137
1998	311,593	312,111	314,322	313,833	309,945	309,235	309,049	308,747	309,706	312,807	316,840	321,718
1999	322,137	322,382	323,161	322,162	320,783	320,211	320,672	318,944	321,349	323,365	327,135	329,320
2000	328,307	328,767	330,876	330,807	327,597	325,012	324,843	326,240	325,212	327,219	329,092	332,410
2001	332,107	335,449	336,131	337,472	336,755	333,522	332,274	332,148	333,417	336,573	337,549	338,625
2002	339,423	338,465	337,478	337,376	336,131	335,547	335,236	335,717	336,561	337,923	338,350	339,827
2003[1]	340,752	341,019	337,647	337,234	334,285	333,233	331,560	332,034	332,181	331,913	334,355	339,989

[1] Preliminary.   Source: National Agricultural Statistics Service, U.S. Department of Agriculture (NASS-USDA)

EGGS

Eggs Laid Per Hundred Layers in the United States   In Number of Eggs

Year	Jan.	Feb.	Mar.	Apr.	May	June	July	Aug.	Sept.	Oct.	Nov.	Dec.	Average
1994	2,199	1,987	2,246	2,160	2,204	2,142	2,222	2,230	2,152	2,227	2,180	2,176	2,177
1995	2,130	1,919	2,173	2,092	2,137	2,075	2,137	2,135	2,065	2,140	2,108	2,183	2,108
1996	2,141	1,996	2,178	2,105	2,153	2,099	2,180	2,172	2,094	2,171	2,124	2,199	2,134
1997	2,161	1,943	2,176	2,093	2,156	2,093	2,155	2,165	2,096	2,172	2,122	2,193	2,127
1998	2,169	1,950	2,187	2,117	2,153	2,088	2,175	2,165	2,082	2,157	2,109	2,190	2,129
1999	2,165	1,946	2,185	2,110	2,166	2,104	2,158	2,177	2,128	2,192	2,138	2,214	2,140
2000	2,178	2,016	2,186	2,130	2,177	2,093	2,169	2,181	2,101	2,173	2,125	2,193	2,144
2001	2,165	1,943	2,178	2,106	2,160	2,100	2,166	2,170	2,103	2,180	2,130	2,188	2,132
2002	2,143	1,947	2,198	2,110	2,173	2,125	2,190	2,188	2,119	2,192	2,139	2,189	2,143
2003[1]	2,168	1,959	2,181	2,123	2,180	2,122	2,214	2,202	2,127	2,218	2,166	2,223	2,157

[1] Preliminary.   *Source: National Agricultural Statistics Service, U.S. Department of Agriculture (NASS-USDA)*

Egg-Type Chicks Hatched by Commercial Hatcheries in the United States   In Thousands

Year	Jan.	Feb.	Mar.	Apr.	May	June	July	Aug.	Sept.	Oct.	Nov.	Dec.	Total
1994	33,236	31,086	33,489	35,657	35,322	31,985	29,613	31,295	31,587	32,066	26,075	30,166	381,577
1995	32,374	32,743	36,019	35,078	37,540	34,996	29,572	31,442	33,586	33,383	29,129	30,639	396,501
1996	31,580	34,608	36,890	35,740	38,028	33,017	31,920	31,782	31,930	32,319	30,947	32,879	401,640
1997	33,752	35,655	37,347	38,842	39,020	36,796	33,772	33,061	37,118	35,262	28,122	35,796	424,543
1998	37,168	34,597	40,604	39,057	39,206	39,323	35,576	33,398	37,959	34,667	31,217	35,501	438,273
1999	35,242	36,367	41,172	42,285	40,726	41,439	34,275	35,518	39,287	39,044	32,802	33,564	451,721
2000	34,181	34,659	38,877	36,653	41,185	37,268	33,240	34,328	36,325	36,080	32,438	35,178	430,412
2001	36,728	37,836	41,015	42,789	42,655	40,822	38,651	34,987	37,140	35,825	32,355	31,870	452,673
2002	35,647	34,465	36,977	38,088	38,751	35,136	35,573	35,681	35,734	32,149	31,146	31,973	421,320
2003[1]	33,499	29,988	36,726	37,531	38,206	36,344	35,593	33,179	35,777	34,999	30,129	33,856	415,827

[1] Preliminary.   *Source: National Agricultural Statistics Service, U.S. Department of Agriculture (NASS-USDA)*

Cold Storage Holdings of Frozen Eggs in the United States, on First of Month   In Millions of Pounds[2]

Year	Jan.	Feb.	Mar.	Apr.	May	June	July	Aug.	Sept.	Oct.	Nov.	Dec.
1994	13.7	14.8	15.8	15.6	16.3	15.2	15.4	19.0	19.7	17.8	20.0	19.1
1995	19.5	19.5	18.3	18.5	17.3	18.1	22.9	20.6	18.0	16.2	14.4	12.5
1996	13.8	15.6	16.2	12.4	11.5	11.4	11.7	13.5	15.0	14.9	12.6	10.4
1997	10.2	11.0	11.5	8.5	8.5	8.2	8.3	8.9	11.1	10.8	10.9	10.3
1998	9.7	12.0	12.3	10.4	9.2	12.9	10.2	11.8	9.0	8.2	9.0	9.3
1999	11.0	11.0	10.8	9.2	9.4	9.7	11.3	11.1	8.8	9.5	9.0	8.5
2000	10.1	17.6	14.8	14.0	12.8	13.5	14.1	14.4	14.9	14.4	16.6	15.4
2001	15.0	16.9	15.5	14.6	15.9	15.8	14.4	16.7	17.8	17.7	15.5	13.9
2002	13.7	13.1	13.9	11.7	10.2	11.1	12.7	12.9	13.2	13.2	13.1	11.2
2003[1]	13.5	15.3	17.1	17.0	15.7	17.7	18.0	18.6	18.0	16.6	16.9	14.9

[1] Preliminary.   [2] Converted on basis 39.5 pounds frozen eggs equals 1 case.   *Source: National Agricultural Statistics Service, U.S. Department of Agriculture (NASS-USDA)*

Electric Power

The modern electric utility industry began in the 1800s. In 1807, Humphry Davy constructed a practical battery and demonstrated both incandescent and arc light. In 1831, Michael Faraday built the first electric generator proving that rotary mechanical power could be converted into electric power. In 1879, Thomas Edison perfected a practical incandescent light bulb. The electric utility industry evolved from gas and electric carbon-arc commercial and street lighting systems. In 1882, in New York City, Thomas Edison's Pearl Street electricity generating station established the industry by displaying the four key elements of a modern electric utility system: reliable central generation, efficient distribution, a successful end use, and a competitive price.

Electricity is measured in units called watts and watt-hours. Electricity must be used shortly after it is generated and cannot be stored to any significant degree. That means the power utilities must match the level of electricity generation to the level of demand in order to avoid wasteful over-production. The power industry has been deregulated to some degree in the past decade and now major utility companies sell power back and forth across major national grids in order to meet supply and demand needs. The quick changes in the supply-demand situation means that the price of electricity can be volatile.

Electricity futures trade at the New York Mercantile Exchange (NYMEX). The futures contract is a financially settled contract, which is priced based on electricity prices in the PJM western hub at 111 delivery points, mainly on the utility transmission systems of Pennsylvania Electric Co. and the Potomac Electric Co. The contract is priced in dollars and cents per megawatt hours.

Supply – US electricity production in 2002 was approximately 2.6 trillion kilowatt-hours, little changed from the 2001 level. The 2001-2002 levels were down from the 3.0 3.1 trillion kilowatt-hour range seen in the 1996-2000 period. The lower supply and demand for electricity in 2001 and 2002 was caused by the weaker US economy since there is a direct correlation between economic growth and electricity generation and usage.

US electricity generation in 2001 required the use of 2.686 trillion cubic feet of natural gas, 806 million short tons of coal, and 126 million barrels of fuel oil. In terms of kilowatt-hours, coal is the most widely used source of electricity production, accounting for about 56% of US electricity production. The other fuels in order of electricity production share are nuclear (23%), natural gas (9%), hydro (9%), and fuel oil (3%). Alternative sources of fuel for electricity generation that are gaining favor include biomass, wind, and fuel cells.

Demand – Residential use of electricity accounts for the largest single category of electricity demand with usage of 1.141 trillion kilowatt hours in 1999, followed by industrial (1.018 trillion kilowatt hours), commercial (971 billion kilowatt hours), public authorities other than street lighting (91 billion kilowatt hours), and street and highway lighting (16 billion kilowatt hours).

World Electricity Production (Monthly Average) In Millions of Kilowatt Hours

Year	Australia	Canada	China	Germany	India	Italy	Japan	Rep. of Korea	Russia	South Africa	Ukraine	United Kingdom	United States
1994	13,959	44,954	75,312	37,786	29,250	19,323	80,361	13,749	72,993	15,825	16,910	27,042	271,150
1995	14,449	45,206	83,977	44,754	31,656	20,228	82,490	15,388	71,669	16,016	16,193	27,970	279,820
1996	14,806	46,307	90,109	46,277	32,991	20,340	84,113	17,125	70,600	16,096	15,166	27,191	287,250
1997	15,256	47,929	94,539	45,961	35,146	20,898	86,676	18,704	69,511	16,108	14,834	27,012	291,185
1998	14,737	45,259	97,183	46,367	37,379	21,659	76,763	17,942	68,930	17,119	14,402	27,914	301,489
1999	15,399	46,496	100,345	45,820	40,148	22,136	76,755	19,944	70,611	16,961	14,342	28,095	308,712
2000	15,712	48,563	109,426	46,417	41,725	22,986	78,391	22,200	73,117	17,557	14,287	28,484	316,662
2001	15,495	47,009	118,439	47,107	42,434	23,242	77,742	23,768	74,031	17,508	14,414	28,825	314,876
2002	15,646	49,521	133,513	45,375	44,141	23,660	77,521	25,500	74,078	18,142	14,477		292,134
2003[2]	15,659		149,680		44,907	24,752	75,394	26,476	73,295	17,534	15,299		

[1] Preliminary.   [2] Estimate.   *Source: United Nations*

Installed Capacity, Capability & Peak Load of the U.S. Electric Utility Industry In Millions of Kilowatt Hours

Year	Total Electric Utility Industry	Hydro	Gas, Turbine & Steam	Nuclear Power	Internal Combustion	Investor Owned	Cooperative	Subtotal Gov't	Municipal Utilities	Federal	Power Districts, State Projects	Capability at Winter Peak Load	Non-Coincident Winter Peak Load	Capacity Margin Non-Coincident Peak Load (%)	Total Electric Utility Industry Generation	Annual Peak Load Factor (%)
1990	735.1	87.2	531.1	108.0	8.7	568.8	26.3	139.9	40.1	65.4	34.4	696.8	484.0	20.4	2,808.2	60.4
1991	740.0	88.7	534.1	108.4	8.8	573.0	26.5	140.5	40.4	65.6	34.5	703.2	485.4	20.2	2,825.0	60.9
1992	741.7	89.7	534.5	107.9	9.6	572.9	26.0	142.7	41.6	66.1	35.0	707.8	493.0	21.1	2,797.2	61.1
1993	744.7	90.2	536.9	107.8	9.8	575.2	26.1	143.4	41.8	66.1	35.5	712.0	521.7	17.1	2,882.5	61.0
1994	746.0	90.3	537.9	107.9	9.9	574.8	26.4	144.7	42.0	66.3	36.4	715.1	518.3	16.7	2,910.7	61.2
1995	750.5	91.1	541.6	107.9	9.9	578.7	27.1	144.8	42.2	65.9	36.6	727.7	544.7	13.2	2,994.5	59.8
1996	756.5	91.0	546.6	109.0	9.9	582.2	27.2	147.1	43.0	67.2	36.9	740.5	545.1	14.9	3,073.1	61.0
1997	759.9	92.5	549.7	107.6	10.0	582.5	28.0	149.4	43.8	68.9	36.7	743.8	560.2	13.4	3,119.1	61.3
1998	728.3	91.2	522.1	104.8	10.2	531.3	32.5	164.5	50.5	68.7	45.3	835.3	652.4	12.0	3,212.2	62.0
1999[1]	678.0	89.8	476.3	102.3	9.6	483.7	34.6	159.6	50.2	68.7	40.7	848.9	656.3	10.3	3,173.7	61.2

[1] Preliminary.   *Source: Edison Electric Institute (EEI)*

ELECTRIC POWER

Available Electricity and Energy Sales in the United States   In Billions of Kilowatt Hours

	Net Generation — Electric Utility Industry								Sales to Ultimate Customers								
Year	Total[2]	Hydro	Natural Gas	Coal	Fuel Oil	Nu-clear	Other Source[3]	Total	Total Million $	Total	Resi-den-tial	Inter-depart-mental	Com-mercial	Indust-rial	Street & Highway Lighting	Other Public Auth.	Rail ways & Rail-roads
1987	2,572	249.7	272.6	1,464	118.5	455.3	12.3	2,719	155,734	2,441	846	4.5	658.4	844	14.4	63.0	4.9
1988	2,704	222.9	252.8	1,541	148.9	527.0	12.0	2,879	162,449	2,561	886	4.2	697.8	882	14.6	64.6	5.1
1989	2,784	265.1	266.6	1,554	158.3	529.4	11.3	2,985	169,903	2,636	899	4.3	715.9	913	14.6	69.3	5.3
1990	2,808	279.9	264.1	1,560	117.0	576.9	10.7	3,041	176,929	2,705	916	4.2	738.9	932	15.2	72.8	5.3
1991	1,825	275.5	264.2	1,551	111.5	612.6	10.1	3,071	186,359	2,762	955	2.6	765.7	947	15.6	76.1	5.3
1992	2,797	239.6	263.9	1,576	88.9	618.8	10.2	3,083	188,480	2,763	936	2.6	761.3	973	15.8	77.2	5.2
1993	2,883	265.1	258.9	1,639	99.5	610.3	9.6	3,197	198,220	2,861	995	2.7	794.6	977	18.1	69.7	5.4
1994	2,911	243.7	291.1	1,635	91.0	640.4	8.9	3,254	202,706	2,935	1,008	3.0	820.3	1,008	18.5	70.6	5.8
1995	2,995	293.7	307.3	1,653	60.8	673.4	6.4	3,358	207,717	3,013	1,043	2.1	862.7	1,013	17.9	69.9	5.5
1996	3,073	324.5	262.3	1,737	67.0	674.7	7.2	3,447	212,455	3,101	1,083	2.5	887.4	1,034	18.0	70.3	5.3
1997	3,119	333.5	283.1	1,789	77.1	629.4	7.5	3,494	215,059	3,146	1,076	2.6	928.6	1,038	19.7	75.6	5.3
1998	3,212	304.4	309.2	1,807	110.2	673.7	7.2	3,618	218,346	3,264	1,130	[4]	979.4	1,051	16.3	87.2	[4]
1999	3,174	293.9	296.4	1,768	86.9	725.0	3.7	3,705	219,873	3,312	1,145	[4]	1,002.0	1,058	15.9	90.9	[4]
2000[1]	3,015	248.0	291.0	1,697	72.0	705.0	2.0	3,800	228,313	3,413	1,193	[4]	1,037.9	1,071	[4]	110.6	[4]

[1] Preliminary.   [2] Includes internal combustion.   [3] Includes electricity produced from geothermal, wood, waste, wind, solar, etc.   [4] Included in Other.
NA = Not available.   Source: Edison Electric Institute (EEI)

Electric Power Production by Electric Utilities in the United States   In Millions of Kilowatt Hours

Year	Jan.	Feb.	Mar.	Apr.	May	June	July	Aug.	Sept.	Oct.	Nov.	Dec.	Total
1989	232,747	219,826	226,742	208,042	220,124	235,689	257,050	258,687	227,150	219,910	219,300	259,038	2,784,304
1990	237,289	212,880	226,034	211,070	222,908	249,175	266,375	268,527	237,017	224,694	213,748	237,434	2,808,151
1991	248,455	210,821	221,400	209,004	234,373	248,427	271,976	268,115	233,885	223,430	221,377	233,760	2,825,023
1992	243,970	217,761	224,665	210,837	220,355	236,842	266,148	255,203	234,760	221,289	221,263	244,126	2,797,219
1993	245,782	224,617	234,801	211,374	222,396	249,633	282,292	279,132	236,603	223,629	225,855	246,412	2,882,525
1994	261,697	225,011	231,544	214,817	227,703	263,859	278,149	274,645	237,663	227,972	224,745	242,906	2,910,712
1995	253,077	228,127	233,675	217,381	236,381	256,083	292,827	304,709	245,574	234,409	234,117	258,170	2,994,529
1996	268,713	245,388	247,989	226,423	251,570	268,644	289,329	290,458	250,672	240,674	241,077	258,138	3,077,442
1997	273,410	233,907	244,659	230,512	243,143	266,588	304,628	294,557	266,649	253,267	243,726	267,477	3,122,523
1998	265,435	235,340	256,575	232,457	265,077	291,029	317,521	312,538	279,198	251,380	239,089	266,532	3,212,171
1999	275,230	239,825	258,678	238,969	255,266	281,233	318,745	307,835	261,347	243,212	235,129	258,205	3,173,674
2000	265,991	237,324	241,397	227,031	253,890	268,128	279,421	286,682	245,137	228,389	226,765	255,229	3,015,383
2001	236,467	199,802	211,942	197,499	215,508	233,622	253,400	258,901	214,236	204,307	192,518	211,742	2,629,944
2002	215,684	187,929	200,833	194,038	208,436	227,940	248,962	241,449	215,408	201,705	194,205	212,868	2,549,457
2003[1]	219,933	193,289	197,193	186,681	206,434	217,934	242,259	241,738	208,026	198,244			2,534,077

[1] Preliminary.   Source: Energy Information Administration, U.S. Department of Energy (EIA-DOE)

Use of Fuels for Electric Generation in the United States

	Consumption of Fuell			Total Fuel in Coal Equivalent[3] (Thousand Short Tons)	Net Generation by Fuels4 (Million Kilowatthour)	Pounds of Coal Per Kilowatthour (Pounds)	Cost of Fossil-fuel at Elec. Util. Cents/MBTU	Average Cost of Fuel Per Kiliowatthour (Cents)	Heat Rate BTU Per kilowatthour	Cost Per Million BTU Consumed (Cents)
Year	Coal (Thousand Short Tons)	Fuel Oil (Thousand Barels)[2]	Gas (Million Cubic Feet)							
1989	766,888	267,451	2,787,012	1,004,964	1,978,577	.987	167.5	1.79	10,312	174.0
1990	773,549	200,152	2,787,332	988,300	1,940,712	.997	168.9	1.80	10,366	174.1
1991	772,268	188,494	2,789,014	987,469	1,926,801	.996	160.3	1.75	10,322	169.6
1992	779,860	152,329	2,765,608	983,484	1,928,683	.990	159.0	1.72	10,340	166.6
1993	813,508	168,556	2,682,440	1,017,086	1,997,605	.993	159.5	1.72	10,351	166.6
1994	817,270	155,377	2,987,146	1,033,575	2,017,646	.999	152.6	1.59	10,425	152.6
1995	829,007	105,956	3,196,507	1,039,174	2,021,064	1.003	145.3	1.48	10,173	145.2
1996	874,681	116,680	2,732,107	1,063,755	2,066,666	1.007	151.9	1.55	10,176	151.9
1997	900,361	132,147	2,968,453	1,103,037	2,148,756	1.005	152.2	1.53	10,081	152.2
1998	910,867	187,461	3,258,054	1,147,317	2,226,860	.996	143.8	1.49	10,360	143.8
1999	894,120	151,868	3,113,419	1,113,614	2,150,989	1.012	144.1	1.48	10,301	144.1
2000	859,335	125,788	3,043,094				173.8			
2001	806,269	133,456	2,686,287				173.0			
2002[1]	767,803	99,219	2,259,684				151.5			

[1] Preliminary.   [2] 42-gallon barrels.   [3] Coal equivalents are calculated on the basis of Btu instead of generation data.   [4] Excludes wood & waste fuels.
Source: Edison Electric Institute (EEI)

Fertilizer

Fertilizer is a natural or synthetic chemical substance or mixture that enriches soil to promote plant growth. The three primary nutrients that fertilizers provide are nitrogen, potassium, and phosphorus. In ancient times, and still today, many commonly used fertilizers contain one or more of the three primary ingredients: manure (containing nitrogen), bones (containing small amounts of nitrogen and large quantities of phosphorus), and wood ash (containing potassium).

At least fourteen different nutrients have been found essential for crops. These include three organic nutrients (carbon, hydrogen, and oxygen, which are taken directly from air and water), three primary chemical nutrients (nitrogen, phosphorus, and potassium), and three secondary chemical nutrients (magnesium, calcium, and sulfur). The others are micronutrients or trace elements include iron, manganese, copper, zinc, boron, and molybdenum.

Prices – The price of ammonia, a key source of ingredients for fertilizers, in 2002 fell to a 4-year low of $137 per metric ton from $183 in 2001, and was well below the 10-year average price of $161 per metric ton. The average price of phosphate rock in the US rose 3% to $27.69 per metric ton from $26.81 per metric ton in 2001 and was above the 10-year average price of $24.98 per metric ton. The average price of potash in the US fell to a 3-year low of $155.00 per metric ton from $165.00 in 2001, and was right on the 10-year average price.

Supply – World production of nitrogen in 2002 rose +3.8% to a record high 109.000 million metric tons. The world's largest producers of nitrogen in 2002 were China with 27.6% of world production, the US (9.9%), India (9.0%),

and Russia (7.9%). US nitrogen production in 2002 rose +16% to 10.800 million metric tons.

World production of phosphate rock, basic slag and guano rose +7.1% to a 4-year high of 135.000 million metric tons in 2002 from 126.000 million metric tons in 2001. The world's largest producers are the US with 26.7% of world production in 2002, China (17.0%), Morocco (17.0%), and Russia (7.9%). US production in 2002 rose +13.2% to 36.100 million metric tons from the record low of 31.900 million in 2001.

World production of marketable potash rose by +0.4% to 26.500 million metric tons in 2002 from 26.400 million metric tons in 2001. The world's largest producers of potash in 2002 were Canada with 30.9% of world production, Russia (16.6%), Belarus (14.3%), and Germany (13.0%). US production of potash in 2002 was unchanged from 2001 at 1.200 million metric tons and accounted for only 4.5% of world production.

Demand – US consumption of nitrogen in 2002 rose +3.8% to 11.000 million metric tons. US consumption of phosphate rock in 2002 rose +5.9% to 37.400 million metric tons. US consumption of potash in 2002 was unchanged from 2001 at 5.300 million metric tons.

Trade – US imports of nitrogen in 2002 rose +2.6% to 4.670 million metric tons and the US relied on imports for 29% of consumption. US imports of phosphate rock in 2002 rose +8.0% to 2.700 million metric tons from 2.500 million metric tons in 2001. US imports of potash rose +7.7% to 4.620 million metric tons in 2002, and imports accounted for 80% of US consumption.

World Production of Ammonia   In Thousands of Metric Tons of Contained Nitrogen

Year	Canada	China	France	Germany	India	Indo-nesia	Japan	Mexico	Nether-lands	Poland	Russia	United States	World Total
1994	3,470	20,100	1,480	2,170	7,503	3,012	1,483	2,030	2,479	1,230	7,300	13,300	93,600
1995	3,773	22,600	1,470	2,518	8,287	3,336	1,584	1,992	2,580	1,726	7,900	13,000	100,000
1996	3,840	25,200	1,570	2,485	8,549	3,647	1,490	2,054	2,652	1,713	7,900	13,400	105,000
1997	4,081	24,700	1,757	2,471	9,328	3,770	1,509	1,448	2,478	1,824	7,150	13,300	103,000
1998	3,900	25,800	1,570	2,512	10,240	3,600	1,389	1,449	2,350	1,683	6,500	13,800	104,000
1999	4,135	28,300	1,580	2,406	10,376	3,450	1,385	1,003	2,430	1,474	7,633	12,900	107,000
2000	4,130	27,700	1,620	2,599	10,148	3,620	1,410	701	2,540	1,862	8,735	11,800	108,000
2001[1]	3,439	28,200	1,380	2,522	10,081	3,655	1,318	548	1,940	1,735	8,690	9,350	105,000
2002[2]	3,594	30,100	1,050	2,560	9,827	4,200	1,188	537	1,970	1,311	8,600	10,800	109,000

[1] Preliminary.   [2] Estimate.   *Source: U.S. Geological Survey (USGS)*

Salient Statistics of Nitrogen[3] (Ammonia) in the United States   In Thousands of Metric Tons

Year	Net Import Reliance as a % of Apparent Consumption	Production[3] (Fixed) Fertilizer	Production[3] (Fixed) Non-fertilizer	Total	Imports[4] (Fixed)	Exports	Produced	Nitrogen[5] Compounds Consumption	Stocks, Dec. 31- Ammonia	Stocks, Dec. 31- Fixed Nitrogen Compounds	Ammonia Consumption (Apparent)	Urea FOB Gulf[6] Coast	Urea FOB Corn Belt	Ammonium Nitrate: FOB Corn Belt	Ammonia FOB Gulf Coast
1995	15	11,600	1,410	13,010	2,630	319	10,400	10,700	959	1,580	15,300	217-222	220-235	162-170	191
1996	19	11,500	1,720	13,220	3,390	435	11,502	11,100	881	1,390	16,400	188-190	197-210	160-170	190
1997	16	11,400	1,900	13,300	3,530	395	11,441	11,300	1,530	2,220	15,800	102-103	125-135	122-125	173
1998	19	11,800	1,950	13,800	3,460	614	11,712	11,300	1,050	1,270	17,100	82-85	110-125	110-115	121
1999	21	11,400	1,550	12,900	3,890	562	11,303	11,500	996	1,240	16,300	107-110	115-125	110-115	109
2000	20	10,300	1,510	11,800	3,880	662	10,272	12,500	1,120	1,400	14,900	158-161	175-180	140-150	169
2001[1]	29	8,420	929	9,350	4,550	647	7,852	10,600	916	1,340	13,500	104-108	130-135	120-130	183
2002[2]	29	9,730	1,100	10,800	4,670	437	8,474	11,000	771	1,100	15,200	128-132	150-160	120-130	137

[1] Preliminary.   [2] Estimate.   [3] Anhydrous ammonia, synthetic.   [4] For consumption.   [5] Major downstream nitrogen compounds.   [6] Granular.

E = Net exporter.   *Source: U.S. Geological Survey (USGS)*

FERTILIZER

World Production of Phosphate Rock, Basic Slag & Guano   In Thousands of Metric Tons (Gross Weight)

Year	Brazil	China	Egypt	Israel	Jordan	Morocco	Russia	Senegal	Syria	Togo	Tunisia	United States	World Total
1993	3,419	21,200	1,585	3,680	4,129	18,193	9,400	1,667	931	1,794	5,500	35,494	119,000
1994	3,937	24,100	632	3,961	4,217	19,764	8,000	1,587	1,203	2,149	5,699	41,100	127,000
1995	3,888	19,300	765	4,063	4,984	20,684	9,000	1,500	1,551	2,570	7,241	43,500	131,000
1996	3,823	21,000	808	3,839	5,355	20,855	8,300	1,340	2,189	2,731	7,167	45,400	135,000
1997	4,276	24,500	1,067	4,047	5,896	23,084	9,800	1,565	2,392	2,631	6,941	45,900	143,000
1998	4,421	25,000	1,076	4,067	5,925	23,587	10,100	1,478	2,496	2,250	7,901	44,200	144,000
1999	4,344	20,000	1,018	4,128	6,014	22,163	11,400	1,814	2,084	1,600	8,006	40,600	134,000
2000	4,725	19,400	1,096	4,110	5,526	21,463	11,100	1,739	2,166	1,400	8,339	38,600	132,000
2001[1]	4,805	21,000	972	3,511	5,843	21,983	10,500	1,708	2,043	1,060	8,144	31,900	126,000
2002[2]	4,850	23,000	1,500	3,500	7,179	23,000	10,700	1,500	2,400	1,281	7,750	36,100	135,000

[1] Preliminary.   [2] Estimate.   *Source: U.S. Geological Survey (USGS)*

Salient Statistics of Phosphate Rock in the United States   In Thousands of Metric Tons

Year	Mine Production	Marketable Production	Value Million Dollars	Imports For Consumption	Exports	Apparent Consumption	Stocks, Dec. 31 (Producer)	Price - $ Avg. Per Metric Ton (FOB Mine)	Avg. Price of Florida & N. Carolina - $/Tonne - FOB Mine (-60% to +74%) - Domestic	Export	Average
1993	107,000	35,500	759	534	3,200	38,300	9,220	21.38	21.26	28.51	21.89
1994	157,000	41,100	869	1,800	2,800	42,900	5,980	21.14	21.79	25.60	22.08
1995	165,000	43,500	947	1,800	2,760	42,700	5,710	21.75	21.29	28.35	21.75
1996	179,000	45,400	1,060	1,800	1,570	43,700	6,390	23.40	22.90	35.82	23.40
1997	166,000	45,900	1,080	1,830	335	43,600	7,910	24.50	24.40	34.80	24.50
1998	170,000	44,200	1,130	1,760	378	45,000	7,920	25.87	25.46	42.70	25.87
1999	161,000	40,600	1,240	2,170	272	43,500	6,920	31.49	30.56	41.96	31.49
2000	163,000	38,600	932	1,930	299	39,000	8,170	24.29	24.20	40.38	24.29
2001[1]	130,000	31,900	856	2,500	9	35,300	7,510	26.81	26.81	38.58	26.81
2002[2]	154,000	36,100	993	2,700	39	37,400	8,860	27.69	27.69	W	27.69

[1] Preliminary.   [2] Estimate.   *Source: U.S. Geological Survey (USGS)*

World Production of Marketable Potash   In Thousands of Metric Tons (K$_2$O Equivalent)

Year	Belarus	Brazil	Canada	China	France	Germany	Israel	Jordan	Russia	Spain	United Kingdom	United States	World Total
1993	1,947	168	3,836	25	890	2,861	1,309	822	2,628	661	555	1,510	20,400
1994	3,021	234	8,037	74	870	3,286	1,259	930	2,498	684	580	1,400	23,100
1995	3,211	215	9,066	80	799	3,278	1,330	1,075	2,800	760	582	1,480	24,800
1996	2,716	243	8,120	110	751	3,332	1,500	1,080	2,620	717	618	1,390	23,300
1997	3,247	280	8,989	115	725	3,423	1,488	850	3,400	639	565	1,400	25,200
1998	3,451	326	9,201	120	453	3,582	1,668	916	3,500	597	608	1,300	26,000
1999	4,553	348	8,475	260	345	3,543	1,702	1,080	4,200	656	495	1,200	27,200
2000	3,786	352	9,202	380	320	3,407	1,747	1,160	3,700	653	600	1,300	27,000
2001[1]	3,700	352	8,224	385	244	3,550	1,774	1,177	4,300	471	532	1,200	26,400
2002[2]	3,800	352	8,200	450	130	3,450	1,930	1,200	4,400	407	540	1,200	26,500

[1] Preliminary.   [2] Estimate.   *Source: U.S. Geological Survey (USGS)*

Salient Statistics of Potash in the United States   In Thousands of Metric Tons (K$_2$O Equivalent)

Year	Net Import Reliance as a % of Consumption	Production	Sales by Producers	Value Million Dollars	Imports For Consumption	Exports	Apparent Consumption	Producer Stocks Dec. 31	----- $ Per Ton ----- Avg. Value Per Ton of Product ($)	Avg. Value of K$_2$O Equiv.	Avg. Price[3] $ Per Tonne
1993	72	1,510	1,480	286.0	4,360	415	5,430	305	94.36	192.72	130.74
1994	76	1,400	1,470	284.0	4,800	464	5,810	234	95.93	193.50	125.34
1995	75	1,480	1,400	284.0	4,820	409	5,820	312	98.58	202.43	137.99
1996	77	1,390	1,430	299.0	4,940	481	5,890	265	101.08	208.57	134.07
1997	80	1,400	1,400	320.0	5,490	466	6,500	200	110.00	230.00	138.00
1998	80	1,300	1,300	330.0	4,780	477	5,600	300	115.00	250.00	145.00
1999	80	1,200	1,200	280.0	4,470	459	5,100	300	110.00	230.00	150.00
2000	70	1,300	1,200	290.0	4,600	367	5,600		110.00	230.00	157.50
2001[1]	80	1,200	1,100	260.0	4,540	366	5,300		110.00	230.00	165.00
2002[2]	80	1,200	1,200	280.0	4,620	371	5,300		110.00	230.00	155.00

[1] Preliminary.   [2] Estimate.   [3] Unit of K$_2$O, standard 60% muriate F.O.B. mine.   *Source: U.S. Geological Survey (USGS)*

Fish

Fish is the primary source of protein for a large proportion of the world's population. The worldwide yearly harvest of all sea fish (including aquaculture) is between 85 and 130 million metric tons. There are approximately 20,000 species of fish, of which 9,000 are regularly caught, with only 22 species harvested in large amounts. Ground-fish, which are fish that live near or on the ocean floor, account for nearly 10% of the world's fishery harvest, and include cod, haddock, pollock, flounder, halibut and sole. Large pelagic fish such as tuna, swordfish, marlin, and mahi-mahi, account for nearly 5% of world harvest. The fish eaten most often in the United States is canned tuna.

Rising global demand for fish has increased the pressure to harvest more fish, to the point where all 17 of the world's major fishing areas have either reached or exceeded their limits. Atlantic stocks of cod, haddock and blue-fin tuna are all seriously depleted, while in the Pacific, anchovies, salmon and halibut are all being over-fished. Aquaculture, or fish farming, reduces pressure on wild stocks and now accounts for nearly 20% of world harvest.

Over 30% of the fish harvested is processed directly into fishmeal and fish oil. Fishmeal is used primarily in animal feed. Fish oil is used in both animal feed and human food products.

Supply – Of the US supply of fishery products of 18.119 billion pounds in 2001, the latest full reporting year, 52.4% came from the domestic catch, which rose to 9.492 billion pounds in 2001 from 9.068 billion pounds in 2000. Of the domestic catch, 6.162 billion pounds of the catch was finfish, 1.152 billion pounds shellfish, and 2.178 billion pounds for industrial use. The principal species of US fishery landings in 2001 were Pollock (with 3.188 billion pounds landed), Menhaden (1.741 billion pounds), Pacific Salmon (723 million pounds), Flounder (352 million pounds), Sea Herring (300 million pounds), and crabs (272 million pounds).

World fishmeal production in 2002/3 fell –0.8% to 6.360 million metric tons. The world's largest producers of fishmeal in 2001/2 were Peru with 24% of world production, Chile (12.1%), European Union (8.6%), and the US (5.3%). World production of fish oil in 2002/3 rose +7.4% to 1.024 million metric tons. The world's largest producers of fish oil are Peru (with 17.1% of world production), Chile (16.0%), and the US (11.7%).

Trade – US imports of fishery products in 2001 rose to a 14-year high of 8.627 billion pounds.

Fishery Products -- Supply in the United States   In Millions of Pounds[2]

| | | | | | --------- Domestic Catch --------- | | | | | --------- Imports --------- | | | | |
Year	Grand Total	- For Human Food - Finfish	Shellfish[3]	For Industrial Use[4]	Total	% of Grand Total	- For Human Food - Finfish	Shellfish[3]	For Industrial Use[4]	Total	% of Grand Total	- For Human Food - Finfish	Shellfish[3]	For Industrial Use[4]
1995	16,484	10,692	2,891	2,900	9,788	59.4	6,414	1,252	2,121	6,696	40.6	4,278	1,639	779
1996	16,474	10,699	2,927	2,848	9,565	58.1	6,205	1,271	2,089	6,909	41.9	4,494	1,656	759
1997	17,133	10,580	3,160	3,393	9,843	57.5	5,969	1,277	2,598	7,290	42.5	4,612	1,883	795
1998	16,898	10,837	3,338	2,723	9,194	54.4	5,935	1,238	2,021	7,704	45.6	4,901	2,100	702
1999	17,378	10,831	3,630	2,916	9,339	53.7	5,490	1,341	2,507	8,039	46.3	5,341	2,289	409
2000	17,339	11,006	3,734	2,599	9,068	52.3	5,637	1,275	2,157	8,271	47.7	5,369	2,459	442
2001[1]	18,119	11,330	3,977	2,812	9,492	52.4	6,162	1,152	2,178	8,627	47.6	5,168	2,828	634

[1] Preliminary.   [2] Live weight, except percent.   [3] For univalue and bivalues mollusks (conchs, clams, oysters, scallops, etc.) the weight of meats, excluding the shell is reported.   [4] Fish meal and sea herring.   *Source: Fisheries Statistics Division, U.S. Department of Commerce*

Fisheries -- Landings of Principal Species in the United States   In Millions of Pounds

| | ---------- Fish ---------- | | | | | | | | | ---------- Shellfish ---------- | | | | |
Year	Cod, Atlantic	Flounder	Halibut	Herring, Sea	Man-haden	Pollock	Salmon, Pacific	Tuna	Whiting	Clams (Meats)	Crabs	Lobsters (American)	Oysters ------ (Meats) ------	Scallops	Shrimp
1995	30	423	45	265	1,847	2,853	1,137	14	34	134	364	66	40	20	307
1996	31	460	49	318	1,755	2,630	877	85	35	123	392	71	38	18	317
1997	29	566	70	348	2,028	2,522	568	83	34	114	430	84	40	15	290
1998	25	391	73	272	1,706	2,729	644	85	33	108	553	80	34	13	278
1999	21	331	80	267	1,989	2,336	815	58	31	112	458	87	27	27	304
2000	25	413	75	235	1,760	2,616	629	51	27	118	299	83	41	33	332
2001[1]	33	352	78	300	1,741	3,188	723	52	28	123	272	74	33	47	324

[1] Preliminary.   *Source: National Marine Fisheries Service, U.S. Department of Commerce*

U.S. Fisheries: Quantity & Value of Domestic Catch & Consumption & World Fish Oil Production

| | ---------- Disposition ---------- | | | | | For Human Food | For Industrial Products | Ex-vessel Value[3] | Average Price | Fish Per Capita Cunsumption | World[2] Fish Oil Production |
Year	Fresh & Frozen	Canned	Cured	For Meal, Oil, Etc.	Total	---------- Millions of Pounds ----------		- Million $ -	- Cents/Lb. -	- Pounds -	- 1,000 Tons -
1995	7,099	769	90	1,830	9,788	7,667	2,121	3,770	38.5	NA	1,302
1996	7,054	678	93	1,740	9,565	7,474	2,091	3,487	36.5	NA	1,337
1997	6,873	648	108	2,213	9,842	7,244	2,598	3,448	35.0	NA	1,214
1998	6,870	516	129	1,679	9,194	7,173	2,021	3,128	34.0	NA	886
1999	6,416	712	133	2,078	9,339	6,832	2,507	3,467	37.1	NA	1,413
2000	6,657	530	119	1,763	9,069	6,912	2,157	3,550	39.1	NA	1,422
2001[1]	7,085	536	123	1,748	9,492	7,314	2,178	3,228	34.0	NA	1,132

[1] Preliminary.   [2] Crop years on a marketing year basis.   [3] At the Dock Prices.   *Source: Fisheries Statistics Division, U.S. Department of Commerce*

FISH

Imports of Seafood Products into the United States   In Thousands of Pounds

	Fresh			Frozen							Canned	Prepared
Year	Atlantic Salmon	Pacific Salmon	Shrimp	Trout	Atlantic Salmon	Pacific Salmon	Shrimp	Oysters[2]	Mussels[3]	Clams[4]	Salmon	Shrimp[5]
1996	116,606	43,962	----	4,552	10,752	8,514	507,823	14,222	21,241	6,596	4,182	74,648
1997	150,135	38,999	----	5,403	14,956	25,662	572,111	14,531	26,903	5,703	3,675	76,213
1998	190,131	38,486	----	5,670	19,092	17,134	599,466	18,049	34,099	6,541	3,430	95,942
1999	217,948	26,467	----	5,259	24,222	16,596	617,089	18,325	34,969	7,537	5,627	114,191
2000	257,218	19,908	----	7,083	32,089	12,866	621,231	20,810	43,141	8,074	8,893	139,526
2001	316,837	17,472	----	7,382	41,176	10,515	714,706	18,438	39,973	8,007	11,298	167,877
2002	356,164	23,210	----	9,887	56,883	18,317	730,002	19,084	45,695	7,457	16,378	216,439
2003[1]	349,474	22,462	----	9,023	64,999	26,658	878,124	22,257	43,236	8,752	25,177	234,084

[1] Preliminary.   [2] Oysters fresh or prepared.   [3] Mussels fresh or prepared.   [4] Clams, fresh or prepared.   [5] Shrimp, canned, breaded or prepared.
NA = Not available.   *Source: Bureau of the Census, U.S. Department of Commerce*

Exports of Seafood Products into the United States   In Thousands of Pounds

	Fresh			Frozen							Canned	Prepared
Year	Atlantic Salmon	Pacific Salmon	Shrimp	Trout	Atlantic Salmon	Pacific Salmon	Shrimp	Oysters[2]	Mussels[3]	Clams[4]	Salmon	Shrimp[5]
1996	7,280	42,999	----	1,867	322	223,346	11,180	2,097	1,603	5,126	94,842	17,665
1997	7,504	25,529	----	1,709	322	152,516	11,967	2,890	1,157	4,916	81,407	14,826
1998	7,978	34,645	----	1,453	243	105,869	11,323	2,496	1,347	5,375	77,201	13,882
1999	10,717	40,683	----	1,697	182	157,278	13,607	2,727	1,861	5,240	113,556	13,153
2000	15,942	38,750	----	1,816	299	161,515	15,162	3,229	1,513	3,413	81,098	14,229
2001	18,417	20,651	----	1,077	84	167,933	13,905	3,915	1,485	3,939	109,109	13,640
2002	8,456	29,672	----	1,163	84	132,646	13,890	3,896	1,178	3,861	95,955	13,148
2003[1]	11,337	38,902	----	2,592	99	150,766	16,466	5,827	1,337	4,003	94,338	14,307

[1] Preliminary.   [2] Oysters fresh or prepared.   [3] Mussels fresh or prepared.   [4] Clams, fresh or prepared.   [5] Shrimp, canned, breaded or prepared.
NA = Not available.   *Source: Bureau of the Census, U.S. Department of Commerce*

World Production of Fish Meal   In Thousands of Metric Tons

Year	Chile	Spain	Denmark	EU-12	FSU-12	Iceland	Japan	Norway	Peru	South Africa	Thailand	United States	World Total
1995-6	1,387.6	76.4	322.9	532.5	209.8	271.0	195.0	233.8	1,702.7	49.6	380.9	331.1	6,332.9
1996-7	1,209.9	86.1	334.6	555.5	206.3	272.5	363.5	259.7	2,150.5	52.6	384.4	366.1	6,992.7
1997-8	708.5	92.8	317.2	544.7	206.7	221.6	383.4	296.7	697.2	89.3	403.8	339.9	5,218.4
1998-9	823.4	86.1	319.1	542.7	147.1	240.6	388.5	352.6	1,597.4	76.2	398.0	389.9	6,324.6
1999-00	890.0	81.5	314.2	531.1	148.8	281.2	390.0	315.0	2,449.4	113.7	392.4	346.8	7,334.3
2000-1[1]	731.0	88.0	311.9	534.4	137.4	284.0	350.0	238.8	2,144.2	97.8	385.0	337.1	6,771.8
2001-2[2]	766.0	90.0	308.2	535.8	147.2	311.0	323.0	222.9	1,688.1	115.8	390.0	347.6	6,412.5
2002-3[3]	770.0	92.0	310.0	544.5	147.2	305.0	338.0	232.0	1,550.0	116.0	400.0	338.0	6,360.0

[1] Preliminary.   [2] Estimate.   [3] Forecast.   *Source: The Oil World*

World Production of Fish Oil   In Thousands of Metric Tons

Year	Canada	Chile	China	Denmark	Iceland	Japan	Norway	Peru	South Africa	FSU-12	United States	World Total	Fish Oil CIF[4]
1995-6	10.6	280.2	12.0	120.0	120.5	45.8	93.7	410.0	3.7	43.0	110.4	1,363.4	461
1996-7	4.8	192.6	9.0	138.0	143.2	47.6	86.4	413.3	4.1	41.0	119.8	1,289.0	502
1997-8	4.5	91.4	7.2	126.7	95.1	70.7	89.0	86.3	7.8	14.3	101.3	825.5	722
1998-9	3.3	176.8	28.8	135.2	92.1	72.8	99.2	376.5	6.8	14.5	141.6	1,277.3	408
1999-00	3.7	166.0	26.7	139.7	98.0	69.7	98.3	699.4	8.9	12.0	81.3	1,533.3	268
2000-1[1]	4.1	142.9	26.3	121.3	99.0	65.0	66.4	400.8	7.9	11.1	123.3	1,217.3	375
2001-2[2]	4.3	140.2	28.0	112.7	85.0	65.0	61.2	179.5	10.0	11.0	106.0	953.4	593
2002-3[3]	4.5	164.0	30.0	124.0	89.0	67.0	78.0	175.0	9.0	11.0	120.0	1,023.7	

[1] Preliminary.   [2] Estimate.   [3] Forecast.   [4] Any origin, N.W. Europe.   NA = Not available.   *Source: The Oil World*

Monthly Production of Catfish--Round Weight Processed, in the US   In Thousands of Pounds (Live Weight)

Year	Jan.	Feb.	Mar.	Apr.	May	June	July	Aug.	Sept.	Oct.	Nov.	Dec.	Total
1996	38,475	38,004	46,376	38,557	39,583	36,810	39,025	40,463	38,807	42,070	37,210	36,874	472,254
1997	42,409	45,067	48,431	45,721	43,409	42,282	43,376	44,154	43,472	46,275	40,137	40,216	524,949
1998	46,723	47,606	53,761	49,393	45,218	46,244	46,383	47,739	46,579	47,904	43,224	43,581	564,355
1999	48,723	48,891	56,310	46,830	47,703	48,445	50,074	50,372	50,414	52,407	48,118	48,341	596,628
2000	50,552	50,942	56,856	48,781	48,424	48,011	49,023	53,204	49,422	51,412	45,535	41,441	593,603
2001	46,999	50,257	57,766	52,478	51,736	47,883	47,829	51,690	49,699	52,264	44,670	43,837	597,108
2002	52,551	52,856	58,340	50,694	52,902	49,450	52,363	54,383	53,366	56,576	50,072	48,048	631,601
2003[1]	55,523	55,461	65,007	57,105	58,424	52,441	54,089	54,153	51,885	57,652	51,246	48,518	661,504

[1] Preliminary.   *Source: Economic Research Service, U.S. Department of Agriculture (ERS-USDA)*

Average Price Paid to Producers for Farm-Raised Catfish in the US   In Cents Per Pound (Live Weight)

Year	Jan.	Feb.	Mar.	Apr.	May	June	July	Aug.	Sept.	Oct.	Nov.	Dec.	Average
1996	77.0	78.0	78.0	78.0	79.0	79.0	79.0	78.0	77.0	76.0	75.0	73.0	77.3
1997	73.0	73.0	73.0	73.0	73.0	72.0	71.0	70.0	69.0	69.0	69.0	69.0	71.2
1998	69.0	73.0	78.0	79.0	79.0	78.0	76.0	74.0	73.0	71.0	70.0	70.0	74.2
1999	70.3	71.4	73.2	75.6	77.7	77.5	76.8	74.3	72.8	71.6	71.3	71.6	73.7
2000	74.4	78.8	78.9	78.9	78.5	78.6	76.0	74.1	72.7	71.0	69.6	68.2	75.0
2001	69.3	69.6	69.7	69.4	68.7	66.9	66.6	62.1	61.0	59.6	56.6	55.4	64.5
2002	54.9	55.5	56.5	56.1	57.4	58.8	59.0	58.2	57.6	56.8	56.0	54.4	56.8
2003[1]	52.9	54.4	58.5	63.0	61.8	58.6	56.4	55.2	56.0	56.7	61.0	62.9	58.1

[1] Preliminary.   *Source: Economic Research Service, U.S. Department of Agriculture (ERS-USDA)*

Sales of Fresh Catfish in the United States   In Thousands of Pounds

Year	Jan.	Feb.	Mar.	Apr.	May	June	July	Aug.	Sept.	Oct.	Nov.	Dec.	Total
Whole
1998	3,700	4,049	4,308	3,856	3,421	3,340	3,342	3,270	3,332	3,431	3,152	3,254	42,455
1999	3,650	3,957	4,467	3,459	3,492	3,380	3,471	3,271	3,583	3,561	3,209	3,313	42,813
2000	3,496	3,396	4,031	3,655	3,483	3,581	3,491	3,545	3,246	3,504	2,971	2,993	41,392
2001	3,516	3,242	4,260	3,644	3,271	3,166	3,233	3,204	3,174	3,294	2,865	2,803	39,672
2002	3,713	3,656	3,826	3,373	3,644	3,313	3,477	3,733	3,418	3,822	3,031	2,986	41,992
2003[1]	3,833	3,785	4,339	3,643	3,692	3,266	3,553	3,510	3,233	3,231	2,798	2,693	41,576
Fillets[2]
1998	4,292	4,784	5,130	4,634	4,371	4,220	4,542	4,622	4,626	4,588	4,092	3,975	53,876
1999	4,581	5,030	5,768	4,897	4,918	4,707	4,846	5,002	4,550	4,811	4,171	4,142	57,423
2000	4,686	4,853	5,957	5,206	5,099	4,792	4,650	4,899	4,650	5,283	4,355	4,099	58,529
2001	4,884	6,112	6,751	5,709	5,587	5,122	5,191	5,313	5,264	5,273	4,463	4,489	64,158
2002	5,684	6,132	6,010	5,236	5,682	5,093	5,327	5,442	5,317	5,420	4,447	4,119	63,909
2003[1]	5,362	5,158	6,715	5,700	6,364	5,737	5,984	6,013	5,308	6,082	5,187	4,710	68,320
Other[3]
1998	1,499	1,712	1,721	1,509	1,395	1,453	1,246	1,369	1,314	1,345	1,117	1,081	16,761
1999	1,243	1,614	1,724	1,153	1,227	1,126	1,305	1,495	1,354	1,676	1,299	1,227	16,443
2000	1,429	1,437	1,685	1,547	1,364	1,299	1,340	1,438	1,332	1,473	1,271	1,198	16,813
2001	1,443	1,292	2,156	1,309	1,282	1,298	1,375	1,436	1,449	1,430	1,223	1,252	16,945
2002	1,526	1,446	1,375	1,356	1,732	1,527	1,576	1,569	1,441	1,596	1,165	1,205	17,514
2003[1]	1,668	1,532	1,599	1,458	1,472	1,319	1,425	1,366	1,473	1,361	1,138	1,134	16,945

[1] Preliminary.   [2] Includes regular, shank and strip fillets; excludes breaded products.   [3] Includes steaks, nuggets and all other products not reported.
Source: Economic Research Service, U.S. Department of Agriculture (ERS-USDA)

Prices of Fresh Catfish in the United States   In Dollars per Pound

Year	Jan.	Feb.	Mar.	Apr.	May	June	July	Aug.	Sept.	Oct.	Nov.	Dec.	Average
Whole
1998	1.52	1.57	1.63	1.61	1.65	1.60	1.60	1.63	1.59	1.59	1.56	1.52	1.59
1999	1.54	1.55	1.57	1.59	1.63	1.60	1.59	1.63	1.61	1.63	1.59	1.59	1.59
2000	1.63	1.67	1.69	1.70	1.68	1.63	1.65	1.70	1.67	1.64	1.62	1.58	1.66
2001	1.59	1.68	1.63	1.65	1.65	1.62	1.59	1.55	1.53	1.49	1.42	1.37	1.56
2002	1.36	1.35	1.30	1.34	1.36	1.37	1.35	1.32	1.32	1.28	1.24	1.25	1.32
2003[1]	1.28	1.30	1.35	1.37	1.36	1.39	1.33	1.33	1.34	1.36	1.40	1.43	1.35
Fillets[2]
1998	2.71	2.75	2.85	2.86	2.86	2.85	2.84	2.82	2.78	2.78	2.75	2.73	2.80
1999	2.73	2.71	2.76	2.75	2.84	2.86	2.86	2.85	2.85	2.83	2.84	2.83	2.81
2000	2.82	2.87	2.89	2.88	2.88	2.90	2.90	2.88	2.85	2.83	2.83	2.81	2.86
2001	2.80	2.79	2.80	2.80	2.80	2.78	2.77	2.75	2.69	2.63	2.60	2.55	2.73
2002	2.52	2.49	2.49	2.51	2.53	2.55	2.55	2.54	2.54	2.52	2.49	2.47	2.52
2003[1]	2.44	2.45	2.44	2.49	2.51	2.50	2.48	2.48	2.49	2.49	2.50	2.54	2.48
Other[3]
1998	1.61	1.65	1.72	1.78	1.78	1.76	1.79	1.71	1.72	1.69	1.73	1.69	1.72
1999	1.61	1.55	1.59	1.70	1.74	1.76	1.66	1.62	1.66	1.57	1.65	1.66	1.65
2000	1.66	1.69	1.69	1.66	1.71	1.71	1.72	1.69	1.62	1.68	1.71	1.68	1.69
2001	1.64	1.68	1.57	1.64	1.69	1.64	1.61	1.57	1.52	1.59	1.59	1.53	1.61
2002	1.53	1.57	1.54	1.51	1.45	1.51	1.51	1.50	1.54	1.48	1.55	1.46	1.51
2003[1]	1.40	1.41	1.51	1.53	1.47	1.54	1.52	1.58	1.50	1.58	1.60	1.64	1.52

[1] Preliminary.   [2] Includes regular, shank and strip fillets; excludes breaded products.   [3] Includes steaks, nuggets and all other products not reported.
Source: Economic Research Service, U.S. Department of Agriculture (ERS-USDA)

Flaxseed and Linseed Oil

Flaxseed, also called linseed, is an ancient crop that was cultivated by the Babylonians around 3,000 BC. Flaxseed is used for fiber in textiles and to produce oil. Flaxseeds contain approximately 35% oil, of which 60% is omega-3 fatty acid. Flaxseed or linseed oil is obtained through either expeller extraction or solvent extraction method. Manufacturers filter the processed oil to remove some impurities and then sell it as unrefined. Unrefined oil retains its full flavor, aroma, color, and naturally occurring nutrients. Flaxseed oil is used for cooking and as a dietary supplement as well as for animal feed. Industrial linseed oil is not for internal consumption due to possible poisonous additives and is used for making putty, sealants, linoleum, wood preservation, varnishes, and oil paints.

Flaxseed futures and options trade at the Winnipeg Commodity Exchange. The futures contract calls for the delivery of 20 metric tons of flaxseed. The contract is now priced in US dollars per metric ton.

Prices – Flaxseed prices received by US farmers in December 2003 ended the calendar year at $5.97 per bushel, slightly higher than the 2002/3 marketing year (July/June) average of $5.91 and far higher than $4.53 in 2001/2 and $3.57 in 2000/1.

Supply – World production of flaxseed in 2002/3 fell to 2.064 million metric tons from 2.159 million in 2001/2 and was sharply below the recent peak of 2.868 million in 1999/00. By far, the world's largest producer of flaxseed is Canada with 35% of world production (2002/3), followed by China (23%), the US (16%), and India (10%). Chinese production in 2002/3 rose by 11% to 465,000 metric tons from 2001/2, while Canadian production fell 5% to 730,000 metric tons. US production rose by 10% to 319,000 metric tons. North Dakota is the king of US flaxseed production, accounting for 97% of US production. The 2003/4 US flaxseed crop promises to be small since farmers harvested only 572,000 acres, down from 704,000 in 2002/3. US production of linseed oil in 2002/3 rose slightly to 198 million pounds from 195 million in 2001/2.

Demand – The demand (distribution) breakdown for the US flaxseed supply of 16.507 million bushels in 2002/3 was 10.150 million bushels for crushing into flaxseed oil and meal (accounting for 62% of overall supply), 3.150 million bushels for export (19%), 2.842 million as residual consumption (17%), and 365,000 bushels for seed (2%). US consumption of linseed oil in 2002/3 rose by 4% to 94.9 million pounds from 91.3 million in 2001/2.

Trade – US exports of flaxseed in 2002/3 rose sharply by 32% to 3.150 million bushels from 2.386 million in 2001/2. US imports of flaxseed in 2002/3 fell even more sharply by 56% to 844,000 bushels from 1.903 million in 2001/2. The US is a net exporter of flaxseed, exporting more than three times what it imports.

World Production of Flaxseed   In Thousands of Metric Tons

Year	Argen-tina	Aust-ralia	Bang-ladesh	Canada	China	Egypt	France	Hungary	India	Rom-ania	United States	Former USSR	World Total
1993-4	112	8	49	627	410	22	27	4	330	28	88	120	2,191
1994-5	152	6	48	960	511	18	44	4	325	7	74	110	2,474
1995-6	149	15	49	1,105	420	16	27	4	308	5	56	113	2,518
1996-7	72	7	46	851	480	17	29	4	319	5	41	86	2,300
1997-8	75	9	50	1,038	393	19	31	----	275	5	62	47	2,370
1998-9	85	10	50	1,210	523	24	29	1	265	3	170	55	2,828
1999-00	47	9	46	1,100	404	30	34	2	289	3	200	46	2,868
2000-1[1]	22	9	48	775	520	30	38	1	240	1	273	76	2,358
2001-2[2]	16	9	50	770	420	26	31	1	240	2	291	82	2,159
2002-3[3]	9	6	50	730	465	19	31	1	200	3	319	61	2,064

[1] Preliminary.   [2] Estimate.   [3] Forecast.   *Source: The Oil World*

Supply and Distribution of Flaxseed in the United States   In Thousands of Bushels

Crop Year Beginning June 1	Planted	Harvested	Yield Per Acre (Bushels)	Beginning Stocks	Pro-duction	Imports	Total Supply	Seed	Crush	Exports	Residual	Total Distribution
	---- 1,000 Acres ----			---- Supply ----				---- Distribution ----				
1994-5	178	171	17.1	1,155	2,922	6,005	10,082	134	8,550	72	156	8,912
1995-6	165	147	15.0	1,170	2,212	7,248	10,630	78	9,000	119	203	9,400
1996-7	96	92	17.4	1,230	1,602	8,390	11,222	122	10,000	144	503	10,769
1997-8	151	146	16.6	453	2,420	9,636	12,509	272	10,500	174	382	11,328
1998-9	336	329	20.4	1,181	6,708	5,992	13,881	313	10,600	476	333	11,723
1999-00	387	382	20.6	2,158	7,864	6,629	16,651	434	11,500	215	2,735	14,884
2000-1	536	517	20.8	1,767	10,730	2,850	15,347	474	12,000	1,015	572	14,039
2001-2[1]	585	578	19.8	1,308	11,455	1,903	14,666	636	10,000	2,386	751	13,773
2002-3[2]	785	704	17.9	893	12,569	2,650	18,157	472	10,300	2,900	890	14,562
2003-4[3]	595	583	17.9		10,426							

[1] Preliminary.   [2] Estimate.   [3] Forecast.   *Source: Economic Research Service, U.S. Department of Agriculture*

Production of Flaxseed in the United States, by States   In Thousands of Bushels

Crop Year	Minne- sota	North Dakota	South Dakota	Other States	Total	Crop Year	Minne- sota	North Dakota	South Dakota	Other States	Total
1994	126	2,450	304	42	2,922	1999	300	6,867	357	340	7,864
1995	171	1,725	260	55	2,211	2000	198	9,975	361	196	10,730
1996	60	1,386	126	30	1,602	2001	52	10,900	323	180	11,455
1997	96	1,997	252	75	2,420	2002	90	12,240	44	195	12,569
1998	402	5,817	294	165	6,708	2003[1]	161	9,900	144	221	10,426

[1] Preliminary.   Source: National Agricultural Statistics Service, U.S. Department of Agriculture (NASS-USDA)

Factory Shipments of Paints, Varnish and Lacquer in the United States   In Millions of Dollars

Year	First Quarter	Second Quarter	Third Quarter	Fourth Quarter	Total	Year	First Quarter	Second Quarter	Third Quarter	Fourth Quarter	Total
1994	3,039.8	3,783.0	3,736.2	3,240.8	13,800	1999	3,926.2	4,452.2	4,216.5	3,925.7	16,521
1995	3,330.3	3,838.0	3,814.5	3,423.4	14,406	2000	4,073.1	4,573.5	4,082.0	3,474.7	16,203
1996	3,438.6	4,161.9	3,954.9	3,428.9	14,984	2001	3,625.0	4,345.4	4,094.5	3,652.6	15,718
1997	3,515.2	4,023.4	3,924.1	3,323.0	14,786	2002	3,729.9	4,440.7	4,251.4	3,600.7	16,023
1998	3,600.7	4,216.4	4,063.9	3,804.4	15,685	2003[1]	3,790.7	4,450.2	4,168.2	3,715.6	16,125

[1] Preliminary.   Source: Bureau of the Census, U.S. Department of Commerce

Consumption of Linseed Oil (Inedible Products) in the United States   In Millions of Pounds

Year	July	Aug.	Sept.	Oct.	Nov.	Dec.	Jan.	Feb.	Mar.	Apr.	May	June	Total
1996-7	9.0	10.8	7.8	6.0	6.7	6.1	6.7	7.1	6.3	8.3	8.9	8.5	92.3
1997-8	8.9	7.7	8.6	6.7	7.5	6.4	8.0	6.0	6.2	5.9	6.8	5.7	84.3
1998-9	7.2	6.8	6.4	5.6	4.6	6.6	5.9	4.7	6.8	6.4	5.6	7.9	74.6
1999-00	5.4	6.2	5.5	5.2	5.6	4.5	4.2	6.1	5.8	7.0	7.6	6.6	69.8
2000-1	6.5	7.2	7.3	7.5	6.5	5.7	8.0	6.7	7.7	7.6	9.3	9.4	89.3
2001-2	9.6	8.4	9.2	7.4	5.3	5.0	8.2	7.1	6.9	8.0	7.7	8.7	91.3
2002-3	11.7	9.6	10.0	7.0	5.7	7.3	6.8	6.4	8.7	8.5	6.6	6.7	94.9
2003-4[1]	7.9	6.9	6.0	6.8	3.5	5.0	5.6						71.5

[1] Preliminary.   Source: Bureau of the Census, U.S. Department of Commerce

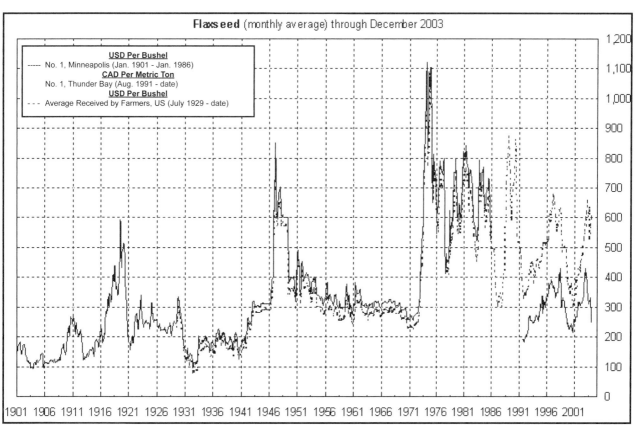

Flaxseed (monthly average) through December 2003

USD Per Bushel
----- No. 1, Minneapolis (Jan. 1901 - Jan. 1986)
CAD Per Metric Ton
No. 1, Thunder Bay (Aug. 1991 - date)
USD Per Bushel
- - - Average Received by Farmers, US (July 1929 - date)

FLAXSEED AND LINSEED OIL

Supply and Distribution of Linseed Oil in the United States   In Millions of Pounds

Crop Year Beginning June 1	Stocks June 1	Pro- duction	Total	Exports	Domestic	Total Disappearance	Average Price at Minneapolis Cents/Lb.
		Supply			Disappearance		
1993-4	54	174	228	7	162	165	31.8
1994-5	63	172	235	24	166	190	33.7
1995-6	45	180	225	26	149	175	36.5
1996-7	50	200	250	66	149	215	36.0
1997-8	35	205	240	58	140	198	37.8
1998-9	35	207	249	63	138	201	37.5
1999-00	45	224	272	76	147	223	37.8
2000-1	49	234	293	100	150	250	36.0
2001-2[1]	43	195	238	90	103	193	36.0
2002-3[2]	45	201	246	92	109	201	33.0

[1] Preliminary.   [2] Forecast.   Source: Economic Research Service, U.S. Department of Agriculture (ERS-USDA)

World Production and Price of Linseed Oil   In Thousands of Metric Tons

Year	Argentina	Bang- ladesh	Belgium	China	Egypt	Germany	India	Japan	United Kingdom	United States	Former USSR	World Total	Rotterdam Ex-Tank $/Tonne
1993-4	32.2	12.7	28.8	121.8	8.6	77.2	90.7	30.7	35.2	78.7	11.2	617.9	476
1994-5	46.8	13.0	35.2	137.4	8.2	104.0	91.4	29.2	41.4	81.7	10.6	697.5	657
1995-6	47.5	13.0	44.3	125.1	8.0	72.0	88.1	30.0	28.9	80.0	12.7	665.3	579
1996-7	17.1	12.5	52.1	142.5	9.6	52.2	90.0	31.0	34.1	97.9	16.5	676.7	560
1997-8	24.1	13.4	54.7	120.0	11.1	66.9	84.3	31.3	35.1	100.7	7.2	678.6	686
1998-9	24.5	13.6	59.2	150.0	15.2	74.1	80.1	26.5	34.3	107.6	10.7	731.2	575
1999-00	13.1	12.6	68.8	118.3	15.0	73.6	85.9	23.8	34.1	124.9	7.9	709.6	413
2000-1	6.2	12.9	75.2	134.5	23.0	63.4	74.7	21.1	17.0	114.7	15.1	668.3	378
2001-2[1]	3.8	13.5	95.0	125.8	16.4	57.3	73.7	18.9	9.9	98.8	17.8	632.4	454
2002-3[2]	2.0	13.6	88.9	124.9	15.8	55.0	65.0	11.2	8.1	107.3	11.8	602.7	

[1] Preliminary.   [2] Forecast.   Source: The Oil World

Average Price Received by Farmers for Flaxseed in the United States   In Dollars Per Bushel

Year	July	Aug.	Sept.	Oct.	Nov.	Dec.	Jan.	Feb.	Mar.	Apr.	May	June	Average
1994-5	4.28	4.52	4.54	4.49	4.51	4.71	4.76	4.94	5.13	5.10	4.91	5.03	4.74
1995-6	5.11	5.21	5.11	5.11	5.17	5.03	5.26	5.21	5.28	5.31	6.13	5.90	5.32
1996-7	6.19	6.15	5.89	6.49	6.38	6.77	6.43	6.74	6.66	6.43	6.45	5.99	6.38
1997-8	6.07	5.53	5.72	5.81	5.71	5.72	5.82	6.27	6.26	6.23	6.33	6.17	5.97
1998-9	6.17	5.45	5.09	4.86	4.97	5.00	5.05	5.05	4.94	4.93	4.89	4.38	5.07
1999-00	4.40	3.86	4.00	3.76	3.66	3.61	3.75	3.43	3.70	3.66	3.77	3.64	3.77
2000-1	3.25	3.05	3.10	3.17	3.39	4.45	3.42	3.43	3.90	3.68	3.91	4.10	3.57
2001-2	4.28	4.09	4.10	4.21	4.33	4.55	4.22	4.75	4.75	4.80	5.02	5.29	4.53
2002-3	5.38	5.27	5.55	5.76	6.04	5.92	5.71	6.25	6.48	6.58	6.04	6.04	5.92
2003-4[1]	6.38	5.30	5.43	5.77	6.06	6.22	6.09	6.20					5.93

[1] Preliminary.   Source: National Agricultural Statistics Service, U.S. Department of Agriculture (NASS-USDA)

Stocks of Linseed Oil (Crude and Refined) at Factories and Warehouses in the US   In Millions of Pounds

Year	July 1	Aug. 1	Sept. 1	Oct. 1	Nov. 1	Dec. 1	Jan. 1	Feb. 1	Mar. 1	Apr. 1	May 1	June 1
1994-5	60.3	56.5	49.4	60.6	48.1	39.3	38.6	38.9	31.0	35.7	37.9	44.8
1995-6	39.5	44.6	37.4	46.0	48.0	44.5	45.3	58.9	64.0	62.0	60.6	47.2
1996-7	51.3	50.9	59.0	46.1	38.8	41.8	49.2	48.1	53.9	50.5	44.5	45.6
1997-8	39.9	35.2	40.3	33.3	38.6	40.3	46.9	60.8	55.8	63.1	54.6	49.4
1998-9	49.6	45.3	38.5	55.4	35.7	44.5	53.2	68.2	54.6	68.2	65.3	76.2
1999-00	68.7	65.5	68.9	74.0	92.4	69.6	72.0	69.5	65.7	53.9	49.1	44.2
2000-1	39.5	42.5	41.3	54.3	58.7	87.0	61.6	50.1	50.5	51.2	39.2	44.8
2001-2	29.1	30.2	22.6	38.4	32.4	29.9	33.4	36.6	26.8	33.4	32.3	31.1
2002-3	27.8	17.7	12.8	21.8	30.5	29.0	31.9	35.9	34.6	36.2	33.7	33.7
2003-4[1]	30.2	27.2	22.3	78.5	42.0	35.0	40.0	43.4				

[1] Preliminary.   Source: Bureau of the Census, U.S. Department of Commerce

Wholesale Price of Raw Linseed Oil at Minneapolis in Tank Cars   In Cents Per Pound

Year	July	Aug.	Sept.	Oct.	Nov.	Dec.	Jan.	Feb.	Mar.	Apr.	May	June	Average
1994-5	30.31	32.00	32.00	33.50	35.00	35.00	35.00	35.00	35.00	35.00	35.00	35.00	33.98
1995-6	35.00	35.50	37.00	37.00	37.00	37.00	37.00	37.00	37.00	37.00	37.00	37.00	36.71
1996-7	37.00	37.20	37.50	37.00	33.75	32.12	36.00	36.00	36.00	36.00	36.00	36.00	35.88
1997-8	36.00	36.00	36.00	37.00	37.00	37.00	36.00	36.00	36.00	36.00	37.00	37.00	36.42
1998-9	37.00	37.00	37.00	37.00	37.00	37.00	36.00	36.00	36.00	36.00	36.00	36.00	36.50
1999-00	36.00	36.00	36.00	36.00	36.00	36.00	36.00	36.00	36.00	36.00	36.00	36.00	36.00
2000-1	36.00	36.00	36.00	36.00	36.00	36.00	36.00	36.00	36.00	36.00	36.00	32.00	35.67
2001-2	35.50	38.00	39.00	39.00	39.00	39.00	39.00	39.00	39.00	39.00	39.65	40.35	38.79
2002-3	40.00	38.00	41.00	31.75	41.00	41.00	41.00	41.00	41.00	41.00	41.19	41.75	39.97
2003-4[1]	41.75	41.75	42.00										41.83

[1] Preliminary.   *Source: Economic Research Service, U.S. Department of Agriculture (ERS-USDA)*

Average Open Interest of Flaxseed Futures in Winnipeg   In Contracts

Year	Jan.	Feb.	Mar.	Apr.	May	June	July	Aug.	Sept.	Oct.	Nov.	Dec.
1994	6,118	6,201	5,946	5,519	4,683	3,945	4,301	4,654	4,997	3,077	4,888	5,251
1995	6,242	8,731	7,505	7,121	8,107	7,212	6,436	5,557	6,230	5,245	5,937	4,414
1996	6,059	6,056	4,402	5,192	6,970	4,435	3,102	2,989	3,257	3,438	4,326	5,119
1997	5,420	5,356	5,591	5,151	4,923	4,075	3,891	4,031	7,131	8,284	7,255	7,955
1998	10,059	10,190	9,707	8,540	6,480	6,874	6,030	6,767	7,421	7,221	7,564	5,828
1999	4,372	4,552	4,533	4,238	3,719	2,456	2,149	2,758	3,725	4,236	4,493	4,276
2000	4,365	4,907	5,588	6,218	5,066	3,696	3,152	3,585	3,936	4,666	4,922	4,914
2001	4,101	3,476	4,270	3,043	3,169	3,661	2,745	2,350	2,400	3,158	2,726	3,031
2002	2,225	1,981	1,921	1,787	1,270	935	612	699	776	704	424	249
2003	235	316	477	604	394	489	298	305	253	193	94	49

Source: Winnipeg Commodity Exchange (WCE)

Volume of Trading of Flaxseed Futures in Winnipeg   In Contracts

Year	Jan.	Feb.	Mar.	Apr.	May	June	July	Aug.	Sept.	Oct.	Nov.	Dec.	Total
1994	10,671	7,839	9,929	8,553	6,103	9,389	7,580	4,455	6,580	12,415	15,820	6,004	105,338
1995	10,707	15,819	10,676	15,315	12,569	9,235	6,579	5,922	11,790	11,051	15,064	7,798	132,525
1996	9,617	8,301	4,110	13,531	10,855	7,997	6,517	4,153	5,430	11,126	7,532	10,720	99,889
1997	7,640	6,486	7,123	10,912	6,256	7,851	7,662	7,081	20,967	23,418	20,049	15,311	140,756
1998	15,713	19,906	8,275	9,060	5,231	7,642	4,468	4,062	7,328	13,085	13,824	6,958	115,552
1999	4,855	8,922	4,383	8,460	5,241	5,891	4,863	2,833	5,852	12,078	7,710	7,345	78,433
2000	9,022	9,340	9,292	12,604	7,372	7,393	2,676	2,525	9,822	11,915	14,436	7,819	100,040
2001	8,232	6,428	6,928	7,117	6,514	6,745	4,344	2,620	5,242	7,291	4,689	6,326	72,476
2002	2,990	2,838	2,519	3,832	3,320	3,018	1,153	810	777	3,030	955	344	25,586
2003	333	724	412	368	452	738	343	96	491	273	183	25	4,438

Source: Winnipeg Commodity Exchange (WCE)

Fruits

A fruit is any seed-bearing structure produced from a flowering plant. A widely used classification system divides fruit into fleshy or dry types. Fleshy fruits are juicy and include peaches, mangos, apples, and blueberries. Dry fruits include tree nuts such as almonds, walnuts, and pecans. Some foods that are commonly called vegetables, such as tomatoes, squash, peppers and eggplant, are technically fruits because they develop from the ovary of a flower.

Worldwide, over 430 million tons of fruit are produced each year and are grown everywhere except the Arctic and the Antarctic. The tropics, because of their abundant moisture and warm temperatures, produce the most diverse and abundant fruits. Mexico and Chile produce more than half of all the fresh and frozen fruit imported into the US. In the US, the top three fruits produced are oranges, grapes, and apples. Virtually all US production of almonds, pistachios, and walnuts occurs in California, which leads the US in tree nut production.

Prices – Fruit prices were strong in 2001, the last reporting year, with the fresh fruit CPI index rising +2.6% to 265.1 and the processed fruit CPI index rising +2.0% to 109.0. The largest price increases in 2001 were seen in navel oranges which rallied 18% to 72.2 cents per pound, grapefruit which rallied +6.7% to 65.1 cents per pound, and seed-less grapes which rallied +6.0% to $1.85 per pound. The largest declines were seen in Valencia oranges, which fell –14.1% to 52.4 cents per pound, and Delicious apples, which fell 5.5% to 86.8 cents per pound.

Supply – US commercial production of selected fruits in 2001, the last reporting year, fell –8.8% to 32.992 million tons from 36.182 million tons in 2000. Oranges accounted for 37% of that US fruit production figure, followed by grapes at 20%, and apples at 15%. The value of US fruit production in 2001 was $11.694 billion.

Demand – US per capita fresh fruit consumption in 2001 fell 3.0% to 97.53 pounds from 100.50 pounds in 2000 and the record high of 101.58 pounds in 1998. The highest per capita consumption categories for non-citrus fruits in 2001 were bananas (26.53 pounds), apples (15.81 pounds), grapes (7.59 pounds), nectarines and peaches (5.25 pounds), and strawberries (4.23 pounds). Per capital consumption of citrus fruits was the highest for oranges (12.32 pounds), followed by grapefruit (4.82 pounds) and lemons (2.96 pounds).

The utilization breakdown for 2001 shows that 39% of total US fruit utilization went for fresh fruit, 21% for wine, 14% for dried fruit, 11% for canned fruit, 9% for juice, and 4% for frozen fruit.

Commercial Production for Selected Fruits in the United States   In Thousands of Short Tons

Year	Apples	Cherries[2]	Cran-berries	Grapes	Grape-fruit	Lemons	Nect-arines	Oranges	Peaches	Pears	Pine-apples	Prunes & Plums	Straw-berries	Tangelos	Tang-erines	Total All Fruits
1996	5,191	290	234	5,554	2,718	992	247	11,426	1,052	821	347	952	813	110	349	30,904
1997	5,162	373	275	7,291	2,885	962	264	12,692	1,312	1,043	324	899	814	178	425	35,507
1998	5,823	371	272	5,820	2,593	897	224	13,670	1,200	970	332	559	820	128	360	34,582
1999	5,315	344	318	6,236	2,513	747	274	9,824	1,263	1,016	352	735	916	115	327	30,802
2000	5,332	351	286	7,688	2,763	840	267	12,997	1,300	967	354	902	979	99	458	36,105
2001	4,714	415	267	6,570	2,462	996	275	12,221	1,217	1,002	323	651	826	95	373	32,908
2002[1]	4,263	213	284	7,339	2,424	801	300	12,374	1,288	869	320	736	943	97	420	33,264

[1] Preliminary.   [2] Sweet and tart.   [3] Utilized production.   *Source: Economic Research Service, U.S. Department of Agriculture (ERS-USDA)*

Utilized Production for Selected Fruits in the United States   In Thousands of Short Tons

	---- Utilized Production ----				---- Value of Production ----			
Year	Citrus[2]	Noncitrus	Tree Nuts[3]	Total	Citrus[2]	Noncitrus	Tree Nuts[3]	Total
	In Thousands of Short Tons				In Thousands of Dollars			
1996	15,712	16,103	831	32,646	2,517,394	7,265,788	1,663,574	11,446,756
1997	17,271	18,363	1,210	36,844	2,582,767	8,158,095	2,093,697	12,834,559
1998	17,770	16,545	908	35,223	2,600,066	7,257,288	1,365,349	11,222,703
1999	13,633	17,331	1,288	32,252	2,431,179	8,070,840	1,505,926	12,007,945
2000	17,276	18,923	1,086	37,209	2,513,174	7,930,668	1,496,584	11,898,193
2001	16,216	16,734	1,304	34,254	2,319,917	7,924,741	1,513,063	11,743,693
2002[1]	16,194	17,126	1,448	34,856	2,610,559	8,136,447	2,053,290	12,819,421

[1] Preliminary.   [2] Year harvest was completed.   [3] Tree nuts on an in-shell equivalent.
Source: Economic Research Service, U.S. Department of Agriculture (ERS-USDA)

Annual Average Retail Prices for Selected Fruits in the United States   In Dollars Per Pound

							---- Oranges ----	
Year	Red Delicious Apples	Bananas	Anjou Pears	Thompson Seedless Grapes	Lemons	Grapefruit	Navel	Valen-cias
1996	.930	.490	.916	1.685	1.114	.574	.707	.703
1997	.907	.487	.985	1.712	1.154	.520	.592	.682
1998	.943	.494	1.089	1.589	1.198	.599	.565	.657
1999	.897	.491	.950	1.841	1.236	.612	.843	.947
2000	.919	.501	.986	1.745	1.289	.610	.613	.610
2001	.868	.507	.966	1.850	1.265	.651	.722	.524
2002[1]	.948	.508	.997	1.887	1.391	.648	.836	.565

[1] Estimate.   *Source: Economic Research Service, U.S. Department of Agriculture (ERS-USDA)*

Utilization of Noncitrus Fruit Production, and Value in the U.S.   1,000 Short Tons (Fresh Equivalent)

Year	Utilized Pro- duction	Fresh	Canned	Dried	Processed Juice	Frozen	Wine	Other	Value of utilized Production $1,000
1993	16,554	6,391	2,042	2,339	1,749	627	3,029	181	6,130,119
1994	17,339	6,710	2,090	2,816	1,886	665	2,711	228	6,268,176
1995	16,348	6,285	1,753	2,400	1,857	647	2,992	205	6,815,962
1996	16,103	6,313	1,873	2,275	1,582	664	3,043	180	7,265,788
1997	18,363	6,643	2,130	2,660	1,675	699	4,035	247	8,158,095
1998	16,545	6,505	1,845	1,911	1,786	713	3,315	198	7,257,288
1999	17,331	6,674	1,986	2,150	1,887	719	3,351	248	8,070,840
2000	18,847	7,002	1,812	3,023	1,713	695	4,130	193	7,888,435
2001	16,734	6,477	1,860	2,290	1,462	669	3,569	169	7,910,713
2002[1]	17,215	6,607	1,720	2,610	1,281	576	3,999	137	8,163,929

[1] Preliminary.   Source: Economic Research Service, U.S. Department of Agriculture (ERS-USDA)

Average Price Indexes for Fruits in the United States

Year	Index of all Fruit and Nut Prices Received by Growers (1990-92=100)	Producer Price Index Fresh Fruit	Dried Fruit	Canned Fruits and Juices	Frozen Fruits and Juices	Consumer Price Index Fresh Fruit	Processed Fruit
		1982 = 100				1982-84 = 100	
1993	93	84.5	113.0	126.1	110.9	188.8	132.3
1994	90	82.7	116.1	126.0	111.9	201.2	133.1
1995	97	85.8	116.1	129.4	115.8	219.0	137.2
1996	118	100.8	119.1	137.5	123.9	234.4	145.2
1997	110	101.3	119.8	137.5	117.3	236.3	148.8
1998	111	90.5	119.3	138.6	----	246.5	101.9
1999	115	103.2	116.2	130.0	----	266.3	105.4
2000	99	91.4	117.9	131.7	----	258.3	106.9
2001	109	97.7	118.5	143.4	----	269.3	109.0
2002[1]	112	91.5	----	141.7	----	276.5	111.5

[1] Estimate.   Source: Economic Research Service, U.S. Department of Agriculture (ERS-USDA)

Fresh Fruit: Per Capita Consumption[1] in the United States   In Pounds

Year	Citrus Fruit Oranges	Tangerines and Tangelos	Lemons	Grapefruit	Total	Noncitrus Fruit Apples	Apricots	Avacados	Bananas	Cherries	Cran- berries
1993	14.15	1.86	2.64	6.20	25.81	19.00	.13	1.33	26.60	.43	.07
1994	12.94	2.09	2.66	6.07	24.74	19.36	.15	1.35	27.78	.52	.08
1995	11.83	1.99	2.84	6.00	23.86	18.69	.10	1.58	27.08	.29	.08
1996	12.58	2.15	2.86	5.85	24.60	18.67	.09	1.58	27.60	.40	.08
1997	13.91	2.52	2.76	6.18	26.54	18.09	.14	1.73	27.16	.60	.07
1998	14.61	2.17	2.46	5.94	26.61	18.98	.12	1.52	28.01	.52	.08
1999	8.38	2.21	2.61	5.75	20.31	18.50	.12	1.92	30.70	.63	.11
2000	11.74	2.84	2.44	5.11	23.42	17.46	.15	2.21	28.44	.60	.14
2001	11.88	2.95	2.96	4.82	24.11	15.59	.08	2.50	26.61	.77	.13
2002[2]	10.63	2.98	3.33	4.82	22.85	15.97	.09	2.33	26.73	.70	.11

[1] All data on calendar-year basis except for citrus fruits; apples, August; grapes and pears, July; grapefruit, September; lemons, August of prior year; all other citrus, November.   [2] Preliminary.   Source: Economic Research Service, U.S. Department of Agriculture (ERS-USDA)

Fresh Fruit: Per Capita Consumption[1] in the United States   In Pounds

Year	Noncitrus Fruit Continued Grapes	Kiwifruit	Mangos	Nectarines & Peaches	Pears	Pine- apples	Papaya	Plums & Prunes	Straw- berries	Total Noncitrus	Total Fruit
1994	7.25	.57	.97	5.42	3.44	2.02	.30	1.60	4.05	75.13	99.87
1995	7.42	.55	1.12	5.33	3.36	1.91	.37	.93	4.06	73.18	97.04
1996	6.82	.54	1.34	4.38	3.05	1.90	.54	1.43	4.27	72.96	97.56
1997	7.89	.48	1.44	5.51	3.39	2.34	.47	1.51	4.05	75.13	101.70
1998	7.14	.55	1.49	4.77	3.29	2.75	.47	1.18	3.88	75.07	101.68
1999	8.01	.55	1.62	5.37	3.33	3.03	.62	1.28	4.52	80.63	100.94
2000	7.28	.56	1.75	5.40	3.21	3.22	.68	1.19	4.81	77.35	100.77
2001	7.61	.57	1.79	5.24	3.07	3.16	.78	1.32	4.17	73.73	97.84
2002[2]	8.58	.49	1.97	5.34	2.91	3.81	.79	1.25	4.89	76.37	99.22

[1] All data on calendar-year basis except for citrus fruits; apples, August; grapes and pears, July; grapefruit, September; lemons, August of prior year; all other citrus, November.   [2] Preliminary.   Source: Economic Research Service, U.S. Department of Agriculture (ERS-USDA)

Gas

Natural gas is a fossil fuel that is colorless, shapeless, and odorless in its pure form. It is a mixture of hydrocarbon gases formed primarily of methane, but it can also include ethane, propane, butane, and pentane. Natural gas is combustible, clean burning, and gives off a great deal of energy. In about 500 BC, the Chinese discovered that the energy in natural gas could be harnessed. They passed it through crude bamboo-shoot pipes and then burned it to boil sea water to create potable fresh water. Around 1785, Britain became the first country to commercially use natural gas produced from coal for streetlights and indoor lights. In 1821, William Hart dug the first well specifically intended to obtain natural gas, and is regarded by many as the "father of natural gas" in America. There is a vast amount of natural gas estimated to still be in the ground in the US, concentrated in Texas and the Gulf of Mexico.

In the US, the industrial sector accounts for 43% of natural gas used, with the residential sector coming in second. The major industries using natural gas include pulp and paper, metals, chemicals, petroleum refining, stone, clay and glass, plastic, and food processing. Natural gas as a source of energy has always been much cheaper than electricity for residential consumers. Natural gas costs less than 30% of the cost of electricity per Btu. Natural gas accounts for roughly one-quarter of all US energy consumption.

Natural gas futures and options are traded on the New York Mercantile Exchange (NYMEX). The NYMEX natural gas futures contract calls for the delivery of natural gas representing 10,000 million British thermal units (mmBtu) at the Henry Hub in Louisiana, which is the nexus of 16 intrastate and inter-state pipelines. The contract is priced in term of dollars per mmBtu. NYMEX also has basic swap futures contracts available for 30 different natural gas pricing locations against the benchmark Henry Hub location. Natural gas futures are also listed in London on the International Petroleum Exchange (IPE).

Prices – NYMEX natural gas futures on the nearest-futures chart in 2003 showed an upward spike to a record high of $11.90 per mmBtu related to the start of the Iraq war, but then quickly settled back down to the $5-7 area through Q2 and Q3 2003. Natural gas prices then moved higher in December to post a 10-month high of $7.55 and closed the year at $6.19, up 16% from the 2002 close of $5.34. The rally late in the year was generally attributed to higher demand with the stronger economy, the weak dollar, and early cold weather in the US. However, inventories were also rising during that period and federal authorities started an investigation into allegations of price manipulation.

Supply – The US recovered 24,130 billion cubic feet of natural gas in 2002, down 1.4% from 2001. The world's largest natural gas producers are Russia (with about 34% of world production), the US (30%), and Canada (10%).

World Production of Natural Gas (Monthly Average Marketed Production[3])   (In Terajoule[4])

Year	Australia	Canada	China	Germany	Indonesia	India	Italy	Mexico	Netherlands	Romania	Russia	United Kingdom	United States
1994	87,178	480,577	57,036	52,911	190,775	55,355	64,122	95,250	207,317	51,720	1,657,151	214,710	1,703,771
1995	96,912	511,447	58,261	55,714	203,633	72,796	63,371	93,473	209,229	50,401	1,891,583	246,818	1,683,674
1996	99,461	530,891	72,609	62,479	248,574	74,776	63,436	106,214	236,803	48,023	1,844,954	293,536	1,706,764
1997	99,077	537,295	81,954	61,804	248,585	84,892	61,173	109,568	209,526	41,547	1,771,467	299,503	1,711,134
1998	95,265	538,273	84,033	60,748	274,281	88,195	60,159	182,615	198,554	32,932	1,665,726	314,506	1,722,107
1999	92,440	569,819	79,523	62,651	282,485	91,468	56,616	182,610	186,672	38,952	1,807,313	345,040	1,704,788
2000	92,746	588,447	90,287	59,164	267,707	94,783	54,289	178,861	178,989	38,254	1,898,046	377,565	1,726,861
2001	96,523	594,397	98,431	60,463	258,122	91,063	48,008	171,940	192,180	40,422	1,887,953	370,237	1,759,236
2002[1]	96,841		106,720	61,147	276,990	92,568	45,782	168,675	186,206	38,004	1,934,011	397,129	1,722,443
2003[2]	93,959		109,099			99,711	42,097	173,896		36,600	1,962,552		

[1] Preliminary.   [2] Estimate.   [3] Compares all gas collected & utilized as fuel or as a chemical industry raw material, including gas used in oilfields and/or gasfields as a fuel by producers.   [4] Terajoule = 10 to the 12th power Joule = approximately 10 to the 9th power BTU.   NA = Not available.
Source: United Nations

Marketed Production of Natural Gas in the United States, by States   (In Million Cubic Feet)

Year	Alaska	California	Colorado	Kansas	Louisiana	Michigan	Mississippi	New Mexico	Oklahoma	Texas	Wyoming	Total
1993	430,350	315,851	400,985	686,347	4,991,138	204,635	80,695	1,409,429	2,049,942	6,249,624	634,957	18,981,915
1994	555,402	309,427	453,207	712,730	5,169,705	222,657	63,448	1,557,689	1,934,864	6,353,844	696,018	19,709,525
1995	469,550	279,555	523,084	721,436	5,108,366	238,203	95,533	1,625,837	1,811,734	6,330,048	673,775	19,506,474
1996	480,828	286,494	572,071	712,796	5,289,742	245,740	103,263	1,554,087	1,734,887	6,470,620	666,036	19,812,241
1997	468,311	285,690	637,375	687,215	5,229,821	305,950	107,300	1,558,633	1,703,888	6,453,873	738,368	19,866,093
1998	466,648	315,277	696,321	603,586	5,277,188	278,076	108,068	1,501,098	1,669,367	6,408,444	903,836	19,961,348
1999	462,967	382,715	722,738	553,419	5,275,730	277,364	111,021	1,511,671	1,594,002	6,211,613	971,230	19,804,848
2000	458,995	376,580	752,985	525,729	5,068,863	296,556	88,558	1,695,295	1,612,890	6,205,249	1,088,328	20,197,511
2001	471,440	377,824	696,237	480,145	5,456,463	275,036	107,541	1,689,125	1,615,384	6,335,794	1,363,879	20,630,412
2002[1]	464,669	360,559	605,384	450,801	1,537,769	275,363	112,812	1,579,130	1,623,152	5,251,807	1,436,692	19,968,906

[1] Preliminary.   *Source: Energy Information Administration, U.S. Department of Energy (EIA-DOE)*

World Production of Natural Gas Plant Liquids   (Thousand Barrels per Day)

Year	Algeria	Canada	Mexico	Saudi Arabia	Russia	United States	Persian Gulf[2]	OAPEC[3]	OPEC[4]	World
1994	140	529	461	698	200	1,727	1,071	1,267	1,465	5,299
1995	145	581	447	701	180	1,762	1,106	1,301	1,506	5,492
1996	150	596	423	697	185	1,830	1,082	1,295	1,501	5,585
1997	160	636	388	712	195	1,817	1,152	1,384	1,589	5,729
1008	155	651	424	755	220	1,759	1,225	1,449	1,662	5,883
1999	190	653	439	666	231	1,850	1,153	1,412	1,648	5,995
2000	230	699	438	705	232	1,911	1,253	1,578	1,798	6,289
2001	250	709	433	680	237	1,868	1,347	1,706	1,933	6,601
2002	250	698	408	810	236	1,880	1,508	1,873	2,098	6,812
2003[1]	250	725	418	1,011	257	1,720	1,756	2,119	2,328	7,102

[1] Preliminary.   [2] Bahrain, Iran, Iraq, Kuwait, Qatar, Saudi Arabia and the United Arab Emirates.   [3] Organization of Arab Petroleum Exporting Countries.   [4] Organization of Pertroleum Exporting Countries.   *Source: Energy Information Administration, U.S. Department of Energy (EIA-DOE)*

Recoverable Reserves and Deliveries of Natural Gas in the United States   (in Billions of Cubic Feet)

Year	Gross Withdrawals	Recoverable Reserves of Natural Gas Dec. 31[2]	Residential	Commercial	Deliveries — Electric Utility Plants[3]	Industrial	Total Deliveries	Consumption — Lease & Plant Fuel	Used as Pipeline Fuel	Heating Value BTU per Cubic Foot
1993	22,726	162,415	4,956	2,863	2,682	7,981	18,483	1,172	624	1,027
1994	23,581	163,837	4,848	2,897	2,987	8,167	18,899	1,124	685	1,028
1995	23,744	165,146	4,850	3,034	3,197	8,580	19,660	1,220	700	1,027
1996	24,114	166,474	5,241	3,161	2,732	8,870	20,006	1,250	711	1,027
1997	24,213	167,223	4,984	3,215	4,065	8,511	20,782	1,203	751	1,026
1998	24,108	164,041	4,520	2,999	4,588	8,320	20,436	1,173	635	1,031
1999	23,823	167,406	4,726	3,045	4,820	8,079	20,679	1,079	645	1,027
2000	24,174	177,427	4,996	3,218	5,206	8,142	21,538	1,151	642	1,025
2001	24,476	183,460	4,776	3,037	5,343	7,363	20,477	1,089	624	1,028
2002[1]	24,130	186,946	4,906	3,154	5,672	7,222	20,969	1,053	635	

[1] Preliminary.   [2] Estimated proved recoverable reserves of dry natural gas.   [3] Figures include gas other than natural (impossible to segregate); therefore, shown separately from other consumption.   *Source: Energy Information Administration, U.S. Department of Energy (EIA-DOE)*

Gas Utility Sales in the United States by Types and Class of Service   (In Trillions of BTUs)

Year	Total Utility Sales	Number of Customers (Millions)	Residential	Commercial	Class by Service — Industrial	Electric Generation	Other	Total	Residential	Commercial	Revenue - Million $ From Sales to Customers — industrial	Electric Generation	Other
1992	9,907	56.1	4,694	2,209	1,959	813	231	46,178	26,702	10,865	5,837	2,077	698
1993	10,151	57.0	5,054	2,397	2,009	524	168	50,137	29,787	12,076	6,162	1,480	632
1994	9,248	57.9	4,845	2,253	1,690	420	159	49,852	30,552	12,276	5,529	1,170	597
1995	9,221	58.7	4,803	2,281	1,591	328	218	46,436	28,742	11,573	4,816	836	549
1996	9,532	59.8	5,198	2,395	1,519	271	148	51,115	32,021	12,726	5,039	783	545
1997	8,880	59.8	5,013	2,234	1,279	245	123	51,531	33,175	12,632	4,518	766	488
1998	8,630	60.4	4,828	2,157	1,153	336	117	47,930	31,333	11,523	3,779	899	391
1999[1]	8,889	64.0	4,865	2,087	1,200	644	69	48,423	31,472	11,133	3,883	1,664	272
2000[2]	9,052	64.1	4,941	2,116	1,382	522	91	59,667	37,446	13,648	6,011	2,058	504

[1] Preliminary.   [2] Estimate.   *Source: American Gas Association (AGA)*

Salient Statistics of Natural Gas in the United States

Year	Marketed Production	Extraction Loss	Dry Production	Storage Withdrawals	Imports (Consumed)	Total Supply	Consumption	Exports	Added to Storage	Total Disposition	Wellhead Price	Imports	Exports	Residential	Commercial	Industrial	Electric Utilities
	In Billions of Cubic Feet										USD Per Thousand Cubic Feet						
1993	18,982	886	18,095	2,799	2,350	23,578	20,790	140	2,835	22,726	2.04	2.03	2.59	6.16	5.22	3.07	2.61
1994	19,710	889	18,821	2,579	2,624	24,207	21,247	162	2,865	23,581	1.85	1.87	2.50	6.41	5.44	3.05	2.28
1995	19,506	908	18,599	3,025	2,841	24,837	22,207	154	2,610	23,744	1.55	1.49	2.39	6.06	5.05	2.71	2.02
1996	19,812	958	18,854	2,981	2,937	25,635	22,610	153	2,979	24,114	2.17	1.97	2.97	6.34	5.40	3.42	2.69
1997	19,866	964	18,902	2,894	2,994	25,502	22,737	157	2,870	24,213	2.32	2.17	3.02	6.94	5.80	3.59	2.78
1998	19,961	938	19,024	2,432	3,152	24,859	22,246	159	2,961	24,108	1.96	1.97	2.45	6.82	5.48	3.14	2.40
1999	19,805	973	18,832	2,808	3,586	25,055	22,405	163	2,636	23,823	2.19	2.24	2.61	6.69	5.33	3.12	2.62
2000	20,198	1,016	18,182	3,550	3,782		23,368	244	2,721	24,174	3.69	3.95	4.10	7.76	6.59	4.45	4.38
2001[1]	20,630	954	19,676	2,344	3,977		22,246	373	3,509	24,476	4.02	4.43	4.19	9.64	8.43	5.28	4.61
2002[2]	19,969	922	19,047	3,126	4,008		22,534	516	2,679	24,130	2.95	3.15	3.41	7.88	6.57	3.99	3.78

[1] Preliminary.   [2] Estimate.   *Source: Energy Information Administration, U.S. Department of Energy (EIA-DOE)*

GAS

Average Open Interest of Natural Gas Futures in New York   In Contracts

Year	Jan.	Feb.	Mar.	Apr.	May	June	July	Aug.	Sept.	Oct.	Nov.	Dec.
1994	127,254	128,336	118,480	119,908	120,894	120,956	111,044	135,652	156,238	145,766	139,471	139,054
1995	148,448	151,882	157,097	150,101	148,797	144,402	143,942	140,297	135,226	133,969	140,301	166,227
1996	155,024	150,521	149,809	159,132	147,616	156,959	151,913	135,191	138,657	144,944	147,854	151,498
1997	156,231	162,567	171,467	181,745	206,685	197,637	199,296	213,640	235,509	242,184	231,556	210,259
1998	192,652	198,853	203,402	251,344	255,837	264,517	255,878	273,350	275,868	252,827	236,292	240,832
1999	244,472	268,649	284,312	315,336	332,398	330,725	316,034	353,767	336,622	316,157	309,130	292,161
2000	262,845	266,826	295,176	313,739	342,455	347,353	330,604	339,025	373,654	369,448	389,363	377,470
2001	364,532	346,343	360,032	380,632	421,145	456,512	473,675	497,972	494,475	488,187	455,766	415,882
2002	458,924	491,215	527,765	559,413	556,277	526,016	494,133	437,285	419,532	413,312	393,953	391,424
2003	415,642	420,329	367,673	354,154	365,838	366,610	357,299	343,622	354,568	352,685	356,622	341,871

Source: New York Mercantile Exchange (NYMEX)

Volume of Trading of Natural Gas Futures in New York   (In Thousands of Contracts)

Year	Jan.	Feb.	Mar.	Apr.	May	June	July	Aug.	Sept.	Oct.	Nov.	Dec.	Total
1994	667.6	470.9	373.5	344.7	411.1	465.8	438.8	724.2	578.7	594.2	621.9	721.8	6,413.2
1995	733.0	557.8	676.1	524.5	621.3	622.5	641.8	745.6	548.3	664.4	763.0	988.5	8,086.7
1996	887.2	655.7	694.6	620.0	590.7	681.3	829.0	628.8	679.1	924.4	802.8	820.4	8,813.9
1997	922.8	693.6	664.7	836.3	945.4	803.7	812.9	1,313.8	1,377.1	1,394.0	1,104.8	1,054.6	11,923.6
1998	1,005.6	1,089.1	1,193.5	1,625.9	1,245.2	1,568.8	1,310.4	1,237.0	1,656.3	1,339.5	1,243.1	1,464.0	15,978.3
1999	1,296.7	1,158.6	1,788.5	1,655.8	1,465.3	1,474.2	1,865.8	1,892.1	1,978.6	1,676.5	1,552.3	1,360.7	19,165.1
2000	1,388.8	1,470.9	1,505.0	1,179.3	1,822.2	1,853.7	1,331.4	1,483.9	1,510.2	1,594.9	1,759.5	975.1	17,875.0
2001	1,044.4	1,044.6	1,131.7	1,144.8	1,632.5	1,536.9	1,350.3	1,510.9	901.1	1,639.7	1,891.7	1,639.6	16,468.4
2002	1,942.5	1,668.6	2,381.1	2,421.7	2,281.4	1,911.7	2,266.1	2,115.6	1,990.0	2,103.4	1,569.2	1,706.4	24,357.8
2003	2,134.4	1,909.1	1,362.4	1,321.3	1,521.7	1,584.8	1,543.7	1,315.3	1,503.7	1,948.9	1,376.6	1,515.2	19,037.1

Source: New York Mercantile Exchange (NYMEX)

Average Price of Natural Gas at Henry Hub   In Dollars Per MMBtu

Year	Jan.	Feb.	Mar.	Apr.	May	June	July	Aug.	Sept.	Oct.	Nov.	Dec.	Average
1994	2.49	2.59	2.08	2.05	1.87	1.96	1.88	1.59	1.48	1.54	1.54	1.69	1.90
1995	1.51	1.58	1.54	1.63	1.64	1.62	1.44	1.56	1.64	1.77	2.04	2.71	1.72
1996	2.93	4.82	2.95	2.23	2.24	2.49	2.48	2.03	1.84	2.37	3.03	3.91	2.78
1997	3.31	2.22	1.89	2.03	2.24	2.20	2.19	2.48	2.85	3.04	3.02	2.36	2.49
1998	2.10	2.22	2.24	2.43	2.14	2.17	2.17	1.85	2.02	1.89	2.10	1.72	2.09
1999	1.85	1.77	1.79	2.15	2.25	2.30	2.31	2.79	2.54	2.72	2.35	2.36	2.27
2000	2.42	2.65	2.79	3.03	3.58	4.28	3.96	4.41	5.11	5.02	5.54	8.95	4.31
2001	8.18	5.62	5.16	5.16	4.21	3.71	3.11	2.95	2.15	2.45	2.35	2.43	3.96
2002	2.25	2.31	3.03	3.42	3.49	3.22	2.98	3.09	3.55	4.12	4.04	4.75	3.35
2003	5.49	7.41	6.08	5.27	5.81	5.83	5.03	4.97	4.61	4.66	4.47	6.13	5.48

Source: Energy Information Administration, U.S. Department of Energy (EIA-DOE)

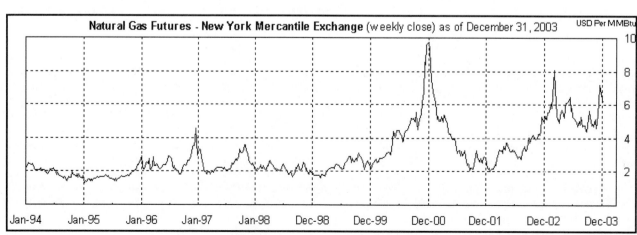

Natural Gas Futures - New York Mercantile Exchange (weekly close) as of December 31, 2003   USD Per MMBtu

Gasoline

Gasoline is a complex mixture of hundreds of lighter liquid hydrocarbons and is used chiefly as a fuel for internal-combustion engines. Gasoline is the single largest volume refined product sold in the US. Petroleum crude, or crude oil, is still the most economical source of gasoline with refineries turning more than half of every barrel of crude oil into gasoline. The three basic steps to all refining operations are the separation process (separating crude oil into various chemical components), conversion process (breaking the chemicals down into molecules called hydrocarbons), and treatment process (transforming and combining hydrocarbon molecules and other additives). Another process, called *hydro treating,* removes a significant amount of sulfur from finished gasoline as is currently required by the state of California.

Octane is a measure of a gasoline's ability to resist pinging or knocking noise from an engine. Most gasoline stations offer three octane grades of unleaded fuel—regular at 87 (R+M)/2, midgrade at 89 (R+M)/2, and premium at 93 (R+M)/2. Higher octane ratings mean less engine knock. Additional refining steps are needed to increase the octane. This does not make the gasoline any cleaner or better, but yields a different blend of hydrocarbons that burn more slowly. The additional refining steps also increase the price per gallon.

In an attempt to improve air quality and reduce harmful emissions from internal combustion engines, Congress in 1990 amended the Clean Air Act to mandate the addition of ethanol to gasoline. Some 2 billion gallons of ethanol is now added to gasoline each year in the US. The most common blend is E10, which contains 10% ethanol and 90% gasoline and that mixture is approved by all auto manufacturers for use in US vehicles. Ethanol is an alcohol-based fuel produced by fermenting and distilling crops such as corn, barley, wheat and sugar.

Unleaded gasoline futures and options trade at the New York Mercantile Exchange (NYMEX). The NYMEX gasoline futures contract calls for the delivery of 1,000 barrels (42,000 gallons) of unleaded gasoline in the New York harbor and is priced in terms of dollars and cents per gallon.

Prices – Gasoline prices generally followed crude oil prices during 2003, rallying early in the year ahead of the Iraq war, dipping in spring, and then showing a sustained rally late in the year on tight supplies and strong demand. NYMEX unleaded gasoline futures closed 2003 at $1.02 per gallon, mildly higher than the 92-cent close in 2002. However, that was at the upper end of the range seen in the past two decades. The retail price of regular unleaded gasoline averaged $1.61 per gallon in 2003 (through October), the highest level of the past three decades and up from $1.36 in 2002. The retail price of aviation gasoline rose to an average $1.50 in 2003 from $1.29 in 2002.

Supply – US production of gasoline in 2003 averaged 8.467 million barrels per day, slightly lower than 8.475 million barrels per day in 2002. Gasoline stocks in September 2003 were tight at 145 million barrels, down from 162 million in 2002 and 2001.

Demand – US consumption of finished motor gasoline in 2003 averaged 8.929 million barrels per day, up +0.9% from 2002. Gasoline accounts for about one-half of US national oil consumption.

Average Spot Price of Unleaded Gasoline in New York   In Cents Per Gallon

Year	Jan.	Feb.	Mar.	Apr.	May	June	July	Aug.	Sept.	Oct.	Nov.	Dec.	Average
1994	42.40	43.75	44.04	48.98	50.62	52.84	54.52	55.61	46.53	51.14	52.32	46.87	49.14
1995	50.99	51.43	50.74	61.01	64.76	59.47	51.45	53.45	56.10	48.89	51.15	53.44	54.41
1996	50.70	53.26	58.56	69.17	65.10	58.03	61.65	61.17	62.43	65.52	69.23	68.58	61.95
1997	67.64	62.49	61.28	58.59	62.08	55.17	58.58	70.42	62.17	58.35	55.60	51.75	60.34
1998	47.85	45.14	44.13	46.98	48.26	43.95	42.29	40.14	42.70	43.71	36.78	30.92	42.74
1999	34.24	31.81	42.33	50.11	48.86	48.65	58.35	63.89	69.37	62.63	69.57	70.55	54.20
2000	70.43	81.30	89.11	73.15	89.06	96.18	86.76	86.97	96.04	94.71	93.94	73.66	85.94
2001	83.32	82.56	78.18	94.95	92.37	71.85	68.31	77.18	75.00	59.79	51.34	51.85	73.89
2002	54.30	55.41	69.64	74.66	70.32	71.65	76.62	76.75	78.36	82.34	76.08	80.56	72.22
2003	87.56	99.62	95.51	80.08	76.16	80.65	87.17	100.42	90.41	87.12	87.33	88.37	88.37

Source: Energy Information Administration, U.S. Department of Energy (EIA-DOE)

Average Open Interest of Unleaded Regular Gasoline Futures in New York   In Contracts

Year	Jan.	Feb.	Mar.	Apr.	May	June	July	Aug.	Sept.	Oct.	Nov.	Dec.
1994	135,366	120,204	118,977	122,092	96,525	89,854	86,401	76,213	67,881	70,258	71,245	63,679
1995	61,015	67,631	65,201	76,323	76,269	69,676	64,379	58,426	62,089	58,782	57,902	70,098
1996	64,561	64,990	70,100	71,895	66,172	52,882	55,394	55,618	57,119	59,993	58,416	62,760
1997	68,188	84,693	92,520	97,619	90,407	78,492	83,082	103,538	103,250	94,602	92,852	103,497
1998	106,353	102,656	108,667	117,521	107,235	100,792	89,846	86,902	85,188	81,991	87,306	103,079
1999	105,532	113,683	111,449	110,531	107,644	102,927	113,619	120,468	120,328	111,758	109,428	96,652
2000	89,049	103,586	105,448	105,133	103,831	96,772	80,886	66,598	74,735	80,446	88,509	92,041
2001	117,540	126,762	124,631	124,162	111,576	103,058	101,249	92,156	87,841	102,414	115,699	126,634
2002	136,795	139,191	133,649	129,274	120,224	114,663	106,463	94,648	95,754	100,427	105,175	109,737
2003	117,558	124,288	113,380	98,627	96,405	93,285	95,433	99,394	85,457	90,007	95,002	105,895

Source: New York Mercantile Exchange (NYMEX)

GASOLINE

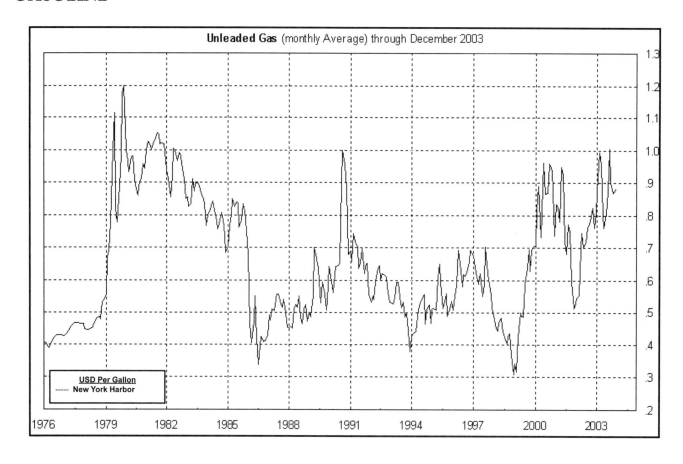

Unleaded Gas (monthly Average) through December 2003

USD Per Gallon
----- New York Harbor

Volume of Trading of Unleaded Regular Gasoline Futures in New York   In Thousands of Contracts

Year	Jan.	Feb.	Mar.	Apr.	May	June	July	Aug.	Sept.	Oct.	Nov.	Dec.	Total
1994	634.0	526.5	615.6	677.9	637.0	673.0	602.0	748.4	569.4	684.7	582.4	520.0	7,470.8
1995	592.3	506.6	736.7	663.7	780.6	680.8	565.7	556.6	573.6	473.0	480.5	461.7	7,071.8
1996	543.8	449.5	570.3	676.2	623.3	468.0	533.8	463.8	469.0	527.6	487.6	499.3	6,312.3
1997	590.1	563.2	605.1	623.2	618.3	555.5	721.4	795.4	664.9	613.6	509.9	614.6	7,475.1
1998	613.6	612.3	766.4	789.3	681.1	753.1	680.6	592.0	654.2	670.2	577.8	601.7	7,992.3
1999	561.5	619.7	876.4	741.5	721.1	737.7	822.0	800.4	751.3	705.1	748.8	615.7	8,701.2
2000	693.6	721.9	921.6	730.0	927.5	838.5	650.6	677.2	641.2	635.7	612.1	595.1	8,645.2
2001	825.2	701.2	809.2	981.0	1,056.5	895.0	737.3	790.8	581.9	664.9	613.3	567.2	9,223.5
2002	795.0	744.7	942.7	1,019.3	985.2	834.5	967.8	893.6	867.6	1,105.0	865.9	958.4	10,979.7
2003	1,054.1	968.7	1,010.9	909.0	933.7	944.0	987.5	1,021.5	943.0	877.1	760.8	761.6	11,172.1

Source: New York Mercantile Exchange (NYMEX)

Production of Finished Motor Gasoline in the United States   In Thousand Barrels per Day

Year	Jan.	Feb.	Mar.	Apr.	May	June	July	Aug.	Sept.	Oct.	Nov.	Dec.	Average
1994	7,097	6,790	6,760	7,195	7,348	7,455	7,380	7,432	7,385	7,151	7,849	7,867	7,312
1995	7,303	7,243	7,168	7,529	7,678	7,843	7,747	7,642	7,785	7,544	7,739	7,821	7,588
1996	7,333	7,303	7,242	7,475	7,724	7,820	7,811	7,696	7,585	7,496	7,835	7,784	7,647
1997	7,308	7,315	7,322	7,822	8,056	8,180	7,947	8,048	8,147	8,039	7,984	8,143	7,870
1998	7,749	7,485	7,591	8,029	8,057	8,372	8,287	8,200	8,029	7,995	8,263	8,395	8,082
1999	7,886	7,607	7,531	8,138	8,207	8,402	8,280	8,183	8,187	8,266	8,142	8,471	8,111
2000	7,798	7,658	8,032	8,130	8,398	8,550	8,320	8,251	8,358	8,031	8,394	8,298	8,186
2001	7,888	7,822	8,011	8,450	8,651	8,637	8,481	8,277	8,381	8,446	8,366	8,301	8,312
2002	8,160	8,117	8,072	8,626	8,729	8,661	8,665	8,666	8,320	8,190	8,738	8,734	8,475
2003[1]	8,038	8,031	7,917	8,449	8,780	8,694	8,653	8,773	8,524	8,578	8,764	8,759	8,497

[1] Preliminary.   *Source: Energy Information Administration, U.S. Department of Energy (EIA-DOE)*

108

Disposition of Finished Motor Gasoline, Total Product Supplied in the U.S.   In Thousand Barrels per Day

Year	Jan.	Feb.	Mar.	Apr.	May	June	July	Aug.	Sept.	Oct.	Nov.	Dec.	Average
1994	6,980	7,275	7,395	7,564	7,644	7,922	7,884	7,975	7,615	7,548	7,464	7,924	7,601
1995	7,163	7,481	7,788	7,651	7,894	8,220	7,888	8,187	7,786	7,781	7,866	7,742	7,789
1996	7,254	7,552	7,729	7,869	7,998	8,089	8,135	8,216	7,641	8,038	7,875	7,775	7,891
1997	7,312	7,651	7,808	8,067	8,128	8,260	8,471	8,195	8,004	8,166	7,955	8,093	8,017
1998	7,590	7,755	7,956	8,137	8,070	8,437	8,659	8,500	8,308	8,405	8,136	8,401	8,253
1999	7,701	8,001	8,120	8,500	8,420	8,600	8,942	8,579	8,305	8,542	8,240	8,859	8,431
2000	7,653	8,291	8,305	8,375	8,661	8,824	8,642	8,921	8,518	8,417	8,384	8,670	8,472
2001	8,099	8,234	8,532	8,575	8,706	8,690	9,023	8,953	8,557	8,655	8,677	8,585	8,610
2002	8,227	8,607	8,655	8,766	9,078	9,140	9,143	9,313	8,687	8,814	8,829	8,893	8,848
2003[1]	8,504	8,540	8,585	8,785	9,097	9,165	9,209	9,410	8,927	9,037	8,949	9,004	8,934

[1] Preliminary.   Source: Energy Information Administration, U.S. Department of Energy (EIA-DOE)

Stocks of Finished Gasoline[2] on Hand in the United States, at End of Month   In Millions of Barrels

Year	Jan.	Feb.	Mar.	Apr.	May	June	July	Aug.	Sept.	Oct.	Nov.	Dec.
1994	194.1	186.2	175.6	176.4	179.0	176.9	172.9	167.6	169.2	161.7	176.6	175.9
1995	182.7	180.0	167.8	167.1	167.1	163.5	166.0	154.6	158.9	155.6	155.6	161.3
1996	168.7	168.4	158.3	159.8	161.8	163.8	163.7	154.9	161.3	149.1	150.7	157.0
1997	164.9	161.3	153.8	152.0	157.8	163.9	150.6	149.6	158.1	158.0	161.1	166.1
1998	175.3	172.8	166.4	168.3	174.9	177.7	172.5	168.8	164.7	160.0	167.5	172.0
1999	185.2	178.4	167.8	168.9	176.5	172.3	163.6	158.6	159.2	158.8	160.5	151.6
2000	165.3	156.4	157.1	160.6	162.2	164.5	164.6	151.0	154.2	147.4	156.7	153.0
2001	158.7	154.6	144.7	150.3	160.1	169.4	162.3	150.6	158.0	160.2	161.2	161.5
2002	169.7	165.5	159.8	167.0	168.3	167.6	164.8	157.3	157.4	148.2	158.0	161.9
2003[1]	158.4	152.1	145.0	151.9	156.1	153.4	149.6	144.7	144.8	140.3	145.9	

[1] Preliminary.   [2] Includes oxygenated and other finished.   Source: Energy Information Administration, U.S. Department of Energy (EIA-DOE)

Average Refiner Price of Finished Motor Gasoline to End Users[1] in the U.S.   In Cents Per Gallon

Year	Jan.	Feb.	Mar.	Apr.	May	June	July	Aug.	Sept.	Oct.	Nov.	Dec.	Average
1994	66.8	67.6	67.3	69.5	71.1	74.1	77.0	81.5	79.6	76.9	77.5	75.1	73.8
1995	74.5	73.3	73.1	77.3	83.4	83.9	80.0	76.9	75.8	73.6	71.8	73.0	76.5
1996	74.6	74.8	79.8	88.1	92.7	90.3	87.5	84.9	84.4	84.4	86.7	85.9	84.7
1997	86.6	86.1	84.3	83.9	84.5	83.3	81.5	86.8	87.2	84.3	81.6	77.8	83.9
1998	73.3	69.0	65.6	67.4	71.0	70.4	69.4	66.7	65.4	66.4	64.0	60.0	67.3
1999	59.2	56.8	65.1	79.0	78.2	75.6	80.6	86.5	88.8	87.1	88.4	90.3	78.1
2000	91.7	98.7	113.1	108.7	110.3	121.3	117.3	110.3	117.5	115.5	113.5	106.3	110.6
2001	106.8	106.7	103.9	117.7	130.1	120.7	103.2	102.5	1,009.2	89.9	76.9	68.5	103.2
2002	70.6	71.8	87.2	100.4	99.9	99.1	100.3	100.1	100.1	104.0	101.2	98.1	94.7
2003[2]	106.0	122.1	130.0	120.1	110.0	109.3	110.6	123.1	126.5	115.0	109.5		116.6

[1] Excludes aviation and taxes.   [2] Preliminary.   Source: Energy Information Administration, U.S. Department of Energy (EIA-DOE)

Unleaded Gasoline Futures - New York Mercantile Exchange (weekly close) as of Dec. 31, 2003   USD Per Gallon

GASOLINE

Average Retail Price of Unleaded Premium Motor Gasoline[2] in the United States   In Cents per Gallon

Year	Jan.	Feb.	Mar.	Apr.	May	June	July	Aug.	Sept.	Oct.	Nov.	Dec.	Average
1994	124.0	124.5	124.3	126.0	127.4	130.0	132.7	136.7	136.4	134.5	135.4	133.7	130.5
1995	132.4	131.6	130.6	132.5	138.3	141.1	138.4	135.2	133.2	131.5	129.2	129.0	133.6
1996	131.7	131.1	134.8	143.1	150.7	148.1	145.3	142.1	141.7	140.8	142.8	143.8	141.3
1997	144.1	143.4	141.5	141.3	140.9	141.1	138.8	143.3	145.8	142.6	139.7	136.3	141.6
1998	131.9	127.1	122.9	123.7	127.5	127.9	126.8	124.4	123.0	123.6	122.5	118.7	125.0
1999	117.1	115.5	118.6	136.7	137.0	133.9	137.8	144.1	146.8	146.4	145.4	148.6	135.7
2000	148.6	155.1	172.3	169.8	168.2	178.6	177.3	168.9	176.4	174.4	173.8	167.9	169.3
2001	165.7	167.1	163.8	174.8	193.4	188.1	169.5	163.6	172.6	156.0	142.7	131.2	165.7
2002	132.3	133.0	145.0	162.2	162.5	160.8	160.7	162.0	161.9	164.3	164.3	158.9	157.8
2003[1]	166.6	182.8	192.4	184.6	172.9	170.0	171.0	180.8	191.1	178.9	172.4	168.6	177.7

[1] Preliminary.   [2] Including taxes.   *Source: Energy Information Administration, U.S. Department of Energy (EIA-DOE)*

Average Retail Price of Unleaded Regular Motor Gasoline[2] in the United States   In Cents per Gallon

Year	Jan.	Feb.	Mar.	Apr.	May	June	July	Aug.	Sept.	Oct.	Nov.	Dec.	Average
1994	104.3	105.1	104.5	106.4	108.0	110.6	113.6	118.2	117.7	115.2	116.3	114.3	111.2
1995	112.9	112.0	111.5	114.0	120.0	122.6	119.5	116.4	114.8	112.7	110.1	110.1	114.7
1996	112.9	112.4	116.2	125.1	132.3	129.9	127.2	124.0	123.4	122.7	125.0	126.0	123.1
1997	126.1	125.5	123.5	123.1	122.6	122.9	120.5	125.3	127.7	124.2	121.3	117.7	123.4
1998	113.1	108.2	104.1	105.2	109.2	109.4	107.9	105.2	103.3	104.2	102.8	98.6	105.9
1999	97.2	95.5	99.1	117.7	117.8	114.8	118.9	125.5	128.0	127.4	126.4	129.8	116.5
2000	130.1	136.9	154.1	150.6	149.8	161.7	159.3	151.0	158.2	155.9	155.5	148.9	151.0
2001	147.2	148.4	144.7	156.4	172.9	164.0	148.2	142.7	153.1	136.2	126.3	113.1	146.1
2002	113.9	113.0	124.1	140.7	142.1	140.4	141.2	142.3	142.2	144.9	144.8	139.4	135.8
2003[1]	147.3	164.1	174.8	165.9	154.2	151.4	152.4	162.8	172.8	160.3	153.5	149.4	159.1

[1] Preliminary.   [2] Including taxes.   *Source: Energy Information Administration, U.S. Department of Energy (EIA-DOE)*

Average Retail Price of All-Types[2] Motor Gasoline[3] in the United States   In Cents per Gallon

Year	Jan.	Feb.	Mar.	Apr.	May	June	July	Aug.	Sept.	Oct.	Nov.	Dec.	Average
1994	110.9	111.4	110.9	112.8	114.3	116.7	119.9	124.3	123.7	121.2	122.2	120.3	117.4
1995	119.0	118.1	117.3	119.7	125.6	128.1	125.2	122.2	120.6	118.5	116.1	116.0	120.5
1996	118.6	118.1	121.9	130.5	137.8	135.4	132.8	129.8	129.3	128.7	130.8	131.8	128.8
1997	131.8	131.2	129.3	128.8	128.4	128.6	126.3	131.0	133.4	130.0	127.1	123.6	129.1
1998	118.6	113.7	109.7	110.6	114.6	114.8	113.4	110.8	109.1	109.9	108.6	104.6	111.5
1999	103.1	101.4	104.8	123.2	123.3	120.4	124.4	130.9	133.4	132.9	131.9	135.3	122.1
2000	135.6	142.2	159.4	156.1	155.2	166.6	164.2	155.9	163.5	161.3	160.8	154.4	156.3
2001	152.5	153.8	150.3	161.7	181.2	173.1	156.5	150.9	160.9	144.2	132.4	120.0	153.1
2002	120.9	121.0	132.4	149.3	150.8	148.9	149.6	150.8	150.7	153.5	153.4	147.7	144.1
2003[1]	155.7	168.6	179.1	170.4	158.7	155.8	156.7	167.1	177.1	164.6	157.8	153.8	163.8

[1] Preliminary.   [2] Also includes types of motor oil not shown separately.   [3] Including taxes.   *Source: Energy Information Administration, U.S. Department of Energy (EIA-DOE)*

Average Refiner Price of Finished Aviation Gasoline to End Users[2] in the U.S.   In Cents per Gallon

Year	Jan.	Feb.	Mar.	Apr.	May	June	July	Aug.	Sept.	Oct.	Nov.	Dec.	Average
1994	88.6	88.4	89.0	91.3	92.3	95.6	95.9	101.7	101.1	100.0	100.0	99.2	95.6
1995	99.6	99.8	99.0	101.3	105.8	106.4	101.8	99.2	101.3	96.8	95.4	96.0	100.5
1996	97.6	100.6	105.0	111.2	114.4	113.5	113.7	114.4	114.3	115.0	115.1	115.3	111.6
1997	113.7	114.9	113.8	114.7	115.7	114.6	112.5	114.6	115.6	113.9	113.0	107.7	113.8
1998	104.3	101.1	98.2	98.6	99.9	99.0	98.4	95.9	94.1	95.1	93.2	88.5	97.2
1999	87.1	85.1	90.1	101.4	104.2	104.1	107.9	113.2	115.4	117.6	116.4	119.6	105.9
2000	118.7	119.5	129.1	124.3	126.8	139.8	142.6	NA	138.2	134.9	134.9	126.1	130.6
2001	128.5	129.2	124.5	134.9	150.9	145.1	134.6	136.3	142.4	125.3	119.4	115.8	132.3
2002	111.8	110.6	122.6	129.8	128.9	127.3	139.2	136.9	139.1	143.0	141.8	139.8	128.8
2003[1]	139.7	NA	NA	NA	139.8	145.1	151.9	162.2	158.9	150.8			149.8

[1] Preliminary.   [2] Excluding taxes.   NA = Not available.   *Source: Energy Information Administration, U.S. Department Energy (EIA-DOE)*

Gold

Gold is a dense, bright yellow metallic element with a high luster. Gold is an inactive substance and is unaffected by air, heat, moisture, and most solvents. Gold has been coveted for centuries for its unique blend of rarity, beauty, and near indestructibility. It is known that the Egyptians mined gold before 2,000 BC. The first pure gold coin was made on the orders of King Croesus of Lydia in the sixth century BC.

In 1792, the United States first assigned a formal monetary role for gold when Congress put the nation's currency on a bimetallic standard, backing it with gold and silver. Under the gold standard, the US governance was willing to exchange its paper currency for a set amount of gold, thus ensuring that the paper currency was backed by a physical asset with real value. However, President Nixon in 1971 severed the convertibility between the US dollar and gold, which led to the breakdown of the Bretton Woods international payments system. That meant that the prices of gold and of paper currencies floated freely according to supply and demand factors in their own markets. The US and other central banks now only hold physical gold reserves as a psychological backing for their paper currencies. World central banks hold a little over 1 billion troy ounces of gold, which equates to roughly $400 billion worth of gold (assuming a gold price of $400 per ounce). The US holds the most gold with roughly 262 million troy ounces, followed by Germany (112 million), and France (97 million). Although the US holds roughly $100 billion worth of gold, that is a mere fraction of the total US debt or the amount of outstanding US currency, illustrating that gold now plays an insignificant role in backing the dollar or paper currencies.

Gold is found in nature in quartz veins and secondary alluvial deposits as a free metal. Gold is produced from mines on every continent with the exception of Antarctica, where mining is forbidden. Because it is virtually indestructible, all the gold that has ever been mined still exists above ground in some form or another. South Africa remains the world's largest producing nation. The largest producer of gold in the US by far is the state of Nevada, with Alaska and California running a distant second and third.

Gold is a vital industrial commodity. Pure gold is one of the most malleable and ductile of all the metals. It is a good conductor of heat and electricity. Gold melts at 1,064 degrees Celsius and boils at about 2,808 degrees Celsius. The prime industrial use of gold is in electronics. Another important sector is dental gold where it has been used for almost 3,000 years. Other applications for gold include decorative gold leaf, reflective glass, and jewelry.

Gold futures and options are traded on the COMEX division of the New York Mercantile Exchange. Gold futures are traded on the Bolsa de Mercadorias and Futuros (BM&F) and on the Tokyo Commodity Exchange (TOCOM), the Chicago Board of Trade (CBOT) and he Korea Futures Exchange (KOFEX). The COMEX gold futures contract calls for the delivery of 100 troy ounces of gold (0.995 fineness), and the contract trades in terms of dollars and cents per troy ounce.

Prices – Comex gold futures prices rallied early in 2003 on geopolitical concerns caused by the war with Iraq, but then fell back through early April. Gold prices in August then began a steady rally that took the contract to an 8-year high of $417 in the last week of December. That was only mildly below the 14-year high of $425 posted in February 1990. The record high for cash gold prices was $675.75 posted in September 1980. Bullish factors for gold in the latter half of 2003 centered on the weak dollar and improved industrial demand with the rebounding global economy. The weak dollar was a key reason for gold's strength, since the dollar depreciated not only against other world paper currencies but also against a store of wealth such as gold.

Supply – World mine production of gold fell -1.9% in 2002 to 2.550 million kilograms (1 kilogram = 32.1507 troy ounces) from 2.600 million in 2001. The world's largest producers of gold are South Africa (with 16% of world production), followed by the US (12%), Australia (11%), China (7.5%), Russia (6.2%), and Canada (5.8%). US gold mine production in 2002 fell to 298,000 kilograms from 335,000 kilograms in 2001. US refinery production in 2002 was 196,000 kilograms for domestic and foreign ores and 78,100 kilograms from secondary (old scrap).

Demand – US consumption of gold in 2002 fell to 163,000 kilograms from 179,000 kilograms in 2001.

Trade – US exports of gold in 2002 (including coinage) fell sharply to 257,000 kilograms from 489,000 kilograms in 2001. US imports of gold for consumption in 2002 rose to 217,000 kilograms from 194,000 kilograms in 2001.

World Mine Production of Gold   In Kilograms (1 Kilogram = 32.1507 Troy Ounces)

Year	Aust-ralia	Brazil	Canada	Chile	China	Ghana	Indo-nesia	Papua N. Guinea	Russia	South Africa	United States	Uzbek-istan	World Total
1993	247,196	69,894	152,929	33,638	130,000	38,911	42,097	61,671	149,500	619,201	331,000	70,000	2,280,000
1994	256,188	72,397	146,428	38,786	132,000	43,478	42,600	59,286	146,600	580,201	327,000	65,000	2,250,000
1995	253,504	64,424	152,032	44,585	140,000	53,087	64,031	53,405	132,170	523,809	317,000	65,000	2,230,000
1996	289,530	60,011	166,378	53,174	145,000	49,211	83,564	51,119	123,300	496,846	326,000	72,000	2,290,000
1997	314,500	58,488	171,479	49,459	175,000	54,662	86,927	45,418	124,000	491,680	362,000	81,700	2,450,000
1998	310,070	49,567	165,599	44,980	178,000	72,541	124,018	61,641	114,900	465,100	366,000	80,000	2,500,000
1999	301,070	52,634	157,617	48,069	173,000	79,946	127,184	65,747	125,870	451,300	341,000	85,000	2,570,000
2000	296,410	50,393	156,207	54,143	180,000	72,100	124,596	74,540	143,000	430,800	353,000	85,000	2,590,000
2001[1]	285,030	53,207	158,875	42,673	185,000	68,700	166,091	67,043	152,500	394,800	335,000	87,000	2,600,000
2002[2]	273,010	50,500	148,860	40,000	190,000	69,707	135,000	65,200	158,000	399,234	298,000	90,000	2,550,000

[1] Preliminary.   [2] Estimate.   *Source: U.S. Geological Survey (USGS)*

GOLD

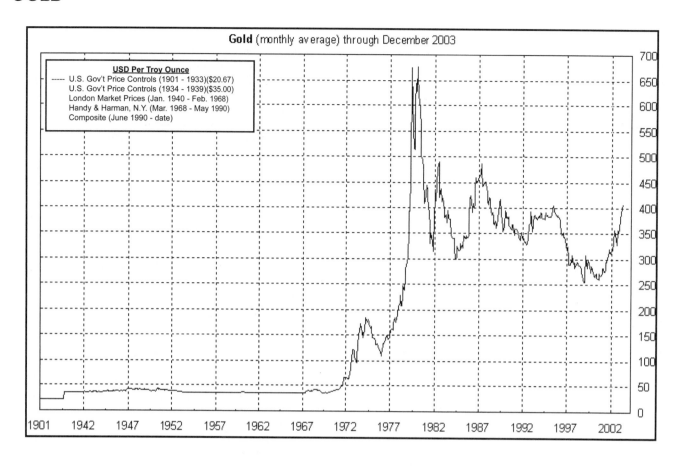

Gold (monthly average) through December 2003

USD Per Troy Ounce
- - - - U.S. Gov't Price Controls (1901 - 1933)($20.67)
U.S. Gov't Price Controls (1934 - 1939)($35.00)
London Market Prices (Jan. 1940 - Feb. 1968)
Handy & Harman, N.Y. (Mar. 1968 - May 1990)
Composite (June 1990 - date)

Salient Statistics of Gold in the United States   In Kilograms (1 Kilogram = 32.1507 Troy Ounces)

Year	Mine Production	Value Million $	Refinery Production Domestic Secondary & Foreign Ores	(Old Scrap)	Exports (Excluding Coinage)	Imports for Con-sumption	Stocks, Dec. 31 Treasury Depar tment[3]	Futures Exchange	Industry	Official World Reserves[4]	Consumption Dental	Industrial[5]	Jewelry & Arts	Total
1993	331,013	3,840.0	243,000	152,000	792,680	169,305	8,143,000	78,514	34,400	34,900	6,173	19,663	65,600	91,400
1994	327,000	4,050.0	241,000	148,000	471,000	114,000	8,142,000	49,100	32,700	34,800	5,430	17,013	53,700	76,100
1995	317,000	3,950.0	NA	NA	347,000	126,000	8,140,000	45,400	NA	34,600	NA	NA	NA	NA
1996	326,000	4,090.0	NA	NA	471,000	159,000	8,140,000	20,700	NA	34,400	NA	NA	NA	NA
1997	362,000	3,870.0	270,000	100,000	476,000	209,000	8,140,000	15,200	17,300	34,000	NA	NA	NA	137,000
1998	366,000	3,480.0	277,000	163,000	522,000	278,000	8,130,000	25,200	16,600	33,600	NA	NA	NA	219,000
1999	341,000	3,070.0	265,000	143,000	523,000	221,000	8,170,000	37,900	14,700	33,500	NA	NA	NA	245,000
2000	353,000	3,180.0	197,000	81,600	547,000	223,000	8,140,000	52,900	9,300	33,000	NA	NA	NA	183,000
2001[1]	335,000	2,940.0	191,000	82,700	489,000	194,000	8,120,000	38,000	3,700	33,000	NA	NA	NA	179,000
2002[2]	298,000	2,980.0	196,000	78,100	257,000	217,000	8,140,000	63,900	3,500	32,200	NA	NA	NA	163,000

[1] Preliminary.   [2] Estimate.   [3] Includes gold in Exchange Stabilization Fund.   [4] Held by market economy country central banks and governments andinternational monetary orgainzations.   [5] Including space and defense.   NA = Not available.   *Source: U.S. Geological Survey (USGS)*

Monthly Average Gold Price (Handy & Harman) in New York   In Dollars Per Troy Ounce

Year	Jan.	Feb.	Mar.	Apr.	May	June	July	Aug.	Sept.	Oct.	Nov.	Dec.	Average
1994	387.02	382.01	384.13	378.20	381.21	385.64	385.44	380.43	391.80	389.77	349.43	379.60	384.14
1995	378.55	376.51	382.12	391.11	385.46	387.56	386.40	383.63	382.22	383.14	385.53	387.42	384.22
1996	399.59	404.73	396.21	392.96	391.98	385.58	383.69	387.43	382.97	381.07	378.46	369.02	387.81
1997	355.10	346.71	351.67	344.47	343.75	340.75	324.08	324.03	322.74	324.87	307.10	288.65	331.16
1998	289.18	297.49	295.90	308.40	299.39	292.31	292.79	283.76	289.01	295.92	293.89	291.29	294.12
1999	287.05	287.22	285.96	282.45	276.94	261.31	255.81	256.56	265.23	310.72	292.74	283.69	278.81
2000	284.26	299.60	286.39	279.75	275.10	285.73	281.01	274.44	273.53	270.00	266.05	271.68	278.96
2001	265.58	261.99	263.03	260.56	272.07	270.23	267.53	272.40	283.78	283.06	276.49	275.98	271.06
2002	281.47	295.40	294.06	302.68	314.08	321.81	313.51	310.18	319.49	316.56	319.14	333.21	310.13
2003[1]	356.91	359.60	340.55	328.25	355.03	356.35	351.01	359.91	379.07	378.92	389.13		359.52

[1] Preliminary.   *Source: U.S. Geological Survey (USGS)*

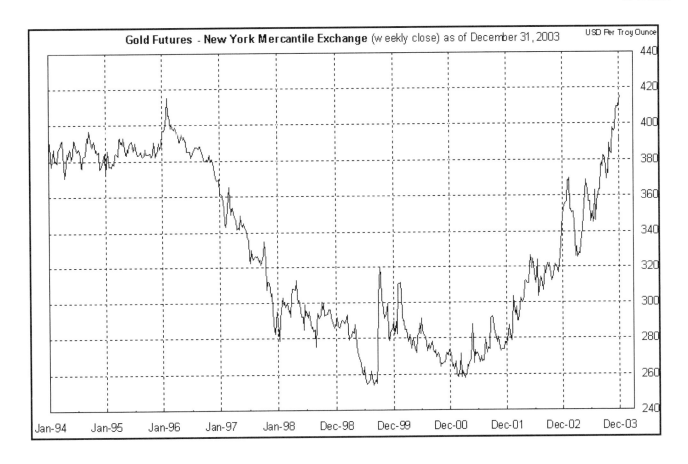

Average Open Interest of Gold in New York (NYMEX)   In Thousands of Contracts

Year	Jan.	Feb.	Mar.	Apr.	May	June	July	Aug.	Sept.	Oct.	Nov.	Dec.
1994	156,045	139,354	146,269	144,386	147,738	146,255	148,915	155,641	167,981	166,041	166,536	178,998
1995	184,549	170,972	168,651	191,667	173,805	174,075	175,727	176,135	185,128	185,854	170,674	141,751
1996	210,695	226,160	203,968	201,826	203,056	192,423	185,374	159,435	185,907	192,606	187,145	185,994
1997	199,710	190,524	167,595	157,176	160,512	170,640	207,352	198,099	201,267	188,365	212,757	188,558
1998	180,994	171,507	183,358	180,267	158,157	172,250	169,180	192,623	183,351	186,680	164,304	153,063
1999	179,726	185,345	178,456	198,202	193,978	207,122	205,687	193,023	206,186	216,034	189,433	156,754
2000	149,606	158,026	160,325	155,188	162,516	144,099	133,087	126,893	132,731	132,546	134,630	113,830
2001	134,401	142,673	126,558	120,111	118,426	116,788	114,098	116,687	125,907	125,639	114,238	111,622
2002	124,222	142,763	142,638	159,892	190,845	174,123	166,042	146,596	167,620	162,456	164,581	191,594
2003	221,495	210,247	186,656	176,033	191,459	198,808	199,741	224,694	284,906	258,238	275,346	277,073

Source: New York Mercantile Exchange (NYMEX), COMEX division

Volume of Trading of Gold Futures in New York (NYMEX)   In Thousands of Contracts

Year	Jan.	Feb.	Mar.	Apr.	May	June	July	Aug.	Sept.	Oct.	Nov.	Dec.	Total
1994	981.8	584.0	889.5	589.2	922.6	740.2	723.8	626.0	645.6	651.2	687.8	461.5	8,503.2
1995	881.9	420.0	1,087.5	613.0	777.0	588.1	669.9	500.5	495.5	387.7	982.5	378.1	7,781.6
1996	1,384.7	987.5	943.6	647.1	858.5	582.1	749.8	541.9	541.9	528.5	795.2	458.8	8,694.5
1997	1,102.8	830.2	899.4	508.5	762.1	522.7	1,147.5	667.8	715.8	988.0	808.8	588.1	9,541.9
1998	1,078.2	534.2	877.2	698.1	845.2	718.7	712.4	680.0	851.7	769.6	705.6	519.0	8,990.1
1999	860.8	517.4	1,147.6	561.1	1,069.6	573.6	964.3	709.6	1,067.3	993.8	674.7	436.1	9,575.8
2000	616.4	833.5	767.7	362.2	701.5	625.5	532.5	374.4	403.2	424.9	625.7	349.0	6,643.5
2001	755.2	483.3	766.6	438.1	971.6	481.4	578.3	547.4	341.0	481.4	573.6	367.4	6,785.3
2002	733.6	613.2	717.7	559.8	1,089.6	775.5	998.9	585.8	621.8	669.0	844.8	808.5	9,018.2
2003	1,260.1	1,007.5	987.6	667.8	1,160.3	824.3	1,191.7	837.5	1,034.0	1,091.3	1,397.3	776.3	12,235.5

Source: New York Mercantile Exchange (NYMEX), COMEX division

GOLD

Commodity Exchange, Inc. (COMEX) Depository Warehouse Stocks of Gold   In Thousands of Troy Ounces

Year	Jan. 1	Feb. 1	Mar. 1	Apr. 1	May 1	June 1	July 1	Aug. 1	Sept. 1	Oct. 1	Nov. 1	Dec. 1
1993	1,507	1,340	1,365	1,426	1,383	2,231	2,247	2,448	2,437	2,425	2,349	2,552
1994	2,524	2,955	2,958	2,862	2,802	2,434	2,665	2,574	2,030	1,904	1,843	1,867
1995	1,577	1,498	1,386	1,360	1,391	1,488	1,505	1,608	1,448	1,745	1,395	1,315
1996	1,460	1,869	1,412	1,429	1,335	1,711	1,263	1,273	1,402	1,283	1,060	1,104
1997	666	837	583	1,000	946	878	850	914	733	894	615	761
1998	488	446	481	720	658	1,077	1,055	1,092	911	958	827	819
1999	809	809	860	1,034	896	879	818	936	1,198	928	874	1,137
2000	1,219	1,393	1,374	1,968	1,967	1,901	1,890	2,013	1,961	1,918	1,865	1,864
2001	1,701	1,775	1,654	1,302	858	864	891	901	794	824	1,165	1,426
2002	1,220	1,187	1,286	1,322	1,372	1,764	1,851	1,836	1,915	1,892	1,995	2,046

Source: New York Mercantile Exchange (NYMEX), COMEX division

Central Gold Bank Reserves   In Millions of Troy Ounces

Year	Belgium	Canada	France	Germany	Italy	Japan	Netherlands	Switerland	United Kingdom	United States	Industrial Total	Developing Oil	Developing Non-Oil	IMF[2]	Bank for Int'l Settlements	World Total
1992	25.0	9.9	81.9	95.2	66.7	24.2	43.9	83.3	18.6	261.8	877.4	42.0	100.3	103.4	6.8	1,129.9
1993	25.0	6.1	81.9	95.2	66.7	24.2	35.1	83.3	18.5	261.8	860.4	42.4	108.1	103.4	8.6	1,123.0
1994	25.0	3.9	81.9	95.2	66.7	24.2	34.8	83.3	18.4	261.7	856.9	42.4	106.6	103.4	7.0	1,116.2
1995	20.5	3.4	81.9	95.2	66.7	24.2	34.8	83.3	18.4	261.7	848.7	41.9	111.9	103.4	7.3	1,113.2
1996	15.3	3.1	81.9	95.2	66.7	24.2	34.8	83.3	18.4	261.7	840.1	42.5	115.5	103.4	6.6	1,108.2
1997	15.3	3.1	81.9	95.2	66.7	24.2	27.1	83.3	18.4	261.6	821.9	42.3	115.8	103.4	6.2	1,089.7
1998	9.5	2.5	102.4	119.0	83.4	24.2	33.8	83.3	23.0	261.6	809.0	41.6	115.7	103.4	6.4	1,076.1
1999	8.3	1.8	97.2	111.5	78.8	24.2	31.6	83.3	20.6	261.7	810.4	41.2	112.9	103.4	6.5	1,074.5
2000	8.3	1.2	97.3	111.5	78.8	24.6	29.3	78.8	16.5	261.6	796.5	41.6	112.0	103.4	6.5	1,060.1
2001[1]	8.0	1.2	97.0	112.0	79.0	24.6	29.0	74.6	13.4	261.6	791.3	42.3	111.3	103.4	6.5	1,054.7

[1] Preliminary.   [2] International Monetary Fund.   *Source: American Metal Market (AMM)*

Mine Production of Recoverable Gold in the United States   In Kilograms

Year	Arizona	California	Idaho	Montana	Nevada	Alaska	Colorado	South Dakota	New Mexico	Utah	Other States	Total
1993	2,710	35,800	4,324	14,300	211,000	2,780	W	19,200	995	W	39,891	331,000
1994	2,050	30,100	3,610	12,600	214,000	5,660	4,420	W	W	W	33,560	306,000
1995	1,920	25,600	8,850	12,400	210,000	4,410	W	W	W	W	53,820	317,000
1996	1,740	23,800	7,410	9,110	213,000	5,020	W	W	W	W	57,920	318,000
1997	2,140	24,200	7,490	10,200	243,000	18,400	W	16,400	W	W	40,170	362,000
1998	1,840	18,700	W	8,200	273,000	18,300	W	12,100	W	W	33,860	366,000
1999	786	17,500	W	7,540	9,310	16,200	W	10,300	W	W	279,364	341,000
2000	442	17,200	W	9,310	268,000	15,600	W	8,230	W	W	34,218	353,000
2001	W	13,800	W	W	253,000	16,700	W	W	W	W	51,500	335,000
2002[1]	W	9,180	W	W	240,000	W	W	W	W	W	48,820	298,000

[1] Preliminary.   W = Withheld proprietary data, included in Other States.   *Source: U.S. Geological Survey (USGS)*

Consumption of Gold, By End-Use in the United States   In Kilograms

Year	Jewelry and the Arts — Gold-Filled & Other	Electro-plating	Karat Gold	Total	Dental	Industrial — Gold-Filled & Other	Electro-plating	Karat Gold	Total	Grand Total
1987	9,256	3,133	58,635	71,024	6,944	21,010	12,343	1,892	35,245	113,319
1988	7,598	1,469	57,959	67,027	7,576	21,034	15,088	1,104	37,226	111,836
1989	7,364	1,283	60,877	69,524	7,927	15,723	20,684	1,215	37,621	115,078
1990	8,132	429	69,952	78,514	8,700	12,725	17,251	1,020	30,996	118,216
1991	3,848	373	79,875	84,096	8,485	8,102	12,624	1,068	21,793	114,375
1992	3,546	581	79,381	83,508	6,543	8,802	10,476	1,082	20,360	110,410
1993	3,530	373	61,700	65,600	6,170	9,470	9,090	1,100	19,700	91,400
1994	3,650	369	49,700	53,700	5,430	7,450	9,470	96	17,000	76,100
1995	NA	NA	NA	NA	NA	NA	NA	NA	NA	NA
1996	NA	NA	NA	NA	NA	NA	NA	NA	NA	NA

[1] Preliminary.   **Source: U.S. Geological Survey (USGS)**

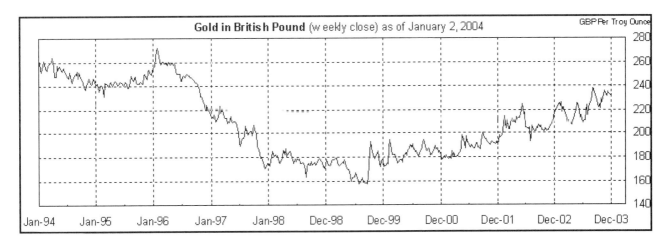

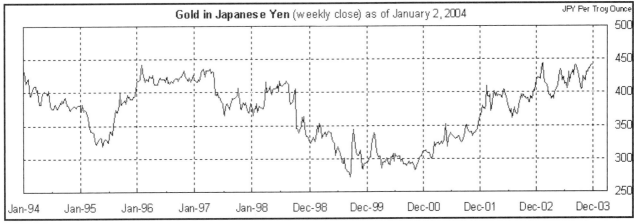

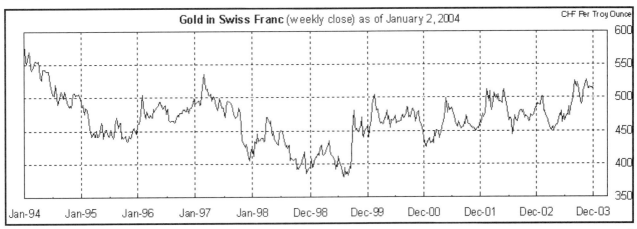

Grain Sorghum

Grain sorghums include milo, kafir, durra, feterita, and kaoliang. Grain sorghums are tolerant of drought by going into dormancy during dry and hot conditions and then resuming growth as conditions improve. Grain sorghums are a staple food in China, India, and Africa but in the US they are mainly used as livestock feed. The two key US producing states are Texas and Kansas, each with about one-third of total US production. US sorghum production has become more popular with the breeding of dwarf grain sorghum hybrids which are only about 3 feet tall (versus up to 10 feet tall for wild sorghum) and are easier to harvest with a combine. The U.S. sorghum crop year begins September 1.

Prices – Grain sorghum prices (No. 2 yellow in Kansas City) in 2003 were on track to average above $4 per hundred pounds, the highest level since 1997/8 when prices averaged $4.18.

Supply – World production of sorghum in 2003/4 was forecast to rise to 53.730 million metric tons, up 4.5% from 51.403 million in 2002/3. World ending stocks in 2003/4 are forecasted at 3.864 million metric tons, up 18% from 3.281 million in 2002/3. The world's largest producers of grain sorghum in 2002/3 were the US with 9.392 million metric tons of production (accounting for 18% of world production), Nigeria with 7.850 million metric tons (15%), India with 7.060 million (14%), and Mexico with 6.338 million (12%). US production in 2003/4 was forecast at 10.446 million metric tons, up 11% from 9.392 million in 2002/3. US ending stocks in 2003/4 are forecasted to rise to 1.378 million metric tons from 1.093 million in 2002/3.

Demand – World consumption of grain sorghum was forecast to rise slightly by 0.4% to 53.147 million metric tons in 2003/4 from 52.949 million in 2002/3. Forecasted consumption of 53.147 million metric tons in 2003/4 will be slightly below forecasted production of 53.730 million in 2003/4, a slightly bullish factor for prices. In 2002/3, consumption of 52.949 million was well above production of 51.403 million, a bearish factor for prices. The world's main consumers of sorghum are Mexico, Nigeria, and India.

Trade – World trade in grain sorghum was forecast to rise to 6.205 million metric tons in 2003/4 from 5.849 million in 2002/3. The world's main exporter by far is the US. US exports are forecasted to rise to 5.200 million metric tons from 4.911 million in 2002/3, accounting for 84% of world exports. The U.S. generally consumes only about half its production and exports the balance. The world's two main importers are Mexico and Japan.

World Supply and Demand Grain Sorghum   In Thousands of Metric Tons

Year	Exports Argentina	Exports Non-U.S.	Exports U.S.	Exports Total	Imports Japan	Imports Mexico	Imports Unaccounted	Imports Total	Total Production	Utilization China	Utilization Mexico	Utilization U.S.	Utilization Total	Ending Stocks Non-U.S.	Ending Stocks U.S.	Ending Stocks Total
1998-9	565	1,467	4,996	6,463	2,453	3,291	71	6,463	59,905	4,134	9,746	7,798	59,046	3,773	1,655	5,428
1999-00	920	1,660	6,484	8,144	2,206	4,890	54	8,144	59,044	3,319	11,200	8,628	60,364	3,225	1,661	4,886
2000-1	439	1,607	6,009	7,616	1,983	5,037	120	7,616	52,818	2,561	11,200	6,543	54,165	2,478	1,061	3,539
2001-2[1]	419	1,090	6,142	7,232	1,776	4,837	281	7,232	57,660	2,700	10,750	6,440	56,325	3,325	1,549	4,874
2002-3[2]	600	1,134	4,715	5,849	1,562	3,394	24	5,849	52,027	2,700	9,900	5,134	53,638	2,170	1,093	3,263
2003-4[3]	500	1,021	5,334	6,355	1,500	3,100	235	6,355	54,720	2,500	8,800	4,827	54,022	2,583	1,378	3,961

[1] Preliminary. [2] Estimate. [3] Forecast. *Source: Foreign Agricultural Service, U.S. Department of Agriculture (FAS-USDA)*

Salient Statistics of Grain Sorghum in the United States

Year	Acreage Planted[4] for All Purposes (1,000 Acres)	Acreage Harvested (1,000 Acres)	For Grain Production 1,000 Bushels	For Grain Yield Per Harvested Acre Bushels	For Grain Price in Cents Per Bushel	For Grain Value of Production Million $	For Silage Acreage Harvested 1,000 Acres	For Silage Production 1,000 Tons	For Silage Yield Per Harvested Acre	Sorghum Grain Stocks Dec. 1 On Farms 1,000 Bushels	Sorghum Grain Stocks Dec. 1 Off Farms 1,000 Bushels	Sorghum Grain Stocks June 1 On Farms 1,000 Bushels	Sorghum Grain Stocks June 1 Off Farms 1,000 Bushels
1998-9	9,626	7,723	519,933	67.3	166	905.5	308	3,526	11.4	95,900	239,416	27,400	88,680
1999-00	9,288	8,544	595,166	69.7	157	937.4	320	3,716	11.6	90,300	259,136	27,300	99,606
2000-1	9,195	7,723	470,070	60.9	189	847.1	265	2,863	10.8	74,300	187,681	19,000	57,411
2001-2[1]	10,252	8,584	514,524	59.9	194	979.8	336	3,728	11.1	72,400	241,477	17,300	88,178
2002-3[2]	9,580	7,299	369,758	50.7	232	876.5	352	3,360	9.5	53,600	178,252	11,150	70,744
2003-4[3]	9,420	7,798	411,237	51.0	220-250	965.8	343	3,552	10.4	45,200	188,507		

[1] Preliminary. [2] Estimate. [3] Forecast. NA = Not available. *Source: Economic Research Service, U.S. Department of Agriculture (ERS-USDA)*

Production of All Sorghum for Grain in the United States, by States   In Thousands of Bushels

Year	Arkansas	Colorado	Illinois	Kansas	Louisiana	Mississippi	Missouri	Nebraska	New Mexico	Oklahoma	South Dakota	Texas	Total
1998	6,890	10,545	7,918	264,000	7,500	2,340	26,560	56,400	2,925	15,300	9,940	105,800	519,933
1999	9,750	8,610	9,215	258,400	19,270	4,872	22,010	42,770	7,425	18,000	4,640	185,850	595,166
2000	9,940	6,720	8,075	188,800	17,845	6,708	24,840	35,000	1,625	13,680	5,880	143,350	470,070
2001	14,620	9,460	8,085	232,500	17,850	7,134	20,680	35,700	6,300	15,120	8,850	130,000	514,524
2002	17,710	1,800	6,391	135,000	13,365	6,237	15,725	15,000	2,800	14,850	3,060	130,050	369,758
2003[1]	17,220	4,320	8,610	130,500	14,025	6,132	16,170	31,000	1,674	9,250	6,750	153,900	411,237

[1] Preliminary. *Source: National Agricultural Statistics Service, U.S. Department of Agriculture (NASS-USDA)*

Grain Sorghum Quarterly Supply and Disappearance in the United States   In Millions of Bushels

Crop Year Beginning Sept. 1	Beginning Stocks	Pro- duction	Imports	Total Supply	Food Alcohol & Industrial	Seed	Feed & Residual	Total	Export	Total	Gov't Owned[3]	Privately Owned[4]	Total Stocks
2000-1	65.0	471.0	0	536.0	35.0	1.0	220.0	494.0	237.0	731.0			42.0
Sept.-Nov.	65.0	471.0	0	536.0	17.0	0	194.0	274.0	63.0	337.0			262.0
Dec.-Feb.	262.0	----	0	262.0	11.0	0	15.0	95.0	69.0	164.0			167.0
Mar.-May	167.0	----	0	167.0	4.0	1.0	23.0	91.0	63.0	154.0			76.0
June-Aug.	76.0	----	0	767.0	3.0	0	-10.0	35.0	42.0	77.0			42.0
2001-2	42.0	515.0	0	556.0	45.0	0	208.0	495.0	242.0	737.0			61.0
Sept.-Nov.	42.0	515.0	0	556.0	15.0	0	164.0	242.0	63.0	305.0			314.0
Dec.-Feb.	314.0	----	0	314.0	15.0		26.0	120.0	78.0	198.0			194.0
Mar.-May	194.0	----	0	194.0	10.0		26.0	89.0	53.0	142.0			105.0
June-Aug.	105.0	----	0	105.0	5.0		-8.0	45.0	47.0	92.0			61.0
2002-3[1]	61.0	370.0	0	431.0	45.0		158.0	388.0	186.0	574.0			43.0
Sept.-Nov.	61.0	370.0	0	431.0	15.0		133.0	199.0	51.0	250.0			232.0
Dec.-Feb.	232.0	----	0	232.0	15.0		7.0	69.0	47.0	116.0			163.0
Mar.-May	163.0	----	0	163.0	10.0		31.0	81.0	40.0	121.0			82.0
June-Aug.	82.0	----	0	82.0	5.0		-13.0	39.0	48.0	87.0			43.0
2003-4[2]	43.0	411.0	0	454.0	25.0		165.0	400.0	210.0	610.0			54.0
Sept.-Nov.	43.0	411.0	0	454.0	7.0		154.0	221.0	60.0	281.0			234.0

[1] Preliminary.   [2] Forecast.   [3] Uncommitted inventory.   [4] Includes quantity under loan & farmer-owned reserve.   *Source: Economic Research Service, U.S. Department of Agriculture (ERS-USDA)*

Average Price of Sorghum Grain, No. 2, Yellow in Kansas City   In Dollars Per Hundred Pounds (Cwt.)

Year	Sept.	Oct.	Nov.	Dec.	Jan.	Feb.	Mar.	Apr.	May	June	July	Aug.	Average
1996-7	5.29	4.64	4.31	4.22	4.24	4.46	4.88	4.83	4.63	4.48	4.48	4.18	4.55
1997-8	4.13	4.36	4.30	4.26	4.33	4.36	4.40	4.10	4.09	4.03	4.03	3.74	4.18
1998-9	2.98	3.17	3.45	3.41	3.41	3.43	3.48	3.37	3.35	3.32	2.92	2.92	3.30
1999-00	2.97	2.71	2.75	2.87	3.20	3.28	3.51	3.53	3.75	3.18	2.71	2.76	3.10
2000-1	2.67	3.14	3.41	3.66	3.64	3.63	3.56	3.45	3.30	3.26	3.59	3.65	3.41
2001-2	3.55	3.38	3.44	3.59	3.61	3.55	3.58	3.47	3.44	3.57	3.97	4.60	3.65
2002-3	4.86	4.70	4.72	4.62	4.52	4.43	4.07	4.24	4.12	4.06	3.71	4.00	4.34
2003-4[1]	4.15	4.18	4.50										4.28

[1] Preliminary.   *Source: Economic Research Service, U.S. Department of Agriculture (ERS-USDA)*

Exports of Grain Sorghum, by Country of Destination from the United States   In Metric Tons

Year Beginning Oct. 1	Canada	Ecuador	Ethiopia	Israel	Japan	Jordan	Mexico	South Africa	Spain	Sudan	Turkey	World Total
1996-7	3,347	0	10,020	456,271	2,207,304	0	2,091,131	0	125,827	8,000	138,590	5,210,569
1997-8	5,076	0	49,999	82,583	1,451,123	0	3,287,628	0	203,896	0	94	5,164,844
1998-9	3,484	0	0	92,335	1,480,220	0	3,290,663	0	196,110	0	101	5,194,028
1999-00	4,061	0	21,940	167,816	1,045,253	0	4,773,760	12,857	178,829	0	0	6,297,344
2000-1	4,170	0	24,117	82,776	853,211	0	4,864,414	0	0	0	0	5,866,340
2001-2[1]	4,912	0	0	25,082	1,233,799	0	4,695,814	37,272	8,193	0	0	6,014,304
2002-3[2]	5,921	91	48,000	65,725	1,059,424	0	3,160,313	43,918	266,892	5,880	0	4,724,964

[1] Preliminary.   [2] Estimate.   *Source: Economic Research Service, U.S. Department of Agriculture (ERS-USDA)*

Grain Sorghum Price Support Program and Market Prices in the United States

Year	Price Support Quantity	Price Support % of Pro- duction	Aquired by CCC	Owned by CCC at Year End	Basic Loan Rate	Target Price	Findley Loan Rate	Effective Base[3] Million Acres	Partici- pation Rate[4] % of Base	No. 2 Yellow Kansas City	No. 2 Yellow Texas High Plains	No. 2 Yellow Los Angeles	No. 2 Yellow Gulf Ports
	Million Cwt.				\$ Per Bushel					\$ Per Cwt.			
1995-6	4.0	1.6			1.84	2.61	1.80	13.3	76.9	6.66	7.30	----	7.19
1996-7	11.4	2.6			[5]	NA	1.81	13.2	98.8	4.55	5.02	----	5.03
1997-8	9.8	2.8	.1	.1	[5]	NA	1.76	13.1	98.8	4.11	4.72	----	4.76
1998-9	12.0	4.1	.6	.2	[5]	NA	1.74	13.6	98.8	3.29	3.78	----	3.97
1999-00	9.6	2.9	.5		[5]	NA	1.74	13.7	98.8	3.10	3.36	----	3.79
2000-1[1]	8.6	3.3	.4		[5]	NA	1.71	13.6		3.41	3.87	----	4.35
2001-2[2]						NA	1.71	13.6		3.90	----	4.23	

[1] Preliminary.   [2] Estimate.   [3] National effective crop acreage base as determined by ASCS.   [4] Percentage of effective base acres enrolled in acreage reduction programs.   [5] Beginning with the 1996-7 marketing year, target prices are no longer applicable.   *Source: Economic Research Service, U.S. Department of Agriculture (ERS-USDA)*

Hay

Hay is a catchall term for forage plants, typically grasses such as timothy and Sudan-grass, and legumes such as alfalfa and clover. Hay is generally used to make cured feed for livestock. Curing, which is the proper drying of hay, is necessary to prevent spoilage. Hay, when properly cured, contains about 20% moisture. If hay is dried excessively, however, there is a loss of protein, which makes it less effective as livestock feed. Hay is harvested in virtually all of the lower 48 states, but the top producing states are Texas (with 9% of US production), California (6%), Missouri (5%), and Minnesota (4%).

Prices – Hay prices as of December 2003 were $81.30 per ton, down from the $94.00 average price seen in 2002/3 and from $96.50 seen in 2001/2.

Supply – US hay production in 2003/4 was forecast at 160.7 million tons, up from 151.0 million tons in 2002/3 and 156.8 million in 2001/2. That production is well above the annual production average of 151 million tons seen in the 1990's. Higher production in 2003/4 is expected due to a rise in yields to 2.50 tons per acre versus the previous year's 2.34 tons. Acres harvested in 2003/4 is actually expected to decline to 64.379 million acres from 64.497 million in 2002/3. However, that is still significantly above the average 60.6 million acres harvested in the 1990's. Carry-over in 2002/3 was slightly higher at 22.5 million tons, up from 21.1 million tons in 2001/2.

Salient Statistics of All Hay in the United States

Crop Year Beginning May 1	Acres Harvested 1,000 Acres	Yield Per Acre Tons	Pro- duction	Carryover May 1	Disap- pearance	Supply	Disap- pearance	Animal Units Fed[3]	Farm Price $ Per Ton	Farm Pro- duction Value Million $	Alfalfa (Certified)	Timothy	Red Clover	Sudan- Grass
				--- Millions of Tons ---		Per Animal Unit In Tons		Millions			--- Dollars Per Cwt. ---			
1997-8	61,084	2.50	152.5	17.4	148.1	2.27	1.98	74.9	100.0	13,250	282.00	73.00	184.00	51.40
1998-9	60,076	2.53	151.8	21.8	148.8	2.33	2.00	74.5	85.0	11,607	288.00	71.20	194.00	53.70
1999-00	63,220	2.53	159.7	24.8	155.7	2.52	2.12	73.3	76.7	11,014	287.00	78.80	178.00	52.20
2000-1	59,854	2.54	151.9	28.8	159.6	2.49	2.20	72.5	85.4	11,417	277.00	115.00	143.00	53.00
2001-2[1]	63,521	2.47	156.8	21.1	159.6	2.46	2.15	72.0	96.5	12,597	278.00	105.00	132.00	53.00
2002-3[2]	64,497	2.34	151.0	22.5		2.40	NA		93.8	12,450	157.00	90.00	130.00	56.00

Retail Price Paid by Farmers for Seed, April 15 (columns: Alfalfa (Certified), Timothy, Red Clover, Sudan-Grass)

[1] Preliminary. [2] Estimate. [3] Roughage-consuming animal units fed annually. NA = Not available. *Source: Economic Research Service, U.S. Department of Agriculture (ERS-USDA)*

Production of All Hay in the United States, by States   In Thousands of Tons

Year	California	Idaho	Iowa	Minnesota	Missouri	New York	North Dakota	Ohio	Oklahoma	South Dakota	Texas	Wisconsin	Total
1998	8,554	5,549	5,332	7,110	7,703	7,680	4,190	3,875	3,380	8,160	6,870	6,370	151,780
1999	8,782	5,132	5,970	7,130	7,225	7,700	5,511	3,060	5,000	9,440	13,135	7,510	159,707
2000	8,568	5,292	6,000	6,840	6,657	6,055	5,110	4,521	4,659	7,393	8,880	6,000	151,921
2001	8,915	4,938	5,565	6,195	7,853	7,578	5,065	4,275	4,025	9,150	10,837	4,790	156,764
2002	9,594	5,608	5,645	6,610	7,840	5,950	3,920	3,750	5,030	4,800	13,850	5,340	150,962
2003[1]	9,310	4,950	5,515	5,245	8,168	7,600	4,598	3,974	4,992	7,210	12,388	4,380	157,123

[1] Preliminary. *Source: Agricultural Statistics Board, U.S. Department of Agriculture (ASB-USDA)*

Hay Production and Farm Stocks in the United States   In Thousands of Short Tons

Year	Alfalfa & Mixtures	All Others	All Hay	Corn for Silage[1]	Sorghum Silage[1]	Farm Stocks May 1	Farm Stocks Dec. 1
1998	82,310	69,470	151,780	95,479	3,526	21,827	112,066
1999	84,385	75,322	159,707	95,633	3,716	24,817	108,922
2000	80,347	71,574	151,921	102,156	2,773	28,817	105,582
2001	80,327	76,437	156,764	102,077	3,728	21,106	110,510
2002	73,824	77,138	150,962	104,979	3,360	22,494	103,692
2003[2]	76,307	80,816	157,123	105,864	3,552	22,168	110,752

[1] Not included in all tame hay. [2] Preliminary. *Source: Agricultural Statistics Board, U.S. Department of Agriculture (ASB-USDA)*

Mid-Month Price Received by Farmers for All Hay (Baled) in the United States   In Dollars Per Ton

Year	May	June	July	Aug.	Sept.	Oct.	Nov.	Dec.	Jan.	Feb.	Mar.	Apr.	Average[2]
1998-9	103.0	91.8	88.6	88.5	86.5	85.2	81.4	77.5	78.5	79.0	78.5	81.9	85.0
1999-00	91.6	81.7	78.4	77.4	74.5	73.7	74.0	71.1	71.8	72.6	74.8	78.2	76.7
2000-1	91.0	82.5	80.2	80.5	83.0	84.9	84.0	84.9	85.2	86.8	87.2	94.8	85.4
2001-2	106.0	95.8	96.3	97.4	99.0	98.0	95.9	95.6	91.7	91.7	92.3	98.3	96.5
2002-3	103.0	95.8	93.6	92.4	93.0	93.8	93.2	91.1	91.4	91.4	92.8	94.5	93.8
2003-4[1]	99.2	94.6	89.0	85.3	84.2	84.4	80.7	81.3	79.3	79.9			85.8

[1] Preliminary. [2] Marketing year average. *Source: Economic Research Service, U.S. Department of Agriculture (ERS-USDA)*

Heating Oil

Heating oil is a petroleum product. Heating oil is also known as No. 2 fuel oil and accounts for about 25% of the yield from a barrel of crude oil. That is the second largest "cut" after gasoline. The price to consumers of home heating oil is generally comprised of 42% for crude oil, 12% for refining costs, and 46% for marketing and distribution costs (source: EIA's Petroleum Marketing Monthly, 2001). Generally, a $1 increase in the price of crude oil translates into a 2.5-cent per gallon rise in heating oil. Because of this, heating oil prices are highly correlated with crude oil prices, although heating oil prices are also subject to swift supply and demand shifts due to weather or refinery shutdowns.

The primary use for heating oil is residential space heating. In the US, approximately 8.1 million households use heating oil as their main heating fuel. Most of the demand for heating oil occurs from October through March. The Northeast region, which includes the New England and the Central Atlantic States, is most reliant on heating oil. This region consumes approximately 70% of US heating oil. However, demand for heating oil has been dropping as households switch to a more convenient heating source like natural gas. In fact, demand for heating oil is down by about 10 billion gallons/year from its peak use in 1976 (source: American Petroleum Institute).

The US has two suppliers of heating oil, domestic refineries and imports from foreign countries. Refineries produce approximately 85 % of US heating oil as part of the "distillate fuel oil" product family, which includes heating oils and diesel fuel. The remainder of US heating oil is imported from Canada, the Virgin Islands, and Venezuela.

Recently, a team of Purdue University researchers developed a way to make home heating oil from a mixture of soybean oil and conventional fuel oil. The oil blend is made by replacing 20% of the fuel oil with soybean oil, potentially saving 1.3 billion gallons of fuel oil per year. This soybean heating oil can be used in conventional furnaces without altering existing equipment. The soybean heating oil is relatively easy to produce and creates no sulfur emissions.

The "crack-spread" is the processing margin earned when refiners buy crude oil and refine it into heating oil and gasoline. The crack-spread ratio commonly used in the industry is the 3-2-1, which involves buying 1 heating oil contract and 2 gasoline futures contracts, and then selling 3 crude oil contracts. As long as the crack spread is positive, it is profitable for refiners to buy crude oil and refine it into products. The NYMEX has a crack-spread calculator on their web site at www.nymex.com.

Heating oil futures and options trade at the New York Mercantile Exchange (NYMEX). The heating oil futures contract calls for the delivery of 1,000 barrels of fungible No. 2 heating oil in the New York harbor. In London, gas/oil futures and options are traded on the International Petroleum Exchange (IPE).

Prices – NYMEX heating oil futures prices on the nearest-futures chart posted a record high (going back to the 1982 start of the NYMEX futures contract) of $1.31 in February 2003 in conjunction with the Iraq war, but then quickly fell back as it became clear that the Iraq war would be short and would not create major oil supply disruptions in the Persian Gulf and Middle East. Heating oil prices then entered a sustained rally in Q3-2003 and closed the year at 91 cents, little changed from the 2002 close of 92 cents. Still, heating oil prices closed 2003 at the upper end of the price range seen over the last 20 years. Bullish factors were basically the same as for crude oil (weak dollar, higher global economic growth, tight inventories) but were also boosted by a cold start to winter which boosted demand for heating oil in the northeastern US which is the primary consumer of heating oil for home heating.

Supply – Production of distillate fuel oil in the US in 2003 averaged 3.7 million barrels per day, up 3.0% from 3.592 million in 2002. Stocks of distillate fuel oil in October 2003, the latest reporting month, were 130.9 million barrels, up from 124.4 million barrels in December 2002. US production of residual fuel in 2003 rose to an average 657,000 barrels per day, up 9.2% from 601,000 in 2002. US stocks of residual fuel oil in July 2003 rose to 35.6 million barrels from 32.7 million a year earlier.

Demand – US usage of distillate fuel oil in the US in 2003 averaged 3.944 million barrels per day, up 4.4% from 3.776 million in 2002.

Trade – US imports of distillate fuel oil in 2003 rose to an average 337,000 barrels per day, up 26% from 267,000 in 2002. US exports of distillate fuel oil in 2003 fell slightly to 109,000 per day from 112,000 in 2002.

Average Price of #2 Heating Oil   In Cents Per Gallon

Year	Jan.	Feb.	Mar.	Apr.	May	June	July	Aug.	Sept.	Oct.	Nov.	Dec.	Average
1994	49.93	55.81	49.18	48.01	47.98	49.37	49.93	49.51	47.90	48.23	49.62	48.41	49.49
1995	47.98	47.64	45.95	49.40	50.31	47.75	46.65	49.14	50.21	48.89	51.89	57.76	49.46
1996	55.64	61.24	65.19	67.90	57.59	51.56	55.58	60.42	67.61	72.34	70.13	72.13	63.11
1997	69.90	61.15	54.83	57.74	56.31	52.32	53.11	54.02	53.19	57.24	56.23	51.09	56.43
1998	46.59	44.26	42.12	42.97	41.07	37.88	36.24	34.48	40.15	38.29	35.59	31.38	39.25
1999	33.41	30.48	38.74	43.07	41.68	43.36	50.02	54.81	60.27	58.34	64.89	67.36	48.87
2000	91.32	94.37	77.29	75.32	75.88	78.32	78.14	89.13	98.87	97.46	102.70	94.08	87.74
2001	84.30	78.55	74.17	78.02	77.11	75.74	69.88	73.41	71.65	62.63	54.37	52.60	71.04
2002	53.52	54.03	63.52	66.60	66.54	64.50	67.79	69.81	77.25	76.55	72.14	81.70	67.83
2003	90.09	112.84	99.70	79.75	74.31	75.95	79.03	81.61	73.54	81.97	83.35	89.04	85.10

Source: Energy Information Administration, U.S. Department of Energy (EIA-DOE)

HEATING OIL

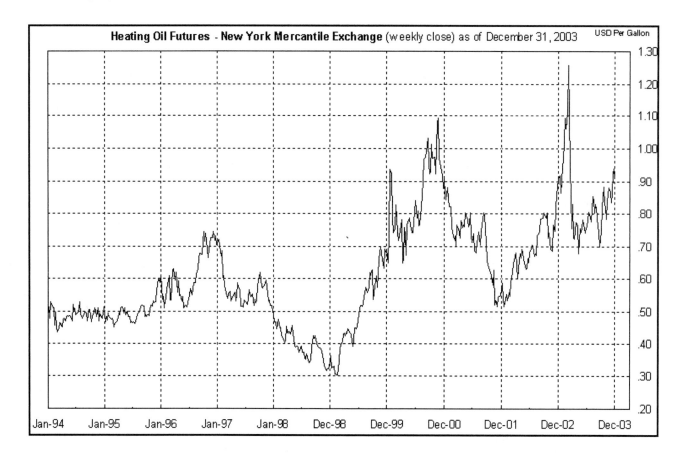

Average Open Interest of #2 Heating Oil Futures in New York   In Contracts

Year	Jan.	Feb.	Mar.	Apr.	May	June	July	Aug.	Sept.	Oct.	Nov.	Dec.
1994	196,390	185,607	186,539	164,417	140,658	129,005	124,764	149,571	172,071	165,475	152,570	148,298
1995	128,664	112,508	118,700	121,974	115,501	122,163	136,722	140,214	149,934	152,244	139,232	138,596
1996	114,324	95,745	90,080	94,161	98,038	97,699	109,524	119,366	138,513	141,217	127,512	108,558
1997	100,333	105,223	122,149	139,981	135,523	141,864	151,403	149,243	151,407	141,008	126,528	145,153
1998	171,177	163,114	177,158	174,587	176,663	196,903	205,071	198,527	188,096	188,019	192,835	184,100
1999	167,686	160,388	166,472	172,127	170,842	168,307	182,383	188,726	192,883	179,040	165,334	146,997
2000	135,431	132,407	108,646	100,389	117,055	129,872	153,914	169,092	177,997	168,388	155,475	142,145
2001	138,980	127,219	120,899	127,395	130,328	141,436	149,577	145,605	145,692	155,540	162,392	153,850
2002	166,824	173,110	160,205	144,936	139,979	136,201	131,742	141,084	147,692	153,739	161,137	156,268
2003	178,932	174,224	134,616	111,706	118,822	124,675	127,273	146,821	150,893	156,142	145,857	146,085

Source: New York Mercantile Exchange (NYMEX)

Volume of Trading of #2 Heating Oil Futures in New York   In Thousand of Contracts

Year	Jan.	Feb.	Mar.	Apr.	May	June	July	Aug.	Sept.	Oct.	Nov.	Dec.	Total
1994	1,085.7	875.7	766.8	631.7	629.3	723.7	612.3	783.2	706.8	721.4	652.3	798.1	8,986.8
1995	779.8	608.7	716.0	622.8	729.8	618.8	612.7	563.6	714.2	650.8	659.5	990.1	8,266.8
1996	977.2	768.1	666.2	586.5	530.9	402.0	530.2	624.4	766.5	1,014.2	725.0	750.7	8,341.9
1997	794.4	719.0	588.6	710.1	592.0	679.4	679.6	694.7	828.3	742.7	619.3	722.9	8,371.0
1998	793.6	641.8	776.4	578.4	688.5	904.9	720.2	683.0	748.2	768.2	766.5	793.9	8,863.8
1999	738.9	662.3	973.3	706.3	768.1	802.7	770.4	707.9	720.1	819.6	818.6	712.7	9,200.7
2000	914.0	770.3	645.2	556.1	673.3	705.9	663.0	1,004.4	954.9	878.1	939.0	927.3	9,631.4
2001	914.4	650.7	758.0	728.6	722.8	849.9	712.9	745.8	694.0	853.8	835.5	798.1	9,264.5
2002	998.5	810.8	885.5	844.1	789.8	720.1	798.8	866.0	794.4	1,017.9	1,039.5	1,129.9	10,695.2
2003	1,340.1	1,158.9	965.9	757.7	811.6	802.9	849.9	891.3	1,118.5	1,095.5	817.3	971.8	11,581.7

Source: New York Mercantile Exchange (NYMEX)

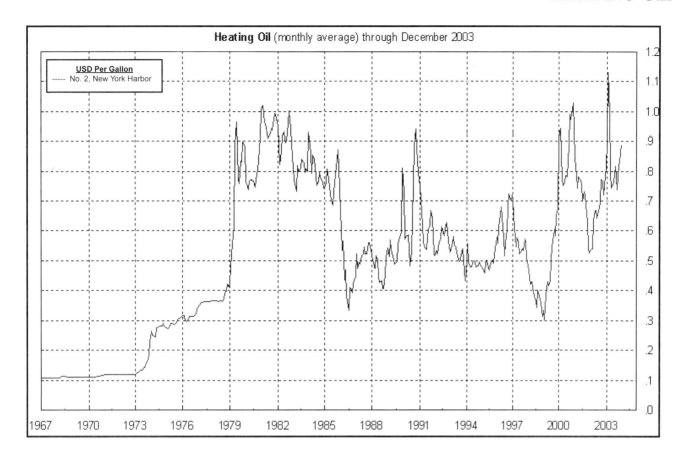

Heating Oil (monthly average) through December 2003

USD Per Gallon
----- No. 2, New York Harbor

Stocks of Distillate and Residual Fuel in the United States, on First of Month   In Millions of Barrels

Year	Jan.	Feb.	Mar.	Apr.	May	June	July	Aug.	Sept.	Oct.	Nov.	Dec.	Residual Fuel Oil Stocks Jan. 1	July 1
1994	140.9	117.5	102.9	99.4	102.6	112.4	119.5	134.2	138.6	144.7	146.0	147.3	44.2	39.4
1995	145.2	140.2	122.1	115.4	114.6	118.3	114.7	125.0	130.9	131.7	131.4	135.4	41.9	36.0
1996	130.2	113.8	97.3	89.7	90.1	95.7	101.6	106.8	110.3	115.0	114.7	121.8	36.8	34.8
1997	126.7	111.3	105.9	101.8	97.5	108.4	118.2	123.0	132.9	138.9	136.2	140.5	45.9	39.2
1998	139.0	133.1	127.9	124.4	125.7	136.8	139.1	148.8	150.5	152.5	147.5	154.6	40.4	39.8
1999	156.2	147.9	142.3	125.7	125.3	134.8	133.2	138.1	142.0	145.2	137.6	140.6	44.9	42.5
2000	124.1	106.7	105.2	96.0	100.1	105.4	106.4	112.9	111.0	115.3	116.5	121.1	35.8	37.0
2001	118.0	118.2	117.0	105.0	104.9	107.1	113.9	125.2	122.0	127.0	128.9	138.9	36.2	41.7
2002	144.5	137.8	130.0	123.0	122.6	127.4	130.9	133.4	130.6	126.9	121.4	124.4	41.0	32.7
2003[1]	134.1	112.2	97.2	98.5	97.1	106.1	111.8	117.7	126.4	130.9	131.4	137.2	31.3	35.6

[1] Preliminary.   *Source: Energy Information Administration; U.S. Department of Energy (EIA-DOE)*

Production of Distillate Fuel Oil in the United States   In Thousand Barrels per Day

Year	Jan.	Feb.	Mar.	Apr.	May	June	July	Aug.	Sept.	Oct.	Nov.	Dec.	Average
1994	3,114	3,018	3,096	3,249	3,317	3,285	3,191	3,187	3,285	3,203	3,270	3,232	3,205
1995	3,054	2,954	3,157	3,126	3,111	3,109	3,056	3,145	3,287	3,169	3,341	3,344	3,155
1996	3,110	3,145	3,110	3,305	3,258	3,291	3,139	3,295	3,403	3,626	3,665	3,558	3,325
1997	3,119	3,089	3,258	3,291	3,525	3,517	3,362	3,427	3,452	3,488	3,543	3,578	3,389
1998	3,323	3,280	3,397	3,468	3,560	3,520	3,569	3,482	3,399	3,215	3,438	3,431	3,424
1999	3,176	3,253	3,183	3,407	3,458	3,374	3,521	3,419	3,482	3,506	3,608	3,401	3,399
2000	3,123	3,348	3,342	3,533	3,650	3,481	3,520	3,678	3,844	3,774	3,785	3,872	3,580
2001	3,609	3,612	3,483	3,650	3,652	3,702	3,837	3,654	3,625	3,796	3,968	3,744	3,695
2002	3,508	3,498	3,360	3,647	3,709	3,679	3,561	3,538	3,536	3,380	3,768	3,922	3,592
2003[1]	3,403	3,455	3,743	3,817	3,860	3,728	3,673	3,750	3,721	3,750	3,800	3,845	3,712

[1] Preliminary.   *Source: Energy Information Administration, U.S. Department of Energy (EIA-DOE)*

HEATING OIL

Imports of Distillate Fuel Oil in the United States   In Thousand Barrels per Day

Year	Jan.	Feb.	Mar.	Apr.	May	June	July	Aug.	Sept.	Oct.	Nov.	Dec.	Average
1996	243	271	253	258	215	185	194	195	187	246	192	253	224
1997	293	246	245	256	220	219	223	202	210	213	161	232	227
1998	195	213	237	209	185	202	229	181	203	239	179	245	210
1999	304	322	248	213	261	238	234	273	249	216	265	188	250
2000	218	510	260	234	316	258	199	234	283	259	332	447	295
2001	789	635	348	288	310	302	209	212	317	253	244	241	344
2002	298	248	234	219	193	204	188	205	196	350	373	496	267
2003[1]	324	498	460	246	287	337	299	375	352	293	256	305	336

[1] Preliminary.   Source: Energy Information Administration, U.S. Department of Energy (EIA-DOE)

Exports of Distillate Fuel Oil in the United States   In Thousand Barrels per Day

Year	Jan.	Feb.	Mar.	Apr.	May	June	July	Aug.	Sept.	Oct.	Nov.	Dec.	Average
1996	216	256	139	166	176	81	134	182	256	300	171	206	190
1997	133	107	120	166	153	174	151	185	160	133	149	192	152
1998	131	120	135	168	227	152	124	105	133	139	110	108	138
1999	117	116	159	191	187	180	123	130	162	192	170	212	162
2000	132	112	211	178	127	149	132	253	194	255	191	135	173
2001	67	77	75	107	146	120	113	140	152	99	132	202	119
2002	109	279	67	68	74	93	44	119	127	96	114	171	112
2003[1]	119	132	161	139	162	101	103	68	43	62	81	100	106

[1] Preliminary.   Source: Energy Information Administration, U.S. Department of Energy (EIA-DOE)

Disposition of Distillate Fuel Oil, Total Product Supplied in the U.S.   In Thousand Barrels per Day

Year	Jan.	Feb.	Mar.	Apr.	May	June	July	Aug.	Sept.	Oct.	Nov.	Dec.	Average
1996	3,681	3,722	3,453	3,385	3,118	3,194	3,046	3,184	3,178	3,575	3,460	3,434	3,368
1997	3,780	3,422	3,515	3,523	3,240	3,235	3,279	3,124	3,302	3,659	3,411	3,665	3,430
1998	3,566	3,598	3,606	3,465	3,268	3,574	3,294	3,446	3,377	3,547	3,320	3,484	3,461
1999	3,788	3,542	3,785	3,415	3,314	3,407	3,479	3,437	3,431	3,749	3,608	3,892	3,572
2000	3,818	3,794	3,693	3,455	3,681	3,549	3,369	3,726	3,786	3,712	3,829	4,250	3,722
2001	4,325	4,212	4,143	3,834	3,746	3,659	3,569	3,829	3,624	3,888	3,746	3,604	3,847
2002	3,940	3,714	3,750	3,821	3,679	3,587	3,683	3,728	3,730	3,808	3,929	3,934	3,776
2003[1]	4,325	4,359	4,000	3,972	3,692	3,775	3,678	3,778	3,878	3,966	3,782	4,064	3,939

[1] Preliminary.   Source: Energy Information Administration, U.S. Department of Energy (EIA-DOE)

Production of Residual Fuel Oil in the United States   In Thousands Barrels per Day

Year	Jan.	Feb.	Mar.	Apr.	May	June	July	Aug.	Sept.	Oct.	Nov.	Dec.	Average
1996	774	776	701	671	732	731	646	732	713	693	712	753	719
1997	800	789	639	617	618	727	645	643	688	711	786	810	705
1998	765	672	790	857	766	739	778	782	749	676	753	805	762
1999	775	726	683	679	725	706	736	701	702	658	596	690	698
2000	640	627	649	620	640	679	741	760	702	747	778	768	696
2001	809	743	750	817	786	783	639	622	653	710	685	655	721
2002	625	613	617	601	582	540	566	583	607	593	648	641	601
2003[1]	660	682	653	634	731	668	634	663	662	661	616	686	663

[1] Preliminary.   Source: Energy Information Administration U.S. Department of Energy (EIA-DOE)

Supply and Disposition of Residual Fuel Oil in the United States

	Supply		Disposition			Ending	Average
	Total Production	Imports	Stock Change	Exports	Product Supplied	Stocks Million Barrels	Sales to End Users[3] Cents per Gallon
Year	Thousand Barrels Per Day						
1996	726	248	24	102	848	46	45.5
1997	708	194	-15	120	797	40	42.3
1998	762	275	12	138	887	45	30.5
1999	698	237	-25	129	830	36	37.4
2000	696	352	1	139	909	36	60.2
2001	721	295	13	191	811	41	53.1
2002	601	249	-27	177	700	31	56.8
2003[1]	663	325	18	197	772	38	

[1] Preliminary.   [2] Less than +500 barrels per day and greater than -500 barrels per day.   [3] Refiner price excluding taxes.
Source: Energy Information Administration, U.S. Department of Energy (EIA-DOE)

Hides and Leather

Hides and leather have been used since ancient times for boots, clothing, shields, armor, tents, bottles, buckets, and cups. Leather is produced through the tanning of hides, pelts, and skins of animals. Dating back at least 7,000 years, remains of leather have been found in the Middle East. The leather-tanning craft can be traced back for almost 500,000 years.

Today, most leather is made of cowhide but it is also made from the hides of lamb, deer, ostrich, and even stingray. Cattle hides are the most valuable byproduct of the meat packing industry. US exports of cowhides bring more than $1 billion in foreign trade, and US finished leather production is worth about $4 billion.

Prices – The price of wholesale cattle hides (packer heavy native steers FOB Chicago) in 2003 rose +2.3% to 84.00 cents per pound from 82.13 cents in 2002, slightly above the 10-year average price of 83.12 cents per pound.

Supply – World production of bovine hides and skins in 2000, the last reporting year, rose slightly by +0.2% to 4.139 million metric tons from the previous year. The world's largest producers of bovine hides and skins is the US with 24% of world production in 2000, Brazil with 16% and Argentina with 7%. US new supply of cattle hides from domestic slaughter in 2001 fell –2.9% to 35.370 million hides from 36.416 million in 2000.

US production of leather footwear has been dropping off sharply in recent years due to the movement of production offshore to lower cost producers. US production of leather footwear in 2002 fell to 41.2 million pairs from 55.6 million in 2001 and was only about one-fourth of the production level seen 10 years earlier.

Demand – World consumption of cowhides and skins in 2000, the last reporting year for the data series, rose +1.4% to 4,774 metric tons, which was the highest level seen in the data series which goes back to 1983. The world's largest consumers of cowhides and skins are the US with 13.0% of world consumption in 2000, Italy (10.6%), Brazil (8.9%), Mexico, (6.0%), Argentina (6.0%), and South Korea (5.9%).

Trade – US net exports of cattle hides in 2001 rose +10.6% to a 12- year high of 21.750 million hides from 19.670 million in 2000. The total value of US leather exports rose to a record high $1.221 billion in 2001. The largest destinations for US exports are South Korea (which took 28.0% of US exports in 2000), Taiwan (10.8%), Mexico (6.2%), and Italy (5.3%).

World imports of cowhides and skins in 2000 rose to a record high of 2,058 metric tons from 2,002 metric tons in 1999. The world's largest importers of cowhides and skins are South Korea (with 12.6% of world imports in 2000), Italy (10.7%) and Taiwan (6.9%).

World Production of Cattle and Buffalo Hides — In Thousands of Metric Tons

Year	Argentina	Australia	Brazil	Canada	Colombia	France	Germany	Italy	Mexico	Russia	United Kingdom	United States	World Total
1992	351	215	420	82	80	177	198	154	160	320	94	938	6,799
1993	357	212	461	76	81	162	198	150	161	315	96	921	6,835
1994	356	207	448	77	77	160	190	149	165	376	96	974	7,060
1995	347	207	475	79	81	159	176	150	170	376	107	1,011	7,658
1996	388	198	496	88	84	164	176	150	160	357	67	1,065	7,539
1997	384	211	515	91	81	163	176	148	161	294	67	1,174	7,872
1998	338	230	637	94	81	154	161	142	170	275	67	1,070	7,950
1999	364	230	667	99	86	151	160	145	170	229	64	1,099	8,061
2000[1]	369	230	670	98	84	150	160	143	175	233	68	1,120	8,173
2001[2]	369	230	670	98	84	150	160	145	176	232	61	1,120	8,221

[1] Preliminary. [2] Forecast. *Source: Food and Agricultural Organization of the United Nations (FAO-UN)*

Salient Statistics of Hides and Leather in the United States — In Thousands of Equivalent Hides

Year	Federally Inspected	Unin-spected[4]	Total Production	Net Exports	Heavy Native Cows[2]	Heavy Native Steers[3]	All U.S. Tanning	Cattle-hide	Value of Leather Exports $1,000	Men	Women	Pro-duction[5]	Exports
	----- New Supply of Cattle Hides ----- Domestic Slaughter — Thousands of Equivalent Hides				Wholesale Prices -- Cents Per Pound --		Production — In 1,000 Equiv. Hides			Wholesale Leather Indexes- Upper — 1982 = 100		Footwear — Million Pairs	
1993	32,593	731	33,324	17,117	82.16	78.9	18,057	16,931	764,120	142.8	126.9	171,733	20,700
1994	33,483	713	34,196	16,259	94.99	87.3	18,842	18,117	811,951	144.7	127.2	163,000	22,505
1995	34,879	760	35,639	18,336	93.89	87.6	18,092	17,480	870,247	150.1	129.0	147,550	20,571
1996	36,583	177	36,760	18,626	92.15	86.4	18,769	18,135	950,510	152.4	132.1	127,315	23,726
1997	35,567	751	36,318	17,562	90.99	86.1	19,592	18,930	1,145,664	156.4	132.2	124,444	21,958
1998	34,787	677	35,464	15,937	75.45	69.5	20,297	19,706	1,289,547	158.0	132.4	108,536	19,009
1999	35,486	664	36,150	15,700	73.80	73.1	21,342	20,620	1,137,534	157.0	133.0	78,581	18,176
2000	35,631	615	36,246	19,670	83.41	81.2	17,332	16,746	1,125,957	157.2	133.6	58,870	20,157
2001	34,771	599	35,370	21,750		89.8	14,212	13,779	1,221,131	158.4	133.8	54,757	19,472
2002[1]	35,120	614	35,735	19,484		82.3		16,403	1,161,943	158.8	133.5		21,582

[1] Preliminary. [2] Central U.S., heifers. [3] F.O.B. Chicago. [4] Includes farm slaughter; diseased & condemned animals & hides taken off fallen animals. [5] Other than rubber. *Sources: Leather Industries of America (LIA); Bureau of Labor Statistics, U.S. Department of Commerce (BLS)*

HIDES AND LEATHER

Production of All Footwear (Shoes, Sandals, Slippers, Athletic, Etc.) in the U.S.   In Millions of Pairs

Year	First Quarter	Second Quarter	Third Quarter	Fourth Quarter	Total	Year	First Quarter	Second Quarter	Third Quarter	Fourth Quarter	Total
1993	43.3	44.6	42.8	41.0	171.7	1998	32.8	31.8	29.3	28.6	108.5
1994	42.5	40.8	40.1	39.5	163.0	1999	26.7	26.1	24.5	21.7	78.6
1995	37.2	38.3	34.8	36.7	147.0	2000	----	----	----	----	68.7
1996	33.2	31.8	29.7	33.2	128.0	2001	----	----	----	----	55.6
1997	31.4	33.1	28.6	30.6	124.4	2002[1]	----	----	----	----	41.2

[1] Preliminary.   *Source: Bureau of the Census, U.S. Department of Commerce*

Average Factory Price[2] of Footwear in the United States   In Dollars Per Pair

Year	First Quarter	Second Quarter	Third Quarter	Fourth Quarter	Total	Year	First Quarter	Second Quarter	Third Quarter	Fourth Quarter	Total
1993	21.62	21.67	21.37	21.79	21.61	1998	24.39	24.21	20.27	19.78	21.84
1994	25.77	23.60	21.49	22.44	23.22	1999	23.33	22.70	19.90	19.50	21.19
1995	19.61	21.46	25.37	21.26	21.79	2000	----	----	----	----	24.14
1996	23.65	22.78	22.14	20.38	22.07	2001	----	----	----	----	25.66
1997	22.42	21.56	22.21	22.24	22.11	2002[1]	----	----	----	----	24.29

[1] Preliminary.   [2] Average value of factory shipments per pair.   *Source: Bureau of the Census, U.S. Department of Commerce*

Imports and Exports of All Cattle Hides in the United States   In Thousands of Hides

Year	Imports Total	Imports From Canada	Total	Canada	Italy	Japan	Rep. of Korea	Mexico	Portugal	Romania	Spain	Taiwan	Thailand
1993	1,660	1,597	18,777	965	354	4,167	7,919	2,217	79	1	60	1,950	386
1994	1,731		17,990	995	309	3,133	7,472	1,553	168	72	141	2,491	332
1995	1,759		20,095	952	332	3,246	8,283	899	111	63	215	3,017	781
1996	1,702		20,328	1,149	522	2,372	7,956	2,123	64	171	189	2,871	455
1997	1,633		19,195	1,320	469	1,802	7,470	2,501	55		148	2,866	323
1998	1,930		17,867	1,126	1,164	1,407	4,897	2,846	91		440	2,701	336
1999	1,921		17,621	829	738	1,252	6,038	2,723	46		262	2,863	343
2000	1,988		21,658	875	1,163	1,529	7,673	2,196	37		189	2,844	562
2001	1,721		23,471	716	920	1,343	7,602	1,647	54		159	2,751	888
2002[1]	1,299		20,784	837	1,099	584	5,812	1,470	14		189	2,145	914

U.S. Exports - by Country of Destination

[1] Preliminary.   *Source: Leather Industries of America*

Imports of Bovine Hides and Skins by Selected Countries   In Metric Tons

Year	Brazil	Canada	Hong Kong	Italy	Japan	Mexico	Portugal	Rep. of Korea	Spain	Taiwan	Turkey	United States	World Total
1992	11	17	80	131	188	71	32	385	26	91	28	65	1,266
1993	21	26	81	141	188	71	39	372	35	94	37	57	1,426
1994	16	28	95	243	139	60	56	356	29	112	17	49	1,556
1995	33	35	100	250	152	30	43	342	42	112	43	57	1,715
1996	20	34	79	263	123	71	42	341	33	124	50	60	1,692
1997	13	39	64	254	114	96	37	323	44	140	68	60	1,985
1998	10	42	71	249	96	110	39	229	44	142	45	59	1,876
1999[1]	8	34	91	215	95	115	42	254	29	142	55	57	2,002
2000[2]	8	36	93	220	95	115	43	260	30	142	60	57	2,058

[1] Preliminary.   [2] Forecast.   *Source: Foreign Agricultural Service, U.S. Department of Agriculture (FAS-USDA)*

Exports of Bovine Hides and Skins by Selected Countries   In Metric Tons

Year	Australia	Brazil	Canada	Germany	Hong Kong	Italy	Netherlands	New Zealand	Poland	Russia	United Kingdom	United States	World Total
1992	144	71	74	38	75	9	66	31	17	28	19	610	1,261
1993	142	76	87	40	76	7	35	21	5	150	25	581	1,374
1994	96	84	79	24	93	10	37	22	2	216	22	455	1,271
1995	85	148	90	34	100	10	47	22	2	195	22	510	1,351
1996	93	174	97	33	72	20	47	28	3	212	24	506	1,423
1997	115	216	97	35	60	16	48	27	3	210	25	473	1,475
1998	111	220	86	31	69	24	32	28	6	202	17	443	1,400
1999[1]	115	230	83	28	90	7	30	30	7	190	15	436	1,389
2000[2]	108	250	85	31	92	8	25	30	7	170	15	427	1,399

[1] Preliminary.   [2] Forecast.   *Source: Foreign Agricultural Service, U.S. Department of Agriculture (FAS-USDA)*

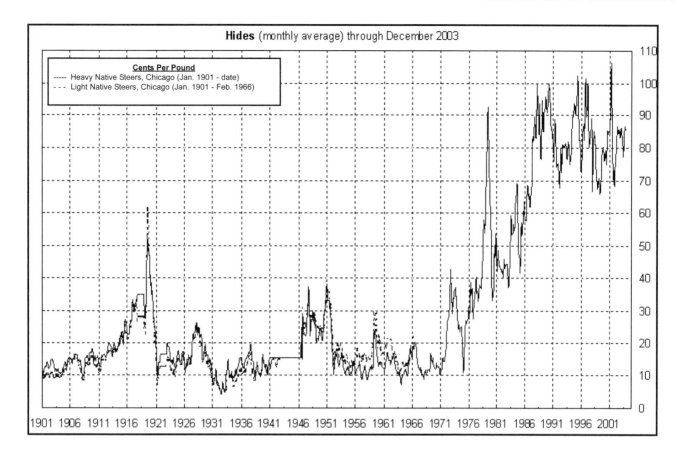

Hides (monthly average) through December 2003

Cents Per Pound
----- Heavy Native Steers, Chicago (Jan. 1901 - date)
- - - Light Native Steers, Chicago (Jan. 1901 - Feb. 1966)

Utilization of Bovine Hides and Skins by Selected Countries   In Metric Tons

Year	Argentina	Brazil	Colombia	Germany	Italy	Japan	Mexico	Rep. of Korea	Spain	Taiwan	Turkey	United States	World Total
1991	308	396	98	143	435	253	225	400	119	101	78	491	4,009
1992	298	382	97	129	435	229	231	400	98	91	90	528	3,977
1993	302	510	94	100	435	226	232	385	98	94	95	554	4,322
1994	304	505	96	83	550	200	226	374	94	112	85	536	4,282
1995	300	493	89	79	570	191	200	355	98	112	100	523	4,365
1996	308	461	91	80	615	165	230	353	95	124	110	548	4,332
1997	332	387	89	101	570	150	251	347	106	140	120	572	4,609
1998	285	412	91	100	540	135	275	265	108	142	100	603	4,584
1999[1]	300	415	89	102	500	130	280	280	104	142	110	623	4,707
2000[2]	285	425	89	103	505	130	285	283	108	142	120	623	4,774

[1] Preliminary.   [2] Forecast.   *Source: Foreign Agricultural Service, U.S. Department of Agriculture (FAS-USDA)*

Wholesale Price of Hides (Packer Heavy Native Steers) F.O.B. Chicago   In Cents Per Pound

Year	Jan.	Feb.	Mar.	Apr.	May	June	July	Aug.	Sept.	Oct.	Nov.	Dec.	Average
1994	75.07	75.08	79.00	84.75	87.33	88.77	90.38	89.76	93.90	93.67	93.19	91.13	86.84
1995	90.10	91.42	97.99	102.32	99.64	92.45	85.74	82.46	82.45	82.16	78.02	73.02	88.15
1996	73.67	75.11	77.96	84.58	87.56	82.51	89.45	96.06	98.91	101.51	94.60	90.65	87.71
1997	89.77	93.47	99.44	99.40	89.44	81.45	80.20	83.92	84.86	86.35	89.20	82.61	88.34
1998	66.88	77.33	82.61	83.72	85.05	83.13	81.17	81.11	75.23	67.95	67.53	68.26	76.66
1999	69.42	69.97	70.84	67.36	65.96	66.89	68.17	72.41	77.52	80.43	79.67	78.00	72.22
2000	75.92	76.29	77.86	78.83	79.24	75.18	77.25	81.64	85.60	84.89	84.41	85.31	80.20
2001	85.33	84.12	93.02	102.64	106.19	97.31	87.59	77.28	73.51	70.58	73.30	69.16	85.00
2002	68.23	72.39	80.41	83.21	84.32	86.72	84.43	85.77	85.84	85.75	83.35	85.18	82.13
2003	83.77	85.81	86.04	85.81	79.42	77.64	80.53	84.09	86.78	86.13	85.89	86.05	84.00

Source: National Agricultural Statistics Service, U.S. Department of Agriculture (NASS-USDA)

Hogs

Hogs are generally bred twice a year in a continuous cycle designed to provide a steady flow of production. The gestation period for hogs is 3-1/2 months and the average litter size is 9-10 pigs. The pigs are weaned at 3-4 weeks of age. The pigs are then fed so as to maximize weight gain. The feed consists primarily of grains such as corn, barley, milo, oats, and wheat. Protein is added from oilseed meals. Hogs typically gain 3.1 pounds per pound of feed. The time from birth to slaughter is typically 6 months. Hogs are ready for slaughter at about 254 pounds, producing a dressed carcass weight of around 190 pounds and an average 88.6 pounds of lean meat. The lean meat consists of 21% ham, 20% loin, 14% belly, 3% spareribs, 7% Boston butt roast and blade steaks, and 10% picnic, with the remaining 25% going into jowl, lean trim, fat, miscellaneous cuts, and trimmings (USDA). Futures on lean hogs are traded at the Chicago Mercantile Exchange. The futures contract is settled in cash based on the CME Lean Hog Index price, meaning that no physical delivery of hogs occurs.

Prices – Lean hog prices on the weekly nearest futures chart moved sideways in the first quarter of 2003 in the narrow range of about 48-55 cents/pound. Hog prices then rallied sharply in the April-June period to post a 2-year high of 68.20 cents in mid-June. Prices then trended lower through the rest of the year and closed the year at 55.42 cents. That close was very close to the average price of 55 cents seen over the past 3 years.

The decline in hog prices in the latter half of the year was due mainly to higher than expected hog counts and slaughter rates, which put downward pressure on cash pork prices. Furthermore, hogs coming to market were several pounds heavier on average than in the previous year. Downward pressure on hog prices also stemmed from a sharp increase in the number of feeder pigs and market hogs being imported from Canada (7 million in 2003, up 1.25 million from 2002, USDA). Offsetting the bearish supply situation was an increase in US consumer demand for pork, boosted in the latter half of 2003 by some switching away from beef. The switch from beef to pork was due to high beef prices into November and then by beef safety concerns after US mad cow scare hit in late December.

Supply – World production of pork in 2003 totaled 87.204 million metric tons, according to the USDA, up by 1.4% from 86.030 million tons in 2002. The USDA is forecasting a continued rise in production to 88.303 million tons in 2004. The US in 2003 produced 8.931 million metric tons of pork, up slightly from 8.929 million tons in 2002. US pork production in 2003 accounted for about 10% of world production. China was the world's largest pork producer in 2003 at 44.100 million metric tons, followed by the European Union at 17.850 million tons, and then the US.

Demand – World consumption of pork in 2003 totaled 86.732 million metric tons, up from 85.639 million in 2002. China is the largest consumer of pork at 43.856 million tons, followed by the European Union at 16.940 million tons, and the US at 8.733 million tons. The US accounts for about 10% of world pork consumption.

Trade – World pork exports in 2003 reached a record 4.061 million metric tons, up 1.3% from 4.008 million tons in 2002. The largest exporters of pork in 2003 were the European Union (1.000 million tons), Canada (975,000 tons), the US (762,000 tons), and Brazil (620,000 tons). The largest export markets for US pork products in 2003 were Japan (accounting for 49% of US exports), Mexico (accounting for 19% of US exports), and Canada (accounting for 11% of US exports). World imports in 2003 fell 4.3% to 3.591 million tons from 3.752 million tons in 2002 and a continued slight decline to 3.584 million is expected in 2004. The world's largest importers of pork in 2003 were Japan (1.150 million tons), Russia (600,000 tons), the US (567,000 tons), and Mexico (335,000 tons).

Salient Statistics of Pigs and Hogs in the United States

	Pig Crop						Value of Hogs on Farms, Dec. 1		Hog Marketings	Quantity Produced	Value of Pro-	Hogs Slaughtered in Thousand Head				
	Spring[3]			Fall[4]								Commercial				
Year	Sows Farrowed	Pig Crop	Pigs Per Litter	Sows Farrowed	Pig Crop	Pigs Per Litter	$ Per Head	Total Million $	Thousand Head	(Live Wt.) Mill. Lbs.	duction Mil. $	Federally Inspected	Other	Total	Farm	Total
	--- 1,000 Head ---			--- 1,000 Head ---												
1994	6,257	51,217	8.18	6,139	50,262	8.19	53.2	3,178	100,747	24,437	9,692	93,435	2,261	95,696	208	95,905
1995	6,046	50,077	8.28	5,843	48,739	8.35	70.7	4,115	102,684	24,426	9,829	94,203	2,123	96,325	210	96,535
1996	5,648	47,887	8.46	5,449	46,571	8.55	94.0	5,281	101,852	23,267	12,013	90,534	1,860	92,394	175	92,569
1997	5,595	48,393	8.65	5,885	51,190	8.70	82.0	4,986	104,301	23,979	12,552	90,228	1,733	91,960	161	92,121
1998	6,015	52,469	8.73	6,047	52,536	8.69	44.0	2,766	117,240	25,715	8,674	99,285	1,745	101,029	163	101,192
1999	5,877	51,519	8.77	5,764	50,835	8.82	72.0	4,254	121,137	25,791	7,766	99,739	1,806	101,544	141	101,685
2000	5,683	50,087	8.81	5,727	50,660	8.85	77.0	4,542	118,418	25,717	10,791	96,436	1,540	97,976	125	98,101
2001	5,619	49,472	8.81	5,767	51,031	8.85	77.0	4,590	119,262	25,884	11,430	96,528	1,434	97,962	119	98,081
2002[1]	5,779	50,752	8.78	5,704	50,592	8.87	71.0	4,201	123,677	26,254	8,679	98,915	1,348	100,263	114	100,377
2003[2]	5,645	49,942	8.85	5,660	50,464	8.92						99,535	1,242	100,777		

[1] Preliminary. [2] Estimate. [3] December-May. [4] June-November. *Source: Economic Research Service, U.S. Department of Agriculture (ERS-USDA)*

World Hog Numbers in Specified Countries as of January 1   In Thousands of Head

Year	Brazil	Canada	China	Denmark	France	Germany	Philippines	Poland	Russia	Spain	Ukraine	United States	World Total
1992	33,050	10,498	369,646	9,767	12,067	26,063	8,022	20,725	35,384	17,209	17,839	57,469	728,789
1993	31,050	10,577	384,210	10,345	13,015	26,514	7,954	21,059	31,520	18,260	16,175	58,202	740,758
1994	31,200	10,534	393,000	10,870	14,791	26,075	8,227	17,422	28,600	18,234	15,298	57,940	743,930
1995	31,338	11,291	414,619	10,864	14,593	24,698	8,941	19,138	24,859	18,295	13,946	59,738	758,461
1996	32,068	11,588	345,848	10,709	14,520	23,737	9,023	20,343	22,630	18,600	13,144	58,201	782,425
1997	31,369	11,480	362,836	11,081	14,968	24,283	9,750	17,697	19,500	18,651	11,236	56,124	695,133
1998	31,427	11,985	400,348	11,442	15,473	24,845	10,210	18,498	16,579	18,970	9,479	61,158	731,575
1999	31,427	12,409	422,563	11,991	15,869	26,299	10,398	19,275	16,400	21,715	10,083	62,206	762,206
2000[1]	31,860	12,242	430,198	11,914	15,991	26,043	10,764	18,224	16,100	22,597	10,073	59,342	774,451
2001[2]	32,440	12,137	446,815	12,125	15,911	25,862	11,715	16,988	15,780	22,700	7,652	59,138	652,022

[1] Preliminary.   [2] Forecast.   *Source: Foreign Agricultural Service, U.S. Department of Agriculture (FAS-USDA)*

Hogs and Pigs on Farms in the United States on December 1   In Thousands of Head

Year	Georgia	Illinois	Indiana	Iowa	Kansas	Minnesota	Missouri	Nebraska	North Carolina	Ohio	South Dakota	Wisconsin	Total
1994	1,020	5,350	4,500	14,500	1,310	4,850	3,500	4,350	7,000	1,800	1,740	1,040	59,990
1995	900	4,800	4,000	13,400	1,230	4,950	1,100	4,050	8,200	1,800	1,450	900	58,264
1996	800	4,400	3,750	12,200	1,450	4,850	3,450	3,600	9,300	1,500	1,200	800	56,171
1997	520	4,700	3,950	14,600	1,530	5,700	3,550	3,500	9,600	1,700	1,400	740	61,158
1998	480	4,850	4,050	15,300	1,590	5,700	3,300	3,400	9,700	1,700	1,400	690	62,206
1999	480	4,050	3,250	15,400	1,460	5,500	3,150	3,000	9,500	1,480	1,260	570	59,342
2000	380	4,150	3,350	15,100	1,520	5,800	2,900	3,050	9,300	1,490	1,320	610	59,138
2001	315	4,250	3,200	15,400	1,570	5,800	3,000	2,900	9,800	1,430	1,290	540	59,804
2002	345	4,150	3,200	15,600	1,530	6,000	2,950	2,950	9,700	1,440	1,310	520	59,513
2003[1]	295	3,950	3,100	15,800	1,630	6,400	2,950	2,900	9,900	1,520	1,260	490	60,040

[1] Preliminary.   *Source: National Agricultural Statistics Service, U.S. Department of Agriculture (NASS-USDA)*

Hog-Corn Price Ratio[1] in the United States

Year	Jan.	Feb.	Mar.	Apr.	May	June	July	Aug.	Sept.	Oct.	Nov.	Dec.	Average
1994	16.1	17.2	16.2	16.1	16.4	16.4	18.4	19.4	16.2	15.4	14.1	14.5	16.4
1995	16.8	17.5	16.4	15.1	15.3	16.8	17.6	18.5	18.0	16.4	13.9	14.2	16.4
1996	13.8	13.8	13.9	12.9	13.7	13.4	13.2	13.9	15.4	19.3	20.5	21.1	15.4
1997	20.0	19.9	17.7	19.2	21.6	22.6	24.3	22.1	20.0	18.6	18.0	16.5	20.0
1998	14.1	14.1	13.7	14.8	18.1	18.6	16.8	18.6	16.1	14.6	9.7	7.3	14.7
1999	12.8	13.5	13.6	14.8	18.4	17.3	18.2	20.7	19.4	20.2	19.6	19.6	17.3
2000	19.3	20.2	20.5	23.3	22.9	25.6	29.5	28.8	25.8	23.8	19.8	20.2	23.3
2001	18.8	20.0	23.5	25.3	27.7	29.7	27.6	26.6	23.7	21.8	18.9	16.8	23.4
2002	19.1	19.9	18.6	16.6	17.2	18.2	18.4	13.4	10.7	13.2	12.2	13.1	15.9
2003[2]	14.2	14.7	14.9	14.9	17.4	19.2	19.7	18.4	18.0	17.4	15.8	14.7	16.6

[1] Bushels of corn equal in value to 100 pounds of hog, live weight.   [2] Preliminary.   *Source: Economic Research Service, U.S. Department of Agriculture (ERS-USDA)*

Cold Storage Holdings of Frozen Pork[2] in the United States, on First of Month   In Millions of Pounds

Year	Jan.	Feb.	Mar.	Apr.	May	June	July	Aug.	Sept.	Oct.	Nov.	Dec.
1994	299.2	348.8	356.9	393.1	429.7	437.6	410.8	393.7	364.0	352.7	385.4	383.2
1995	365.3	389.6	395.1	416.8	422.3	434.9	431.1	408.3	354.0	332.6	321.6	347.1
1996	334.8	382.2	385.5	352.9	385.5	381.3	351.8	322.7	322.9	340.3	333.3	316.4
1997	313.8	342.2	383.9	404.7	440.2	413.4	406.2	388.7	371.8	346.6	354.2	334.1
1998	346.4	446.1	464.5	458.8	487.0	477.4	426.8	414.6	392.6	388.9	411.9	443.4
1999	503.5	510.3	540.9	552.8	596.9	572.7	528.6	494.6	432.6	430.6	438.1	422.5
2000	415.4	481.4	523.5	534.7	532.1	537.9	495.5	478.5	455.6	439.5	438.6	445.6
2001	411.5	471.4	468.3	432.3	432.6	421.5	374.1	339.5	332.6	366.9	430.6	432.7
2002	465.0	503.9	510.9	531.5	567.7	548.0	497.8	472.2	464.4	480.2	489.8	463.9
2003[1]	468.5	512.7	519.7	530.5	520.0	499.7	455.0	440.7	430.2	435.2	446.8	438.9

[1] Preliminary.   [2] Excludes lard.   *Source: Economic Research Service, U.S. Department of Agriculture (ERS-USDA)*

HOGS

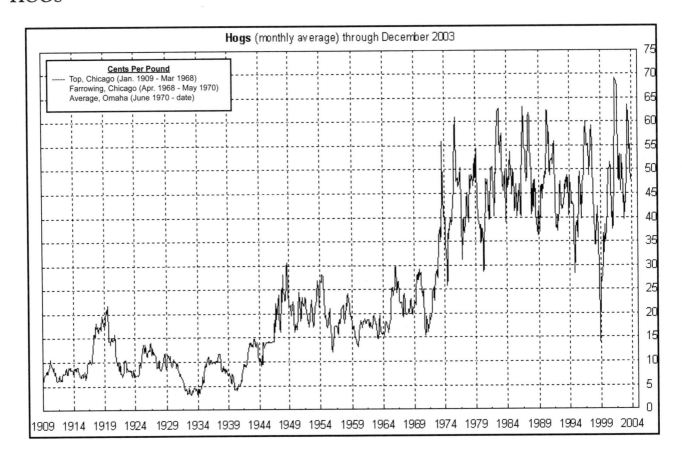

Hogs (monthly average) through December 2003

Cents Per Pound
- - - - Top, Chicago (Jan. 1909 - Mar 1968)
Farrowing, Chicago (Apr. 1968 - May 1970)
Average, Omaha (June 1970 - date)

Average Price of Hogs, National Base 51-52% lean[2] In Dollars Per Hundred Pounds (Cwt.)

Year	Jan.	Feb.	Mar.	Apr.	May	June	July	Aug.	Sept.	Oct.	Nov.	Dec.	Average
1994	43.99	48.12	44.30	42.72	42.27	42.76	42.62	42.37	35.49	32.56	28.25	31.59	39.75
1995	37.82	39.09	37.94	35.88	37.35	43.03	47.18	49.46	48.67	45.42	40.02	43.80	42.14
1996	42.39	46.93	49.06	50.88	58.29	56.45	59.47	60.49	54.60	55.41	54.42	55.47	53.66
1997	52.96	51.36	48.52	54.41	57.84	57.43	58.89	54.17	49.45	46.12	44.86	40.33	51.36
1998	35.60	34.53	37.22	37.22	45.51	45.32	39.85	37.98	32.00	29.60	19.95	16.62	34.28
1999	28.58	29.65	28.25	31.69	38.45	35.39	32.84	38.56	35.71	35.84	35.34	37.70	34.00
2000	38.32	41.58	43.52	49.59	50.21	51.48	50.45	45.35	43.49	43.09	37.84	41.40	44.69
2001	38.61	41.47	48.41	49.28	52.34	54.53	53.75	52.47	46.93	41.27	35.49	35.14	45.81
2002	40.16	40.65	37.47	32.97	34.64	37.32	40.53	34.00	26.98	31.69	29.99	32.35	34.90
2003[1]	34.39	35.64	36.11	36.42	43.62	47.88	44.98	41.90	41.82	38.63	36.02	36.02	39.45

[1] Preliminary.   [2] Data Prior to January 1998 are for Sioux City.   *Source: Economic Research Service, U.S. Department of Agriculture (ERS-USDA)*

Average Price Received by Farmers for Hogs in the United States   In Cents Per Pound

Year	Jan.	Feb.	Mar.	Apr.	May	June	July	Aug.	Sept.	Oct.	Nov.	Dec.	Average
1994	43.5	47.9	44.4	42.7	42.7	42.7	42.2	41.8	35.4	31.8	28.0	30.9	39.5
1995	36.8	39.1	37.8	35.6	37.1	42.2	46.3	48.6	48.4	45.7	39.9	43.5	41.8
1996	42.6	46.5	48.7	49.7	56.8	56.4	58.6	59.7	54.7	55.6	54.4	55.6	53.3
1997	53.8	52.8	49.4	53.8	58.2	57.8	58.9	55.3	50.4	47.3	45.1	41.6	52.0
1998	36.0	35.9	34.9	35.6	42.4	42.5	36.9	35.2	29.5	27.8	18.9	15.0	32.6
1999	26.5	27.7	28.0	30.1	36.6	34.1	31.6	36.2	33.9	34.2	33.4	35.6	32.3
2000	36.8	39.9	41.7	47.4	48.3	48.9	48.3	43.8	41.6	41.4	36.8	39.8	42.9
2001	37.2	39.2	45.9	47.8	50.4	52.2	51.7	50.8	45.2	40.2	35.0	33.3	44.1
2002	37.7	38.5	36.0	31.7	33.2	35.8	39.2	31.9	26.5	30.8	27.8	30.3	33.3
2003[1]	33.0	34.3	34.7	34.8	41.3	45.0	42.8	39.5	39.6	36.8	34.8	34.2	37.6

[1] Preliminary.   *Source: Economic Research Service, U.S. Department of Agriculture (ERS-USDA)*

Quarterly Hogs and Pigs Report in the United States, 10 States — In Thousands of Head

Year[2]	Inventory[3]	Breeding[3]	Market[3]	Farrowings	Pig Crop	Year[2]	Inventory[3]	Breeding[3]	Market[3]	Farrowings	Pig Crop
1994	57,904	7,130	50,739	12,376	101,400	1999	62,206	6,682	55,523	11,641	102,354
I	57,904	7,130	50,739	2,885	23,368	I	62,206	6,682	55,523	2,891	25,247
II	57,350	7,210	50,140	3,390	27,984	II	60,191	6,527	53,663	2,986	26,272
III	60,715	7,565	53,150	3,107	25,547	III	60,896	6,515	54,380	2,920	25,862
IV	62,320	7,415	54,905	2,997	24,517	IV	60,776	6,301	54,474	2,844	24,973
1995	59,990	7,060	52,930	11,847	98,516	2000	59,342	6,234	53,109	11,410	100,747
I	59,990	7,060	52,930	2,886	23,851	I	59,342	6,234	53,109	2,798	24,522
II	58,465	6,998	51,467	3,170	26,373	II	57,782	6,190	51,593	2,885	25,565
III	59,560	7,180	52,380	2,976	24,813	III	59,117	6,234	52,884	2,889	25,548
IV	60,540	6,898	53,642	2,815	23,479	IV	59,495	6,246	53,250	2,838	25,112
1996	58,264	6,839	51,425	11,114	94,458	2001	59,138	6,270	52,868	11,385	100,503
I	58,264	6,839	51,425	2,735	23,054	I	59,138	6,270	52,868	2,748	23,963
II	55,741	6,701	49,040	2,930	24,833	II	57,524	6,232	51,292	2,870	25,509
III	56,038	6,682	49,356	2,718	23,244	III	58,603	6,186	52,417	2,878	25,539
IV	56,961	6,577	50,384	2,731	23,327	IV	59,777	6,158	53,619	2,889	25,492
1997	56,124	6,578	49,546	11,480	99,583	2002	59,804	6,209	53,594	11,483	101,345
I	56,141	6,667	49,474	2,684	23,164	I	59,804	6,209	53,594	2,836	24,794
II	55,049	6,637	48,412	2,911	25,229	II	59,248	6,236	53,011	2,943	25,959
III	57,366	6,789	50,577	2,946	25,696	III	60,288	6,209	54,078	2,887	25,700
IV	60,456	6,858	53,598	2,939	25,494	IV	60,725	6,054	54,670	2,817	24,892
1998	61,158	6,957	54,200	12,062	104,981	2003[1]	59,513	6,012	53,501	11,307	125,556
I	61,158	6,957	54,200	2,929	25,480	I	59,513	6,012	53,501	2,765	24,359
II	60,163	6,942	53,220	3,086	26,989	II	58,207	6,021	52,186	2,881	25,583
III	62,213	6,958	55,254	3,054	26,634	III	59,586	5,960	53,626	2,825	25,150
IV	63,488	6,875	56,612	2,993	25,878	IV	60,103	5,902	54,201	2,836	50,464

[1] Preliminary. [2] Quarters are Dec. preceding year-Feb.(I), Mar.-May(II), June-Aug.(III) and Sept.-Nov.(IV). [3] Beginning of period.
Source: National Agricultural Statistics Service, U.S. Department of Agriculture (NASS-USDA)

Federally Inspected Hog Slaughter in the United States — In Thousands of Head

Year	Jan.	Feb.	Mar.	Apr.	May	June	July	Aug.	Sept.	Oct.	Nov.	Dec.	Total
1994	7,285	6,783	8,148	7,609	7,383	7,452	6,941	7,997	8,192	8,585	8,516	8,547	93,435
1995	7,882	7,157	8,628	7,379	8,012	7,731	6,918	8,083	7,752	8,358	8,424	7,881	94,203
1996	8,129	7,506	7,549	7,886	7,485	6,395	7,187	7,509	7,541	8,423	7,469	7,455	90,534
1997	7,610	6,836	7,437	7,590	6,971	6,859	7,169	7,197	7,872	8,625	7,601	8,461	90,228
1998	8,454	7,590	8,335	8,198	7,443	7,596	8,130	8,024	8,443	9,192	8,650	9,231	99,285
1999	8,373	7,746	8,945	8,386	7,303	8,176	7,778	8,256	8,501	8,806	8,750	8,719	99,739
2000	8,010	7,955	8,695	7,108	7,816	7,823	7,235	8,481	7,992	8,746	8,633	7,943	96,436
2001	8,521	7,491	8,207	7,722	7,836	7,368	7,333	8,247	7,687	9,210	8,610	8,298	96,528
2002	8,552	7,400	7,879	8,321	8,215	7,425	7,957	8,425	8,384	9,276	8,548	8,534	98,915
2003[1]	8,680	7,580	8,052	8,230	7,705	7,649	7,995	7,936	8,445	9,534	8,490	9,236	99,532

[1] Preliminary. *Source: National Agricultural Statistics Service, U.S. Department of Agriculture (NASS-USDA)*

Average Live Weight of all Hogs Slaughtered Under Federal Inspection — In Pounds Per Head

Year	Jan.	Feb.	Mar.	Apr.	May	June	July	Aug.	Sept.	Oct.	Nov.	Dec.	Average
1994	254	254	254	256	255	256	252	252	255	259	261	260	256
1995	258	256	257	258	258	258	256	253	252	255	259	258	257
1996	257	254	255	255	255	256	251	250	250	255	258	257	254
1997	257	256	256	256	256	257	253	252	255	257	261	260	256
1998	259	258	257	257	256	255	252	252	253	257	262	261	257
1999	259	259	259	260	260	260	257	254	256	259	262	262	259
2000	262	262	263	263	264	263	260	258	260	263	266	265	262
2001	265	264	264	265	264	264	261	258	262	267	269	268	264
2002	268	267	267	268	267	266	261	259	261	264	268	268	265
2003[1]	268	267	268	268	268	266	263	261	263	268	270	269	267

[1] Preliminary. *Source: Economic Research Service, U.S. Department of Agriculture (ERS-USDA)*

HOGS

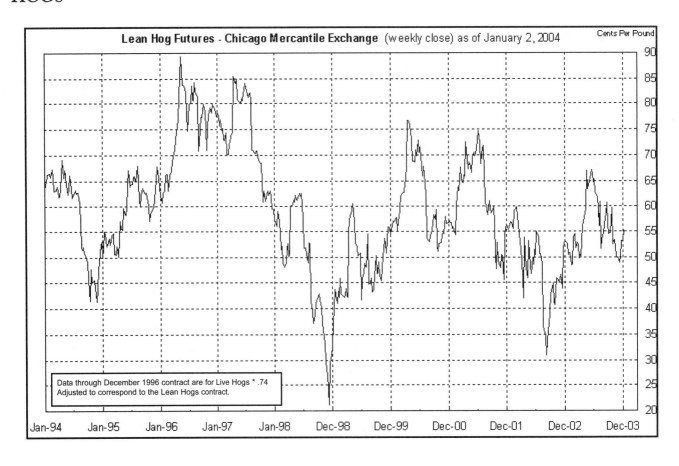

Lean Hog Futures - Chicago Mercantile Exchange (weekly close) as of January 2, 2004

Data through December 1996 contract are for Live Hogs * .74
Adjusted to correspond to the Lean Hogs contract.

Average Open Interest of Lean Hog[1] Futures in Chicago   In Contracts

Year	Jan.	Feb.	Mar.	Apr.	May	June	July	Aug.	Sept.	Oct.	Nov.	Dec.
1994	31,899	32,123	31,012	31,713	30,889	27,327	26,414	25,335	28,957	32,077	36,304	33,516
1995	36,705	30,958	30,736	28,035	28,294	28,729	29,959	31,599	34,183	31,312	31,519	35,127
1996	35,253	34,823	38,730	42,900	41,916	36,620	35,616	32,541	32,591	34,329	33,148	32,163
1997	33,105	33,953	31,289	34,071	41,978	37,398	36,141	33,712	31,483	36,928	39,363	39,394
1998	45,908	42,241	38,965	33,610	34,257	32,456	32,085	31,199	34,165	34,051	42,224	45,241
1999	46,003	44,211	43,803	48,277	55,951	52,398	54,723	49,915	53,055	54,089	54,432	50,691
2000	49,209	54,094	57,472	68,535	64,938	54,208	45,730	38,233	38,802	38,254	40,075	45,141
2001	41,425	41,892	48,381	45,296	41,910	45,715	51,661	47,760	42,072	36,983	32,821	27,687
2002	28,720	31,662	33,056	33,472	33,161	28,719	29,338	32,030	36,136	35,245	42,852	43,974
2003	40,660	39,862	40,446	37,883	43,672	47,338	39,706	37,700	49,469	46,295	43,552	43,352

[1] Data thru October 1995 are Live Hogs, November 1995 thru December 1996 are Live Hogs and Lean Hogs.
Source: Chicago Mercantile Exchange (CME)

Volume of Trading of Lean Hog[1] Futures in Chicago   In Contracts

Year	Jan.	Feb.	Mar.	Apr.	May	June	July	Aug.	Sept.	Oct.	Nov.	Dec.	Total[2]
1994	144,701	96,736	146,934	93,105	127,381	144,373	116,181	122,058	110,697	128,980	150,744	172,132	1,554.0
1995	155,766	115,800	181,919	116,767	145,350	155,295	139,013	144,590	135,262	132,122	142,460	136,191	1,700.7
1996	177,299	138,002	150,117	216,476	208,696	177,359	185,872	157,540	158,077	203,789	170,586	152,098	2,095.9
1997	180,241	159,600	200,118	212,810	222,759	188,615	181,637	146,297	149,950	175,135	152,876	130,871	2,100.9
1998	180,241	182,698	174,752	132,952	155,737	167,767	185,427	157,973	164,964	173,163	218,950	241,767	2,136.3
1999	218,608	171,108	196,825	189,773	214,852	237,240	239,096	167,787	190,238	187,794	205,505	139,270	2,358.1
2000	175,399	186,352	231,532	158,765	218,222	235,036	172,725	145,849	146,240	142,240	153,043	146,404	2,111.8
2001	183,493	159,020	197,004	142,892	165,220	184,421	198,503	164,712	152,178	177,601	163,798	129,497	2,018.3
2002	145,266	120,994	168,929	196,956	163,816	158,074	166,064	140,154	174,797	167,065	165,039	164,106	1,931.3
2003	186,436	137,479	186,511	156,370	209,740	210,901	199,782	124,677	232,705	207,247	164,190	148,117	2,164.2

[1] Data thru October 1995 are Live Hogs, November 1995 thru December 1996 are Live Hogs and Lean Hogs.   [2] In thousands of contracts.
Source: Chicago Mercantile Exchange (CME)

Honey

Honey is the thick, supersaturated sugar solution produced by bees to feed their larvae. It is composed of fructose, glucose and water in varying proportions and also contains several enzymes and oils. The color of honey varies due to the source of nectar and age of the honey. Light colored honeys are usually of higher quality than darker honeys. The average honeybee colony can produce more than 700 pounds of honey per year but only 10 percent is usually harvested by the beekeeper. The rest of the honey is consumed by the colony during the year. American per capita honey consumption is 1 pound per person per year. Honey is said to be humanity's oldest sweet, and beeswax was the first plastic.

Honey is used in many ways, including direct human consumption, for baking, and as medicine. Honey has several healing properties. Its high sugar content nourishes injured tissues, thus enhancing faster healing time. Honey's phytochemicals create a form of hydrogen peroxide that cleans out the wound, and the thick consistency protects the wound from contact with air Honey has also proven superior to antibiotic ointments for reducing rates of infection in people with burns.

Prices – US average domestic honey prices in 2001 rose to 70.4 cents per pound from the 7-year low of 59.7 cents posted in 2000. The value of US honey production in 2002 was $222 million, up sharply from $132 million in 2001.

Supply – World production of honey in 2000, the latest reporting year for the series, rose +1.4% to 1.241 million metric tons from 1.224 million metric tons in 1999. World honey production has been stable in the 1.0-1.2 million metric ton range over the last 15 years. The world's largest producer of honey by far is China with 256,000 metric tons of production in 2000, representing 21% of total world production.

US production of honey in 2002 fell –7.7% to 171.1 million pounds from 185.5 million in 2001, and was sharply below the recent 9-year high of 220.3 million pounds posted in both 1998 and 2000. Stocks in 2002 (Jan 1) fell to a 22-year low of 39.0 million pounds from 64.6 million pounds in 2001. The drop in production in 2002 was mostly due to a sharp decline in yield per colony to a 12-year low of 67.8 pounds per colony, down from 74.0 in 2001 and 84.1 pounds in 2000. The number of colonies in 2002, however rose +0.7% to 2.524 million.

Trade – The US imports almost as much honey as it produces, with imports in 2001 at 145.0 million pounds, down from 198.5 million pounds in 2000. US exports of honey are small and totaled only 7.4 million pounds in 2001, accounting for only 4% of US production.

World Production of Honey   In Metric Tons

Year	Argentina	Australia	Brazil	Canada	China	Germany	Japan	Mexico	Russia	United States	Total
1996	57,000	26,000	18,000	27,000	189,000	15,000	3,000	49,000	46,000	90,000	1,091,000
1997	70,000	27,000	18,000	31,000	215,000	15,000	3,000	54,000	49,000	89,000	1,148,000
1998	65,000	22,000	18,000	46,000	211,000	16,000	3,000	55,000	50,000	100,000	1,178,000
1999	93,000	19,000	20,000	37,000	236,000	20,000	3,000	55,000	51,000	94,000	1,234,000
2000	93,000	21,000	22,000	32,000	252,000	20,000	3,000	59,000	54,000	100,000	1,246,000
2001	80,000	22,000	22,000	35,000	255,000	2,600	3,000	59,000	53,000	84,000	1,255,000
2002[1]	85,000	22,000	22,000	33,000	258,000	22,000	3,000	55,000	55,000	90,000	1,270,000

[1] Preliminary.   Source: Foreign Agricultural Service, U.S. Department of Agriculture (FAS-USDA)

Salient Statistics of Honey in the United States   In Millions of Pounds

Year	Number of Colonies (1,000)	Yield Per Colony Pounds	Stocks Jan. 1	Total U.S. Production	Imports for Consumption	Domestic Disappearance	Exports	Total Supply	Program Activity — Placed Under Loan	CCC Take Over	Net Gov't Expenditure[3] Mil. $	Domestic Avg. Price All Honey - Cents Per Pound -	National Avg. Price Support	Per Capita Consumption Pounds
1998	2,633	83.7	69.1	220.3	132.4	332.9	10.4	397.5	----	----	----	65.5	----	----
1999	2,688	76.4	79.4	205.3	182.5		11.1		----	----	----	60.1	----	----
2000	2,620	84.1	85.3	220.3	198.5		10.1		----	----	----	59.7	----	----
2001	2,506	74.0	64.6	185.5	144.8		7.4		----	----	----	70.4	----	----
2002[1]	2,574	66.7	39.4	171.7	202.5		7.3		----	----	----	132.7	----	----
2003[2]	2,590	69.9	40.7	181.1								140.4		

[1] Preliminary.   [2] Forecast.   [3] Fiscal year.   Source: Economic Research Service, U.S. Department of Agriculture (ERS-USDA)

Production and Yield of Honey in the United States

Year	Production in Thousands of Pounds — California	Florida	Minnesota	North Dakota	South Dakota	Total	Value of Production $1,000	Yield per Colony in Pounds — California	Florida	Minnesota	North Dakota	South Dakota	Average
1998	37,350	22,540	11,060	29,440	21,375	220,316	144,304	83	98	79	128	95	83.7
1999	30,300	23,256	11,890	26,775	23,296	205,250	126,075	60	102	82	105	104	76.4
2000	30,800	24,360	13,500	34,500	28,435	220,339	132,742	70	105	90	115	121	84.1
2001	27,625	22,000	10,935	26,880	15,275	185,461	132,225	65	100	81	96	65	74.0
2002	23,500	20,460	8,541	24,000	11,475	171,718	228,338	50	93	73	75	51	66.7
2003[1]	32,160	14,910	9,960	29,580	14,000	181,096	255,791	67	71	83	87	70	69.9

[1] Preliminary.   Source: National Agricultural Statistics Service, U.S. Department of Agriculture (NASS-USDA)

Interest Rates, U.S.

US interest rates can be characterized in two main ways, credit quality and maturity. Credit quality refers to level of risk associated with a particular borrower, with US Treasury securities carrying the lowest risk. Maturity refers to the point in time when the security matures and must be repaid. Treasury securities, for example, carry the full spectrum of maturities, from short-term cash management bills, to T-bills (3-months, 6-months, and 4-weeks), T-notes (2-year, 3-year, 5-year and 10-years), and 30-year T-bonds. The most active futures markets are Treasury note and bond futures traded at the Chicago Board of Trade (CBOT) and Eurodollar futures traded at the Chicago Mercantile Exchange (CME).

Fed policy – US interest rates during 2003 trended lower early in the year due to weak economic growth tied to the impending Iraq war. Interest rates then moved higher over the summer after the economy started to recover. The Federal Open Market Committee (FOMC) came into 2003 with its overnight federal funds rate at 1.25% but the FOMC then cut its funds rate target by another 0.25% to a 45-year low of 1.00% on June 25 to ensure an economic recovery. As 2003 ended, the market was expecting the Fed to raise its funds rate target by 25 bp by summer 2004 and by another 25 bp by autumn 2004.

The Fed's extraordinarily accommodative monetary policy during 2003 was designed to ensure that the US economy would get back on its feet. The US economy had taken some major hits in the previous two years, with the stock market bubble bursting in 2000, the 9/11 terrorist attack in September 2001, and the corporate scandals seen through 2002 and 2003. Those external shocks, combined with the impending war with Iraq in early 2003, caused concern that the US might slip into another recession and that deflation could become a serious problem. But by late 2003, the Fed's extremely stimulative monetary policy, combined with the expansive fiscal policy, helped create an economic boom and US GDP soared to +8.2% by Q3.

Treasury supply – The Treasury in 2003 made some substantial changes to its debt auction schedule due to the US budget deficit, which soared to $401 billion in fiscal 2003 and is expected to be near $480 billion in fiscal 2004. The higher budget deficit is due to three main factors: (1) lower revenues with the weak economy, (2) high expenses from the war on terror and the wars in Afghanistan and Iraq, and (3) the Bush tax cuts. The Treasury in 2003 revised its auction mix by (1) selling 5-year T-notes monthly versus its previous pattern of eight sales per year, (2) reinstating a quarterly sale of 3-year T-notes (after a 5-year hiatus), (3) increasing the frequency of 10-year T-note sales to eight per year from four per year, and (4) increasing the frequency of inflation-indexed 10-year T-notes to four per year.

Treasury yield curve – The Treasury yield curve was extremely steep during 2003. The Fed's extraordinarily easy monetary policy and the funds rate target of 1.00% kept short-term interest rates locked down to extremely low levels. Longer-term rates, however, were higher as the market discounted a return to a more normal inflation and interest rate situation in coming years. The spread between the 10-year T-note and the 2-year T-note, a widely-watched indicator of yield curve steepness, rose to 2.73 percentage points in July 2003, which was a record high going back to the beginning of the data series in 1977.

U.S. Producer Price Index[2] for All Commodities   1982 = 100

Year	Jan.	Feb.	Mar.	Apr.	May	June	July	Aug.	Sept.	Oct.	Nov.	Dec.	Average
1995	122.9	123.5	123.9	124.6	124.9	125.3	125.3	125.1	125.2	125.3	125.4	125.7	124.8
1996	126.3	126.2	126.4	127.4	128.1	128.0	128.0	128.3	128.2	128.0	128.2	129.1	127.7
1997	129.7	128.5	127.3	127.0	127.4	127.2	126.9	127.2	127.5	127.8	127.9	126.8	127.6
1998	125.4	125.0	124.7	124.9	125.1	124.8	124.9	124.2	123.8	124.0	123.6	122.8	124.4
1999	122.9	122.3	122.6	123.6	124.7	125.2	125.7	126.9	128.0	127.7	128.3	127.8	125.5
2000	128.3	129.8	130.8	130.7	131.6	133.8	133.7	132.9	134.7	135.4	135.0	136.2	132.7
2001	140.0	137.4	135.9	136.4	136.8	135.5	133.4	133.4	133.3	130.3	129.8	128.1	134.2
2002	128.5	128.4	129.8	130.8	130.8	130.9	131.2	131.5	132.3	133.2	133.1	132.9	131.1
2003[1]	135.3	137.6	141.2	136.8	136.7	138.0	137.7	138.0	138.5	139.4	138.9	139.4	138.1

[1] Preliminary.   [2] Not seasonally adjusted.   *Source: Bureau of Labor Statistics, U.S. Department of Commerce (BLS)*

U.S. Consumer Price Index[2] for All Urban Consumers   1982-84 = 100

Year	Jan.	Feb.	Mar.	Apr.	May	June	July	Aug.	Sept.	Oct.	Nov.	Dec.	Average
1995	150.3	150.9	151.4	151.9	152.2	152.5	152.5	152.9	153.2	153.7	153.6	153.5	152.4
1996	154.4	154.9	155.7	156.3	156.6	156.7	157.0	157.3	157.8	158.3	158.6	158.6	156.9
1997	159.1	159.6	160.0	160.2	160.1	160.3	160.5	160.8	161.2	161.6	161.5	161.3	160.5
1998	161.6	161.9	162.2	162.5	162.8	163.0	163.2	163.4	163.6	164.0	164.0	163.9	163.0
1999	164.3	164.5	165.0	166.2	166.2	166.2	166.7	167.1	167.9	168.2	168.3	168.3	166.6
2000	168.8	169.8	171.2	171.3	171.5	172.4	172.8	172.8	173.7	174.0	174.1	174.0	172.2
2001	175.1	175.8	176.2	176.9	177.7	178.0	177.5	177.5	178.3	177.7	177.4	176.7	177.1
2002	177.1	177.8	178.8	179.8	179.8	179.9	180.1	180.7	181.0	181.3	181.4	181.6	179.9
2003[1]	182.2	183.3	183.9	183.3	183.3	183.6	183.9	184.5	185.0	185.0	184.6	185.0	184.0

[1] Preliminary.   [2] Not seasonally adjusted.   *Source: Bureau of Labor Statistics, U.S. Department of Commerce (BLS)*

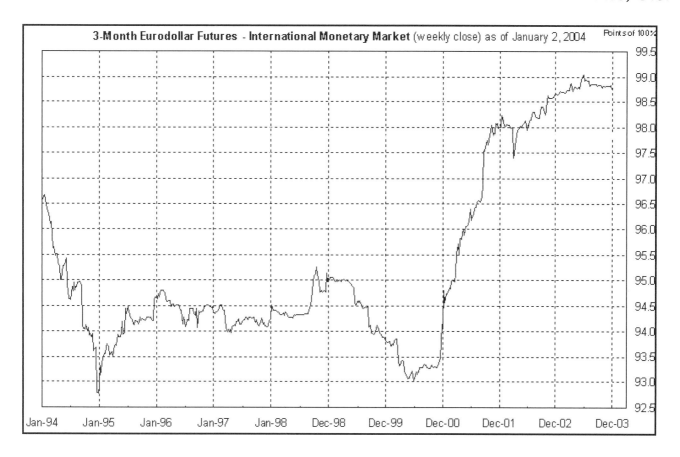

Average Open Interest of 3-month Eurodollar Futures in Chicago   In Thousands of Contracts

Year	Jan.	Feb.	Mar.	Apr.	May	June	July	Aug.	Sept.	Oct.	Nov.	Dec.
1994	2,300.5	2,529.5	2,568.1	2,627.3	2,734.3	2,565.2	2,599.1	2,703.8	2,699.6	2,561.2	2,660.3	2,606.3
1995	2,443.6	2,535.4	2,463.9	2,447.4	2,503.3	2,390.8	2,279.5	2,374.6	2,347.2	2,290.3	2,405.5	2,480.5
1996	2,519.4	2,638.6	2,511.4	2,483.5	2,571.8	2,590.1	2,504.4	2,485.5	2,392.4	2,349.7	2,378.2	2,225.7
1997	2,190.8	2,333.2	2,423.1	2,523.1	2,671.3	2,706.5	2,699.2	2,788.0	2,769.3	2,815.1	2,799.5	2,661.6
1998	2,713.4	2,821.5	2,797.9	2,892.6	3,089.0	3,093.9	3,027.7	3,223.0	3,359.9	3,303.4	3,297.4	3,000.1
1999	2,917.9	3,039.5	2,973.5	2,894.7	3,183.2	3,208.8	3,064.4	3,115.6	2,904.0	2,918.2	2,879.7	2,859.4
2000	2,971.3	3,261.4	3,138.7	3,156.6	3,331.7	3,272.1	3,160.3	3,225.7	3,181.8	3,067.2	3,201.1	3,349.7
2001	3,576.4	3,878.6	4,117.4	4,109.3	4,316.3	4,471.7	4,452.4	4,753.5	4,567.8	4,524.0	4,950.8	4,559.1
2002	4,592.0	4,937.0	4,727.9	4,411.6	4,421.0	4,295.5	4,123.7	4,482.4	4,243.4	4,237.9	4,553.7	4,072.5
2003	4,007.1	4,500.1	4,517.3	4,448.6	5,098.7	5,514.2	5,218.4	5,277.9	5,034.1	4,935.4	5,024.2	4,936.1

Source: International Monetary Market (IOM), division of the Chicago Mercantile Exchange (CME)

Volume of Trading of 3-month Eurodollar Futures in Chicago   In Thousands of Contracts

Year	Jan.	Feb.	Mar.	Apr.	May	June	July	Aug.	Sept.	Oct.	Nov.	Dec.	Total
1994	6,075	8,745	9,469	9,639	11,494	9,348	7,810	7,128	7,641	7,992	9,715	9,766	104,823
1995	10,341	10,429	9,549	6,069	9,897	10,105	6,670	7,013	7,171	6,478	6,055	5,952	95,730
1996	7,486	9,267	9,526	6,872	7,414	7,415	8,323	6,968	8,232	7,014	5,057	5,308	88,883
1997	7,903	6,918	8,936	9,352	8,447	8,050	7,292	9,295	7,635	12,570	6,314	7,058	99,770
1998	10,908	7,861	8,842	9,488	7,202	8,350	5,452	9,811	13,594	11,757	9,628	6,579	109,473
1999	7,471	7,675	8,719	7,347	8,957	9,650	7,746	8,898	7,629	7,501	6,223	5,604	93,418
2000	8,380	9,723	10,198	10,172	10,261	9,791	7,385	7,010	8,205	9,276	7,561	10,152	108,115
2001	17,515	12,908	15,479	15,192	15,691	14,310	12,673	14,948	16,776	14,139	21,150	13,234	184,015
2002	19,487	14,491	17,987	17,947	18,717	17,932	20,367	17,758	15,310	18,496	13,349	10,240	202,081
2003	13,534	12,315	18,275	15,393	19,403	21,163	18,733	18,724	18,817	20,004	15,432	16,978	208,771

Source: International Monetary Market (IOM), division of the Chicago Mercantile Exchange (CME)

INTEREST RATES, U.S.

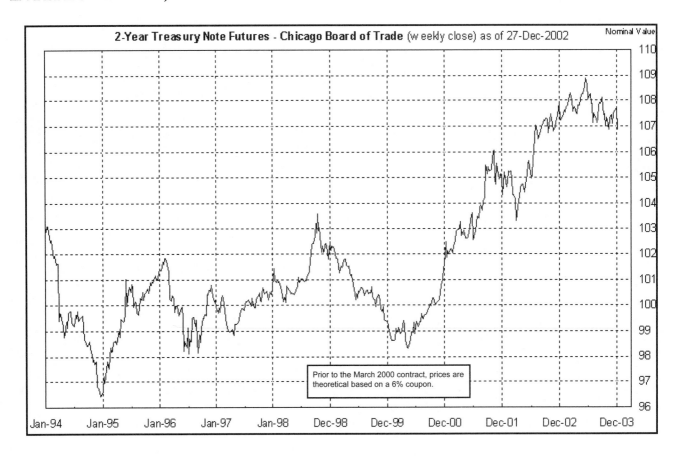

Average Open Interest of 2-Year U.S. Treasury Note Futures in Chicago   In Contracts

Year	Jan.	Feb.	Mar.	Apr.	May	June	July	Aug.	Sept.	Oct.	Nov.	Dec.
1994	24,696	36,184	39,818	37,306	36,331	32,673	29,963	33,038	36,606	31,385	35,929	40,344
1995	43,794	41,932	33,705	29,109	26,227	18,721	19,346	18,657	16,756	17,057	25,740	19,362
1996	20,194	26,865	21,125	17,494	16,606	17,547	15,758	16,849	17,792	17,730	19,247	20,309
1997	20,599	23,027	22,750	24,090	29,379	33,225	36,047	47,253	44,003	40,960	37,785	37,701
1998	39,649	40,462	40,840	40,899	46,833	47,241	44,701	48,888	47,030	37,245	38,222	40,303
1999	39,971	40,747	40,339	40,078	34,731	35,959	35,349	37,624	38,693	38,157	38,702	34,135
2000	34,325	43,026	44,512	43,772	49,033	51,216	55,806	53,449	47,912	53,338	60,894	77,860
2001	82,168	79,389	81,688	72,517	66,185	63,601	56,610	72,951	74,353	65,433	72,697	71,270
2002	86,505	103,331	103,568	87,850	102,040	105,931	99,383	107,955	110,434	108,089	115,503	113,618
2003	107,084	114,234	123,909	108,979	120,264	118,776	112,052	149,099	151,922	144,646	149,014	156,506

Source: Chicago Board of Trade (CBT)

Volume of Trading of 2-Year U.S. Treasury Note Futures in Chicago   In Contracts

Year	Jan.	Feb.	Mar.	Apr.	May	June	July	Aug.	Sept.	Oct.	Nov.	Dec.	Total
1994	39,855	99,669	127,658	38,595	90,394	102,460	43,231	65,330	98,060	31,830	94,659	104,291	936,032
1995	60,170	93,842	131,682	29,273	73,610	68,363	34,073	68,666	37,805	34,181	81,013	49,033	761,711
1996	38,710	98,916	51,861	28,135	60,097	46,049	37,971	61,838	58,688	25,530	69,046	61,006	637,847
1997	32,403	93,921	79,008	44,548	100,191	102,651	53,120	138,498	96,988	68,512	107,780	100,630	1,018,250
1998	77,139	104,312	107,051	52,038	140,903	123,312	59,360	177,445	160,102	93,117	140,650	72,923	1,308,352
1999	64,460	132,651	66,958	62,860	132,319	93,555	46,547	139,182	71,284	43,987	124,064	72,262	1,050,129
2000	51,539	159,339	97,880	76,889	160,157	105,192	43,017	180,980	107,353	97,403	287,602	126,469	1,493,820
2001	174,603	299,158	160,898	194,758	273,983	163,314	93,386	316,446	198,066	122,944	303,778	160,646	2,461,980
2002	195,004	332,884	290,410	159,242	376,968	242,925	177,001	376,991	253,009	174,779	387,153	232,287	3,198,653
2003	146,797	392,934	292,515	153,316	513,945	339,209	274,095	513,993	522,811	281,118	496,714	488,459	4,415,906

Source: Chicago Board of Trade (CBT)

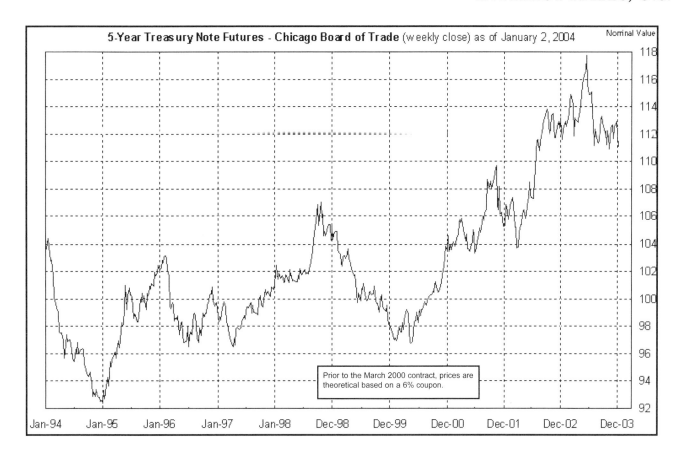

5-Year Treasury Note Futures - Chicago Board of Trade (weekly close) as of January 2, 2004   Nominal Value

Prior to the March 2000 contract, prices are theoretical based on a 6% coupon.

Average Open Interest of 5-Year U.S. Treasury Note Futures in Chicago   In Contracts

Year	Jan.	Feb.	Mar.	Apr.	May	June	July	Aug.	Sept.	Oct.	Nov.	Dec.
1994	200,812	213,037	200,626	185,083	192,659	186,026	189,828	182,027	181,518	181,578	176,322	205,150
1995	206,539	210,192	199,357	200,087	213,531	189,332	176,329	173,897	163,419	162,121	177,915	171,023
1996	163,026	184,523	200,253	191,690	179,951	177,370	174,484	179,599	154,764	138,246	155,820	154,764
1997	176,691	208,928	219,540	235,543	227,882	225,691	226,306	225,792	234,309	233,480	248,377	257,886
1998	257,094	270,048	282,327	277,540	274,145	257,193	264,756	389,118	382,855	383,809	353,399	326,860
1999	290,373	268,561	247,526	246,916	311,106	348,627	325,348	341,495	298,861	328,581	272,628	288,523
2000	387,008	475,464	420,789	417,929	428,239	379,628	402,658	405,087	372,779	373,698	381,432	380,248
2001	377,692	391,989	374,481	376,929	436,278	421,968	460,960	483,252	451,429	463,247	554,640	491,105
2002	507,207	576,204	585,576	632,211	656,402	594,924	554,875	652,799	655,029	662,475	720,688	692,750
2003	685,117	743,152	777,801	835,470	856,337	827,497	781,691	840,392	737,028	819,361	925,644	880,093

Source: Chicago Board of Trade (CBT)

Volume of Trading of 5-Year U.S. Treasury Note Futures in Chicago   In Thousands of Contracts

Year	Jan.	Feb.	Mar.	Apr.	May	June	July	Aug.	Sept.	Oct.	Nov.	Dec.	Total
1994	696	1,235	1,295	917	1,202	1,155	835	945	1,107	841	1,157	1,078	12,463
1995	988	1,296	1,387	783	1,291	1,403	829	1,100	1,009	770	996	785	12,637
1996	837	1,312	1,085	816	1,135	878	882	1,062	979	690	831	957	11,463
1997	928	1,157	1,271	984	1,191	1,144	761	1,245	1,244	1,314	1,068	1,183	13,489
1998	1,452	1,482	1,391	1,155	1,281	1,377	944	2,481	1,913	1,583	1,723	1,279	18,060
1999	1,120	1,554	1,337	1,115	1,906	1,544	1,166	2,164	1,034	1,245	1,607	1,193	16,984
2000	1,801	2,874	2,010	1,708	2,548	1,757	1,189	2,253	1,516	1,774	2,260	1,643	23,332
2001	2,423	2,592	2,281	2,063	3,222	2,264	1,702	2,697	2,617	2,526	4,053	2,684	31,122
2002	2,868	3,826	3,848	3,092	4,638	4,096	4,437	5,354	4,859	5,027	5,013	3,453	50,512
2003	4,436	5,178	5,534	4,624	7,268	6,166	6,463	7,090	7,454	6,364	6,885	6,286	73,746

Source: Chicago Board of Trade (CBT)

INTEREST RATES, U.S.

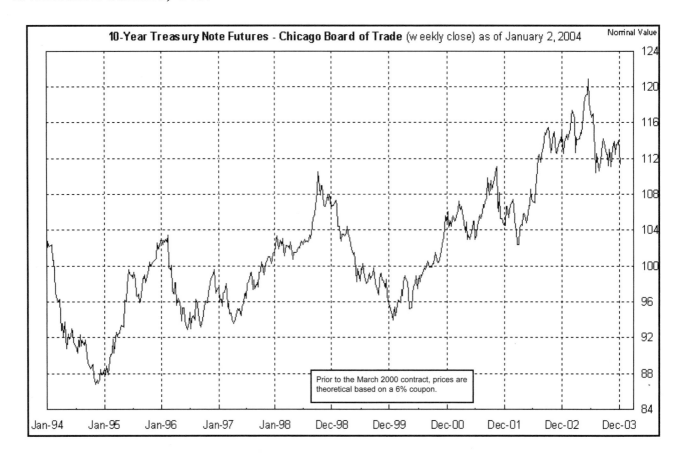

10-Year Treasury Note Futures - Chicago Board of Trade (weekly close) as of January 2, 2004   Nominal Value

Prior to the March 2000 contract, prices are theoretical based on a 6% coupon.

Average Open Interest of 10-year U.S. Treasury Note Futures in Chicago   In Contracts

Year	Jan.	Feb.	Mar.	Apr.	May	June	July	Aug.	Sept.	Oct.	Nov.	Dec.
1994	264,848	258,643	300,080	328,821	294,091	254,612	232,373	253,233	273,564	277,313	301,000	271,992
1995	282,978	285,187	265,747	263,816	273,945	289,052	306,046	323,078	277,011	278,832	270,527	249,073
1996	260,374	297,850	285,501	319,234	331,032	293,416	302,330	326,391	291,208	284,581	313,298	303,702
1997	332,285	343,661	323,982	348,683	350,814	336,927	363,744	407,147	387,284	398,645	404,980	374,448
1998	430,335	507,986	474,916	494,417	533,214	513,369	512,173	604,862	555,268	482,928	508,299	503,533
1999	528,538	549,518	515,404	510,091	541,057	574,514	588,272	623,806	607,305	653,080	582,003	487,888
2000	595,180	653,822	571,932	615,618	621,361	583,900	608,358	602,068	547,582	564,606	555,189	508,888
2001	550,287	541,619	560,035	595,103	628,693	512,127	550,155	627,305	610,435	590,328	661,963	559,949
2002	572,937	643,864	679,635	699,051	806,458	792,956	877,642	958,338	888,696	970,176	938,028	751,575
2003	772,919	896,941	914,943	897,057	968,072	993,643	1,009,484	1,032,497	856,204	985,673	1,140,655	965,049

Source: Chicago Board of Trade (CBT)

Volume of Trading of 10-year U.S. Treasury Note Futures in Chicago   In Thousands of Contracts

Year	Jan.	Feb.	Mar.	Apr.	May	June	July	Aug.	Sept.	Oct.	Nov.	Dec.	Total
1994	1,484	1,936	2,572	2,213	2,399	2,250	1,622	2,029	1,933	1,635	2,254	1,750	24,078
1995	1,753	1,979	2,459	1,368	2,236	2,496	1,589	2,029	1,859	1,460	1,731	1,488	22,445
1996	1,649	2,313	2,076	1,632	2,211	1,716	1,556	1,866	1,810	1,495	1,905	1,711	21,940
1997	1,781	1,940	2,052	1,703	2,026	1,942	1,510	2,536	2,063	2,594	1,826	1,991	23,962
1998	2,394	2,749	2,817	2,342	2,696	2,682	1,704	3,632	3,560	2,883	2,912	2,112	32,483
1999	2,269	3,562	2,994	2,145	3,519	3,153	2,438	3,736	2,509	2,471	3,202	2,048	34,046
2000	3,557	4,975	3,750	3,530	4,712	3,706	2,581	4,460	3,780	3,824	4,514	3,313	46,701
2001	4,633	4,915	4,501	4,299	5,483	4,084	3,493	5,683	4,390	4,145	7,270	4,690	57,586
2002	5,540	6,407	6,521	5,463	8,309	7,548	8,981	10,590	8,529	11,199	9,679	7,020	95,786
2003	9,121	10,746	11,321	9,377	13,817	12,149	15,285	14,249	13,707	13,587	12,475	10,912	146,745

Source: Chicago Board of Trade (CBT)

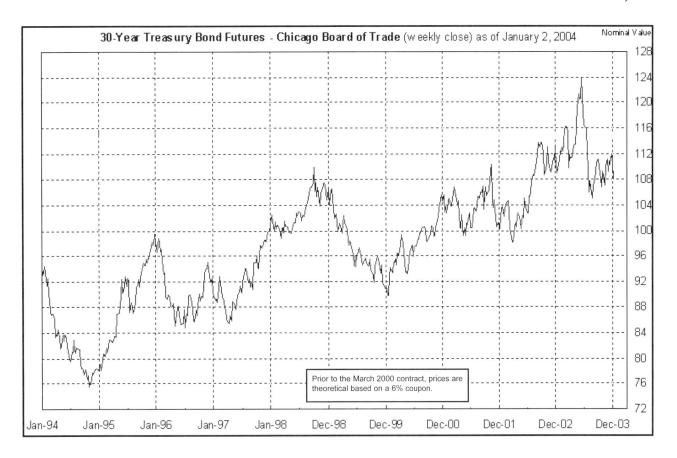

30-Year Treasury Bond Futures - Chicago Board of Trade (weekly close) as of January 2, 2004

Prior to the March 2000 contract, prices are theoretical based on a 6% coupon.

Average Open Interest of 30-year U.S. Treasury Bond Futures in Chicago   In Contracts

Year	Jan.	Feb.	Mar.	Apr.	May	June	July	Aug.	Sept.	Oct.	Nov.	Dec.
1994	380,057	422,902	454,539	500,790	497,296	421,286	441,884	451,462	447,924	436,684	449,642	397,554
1995	384,356	389,908	369,989	367,964	399,500	421,234	438,267	381,237	361,394	395,346	447,409	426,384
1996	382,001	403,403	395,338	381,926	413,944	443,644	464,145	471,203	420,622	409,950	463,731	479,086
1997	497,539	545,775	509,573	493,511	554,418	480,669	530,011	608,474	624,231	723,321	719,186	737,703
1998	744,894	764,309	766,233	806,559	888,215	1,040,659	1,084,889	1,061,223	837,986	769,932	782,677	662,025
1999	657,180	801,115	664,131	618,453	717,453	674,225	672,983	748,974	647,816	621,816	637,656	561,919
2000	637,023	612,298	530,957	503,412	434,771	390,928	394,075	440,437	402,156	399,880	443,282	445,386
2001	413,244	479,165	519,987	509,558	503,194	455,799	458,613	531,098	525,972	567,177	602,647	478,418
2002	468,455	520,573	479,939	463,100	472,778	458,020	427,896	465,971	496,815	467,440	459,877	440,225
2003	420,797	506,910	487,277	449,286	566,887	596,186	554,632	521,928	423,995	443,177	489,185	471,848

Source: Chicago Board of Trade (CBT)

Volume of Trading of 30-year U.S. Treasury Bond Futures in Chicago   In Thousands of Contracts

Year	Jan.	Feb.	Mar.	Apr.	May	June	July	Aug.	Sept.	Oct.	Nov.	Dec.	Total
1994	7,288	8,430	10,837	9,557	9,999	9,804	6,987	7,910	7,913	7,004	8,533	5,699	99,960
1995	7,058	7,714	9,624	5,835	8,722	8,447	5,790	7,084	7,317	6,927	6,626	5,232	86,376
1996	7,529	8,781	7,199	6,011	7,932	6,521	6,422	6,626	6,926	6,772	7,298	6,708	84,725
1997	8,105	7,523	7,493	7,520	8,339	7,400	7,680	10,228	8,356	12,468	7,736	6,980	99,828
1998	9,595	9,368	9,764	8,517	9,054	10,209	8,071	12,025	11,159	10,698	8,155	5,609	112,224
1999	8,075	10,031	8,667	7,197	9,556	8,072	6,415	7,995	6,560	6,301	6,909	4,263	90,042
2000	7,966	8,157	5,379	5,282	5,973	4,459	3,080	4,710	4,529	4,460	5,073	3,682	62,751
2001	5,123	5,546	5,196	4,584	6,022	4,233	3,347	4,966	4,331	4,599	6,746	3,886	58,579
2002	4,133	4,721	4,505	3,933	5,191	4,722	5,158	5,667	4,534	5,190	4,723	3,606	56,082
2003	3,625	4,841	5,107	3,795	7,188	5,896	6,352	6,198	5,738	5,122	4,823	4,835	63,522

Source: Chicago Board of Trade (CBT)

INTEREST RATES, U.S.

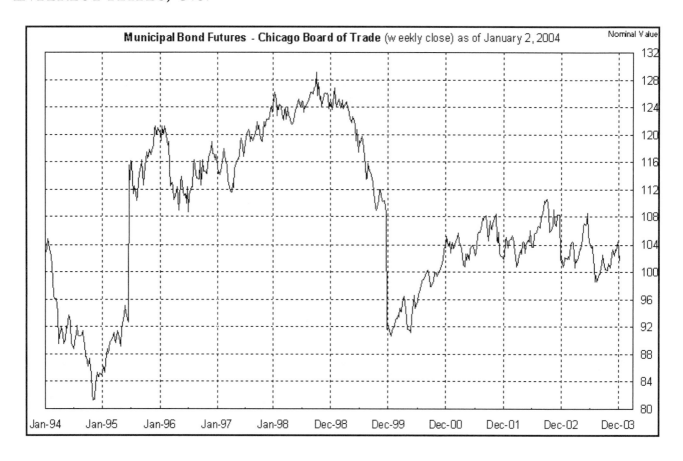

Municipal Bond Futures - **Chicago Board of Trade** (weekly close) as of January 2, 2004 — Nominal Value

U.S. Federal Funds Rate   In Percent

Year	Jan.	Feb.	Mar.	Apr.	May	June	July	Aug.	Sept.	Oct.	Nov.	Dec.	Average
1994	3.05	3.25	3.34	3.56	4.01	4.25	4.26	4.47	4.73	4.76	5.29	5.45	4.20
1995	5.53	5.92	5.98	6.05	6.01	6.00	5.85	5.74	5.80	5.76	5.80	5.60	5.84
1996	5.56	5.22	5.31	5.22	5.56	5.27	5.40	5.22	5.30	5.24	5.31	5.29	5.30
1997	5.25	5.19	5.39	5.51	5.50	5.56	5.52	5.54	5.54	5.50	5.52	5.50	5.46
1998	5.56	5.51	5.49	5.45	5.49	5.56	5.54	5.55	5.51	5.07	4.83	4.68	5.35
1999	4.63	4.76	4.81	4.74	4.74	4.76	4.99	5.07	5.22	5.20	5.42	5.30	4.97
2000	5.46	5.73	5.85	6.02	6.27	6.53	6.54	6.50	6.52	6.51	6.51	6.40	6.24
2001	5.98	5.49	5.31	4.80	4.21	3.97	3.77	3.65	3.07	2.49	2.09	1.82	3.89
2002	1.73	1.74	1.73	1.75	1.75	1.75	1.73	1.74	1.75	1.75	1.34	1.24	1.67
2003	1.24	1.26	1.25	1.26	1.26	1.22	1.01	1.03	1.01	1.01	1.00	0.98	1.13

Source: Bureau of Economic Analysis, U.S. Department of Commerce (BEA)

U.S. Municipal Bond Yield[1]   In Percent

Year	Jan.	Feb.	Mar.	Apr.	May	June	July	Aug.	Sept.	Oct.	Nov.	Dec.	Average
1994	5.31	5.40	5.91	6.23	6.19	6.11	6.23	6.21	6.28	6.52	6.97	6.80	6.18
1995	6.53	6.22	6.10	6.02	5.95	5.84	5.92	6.06	5.91	5.80	5.64	5.45	5.95
1996	5.43	5.43	5.79	5.94	5.98	6.02	5.92	5.76	5.87	5.72	5.59	5.64	5.76
1997	5.72	5.63	5.76	5.88	5.70	5.53	5.35	5.41	5.39	5.38	5.33	5.19	5.52
1998	5.06	5.10	5.21	5.23	5.20	5.12	5.14	5.10	4.99	4.93	5.03	4.98	5.09
1999	5.02	5.03	5.10	5.08	5.18	5.37	5.36	5.58	5.69	5.92	5.86	5.95	5.43
2000	6.08	6.00	5.83	5.75	6.00	5.80	5.63	5.51	5.56	5.59	5.54	5.22	5.71
2001	5.10	5.18	5.13	5.27	5.29	5.20	5.20	5.03	5.09	5.05	5.04	5.25	5.15
2002	5.16	5.11	5.29	5.22	5.19	5.09	5.02	4.95	4.74	4.88	4.95	4.85	5.04
2003	4.90	4.81	4.76	4.74	4.41	4.33	4.74	5.10	4.92	4.89	4.73	4.65	4.75

[1] 20-bond average.   *Source: Bureau of Economic Analysis, U.S. Department of Commerce (BEA)*

INTEREST RATES, U.S.

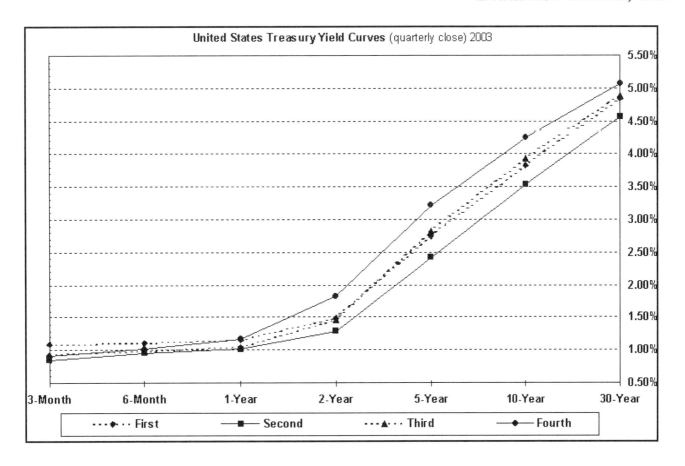

U.S. Industrial Production Index[1]   1997 = 100

Year	Jan.	Feb.	Mar.	Apr.	May	June	July	Aug.	Sept.	Oct.	Nov.	Dec.	Average
1994	105.7	106.2	107.0	107.4	108.1	108.6	109.1	109.2	109.3	109.9	110.6	111.6	108.6
1995	111.9	111.6	111.7	111.4	111.5	111.7	111.7	112.6	113.0	112.5	112.7	112.8	114.5
1996	112.4	113.8	113.2	114.3	114.8	115.5	115.5	115.8	116.0	116.2	120.6	120.9	119.5
1997	121.3	122.1	122.5	123.1	123.3	123.5	124.5	125.2	125.6	129.3	129.9	130.3	127.0
1998	130.3	130.2	130.7	131.3	131.9	130.6	130.5	132.4	131.9	134.1	133.8	133.8	132.4
1999	134.1	134.5	135.1	135.5	136.2	136.6	137.4	137.7	138.1	139.1	141.9	142.8	139.2
2000	143.6	144.3	145.2	146.3	147.2	147.9	147.6	148.7	148.8	146.3	145.8	145.1	145.7
2001	143.9	143.5	142.9	142.0	141.6	140.3	140.4	140.0	138.5	137.7	108.8	108.3	111.5
2002	109.0	109.2	109.6	110.1	110.4	110.8	111.6	111.3	111.2	111.0	111.2	110.6	110.9
2003[2]	111.2	111.6	110.8	110.1	110.0	110.0	110.8	110.9	111.5	111.9	113.1	113.2	111.3

[1] Total Index of the Federal Reserve Index of Quantity Output, seasonally adjusted.   [2] Preliminary.

Source: Bureau of Economic Analysis, U.S. Department of Commerce (BEA)

U.S. Gross National Product, National Income, and Personal Income   In Billions of Constant Dollars[1]

Year	Gross Domestic Product					National Income					Personal Income				
	First Quarter	Second Quarter	Third Quarter	Fourth Quarter	Annual Average	First Quarter	Second Quarter	Third Quarter	Fourth Quarter	Annual Average	First Quarter	Second Quarter	Third Quarter	Fourth Quarter	Annual Average
1994	6,888	7,016	7,096	7,218	7,054	5,373	5,525	5,609	5,720	5,557	5,714	5,861	5,935	6,042	5,888
1995	7,298	7,343	7,433	7,529	7,401	5,775	5,834	5,920	5,978	5,877	6,110	6,163	6,226	6,305	6,201
1996	7,630	7,783	7,859	7,981	7,813	6,067	6,178	6,255	6,343	6,210	6,405	6,509	6,597	6,678	6,547
1997	8,124	8,280	8,391	8,479	8,318	6,455	6,556	6,676	6,787	6,618	6,792	6,879	6,979	7,098	6,937
1998	8,628	8,697	8,817	8,985	8,782	6,874	6,986	7,109	7,197	7,041	7,255	7,383	7,491	7,576	7,426
1999	9,093	9,172	9,317	9,516	9,274	7,343	7,406	7,476	7,650	7,462	7,656	7,722	7,808	7,960	7,787
2000	9,650	9,821	9,875	9,954	9,825	7,860	7,955	8,048	8,075	7,984	8,212	8,350	8,488	8,577	8,407
2001	10,028	10,050	10,098	10,153	10,082	8,092	8,110	8,089	8,197	8,122	8,658	8,676	8,706	8,701	8,685
2002	10,313	10,377	10,506	10,589	10,446	8,269	8,328	8,350	8,414	8,340	8,803	8,914	8,959	9,013	8,922
2003[2]	10,688	10,803	11,063		10,852	8,496	8,618	8,796		8,637	9,080	9,156	9,249		9,162

[1] Seasonally adjusted at annual rates.   [2] Preliminary.   *Source: Bureau of Economic Analysis, U.S. Department of Commerce (BEA)*

INTEREST RATES, U.S.

U.S. Money Supply M1[2]   In Billions of Dollars

Year	Jan.	Feb.	Mar.	Apr.	May	June	July	Aug.	Sept.	Oct.	Nov.	Dec.	Average
1994	1,131.8	1,136.3	1,140.3	1,141.2	1,143.2	1,145.3	1,149.7	1,150.0	1,151.3	1,150.0	1,150.2	1,150.5	1,145.0
1995	1,151.0	1,147.0	1,146.4	1,149.8	1,144.8	1,143.5	1,145.0	1,145.1	1,140.7	1,136.2	1,133.3	1,127.0	1,142.5
1996	1,122.8	1,118.3	1,122.1	1,124.8	1,116.4	1,114.8	1,111.5	1,100.7	1,095.0	1,086.4	1,081.6	1,079.3	1,106.1
1997	1,080.9	1,077.6	1,070.3	1,062.7	1,062.9	1,064.6	1,065.9	1,072.8	1,066.6	1,066.4	1,068.8	1,072.5	1,069.3
1998	1,073.7	1,077.7	1,076.5	1,076.7	1,076.6	1,075.6	1,074.9	1,073.3	1,078.9	1,085.2	1,092.7	1,096.1	1,079.8
1999	1,095.8	1,096.6	1,097.4	1,101.2	1,100.7	1,098.8	1,097.7	1,097.3	1,096.6	1,101.5	1,109.8	1,124.0	1,101.5
2000	1,120.3	1,108.6	1,108.9	1,111.9	1,104.8	1,104.3	1,103.1	1,101.4	1,098.7	1,099.0	1,092.4	1,087.9	1,103.4
2001	1,095.3	1,099.4	1,107.7	1,110.6	1,115.6	1,123.6	1,135.6	1,147.3	1,199.2	1,161.5	1,164.9	1,177.2	1,136.5
2002	1,182.7	1,184.6	1,188.4	1,177.5	1,182.0	1,186.3	1,192.6	1,181.1	1,188.7	1,200.0	1,202.6	1,215.0	1,190.1
2003[1]	1,218.4	1,232.9	1,238.2	1,243.4	1,255.5	1,268.7	1,273.3	1,282.3	1,282.3	1,284.6	1,283.8	1,293.0	1,263.0

[1] Preliminary.   [2] M1 -- The sum of currency held outside the vaults of depository institutions, Federal Reserve Banks, and the U.S. Treasury; travelers checks; and demand and other checkable deposits issued by financial institutions (except demand deposits due to the Treasury and depository institutions), minus cash items in process of collection and Federal Reserve float. Seasonally adjusted.
Source: Board of Governors of the Federal Reserve System

U.S. Money Supply M2[2]   In Billions of Dollars

Year	Jan.	Feb.	Mar.	Apr.	May	June	July	Aug.	Sept.	Oct.	Nov.	Dec.	Average
1994	3,485.1	3,485.7	3,491.6	3,496.2	3,504.3	3,492.6	3,497.3	3,494.8	3,495.4	3,495.0	3,497.1	3,496.3	3,494.3
1995	3,501.8	3,499.4	3,500.6	3,510.6	3,532.5	3,557.8	3,577.9	3,599.5	3,610.2	3,622.2	3,631.2	3,640.2	3,565.3
1996	3,658.0	3,673.3	3,698.6	3,709.9	3,720.5	3,734.2	3,748.4	3,756.6	3,767.7	3,780.8	3,794.6	3,815.5	3,738.2
1997	3,829.8	3,840.9	3,856.3	3,873.2	3,884.9	3,903.1	3,922.7	3,951.9	3,970.4	3,989.1	4,011.0	4,031.0	3,922.0
1998	4,055.3	4,088.2	4,114.9	4,140.1	4,159.4	4,183.9	4,203.7	4,230.2	4,271.5	4,312.3	4,351.9	4,383.7	4,207.9
1999	4,407.3	4,434.1	4,444.5	4,475.3	4,494.3	4,514.8	4,538.8	4,560.8	4,577.1	4,595.5	4,619.8	4,649.4	4,526.0
2000	4,678.2	4,692.3	4,723.1	4,775.3	4,766.8	4,783.6	4,798.9	4,833.2	4,863.9	4,881.1	4,892.8	4,933.3	4,801.9
2001	4,989.7	5,029.2	5,088.6	5,152.8	5,154.7	5,193.0	5,224.5	5,257.2	5,368.5	5,360.3	5,403.3	5,452.8	5,222.9
2002	5,480.3	5,510.4	5,521.5	5,527.6	5,558.6	5,580.6	5,623.0	5,658.3	5,684.9	5,730.7	5,777.2	5,805.8	5,621.6
2003[1]	5,838.2	5,881.0	5,906.4	5,949.7	5,998.5	6,035.7	6,079.5	6,118.1	6,096.3	6,080.3	6,076.0	6,070.8	6,010.9

[1] Preliminary.   [2] M2 -- M1 plus savings deposits (including money market deposit accounts) and small-denomination (less than $100,000) time deposits issued by financial institutions; and shares in retail money market mutual funds (funds with initial investments of less than $50,000), net of retirement accounts. Seasonally adjusted.   *Source: Board of Governors of the Federal Reserve System*

U.S. Money Supply M3[2]   In Billions of Dollars

Year	Jan.	Feb.	Mar.	Apr.	May	June	July	Aug.	Sept.	Oct.	Nov.	Dec.	Average
1994	4,275.2	4,259.8	4,271.2	4,282.4	4,292.7	4,290.7	4,310.5	4,311.4	4,320.0	4,331.7	4,346.3	4,360.2	4,304.3
1995	4,383.7	4,385.1	4,405.7	4,428.3	4,466.3	4,504.5	4,531.5	4,566.0	4,585.1	4,602.8	4,614.6	4,625.4	4,508.2
1996	4,658.8	4,687.4	4,723.0	4,741.2	4,777.1	4,800.4	4,825.9	4,845.3	4,873.2	4,913.6	4,932.7	4,972.1	4,812.6
1997	4,999.9	5,028.8	5,066.9	5,107.2	5,132.7	5,162.9	5,221.3	5,277.3	5,317.4	5,362.3	5,403.6	5,446.0	5,210.5
1998	5,493.0	5,526.1	5,595.7	5,634.0	5,671.7	5,710.8	5,733.6	5,799.6	5,866.6	5,937.3	5,995.4	6,036.2	5,750.0
1999	6,063.4	6,111.4	6,117.1	6,156.6	6,185.1	6,219.1	6,249.0	6,281.0	6,305.8	6,360.6	6,447.5	6,535.1	6,252.6
2000	6,585.1	6,614.3	6,686.8	6,751.1	6,760.0	6,804.4	6,855.2	6,927.1	6,984.0	7,006.8	7,024.2	7,102.3	6,841.8
2001	7,213.1	7,279.2	7,351.8	7,486.7	7,543.5	7,618.4	7,657.8	7,666.2	7,821.8	7,864.9	7,943.4	8,012.2	7,621.6
2002	8,033.2	8,077.6	8,097.4	8,119.3	8,155.4	8,166.6	8,208.5	8,271.6	8,308.0	8,335.9	8,467.5	8,540.6	8,231.8
2003[1]	8,550.6	8,587.8	8,619.4	8,655.9	8,711.3	8,761.5	8,837.9	8,876.2	8,865.2	8,835.6	8,821.9	8,813.6	8,744.7

[1] Preliminary.   [2] M3 -- M2 plus large-denomination ($100,000 or more) time deposits; repurchase agreements issued by depository institutions; Eurodollar deposits, specifically, dollar-denominated deposits due to nonbank U.S. addresses held at foreign offices of U.S. banks worldwide and all banking offices in Canada and the United Kingdom; and institutional money market mutual funds (funds with initial investments of $50,000 or more). Seasonally adjusted.   *Source: Board of Governors of the Federal Reserve System*

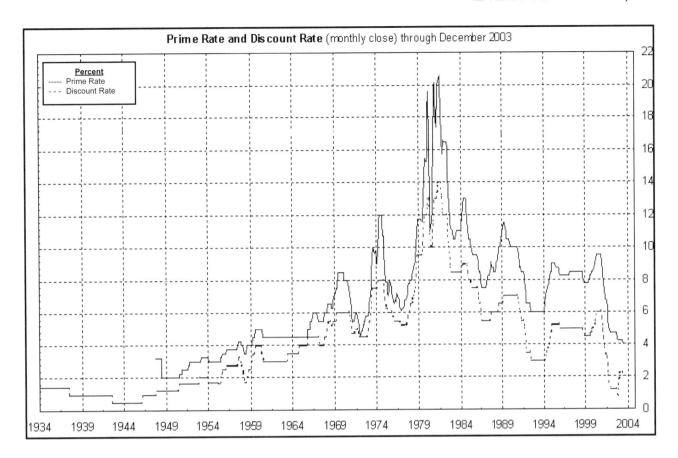

Prime Rate and Discount Rate (monthly close) through December 2003

Percent
----- Prime Rate
- - - Discount Rate

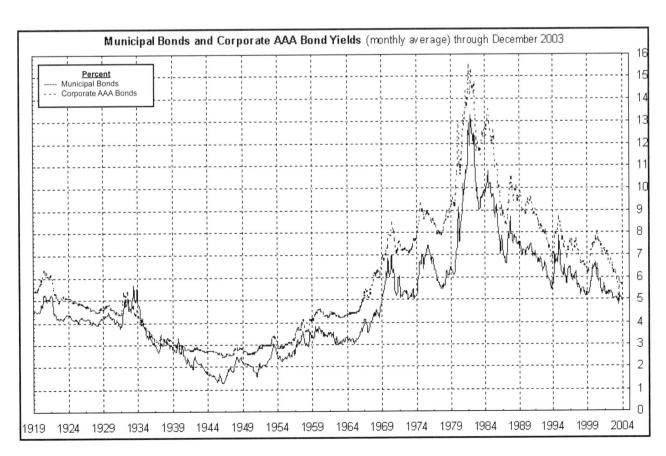

Municipal Bonds and Corporate AAA Bond Yields (monthly average) through December 2003

Percent
----- Municipal Bonds
- - - Corporate AAA Bonds

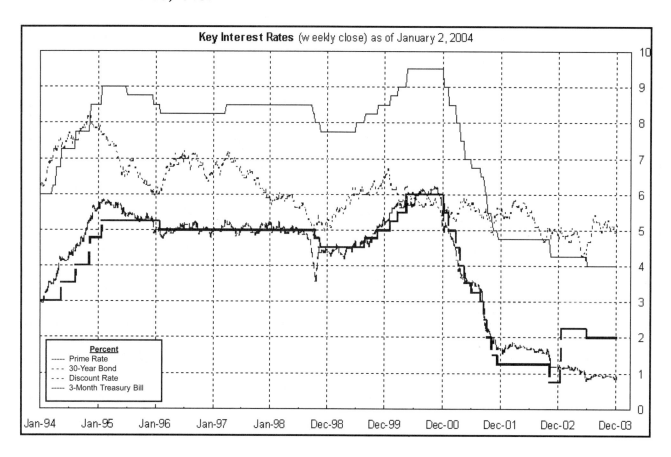

Key Interest Rates (weekly close) as of January 2, 2004

Percent
- Prime Rate
- 30-Year Bond
- Discount Rate
- 3-Month Treasury Bill

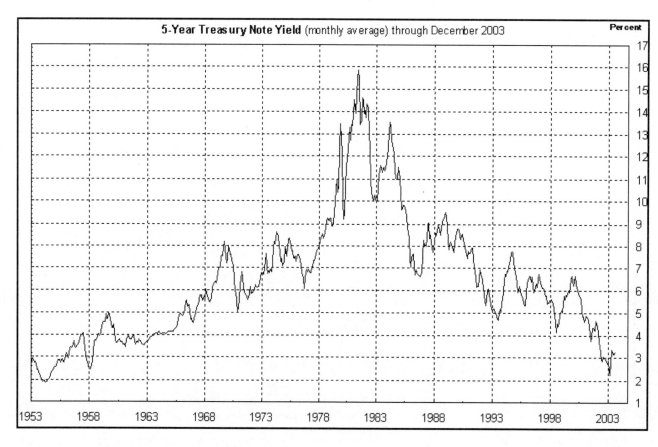

5-Year Treasury Note Yield (monthly average) through December 2003

Interest Rates, Worldwide

Interest rate futures contracts are widely traded throughout the world. The most popular futures contracts for each country are generally the 10-year government bond and the 3-month interest contract. In Europe, futures on German interest rates are traded at the all-electronic Eurex Exchange in Frankfurt. Futures on UK interest rates are traded at the Liffe Exchange in London. Futures on Canadian interest rates are traded at the Montreal Exchange. Futures on Japanese interest rates are traded at the Singapore Exchange (Simex) and at the Tokyo Stock Exchange. A variety of other interest rate futures contracts are traded throughout the rest of the world (please see the front of this Yearbook for a complete list).

Euro-Zone – The 10-year German Bund futures contract traded at the Eurex and rallied sharply and posted a record high of 120.00 in June 2003. However, the Bund then backed off through November and traded sideways into December, finally closing the year at 112.53, only slightly above the 2002 close of 112.23. The Bund in 2003 basically tracked the movement in US T-Notes, rallying early in the year on the Iraq war and then trailing off later in the year due to the upward rebound in the European and general world economies. The 3-month Euribor contract rallied sharply into June and then traded sideways for the remainder of the year in the narrow range between 97.80 (2.20%) and 98.00 (2.00%) on the weekly nearest futures chart.

The European Central Bank (ECB) in 2003 cut its key refinancing rate by a total of 75 basis points, with a 25 basis point cut to 2.50% on March 7 and a 50 basis point cut to 2.00% on June 6. Despite the 75 basis point rate cut, the ECB's key rate of 2.00% in the latter half of the year was still a full 100 basis points higher than the US Federal Reserve's federal funds target rate of 1.00%, even though the European economy during 2003 was weaker than the US economy. That left the ECB open to charges of being overly hawkish with its monetary policy. Moreover, the sharp rally in the euro during the year also had the effect of dampening the European economy via lower exports. The euro ended 2003 more than 50% above its record low against the dollar in 2000 and was up 34% from its 2002 average. As 2003 ended, the ECB was under pressure to counteract the impact on the strong euro, either through talking down the euro, through currency intervention, or through some easing of monetary policy.

UK – The 10-year Gilt contract traded at the Liffe Exchange in London and rallied into June to post a record high of 124.77 but then sold off sharply through November, finally closing the year near 117.07. Gilts in the latter half of 2003 were much weaker than the German Bund because the UK economy in 2003 proved to be much stronger than in continental Europe. The Bank of England in early 2003 cut its base rate by a total of 50 basis points with a 25 basis point cut on February 6 to 3.75% and another 25 basis point cut on July 10 to 3.50%. However, the BOE was then forced to raise the base rate by 25 basis points to 3.75% on November 6 due to the strong UK economy, strong consumer credit growth, and a torrid real estate sector. With its base rate at 3.75%, the UK key reference rate was a hefty 275 basis points above the Federal Reserve's 1.00% federal funds rate target.

Canada – The Canadian 10-year T-note futures contract traded at the Montreal Exchange and rallied in April and May to peak at a record high of 114.09 in June. The contract then fell back into the relatively narrow trading range of 107-110 through the remainder of the year, tracking US T-Note prices fairly closely. The 3-month Bankers Acceptance futures contract traded at the Montreal Exchange and rallied from April through October and closed the year near 1-3/4 year highs of 97.425 (or 2.575%). The Bank of Canada in 2003 raised its overnight target range by a total of 50 basis points in early 2003 (+25 basis points on March 4 and +25 basis points on April 15) to 3.25%, but then reversed that with a 50 basis point rate cut during mid-year (-25 basis points on July 15 and –25 basis points on September 3). The Canadian economy was hurt during the year by the impact from mad cow disease and from the SARS outbreak that hit Toronto. In addition, the Canadian dollar rallied sharply against the US dollar during 2003, causing concern about lower exports to the US. However, as 2003 ended, the Bank of Canada was fairly confident about the prospects for the Canadian economy.

Japan – The 10-year JGB futures contract at the Simex rallied steadily in early 2003 to post a 145.03 on the weekly nearest futures chart. However, the contract then sold off sharply in the July-September period as signs finally emerged of a recovery in the Japanese economy. JGBs finally closed the year at 137.41, about 4-1/2 points lower than the 2002 close of 141.98. The 3-month Euroyen contract at the Simex traded sideways all year in the extraordinarily narrow range of 99.90 to 99.95 (10-15 basis points). Short-term rates were locked near zero due to the Bank of Japan's continued zero-interest-rate monetary policy. The Bank of Japan (BOJ) in 2003 left its monetary policy unchanged all year with its overnight rate set only a few basis points above zero. The Bank of Japan in 2003 finally appeared to be making a little headway in stimulating the economy and trying to get a sustainable economic expansion going. The 1990's were basically a lost decade for Japan which suffered from the severe hangover from the real estate and stock market bubble of the late 1980's. Japanese monetary policy was basically caught in a classic liquidity trap through 2003 whereby even zero interest rates and a huge amount of excess reserves were ineffective in stimulating the economy because of the crippled banking system and the lack of credit demand from Japanese consumers and businesses. However, as 2003 ended, the Japanese government was making some headway on reforming the Japanese banking system and the Japanese economy was picking up, raising hopes that the Japanese economy in 2004 might finally display the long-awaited recovery.

INTEREST RATES, WORLDWIDE

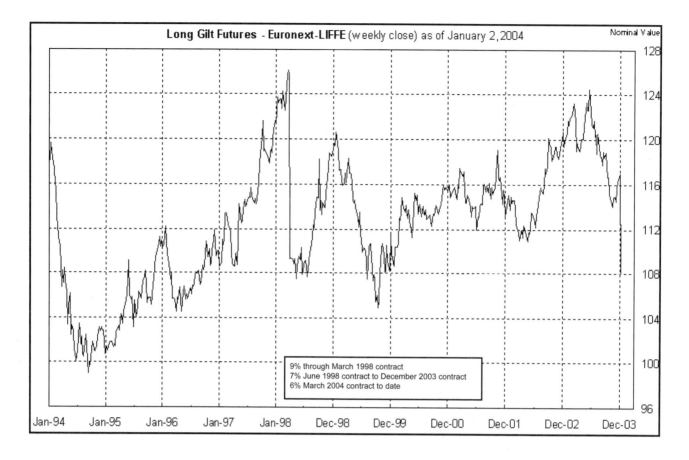

Long Gilt Futures - Euronext-LIFFE (weekly close) as of January 2, 2004

Nominal Value

9% through March 1998 contract
7% June 1998 contract to December 2003 contract
6% March 2004 contract to date

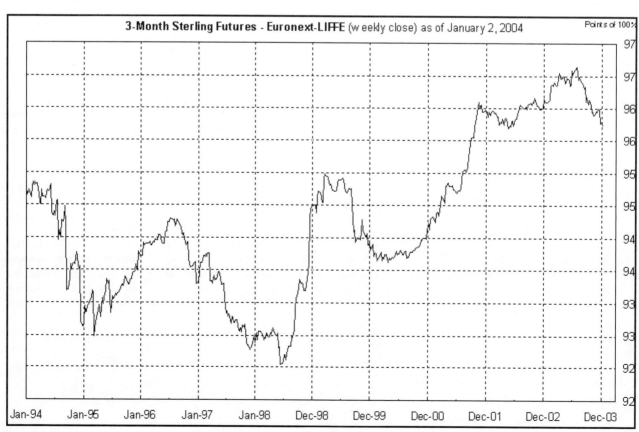

3-Month Sterling Futures - Euronext-LIFFE (weekly close) as of January 2, 2004

Points of 100%

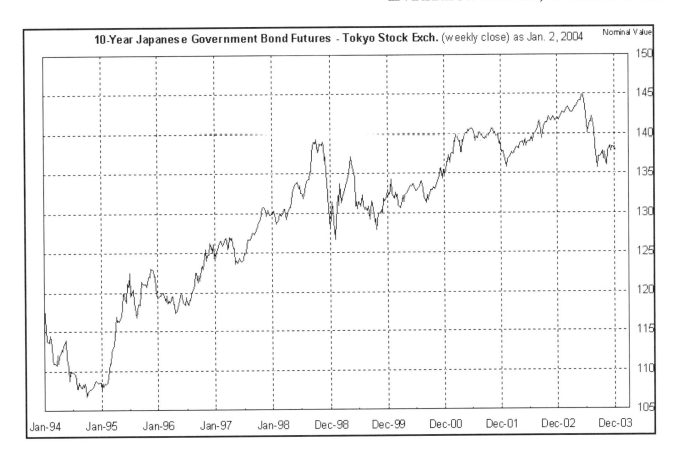

10-Year Japanese Government Bond Futures - Tokyo Stock Exch. (weekly close) as Jan. 2, 2004

Nominal Value

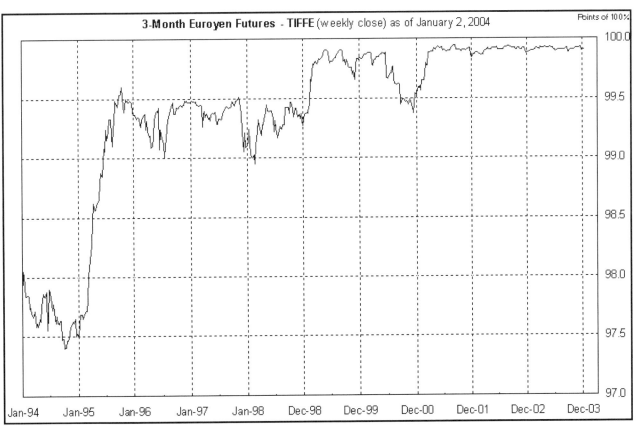

3-Month Euroyen Futures - TIFFE (weekly close) as of January 2, 2004

Points of 100%

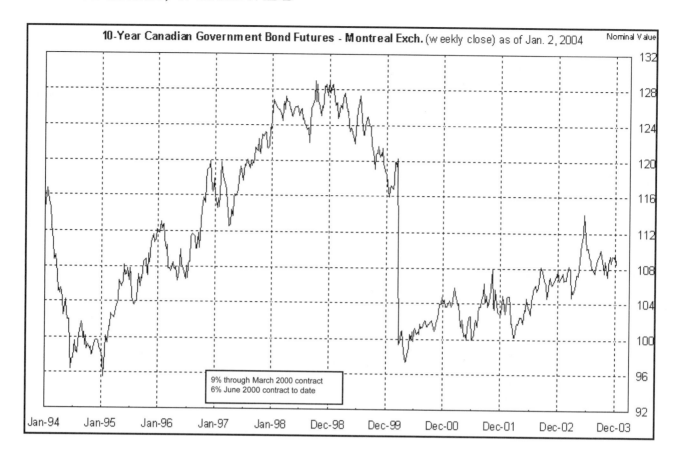

10-Year Canadian Government Bond Futures - Montreal Exch. (weekly close) as of Jan. 2, 2004

9% through March 2000 contract
6% June 2000 contract to date

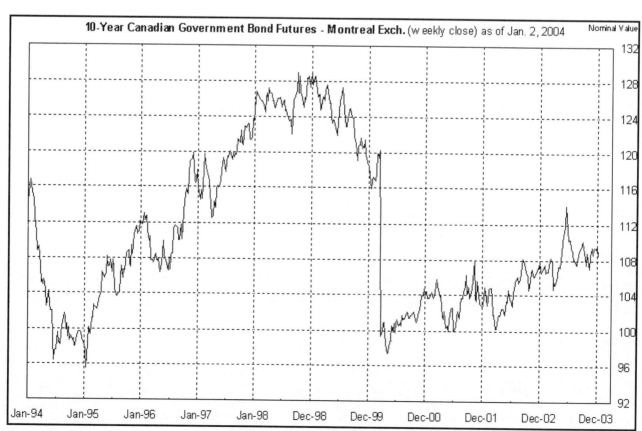

10-Year Canadian Government Bond Futures - Montreal Exch. (weekly close) as of Jan. 2, 2004

Australia -- Economic Statistics   Percentage Change from Previous Period

Year	Real GDP	Nominal GDP	Real Private Consump-tion	Real Public Consump-tion	Grossed Fixed Invest-ment	Real Total Domestic Demand	Real Exports of Goods & Services	Real Imports of Goods & Services	Consumer Prices[1]	Unem-ployment Rate
1996	4.1	5.1	3.2	2.9	4.2	3.1	10.6	8.3	2.6	8.2
1997	3.7	5.4	4.0	2.6	9.4	3.2	11.5	10.5	.3	8.3
1998	5.4	5.7	4.5	3.4	8.8	6.9	-.2	6.0	.9	7.8
1999	4.4	5.2	4.9	2.9	6.9	5.4	4.6	9.2	1.5	7.0
2000	3.0	7.4	3.2	5.8	-.4	2.0	10.8	7.1	4.5	6.3
2001	2.7	5.8	3.0	1.6	-1.7	1.6	1.4	-4.1	4.4	6.8
2002	3.3	6.2	4.1	4.0	13.6	5.8	-.1	12.0	3.0	6.3
2003[2]	2.4	5.3	3.8	3.0	7.5	5.3	-2.7	9.4	2.8	6.0
2004[3]	3.7	6.1	3.6	3.5	3.6	3.6	7.1	6.8	2.0	5.9

[1] National accounts inplicit private consumption deflator.   [2] Estimate.   [3] Projection.   Source: Organization for Economic Co-opertation and Development (OECD)

Canada -- Economic Statistics   Percentage Change from Previous Period

Year	Real GDP	Nominal GDP	Real Private Consump-tion	Real Public Consump-tion	Grossed Fixed Invest-ment	Real Total Domestic Demand	Real Exports of Goods & Services	Real Imports of Goods & Services	Consumer Prices[1]	Unem-ployment Rate
1996	1.6	3.3	2.6	-1.2	4.4	1.3	5.6	5.1	1.6	9.6
1997	4.2	5.5	4.6	-1.0	15.2	6.2	8.3	14.2	1.6	9.1
1998	4.1	3.7	2.8	3.2	2.4	2.5	9.1	5.1	1.0	8.3
1999	5.5	7.4	3.8	2.1	7.3	4.3	10.7	7.8	1.7	7.6
2000	5.3	9.5	4.0	2.6	5.5	4.8	8.8	8.0	2.7	6.8
2001	1.9	3.0	2.6	3.7	4.3	1.4	-3.1	-5.0	2.5	7.2
2002	3.3	4.3	3.4	3.0	1.3	3.8	-.1	.6	2.2	7.6
2003[2]	1.8	5.4	3.4	3.1	3.3	4.1	-1.8	3.8	2.8	7.8
2004[3]	2.8	4.4	3.1	3.4	4.9	3.1	5.0	6.2	1.4	7.8

[1] National accounts inplicit private consumption deflator.   [2] Estimate.   [3] Projection.   Source: Organization for Economic Co-opertation and Development (OECD)

France -- Economic Statistics   Percentage Change from Previous Period

Year	Real GDP	Nominal GDP	Real Private Consump-tion	Real Public Consump-tion	Grossed Fixed Invest-ment	Real Total Domestic Demand	Real Exports of Goods & Services	Real Imports of Goods & Services	Consumer Prices[1]	Unem-ployment Rate
1996	1.0	2.5	1.3	2.2	-.1	.7	3.2	1.6	2.1	12.0
1997	1.9	3.2	.2	2.1	-.2	.7	12.0	7.3	1.3	12.1
1998	3.6	4.5	3.6	-.1	7.2	4.2	8.3	11.6	.7	11.5
1999	3.2	3.7	3.5	1.5	8.3	3.7	4.2	6.2	.6	10.7
2000	4.2	5.0	2.9	3.0	8.4	4.5	13.4	15.3	1.8	9.4
2001	2.1	3.8	2.8	2.9	2.1	2.0	1.8	1.4	1.8	8.7
2002	1.3	3.2	1.5	4.1	-1.4	1.1	1.3	.8	1.9	9.0
2003[2]	.1	1.6	1.6	2.0	-1.1	1.1	-2.2	1.2	2.0	9.6
2004[3]	1.7	3.0	1.6	1.5	1.6	1.7	4.6	5.0	1.4	9.8

[1] National accounts inplicit private consumption deflator.   [2] Estimate.   [3] Projection.   Source: Organization for Economic Co-opertation and Development (OECD)

Germany[2] -- Economic Statistics   Percentage Change from Previous Period

Year	Real GDP	Nominal GDP	Real Private Consump-tion	Real Public Consump-tion	Grossed Fixed Invest-ment	Real Total Domestic Demand	Real Exports of Goods & Services	Real Imports of Goods & Services	Consumer Prices[1]	Unem-ployment Rate
1996	.8	1.8	.9	1.8	-.7	.3	5.3	3.3	1.2	8.4
1997	1.5	2.2	.7	.3	.9	.7	11.4	8.4	1.5	9.2
1998	1.7	2.8	1.7	1.9	2.3	2.2	6.4	8.6	.6	8.7
1999	1.9	2.4	3.6	.8	3.8	2.7	5.1	8.1	.6	8.0
2000	3.1	2.8	2.2	1.0	3.2	2.0	14.4	11.0	1.4	7.3
2001	1.0	2.3	1.5	1.0	-3.9	-.7	6.1	1.2	1.9	7.4
2002	.2	1.8	-1.0	1.7	-6.5	-1.6	3.4	-1.6	1.3	8.1
2003[2]	.0	.9	.7	.8	-2.1	.8	.3	2.9	.9	8.9
2004[3]	1.4	2.7	1.2	.1	1.4	1.2	4.6	4.4	.8	9.1

[1] National accounts inplicit private consumption deflator.   [2] Data are for Western Germany only, except for foreign trade statistics.   [3] Estimate.
[4] Projection.   Source: Organization for Economic Co-operation and Development (OECD)

INTEREST RATES, WORLDWIDE

Italy -- Economic Statistics — Percentage Change from Previous Period

Year	Real GDP	Nominal GDP	Real Private Consumption	Real Public Consumption	Grossed Fixed Investment	Real Total Domestic Demand	Real Exports of Goods & Services	Real Imports of Goods & Services	Consumer Prices[1]	Unemployment Rate
1996	1.0	6.4	1.3	1.0	3.4	.8	.6	-.3	4.0	11.7
1997	2.0	4.5	3.2	.2	2.1	2.7	6.4	10.1	1.9	11.8
1998	1.7	4.5	3.2	.2	3.8	3.1	3.4	8.9	2.0	11.9
1999	1.7	3.2	2.6	1.3	5.0	3.2	.1	5.6	1.7	11.5
2000	3.3	5.4	2.7	1.6	7.5	2.4	11.7	8.9	2.6	10.7
2001	1.7	4.5	1.1	3.6	2.4	1.7	1.1	1.0	2.3	9.6
2002	.4	3.1	.4	1.7	.7	1.1	-1.0	1.5	2.6	9.1
2003[2]	.5	3.2	1.9	1.3	-2.1	1.7	-2.6	1.6	2.8	8.9
2004[3]	1.6	3.6	1.7	.8	2.3	1.8	4.9	5.5	2.0	8.9

[1] National accounts inplicit private consumption deflator.   [2] Estimate.   [3] Projection.   *Source: Organization for Economic Co-opertation and Development (OECD)*

Japan -- Economic Statistics — Percentage Change from Previous Period

Year	Real GDP	Nominal GDP	Real Private Consumption	Real Public Consumption	Grossed Fixed Investment	Real Total Domestic Demand	Real Exports of Goods & Services	Real Imports of Goods & Services	Consumer Prices[1]	Unemployment Rate
1996	3.4	2.6	2.4	2.9	6.4	3.9	6.5	13.2	.1	3.4
1997	1.8	2.2	.9	1.0	.9	.9	11.3	1.2	1.7	3.4
1998	-1.1	-1.2	-.1	2.1	-3.9	-1.5	-2.3	-6.8	.7	4.1
1999	.1	-1.4	.2	4.4	-.9	.2	1.5	3.0	-.3	4.7
2000	2.8	.9	1.0	4.7	2.9	2.4	12.3	9.4	-.7	4.7
2001	.4	-1.2	1.7	2.5	-1.2	1.1	-6.0	.1	-.7	5.0
2002	.2	-1.5	1.3	2.3	-4.7	-.5	8.1	2.0	-.9	5.4
2003[2]	2.7	.1	1.1	1.6	4.4	2.3	7.5	4.5	-.2	5.3
2004[3]	1.8	.4	1.1	2.0	.2	1.1	9.5	5.2	-.2	5.2

[1] National accounts inplicit private consumption deflator.   [2] Estimate.   [3] Projection.   *Source: Organization for Economic Co-opertation and Development (OECD)*

Switzerland -- Economic Statistics — Percentage Change from Previous Period

Year	Real GDP	Nominal GDP	Real Private Consumption	Real Public Consumption	Grossed Fixed Investment	Real Total Domestic Demand	Real Exports of Goods & Services	Real Imports of Goods & Services	Consumer Prices[1]	Unemployment Rate
1996	.3	.7	.7	2.0	-2.4	.1	2.4	1.9	.8	3.8
1997	1.7	1.5	1.4	.0	1.5	.8	8.4	6.1	.5	4.0
1998	2.4	2.3	2.3	1.3	4.5	3.5	5.4	8.3	.0	3.4
1999	1.5	2.2	2.2	1.2	2.7	2.5	5.1	7.4	.8	2.9
2000	3.2	4.4	2.0	2.1	5.8	2.5	10.1	8.4	1.6	2.5
2001	.9	2.0	2.1	2.4	-3.3	.7	.0	-.3	1.0	2.5
2002	.2	.8	.7	1.9	-4.1	-1.2	-.4	-3.5	.6	3.1
2003[2]	-.5	-.6	.4	.9	-2.1	-1.4	-.5	-2.4	.6	3.9
2004[3]	1.2	1.0	1.2	.4	.6	1.3	3.8	4.4	.3	3.9

[1] National accounts inplicit private consumption deflator.   [2] Estimate.   [3] Projection.   *Source: Organization for Economic Co-opertation and Development (OECD)*

United Kingdom -- Economic Statistics — Percentage Change from Previous Period

Year	Real GDP	Nominal GDP	Real Private Consumption	Real Public Consumption	Grossed Fixed Investment	Real Total Domestic Demand	Real Exports of Goods & Services	Real Imports of Goods & Services	Consumer Prices[1]	Unemployment Rate
1996	2.7	6.1	3.6	.7	5.7	3.0	8.6	9.7	2.9	8.0
1997	3.3	6.2	3.6	-.3	6.8	3.6	8.4	9.8	2.8	6.9
1998	3.1	6.0	3.9	1.3	12.7	4.9	2.8	9.3	2.7	6.2
1999	2.8	5.2	4.4	3.2	1.6	3.8	4.3	7.9	2.3	6.0
2000	3.8	5.2	4.6	1.9	3.6	3.8	9.4	9.1	2.1	5.5
2001	2.1	4.5	3.1	1.7	3.6	2.7	2.5	4.5	2.1	5.1
2002	1.7	5.0	3.6	2.4	1.8	2.9	-.9	3.6	2.2	5.2
2003[2]	1.9	4.8	2.4	3.4	2.9	2.4	-.9	1.1	2.8	5.0
2004[3]	2.7	4.9	2.4	1.7	4.9	3.0	6.5	7.0	2.6	4.9

[1] National accounts inplicit private consumption deflator.   [2] Estimate.   [3] Projection.   *Source: Organization for Economic Co-opertation and Development (OECD)*

Iron and Steel

Iron is a soft, malleable, and ductile metallic element. Next to aluminum, iron is the most abundant of all metals. Pure iron melts at about 1535 degrees Celsius and boils at 2750 degrees Celsius. Archaeologists in Egypt discovered the earliest iron implements dating to about 3000 BC, and iron ornaments were used even earlier.

Steel is an alloy of iron and carbon, often with an admixture of other elements. The physical properties of various types of steel and steel alloys depend primarily on the amount of carbon present and how it is distributed in the iron. Steel is marketed in a variety of sizes and shapes, such as rods, pipes, railroad rails, tees, channels, and I-beams. Steel mills roll and form heated ingots into the required shapes. The working of steel improves the quality of the steel by refining its crystalline structure and making the metal tougher. There are five classifications of steel: carbon steels, alloy steels, high-strength low-ally steels, stainless steel, and tool steels.

Prices – Steel prices in 2003 recovered sharply, mainly due to import tariffs imposed by President Bush, which allowed US producers to push prices higher. The average wholesale price of No. 1 heavy melting steel scrap rose to $114.03 per metric ton from the depressed levels of $89.78 seen in 2002 and $74.17 seen in 2001.

Supply – World production of iron ore in 2001 fell slightly to 1.060 billion metric tons from 1.080 billion in 2000. The world's largest producers of iron ore in 2001 were China with 20.8% of world production, followed closely by Brazil (19.8%), and Australia (17.1%). The US accounted for only 4.4% of world iron ore production in 2001. World production of raw steel (ingots and castings) in 2002 fell −0.1% to 846.972 million metric tons, with the largest producers being China (with 17.6% of world production), Japan (12.1%), and the US (10.6%).

US production of steel in 2003 was on track to match or fall slightly below the 2002 production level of 100.976 million short tons, which was up from the 10-year low of 98.889 million short tons in 2001. US production of pig iron (excluding ferro-alloys) in 2003 was on track to fall -3.7% to 42.712 million short tons.

Demand – US consumption of ferrous scrap and pig iron fell −5.0% in 2002 to 113.000 million metric tons from 119.000 million metric tons in 2001. The largest consumers of ferrous scrap and pig iron in 2002 were the manufacturers of pig iron and steel ingots and castings with 87% of consumption at 98.000 million metric tons. Iron foundries and miscellaneous users accounted for 11% of consumption and manufacturers of steel castings (scrap) accounted for 2% of consumption.

Trade – The US imported 10.70 million metric tons of iron ore in 2001, down sharply from 15.700 million metric tons in 2000. The bulk of 2001 imports came from Canada (4.530 million metric tons) and Brazil (4.260 million metric tons).

World Production of Raw Steel (Ingots and Castings)   In Thousands of Metric Tons

Year	Brazil	Canada	China	France	Germany	Italy	Japan	Rep. of Korea	Russia	Ukraine	United Kingdom	United States	World Total
1993	25,207	14,387	89,539	17,106	37,625	25,720	99,623	33,026	58,346	32,609	16,625	88,793	727,549
1994	25,747	13,897	92,613	18,031	40,837	26,151	98,295	33,745	48,812	24,081	17,286	91,244	725,107
1995	25,076	14,415	95,360	18,100	42,051	27,766	101,640	36,772	51,589	22,309	17,604	95,191	752,260
1996	25,237	14,735	101,237	17,633	39,793	23,910	98,801	38,903	49,253	22,332	17,992	95,535	749,992
1997	26,153	15,554	108,911	19,767	45,007	25,842	104,545	42,554	48,502	25,629	18,489	98,486	798,892
1998	25,800	15,930	115,590	20,126	44,046	25,798	93,548	39,896	43,822	23,461	17,066	98,600	770,000
1999	24,996	16,300	124,260	20,211	42,056	24,964	94,192	41,042	51,524	27,390	16,634	97,400	784,000
2000	27,865	15,900	128,500	21,002	46,376	26,544	106,444	43,107	59,098	31,780	15,022	102,000	845,000
2001[1]	26,717	16,300	151,630	19,431	44,775	26,483	102,866	43,852	59,030	33,110	13,610	90,100	847,000
2002[2]	29,604	16,300	181,550	20,524	44,999	25,930	107,745	45,390	59,777	34,538	11,718	91,600	898,000

[1] Preliminary.   [2] Estimate.   *Source: U.S. Geological Survey (USGS)*

Average Wholesale Prices of Iron and Steel in the United States

	No. 1 Heavy Melting Steel Scrap		Hot Rolled Sheet[2]	Sheet Bars		Pittsburg Prices					
	Pittsburg	Chicago		Hot Rolled	Cold Finished	Hot Rolled Strip	Carbon Steel Plates	Cold Rolled Strip	Galvanized Sheets	Railroad Steel Scrap[3]	Used Steel Cans[4]
Year	---- $ Per Gross Ton ----			----- Cents Per Pound -----						----- $ Per Gross Ton -----	
1994	136.76	131.91	22.93	----	25.70	23.50	27.61	39.40	32.24	169.00	102.33
1995	142.34	143.17	25.32	----	25.70	24.88	29.98	39.40	34.47	169.00	126.32
1996	137.28	136.07	23.94	----	26.46	25.00	31.58	----	35.05	169.00	121.27
1997	133.38	139.40	18.12	----	25.65	----	32.00	----	28.62	169.00	108.13
1998	110.10	118.76	15.57	----	25.50	----	22.50	----	24.11	164.29	109.44
1999	97.86	102.49	14.74	----	23.50	----	14.00	----	21.20	150.00	68.94
2000	103.73	96.07	15.67	----	23.08	----	15.69	----	21.38	150.00	82.23
2001	79.34	74.17	11.71	----	22.76	----	12.94	----	16.41	NA	68.52
2002	101.06	89.92	16.46	----	23.26	----	----	----	22.00	NA	66.71
2003[1]	128.32	113.82	14.80	----	25.15	----	----	----	20.08	----	116.21

[1] Preliminary.   [2] 10 gauge; thru 1992,list prices;1993 to date, market prices.   [3] Specialties scrap.   [4] Consumer buying prices.
NA = Not available.   *Source: American Metal Market (AMM)*

IRON AND STEEL

Salient Statistics of Steel in the United States   In Thousands of Short Tons

Year	Pig Iron Production	Producer Price Index for Steel Mill Products (1982=100)	Raw Steel Production — By Type of Furnace — Basic Oxygen	Open Hearth	Electric[2]	Stainless	Carbon	Alloy	Total	Net Shipments Steel Mill Products	Total Steel Products — Exports	Imports
1994	54,426	113.4	61,028	----	39,551	2,022	89,535	9,022	100,579	95,084	4,852	32,705
1995	56,097	120.1	62,523	----	42,407	2,265	92,656	10,009	104,930	97,494	8,157	27,270
1996	54,485	115.7	60,433	----	44,876	2,061	93,649	9,599	105,309	100,878	6,168	32,115
1997	54,679	116.4	61,053	----	47,508	2,382	95,933	10,246	108,561	105,858	7,369	34,389
1998	53,164	113.8	59,686	----	49,067	2,214	97,054	9,484	108,752	102,420	5,520	41,520
1999	51,002	105.3	57,722	----	49,673	2,086	98,694	5,421	107,395	106,201	5,426	35,731
2000	52,787	108.4	59,485	----	52,756	2,104	102,141	5,379	111,903	109,050	6,529	37,957
2001	46,424	101.3	52,204	----	47,118	1,836	92,946	4,666	99,322	99,448	6,144	30,080
2002	44,341	104.8	50,114	----	51,564	1,894	92,518	4,779	101,679	99,191	6,009	32,686
2003[1]	43,122	109.6	50,942	----	48,751	1,952	98,772	4,901	99,693	105,625	8,220	23,125

[1] Preliminary.   [2] Includes crucible steels.   Sources: American Iron & Steel Institute (AISI); U.S. Geological Survey (USGS)

Production of Steel Ingots, Rate of Capability Utilization[1] in the United States   In Percent

Year	Jan.	Feb.	Mar.	Apr.	May	June	July	Aug.	Sept.	Oct.	Nov.	Dec.	Average
1994	87.7	92.2	91.3	91.4	91.2	88.7	87.1	87.7	90.0	92.0	92.6	94.3	93.0
1995	93.8	95.6	96.0	92.9	91.6	90.1	86.8	88.3	93.6	90.3	92.1	90.2	91.7
1996	92.2	92.6	93.8	90.5	89.7	91.3	86.6	87.1	87.7	88.0	87.0	87.9	89.5
1997	85.3	89.3	89.6	89.2	87.9	87.0	85.1	86.4	91.2	86.9	89.6	86.3	89.4
1998	90.0	95.2	93.1	92.5	89.1	86.1	83.0	86.4	83.0	81.0	74.4	74.8	85.7
1999	77.2	79.5	81.7	81.8	81.7	79.7	79.4	82.8	82.3	88.2	89.1	88.5	82.7
2000	89.7	89.4	91.2	92.0	91.3	89.6	85.3	83.5	82.7	81.0	75.1	72.0	85.2
2001	77.6	82.3	81.8	82.9	81.5	81.6	79.8	80.4	80.5	77.5	73.5	65.9	78.8
2002	84.5	88.4	86.7	90.3	89.4	92.5	86.8	91.0	94.0	90.8	86.8	83.9	88.8
2003[2]	83.1	87.3	85.0	87.8	81.1	86.2	78.9	78.3	80.7	82.8	83.9	81.9	83.1

[1] Based on tonnage capability to produce raw steel for a full order book.   [2] Preliminary.   Sources: American Iron and Steel Institute (AISI); U.S. Geological Survey (USGS)

Production of Steel Ingots in the United States   In Thousands of Short Tons

Year	Jan.	Feb.	Mar.	Apr.	May	June	July	Aug.	Sept.	Oct.	Nov.	Dec.	Total
1994	8,003	7,598	8,323	8,180	8,437	7,941	7,996	8,053	7,993	8,477	8,256	8,684	100,579
1995	8,918	8,211	9,131	8,548	8,696	8,286	8,308	8,455	8,668	8,685	8,574	8,678	103,142
1996	8,981	8,438	9,136	8,588	8,798	8,661	8,585	8,627	8,407	8,702	8,276	8,689	104,356
1997	8,735	8,266	9,175	8,882	9,048	8,662	8,692	8,818	9,006	9,128	9,116	9,071	107,488
1998	9,510	9,087	9,839	9,524	9,483	8,863	8,832	9,194	8,548	8,681	7,710	8,013	107,643
1999	8,422	7,837	8,854	8,643	8,914	8,413	8,619	8,993	8,650	9,574	9,357	9,604	105,882
2000	9,838	9,170	10,009	9,843	10,097	9,592	9,411	9,213	8,830	8,978	8,054	7,982	111,015
2001	8,475	8,122	8,932	8,685	8,832	8,550	8,459	8,525	8,263	8,125	7,226	6,695	98,889
2002	8,050	7,609	8,261	8,214	8,401	8,414	8,510	8,918	8,916	9,015	8,340	8,329	100,976
2003[1]	8,617	8,175	8,817	8,692	8,047	8,534	8,163	8,096	8,026	8,514	8,347	8,414	100,442

[1] Preliminary.   Source: American Iron and Steel Institute (AISI)

Shipments of Steel Products[1] by Market Classifications in the United States   In Thousands of Short Tons

Year	Appliances Utensils & Cutlery	Automotive	Containers, Packaging & Shipping Materials	Construction Including Maint.	Contractors Products	Electrical Equipment	Export	Machinery, Industrial Equipment & Tools	Oil and Gas	Rail Transportaion	Steel for Converting & Processing[2]	Steel Service Center & Distributors	All Other[3]	Total Shipments
1994	1,736	14,753	4,495	10,935	3,348	2,299	1,710	2,427	1,703	1,248	10,502	24,153	15,775	95,084
1995	1,589	14,622	4,139	11,761	3,337	2,397	4,442	2,310	2,643	1,373	10,440	23,751	14,690	97,494
1996	1,713	14,665	4,101	15,561	5	2,401	2,328	2,410	3,254	1,400	10,245	27,124	15,676	100,878
1997	1,635	15,251	4,163	15,885	5	2,434	2,610	2,355	3,811	1,410	11,263	27,800	17,241	105,858
1998	1,729	15,842	3,829	15,289	5	2,255	2,556	2,147	2,649	1,657	9,975	27,751	16,741	102,420
1999	1,712	15,639	3,768	14,685	5	2,260	2,292	1,547	1,544	876	7,599	21,439	32,840	106,201
2000	1,530	14,697	3,684	14,763	5	2,039	2,752	1,513	2,268	994	7,753	22,537	35,093	109,624
2001	1,675	12,767	3,193	16,339	5	1,694	2,281	1,210	2,134	720	7,462	23,887	26,086	99,448
2002	1,734	12,562	3,251	15,729	5	1,336	1,844	1,137	1,658	751	7,201	22,828	29,160	99,191
2003[4]	1,891	11,937	2,949	14,403	5	1,200	2,572	1,108	1,800	799	6,798	24,266	35,905	105,628

[1] All grades including carbon, alloy and stainless steel.   [2] Net total after deducting shipments to reporting companines for conversion or resale.

[3] Includes agricultural; bolts, nuts rivets & screws; forgings (other than automotive); shipbuilding & marine equipment; aircraft; mining, quarrying & lumbering; other domestic & commercial equipment machinery; ordnance & other direct military; and shipments of non-reporting companies.

[4] Preliminary.   Source: American Iron and Steel Institute (AISI)

Net Shipments of Steel Products[1] in the United States   In Thousands of Short Tons

Year	Cold Finished Bars	Rails & Accessories	Wire Drawn	Tin Mill Products	Plates (Cut & Coils)	Sheet & Strip Galv. (Hot Dipped)	Hot Rolled Bars	Pipe & Tubing	Structural Shapes & Steel Piling	Reinforcing Bars	Hot Rolled Sheets	Cold Rolled Sheets	Carbon	Alloy	Stainless
1994	1,786	631	788	4,137	8,556	10,943	7,088	4,966	5,942	4,929	15,654	13,016	88,505	4,859	1,720
1995	1,782	630	654	3,942	9,043	11,329	6,902	5,437	6,278	5,048	16,978	12,347	90,485	5,115	1,894
1996	1,685	722	652	4,108	8,672	11,456	6,999	5,895	6,140	5,762	17,466	14,089	93,019	5,948	1,912
1997	1,809	875	619	4,057	8,855	12,439	8,153	6,548	6,029	6,188	18,221	13,322	97,509	6,282	2,067
1998	1,780	938	725	3,714	8,864	13,481	8,189	5,409	5,595	5,909	15,715	13,185	94,536	5,847	2,037
1999	1,775	646	611	3,771	8,200	14,870	8,078	4,772	5,995	6,183	17,740	13,874	98,694	5,421	2,086
2000	1,756	783	579	3,742	8,898	14,917	7,901	5,385	7,402	6,893	19,236	14,802	102,141	5,379	2,104
2001	1,369	630	481	3,202	8,349	14,310	7,032	5,377	6,789	6,976	18,866	12,352	92,314	4,789	1,837
2002	1,404	789	733	3,419	8,769	14,944	6,581	4,809	6,729	6,359	19,243	12,673	92,518	4,779	1,894
2003[2]	1,426	739	684	3,513	9,230	15,221	6,486	4,597	7,437	7,970	22,218	13,485	98,772	4,901	1,952

[1] All grades, including carbon, alloy and stainless steel.   [2] Preliminary.   *Source: American Iron and Steel Institute (AISI)*

World Production of Pig Iron (Excludes Ferro-Alloys)   In Thousands of Metric Tons

Year	Belgium	Brazil	China	France	Germany	India	Italy	Japan	Russia	Ukraine	United Kingdom	United States	World Total
1993	8,178	23,982	87,390	12,679	26,970	15,674	11,066	73,738	40,871	26,999	11,534	48,200	531,000
1994	8,974	25,177	97,410	13,293	29,923	17,808	11,157	73,776	36,116	21,200	11,943	49,400	544,000
1995	9,199	25,090	105,293	12,860	29,828	18,626	11,684	74,905	39,762	20,000	12,238	50,900	536,000
1996	8,628	23,978	107,225	12,108	30,012	19,864	10,347	74,597	36,061	18,143	12,830	49,400	549,000
1997	8,077	25,336	115,110	13,424	30,939	19,898	11,348	78,519	37,327	20,561	13,057	49,600	577,000
1998	8,730	25,111	118,600	13,603	30,162	20,194	10,704	74,981	34,827	20,840	12,574	48,200	572,000
1999	8,472	25,060	125,390	13,854	27,931	20,139	10,509	74,520	40,854	21,937	12,399	46,300	578,000
2000	8,472	27,723	131,010	13,621	30,846	21,321	11,223	81,071	44,618	25,700	10,891	47,900	616,000
2001[1]	7,732	27,441	155,540	12,004	29,184	21,900	10,650	78,836	44,980	26,400	9,861	42,100	616,000
2002[2]	8,053	27,781	170,750	13,217	29,419	22,000	9,736	80,979	46,060	27,560	8,579	40,200	642,000

[1] Preliminary.   [2] Estimate.   *Source: U.S. Geological Survey (USGS)*

Production of Pig Iron (Excludes Ferro-Alloys) in the United States   In Thousands of Short Tons

Year	Jan.	Feb.	Mar.	Apr.	May	June	July	Aug.	Sept.	Oct.	Nov.	Dec.	Total
1994	3,970	3,858	3,957	4,099	4,394	4,519	4,518	4,446	4,320	4,564	4,619	4,928	54,426
1995	4,820	4,453	4,916	4,568	4,674	4,499	4,576	4,688	4,727	4,687	4,738	4,762	56,115
1996	4,811	4,476	4,813	4,430	4,556	4,578	4,524	4,498	4,404	4,443	4,307	4,523	54,485
1997	4,489	4,243	4,713	4,440	4,690	4,452	4,420	4,443	4,605	4,662	4,717	4,861	54,680
1998	4,955	4,433	4,881	4,600	4,731	4,299	4,418	4,502	4,170	4,212	3,837	4,119	53,174
1999	4,140	3,802	4,257	4,157	4,352	4,045	4,204	4,280	4,167	4,572	4,447	4,722	51,145
2000	4,571	4,325	4,793	4,741	4,887	4,577	4,454	4,387	4,262	4,138	3,675	3,781	52,591
2001	3,808	3,691	4,255	4,183	4,278	4,143	4,048	4,121	3,920	3,837	3,202	2,965	46,451
2002	3,493	3,308	3,616	3,480	3,584	3,612	3,854	3,983	4,006	4,018	3,710	3,677	44,341
2003[1]	3,832	3,631	3,906	3,810	3,381	3,569	3,395	3,253	3,289	3,527	3,530	3,733	42,856

[1] Preliminary.   *Source: American Iron and Steel Institute*

Salient Statistics of Ferrous Scrap and Pig Iron in the United States   In Thousands of Metric Tons

| | Consumption: Ferrous Scrap & Pig Iron Charged To | | | | | | | | | | | Stocks -- Dec. 31 | | | |
| | Mfg. of Pig Iron & Steel Ingots & Castings | | | Iron Foundries & Misc. Users | | | Mfg. of Steel Castings | All Uses | | | Imports of | Exports of | Ferrous Scrap & Pig Iron at Consumers | | |
Year	Scrap	Pig Iron	Total	Scrap	Pig Iron	Total	(Scrap)	Ferrous Scrap	Pig Iron	Grand Total	Scrap[2]	Scrap[3]	Scrap	Pig Iron	Total Stocks
1993	53,084	48,092	101,176	12,658	676	13,334	1,900	68,000	48,777	116,777	1,390	9,805	3,725	220	3,945
1994	53,801	50,257	104,057	14,000	1,000	15,000	2,000	70,000	51,000	121,000	1,740	8,813	4,100	400	4,500
1995	56,000	51,000	107,000	13,000	1,100	14,100	2,000	72,000	52,000	124,000	2,090	10,400	4,200	620	4,820
1996	56,000	50,000	106,000	13,000	1,100	14,100	2,700	72,000	52,000	124,000	2,600	8,440	5,200	600	5,800
1997	58,000	51,000	109,000	13,000	1,200	14,200	1,800	73,000	52,000	125,000	2,870	8,930	5,500	510	6,010
1998	58,000	49,000	107,000	13,000	1,200	14,200	2,000	73,000	50,000	123,000	3,060	5,570	5,300	570	5,870
1999	56,000	48,000	104,000	13,000	1,100	14,100	1,900	71,000	49,000	120,000	3,670	5,520	5,500	720	6,220
2000	59,000	49,000	108,000	13,000	1,200	14,200	2,200	74,000	50,000	124,000	3,350	5,760	5,300	800	6,100
2001	57,000	47,000	104,000	12,000	1,100	13,100	2,200	71,000	48,000	119,000	2,630	7,440	4,900	790	5,690
2002[1]	56,000	42,000	98,000	11,000	1,500	12,500	1,800	69,000	44,000	113,000	3,130	8,950	5,100	800	5,900

[1] Preliminary.   [2] Includes tinplate and terneplate.   [3] Excludes used rails for rerolling and other uses and ships, boats, and other vessels for scrapping.
Source: U.S. Geological Survey (USGS)

IRON AND STEEL

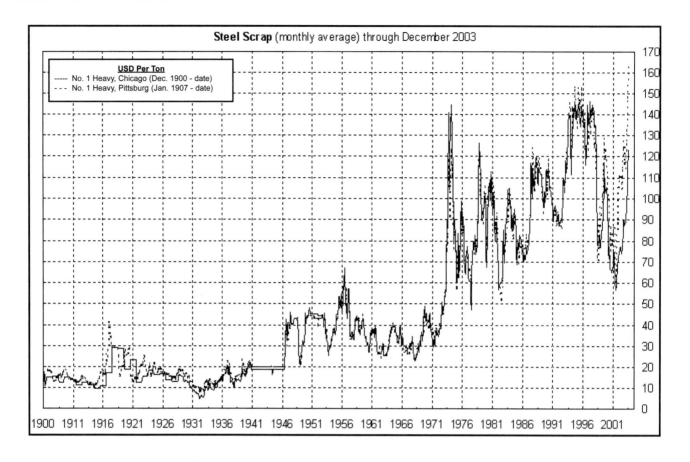

Steel Scrap (monthly average) through December 2003

USD Per Ton
----- No. 1 Heavy, Chicago (Dec. 1900 - date)
- - - No. 1 Heavy, Pittsburg (Jan. 1907 - date)

Consumption of Pig Iron in the U.S., by Type of Furnace or Equipment   In Thousands of Metric Tons

Year	Open Hearth	Electric	Cupola	Basic Oxygen Process	Air & Other Furnace	Direct Casting	Total
1993	----	519	292	47,848	34	84	48,777
1994	----	1,700	520	49,138	4	39	51,401
1995	----	1,700	500	50,000	W	72	52,272
1996	----	2,200	530	49,000	W	42	52,000
1997	----	2,400	400	50,000	W	41	52,000
1998	----	4,000	590	46,000	W	36	50,000
1999	----	3,100	520	45,000	W	36	49,000
2000	----	2,900	530	47,000	W	35	50,000
2001[1]	----	2,700	500	45,000	W	36	48,000
2002[2]	----	3,200	520	40,000	W	36	44,000

[1] Preliminary.   [2] Estimate.   W = Withheld.   *Source: U.S. Geological Survey (USGS)*

Wholesale Price of No. 1 Heavy Melting Steel Scrap in Chicago   In Dollars Per Metric Ton

Year	Jan.	Feb.	Mar.	Apr.	May	June	July	Aug.	Sept.	Oct.	Nov.	Dec.	Average
1994	138.00	138.00	138.00	138.00	123.64	110.50	117.20	133.63	134.50	132.50	137.50	141.50	131.91
1995	152.05	147.50	140.20	141.50	144.50	141.64	141.50	149.76	144.90	141.50	136.50	136.50	143.17
1996	143.41	144.50	139.50	139.50	142.50	139.50	134.50	136.95	140.35	130.89	120.76	120.50	136.07
1997	131.14	143.50	139.70	132.59	136.50	136.50	143.50	146.50	139.60	139.63	142.50	142.50	139.51
1998	144.29	140.39	135.50	133.50	135.30	135.50	131.50	120.88	107.79	85.64	78.71	76.68	118.81
1999	89.66	101.50	90.89	90.50	100.00	104.32	100.98	105.95	106.50	106.50	113.40	120.17	102.49
2000	120.50	111.10	110.50	108.15	101.50	94.59	92.50	92.50	92.50	82.59	72.80	74.20	96.07
2001	83.55	74.50	74.50	74.50	73.23	72.50	75.93	76.50	76.50	72.54	67.50	67.50	74.17
2002	70.21	75.03	75.50	85.05	93.09	97.10	97.50	97.50	100.50	98.85	93.50	93.50	89.78
2003	96.93	101.97	105.07	105.50	101.69	96.88	101.05	116.79	122.02	122.50	138.22	159.74	114.03

Source: American Metal Market (AMM)

World Production of Iron Ore[3]   In Thousands of Metric Tons (Gross Weight)

Year	Australia	Brazil	Canada	China	India	Maur- itania	Russia	South Africa	Sweden	Ukraine	United States	Vene- zuela	World Total
1993	120,534	150,000	31,830	234,660	57,375	9,360	76,100	29,385	18,728	65,500	55,676	16,871	953,316
1994	128,493	177,331	37,703	240,200	60,473	11,440	73,300	30,489	19,663	51,300	58,454	18,318	991,858
1995	142,936	183,839	38,560	249,350	65,173	11,610	78,300	31,946	19,058	50,400	62,501	18,955	1,034,539
1996	147,100	174,157	34,400	249,550	66,657	11,360	72,100	30,830	21,020	47,600	62,083	18,480	1,018,436
1997	157,766	184,970	37,277	268,000	69,153	11,700	70,000	33,225	21,893	53,000	62,971	18,503	1,070,000
1998	155,731	197,500	37,808	247,000	72,532	11,400	72,343	32,948	20,930	50,758	62,931	16,553	1,050,000
1999	154,268	194,000	33,900	237,000	70,220	10,400	81,311	29,508	18,558	47,769	57,749	14,051	1,020,000
2000	167,935	210,000	33,740	223,000	75,950	10,400	86,630	33,707	20,557	55,883	63,089	17,353	1,060,000
2001[1]	181,553	210,000	27,119	220,000	79,200	10,300	82,500	34,757	19,486	54,650	46,192	16,902	1,040,000
2002[2]	182,704	210,000	30,969	231,000	80,000	9,600	84,236	36,484	20,000	58,900	51,570	18,000	1,080,000

[1] Preliminary.   [2] Estimate.   [3] Iron ore, iron ore concentrates and iron ore agglomerates.   *Source: U.S. Geological Survey (USGS)*

Salient Statistics of Iron Ore[3] in the United States   In Thousands of Metric Tons

Year	Net Import Reliance as a % of Apparent Con- sumption	Production Total	Production Lake Superior	Production Other Regions	Ship- ments	Value Million $ (at Mine)	Average Value $ at Mine Per Ton	Stocks -- Dec. 31 Mines	Stocks -- Dec. 31 Con suming Plants	Stocks -- Dec. 31 Lake Erie Docks	Imports	Exports	Con- sumption	Value Million $ Imports
1993	14	55,661	54,814	848	56,300	1,380.0	24.50	2,500	16,500	2,290	14,100	5,060	76,800	419.0
1994	18	58,215	57,848	367	57,600	1,410.0	24.49	2,790	16,300	2,230	17,500	4,980	80,200	499.0
1995	14	60,898	60,462	435	61,100	1,700.0	28.00	4,240	17,100	2,140	17,600	5,270	83,100	491.0
1996	14	62,132	61,748	383	62,200	1,750.0	28.07	4,650	18,800	2,260	18,400	6,260	79,600	556.0
1997	14	63,000	62,600	327	62,800	1,860.0	29.60	4,860	20,200	2,890	18,500	6,340	79,500	551.0
1998	17	62,900	62,591	327	63,200	1,970.0	31.14	6,020	20,500	4,080	16,900	6,000	78,200	517.0
1999	17	57,410	57,410	NA	58,500	1,550.0	26.47	5,710	17,900	2,770	14,300	6,120	75,100	399.0
2000	19	62,983	62,983	NA	61,000	1,560.0	25.57	9,150	16,800	2,860	15,700	6,150	76,500	420.0
2001[1]	15	46,100	46,100	NA	50,600	1,210.0	23.87	3,800	12,300	1,960	10,700	5,610	67,300	293.0
2002[2]	11	51,500	51,500	NA	51,500	1,340.0	26.04	3,210	12,400	1,820	12,500	6,750	59,000	313.0

[1] Preliminary.   [2] Estimate.   [3] Usable iron ore exclusive of ore containing 5% or more manganese and includes byproduct ore.
NA = Not available.   *Source: U.S. Geological Survey (USGS)*

U.S. Imports (for Consumption) of Iron Ore[2]   In Thousands of Metric Tons

Year	Australia	Brazil	Canada	Chile	Maur- itania	Peru	Sweden	Vene- zuela	Total
1993	254	2,872	7,442	68	206	1	60	3,170	14,097
1994	675	3,610	10,073	134	124	2	45	2,778	17,466
1995	570	4,810	9,050	57	317	54	47	2,500	17,600
1996	511	5,170	9,800	164	275	43	48	2,140	18,400
1997	742	4,970	10,000	228	----	252	149	2,090	18,600
1998	807	5,980	8,520	48	----	126	373	970	16,900
1999	694	5,540	6,860	69	----	63	421	327	14,300
2000	755	6,090	7,990	135	----	40	250	349	15,700
2001	576	4,260	4,530	711	----	71	70	87	10,700
2002[1]	567	5,750	5,540	319	----	86	44	----	12,500

[1] Preliminary.   [2] Including agglomerates.   *Source: U.S. Geological Survey (USGS)*

Total[1] Iron Ore Stocks in the United States, at End of Month   In Thousands of Metric Tons

Year	Jan.	Feb.	Mar.	Apr.	May	June	July	Aug.	Sept.	Oct.	Nov.	Dec.
1994	19,013	17,816	15,950	14,880	15,251	16,592	17,864	18,931	20,554	20,760	21,552	21,339
1995	20,316	19,361	18,193	18,293	19,371	20,905	22,336	23,632	23,414	24,389	24,123	23,576
1996	22,277	20,744	19,779	20,104	23,426	21,822	22,445	23,663	24,116	24,866	25,465	25,701
1997	25,913	25,262	24,745	24,812	25,001	25,620	26,076	26,971	27,562	28,029	28,053	27,912
1998	27,977	26,317	24,039	25,251	25,576	26,197	27,605	29,037	30,301	30,095	30,199	30,624
1999	29,631	28,463	28,614	28,292	29,151	29,021	28,857	27,840	26,506	25,528	25,290	26,371
2000	24,885	24,810	23,556	23,714	24,032	24,613	24,993	26,278	26,815	27,530	27,987	28,779
2001	27,583	26,076	24,570	23,800	23,600	21,664	21,010	20,440	20,050	19,660	18,690	18,000
2002	16,980	15,970	14,660	14,920	15,680	16,090	16,120	16,080	15,520	15,790	16,740	17,410
2003[2]	17,640	19,790	21,100	18,560	17,690	17,880	17,950	18,360	17,220	15,790		

[1] All stocks at mines, furnace yards and at U.S. docks.   [2] Preliminary.   *Source: U.S. Geological Survey (USGS)*

Lard

Lard is the layer of fat found along the back and underneath the skin of a hog. The hog's fat is purified by washing it with water, melting it under constant heat, and straining it several times. Lard is an important byproduct of the meatpacking industry. It is valued highly as cooking oil because there is very little smoke when it is heated. However, demand for lard in cooking is declining because of the trend toward healthier eating. Lard is also used for medicinal purposes such as ointments, plasters, liniments, and occasionally as a laxative for children. Lard production is directly proportional to commercial hog production, meaning the largest producers of hogs are the largest producers of lard.

Prices – The average wholesale price of lard in early 2003 fluctuated in the range of 16.7-18.6 cents/pound. That was higher than the average prices seen in the past 4 years but below the recent average yearly high price of 23.39 cents

seen in 1997.

Supply – World production of lard was 7.016 million metric tons in the latest reporting year, up 2.3% from the 2001/2 level of 6.858 million tons. China is by far the largest consumer of lard at 3.023 million metric tons, followed by the US (506 million tons), Germany (427 million tons), and the former USSR (343 million tons). US production of lard in 2001/2 was 1,058 million pounds, with about 963 million pounds of that production going to domestic use and about 103.0 million pounds to exports (down from 174 million in 2000/1).

Demand – US consumption of lard was on track to hit about 330 million pounds in 2003, which would be up 9% from the 2002 level of 303.2 million pounds. Still, that is much lower than the levels over 400 million pounds seen prior to 1998.

World Production of Lard   In Thousands of Metric Tons

Year	Brazil	Canada	China	France	Germany	Italy	Japan	Poland	Romania	Spain	United States	Former USSR	World Total
1994-5	181.6	86.3	1,931.8	153.2	404.8	191.3	83.8	267.9	106.9	196.7	471.2	414.0	5,640.7
1995-6	194.3	83.0	2,136.6	154.6	405.6	198.5	76.3	284.9	105.1	206.5	449.3	385.0	5,860.4
1996-7	197.4	83.1	2,400.2	157.3	396.5	197.6	74.1	259.4	99.1	211.8	437.0	351.5	6,065.0
1997-8	214.3	91.5	2,624.8	162.3	413.4	194.0	67.9	266.4	96.9	238.5	478.9	339.7	6,406.1
1998-9	234.3	99.3	2,665.5	167.4	444.5	201.3	66.4	270.1	92.9	258.1	501.7	337.4	6,597.9
1999-00	250.5	109.2	2,771.4	164.7	423.5	200.9	65.1	254.7	81.1	262.0	491.6	346.3	6,680.1
2000-1[1]	262.1	113.7	2,832.1	155.7	415.2	195.9	62.3	240.1	72.7	264.9	488.6	334.9	6,690.3
2001-2[2]	270.3	119.7	2,918.6	157.1	422.4	199.3	61.8	244.1	69.5	266.9	508.1	338.9	6,857.6
2002-3[3]	277.8	121.7	3,022.6	159.3	426.6	202.5	63.5	249.6	69.0	276.8	506.0	342.9	7,016.0

[1] Preliminary.   [2] Estimate.   [3] Forecast.   *Source: The Oil World*

Supply and Distribution of Lard in the United States   In Millions of Pounds

	Supply			Disappearance						
Year	Production	Stocks Oct. 1	Total Supply	Domestic	Baking & Frying Fats	Margarine[2]	Exports	Total Disappearance	Direct Use	Per Capita (Lbs.)
1994-5	1,052.4	34.4	1,089.0	924.4	332.2	43.0	140.4	1,064.7	561.9	3.4
1995-6	1,012.6	24.3	1,038.8	921.8	295.9	33.0	94.3	1,016.1	593.0	3.5
1996-7	979.0	22.7	1,002.9	879.6	262.0	15.0	103.3	982.9	602.4	3.5
1997-8	1,064.7	19.9	1,086.7	924.6	285.0	17.0	121.8	1,046.4	623.3	3.4
1998-9	1,106.1	40.4	1,148.4	987.6	250.0	26.0	139.9	1,127.5	654.0	3.6
1999-00	1,091.0	20.8	1,097.8	917.8	234.0	14.0	155.0	1,072.8	675.0	3.5
2000-1	1,058.0	27.0	1,087.0	895.0	NA	5.0	174.0	1,069.0	644.0	2.3
2001-2[1]	1,058.0	18.0	1,080.0	963.0	NA	14.0	103.0	1,066.0	661.0	2.3
2002-3[2]	1,083.0	18.0	1,109.0	1,012.0			84.0	1,096.0	706.0	2.4

[1] Preliminary.   [2] Forecast.   [3] Includes edible tallow.   NA = not avaliable.   *Source: Economic Research Service, U.S. Department of Agriculture (ERS-USDA)*

Consumption of Lard (Edible and Inedible) in the United States   In Millions of Pounds

Year	Jan.	Feb.	Mar.	Apr.	May	June	July	Aug.	Sept.	Oct.	Nov.	Dec.	Total
1995	37.5	34.7	41.2	36.2	42.2	44.4	34.9	35.9	35.9	40.1	38.9	36.8	458.7
1996	30.5	35.4	36.7	46.9	36.8	31.4	32.6	33.9	30.9	34.5	34.7	33.6	417.9
1997	26.5	30.5	31.0	36.5	39.9	36.2	36.1	35.0	37.4	39.0	41.5	40.4	429.8
1998	34.1	29.9	31.1	29.6	28.5	35.9	33.0	33.0	37.1	37.7	38.9	33.9	402.7
1999	34.6	30.2	28.8	31.1	30.5	32.9	28.9	33.0	29.2	31.2	31.3	30.3	372.1
2000	27.3	25.7	29.1	23.3	30.3	27.6	24.4	31.3	31.1	32.6	29.6	31.7	343.9
2001	27.8	22.2	28.3	24.5	22.5	23.3	21.8	27.1	23.2	27.9	26.7	24.4	299.8
2002	26.4	26.1	21.8	26.7	24.8	21.2	22.9	26.4	23.6	26.4	28.1	28.7	303.2
2003[1]	22.6	22.3	23.4	21.4	23.3	24.0	23.0	21.4	22.5	24.3	20.2	21.0	269.5

[1] Preliminary.   *Source: Bureau of the Census, U.S. Department of Commerce*

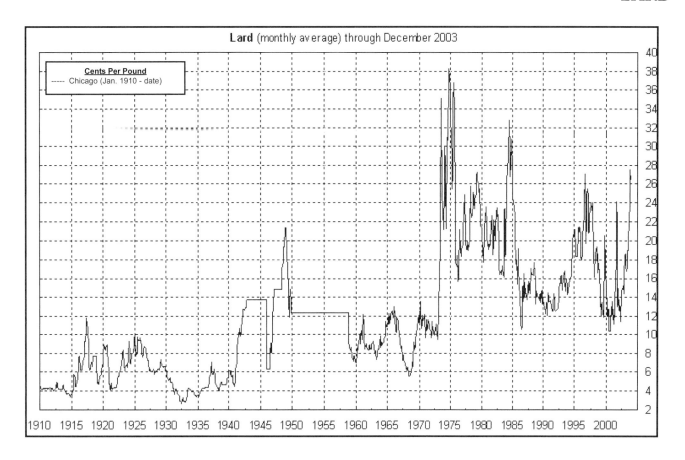

Lard (monthly average) through December 2003

Cents Per Pound
----- Chicago (Jan. 1910 - date)

Average Wholesale Price of Lard, Loose, Tank Cars, in Chicago   In Cents Per Pound

Year	Jan.	Feb.	Mar.	Apr.	May	June	July	Aug.	Sept.	Oct.	Nov.	Dec.	Average
1994	14.50	14.62	15.35	15.74	15.75	16.25	17.24	18.91	20.14	20.39	20.35	20.91	17.51
1995	21.21	21.13	19.25	18.34	18.25	19.02	20.25	21.30	21.48	20.90	21.38	21.35	20.32
1996	20.52	18.17	18.01	18.67	20.47	22.61	24.55	26.30	27.09	23.11	19.70	22.17	21.78
1997	24.93	25.47	24.69	20.82	20.94	22.68	23.83	23.95	23.14	23.41	23.97	22.85	23.39
1998	19.09	16.03	17.36	17.64	18.66	19.38	17.93	18.65	16.58	17.39	17.60	16.27	17.72
1999	16.89	13.91	11.98	13.12	13.43	12.98	11.87	13.89	17.44	20.55	17.74	16.12	14.99
2000	15.66	12.38	11.99	11.96	12.68	12.64	10.32	10.35	11.14	13.04	12.06	12.14	12.20
2001	13.57	11.92	11.07	12.09	11.84	13.38	18.05	24.11	22.00	13.04	13.18	14.92	14.93
2002	12.69	12.50	13.07	12.42	11.38	14.64	14.60	15.00	15.21	14.39	16.28	18.42	14.22
2003	18.61	17.11	16.85	16.72	17.29	18.90	18.93	20.08	23.98	27.50	26.40	25.18	20.63

Source: Economic Research Service, U.S. Department of Agriculture (ERS-USDA)

United States Cold Storage Holdings of all Lard[1], on First of Month   In Millions of Pounds

Year	Jan.	Feb.	Mar.	Apr.	May	June	July	Aug.	Sept.	Oct.	Nov.	Dec.
1994	37.7	38.0	31.8	28.8	25.1	27.4	27.0	25.5	29.7	34.4	34.0	35.8
1995	40.6	50.3	46.4	43.0	36.8	27.1	25.8	22.1	30.2	24.3	19.9	21.6
1996	38.4	38.6	25.8	28.8	21.5	23.2	23.7	30.5	20.7	22.7	20.1	18.8
1997	18.9	16.3	18.5	19.2	18.9	18.7	23.0	23.2	21.5	19.9	21.3	19.7
1998	22.2	30.1	38.3	42.5	41.6	47.6	43.7	44.8	38.8	40.4	34.8	26.3
1999	28.4	30.4	30.6	34.0	27.1	39.9	30.7	25.5	29.4	20.8	19.1	22.8
2000	26.7	27.8	29.2	30.1	20.2	22.5	18.9	19.3	17.3	17.4	16.3	16.8
2001	16.0	14.9	14.9	17.9	13.7	13.1	10.3	12.4	11.8	13.6	13.0	11.7
2002	13.2	18.0	16.4	16.5	20.3	22.4	18.9	18.3	12.0	10.5	14.6	11.3
2003[2]	10.5	14.0	19.6	18.7	16.5	13.5	11.9	9.7	8.4	9.3	10.1	12.4

[1] Stocks in factories and warehouses (except that in hands of retailers).   [2] Preliminary.   *Source: Bureau of the Census, U.S. Department of Commerce*

Lead

Lead is a dense, toxic, bluish-gray metallic element, and is the heaviest stable element. Lead was one of the first known metals. The ancients used lead in face powders, rouges, mascaras, paints, condiments, wine preservatives, and water supply plumbing. The Romans were slowly poisoned from lead because of its diverse daily usage.

Lead is usually found in ore with zinc, silver, and most often copper. The most common lead ore is galena, containing 86.6% lead. Cerussite and angleside are other common varieties of lead. More than half of the lead currently used comes from recycling.

Lead is used in building construction, bullets and shot, tank and pipe lining, storage batteries, and electric cable sheathing. Lead is used extensively as a protective shielding for radioactive material, i.e., X-ray apparatus, because of its high density and nuclear properties. Lead is also part of solder, pewter, and fusible alloys.

Lead futures and options trade at the London Metal Exchange (LME). The lead futures contract calls for the delivery of 25 metric tons of at least 99.970% purity lead ingots (pigs). The contract is priced in terms of US dollars per metric ton. Lead first started trading on the LME in 1903.

Prices – Lead prices took off in the latter half of 2003 along with the rest of the basic metals complex. Lead prices between 2000 and the middle of 2003 bounced back and forth within a range of approximately $400 to $520 per metric ton. However, in mid-2003, lead prices entered a major bull market and rallied from the $500 area all the way up to approximately $850 by the end of the year, a rally of about 70%.

Supply – World smelter production of lead (both primary and secondary) in 2002 fell –1.2% to 6.390 million metric tons from 6.470 million metric tons in 2001, but was only modestly lower than the record production level of 6.580 million metric tons in 2000. The world's largest smelter producers of lead (both primary and secondary) in 2002 were the US with 21.6% of world production, followed by China with 20%, Germany with 6.1%, and the UK with 5.8%.

US mine production of recoverable lead fell to a 6-year low of 440,000 metric tons in 2002 from 454,000 in 2001. Missouri was responsible for 97% of US production, with the remainder produced mainly by Idaho and Montana. Lead recovered from scrap in the US (secondary production) fell to a 6-year low of 1.106 million metric tons in 2002 from 1.113 million metric tons in 2001. That is more than twice the amount of lead produced in the US from mines (primary production). The value of US refined lead production in 2002 was $252 million, down from $279 million in 2001 and well below the record high of $668 million posted back in 1979.

Demand – US lead consumption in 2002 rose slightly to 1.673 million metric tons from 1.652 million metric tons in 2001, and that was only slightly below the record consumption level of 1.680 million metric tons posted in 1999.

Trade – The US relied on imports for 18% of its lead consumption in 2002. US imports of lead pigs and bars in 2002 fell to a 9-year low of 210,000 metric tons. US lead exports in 2002 were comprised by ore concentrate (241,000 metric tons), scrap (106,000 metric tons), unwrought lead (31,400 metric tons), and wrought lead (11,700 metric tons).

World Smelter (Primary and Secondary) Production of Lead   In Thousands of Metric Tons

Year	Aus-tralia[3]	Belgium[4]	Canada[3]	China[2]	France	Germany	Italy	Japan	Mexico[3]	Spain	United Kingdom[3]	United States	World Total
1993	243.0	131.1	217.0	412.0	258.7	334.2	182.8	309.5	188.0	123.0	363.8	1,230	5,420
1994	237.0	123.5	251.6	467.9	260.5	331.7	205.9	292.2	171.0	140.0	352.5	1,280	5,360
1995	241.0	122.0	281.4	608.0	296.7	311.2	180.4	287.6	176.0	80.0	320.7	1,390	5,590
1996	228.0	125.0	309.4	706.0	302.8	238.1	209.8	287.4	160.0	86.0	345.6	1,400	5,630
1997	238.0	110.8	271.4	707.0	302.3	329.2	211.6	296.8	178.0	74.9	391.0	1,450	5,880
1998	206.0	91.5	265.5	757.0	318.0	380.2	199.3	302.1	173.0	90.0	348.9	1,450	5,970
1999	272.8	103.2	266.4	918.0	279.0	373.6	215.3	293.4	121.0	96.0	348.1	1,460	6,170
2000	251.8	118.0	284.8	1,100.0	258.0	415.0	235.0	311.7	153.0	120.0	337.2	1,470	6,580
2001[1]	303.0	96.0	230.9	1,200.0	238.0	374.0	203.0	302.4	154.0	98.0	366.0	1,390	6,470
2002[2]	211.0	96.0	251.3	1,250.0	204.0	390.0	205.0	280.4	155.0	98.0	370.0	1,380	6,390

[1] Preliminary.   [2] Estimate.   [3] Refonded & bullion.   [4] Includes scrap.   *Source: U.S. Geological Survey (USGS)*

Consumption of Lead in the United States, by Products   In Metric Tons

Year	Ammun-ition	Bearing Metals	Pipes, Traps & Bends[2]	Cable Covering	Calking Lead	Casting Metals	Other Metal Products[3]	Total Other Oxides[4]	Sheet Lead	Solder	Storage Battery Grids, Post, etc.	Storage Battery Oxides	Brass and Bronze	Total Consumption
1993	65,100	4,830	5,740	17,165	961	18,500	5,360	63,600	21,200	14,400	677,000	374,000	5,750	1,290,000
1994	62,400	5,560	3,370	16,000	764	18,900	5,330	62,700	21,500	12,200	797,000	425,000	6,320	1,450,000
1995	70,900	6,490	2,210	5,640	935	18,100	5,220	61,700	27,900	16,200	711,000	618,000	5,260	1,560,000
1996	52,100	4,350	1,810	W	767	18,900	5,220	62,100	19,400	9,020	635,000	706,000	5,460	1,540,000
1997	52,400	2,490	1,860	4,930	1,390	34,000	7,570	67,000	19,100	9,580	634,000	761,000	4,410	1,620,000
1998	52,800	2,210	3,130	4,630	1,350	32,600	8,160	53,400	15,500	10,900	685,000	742,000	3,460	1,630,000
1999	58,300	1,570	2,020	2,410	971	34,300	7,130	58,200	15,400	13,100	765,000	707,000	3,940	1,680,000
2000	63,700	1,490	2,010	W	1,140	35,100	25,800	52,400	23,800	11,500	796,000	690,000	3,670	1,720,000
2001	53,600	837	2,370	W	927	31,800	17,100	43,900	22,400	6,120	655,000	694,000	2,590	1,550,000
2002[1]	57,600	406	2,250	W	1,060	34,800	24,200	51,900	25,600	6,450	554,000	641,000	2,730	1,440,000

[1] Preliminary.   [2] Including building.   [3] Including terne metal, type metal, and lead consumerd in foil, collapsible tubes, annealing, plating, galvanizing and fishing weights.   [4] Includes paints, glass and ceramic products, and other pigments and chemicals.   W = Withheld proprietary data.
Source: U.S. Geological Survey (USGS)

156

Salient Statistics of Lead in the United States   In Thousands of Metric Tons

Year	Net Import Reliance as a % of Apparent Consumption	Production — of Refined Lead From — Domestic Ores[3]	Foreign Ores[3]	Total Primary	Total Value of Refined Million $	As Soft Lead	In Anti-monial Lead	In Other Alloys	Total	Total Value of Secondary Million $	Stocks, Dec. 31 Primary	Con-sumer[4]	Average Price New York	London[5]
1993	15	310.7	24.9	335.6	234.4	444.0	417.0	17.0	893.0	625.0	14.3	80.5	31.74	18.42
1994	19	328.0	23.4	351.4	288.0	527.0	371.0	16.1	931.0	763.0	9.3	68.8	37.17	24.83
1995	17	374.0	W	374.0	348.0	584.0	400.0	19.2	1,020.0	951.0	14.2	79.4	42.28	28.08
1996	17	326.0	W	326.0	351.0	625.0	420.0	9.2	1,070.0	1,150.0	8.1	72.1	48.83	31.22
1997	14	343.0	W	343.0	352.0	663.0	411.0	14.2	1,110.0	1,130.0	11.9	89.1	46.54	28.29
1998	21	337.0	W	337.0	336.0	667.0	417.0	16.1	1,120.0	1,110.0	10.9	77.9	45.27	23.96
1999	20	350.0	W	350.0	337.0	635.0	444.0	18.1	1,110.0	1,070.0	12.3	78.7	43.72	22.78
2000	24	341.0	W	341.0	328.0	651.0	428.0	36.8	1,130.0	1,090.0	18.6	106.0	43.57	20.57
2001[1]	20	290.0	W	290.0	279.0	734.0	291.0	75.9	1,100.0	1,060.0	W	100.0	43.64	21.58
2002[2]	18	262.0	W	262.0	252.0	754.0	289.0	71.9	1,120.0	1,070.0	W	105.0	43.56	20.52

[1] Preliminary.   [2] Estimate.   [3] And base bullion.   [4] Also at secondary smelters.   [5] LME data in dollars per metric ton beginning July 1993.
W = Withheld Proprietary data.   E = Net exporter.   Source: U.S. Geological Survey (USGS)

United States Foreign Trade of Lead   In Thousands of Metric Tons

Year	Exports Ore Concentrate	Un-wrought Lead[3]	Wrought Lead[4]	Scrap	Ash & Re-sidues	Imports for Consumption Ores, Flue Dust or Fume & Mattes	Base Bullion	Pigs & Bars	Re-claimed Scrap, etc.	Value Million $	General Imports From: Ore, Flue Dust & Matte Australia	Canada	Peru	Pigs & Bars Canada	Mexico	Peru
1993	41.8	51.4	7.1	54.1	1.7	0.5	----	195.6	0.1	99.4	----	55.7	13.6	130.8	40.3	18.3
1994	38.7	48.2	5.3	88.1	20.6	0.5	0.6	230.8	0.1	146.6	0.5	0.2	----	159.0	31.9	25.6
1995	65.5	48.2	9.0	105.0	8.0	2.6	0.0	264.0	0.1	191.7	1.5	----	0.1	182.0	54.3	22.1
1996	59.7	44.0	16.7	85.3	19.4	6.6	0.0	268.0	0.2	217.0	----	4.4	----	192.0	56.9	17.1
1997	42.2	37.4	15.9	88.4	16.8	17.8	0.0	265.0	0.1	200.3	----	0.8	3.4	186.0	70.4	6.4
1998	72.4	24.1	15.4	99.2	9.0	32.7	0.5	267.0	[6]	191.9	2.4	6.5	18.5	181.0	63.6	11.4
1999	93.5	23.4	13.9	117.0	1.4	12.3	0.1	311.0	----	196.5	0.1	1.2	8.8	198.0	27.2	6.9
2000	117.0	21.4	27.2	71.6	11.3	31.2	0.1	356.0	0.0	217.1	----	[6]	10.8	216.0	18.4	1.8
2001[1]	181.0	17.0	17.7	108.0	14.2	2.2	----	271.0	10.2	166.8	----	----	----	167.0	12.4	2.3
2002[2]	241.0	31.4	11.7	106.0	----	0.0	----	210.0	2.6	124.9	----	----	----	172.0	7.5	----

[1] Preliminary.   [2] Estimate.   [3] And lead alloys.   [4] Blocks, pigs, etc.   [5] Formerly drosses & flue dust.   [6] Less than 1/2 unit.   NA = Not avaliable.
Source: U.S. Geological Survey (USGS)

Annual Mine Production of Recoverable Lead in the United States   In Metric Tons

Year	Total	Idaho	Missouri	Montana	Other States	Missouri's % of Total
1993	353,607	W	276,569	W	77,800	78%
1994	363,443	W	290,738	9,940	63,100	80%
1995	386,000	W	359,000	8,350	18,200	93%
1996	426,000	W	397,000	7,970	21,200	93%
1997	448,000	W	412,000	9,230	26,600	92%
1998	481,000	W	439,000	7,310	35,100	91%
1999	503,000	W	464,000	7,950	31,200	92%
2000	449,000	W	410,000	W	38,700	91%
2001[1]	454,000	W	423,000	W	30,900	93%
2002[2]	440,000	W	428,000	W	12,300	97%

[1] Preliminary.   [2] Estimate.   W = Withheld, included in Other States.   NA = Not Avaliable.   Source: U.S. Geological Survey (USGS)

Mine Production of Recoverable Lead in the United States   In Thousands of Metric Tons

Year	Jan.	Feb.	Mar.	Apr.	May	June	July	Aug.	Sept.	Oct.	Nov.	Dec.	Total
1994	27.6	28.8	33.0	31.3	32.4	29.1	29.4	30.4	31.2	28.0	31.7	29.9	363.4
1995	29.6	30.3	35.2	28.9	32.7	34.8	32.5	33.5	29.9	34.1	31.6	32.1	385.0
1996	36.9	36.4	35.6	35.9	37.5	33.8	35.6	34.1	26.9	35.2	33.6	35.7	426.0
1997	36.7	36.7	37.2	38.6	38.6	35.1	33.4	33.7	34.4	35.4	31.7	32.8	448.0
1998	37.4	35.4	37.8	37.3	35.7	34.7	34.3	35.6	36.1	40.3	37.8	39.2	449.0
1999	41.2	42.1	44.4	43.1	41.7	42.6	47.2	43.6	41.5	41.2	37.8	38.1	505.0
2000	35.1	36.7	43.0	37.5	37.4	37.8	33.0	36.8	36.8	32.4	38.8	36.9	447.0
2001	42.9	37.8	39.4	33.7	35.0	32.2	38.2	39.6	32.4	39.5	32.1	35.4	450.0
2002	39.5	35.5	41.2	36.1	39.3	36.1	35.0	39.6	33.2	34.8	34.1	34.2	438.6
2003[1]	39.0	34.9	38.5	36.2	38.8	39.2	41.3	38.0	38.3	37.2	37.7		457.2

[1] Preliminary.   Source: U.S. Geological Survey (USGS)

LEAD

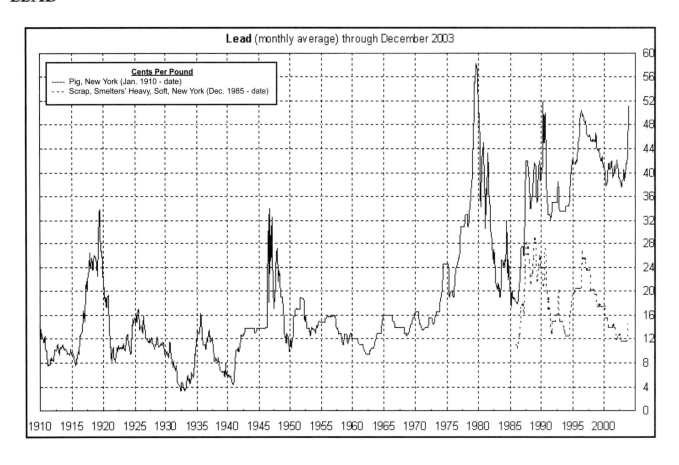

Lead (monthly average) through December 2003

Cents Per Pound
— Pig, New York (Jan. 1910 - date)
- - - Scrap, Smelters' Heavy, Soft, New York (Dec. 1985 - date)

Average Price of Pig Lead, U.S. Primary Producers (Common Corroding)[1]   In Cents Per Pound

Year	Jan.	Feb.	Mar.	Apr.	May	June	July	Aug.	Sept.	Oct.	Nov.	Dec.	Average
1994	34.00	34.00	34.00	34.00	34.00	35.73	37.70	38.00	40.00	42.00	43.70	44.00	37.59
1995	44.00	44.00	42.00	42.00	42.00	42.00	42.00	43.65	44.00	44.00	46.10	48.00	43.65
1996	48.00	49.50	50.96	52.00	52.00	52.00	50.29	49.18	50.00	50.00	50.00	50.00	50.33
1997	50.00	50.00	48.70	48.00	48.00	48.00	48.00	48.00	48.00	48.00	48.00	48.00	48.39
1998	48.00	48.00	48.00	48.00	48.00	48.00	48.00	48.00	48.00	48.00	45.47	45.00	47.54
1999	45.00	45.00	45.00	45.00	45.00	45.00	45.00	45.00	45.00	45.00	45.00	45.00	45.00
2000	45.00	45.00	45.00	45.00	45.00	45.00	45.00	45.00	45.00	45.00	45.00	45.00	45.00
2001	45.00	45.00	45.00	45.00	45.00	45.00	45.00	45.00	45.00	45.00	45.00	45.00	45.00
2002	45.00	45.00	45.00	45.00	45.00	45.00	45.00	45.00	45.00	45.00	45.00	45.00	45.00
2003	23.14	24.65	23.81	23.13	24.56	24.77	26.93	26.05	27.23	30.16	32.09	35.46	26.83

[1] New York Delivery.   Source: American Metal Market (AMM)

Refiners Production[1] of Lead in the United States   In Metric Tons

Year	Jan.	Feb.	Mar.	Apr.	May	June	July	Aug.	Sept.	Oct.	Nov.	Dec.	Total
1994	29,908	30,685	31,420	29,059	31,588	31,707	30,661	27,335	31,185	32,874	29,301	30,447	366,170
1995	32,100	29,100	32,600	32,300	32,600	28,300	31,000	29,300	30,600	34,200	30,100	31,500	374,000
1996	34,700	30,400	30,900	28,600	27,500	21,700	25,500	24,700	25,400	25,300	26,100	25,500	326,000
1997	28,800	28,500	31,900	30,400	30,800	28,700	25,900	28,000	21,600	30,500	29,000	28,700	343,000
1998	29,200	25,900	30,000	29,700	29,500	20,300	28,900	NA	NA	NA	NA	NA	337,000
1999	NA	NA	NA	NA	NA	NA	NA	NA	NA	NA	NA	NA	350,000
2000	NA	NA	NA	NA	NA	NA	NA	NA	NA	NA	NA	NA	341,000
2001	NA	NA	NA	NA	NA	NA	NA	NA	NA	NA	NA	NA	290,000
2002	NA	NA	NA	NA	NA	NA	NA	NA	NA	NA	NA	NA	262,000
2003[2]	NA	NA	NA	NA	NA	NA	NA	NA	NA	NA	NA		

[1] Represents refined lead produced from domestic ores by primary smelters plus small amounts of secondary material passing through these smelters.
Includes GSA metal purchased for remelt.   [2] Preliminary.   *Source: U.S. Geological Survey (USGS)*

Total Stocks of Lead[1] in the United States at Refiners, at End of Month   In Metric Tons

Year	Jan.	Feb.	Mar.	Apr.	May	June	July	Aug.	Sept.	Oct.	Nov.	Dec.
1994	11,964	12,633	12,048	11,445	11,598	10,251	12,368	9,256	8,897	10,659	9,060	9,271
1995	8,200	9,750	11,500	14,500	16,700	16,200	21,300	14,000	12,800	9,820	9,830	14,200
1996	15,000	15,000	15,000	15,000	15,000	19,600	19,900	14,200	12,200	7,060	7,830	8,160
1997	8,460	11,800	21,400	19,900	15,000	10,900	6,530	7,790	5,370	7,310	8,710	11,900
1998	13,000	15,900	18,700	20,900	11,400	11,400	13,700	NA	NA	NA	NA	10,900
1999	NA	NA	NA	NA	NA	NA	NA	NA	NA	NA	NA	12,300
2000	NA	NA	NA	NA	NA	NA	NA	NA	NA	NA	NA	18,600
2001	NA	NA	NA	NA	NA	NA	NA	NA	NA	NA	NA	NA
2002	NA	NA	NA	NA	NA	NA	NA	NA	NA	NA	NA	NA
2003[2]	NA	NA	NA	NA	NA	NA	NA	NA	NA	NA	NA	

[1] Primary refineries.   [2] Preliminary.   *Source: U.S. Geological Survey (USGS)*

Total[1] Lead Consumption in the United States   In Thousands of Metric Tons

Year	Jan.	Feb.	Mar.	Apr.	May	June	July	Aug.	Sept.	Oct.	Nov.	Dec.	Total
1994	107.0	115.2	112.8	111.6	113.5	115.2	114.3	115.5	115.9	121.2	118.7	113.0	1,384
1995	119.0	119.0	119.0	109.0	110.0	113.0	115.0	105.0	115.0	116.0	118.0	116.0	1,370
1996	107.0	100.0	106.0	111.0	113.0	106.0	104.0	146.0	140.0	147.0	163.0	143.0	1,530
1997	139.0	138.0	138.0	140.0	137.0	141.0	116.0	119.0	122.0	123.0	117.0	117.0	1,600
1998	116.0	115.0	119.0	128.0	127.0	129.0	128.0	128.0	129.0	129.0	134.0	125.0	1,550
1999	128.0	129.0	130.0	127.0	128.0	130.0	137.0	136.0	141.0	136.0	140.0	133.0	1,680
2000	139.0	139.0	139.0	139.0	140.0	140.0	135.0	141.0	139.0	139.0	136.0	132.0	1,660
2001	145.0	135.0	133.0	130.0	138.0	136.0	135.0	136.0	142.0	146.0	138.0	138.0	1,652
2002	132.0	131.0	133.0	142.0	142.0	144.0	143.0	145.0	141.0	145.0	142.0	133.0	1,673
2003[2]	134.0	129.0	126.0	120.0	121.0	121.0	121.0	122.0	123.0	127.0	120.0		1,488

[1] Represents total consumption of primary & secondary lead as metal, in chemicals, or in alloys.   [2] Preliminary.   *Source: U.S. Geological Survey (USGS)*

Lead Recovered from Scrap in the United States   In Thousands of Metric Tons (Lead Content)

Year	Jan.	Feb.	Mar.	Apr.	May	June	July	Aug.	Sept.	Oct.	Nov.	Dec.	Total
1994	74.0	76.0	84.2	81.7	81.1	79.0	78.9	79.8	78.4	76.4	81.0	80.4	949.0
1995	82.5	80.8	84.4	72.8	73.7	72.5	79.9	71.5	82.3	80.0	82.3	82.1	945.0
1996	75.7	76.2	84.2	83.7	84.7	80.7	81.2	89.0	92.1	98.8	97.3	93.2	1,100.0
1997	88.0	89.8	91.7	86.0	88.2	85.7	86.7	94.7	97.3	96.2	95.2	91.7	1,110.0
1998	95.0	92.0	92.6	94.1	92.5	89.7	89.3	95.7	94.4	95.0	95.1	90.7	1,110.0
1999	89.5	89.1	88.9	91.0	90.2	91.1	81.3	91.9	91.6	93.5	91.4	93.1	1,110.0
2000	91.0	88.0	91.1	91.4	90.5	91.3	88.6	95.1	94.0	96.0	95.4	93.7	1,110.0
2001	90.3	90.4	86.7	92.6	93.7	93.6	90.4	95.1	93.9	96.7	94.6	94.6	1,112.6
2002	89.3	82.3	88.2	93.1	93.9	93.6	88.0	96.1	93.3	97.5	95.0	95.7	1,106.0
2003[1]	95.7	83.6	86.2	85.1	94.0	94.8	95.7	93.9	93.3	102.0	93.7		1,110.5

[1] Preliminary.   *Source: U.S. Geological Survey (USGS)*

Domestic Shipments[1] of Lead in the United States, by Refiners   In Thousands of Short Tons

Year	Jan.	Feb.	Mar.	Apr.	May	June	July	Aug.	Sept.	Oct.	Nov.	Dec.	Total
1988	33.5	29.5	39.2	33.0	41.4	44.7	32.0	34.7	33.7	43.0	38.5	35.5	438.7
1989	29.3	28.5	32.2	35.7	45.1	36.4	32.8	41.5	40.0	44.2	40.2	31.1	437.1
1990	39.3	33.9	39.1	33.5	38.4	32.9	32.6	38.9	36.6	38.9	37.9	31.7	433.7
1991	35.4	33.8	34.3	39.8	33.9	26.0	31.8	37.9	35.1	35.7	28.7	26.7	399.2
1992	31.3	23.9	30.4	26.3	25.6	27.2	27.3	28.7	26.3	28.5	26.3	21.7	323.5
1993	24.6	23.6	32.5	30.0	31.3	35.1	28.9	34.0	35.5	35.5	31.7	33.5	376.2
1994	35.9	32.8	35.2	32.7	34.7	36.7	31.6	33.4	34.8	34.3	34.0	33.3	409.3
1995	36.5	30.3	35.1	31.1	33.7	31.9	28.6	40.3	34.9	40.9	33.2	29.8	406.4
1996	37.2	32.4	29.5	30.2	29.4	26.7	27.7	33.5	30.1	33.5	28.1	27.6	366.0
1997[2]	31.5	27.8	24.7	35.2	39.2	36.1	33.4	29.4	26.4	31.5	30.4	28.1	377.8

[1] Includes GSA metal.   [2] Preliminary.   *Source: American Metal Market (AMM)*

Lumber & Plywood

Humans have utilized lumber for construction for thousands of years, but due to the heaviness of timber and the manual methods of harvesting, large-scale lumbering didn't occur until the mechanical advances of the Industrial Revolution. Total world harvest, including softwood and hardwood, is currently around 4 billion cubic meters per year.

Lumber is produced from both hardwood and softwood. Hardwood lumber comes from deciduous trees that have broad leaves. Most hardwood lumber is used for miscellaneous industrial applications, primarily wood pallets, and includes oak, gum, maple, and ash. Hardwood species with beautiful colors and patterns are used for such high-grade products as furniture, flooring, paneling, and cabinets and include black walnut, black cherry, and red oak. Wood from cone-bearing trees is called softwood, regardless of its actual hardness. Most lumber from the US is softwood. Softwoods, such as southern yellow pine, Douglas fir, ponderosa pine, and true firs, are primarily used as structural lumber such as 2 x 4s and 2 x 6s, poles, paper and cardboard.

Plywood consists of several thin layers of veneer bonded together with adhesives. The veneer sheets are layered so that the grain of one sheet is perpendicular to that of the next, which makes plywood exceptionally strong for its weight. Most plywood has from thee to nine layers of wood. Plywood manufacturers use both hard and soft woods, although hardwoods serve primarily for appearance and are not as strong as those made from softwoods. Plywood is primarily used in construction, particularly for floors, roofs, walls, and doors. Homebuilding and remodeling account for two-thirds of US lumber consumption. The price of lumber and plywood is highly correlated with the strength of the US home-building market.

The forest and wood products industry is dominated by Weyerhaeuser Company (ticker symbol WY), which has nearly $20 billion in annual sales and a market capitalization of over $13 billion. Weyerhaeuser is a forest products conglomerate that engages not only in growing and harvesting timber, but also in the production and distribution of forest products, real estate development, and construction of single-family homes. Forest products include wood products, pulp and paper, and containerboard. The timberland segment of the business manages 7.2 million acres of company-owned land and 800,000 acres of leased commercial forestlands in North America. The company's Canadian division has renewable, long-term licenses on about 35 million acres of forestland in five Canadian provinces. In order to maximize its long-term yield from its acreage, Weyerhaeuser engages in a number of forest management activities such as extensive planting, suppression of non-merchantable species, thinning, fertilization, and operational pruning.

Lumber futures and options are traded on the Chicago Mercantile Exchange (CME). The CME's lumber futures contract calls for the delivery of 111,000 board feet (one 73 foot rail car) of random length 8 to 12 foot 2 x 4s, the type used in construction. The contract is priced in terms of dollars per thousand board feet.

Prices – Lumber futures prices rallied through most of 2003, with the market posting a new 2-1/2 year high late in the year. Lumber prices closed 2003 at $312.60, up 44% from the 2002 close of $217.70. The market was driven by the extremely strong US home-building market seen all year. Despite the rally, the market remained slightly below the 3-year high of $376.00 posted in May 2001 and well below the record high of $493.50 posted in March 1993.

Supply – US softwood lumber production in 2003 was on track to fall 1.2% to 35.607 billion board feet from 36.025 billion in 2002. The US leads the world in the production of industrial round wood with 405 million cubic meters of production in 2002, followed by Canada with 197 million cubic meters and Russia with 128 million cubic meters.

The US also leads the world in the production of plywood with 15.494 million cubic meters of production in 2002, followed by Canada with 2.475 million cubic meters and Russia with 1.808 million cubic meters.

Trade – US imports of softwood in 2002 rose to 20.986 billion board feet from 20.075 billion board feet in 2001. US imports of hardwood in 2002 rose to 739 million board feet from 645 million board feet in 2001. Total US lumber imports in 2002 rose to 21.774 billion board feet from 20.737 billion in 2001. The majority of US imports were of spruce with 1.046 billion board feet in 2002, and cedar came in second with 648 million board feet.

US exports of softwood in 2002 fell to 848 million board feet from 968 million board feet in 2001. US exports of hardwood in 2002 fell to 1.219 billion board feet from 1.222 billion board feet in 2001. Total US exports in 2002 fell to 2.312 billion board feet from 2.351 billion board feet in 2001. The largest US export of softwood was of southern pine with 205 million board feet in 2002, followed by Douglas fir with 111 million board feet.

World Production of Industrial Roundwood by Selected Countries   In Thousands of Cubic Meters

Year	Austria	Canada	Czech Repulic	Finland	France	Germany	Poland	Romania	Russia	Spain	Sweden	Turkey	United States
1993	9,707	169,770	9,706	38,083	29,563	29,357	15,940	7,740	136,030	11,419	50,200	9,408	401,520
1994	11,701	177,346	11,172	44,644	32,442	36,018	16,711	9,640	83,650	12,990	52,100	9,211	410,781
1995	11,346	183,027	11,716	46,124	33,561	36,914	19,240	10,015	83,050	12,997	59,800	10,745	408,948
1996	11,812	177,943	11,882	42,178	30,643	34,538	18,824	9,441	73,005	12,433	52,500	10,229	406,625
1997	11,902	183,531	12,881	47,757	32,162	35,488	20,097	9,837	67,508	12,433	56,400	9,773	416,092
1998	10,858	173,901	13,171	49,541	32,718	36,441	21,793	8,629	77,400	13,164	54,700	9,979	422,034
1999	10,988	190,846	13,363	49,593	33,237	35,063	22,842	9,484	94,600	13,160	52,800	10,065	425,659
2000	10,416	197,373	13,501	50,147	43,440	51,088	24,489	10,116	105,800	12,721	57,400	10,429	427,654
2001[1]	10,562	197,373	13,364	47,727	37,471	36,502	23,375	9,806	118,700	13,276	57,300	9,976	398,225
2002[2]	11,809	197,373	13,534	48,529	33,500	37,755	25,040	12,092	128,100	13,850	61,600	11,305	404,735

[1] Preliminary.   [2] Estimate.   NA = Not available.   *Source: Food and Agriculture Organization of the United Nations (FAO-UN)*

Lumber Production and Consumption in the United States   In Millions of Board Feet

| | Production | | | | | | Domestic Consumption | | | | | | | |
| | Softwood | | | | | | Softwood | | | | | | | |
Year	California Redwood	Inland Region	Southern Pine	West Coast	Total	Total Hardwood	Inland Region	Southern Pine	West Coast	Softwood Imports	Total	U.S. Hardwood	Hardwood Imports	Total Lumber
1995	1,305	7,015	14,708	7,452	32,233	12,434	6,956	14,384	6,530	17,396	47,749	11,372	380	59,501
1996	1,371	7,079	15,262	7,745	33,266	NA	7,073	15,112	6,821	18,214	49,883	NA	NA	NA
1997	1,511	7,383	16,113	7,772	34,667	NA	7,180	15,993	7,012	18,002	50,863	NA	NA	NA
1998	1,391	7,298	16,151	7,797	34,677	NA	7,256	15,788	7,502	18,686	52,209	NA	NA	NA
1999	1,325	7,580	16,922	8,625	36,605	NA	7,445	16,525	8,115	19,178	54,262	NA	NA	NA
2000	1,320	7,078	16,672	8,782	35,967	NA	6,926	16,374	8,300	19,449	53,934	NA	NA	NA
2001	1,121	6,563	16,094	8,764	34,577	NA	6,490	15,937	8,471	20,075	53,828	NA	NA	NA
2002	1,035	6,760	16,686	9,244	35,831	NA	6,643	16,571	8,966	20,986	56,054	NA	NA	NA
I	245	1,650	4,068	2,264	8,741	NA	1,616	4,060	2,117	5,170	13,645	NA	NA	NA
II	294	1,767	4,526	2,401	9,549	NA	1,761	4,420	2,330	5,716	14,998	NA	NA	NA
III	269	1,730	4,333	2,356	9,230	NA	1,715	4,343	2,326	5,104	14,269	NA	NA	NA
IV	227	1,613	3,759	2,223	8,311	NA	1,551	3,748	2,193	4,996	13,142	NA	NA	NA
2003[1] I	194	1,752	3,985	2,370	8,819	NA	1,678	3,897	2,200	4,725	13,101	NA	NA	NA
II	216	1,656	4,383	2,397	9,193	NA	1,737	4,336	2,336	5,622	14,689	NA	NA	NA
III	234	1,675	4,152	2,496	9,091	NA	1,706	4,258	2,455	5,511	14,621	NA	NA	NA

[1] Preliminary.   NA = Not available.   *Source: American Forest & Paper Association (AFPA)*

U.S. Housing Starts: Seasonally Adjusted Annual Rate   In Thousands of Units

Year	Jan.	Feb.	Mar.	Apr.	May	June	July	Aug.	Sept.	Oct.	Nov.	Dec.	Average
1994	1,272	1,337	1,564	1,465	1,526	1,409	1,439	1,450	1,474	1,450	1,511	1,455	1,446
1995	1,407	1,316	1,249	1,267	1,314	1,281	1,461	1,416	1,369	1,369	1,452	1,431	1,354
1996	1,467	1,491	1,424	1,516	1,504	1,467	1,472	1,557	1,475	1,392	1,489	1,370	1,477
1997	1,355	1,486	1,457	1,492	1,442	1,494	1,437	1,390	1,546	1,520	1,510	1,566	1,474
1998	1,525	1,584	1,567	1,540	1,536	1,641	1,698	1,614	1,582	1,715	1,660	1,792	1,621
1999	1,804	1,738	1,737	1,561	1,649	1,562	1,704	1,657	1,628	1,636	1,663	1,769	1,676
2000	1,744	1,822	1,630	1,626	1,573	1,560	1,477	1,531	1,508	1,527	1,559	1,532	1,591
2001	1,666	1,623	1,592	1,636	1,604	1,633	1,664	1,562	1,582	1,531	1,604	1,583	1,607
2002	1,713	1,788	1,675	1,587	1,735	1,709	1,666	1,630	1,810	1,653	1,760	1,847	1,714
2003[1]	1,822	1,640	1,748	1,630	1,738	1,845	1,892	1,826	1,905	1,977	2,054		1,825

[1] Preliminary.   Total Privately owned.   Source: American Forest & Paper Association (AF&PA)

Stocks (Gross) of Softwood Lumber in the United States, on First of Month   In Millions of Board Feet

Year	Jan.	Feb.	Mar.	Apr.	May	June	July	Aug.	Sept.	Oct.	Nov.	Dec.
1994	4,207	4,512	4,656	4,816	4,883	4,649	4,738	4,432	4,349	4,539	4,235	4,294
1995	4,403	4,336	4,344	4,653	4,352	4,663	4,508	4,323	4,342	4,359	4,361	4,335
1996	4,293	4,435	4,459	4,357	4,251	4,153	4,156	4,038	3,918	3,965	3,939	3,906
1997	3,973	4,019	4,113	4,067	3,963	4,017	3,915	3,871	3,875	3,927	3,925	3,865
1998	3,884	3,970	4,048	4,062	4,158	4,084	NA	NA	NA	NA	NA	NA
1999	3,519	3,595	3,688	3,726	3,698	3,581	3,512	3,485	3,533	3,491	3,562	3,536
2000	3,639	3,704	3,811	3,887	3,960	2,738	3,902	3,936	3,878	3,848	3,957	3,875
2001	3,919	3,864	4,013	3,951	4,095	3,955	NA	3,961	3,938	4,076	4,100	4,248
2002	4,784	3,735	3,826	3,756	3,273	3,316	3,242	3,230	3,136	3,098	3,173	3,127
2003[1]	3,175	3,177	3,202	3,249	3,308	3,211	3,075	3,085	3,081	3,158		

[1] Preliminary.   NA = Not available.   *Source: American Forest & Paper Association (AFPA)*

Lumber (Softwood)[2] Production in the United States   In Millions of Board Feet

Year	Jan.	Feb.	Mar.	Apr.	May	June	July	Aug.	Sept.	Oct.	Nov.	Dec.	Total
1994	3,839	3,662	4,097	3,735	3,972	4,113	3,785	4,124	4,135	4,145	3,636	3,851	47,094
1995	4,084	3,577	3,931	3,675	3,805	3,897	3,641	3,866	3,757	4,105	3,549	3,297	45,184
1996	2,600	2,606	2,757	2,903	2,833	2,819	2,942	3,077	2,858	3,179	2,758	2,424	33,756
1997	3,012	2,791	2,866	3,149	2,890	3,027	3,097	2,889	2,905	3,094	2,536	2,487	34,743
1998	2,767	2,760	2,928	3,084	2,647	3,051	3,079	2,930	2,953	3,167	2,667	2,754	34,787
1999	2,783	2,921	3,190	3,227	3,071	3,318	3,115	3,054	2,992	3,096	2,954	2,795	36,516
2000	3,020	3,128	3,474	3,058	3,276	3,249	2,730	2,971	2,839	3,041	2,761	2,342	35,889
2001	2,832	2,457	2,918	2,928	NA	3,032	2,812	3,240	2,743	3,188	2,740	2,372	34,104
2002	3,019	2,761	3,074	3,284	3,126	3,200	3,104	3,128	2,862	3,386	2,599	2,482	36,025
2003[1]	2,971	2,801	2,937	2,994	2,931	3,109	3,088	2,981	3,052	3,241			36,126

[1] Preliminary.   [2] Data prior to 1996 are Softwood and Hardwood.   *Source: American Forest & Paper Association (AFPA)*

LUMBER & PLYWOOD

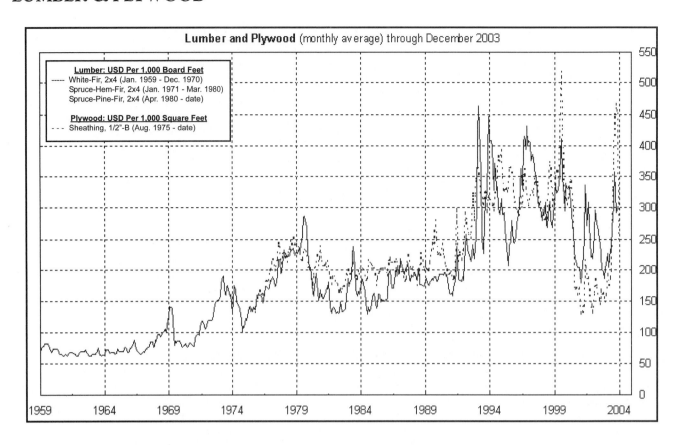

Lumber and Plywood (monthly average) through December 2003

Lumber: USD Per 1,000 Board Feet
----- White-Fir, 2x4 (Jan. 1959 - Dec. 1970)
Spruce-Hem-Fir, 2x4 (Jan. 1971 - Mar. 1980)
Spruce-Pine-Fir, 2x4 (Apr. 1980 - date)

Plywood: USD Per 1,000 Square Feet
- - - Sheathing, 1/2"-B (Aug. 1975 - date)

Lumber (Softwood)[2] Shipments in the United States   In Millions of Board Feet

Year	Jan.	Feb.	Mar.	Apr.	May	June	July	Aug.	Sept.	Oct.	Nov.	Dec.	Total
1994	3,576	3,663	3,912	3,761	4,192	4,091	4,039	4,163	3,914	4,321	3,603	3,696	46,931
1995	3,971	3,584	3,855	3,831	3,765	4,026	3,826	3,870	3,760	4,055	3,478	3,367	45,388
1996	2,460	2,581	2,863	3,002	2,934	2,813	3,058	3,196	2,813	3,206	2,792	2,353	34,071
1997	2,966	2,697	2,890	3,253	2,834	3,126	3,139	2,885	2,852	3,096	2,598	2,461	34,797
1998	2,685	2,685	2,863	3,019	2,684	3,175	3,132	2,963	2,948	3,205	2,703	2,865	34,927
1999	2,689	2,829	3,177	3,227	3,071	3,383	3,141	3,004	3,037	3,021	2,944	2,691	36,214
2000	2,953	3,039	3,394	2,974	3,292	3,309	2,686	3,027	2,871	2,931	2,752	2,444	35,672
2001	2,859	2,372	2,981	2,974	NA	2,961	2,936	3,279	2,644	3,166	2,732	2,396	34,145
2002	3,032	2,815	3,049	3,212	3,064	3,260	3,234	3,111	2,858	3,299	2,675	2,501	36,110
2003[1]	3,018	2,742	2,843	3,134	2,969	3,173	3,209	3,137	3,030	3,413			36,802

[1] Preliminary.   [2] Data prior to 1996 are Softwood and Hardwood.   *Source: American Forest & Paper Association (AFPA)*

Imports and Exports of Lumber in the United States, by Type   In Millions of Board Feet

			Imports[2]						Exports[2]						
		Software					Total	Total	Softwood					Total	Total
		Douglas							Douglas		Ponderosa/ White	Southern			
Year	Cedar	Fir	Hemlock	Pine	Spruce	Total	Hardwood	Lumber	Fir	Hemlock	Pine	Pine	Total	Hardwood	Lumber
1994	703	336	399	97	2,949	16,380	394	16,787	592	283	157	357	2,187	1,041	3,333
1995	768	395	258	97	2,828	17,395	380	17,787	638	227	107	335	1,988	1,101	3,193
1996	727	264	257	133	1,989	18,214	397	18,641	685	195	97	315	1,935	1,141	3,173
1997	586	264	250	314	1,040	18,014	465	18,506	436	105	122	299	1,820	1,281	3,189
1998	514	417	268	363	849	18,686	589	19,306	252	39	113	279	1,265	1,119	2,601
1999	591	426	259	449	803	19,178	708	19,903	249	54	140	326	1,431	1,242	2,867
2000	694	455	184	450	812	19,449	795	20,268	232	46	116	298	1,355	1,319	2,822
2001	667	471	199	365	838	20,075	645	20,737	168	26	86	232	968	1,222	2,351
2002	648	385	69	445	1,046	20,986	739	21,774	111	19	83	205	848	1,219	2,313
2003[1] I	140	65	11	108	186	4,725	184	4,923	31	6	27	34	254	320	621
II	157	98	12	134	225	5,622	191	5,826	23	4	24	29	242	314	613
III	131	110	14	118	208	5,511	191	5,711	20	4	25	33	238	300	593

[1] Preliminary.   [2] Includes sawed timber, board planks & scantlings, flooring, box shook and railroad ties.
Source: American Forest & Paper Association (AFPA)

Average Open Interest of Random Lumber[1] Futures in Chicago   In Contracts

Year	Jan.	Feb.	Mar.	Apr.	May	June	July	Aug.	Sept.	Oct.	Nov.	Dec.
1994	2,571	2,814	2,638	2,563	1,936	1,838	1,705	1,854	2,102	2,169	1,702	1,967
1995	1,757	1,923	2,142	2,509	2,742	3,252	2,896	2,918	2,809	3,039	2,626	2,940
1996	3,378	4,040	3,752	4,395	5,666	4,972	3,280	5,243	4,743	4,797	4,341	3,691
1997	3,745	3,211	3,048	3,337	2,895	3,137	2,767	3,119	3,267	4,006	3,606	4,068
1998	4,249	3,332	3,394	4,102	4,353	4,773	4,048	4,081	3,466	4,295	3,434	3,893
1999	4,864	5,497	4,698	4,456	4,927	6,405	6,263	4,882	3,457	3,704	2,963	2,868
2000	3,004	3,131	2,728	3,175	3,171	3,218	3,064	3,638	3,845	4,277	4,208	4,405
2001	4,605	4,494	3,654	3,644	3,867	3,733	2,612	2,949	2,148	2,102	2,173	2,416
2002	2,106	2,382	2,441	2,011	1,502	2,136	1,879	2,265	2,654	2,974	3,315	3,249
2003	3,238	3,222	2,521	2,804	2,937	3,188	2,370	2,827	3,492	3,033	1,824	1,887

[1] July 1995 thru March 1996, Lumber and Random Lumber.   *Source: Chicago Mercantile Exchange (CME)*

Volume of Trading of Random Lumber[1] Futures in Chicago   In Contracts

Year	Jan.	Feb.	Mar.	Apr.	May	June	July	Aug.	Sept.	Oct.	Nov.	Dec.	Total
1994	16,837	15,204	17,323	17,380	14,996	14,348	11,542	13,327	14,856	13,032	10,997	13,121	172,963
1995	12,150	12,909	15,088	12,139	14,536	20,126	13,766	16,919	15,718	18,981	15,551	14,803	182,686
1996	22,954	19,960	20,956	27,094	28,271	26,100	19,302	27,792	31,982	32,042	25,236	22,525	304,214
1997	28,561	20,946	21,071	24,624	18,248	24,797	20,308	18,503	21,736	24,416	15,131	21,977	260,318
1998	19,556	20,339	20,881	24,673	20,519	24,112	21,763	20,453	19,412	19,578	22,002	16,559	249,847
1999	25,962	22,184	28,151	22,618	23,835	30,410	30,791	25,683	24,177	18,125	20,802	15,118	287,856
2000	19,871	19,486	18,936	16,136	21,003	18,057	16,636	16,563	19,037	17,155	20,706	17,582	221,168
2001	21,567	15,076	24,561	22,458	23,681	18,878	15,210	16,440	12,882	11,608	11,989	12,490	206,840
2002	15,328	13,239	16,401	13,910	12,427	11,950	12,046	10,154	13,518	13,442	15,828	16,180	164,423
2003	24,241	17,533	17,027	11,573	20,132	21,840	21,097	22,418	22,891	19,387	12,480	13,272	223,891

[1] July 1995 thru March 1996, Lumber and Random Lumber.   *Source: Chicago Mercantile Exchange (CME)*

LUMBER & PLYWOOD

Production of Plywood by Selected Countries   In Thousands of Cubic Meters

Year	Austria	Canada	Finland	France	Germany	Italy	Japan	Poland	Romania	Russia	Spain	Sweden	United States
1996	150	2,114	824	536	512	402	4,421	173	98	666	210	132	18,554
1997	150	2,128	908	539	448	414	NA	226	87	884	210	123	17,554
1998	150	2,049	992	541	428	420	NA	178	76	1,102	382	114	17,468
1999	155	2,229	1,076	546	364	450	NA	223	65	1,324	382	105	17,551
2000	155	2,244	1,096	558	357	450	NA	261	72	1,484	380	110	17,271
2001[1]	186	2,326	1,140	509	321	418	NA	242	79	1,590	380	106	15,417
2002[2]	186	2,475	1,240	549	270	450	NA	270	90	1,808	360	79	15,494

[1] Preliminary.   [2] Estimate.   NA = Not available.   *Source: Food and Agricultural Organization of the United Nations (FAO-UN)*

Imports of Plywood by Selected Countries   In Thousands of Cubic Meters

Year	Austria	Belgium	Canada	Denmark	France	Germany	Italy	Japan	Netherlands	Sweden	Switzerland	United Kingdom	United States
1996	99	586	239	168	347	975	295	5,314	260	150	129	965	1,406
1997	110	684	256	226	353	1,095	312	5,326	394	148	138	967	1,592
1998	121	539	273	302	359	1,105	378	NA	528	147	143	969	1,964
1999	136	530	222	222	365	1,021	367	NA	558	152	150	972	2,494
2000	151	534	230	247	348	1,149	422	NA	594	178	153	1,041	2,385
2001[1]	150	526	520	270	358	1,088	425	NA	601	157	143	1,145	3,010
2002[2]	167	500	490	270	347	935	488	NA	601	152	142	1,139	3,891

[1] Preliminary.   [2] Estimate.   NA = Not available.   *Source: Food and Agricultural Organization of the United Nations (FAO-UN)*

Exports of Plywood by Selected Countries   In Thousands of Cubic Meters

Year	Austria	Baltic States	Belgium	Canada	Finland	France	Germany	Italy	Netherlands	Poland	Russia	Spain	United States
1996	163	187	88	360	618	180	135	117	80	76	382	77	1,135
1997	172	198	101	557	725	201	152	125	68	95	559	77	984
1998	180	NA	371	755	832	222	166	139	56	93	736	331	833
1999	192	NA	403	956	939	243	160	139	51	95	913	220	712
2000	246	NA	380	941	1,006	231	210	146	55	109	974	152	673
2001[1]	297	NA	378	1,030	1,009	200	232	125	57	128	1,032	140	530
2002[2]	288	NA	357	1,056	1,117	188	153	140	57	138	1,157	125	523

[1] Preliminary.   [2] Estimate.   NA = Not available.   *Source: Food and Agricultural Organization of the United Nations (FAO-UN)*

Imports of Industrial Roundwood by Selected Countries   In Thousands of Cubic Meters

Year	Austria	Belgium	Canada	Finland	France	Germany	Italy	Norway	Poland	Portugal	Spain	Sweden	United States
1996	4,451	2,391	6,088	6,575	1,601	1,263	4,936	2,476	393	1,065	1,902	5,018	524
1997	5,277	2,823	6,685	6,734	1,806	1,770	4,504	2,855	288	1,679	2,116	7,655	582
1998	5,113	2,823	6,955	9,235	1,980	2,255	5,223	3,494	371	2,122	4,136	9,172	970
1999	7,093	3,393	6,157	10,160	2,154	2,722	4,952	3,037	590	1,432	3,228	10,280	1,422
2000	8,451	3,992	6,508	9,875	2,012	3,549	5,805	3,315	732	1,340	3,771	11,721	7,038
2001[1]	7,630	4,505	7,557	11,869	1,994	3,493	5,211	2,772	882	1,109	4,128	9,505	6,201
2002[2]	7,225	2,645	7,458	12,586	1,934	2,459	5,277	2,734	726	1,067	4,080	9,544	6,618

[1] Preliminary.   [2] Estimate.   *Source: Food and Agricultural Organization of the United Nations (FAO-UN)*

Exports of Industrial Roundwood by Selected Countries   In Thousands of Cubic Meters

Year	Canada	Czech Republic	Estonia	France	Germany	Hungary	Latvia	Lithuania	Russia	Slovakia	Sweden	Switzerland	United States
1996	955	2,687	1,898	2,227	2,992	555	1,467	952	15,915	529	1,621	979	11,937
1997	701	2,657	2,915	2,282	4,032	701	2,124	765	17,845	850	1,393	1,147	10,864
1998	2,029	2,497	3,792	2,857	4,871	1,204	2,760	792	19,972	714	1,420	1,006	12,290
1999	2,213	2,626	3,903	3,093	4,552	1,079	2,953	938	27,600	1,193	1,315	1,220	11,739
2000	2,903	1,857	4,257	5,522	5,558	1,282	4,190	1,200	30,835	1,550	1,431	3,754	11,952
2001[1]	3,835	2,276	3,482	5,116	4,906	1,227	3,990	1,314	31,693	1,550	1,303	3,149	11,412
2002[2]	4,905	2,302	3,132	3,916	4,427	1,210	4,225	1,420	36,546	1,184	1,747	3,150	11,001

[1] Preliminary.   [2] Estimate.   *Source: Food and Agricultural Organization of the United Nations (FAO-UN)*

164

Magnesium

Magnesium is a silvery-white, light, and fairly tough, metallic element and is relatively stable. Magnesium is one of the alkaline earth metals and has the atomic symbol Mg and atomic number 12. Magnesium is the eighth most abundant element in the earth's crust and the third most plentiful element found in seawater. Magnesium is ductile and malleable when heated, and with the exception of beryllium, is the lightest metal that remains stable under ordinary conditions. First isolated by the British chemist Sir Humphrey Davy in 1808, magnesium today is obtained mainly by electrolysis of fused magnesium chloride.

Magnesium compounds, primarily magnesium oxide, are used in the refractory material that line the furnaces used to produce iron and steel, nonferrous metals, glass, and cement. Magnesium oxide and other compounds are also used in the chemical, agricultural, and construction industries. Magnesium's principal use is as an alloying addition for aluminum. These aluminum-magnesium alloys are used primarily in beverage cans. Due to their lightness and considerable tensile strength, the alloys are also used in structural components in airplanes and automobiles.

Prices – The price of magnesium in 2002 fell into the range of $1.10-1.22 per pound from $1.21-1.28 in 2001. The 2002 level was a 22-year low going back to 1980 when the price range was $1.07-$1.25.

Supply – World primary production of magnesium in 2002 rose slightly by +0.2% to a record high of 429,000 metric tons from 428,000 metric tons in 2001. The world's largest primary producers of magnesium are China with 230,000 metric tons of production in 2002, the US with production of 106,000 metric tons (in the latest data available for 1998), and Canada with 80,000 metric tons.

World secondary production of magnesium in 2001 fell –18% to a 13-year low of 75,700 metric tons from 92,300 metric tons in 2000. The largest secondary producer of magnesium by far is the US with 87% of world production in 2001, followed by Japan with 10.3% of world secondary production. US secondary production of magnesium in 2001 fell 20% to 65,800 metric tons, which is about two-thirds that of US primary production.

Demand – US consumption of magnesium for structural products in 2002 rose +0.6% to 48,302 metric tons from 47,992 metric tons in 2001. Of the structural product consumption category, 96% was for castings and the remaining 4% was for wrought products. US consumption of magnesium for aluminum alloys fell –0.3% to 34,900 metric tons from 35,000 metric tons in 2001. The consumption category for magnesium of "other uses" rose by +1.6% in 2002 to 12,900 metric tons.

Trade – US exports of magnesium in 2002 rose +29.6% to 25,400 metric tons from 19,600 metric tons in 2001, which was a 26-year low going back to 1976. US imports of magnesium in 2002 rose +28.5% to 88,000 metric tons from 68,500 metric tons in 2001.

World Production of Magnesium (Primary and Secondary)   In Metric Tons

| | Primary Production | | | | | | | | Secondary Production | | | | |
Year	Brazil	Canada	China	France	Norway	Russia	United States	World Total	Japan	United Kingdom	United States	Former USSR	World Total
1993	9,700	23,000	11,800	10,982	27,300	30,000	132,000	269,000	13,215	1,000	58,900	6,000	80,700
1994	9,700	28,900	24,000	12,280	27,635	35,400	128,000	282,000	19,009	1,000	62,100	5,000	88,700
1995	9,700	48,100	93,600	14,450	28,000	37,500	142,000	395,000	11,767	1,000	65,100	6,000	85,500
1996	9,000	54,000	73,100	14,000	37,800	35,000	133,000	378,000	8,175	1,000	71,200	6,000	88,000
1997	9,000	57,700	75,990	13,740	34,200	39,500	125,000	384,000	10,934	1,000	77,600	NA	91,100
1998	9,000	77,100	70,500	14,000	35,400	41,500	106,000	396,000	7,807	1,000	77,100	NA	87,500
1999	8,000	73,700	120,000	16,200	40,800	45,000	W	341,000	7,732	500	86,100	NA	96,000
2000	5,700	85,700	190,000	16,500	41,400	45,000	W	428,000	7,900	500	82,300	NA	92,300
2001[1]	5,500	83,400	200,000	4,000	36,000	48,000	W	428,000	7,800	500	65,800	NA	75,700
2002[2]	6,000	80,000	230,000	----	10,000	50,000	W	429,000	----	----	----	----	----

[1] Preliminary.   [2] Estimate.   W = Withheld proprietary data.   *Source: U.S. Geological Survey (USGS)*

Salient Statistics of Magnesium in the United States   In Metric Tons

| | Production | | | | | | | | Domestic Consumption of Primary Magnesium | | | | | |
| | | Secondary | | | | | | | Structural Products | | | | | |
Year	Primary (Ingot)	New Scrap	Old Scrap	Total	Total Exports[3]	Imports for Consumption	Stocks Dec. 31[4]	$ Price Per Pound[5]	Castings	Wrought	Total	Aluminum Alloys	Other Uses[6]	Total
1993	132,144	28,313	30,577	58,890	38,815	37,248	26,000	1.43-1.46	12,543	9,870	22,413	46,498	32,202	78,700
1994	128,000	32,500	29,600	62,100	45,200	29,100	20,030	1.63	15,676	7,690	23,366	61,100	27,900	89,000
1995	142,000	35,400	29,800	65,100	38,300	34,800	21,193	1.93-2.25	15,231	8,510	23,741	60,200	25,100	85,300
1996	133,000	41,100	30,100	71,200	40,500	46,600	25,000	1.70-1.80	16,400	8,080	24,480	52,300	25,500	77,800
1997	125,000	47,000	30,500	77,600	40,500	65,100	23,000	1.60-1.70	20,643	6,840	27,400	50,000	23,000	73,000
1998	106,000	45,200	31,800	77,100	35,400	82,500	27,000	1.52-1.62	27,057	7,100	34,157	52,000	20,900	72,900
1999	W	52,000	34,200	86,100	29,100	90,700	W	1.40-1.55	49,181	9,380	58,561	57,800	14,900	72,700
2000	W	52,200	30,100	82,300	23,800	91,400	W	1.23-1.30	29,457	2,120	31,577	55,400	17,400	72,800
2001[1]	W	38,600	27,200	65,800	19,600	68,500	W	1.21-1.28	44,712	3,280	47,992	35,000	12,700	47,700
2002[2]	W	47,100	26,400	73,600	25,400	88,000	W	1.10-1.22	46,362	1,940	48,302	34,900	12,900	47,800

[1] Preliminary.   [2] Estimate.   [3] Metal & alloys in crude form & scrap.   [4] Estimate of Industry Stocks, metal.   [5] Magnesium ingots (99.8%), f.o.b. Valasco, Texas.   [6] Distributive or sacrificial purposes.   W = Withheld proprietary data.   *Source: U.S. Geological Survey (USGS)*

Manganese

Manganese is a silvery-white, very brittle, metallic element used primarily in making alloys. Its atomic symbol is Mn and its atomic number is 25. Manganese was first distinguished as an element and isolated in 1774 by Johan Gottlieb Gahn. Manganese dissolves in acid and corrodes in moist air.

Manganese is distributed over the world in the form of ores such as rhodochrosite, franklinite, psilomelane, and manganite. Pyrolusite is the principal ore of manganese. Pure manganese is produced by igniting pyrolusite with aluminum powder or by electrolyzing manganese sulfate.

Manganese is used primarily in the steel industry for creating alloys, the most important ones being ferromanganese and spiegeleisen. In steel, manganese improves forging and rolling qualities, strength, toughness, stiffness, wear resistance, and hardness. Manganese is also used in plant fertilizers, animal feed, pigments, and dry cell batteries.

Prices – The average price of ferromanganese (high carbon, FOB plant) in 2001 fell –9.1% to $447.44 per gross ton from $492.40 in 2000. The 2001 price of $447.44 was well below the 10-year average price of $522.73.

Supply – World production of manganese ore in 2001 was unchanged from 2000 at 19.1 million metric tons. That was only moderately above the record low of 17.8 million

metric tons for the data series, which goes back to 1970. The world's largest producers of manganese ore are South Africa with 17.1% of world production in 2001, Ukraine with 14.1%, China with 13.1%, Brazil with 11.5%, and Australia with 10.8%. China's production has dropped sharply in the last several years from 6.0 million metric tons in 1997 to 2.500 million in 2001.

Demand – US consumption of manganese ore in 2001 fell –12.6% to 425,000 metric tons from 486,000 metric tons in 2000. US consumption of ferromanganese in 2001 fell –11.3% to 266,000 metric tons from 300,000 metric tons in 2000.

Trade – The US relies on imports for 100% of its manganese consumption. It has been that way since 1985 when the percentage rose to 100% from 97-99% during the 1970s when the US still produced some manganese. US imports of manganese ore for consumption in 2001 fell –19.9% to 358,000 metric tons from 447,000 metric tons in 2000. US imports of ferromanganese for consumption in 2001 fell -19.6% to 251,000 metric tons from 312,000 metric tons in 2000. US imports of silico-manganese in 2001 fell –17.8% to 310,000 metric tons from 377,000 in 2000. The primary sources of US imports of manganese ore are Gabon with 65.4% of US imports in 2002, followed by South Africa with 19.5%, Australia (8.6%), and Brazil (6.0%).

World Production of Manganese Ore — In Thousands of Metric Tons (Gross Weight)

Year	Australia[2] 37-53[4]	Brazil 30-50	China 30	Gabon 50-53	Georgia 29-30	Ghana 30-50	Hungary[3] 30-33	India 10-54	Mexico 27-50	Morocco 50-53	South Africa 30-48+	Ukraine 29-30	World Total
1993	2,092	1,837	5,860	1,290	300	295	59	1,655	363	43	2,507	3,800	20,500
1994	1,920	2,199	3,570	1,436	150	270	55	1,632	307	31	2,851	2,979	18,000
1995	2,180	2,398	6,900	1,930	100	217	----	1,764	472	----	3,199	3,200	23,300
1996	2,109	2,506	7,600	1,983	97	448	----	1,797	485	----	3,240	3,070	24,300
1997	2,136	2,124	6,000	1,904	----	437	----	1,596	534	----	3,121	3,040	21,900
1998	1,500	1,940	5,300	2,092	----	537	----	1,557	510	----	3,044	2,226	19,900
1999	1,892	1,656	3,190	1,908	----	639	----	1,500	459	----	3,122	1,985	17,800
2000	1,614	1,925	3,500	1,743	----	896	----	1,550	435	----	3,635	2,741	19,600
2001	2,069	1,863	4,300	1,791	----	1,077	----	1,600	277	----	3,266	2,700	20,800
2002[1]	2,187	2,000	4,500	1,856	----	1,136	----	1,700	233	----	3,322	2,736	21,900

[1] Preliminary.   [2] Metallurgical Ore.   [3] Concentrate.   [4] Ranges of percentage of manganese.   *Source: U.S. Geological Survey (USGS)*

Salient Statistics of Manganese in the United States — In Thousands of Metric Tons (Gross Weight)

Year	Net Import Reliance as a % of Apparent Consumption	Manganese Ore (35% or More Manganese) Imports for Consumption	Exports	Consumption	Stocks, Dec. 31[3]	Ferromanganese Imports for Consumption	Exports	Consumption	Avg. Price Mn. Metallurgical Ore $ Lg. Ton Unit[4]	Silicomanganese Exports	Imports
1993	100	232	16	389	302	347	18	341	2.60	9.4	316.0
1994	100	331	15	449	269	336	11	347	2.40	6.8	273.0
1995	100	394	15	486	309	310	11	348	2.40	7.8	305.0
1996	100	478	32	478	319	374	10	326	2.55	5.3	323.0
1997	100	355	84	510	241	304	12	337	2.44	5.4	306.0
1998	100	332	8	499	163	339	14	290	2.40	6.7	346.0
1999	100	460	4	479	172	312	12	281	2.26	3.7	301.0
2000	100	447	10	486	226	312	8	300	2.39	1.9	378.0
2001[1]	100	358	9	425	138	251	9	266	2.44	3.6	269.0
2002[2]	100	427	15	360	151	275	9	253	2.30	0.5	247.0

[1] Preliminary.   [2] Estimate.   [3] Including bonded warehouses; excludes Gov't stocks; also excludes small tonnages of dealers' stocks.   [4] 46-48% Mn, C.I.F. U.S. Ports.   *Source: U.S. Geological Survey (USGS)*

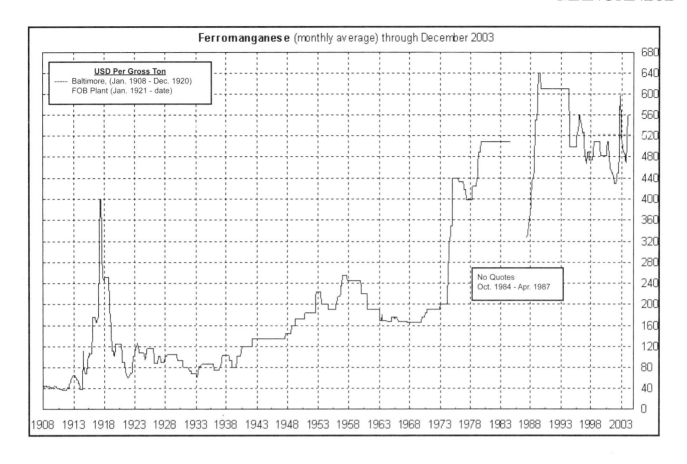

Ferromanganese (monthly average) through December 2003

USD Per Gross Ton
----- Baltimore, (Jan. 1908 - Dec. 1920)
FOB Plant (Jan. 1921 - date)

No Quotes
Oct. 1984 - Apr. 1987

Imports[3] of Manganese Ore (20% or More Mn) in the United States   In Metric Tons (Mn Content)

Year	Australia	Brazil	Gabon	Mexico	Morocco	South Africa	Total	Customs Value Thous. $
1993	30,171	5,573	66,659	7,317	43	6,006	115,770	24,927
1994	23,200	4,530	112,000	13,700	56	7,780	161,000	29,800
1995	31,600	7,080	104,000	23,600	37	13,100	187,000	33,300
1996	48,900	5,640	140,000	16,100	9	20,800	231,000	42,400
1997	16,400	9,100	99,400	30,100	37	----	156,000	30,800
1998	18,700	12,100	94,900	14,600	----	13,800	160,000	27,800
1999	23,500	1	142,000	9,130	----	39,100	224,000	37,200
2000	18,100	3,250	188,000	3,250	----	----	219,000	32,100
2001[1]	18,000	3,480	158,000	1,720	----	17,400	199,000	28,000
2002[2]	18,400	12,900	140,000	1,100	----	41,800	214,000	29,200

[1] Preliminary.   [2] Estimate.   [3] Imports for consumption.   *Source: U.S. Geological Survey (USGS)*

Average Price of Ferromanganese   In Dollars Per Gross Ton

Year	Jan.	Feb.	Mar.	Apr.	May	June	July	Aug.	Sept.	Oct.	Nov.	Dec.	Average
1994	610.00	610.00	610.00	610.00	610.00	527.50	500.00	500.00	500.00	500.00	500.00	500.00	548.13
1995	500.00	500.00	500.00	500.00	500.00	500.00	500.00	518.75	525.00	525.00	542.50	560.00	514.27
1996	560.00	552.50	550.00	550.00	541.00	535.00	533.13	527.50	527.50	527.50	501.25	477.50	531.91
1997	477.50	467.50	470.00	482.50	490.00	490.00	490.00	492.50	475.00	475.00	475.00	475.00	480.00
1998	175.00	175.00	175.00	190.00	190.00	510.00	510.00	510.00	510.00	510.00	510.00	510.00	497.92
1999	510.00	510.00	510.00	510.00	510.00	498.75	482.50	482.50	482.50	482.50	482.50	482.50	495.21
2000	482.50	482.50	482.50	482.50	482.50	482.50	501.63	505.00	509.00	510.00	510.00	477.50	492.40
2001	473.93	467.89	460.00	454.29	450.00	450.00	446.90	444.57	430.79	430.00	430.00	430.00	447.44
2002	430.00	430.00	437.14	447.73	449.55	456.75	481.82	556.14	597.00	589.67	552.89	518.93	495.64
2003	509.52	510.00	502.38	497.61	492.50	481.79	477.27	470.00	478.57	497.83	516.67	559.76	499.49

Domestic standard, high carbon, FOB plant, carloads.   *Source: American Metal Market (AMM)*

Meats

US commercial red meat includes beef, veal, lamb, and pork. Red meat is a good source of iron, vitamin B12, and protein, and eliminating it from the diet can lead to iron and zinc deficiencies. Today, red meat is far leaner than it was 30 years ago due to newer breeds of livestock that carry less fat. The leanest cuts of beef include tenderloin, sirloin, and flank. The leanest cuts of pork include pork tenderloin, loin chops, and rib chops.

The USDA (United States Department of Agriculture) grades various cuts of meat. "Prime" is the highest USDA grade for beef, veal, and lamb. "Choice" is the grade designation below Prime for beef, veal, and lamb. "Commercial" and "Cutter" grades are one of the lower designations for beef, usually sold as ground meat, sausage, and canned meat. "Canner" is the lowest USDA grade designation for beef and is used primarily in canned meats not sold at retail.

Supply – World meat production is led by China with 49.800 million metric tons of production in 2003, up 2.5% from 48.600 million metric tons in 2002. US meat production is the second largest in the world at 20.501 million metric tons in 2003, down –3.8% from 21.306 million metric tons in 2002. Brazil is the third largest producer with 9.815 million metric tons in 2003, up 3.4% from 9.492 million metric tons in 2002.

US meat production involves mostly the production of beef which accounts for 56.5% of red meat production in 2003. Pork accounts for 42.6% of red meat production. Veal accounts for only 0.4% and lamb and mutton account for only 0.5% of US red meat production.

Demand – US consumption of red meats in 2003 fell to 46.269 billion pounds from 47.596 billion pounds in 2002. US per capita consumption of red meat in 2003 was 116.0 pounds per year per person, down from 121.0 pounds in 2002 showing the trend toward healthier foods. Per capital red meat consumption in 2003 was an all-time record low for Americans going back to the beginning of data availability in 1970. The break-down on the per capita red meat consumption figures show per capita consumption of 64.0 pounds of beef (a record low), 1.0 pound of veal, 1.0 pound of lamb and mutton, and 50.0 pounds of pork (matching the record low posted in 2001).

Trade – The world's largest importers of red meat are Japan with 2.010 million metric tons, the US with 1.990 million metric tons, and Russia with 1.450 million metric tons. The world's largest exporters of red meat are the US with 1.874 million metric tons of exports, Australia with 1.583 million metric tons, Canada with 1.415 metric tons, and Brazil with 1.355 million metric tons. Brazil's export figures have been rising sharply, having more than quadrupled from 6 years ago. The US export figure of 1.874 million metric tons of exports in 2003 were an all-time record high.

World Total Meat Production[3]   In Thousands of Metric Tons

Year	Argentina	Australia	Brazil	Canada	China[4]	France	Germany	Italy	Mexico	Russia	United Kingdom	United States	World Total
1996	2,636	2,650	7,750	2,223	36,947	3,973	5,161	2,668	2,832	4,487	2,088	19,634	123,100
1997	3,033	2,914	7,590	2,332	42,500	4,046	5,053	2,632	2,875	4,086	2,183	19,667	128,993
1998	2,648	2,973	7,830	2,487	45,982	4,065	5,244	2,595	2,852	3,775	2,367	20,541	134,134
1999	2,890	2,940	8,105	2,788	47,670	4,086	5,532	2,707	2,999	3,544	2,238	20,994	138,496
2000	2,928	2,986	8,530	2,884	48,292	3,966	5,331	2,692	3,045	3,494	2,134	20,992	138,658
2001	2,640	2,428	9,125	2,979	47,333	3,740	5,195	2,475	2,990	3,320	1,642	20,674	132,116
2002	2,700	2,496	9,805	3,149	49,112	NA	NA	NA	3,015	3,370	NA	21,356	137,063
2003[1]	2,650	2,307	10,130	3,120	50,120	NA	NA	NA	3,050	3,405	NA	21,157	136,993
2004[2]	2,750	2,325	10,520	3,370	51,198	NA	NA	NA	3,070	3,400	NA	20,627	138,350

[1] Preliminary.   [2] Forecast.   [3] Data through 2000, includes beef, veal, pork, sheep and goat meat. Beginning 2001, excludes sheep and goat.
[4] Predominately pork production.   *Source: Foreign Agricultural Service, U.S. Department of Agriculture (FAS-USDA)*

Production and Consumption of Red Meats in The United States

	Beef			Veal			Lamb & Mutton			Pork (Excluding Lard)			All Meats		
	Commercial Production	Consumption		Commercial Production	Consumption		Commercial Production	Consumption		Commercial Production	Consumption		Commercial Production	Consumption	
		Total	Per Capita		Total	Per Capita		Total	Per Capita		Total	Per Capita		Total	Per Capita
Year	-- Million Pounds --		Lbs.[4]	- Million Pounds -		Lbs.[4]	- Million Pounds -		Lbs.[4]	-- Million Pounds --		Lbs.[4]	-- Million Pounds --		Lbs.[4]
1996	25,419	25,863	97.4	378	378	1.4	268	334	1.1	17,117	16,795	63.3	43,182	43,370	163.2
1997	25,490	25,611	95.9	334	333	1.2	260	332	1.1	17,274	16,823	61.4	43,358	43,099	159.6
1998	25,760	26,305	93.3	262	265	1.0	251	360	1.0	19,011	18,309	65.3	45,284	45,239	160.6
1999	26,493	26,936	68.0	235	235	1.0	248	358	1.0	19,308	18,954	53.0	46,284	46,483	122.0
2000	26,888	27,338	68.0	225	225	1.0	234	354	1.0	18,952	18,643	51.0	46,299	46,560	121.0
2001	26,212	27,026	66.0	205	204	1.0	227	368	1.0	19,160	18,492	50.0	45,804	46,089	118.0
2002[1]	27,192	27,878	68.0	205	204	1.0	223	383	1.0	19,685	17,147	52.0	47,305	47,612	121.0
2003[2]	26,402	26,869	65.0	198	200	1.0	204	355	1.0	19,890	19,424	52.0	46,694	46,848	118.0
2004[3]	25,505	26,285	62.0	197	197	1.0	198	356	1.0	19,772	19,452	51.0	45,672	46,270	115.0

[1] Preliminary.   [2] Estimate.   [3] Forecast.   [4] Data through 1998, are for Carcass weight. Beginning 1998, data are for Retail-weight basis.
Source: Economic Research Service, U.S. Department of Agriculture (ERS-USDA)

Total Red Meat Imports[3] (Carcass Weight Equivalent) of Principal Countries   In Thousands of Metric Tons

Year	Canada	France	Germany	Hong Kong	Italy	Japan	Rep. of Korea	Nether-lands	Russia	Singa-pore	United Kingdom	United States	Total
1995	283	39	150	223	37	1,840	239	25	1,084	28	294	1,284	6,465
1996	270	44	139	195	61	1,993	271	31	1,584	38	276	1,249	6,452
1997	303	47	132	217	64	1,767	303	56	1,951	36	293	1,383	6,707
1998	296	44	125	267	57	1,784	191	32	1,429	31	255	1,557	6,645
1999	319	53	135	284	61	1,980	398	25	1,705	39	250	1,729	6,405
2000	331	53	138	319	61	2,110	498	21	1,033	38	260	1,865	8,465
2001	390	19	72	332	56	2,065	369	32	1,210	32	164	1,866	7,984
2002	407	NA	NA	350	NA	1,832	575	NA	1,338	NA	NA	1,939	5,228
2003[1]	385	NA	NA	370	NA	1,975	580	NA	1,410	NA	NA	1,801	5,151
2004[2]	250	NA	NA		NA	885	435	NA	705	NA	NA	1,556	5,462

[1] Preliminary.   [2] Forecast.   [3] Data through 2000, includes beef, veal, pork, sheep and goat meat. Beginning 2001, excludes sheep and goat.
Source: Foreign Agricultural Service, U.S. Department of Agriculture (FAS-USDA)

Total Red Meat Exports[3] (Carcass Weight Equivalent) of Principal Countries   In Thousands of Metric Tons

Year	Argentina	Australia	Brazil	Canada	China	Denmark	France	India	Ireland	Nether-lands	New Zealand	United States	World Total
1995	522	1,374	320	576	328	399	302	206	367	136	864	1,186	8,219
1996	498	1,311	304	703	280	387	290	220	305	195	861	1,294	8,361
1997	460	1,465	314	802	267	531	282	231	271	202	979	1,446	9,003
1998	304	1,596	411	860	242	490	214	263	308	150	956	1,546	8,898
1999	360	1,671	573	1,046	141	594	333	236	369	209	892	1,677	10,065
2000	358	1,762	655	1,181	133	590	222	376	284	214	905	1,705	10,022
2001	168	1,464	1,085	1,302	199	555	185	370	77	147	516	1,737	8,924
2002	348	1,444	1,281	1,410	269	NA	NA	416	NA	NA	503	1,819	6,386
2003[1]	330	1,333	1,570	1,240	240	NA	NA	465	NA	NA	535	1,918	6,400
2004[2]	350	1,300	1,370	615	38	NA	NA	520	NA	NA	535	1,207	6,934

[1] Preliminary.   [2] Forecast.   [3] Data through 2000, includes beef, veal, pork, sheep and goat meat. Beginning 2001, excludes sheep and goat.
Source: Foreign Agricultural Service, U.S. Department of Agriculture (FAS-USDA)

United States Meat Imports by Type of Product   In Metric Tons

Year	Beef and Veal Fresh	Beef and Veal Frozen	Beef and Veal Other Prepared or Preserved	Lamb, Mutton and Goat, Except Canned	Pork Fresh and Chilled	Pork Frozen	Pork Other Prepared or Preserved	Variety Meats, Fresh, hilled and Frozen	Other Livestock Meats NSE	Total
1993	157,471	561,906	73,880	24,468	126,831	80,821	94,238	25,400	13,371	1,158,385
1994	179,121	535,328	74,704	23,276	130,648	78,378	94,013	27,511	13,012	1,155,990
1995	175,540	466,378	65,399	29,844	133,101	61,286	79,155	26,081	12,539	1,049,324
1996	227,874	412,805	66,719	33,009	125,220	58,336	72,650	32,579	13,744	1,042,934
1997	262,985	469,949	63,181	37,848	126,061	65,000	72,903	44,317	14,215	1,156,457
1998	295,820	527,063	68,884	51,630	146,965	70,227	76,230	47,031	13,058	1,296,907
1999	337,899	542,524	82,669	50,209	188,556	77,638	84,207	51,640	13,625	1,428,966
2000	336,117	608,737	73,750	59,968	229,395	91,446	92,672	57,388	14,281	1,563,753
2001[1]	368,529	618,897	73,713	66,785	240,275	84,687	83,724	62,541	16,723	1,615,873

[1] Preliminary.   NSE = Not specified elsewhere.   *Source: Foreign Agricultural Service, U.S. Department of Agriculture (FAS-USDA)*

United States Meat Exports by Type of Product   In Metric Tons

Year	Beef and Veal Fresh and Chilled	Beef and Veal Frozen	Beef and Veal Prepared and Preserved	Lamb and Mutton, Fresh or Frozen	Pork Fresh and Chilled	Pork Frozen	Pork Prepared and Preserved	Variety Meats, Fresh, Chilled or Frozen	Other Meats	Total
1993	181,282	229,353	14,477	3,608	59,479	69,562	19,230	356,232	234,899	1,168,121
1994	242,391	275,067	13,419	3,766	80,609	68,805	27,960	394,740	301,112	1,407,868
1995	262,381	319,416	13,651	2,511	100,235	127,835	35,766	465,919	353,207	1,680,921
1996	273,276	324,329	14,577	2,478	101,975	166,058	38,481	495,075	434,759	1,851,007
1997	316,534	359,460	15,227	2,545	134,684	151,121	38,301	469,233	435,258	1,922,362
1998	346,403	352,050	17,966	2,528	147,006	209,134	43,789	495,495	423,980	2,038,352
1999	370,184	414,458	19,323	2,219	160,910	225,492	47,898	522,994	455,561	2,219,038
2000	395,588	417,538	21,791	2,184	208,055	185,241	44,836	600,241	503,942	2,379,414
2001[1]	393,105	362,972	23,932	2,770	227,807	247,461	52,788	682,261	513,969	2,507,064

[1] Preliminary.   *Source: Foreign Agricultural Service, U.S. Department of Agriculture (FAS-USDA)*

MEATS

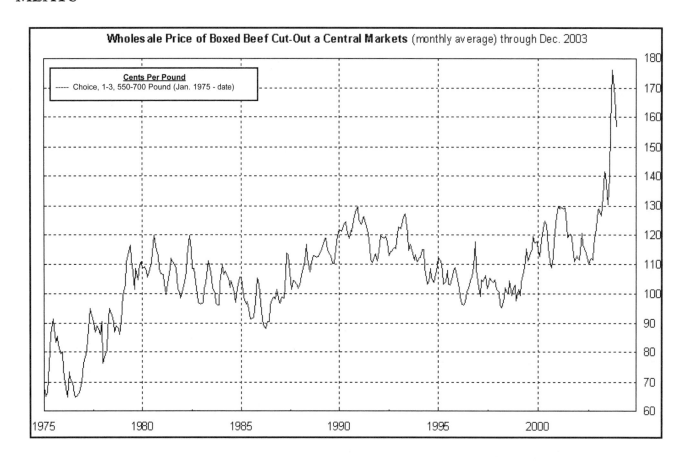

Wholesale Price of Boxed Beef Cut-Out a Central Markets (monthly average) through Dec. 2003

Cents Per Pound
----- Choice, 1-3, 550-700 Pound (Jan. 1975 - date)

Exports and Imports of Meats in the United States (Carcass Weight Equivalent)[4]   In Millions of Pounds

	Exports				Imports			
Year	Beef and Veal	Lamb and Mutton	Pork[4]	All Meat	Beef and Veal	Lamb and Mutton	Pork[4]	All Meat
1994	1,611	9	549	2,169	2,369	49	743	3,161
1995	1,821	6	787	2,614	2,103	64	664	2,832
1996	1,877	6	970	2,853	2,073	73	620	2,764
1997	2,136	5	1,044	3,185	2,343	83	634	3,061
1998	2,171	6	1,229	3,407	2,643	112	705	3,461
1999	2,410	5	1,278	3,693	2,873	112	827	3,812
2000	2,468	6	1,287	3,761	3,031	130	967	4,128
2001	2,269	7	1,559	3,835	3,163	146	951	4,260
2002[1]	2,447	7	1,614	4,068	3,218	160	1,071	4,449
2003[2]	2,565	5	1,645	4,215	3,305	172	1,080	4,557

[1] Preliminary.   [2] Estimate.   [3] Forecast.   [4] Includes meat content of minor meats and of mixed products.   *Source: Economic Research Service, U.S. Department of Agriculture (FAS-USDA)*

Average Wholesale Prices of Meats in the United States   In Cents Per Pound

	Composite Retail Price		Wholesale Value[4]		Net Farm Value of Pork[5]	Cow Beef Canner & Cutter, Central US	Boxed Beef Cut-out, Choice 1-3, Central US, 550-700 Lbs.	Pork Carcass Cut-out, US No. 2	Lamb Carcass, Choice-Prime, East Coast, 55-65 Lbs.	Pork Loins, Central US, 14-18 Lbs.	Skinned Ham, Central US, 20-26 Lbs.	Pork Bellies, Central US, 12-14 Lbs.
Year	of Beef, Choice, Grade 3	of Pork[3]	Beef	Pork								
1995	284.30	194.80	163.90	98.80	66.70	68.22	106.68	59.98	163.45	107.74	58.56	43.04
1996	280.20	220.90	158.10	117.20	84.60	58.18	103.09	72.39	177.58	118.49	72.41	69.97
1997	279.53	231.54	----	----	----	64.30	103.26	70.87	178.99	108.06	62.75	71.41
1998	277.12	239.18	----	----	----	61.33	99.82	52.80	156.75	99.75	44.75	51.94
1999	287.77	241.44	----	----	----	66.51	111.06	53.45	170.29	100.38	45.18	57.12
2000	306.42	258.19	----	----	----	72.57	117.51	64.07	177.78	117.13	52.02	77.46
2001	337.78	269.38	----	----	----	79.50	122.61	66.83	148.96	116.97	56.86	78.61
2002[1]	331.54	265.76	----	----	----	NA	114.42	53.49	151.28	97.98	41.14	69.91
2003[2]	374.62	265.82	----	----	----	NA	143.58	58.87	185.21	100.96	45.48	86.42

[1] Preliminary.   [2] Estimate.   [3] Sold as retail cuts (ham, bacon, loin, etc.).   [4] Quantity equivalent to 1 pound of retail cuts.   [5] Portion of gross farm value minus farm by-product allowance.   *Source: Economic Research Service, U.S. Department of Agriculture (ERS-USDA)*

Average Wholesale Price of Boxed Beef Cut-Out[1], Choice, at Central Markets   In Cents Per Pound

Year	Jan.	Feb.	Mar.	Apr.	May	June	July	Aug.	Sept.	Oct.	Nov.	Dec.	Average
1994	112.11	112.23	115.03	114.98	108.85	102.92	104.19	108.38	105.49	103.63	106.66	107.22	108.47
1995	112.17	111.12	107.87	103.03	104.21	107.65	103.03	102.55	105.82	107.77	108.88	106.08	106.68
1996	101.71	98.86	96.36	96.01	96.90	100.70	101.53	104.43	105.93	109.10	117.53	108.03	103.09
1997	101.90	98.98	104.87	104.17	105.97	101.83	102.38	105.14	104.06	103.72	104.63	101.50	103.26
1998	100.26	96.27	95.34	98.32	102.09	100.38	99.96	104.28	99.28	102.08	102.61	97.49	99.86
1999	101.37	99.37	103.62	107.55	110.89	115.39	111.14	114.00	115.13	119.21	117.38	117.71	111.05
2000	114.74	112.59	118.42	123.45	124.88	123.30	115.85	111.20	108.68	112.58	118.05	126.41	117.51
2001	129.78	128.87	129.58	128.93	129.03	126.82	118.93	120.20	119.30	115.93	110.95	113.04	122.61
2002	111.99	111.53	120.54	116.61	115.14	114.06	109.88	110.93	111.83	111.64	116.41	122.45	114.42
2003[2]	128.59	128.77	126.35	133.03	141.44	141.16	130.13	139.91	156.64	176.06	167.15	153.71	143.58

[1] Choice 1-3, 550-700 pounds.   [2] Preliminary.   *Source: Economic Research Service, U.S. Department of Agriculture (ERS-USDA)*

Production (Commercial) of All Red Meats in the United States   In Millions of Pounds (Carcass Weight)

Year	Jan.	Feb.	Mar.	Apr.	May	June	July	Aug.	Sept.	Oct.	Nov.	Dec.	Total
1994	3,366	3,126	3,591	3,382	3,431	3,615	3,361	3,756	3,720	3,795	3,666	3,714	42,523
1995	3,560	3,210	3,751	3,304	3,758	3,798	3,424	3,860	3,697	3,795	3,748	3,553	43,458
1996	3,823	3,519	3,512	3,690	3,767	3,439	3,585	3,707	3,396	3,827	3,435	3,432	43,132
1997	3,735	3,278	3,444	3,592	3,571	3,492	3,657	3,619	3,665	4,005	3,453	3,715	43,226
1998	3,836	3,476	3,726	3,701	3,582	3,732	3,781	3,770	3,827	4,033	3,725	3,945	45,134
1999	3,833	3,535	4,016	3,824	3,604	3,940	3,781	3,913	3,933	4,002	3,895	3,862	46,138
2000	3,784	3,767	4,044	3,460	3,878	3,941	3,644	4,113	3,861	4,096	3,919	3,619	46,126
2001	3,935	3,761	3,761	3,506	3,881	3,758	3,643	4,060	3,664	4,264	3,970	3,813	46,016
2002	4,081	3,501	3,677	3,902	4,018	3,813	4,016	4,141	3,873	4,382	3,908	3,859	47,171
2003[1]	4,075	3,496	3,705	3,845	3,944	3,948	4,046	3,913	4,007	4,155	3,524	3,876	46,534

[1] Preliminary.   *Source: Economic Research Service, U.S. Department of Agriculture (ERS-USDA)*

Cold Storage Holdings of All[2] Meats in the United States, on First of Month   In Millions of Pounds

Year	Jan.	Feb.	Mar.	Apr.	May	June	July	Aug.	Sept.	Oct.	Nov.	Dec.
1994	726.7	807.7	800.5	842.5	858.0	837.5	822.6	816.2	771.9	788.5	822.7	827.5
1995	802.0	838.7	833.8	834.0	852.7	831.2	820.8	803.6	733.4	711.3	732.3	757.0
1996	749.7	779.5	781.6	729.3	748.6	716.2	687.9	642.7	657.4	678.4	655.5	627.1
1997	621.3	655.9	669.9	719.5	752.5	719.7	742.9	726.3	731.5	728.2	739.1	741.0
1998	722.4	802.8	825.8	816.3	849.3	814.3	771.0	747.2	728.2	738.8	794.9	794.1
1999	821.0	833.0	863.1	883.5	936.4	901.2	843.9	810.4	834.9	746.3	780.3	750.5
2000	748.3	853.1	913.9	934.3	951.3	963.5	926.7	896.2	881.0	871.1	868.0	883.0
2001	836.2	907.8	852.6	787.9	771.4	772.5	742.2	717.4	732.6	775.3	849.0	880.9
2002	946.8	982.6	970.7	961.9	996.6	973.0	918.0	912.6	950.7	997.8	1,038.9	997.7
2003[1]	1,011.5	1,015.2	978.5	951.9	926.7	901.5	842.5	825.0	817.3	832.2	836.9	828.1

[1] Preliminary.   [2] Includes beef and veal, mutton and lamb, pork and products, rendered pork fat, and miscellaneous meats. Excludes lard.
Source: Economic Research Service, U.S. Department of Agriculture (ERS-USDA)

Cold Storage Holdings of Frozen Beef in the United States, on First of Month   In Millions of Pounds

Year	Jan. 1	Feb. 1	Mar. 1	Apr. 1	May 1	June 1	July 1	Aug. 1	Sept. 1	Oct. 1	Nov. 1	Dec. 1
1994	401.0	430.2	414.4	423.2	399.5	367.9	379.4	388.9	377.2	406.8	410.6	419.5
1995	411.2	420.3	407.7	385.4	392.2	359.1	352.3	359.3	344.9	347.7	381.6	381.4
1996	389.6	367.9	362.6	347.3	335.6	307.4	306.7	291.1	305.2	312.2	295.9	288.1
1997	284.9	290.3	261.7	290.4	285.4	278.7	305.6	302.8	324.6	349.1	351.6	378.2
1998	350.2	331.1	334.9	329.7	335.5	310.2	316.5	303.0	306.7	323.1	358.2	328.2
1999	296.4	301.1	300.1	309.2	316.8	306.7	293.1	292.7	377.9	294.4	322.5	308.9
2000	314.2	350.9	369.0	378.2	396.1	401.1	405.1	391.5	398.8	405.7	404.4	411.8
2001	401.7	410.9	360.2	332.6	315.3	325.1	340.8	351.4	373.2	382.8	395.1	427.6
2002	460.7	455.5	439.0	410.5	405.7	401.8	396.9	416.5	461.8	494.9	525.2	512.6
2003[1]	524.6	482.4	442.1	403.1	389.6	385.1	371.5	368.2	371.0	379.8	375.2	373.8

[1] Preliminary.   *Source: Economic Research Service, U.S. Department of Agriculture (ERS-USDA)*

Mercury

Mercury was known to the ancient Hindus and Chinese, and was also found in Egyptian tombs dating back to the 1500s BC. The ancient Greeks used Mercury in ointments, and the Romans used it in cosmetics. Alchemists thought mercury turned into gold when it hardened.

Mercury, also called quicksilver, is a heavy, silvery, toxic, transitional metal. Mercury is the only common metal that is liquid at room temperatures. When subjected to a pressure of 7,640 atmospheres (7.7 million millibars), mercury becomes a solid. Mercury dissolves in nitric or concentrated sulfuric acid, but is resistant to alkalis. It is a poor conductor of heat. Mercury has superconductivity when cooled to sufficiently low temperatures. It has a freezing point of about –39 degrees Celsius and a boiling point of about 357 degrees Celsius. The atomic symbol for mercury is Hg and its atomic number is 80.

Mercury is found in its pure form or combined in small amounts with silvers, but is found most often in the ore cinnabar, a mineral consisting of mercuric sulfide. By heating the cinnabar ore in air until the mercuric sulfide breaks down, pure mercury metal is produced. Mercury forms alloys called amalgams with all common metals except iron and platinum. Most mercury produced is used for the manufacture of industrial chemicals and for electrical and electronic applications. Other uses for mercury include its use in gold recovery from ores, barometers, diffusion pumps, laboratory instruments, mercury-vapor lamps, pesticides, batteries, and catalysts. A decline in mercury production and usage since the 1970s reflects a trend for using mercury substitutes due to its toxicity.

Prices – The average free market price of mercury in 2003 rose sharply by 19.5% from 2002 to a 6-year high of $184.07 per flask (34.5 kilograms). That was right on the 10-year average price.

Supply – World mine production of mercury in 2002 rose +20.8% to 1,800 metric tons from 1,490 metric tons in 2001. The world's largest miners of mercury are Algeria with 44.4% of world production in 2002, followed by Spain (16.7%), and China and Kyrgyzstan (both with 13.9%). World mercury resources are estimated in excess of 500,000 tons, mostly in Kyrgyzstan and Spain, which if accurate, suggests a potential supply sufficient to last at least a century, based on declining world usage rates.

Demand – The breakdown of domestic consumption of mercury by particular categories is no longer available, but the data as of 1997 showed that chlorine and caustic soda accounted for 46% of US mercury consumption, followed by wiring devices and switches (17%), dental equipment (12%), electrical lighting (8%), and measuring control instruments (7%). Substitutes for mercury include lithium and composite ceramic materials.

Trade – US foreign trade in mercury is small. US imports of mercury in 2002 more than doubled to 209 metric tons from 100 metric tons in 2001. At the same time, the US exported 201 metric tons of mercury in 2002, up from 108 metric tons in 2000. The imports were mostly from Chile and Peru. Exports are scattered, but India and the Netherlands were generally the largest takers.

World Mine Production of Mercury   In Metric Tons (1 tonne = 29.008216 flasks)

Year	Algeria	China	Finland	Kyrgyz-stan	Mexico	Spain	Tajik-istan	Turkey	Ukraine	United States	World Total
1994	414	470	83	379	12	393	55	----	50	W	1,960
1995	292	780	90	380	15	1,497	50	----	40	W	3,190
1996	368	510	88	584	15	862	45	----	30	W	2,560
1997	447	830	63	550	15	389	40	----	25	W	2,410
1998	224	230	54	250	15	675	35	----	20	NA	1,580
1999	240	200	40	300	15	433	35	----	NA	NA	1,310
2000	216	200	76	257	15	500	40	----	NA	NA	1,350
2001[1]	320	190	71	300	15	500	40	----	----	NA	1,490
2002[2]	800	250	70	250	15	300	20	----	----	NA	1,800

[1] Preliminary. [2] Estimate. W = Withheld to avoid disclosing company proprietary data. NA = Not available. *Source: U.S. Geological Survey (USGS)*

Salient Statistics of Mercury in the United States   In Metric Tons

Year	Priducing Mines	Secondary Production Industrial	Secondary Production Government[3]	NDS[4] Shipments	Consumer & Dealer Stocks, Dec. 31	Industrial Demand	Exports	Imports
1994	7	466	----	86	469	483	316	129
1995	8	534	----	----	321	436	179	377
1996	6	446	----	----	446	372	45	340
1997	5	389	----	----	203	346	134	164
1998	NA	NA	----	----	NA	NA	63	128
1999	NA	NA	----	----	NA	NA	181	62
2000	NA	NA	----	----	NA	NA	182	103
2001[1]	NA	NA	----	----	NA	NA	108	100
2002[2]	NA	NA	----	----	NA	NA	201	209

[1] Preliminary. [2] Estimate. [3] Secondary mercury shipped from the Department of Energy. [4] National Defense Stockpile. NA = Not available.
Source: U.S. Geological Survey (USGS)

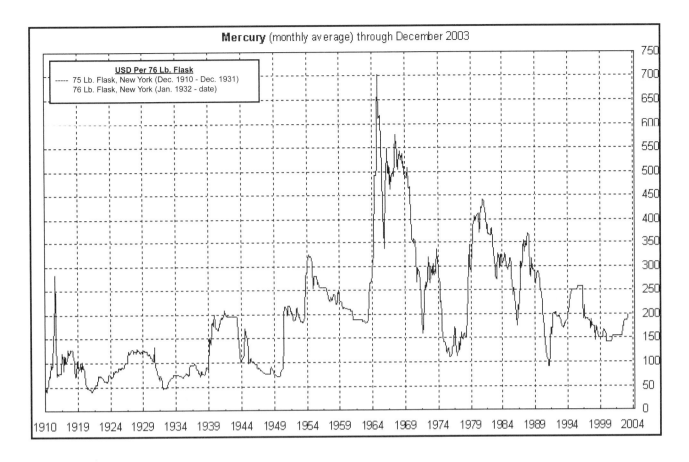

Mercury (monthly average) through December 2003

USD Per 76 Lb. Flask
------ 75 Lb. Flask, New York (Dec. 1910 - Dec. 1931)
     76 Lb. Flask, New York (Jan. 1932 - date)

Average Price of Mercury in New York   In Dollars Per Flask of 76 Pounds (34.5 Kilograms)

Year	Jan.	Feb.	Mar.	Apr.	May	June	July	Aug.	Sept.	Oct.	Nov.	Dec.	Average
1994	175.00	175.00	179.78	180.00	180.95	186.64	196.50	200.00	203.10	205.00	217.50	230.71	194.18
1995	235.00	240.00	241.30	250.00	250.00	250.00	250.00	250.00	250.00	250.00	250.00	250.00	247.19
1996	250.00	250.00	261.67	268.33	265.00	265.00	265.00	265.00	265.00	265.00	262.63	235.48	259.84
1997	233.98	232.76	228.88	228.64	220.00	199.05	200.00	198.10	190.83	198.83	191.47	187.00	209.13
1998	187.00	187.00	187.00	187.00	187.00	181.55	175.00	175.00	175.00	175.00	175.00	175.00	180.55
1999	175.00	152.63	150.00	150.00	150.00	150.00	150.00	150.00	150.00	150.00	150.00	150.00	152.09
2000	150.00	157.88	167.50	167.50	167.50	158.23	142.00	142.00	142.00	142.00	142.00	142.00	151.90
2001	142.00	142.00	142.00	142.00	142.00	143.71	154.00	154.00	154.00	154.00	154.00	154.00	148.12
2002	154.00	154.00	154.00	154.00	154.00	154.00	154.00	154.00	154.00	154.00	154.00	154.00	154.00
2003	165.43	175.00	175.00	175.00	185.23	187.50	187.50	187.50	187.50	187.50	195.63	200.00	184.07

Source: American Metal Market (AMM)

Mercury Consumed in the United States   In Metric Tons

Year	Batteries[3]	Chlorine & Caustic Soda	Catalysts, Misc.	Dental Equip.	Electrical Lighting[3]	General Lab Use	Measuring Contraol Instrument	Paints	Wiring Devices & Switches[3]	Other Uses	Total
1988	448	354	86	53	31	26	77	197	176	55	1,503
1989	250	379	40	39	31	18	87	192	141	32	1,212
1990	106	247	29	44	33	32	108	14	70	38	720
1991	18	184	26	41	39	30	90	6	71	49	554
1992	13	209	20	42	55	28	80	-----	82	92	621
1993	10	180	18	35	38	26	65	-----	83	103	558
1994	6	135	25	24	27	24	53	-----	79	110	483
1995	-----	154	-----	32	30	-----	43	-----	84	93	436
1996[1]	-----	136	-----	31	29	-----	41	-----	49	86	372
1997[2]	-----	160	-----	40	29	-----	24	-----	57	36	346

[1] Preliminary.   [2] Estimate.   W = Withheld proprietary data.   *Source: U.S. Geological Survey (USGS)*

Milk

Evidence of man's use of animal milk as food was discovered in a temple in the Euphrates Valley near Babylon, dating back to 3,000 BC. Humans drink the milk produced from a variety of domesticated mammals, including cows, goats, sheep, camels, reindeer, buffaloes, and llama. In India, half of all milk consumed is from water buffalo. Camels' milk spoils slower than other types of milk in the hot desert. But the vast majority of milk used for commercial production and consumption comes from cows.

Milk directly from a cow in its natural form is called raw milk. Raw milk is processed by spinning it in a centrifuge, homogenizing it to create a consistent texture (i.e., by forcing hot milk under high pressure through small nozzles), and then sterilizing it through pasteurization (i.e., heating to a high temperature for a specified length of time to destroy pathogenic bacteria). Condensed, powdered, and evaporated milk are produced by evaporating some or all of the water content. Whole milk contains 3.5% milk fat. Lower-fat milks include 2% low-fat milk, 1% low-fat milk, and skim milk, which has only 1/2 gram of milk fat per serving.

The Chicago Mercantile Exchange has three different milk futures contracts: Milk Class III which is milk used in the manufacturing of cheese, Milk Class IV which is milk used in the production of butter and all dried milk products, and Nonfat Dry Milk which is used in commercial or consumer cooking or to reconstitute nonfat milk by the consumer. The Milk Class III contract has the largest volume and open interest.

Prices – The average price received by farmers of all milk sold to plants was $12.51 per hundred pounds in 2003, up from $12.10 in 2002 but well below the record $15.43 in 1998. The average price received by farmers for fluid grade milk averaged $12.53 per hundred pounds in 2003, up from $12.10 in 2002 but much lower than the record high of $15.47 posted in 1998. The average price received by farmers for manufacturing grade milk was $11.73 per hundred pounds in 2003, up from $10.92 in 2002 but below the record of $14.36 in 1998.

Supply – India is the world's largest producer of milk with 85.000 million metric tons of production in 2003. The second and third largest producers are the US with 77.970 million metric tons of production and Russia with 33.200 million metric tons. US milk production in 2003 was forecast at 169.684 billion pounds, slightly below the 2002 level of 169.8 billion pounds.

The number of dairy cows on US farms has fallen in the past 3 decades from the 12 million level seen in 1970, but has stabilized in the past 6 years in the range of 9.1-9.2 million. Dairy farmers have been able to increase milk production even with fewer cows because of a dramatic increase in milk yield per cow. In 2002, the average cow produced 18,573 pounds of milk per year, up sharply by 26% from 14,782 pounds in 1990, by 56% from 11,891 pounds in 1980, and by 90% from 9,751 pounds in 1970.

Demand – Per capita consumption of milk has fallen in the past several decades and hit 208 pounds per year in 2001, down fairly sharply from 233 pounds in 1990 and 277 pounds in 1970.

Trade – US imports of milk totaled 4.888 billion pounds in 2003, down from 5.104 billion in 2002.

World Fluid Milk Production (Cow's Milk)   In Thousands of Metric Tons

Year	Brazil	France	Germany	India	Italy	Nether-lands	New Zealand	Poland	Russia	Ukraine	United Kingdom	United States	World Total
1996	19,480	25,795	28,776	69,000	11,621	11,023	10,405	11,720	35,800	16,000	14,672	69,857	364,321
1997	20,600	24,893	28,702	72,000	10,818	10,922	11,500	12,010	34,100	14,730	14,857	70,802	365,609
1998	21,630	24,793	28,378	74,500	10,736	11,000	11,640	12,530	33,000	14,550	14,218	71,373	368,028
1999	21,700	24,892	28,400	77,000	10,444	11,174	11,070	12,099	32,000	13,362	14,584	73,807	371,572
2000	22,134	24,890	28,400	79,250	10,350	10,800	12,235	11,830	31,900	12,658	14,200	76,004	375,676
2001	22,300	24,890	28,400	81,000	10,350	10,500	13,162	11,924	33,000	13,444	14,300	74,996	378,823
2002[1]	22,635	NA	NA	82,000	NA	NA	13,925	12,030	33,250	14,000	NA	77,035	NA
2003[2]	23,000	NA	NA	85,000	NA	NA	14,204	12,230	33,200	14,300	NA	77,970	NA

[1] Preliminary.   [2] Forecast.   *Source: Foreign Agricultural Service, U.S. Department of Agriculture (FAS-USDA)*

Salient Statistics of Milk in the United States   In Millions of Pounds

Year	Number of Milk Cows on Farms[3] (Thousands)	Production Per Cow[4] (Pounds)	Production Total[4]	Beginning Stocks[5]	Imports	Total Supply	Exports[5]	Fed to Calves	Humans	Total Use	All Milk, Wholesale	Milk, Eligible for Fluid Market	Milk, Manufacturing Grade	Per Capita Consumption[6] (Fluid Milk in Lbs.)
1997	9,252	16,871	156,091	4,700	2,700	163,491	2,094	1,138	154,816	158,048	13.33	13.38	12.78	216
1998	9,154	17,189	157,348	4,900	4,600	166,848	1,408	1,162	157,352	159,922	15.43	15.47	14.36	213
1999	9,156	17,772	162,716	5,300	4,700	172,716	1,303	1,109	163,316	165,728	14.37	14.43	13.78	213
2000	9,206	18,202	167,658	6,186	4,445	178,289	----	1,107	----	----	12.33	12.38	10.54	210
2001	9,114	18,158	165,336	7,010	5,716	178,062	----	1,084	----	----	14.98	14.99	14.78	208
2002[1]	9,141	18,573	169,758	7,259	5,103	182,120	----	980	----	----	12.10	12.10	10.92	----
2003[2]	9,084	18,747	170,312	9,889	4,895	185,096	----	----	----	----	12.51	12.53	11.73	----

[1] Preliminary.   [2] Estimate.   [3] Average number on farms during year including dry cows, excluding heifers not yet fresh.   [4] Excludes milk sucked by calves.   [5] Government and commercial.   [6] Product pounds of commercial sales and on farm consumption.   *Source: Economic Research Service, U.S. Department of Agriculture (ERS-USDA)*

Utilization of Milk in the United States — In Millions of Pounds (Milk Equivalent)

Year	Butter from Whey Cream	Creamery Butter[2]	Cheese[3] (American and other)	Cottage Cheese (Creamed)	Canned Milk[4]	Bulk Condensed Whole Milk Unsweet-ened	Bulk Condensed Whole Milk Sweet-ened	Dry Whole Milk Products	Ice Cream[5]	Other Frozen Dairy Products	Other Manu-factured Por-ducts[6]	Used on Farms Farm-Churned Butter	Total
1996	4,911	26,187	53,937	461	1,013	242	266	983	2,058	13,190	217	301	1,476
1997	4,966	25,714	55,719	NA	1,208	227	314	898	2,112	13,859	686	256	1,394
1998	5,094	26,211	56,827	NA	1,017	222	186	1,050	2,151	14,301	697	244	1,406
1999	5,392	28,657	60,154	NA	1,037	216	171	868	2,305	14,370	682	219	1,328
2000	5,538	28,059	62,257	NA	965	180	163	815	2,218	14,447	700	196	1,303
2001[1]	5,525	27,675	61,088	NA	991	171	163	304	2,240	14,774	701	180	1,264

[1] Preliminary. [2] Excludes whey butter. [3] American and other. [4] Includes evaporated and sweetened condensed. [5] Milk equivalent of butter and condensed milk used in ice cream. [6] Whole milk equivalent of dry cream, malted milk powder, part-skim milk, dry or concentrated ice cream mix, dehydrated butterfat and other miscellaneous products using milkfat. Source: National Agricultural Statistics Service, U.S. Department of Agriculture (NASS-USDA)

Milk-Feed Price Ratio[1] in the United States — In Pounds

Year	Jan.	Feb.	Mar.	Apr.	May	June	July	Aug.	Sept.	Oct.	Nov.	Dec.	Average
1996	2.59	2.42	2.35	2.17	2.10	2.17	2.19	2.28	2.64	2.98	2.85	2.70	2.45
1997	2.44	2.35	2.27	2.14	2.07	2.12	2.24	2.35	2.44	2.63	2.73	2.80	2.38
1998	2.75	2.77	2.73	2.70	2.58	2.89	3.00	3.60	3.98	4.18	4.22	4.27	3.31
1999	4.09	3.67	3.57	2.97	2.89	3.17	3.61	3.85	4.09	3.96	3.87	3.24	3.58
2000	3.07	2.94	2.91	2.84	2.63	2.96	3.29	3.38	3.34	3.12	3.03	3.04	3.05
2001	3.08	3.03	3.24	3.29	3.41	3.74	3.60	3.62	3.75	3.55	3.29	2.99	3.38
2002	3.03	3.00	2.89	2.81	2.64	2.54	2.34	2.27	2.30	2.46	2.44	2.44	2.60
2003[2]	2.40	2.35	2.27	2.25	2.19	2.23	2.58	2.88	3.11	3.24	3.05	2.81	2.61

[1] Pounds of 16% protein mixed dairy feed equal in value to one pound of whole milk. [2] Preliminary. Source: Economic Research Service, U.S. Department of Agriculture (ERS-USDA)

Milk Production[1] in the United States — In Millions of Pounds

Year	Jan.	Feb.	Mar.	Apr.	May	June	July	Aug.	Sept.	Oct.	Nov.	Dec.	Total
1997	13,126	12,141	13,694	13,406	13,902	13,375	13,319	13,059	12,427	12,814	12,362	12,977	156,602
1998	13,282	12,188	13,694	13,510	14,015	13,296	13,162	12,942	12,415	12,956	12,611	13,370	157,441
1999	13,628	12,607	14,270	13,938	14,458	13,633	13,444	13,357	12,970	13,412	13,140	13,854	162,711
2000	14,263	13,606	14,761	14,390	14,791	14,008	14,117	13,798	13,246	13,708	13,212	13,758	167,658
2001	13,998	12,894	14,375	14,078	14,646	13,957	13,877	13,564	13,129	13,611	13,305	13,902	165,336
2002	14,304	13,229	14,864	14,580	15,118	14,317	14,196	14,128	13,467	13,866	13,478	14,211	169,758
2003[2]	14,584	13,441	15,044	14,634	15,003	14,328	14,263	14,015	13,468	13,898	13,470	14,164	170,312

[1] Excludes milk sucked by calves. [2] Preliminary. Source: Economic Research Service, U.S. Department of Agriculture (ERS-USDA)

Average Price Received by U.S. Farmers for All Milk (Sold to Plants) — In Dollars Per Hundred Pounds (Cwt.)

Year	Jan.	Feb.	Mar.	Apr.	May	June	July	Aug.	Sept.	Oct.	Nov.	Dec.	Average
1997	13.40	13.50	13.50	13.20	12.70	12.20	12.10	12.70	13.10	14.10	14.70	14.80	13.33
1998	14.70	14.70	14.40	14.00	13.30	14.10	14.20	15.50	16.70	17.70	17.80	18.00	15.43
1999	17.40	15.50	15.00	12.60	12.70	13.10	13.80	15.10	15.70	14.90	14.40	12.20	14.37
2000	12.00	11.80	11.90	11.90	12.00	12.30	12.60	12.50	12.90	12.50	12.60	13.00	12.33
2001	13.20	13.00	13.90	14.60	15.50	16.20	16.20	16.50	17.10	15.60	14.40	13.50	14.98
2002	13.40	13.10	12.70	12.50	12.10	11.50	11.10	11.30	11.60	12.10	11.90	11.90	12.10
2003[1]	11.70	11.40	11.00	11.00	11.10	11.10	12.00	13.20	14.40	15.00	14.50	13.70	12.51

[1] Preliminary. Source: Economic Research Service, U.S. Department of Agriculture (ERS-USDA)

Average Farm Price of Milk Eligible for Fluid Market — In Dollars Per Hundred Pounds (Cwt.)

Year	Jan.	Feb.	Mar.	Apr.	May	June	July	Aug.	Sept.	Oct.	Nov.	Dec.	Average
1997	13.40	13.50	13.60	13.20	12.80	12.30	12.20	12.80	13.10	14.10	14.70	14.80	13.38
1998	14.70	14.80	14.50	14.00	13.30	14.10	14.20	15.50	16.80	17.80	17.80	18.10	15.47
1999	17.50	15.60	15.10	12.60	12.80	13.20	13.90	15.00	15.70	15.00	14.50	12.30	14.43
2000	12.00	11.90	12.00	11.90	12.10	12.30	12.60	12.50	13.00	12.60	12.60	13.10	12.38
2001	13.20	13.10	13.90	14.60	15.50	16.20	16.20	16.50	17.10	15.60	14.50	13.50	14.99
2002	13.40	13.10	12.70	12.50	12.10	11.50	11.10	11.30	11.60	12.10	11.90	11.90	12.10
2003[1]	11.80	11.40	11.00	11.10	11.10	11.10	12.00	13.20	14.40	15.00	14.50	13.80	12.53

[1] Preliminary. Source: Economic Research Service, U.S. Department of Agriculture (ERS-USDA)

Molasses

Molasses, also called treacle, is a dark brown viscous liquid obtained as a by-product in the processing of both beet and cane sugar. Molasses is the syrup remaining from the crystallization of sugar cane and sugar beet juice.

Sugar cane molasses accounts for approximately 80% of molasses production. Beet molasses is a product of the sugar beet industry, and accounts for approximately 20% of molasses production. In sugar refining, blackstrap molasses is obtained after the last of three boiling or extraction processes that sugar cane goes through to produce molasses. The third and final separation is called blackstrap molasses, which is a thick dark liquid syrup. Blackstrap molasses is used worldwide mostly as a feed supplement for livestock. Other uses for molasses include cooking or baking and the production of alcohol.

Prices – The price of molasses fell in 2003 due to the plunge in sugar prices during the year, which closed the year near 20-year lows. Molasses and sugar prices show a fairly high correlation since molasses is a by-product of sugar production. In fact, statistical analysis of CRB data shows a correlation factor of 0.64 between molasses and sugar prices over the past 3 decades. The wholesale price of blackstrap molasses (cane) at Orleans fell to $58.07 per ton in 2003 from $64.67 in 2002 and the 7-year high of 67.95 posted in 2001. The 2003 price of $58.07 per ton translates into a per gallon price of 34 cents per gallon (dollars per ton divided by 171 equals cents per gallon).

Supply – The production of molasses is highly correlated with the production of sugar, and by extension sugarcane and sugar beets. The largest producers of sugarcane are India, Brazil, China, and Thailand. US production of sugarcane amounts to less than 3% of world production. However, when it comes to using sugar beets to produce sugar, the US is in the top tier of producers along with Germany and France.

World Production of Sugarcane, by Selected Countries   In Thousands of Metric Tons

Crop Year	Australia	Brazil	China	Cuba	India	Indonesia	Mexico	Pakistan	Philippines	South Africa	Thailand	United States	World Total
1990-1	25,140	75,000	57,620	67,500	135,494	28,074	36,000	22,604	18,600	18,083	40,563	24,018	707,497
1991-2	21,306	87,000	67,898	62,000	148,814	28,100	35,300	24,796	22,816	20,078	47,505	26,272	753,303
1992-3	29,400	90,000	73,011	47,150	123,985	32,000	39,700	27,276	23,850	12,955	34,711	26,264	719,671
1993-4	31,951	91,000	63,549	46,000	116,638	33,000	34,100	34,182	22,753	11,244	37,569	26,680	706,433
1994-5	34,860	110,000	60,300	39,000	159,593	30,545	40,134	34,193	18,415	15,683	50,459	25,485	783,373
1995-6	37,378	93,000	65,417	45,500	184,708	30,000	42,300	28,151	22,774	16,750	57,693	25,835	842,937
1996-7[1]	39,878	101,000	68,500	45,000	147,858	28,600	42,000	25,580	23,500	22,512	59,000	24,055	845,645
1997-8[2]	40,878	105,000	69,400	45,500	137,184	29,000		31,600			60,000		

[1] Preliminary.   [2] Estimate.   *Source: Economic Research Service, U.S. Department of Agriculture (ERS-USDA)*

World Production of Sugarbeet, by Selected Countries   In Thousands of Metric Tons

Year	Belgium-Luxembourg	China	France	Germany	Italy	Poland	Russia	Spain	Turkey	Ukraine	United Kingdom	United States	World Total
1990-1	6,857	14,525	25,520	30,366	11,600	16,721	31,091	7,358	13,986	44,265	8,000	24,959	303,149
1991-2	6,043	16,289	24,403	25,926	11,400	11,412	24,280	6,679	15,474	36,168	7,672	25,485	277,368
1992-3	6,174	15,069	26,491	27,177	14,762	11,052	25,548	7,234	15,563	28,783	9,180	26,438	274,751
1993-4	6,120	11,938	25,514	28,606	10,510	15,621	25,468	8,622	15,463	33,717	8,988	23,813	272,746
1994-5	5,729	12,406	23,943	24,211	11,905	11,630	13,945	8,100	12,757	28,138	8,360	29,024	247,798
1995-6	6,291	13,984	25,121	26,049	12,932	13,309	19,110	7,450	10,989	28,000	8,360	25,460	257,984
1996-7[1]	6,100	13,900	24,400	27,000	11,150	17,460	16,500	7,700	14,383	25,500	8,432	24,104	254,335
1997-8[2]	6,000	14,000	24,500	26,500	12,500	14,000	17,000	6,800	15,100	25,400	8,400	26,134	256,393

[1] Preliminary.   [2] Estimate.   *Source: Economic Research Service, U.S. Department of Agriculture (ERS-USDA)*

U.S. Annual Average Prices of Molasses, by Types (F.O.B. Tank Car or Truck)   In Dollars Per Short Ton[2]

Year	New Orleans	South Florida	Baltimore	Upper Mississippi	Savannah	California Ports[3]	Houston	Montana, Wyoming & Nebraska	Red River Valley[4]
				Blackstrap				Beet Molasses	
1996	74.88	83.07	91.27	104.71	92.55	97.11	79.41	----	----
1997	58.14	68.00	76.84	90.69	77.51	83.38	62.13	----	----
1998	46.35	59.92	63.37	78.00	68.75	69.30	48.85	----	----
1999	33.77	49.15	51.06	65.50	56.63	58.32	36.30	----	----
2000	44.64	58.34	61.73	71.66	65.42	71.78	48.94	----	----
2001	67.97	76.79	90.12	85.45	83.30	92.82	72.33	----	----
2002	64.57	74.23	87.02	84.01	87.50	84.81	68.76	----	----
2003[1]	57.67	66.72	81.11	78.78	81.18	78.61	62.92	----	----

[1] Preliminary.   [2] To convert dollars per short ton to cents per gallon divide by 171.   [3] Los Angeles and Stockton.   [4] North Dakota and Minnesota.
Source: Agricultural Marketing Service, U.S. Department of Agriculture (AMS-USDA)

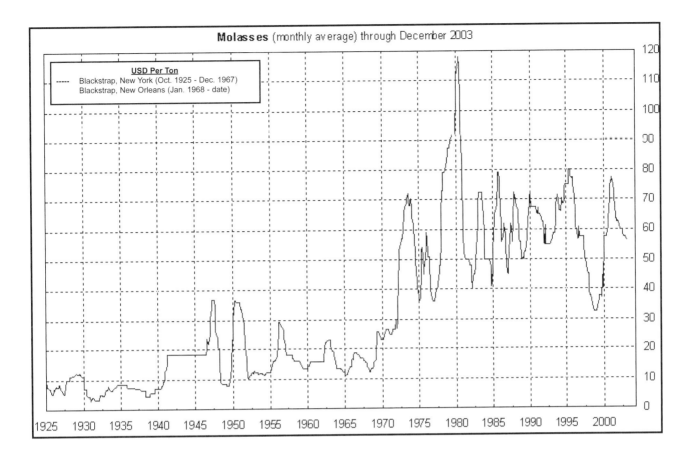

Molasses (monthly average) through December 2003

USD Per Ton
----- Blackstrap, New York (Oct. 1925 - Dec. 1967)
Blackstrap, New Orleans (Jan. 1968 - date)

Salient Statistics of Molasses[3] in the United States   In Metric Tons

	Production											Pro-duction of Edible
	Mainland				In Ship-ments		Inedible Imports From				Total Molasses
		Refiners						Dominican		Mainland	U.S.	(1,000
	Mainland	Black-		Puerto	From	Total				Exports[5]	Supply	Gallons)
Year	Hawaii	Hills[4]	strap	Beet	Rico	Hawaii	Imports	Brazil	Republic	Mexico			
1989	218,009	808,355	122,786	974,179	34,864	169,270	926,870	107,109	147,235	75,634	293,535	2,707,925	1,990
1990	228,968	741,749	105,124	948,820	24,959	214,045	1,078,924	70,986	145,543	88,401	212,263	2,876,399	1,405
1991	188,252	807,652	126,000	1,165,962	27,882	184,337	1,258,637	10,342	137,271	235,244	242,635	3,299,953	1,825
1992	182,849	782,566	123,000	950,312	25,097	183,657	1,115,863	0	127,500	117,722	282,098	2,873,300	1,460
1993	187,915	831,661	113,000	692,465	22,802	190,371	1,040,858	0	163,180	47,596	255,907	2,612,448	1,480
1994	180,884	824,453	114,000	1,200,000	18,531	151,172	1,556,640	0	121,320	197,753	277,098	3,459,167	1,500
1995	146,000	886,826	114,000	1,040,000	16,156	146,000	1,048,726	0	132,983	172,177	274,868	2,960,684	1,500
1996[1]	-----	NA	NA	NA	-----	NA	NA	-----	-----	-----	NA	NA	0
1997[2]	-----	900,000	100,000	1,200,000	-----	100,000	1,583,755	-----	-----	-----	300,000	3,583,755	0

[1] Preliminary.   [2] Estimate.   [3] Feed and industrial molasses.   [4] Includes high-test molasses from frozen cane.   [5] Excluding exports from Hawaii and Puerto Rico.   NA = Not available.   Source: Agricultural Marketing Service, U.S. Department of Agriculture (AMS-USDA)

Wholesale Price of Blackstrap Molasses (Cane) at New Orleans   In Dollars Per Short Ton

Year	Jan.	Feb.	Mar.	Apr.	May	June	July	Aug.	Sept.	Oct.	Nov.	Dec.	Average
1994	57.75	57.50	59.38	62.50	68.00	70.00	70.63	71.25	69.38	67.50	66.25	66.25	65.53
1995	69.00	70.31	68.75	68.75	68.75	69.38	74.25	75.00	75.00	75.00	75.00	75.00	72.00
1996	80.00	80.00	80.00	78.00	77.50	77.50	77.50	77.50	75.00	70.00	65.63	60.75	74.88
1997	60.00	60.00	59.00	56.56	56.88	60.31	57.50	57.50	57.50	57.50	57.50	57.50	58.14
1998	57.50	55.63	51.00	50.00	50.00	46.00	45.00	45.00	45.00	37.50	37.50	37.50	46.35
1999	37.50	36.25	35.00	34.38	32.50	32.50	32.50	32.50	32.50	32.50	33.75	33.75	33.80
2000	35.25	36.11	37.50	37.50	63.75	66.25	70.75	73.75	76.25	77.50	77.50	75.00	67.95
2001	57.50	57.50	59.38	60.25	63.75	66.25	63.50	62.50	62.50	62.50	60.00	60.00	64.67
2002	72.50	70.60	67.50	67.50	64.40	62.50	63.50	62.50	62.50	62.50	60.00	60.00	64.67
2003[1]	60.00	60.00	60.00	58.75	57.50	57.50	57.50	57.50	57.50	56.25	56.25	53.75	57.71

[1] Preliminary.   Source: Agricultural Marketing Service, U.S. Department of Agriculture (AMS-USDA)

Molybdenum

Molybdenum is a silvery-white, hard, malleable, metallic element with the symbol Mo and atomic number 42. Molybdenum melts at about 2610 degrees Celsius and boils at about 4640 degrees Celsius. Swedish chemist Carl Wilhelm Scheele discovered molybdenum in 1778.

Molybdenum occurs in nature in the form of molybdenite and wulfenite. Contributing to the growth of plants, it is an important trace element in soils. Approximately 70% of the world supply of molybdenum is obtained as a by-product of copper mining. Molybdenum is chiefly used as an alloy to strengthen steel and resist corrosion. It is used for structural work, aircraft parts, and forged automobile parts because it withstands high temperatures and pressures and adds strength. Other uses include lubricants, a refractory metal in chemical applications, electron tubing, and a catalyst.

Prices – The US merchant price of molybdic oxide in 2001 fell to $2.37 per pound from $2.74 per pound in 2000. That was well below the 10-year average price of $3.84. There was an upward spike in prices in the first half of 1995 to a peak of $17.00 per pound in February 1995, which skewed the 10-year average price figure higher.

Supply – World production of molybdenum in 2001 fell –2.3% to 130,000 metric tons from 133,000 metric tons in 2000. The world's largest producers of molybdenum are the US with 28.9% of world production, Chile with 25.4%, and China with 21.7%. Chile's production has increased sharply in recent years and its 2001 production level of 33,000 metric tons was more than double that seen 10 years earlier.

US production of molybdenum concentrate in 2001 fell –8.1% to an 8-year low of 37,600 metric tons. US production of molybdenum primary products in 2001 fell –20.3% to 15,700 metric tons, with 14,900 metric tons of that production in molybdic oxide and 771 metric tons in molybdenum metal powder.

Demand – US consumption of molybdenum concentrate fell –1.5% to 33,300 metric tons in 2001 from 33,800 metric tons in 2000. US consumption of molybdenum concentrate has more than doubled over the last 10 years. US consumption of molybdenum primary products fell by 11.5% to 16,200 metric tons in 2001 from 18,300 metric tons in 2000.

Trade – US imports of molybdenum concentrate for consumption in 2001 fell –1.8% to 6,010 metric tons from 6,120 metric tons in 2000.

World Mine Production of Molybdenum   In Metric Tons (Contained Molybdenum)

Year	Bulgaria	Canada[3]	Chile	China	Iran	Kazak-hstan	Mexico	Mongolia	Peru	Russia	United States	Uzbek-isten	World Total
1996	400	8,789	17,415	29,600	560	100	4,210	2,201	3,711	2,000	56,000	500	127,000
1997	----	8,223	21,339	33,300	600	100	4,842	2,000	3,835	2,000	60,100	500	139,000
1998	----	8,469	25,297	30,000	1,400	100	5,949	2,000	4,344	2,000	53,343	500	136,000
1999	----	6,250	27,309	29,700	1,600	155	7,961	1,910	5,470	2,400	42,400	500	129,000
2000	----	6,830	33,187	28,800	1,600	215	6,886	1,335	7,190	2,400	40,900	500	133,000
2001[1]	----	7,556	33,492	28,200	1,700	225	5,518	1,514	9,500	2,600	37,600	500	132,000
2002[2]	----	7,521	29,466	29,300	1,700	230	3,428	1,590	9,500	2,900	32,600	500	123,000

[1] Preliminary.   [2] Estimate.   [3] Shipments.   *Source: U.S. Geological Survey (USGS)*

Salient Statistics of Molybdenum in the United States   In Metric Tons (Contained Molybdenum)

| | Concentrate | | | | | | | Primary Products[4] | | | | | | |
| | | Shipments | | | | | | Net Production | | | Shipments | | |
Year	Pro-duction	Total (Includes Exports)	Value Million $	For Exports	Con-sumption	Imports For Con-sumption	Stocks, Dec. 31[3]	Grand Total	Molybolic Oxide[5]	Moly-bolic Metal Powder	Price Average Value $ / Kg.[6]	To Domestic Dest-inations	Oxide for Exports (Groos Weight)	Con-sumption	Producer Stocks, Dec. 31
1996	56,000	35,800	456.0	19,700	24,500	5,480	2,470	24,100	20,400	1,970	8.30	24,100	1,790	20,900	5,780
1997	60,100	32,100	406.0	20,000	24,300	6,330	3,660	25,900	22,700	2,000	9.46	25,900	1,240	20,000	6,500
1998	53,300	52,100	200.0	----	35,900	6,570	6,270	33,900	31,600	2,270	5.90	38,000	1,100	18,800	7,780
1999	42,400	42,800	251.0	----	34,500	6,390	4,580	19,200	17,400	1,880	5.90	39,000	1,130	18,700	5,340
2000	40,900	40,400	210.0	----	33,800	6,120	4,030	19,700	17,500	2,190	5.64	34,600	1,190	18,300	5,360
2001[1]	37,600	37,000	192.0	----	33,300	6,010	4,210	15,700	14,900	771	5.20	32,600	940	15,800	5,600
2002[2]	32,600	32,300	236.0	----	20,000	4,710	3,950	10,500	10,000	513	8.30	27,500	1,670	14,400	4,300

[1] Preliminary.   [2] Estimate.   [3] At mines & at plants making molybdenum products.   [4] Comprises ferromolybdenum, molybdic oxide, & molybdenum salts & metal.   [5] Includes molybdic oxide briquets, molybdic acid, molybdenum trioxide, all other.   [6] U.S. producer price per kilogram of molybdenum oxide contained in technical-grade molybdic oxide.   W = Withheld proprietary data.   *Source: U.S. Geological Survey (USGS)*

US Merchant Price of Molybdic Oxide   In Dollars Per Pound

Year	Jan.	Feb.	Mar.	Apr.	May	June	July	Aug.	Sept.	Oct.	Nov.	Dec.	Average
1997	4.25	4.60	4.57	4.55	4.55	4.55	4.55	4.55	4.55	4.38	4.33	4.20	4.47
1998	4.10	4.10	4.17	4.51	4.05	4.00	4.00	4.00	4.00	4.00	4.00	4.00	4.08
1999	3.53	2.73	2.73	2.73	2.73	2.73	2.73	2.73	2.73	2.73	2.73	2.73	2.79
2000	2.86	3.55	3.40	2.55	2.55	2.55	2.55	2.64	2.70	2.70	2.70	2.39	2.74
2001	2.38	2.38	2.38	2.38	2.38	2.38	2.38	2.38	2.38	2.40	2.33	2.33	2.37
2002	2.33	2.33	2.33	2.75	2.99	6.93	5.32	4.75	4.73	4.70	3.82	3.48	3.87
2003	3.63	3.74	4.62	5.20	5.20	5.77	5.86	5.60	5.84	6.25	6.25	6.25	5.35

Source: American Metal Market (AMM)

Nickel

Nickel (atomic symbol Ni) is a hard, malleable, ductile metal that has a silvery tinge that can take on a high polish. Nickel is somewhat ferromagnetic and is a fair conductor of heat and electricity. Nickel is primarily used in the production of stainless steel and other corrosion-resistant alloys. Nickel is used in coins to replace silver, in rechargeable batteries, and in electronic circuitry. Nickel plating techniques, like electro-less coating or single-slurry coating, are employed in such applications as turbine blades, helicopter rotors, extrusion dies, and rolled steel strip.

Nickel futures and options trade at the London Metal Exchange (LME). The nickel futures contract calls for the delivery of 6 metric tons of primary nickel with at least 99.80% purity in the form of full plate, cut cathodes, pellets or briquettes. The contract is priced in terms of US dollars per metric ton.

Prices – Nickel prices in 2003 staged an impressive rally along with the rest of the basic metals complex, nearly quadrupling from the lows seen in late 2001. Nickel prices hit bottom in late 2001 at around $4500 per metric ton. But then the market really took off in mid-2003 with a rally from the $9,000 per metric ton area up to a high of nearly $18,000 by the end of the year.

Supply – World mine production of nickel in 2001, the latest reporting year for the data series, rose +3.1% to a record 1.330 million metric tons. That is approximately double the production seen in 1970. The world's largest mine producers of nickel in 2001 were Russia (with 24.4% of world production), Australia (14.8%), Canada (14.5%), New Caledonia (8.8%), and Indonesia (7.7%). In 2001, US secondary nickel production rose to a record high of 101,000 metric tons from 84,000 metric tons in 2000.

Demand – US consumption of nickel in 2001 fell to 188,000 metric tons from 189,000 metric tons in 2000, but was only mildly below the record high production level of 191,000 metric tons posted in 1997. The primary US nickel consumption use is for stainless and heat-resisting steels, which accounted for 64% of US consumption in 2001. Other sectors were super alloys (9.8%), nickel alloys (9.7%), electroplating anodes (6.6%), alloy steels (4.1%), copper base alloys (3.7%), chemicals (0.9%), and cast irons (0.5%).

Trade – The US relied on imports for 56% of its nickel consumption in 2001. US imports of primary and secondary nickel in 2001 fell to a 7-year low of 144,760 metric tons from 166,700 metric tons in 2000. US exports of primary and secondary nickel in 2001 were 57,050 metric tons, only mildly below the record high of 58,050 metric tons posted in 2001.

World Mine Production of Nickel — In Metric Tons (Contained Nickel)

Year	Australia[3]	Botswana	Brazil	Canada	China	Dominican Republic	Greece	Indonesia	New Caledonia	Phillippines	Russia	South Africa	World Total
1995	98,467	21,107	29,124	181,820	41,800	46,523	19,947	88,183	119,905	15,075	251,000	29,803	1,040,000
1996	113,134	21,910	25,245	192,649	43,800	45,168	21,600	87,911	122,486	14,539	230,000	34,830	1,060,000
1997	123,372	19,860	31,936	190,529	46,600	49,152	18,419	71,127	136,467	18,137	280,000	34,830	1,140,000
1998	143,513	21,700	36,764	208,201	48,700	40,311	16,985	74,063	125,319	23,713	290,000	36,679	1,180,000
1999	119,226	33,733	41,522	186,236	49,500	39,997	16,050	89,111	110,062	20,689	300,000	36,202	1,160,000
2000[1]	165,700	34,465	45,317	190,793	50,300	39,943	19,535	98,200	128,789	17,388	315,000	36,616	1,290,000
2001[2]	197,000	26,200	45,400	193,361	51,500	31,000	20,830	102,000	117,554	27,359	325,000	36,443	1,330,000

[1] Preliminary. [2] Estimate. [3] Content of nickel sulfate and concentrates. *Source: U.S. Geological Survey (USGS)*

Salient Statistics of Nickel in the United States — In Metric Tons (Contained Nickel)

Year	Net Import Reliance as a % of Apparent Consumption	Production Plant[4]	Production Secondary[5]	Alloy Sheets	Cast Irons	Copper Base Alloys	Electroplating Anodes	Nickel Alloys	Stainless & Heat Resisting Steels	Super Alloys	Chemicals	Apparent Consumption	Stocks, Dec. 31 At Consumers' Plants	Stocks, Dec. 31 At Producer Plants	Primary & Secondary Nickel Exports	Primary & Secondary Nickel Imports	Avg. Price LME[6] $/Lb.
1995	60	8,290	64,600	9,570	491	8,510	15,600	21,800	103,000	14,100	5,210	181,000	12,300	12,700	51,550	156,930	3.73
1996	59	15,100	59,300	6,240	563	7,300	16,200	19,700	94,000	12,600	5,310	183,000	12,900	13,300	46,700	150,060	3.40
1997	56	16,000	68,400	9,290	654	6,530	15,900	19,400	105,000	19,000	3,720	191,000	16,070	12,600	56,600	158,000	3.14
1998	64	4,290	63,100	9,590	908	7,470	16,400	17,500	93,000	18,600	1,970	186,000	15,960	13,100	43,540	156,500	2.10
1999	63	----	71,000	8,100	495	10,500	15,400	15,200	102,000	18,900	1,580	190,000	10,050	12,700	38,840	148,480	2.73
2000[2]	58	----	84,000	7,700	198	9,940	15,700	18,200	108,000	19,400	991	189,000	14,260	12,300	58,050	166,700	3.92
2001[3]	56	----	101,000	7,620	892	6,880	12,500	18,200	121,000	18,400	1,630	188,000	13,900	12,600	57,050	144,760	2.70

[1] Exclusive of scrap. [2] Preliminary. [3] Estimate. [4] Smelter & refinery. [5] From purchased scrap (ferrous & nonferrous). W = Withheld proprietary data. NA = Not avaliable. *Source: U.S. Geological Survey (USGS)*

Average Price of Nickel[1] in the United States — In Cents Per Pound

Year	Jan.	Feb.	Mar.	Apr.	May	June	July	Aug.	Sept.	Oct.	Nov.	Dec.	Average
1999	NA	NA	NA	NA	NA	NA	NA	316.00	339.00	353.00	381.00	390.00	355.80
2000	403.00	456.00	493.00	469.00	474.00	346.00	399.00	385.00	413.00	380.00	360.00	358.00	411.33
2001	344.00	336.00	316.00	296.00	339.00	343.00	295.00	278.00	252.00	243.00	253.00	266.00	296.75
2002	266.00	266.00	266.00	266.00	295.00	331.00	341.00	342.00	332.00	321.00	354.00	363.00	311.92
2003	376.67	416.01	408.76	391.72	409.63	439.13	438.50	464.67	492.62	540.81	583.21	674.78	469.71

[1] Plating material, briquettes. *Source: American Metal Market (AMM)*

Oats

Oats are seeds or grains of a genus of plants that thrive in cool, moist climates. There are about 25 species of oats that grow worldwide in the cooler temperate regions. The oldest known cultivated oats were found inside caves in Switzerland and are believed to be from the Bronze Age. Oats are usually sown in early spring and harvested in mid to late summer, but in southern regions of the northern hemisphere, they may be sown in the fall. Oats are used in many processed foods such as flour, livestock feed, and furfural, a chemical used as a solvent in various refining industries. Oat futures and options are traded on the Chicago Board of Trade (CBOT) and the Winnipeg Commodity Exchange (WCE).

Prices – Oat prices on the CBOT weekly nearest futures chart started the year near $2.18 per bushel, but then fell sharply in the first half of the year to post a 2-1/2 year low of $1.23 per bushel in late July. Oat prices then traded sideways in a narrow range between about $1.30-$1.50 through the remainder of the year, with an upturn at the end of the year producing a close for 2003 of $1.52, a 6-month high. Prices were pressured early in the year by predictions of a large US crop harvest, lower US consumption figures, and lower export demand. However, prices recovered later in the year on short-covering, some foreign buying, and the weak dollar.

Supply – World oat production in 2003/4 (June/May) was forecast at 26.848 million metric tons, up 4.6% from 25.660 million in 2002/3 but down from 27.096 million in 2001/2. World ending stocks for 2003/4 are forecasted at 4.026 million metric tons, up from 3.376 million in 2002/3. The world's largest oat producing countries in 2002/3 were the European Union with 7.228 million metric tons of production (28% of world production), Russia with 5.700 million (22%), Canada with 2.911 million (11%), and the US coming in fourth with 1.722 million metric tons (7%). US production of oats in 2003/4 was forecast at 2.100 million metric tons, up 22% from 1.722 million in 2002/3 and by an overall 24% from 1.699 million in 2001/2. US ending stocks for 2003/4 are forecasted at 1.081 million metric tons, up sharply from 723,000 in 2002/3. US farmers planted 4.601 million acres with oats in 2003/4, down from 4.995 million in 2002/3, but acres harvested rose to 2.224 million acres in 2003/4 from 2.093 million. Yields rose sharply in 2003 to 65.0 bushels per acre from 56.7 bushels in 2002/3. The largest US oat-producing states in 2003 were North Dakota (with 15% of US production), Minnesota (13%), South Dakota (10.8%), and Wisconsin (10.7%).

Demand – World consumption of oats in 2003/4 was forecast at 26.198 million metric tons, down slightly from 26.226 million in 2002/3. The fact that consumption is lower than production suggests an oversupply of oats, a bearish factor for oat prices.

Trade – Most of the world's oats production is consumed domestically and world trade is small at only 7% of overall world production. World trade in oats in 2003/4 was forecast to rise to 26.848 million metric tons from 25.660 million in 2002/3. The world's largest oat exporters are Canada with 1.057 million metric tons in 2002/3 and the European Union with 800,000 metric tons. The world's largest importer is the US with 1.777 million metric tons, with most of those oats coming from Canada.

World Production of Oats   In Thousands of Metric Tons

Year	Argentina	Australia	Canada	China	France	Germany	Italy	Poland	Sweden	Turkey	United States	Ex-USSR	World Total
1994-5	357	924	3,638	600	681	1,663	355	1,243	991	300	3,322	13,903	32,967
1995-6	260	1,875	2,858	640	617	1,421	301	1,495	947	275	2,338	10,843	28,663
1996-7	310	1,653	4,361	600	622	1,606	350	1,581	1,200	275	2,224	10,430	30,637
1997-8	517	1,634	3,485	400	564	1,599	311	1,630	1,275	280	2,428	11,560	30,903
1998-9	383	1,798	3,958	650	658	1,279	280	1,460	1,136	310	2,409	6,490	25,911
1999-00	555	1,118	3,641	600	550	1,340	350	1,446	1,200	250	2,122	5,740	24,000
2000-1	645	1,050	3,389	600	460	1,090	460	1,070	1,150	250	2,171	7,500	26,170
2001-2[1]	645	1,439	2,691	600	490	1,150	310	1,305	960	250	1,699	6,580	27,040
2002-3[2]	485	926	2,911	600	770	1,020	330	1,480	1,180	250	1,722	7,340	25,630
2003-4[3]	400	1,600	3,700	600	560	1,200	300	1,200	1,090	250	2,100	6,740	26,160

[1] Preliminary.   [2] Estimate.   [3] Forecast.   *Source: Foreign Agricultural Service, U.S. Department of Agriculture (FAS-USDA)*

Official Oats Crop Production Reports in the United States   In Thousands of Bushels

Year	July 1	Aug. 1	Sept. 1	Oct. 1	Dec. 1	Final	Year	July 1	Aug. 1	Sept. 1	Oct. 1	Dec. 1	Final
1992	256,381	276,381	----	----	----	294,229	1998	183,201	177,211	----	----	----	165,981
1993	262,860	249,830	249,830	208,138	----	206,770	1999	----	162,096	----	----	----	146,218
1994	248,151	247,753	247,753	229,717	----	229,008	2000	151,380	152,745	----	----	----	149,545
1995	181,508	186,167	186,167	----	----	162,027	2001	132,150	135,445	----	----	----	117,024
1996	154,968	157,663	----	----	----	153,245	2002	147,584	142,580	----	----	----	118,628
1997	182,672	187,127	----	----	----	167,246	2003[1]	147,895	151,345	----	----	----	145,000

[1] Preliminary.   *Source: National Agricultural Statistics Service, U.S. Department of Agriculture (NASS-USDA)*

Oat Stocks in the United States   In Thousands of Bushels

	On Farms				Off Farms				Total Stocks			
Year	Mar. 1	June 1	Sept. 1	Dec. 1	Mar. 1	June 1	Sept. 1	Dec. 1	Mar. 1	June 1	Sept. 1	Dec. 1
1994	85,050	53,940	144,300	113,400	61,502	51,583	75,551	78,664	146,552	105,523	219,851	192,064
1995	78,400	46,750	107,200	87,200	70,575	53,848	72,967	65,804	148,975	100,598	180,167	153,004
1996	57,350	32,600	93,400	80,650	55,268	33,708	38,716	45,218	112,618	66,308	132,116	125,868
1997	56,200	33,100	107,950	83,200	39,362	33,576	48,972	61,051	95,562	66,676	156,922	144,251
1998	58,800	34,500	110,300	81,500	52,418	39,498	51,502	61,835	111,218	73,998	161,802	143,335
1999	61,700	40,700	97,300	79,800	50,850	40,678	51,151	53,872	112,550	81,378	148,451	133,672
2000	53,300	36,000	101,200	86,900	48,500	40,031	49,177	57,237	101,800	76,031	150,377	144,137
2001	55,800	32,050	74,800	58,100	54,128	40,677	41,592	56,117	109,928	72,727	116,392	114,217
2002	40,200	28,650	70,500	52,500	53,158	34,552	41,212	51,284	93,358	63,202	111,712	103,784
2003[1]	35,000	20,600	82,100	64,300	47,879	29,233	49,637	54,918	82,879	49,833	131,737	119,218

[1] Preliminary.   Source: National Agricultural Statistics Service, U.S. Department of Agriculture (NASS-USDA)

Supply and Utilizationof Oats in the United States   In Millions of Bushels

	Acreage		Yield Per	Pro-		Total	Feed &	Food, Alcohol &			Total	Ending	Findley Farm	Loan	Target
Year	Planted	Harvested	Acre	duction	Imports	Supply	Residual	Industrial	Seed	Exports	Use	Stocks	Price	Rate	Price
	1,000 acres		(Bushels)		In Millions of Bushels								Dollars Per Bushel		
1994-5	6,637	4,008	57.1	228.8	93.2	427.6	242.6	70.0	13.4	1.0	327.0	100.6	1.22	.97	1.45
1995-6	6,225	2,952	54.6	161.1	80.5	342.2	194.9	67.0	12.0	2.1	275.9	66.3	1.67	.97	1.45
1996-7	4,638	2,655	57.7	153.2	97.5	317.1	171.7	63.0	13.1	2.5	250.4	66.7	1.96	1.03	NA
1997-8	5,068	2,813	59.5	167.2	98.4	332.3	184.6	59.0	12.6	2.1	258.3	74.0	1.60	1.11	NA
1998-9	4,892	2,755	60.2	166.0	108.0	347.7	195.6	57.0	12.0	1.7	266.3	81.4	1.10	1.11	NA
1999-00	4,670	2,453	59.6	146.2	99.0	326.0	180.0	56.8	11.2	1.8	250.0	76.0	1.12	1.13	NA
2000-1	4,477	2,329	64.2	149.5	106.0	332.0	189.0	57.0	11.0	1.7	259.0	73.0	1.10	1.16	NA
2001-2	4,403	1,905	61.4	117.0	96.0	286.0	148.0	59.0	13.0	2.8	223.0	63.0	1.59	1.21	NA
2002-3[1]	4,995	2,093	56.7	118.6	95.0	277.0	152.0			2.7	227.0	50.0	1.81	1.35	1.40
2003-4[2]	4,601	2,224	65.0	145.0	90.0	284.0	135.0			2.0	210.0	74.0	1.40-1.50	1.35	1.40

[1] Preliminary.   [2] Forecast.   NA = Not available.   Source: Economic Research Service, U.S. Department of Agriculture (ERS-USDA)

Production of Oats in the United States, by States   In Thousands of Bushels

Year	Illinois	Iowa	Michigan	Minnesota	Nebraska	New York	North Dakota	Ohio	Penn-slyvania	South Dakota	Texas	Wisconsin	Total
1994	5,490	26,660	6,270	24,750	7,500	7,040	33,550	6,720	8,480	31,360	5,200	25,380	229,008
1995	5,360	14,625	5,130	18,000	4,500	5,310	21,600	6,900	9,440	11,500	5,040	18,700	162,027
1996	4,620	12,920	3,600	15,120	7,455	3,850	19,000	5,130	7,560	21,600	3,400	17,400	153,245
1997	5,550	16,790	4,880	17,400	5,850	5,850	18,700	6,660	8,990	14,850	6,760	20,160	167,246
1998	3,920	10,915	4,800	19,530	5,320	6,510	25,200	6,500	8,480	20,100	6,890	18,300	165,981
1999	4,260	11,375	4,875	17,700	4,650	4,760	16,830	7,000	7,975	12,800	4,840	18,600	146,218
2000	4,015	12,060	4,800	22,320	1,890	3,900	19,845	6,840	8,265	13,420	4,300	19,040	149,545
2001	3,200	9,100	3,520	12,600	3,660	5,520	14,880	6,205	7,475	7,800	7,200	12,480	117,024
2002	3,450	13,300	4,160	15,960	2,365	3,630	12,760	3,720	7,015	4,500	7,040	15,000	118,628
2003[1]	4,450	10,790	5,250	18,815	6,570	4,410	21,240	3,960	6,490	15,640	6,300	15,410	145,000

[1] Preliminary.   Source: National Agricultural Statistics Service, U.S. Department of Agriculture (NASS-USDA)

Average Cash Price of No. 2 Heavy White Oats in Toledo   In Dollars Per Bushel

Year	June	July	Aug.	Sept.	Oct.	Nov.	Dec.	Jan.	Feb.	Mar.	Apr.	May	Average
1994-5	1.35	1.26	1.26	1.32	1.35	1.28	1.27	1.34	1.45	1.43	1.48	1.59	1.37
1995-6	1.65	1.76	1.83	1.90	1.76	1.91	2.21	2.14	2.06	2.17	2.32	2.05	1.98
1996-7	NQ	2.45	2.34	2.19	2.02	1.96	1.96	1.99	2.16	2.26	2.12	2.08	2.14
1997-8	2.12	1.79	1.84	1.80	1.77	NQ	NQ	NQ	NQ	NQ	NQ	NQ	1.86
1998-9	NQ	NQ	NQ	NQ	NQ	NQ	NQ	NQ	NQ	NQ	NQ	NQ	NQ
1999-00	NQ	NQ	NQ	NQ	NQ	NQ	NQ	NQ	NQ	NQ	NQ	NQ	NQ
2000-1	NQ	NQ	NQ	NQ	NQ	NQ	NQ	NQ	NQ	NQ	NQ	NQ	NQ
2001-2	NQ	NQ	NQ	NQ	NQ	NQ	NQ	NQ	NQ	NQ	NQ	NQ	NQ
2002-3	NQ	NQ	NQ	NQ	NQ	NQ	NQ	NQ	NQ	NQ	NQ	NQ	NQ
2003-4[1]	NQ	NQ	NQ	NQ	NQ	NQ	NQ						

[1] Preliminary.   NQ = No quotes.   Source: Economic Research Service, U.S. Department of Agriculture (ERS-USDA)

OATS

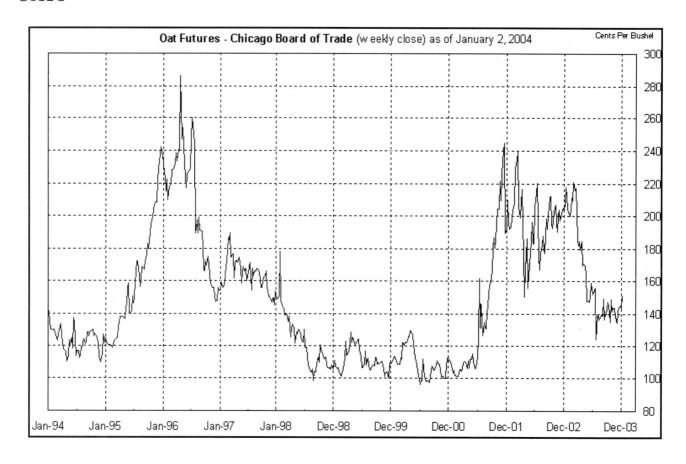

Volume of Trading in Oats Futures in Chicago   In Contracts

Year	Jan.	Feb.	Mar.	Apr.	May	June	July	Aug.	Sept.	Oct.	Nov.	Dec.	Total
1994	47,980	57,060	39,800	53,820	34,300	69,760	20,760	39,340	28,840	24,900	56,940	19,680	493,180
1995	13,512	37,014	29,490	45,536	34,116	107,082	29,862	45,677	31,676	38,641	52,321	47,005	511,932
1996	61,451	52,079	34,608	77,395	47,161	34,498	38,960	33,316	30,801	37,579	37,856	16,154	501,858
1997	34,238	51,608	39,607	41,988	27,028	29,632	25,473	26,486	21,241	42,630	38,187	19,214	397,332
1998	21,150	51,247	25,551	65,381	23,490	55,376	29,870	42,156	27,131	31,426	51,172	18,924	442,874
1999	23,747	35,706	43,671	44,974	22,399	40,722	35,812	27,928	17,893	16,155	42,029	20,370	371,406
2000	27,073	43,332	29,707	31,653	38,647	50,461	30,885	42,814	21,846	21,476	48,890	15,406	402,190
2001	26,377	38,040	24,903	41,482	20,516	41,926	50,440	22,883	31,252	50,580	53,578	38,877	440,854
2002	41,516	46,435	30,662	51,889	32,386	39,229	35,217	29,647	23,968	32,847	35,412	15,932	415,140
2003	26,149	31,892	27,766	26,022	20,442	24,113	23,230	21,562	26,658	33,621	30,273	27,170	318,898

Source: Chicago Board of Trade (CBT)

Average Open Interest of Oats in Chicago   In Contracts

Year	Jan.	Feb.	Mar.	Apr.	May	June	July	Aug.	Sept.	Oct.	Nov.	Dec.
1994	21,193	20,137	20,194	19,882	18,312	14,575	11,710	13,923	14,743	16,266	15,354	13,376
1995	13,133	13,231	13,000	15,426	16,054	13,611	11,019	11,348	11,012	11,970	12,542	13,003
1996	13,253	14,095	14,231	14,497	13,897	11,697	11,336	11,803	11,457	11,918	11,150	8,550
1997	8,088	9,650	12,649	11,024	9,830	9,395	8,131	8,606	8,618	10,953	11,816	10,964
1998	12,782	15,368	16,553	17,748	17,441	16,437	14,255	15,052	14,771	16,263	18,466	17,048
1999	17,126	17,019	16,677	15,398	13,491	12,705	11,927	11,670	9,802	10,638	12,754	12,360
2000	15,343	17,521	17,719	18,183	176,686	16,178	15,550	15,225	13,176	13,985	14,377	14,119
2001	14,093	15,060	14,873	14,962	14,875	13,695	11,861	11,707	10,059	12,111	14,453	12,142
2002	12,640	13,137	11,833	10,976	9,047	10,381	10,230	10,970	9,881	9,550	9,134	6,008
2003	6,929	6,715	5,945	6,135	5,833	5,640	5,811	5,958	6,261	6,194	6,268	5,122

Source: Chicago Board of Trade (CBT)

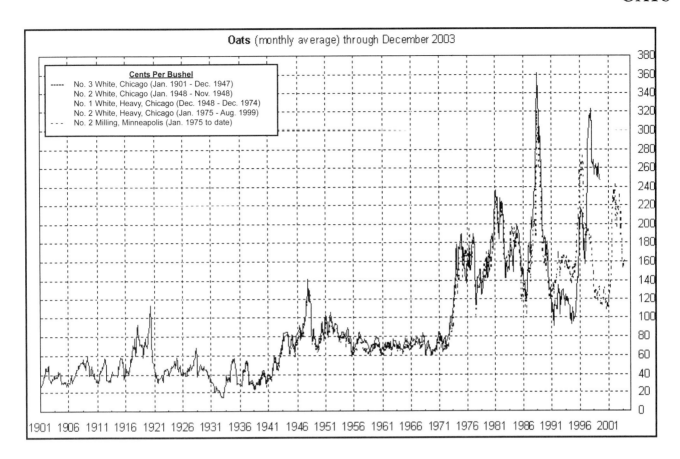

Average Cash Price of No. 2 Heavy White Oats in Minneapolis   In Dollars Per Bushel

Year	June	July	Aug.	Sept.	Oct.	Nov.	Dec.	Jan.	Feb.	Mar.	Apr.	May	Average
1994-5	1.47	1.36	1.44	1.44	1.44	1.41	NQ	1.46	1.42	1.54	1.62	1.76	1.36
1995-6	1.73	1.92	1.96	2.04	2.11	2.63	2.50	2.40	2.31	2.47	2.56	2.68	2.28
1996-7	2.11	2.48	2.36	2.08	2.06	1.87	1.86	1.89	1.94	1.99	1.88	1.81	2.03
1997-8	1.89	1.76	1.80	1.78	1.75	1.65	1.71	1.68	1.59	1.65	1.54	1.58	1.70
1998-9	1.52	1.42	1.21	1.30	1.29	1.32	1.31	1.33	1.26	1.35	1.36	1.39	1.34
1999-00	1.34	1.25	1.20	1.17	1.20	1.20	1.28	1.21	1.19	1.34	1.45	NQ	1.26
2000-1	.73	.72	.69	.68	.70	.72	.70	.70	.75	.77	.80	.82	.73
2001-2	.83	.95	1.08	1.04	1.29	1.41	1.48	1.41	1.47	1.51	1.31	1.29	1.26
2002-3	1.40	1.24	1.23	1.36	1.36	1.33	1.36	1.44	1.28	1.28	1.22	1.08	1.30
2003-4[1]	1.05	NQ	.98	1.01	1.00	.99	1.04						1.01

[1] Preliminary.   NQ = No quote.   *Source: Economic Research Service, U.S. Department of Agriculture (ERS-USDA)*

Average Price Received by U.S. Farmers for Oats   In Dollars Per Bushel

Year	June	July	Aug.	Sept.	Oct.	Nov.	Dec.	Jan.	Feb.	Mar.	Apr.	May	Average
1994-5	1.31	1.20	1.16	1.18	1.21	1.18	1.18	1.22	1.22	1.33	1.36	1.41	1.22
1995-6	1.38	1.52	1.48	1.43	1.50	1.72	1.91	1.93	1.96	2.04	2.13	2.48	1.46
1996-7	2.17	2.13	2.00	1.83	1.84	1.85	1.72	1.83	1.81	1.91	1.87	1.86	1.96
1997-8	1.81	1.68	1.57	1.47	1.62	1.66	1.57	1.60	1.60	1.64	1.61	1.53	1.61
1998-9	1.39	1.19	1.02	1.07	1.09	1.10	1.19	1.20	1.20	1.20	1.18	1.31	1.18
1999-00	1.22	1.08	.97	1.08	1.06	1.12	1.18	1.20	1.27	1.28	1.35	1.31	1.18
2000-1	1.24	1.07	.93	.95	1.08	1.22	1.14	1.21	1.28	1.24	1.28	1.28	1.16
2001-2	1.38	1.33	1.25	1.39	1.64	1.79	1.92	1.93	1.91	1.99	1.99	1.99	1.71
2002-3	1.95	1.69	1.67	1.80	1.80	1.91	1.95	2.04	2.11	2.08	1.99	1.95	1.91
2003-4[1]	1.84	1.47	1.39	1.38	1.44	1.32	1.58	1.46	1.51				1.49

[1] Preliminary.   *Source: National Agricultural Statistics Service, U.S. Department of Agriculture (NASS-USDA)*

Olive Oil

Olive oil is derived from the fruit of the olive tree, which originated in the Mediterranean area. Olives designated for oil are picked before ripening in the fall and is usually done by hand. The olives are then weighed and washed in cold water. The olives, along with their oil-rich pits, are then crushed and kneaded until a homogeneous paste is formed. The paste is spread by hand onto metal plates, which are then stacked and pressed hydraulically to yield a liquid. The liquid is then centrifuged to separate the oil. It takes 1,300 to 2,000 olives to produce 1 quart of olive oil. The best olive oil is still produced from the first pressing, which is usually performed within 24 to 72 hours after harvest and is called *extra virgin* olive oil.

Supply – World production of olive oil (pressed oil) in 2002/3 fell –11.2% to 2.471 million metric tons from the record-high production level of 2.784 million metric tons in 2001/2. The world's largest producers of olive oil are Spain (with 36% of world production), Italy (22%), Greece (15%), Turkey (8%), and Syria (7%). Production levels in various countries are highly volatile from year-to-year depending on various weather and crop conditions.

Demand – World consumption of olive oil in 2002/3 rose +1.8% to 2.805 million metric tons. The US is the world's largest consumer of olive oil with 7.9% of world consumption in 2002/3. US consumption of olive oil is on an upward trend, reaching a record 220,300 metric tons in 2002-03, up from 211,500 metric tons in 2001/2 and double that seen a decade earlier.

Trade – World olive oil imports in 2002/3 fell –0.1% to 491,400 metric tons. The US was the world's largest importer in 2002/3 with 220,200 metric tons, representing 45% of world imports. The world's largest exporters are Italy (with 36% of world exports), Spain (21%), and Turkey (16%).

World Production of Olive Oil (Pressed Oil) In Thousands of Metric Tons

Year	Algeria	Argentina	Greece	Italy	Jordan	Libya	Morocco	Portugal	Spain	Syria	Tunisia	Turkey	World Total
1995-6	23.0	11.5	362.0	540.0	15.5	4.0	40.0	48.6	320.0	84.0	64.5	45.5	1,598.4
1996-7	46.0	12.0	469.8	317.0	25.5	10.0	121.0	48.8	1,027.5	138.0	288.5	222.0	2,771.6
1997-8	6.5	8.5	405.0	585.0	16.0	6.0	75.0	45.5	1,212.0	78.0	99.0	45.0	2,615.5
1998-9	54.5	7.0	511.0	427.2	23.5	8.0	71.0	40.3	804.0	129.0	231.0	188.0	2,537.1
1999-00	33.5	11.5	454.0	670.0	7.0	7.0	45.0	58.3	694.1	88.0	225.0	61.0	2,412.4
2000-1[1]	26.5	3.0	467.0	508.0	29.5	4.0	39.5	28.5	1,040.0	183.0	141.0	197.5	2,731.7
2001-2[2]	25.5	10.0	390.0	490.0	16.0	7.0	66.0	38.7	1,468.0	104.0	40.0	71.0	2,783.6
2002-3[3]	25.0	8.0	378.0	550.0	28.0	6.5	55.0	46.0	890.0	162.5	54.0	192.5	2,470.7

[1] Preliminary. [2] Estimate. [3] Forecast. *Source: The Oil World*

World Imports and Exports of Olive Oil (Pressed Oil) In Thousands of Metric Tons

	Imports							Exports					
Year	Australia	Brazil	Italy	Japan	Spain	United States	World Total	Greece	Italy	Spain	Tunisia	Turkey	World Total
1995-6	16.7	18.8	47.0	16.1	26.4	113.6	318.4	7.8	98.0	54.4	33.1	28.9	307.9
1996-7	19.0	26.3	108.1	24.3	35.2	148.1	461.8	9.3	136.8	72.0	101.4	46.6	460.5
1997-8	17.7	28.9	89.4	35.5	28.0	161.0	467.8	9.3	140.2	82.0	126.8	42.2	469.4
1998-9	23.7	23.5	150.4	28.1	76.8	169.9	570.7	6.3	141.6	70.9	172.5	99.0	572.9
1999-00	24.2	25.6	105.2	27.2	23.4	189.3	504.8	9.4	180.0	97.2	122.4	25.8	502.1
2000-1[1]	29.5	24.7	110.5	29.6	13.3	212.5	551.6	6.7	198.1	100.7	101.0	77.5	559.5
2001-2[2]	26.4	24.0	51.4	31.2	6.6	218.1	492.0	9.9	204.9	120.3	33.0	39.8	486.4
2002-3[3]	27.6	24.9	38.0	32.0	16.2	220.2	491.4	9.5	175.0	105.4	22.2	80.3	491.8

[1] Preliminary. [2] Estimate. [3] Forecast. *Source: The Oil World*

World Consumption and Ending Stocks of Olive Oil (Pressed Oil) In Thousands of Metric Tons

	Consumption							Ending Stocks					
Year	Brazil	Morocco	Syria	Tunisia	Turkey	United States	World Total	Greece	Italy	Spain	Syria	Turkey	World Total
1995-6	18.8	32.9	98.5	32.4	64.7	110.5	1,884.6	30.9	81.4	88.4	12.0	23.0	320.1
1996-7	26.3	57.2	103.9	89.1	83.4	130.9	2,246.3	115.0	47.4	273.0	50.0	115.0	846.7
1997-8	28.9	61.3	106.9	61.0	82.9	154.8	2,406.9	118.3	204.1	533.1	24.0	35.0	1,053.7
1998-9	23.5	62.5	107.8	64.8	74.3	160.9	2,534.6	132.0	120.8	574.4	46.0	50.0	1,054.0
1999-00	25.6	55.7	99.0	66.3	76.3	180.1	2,607.3	143.0	173.9	340.0	36.6	9.9	861.9
2000-1[1]	24.7	46.6	114.6	65.3	79.9	205.5	2,739.1	142.0	136.0	287.9	95.0	50.0	846.6
2001-2[2]	24.0	66.5	115.9	35.3	71.1	211.5	2,754.6	162.0	69.0	476.0	70.7	12.0	881.1
2002-3[3]	24.9	57.3	120.1	29.9	84.8	220.3	2,804.8	128.6	55.0	150.0	85.0	41.7	546.6

[1] Preliminary. [2] Estimate. [3] Forecast. *Source: The Oil World*

Onions

Onions are the bulbs of plants in the lily family. Onions can be eaten raw, cooked, pickled, used as a flavoring or seasoning, or dehydrated. Onions, by value, rank in the top 10 vegetables produced in the US. Since 1629, onions have been cultivated in the US, but are believed to be indigenous to Asia.

Onions that are planted as a winter crop in warm areas are milder in taste and odor than onions planted during the summer in cooler regions. The two main types of onions produced in the US are yellow and white onions. Yellow varieties comprise approximately 75% of all onions grown for bulb production in the US.

Prices – Onion prices in 2003 rallied to a record yearly average of $19.53 per hundred pounds, up 66% from $11.73 in 2002. The record high yearly average price in 2003 was due to an upward spike in April to $39.80. Prices, however, fell back to the $14 area by late in 2003.

Supply – US production in 2002 was little changed at 6.761 billion pounds. The farm value of the US production crop in 2002 was $716 million, up from $698 million in 2001. US farmers harvested 160,220 acres in 2002, which was a 9-year low. The yield per acre in 2002 was 42,200 pounds per acre.

Demand – US per capita consumption of onions in 2003 rose to 19.5 pounds from 19.3 pounds in 2002.

Trade – US exports of fresh onions in 2002 totaled 700 million pounds, and imports were not far behind at 610 million pounds.

Salient Statistics of Onions in the United States

Crop Year	Harvested Acres	Yield Per Acre	Production 1,000 Cwt.	Price Per Cwt.	Farm Value $1,000	Jan. 1 Pack Frozen	Annual Pack Frozen	Imports Canned	Exports (Fresh)	Imports (Fresh)	Per Capita[3] Utilization -- Lbs., Farm Weight -- All	Fresh
						In Millions of Pounds						
1998	171,340	393	67,282	13.80	838,441	42.2	270.9	3.5	628.8	598.5	19.4	18.3
1999	173,400	424	73,562	9.78	635,128	40.3	310.5	5.2	667.7	583.9	20.7	18.4
2000	166,170	432	71,721	11.30	736,369	58.3	226.2	5.0	763.5	476.9	20.1	18.3
2001	161,590	419	67,653	11.40	697,950	54.9		5.0	708.3	632.6	19.4	18.3
2002[1]	160,220	424	67,928	12.40	767,913	36.9			637.2	595.4	19.3	18.3
2003[2]	159,490	437	69,727	15.00	958,032					646.3	19.5	18.3

[1] Preliminary. [2] Forecast. [3] Includes fresh and processing. *Source: Economic Research Service, U.S. Department of Agiculture (ERS-USDA)*

Production of Onions in the United States   In Thousands of Hundredweight (Cwt.)

	Spring				Summer										
Year	Arizona	California	Texas	Total (All)	California	Colorado	Idaho	Michigan	Minne-sota	New Mexico	New York	Oregon (Malheur)	Texas	Total (All)	Grand Total
1998	1,175	4,050	2,907	10,356	14,388	6,080	4,640	1,092	150	----	3,750	6,120	----	55,668	66,024
1999	1,635	3,212	3,620	11,222	16,965	5,438	5,530	1,080	118	----	3,528	8,643	----	62,340	73,562
2000	1,376	3,089	4,185	11,812	16,154	4,083	4,810	945	19	----	4,674	6,960	----	59,909	71,721
2001	1,290	2,666	4,615	11,136	12,069	4,140	4,992	999	73	----	4,224	7,006	----	56,517	67,653
2002	690	2,945	4,725	9,798	12,464	4,400	5,056	897	78	----	2,829	7,800	----	58,130	67,928
2003[1]	750	3,283	3,520	9,741	13,527	3,936	4,920	1,152	65	----	3,808	7,080	----	59,986	69,727

[1] Preliminary. *Source: Agricultural Statistics Board, U.S. Department of Agiculture (ASB-USDA)*

Cold Storage Stocks of Frozen Onions in the United States, on First of Month   In Thousands of Pounds

Year	Jan.	Feb.	Mar.	Apr.	May	June	July	Aug.	Sept.	Oct.	Nov.	Dec.
1998	31,187	28,724	27,710	24,428	23,443	22,787	22,179	21,468	18,755	24,553	27,070	25,965
1999	24,596	24,665	27,280	27,972	33,113	35,809	35,605	33,171	31,675	31,338	35,573	41,677
2000	41,236	40,730	44,029	45,874	52,691	55,340	53,537	42,910	40,792	34,318	37,408	39,909
2001	40,420	39,722	39,407	36,925	36,503	38,705	38,275	29,993	28,912	26,133	27,726	28,987
2002	29,893	33,646	34,851	35,477	40,789	41,066	40,762	33,370	36,895	36,120	39,796	39,310
2003[1]	39,480	39,764	38,126	37,569	35,623	35,617	36,529	35,590	35,907	33,846	38,693	39,467

[1] Preliminary. *Source: National Agricultural Statistics Service, U.S. Department of Agiculture (NASS-USDA)*

Average Price Received by Growers for Onions in the United States   In Dollars Per Hundred Pounds (Cwt.)

Year	Jan.	Feb.	Mar.	Apr.	May	June	July	Aug.	Sept.	Oct.	Nov.	Dec.	Season Average
1998	10.50	14.00	19.40	19.20	15.80	14.00	19.10	14.00	12.90	12.70	14.00	16.00	13.80
1999	16.10	13.10	10.00	14.60	13.00	15.00	15.70	13.10	10.10	8.18	7.47	6.95	9.78
2000	5.86	4.86	4.38	10.00	12.50	12.10	13.30	12.10	10.60	10.10	10.70	11.10	11.30
2001	11.40	10.60	10.70	12.80	15.50	15.30	15.50	12.30	10.70	9.20	7.41	9.35	11.60
2002	9.48	8.27	6.92	16.20	16.10	15.60	15.10	12.20	10.00	9.61	9.79	11.50	12.40
2003[1]	12.30	14.90	21.80	39.80	35.00	22.20	17.50	14.10	13.10	13.40	14.70	16.10	15.00

[1] Preliminary. *Source: Economic Research Service, U.S. Department of Agiculture (ERS-USDA)*

Oranges and Orange Juice

The orange tree is a semi-tropical, non-deciduous tree, and the fruit is technically a hesperidium, a kind of berry. The orange originated in India and was called *na rangi* in Sanskrit. The original fruit was bitter compared to modern varieties. The three major varieties of oranges include the sweet orange, the sour orange, and the mandarin orange (or tangerine). In the US, only sweet oranges are grown commercially. Those include Hamlin, Jaffa, navel, Pineapple, blood orange, and Valencia. Sour oranges are mainly used in marmalade and as an ingredient in liqueurs such as triple sec and curacao.

Frozen Concentrated Orange Juice (FCOJ) was developed in 1945, which led to oranges becoming the main fruit crop in the US. The world's largest producer of orange juice is Brazil, followed by Florida. Two to four medium-sized oranges will produce about 1 cup of juice, and modern mechanical extractors can remove the juice from 400 to 700 oranges per minute. Before juice extraction, orange oil is recovered from the peel. Orange oil is used to produce flavors, perfumes, wood furniture conditioners, and cleaning agents. Approximately 50% of the orange weight is juice, the remainder is peel, pulp, and seeds, which are dried to produce nutritious cattle feed.

Frozen concentrated orange juice future and options are traded on the NYCE division of the New York Board of Trade (NYBOT). The NYCE orange juice futures contract calls for the delivery of 15,000 pounds of orange solids and is priced in terms of cents per pound.

Prices – NYCE orange juice futures in 2003 were locked in a sustained bear market that lasted all year and produced new 3-decade lows. Orange juice prices fell to levels not seen since the 1970's, producing some serious financial problems for orange producers. Orange juice futures closed 2003 on the year's low at 60.75 cents per pound, down 34% from the 2002 close of 92.20 cents. Bearish factors centered on weak demand with the emphasis on low-carbohydrate diets and a bumper crop in Florida in 2003.

Supply – World production of oranges in the 2001/2 marketing year rose +7.1% to 48.301 million metric tons from 45.108 million in 2000-1. The world's largest producers of oranges are Brazil with 37% of world production, followed by the US (24%), and Mexico (8%).

US production of oranges in 2002/3 fell -5.9% 267.0 million boxes. Florida production fell -11.7% to 203.0 million boxes, while California production rose by 20.4% to 62.0 million boxes. California oranges go mostly to the fresh market while about 90% of Florida's oranges are processed for frozen orange juice concentrate. Florida produces approximately 70% of US oranges. The orange juice yield in 2002/3 was 1.54 gallons per box, which was a 7-year low.

World Production of Oranges — In Thousands of Metric Tons

Year	Argentina	Australia	Brazil	Egypt	Greece	Italy	Mexico	Morocco	South Africa	Spain	Turkey	United States	World Total
1992-3	660	578	14,484	1,771	1,042	2,111	2,913	874	712	2,926	820	10,074	41,582
1993-4	746	651	13,710	1,324	854	2,100	3,174	916	739	2,509	840	9,462	39,595
1994-5	712	416	16,520	1,513	865	1,710	3,500	657	770	2,644	920	10,641	43,539
1995-6	703	589	16,973	1,360	838	1,770	2,600	870	850	2,440	880	10,454	43,066
1996-7	640	543	16,450	1,360	850	1,770	2,600	870	850	2,440	880	10,747	42,932
1997-8	921	448	15,912	1,350	987	2,100	3,331	1,131	961	2,744	740	12,493	46,300
1998-9	660	515	17,952	1,442	795	1,422	2,903	900	1,048	2,442	970	8,989	43,768
1999-00[1]	789	624	17,136	1,637	1,040	1,750	3,385	845	1,119	2,828	1,100	11,875	48,391
2000-1[2]	913	437	14,729	1,610	1,100	1,800	3,885	693	1,150	2,688	1,070	11,225	45,108
2001-2[3]	780	591	17,993	1,642	800	1,935	3,800	680	1,220	2,807	1,040	11,337	48,301

[1] Preliminary. [2] Estimate. [3] Forecast. NA = Not available. *Source: Foreign Agricultural Service, U.S. Department of Agriculture (FAS-USDA)*

Salient Statistics of Oranges & Orange Juice in the United States

						Florida Crop Processed				Frozen Concentrated Orange Juice - Florida			
	Production[4]			Farm Price $ Per	Farm Value	Frozen Concen-trates	Chilled Products	Total Pro-cessed	Yield Per Box Gallons[5]	Carry-in	Pack	Total Supply	Total Season Movement
	California	Florida	Total U.S.										
Year	Million Boxes			Box	Million $	Million Boxes				In Millions of Gallons (42 Deg. Brix)			
1993-4	63.6	174.4	240.5	6.37	1,541.3	111.7	51.0	174.4	1.6	53.5	261.7	315.2	256.6
1994-5	56.0	205.5	263.6	6.08	1,624.1	144.7	54.8	199.8	1.5	58.6	274.2	332.8	290.4
1995-6	58.0	203.3	263.9	6.85	1,821.6	132.9	64.5	197.7	1.5	42.4	284.5	326.9	285.7
1996-7	64.0	226.2	293.0	6.16	1,836.7	153.8	65.7	220.4	1.6	41.2	289.6	342.9	273.9
1997-8	69.0	244.0	315.5	6.13	1,965.4	160.9	74.8	236.6	1.6	69.7	290.2	359.9	263.8
1998-9	36.0	186.0	224.6	7.41	1,687.9	97.2	80.1	175.1	1.6	104.7	216.9	321.6	209.1
1999-00	64.0	233.0	299.8	5.56	1,666.1	134.2	90.1	226.7	1.5	105.2	254.0	359.2	239.7
2000-1[1]	54.5	223.3	280.9	5.88	1,682.8	124.1	89.6	215.9	1.6	112.6	245.2	357.8	226.0
2001-2[2]	51.5	230.0	283.8	6.37	1,846.2	136.0	85.9	223.2	1.6	128.3	253.2	381.5	249.9
2002-3[3]	62.0	203.0	267.0	5.97	1,611.8	102.1	92.5	196.1	1.5	120.2	203.3	323.5	200.2

[1] Preliminary. [2] Estimate. [3] Forecast. [4] Fruit ripened on trees, but destroyed prior to picking not included. [5] 42 deg. Brix equivalent.
Source: Economic Research Service, U.S. Department of Agriculture (ERS-USDA); Florida Department of Citrus

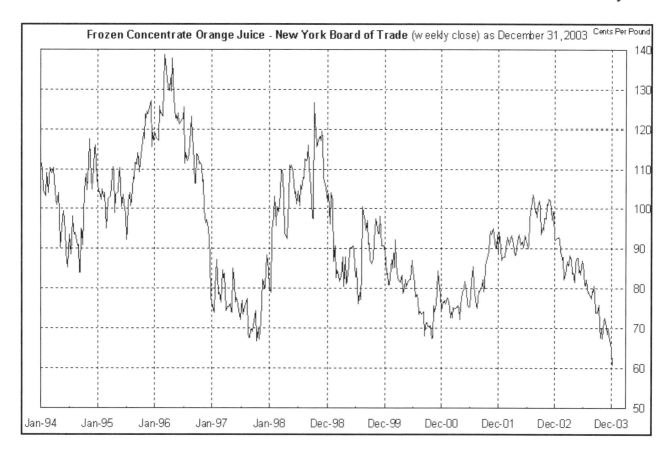

Frozen Concentrate Orange Juice - New York Board of Trade (weekly close) as December 31, 2003. Cents Per Pound

Average Open Interest of Frozen Concentrated Orange Juice Futures in New York — In Contracts

Year	Jan.	Feb.	Mar.	Apr.	May	June	July	Aug.	Sept.	Oct.	Nov.	Dec.
1994	17,544	18,137	19,073	21,607	21,450	23,530	24,829	21,874	22,739	23,385	26,859	26,413
1995	27,439	25,885	26,407	30,172	27,057	26,844	23,537	17,881	20,918	22,460	26,303	24,202
1996	22,943	21,670	25,232	23,788	21,724	20,934	20,159	19,834	18,029	18,000	22,513	26,405
1997	29,171	26,929	26,331	28,955	29,868	33,639	31,799	34,339	36,057	40,365	41,811	46,169
1998	38,885	37,893	36,843	33,146	35,749	32,608	25,503	26,394	28,017	26,506	21,984	24,562
1999	25,917	28,965	28,707	31,199	26,669	28,362	28,087	30,021	28,922	27,498	26,893	25,887
2000	23,727	24,647	19,684	22,475	23,456	27,087	27,386	30,272	30,090	32,328	30,192	30,757
2001	28,852	28,011	28,073	27,794	24,199	24,428	22,591	22,073	17,789	18,026	21,506	19,275
2002	15,716	16,593	18,515	22,328	23,498	26,581	28,137	33,206	27,323	23,758	22,651	23,461
2003	25,080	26,588	22,707	21,466	20,634	23,794	25,467	26,518	27,788	30,767	31,575	36,371

Source: New York Board of Trade (NYBOT)

Volume of Trading of Frozen Concentrated Orange Juice Futures in New York — In Contracts

Year	Jan.	Feb.	Mar.	Apr.	May	June	July	Aug.	Sept.	Oct.	Nov.	Dec.	Total
1994	46,166	51,123	43,075	55,955	48,236	60,110	37,069	55,711	52,209	73,155	54,978	76,037	653,824
1995	50,875	66,370	51,292	78,288	32,607	80,165	41,357	67,528	38,781	64,904	45,688	71,077	688,932
1996	59,666	82,057	46,272	65,752	62,247	44,827	40,884	58,346	44,239	40,680	39,291	70,676	654,937
1997	84,982	89,875	66,340	82,772	62,890	78,690	47,242	118,286	55,081	108,413	100,941	134,349	1,029,861
1998	96,020	81,554	66,235	101,651	70,909	79,319	48,844	85,544	81,187	98,639	29,541	75,171	914,614
1999	64,149	92,868	40,027	92,522	49,180	78,627	48,177	99,531	49,323	71,914	42,532	68,734	797,584
2000	45,680	78,532	33,617	71,024	50,475	80,372	46,548	67,312	38,485	64,831	45,966	89,362	712,204
2001	46,655	66,561	27,994	63,012	38,447	66,773	40,870	64,860	22,246	68,364	23,376	48,338	577,496
2002	31,709	50,898	30,316	58,644	37,283	52,238	45,316	78,111	36,053	71,635	24,111	61,443	577,757
2003	45,945	63,224	23,926	70,846	35,791	64,209	27,056	73,792	40,782	87,055	42,084	78,005	652,715

Source: New York Board of Trade (NYBOT)

ORANGES AND ORANGE JUICE

Cold Storage Stocks of Orange Juice Concentrate in the U.S., on First of Month   In Millions of Pounds

Year	Jan.	Feb.	Mar.	Apr.	May	June	July	Aug.	Sept.	Oct.	Nov.	Dec.
1994	955.5	1,248.9	1,429.0	1,273.8	1,499.6	1,615.2	1,521.8	1,449.1	1,257.5	1,119.6	1,026.1	1,055.9
1995	1,353.1	1,704.0	1,685.1	1,773.3	1,864.6	1,833.8	1,631.6	1,424.1	1,233.7	1,038.3	830.3	897.7
1996	1,050.6	1,295.4	1,353.0	1,322.3	1,443.9	1,596.9	1,535.0	1,423.6	1,238.6	965.6	732.7	691.0
1997	1,069.4	1,522.6	1,677.6	1,752.9	1,993.4	2,176.0	1,977.7	1,761.8	1,571.8	1,287.8	1,140.9	1,214.4
1998	1,503.4	1,945.9	2,029.7	2,025.0	2,487.0	2,627.5	2,457.7	2,249.0	2,025.1	1,803.9	1,470.7	1,540.2
1999	1,791.9	1,999.4	2,204.2	2,191.3	2,485.7	2,115.6	1,969.7	1,823.0	1,618.5	1,443.4	1,182.0	1,102.7
2000	1,330.7	1,540.6	1,632.7	1,857.9	1,812.5	1,965.6	2,037.9	1,843.7	1,457.7	1,346.6	1,169.4	1,202.0
2001	1,382.0	1,610.8	1,825.1	1,735.5	1,872.2	2,061.8	2,035.6	1,913.2	1,691.1	1,537.7	1,398.9	1,406.7
2002	1,571.7	1,721.3	1,770.9	1,794.4	1,886.0	1,982.8	1,934.0	1,870.9	1,680.9	1,543.6	1,409.6	1,471.2
2003[1]	1,673.6	1,851.9	1,833.4	1,856.6	1,936.9	2,102.6	2,021.2	1,848.9	1,672.2	1,529.8	1,335.6	1,428.5

[1] Preliminary.   Source: Agricultural Statistics Board, U.S. Department of Agriculture (ASB-USDA)

Producer Price Index of Frozen Orange Juice Concentrate   1982 = 100

Year	Jan.	Feb.	Mar.	Apr.	May	June	July	Aug.	Sept.	Oct.	Nov.	Dec.	Average
1994	107.9	104.8	104.2	104.2	102.7	101.2	100.2	100.1	99.9	99.8	100.7	100.5	102.2
1995	107.4	105.4	107.6	107.6	109.1	109.1	109.1	105.3	101.0	101.6	106.1	107.3	106.4
1996	109.4	112.5	117.2	119.5	119.5	119.5	115.3	113.6	113.6	112.8	112.8	108.8	114.5
1997	106.9	106.9	106.0	107.6	107.7	107.3	105.3	105.8	102.7	101.4	95.0	94.2	103.9
1998	94.9	101.2	104.1	103.2	108.8	109.1	109.5	109.6	109.5	110.2	119.1	121.2	108.4
1999	119.7	118.6	118.0	115.5	113.3	113.2	112.5	111.3	112.4	112.5	113.1	112.4	114.4
2000	110.0	108.9	108.0	107.1	106.9	106.6	105.4	104.8	101.5	100.4	99.8	99.1	104.9
2001	98.9	99.2	98.3	96.8	96.8	97.4	97.3	97.2	97.3	97.3	99.6	102.5	98.2
2002	103.0	102.9	103.1	102.9	102.8	103.2	103.2	103.5	107.4	107.4	109.7	110.2	104.9
2003[1]	110.2	110.2	110.7	110.4	108.5	109.4	109.1	108.9	106.7	106.1	104.0	100.8	107.9

[1] Preliminary.   Source: Bureau of Labor Statistics, U.S. Department of Labor (BLS)

Average Price of Oranges (Equivalent On-Tree) Received by Growers in the U.S.   In Dollars Per Box

Year	Jan.	Feb.	Mar.	Apr.	May	June	July	Aug.	Sept.	Oct.	Nov.	Dec.	Average
1994	3.76	3.90	4.66	4.83	5.04	4.94	4.08	4.24	3.44	2.92	3.44	3.43	4.06
1995	3.43	3.59	4.22	4.61	4.90	5.63	7.44	7.30	7.26	7.90	3.57	3.55	5.28
1996	3.97	4.39	5.20	6.11	6.63	6.72	6.97	8.15	13.70	10.94	4.17	3.52	6.71
1997	3.59	3.67	4.82	4.68	4.74	4.62	6.48	7.45	7.15	4.48	3.09	3.14	4.83
1998	3.14	3.55	5.05	5.44	5.70	6.05	6.77	5.56	5.64	5.98	5.03	4.82	5.23
1999	4.52	4.99	5.90	5.96	6.48	8.04	8.58	6.66	9.96	9.50	4.70	3.42	6.56
2000	3.35	3.18	3.24	4.20	4.39	4.34	2.45	0.35	0.29	1.43	3.20	2.95	2.78
2001	2.85	3.20	4.93	4.84	4.64	4.47	4.63	5.01	6.20	4.99	2.90	3.20	4.32
2002	3.75	4.05	4.64	4.65	4.47	4.00	4.06	6.61	5.33	5.18	3.11	3.23	4.42
2003[1]	3.00	3.14	4.59	4.46	4.57	4.49	4.35	4.27	2.80	5.76	2.23	2.44	3.84

[1] Preliminary.   Source: Economic Research Service, U.S. Department of Agriculture (ERS-USDA)

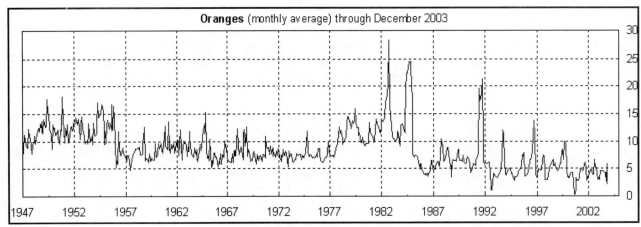

Oranges (monthly average) through December 2003

Palm Oil

Palm oil is an edible vegetable oil produced from the flesh of the fruit of the oil palm tree. The oil palm tree is a tropical palm tree that is a native of the west coast of Africa and is different from the coconut palm tree. The fruit of the oil palm tree is reddish, about the size of a large plum, and grows in large bunches. A single seed, the palm kernel, is contained in each fruit. Oil is extracted from both the pulp of the fruit (becoming palm oil) and the kernel (palm kernel oil), with 1 metric ton of palm kernel oil obtained for every 10 metric tons of palm oil.

Palm oil is commercially used in soap, ointments, cosmetics, detergents, and machinery lubricants. It is also used worldwide as cooking oil, shortening, and margarine. Palm kernel oil is a lighter oil and is used exclusively for food use. Crude palm oil and crude palm kernel oil are traded on the Kuala Lumpur Commodity Exchange (KLSE).

Prices – Palm oil prices in September 2003 were 32.25 cents/pound, slightly above the running average for calendar 2003 of 31.76 cents. That was sharply higher than 23.31 cents in 2002 and 15.73 cents in 2001.

Supply – World production of palm oil in 2003/4 rose by 3% to 28.13 million metric tons from 27.21 million in 2002/3. Palm oil is the world's second largest vegetable oil crop, running only slightly below soybean oil production of 31.98 million metric tons in 2003/4. The large production year in 2003/4 for palm oil outpaced demand and that led to an 11% increase in stocks to 2.31 million metric tons from 2.09 million in 2002/3, although that is still a relatively tight stocks level compared to the 1999 to 2002 period.

The world's largest producer of palm oil by far is Malaysia with 48% of world production and Indonesia is the second largest producer with 36% of world production. Together they account for 84% of world production. Malaysian production in 2002/3 rose by 6% to 12.520 million metric tons from 11.856 million in 2001/2. Indonesian production in 2002/3 rose by 8% to 9.480 million metric tons from 8.790 million in 2001/2.

Trade – World palm oil exports in 2002/3 rose by 6.5% to 20.220 million metric tons. The world's largest exporters are Malaysia with a 58% market share of world exports, followed by Indonesia with a 32% share. The world's largest importers are India with a 16% share of world imports, followed by Germany (9%) and China (8%).

World Production of Palm Oil   In Thousands of Metric Tons

Crop Year	Brazil	Came-roon	Colom-bia	Costa Rica	Ecuador	Ghana	Indo-nesia	Ivory Coast	Malay-sia	Nigeria	Papua/N Guinea	Thailand	World Total
1993-4	80	90	348	84	166	50	3,630	305	7,103	640	212	311	13,793
1994-5	85	125	391	88	194	74	4,144	282	7,771	661	223	346	15,073
1995-6	90	130	393	93	220	79	4,587	277	8,264	667	236	369	16,152
1996-7	90	161	440	97	200	83	5,078	258	9,000	678	248	438	17,569
1997-8	88	140	439	108	205	107	5,320	270	8,509	688	206	469	17,305
1998-9	91	134	466	116	247	110	6,011	265	9,759	713	257	540	19,502
1999-00	105	138	513	136	233	109	6,855	283	10,492	735	300	533	21,281
2000-1[1]	109	143	561	138	196	108	7,725	226	11,940	763	334	597	23,730
2001-2[2]	115	144	517	140	213	108	8,790	238	11,856	774	338	597	24,747
2002-3[3]	128	146	572	143	255	111	9,480	254	12,520	782	310	613	26,251

[1] Preliminary.   [2] Estimate.   [3] Forecast.   *Source: The Oil World*

World Trade of Palm Oil   In Thousands of Metric Tons

Crop Year	Imports							Exports					
	China	Germany	India	Nether-lands	Pakistan	United Kingdom	World Total	Hong Kong	Indo-nesia	Malay-sia	Papua/N Guinea	Singa-pore	World Total
1993-4	1,653	427	200	443	1,080	365	10,346	234	1,965	6,737	210	829	10,391
1994-5	1,786	412	480	443	1,215	462	10,674	145	1,904	6,728	178	829	10,573
1995-6	1,178	446	970	544	1,166	500	10,558	160	2,082	6,896	191	829	10,582
1996-7	1,851	498	1,300	649	1,020	516	11,751	145	2,419	7,794	203	829	11,974
1997-8	1,490	370	1,684	670	1,210	457	11,971	120	2,459	7,847	207	253	11,795
1998-9	1,433	406	2,762	738	1,053	528	12,962	113	3,219	8,482	248	289	13,246
1999-00	1,474	431	3,482	780	1,086	558	14,774	130	3,898	9,101	292	251	14,722
2000-1[1]	2,147	497	3,856	907	1,191	610	17,369	180	4,577	10,767	334	228	17,311
2001-2[2]	2,600	592	3,233	1,071	1,333	721	18,683	302	6,024	10,939	322	217	18,977
2002-3[3]	2,800	644	3,750	1,123	1,315	732	20,390	330	6,450	11,680	325	243	20,220

[1] Preliminary.   [2] Estimate.   [3] Forecast.   *Source: The Oil World*

PALM OIL

Supply and Distribution of Palm Oil in the United States   In Thousands of Metric Tons

Year Beginning Oct. 1	Stocks Oct. 1	Imports	Total Supply	Edible Products	Inedible Products	Total End Products	Total Disappearance	Exports	U.S. Import Value[4]	Malaysia, F.O.B., RBD	Palm Kernal Oil, Malaysia, C.I.F. Rotterdam
				Consumption					**Prices**		
				------ In Millions of Pounds ------					---------- U.S. $ Per Metric Ton ----------		
1993-4	14.9	167.0	181.9	86.2	118.2	204.4	162.0	3.6	370	451	566
1994-5	16.4	98.7	115.1	38.1	113.6	151.7	101.8	5.9	538	647	680
1995-6	7.4	106.9	114.3	6.7	103.9	110.6	91.1	9.2	511	545	729
1996-7	14.0	146.4	160.4	W	91.8	W	164.6	4.2	432	544	680
1997-8	21.4	128.0	149.4	W	93.8	W	155.3	4.4	464	640	653
1998-9	16.1	128.8	144.9	W	72.4	W	173.2	5.2	----	514	708
1999-00	21.1	156.6	177.7	W	55.0	W	183.4	3.4	----	338	533
2000-1[1]	25.7	175.5	201.2	W	36.0	W	167.7	6.0	----	272	313
2001-2[2]	27.5	218.7	246.2	W	22.6	75.1	215.9	6.2	----	359	379
2002-3[3]	26.0	195.0	221.0	W	W	76.7	185.0	7.1	----	438	455

[1] Preliminary.   [2] Estimate.   [3] Forecast.   [4] Market value in the foreign country, excluding import duties, ocean freight and marine insurance.
Sources: The Oil World; Economic Research Service, U.S. Department of Agriculture (ERS-USDA)

Average Wholesale Palm Oil Prices, CIF, Bulk, U.S. Ports   In Cents Per Pound

Year	Jan.	Feb.	Mar.	Apr.	May	June	July	Aug.	Sept.	Oct.	Nov.	Dec.	Average
1994	21.91	21.67	21.72	23.08	26.27	28.94	27.44	30.18	32.15	31.93	34.95	36.83	28.09
1995	34.26	33.82	36.18	35.56	32.80	33.06	33.68	32.59	30.86	31.45	31.96	30.00	33.02
1996	27.08	26.52	26.33	27.52	28.57	25.43	24.78	24.46	27.24	26.13	26.95	27.45	26.54
1997	28.68	29.25	28.00	28.18	28.93	27.25	26.17	25.55	25.37	27.33	27.28	25.05	27.25
1998	29.30	29.59	30.53	32.10	31.11	31.42	32.33	33.14	33.14	33.06	33.30	34.00	31.92
1999	31.06	28.58	25.52	25.52	24.50	21.30	18.15	18.70	21.00	20.00	20.00	20.00	22.86
2000	18.65	17.66	17.73	18.21	18.12	16.52	16.85	16.23	15.90	13.19	13.56	12.75	16.28
2001	18.05	18.05	13.50	13.50	12.50	13.00	15.50	18.00	16.75	15.60	16.85	17.45	15.73
2002	17.75	17.06	17.30	17.75	18.85	21.44	20.50	21.85	32.00	31.75	31.75	31.75	23.31
2003	31.75	31.75	31.35	31.25	31.25	31.75	32.25	32.25	32.25				31.76

Source: Economic Research Service, U.S. Department of Agriculture (ERS-USDA)

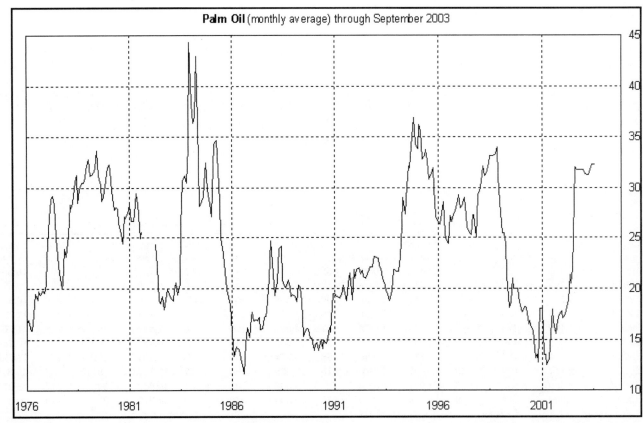

Palm Oil (monthly average) through September 2003

Paper

The earliest known paper, still in existence, was made from cotton rags around 150 AD. Around 800 AD, paper made its appearance in Egypt but was not manufactured there until 900 AD. The Moors introduced the use of paper to Europe, and around 1150, the first papermaking mill was established in Spain, followed by England in 1495, and the US in 1690.

During the 17th and 18th centuries, the increased usage of paper created a shortage of cotton rags, which were the only source for papermaking. The solution to this problem lead to the introduction of the ground-wood process of pulp making in 1840 and the first chemical pulp process 10 years later.

Today, the paper and paperboard industries, including newsprint, are economically sensitive. As the economy strengthens, paper use increases, and as the economy weakens, paper use declines.

Prices – The index price for paperboard was on track to fall –0.6% to 163.3 in 2003, but remained above the 10-year average of 160.4. The producer price index of standard newsprint paper was on track to rise +5.4% to 111.5 in 2003 from the 17-year low of 105.7 posted in 2002. The 2003 price was still well below the 10-year average price of 132.1.

Supply – US production of paper and paperboard in 2002 rose slightly by +0.4% to 81.792 million metric tons from 81.438 million in 2001, which was an 8-year low. The US is by far the world's largest producer of paper and paperboard, followed by Canada with 20.226 million metric tons and Germany with 18.526 million metric tons.

US production of newsprint rose to 428,000 metric tons per month in 2003, up from 330,800 metric tons per month in 2002. US production of newsprint is second, next to Canada, which had production of 718,100 metric tons per month in 2003.

Production of Paper and Paperboard by Selected Countries   In Thousands of Metric Tons

Year	Austria	Canada	Finland	France	Germany	Italy	Nether-lands	Norway	Russia	Spain	Sweden	United Kingdom	United States
1997	3,884	18,730	12,519	8,867	15,911	7,929	3,130	2,162	2,960	3,668	9,654	6,476	86,921
1998	4,009	18,875	12,703	9,161	16,311	8,254	3,180	2,260	3,595	3,545	9,879	6,477	86,451
1999	4,142	20,280	12,947	9,603	16,742	8,568	3,256	2,241	4,535	4,435	10,071	6,576	88,776
2000	4,386	20,921	13,509	10,006	18,182	9,129	3,332	2,300	5,310	4,765	10,786	6,868	86,545
2001	4,250	19,834	12,502	9,625	17,879	8,926	3,174	2,220	5,625	5,131	10,534	6,467	81,438
2002[1]	4,419	20,226	12,776	9,798	18,526	9,273	3,346	2,114	5,915	5,365	10,724	6,481	81,792

[1] Preliminary.   Source: Food and Agriculture Organization of the United Nations (FAO-UN)

Production of Newsprint by Selected Countries (Monthly Average)   In Thousands of Metric Tons

Year	Australia	Brazil	Canada	China	Finland	France	Germany	India	Japan	Rep. of Korea	Russia	Sweden	United States
1997	34.0	22.1	767.1	68.7	122.5	65.3	134.8	23.3	266.0	132.7	99.8	200.9	545.3
1998	33.9	22.7	718.6	70.8	123.6	75.7	135.8	28.8	272.0	141.7	116.2	206.5	541.7
1999	31.8	20.2	767.0	93.4	124.2	79.2	136.9	32.4	274.6	144.8	135.0	209.0	543.0
2000	32.7	22.2	768.0	121.0	116.1	86.6	150.5	48.9	284.9	151.5	141.5	211.5	547.5
2001	32.3	19.2	697.8	127.4	108.0	86.0	170.5	53.0	288.7	136.6	144.3	205.3	480.8
2002[1]	34.0	15.0	705.0	117.0	88.7	82.0	173.5	49.6	299.7	137.9		153.3	330.8
2003[2]	34.5	15.3	718.1	171.2	78.1	31.6	177.2	57.0	290.8	132.0		211.0	428.0

[1] Preliminary.   [2] Estimate.   Source: United Nations

Index Price of Paperboard   1982 = 100

Year	Jan.	Feb.	Mar.	Apr.	May	June	July	Aug.	Sept.	Oct.	Nov.	Dec.	Average
1997	147.1	144.2	139.7	137.2	136.8	137.5	137.8	143.8	148.4	150.1	154.4	156.1	144.4
1998	155.9	156.1	156.0	155.2	154.2	153.7	152.2	150.9	149.0	146.9	144.7	143.6	151.6
1999	142.2	142.3	146.4	148.1	149.3	149.5	154.5	158.6	161.0	162.1	162.2	162.3	153.2
2000	163.1	163.6	173.6	176.6	180.4	180.3	180.9	181.2	180.9	180.4	180.2	179.5	176.7
2001	179.4	176.6	175.8	175.2	174.1	172.4	172.3	169.8	169.0	167.1	166.8	167.0	172.1
2002	165.0	164.0	162.6	162.8	161.1	161.1	161.8	165.8	166.7	167.1	167.3	166.6	164.3
2003[1]	166.8	166.5	164.4	163.5	163.6	163.4	162.5	162.5	160.1	160.0	159.7	159.9	162.7

[1] Preliminary.   Source: Bureau of Labor Statistics, U.S. Department of Commerce (BLS) (0914)

Producer Price Index of Standard Newsprint   1982 = 100

Year	Jan.	Feb.	Mar.	Apr.	May	June	July	Aug.	Sept.	Oct.	Nov.	Dec.	Average
1997	121.1	120.9	123.1	128.6	135.9	137.2	138.6	139.4	139.4	139.4	141.3	141.8	133.9
1998	142.2	142.5	141.8	142.3	140.0	140.3	143.4	143.1	144.6	147.6	147.6	145.0	143.4
1999	143.0	135.9	128.1	125.0	117.8	117.7	110.3	111.7	111.4	NA	NA	NA	122.3
2000	117.2	116.8	116.5	118.3	123.1	127.1	127.6	130.7	131.5	139.4	141.2	140.5	127.5
2001	140.6	141.4	143.0	150.9	146.8	148.5	146.6	142.4	134.5	130.1	121.6	117.3	138.6
2002	113.6	106.2	106.5	105.7	98.9	100.5	101.0	101.8	104.7	112.2	109.6	107.9	105.7
2003[1]	106.1	107.4	106.3	110.2	112.6	112.5	111.0	114.3	116.5	117.0	114.4	113.3	111.8

[1] Preliminary.   NA = Not available.   Source: Bureau of Labor Statistics, U.S. Department of Commerce (BLS) (0913-02)

Peanuts and Peanut Oil

Peanuts are the edible seeds of a plant member of the pea family. Although called a nut, the peanut is actually a legume. Ancient South American Inca Indians were the first to grind peanuts to make peanut butter. The peanut originated in Brazil and was brought to the US via Africa. The first major use of peanuts was as feed for pigs. It wasn't until the Civil War that peanuts were used as human food, when both Northern and Southern troops used the peanut as a food source during hard times. In 1903, Dr. George Washington Carver, a talented botanist who is considered the "father of commercial peanuts", introduced peanuts as a rotation crop in cotton-growing areas. Carver discovered over 300 uses for the peanut including shaving cream, leather dye, coffee, ink, cheese, and shampoo.

Peanuts come in many varieties, but there are four basic types grown in the US: Runner, Spanish, Valencia, and Virginia. Over half of Runner peanuts are used to make peanut butter. Spanish peanuts are primarily used to make candies and peanut oil. Valencia peanuts are the sweetest of the four types. Virginia peanuts are mainly roasted and sold in and out of the shell.

Peanut oil is extracted from shelled and crushed peanuts through hydraulic pressing, expelled pressing, or solvent extraction. Crude peanut oil is used as a flavoring agent, salad oil, and light cooking oil. Refined, bleached and deodorized peanut oil is used for cooking and in margarines and shortenings. The by-product called press cake is used for cattle feed along with the tops of the plants, after the pods are removed. The dry shells can be burned as fuel.

Prices – The average price received by farmers for peanuts (in the shell) as of December 2003 was very depressed at 18.9 cents/pound. That was just 0.1 cent above the 2002/3 average of 18.8 cents, which was the weakest average price seen since 1974/5. Peanut prices were hurt in 2003 by an oversupply situation due to a 10% boost in production. That led to a 25% increase in stocks as demand failed to keep up with supply.

Supply – Peanut production in 2003/4 was forecast by the USDA at 33.45 million metric tons, up 10.4% from 30.31 million in 2002/3. The big boost in production led to a 25% increase in stocks in 2003/4 to 640,000 metric tons from 510,000 in 2002/3. The world's largest peanut producer is China with 45% of world production in 2003/4, followed by India with 22% and the US with 6%. India saw a sharp 44% jump in production to 7.50 million metric tons in 2003/4 versus 5.20 million in 2002/3, whereas Chinese production was only slightly higher by +1.3% to 15.10 million. World peanut oil production in 2003/4 rose by 13% to 4.91 million metric tons from 4.34 million in 2002/3. Peanut oil accounted for only about 5% of world vegetable oil production in 2003/4.

US peanut production in 2003/4 rose sharply by 23% to 1.86 million metric tons from 1.51 million in 2002/3. The largest peanut producing states in the US are Georgia (with about 44% of US production), Texas (19%), Alabama (13%), Florida (8%), and North Carolina (7%).

Demand – Of world peanut production, 47% of that production was forecast to go towards crushing of peanuts into oil and meal in 2003/4. Specifically, crush demand in 2003/4 was forecasted 15.82 million metric tons, up 13% from 14.04 million in 2002/3. World consumption of peanut meal in 2003/4 was forecast at 6.05 million metric tons, up 12% from 5.40 million in 2002/3. World consumption of peanut oil was forecast at 4.86 million in 2003/4, up 11% from 4.36 million in 2002/3.

There are three main types of peanuts grown in the US. The most popular type is Runner peanuts with 82% of US production, followed by Virginia peanuts with 15% of production, and Spanish peanuts with 3% of production. The primary use for both Runner and Virginia peanuts is the production of peanut butter (55% for Runner and 46% for Virginia). The second largest use for Virginia peanuts is for peanut snacks (42%), while the second largest use for Runner peanuts is candy (24%). The main use for Spanish peanuts is for candy (44%).

Trade – World exports of peanuts in 2003/4 was forecast at 1.54 million metric tons, up 16% from 1.33 million in 2002/3. Exports accounted for only 4.6% of overall world production, showing that peanuts are generally consumed where they are produced. US exports of peanuts in 2003/4 fell sharply to 141,000 metric tons from 269,000 in 2002/3.

World Production of Peanuts (in the Shell)   In Thousands of Metric Tons

Year	Argentina	Burma	China	India	Indonesia	Nigeria	Senegal	South Africa	Sudan	Thailand	United States	Zaire	World Total
1994-5	238	445	9,682	8,255	1,085	650	720	105	390	150	1,927	581	27,366
1995-6	462	501	10,200	7,400	1,055	800	827	193	370	147	1,570	585	27,467
1996-7	300	593	10,140	9,024	985	950	646	140	370	147	1,661	570	28,958
1997-8	625	559	9,648	7,580	990	1,250	506	97	370	130	1,605	400	27,289
1998-9	340	540	11,886	7,450	930	1,430	541	138	370	135	1,798	410	29,765
1999-00	420	560	12,640	5,500	1,020	1,450	760	170	370	140	1,740	400	28,990
2000-1	400	640	14,440	5,700	1,040	1,470	1,000	150	370	140	1,480	380	31,110
2001-2	360	730	14,420	7,600	1,030	1,490	900	150	370	130	1,940	370	33,630
2002-3[1]	220	700	14,900	5,200	1,040	1,510	260	150	370	130	1,510	360	30,310
2003-4[2]	220	710	15,100	7,500	1,040	1,510	450	150	370	130	1,860	410	33,450

[1] Preliminary.   [2] Estimate.   *Source: Foreign Agricultural Service, U.S. Department of Agriculture (FAS-USDA)*

Salient Statistics of Peanuts in the United States

Crop Year	Agreage Planted	Acreage Harvested for Nuts	Average Yield Per Acre	Pro- duction	Season Farm Price	Farm Value Million	----- Thousand Pounds (Year Beginning August 1) -----			
							------------ Exports -------------		------------- Imports -------------	
	----- 1,000 Acres -----		In Lbs.	1,000 Lbs.	Cents/Lb.	Dollars	Unshelled	Shelled	Unshelled	Shelled
1994-5	1,641.0	1,618.5	2,624	4,247,455	28.9	1,229.0	878,000	583,142	74,000	55,385
1995-6	1,537.5	1,517.0	2,282	3,461,475	29.3	1,013.3	826,000	564,021	153,000	108,303
1996-7	1,401.5	1,380.0	2,653	3,661,205	28.1	1,029.8	668,000	440,438	127,000	95,041
1997-8	1,434.0	1,413.8	2,503	3,539,380	28.3	1,001.6	682,000	455,264	141,000	101,792
1998-9	1,521.0	1,467.0	2,702	3,963,440	28.4	1,126.0	562,000	----	155,000	----
1999-00	1,534.5	1,436.0	2,667	3,829,490	25.4	971.6	727,000	----	178,000	----
2000-1	1,536.8	1,336.0	2,444	3,265,505	27.4	896.1	527,000	----	216,000	----
2001-2	1,541.2	1,411.9	3,029	4,276,704	23.4	1,000.5	713,000	----	203,000	----
2002-3[1]	1,358.0	1,296.7	2,561	3,320,490	18.2	599.6	490,000	----	75,000	----
2003-4[2]	1,344.0	1,312.0	3,159	4,144,150	18.8	779.2	500,000	----	65,000	----

[1] Preliminary.   [2] Estimate.   *Source: Economic Research Service, U.S. Department of Agriculture (ERS-USDA)*

Supply and Disposition of Peanuts (Farmer's Stock Basis) & Support Program in the United States

Crop Year	----------------------- Supply -----------------------				------------------------------ Disposition ------------------------------					-------- Government Support Program --------			
	Pro- duction	Imports	Stocks Aug. 1	Total	Exports	Crushed fior Oil	Seed, Loss & Residual	Food	Total Disap- pearance	Support Price	Addi- tional	Amount Put --- Under Support ---	
												Quantity Mil. Lbs.	% of Pro- duction
	------------------------ In Millions of Pounds ------------------------									---- Cents per Lb. ----			
1995-6	3,461	153	1,198	4,812	826	999	238	1,993	4,054	33.92	6.6	818	24.0
1996-7	3,661	127	758	4,546	668	692	363	2,029	3,750	30.50	6.6	320	8.7
1997-8	3,539	141	795	4,475	682	544	303	2,099	3,627	30.50	6.6	417	11.8
1998-9	3,963	155	848	4,966	562	460	374	2,153	3,574	30.50	8.8	----	----
1999-00	3,829	178	1,392	5,399	727	713	493	2,233	4,166	30.50	8.8	----	----
2000-1	3,266	216	1,233	4,715	527	548	364	2,179	3,618	30.50	6.6	----	----
2001-2	4,277	203	1,097	5,576	713	693	483	2,211	4,100	30.50	6.6	----	----
2002-3[1]	3,320	75	1,476	4,872	490	857	422	2,228	3,997	NA	NA	----	----
2003-4[2]	4,144	65	875	4,892	500	656	378	2,283	3,817	NA	NA	----	----

[1] Preliminary.   [2] Estimate.   *Source: Economic Research Service, U.S. Department of Agriculture (ERS-USDA)*

Production of Peanuts (Harvested for Nuts) in the United States, by States   In Thousands of Pounds

Year	Alabama	Florida	Georgia	New Mexico	North Carolina	Okla homa	South Carolina	Texas	Virgina	Total
1994	446,220	207,480	1,862,630	51,660	485,465	261,000	36,250	605,570	291,180	4,247,455
1995	483,360	193,590	1,414,880	43,000	347,040	201,880	30,800	540,000	206,925	3,461,475
1996	449,805	236,160	1,433,770	37,950	367,500	195,210	32,550	689,000	219,260	3,661,205
1997	372,490	228,060	1,333,830	46,710	329,640	184,800	30,450	822,150	191,250	3,539,380
1998	432,415	233,100	1,511,655	62,040	397,155	159,750	28,175	917,900	221,250	3,963,440
1999	448,050	260,380	1,400,800	61,600	298,840	189,600	25,300	926,800	218,120	3,829,490
2000	271,180	213,710	1,328,400	54,990	338,250	120,600	29,500	698,500	210,375	3,265,505
2001	532,325	250,100	1,711,620	67,044	356,475	197,890	30,600	895,900	234,750	4,276,704
2002	379,250	197,800	1,313,000	54,000	210,000	159,600	19,140	868,000	119,700	3,320,490
2003[1]	508,750	345,000	1,863,000	45,900	320,000	98,000	57,800	810,000	95,700	4,144,150

[1] Preliminary.   *Source: Agricultural Statistics Board, U.S. Department of Agriculture (ASB-USDA)*

Supply and Reported Uses of Shelled Peanuts and Products in the United States   In Thousands of Pounds

Crop Year Beginning Aug. 1	Shelled Peanuts --- Stocks, Aug. 1 ---		Shelled Peanuts ------- Production -------		------------------------- Reported Used (Shelled Peanuts -- Raw Basis) -------------------------						Shelled Peanuts Crushed[6]	Crude Oil Pro- duction	Cake & Meal Pro- duction
					------------------------- Edible Grades Used In -------------------------								
	Edible	Oil Stock[2]	Edible	Oil Stock[2]	Candy[3]	Snacks[4]	Sandwich Spread	Butter[5]	Other Products	Total			
1994-5	679,639	42,054	1,741,824	511,635	349,630	301,548	----	709,823	36,854	1,397,855	738,221	314,189	415,394
1995-6	752,814	58,188	1,253,451	491,818	350,663	277,089	----	728,076	32,015	1,387,843	751,281	320,909	420,919
1996-7	370,431	126,318	1,692,581	305,674	360,846	290,102	----	727,531	33,825	1,412,304	520,413	220,877	294,590
1997-8	498,954	41,000	1,694,016	290,882	351,017	306,908	----	760,230	35,471	1,453,626	409,249	175,853	228,276
1998-9	580,370	14,091	2,227,037	310,459	380,177	349,806	----	744,706	22,131	1,496,820	345,825	145,254	192,425
1999-00	855,572	16,587	2,157,828	448,875	354,953	394,121	----	772,104	20,227	1,541,405	536,164	228,839	291,491
2000-1	707,672	14,463	1,939,736	337,324	355,610	361,516	----	753,239	19,998	1,490,363	411,558	178,523	230,099
2001-2	680,850	16,648	2,090,776	485,092	349,729	360,916	----	818,927	17,284	1,546,856	521,173	230,791	296,874
2002-3[1]	504,131	20,512	1,982,254	574,817	354,115	344,639	----	827,163	25,036	1,550,953	585,642	259,360	322,998

[1] Preliminary.   [2] Includes straight run oil stock peanuts.   [3] Includes peanut butter made by manufacturers for own use in candy.   [4] Formerly titled Salted Peanuts.   [5] Includes peanut butter made by manufacturers for own use in cookies and sandwiches, but excludes peanut butter used in candy.
[6] All crushings regardless of grade.   *Source: National Agricultural Statistics Service, U.S. Department of Agriculture (NASS-USDA)*

PEANUTS AND PEANUT OIL

Shelled Peanuts (Raw Basis) Used in Primary Products, by Type   In Thousands of Pounds

	---------- Virginia ----------				---------- Runner ----------				---------- Spanish ----------			
Year	Candy[2]	Snack Peanuts	Peanut Butter[3]	Total	Candy[2]	Snack Peanuts	Peanut Butter[3]	Total	Candy[2]	Snack Peanuts	Peanut Butter[3]	Total
1994-5	26,857	97,389	51,354	190,916	302,697	185,377	644,711	1,152,110	20,076	18,782	13,758	54,829
1995-6	25,176	93,041	71,310	203,183	304,285	169,142	634,350	1,123,719	21,202	14,906	22,416	60,941
1996-7	24,158	91,882	64,274	193,166	318,924	176,851	634,387	1,149,347	17,764	21,369	28,870	69,791
1997-8	48,428	80,309	59,228	182,100	302,791	206,718	676,839	1,206,946	19,798	19,581	24,163	64,580
1998-9	36,178	99,401	57,864	196,935	321,838	234,486	670,705	1,244,748	22,161	15,919	16,137	55,137
1999-00	23,173	100,384	73,926	200,804	315,467	278,440	690,564	1,300,393	16,313	15,297	7,614	40,208
2000-1	19,101	100,650	102,050	225,072	320,304	247,739	643,229	1,227,156	16,205	13,127	7,960	38,135
2001-2	26,640	97,046	106,573	233,356	303,668	250,079	702,454	1,269,776	19,421	13,791	9,900	43,724
2002-3[1]	26,924	75,091	78,394	184,596	312,090	257,095	732,103	1,321,490	15,101	12,453	16,666	44,867

[1] Preliminary.   [2] Includes peanut butter made by manufacturers for own use in candy.   [3] Includes peanut butter made by manufacturers for own use in cookies and sandwiches, but excludes peanut butter used in candy.   Source: National Agricultural Statistics Service, U.S. Department of Agriculture (NASS-USDA)

Production, Consumption, Stocks and Foreign Trade of Peanut Oil in the U.S.   In Millions of Pounds

Crop Year Beginning Aug. 1	-------- Production --------		-------- Consumption --------		-------- Stocks Dec. 31 --------		Imports for Consumption	Exports
	Crude	Refined	In Refining	In End Products	Crude	Refined		
1995-6	329.0	125.7	129.9	126.0	19.9	2.8	3.2	47.8
1996-7	233.9	133.5	138.9	138.4	85.6	2.8	1.6	35.1
1997-8	144.3	104.0	111.6	121.6	42.6	3.0	6.6	8.8
1998-9	172.9	118.3	123.7	180.1	47.2	3.8	30.3	4.3
1999-00	262.9	195.9	238.9	260.4	19.7	1.7	9.6	5.8
2000-1	222.1	206.3	258.9	277.3	23.1	1.9	19.5	5.5
2001-2	278.5	179.1	291.9	282.5	8.2	1.7		
2002-3[1]	267.7	166.3	W	277.6	52.9	3.5		
2003-4[2]	202.2	125.5	W	227.8	23.0	1.8		

[1] Preliminary.   [2] Forecast.   Source: Bureau of the Census, U.S. Department of Commerce

Production of Crude Peanut Oil in the United States   In Millions of Pounds

Year	Jan.	Feb.	Mar.	Apr.	May	June	July	Aug.	Sept.	Oct.	Nov.	Dec.	Total
1994	18.1	18.3	21.2	18.7	25.6	15.4	21.7	16.8	17.2	11.9	18.4	24.2	227.5
1995	27.9	28.6	42.7	36.9	39.2	29.2	26.9	26.3	17.4	13.2	19.5	24.3	332.0
1996	29.2	31.9	36.8	36.8	36.7	33.3	31.4	31.5	27.1	21.1	20.6	21.8	358.2
1997	19.9	16.1	18.8	17.9	13.3	15.9	9.9	12.1	6.1	12.2	11.6	14.0	167.7
1998	16.0	14.5	14.3	13.0	10.8	10.0	9.5	6.3	5.8	6.9	13.6	13.9	134.5
1999	16.2	18.2	15.8	18.2	16.4	20.7	20.8	17.8	16.3	13.5	22.6	22.7	219.2
2000	35.2	32.1	27.4	31.9	30.4	28.0	24.1	28.8	21.5	25.4	16.4	15.2	316.3
2001	17.3	15.7	20.1	15.3	12.4	19.1	16.3	16.7	12.9	17.1	13.8	25.6	202.4
2002	24.8	25.5	32.8	28.5	33.8	24.3	22.6	27.7	27.2	26.5	24.9	20.2	319.0
2003[1]	21.7	16.6	19.4	20.5	20.0	23.2	19.8	17.3	18.3	24.1	15.6	13.2	229.6

[1] Preliminary.   Source: Bureau of the Census, U.S. Department of Commerce

Average Price of Peanut Meal 50% Southeast Mills   In Dollars Per Short Ton

Year	Oct.	Nov.	Dec.	Jan.	Feb.	Mar.	Apr.	May	June	July	Aug.	Sept.	Average
1994-5	151.25	147.50	127.00	105.00	107.50	119.00	125.00	123.75	134.00	138.75	136.25	142.00	128.94
1995-6	132.50	175.00	204.00	220.00	215.00	210.00	210.00	212.00	210.00	224.25	227.00	192.80	202.70
1996-7	170.00	146.13	172.67	221.00	228.13	225.00	233.75	222.00	235.00	220.00	213.00	210.00	232.00
1997-8	210.00	210.00	210.00	210.00	210.00	210.00	210.00	210.00	210.00	210.00	207.50	205.00	209.60
1998-9	161.00	100.00	103.75	105.00	102.50	91.25	94.50	93.75	100.00	100.00	105.00	102.50	104.94
1999-00	98.00	103.00	103.00	104.00	104.75	110.00	115.00	115.00	119.60	118.00	118.00	118.00	108.15
2000-1	118.00	118.00	118.00	142.50	120.00	118.00	110.75	112.50	NA	123.50	130.50	126.25	121.64
2001-2	115.00	111.25	100.00	102.50	100.00	105.00	110.00	105.00	NA	130.00	135.00	136.88	113.69
2002-3	NA	130.00	122.50	118.50	114.25	124.00	125.00	135.00	135.00	135.75	130.00	130.00	127.27
2003-4[1]	147.10	161.00	163.25	163.35									158.68

[1] Preliminary.   NA = Not available.   Source: Agricultural Marketing Service, U.S. Department of Agriculture (AMS-USDA)

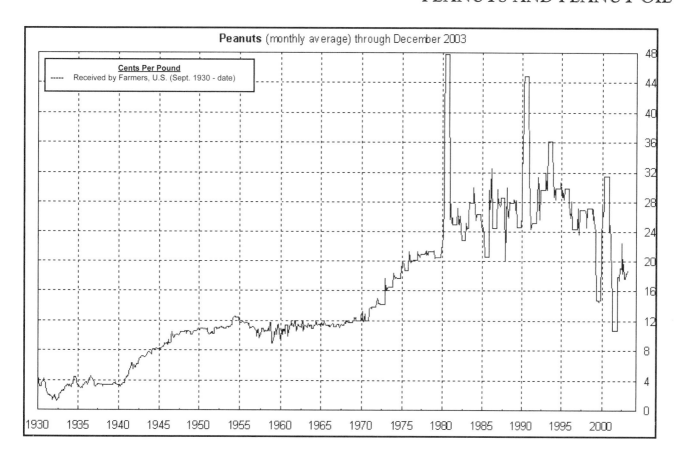

Peanuts (monthly average) through December 2003

Cents Per Pound
----- Received by Farmers, U.S. (Sept. 1930 - date)

Average Price Received by Producers for Peanuts (in the Shell) in the U.S.   In Cents Per Pound

Year	Aug.	Sept.	Oct.	Nov.	Dec.	Jan.	Feb.	Mar.	Apr.	May	June	July	Average[1]
1994-5	NQ	30.6	28.6	25.9	25.8	25.7	NQ	NQ	NQ	NQ	NQ	NQ	27.9
1995-6	30.6	29.7	28.6	29.5	28.3	29.8	NQ	NQ	NQ	NQ	NQ	NQ	29.4
1996-7	NQ	27.6	25.8	27.1	28.1	24.3	NQ	NQ	NQ	NQ	NQ	NQ	26.6
1997-8	23.3	27.1	25.4	25.0	30.7	24.7	NQ	NQ	NQ	NQ	NQ	NQ	26.0
1998-9	NQ	26.8	26.3	24.6	27.2	NQ	NQ	NQ	NQ	NQ	NQ	NQ	26.2
1999-00	25.7	27.0	25.4	24.1	21.8	14.9	NQ	NQ	NQ	NQ	NQ	NQ	23.2
2000-1	NQ	27.7	26.5	26.1	27.3	31.4	NQ	NQ	NQ	NQ	NQ	NQ	27.8
2001-2	24.1	24.9	22.8	21.0	19.5	13.5	10.7	NQ	NQ	NQ	NQ	NQ	19.5
2002-3	NQ	17.9	17.9	18.0	17.5	19.1	19.6	22.5	18.4	19.6	17.7	NQ	18.8
2003-4[2]	NQ	18.3	18.5	18.4	19.6	20.7	21.3						19.5

[1] Weighted average by sales.   [2] Preliminarly.   NQ = No quote.   *Source: National Agricultural Statistics Service,*
U.S. Department of Agriculture (NASS-USDA)

Average Price of Domestic Crude Peanut Oil (in Tanks) F.O.B. Southeast Mills   In Cents Per Pound

Year	Oct.	Nov.	Dec.	Jan.	Feb.	Mar.	Apr.	May	June	July	Aug.	Sept.	Average
1994-5	46.00	50.88	53.80	50.25	41.83	41.00	41.25	40.25	39.00	39.13	41.50	41.30	43.85
1995-6	42.50	41.63	39.20	37.25	36.00	36.60	39.25	42.80	43.00	43.00	42.60	40.80	40.39
1996-7	41.50	39.20	40.75	43.50	43.88	44.75	45.00	46.20	47.88	48.06	48.00	47.25	44.66
1997-8	49.63	51.00	51.25	51.60	51.00	51.00	50.00	47.20	45.50	44.00	43.75	43.88	48.32
1998-9	45.40	45.00	44.25	44.00	39.75	34.75	35.20	35.00	37.75	39.00	38.75	38.00	39.74
1999-00	40.40	41.00	35.40	33.00	32.50	31.60	33.00	36.25	36.00	35.63	35.00	34.90	35.39
2000-1	34.63	35.50	36.40	37.25	37.00	35.90	34.00	33.00	33.00	33.00	34.00	34.00	34.81
2001-2	36.25	37.00	37.00	35.00	28.00	27.50	27.00	27.00	30.00	34.00	35.20	36.25	32.52
2002-3	NA	42.00	43.67	45.75	46.00	47.00	50.25	52.75	56.60	58.25	60.00	60.67	51.18
2003-4[1]	61.60	63.25	64.50	65.00									63.59

[1] Preliminary.   *Source: Agricultural Marketing Service, U.S. Department of Agriculture (AMS-USDA)*

Pepper

The pepper plant is a perennial climbing shrub that originated in India and Sri Lanka. Pepper is considered the world's most important spice and has been used to flavor foods for over 3,000 years. Pepper was once considered so valuable that it was used to ransom Rome from Attila the Hun. Black pepper alone accounts for nearly 35% of the world's spice trade. Unlike many other popular herbs and spices, pepper can only be cultivated in tropical climates. The pepper plant produces a berry called a peppercorn. Both black and white pepper are obtained from the same plant. The colors of pepper are determined by the maturity of the berry at harvest and by the different processing methods.

Black pepper is picked when the berries are still green and immature. The peppercorns are then dried in the sun until they turn black. White pepper is picked when the berries are fully ripe and bright red. The red peppercorns are then soaked, washed to remove the skin of the berry, and dried to produce a white to yellowish-white peppercorn. Black pepper has a slightly hotter flavor and stronger aroma than white pepper. Piperine, an alkaloid of pyridine, is the active ingredient in pepper that makes it hot.

Black pepper oil is obtained from crushed berries using solvent extraction. Black pepper oil is used in the treatment of pain, chills, flue, muscular aches, and in some perfumes. It is also helpful in promoting digestion in the colon.

The world's key pepper varieties are known by their place of origin. Some popular types of pepper are: Lampong Black and Muntok White from Indonesia, Brazilian black, and Malabar Black and Tellicherry from India.

Prices – Average black pepper prices in 2002 fell sharply to 92.3 cents per pound from 116.2 cents in 2001 and the 1999 record high of 254.5 cents. Average white pepper prices in 2002 fell to 117.6 cents per pound from 132.6 cents in 2001, and were down sharply from the 1998 record of 356.5 cents.

Trade – The world's largest exporter of pepper by far is Indonesia with 47,502 metric tons of exports in 2000, the latest reporting year. After Indonesia, the largest exporters are Vietnam with 23,543 metric tons (5-yr average), Malaysia with 21,804 metric tons, Brazil with 20,469 metric tons, and India with 19,125 metric tons.

US imports of black pepper in 2000 fell –8.6% to 43,479 metric tons from 47,591 metric tons in 1999, which was a record high. The primary source of US imports of black pepper was Indonesia, which accounted for 36% of US imports, followed by India with 25%, Brazil with 18%, and Malaysia with 10%.

US imports of white pepper in 2000 rose +7.7% to a record high of 7,311 metric tons. The primary source of US imports of white pepper was Indonesia, which accounted for 87% of US imports, followed by 3% shares each from Singapore, Malaysia and China.

World Exports of Pepper (Black and White) and Prices in the United States   In Metric Tons

| | | | | | | | | | New York Spot Prices (Cents Per Pound) | | | | |
| | | | | | | | | | Indonesian | | | Indian | |
Year	Brazil	India	Indo-nesia	Mada-gascar	Malay-sia	Mexico	Sri Lanka	Vietnam	Lampong Black	Muntok White	Brazilian Black	Malabar Black	Telli-cherry[2]
1993	26,254	47,677	27,684	2,001	16,737	2,430	5,032	20,138	62.5	114.6	62.3	62.3	84.0
1994	22,231	36,536	36,036	2,066	23,275	2,615	1,850	16,000	95.3	151.9	95.0	95.0	110.7
1995	22,158	25,270	57,781	1,274	14,869	3,085	2,082	17,900	116.8	182.3	116.8	116.8	150.9
1996	24,178	47,211	36,849	1,570	28,124	4,200	2,612	25,300	114.8	178.9	114.8	114.8	140.0
1997	13,962	35,403	33,386	894	29,000	4,210	3,485	24,713	206.7	304.6	206.7	206.7	225.8
1998	17,249	32,859	38,723	339	18,717	3,365	5,493	15,000	239.5	356.5	239.5	239.5	286.6
1999	19,617	35,635	36,293	619	21,804	4,026	3,754	34,800	254.5	334.9	254.5	254.5	296.3
2000	20,469	19,125	47,502	588	23,684	4,534	4,855	----	228.1	227.1	228.1	228.1	282.6
2001[1]	36,975	19,641	53,432	635	25,537	4,658	2,161	----	116.2	132.6	116.2	116.2	179.3
2002[1]									92.9	120.5	92.9	92.9	127.8

[1] Preliminary.   [2] Extra bold.   *Source: Foreign Agricultural Service, U.S. Department of Agriculture (FAS-USDA)*

United States Imports of Unground Pepper from Specified Countries   In Metric Tons

| | Black Pepper | | | | | | | White Pepper | | | | | |
Year	Brazil	India	Indo-nesia	Malay-sia	Singa-pore	Sri Lanka	Total	Brazil	China	Indo-nesia	Malay-sia	Singa-pore	Total
1991	15,069	2,308	11,330	8,154	391	396	38,860	2	7	4,938	37	96	5,174
1992	6,601	9,892	20,768	2,073	52	310	40,590	51	2	5,089	29	261	5,544
1993	4,580	21,985	7,666	209	----	539	35,969	322	114	4,304	137	363	5,481
1994	8,215	21,097	11,877	829	90	386	43,011	312	756	3,974	228	302	6,102
1995	3,165	10,836	19,630	268	30	327	34,465	414	280	4,037	164	211	5,266
1996	4,267	18,350	17,213	1,084	101	411	41,602	519	54	4,370	150	391	5,765
1997	4,328	23,404	13,610	2,203	678	285	45,319	75	522	3,755	199	750	5,751
1998	5,806	15,540	13,045	422	185	578	36,508	32	108	4,571	195	203	5,393
1999	7,093	24,931	8,429	2,392	525	441	47,591	32	451	5,202	420	342	6,789
2000[1]	7,853	10,981	15,713	4,148	306	516	43,479	15	210	6,345	185	215	7,311

[1] Preliminary.   *Source: Foreign Agricultural Service, U.S. Department of Agriculture (FAS-USDA)*

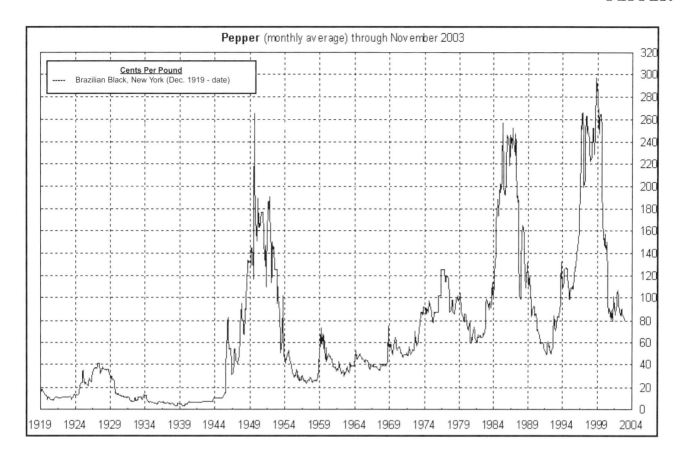

Average Black Pepper in New York (Brazilian)   In Cents Per Pound

Year	Jan.	Feb.	Mar.	Apr.	May	June	July	Aug.	Sept.	Oct.	Nov.	Dec.	Average
1994	69.3	74.3	82.0	82.8	82.0	86.5	87.8	97.8	112.2	131.5	123.5	110.4	95.0
1995	111.0	110.0	114.2	124.8	127.3	126.0	127.0	126.3	118.2	113.5	104.8	99.0	116.8
1996	99.3	103.3	109.2	108.3	111.2	109.5	108.0	119.8	126.5	127.5	127.6	128.0	114.8
1997	138.6	151.8	149.0	161.8	173.4	193.8	229.5	255.0	251.3	264.8	266.3	245.0	206.7
1998	199.4	205.5	243.8	262.8	262.8	247.5	253.0	253.8	246.3	243.0	231.3	225.0	239.5
1999	222.5	225.8	252.5	248.0	252.5	250.0	229.0	249.3	263.8	282.0	297.5	281.0	254.5
2000	260.0	256.3	246.0	260.0	265.0	265.0	263.8	252.5	205.0	167.5	147.5	149.0	228.1
2001	157.5	146.3	144.0	150.0	143.8	123.0	97.3	87.0	90.0	89.3	81.6	85.3	116.2
2002	85.0	80.0	81.4	100.5	101.0	92.0	84.8	86.8	93.5	103.5	106.0	100.8	92.9
2003	93.8	89.0	88.5	85.5	83.8	89.0	90.0	86.6	83.5	81.6	80.0		86.5

Source: Foreign Agricultural Service, U.S. Department of Agriculture (FAS-USDA)

Average White Pepper in New York (Indonesian)[1]   In Cents Per Pound

Year	Jan.	Feb.	Mar.	Apr.	May	June	July	Aug.	Sept.	Oct.	Nov.	Dec.	Average
1994	144.5	139.5	141.3	140.8	137.0	143.3	143.4	156.3	159.2	167.5	176.5	173.0	151.9
1995	179.5	175.8	168.0	181.3	195.0	184.2	187.5	190.8	191.0	182.0	178.5	174.2	182.3
1996	174.5	177.5	181.6	179.5	172.6	164.8	154.0	169.6	181.5	193.5	191.8	205.8	178.9
1997	256.0	264.5	255.0	250.0	241.0	248.8	280.3	324.0	332.5	362.0	433.8	407.5	304.6
1998	348.0	346.3	362.5	390.0	393.0	358.8	354.0	356.3	348.8	340.0	340.0	340.0	356.5
1999	361.3	355.0	365.0	355.0	352.5	335.0	310.0	313.8	325.0	327.0	316.3	303.0	334.9
2000	295.0	293.8	264.0	253.8	246.3	242.0	226.3	227.5	205.0	171.3	150.0	150.0	227.1
2001	159.0	151.3	144.0	133.8	130.0	127.0	122.5	129.6	128.0	125.5	120.0	120.0	132.6
2002	111.3	100.3	95.6	108.8	108.0	105.0	104.5	118.8	130.0	154.0	157.5	153.0	120.6
2003	152.4	148.8	150.0	150.0	142.6	133.0	133.0	138.2	137.5	133.6	127.5		140.6

[1] Muntok White.   *Source: Foreign Agricultural Service, U.S. Department of Agriculture (FAS-USDA)*

Petroleum

Petroleum directly out of the ground is called crude oil. Crude oil was formed over millions of years ago from the remains of tiny aquatic plants and animals that lived in ancient seas. It was believed that crude oil had medicinal benefits by ancient Persians, 10th century Sumatrans, and pre-Columbian Indians. Around 4,000 BC in Mesopotamia, bitumen, a tarry crude, was used as caulking for ships, a setting for jewels and mosaics, and an adhesive to secure weapon handles. The walls of Babylon and the famed pyramids were held together with it, and Egyptians used it for embalming. During the 19th century, an oil find was often met with dismay. Pioneers who dug wells to find water or brine, were disappointed when they struck oil. It wasn't until 1854, with the invention of the kerosene lamp, that the first large-scale demand for petroleum was created. Surprisingly, crude oil is an abundant commodity. The world has produced approximately 650 billion barrels of oil, but another trillion barrels of proved reserves have yet to be produced. Crude oil was the world's first trillion-dollar industry and accounts for the single largest product in world trade.

Futures and options on crude oil trade at the New York Mercantile Exchange (NYMEX) and at the International Petroleum Exchange in London (IPE). NYMEX trades two main types of crude oil: light sweet crude oil and Brent crude oil. The light sweet futures contract calls for the delivery of 1,000 barrels of crude oil in Cushing, Oklahoma. Light sweet crude is preferred by refiners because of its low sulfur content and relatively high yield of high-value products such as gasoline, diesel fuel, heating oil, and jet fuel. The Brent blend crude is based on a light, sweet North Sea crude oil. Brent blend crude production is approximately 500,000 barrels per day, and is shipped from Sullom Voe in the Shetland Islands.

Prices – NYMEX crude oil prices on the weekly nearest-futures chart rallied early in 2003 and posted a 13-year high of $39.99 per barrel in late February 2003 due to the war with Iraq and concerns about supply disruptions in the Middle East. After it became clear that the war would be relatively short, crude oil prices fell sharply and hit a 1-1/4 year low of $25.04 in late April. Prices then rallied fairly steadily in the fourth quarter of 2003 and ended the year near $33 per barrel, little changed from the close in 2002 but still at the upper end of the price ranges seen in the last two decades. Bullish factors supporting prices later in year included the weak dollar (which boosts the real value of crude oil priced in dollars), much stronger demand as the US economy revved up in Q3 and Q4, weak production from Iraq as the US struggled to revive the moribund Iraqi oil production machinery, OPEC's relative discipline in limiting production, and tight inventories which dropped to the lowest level in decades. OPEC blamed the Q4 rally in crude oil prices on the weak dollar and stronger demand, rather than a shortage of supply. OPEC late in the year therefore refused to boost production even though prices rose above OPEC's target range of $22-28 for a basket of OPEC crude. NYMEX crude oil trades about $2 higher than the OPEC basket price due to higher quality and transport costs. OPEC produces about one-third of world demand for oil.

Supply – World crude oil production in 2002, the last full reporting year, fell –1.7% to 66.819 million barrels per day. The world's largest oil producers in 2002 were Saudi Arabia (with 11.4% of world production in 2002), Russia (11.1%), the United States (8.7%), Iran (5.2%), and China (5.0%). US production in 2002 rose +0.3% to 5.817 million barrels per day, with Alaskan production of 984,000 barrels per day accounting for 17% of total US production. Production of oil in Alaska has been declining. In 1988 it was 2.02 million barrels per day, more than double current production levels.

Demand – US demand for crude oil in 2002 fell –1.3% to 14.926 million barrels per day, which accounted for 22% of total world production even though the US only accounts for about 5% of world population. Most of that demand went for US refinery production into products such as gasoline and diesel fuel, aviation fuel, heating oil, kerosene, asphalt, and lubricants.

Trade – The US is highly dependent on imports of crude oil to meet its energy needs. US imports in 2002, the latest full reporting year, fell –3.0% to 9.047 million barrels per day, accounting for 61% of US usage. US exports of crude oil have dropped sharply in the past several years and totaled a miniscule 9,000 barrels per day in 2002 versus 118,000 barrels as recently as 1999.

World Production of Crude Petroleum   In Thousands of Barrels Per Day

Year	Canada	China	Indo-nesia	Iran	Kuwait	Mexico	Nigeria	Russia	Saudi Arabia	United Kingdom	United States	Vene-zuela	World Total
1994	1,746	2,939	1,510	3,618	2,025	2,685	1,931	6,135	8,120	2,375	6,662	2,588	60,991
1995	1,805	2,990	1,503	3,643	2,057	2,618	1,993	5,995	8,231	2,489	6,560	2,750	62,335
1996	1,837	3,131	1,547	3,686	2,062	2,855	2,188	5,850	8,218	2,568	6,465	3,053	63,711
1997	1,893	3,200	1,520	3,664	2,083	3,023	2,317	5,920	8,562	2,517	6,452	3,315	65,690
1998	1,981	3,198	1,518	3,634	2,085	3,070	2,153	2,854	8,389	2,616	6,252	3,167	66,921
1999	1,907	3,206	1,472	3,557	1,898	2,906	2,130	6,079	7,833	2,684	5,881	2,826	65,848
2000	1,977	3,249	1,423	3,696	2,126	3,012	2,144	6,479	8,404	2,275	5,822	2,949	68,342
2001	2,029	3,303	1,369	3,724	2,026	3,127	2,256	7,049	8,031	2,282	5,801	2,880	68,057
2002[1]	2,171	3,390	1,267	3,444	1,894	3,177	2,118	7,408	7,634	2,292	5,746	2,604	66,842
2003[2]	2,306	3,409	1,171	3,778	2,178	3,371	2,241	8,182	8,848	2,073	5,738	2,335	69,430

Includes lease condensate.   [1] Preliminary.   [2] Estimate.   *Source: Energy Information Administration, U.S. Department of Energy (EIA-DOE)*

Refiner Sales Prices of Residual Fuel Oil   In Cents Per Gallon

Year	Jan.	Feb.	Mar.	Apr.	May	June	July	Aug.	Sept.	Oct.	Nov.	Dec.	Average
1998	35.2	30.7	29.4	32.9	31.9	29.3	30.7	26.9	29.9	31.0	27.3	24.0	29.9
1999	27.5	21.8	27.2	30.9	34.6	35.0	38.6	44.8	49.8	47.3	48.5	50.3	38.2
2000	55.3	59.2	53.2	52.3	58.9	65.8	65.1	61.5	71.9	73.7	71.3	66.6	62.7
2001	64.5	61.9	57.2	57.3	58.2	53.0	50.0	50.4	51.2	44.8	40.5	40.0	51.7
2002	50.8	51.2	53.2	59.1	64.0	63.5	63.9	67.4	67.8	72.7	73.6	73.9	63.9
2003[1]	86.1	95.6	97.4	78.1	74.9	71.9	74.5	75.4	72.0	70.7	76.7		79.4

Sulfur 1% or less, excluding taxes.   [1] Preliminary.   *Source: Energy Information Administration, U.S. Department of Energy (EIA-DOE)*

Refiner Sales Prices of No. 2 Fuel Oil   In Cents Per Gallon

Year	Jan.	Feb.	Mar.	Apr.	May	June	July	Aug.	Sept.	Oct.	Nov.	Dec.	Average
1998	48.9	47.7	44.9	44.9	43.4	39.9	38.8	36.9	41.8	41.2	38.9	34.6	42.2
1999	36.3	33.1	39.8	44.7	43.8	44.7	51.2	56.2	60.9	61.0	66.2	67.8	49.3
2000	84.1	92.4	79.6	76.4	78.4	80.3	81.0	88.3	100.9	98.8	100.4	94.1	88.6
2001	90.3	82.5	76.3	79.2	82.7	79.3	72.8	77.0	79.0	68.5	60.6	56.6	75.6
2002	57.5	57.7	64.6	68.3	68.4	65.8	68.7	71.3	78.3	79.6	74.8	80.8	69.3
2003[1]	89.5	107.8	104.5	82.4	75.5	76.8	78.9	83.7	77.4	84.2	84.2		85.9

Excluding taxes.   [1] Preliminary.   *Source: Energy Information Administration, U.S. Department of Energy (EIA-DOE)*

Refiner Sales Prices of No. 2 Diesel Fuel   In Cents Per Gallon

Year	Jan.	Feb.	Mar.	Apr.	May	June	July	Aug.	Sept.	Oct.	Nov.	Dec.	Average
1998	49.6	48.3	45.8	48.2	47.0	43.6	42.6	41.4	45.6	45.5	41.4	35.6	44.4
1999	36.2	35.1	43.2	48.8	47.9	50.4	56.4	61.6	64.9	65.0	69.9	70.5	54.6
2000	77.7	85.2	85.1	79.9	81.4	82.4	83.6	92.1	105.0	104.0	103.2	93.8	89.8
2001	90.7	85.8	78.1	82.6	89.8	85.3	75.5	80.8	84.1	71.4	61.6	54.7	78.4
2002	54.6	56.8	66.7	70.9	70.6	68.2	71.0	75.7	83.6	86.1	78.7	82.0	72.4
2003[1]	89.2	108.1	102.1	86.7	79.3	81.1	83.8	88.9	80.7	87.1	86.5		88.5

Excluding taxes.   [1] Preliminary.   *Source: Energy Information Administration, U.S. Department of Energy (EIA-DOE)*

Refiner Sales Prices of Kerosine-Type Jet Fuel   In Cents Per Gallon

Year	Jan.	Feb.	Mar.	Apr.	May	June	July	Aug.	Sept.	Oct.	Nov.	Dec.	Average
1998	53.4	50.2	45.7	46.6	46.9	43.5	43.8	42.9	44.6	45.8	43.1	36.5	45.0
1999	37.3	35.2	39.5	46.6	46.8	48.6	53.7	59.1	62.7	63.8	66.5	72.1	53.3
2000	80.4	83.6	83.4	77.4	77.9	79.9	83.6	87.9	105.1	104.4	105.1	99.0	88.0
2001	88.2	86.8	80.5	79.5	83.5	82.6	75.9	77.6	80.7	68.5	61.9	55.3	76.3
2002	57.3	57.4	64.2	69.5	69.6	67.9	71.5	74.0	81.6	83.8	74.9	79.9	71.3
2003[1]	89.5	102.8	101.7	82.6	75.1	77.0	81.4	86.3	80.9	83.9	87.1		86.2

Excluding taxes.   [1] Preliminary.   *Source: Energy Information Administration, U.S. Department of Energy (EIA-DOE)*

Refiner Sales Prices of Propane   In Cents Per Gallon

Year	Jan.	Feb.	Mar.	Apr.	May	June	July	Aug.	Sept.	Oct.	Nov.	Dec.	Average
1998	35.4	33.1	31.2	30.3	29.3	26.6	25.7	25.7	26.3	27.6	27.7	25.7	28.8
1999	26.5	26.1	26.8	28.7	29.1	29.1	34.7	38.3	42.6	43.7	42.6	41.8	34.2
2000	49.4	60.2	52.9	48.8	49.3	53.9	54.8	60.3	65.9	64.3	63.3	76.7	59.5
2001	86.4	66.9	60.1	58.6	56.2	48.7	43.6	45.6	46.4	46.1	41.6	38.1	54.1
2002	37.6	36.6	39.9	41.7	40.8	37.9	37.5	41.5	47.0	48.9	49.4	53.2	43.1
2003[1]	60.5	72.8	69.1	53.9	54.3	57.5	55.9	58.5	56.6	59.7	58.7		59.8

Consumer Grade, Excluding taxes.   [1] Preliminary.   *Source: Energy Information Administration, U.S. Department of Energy (EIA-DOE)*

Supply and Disposition of Crude Oil in the United States   In Thousands of Barrels Per Day

Yearly Average	-- Field Production --		----- Imports -----		Unaccounted for Crude Oil	---- Stock Withdrawal[3] ----		Refinery Inputs	Exports	----- Ending Stocks -----		
	Total Domestic	Alaskan	Total	SPR[2]	Other		SPR[2]	Other			Total	SPR[2]	Other Primary
	In Thousands of Barrels Per Day										In Millions of Barrels		
1996	6,465	1,393	7,508	0	7,508	215	-71	-53	14,195	110	850	566	284
1997	6,452	1,296	8,225	0	8,225	145	-7	57	14,662	108	868	563	305
1998	6,252	1,175	8,706	0	8,706	115	22	52	14,889	110	895	571	324
1999	5,881	1,050	8,731	8	8,722	191	-11	-107	14,804	118	852	567	284
2000	5,822	970	9,071	8	9,062	155	-73	3	15,067	50	826	541	286
2001	5,801	963	9,328	11	9,318	117	26	73	15,128	20	862	550	312
2002	5,746	984	9,140	16	9,124	110	134	-94	14,947	9	877	599	278
2003[1]	5,737	974	9,646	0	9,646	14	108	-27	15,303	12	906	638	268

[1] Preliminary.   [2] Strategic Petroleum Reserve.   [3] A negative number indicates a decrease in stocks and a positive number indicates an increase.
Source: Energy Information Administration, U.S. Department of Energy (EIA-DOE)

PETROLEUM

Crude Petroleum Refinery Operations Ratio[1] in the United States   In Percent of Capacity

Year	Jan.	Feb.	Mar.	Apr.	May	June	July	Aug.	Sept.	Oct.	Nov.	Dec.	Average
1994	89.8	88.7	87.6	92.4	95.4	95.8	95.5	96.4	94.4	89.8	92.7	92.6	92.6
1995	89.6	87.9	86.7	90.5	94.0	95.6	94.0	94.0	95.6	90.5	92.1	93.3	92.0
1996	90.6	89.1	90.6	93.7	94.4	95.4	93.9	95.0	95.5	94.6	94.7	94.3	93.5
1997	89.3	87.3	90.7	92.6	97.3	97.7	97.1	98.6	99.7	96.7	95.6	97.2	95.0
1998	93.3	91.3	94.4	96.4	97.1	98.9	99.2	99.8	95.0	89.7	94.7	95.1	95.4
1999	90.4	90.0	90.9	94.6	93.9	93.5	94.9	95.5	94.1	91.1	92.0	90.4	92.7
2000	85.7	86.4	89.8	92.6	94.7	96.2	96.9	95.9	94.3	92.4	92.7	94.0	92.6
2001	90.2	90.5	89.4	94.9	96.4	95.6	93.9	93.3	92.2	92.0	92.2	90.2	92.6
2002	87.7	86.6	87.9	93.0	91.5	93.1	93.5	92.9	90.4	87.5	92.6	91.1	90.7
2003[2]	87.2	87.3	90.5	94.0	95.8	94.5	94.0	94.9	93.0	92.4	93.5		92.5

[1] Based on the ration of the daily average crude runs to stills to the rated capacity of refineries per day.   [2] Preliminary.
Source: Energy Information Administration, U.S. Department of Energy (EIA-DOE)

Crude Oil Refinery Inputs in the United States   In Thousands of Barrels Per Day

Year	Jan.	Feb.	Mar.	Apr.	May	June	July	Aug.	Sept.	Oct.	Nov.	Dec.	Average
1994	13,286	13,130	12,985	13,809	14,272	14,351	14,344	14,491	14,234	13,529	13,968	13,951	13,866
1995	13,604	13,365	13,480	13,817	14,303	14,553	14,403	14,276	14,402	13,598	13,833	14,011	13,973
1996	13,708	13,529	13,755	14,263	14,401	14,535	14,319	14,423	14,483	14,276	14,276	14,194	14,195
1997	13,632	13,425	14,047	14,283	15,083	15,139	14,958	15,217	15,297	14,790	14,654	14,898	14,662
1998	14,313	14,034	14,590	14,961	15,104	15,368	15,496	15,660	14,854	14,001	14,769	14,832	14,889
1999	14,442	14,309	14,498	15,094	14,973	14,959	15,237	15,299	15,107	14,589	14,704	14,410	14,804
2000	13,779	14,028	14,613	15,053	15,494	15,643	15,819	15,640	15,407	15,029	15,023	15,232	15,067
2001	14,789	14,813	14,649	15,536	15,763	15,650	15,369	15,259	15,005	15,002	15,001	14,688	15,128
2002	14,487	14,306	14,526	15,325	15,301	15,397	15,430	15,338	14,861	14,303	15,155	14,900	14,947
2003[1]	14,337	14,382	14,929	15,575	15,919	15,618	15,549	15,685	15,444	15,342	15,455	15,343	15,303

[1] Preliminary.   *Source: Energy Information Administration, U.S. Department of Energy (EIA-DOE)*

Production of Major Refined Petroleum Products in Continental United States   In Millions of Barrels

| | | ---------- Fuel Oil ---------- | | | | | | Natural | | ------------ Liquified Gasses ------------ | | |
Year	Asphalt	Aviation Gasoline	Distillate	Residual	Gasoline	Jet Fuel	Kero-sene	Gas Plant Liquids	Lubri-cants	Total	at L.P.G.[2]	at L.P.G.[3]
1994	164.8	7.9	1,169.7	301.4	2,621	528.4	21.1	630.2	62.1	734.2	511.1	223.2
1995	170.4	7.8	1,151.7	287.6	2,722	516.8	19.2	643.2	63.7	759.9	521.1	238.8
1996	167.8	7.3	1,213.6	265.5	2,769	554.5	22.8	669.8	63.3	789.1	546.7	242.5
1997	177.0	7.2	1,238.0	258.3	2,826	567.3	23.9	663.3	65.9	799.4	547.3	252.2
1998	179.7	7.3	1,248.6	278.0	2,865	554.6	28.6	639.9	67.2	771.2	526.3	244.9
1999	184.3	7.5	1,240.8	254.8	2,896	571.3	24.4	675.1	66.8	811.0	564.5	246.5
2000	180.6	6.2	1,189.9	234.3	2,664	536.6	20.4	649.4	60.9	788.0	545.5	242.5
2001	177.3	6.5	1,348.4	262.8	2,913	558.2	26.7	680.3	64.1	810.1	569.1	241.0
2002	179.9	6.4	1,309.8	218.8	2,983	552.3	20.8	686.5	63.3	822.5	576.8	245.7
2003[1]	181.0	5.8	1,355.5	241.8	2,992	543.1	20.4	626.7	60.6	766.1	526.4	239.6

[1] Preliminary.   [2] Gas processing plants.   [3] Refineries.   *Source: Energy Information Administration, U.S. Department of Energy (EIA-DOE)*

Stocks of Petroleum and Products in the United States on January 1   In Millions of Barrels

| | | | | | | ----- Fuel Oil ----- | | | | | | | --- Motor Gasoline --- | |
Year	Crude Petroleum	Strategic Reserve	Total	Asphalt	Aviation Gasoline	Distillate	Residual	Finished Gasoline	Jet Fuel	Kero-sene	Liduified Gases[2]	Lubri-cants	Total	Finished[3]
1994	922.5	587.1	465.8	19.1	1.8	140.9	44.2	185.7	40.4	4.1	106.6	11.8	226	187
1995	928.9	591.7	468.0	18.6	2.3	145.2	41.9	175.9	46.8	8.0	108.0	11.5	215	176
1996	895.0	591.6	401.2	22.5	2.3	130.2	37.2	161.3	40.0	7.2	93.1	13.0	206	161
1997	849.7	565.8	452.6	20.5	2.3	126.7	45.9	157.0	39.9	7.0	86.2	12.7	202	157
1998	868.1	563.4	451.6	22.1	1.7	138.4	40.5	166.4	44.0	7.3	89.5	12.9	213	166
1999	894.9	571.4	407.1	21.4	1.8	156.1	44.9	171.8	44.7	6.9	115.1	13.2	219	172
2000	851.7	567.2	407.1	16.9	1.6	125.5	35.8	154.1	40.5	4.9	89.3	11.8	196	154
2001	826.2	540.7	415.7	25.0	1.3	118.0	36.2	153.0	44.5	4.1	82.5	12.1	207	153
2002	862.2	550.2	445.6	20.6	1.5	144.5	41.0	161.5	42.0	5.4	120.9	13.8	214	161
2003[1]	876.7	599.1	425.1	21.3	1.4	134.1	31.3	161.9	39.2	5.5	105.7	12.0	199	162

[1] Preliminary.   [2] Includes ethane & ethylene at plants and refineries.   [3] Includes oxygenated.   *Source: Energy Information Administration, U.S. Department of Energy (EIA-DOE)*

Stocks of Crude Petroleum in the United States, on First of Month   In Millions of Barrels

Year	Jan.	Feb.	Mar.	Apr.	May	June	July	Aug.	Sept.	Oct.	Nov.	Dec.
1994	922.5	925.3	922.6	932.6	930.6	922.7	919.6	924.2	920.2	927.0	934.9	938.0
1995	922.2	920.8	931.0	929.4	924.1	919.6	907.3	899.5	897.5	902.8	910.6	894.9
1996	894.9	894.7	892.9	888.8	889.7	889.7	898.9	891.3	890.8	875.8	881.5	869.1
1997	849.7	865.9	862.1	877.6	883.9	890.5	885.3	873.0	864.2	866.6	879.3	886.9
1998	868.1	884.3	885.7	899.8	914.6	916.1	896.4	902.6	893.5	873.0	897.4	906.2
1999	894.4	896.6	897.4	908.0	902.3	914.8	902.8	906.0	889.1	878.0	875.7	866.2
2000	851.6	852.4	855.2	866.5	873.2	864.1	859.5	852.6	858.7	848.2	842.4	833.9
2001	826.2	836.0	824.2	850.8	873.0	871.7	851.5	856.6	851.6	854.1	858.4	859.5
2002	862.2	874.9	887.4	895.0	891.3	898.3	894.1	882.8	878.5	857.8	881.1	884.0
2003[1]	876.7	872.2	869.6	879.7	889.8	886.7	891.7	895.6	896.0	908.9	924.6	913.9

[1] Preliminary.   *Source: Energy Information Administration; U.S. Department of Energy (EIA-DOE)*

Production of Crude Petroleum in the United States   In Thousands of Barrels Per Day

Year	Jan.	Feb.	Mar.	Apr.	May	June	July	Aug.	Sept.	Oct.	Nov.	Dec.	Average
1994	6,817	6,770	6,746	6,612	6,688	6,611	6,501	6,544	6,609	6,658	6,628	6,760	6,662
1995	6,682	6,794	6,600	6,604	6,629	6,579	6,449	6,447	6,416	6,421	6,585	6,530	6,560
1996	6,495	6,577	6,571	6,444	6,394	6,458	6,338	6,360	6,482	6,481	6,476	6,506	6,465
1997	6,402	6,514	6,452	6,441	6,474	6,442	6,409	6,347	6,486	6,467	6,459	6,531	6,452
1998	6,541	6,476	6,408	6,483	6,347	6,267	6,194	6,203	5,789	6,143	6,140	6,043	6,252
1999	5,963	5,966	5,883	5,887	5,875	5,760	5,798	5,780	5,804	5,947	5,960	5,959	5,881
2000	5,784	5,852	5,918	5,854	5,847	5,823	5,739	5,789	5,758	5,809	5,833	5,855	5,822
2001	5,799	5,780	5,880	5,863	5,829	5,766	5,749	5,725	5,709	5,746	5,881	5,887	5,801
2002	5,848	5,871	5,883	5,859	5,924	5,915	5,770	5,811	5,411	5,363	5,597	5,699	5,746
2003[1]	5,842	5,915	5,890	5,813	5,783	5,746	5,662	5,642	5,657	5,642	5,637	5,629	5,737

[1] Preliminary.   *Source: Energy Information Administration, U.S. Department of Energy (EIA-DOE)*

U.S. Foreign Trade of Petroleum and Products   In Thousands of Barrels Per Day

	----- Exports -----		-------------------------- Imports --------------------------					------ Exports ------		-------------------------- Imports --------------------------				
Year	Total[2]	Petroleum Products	Crude	Petroleum Products	Distillate Fuel Oil	Residual Fuel Oil	Net Imports[3]	Year	Total[2]	Petroleum Products	Crude	Petroleum Products	Distillate Fuel Oil	Residual Fuel Oil	Net Imports[3]
1984	722	541	3,426	2,011	272	681	4,715	1994	942	843	7,063	1,933	203	314	8,054
1985	781	577	3,201	1,866	200	510	4,286	1995	949	855	7,230	1,605	193	187	7,886
1986	785	631	4,178	2,045	247	669	5,439	1996	981	871	7,508	1,971	230	248	8,498
1987	764	613	4,674	2,004	255	565	5,914	1997	1,003	896	8,225	1,936	228	194	9,158
1988	815	661	5,107	2,295	302	644	6,587	1998	945	835	8,706	2,002	210	275	9,764
1989	859	717	5,843	2,217	306	629	7,202	1999	940	822	8,731	2,122	250	237	9,912
1990	857	748	5,894	2,123	278	504	7,161	2000	1,040	990	9,071	2,389	295	352	10,419
1991	1,001	885	5,782	1,844	205	453	6,626	2001	971	951	9,328	2,543	344	295	10,900
1992	950	861	6,083	1,805	216	375	6,938	2002	984	975	9,140	2,390	267	249	10,546
1993	1,003	904	6,787	1,833	184	373	7,618	2003[1]	1,017	1,005	9,646	2,608	335	325	11,237

[1] Preliminary.   [2] Includes crude oil.   [3] Equals imports minus exports.   *Source: Energy Information Administration, U.S. Department of Energy (EIA-DOE)*

Domestic First Purchase Price of Crude Petroleum at Wells[1]   In Dollars Per Barrel

Year	Jan.	Feb.	Mar.	Apr.	May	June	July	Aug.	Sept.	Oct.	Nov.	Dec.	Average
1994	10.49	10.71	10.94	12.31	14.02	14.93	15.34	14.50	13.62	13.84	14.14	13.43	13.19
1995	14.00	14.69	14.68	15.84	15.85	15.02	14.01	14.13	14.49	13.68	14.03	15.02	14.62
1996	15.43	15.54	17.63	19.58	17.94	16.94	17.63	18.29	19.93	21.09	20.20	21.34	18.46
1997	21.76	19.38	17.85	16.64	17.24	15.90	15.91	16.21	16.44	17.68	16.84	15.06	17.23
1998	13.48	12.16	11.53	11.64	11.49	10.00	10.46	10.18	11.28	11.32	9.65	8.05	10.87
1999	8.57	8.60	10.76	12.82	13.92	14.39	16.12	17.58	20.03	19.71	21.35	22.55	15.56
2000	23.53	25.48	26.19	23.20	25.58	27.62	26.81	27.91	29.72	29.65	30.36	24.46	26.72
2001	24.58	25.27	23.02	23.41	24.06	23.43	22.94	23.08	22.37	18.73	16.49	15.54	21.84
2002	15.89	16.92	20.04	22.14	23.51	22.59	23.51	24.76	26.08	25.29	23.38	25.29	22.51
2003[2]	28.35	31.85	30.09	25.46	24.96	26.83	27.53	27.94	25.23	26.52	27.22		27.45

[1] Buyers posted prices.   [2] Preliminary.   *Source: Energy Information Administration, U.S. Department of Energy (EIA-DOE)*

PETROLEUM

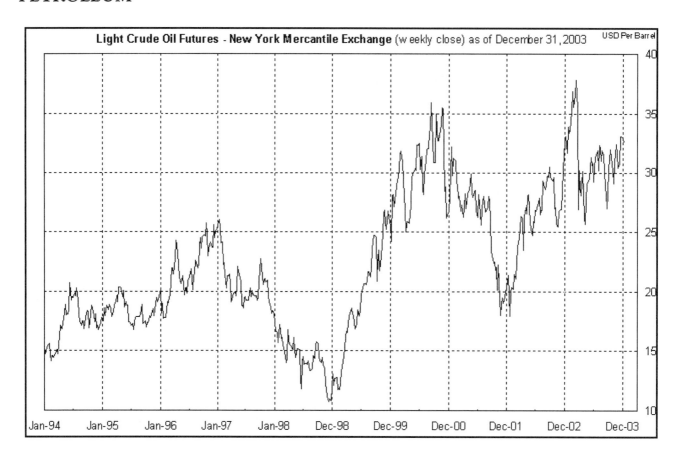

Volume of Trading of Crude Oil Futures in New York   In Thousands of Contracts

Year	Jan.	Feb.	Mar.	Apr.	May	June	July	Aug.	Sept.	Oct.	Nov.	Dec.	Total
1994	2,296	1,933	2,228	2,382	2,602	2,576	2,187	2,544	1,897	2,195	2,196	1,778	26,812
1995	2,133	1,657	2,290	2,220	2,409	2,172	1,749	1,794	1,968	1,835	1,739	1,647	23,614
1996	2,260	1,928	2,399	2,490	2,161	1,602	1,732	1,657	1,913	2,098	1,643	1,604	23,488
1997	1,950	1,974	2,087	2,034	2,135	2,099	2,221	2,054	2,028	2,574	1,770	1,847	24,771
1998	2,468	2,208	2,903	2,451	2,604	3,079	2,375	2,067	2,618	2,592	2,553	2,577	30,496
1999	2,534	2,326	3,768	3,167	3,038	3,307	3,471	3,355	3,388	3,571	3,465	2,470	37,860
2000	3,139	3,077	3,380	2,579	3,002	3,232	2,750	3,149	3,712	3,418	2,824	2,620	36,883
2001	3,035	2,855	3,449	3,312	3,469	3,572	3,170	3,316	2,773	2,913	3,210	2,455	37,531
2002	3,481	3,150	3,790	4,315	4,317	3,429	3,466	3,883	3,939	4,397	3,478	4,034	45,679
2003	4,553	4,039	4,151	3,355	3,329	3,534	3,401	3,732	3,826	4,248	3,624	3,646	45,437

Source: New York Mercantile Exchange (NYMEX)

Average Open Interest of Crude Oil Futures in New York   In Contracts

Year	Jan.	Feb.	Mar.	Apr.	May	June	July	Aug.	Sept.	Oct.	Nov.	Dec.
1994	427,705	438,929	424,462	410,974	427,071	414,257	409,251	396,657	395,194	413,206	388,932	391,151
1995	373,798	379,329	353,805	364,929	350,826	346,051	357,718	343,636	342,360	334,170	329,786	348,954
1996	389,935	400,236	427,306	460,841	424,994	376,164	367,405	364,458	395,358	410,387	385,415	368,331
1997	365,522	384,737	408,751	409,719	401,663	397,245	411,292	424,529	405,389	419,821	404,597	424,333
1998	424,810	445,167	468,438	463,961	450,611	467,998	476,516	486,499	486,047	481,657	487,175	501,591
1999	501,655	524,677	581,072	611,727	594,032	582,058	601,212	584,962	622,257	595,743	564,488	531,567
2000	512,049	519,090	513,359	467,259	453,042	462,476	432,571	416,934	461,298	478,242	479,008	438,118
2001	432,892	437,188	432,627	419,904	442,950	462,321	451,005	461,851	434,967	430,774	435,178	436,332
2002	448,063	454,154	497,405	488,061	512,413	474,087	457,033	454,219	505,530	528,548	482,227	531,078
2003	608,254	640,979	568,526	495,456	478,886	494,078	517,539	542,573	507,191	532,024	550,369	579,603

Source: New York Mercantile Exchange (NYMEX)

Plastics

Plastics are moldable, chemically fabricated materials produced mostly from fossil fuels, such as oil, coal, or natural gas. The word plastic is derived from the Greek *plastikos*, meaning to mold, and the Latin *plasticus*, meaning capable of molding. The first commercially successful thermosetting synthetic resin was created by Leo Baekeland in 1909, and over 50 families of plastics have been produced since then.

All plastics can be divided into either thermoplastics or thermosetting plastics. The difference between the two is the way in which they respond to heat. Thermoplastics can be repeatedly softened by heat and hardened by cooling. Thermosetting plastics harden permanently after being heated once.

Prices – Plastics prices in 2003 rebounded sharply higher along with the US economy after the weak prices seen in 2001 and 2002 during the US economic slump. Specifically, the average producer price index of plastic resins and materials in the US in 2003 (through Oct) rose +12.2% to 146.7 from the 4-year low of 130.7 posted in 2002. The average producer price index of thermoplastic resins in the US in 2003 (through October) rose +14.0% to 147.2 from the 4-year low of 129.1 posted in 2002. The average producer price index of styrene plastic materials (also a thermoplastic) in the US in 2003 (through October) rose +23.9% to 118.3 from the 23-year low of 95.5 posted in 2002. The average producer price index of thermosetting resins in the US in 2003 (through October) rose +5.3% to 154.3 from the

3-year low of 146.5 posted in 2002.

Supply – Total US plastics production in 2002 rose +6.2% to a record high of 108.262 billion pounds, despite weak US economic demand during 2001-2002. The 2002 production level was more than twice that seen as recently as 1986, which shows that plastics continue to represent a growth industry.

By sector, the thermoplastics sector is by far the largest, with 2002 production of 86.762 billion pounds up +6.2% from 2001 and accounting for 80% of total US plastic production. The thermosetting plastic sector (polyester unsaturated, phenolic, and epoxy) production in 2002 rose +5.1% to 7.893 billion pounds and accounted for 7% of total US plastics production. The category of "other plastics" rose +12.6% to 13.607 billion pounds and accounted for 13% of total US plastics production.

Demand – The breakdown by market for the usage of plastic resins shows that the largest single consumption category is packaging with 23.616 billion pounds of usage in 2002, accounting for 28.7% of total US consumption. After packaging, the largest categories are building and construction (16.8% of US consumption), and commercial and industrial (14.4%).

Trade – US exports of plastics in 2002 totaled 9.820 billion pounds, up 8.1% from 9.084 billion pounds in 2001. US exports accounted for 11.9% of US supply disappearance in 2002.

Plastics Production by Resin in the United States In Millions of Pounds

| | Thermosets | | | | Thermoplastics | | | | | | | | | | | |
Year	Polyester Unsaturated	Phenlic	Epoxy	Total Thermosets	Thermo-plastic Polyester	Polyvinyl Chloride	Poly-styrene	Poly-propylene	Nylon	Low Density Polye-thylene[1]	High Density Polye-thylene	Total Thermo-plastics	Total Selected Plastics	Other Plastics	Total Plastics
1993	1,264	3,078	512	6,868	2,549	10,257	5,382	8,628	768	12,067	9,941	51,159	58,027	10,777	68,854
1994	1,468	3,229	601	7,513	3,196	11,712	5,848	9,539	943	12,600	11,117	56,794	64,307	11,664	75,971
1995	1,577	3,204	632	7,519	3,785	12,295	5,656	10,890	1,020	12,886	11,211	59,331	66,850	11,834	78,684
1996	1,557	3,476	662	8,129	4,031	13,220	6,065	11,991	1,103	14,145	12,373	64,526	72,655	11,640	84,295
1997	1,621	3,734	654	8,647	4,260	14,084	6,380	13,320	1,222	14,579	12,557	67,872	76,519	12,287	88,806
1998	1,713	3,940	639	9,163	4,423	14,502	6,237	13,825	1,285	14,805	12,924	71,209	78,659	13,026	91,685
1999	2,985	4,388	657	8,030	6,735	14,912	7,075	15,493	1,349	15,807	13,864	78,457	86,487	13,467	99,954
2000	3,149	3,965	669	7,783	7,239	14,364	6,676	15,583	1,395	19,588	16,439	84,553	92,336	13,604	105,940
2001	3,021	3,894	597	7,512	6,972	14,626	6,223	16,135	1,159	18,389	15,195	81,726	89,238	12,720	101,958
2002	3,197	4,076	620	7,893	7,480	15,250	6,768	17,084	1,284	19,515	16,190	86,762	94,655	13,607	108,262

[1] Includes LDPE and LLDPE.   *Source: American Plastics Council (APC)*

Total Resin Sales and Captive Use by Important Markets In Millions of Pounds (Dry Weight Basis)

Year	Adhesive, Inks & Coatings	Building & Construction	Consumer & Industrial	Electrical & Electronics	Exports	Furniture & Furnishings	Industrial & Machinary	Packaging	Transportation	Other	Total
1993	1,572	12,885	6,015	2,981	6,632	2,759	768	19,569	3,221	7,234	63,636
1994	1,789	14,715	9,266	3,325	6,889	3,118	836	19,551	3,795	7,515	70,799
1995	1,795	13,551	8,921	2,872	7,162	3,189	805	17,107	3,376	7,421	66,200
1996	1,833	15,413	9,662	3,022	7,997	3,468	965	18,691	3,469	8,701	73,221
1997	1,713	11,418	10,357	2,806	8,647	3,099	729	19,135	3,411	8,640	69,955
1998	1,758	12,077	11,031	2,816	8,208	3,293	710	19,396	3,588	9,211	71,994
1999	1,753	13,793	11,645	3,036	8,424	2,885	802	21,210	3,632	10,189	77,123
2000	1,715	13,520	11,505	2,924	9,432	2,993	783	21,289	3,872	9,456	77,640
2001	1,675	13,231	11,219	2,352	9,084	2,879	647	22,574	3,595	10,134	77,390
2002	1,664	13,839	11,861	2,433	9,820	3,076	663	23,616	3,753	11,600	82,324

[1] Included in other.   *Source: American Plastics Council (APC)*

PLASTICS

Average Producer Price Index of Plastic Resins and Materials (066) in the United States   (1982 = 100)

Year	Jan.	Feb.	Mar.	Apr.	May	June	July	Aug.	Sept.	Oct.	Nov.	Dec.	Average
1994	115.0	114.7	114.5	116.5	117.7	119.1	119.6	121.5	126.3	131.9	134.1	138.1	122.4
1995	142.5	144.1	145.9	148.5	149.0	148.9	147.0	144.8	142.7	139.2	135.8	132.2	143.4
1996	129.9	128.4	128.4	127.7	130.6	132.1	133.2	135.2	137.9	138.0	138.0	137.7	133.1
1997	137.0	137.5	138.7	138.9	139.1	139.6	139.3	137.4	136.0	135.9	134.6	133.9	137.3
1998	134.0	132.2	131.0	130.7	128.8	126.8	125.0	123.7	119.6	118.6	117.1	115.9	125.3
1999	115.9	115.8	117.3	118.6	122.1	123.1	127.9	130.0	133.8	135.6	135.8	134.3	125.8
2000	133.2	135.7	139.4	143.7	147.4	147.8	146.4	146.3	142.4	140.7	138.8	137.3	141.6
2001	137.8	139.3	141.4	141.9	139.9	137.6	135.1	131.3	126.8	128.3	126.6	123.9	134.2
2002	122.0	121.3	123.1	125.4	128.0	130.1	135.3	136.4	136.7	138.2	137.0	135.3	130.7
2003[1]	137.2	141.8	149.6	153.2	152.4	149.2	144.9	143.6	144.8	145.4	145.8	145.4	146.1

[1] Preliminary.   Source: Bureau of Labor Statistics, U.S. Department of Commerce (BLS)

Average Producer Price Index of Thermoplastic Resins (0662) in the United States   (1982 = 100)

Year	Jan.	Feb.	Mar.	Apr.	May	June	July	Aug.	Sept.	Oct.	Nov.	Dec.	Average
1994	113.0	112.7	112.5	115.0	116.2	117.9	118.4	120.1	125.4	131.6	133.9	138.4	121.3
1995	143.1	145.0	147.1	150.3	151.0	151.2	148.7	146.2	143.7	139.6	135.5	131.1	144.4
1996	128.4	126.7	126.8	125.9	129.4	131.1	132.5	134.8	137.8	137.9	137.9	137.6	132.2
1997	136.7	137.3	138.6	138.8	139.0	139.7	139.3	137.0	135.5	135.3	133.8	133.0	137.0
1998	133.0	130.7	129.5	129.2	127.0	124.7	122.5	121.0	116.4	115.3	113.7	112.2	122.9
1999	112.3	112.5	114.4	116.1	120.4	121.6	127.5	129.9	134.5	136.7	137.0	135.2	124.9
2000	133.8	136.0	140.4	145.2	149.3	149.6	147.6	147.4	142.7	140.3	137.9	136.0	142.2
2001	136.3	138.0	140.2	140.8	138.4	135.7	133.1	128.6	123.4	125.7	123.9	120.8	132.1
2002	118.4	117.8	120.3	123.8	126.2	128.6	135.0	135.9	136.2	137.6	136.1	133.8	129.1
2003[1]	136.3	142.2	151.4	155.8	153.6	149.5	144.3	142.8	144.5	145.2	146.2	145.6	146.5

[1] Preliminary.   Source: Bureau of Labor Statistics, U.S. Department of Commerce (BLS)

Average Producer Price Index of Styrene Plastics Materials (0662-06) in the United States   (1982 = 100)

Year	Jan.	Feb.	Mar.	Apr.	May	June	July	Aug.	Sept.	Oct.	Nov.	Dec.	Average
1994	105.8	104.1	104.1	108.1	108.3	109.2	110.4	110.6	116.0	123.3	125.3	126.2	112.6
1995	129.0	127.0	132.5	134.7	135.9	137.5	135.1	133.2	132.1	130.1	127.9	126.1	131.8
1996	125.7	123.5	125.0	118.3	120.1	122.7	123.4	123.3	123.6	122.8	122.0	120.9	122.6
1997	120.6	123.1	123.0	121.6	121.6	121.6	122.7	117.7	118.0	116.5	113.5	113.7	119.5
1998	113.3	113.9	115.5	114.9	114.1	112.8	111.3	111.2	107.6	107.9	107.1	106.3	111.3
1999	103.5	102.4	103.5	104.7	103.0	102.3	103.1	101.5	101.4	99.8	99.4	100.5	102.1
2000	103.0	104.3	110.5	113.0	116.2	116.9	118.5	116.5	115.0	114.1	112.1	110.4	112.5
2001	110.5	109.2	107.9	108.0	101.8	99.9	97.6	95.7	87.3	89.4	90.0	85.4	98.6
2002	85.7	85.8	87.9	88.5	90.4	91.7	93.7	100.6	100.5	108.9	108.1	103.9	95.5
2003[1]	102.9	110.2	119.5	127.2	126.7	119.1	118.0	113.3	120.3	115.0	113.9	111.7	116.5

[1] Preliminary.   Source: Bureau of Labor Statistics, U.S. Department of Commerce (BLS)

Average Producer Price Index of Thermosetting Resins (0663) in the United States   (1982 = 100)

Year	Jan.	Feb.	Mar.	Apr.	May	June	July	Aug.	Sept.	Oct.	Nov.	Dec.	Average
1994	128.2	128.1	128.1	127.8	128.7	129.1	129.7	132.1	134.9	137.7	140.1	141.5	132.2
1995	144.3	145.1	145.4	145.2	144.7	143.5	144.0	143.5	142.9	142.3	142.4	142.1	143.8
1996	141.8	141.9	141.2	141.3	141.4	141.2	140.6	141.5	141.7	142.0	142.0	142.2	141.6
1997	142.1	142.3	142.7	143.1	143.2	143.0	142.8	142.9	143.0	143.1	142.9	142.9	142.8
1998	143.6	144.0	143.2	142.9	142.6	142.7	142.5	142.2	141.2	140.9	140.1	140.3	142.2
1999	139.9	138.1	137.7	137.4	136.9	136.5	136.2	136.5	136.5	136.5	136.3	136.2	137.0
2000	136.8	141.1	141.3	142.8	144.9	146.0	147.6	147.8	147.5	149.5	150.3	151.0	145.6
2001	152.1	152.9	154.5	154.4	154.2	154.2	152.3	151.3	150.4	148.2	146.3	146.1	151.4
2002	146.2	144.6	143.8	141.2	144.1	145.5	145.8	147.6	148.4	150.3	150.3	150.6	146.5
2003[1]	150.4	149.7	151.7	152.0	156.8	157.9	157.1	156.4	155.4	155.6	153.9	154.1	154.3

[1] Preliminary.   Source: Bureau of Labor Statistics, U.S. Department of Commerce (BLS)

Platinum-Group Metals

Platinum is a relatively rare, chemically inert metallic element that is more valuable than gold. Platinum is a grayish-white metal that has a high fusing point, is malleable and ductile, and has a high electrical resistance. Chemically, platinum is relatively inert and resists attack by air, water, single acids, and ordinary reagents. Weighing almost twice as much as gold, platinum is the heaviest of the precious metals. Platinum is the most important of the six-metal group, which also includes ruthenium, rhodium, palladium, osmium, and iridium. The word "platinum" is derived from the Spanish word *platina* meaning silver.

Platinum is one of the world's rarest metals with new mine production totaling only about 5 million troy ounces a year. All the platinum mined to date would fit in the average-size living room. Platinum is mined all over the world with supplies concentrated in South Africa. South Africa accounts for nearly 80% of world supply, followed by Russia, and North America.

Because platinum will never tarnish, lose its rich white luster, or even wear down after many years, it is prized by the jewelry industry. The international jewelry industry is the largest consumer sector for platinum, accounting for 51% of total platinum demand. In Europe and the US, the normal purity of platinum is 95%. Ten tons of ore must be mined and a five-month process is needed to produce one ounce of pure platinum.

The second major consumer sector for platinum is for auto catalysts, with 21% of total platinum demand. Catalysts in autos are used to convert most of vehicle emissions into less harmful carbon dioxide, nitrogen, and water vapor. Platinum is also used in the production of hard disk drive coatings, fiber optic cables, infra-red detectors, fertilizers, explosives, petrol additives, platinum-tipped spark plugs, glassmaking equipment, biodegradable elements for household detergents, dental restorations, and in anti-cancer drugs.

Palladium is very similar to platinum and is part of the same general metals group. Palladium is mined with platinum, but it is somewhat more common because it is also a by-product of nickel mining. The primary use for palladium is in the use of automotive catalysts, with that sector accounting for about 63% of total palladium demand. Other uses for palladium include electronic equipment (21%), dental alloys (12%), and jewelry (4%).

Rhodium, another member of the platinum group, is also used in the automotive industry in pollution control devices. To some extent palladium has replaced rhodium. Iridium is used to process catalysts and it has also found use in some auto catalysts. Iridium and ruthenium are used in the production of polyvinyl chloride. As the prices of these metals change, there is some substitution. Therefore, strength of platinum prices relative to palladium should lead to the substitution of palladium for platinum in catalytic converters.

Platinum futures and options and palladium futures are traded on the New York Mercantile Exchange (NYMEX). Platinum and palladium futures are traded on the Tokyo Commodity Exchange (TOCOM). The NYMEX platinum futures contract calls for the delivery of 50 troy ounces of platinum (0.9995 fineness) and the contract trades in terms of dollars and cents per troy ounce. The NYMEX palladium futures contract calls for the delivery of 50 troy ounces of palladium (0.9995 fineness) and the contract trades in terms of dollars and cents per troy ounce.

Prices – NYMEX platinum futures prices in 2003 on the nearest-futures chart rallied sharply and fairly steadily during the year, finally closing the year at an all-time record high of $811.30 per ounce, up 33% from the 2002 close of $610.50. Palladium prices, by contrast, were relatively weak in 2003, moving generally sideways at the bottom of the plunge in prices seen from the peak of about $1,100 per ounce in early 2001 to the low of $145 seen in April 2003. However, palladium did recover somewhat along with the rest of the metals in late 2003 due to the stronger US economy and the weak dollar, closing the year at $197.50. That was up 36% from the year's low of $145 but was still down 18% from the 2002 close of $241.55.

Supply – World mine production of platinum in 2002, the latest reporting year, rose by 2.2% to 184,000 kilograms from 180,000 in 2001. That was a 17-year high in production, going back to 246,988 kilograms of production in 1985. South Africa is the world's largest producer of platinum by far with 73% of world production, followed by Russia (19%), Canada (4%) and the US (2.4%).

World mine production of palladium rose +2.3% to 181,000 kilograms in 2002 from 177,000 in 2001. The world's largest palladium producers are Russia with 46.4% of world production, followed by South Africa with 35.5%, the US with 8.2%, and Canada with 6.4%.

World production of platinum group metals other than platinum and palladium rose to 57,000 kilograms in 2003 from 51,100 in 2001. South Africa accounted for 73% of that production and Russia accounted for the bulk of the remainder.

US mine production of platinum in 2002 rose by 21.6% to 4,390 kilograms from 3,610 in 2001. US mine production of palladium in 2002 rose by 22.3% to 14,800 kilograms from 12,100 in 2001. US refinery production of scrap platinum in 2002 fell 15.7% to 20,900 kilograms from 24,790 in 2001. Scrap platinum accounts for virtually all of US platinum refinery production since US mine production is miniscule.

Demand – The US automotive industry accounted for 60.3% of US platinum usages in 2001, followed by 10.7% for the electrical industry, 7.6% by the petroleum industry, 7.3% for the jewelry industry, 4.8% by the chemical industry, and 1.8% by the dental and medical industry.

Trade – US platinum imports for consumption rose 11.1% to 297,656 kilograms in 2002 from 267,957 in 2001. The US relied on imports for 93% of its platinum consumption in 2002. US exports of platinum rose 6.1% to 72,838 kilograms in 2002 from 68.625 in 2001.

PLATINUM-GROUP METALS

World Mine Production of Platinum   In Kilograms

Year	Australia	Canada	Colombia[3]	Finland	Japan	Russia	Serbia/Montenegro	South Africa	United States	Zimbabwe	World Total
1994	100	6,000	1,084	60	691	15,000	10	114,000	1,960	7	139,000
1995	100	5,945	973	60	730	27,000	10	102,000	1,590	7	139,000
1996	100	5,155	672	62	816	25,000	10	105,000	1,840	100	139,000
1997	300	4,813	406	60	693	30,000	10	115,861	2,610	345	155,000
1998	150	5,640	411	500	533	30,000	10	116,483	3,240	2,730	160,000
1999	90	5,663	448	500	737	32,000	5	121,304	2,920	479	164,000
2000	171	6,302	339	441	782	35,000	5	114,459	3,110	505	161,000
2001[1]	174	7,410	674	510	550	36,000	5	130,307	3,610	519	180,000
2002[2]	200	7,400	700	500	500	35,000	5	133,796	4,390	1,500	184,000

[1] Preliminary.   [2] Estimate.   [3] Placer platinum.   *Source: U.S. Geological Survey (USGS)*

World Mine Production of Palladium and Other Group Metals   In Kilograms

	Palladium										Other Group Metals		
Year	Australia	Canada	Finland	Japan	Russia	Serbia/Montenegro	South Africa	United States	Zimbabwe	World Total	Russia	South Africa	World Total
1994	400	7,000	100	1,277	40,000	50	47,800	6,440	17	103,000	3,000	22,100	27,100
1995	400	9,319	95	2,174	85,000	50	51,000	5,260	17	153,000	3,600	29,797	34,200
1996	400	8,082	182	2,182	80,000	50	52,600	6,100	120	150,000	3,500	30,363	34,800
1997	400	7,545	180	1,899	70,000	50	55,675	8,430	245	144,000	13,500	25,068	39,200
1998	800	8,905	150	4,151	70,000	50	56,608	10,600	1,855	153,000	13,500	26,862	41,300
1999	816	8,939	150	5,354	75,000	25	58,164	9,800	342	159,000	13,700	37,011	51,500
2000	812	9,949	----	4,712	84,000	25	55,818	10,300	366	166,000	14,100	36,493	51,400
2001[1]	828	11,700	----	4,830	85,000	25	62,601	12,100	371	177,000	14,500	35,839	51,100
2002[2]	800	11,500	----	5,000	84,000	25	64,244	14,800	1,080	181,000	14,500	41,721	57,000

[1] Preliminary.   [2] Estimate.   *Source: U.S. Geological Survey (USGS)*

Platinum-Group Metals Sold to Consuming Industries in the United States   In Kilograms

	Automotive		Chemical		Electrical		Medical		Dental & Decorative		Petroleum		All Platinum-Group Metals			
Year	Platinum	Other[3]	Platinum	Other[3]	Platinum	Other[3]	Platinum	Other[3]	Platinum	Other[3]	Platinum	Other[3]	Platinum	Palladium	Other[3]	Total
1993	19,446	10,124	2,364	3,121	2,125	12,699	687	5,562	1,024	1,422	1,204	709	29,879	26,840	8,544	65,063
1994	21,756	11,413	3,104	1,889	2,790	7,961	902	5,092	1,345	824	1,581	422	34,044	21,509	7,387	62,940
1995	27,990	12,440	2,022	2,395	4,510	18,225	778	6,158	1,337	1,431	3,421	871	43,524	45,188	----	88,712
1996	28,550	19,282	2,115	2,457	4,541	17,665	778	6,285	1,493	1,493	3,514	902	44,489	45,157	----	89,646
1997	28,923	20,402	2,239	2,426	4,945	19,997	840	6,376	2,115	1,617	3,390	871	46,184	50,227	----	96,411
1998	29,483	26,528	2,301	2,488	5,194	20,215	902	6,376	2,333	1,617	3,390	809	47,396	61,827	----	109,223
1999	31,100	29,390	2,364	2,519	5,443	21,148	933	6,065	3,110	1,679	3,514	778	50,310	65,248	----	115,558
2000[1]	32,344	31,100	2,457	2,139	5,691	19,282	964	3,732	3,670	1,400	3,639	660	52,808	61,889	----	114,697
2001[2]	33,411	34,832	2,644	715	5,909	17,354	995	3,670	4,043	1,431	4,199	715	55,399	62,293	----	117,692

[1] Preliminary.   [2] Estimate.   [3] Includes Palladium, iridium, osmium, rhodium, and ruthenium.   *Sources: U.S. Geological Survey (USGS); American Metal Market (AMM)*

Salient Statistics of Platinum and Allied Metals[3] in the United States   In Kilograms

	Net Import Reliance as a % of Apparent Consumption	Mine Production		Refinery Production (Secondary) Total Refined		Refiner, Importer & Dealer Stocks as of Dec. 31				Imports for Consumption		Exports		Apparent Consumption
Year		Platinum	Palladium			Platinum	Palladium	Other[4]	Total	Refined	Total	Refined	Total	
1994	91	1,960	6,440	63,000	63,000	10,304	9,345	123	19,772	167,681	170,907	46,259	88,561	127,000
1995	----	1,590	5,260	NA	NA	----	----	----	----	214,143	220,613	41,825	50,575	----
1996	84	1,840	6,100	NA	NA	----	----	----	----	248,860	255,880	39,709	48,836	----
1997	84	2,610	8,430	NA	NA	14,100	39,300	920	54,320	253,114	258,424	67,656	81,249	----
1998	94	3,240	10,600	NA	NA	13,700	38,800	920	53,420	297,101	303,351	52,716	73,162	----
1999	----	2,920	9,800	23,300	23,300	7,060	28,200	784	36,044	337,973	----	64,165	----	----
2000	83	3,110	10,300	23,780	23,780	5,190	19,000	784	24,974	316,633	----	85,177	----	----
2001[1]	66	3,610	12,100	24,790	24,790	3,680	16,300	784	20,764	267,957	----	68,652	----	----
2002[2]	93	4,390	14,800	20,900	20,900	649	5,870	784	7,303	297,656	----	72,838	----	----

[1] Preliminary.   [2] Estimate.   [3] Includes platinum, palladium, iridium, osmium, rhodium, and ruthenium.   [4] Includes iridium, osmium, rhodium, and ruthenium.   W = Withheld proprietary data.   *Source: U.S. Geological Survey (USGS)*

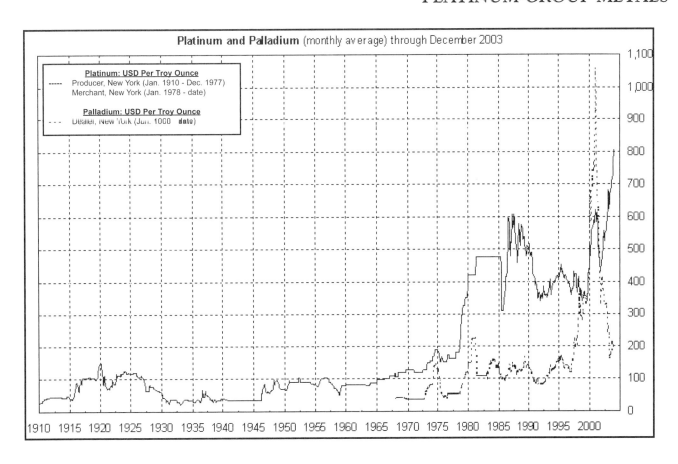

Average Merchant's Price of Platinum in the United States   In Dollars Per Troy Ounce

Year	Jan.	Feb.	Mar.	Apr.	May	June	July	Aug.	Sept.	Oct.	Nov.	Dec.	Average
1994	390.30	393.95	398.29	400.38	395.41	401.42	408.25	411.91	415.93	421.11	415.73	408.83	405.13
1995	414.27	415.22	415.37	446.24	439.02	436.58	435.21	425.61	430.31	414.49	413.55	410.17	424.67
1996	416.59	421.45	412.39	405.71	402.86	393.18	392.00	400.97	391.43	385.53	383.92	372.97	398.24
1997	360.13	362.35	382.82	371.18	385.20	427.12	409.93	423.48	424.00	428.59	396.68	369.55	395.42
1998	375.30	390.56	396.18	412.82	392.60	357.38	379.34	372.24	361.40	347.27	348.42	352.76	373.85
1999	353.53	361.55	370.80	357.30	354.75	357.75	350.30	352.24	365.62	421.52	436.48	438.00	376.44
2000	432.95	517.02	478.28	493.53	519.57	557.45	558.53	572.76	592.53	576.91	592.73	608.28	541.49
2001	623.43	453.56	566.67	589.63	611.07	588.91	643.88	457.37	453.50	437.43	427.25	450.24	531.93
2002	471.52	470.68	511.95	539.20	533.66	554.70	526.32	545.48	556.05	580.11	588.15	594.89	539.39
2003[1]	629.52	681.79	675.00	624.48	649.43	661.43	682.02	692.48	705.33	732.65	760.08	807.10	691.78

[1] Preliminary.   Source: American Metal Market (AMM)

Average Dealer[1] Price of Palladium in the United States   In Dollars Per Troy Ounce

Year	Jan.	Feb.	Mar.	Apr.	May	June	July	Aug.	Sept.	Oct.	Nov.	Dec.	Average
1994	124.40	130.92	132.43	133.22	135.76	137.03	145.28	151.83	152.99	154.90	158.10	153.80	142.56
1995	156.67	157.53	161.18	170.91	160.87	158.59	156.27	138.81	143.76	137.36	135.57	132.37	150.83
1996	130.47	138.77	138.77	137.10	132.83	129.70	132.69	128.12	122.55	118.35	118.21	117.91	128.79
1997	121.48	134.26	151.13	152.75	167.52	203.62	176.84	210.90	190.17	206.52	209.93	200.70	177.15
1998	222.55	237.25	258.01	310.81	353.58	284.34	307.53	287.48	283.88	277.89	281.82	306.73	284.32
1999	317.28	351.38	351.78	358.83	330.70	339.84	333.17	341.64	358.55	387.05	400.38	420.17	357.50
2000	447.45	607.33	687.72	580.00	574.89	640.80	686.63	759.63	731.15	734.91	778.73	887.33	676.55
2001	1054.10	984.37	792.68	699.15	663.41	619.67	525.90	459.83	444.47	340.52	333.14	405.95	610.27
2002	412.62	377.79	377.15	372.50	360.00	339.20	325.41	327.55	330.50	319.09	289.20	243.57	339.55
2003[2]	258.19	255.68	226.38	164.76	168.90	181.76	174.91	185.76	213.24	204.17	200.17	200.86	202.90

[1] Based on wholesale quantities, prompt delivery.   [2] Preliminary.   Source: U.S. Geological Survey (USGS)

PLATINUM-GROUP METALS

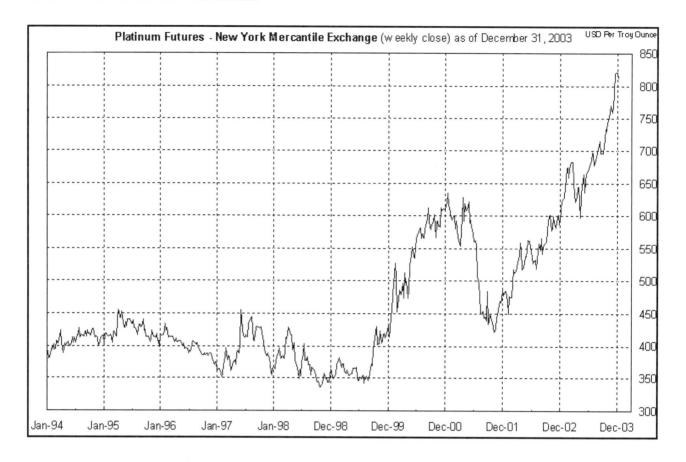

Platinum Futures - New York Mercantile Exchange (weekly close) as of December 31, 2003 — USD Per Troy Ounce

Volume of Trading of Platinum Futures in New York   In Contracts

Year	Jan.	Feb.	Mar.	Apr.	May	June	July	Aug.	Sept.	Oct.	Nov.	Dec.	Total
1994	48,259	65,297	94,426	62,600	65,140	88,300	84,182	75,409	92,439	60,878	77,264	81,611	895,805
1995	61,400	38,594	131,294	69,892	60,382	75,353	53,422	62,451	98,837	55,919	56,339	82,810	846,693
1996	80,545	70,260	86,258	54,151	47,929	88,806	53,312	53,654	90,140	47,116	41,970	88,327	802,468
1997	60,515	83,325	86,242	57,719	67,000	72,481	37,836	36,391	62,462	46,188	28,913	58,625	698,597
1998	38,198	35,538	65,871	36,169	36,208	47,464	35,223	27,505	58,302	44,381	42,658	60,752	528,629
1999	37,700	53,698	68,350	36,900	26,507	75,444	57,536	36,115	102,196	30,637	32,176	40,009	597,268
2000	33,226	31,352	35,013	28,057	22,741	47,197	16,527	14,739	36,643	12,122	12,662	30,645	320,924
2001	19,278	12,885	31,617	14,961	15,714	23,245	14,494	12,477	17,040	9,957	11,401	22,890	205,969
2002	12,848	13,807	24,434	11,066	12,294	27,176	14,198	18,583	29,762	11,834	9,878	33,891	219,771
2003	15,545	15,157	38,170	13,472	18,968	30,961	10,852	11,878	37,686	19,275	14,040	42,301	268,305

Source: New York Mercantile Exchange (NYMEX)

Average Open Interest of Platinum Futures in New York   In Contracts

Year	Jan.	Feb.	Mar.	Apr.	May	June	July	Aug.	Sept.	Oct.	Nov.	Dec.
1994	18,779	19,655	21,673	22,834	21,880	22,835	24,804	25,049	24,245	24,159	26,287	26,661
1995	23,285	23,058	23,470	23,657	20,984	21,533	20,801	25,288	23,489	24,498	22,137	21,534
1996	23,130	21,535	23,156	25,081	26,343	27,720	25,861	25,455	28,511	28,305	27,423	29,143
1997	25,890	26,092	22,364	16,568	18,933	18,440	13,280	14,180	13,639	13,466	12,396	13,501
1998	10,791	10,932	13,220	13,559	12,048	11,471	10,607	9,733	11,950	14,601	15,709	13,289
1999	12,311	14,481	16,493	11,471	12,256	12,436	14,703	13,777	15,014	14,892	13,402	12,017
2000	10,858	10,952	9,218	8,484	9,057	10,585	9,566	9,731	9,716	8,106	8,163	8,507
2001	8,449	7,311	6,855	6,715	7,436	5,751	6,210	5,996	5,646	5,395	6,102	6,033
2002	6,587	6,213	7,121	6,823	6,031	6,901	5,516	6,405	6,930	7,211	7,406	8,388
2003	8,694	8,132	8,034	6,322	6,599	6,847	7,450	8,556	8,794	8,489	9,421	9,434

Source: New York Mercantile Exchange (NYMEX)

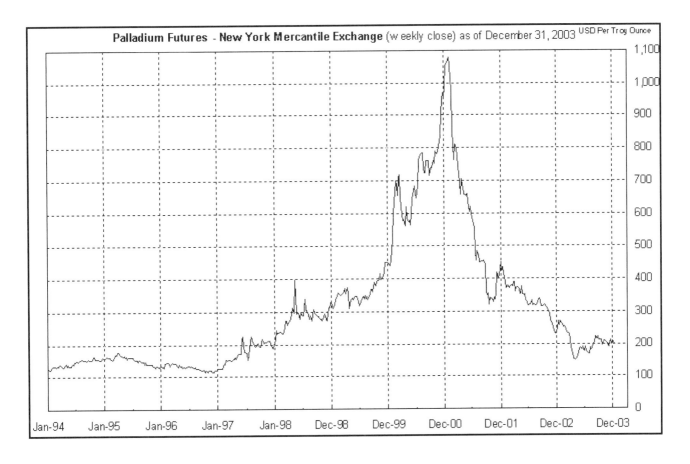

Palladium Futures - New York Mercantile Exchange (weekly close) as of December 31, 2003 USD Per Troy Ounce

Volume of Trading of Palladium Futures in New York   In Contracts

Year	Jan.	Feb.	Mar.	Apr.	May	June	July	Aug.	Sept.	Oct.	Nov.	Dec.	Total
1994	8,250	14,953	6,067	6,676	15,481	6,514	9,024	21,741	15,690	9,603	21,384	8,390	143,773
1995	10,684	17,092	21,001	12,775	17,413	9,615	11,816	18,948	9,754	9,320	16,662	11,633	166,713
1996	13,725	33,519	11,931	16,416	27,467	8,989	9,896	23,740	10,721	8,149	28,870	12,187	205,610
1997	13,908	43,160	22,796	21,604	36,422	17,647	18,097	18,751	8,331	13,094	13,143	11,763	238,716
1998	11,506	17,786	18,678	14,042	17,942	7,370	4,241	8,737	6,214	4,962	12,839	6,933	131,250
1999	3,092	11,614	4,082	7,097	8,890	3,411	5,053	6,868	5,826	3,722	10,670	5,069	75,394
2000	4,584	13,976	2,803	1,833	7,034	2,622	3,120	5,169	2,523	2,460	3,041	1,601	50,766
2001	2,171	6,090	1,397	1,121	3,325	1,013	1,173	3,221	523	1,255	3,261	1,375	25,925
2002	1,275	3,372	1,538	1,527	6,126	2,166	2,154	8,971	1,452	1,710	8,118	2,644	41,053
2003	4,200	7,266	3,256	3,971	8,420	3,430	4,221	15,645	8,152	7,587	18,323	11,142	95,613

Source: New York Mercantile Exchange (NYMEX)

Average Open Interest of Palladium Futures in New York   In Contracts

Year	Jan.	Feb.	Mar.	Apr.	May	June	July	Aug.	Sept.	Oct.	Nov.	Dec.
1994	4,626	4,995	4,672	4,303	5,116	4,530	5,807	6,851	6,625	6,511	7,726	6,917
1995	7,484	7,579	7,102	7,231	6,519	6,413	6,739	6,852	5,950	6,120	6,486	6,090
1996	6,365	7,539	6,682	7,099	8,713	8,143	7,977	8,805	8,129	7,971	8,227	7,727
1997	8,291	10,946	10,528	9,759	9,947	7,072	5,538	4,973	3,822	4,282	4,291	4,030
1998	4,062	4,873	5,220	5,369	4,371	4,219	4,166	3,488	2,959	3,048	2,938	2,700
1999	2,846	3,234	2,957	3,015	2,796	2,757	2,823	2,496	2,755	3,210	3,301	3,045
2000	3,129	3,101	2,367	2,359	2,628	2,015	2,118	1,974	1,757	1,905	1,859	1,837
2001	1,828	1,666	1,525	1,577	1,613	1,385	1,420	1,318	1,383	1,286	1,477	1,244
2002	1,217	1,208	1,042	1,199	1,554	1,806	2,103	2,298	1,878	1,976	1,977	2,025
2003	2,000	2,039	1,948	1,997	2,315	2,609	2,680	3,605	5,184	5,533	6,096	6,707

Source: New York Mercantile Exchange (NYMEX)

Pork Bellies

Pork bellies are the cut of meat from a hog from which bacon is produced. A hog has two bellies, generally weighing 8-18 pounds, depending on the hog's commercial slaughter weight. Slaughter weights average around 255 pounds, equal to a dressed carcass weight of about 190 pounds. Bellies account for about 12% of a hog's live weight, but represent a somewhat larger percentage of 14% of the total cutout value of the realized pork products. Pork bellies can be frozen and stored for up to a year before processing. The pork belly futures contract at the Chicago Mercantile Exchange calls for the physical delivery of 40,000 pounds of frozen pork bellies, which have been slaughtered at USDA federally inspected slaughtering plants. Each deliverable belly typically weighs 12-14 pounds each.

There are definite seasonal patterns in pork belly prices. Bellies are storable and the movement into cold storage builds early in the calendar year, peaking about mid-year. Net withdrawals from storage then carry stocks to a low around October. The cycle then starts again. Retail bacon demand also follows a time worn trend, peaking in the summer when consumer preference shifts to lighter foods and tapering off to a low during the winter months. While demand patterns would suggest the highest prices in the summer and the lowest in the winter, just the opposite is not unusual. Such contra-seasonal price moves can be partially attributed to supply logistics, notably the availability of frozen storage stocks deliverable against futures at CME exchange-approved warehouses. When stocks prove either too large or small, the underlying demand variables for bacon can be relegated to the backburner as a market-moving factor. The fact that no contract months are traded between August and the following February adds to the late fall futures price distortion.

Belly prices (cash and futures) are sensitive to the inventory in cold storage and to the weekly net movement in and out of storage, which affords some insight to demand, although a better measure is the weekly quantity of bellies being sliced into bacon. Higher retail prices tend to encourage placing more supply into storage because of lower retail bacon demand. Bacon is not a necessary foodstuff so demand can be buoyed by favorable consumer disposable income. However, dietary standards have changed dramatically in recent years and do not favor the consumption of high fat and salt content food, like bacon. The U.S. economy stalled in 2002 at least relative to expectations, which would have been expected to reduce consumer bacon demand, but retail prices held firm, especially in the first half of the year. The anticipated 2002 average of $3.25/lb was unchanged from 2001, which was well above the annual average of the 1990's.

Prices – Pork bellies rallied in the first half of 2003 and posted a 7-year high of 103.30 cents/pound in late July on the weekly nearest futures chart. However, prices quickly fell back in August and then remained in the relatively narrow range between 80-94 cents/pound through the remainder of the year, closing at 86.90 cents. In the bigger picture, pork belly prices closed 2003 in the upper one-quarter of the range of roughly 40 cents to $1.00 seen in the past 7 years.

Average Retail Price of Bacon, Sliced   In Dollars Per Pound

Year	Jan.	Feb.	Mar.	Apr.	May	June	July	Aug.	Sept.	Oct.	Nov.	Dec.	Average
1994	2.04	2.02	2.02	2.06	1.99	1.99	2.00	1.99	1.97	1.97	1.92	1.89	1.99
1995	1.93	1.93	1.91	1.89	1.92	1.90	1.91	1.97	2.04	2.12	2.16	2.17	1.99
1996	2.14	2.20	2.20	2.24	2.35	2.49	2.54	2.68	2.81	2.72	2.66	2.64	2.47
1997	2.66	2.65	2.66	2.66	2.63	2.69	2.72	2.76	2.75	2.73	2.67	2.61	2.68
1998	2.64	2.62	2.54	2.44	2.44	2.46	2.52	2.51	2.58	2.57	2.62	2.58	2.54
1999	2.52	2.52	2.51	2.45	2.47	2.50	2.50	2.93	2.58	2.57	2.66	2.75	2.58
2000	2.75	2.87	2.93	2.95	3.01	3.13	3.17	3.20	3.21	3.07	3.05	3.03	3.03
2001	2.99	3.07	3.16	3.11	3.26	3.25	3.32	3.47	3.49	3.34	3.30	3.30	3.25
2002	3.27	3.32	3.27	3.26	3.18	3.19	3.23	3.29	3.16	3.24	3.21	3.24	3.24
2003[1]	3.20	3.28	3.22	3.29	3.09	3.14	3.16	3.23	3.22	3.16	3.23	3.18	3.20

[1] Preliminary.   Source: Economic Research Service, U.S. Department of Agriculture (ERS-USDA)

Frozen Pork Belly Storage Stocks in the United States, on First of Month   In Thousands of Pounds

Year	Jan.	Feb.	Mar.	Apr.	May	June	July	Aug.	Sept.	Oct.	Nov.	Dec.
1994	53,168	55,999	54,921	63,099	72,230	79,018	73,583	57,747	30,636	18,260	22,656	40,725
1995	61,073	62,776	64,228	78,975	78,539	77,919	67,607	47,055	17,435	6,255	13,478	37,092
1996	47,587	46,498	46,381	47,655	57,174	63,522	56,767	28,533	18,996	12,702	16,206	30,943
1997	37,930	38,030	44,277	54,767	54,015	55,274	52,274	33,657	18,346	11,148	14,408	25,365
1998	44,763	55,249	55,368	54,441	58,600	59,462	52,010	31,433	14,786	9,452	16,440	41,711
1999	72,657	82,605	93,323	106,194	109,521	108,257	93,383	69,675	34,814	19,273	22,489	26,170
2000	40,300	43,802	49,983	60,527	63,461	68,292	60,097	50,515	33,005	21,341	20,589	38,674
2001	47,099	50,145	47,154	45,440	43,878	46,029	39,552	24,996	12,754	8,960	28,216	36,297
2002	44,301	50,849	57,569	60,721	63,293	62,269	51,019	29,925	14,250	9,452	10,354	18,059
2003[1]	28,254	35,354	38,278	42,971	48,542	45,870	43,504	32,075	17,900	10,180	21,135	33,073

[1] Preliminary.   Source: National Agricultural Statistics Service, U.S. Department of Agriculture (NASS-USDA)

Weekly Pork Belly Storage Movement

2002 Week Ending	In	Out	On Hand	Net Movement	2003 Week Ending	In	Out	On Hand	Net Movement
Jan. 5	2,176	185	28,305	1,991	Jan. 4	2,260	344	15,961	1,916
12	1,621	134	29,792	1,487	11	2,316	82	18,195	2,234
10	1,695	532	33,955	4,163	18	1,189	251	19,133	938
26	1,463	333	35,085	1,130	25	1,033	381	19,755	622
Feb. 2	563	1,128	34,520	-645	Feb. 1	486	239	19,969	247
9	1,187	1,043	3,464	144	8	617	134	20,485	483
16	2,175	140	36,699	2,035	15	345	187	20,622	158
23	1,834	298	38,235	1,536	22	626	48	21,221	278
Mar. 2	1,109	307	39,037	802	Mar. 1	1,004	142	22,083	862
9	529	246	39,320	283	8	1,299	172	23,210	1,127
16	1,651	246	40,725	1,405	15	860	408	23,662	452
23	1,094	81	41,738	1,013	22	125	186	23,601	-61
30	1,094	525	42,307	569	29	245	42	23,805	203
Apr. 6	1,481	1,839	41,949	-358	Apr. 5	316	205	23,916	111
13	989	501	42,437	488	12	440	370	23,986	70
20	1,611	1,108	42,939	503	19	1,719	127	25,578	1,592
27	473	363	43,049	110	26	1,905	166	27,317	1,738
May 4	571	362	43,258	209	May 3	279	157	27,439	122
11	381	277	43,362	104	10	75	634	26,880	-559
18	298	93	43,567	205	17	40	770	26,150	-730
25	432	122	43,877	310	24	637	882	25,905	-245
June 1	165	661	43,381	-496	31	56	955	25,006	-899
8	62	1,607	41,917	-1,545	June 7	102	890	24,218	-788
15	166	2,334	39,749	-2,168	14	251	643	23,826	-392
22	106	3,804	36,050	-3,698	21	345	568	23,603	-223
29	42	3,785	32,307	-3,743	28	168	735	23,036	-567
July 6	215	2,764	29,759	-2,549	July 5	51	771	23,316	-710
13	237	3,441	26,554	-3,204	12	2,770	2,218	25,868	3,552
20	449	4,322	22,681	-3,873	19	50	2,890	24,761	-2,840
27	134	2,979	19,645	-2,845	26	159	3,455	21,465	-3,296
Aug. 3	62	3,803	16,095	-3,741	Aug. 2	106	2,701	18,870	-2,595
10	97	2,765	13,427	-2,668	9	65	2,778	16,157	-2,713
17	159	3,036	10,550	-2,877	16	124	2,496	13,785	-2,372
24	294	3,161	7,683	-2,867	23	184	2,385	11,584	-2,201
31	58	2,441	5,300	-2,383	30	155	2,520	9,219	-2,365
Sept. 7	114	1,851	3,563	-1,737	Sept. 6	82	2,635	6,667	-2,553
14	1,298	1,431	3,430	-133	13	242	1,613	5,296	-1,371
21	545	793	3,182	-248	20	116	1,063	4,349	-947
28	958	664	3,476	294	27	53	881	3,520	-828
Oct. 5	290	244	3,522	46	Oct. 4	145	198	3,467	-53
12	135	527	3,130	-392	11	297	302	3,462	-5
19	53	643	2,540	-590	18	1,840	62	5,240	1,778
26	102	84	2,558	18	25	3,446	40	8,646	3,406
Nov. 2	818	83	3,293	735	Nov. 1	2,074	138	10,582	1,936
9	1,492	65	4,720	1,427	8	1,811	130	12,263	1,681
16	2,278	41	6,957	2,237	15	1,534	158	13,668	1,376
23	943	345	7,655	698	22	2,243	80	15,832	2,163
30	1,313	163	8,805	1,150	29	2,308	41	18,099	2,267
Dec. 7	557	207	9,155	350	Dec. 6	1,828	40	19,887	1,788
14	931	389	9,697	542	13	1,736	40	21,658	1,696
21	2,252	41	11,908	2,211	20	1,359	123	22,898	1,236
28	2,137	397	14,045	2,137	27	2,816	119	25,595	2,697

[1] 57 Chicago and Outside Combined Chicago Mercantile Exchange approved warehouses. *Source: Chicago Mercantile Exchange (CME)*

PORK BELLIES

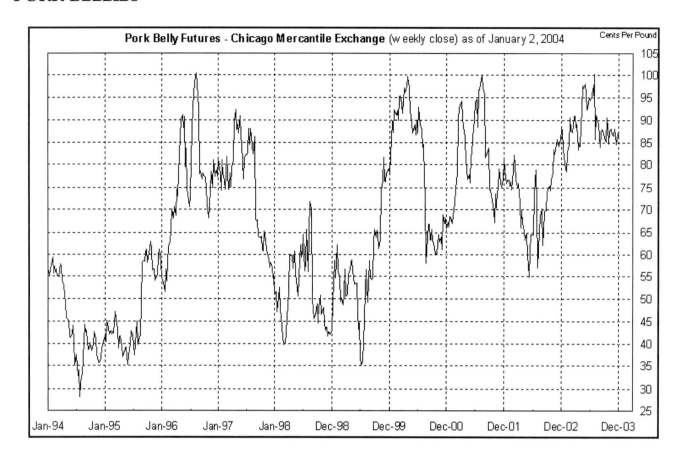

Average Open Interest of Pork Belly Futures in Chicago In Contracts

Year	Jan.	Feb.	Mar.	Apr.	May	June	July	Aug.	Sept.	Oct.	Nov.	Dec.
1994	11,053	10,426	9,375	9,894	8,092	8,248	7,836	7,841	8,398	10,072	10,141	10,216
1995	10,294	9,080	7,809	7,367	8,017	7,036	5,666	4,271	6,246	7,007	7,103	7,282
1996	7,094	8,028	10,521	10,753	10,018	8,136	6,432	6,296	6,056	6,395	6,050	6,480
1997	7,504	7,930	7,260	7,165	8,950	7,203	5,905	4,791	5,242	7,520	8,302	9,009
1998	9,187	9,145	9,082	7,825	6,786	5,406	4,185	3,493	2,933	3,841	4,987	7,085
1999	7,217	6,192	4,623	5,113	6,030	6,639	5,003	2,415	2,320	3,206	4,011	4,868
2000	5,872	6,011	6,320	6,563	5,836	5,306	3,650	1,877	1,860	2,093	2,409	2,610
2001	2,719	2,908	2,935	3,138	2,808	2,354	2,526	2,579	2,695	2,321	2,441	2,451
2002	2,574	2,768	2,879	3,271	3,224	2,821	1,885	986	1,116	1,329	2,020	2,548
2003	2,842	2,805	2,915	3,082	3,383	3,410	2,858	1,632	1,899	1,885	2,075	2,484

Source: Chicago Mercantile Exchange (CME)

Volume of Trading of Pork Belly Futures in Chicago In Contracts

Year	Jan.	Feb.	Mar.	Apr.	May	June	July	Aug.	Sept.	Oct.	Nov.	Dec.	Total
1994	60,316	67,250	58,183	53,839	56,575	58,424	50,450	47,626	38,375	45,525	49,280	47,803	633,646
1995	62,994	54,330	59,324	43,501	49,453	53,571	45,869	36,623	31,112	35,444	47,061	42,631	561,913
1996	48,563	56,623	61,669	61,703	61,868	55,337	55,121	45,399	39,182	48,973	42,709	35,502	612,649
1997	60,761	53,604	56,750	76,072	62,190	54,043	55,043	36,153	31,154	44,277	31,663	33,609	595,319
1998	41,894	50,105	47,249	61,910	36,058	48,913	41,133	33,832	24,006	30,538	30,093	35,521	481,252
1999	39,925	36,293	33,322	31,558	31,321	45,030	36,513	23,536	16,544	20,392	28,920	24,955	368,309
2000	37,650	38,943	39,061	31,464	40,311	31,229	25,051	17,875	10,711	11,854	11,737	13,690	309,576
2001	15,861	16,200	16,675	18,274	18,708	16,989	20,187	18,823	12,719	12,905	15,984	13,034	196,359
2002	16,495	16,650	14,279	17,758	13,648	15,764	16,773	7,490	6,857	8,107	8,659	9,574	152,054
2003	13,635	13,956	13,137	18,279	18,112	16,993	19,540	9,967	7,909	10,235	8,542	11,024	161,329

Source: Chicago Mercantile Exchange (CME)

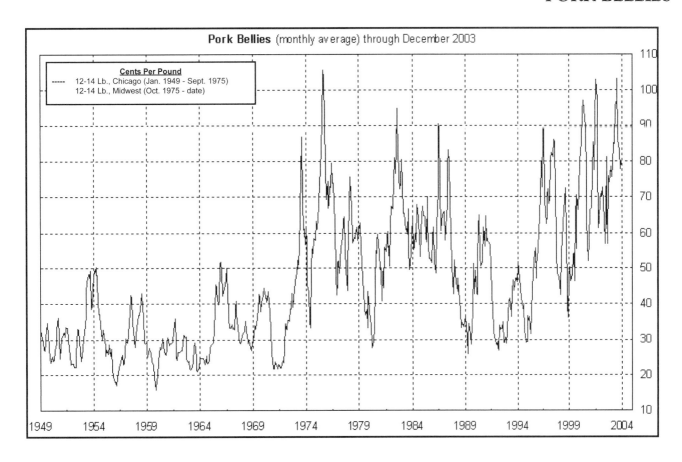

Pork Bellies (monthly average) through December 2003

Cents Per Pound
----- 12-14 Lb., Chicago (Jan. 1949 - Sept. 1975)
12-14 Lb., Midwest (Oct. 1975 - date)

Average Price of Pork Bellies (12-14 Pounds) Midwest   In Cents Per Pound

Year	Jan.	Feb.	Mar.	Apr.	May	June	July	Aug.	Sept.	Oct.	Nov.	Dec.	Average
1994	50.63	51.66	49.68	46.84	41.40	40.39	38.64	39.60	31.50	31.33	29.09	29.29	40.00
1995	36.03	35.80	36.30	33.83	31.70	37.94	43.10	52.42	54.43	56.20	47.28	51.45	43.04
1996	52.33	56.33	64.50	69.86	79.50	72.64	89.49	88.40	68.12	63.07	65.27	70.07	69.97
1997	72.04	68.42	59.05	80.54	82.58	80.68	86.70	85.43	72.25	57.97	53.77	47.52	70.58
1998	43.00	45.89	42.28	54.65	57.87	63.10	68.46	72.99	57.49	42.05	39.13	36.31	51.94
1999	48.80	50.76	46.51	49.23	53.76	53.41	47.78	67.29	57.87	70.83	67.81	71.37	57.12
2000	80.45	82.40	85.00	93.70	97.85	91.99	90.38	75.64	63.94	57.83	51.97	58.36	77.46
2001	66.61	66.68	78.04	85.80	77.91	91.50	102.42	98.39	81.91	61.30	63.68	69.13	78.61
2002	70.87	70.75	72.55	63.48	58.65	65.90	81.06	67.98	57.05	76.24	75.50	78.92	69.91
2003[1]	78.02	79.54	85.80	84.94	96.58	97.05	102.37	85.65	83.15	84.46	78.53	81.00	86.42

[1] Preliminary.   *Source: Economic Research Service, U.S. Department of Agriculture (ERS-USDA)*

Average Price of Pork Loins (12-14 lbs.)[2] Central, U.S.   In Cents Per Pound

Year	Jan.	Feb.	Mar.	Apr.	May	June	July	Aug.	Sept.	Oct.	Nov.	Dec.	Average
1994	103.90	110.75	100.45	101.89	103.99	103.84	109.79	112.86	105.34	95.65	80.00	89.50	101.50
1995	96.94	102.20	95.30	93.33	103.50	118.81	124.65	127.98	117.63	108.23	93.94	110.39	107.74
1996	110.00	116.43	120.49	119.70	131.61	115.73	126.16	118.18	112.28	115.40	115.39	120.45	118.49
1997	112.50	109.50	106.58	117.16	125.68	116.28	122.53	119.28	112.07	99.68	85.99	79.44	108.89
1998	76.50	103.03	104.56	102.51	130.64	113.13	106.51	105.90	97.23	99.63	79.90	72.49	99.34
1999	105.82	92.35	83.47	99.35	107.44	97.62	105.72	111.55	104.99	98.98	94.64	102.75	100.39
2000	99.29	110.66	110.06	127.48	115.38	132.53	131.73	120.45	119.22	119.90	104.19	114.68	117.13
2001	110.80	114.32	128.53	117.98	130.72	132.33	126.41	121.22	116.21	108.69	97.87	98.50	116.97
2002	106.95	105.73	100.08	94.13	101.71	104.80	108.64	97.85	87.17	93.04	82.60	93.03	97.98
2003[1]	91.83	95.75	92.43	96.90	108.93	126.51	102.50	104.85	111.38	97.71	89.06	93.72	100.96

[1] Preliminary.   *Source: Economic Research Service, U.S. Department of Agriculture (ERS-USDA)*

Potatoes

The potato is a member of the nightshade family. The leaves of the potato plant are poisonous and a potato will begin to turn green if left too long in the light. This green skin contains solanine, a substance that can cause the potato to taste bitter and even cause illness in humans. In Peru, the Inca Indians were the first to cultivate potatoes around 200 BC. The Indians developed potato crops because their staple diet of corn would not grow above an altitude of 3,350 meters. In 1536, after conquering the Incas, the Spanish Conquistadors brought potatoes back to Europe. At first, Europeans did not accept the potato due to the fact that it was not mentioned in the Bible and therefore considered an "evil" food. But after Marie Antoinette wore a crown of potato flowers, it finally became a popular food. In 1897, during the Alaskan Klondike gold rush, potatoes were so valued for their vitamin C content that miners traded gold for potatoes. The potato became the first vegetable to be grown in outer space in October 1995.

The potato is a highly nutritious, fat-free, cholesterol-free and sodium-free food, and is an important dietary staple in over 130 countries. A medium-sized potato contains only 100 calories. Potatoes are an excellent source of Vitamin C and provide B vitamins as well as potassium, copper, magnesium, and iron. According to the US Department of Agriculture, "a diet of whole milk and potatoes would supply almost all of the food elements necessary for the maintenance of the human body."

Potatoes are one of the largest vegetable crops grown in the US, and are grown in all fifty states. The US ranks about 4th in world potato production. The top three types of potatoes grown extensively in the US are white, red, and Russets (Russets account for about two-thirds the US crop). Potatoes in the US are harvested in all four seasons, but the vast majority of the crop is harvested in fall. Potatoes harvested in the winter, spring and summer are used mainly to supplement fresh supplies of fall-harvested potatoes and are also important to the processing industries. The four principal categories for US potato exports are frozen, potato chips, fresh, and dehydrated. Fries account for approxi-

mately 95% of US frozen potato exports.

Prices – Potato prices in 2003 fell 9.5% to $6.18 per hundred pounds from $6.82 in 2002. Potato prices in 2003 weakened substantially after the strong run seen in 2000-2002 when prices hit a 14-year high of $6.99 in 2000. Bearish factors centered on weaker demand with the emphasis on lower carbohydrate diets and a 3-year high in stocks.

Supply –The potato crop in 2003 fell slightly by –0.1% to 45.924 billion pounds, which was well below the record high of 51.362 billion pounds posted in 2000. The fall crop was estimated at 41.35 billion pounds, accounting for 90.0% of the total crop. Stocks of the fall crop were estimated at a 3-year high of 26.716 billion pounds. The spring crop in 2003 was estimated at 2.231 billion pounds (4.9% of the total crop), the summer crop at 1.936 billion pounds (4.2% of the total crop), and the winter crop at 403 million pounds (0.9% of the total crop).

For the fall crop, the largest producing states are Idaho (with 29.8% of the fall crop in 2003), Washington (23.1%), Wisconsin (8.2%), North Dakota (6.5%), and Colorado (5.7%). For the spring crop the largest producing states are California (with 34.0% of the spring crop) and Florida (30.6%).

Farmers harvested 1.253 million acres in 2003, which was below the 10-year average of 1.334 million acres. The yield per harvested acre was 36,700 pounds, which was well above the 10-year average of 35,300.

Demand – Total utilization of potatoes in 2002 rose to 45.980 billion pounds from 43.789 billion in 2001. The breakdown shows that the largest consumption category for potatoes is table stock with 31.5% of total consumption, followed by frozen french fries (29.5%), chips and shoestrings (12.2%), and dehydration (12.1%). US per capita consumption of potatoes in 2002 fell to a 3-year low of 137.8 pounds from the 5-year high of 140.1 pounds posted in 2001.

Trade – US exports of potatoes in 2001, the latest reporting year for the series, fell to 555.829 million pounds from 644.190 million in 2000. US imports fell to 420.167 million pounds from 502.706 million in 2000.

Salient Statistics of Potatoes in the United States

Crop Year	Acreage Planted	Acreage Harvested	Yield Per Harvested Acre Cwt.	Total Production	Seed & Feed	Shrinkage & Loss	Sold[2]	Farm Price $/Cwt.	Production[3]	Sales	Stocks on Jan. 1 1,000 Cwt.	Domestic Exports	Imports	Fresh	Total
	---- 1,000 Acres ----			---------- In Thousands of Cwt. ----------					----- Million $ -----			-- Millions of Lbs.--		--- In Pounds ---	
1994	1,416	1,380	339	467,054	5,878	37,166	424,010	5.58	2,590	2,367	238,560	655,026	405,899	49.6	136.7
1995	1,398	1,372	323	443,606	5,745	29,530	408,331	6.77	2,992	2,762	223,550	583,938	458,926	49.2	136.9
1996	1,455	1,426	350	499,254	6,221	41,222	451,190	4.91	2,425	2,220	261,320	564,010	690,768	49.9	145.0
1997	1,384	1,354	345	467,091	5,475	32,183	429,433	5.64	2,623	2,421	246,550	670,270	512,321	48.5	141.4
1998	1,417	1,388	343	475,771	5,766	35,454	434,551	5.56	2,635	2,416	246,230	650,918	737,223	47.0	138.1
1999	1,377	1,332	359	478,216	5,569	35,531	437,116	5.77	2,746	2,522	239,910	599,066	610,538	48.0	136.5
2000	1,384	1,348	381	513,621	5,288	43,688	464,645	5.08	2,591	2,360	275,270	676,577	502,706	47.3	138.7
2001	1,248	1,222	358	437,888	5,387	31,208	401,293	6.99	3,058	2,805	224,680	636,176	487,889	46.4	138.0
2002	1,305	1,270	362	459,802	5,631	30,955	423,216	6.69	3,064	2,832	231,690	693,196	621,475	44.5	132.2
2003[1]	1,275	1,250	367	459,045				5.85	2,687		233,880	589,756	634,971	46.8	137.8

[1] Preliminary.   [2] For all purposes, including food, seed processing & livestock feed.   [3] Farm weight basis, excluding canned and frozen potatoes.

Source: Economic Research Service, U.S. Department of Agriculture (ERS-USDA)

Cold Storage Stocks of All Frozen Potatoes in the United States, on First of Month   In Millions of Pounds

Year	Jan.	Feb.	Mar.	Apr.	May	June	July	Aug.	Sept.	Oct.	Nov.	Dec.
1994	1,006.4	1,019.9	1,057.1	1,054.4	1,050.5	1,118.9	1,099.9	979.8	1,028.2	1,108.7	1,189.0	1,163.5
1995	1,096.6	1,156.0	1,179.9	1,169.0	1,138.0	1,125.4	1,116.5	992.4	992.6	1,145.3	1,225.6	1,174.5
1996	1,123.7	1,147.2	1,172.5	1,164.6	1,112.1	1,076.4	1,059.7	907.1	957.8	1,124.9	1,225.2	1,146.3
1997	1,098.4	1,111.5	1,180.1	1,177.1	1,195.8	1,213.3	1,271.4	1,214.3	1,130.8	1,270.0	1,354.7	1,313.5
1998	1,163.5	1,147.2	1,235.7	1,278.3	1,225.1	1,282.8	1,316.5	1,234.7	1,204.5	1,266.8	1,341.0	1,290.5
1999	1,151.3	1,219.7	1,272.9	1,278.8	1,236.2	1,255.5	1,234.1	1,142.3	1,169.8	1,235.5	1,307.8	1,254.5
2000	1,165.4	1,140.9	1,270.1	1,283.4	1,239.4	1,250.4	1,186.3	1,180.3	1,185.7	1,291.5	1,351.5	1,285.9
2001	1,189.7	1,228.6	1,254.7	1,220.9	1,280.4	1,270.3	1,355.0	1,282.6	1,197.5	1,323.8	1,338.5	1,297.4
2002	1,239.8	1,274.2	1,271.5	1,271.4	1,222.7	1,182.3	1,223.5	1,106.6	1,040.6	1,141.4	1,252.2	1,214.4
2003[1]	1,131.2	1,173.1	1,209.6	1,217.4	1,150.5	1,106.6	1,181.8	1,130.4	1,070.4	1,153.7	1,253.9	1,232.8

[1] Preliminary.   Source: Agricultural Statistics Board, U.S. Department of Agriculture (ASB-USDA)

Potato Crop Production Estimates, Stocks and Disappearance in the United States   In Millions of Cwt.

												Fall Crop 1,000 Cwt.			
	Crop Production Estimates				Total Storage Stocks[2]								Disap-	Dec. 1	Average Price	Value of Sales
	Total Crop			Fall Crop			Following Year					Pro-	pearance			
Year	Oct. 1	Nov. 1	Dec. 1	Oct. 1	Nov. 1	Dec. 1	Jan. 1	Feb. 1	Mar. 1	Apr. 1	May 1	duction	(Sold)	Stocks	$/Cwt.	$ 1,000
1994	----	467.9	----	----	412.4	273.3	238.6	202.5	169.6	129.8	87.6	410,839	380,818	273,290	5.06	1,914,311
1995	----	444.8	----	----	402.4	256.7	223.6	189.4	156.0	115.9	75.9	394,785	370,679	256,710	6.43	2,372,983
1996	----	491.5	----	----	447.9	295.1	261.3	226.1	189.2	147.6	103.2	443,704	408,247	295,100	4.35	1,772,037
1997	----	459.4	----	----	417.5	278.8	246.6	212.6	175.9	134.2	92.8	413,513	387,089	278,830	5.20	2,011,004
1998	----	471.0	----	----	429.0	280.9	246.2	209.6	173.7	131.2	87.9	423,170	392,922	280,910	5.07	1,994,030
1999	----	481.5	----	----	435.6	275.1	239.9	207.2	169.6	128.4	86.9	420,567	390,210	275,100	5.29	2,064,564
2000	----	509.4	----	----	463.4	310.3	275.3	234.3	197.7	153.5	109.2	467,504	420,279	310,300	4.55	1,910,833
2001	----	441.8	----	----	400.7	258.8	224.7	192.2	158.6	120.0	81.2	393,750	358,954	258,750	6.54	2,349,036
2002	----	459.7	----	----	415.0	264.6	231.7	199.3	165.3	125.9	82.9	414,317	379,491	264,585	5.91	2,243,100
2003[1]	----	459.2	----	----	413.5	267.9	233.9	200.5				411,386		267,860		

[1] Preliminary.   [2] Held by growers and local dealers in the fall producing areas.   Source: Agricultural Statistics Board, U.S. Department of Agriculture

Production of Potatoes by Seasonal Groups in the United States   In Thousands of Cwt.

	- Winter -	Spring			Summer			Fall								
Year	Total	Cali-fornia	Florida	Total	New Mexico	Virginia	Total	Colo-rado	Idaho	Maine	Minne-sota	North Dakota	Oregon	Washing-ton	Wis-consin	Total
1994	2,372	7,790	8,588	22,646	1,088	1,425	17,381	25,795	138,801	18,375	20,035	28,200	27,514	88,920	25,740	419,645
1995	2,473	6,230	7,830	20,193	1,344	2,040	17,931	23,808	132,657	17,160	20,790	25,410	24,788	80,850	26,000	403,009
1996	3,273	7,538	7,765	22,417	1,404	1,463	19,176	29,175	142,800	21,175	24,600	28,820	30,124	94,990	33,150	454,388
1997	3,431	8,073	7,150	22,299	1,248	1,268	18,171	24,993	140,314	19,080	20,440	22,000	27,319	88,160	30,175	423,190
1998	2,980	6,198	7,358	21,121	962	1,380	18,933	25,360	138,000	18,060	21,170	28,670	26,229	93,225	30,895	432,737
1999	4,070	7,600	8,820	25,327	1,247	1,050	18,972	25,762	133,330	17,813	18,020	26,400	28,020	95,200	34,000	429,847
2000	4,960	7,426	6,343	21,921	1,050	1,292	19,236	27,972	152,320	17,920	21,240	26,950	30,683	105,000	33,800	467,504
2001	4,115	6,045	7,970	21,814	770	1,386	18,209	21,357	120,200	16,430	18,425	26,400	20,730	94,400	31,955	393,750
2002	4,206	7,695	7,883	23,294	736	1,386	17,985	27,885	133,385	16,960	18,700	23,460	24,936	92,400	31,125	414,317
2003[1]	4,027	8,360	8,008	24,433	532	1,550	19,199	23,652	123,180	17,030	22,330	27,440	20,991	93,150	32,800	411,386

[1] Preliminary.   Source: Agricultural Statistics Board, U.S. Department of Agriculture (ASB-USDA)

Utilization of Potatoes in the United States   In Thousands of Cwt.

		Sales										Non-Sales			
		For Processing							Other Sales		Used on			
Crop Year	Table Stock	Chips, Shoe-strings	For Dehyd-ration	Frozen French Fries	Other Frozen Products	Canned Potatoes	Other Canned Products[2]	Starch & Flour	Live-stock Feed	Seed	Total Sales	Farms Where Grown	Shrink-age & Loss	Total Non-Sales	Total
1993	123,802	48,987	40,795	121,087	25,190	1,879	2,458	1,691	2,498	24,223	392,610	4,808	30,152	36,083	428,693
1994	133,989	49,299	41,381	136,531	26,362	2,503	3,006	2,176	4,147	24,616	424,010	4,732	37,166	43,044	467,054
1995	124,875	47,284	45,065	129,029	27,073	3,342	2,385	1,668	3,224	25,769	409,714	4,792	29,630	35,385	445,099
1996	131,446	48,305	54,261	145,489	28,972	2,785	2,167	1,956	12,073	24,341	451,795	4,797	41,238	47,459	499,254
1997	131,670	48,130	48,389	131,628	33,397	2,822	2,675	1,311	3,603	25,808	429,433	4,167	32,183	37,658	467,091
1998	125,413	51,471	55,522	142,932	24,964	2,730	1,964	1,585	3,111	24,859	434,551	4,358	35,454	41,220	475,771
1999	134,130	52,916	50,831	140,196	23,593	3,311	2,394	1,310	3,141	25,294	437,116	4,415	35,531	41,100	478,216
2000	139,146	52,371	54,880	146,869	26,723	2,368	2,709	1,966	10,096	23,353	464,645	3,792	43,688	48,976	513,621
2001	122,843	54,080	40,745	126,711	23,598	2,590	1,722	1,015	3,496	24,493	401,293	4,146	31,208	36,595	437,888
2002[1]	133,298	51,640	51,334	124,875	28,951	2,744	2,085	1,050	3,104	24,135	423,216	4,164	30,955	36,586	459,802

[1] Preliminary.   [2] Hash, stews and soups.   Source: Agricultural Statistics Board, U.S. Department of Agriculture (ASB-USDA)

POTATOES

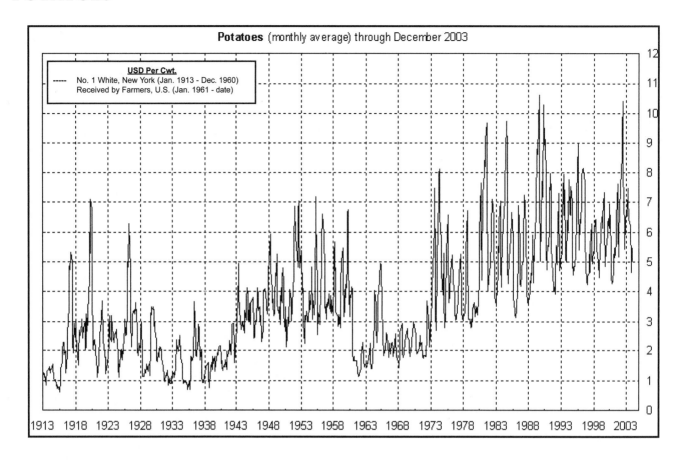

Per Capita Utilization of Potatoes in the United States   In Pounds (Farm Weight)

Year	Total	Fresh	Freezing	Processing — Chips & Shoe-string	Processing — Dehy-drating	Processing — Canning	Total
1995	136.9	49.2	56.2	16.4	13.2	1.9	87.7
1996	145.0	49.9	60.2	16.4	16.7	1.8	95.1
1997	141.4	48.5	59.3	15.9	15.9	1.8	92.9
1998	138.1	47.0	58.2	14.8	16.6	1.5	91.1
1999	136.5	48.0	58.5	15.9	12.3	1.8	88.5
2000	138.7	47.3	57.8	16.0	15.9	1.7	91.4
2001	138.0	46.4	57.9	17.6	14.6	1.5	91.6
2002	132.2	44.5	55.1	16.4	14.8	1.4	87.7
2003[1]	135.1	45.2	55.5	16.7	16.1	1.6	89.9
2004[2]	134.6	45.4	55.2	16.8	15.7	1.5	89.2

[1] Preliminary.   [2] Forecast.   *Source: Agricultural Statistics Board, U.S. Department of Agriculture (ASB-USDA)*

Average Price Received by Farmers for Potatoes in the United States   In Dollars Per Cwt.

Year	Jan.	Feb.	Mar.	Apr.	May	June	July	Aug.	Sept.	Oct.	Nov.	Dec.	Season Average
1994	6.04	6.37	7.75	6.68	6.62	6.80	7.38	6.25	4.95	4.57	4.77	4.85	5.56
1995	4.83	4.97	5.37	5.41	5.86	7.12	8.75	6.64	5.76	6.30	6.39	6.33	6.75
1996	6.65	6.92	7.51	7.82	8.09	8.16	7.79	5.58	4.92	4.75	4.44	4.28	4.91
1997	4.22	4.56	4.64	4.67	5.31	5.67	5.66	6.31	5.08	4.93	5.12	5.36	5.64
1998	5.40	5.94	6.41	6.27	6.45	6.16	5.81	5.46	4.97	4.47	4.86	5.30	5.56
1999	5.50	5.75	6.12	6.50	6.13	6.54	7.35	6.02	5.09	4.86	5.52	5.44	5.77
2000	5.68	5.92	6.26	6.46	6.31	6.14	6.93	5.56	4.49	4.27	4.31	4.48	5.08
2001	4.56	5.26	5.12	5.47	5.24	5.75	6.46	7.61	6.04	5.15	5.96	6.66	6.99
2002	6.90	7.34	8.26	8.00	8.62	9.39	10.40	8.00	6.14	5.44	6.38	6.67	6.82
2003[1]	6.67	6.33	6.68	7.49	7.15	6.47	6.43	6.22	4.93	4.67	5.35	5.60	

[1] Preliminary.   *Source: Agricultural Statistics Board, U.S. Department of Agriculture (ASB-USDA)*

Potatoes Processed[1] in the United States, Eight States   In Thousands of Cwt.

States	Storage Season	to Dec. 1	to Jan. 1	to Feb. 1	to Mar. 1	to Apr. 1	to May 1	to June 1	Entire Season
Idaho and	1994-5	26,620	34,230	42,330	49,890	57,990	66,680	----	90,300
Oregon-	1995-6	27,310	35,040	43,260	51,530	59,060	66,690	----	89,250
Malheur	1996-7	31,060	38,210	45,420	54,640	62,570	70,720	----	96,970
Co	1997-8	26,880	33,950	41,050	49,470	57,620	65,750	----	91,450
	1998-9	27,510	34,700	42,670	51,210	60,040	68,550	70,410	92,000
	1999-00	27,970	34,490	40,790	49,220	57,820	66,080	74,110	88,210
	2000-1	29,290	35,720	43,470	50,580	58,910	66,760	75,270	93,460
	2001-2	20,940	27,330	33,620	40,860	47,710	54,150	61,200	73,390
	2002-3	28,380	34,860	41,200	48,600	56,240	63,840	71,280	85,390
	2003-4	24,310	30,730	36,260					
Maine[2]	1994-5	1,505	1,840	2,265	2,540	2,985	3,330	----	4,770
	1995-6	1,455	1,850	2,430	2,850	3,435	3,965	----	5,725
	1996-7	1,790	2,115	2,820	3,280	3,820	4,420	----	6,495
	1997-8	1,250	1,720	2,265	2,735	3,355	3,900	----	5,870
	1998-9	1,430	1,935	2,530	2,985	3,595	4,180	4,705	5,945
	1999-00	1,270	1,700	2,385	3,070	3,765	4,560	5,150	6,670
	2000-1	1,845	2,475	3,105	3,695	4,225	4,760	5,340	7,015
	2001-2	1,975	2,440	3,110	3,700	4,285	4,775	5,515	7,195
	2002-3	2,230	2,715	3,345	3,905	4,505	5,225	5,905	7,835
	2003-4	1,590	2,095	2,725					
Wash. &	1994-5	28,670	33,480	39,120	46,070	52,940	59,540	----	76,780
Oregon-	1995-6	30,000	35,170	39,460	45,280	51,730	57,360	----	70,250
Other	1996-7	31,670	36,660	41,700	48,740	55,570	62,320	----	80,970
	1997-8	28,580	33,990	38,690	46,400	53,720	59,780	----	76,930
	1998-9	33,630	38,890	45,650	53,290	60,930	67,180	74,190	83,730
	1999-00	33,320	39,620	45,500	53,350	61,080	67,230	74,840	83,210
	2000-1	34,770	40,970	47,720	55,250	62,860	69,850	78,010	91,130
	2001-2	29,320	35,310	40,540	47,910	54,970	61,360	69,400	77,180
	2002-3	33,680	39,490	44,190	51,920	58,710	64,300	71,480	79,110
	2003-4	32,670	38,520	43,600					
Other	1994-5	9,725	13,110	15,630	18,260	21,115	24,060	----	32,260
States[3]	1995-6	12,650	15,630	18,815	21,985	25,510	28,610	----	33,580
	1996-7	13,720	17,000	20,645	24,085	27,650	30,830	----	43,100
	1997-8	11,645	13,960	17,115	19,905	23,515	26,365	----	37,842
	1998-9	11,570	14,465	18,030	20,850	24,850	28,190	31,365	39,865
	1999-00	12,455	15,035	17,950	20,855	24,305	27,220	30,410	36,435
	2000-1	12,665	16,215	18,975	22,095	25,410	28,695	31,765	39,020
	2001-2	13,170	14,925	19,000	22,115	24,655	27,815	30,460	37,740
	2002-3	12,190	14,865	17,865	20,740	23,580	26,000	29,075	36,705
	2003-4	12,570	15,410	18,760					
Total	1994-5	66,520	82,660	99,345	116,760	135,030	153,610	----	204,110
	1995-6	71,415	87,690	103,965	121,645	139,735	156,625	----	198,805
	1996-7	78,240	93,985	110,585	130,745	149,610	168,290	----	227,535
	1997-8	68,355	83,620	99,120	118,510	138,210	155,795	----	212,092
	1998-9	74,140	89,990	108,880	128,335	149,415	168,100	186,670	222,400
	1999-00	75,015	90,845	106,625	126,495	146,970	165,090	184,510	214,525
	2000-1	78,570	95,380	113,270	131,620	151,405	170,065	190,385	230,625
	2001-2	65,405	80,005	96,270	114,585	131,620	148,100	166,575	195,505
	2002-3	76,480	91,930	106,600	125,165	143,035	159,365	177,740	209,040
	2003-4	71,140	86,755	101,345					

[1] Total quantity received and used for processing regardless of the state in which the potatoes were produced. Excludes quantities used for potato chips in Maine, Michigan, Minnesota, North Dakota or Wisconsin.   [2] Includes Maine grown potatoes only.   [3] Michigan, Minnesota, North Dakota and Wisconsin.   *Source: National Agricultural Statistics Service, U.S. Department of Agriculture (NASS-USDA)*

Rayon and Other Synthetic Fibers

World Cellulosic Fiber Production   In Thousands of Metric Tons

Year	Austria	Brazil	China	Czech Republic	Finland	Germany	India	Japan	Taiwan	United Kingdom	United States	Ex-USSR	World Total
1994	134.3	58.6	336.0	33.7	58.5	138.1	239.7	218.9	149.3	67.0	225.0	189.8	2,308
1995	139.4	53.1	435.0	35.0	57.5	143.5	262.1	212.7	139.6	67.1	226.0	188.4	2,423
1996	145.0	34.4	432.0	31.4	49.8	143.6	251.9	198.2	144.7	62.3	213.1	127.3	2,270
1997	145.0	36.4	450.0	27.3	62.0	155.0	242.4	184.1	148.4	70.0	208.1	401.2	2,314
1998	----	29.2	451.5	26.9	----	----	264.4	164.5	142.6	----	165.5	----	2,227
1999	----	34.6	472.1	17.6	----	----	248.5	135.5	143.7	----	134.7	----	2,074
2000	----	36.2	552.3	7.1	----	----	297.5	126.2	141.5	----	158.8	----	2,215
2001	----	28.7	608.6	7.6	----	----	251.9	107.1	127.4	----	103.0	----	2,084
2002[1]	----	32.2	682.0	7.2	----	----	285.9	68.1	114.2	----	80.7	----	2,118
2003[2]	----	38.5	750.0	9.2	----	----	386.9	105.0	145.2	----	96.6	----	2,523

[1] Preliminary.   [2] Producing capacity.   Source: Fiber Economics Bureau, Inc. (FEB)

World Noncellulosic Fiber Production (Except Olefin)   In Thousands of Metric Tons

Year	Brazil	China	West Germany	India	Italy/ Malta	Japan	Rep. of Korea	Mexico	Spain	Taiwan[3]	United States[4]	Ex-USSR	World Total
1994	243.2	2,119.0	807.6	681.1	599.9	1,394.0	1,825.0	484.4	273.6	2,301.5	3,250.3	658.1	17,939
1995	227.4	2,283.7	771.3	738.0	551.3	1,400.0	1,858.2	516.6	252.3	2,410.5	3,238.9	636.1	18,377
1996	229.6	2,729.6	----	916.4	----	1,399.0	2,025.2	584.6	----	2,561.0	3,284.1	1,359.8	19,765
1997	248.3	3,527.2	----	1,240.7	----	1,433.6	2,403.3	612.7	----	2,932.4	3,420.0	----	22,396
1998	268.6	4,406.8	----	1,361.3	----	1,363.6	2,446.0	591.1	----	3,111.5	3,222.7	----	2,354
1999	292.6	5,235.1	----	1,486.1	----	1,299.7	2,592.8	571.2	----	2,927.7	3,169.5	----	24,359
2000	311.1	6,158.4	----	1,568.4	----	1,307.9	2,659.0	586.8	----	3,122.9	3,149.2	----	26,129
2001	288.8	7,322.9	----	1,570.2	----	1,239.5	2,381.2	536.4	----	2,977.5	2,687.6	----	26,039
2002[1]	293.1	8,881.3	----	1,689.9	----	1,129.1	2,341.2	509.6	----	3,089.3	2,787.2	----	27,890
2003[2]	348.2	12,275.0	----	2,037.3	----	1,559.0	2,976.9	669.5	----	3,666.5	3,432.5	----	36,273

[1] Preliminary.   [2] Producing capacity.   [3] Beginning 1995; data for S. Korea and Taiwan.   [4] Beginning 1995; data for USA and Canada.
Source: Fiber Economics Bureau, Inc. (FEB)

World Production of Synthetic Fibers   In Thousands of Metric Tons

Year	Acrylic & Modacrylic	Nylon & Aramid	Polyester	Other Fibers[3]	Yarn & Monofilaments	Staple, Tow & Fiberfill	Total	Europe	Japan	Americas	Other United States	Total	China	Ex-USSR	Cigarette Tow Production
1994	2,543	3,706	11,468	222	9,087	8,852	17,939	545	313	87	959	2,235	78	54	536
1995	2,446	3,740	11,945	247	9,684	8,693	18,377	567	318	96	981	2,308	85	55	550
1996	2,604	3,858	13,047	256	10,529	9,236	19,765	585	316	94	996	2,387	98	25	584
1997	2,706	4,028	15,406	256	12,093	10,303	22,396	610	328	100	1,007	2,431	75	27	582
1998	2,656	3,792	16,539	268	12,959	10,295	23,254	660	300	96	1,018	2,416	60	30	551
1999	2,513	3,800	17,879	294	13,660	10,825	24,485	674	300	96	1,126	2,538	60	30	544
2000	2,670	4,072	19,073	313	14,645	11,484	26,129	728	280	96	1,143	2,580	60	28	570
2001	2,577	3,740	19,381	335	14,725	11,308	26,033	701	273	93	1,016	2,431	67	32	590
2002[1]	2,742	3,905	20,956	349	15,813	12,139	27,952	718	251	96	1,222	2,661	90	34	596
2003[2]	3,264	5,039	27,521	449	21,199	15,074	36,273	724	250	100	1,307	2,790	120	37	-----

Noncellulosic Fiber Production (Except Olefin) — By Fibers / World Total; Glass Fiber Production

[1] Preliminary.   [2] Producing capacity.   [3] Alginate, azion, spandex, saran, etc.   Source: Fiber Economics Bureau, Inc. (FEB)

Artificial (Cellulosic) Fiber Distribution in the United States   In Millions of Pounds

Year	Yarn & Monofilament Domestic	Exports	Total	Imports	Domestic Consumption	Staple & Tow Domestic	Exports	Total	Imports	Domestic Consumption	Glass Fiber Shipments
1995	169.3	7.8	177.1	34.0	203.3	259.8	28.7	288.5	40.8	300.6	2,163.0
1996	168.9	6.3	175.2	39.3	208.2	225.4	20.0	245.4	35.3	260.7	2,196.0
1997	145.9	4.1	150.0	42.9	188.8	205.3	60.1	265.4	51.6	256.9	2,275.0
1998	111.2	3.5	114.7	38.1	149.3	184.4	31.4	215.8	47.4	231.8	----
1999	111.0	3.0	114.0	28.2	139.3	168.8	29.9	198.7	47.5	216.3	----
2000	109.9	5.1	115.0	23.2	133.1	162.3	69.3	231.5	37.5	199.7	----
2001	81.3	6.7	88.0	14.5	95.8	117.2	35.5	152.7	33.9	151.2	----
2002	66.3	2.3	68.6	12.7	79.0	91.1	12.6	103.7	56.2	147.4	----
2003[1]	57.0	2.0	59.0	11.7	68.7	86.7	13.1	99.8	44.5	131.2	----

[1] Preliminary.   Source: Fiber Economice Bureau, Inc. (FEB)

Man-Made Fiber Production in the United States   In Millions of Pounds

| | -- Artificial (Cellulosic) Fibers -- | | | Synthetic (Noncellulosic) Fibers | | | | | | | | | | | |
| | -- Rayon & Acetate -- | | | Yarn & Monofilament | | | | Staple & Tow | | | | | | Total | |
Year	Filament Yarn & Monofil- ament	Staple & Tow	Total Cellu- losic	Nylon	Polyester	Olefin	Total Yarn	Nylon	Polyester	Acrylic & Mod- acrylic	Olefin	Total Staple	Total Noncel- lulosic	Total Manu- factured Fibers	Total Glass Fiber
1994	225	273	498	1,805	1,492	1,839	5,136	935	2,366	442	549	4,292	9,428	9,957	2,159
1995	208	290	498	1,829	1,597	1,870	5,296	874	2,290	432	521	4,117	9,413	9,948	2,282
1996	219	245	464	1,917	1,571	1,951	5,438	883	2,260	465	610	4,217	9,655	9,979	2,326
1997	187	266	453	2,039	1,644	2,058	5,740	797	2,446	461	623	4,327	10,067	10,465	2,408
1998	144	216	360	1,887	1,541	2,212	5,640	799	2,357	346	712	4,214	9,853	10,314	2,490
1999	115	199	314	1,896	1,595	2,278	5,769	787	2,291	316	797	4,192	9,960	10,263	2,570
2000	114	232	345	1,947	1,509	2,406	5,860	733	2,405	339	816	4,293	10,153	10,236	2,738
2001	----	153	153	1,642	1,188	2,238	5,067	606	2,040	280	721	3,646	8,713	----	2,638
2002[1]	----	104	104	1,772	1,218	2,235	5,225	681	2,050	260	749	3,740	8,964	----	2,759
2003[2]	----	100	100	1,762	1,145	2,289	5,195	697	1,886	220	680	3,483	8,678	----	2,789

[1] Preliminary.   [2] Estimate.   *Source: Fiber Economics Bureau, Inc. (FEB)*

Domestic Distribution of Synethic (Noncellulosic) Fibers in the United States   In Millions of Pounds

	Yarn & Monofilament						Dome- stic Con- sumption	Staple & Tow							Dome- stic Con- sump- tion
	Producers' Shipments							Producers' Shipments							
	Domestic							Domestic							
Year	Nylon	Poly- ester	Olefin	Total	Exports	Total	Imports	Nylon	Poly- ester	Acrylic & Mod- acrylic	Olefin	Total	Exports	Total	Imports
1995	1,741	1,440	1,870	5,052	259	5,311	394	5,445	829	2,100	266	458	3,653	399	4,052	625	4,278
1996	1,801	1,429	1,954	5,184	251	5,435	482	5,666	844	2,016	288	515	3,662	465	4,128	608	4,270
1997	1,877	1,528	2,015	5,421	239	5,659	589	6,010	757	2,250	289	542	3,837	392	4,229	673	4,510
1998	1,790	1,426	2,167	5,383	218	5,601	637	6,020	763	2,105	267	596	3,732	340	4,072	777	4,509
1999	1,765	1,463	2,251	5,480	244	5,724	719	6,199	756	2,138	233	726	3,852	338	4,190	788	4,640
2000	1,795	1,353	2,371	5,519	250	5,769	790	6,309	674	2,174	244	757	3,849	327	4,176	727	4,576
2001	1,606	1,189	2,200	4,995	155	5,150	697	5,692	607	1,881	169	673	3,330	308	3,638	757	4,087
2002	1,668	1,113	2,192	4,973	189	5,162	765	5,737	637	1,823	170	723	3,353	353	3,706	875	4,227
2003[1]	1,666	1,051	2,260	4,977	179	5,156	766	5,743	673	1,688	167	635	3,162	246	3,409	829	3,991

[1] Preliminary.   *Source: Fiber Economice Bureau, Inc. (FEB)*

Mill Consumption of Fiber & Products and Per Capita Consumption in the U.S.   In Millions of Pounds

| | Cellulosic Fibers | | | | Noncellulosic Fibers | | | Total Manu- factured Fibers[2] | | | | | Per Capita[4] Mill Consumption (Lbs.) | | | | |
Year	Yarn & Monofil- ament	Staple & Tow	Net Waste	Total Cellu- losic	Noncellu- losic	Net Waste	Total Noncellu- losic		Cotton	Wool	Other Fibers[3]	Grand Total	Man- made Fibers[2]	Cotton	Wool	Other Fibers[3]	Total All Fibers
1994	223	318	3.4	545	9,869	102	9,971	10,516	5,375	172	54.8	16,117	44.5	30.9	1.4	2.7	79.6
1995	203	301	3.9	508	9,723	76	9,799	10,307	5,110	162	65.6	15,645	43.7	29.8	1.4	2.5	77.4
1996	208	261	4.0	473	9,936	100	10,036	10,509	5,340	164	46.0	16,059	44.1	30.2	1.4	1.8	77.5
1997	189	257	2.5	448	10,520	103	10,623	11,071	5,448	164	42.8	16,726	46.5	32.5	1.4	2.0	82.4
1998	149	232	1.4	383	10,529	165	10,694	11,077	5,225	126	44.3	16,472	47.4	34.4	1.3	1.8	84.8
1999	139	216	1.6	357	10,839	177	11,016	11,373	4,996	85	40.4	16,495	49.1	35.3	1.2	1.9	87.5
2000	133	200	1.9	335	10,884	190	11,075	11,409	4,754	83	38.5	16,285	49.7	35.8	1.3	2.2	89.0
2001	96	151	2.4	249	9,820	193	10,013	10,262	3,983	89	30.3	14,365	45.8	33.9	1.4	1.7	82.7
2002[1]	79	147	1.8	228	9,994	190	10,185	10,413	3,609	61	28.9	14,111	46.3	34.2	1.4	2.0	83.8

[1] Preliminary.   [2] Excludes Glass Fiber.   [3] Includes silk, linen, jute and sisal & others.   [4] Mill consumption plus inports less exports of semimanufactured and unmanufactured products.   *Source: Fiber Economics Bureau, Inc. (FEB)*

Producer Price Index of Grey Synthetic Broadwovens   (1982 = 100)

Year	Jan.	Feb.	Mar.	Apr.	May	June	July	Aug.	Sept.	Oct.	Nov.	Dec.	Average
1989	114.3	112.0	112.2	112.2	112.1	113.1	114.7	115.0	115.0	115.8	115.9	115.3	114.0
1990	115.6	115.7	115.6	115.7	115.5	115.6	115.7	115.2	115.3	115.6	115.8	116.1	115.6
1991	115.7	114.7	114.4	114.1	114.3	113.9	114.8	116.4	116.5	116.5	116.8	118.2	115.5
1992	119.0	119.9	120.3	120.9	121.8	122.0	122.6	122.0	121.7	120.8	119.4	119.9	120.9
1993	119.6	119.1	119.1	119.2	117.1	118.4	118.0	118.0	116.9	117.3	115.2	114.5	117.7
1994	113.5	112.8	112.9	113.2	113.2	113.3	113.1	113.3	114.1	111.8	112.9	113.8	113.2
1995	114.8	116.8	116.7	116.3	116.6	117.1	115.4	114.8	116.9	116.4	114.7	116.2	116.1
1996	114.3	114.1	116.9	117.9	116.8	115.7	116.1	117.1	116.9	117.2	116.6	117.0	116.4
1997	117.9	118.3	118.3	117.9	118.4	119.0	118.8	118.5	119.4	118.7	117.6	119.6	118.5
1998[1]	120.1	120.4	119.7	120.2	119.8	119.7	118.0	118.1	116.7	114.2	115.1	115.0	118.1

[1] Preliminary.   *Source: Bureau of Labor Statistics, U.S. Department of Commerce (BLS) (0337-03)*

Rice

Rice is a grain that is cultivated on every continent except Antarctica and is the primary food for half the people in the world. Rice cultivation probably originated as early as 10,000 BC in Asia. Rice is grown at varying altitudes (sea level to about 3,000 meters), in varying climates (tropical to temperate), and on dry to flooded land. The growth duration of rice plants is 3-6 months, depending on variety and growing conditions. Rice is harvested by hand in developing countries or by combines in industrialized countries. Asian countries produce about 90% of rice grown worldwide. Rough rice futures and options are traded on the Chicago Board of Trade (CBOT).

Prices – Rough rice prices on the CBOT nearest futures chart started 2003 near $4 per 100 pounds (cwt or hundredweight). Prices then rallied fairly steadily during the year, more than doubling in price to hit a 5-year high of $9 by the end of the year. Bullish factors centered on strong consumption, a sharp drawdown in stocks, and the weak dollar.

Supply – World rice production in 2003/4 was forecasted to rise to 391.023 million metric tons, up 2.8% from 380.263 million in 2002/3. World ending stocks in 2003/4 are forecasted at 83.997 million metric tons, down sharply from 106.901 million in 2002/3. The world's largest rice producers in 2002/3 were China with 122.180 million met-

ric tons of production (accounting for 32% of world production), followed by Indian (75.700 million or 20%), and Indonesia (33.411 million or 9%). US rice production in 2003/4 was forecast at 6.324 million metric tons, down 3.2% from 6.536 million in 2002/3 and accounting for only about 2% of world production.

Demand – World rice consumption in 2003/4 was forecast to rise to 413.927 million metric tons, up 0.9% from 410.132 million in 2002/3. Consumption in 2003/4 was forecast to exceed production for the third consecutive year, a factor that has led to the sharp drawdown in stocks and the sharp rise in rice prices. US rice consumption in 2003/4 was forecast to rise to 3.853 million metric tons, up 9% from 3.535 million in 2002/3.

Trade – Rice is generally consumed where it is produced, with only about 6% of world rice production moving into world trade. World rice trade in 2003/4 was forecast to fall to 24.737 million metric downs, down 9% from 27.316 million in 2002/3. The world's largest rice exporters in 2002/3 were Thailand (representing 27% of total world exports), India (16%), the US (14.1%), and Vietnam (13.9%). US exports in 2003/4 are forecasted to fall to 3.000 million metric tons from 3.850 million in 2002/3. There are many nations that import rice, the largest being Indonesia, Philippines, Nigeria, and Brazil.

World Rice Supply and Distribution   In Thousands of Metric Tons

	Imports							Utilization			Ending Stocks		
Year	Brazil	Indonesia	European Union	Iran	Saudi Arabia	Unaccounted	Total	China	India	Total	China	India	Total
1998-9	781	3,729	784	1,313	750	1,659	24,941	133,570	81,154	387,467	96,000	12,000	134,743
1999-00	700	1,500	852	1,100	992	1,628	22,846	133,763	82,670	397,777	98,500	17,716	146,992
2000-1	673	1,500	923	765	1,053	1,449	24,442	134,356	75,851	395,389	94,100	25,051	149,565
2001-2[1]	548	3,500	959	964	938	2,332	27,888	134,581	87,351	411,169	82,167	24,480	136,821
2002-3[2]	1,200	2,750	975	900	1,150	1,843	27,357	134,800	83,680	411,398	67,224	11,060	106,269
2003-4[3]	600	2,000	975	1,000	950	1,401	24,712	135,000	85,000	414,106	45,499	12,560	82,596

[1] Preliminary.   [2] Estimate.   [3] Forecast.   *Source: Foreign Agricultural Service, U.S. Department of Agriculture (FAS-USDA)*

World Production of Rough Rice   In Thousands of Metric Tons

Year	Bangladesh	Brazil	Burma	China	India	Indonesia	Japan	Rep. of Korea	Pakistan	Philippines	Thailand	Vietnam	World Total
1998-9	29,784	11,582	16,000	198,714	129,013	50,400	11,201	6,800	7,012	10,268	23,620	30,467	585,712
1999-00	34,602	11,424	17,000	198,480	134,233	52,919	11,470	7,066	7,735	11,957	25,000	31,706	607,545
2000-1	36,547	10,385	18,571	187,909	129,463	50,633	11,863	7,197	7,051	12,515	25,500	31,020	591,159
2001-2[1]	34,503	11,000	17,000	181,000	133,513	51,424	11,332	7,503	5,611	12,692	25,500	31,212	584,865
2002-3[2]	25,360	6,935	10,440	122,180	75,700	33,411	8,089	4,927	4,228	8,450	17,124	21,527	380,846
2003-4[3]	26,000	7,900	10,440	115,000	89,000	34,508	7,080	4,450	4,900	8,840	17,800	21,252	390,433

[1] Preliminary.   [2] Estimate.   [3] Forecast.   *Source: Foreign Agricultural Service, U.S. Department of Agriculture (FAS-USDA)*

World Exports of Rice (Milled Basis)   In Thousands of Metric Tons

Year	Argentina	Australia	Burma	China	European Union	Guyana	India	Pakistan	Thailand	Uruguay	Vietnam	United States	World Total
1998-9	674	667	57	2,708	348	252	2,752	1,838	6,679	681	4,555	2,644	24,941
1999-00	332	617	159	2,951	308	167	1,449	2,026	6,549	642	3,370	2,847	22,846
2000-1	363	618	670	1,847	264	175	1,936	2,417	7,521	806	3,528	2,541	24,442
2001-2[1]	233	360	1,002	1,963	358	150	6,650	1,603	7,245	526	3,245	3,295	27,888
2002-3[2]	160	150	400	2,583	325	175	4,421	1,700	7,552	675	3,795	3,850	27,357
2003-4[3]	300	300	500	2,000	350	175	2,000	1,700	8,250	750	4,000	3,000	24,712

[1] Preliminary.   [2] Estimate.   [3] Forecast.   *Source: Foreign Agricultural Service, U.S. Department of Agriculture (FAS-USDA)*

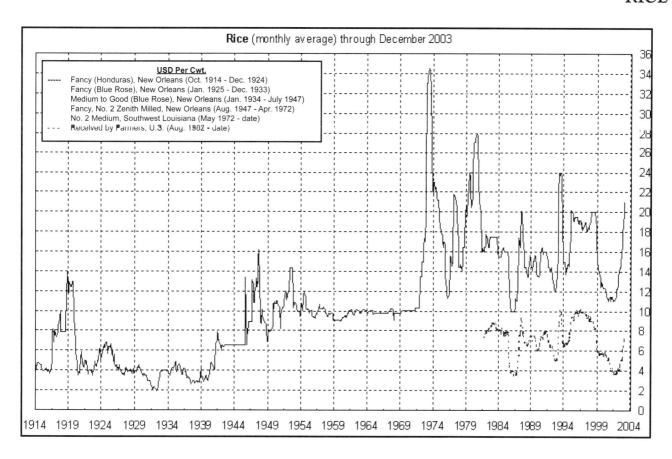

Rice (monthly average) through December 2003

USD Per Cwt.
----- Fancy (Honduras), New Orleans (Oct. 1914 - Dec. 1924)
Fancy (Blue Rose), New Orleans (Jan. 1925 - Dec. 1933)
Medium to Good (Blue Rose), New Orleans (Jan. 1934 - July 1947)
Fancy, No. 2 Zenith Milled, New Orleans (Aug. 1947 - Apr. 1972)
No. 2 Medium, Southwest Louisiana (May 1972 - date)
--- Received by Farmers, U.S. (Aug. 1902 - date)

Average Wholesale Price of Rice No. 2 (Medium)[1] Southwest Louisiana   In Dollars Per Cwt. Bagged

Year	Aug.	Sept.	Oct.	Nov.	Dec.	Jan.	Feb.	Mar.	Apr.	May	June	July	Average
1994-5	18.30	15.88	15.00	15.00	14.00	13.80	14.16	14.38	14.38	14.70	14.75	14.55	14.91
1995-6	15.44	17.50	20.25	20.13	20.00	20.00	19.88	19.25	19.13	19.38	19.40	19.50	19.15
1996-7	19.50	19.50	19.25	19.25	19.00	18.81	19.19	19.25	19.25	19.25	18.40	19.00	19.14
1997-8	18.25	18.35	18.63	19.00	19.00	19.00	19.00	18.20	18.00	18.13	18.50	18.50	18.55
1998-9	18.35	18.75	19.00	19.00	20.00	20.00	20.00	20.00	20.00	20.00	20.00	20.00	19.59
1999-00	18.60	17.50	14.88	14.70	14.67	14.35	14.00	13.83	13.75	13.40	12.50	12.63	14.57
2000-1	13.00	12.34	12.48	12.41	12.38	12.38	12.25	12.00	11.82	11.53	11.25	11.25	12.09
2001-2	11.06	11.50	11.50	11.50	11.08	11.50	11.50	11.44	11.03	11.13	11.13	11.13	11.29
2002-3	11.13	11.50	12.25	12.25	12.25	12.63	13.50	14.05	14.25	14.44	14.50	14.88	13.13
2003-4[2]	16.75	17.70	19.00	19.75	21.08								18.86

[1] U.S. No. 2 -- broken not to exceed 4%.   [2] Preliminary.   Source: Economic Research Service, U.S. Department of Agriculture (ERS-USDA)

Average Price Received by Farmers for Rice (Rough) in the United States   In Dollars Per Cwt.

Year	Aug.	Sept.	Oct.	Nov.	Dec.	Jan.	Feb.	Mar.	Apr.	May	June	July	Average[2]
1994-5	6.87	6.89	6.47	6.53	6.56	6.78	6.71	6.64	6.70	6.75	7.03	7.17	6.78
1995-6	7.64	7.95	8.77	9.12	9.36	9.33	9.10	9.31	9.34	9.69	9.74	9.68	9.15
1996-7	10.10	10.00	9.66	9.41	9.82	9.95	10.10	10.20	10.30	10.20	9.90	10.00	9.96
1997-8	9.94	9.92	10.00	9.82	9.77	9.57	9.75	9.67	9.40	9.38	9.58	9.58	9.70
1998-9	9.01	9.42	9.31	9.02	9.10	9.09	9.02	8.93	8.49	8.21	8.25	8.26	8.89
1999-00	6.91	6.17	5.91	5.96	6.01	5.98	5.82	5.64	5.75	5.62	5.69	5.59	5.93
2000-1	5.72	5.53	5.57	5.72	5.69	5.86	5.72	5.66	5.68	5.40	5.14	5.32	5.61
2001-2	5.10	4.78	4.36	4.08	4.07	4.30	4.16	3.99	3.94	3.98	3.92	3.81	4.21
2002-3	3.71	3.94	3.69	3.70	4.13	4.66	4.24	4.14	4.33	4.58	5.04	5.09	4.27
2003-4[1]	5.27	6.13	6.44	6.99	7.57	8.19	7.55						6.88

[1] Preliminary.   [2] Weighted average by sales.   Source: Economic Research Service, U.S. Department of Agriculture (ERS-USDA)

RICE

Salient Statistics of Rice, Rough & Milled (Rough Equivalent) in the United States   In Millions of Cwt.

Crop Year Beginning Aug. 1	Supply — Stocks Aug. 1	Supply — Pro-duction	Supply — Imports	Supply — Total Supply	Disappearance Domestic — Food	Disappearance Domestic — Brewers	Disappearance Domestic — Seed	Disappearance Domestic — Total	Resi-dual	Exports	Total Disap-pearance	CCC Stocks July 31	Gov. Support — Put Under Price Support	Loan Rate Rough — Long	Loan Rate Rough — Medium	Loan Rate — All Classes	Loan Rate — Milled Long
1998-9	27.9	184.4	10.6	223.0	87.3	16.0	4.4	114.0	11.4	86.8	200.9	0	80.2	6.67	6.14	6.50	10.71
1999-00	22.1	206.0	10.1	238.2	90.1	16.0	4.0	121.9	6.5	88.8	210.7	0	107.6	6.67	6.12	6.50	10.66
2000-1	27.5	190.9	10.9	229.2	110.2	4	4.1	117.5	4	83.2	200.7	0	----	6.66	6.12	6.50	10.71
2001-2	28.5	215.3	13.2	256.9	119.0	4	4.0	123.3	4	94.7	218.0	0	----	6.67	6.09	6.50	10.69
2002-3[1]	39.0	211.0	14.8	264.8	120.0	4	3.7	113.4	4	124.6	238.0	0	----	6.66	6.06	6.50	10.66
2003-4[2]	26.8	199.2	15.5	241.4	122.0	4	4.0	122.0	4	97.0	219.0	0	----	6.64	6.09	6.50	10.65

[1] Preliminary.   [2] Forecast.   [3] Loan rate for each class of rice is the sum of the whole kernels' loan rate weighted by its milling yield (average 56%) and the broken kernels' loan rate weighted by its milling yield (average 12%).   Source: Economic Research Service, U.S. Department of Agriculture (ERS)

Acreage, Yield, Production and Prices of Rice in the United States

Crop Year	Acreage Harvested (1,000 Acres) — Southern States	California	Yield Per Harvested Acre (In Lbs.) — United States	California	Production (1,000 Cwt.) — United States	Southern States	California	Production — United States	Value of Pro-duction $1,000	Wholesale Prices ($ Per Cwt.) — Arkan-sas[2]	Hous-ton[3]	Milled Rice, Average C.I.F. at Rotterdam U.S. No. 2[4] ($ Per Metric Ton)	Thai "A"[5]	Thai "B"[5]
1998-9	2,799	458	3,257	6,850	5,663	153,057	31,386	184,443	1,654,157	19.04	18.05	368	----	333
1999-00	3,007	505	3,512	7,270	5,866	169,337	36,690	206,027	1,231,207	15.01	15.33	272	----	278
2000-1	2,491	548	3,039	7,940	6,281	147,351	43,521	190,872	1,049,961	11.75	14.92	274	----	234
2001-2	2,843	471	3,314	8,170	6,496	176,780	38,490	215,270	925,055	10.85	12.88	208	----	225
2002-3	2,679	528	3,207	8,140	6,578	167,971	42,989	210,960	979,628	13.39	11.76	221	----	NA
2003-4[1]	2,490	507	2,997	7,620	6,645	160,533	38,624	199,157	1,485,031	19.79	16.01			

[1] Preliminary.   [2] F.O.B. mills, Arkansas, medium.   [3] Houston, Texas (long grain).   [4] Milled, 4%, container, FAS.   [5] SWR, 100%, bulk.
NA = Not available.   Source: Economic Research Service, U.S. Department of Agriculture (ERS-USDA)

U.S. Exports of Milled Rice, by Country of Destination   In Thousands of Metric Tons

Year Beginning October	Canada	Haiti	Iran	Ivory Coast	Jamaica	Mexico	Nether-lands	Peru	Saudi Arabia	South Africa	Switzer-land	United Kingdom	Total
1997-8	175.8	160.0	----	32.3	26.7	413.7	54.6	149.3	123.1	74.4	22.8	105.9	3,309
1998-9	174.9	219.9	----	13.9	17.4	353.7	44.0	103.9	113.0	77.9	25.0	110.3	3,076
1999-00	181.1	221.0	----	21.1	38.2	525.8	60.6	19.5	164.8	70.6	30.2	141.9	3,307
2000-1	182.4	212.3	----	22.2	32.0	516.0	50.8	1.0	156.3	65.9	33.2	104.0	3,058
2001-2	174.5	247.1	----	25.0	28.7	740.4	52.9	11.2	97.0	67.3	18.0	106.0	3,536
2002-3[1]	167.0	324.3	10.3	65.8	60.7	740.7	71.0	23.8	97.6	73.1	26.2	126.0	4,471

[1] Preliminary.   Source: Economic Research Service, U.S. Department of Agriculture (ERS-USDA)

U.S. Rice Exports by Export Program   In Thousands of Metric Tons

Fiscal Year	PL 480	Section 416	CCC Credit Pro-grams[2]	CCC African Reliel Exports	EEP[3]	Export Pro-grams[4]	Exports Outside Specified Export Programs	Total U.S. Rice Exports	% Export Programs as a Share of Total Exports
1998	183	0	499	0	0	194	3,116	3,310	6
1999	515	0	192	0	0	561	2,505	3,066	18
2000	216	147	225	0	0	394	2,913	3,307	12
2001	149	31	----	0	0	231	2,827	3,058	8
2002	253	64	----	0	0	374	3,162	3,536	11
2003[1]	239	0	----	0	0	309	4,162	4,471	7

[1] Preliminary.   [2] May not completely reflect exports made under these programs.   [3] Sales not shipments.   [4] adjusted for estimated overlap between CCC export credit and EEP shipments.   Source: Economice Research Service, U.S. Department of Agriculture (ERS-USDA)

Production of Rice (Rough) in the United States, by Type and Variety   In Thousands of Cwt.

Year	Long Grain	Medium Grain	Short Grain	Total	Year	Long Grain	Medium Grain	Short Grain	Total
1994	133,445	63,390	944	197,779	1999	151,863	50,540	3,624	206,027
1995	121,730	51,241	900	173,871	2000	128,756	59,514	2,602	190,872
1996	113,629	56,901	1,069	171,599	2001	167,555	46,105	1,610	215,270
1997	124,485	57,091	1,416	182,992	2002	157,243	52,201	1,516	210,960
1998	139,328	43,404	1,711	184,443	2003[1]	149,011	47,440	2,706	199,157

[1] Preliminary.   Source: National Agricultural Statistics Service, U.S. Department of Agriculture (NASS-USDA)

Rubber

Rubber is a natural or synthetic substance characterized by elasticity, water repellence, and electrical resistance. Pre-Columbian Native South Americans discovered many uses for rubber such as containers, balls, shoes, and for waterproofing fabrics for coats and capes. The Spaniards tried to duplicate these products for many years but were unsuccessful. The first commercial application of rubber began in 1791 when Samuel Peal patented a method of waterproofing cloth by treating it with a solution of rubber and turpentine. In 1839, Charles Goodyear revolutionized the rubber industry with his discovery of a process called vulcanization, which involves combining rubber and sulfur and heating the mixture.

Natural rubber is obtained from latex, a milky white fluid, from the Hevea Brasiliensis tree. The latex is gathered by cutting a chevron shape through the bark of the rubber tree. The latex is collected in a small cup, with approximately 1 fluid ounce per cutting. The cuttings are usually done every other day until the cuttings reach the ground. The tree is then allowed to renew itself before a new tapping is started. The collected latex is strained, diluted with water, and treated with acid to clump the rubber particles together. The rubber is then pressed between rollers to consolidate the rubber into slabs or thin sheets and is air-dried or smoke-dried for shipment.

During World War II, natural rubber supplies from the Far East were terminated, and the rubber shortage accelerated the development of synthetic rubber in the US. Synthetic rubber is produced by chemical reactions, condensation or polymerization, of certain unsaturated hydrocarbons. Synthetic rubber is made of raw material derived from petroleum, coal, oil, natural gas, and acetylene and is almost identical to natural rubber in chemical and physical properties.

Natural rubber and Rubber Index futures are traded on the Osaka Mercantile Exchange (OME). The OME's natural rubber contract is based on the RSS3 ribbed smoked sheet No. 3 while the Rubber Index Futures Contract is based on a composite of 8 component grades from 6 component rubber markets in the world. Rubber futures are also traded on the Shanghai Futures Exchange (SHFE) and the Tokyo Commodity Exchange (TOCOM).

Prices – Spot crude rubber prices (No.1 smoked sheets, ribbed, plantation rubber), basis in New York, rallied sharply to an average 49.14 cents per pound in 2003, up 8% from 41.12 cents in 2002 and up by 45% from the 3-decade low of 33.88 cents posted in 2001. Rubber prices recovered in 2002 and 2003 as the US economic recovery took hold and as auto demand remained strong.

Supply – World production of rubber in 2001/2, the latest full reporting year, rose 5.5% to 7.130 million metric tons from 6.760 million metric tons in 2000/1. The world's largest producers of rubber in 2001/2 were Thailand with 32.0% of world production, Indonesia (22.1%), India (8.9%), Malaysia (7.7%), China (6.3%), and Vietnam (4.4%). World production of synthetic rubber in 2001/2 fell by –3.5% to 10.490 million metric tons. The world's largest producers of synthetic rubber in 2001/2 were the US with 19.7% of world production, Japan (14.0%), Russia (8.8%), and Germany (7.9%).

US production of synthetic rubber in 2002 was set to rebound upward to about 2.2 million metric tons from the 8-year low of 2.064 million metric tons posted in 2001. US production of car and truck tires in 2001 fell to 255.700 million tires from 276.765 million tires in 2000.

Demand – World consumption of natural and synthetic rubber in 2001 fell to 7.070 million metric tons from 7.340 million metric tons in 2000. The largest consumers of natural and synthetic rubber in 2001 were the US with 14% of consumption, Japan with 10%, and France and Germany with a combined 7.5%.

US consumption of natural rubber in 2002 was set to rebound upward from the 9-year low of 974,000 metric tons posted in 2001. US consumption of synthetic rubber in 2002 was on track to increase to at least 1.914 million metric tons from the 11-year low of 1.840 million metric tons in 2001.

Trade – World exports of natural rubber in 2001, the latest reporting year for the series, rose +2.4% to a record 5.070 million metric tons. The world's largest exporters of natural rubber in 2001 were Thailand with 40% of world exports, Indonesia with 29% of world exports. Together, Thailand and Indonesia accounted for 69% of world exports.

US imports of natural rubber in 2002 were on track to rise to 1.09 million metric tons from the 8-year low of 972,000 posted in 2001. US exports of synthetic rubber in 2002 were set to rise to about 875,000 metric tons from 844,400 metric tons in 2001, which would be only moderately below the record export figure of 886,000 seen in 2000 before the world recession hit.

U.S. Imports of Natural Rubber (Includes Latex & Guayule)   In Thousands of Metric Tons

Year	Jan.	Feb.	Mar.	Apr.	May	June	July	Aug.	Sept.	Oct.	Nov.	Dec.	Total
1993	95.3	79.9	93.9	86.3	74.1	81.2	83.6	77.8	69.2	73.4	86.0	86.9	987.6
1994	87.5	74.7	102.6	78.9	88.3	77.8	66.7	85.0	78.8	89.3	70.0	76.0	975.6
1995	81.7	86.9	102.3	90.2	94.1	93.4	78.0	81.0	81.5	89.2	79.1	68.7	1,026.1
1996	105.4	86.1	82.2	90.6	65.1	70.4	79.0	81.0	82.1	113.6	73.5	85.0	1,014.0
1997	94.2	92.0	93.9	88.2	93.0	65.1	76.8	90.1	87.5	86.8	87.6	89.0	1,044.2
1998	104.4	76.6	102.8	81.0	98.0	92.9	96.4	100.8	123.2	104.8	84.5	111.4	1,176.8
1999	91.8	90.7	93.4	101.6	84.8	80.0	76.6	112.2	88.7	127.5	83.1	85.9	1,116.3
2000	127.4	88.2	114.1	107.9	114.9	120.1	65.9	96.2	79.2	96.2	92.2	89.3	1,191.6
2001	85.2	69.1	93.9	80.0	74.9	63.8	101.1	109.2	69.9	92.4	69.2	63.4	972.1
2002[1]	104.8	71.2	79.2	90.8	106.1	92.2							1,088.6

[1] Preliminary.   Source: International Rubber Study Group (IRSG)

RUBBER

World Production[1] of Rubber   In Thousands of Metric Tons

								Natural					Synthetic		
Year	China	India	Indo-nesia	Malaysia	Sri Lanka	Thailand	Vietnam	World Total	Ger-many	Japan	United States	Russia[3]	World Total
1992	309.3	383.0	1,387.0	1,173.2	106.1	1,531.0	114.0	5,440	544.7	1,389.9	2,300.0	1,610.5	9,300
1993	326.1	428.1	1,300.5	1,074.3	104.2	1,553.4	114.0	5,310	569.7	1,309.8	2,180.0	1,102.5	8,600
1994	374.0	464.0	1,358.5	1,100.6	105.3	1,717.9	156.0	5,720	621.6	1,349.0	2,390.0	631.9	8,870
1995	424.0	499.6	1,454.5	1,089.3	105.7	1,804.8	155.0	6,070	480.0	1,497.6	2,530.0	836.9	9,480
1996	430.0	540.1	1,527.0	1,082.5	112.5	1,970.4	220.0	6,440	548.1	1,519.9	2,486.0	775.1	9,760
1997	444.0	580.3	1,504.8	971.1	105.8	2,032.7	212.0	6,470	555.1	1,591.5	2,589.0	724.9	10,080
1998	450.0	591.1	1,714.0	885.7	95.7	2,075.9	218.0	6,850	619.0	1,520.1	2,600.0	621.0	9,880
1999	460.0	620.1	1,599.2	768.9	96.6	2,154.6	230.0	6,810	720.1	1,576.7	2,354.0	737.0	10,390
2000	445.0	629.0	1,501.1	615.4	87.6	2,346.4	291.0	6,760	849.2	1,591.7	2,395.4	837.1	10,870
2001[2]	451.0	631.5	1,576.5	547.0	86.2	2,283.9	317.0	7,130	828.4	1,465.5	2,064.4	919.2	10,490

[1] Including rubber in the form of latex.   [2] Preliminary.   [3] Formerly part of the U.S.S.R., data reported separately until 1992.
Source: International Rubber Study Group (IRSG)

World Consumption of Natural and Synthetic Rubber   In Thousands of Metric Tons

				Natural								Synthetic			
Year	Brazil	France	Ger-many	Japan	United Kingdom	United States	World Total	France	Ger-many	Japan	United Kingdom	United States	World Total
1992	123.4	179.0	212.8	685.4	124.5	910.2	5,320	365.4	506.0	1,080.6	231.0	1,959.6	9,360
1993	131.7	168.5	174.9	631.0	119.0	966.7	5,430	314.7	488.0	1,022.0	211.0	2,001.0	8,630
1994	144.7	179.8	186.4	639.8	135.0	1,001.7	5,650	400.1	512.2	1,026.2	220.0	2,117.6	8,820
1995	155.2	176.0	211.7	692.0	118.0	1,003.9	5,950	430.2	426.4	1,085.0	226.0	2,172.0	9,270
1996	160.7	182.2	193.0	714.5	111.0	1,001.7	6,110	436.1	497.0	1,124.5	230.0	2,186.6	9,590
1997	161.0	192.3	214.0	713.0	119.0	1,044.1	6,470	416.2	509.0	1,163.0	235.0	2,322.7	10,010
1998	185.3	223.0	247.0	707.3	139.0	1,157.4	6,570	451.4	582.0	1,115.7	177.0	2,354.4	9,870
1999	177.6	252.7	226.0	734.2	130.0	1,116.3	6,650	434.3	565.0	1,132.9	189.0	2,217.5	10,280
2000	226.8	308.6	250.0	751.8	133.0	1,194.8	7,340	481.5	632.0	1,137.5	188.0	2,190.3	10,830
2001[1]	217.8	282.0	246.0	729.2	107.0	974.1	7,070	464.5	612.0	1,085.1	167.0	1,839.5	10,340

[1] Preliminary.   *Source: International Rubber Study Group (IRSG)*

World Stocks[1] of Natural & Synthetic Rubber (by Countries) on January 1   In Thousands of Metric Tons

	Total			In Producing Countries				Total		In Consuming Countries (Reported Stocks)			
Year	Synthetic	Africa	Indo-nesia	Malaysia	Sri Lanka	Thai-land	Vietnam	Natural	Brazil	India	Japan	United States	Total
1993	1,004	19.6	110	187.2	16.0	89.0	12.0	560	17.0	90.9	82.9	108.0	442
1994	949	21.6	110	159.2	17.2	115.6	12.0	570	25.0	96.4	85.4	71.3	410
1995	915	17.0	110	187.0	16.5	96.5	19.0	480	17.0	94.1	72.9	45.2	363
1996	988	21.0	110	175.6	17.0	113.0	20.0	490	13.0	127.4	77.1	67.1	414
1997	1,057	20.5	70	190.3	17.6	147.7	28.0	510	13.0	123.4	86.8	79.3	427
1998	1,081	25.5	40	209.5	17.9	159.4	28.0	510	13.0	157.0	87.2	57.2	385
1999	1,116	27.6	30	234.2	18.6	209.5	36.0	750	13.0	194.0	58.0	70.4	406
2000	1,103	27.9	33	236.6	18.6	250.9	16.0	880	34.0	215.1	79.1	46.0	443
2001	1,196	28.7	48	212.7	18.7	188.6	22.0	630	40.0	203.3	95.2	44.6	452
2002[1]	1,189	31.0	45	191.6	19.0	213.0	31.0	650	42.0	225.5	46.9	42.6	429

[1] Preliminary.   *Source: International Rubber Study Group (IRSG)*

Net Exports of Natural Rubber from Producing Areas   In Thousands of Metric Tons

Year	Cam-bodia	Guat-emala[4]	Indo-nesia	Liberia	Malaysia	Nigeria	Sri Lanka	Thai-land	Vietnam	Other Africa[2]	Other Asia[3]	World Total
1992	20.0	15.7	1,268.1	30.0	939.1	70.4	78.6	1,412.9	80.9	135.0	25.9	4,010
1993	21.0	16.9	1,214.3	45.0	769.8	79.7	69.6	1,396.8	96.7	136.0	32.6	3,880
1994	32.0	22.3	1,244.8	10.0	782.1	49.6	69.1	1,605.0	135.5	145.0	28.9	4,250
1995	30.0	23.2	1,323.8	13.0	777.5	99.2	68.2	1,635.5	138.1	140.0	31.1	4,340
1996	31.0	29.2	1,434.3	30.0	709.7	48.8	72.1	1,763.0	194.5	166.7	65.3	4,380
1997	32.0	28.3	1,403.8	67.2	586.8	53.0	61.4	1,837.1	194.2	186.1	58.6	4,580
1998	33.0	25.2	1,641.2	75.0	424.9	74.0	41.4	1,839.4	190.6	182.2	62.8	4,720
1999	34.0	26.7	1,494.6	100.0	435.5	38.0	42.7	1,886.3	230.0	196.5	59.6	4,660
2000	35.0	30.0	1,379.6	105.0	196.4	36.0	32.6	2,166.2	269.0	202.9	54.9	4,950
2001[1]	35.0	32.0	1,453.1	109.0	162.1	30.0	32.0	2,006.4	292.0	208.1	69.5	5,070

[1] Preliminary.   [2] Includes Cameroon, Cote d'Ivoire, Gabon, Ghana and Zaire.   [3] Includes Myanmar, Papua New Guinea and the Philippines.
Source: International Rubber Study Group (IRSG)

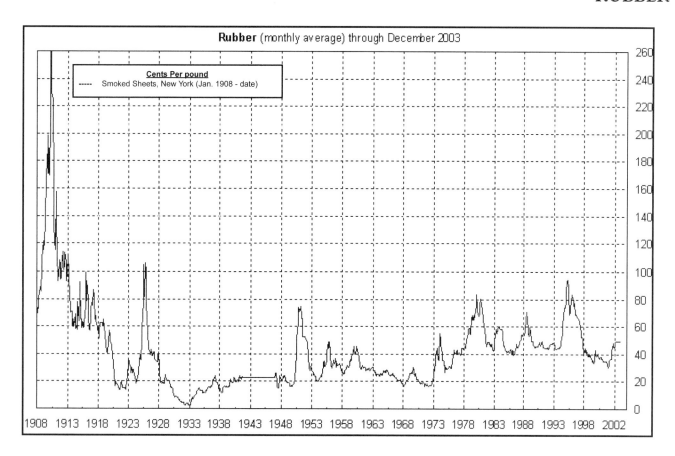

Average Spot Crude Rubber Prices (Smoked Sheets1) in New York   In Cents Per Pound

Year	Jan.	Feb.	Mar.	Apr.	May	June	July	Aug.	Sept.	Oct.	Nov.	Dec.	Average
1994	44.92	46.11	49.62	50.83	51.43	55.13	62.49	66.35	67.15	73.51	71.76	77.35	59.72
1995	85.68	92.61	94.15	93.43	89.50	80.57	72.13	68.54	70.70	73.59	83.19	83.39	82.29
1996	80.25	79.90	79.76	75.08	76.99	75.10	71.03	69.13	68.75	66.32	66.32	66.14	72.90
1997	65.06	64.76	63.53	59.97	57.71	57.30	51.96	52.45	51.89	51.36	47.99	40.53	55.38
1998	40.21	43.96	41.70	41.23	42.65	41.28	40.03	38.58	38.62	40.26	39.96	38.20	40.56
1999	38.99	38.58	36.34	34.98	35.75	34.64	33.60	33.63	34.45	37.58	42.57	38.88	36.67
2000	38.16	40.36	38.17	37.80	37.76	37.07	36.65	37.90	37.35	37.61	37.02	36.90	37.73
2001	35.98	35.66	34.78	34.50	34.80	35.00	34.80	34.48	33.07	31.98	31.14	30.35	33.88
2002	32.21	34.45	36.50	36.38	36.93	43.53	44.32	45.20	47.90	45.70	44.97	45.39	41.12
2003	47.95	49.25	49.25	49.25	49.25	49.25	49.25	49.25	49.25	49.25	49.25	49.25	49.14

[1] No. 1, ribbed, plantation rubber.   *Source: International Rubber Study Group (IRSG)*

Natural Rubber Prices in London   In Euro[1] Per Metric Ton

Year	Jan.	Feb.	Mar.	Apr.	May	June	July	Aug.	Sept.	Oct.	Nov.	Dec.	Average
Buyers' Price RSS 1 (CIF)													
1999	495.8	463.3	430.0	414.4	442.4	435.7	410.2	404.5	419.9	455.4	509.8	484.7	446.4
2000	462.0	518.2	487.6	496.0	500.5	501.8	494.5	529.5	526.2	537.4	518.4	502.4	506.2
2001	490.5	494.0	477.3	479.9	498.8	509.5	493.3	471.3	443.9	440.2	430.3	409.1	469.8
2002	461.8	502.5	522.1	511.9	518.9								503.4
Buyers' Prices RSS 3 (CIF)													
1999	466.4	451.6	417.9	394.0	418.8	425.3	391.1	384.8	398.6	439.0	489.5	453.3	427.1
2000	440.0	498.5	464.8	481.0	483.0	479.3	472.0	509.5	507.3	519.9	498.4	477.9	486.0
2001	464.2	467.3	450.2	455.6	482.5	497.3	477.3	450.7	423.6	418.3	411.4	389.4	449.0
2002	444.2	486.5	511.3	500.2	515.4	959.9	893.4	932.2	981.1				691.6
Sellers' Prices SMR 20 (CIF)													
1999	414.4	411.9	380.5	375.0	396.9	393.5	373.8	388.8	417.0	453.1	518.8	480.0	415.8
2000	471.9	504.4	472.5	466.3	465.0	447.5	435.0	477.0	478.1	486.3	487.0	483.8	472.9
2001	468.8	461.3	433.8	411.9	414.5	418.8	416.3	422.5	400.0	400.0	406.3	397.5	421.0
2002	428.0	461.3	510.6	500.6	503.5	921.3	864.6	898.5	978.9				674.1

[1] Data prior to June 2002 are in British Pound per metric ton.   *Source: International Rubber Study Group (IRSG)*

RUBBER

Consumption of Natural Rubber in the United States   In Thousands of Metric Tons

Year	Jan.	Feb.	Mar.	Apr.	May	June	July	Aug.	Sept.	Oct.	Nov.	Dec.	Total
1993	96.3	76.0	93.4	93.4	67.9	76.8	77.3	84.9	72.0	73.6	82.9	72.2	966.7
1994	92.8	84.9	93.1	82.7	89.6	84.6	76.2	87.8	74.8	90.1	66.4	78.7	1,001.7
1995	70.5	75.8	98.4	90.3	92.2	93.3	85.0	82.7	83.1	89.9	81.4	61.3	1,003.9
1996	102.5	85.8	81.2	87.9	65.6	76.7	81.9	88.1	83.3	108.4	72.1	68.2	1,001.7
1997	94.2	92.0	93.9	88.2	93.0	65.1	76.8	90.1	87.5	86.8	87.5	89.0	1,044.1
1998	104.4	76.6	102.7	81.0	98.0	92.9	96.4	91.7	119.1	104.8	78.4	111.4	1,157.4
1999	92.0	92.0	93.0	88.0	88.0	88.0	92.0	92.0	92.0	100.0	100.0	100.0	1,116.3
2000	110.0	110.0	110.0	114.0	114.0	114.0	80.0	80.0	80.0	93.0	93.0	93.0	1,194.8
2001	85.5	69.4	94.1	80.2	75.1	64.1	101.2	109.3	70.0	92.4	69.4	63.4	974.1
2002[1]	104.9	71.3	79.2	90.4	106.4	92.3	108.7						1,119.8

[1] Preliminary.   Source: International Rubber Study Group (IRSG)

Stocks of Natural Rubber in the United States, on First of Month   In Thousands of Metric Tons

Year	Jan.	Feb.	Mar.	Apr.	May	June	July	Aug.	Sept.	Oct.	Nov.	Dec.
1993	108.0	49.4	53.3	53.7	46.7	52.9	57.3	63.6	56.5	53.7	53.4	56.5
1994	71.3	65.9	55.7	65.2	61.4	60.0	53.2	43.8	41.0	45.0	44.2	47.8
1995	45.2	56.4	67.5	71.4	71.2	72.6	73.0	66.0	64.4	62.8	62.1	59.8
1996	67.1	70.0	70.3	71.2	73.9	73.4	67.1	64.2	57.2	56.0	61.1	62.4
1997	79.3	74.2	74.2	76.9	77.5	62.2	55.2	53.6	52.1	51.2	52.4	55.2
1998	57.2	61.2	65.5	63.5	60.9	66.7	53.6	57.9	54.7	58.3	58.9	66.5
1999	70.4	68.0	66.0	64.0	62.0	60.0	58.0	56.0	54.0	52.0	50.0	48.0
2000	46.0	63.4	41.6	45.7	39.6	40.5	46.6	32.5	48.7	47.9	51.1	50.3
2001	46.6	44.3	44.0	43.8	43.6	43.4	43.1	43.0	42.9	42.8	42.8	42.6
2002[1]	42.6	42.5	42.4	42.4	42.8	42.5	42.4	42.3				

[1] Preliminary.   Source: International Rubber Study Group (IRSG)

Stocks of Synthetic Rubber in the United States, on First of Month   In Thousands of Metric Tons

Year	Jan.	Feb.	Mar.	Apr.	May	June	July	Aug.	Sept.	Oct.	Nov.	Dec.
1993	406.9	345.9	345.7	346.0	340.5	351.8	342.1	341.6	333.6	326.4	319.9	321.4
1994	331.1	313.3	313.3	307.9	306.0	314.2	302.5	323.2	318.5	304.6	299.4	299.5
1995	305.4	307.4	302.8	293.5	319.4	315.6	325.9	349.2	355.7	354.6	347.0	351.5
1996	366.2	355.3	342.0	354.8	365.4	360.0	367.0	377.3	366.0	362.8	354.1	370.6
1997	400.5	400.4	408.4	412.7	411.9	403.5	393.1	376.9	378.4	364.4	365.2	377.7
1998	377.7	382.2	375.7	379.5	387.5	402.8	394.6	406.8	394.2	398.7	395.7	396.5
1999	409.3	404.0	404.0	406.0	399.0	420.0	410.0	419.0	413.0	390.0	391.0	389.0
2000	406.0	416.0	413.0	402.0	405.0	416.0	409.0	418.0	400.0	412.0	407.0	419.0
2001	443.0	451.0	467.0	4,559.0	448.0	433.0	426.0	420.0	394.0	400.0	394.0	379.0
2002[1]	392.0	377.0	379.0	393.0	398.0	384.0	385.0					

[1] Preliminary.   Source: International Rubber Study Group (IRSG)

Production of Synthetic Rubber in the United States   In Thousands of Metric Tons

Year	Jan.	Feb.	Mar.	Apr.	May	June	July	Aug.	Sept.	Oct.	Nov.	Dec.	Total
1993	120.0	160.0	220.0	190.0	200.0	180.0	190.0	180.0	180.0	180.0	190.0	180.0	2,180
1994	180.0	180.0	210.0	200.0	210.0	200.0	200.0	210.0	190.0	210.0	200.0	200.0	2,390
1995	220.0	200.0	210.0	210.0	240.0	220.0	210.0	230.0	210.0	200.0	200.0	190.0	2,530
1996	200.0	190.0	220.0	210.0	200.0	210.0	200.0	210.0	200.0	210.0	220.0	216.0	2,486
1997	220.0	200.0	220.0	230.0	220.0	200.0	220.0	220.0	230.0	210.0	210.0	203.0	2,589
1998	230.0	200.0	230.0	220.0	240.0	210.0	220.0	210.0	230.0	210.0	200.0	210.0	2,610
1999	200.0	181.0	209.0	195.0	205.0	190.0	199.0	192.0	180.0	204.0	197.0	202.0	2,354
2000	202.0	202.0	214.0	193.0	216.0	202.0	198.0	187.0	193.0	197.0	194.0	184.0	2,382
2001	203.0	188.6	184.3	172.1	175.5	162.3	166.7	164.7	174.3	178.6	155.1	139.2	2,064
2002[1]	176.1	171.9	192.3	190.6	187.5	185.0							2,207

[1] Preliminary.   Source: International Rubber Study Group (IRSG)

Consumption of Synthetic Rubber in the United States   In Thousands of Metric Tons

Year	Jan.	Feb.	Mar.	Apr.	May	June	July	Aug.	Sept.	Oct.	Nov.	Dec.	Total
1993	161.3	154.4	189.4	172.8	164.5	173.6	166.0	173.9	162.0	169.4	162.3	151.4	2,001
1994	177.7	160.8	191.8	173.0	173.5	187.5	164.9	187.1	176.0	178.8	175.7	170.8	2,118
1995	188.6	182.2	194.3	179.1	212.7	188.7	160.0	190.7	182.4	178.1	169.7	145.5	2,172
1996	188.0	173.7	186.9	176.8	184.9	178.5	177.0	197.3	182.9	201.0	177.8	165.5	2,187
1997	101.7	181.4	190.0	187.9	192.2	187.7	205.9	208.0	204.2	203.0	181.9	188.8	2,323
1998	196.5	192.5	214.8	194.4	199.8	201.4	192.0	204.5	202.2	200.3	181.2	174.8	2,354
1999	164.0	166.0	195.0	178.0	170.0	186.0	177.0	176.0	191.0	171.0	178.0	161.0	2,113
2000	173.0	185.0	202.0	178.0	194.0	196.0	177.0	189.0	172.0	182.0	168.0	147.0	2,163
2001	170.8	149.6	166.8	153.3	159.8	148.6	156.4	173.0	145.7	162.7	140.8	112.0	1,840
2002[1]	155.5	146.8	153.0	165.8	173.4	160.4	161.5						1,914

[1] Preliminary.   *Source: International Rubber Study Group (IRSG)*

U.S. Exports of Synthetic Rubber   In Thousands of Metric Tons

Year	Jan.	Feb.	Mar.	Apr.	May	June	July	Aug.	Sept.	Oct.	Nov.	Dec.	Total
1993	47.1	34.1	57.7	47.4	52.4	46.9	46.9	43.8	48.8	46.6	49.0	41.9	562.6
1994	48.8	46.4	55.4	57.0	52.4	49.6	50.2	62.8	60.7	59.9	56.9	55.0	655.1
1995	54.9	51.6	62.7	55.6	58.6	58.6	50.0	54.9	53.0	60.4	53.9	52.6	666.8
1996	61.1	57.7	64.0	68.0	48.2	66.8	62.3	57.1	63.9	65.2	58.6	58.6	731.5
1997	63.1	58.2	57.5	74.2	66.9	61.6	64.1	70.0	65.6	65.6	63.0	58.7	768.5
1998	61.1	60.8	62.8	59.8	66.9	61.8	60.1	64.4	63.7	62.3	59.2	59.2	742.1
1999	57.6	63.3	65.0	70.5	64.7	66.0	61.5	68.2	65.1	79.0	70.2	65.7	796.8
2000	64.3	73.4	83.8	70.2	73.2	72.3	72.4	78.6	78.6	75.2	73.3	70.7	886.0
2001	74.6	67.3	76.4	78.2	75.1	69.6	70.6	71.6	68.1	70.7	62.4	59.4	844.4
2002[1]	67.9	71.6	69.5	74.9	78.5	73.6	74.5						875.1

[1] Preliminary.   *Source: International Rubber Study Group (IRSG)*

Production of Tyres (Car and Truck) in the United States   In Thousands of Units

Year	First Quarter	Second Quarter	Third Quarter	Fourth Quarter	Total	Year	First Quarter	Second Quarter	Third Quarter	Fourth Quarter	Total
1985	54,460	49,385	46,468	46,610	196,923	1994	63,586	63,331	57,018	59,442	243,696
1986	49,240	45,687	46,855	48,507	190,289	1995	63,800	63,800	63,800	63,754	255,521
1987	51,205	50,210	49,723	51,839	202,978	1996	64,000	64,000	64,000	63,700	255,723
1988	54,677	52,986	51,195	52,493	211,351	1997	----	----	----	----	263,860
1989	56,716	56,626	50,086	49,444	212,870	1998	----	----	----	----	270,905
1990	55,915	53,856	51,163	49,729	210,663	1999	----	----	----	----	267,652
1991	51,296	52,796	49,183	51,115	202,391	2000	----	----	----	----	276,765
1992	57,890	57,319	57,554	57,487	230,250	2001	65,367	62,809	62,366	56,106	255,700
1993	61,809	60,752	57,702	57,184	237,447	2002[1]	62,937	64,362			

[1] Preliminary.   [2] Estimate.   *Source: International Rubber Study Group IRSG)*

U.S. Foreign Trade of Tyres (Car and Truck)   In Thousands of Units

	Imports					Exports				
Year	First Quarter	Second Quarter	Third Quarter	Fourth Quarter	Total	First Quarter	Second Quarter	Third Quarter	Fourth Quarter	Total
1992	10,760	12,496	11,850	12,285	47,391	6,243	6,475	7,125	6,646	26,489
1993	11,519	13,045	12,688	13,036	50,288	7,266	6,930	7,163	7,133	28,492
1994	13,809	15,352	14,906	14,774	58,841	7,444	8,035	7,945	8,678	32,102
1995	14,883	14,977	13,762	12,718	56,340	8,438	8,502	8,478	9,174	34,592
1996	13,163	13,864	12,543	13,186	52,756	8,244	10,013	8,672	9,401	36,330
1997	13,359	14,487	15,314	16,064	59,434	9,466	11,386	10,456	11,085	42,452
1998	17,046	17,728	18,016	19,346	72,124	12,840	10,678	10,018	10,372	43,923
1999	19,471	22,295	22,194	23,784	87,768	9,874	9,580	10,480	10,537	40,945
2000	24,200	24,698	23,561	22,123	94,019	11,200	10,200	10,200	10,100	44,164
2001[1]	19,563	22,251	22,072	20,956	84,842	10,087	10,362	11,004	10,691	42,144

[1] Preliminary.   [2] Estimate.   *Source: International Rubber Study Group (IRSG)*

Rye

Rye is a cereal grain and a member of the grass family. Hardy varieties of rye have been developed for winter planting. Rye is most widely grown in northern Europe and Asia. In the US, rye is used as an animal feed and as an ingredient in bread and some whiskeys. About a third of the total supply is used as livestock feed, another third as a foodstuff, and the balance as seed and for whisky. The major producing states are North and South Dakota, Oklahoma, and Georgia. The crop year runs from June to May.

Supply – World rye production was forecasted to drop sharply to 14.438 million metric tons in 2003/4, down 30% from 20.599 million in 2002/3. The drop in production should be spread fairly evenly across the major producers, but production in Russia (the world's largest producer) is expected to plunge by 41% to 4.200 million in 2003/4 from 7.150 million in 2002/3. World rye stocks are forecasted to plunge 52% to 4.013 million metric tons in 2003/4 from 8.327 million in 2002/3.

The world's largest producers of rye in 2002/3 were Russia with 7.150 million metric tons of production (accounting for 35% of world production), the European Union (4.718 million or 23%), and Poland (3.822 million or 19%). US rye production in 2003/4 was forecast to rise sharply by 33% to 235,000 metric tons from 177,000 in 2002/3, but that still represents only 1.6% of world production.

Demand – World rye consumption in 2003/4 was forecast at 18.752 million metric tons, significantly higher than the forecasted production of 14.438 million, a bullish factor for rye prices. In 2002/3, consumption of 20.253 million metric tons was just slightly below production of 20.599 million. The world's largest consumers of rye are Russia with 6.150 million metric tons of consumption (or 30% of world consumption), the European Union (4.454 million or 22%), and Poland (4.100 million or 20%). US consumption in 2003/4 was forecast to rise by 2.5% to 331,000 metric tons from 323,000 metric tons in 2002/3.

Trade – World trade in rye in 2003/4 was forecast to fall sharply by 39% to 985,000 metric tons from 1.604 million in 2002/3. There were only three regions with rye exports of consequence in 2002/3 – the European Union with 800,000 metric tons of exports (accounting for 50% of world exports), Russia (414,000 metric tons or 26%), and the Ukraine (265,000 metric tons or 17%). US exports of rye are forecasted at a negligible 5,000 metric tons in 2003/4, up from 2,000 in 2002/3 but accounting for less than 1% of world trade. The world's main rye importers are Japan with 414,000 metric tons in 2002/3 (accounting for 26% of world imports), the European Union with 350,000 (22%), and the US with 109,000 (7%). US imports of rye in 2003/4 are forecasted to fall by 8% to 100,000 metric tons from 109,000 in 2002/3. The US imports about one-third of its rye consumption needs.

World Production of Rye   In Thousands of Metric Tons

Year	Austria	Canada	Czech Republic	Denmark	France	Germany	Poland	Russia	Spain	Turkey	Ukraine	United States	World Total
1994-5	319	397	281	380	182	3,451	5,300	6,000	217	250	941	288	21,571
1995-6	314	310	262	500	198	4,521	6,287	4,100	174	255	1,208	256	21,939
1996-7	151	309	204	343	225	4,214	5,652	5,900	295	245	1,100	227	22,050
1997-8	207	320	259	453	207	4,580	5,300	7,500	212	235	1,348	207	24,433
1998-9	236	408	261	538	216	4,775	5,664	3,300	207	237	1,140	309	20,306
1999-00	220	387	202	250	190	4,330	5,181	4,800	220	250	919	280	19,290
2000-1	180	260	150	260	150	4,150	4,003	5,450	210	250	966	213	19,140
2001-2[1]	210	228	149	330	120	5,130	4,863	6,600	110	250	1,822	177	22,610
2002-3[2]	170	134	119	230	140	3,670	3,822	7,150	170	250	1,500	177	20,290
2003-4[3]	130	330	150	180	120	2,300	3,200	4,200	190	250	800	235	14,110

[1] Preliminary.   [2] Estimate.   [3] Forecast.   Source: Foreign Agricultural Service, U.S. Department of Agriculture (FAS-USDA)

Production of Rye in the United States   In Thousands of Bushels

Year	Georgia	Kansas	Michigan	Minnesota	Nebraska	North Dakota	Oklahoma	Pennsylvania	South Carolina	South Dakota	Texas	Wisconsin	Total
1994	1,890	325	442	810	546	700	945	320	600	1,485	435	875	11,341
1995	1,155	400	544	609	480	726	810	330	440	1,650	380	480	10,064
1996	1,820	150	351	480	323	528	975	216	520	1,476	190	384	8,936
1997	1,430	300	450	400	240	513	1,080	400	250	728	330	432	8,132
1998	1,050	375	420	837	288	2,562	1,540	495	400	1,400	400	360	12,161
1999	1,050	300	756	775	405	1,517	1,045	600	500	1,012	450	384	11,038
2000	1,170	[2]	[2]	[2]	[2]	704	1,470	[2]	[2]	546	[2]	[2]	8,386
2001	875	[2]	[2]	[2]	[2]	340	1,150	[2]	[2]	350	[2]	[2]	6,971
2002	720	[2]	[2]	[2]	[2]	342	1,300	[2]	[2]	270	[2]	[2]	6,955
2003[1]	800	[2]	[2]	[2]	[2]	750	2,160	[2]	[2]	672	[2]	[2]	9,254

[1] Preliminary.   [2] Estimates not published beginning in 2000.   Source: Agricultural Statistics Board, U.S. Department of Agriculture (ASB-USDA)

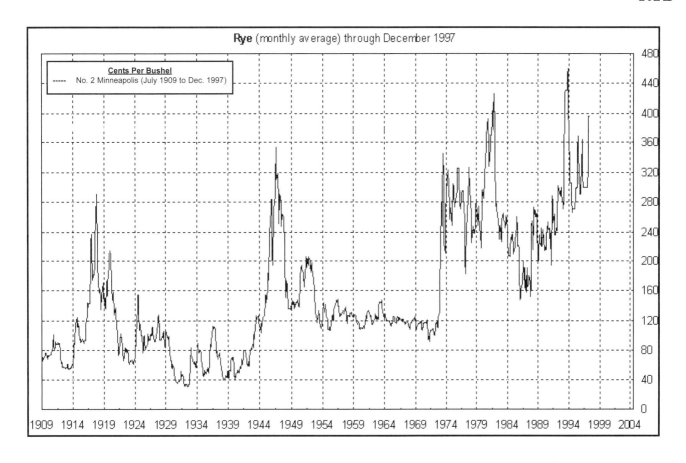

Salient Statistics of Rye in the United States   In Thousands of Bushels

Crop Year Beginning June 1	Supply Stocks June 1	Supply Production	Supply Imports	Supply Total Supply	Domestic Use Food	Domestic Use Industry	Domestic Use Seed	Domestic Use Feed & Residual	Domestic Use Total	Exports	Total Disappearance	Acreage Planted ----- 1,000 Acres -----	Acreage Harvested for Grain	Yield Per Harvested Acre Bushels
1994-5	971	11,341	4,386	16,698	3,312	2,000	3,000	6,900	15,212	35	15,247	1,613	407	27.9
1995-6	1,451	10,064	3,760	15,275	3,318	2,000	3,000	6,018	14,336	41	14,377	1,602	385	26.1
1996-7	898	8,936	4,327	14,161	3,459	2,000	3,000	4,916	13,375	32	13,407	1,457	345	25.9
1997-8	754	8,132	5,562	14,448	3,298	3,000	2,000	5,306	13,604	80	13,684	1,400	316	25.7
1998-9	764	12,161	3,322	16,247	3,639	3,000	3,000	4,392	14,031	33	14,064	1,566	418	29.1
1999-00	2,449	11,038	3,424	16,911	3,300	3,000	3,000	5,736	15,036	286	15,322	1,582	383	28.8
2000-1	1,589	8,386	3,230	13,205	3,300	3,000	3,000	2,307	11,607	390	11,997	1,329	296	28.3
2001-2[1]	1,190	6,971	4,900	13,061	3,300	3,000	3,000	3,000	12,300	200	12,500	1,328	255	27.3
2002-3[2]	568	6,955	5,000	12,523	3,300	3,000	3,000	2,400	11,700	300	12,000	1,395	281	24.8
2003-4[3]	445	9,254										1,368	339	27.3

[1] Preliminary.   [2] Estimate.   [3] Forecast   *Source: Economic Research Service, U.S. Department of Agriculture (ERS-USDA)*

Average Price of Cash Rye No. 2 in Minneapolis   In Cents Per Bushel

Year	July	Aug.	Sept.	Oct.	Nov.	Dec.	Jan.	Feb.	Mar.	Apr.	May	June	Average
1994-5	360	336	305	305	305	305	285	267	270	270	270	270	296
1995-6	287	298	299	300	300	350	368	346	290	290	290	304	310
1996-7	325	364	314	300	300	300	300	300	300	300	300	300	309
1997-8	300	327	395	395	395	395	NQ	NQ	NQ	NQ	NQ	NQ	382
1998-9	NQ	NQ	NQ	NQ	NQ	NQ	NQ	NQ	NQ	NQ	NQ	NQ	NQ
1999-00	NQ	NQ	NQ	NQ	NQ	NQ	NQ	NQ	NQ	NQ	NQ	NQ	NQ
2000-1	NQ	NQ	NQ	NQ	NQ	NQ	NQ	NQ	NQ	NQ	NQ	NQ	NQ
2001-2	NQ	NQ	NQ	NQ	NQ	NQ	NQ	NQ	NQ	NQ	NQ	NQ	NQ
2002-3	NQ	NQ	NQ	NQ	NQ	NQ	NQ	NQ	NQ	NQ	NQ	NQ	NQ
2003-4[1]	NQ	NQ	NQ	NQ	NQ	NQ	NQ						

[1] Preliminary.   NQ = No quote.   *Source: Agricultural Marketing Service, U.S. Department of Agriculture (AMS-USDA)*

Salt

Salt, also known as sodium chloride, is a chemical compound and is an essential element in the diet of humans, animals, and even many plants. Since prehistoric times, salt has been used to preserve foods and was commonly used in the religious rites of the Greeks, Romans, Hebrews, and Christians. Salt, in the form of salt cakes, served as money in ancient Ethiopia and Tibet. As long ago as 1450 BC, Egyptian art shows records of salt production.

Evaporation of salt water from areas near oceans or seas is the simplest method of obtaining salt. In most regions, rock salt is obtained from underground mining or by wells sunk to the deposits. Salt is soluble in water, is slightly soluble in alcohol, but insoluble in concentrated hydrochloric acid. In its crystalline form, salt is transparent and colorless, shining with an ice-like luster.

Prices – Salt prices in 2002 (vacuum and open pan, FOB mine) were unchanged from 2001 at $120.02 per ton, sustaining the recovery from the weak prices seen in 1999-

2000 of $112.49 and $113.95, respectively.

Supply – World production of salt in 2002 fell –3.2% to 210.000 million metric tons from the record high of 217.000 million metric tons in 2001. The world's largest salt producers are the US with 19.2% of world production, China (15.6%), Germany (7.5%), India (6.9%), and Canada (5.9%). US production in 2002 fell -10.0% to 40.300 million metric tons from 44.800 million in 2001.

Demand – US consumption of salt in 2002 fell –16.5% to 45.100 million metric tons from the record high of 54.000 million metric tons in 2001.

Trade – The US relied on imports for 18% of its salt consumption in 2002, up from 17% in 2001. US imports of salt for consumption in 2002 fell 37% to 8.160 million metric tons. US exports of salt were 689,000 metric tons in 2002, with the bulk of those exports (585,000 metric tons) going to Canada.

World Production of All Salt   In Thousands of Metric Tons

Year	Australia	Canada	China	France	Ger-many	India	Italy	Mexico	Poland	Spain	United Kingdom	United States	World Total
1995	8,148	10,957	29,780	7,539	15,224	12,544	3,552	7,670	4,214	4,776	6,650	42,200	199,000
1996	7,905	12,248	29,035	7,860	15,907	14,466	3,541	8,508	4,163	4,000	6,610	42,300	204,000
1997	8,883	13,264	30,830	7,085	15,787	14,251	3,510	7,933	3,859	4,000	6,600	41,500	221,000
1998	9,033	13,296	22,420	7,000	15,700	11,964	3,600	8,412	4,005	3,500	6,600	41,300	200,000
1999	9,888	12,686	28,124	7,000	15,700	14,453	3,600	8,236	4,212	3,200	5,800	45,000	210,000
2000	8,778	12,164	31,280	7,000	15,700	14,453	3,600	8,884	4,307	3,200	5,800	45,600	212,000
2001[1]	9,536	13,725	34,105	7,000	15,700	14,503	3,600	8,501	4,200	3,200	5,800	44,800	217,000
2002[2]	9,887	12,313	32,835	7,000	15,700	14,503	3,600	8,500	4,200	3,200	5,800	40,300	210,000

[1] Preliminary.   [2] Estimate.   Source: U.S. Geological Survey (USGS)

Salient Statistics of the Salt Industry in the United States   In Thousands of Metric Tons

Year	Net Import Reliance as a % of Apparent Consumption	Average Value FOB Mine Vacuum & Open Pan $ Per Ton	Production Total	Production Open & Vacuum Pan	Production Solar	Production Rock	Sold or Used Producers Brine	Sold or Used Producers Open & Vacuum Pan	Sold or Used Producers Rock Salt	Sold or Used Producers Brine	Total Salt	Value[3] Million $	Imports for Consumption	Exports Total	Exports To Canada	Apparent Consumption
1995	14	118.63	42,100	3,950	3,540	14,000	20,600	3,920	13,000	20,500	40,800	1,000.0	7,090	670	558	47,200
1996	19	120.54	42,200	3,920	3,270	13,500	21,500	3,900	14,500	21,500	42,900	1,060.0	10,600	869	710	52,600
1997	17	119.61	41,400	3,980	3,170	12,900	21,400	3,990	12,200	21,400	40,600	993.0	9,160	748	624	49,000
1998	17	114.93	41,200	4,040	3,190	12,900	21,100	4,040	12,700	21,100	40,800	986.0	8,770	731	533	48,800
1999	16	112.49	44,900	4,190	3,580	14,400	22,700	4,190	14,700	22,700	44,400	1,110.0	8,870	892	730	52,400
2000	15	113.95	45,600	4,200	3,810	15,000	22,500	4,190	13,600	22,500	43,300	1,040.0	8,960	642	500	51,600
2001[1]	17	120.02	44,800	4,120	3,310	17,000	20,400	4,090	14,600	20,400	42,200	1,110.0	12,900	1,120	984	54,000
2002[2]	18	120.02	40,300	4,100	3,390	13,500	19,300	4,070	11,400	19,300	37,700	1,010.0	8,160	689	585	45,100

[1] Preliminary.   [2] Estimate.   [3] Values are f.o.b. mine or refinery & do not include cost of cooperage or containers.   Source: U.S. Geological Survey

Salt Sold or Used by Producers in the U.S. by Classes & Consumers or Uses   In Thousands of Metric Tons

Year	Chemical[2]	Tanning Leather	Textile & Dyeing	Meat Packers	Canning	Baking	Agricultural Distribution	Feed Dealers	Feed Manufacturers	Rubber	Oil	Paper & Pulp	Metal Processing	Water Treatment	Grocery Stores	Water Conditioning Distrib.	Ice Control and/or Stabilization
1995	21,100	74	290	410	332	155	726	1,040	407	67	2,420	152	236	413	847	563	12,900
1996	22,400	83	288	407	336	169	661	1,150	403	71	2,430	122	199	534	855	719	17,700
1997	22,400	78	273	416	334	167	307	1,110	683	68	2,440	107	177	471	800	624	15,000
1998	22,000	93	250	440	275	219	362	1,190	536	68	2,320	115	170	531	807	598	9,490
1999	22,400	103	235	405	225	234	254	1,210	533	72	2,430	112	153	899	831	600	15,300
2000	22,400	82	209	402	220	234	262	1,240	540	71	2,510	106	112	589	823	568	19,700
2001	20,100	87	172	411	213	242	280	1,170	533	61	2,260	100	124	512	824	560	16,800
2002[1]	19,500	79	155	395	229	215	245	1,040	507	61	2,010	93	118	662	781	525	13,300

[1] Preliminary.   [2] Chloralkali producers and other chemical.   Source: U.S. Geological Survey (USGS)

Sheep & Lambs

Sheep and lambs are raised for both their wool and meat. In countries that have high wool production, there is also demand for sheep and lamb meat due to the easy availability. Production levels have declined in New Zealand and Australia, but that has been counteracted by a substantial increase in China.

Prices – The average price received by farmers for lambs in the US in 2003 (through November) rose sharply by +28.6% to 94.28 cents per pound from 73.33 cents in 2002 and the 9-year low of 67.61 cents in 2001. The average price received by farmers for sheep in the US (through November) rose by +19.4% to 34.66 cents per pound from the 11-year low of 29.03 cents in 2002. The average wholesale price of slaughter lambs (choice) at San Angelo, Texas in 2003 rose sharply by 26.9% to a record high of 91.74 cents per pound.

Supply – World sheep numbers in 2001 rose +0.7% to an 8-year high of 898.132 million sheep. The world's largest producers of sheep are China with 280.420 million (or 31.2% of world totals), India (20.2%), Australia (13.2%), and New Zealand (5.1%).

The number of sheep and lambs on US farms in 2003 (Jan 1) fell –5.0% to a record low of 6.350 million head, illustrating the downward trend in US sheep production. The US states with the most sheep and lambs were Texas (with 16.5% of the US total), California (12.4%), Wyoming (7.2%), South Dakota (6.0%), and Colorado (5.8%).

World Sheep and Goat Numbers in Specified Countries on January 1   In Thousands of Head

Year	Argentina	Australia	China	India	Kazak-hstan	New Zealand	Romania	Russia	South Africa	Spain	Turkey	United Kingdom	World Total
1992	25,706	161,073	206,210	161,084	34,556	55,162	13,879	55,255	36,076	24,625	44,700	28,932	931,903
1993	24,500	140,542	207,329	162,155	34,420	52,568	12,079	51,368	35,770	24,615	44,600	29,493	900,400
1994	23,500	120,900	217,314	169,569	34,208	50,298	12,276	43,700	33,800	23,872	44,000	29,333	881,258
1995	21,626	121,100	240,528	171,626	25,132	50,135	12,119	34,500	33,385	23,058	43,000	29,484	874,912
1996	17,956	121,200	279,535	173,519	19,600	48,816	11,086	28,336	35,145	21,322	42,400	28,797	897,009
1997	17,295	120,228	236,961	175,976	13,742	47,394	10,317	23,519	35,830	23,981	41,100	28,256	842,179
1998	15,232	117,494	255,055	178,462	10,896	46,970	9,747	20,697	36,821	24,857	39,500	30,027	853,061
1999	13,953	117,091	268,143	180,130	9,556	46,150	9,167	18,213	34,910	24,199	37,300	31,080	897,310
2000[1]	13,800	117,191	271,130	180,885	9,000	45,800	8,700	15,698	35,000	23,700	34,400	30,800	891,751
2001[2]	14,100	118,321	280,420	181,440	8,700	46,000	8,500	15,700	35,220	23,600	31,000	30,600	898,132

[1] Preliminary.   [2] Forecast.   *Source: Foreign Agricultural Service, U.S. Department of Agriculture (FAS-USDA)*

Salient Statistics of Sheep & Lambs in the United States (Average Live Weight)   In Thousands of Head

| | -- Inventory, Jan. 1 -- | | | | --- Marketings[3] --- | | ---------- Slaughter ---------- | | | | Total Disap-pearance | Pro-duction (Live Weight) Mil. Lbs. | Farm Value Jan. 1 | |
Year	Without New Crop Lambs	With New Crop Lambs	Lamb Crop	Total Supply	Sheep	Lambs	Farm	Com-mercial	Total[4]	Net Exports				All Million $	$ Per Head
1995	8,989	8,886	5,606	14,492	990	6,228	69	4,560	4,628	680	5,807	599.4	663.4	74.7
1996	8,465	8,461	5,282	13,743	1,024	6,023	65	4,184	4,249	264	5,488	565.7	732.2	86.5
1997	8,024	8,024	5,356	13,380	1,011	5,709	62	3,907	3,969	----	5,946	591.3	761.7	96.0
1998	7,825	7,825	5,007	12,832	977	5,510	57	3,804	3,861	----	----	555.7	797.8	102.0
1999	7,215	7,215	4,733	11,948	790	5,208	65	3,701	3,766	----	----	533.6	637.6	88.0
2000	7,032	7,032	4,622	11,654	788	4,827	67	3,460	3,527	----	----	508.9	668.8	95.0
2001	6,965	6,965	4,495	11,460	711	4,795	68	3,222	3,290	----	----	495.6	694.5	100.0
2002[1]	6,685	6,685	4,357	11,042	869	4,810	65	3,286	3,351	----	----	484.0	618.1	94.0
2003[2]	6,300	6,300	4,120	10,420									657.7	104.0

[1] Preliminary.   [2] Estimate.   [3] Excludes interfarm sales.   [4] Includes all commercial and farm.   Source: Economic Research Service, U.S. Department of Agriculture (ERS-USDA)

Sheep and Lambs[3] on Farms in the United States on January 1   In Thousands of Head

Year	California	Colorado	Idaho	Iowa	Minnesota	Montana	New Mexico	Ohio	South Dakota	Texas	Utah	Wyoming	Total
1996	1,000	535	273	345	185	465	265	153	500	1,650	395	680	8,461
1997	960	575	285	285	180	432	235	130	450	1,400	375	720	7,937
1998	800	575	285	265	165	415	290	135	420	1,530	420	710	7,825
1999	810	440	265	260	175	380	275	125	420	1,350	400	630	7,215
2000	800	440	275	265	165	370	290	134	420	1,200	400	570	7,032
2001	840	420	275	270	170	360	255	142	420	1,150	390	530	6,965
2002	800	370	260	250	160	335	230	140	400	1,130	365	480	6,685
2003[1]	730	380	260	255	145	310	175	150	380	1,040	310	460	6,300
2004[2]	680	360	260	250	140	300	160	140	370	1,100	265	430	6,090

[1] Preliminary.   [2] Estimate.   [3] Includes sheep & lambs on feed for market and stock sheep & lambs.   Source: Economic Research Service, U.S. Department of Agriculture (ERS-USDA)

SHEEP & LAMBS

Average Wholesale Price of Slaughter Lambs (Choice) at San Angelo Texas   In Dollars Per Cwt.

Year	Jan.	Feb.	Mar.	Apr.	May	June	July	Aug.	Sept.	Oct.	Nov.	Dec.	Average
1995	65.38	75.08	73.75	68.58	77.20	81.63	83.70	87.00	80.00	75.50	72.00	70.50	75.86
1996	74.44	85.63	84.07	83.10	86.17	97.50	92.67	83.75	84.40	82.58	80.00	88.88	85.27
1997	94.63	100.81	97.50	95.50	83.17	83.25	78.94	90.25	85.45	82.75	80.33	83.52	88.01
1998	74.38	74.31	71.50	63.00	73.00	91.21	82.21	82.05	69.50	67.20	63.33	71.44	73.59
1999	69.31	67.88	68.54	70.50	82.70	81.06	77.29	81.17	77.00	74.81	78.00	83.29	75.96
2000	73.71	76.83	78.17	78.25	89.65	78.30	84.17	82.20	82.00	77.50	76.70	75.33	79.40
2001	81.25	87.00	82.63	83.30	86.07	75.21	69.82	54.47	56.50	57.67	59.00	71.60	72.04
2002	65.85	70.00	64.00	65.15	64.06	68.75	75.83	74.35	73.69	76.20	83.00	86.88	72.31
2003[1]	89.25	90.25	96.25	88.13	95.75	97.25	87.88	85.81	91.44	91.31	91.00	96.17	91.71

[1] Preliminary.   Source: Economic Research Service, U.S. Department of Agriculture (ERS-USDA)

Federally Inspected Slaughter of Sheep & Lambs in the United States   In Thousands of Head

Year	Jan.	Feb.	Mar.	Apr.	May	June	July	Aug.	Sept.	Oct.	Nov.	Dec.	Total
1995	373	363	456	420	355	347	296	355	344	356	364	358	4,388
1996	352	353	403	374	313	271	313	315	313	365	324	336	4,032
1997	294	317	386	321	308	293	295	288	310	324	299	337	3,771
1998	301	300	377	367	270	283	269	263	295	312	290	344	3,671
1999	260	291	411	295	260	259	253	283	294	293	317	341	3,557
2000	271	284	334	330	248	247	229	269	257	266	286	287	3,308
2001	258	236	316	275	227	221	229	258	230	274	273	266	3,065
2002	244	244	311	263	267	216	241	246	259	284	255	262	3,092
2003[1]	227	211	252	280	209	216	225	226	241	251	223	246	2,805

[1] Preliminary.   Source: Economic Research Service, U.S. Department of Agriculture (ERS-USDA)

Cold Storage Holdings of Lamb and Mutton in the U.S., on First of Month   In Thousands of Pounds

Year	Jan.	Feb.	Mar.	Apr.	May	June	July	Aug.	Sept.	Oct.	Nov.	Dec.
1995	10,913	11,621	10,825	12,679	14,934	13,992	12,306	10,679	10,240	7,412	7,503	7,846
1996	7,606	9,794	13,017	12,247	13,649	12,187	13,726	13,164	14,645	11,249	10,494	9,788
1997	8,899	9,473	9,862	11,163	13,027	15,220	16,594	18,535	19,383	16,119	16,894	16,534
1998	13,741	13,920	15,284	16,226	16,306	16,666	16,040	16,188	14,530	12,253	12,558	11,914
1999	11,721	10,452	12,134	12,374	13,146	12,313	12,459	11,975	12,240	9,815	9,210	9,446
2000	8,740	10,394	10,335	11,437	13,345	13,137	13,984	13,557	14,042	12,867	12,195	12,486
2001	13,455	13,833	13,141	13,729	13,551	14,586	15,443	15,744	15,266	13,979	13,238	11,336
2002	11,905	13,110	11,269	10,528	13,172	12,938	13,553	14,215	14,458	11,961	12,004	9,255
2003[1]	7,124	6,232	4,063	3,900	5,016	5,838	5,427	5,929	5,855	6,210	4,485	4,883

[1] Preliminary.   Source: Economic Research Service, U.S. Department of Agriculture (ERS-USDA)

Average Price Received by Farmers for Sheep in the United States   In Dollars Per Cwt.

Year	Jan.	Feb.	Mar.	Apr.	May	June	July	Aug.	Sept.	Oct.	Nov.	Dec.	Average
1995	32.80	37.50	31.90	29.50	27.90	28.30	28.60	27.00	26.00	24.50	23.80	26.00	28.65
1996	34.40	33.80	34.00	27.30	25.30	26.60	30.50	29.10	30.20	28.80	29.80	34.20	30.33
1997	41.80	41.30	42.50	37.50	34.00	36.60	39.40	38.40	33.90	35.80	38.90	37.70	38.15
1998	42.00	39.60	41.00	34.40	30.30	30.20	29.40	28.30	26.80	26.10	26.40	30.10	32.05
1999	32.40	30.20	32.70	31.80	31.50	28.90	32.00	29.80	29.20	26.40	30.20	33.40	30.71
2000	36.80	39.50	38.80	35.00	30.50	30.00	34.20	30.70	30.30	29.50	33.60	36.20	33.76
2001	43.30	47.50	46.60	36.90	36.30	31.70	34.10	32.20	29.90	27.20	27.10	34.00	35.57
2002	36.20	34.30	31.80	26.00	25.30	23.50	25.60	25.60	24.50	25.60	31.30	38.70	29.03
2003[1]	41.30	44.00	40.20	30.90	31.10	30.30	28.60	28.30	32.10	34.80	40.10	44.40	35.51

[1] Preliminary.   Source: Economic Research Service, U.S. Department of Agriculture (ERS-USDA)

Average Price Received by Farmers for Lambs in the United States   In Dollars Per Cwt.

Year	Jan.	Feb.	Mar.	Apr.	May	June	July	Aug.	Sept.	Oct.	Nov.	Dec.	Average
1995	67.50	70.40	74.80	74.60	80.40	85.70	85.70	85.60	82.70	77.60	77.10	76.50	78.22
1996	76.10	84.30	86.60	85.90	90.30	100.70	98.30	89.10	88.50	87.00	84.60	88.20	88.30
1997	94.60	99.80	99.70	96.40	90.80	86.50	81.10	92.70	90.20	87.20	83.10	83.90	90.50
1998	78.40	75.00	70.10	66.00	63.00	88.90	81.30	80.10	71.80	67.60	62.60	64.70	72.46
1999	68.20	67.20	67.40	67.40	82.80	81.30	77.00	80.30	75.30	72.60	76.30	77.60	74.45
2000	70.90	72.00	80.20	82.60	96.40	89.70	87.00	83.60	80.80	76.80	71.50	71.80	80.28
2001	74.10	80.10	84.00	84.30	80.00	71.60	64.30	54.80	52.50	51.40	52.80	61.40	67.61
2002	65.50	67.80	66.70	64.70	64.40	72.90	75.60	75.30	76.30	79.60	84.00	87.20	73.33
2003[1]	92.00	92.40	97.10	93.60	97.50	96.70	89.40	87.60	94.70	96.90	99.20	98.40	94.63

[1] Preliminary.   Source: Economic Research Service, U.S. Department of Agriculture (ERS-USDA)

Silk

Silk is a fine, tough, elastic fiber produced by caterpillars, commonly called silkworms. Silk is one of the oldest known textile fibers. Chinese tradition credits Lady Hsi-Ling-Shih, wife of the Emperor Huang Ti, with the discovery of the silkworm and the invention of the first silk reel. Dating to around 3000 BC, a group of ribbons, threads, and woven fragments was found in China. Also found, along the lower Yangzi River, were 7,000 year-old spinning tools, silk thread, and fabric fragments.

Silk filament was first woven into cloth in Ancient China. The Chinese successfully guarded this secret until 300AD, when Japan, and later India, learned the secret. In 550 AD, two Nestorian monks were sent to China to steal mulberry seeds and silkworm eggs, which they hid in their walking staffs, and then brought back to Rome. By the 17th century, France was the silk center of the West. Unfortunately, the silkworm did not flourish in the English climate, nor has it ever flourished in the US.

Sericulture is the term for the raising of silkworms. More than 500 tiny eggs are laid by the blind, flightless moth, Bombyx mori. After hatching, the tiny worms eat chopped mulberry leaves continuously until they are ready to spin their cocoons. After gathering the complete cocoons, the first step in silk manufacturing is to kill the insects inside the cocoons with heat. The cocoons are then placed in boiling water to loosen the gummy substance, sericin, holding the filament together. The filament is unwound, and then rewound in a process called reeling. Each cocoon's silk filament is between 600 and 900 meters long. Four different types of silk thread may be produced: organzine, crepe, tram, and thrown singles. During the last 30 years, in spite of the use of man-made fibers, world silk production has doubled.

Raw silk is traded on the Kansai Agricultural Commodities Exchange (KANEX) in Japan. Dried cocoons are traded on the Chuba Commodity Exchange (CCE). Raw silk and dried cocoons are traded on the Yokohama Commodity Exchange.

Supply – World production of silk in 2000, the latest reporting year, rose +4.8% to 110,000 metric tons, recovering to a 5-year high after hitting a trough of 85,000 metric tons in 1997. China is the world's largest producer of silk by far with 69% of world production. Other producers include India with 14.5% of world production, and North Korea and Turkmenistan, each with 4.5% of world production.

Trade – The world's largest exporters of silk are China with 45.0% of world exports, Hong Kong with 3.2%, and North Korea with 2.8%. The world's largest importers of silk (1999) were Italy (with 15.3% of world imports), Japan (11.7%), India (8.8%), and South Korea (7.0%).

World Production of Raw Silk   In Metric Tons

Year	Brazil	China	India	Iran	Japan	North Korea	South Korea	Kyrgyzstan	Thailand	Turkmenistan	Uzbekistan	Viet Nam	World Total
1993	2,450	76,801	14,168	480	4,254	4,600	683	1,000	1,500	500	2,000	550	109,790
1994	2,450	84,001	14,500	600	2,400	4,700	700	1,000	1,600	500	2,000	600	115,796
1995	2,450	80,001	15,000	600	2,400	4,700	700	1,000	1,600	500	2,000	650	112,350
1996	2,000	51,000	16,000	1,000	3,000	5,000	----	1,000	1,000	5,000	2,000	1,000	88,000
1997	2,000	51,000	16,000	1,000	2,000	4,000	----	1,000	1,000	5,000	2,000	1,000	85,000
1998	2,000	68,000	16,000	1,000	1,000	5,000	----	1,000	1,000	5,000	2,000	1,000	102,000
1999	2,000	70,000	16,000	1,000	1,000	5,000	----	1,000	1,000	5,000	1,000	1,000	98,000
2000	2,000	78,000	15,000	1,000	1,000	5,000	----	1,000	1,000	5,000	1,000	3,000	107,000
2001[1]	2,000	94,000	15,000	1,000	1,000	----	----	1,000	2,000	5,000	1,000	10,000	131,000
2002[2]	1,000	94,000	15,000	1,000	1,000	----	----	----	2,000	4,000	1,000	12,000	132,000

[1] Preliminary.   [2] Estimate.   *Source: Food and Agricultural Organization of the United Nations (FAO-UN)*

World Trade of Silk by Selected Countries   In Metric Tons

Year	Imports							Exports					
	France	Hong Kong	India	Italy	Japan	South Korea	World Total	Brazil	China	Hong Kong	Japan	North Korea	World Total
1992	693	4,400	2,843	4,337	5,137	3,627	28,239	1,552	13,474	4,358	701	800	26,433
1993	1,001	5,475	4,977	5,634	5,982	4,494	36,086	1,495	15,652	7,204	904	1,200	35,634
1994	1,047	6,165	5,750	9,235	5,772	4,128	44,136	1,739	21,004	6,149	1,265	1,400	41,998
1995	663	4,775	4,276	5,612	4,331	3,513	37,854	966	16,788	5,176	925	1,000	40,633
1996	675	3,978	2,980	4,400	6,098	3,737	37,615	1,071	15,791	4,165	946	1,000	38,587
1997	582	4,320	2,437	5,482	4,229	2,796	45,817	905	14,384	4,501	936	1,000	37,233
1998	592	2,030	2,846	4,088	3,357	1,510	31,908	780	12,250	2,105	612	180	29,611
1999	579	1,258	5,120	4,985	3,792	2,265	35,352	408	16,251	1,153	227	130	35,041
2000	481	866	4,732	5,906	4,020	1,843	32,974	370	17,520	936	239	120	34,974
2001[1]	452	256	6,929	4,506	2,823	1,628	27,789	232	14,485	259	124	90	26,592

[1] Preliminary.   *Source: Food and Agricultural Organization of the United Nations (FAO-UN)*

Silver

Silver is a white, lustrous metallic element that conducts heat and electricity better than any other metal. In ancient times, many silver deposits were on or near the earth's surface. Before 2,500 BC, silver mines were worked in Asia Minor. Around 700 BC, ancient Greeks stamped a turtle on their first silver coins. Silver assumed a key role in the US monetary system in 1792 when Congress based the currency on the silver dollar, but then discontinued the use of silver in coinage in 1965. Today Mexico is the only country that uses silver in its circulating coinage.

Silver is the most malleable and ductile of all metals, with the exception of gold. Silver melts at about 962 degrees Celsius and boils at about 2212 degrees Celsius. Silver is not very chemically active, although tarnishing occurs when sulfur and sulfides attack silver, forming silver sulfide on the surface of the metal. Because silver is too soft in its pure form, a hardening agent, usually copper, is mixed into the silver. Copper is usually used as the hardening agent because it does not discolor the silver. The term "sterling silver" means silver that contains at least 925 parts of silver per thousand (92.5%) to 75 parts of copper (7.5%).

Silver is usually found combined with other elements in minerals and ores. In the US, silver is mined in conjunction with lead, copper, and zinc. Most of the world's mined silver comes from Mexico, the US, and Peru. Nevada, Idaho, Alaska, and Arizona are the leading silver-producing states. Industrially, silver is used for jewelry, photography, electrical appliances, glass, and as an antibacterial agent for the health industry.

Silver futures and options are traded on the Comex division of the New York Mercantile Exchange, the Chicago Board of Trade (CBOT), and the London Metal Exchange (LME). Silver futures are traded on the Tokyo Commodity Exchange (TOCOM). The Comex silver futures contract calls for the delivery of 5,000 troy ounces of silver (0.999 fineness) and is priced in terms of dollars and cents per troy ounce.

Prices – Comex silver futures prices showed some strength early in 2003 on the Iraq war but then fell into a trading range through summer. Silver then began a fairly steady bull market in July, rallying to finally post a 3-year high of $5.98 by the end of December. Silver futures closed 2003 at $5.95, up 22% from $4.89 in 2002. Although silver futures closed 2003 at a 3-year high, the market was still well below the 15-year high of $7.26 posted in February 1998. The highest month-end price ever reached for cash silver was $38 per troy ounce back in January 1980. Bullish factors for silver in the latter half of 2003 centered on the weak dollar and the rebound in the US economy, which boosted industrial use of silver.

Supply – World production of silver in 2001, the latest full reporting year, rose +2.2% to 18.700 million metric tons from 18.300 million metric tons in 2000. There are many producing nations for silver, but the largest are Mexico (with 14.8% of world production in 2001), Peru (12.6%), Australia (11.2%), China (9.6%), and the US (9.3%). US production of refined silver in 2003 was on track to fall to 4,900 metric tons, down from 5,441 metric tons in 2002.

Demand – US consumption of silver in 2001 fell 6.8% to 187.4 million troy ounces from 201.1 million in 2000. The largest demand for silver usage by far comes from photographic materials with 54.4% of total usage, followed by electrical contacts and conductors (15.7%), brazing allows and solders (4.5%), catalysts (3.3%), batteries (2.8%), jewelry (2.6%), sterling ware (2.5%), silver plate (2.1%), and mirrors (1.3%). The world's largest consuming nation of silver for industrial purposes is the US with 20.2% of world consumption, followed by India and Japan (both at 14.7%), and Italy (6.5%).

Trade – US exports of silver in 2001 rose to 707,000 troy ounces from 279,000 in 2000, but the 2000 and 2001 levels were sharply lower than the levels seen in the previous several years (e.g., 15.455 million troy ounces in 1999, 72.479 million troy ounces in 1998, and 96.039 million troy ounces in 1997). The largest destination for US silver exports is the UK with 615,000 troy ounces of exports in 2001. US imports of silver ore and concentrates were almost solely from Canada and rose sharply to 7.55 million troy ounces in 2001 from 1.420 million in 2000. US imports of silver bullion fell to 2.935 million troy ounces in 2001 from 3.810 million in 2000. The bulk of those imports came from Canada (1.370 million troy ounces) and Mexico (1.280 million).

World Mine Production of Silver   In Thousands of Kilograms In Metric Tons

Year	Australia	Bolivia	Canada[3]	Chile	China	Kazak-hstan[4]	Rep. of Korea	Mexico	Peru	Poland	Sweden	United States	World Total[2]
1993	1,092	333	896	970	840	500	215	2,136	1,671	767	255	1,640	14,100
1994	1,045	352	768	983	810	506	257	2,215	1,768	1,064	276	1,490	14,000
1995	939	425	1,285	1,041	910	489	299	2,324	1,929	1,001	268	1,560	14,900
1996	1,013	384	1,309	1,047	1,140	468	254	2,528	1,970	935	272	1,570	15,100
1997	1,106	387	1,224	1,091	1,300	690	268	2,679	2,090	1,038	304	2,180	16,500
1998	1,474	404	1,196	1,340	1,300	726	339	2,686	2,025	1,108	299	2,060	17,200
1999	1,720	422	1,174	1,381	1,320	905	489	2,467	2,231	1,100	284	1,950	17,600
2000	2,060	434	1,212	1,242	1,600	927	591	2,620	2,145	1,148	329	1,980	18,400
2001[1]	2,100	408	1,265	1,348	1,910	982	665	2,760	2,353	1,194	306	1,740	19,300
2002[2]	2,077	450	1,344	1,350	2,500	892	650	2,748	2,687	1,200	299	1,420	20,000

[1] Preliminary.   [2] Estimate.   [3] Shipments.   [4] Formerly part of the U.S.S.R.; data not reported separately until 1992.

Source: U.S. Geological Survey (USGS)

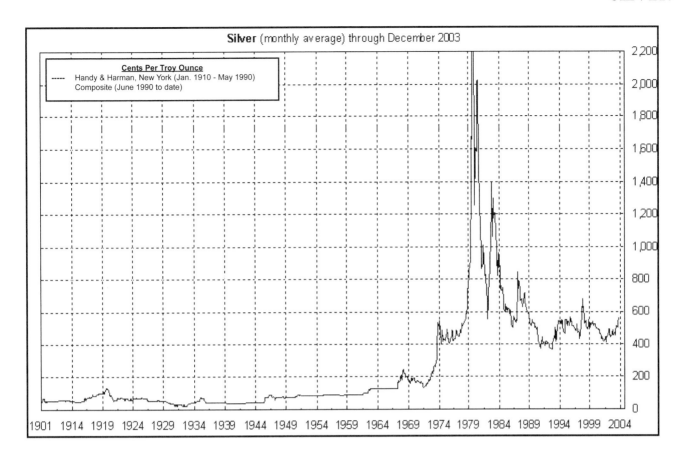

Average Price of Silver in New York (Handy & Harman)   In Cents Per Troy Ounce (.999 Fine)

Year	Jan.	Feb.	Mar.	Apr.	May	June	July	Aug.	Sept.	Oct.	Nov.	Dec.	Average
1994	513.14	527.24	545.11	530.87	543.64	539.34	528.65	519.54	552.88	544.10	519.60	476.88	528.42
1995	476.36	469.53	464.83	552.42	555.25	535.27	517.58	539.59	540.78	534.48	529.30	514.75	519.18
1996	547.03	562.75	551.38	540.14	536.02	513.58	502.95	510.50	501.57	492.76	481.69	480.14	518.34
1997	483.70	508.76	519.88	476.41	475.80	474.60	435.96	451.36	472.69	501.15	507.30	571.53	489.07
1998	584.58	672.61	617.18	628.86	558.65	526.05	546.82	516.45	502.67	500.18	498.39	476.85	552.68
1999	511.61	554.55	519.85	509.21	529.83	507.73	522.81	529.36	527.86	541.67	519.20	521.95	524.75
2000	523.47	529.65	510.15	510.37	504.30	505.20	501.82	492.76	494.50	488.14	471.93	466.40	499.89
2001	470.19	457.34	439.93	439.25	443.59	436.79	425.45	420.72	441.09	441.87	412.35	437.98	438.88
2002	450.17	444.79	457.00	460.50	473.55	492.13	494.57	456.16	458.93	442.28	453.87	465.78	462.39
2003	485.62	468.11	454.74	453.40	475.29	455.62	486.48	502.90	520.62	503.91	520.64	565.33	491.06

Source: American Metal Market (AMM)

Average Price of Silver in London (Spot Fix)   In Pence Per Troy Ounce (.999 Fine)

Year	Jan.	Feb.	Mar.	Apr.	May	June	July	Aug.	Sept.	Oct.	Nov.	Dec.	Average
1994	344.48	354.77	364.74	358.95	360.86	353.28	341.86	336.67	353.15	339.73	326.64	306.49	345.14
1995	302.80	300.36	290.35	341.95	248.74	336.31	323.80	343.72	348.99	340.29	339.90	336.05	329.44
1996	359.20	367.64	362.03	392.85	354.25	334.68	325.81	330.93	322.98	310.78	290.51	289.77	336.79
1997	287.63	311.95	323.99	293.08	291.43	289.16	272.73	280.36	295.67	308.69	300.76	348.90	300.36
1998	359.62	416.55	375.76	378.77	339.42	319.05	331.87	317.74	297.40	295.41	298.72	291.77	335.17
1999	312.69	340.46	320.27	315.12	326.80	315.51	328.86	327.98	322.20	326.42	317.53	319.87	322.75
2000	316.08	327.90	320.87	319.61	330.53	331.24	329.35	327.80	340.75	332.24	327.71	317.47	326.94
2001	315.87	312.57	304.50	304.36	310.19	309.54	300.97	277.97	297.93	289.21	286.92	306.25	302.43
2002	315.08	310.55	318.27	316.61	322.58	329.32	316.07	295.93	292.38	282.49	286.93	291.52	306.48
2003	297.21	289.23	287.39	285.06	292.05	272.79	295.53	313.01	320.30	298.01	306.53		296.10

Source: American Metal Market (AMM)

SILVER

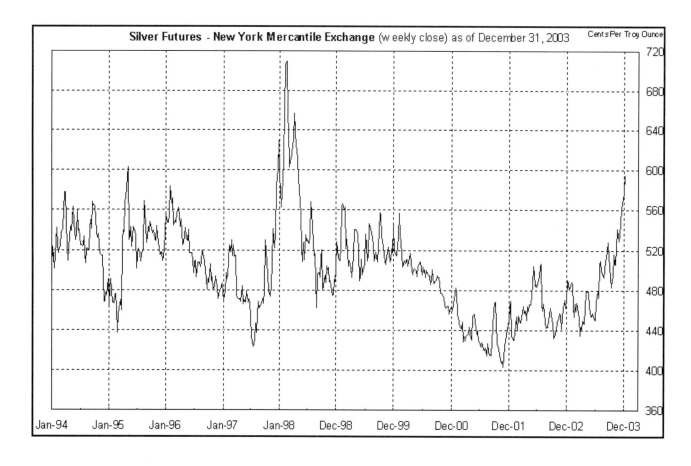

Average Open Interest of Silver Futures in New York (COMEX)　In Contracts

Year	Jan.	Feb.	Mar.	Apr.	May	June	July	Aug.	Sept.	Oct.	Nov.	Dec.
1994	112,584	116,652	112,745	119,314	121,296	126,255	122,138	118,081	113,261	117,224	126,666	134,099
1995	132,158	139,806	132,317	129,063	112,723	108,941	101,842	111,251	95,433	101,763	105,453	95,551
1996	99,316	107,667	92,186	101,011	99,529	110,247	105,627	103,618	93,448	95,809	93,238	83,879
1997	91,385	94,539	90,531	97,434	87,510	90,145	96,777	89,250	79,344	100,464	96,695	93,761
1998	95,717	108,284	91,730	83,045	79,451	91,563	78,353	82,530	74,848	74,451	76,440	78,716
1999	77,946	97,593	82,435	82,824	78,745	78,943	78,151	86,601	77,490	86,577	80,564	70,275
2000	76,187	81,398	75,765	76,213	75,001	76,466	75,199	91,083	73,441	78,222	83,142	73,644
2001	69,408	72,798	74,337	71,589	67,328	67,429	75,019	75,830	65,533	66,530	74,228	66,903
2002	67,442	65,355	67,405	76,158	82,525	100,837	94,731	82,349	80,511	89,094	85,434	78,174
2003	98,561	94,472	84,485	87,445	85,232	80,001	91,544	108,118	110,423	92,216	101,303	103,044

Source: New York Mercantile Exchange (NYMEX), COMEX Division

Volume of Trading of Silver Futures in New York (COMEX)　In Contracts

Year	Jan.	Feb.	Mar.	Apr.	May	June	July	Aug.	Sept.	Oct.	Nov.	Dec.	Total
1994	489,055	555,136	484,134	585,058	516,396	729,414	339,298	535,722	377,540	455,049	589,220	348,323	5,994,345
1995	390,453	501,454	541,807	592,620	500,522	476,481	280,651	655,854	344,182	272,362	447,095	179,755	5,183,236
1996	415,801	583,767	368,175	547,629	334,973	549,631	296,905	460,686	316,366	321,781	415,441	259,653	4,870,808
1997	401,995	530,514	360,871	493,999	280,536	472,306	340,245	425,471	335,400	430,397	488,024	333,762	4,893,520
1998	352,688	550,800	368,127	360,130	310,130	393,971	278,774	367,257	283,475	280,066	319,216	229,982	4,094,616
1999	315,165	550,271	355,559	424,822	274,002	373,662	288,480	422,653	328,907	318,256	344,289	161,434	4,157,500
2000	258,053	425,910	231,336	318,752	216,938	407,455	175,235	370,739	146,007	149,252	303,673	113,667	3,117,017
2001	175,026	302,035	155,658	252,486	204,552	281,846	112,956	267,711	160,329	210,266	266,077	180,256	2,569,198
2002	265,773	271,293	163,898	325,889	243,475	389,798	281,214	296,579	164,537	209,249	292,861	230,998	3,135,564
2003	291,120	409,737	216,660	315,240	251,096	352,729	407,931	442,762	335,508	373,493	464,244	250,835	4,111,355

Source: New York Mercantile Exchange (NYMEX), COMEX division

Mine Production of Recoverable Silver in the United States   In Metric Tons

Year	Arizona	California	Colorado	Idaho	Missouri	Montana	Nevada	New Mexico	South Dakota	Washington	Other States	Total
1997	190	23	W	341	W	W	787	W	4	2	833	2,180
1998	211	11	W	447	W	W	670	W	2	1	723	2,060
1999	183	8	W	416	W	W	597	W	W	W	748	1,950
2000	W	8	3	W	W	W	734	W	W	2	1,240	1,980
2001	W	8	3	W	W	W	544	W	W	W	1,180	1,740
2002[1]	W	3	W	W	W	W	424	W	W	W	994	1,420

[1] Preliminary.   W = Withheld proprietary data; included in Other States.   *Source: U.S. Geological Survey (USGS)*

Consumption of Silver in the United States, by End Use   In Millions of Troy Ounces

Year	Brazing Alloy & Solders	Catalysts	Batteries	Mirrors	Electrical Contacts-Conductors	Photo-graphic Materials	Silver-plate	Jewerly	Sterling Ware	Total Net Industrial Con-sumption	Coinage	Total Con-sumption
1992	7.1	3.8	3.1	1.2	18.3	64.4	2.9	3.0	3.9	118.9	8.1	127.0
1993	7.2	4.0	3.3	1.3	18.8	65.0	3.0	3.3	4.0	121.1	8.9	130.0
1994	7.5	4.2	3.6	1.5	19.5	71.0	3.1	3.7	4.2	130.1	8.1	138.2
1995	7.7	4.9	4.1	1.7	20.9	72.9	3.5	4.1	4.4	136.2	7.5	143.7
1996	8.2	5.5	4.5	2.1	22.3	78.3	3.9	4.4	4.8	146.7	5.0	151.7
1997	8.9	5.7	4.8	2.4	26.5	84.6	4.1	4.9	5.1	160.5	5.3	165.8
1998	9.3	5.9	4.9	2.6	28.4	91.0	4.5	5.5	5.7	172.3	5.6	177.9
1999	9.1	5.9	5.0	2.6	29.2	96.0	4.4	5.7	5.8	178.5	10.0	188.5
2000	8.6	6.3	5.2	2.6	32.7	104.0	4.5	6.1	5.6	191.1	10.0	201.1
2001[1]	8.5	6.1	5.3	2.5	29.5	102.0	4.0	4.9	4.6	NA	NA	187.4

[1] Preliminary.   *Source: The Silver Institute*

Commodity Exchange, Inc. (COMEX) Warehouse of Stocks of Silver   In Thousands of Troy Ounces

Year	Jan. 1	Feb. 1	Mar. 1	Apr. 1	May 1	June 1	July 1	Aug. 1	Sept. 1	Oct. 1	Nov. 1	Dec. 1
1994	251,685	250,730	239,374	240,187	233,950	236,459	246,291	249,417	255,198	259,634	265,710	258,618
1995	260,708	264,045	235,114	211,028	189,668	184,570	181,269	175,764	156,544	156,529	156,110	156,932
1996	159,695	143,426	151,336	139,059	141,789	150,141	168,079	155,441	151,283	141,673	129,911	148,451
1997	204,051	195,450	193,381	191,676	189,498	201,682	184,691	169,079	164,296	138,775	133,470	128,252
1998	110,437	103,778	89,458	86,926	89,715	89,628	85,911	79,136	78,681	73,142	74,260	76,818
1999	75,807	75,108	78,135	79,605	78,819	77,512	73,514	77,592	79,606	79,391	79,155	78,416
2000	75,945	73,948	93,782	104,259	102,589	99,285	102,713	102,291	97,879	99,552	95,749	95,717
2001	93,983	93,195	98,659	96,694	95,745	96,090	98,700	100,494	102,770	101,538	103,982	105,235
2002	104,547	102,395	100,983	102,540	104,526	107,766	105,938	105,563	108,090	107,495	107,440	107,090
2003	107,394	107,610	109,153	108,521	108,168	NA	107,222	105,406	104,862	106,283	118,238	124,498

Source: New York Mercantile Exchange (NYMEX), COMEX Division

Production[2] of Refined Silver in the United States, from All Sources   In Metric Tons

Year	Jan.	Feb.	Mar.	Apr.	May	June	July	Aug.	Sept.	Oct.	Nov.	Dec.	Total
1994	278	327	319	307	209	371	239	288	273	254	297	281	3,443
1995	279	273	340	281	381	355	331	404	364	340	384	351	4,083
1996	373	299	332	321	327	316	354	314	333	344	304	403	4,020
1997	343	262	296	331	250	326	292	344	331	281	340	382	3,778
1998	338	486	426	372	377	374	394	324	463	443	469	447	4,860
1999	424	420	441	356	368	394	404	316	354	371	364	396	4,608
2000	436	1,177	551	399	431	390	361	402	400	469	386	401	5,780
2001	405	343	405	360	360	331	395	380	338	403	442	383	4,545
2002	544	387	465	532	509	398	398	419	473	437	394	485	5,441
2003[1]	483	426	320	412	357	431	430	373	361	810			5,283

[1] Preliminary.   [2] Includes U.S. mine production of recoverable silver plus imports of refined silver.   *Source: U.S. Geological Survey (USGS)*

SILVER

U.S. Exports of Refined Silver to Selected Countries   In Thousands of Troy Ounces

Year	Canada	France	Ger-many	Hong Kong	Japan	Singa-pore	South Korea	Switzer-land	United Arab Emirates	United Kingdom	Uruguay	Other Countries	World Total
1993	4,910	[2]	34	1,002	3,414	2,500	1,492	38	4,403	3,673	530	44	22,673
1994	3,138	[2]	8	456	10,385	16	2,701	14	4,823	4,212	1,489	14	27,889
1995	1,665	431	[2]	[2]	5,819	2,209	2,932	1,177	10,288	63,980	939	5	90,462
1996	489	[2]	2	646	4,662	3,601	383	2,413	15,850	35,366	624	40	93,346
1997	1,861	[2]	2	797	6,044	[2]	547	5,369	16,750	62,693	402	57	99,022
1998	669	2,205	347	45	585	210	----	604	3,569	62,693	688	38	80,375
1999	2,180	2	1	----	585	37	31	624	4,244	7,716	180	5	19,804
2000	1,906	22	2	----	3,504	1	----	727	----	3,311	109	1	12,217
2001	1,598	----	----	11	1,202	2	----	354	----	20,029	105	----	30,960
2002[1]	466	----	1	4	466	10	----	727	----	14,532	----	----	28,196

[1] Preliminary.   [2] Included in other countries, if any.   *Source: American Bureau of Metal Statistics, Inc. (ABMS)*

U.S. Imports of Silver From Selected Countries   In Thousands of Troy Ounces

Year	Canada	Mexico	Other Countries	Total	Canada	Chile	Mexico	Peru	Uruguay	Other Countries	Total
1993	299	836	12	1,147	28,622	1,058	27,241	12,709	[2]	559	70,189
1994	369	3,805	97	4,271	28,678	1,923	22,135	12,663	[2]	742	66,141
1995	338	6,655	243	7,236	27,649	2,003	31,957	13,728	[2]	9,197	84,534
1996	256	4,662	----	4,918	35,365	1,874	30,285	12,153	[2]	3,122	82,799
1997	7	4,437	90	4,533	29,385	608	28,774	8,873	----	518	68,158
1998	24	5,851	427	6,301	34,722	813	41,152	9,388	----	3,945	90,020
1999	11	334	2	347	43,403	1,048	33,115	5,433	----	2,521	85,519
2000	46	----	----	46	38,902	225	44,689	2,787	----	35,899	122,502
2001	243	----	----	243	44,046	2,054	41,152	5,498	----	1,771	94,521
2002[1]	149	1,813	----	1,961	48,868	2,331	67,837	6,430	----	3,778	129,243

[1] Preliminary.   [2] Included in other countries, if any.   *Source: American Bureau of Metal Statistics, Inc. (ABMS)*

World Silver Consumption[1]   In Millions of Troy Ounces

Year	Canada	France	Ger-many	India	Italy	Japan	Mexico	United Kingdom	United States	World Total	Austria	Canada	France	Ger-many	Mexico	United States	World Total	Grand Total
	Industrial Uses										Coinage							
1993	1.6	28.1	45.7	108.8	56.3	105.5	14.9	27.7	131.6	739.1	.5	1.2	2.1	2.8	17.1	9.2	41.5	780.6
1994	1.6	27.2	45.7	93.9	51.6	108.4	14.6	30.4	140.4	722.4	.5	1.5	1.0	7.1	13.0	9.5	43.8	766.2
1995	2.0	30.0	43.6	101.3	49.5	112.7	16.9	31.6	148.7	752.7	.5	.7	1.2	2.4	.6	9.0	24.7	777.4
1996	2.0	26.9	41.0	122.2	51.7	112.1	20.3	33.8	155.0	785.8	.5	.7	.3	4.6	.5	7.1	23.3	809.1
1997	2.2	28.3	42.3	122.9	56.1	119.9	23.3	34.9	166.3	828.2	.4	.6	.3	3.7	.4	6.5	28.5	856.7
1998	2.3	28.4	38.4	114.7	55.9	112.8	21.7	38.6	162.2	800.6	.3	1.1	.3	10.0	.2	7.0	27.8	828.5
1999	2.1	26.6	35.1	121.5	61.8	122.5	22.3	39.3	173.5	839.5	.3	1.4	.3	7.0	.4	10.7	29.2	868.6
2000	2.0	28.8	31.8	131.0	65.1	135.0	17.7	42.7	180.0	876.4	.3	1.0	.4	8.8	.6	13.4	32.2	908.6
2001	2.0	28.7	32.4	154.0	55.5	119.3	16.8	46.0	157.3	838.0	.3	.9	.4	8.1	1.1	12.3	30.5	868.5
2002[2]	2.1	27.1	29.4	118.5	52.8	118.6	17.9	43.6	162.9	806.9	.4	1.0	.5	6.0	1.1	14.2	31.3	838.2

[1] Non-communist areas only.   [2] Preliminary.   *Source: The Silver Institute*

Soybean Meal

Soybean meal is produced through processing and separating soybeans into oil and meal components. By weight, soybean meal accounts for about 35% of the weight of raw soybeans (at 13% moisture). If the soybeans are of particularly good quality, then the processor can get more meal weight by including more hulls in the meal while still meeting the 48% protein minimum. Soybean meal can be further processed into soy flour and isolated soy protein, but the bulk of soybean meal is used as animal feed for poultry, hogs and cattle. Soybean meal accounts for about two-thirds of the world's high-protein animal feed, followed by cottonseed and rapeseed meal, which together account for less than 20%. Soybean meal futures and options are traded on the Chicago Board of Trade (CBOT). The CBOT soybean meal futures contract calls for the delivery of 100 tons of soybean meal produced by conditioning ground soybeans and reducing the oil content of the conditioned product and having a minimum of 48.0% protein, minimum of 0.5% fat, maximum of 3.5% fiber, and maximum of 12.0% moisture.

Soybean crush – The term soybean "crush" refers to both the physical processing of soybeans and also to the dollar-value premium received for processing soybeans into their component products of meal and oil. The conventional model says that processing 60 pounds (one bushel) of soybeans produces 11 pounds of soybean oil, 44 pounds of 48% protein soybean meal, 3 pounds of hulls, and 1 pound of waste. The Gross Processing Margin (GPM) or crush equals (0.22 times Soybean Meal Prices in dollars per ton) + (11 times Soybean Oil prices in cents/pound) – Soybean prices in $/bushel. A higher crush value will occur when the price of the meal and oil products are strong relative to soybeans, e.g., because of supply disruptions or because of an increase in demand for the products. When the crush value is high, companies will have a strong incentive to buy raw soybeans and boost the output of the products. That supply increase will eventually bring the crush value back into line with the long-term equilibrium.

Prices – Soybean meal prices in 2003 rallied sharply by 38% to new 6-year highs, adding to the 15% rally seen in 2002. Despite that rally, the 2003 yearly close near $242

per ton was still well below the 15-year high of $308.5 posted in 1997 and the record high of $336.5 posted in 1988. Bullish factors centered on heavy Chinese buying and tight supplies. In addition, the emergence of mad cow disease in North America in 2003 (Canada in May and the US in December) seems destined to boost demand for soybean meal Rendered beef was already banned from the feed of cattle due to mad cow disease. Then as 2003 ended, it appeared that widespread concern about mad cow disease might cause officials to also ban rendered beef from the feed of other animals including hogs, poultry and pets. That would sharply boost demand for soybean meal due to its high protein content and its ability to quickly fatten up animals.

Supply – World soybean meal production in 2002/3 rose to a record 130.140 million metric tons, up 4.1% from the previous year's 125.030 million tons. The world's largest producers of soybean meal in 2002/03 were the US with 35.489 million tons of production (27%), Brazil with 20.909 million tons (16%), and the European Union with 17.880 million tons (14%). US soybean meal production in 2003/04 was forecasted at 35.340 million short tons, down 7.5% from the preliminary figure of 38.213 million in 2002/03 and down from the record high of 40.292 million short tons in 2001/02.

Demand – World soybean meal consumption in 2002/03 of a record high 129.6 million tons compares with 124.2 million in 2001/02 and less than 100 million as recently as 1997/98. The US is the largest single consumer with about 30 million tons of annual consumption recent years, but collectively the European Union and especially Asia have closed the gap with 29 million and 36 million tons, respectively. Asia's increasing use reflects the expansion in the region's poultry production.

Trade – US exports of soybean meal are forecasted at 4.08 million metric tons in 2003/4, down from 5.47 million metric tons in 2002/3. US exports of soybean meal in 2003/4 were down sharply by 42% from the recent peak of 6.99 million metric tons in 2000/01. The countries that import the largest volume of soybean meal from the US are Canada (17%), Philippines (11%), and Mexico (8%).

World Supply and Distribution of Soybean Meal   In Thousands of Metric Tons

Year Beginning Oct. 1	Production Brazil	China	European Union	United States	Total	Exports Brazil	United States	Total	Imports France	Total	Consumption European Union	United States	Total	Ending Stocks Brazil	United States	Total
1994-5	15,869	6,958	11,984	30,182	89,302	10,445	6,092	32,389	3,792	31,588	25,412	24,081	87,812	984	203	3,729
1995-6	17,040	6,051	11,220	29,508	87,895	11,941	5,446	32,220	3,343	32,823	23,719	24,140	88,754	973	193	3,473
1996-7	15,722	5,963	11,428	31,035	89,607	10,660	6,344	32,593	3,266	34,389	22,340	24,785	91,785	835	191	3,091
1997-8	15,728	6,717	12,126	34,633	103,681	9,588	8,464	41,495	3,647	37,602	24,562	26,213	99,924	975	198	2,955
1998-9	16,595	10,023	12,354	34,285	107,540	9,830	6,461	38,980	4,106	38,970	27,258	27,812	106,340	1,190	300	5,100
1999-00	16,745	11,975	11,231	34,102	107,470	9,932	6,652	35,370	4,154	36,240	26,670	27,529	109,350	903	266	4,150
2000-1	17,863	15,050	13,229	35,730	116,420	10,679	6,988	37,230	4,416	38,330	28,541	28,706	117,880	721	348	3,790
2001-2	19,469	16,300	13,906	36,552	125,300	11,975	6,811	42,360	4,610	43,990	30,919	30,001	126,630	645	218	4,100
2002-3[1]	21,679	21,500	12,635	34,666	131,370	13,750	5,455	44,030	4,695	45,800	30,682	29,380	133,550	649	200	3,700
2003-4[2]	24,970	24,050	13,910	31,529	138,780	16,500	3,856	48,130		48,780	32,517	28,123	139,410	669	181	3,720

[1] Preliminary.   [2] Forecast.   *Source: Foreign Agricultural Service, U.S. Department of Agriculture (FAS-USDA)*

SOYBEAN MEAL

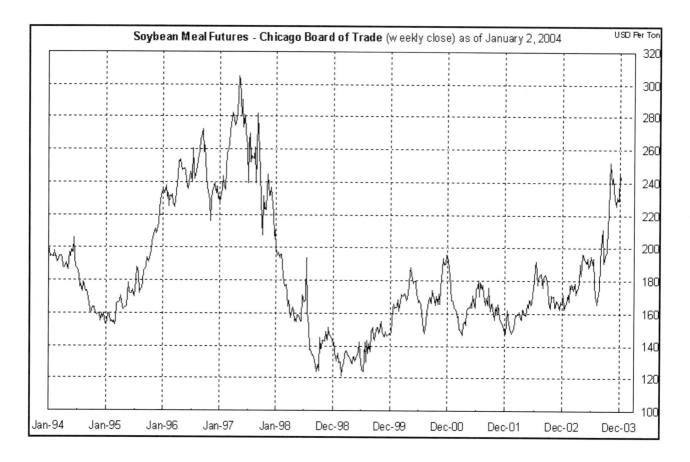

Average Open Interest of Soybean Meal Futures in Chicago   In Contracts

Year	Jan.	Feb.	Mar.	Apr.	May	June	July	Aug.	Sept.	Oct.	Nov.	Dec.
1994	87,612	91,142	82,193	89,453	85,553	81,721	84,461	82,691	85,508	94,483	101,030	98,717
1995	97,661	101,253	101,846	99,898	90,237	86,090	83,712	74,233	79,450	85,290	103,824	110,193
1996	95,903	90,010	87,468	101,204	91,453	88,641	77,961	80,727	93,373	88,969	90,007	84,399
1997	86,204	97,618	107,763	111,413	113,848	110,780	114,372	108,923	111,447	118,409	125,201	116,760
1998	114,243	122,979	131,390	137,251	136,212	136,216	126,108	139,239	140,904	141,426	134,095	122,788
1999	123,041	130,473	121,435	112,155	104,176	108,134	116,464	121,202	120,462	112,426	117,523	104,246
2000	115,285	124,822	120,157	123,957	123,691	112,425	105,230	94,469	105,240	103,263	120,164	127,529
2001	111,880	108,047	107,253	116,888	119,644	135,046	134,982	129,536	123,644	121,845	145,996	147,576
2002	146,674	137,425	134,880	130,138	132,376	143,956	142,728	132,996	137,799	131,249	137,836	140,902
2003	154,821	168,036	157,670	163,532	163,096	154,985	152,121	146,582	153,505	169,709	170,707	176,191

Source: Chicago Board of Trade (CBT)

Volume of Trading of Soybean Meal Futures in Chicago   In Contracts

Year	Jan.	Feb.	Mar.	Apr.	May	June	July	Aug.	Sept.	Oct.	Nov.	Dec.	Total[1]
1994	405,590	339,834	330,694	380,736	467,223	456,279	384,508	354,372	366,263	317,438	370,377	420,500	4,593.8
1995	283,623	307,477	404,387	410,860	532,694	479,589	610,833	491,775	481,949	449,009	523,440	625,606	5,601.2
1996	496,414	442,937	435,764	655,984	439,212	442,370	507,240	490,349	425,850	581,126	491,917	452,139	5,861.3
1997	479,001	481,841	509,515	576,564	581,886	569,760	579,748	452,188	531,299	589,542	561,133	512,471	6,424.9
1998	458,519	454,310	449,806	592,614	499,468	749,765	675,104	536,650	504,088	553,224	521,231	559,067	6,553.8
1999	420,240	509,348	476,104	477,102	390,527	646,806	710,110	597,026	568,859	511,503	572,194	447,078	6,326.9
2000	455,335	537,527	556,010	467,698	566,607	606,190	488,172	469,017	484,617	483,174	690,313	513,328	6,318.0
2001	530,193	431,822	470,608	485,106	584,352	625,089	709,973	630,909	491,398	652,931	659,328	472,063	6,743.8
2002	610,275	398,294	424,684	618,880	567,221	664,687	806,395	673,705	581,155	613,701	657,822	557,688	7,174.5
2003	639,628	551,401	527,723	676,739	599,614	749,844	772,104	692,778	677,194	896,429	700,676	674,315	8,158.4

[1] In thousands of contracts.   *Source: Chicago Board of Trade (CBT)*

Supply and Distribution of Soybean Meal in the United States   In Thousands of Short Tons

Year Beginning Oct. 1	For Stocks Oct. 1	Pro- duction	Total Supply	Domestic	Exports	Total	$ Per Ton Decatur 48% Protein Solvent	Decatur 44% Protein Solvent	Brazil FOB 45-46% Protein	Rotter- dam CIF
		Supply			Distribution			$ Per Metric Ton		
1994-5	150	33,269	33,483	26,542	6,717	33,260	162.55	179	172	184
1995-6	223	32,527	32,826	26,611	6,002	32,613	236.00	260	256	256
1996-7	212	34,211	34,525	27,321	6,994	34,316	270.90	289	289	278
1997-8	210	38,176	38,442	28,894	9,330	38,224	185.28	204	201	197
1998-9	218	37,797	38,114	30,662	7,122	37,784	138.55	153	150	150
1999-00	330	37,591	37,970	30,346	7,331	37,677	167.70	185	182	180
2000-1	293	39,385	39,729	31,643	7,703	39,346	173.60	191	187	188
2001-2[1]	383	40,292	40,818	33,070	7,508	40,578	167.73	180	174	174
2002-3[2]	240	38,213	38,619	32,386	6,013	38,399	181.57	200	198	197
2003-4[3]	220	34,755	35,450	31,000	4,250	35,250	225-245	257	274	275

[1] Preliminary.   [2] Estimate.   [3] Forecast.   Source: Economic Research Service, U.S. Department of Agriculture (ERS-USDA)

U.S. Exports of Soybean Cake & Meal by Country of Destination   In Thousands of Metric Tons

Year	Algeria	Australia	Canada	Dominican Republic	Italy	Japan	Mexico	Nether- lands	Philip- pines	Russia	Spain	Vene- zuela	Total
1993	266.1	94.8	666.8	201.2	108.1	203.2	338.6	829.6	295.7	697.7	360.7	425.1	6,313
1994	233.7	243.2	730.1	209.9	29.3	78.1	481.6	651.4	257.9	159.5	234.9	259.0	5,406
1995	216.7	190.6	809.9	219.8	95.4	247.4	425.8	879.3	593.6	11.5	212.8	181.5	6,370
1996	203.4	157.5	698.8	260.7	96.1	234.1	374.1	501.3	423.4	5.8	51.9	274.9	6,133
1997	250.8	136.7	662.9	261.5	295.8	288.1	220.1	508.5	483.2	8.3	345.0	337.1	7,309
1998	263.2	135.7	791.8	221.8	227.7	267.1	198.6	298.2	758.7	----	296.9	447.1	8,230
1999	213.2	167.1	796.7	309.9	60.9	209.6	425.4	231.5	825.5	289.4	77.7	359.6	6,839
2000	202.0	167.7	827.2	357.4	19.0	219.7	264.5	94.6	851.8	90.1	96.5	248.1	6,462
2001	178.8	157.5	1,050.6	364.9	132.8	279.1	419.8	241.1	689.0	102.2	132.4	137.8	7,426
2002[1]	219.2	243.7	1,133.6	358.8	34.4	116.0	506.5	107.4	756.2	112.8	79.7	60.3	6,672

[1] Preliminary.   Source: The Oil World

Production of Soybean Cake & Meal[2] in the United States   In Thousands of Short Tons

Year	Oct.	Nov.	Dec.	Jan.	Feb.	Mar.	Apr.	May	June	July	Aug.	Sept.	Total	Yield in lbs.
1994-5	2,812.5	2,903.5	3,027.8	3,007.5	2,755.0	3,048.5	2,829.8	2,697.9	2,492.1	2,565.4	2,589.8	2,535.8	33,269	47.33
1995-6	2,893.2	2,948.9	2,972.3	2,945.2	2,652.1	2,757.5	2,683.1	2,534.6	2,566.2	2,656.3	2,513.4	2,404.1	32,527	47.69
1996-7	2,992.8	3,151.8	3,263.8	3,251.7	2,966.8	3,089.1	2,709.1	2,618.1	2,573.2	2,517.4	2,465.2	2,611.0	34,211	47.36
1997-8	3,344.0	3,390.6	3,624.2	3,592.1	3,279.2	3,484.0	3,172.5	2,956.7	2,795.2	2,941.5	2,665.6	2,930.7	37,176	47.41
1998-9	3,365.1	3,368.4	3,422.4	3,214.4	3,027.7	3,302.7	3,044.2	3,024.4	2,844.0	3,011.9	3,003.5	3,167.8	37,797	47.25
1999-00	3,573.4	3,400.4	3,413.5	3,332.8	2,998.2	3,123.6	2,906.1	2,882.5	2,845.4	3,118.8	2,906.8	3,089.7	37,591	47.76
2000-1	3,573.9	3,432.8	3,399.4	3,521.6	3,083.0	3,412.5	3,152.3	3,181.0	3,091.6	3,256.6	3,203.6	3,076.8	39,385	48.06
2001-2	3,534.4	3,538.7	3,655.3	3,703.1	3,313.2	3,589.7	3,315.7	3,344.2	3,194.1	3,085.4	3,106.7	2,911.3	38,213	44.27
2002-3	3,499.3	3,424.7	3,526.8	3,358.4	3,048.4	3,360.1	2,994.7	3,072.4	2,873.4	3,064.4	2,966.6	3,023.5		43.90
2003-4[1]	3,462.1	3,465.9	3,483.7	3,423.4									41,505	

[1] Preliminary.   [2] At oil mills; including millfeed and lecithin.   Sources: Economic Research Service, U.S. Department of Agriculture (ERS-USDA)

Stocks (at Oil Mills)[2] of Soybean Cake & Meal in the U.S., on First of Month   In Thousands of Short Tons

Year	Oct.	Nov.	Dec.	Jan.	Feb.	Mar.	Apr.	May	June	July	Aug.	Sept.
1994-5	149.6	240.9	231.6	241.1	197.7	227.1	173.1	382.7	337.6	222.6	252.0	203.8
1995-6	223.4	196.9	241.3	394.8	302.2	229.9	369.3	382.1	306.8	406.2	298.8	218.3
1996-7	212.4	200.2	291.8	254.4	263.0	198.5	322.6	280.1	256.5	317.3	303.2	257.4
1997-8	206.6	218.2	412.2	262.0	269.3	280.7	238.0	210.4	290.2	193.1	205.3	187.2
1998-9	218.1	271.9	352.3	313.9	380.5	436.4	341.0	316.0	447.7	284.2	394.8	279.4
1999-00	330.2	467.6	460.2	436.5	489.8	482.5	350.2	441.2	325.0	260.2	305.8	225.9
2000-1	292.9	317.4	343.8	423.7	333.9	325.8	309.1	313.3	286.9	341.3	338.1	273.9
2001-2	383.3	305.5	302.9	393.7	289.7	272.0	336.5	253.8	212.7	343.3	202.4	256.5
2002-3	240.0	285.2	371.7	337.0	299.1	259.5	335.7	263.5	311.8	271.6	228.4	266.9
2003-4[1]	219.9	317.8	432.4	280.7								

[1] Preliminary.   [2] Including millfeed and lecithin.   Source: Economic Research Service, U.S. Department of Agriculture (ERS-USDA)

SOYBEAN MEAL

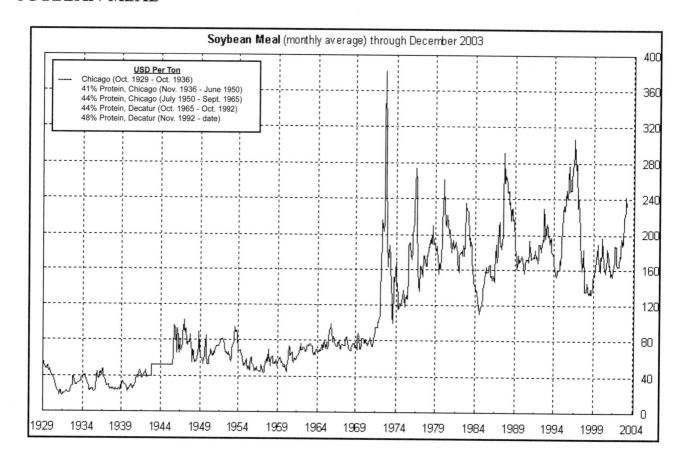

Soybean Meal (monthly average) through December 2003

USD Per Ton
----- Chicago (Oct. 1929 - Oct. 1936)
41% Protein, Chicago (Nov. 1936 - June 1950)
44% Protein, Chicago (July 1950 - Sept. 1965)
44% Protein, Decatur (Oct. 1965 - Oct. 1992)
48% Protein, Decatur (Nov. 1992 - date)

Average Price of Soybean Meal (44% Solvent) in Decatur Illinois   In Dollars Per Short Ton -- Bulk

Year	Oct.	Nov.	Dec.	Jan.	Feb.	Mar.	Apr.	May	June	July	Aug.	Sept.	Average
1992-3	168.6	170.9	176.4	175.6	167.5	172.4	175.6	181.7	181.3	217.6	206.9	186.5	181.8
1993-4	180.6	195.7	192.5	185.9	184.4	182.0	176.4	191.1	183.0	168.1	165.6	162.5	180.7
1994-5	156.4	150.9	145.4	145.1	149.4	145.7	151.0	148.1	149.1	160.1	157.5	171.8	152.5
1995-6	183.4	194.1	213.6	220.5	216.7	215.7	237.9	232.3	227.9	242.3	251.1	265.5	225.1
1996-7	238.0	242.7	240.9	240.7	253.6	270.4	277.7	296.0	275.9	261.5	261.6	265.7	260.4
1997-8	216.0	231.6	214.9	193.1	182.1	165.3	152.8	150.3	157.8	173.3	135.7	126.9	175.0
1998-9	129.4	139.3	139.6	131.0	124.4	127.2	128.6	127.0	131.7	125.7	135.9	144.1	132.0
1999-00	147.2	148.1	145.4	155.0	163.6	166.6	168.1	180.1	170.2	156.8	151.4	166.9	160.0
2000-1	166.0	173.7	187.9	175.6	158.3	149.1	149.7	155.6	163.1	183.9	170.6	163.5	166.4
2001-2	157.7	157.2	146.6	Disc.	Disc.	Disc.	Disc.	Disc.	Disc.	Disc.	Disc.	Disc.	153.8

Source: Economic Research Service, U.S. Department of Agriculture (ERS-USDA)

Average Price of Soybean Meal (48% Solvent) in Decatur Illinois   In Dollars Per Short Ton -- Bulk

Year	Oct.	Nov.	Dec.	Jan.	Feb.	Mar.	Apr.	May	June	July	Aug.	Sept.	Average
1994-5	168.50	161.00	156.90	156.40	151.30	156.90	161.90	159.10	160.40	170.45	166.70	180.99	162.55
1995-6	193.90	204.10	223.60	232.00	228.30	226.57	249.30	244.30	238.80	252.50	261.20	276.40	235.90
1996-7	248.50	251.50	250.60	249.20	262.40	280.50	288.60	306.40	287.90	273.60	273.30	278.30	270.90
1997-8	229.30	245.30	222.50	202.85	192.75	174.20	162.50	160.00	168.55	183.40	146.25	135.80	185.28
1998-9	135.70	144.45	146.40	138.80	132.30	133.00	134.50	133.20	139.10	132.70	141.70	150.65	138.54
1999-00	153.57	154.70	154.00	163.41	170.85	175.50	177.53	189.34	177.45	163.38	157.48	174.60	167.65
2000-1	171.52	179.95	195.65	183.17	166.08	156.32	158.48	165.14	172.60	184.43	178.46	171.67	173.62
2001-2	165.45	166.10	154.18	158.01	153.11	160.49	161.57	164.28	170.33	187.45	186.25	185.45	167.72
2002-3	168.20	163.20	163.60	167.40	176.80	175.40	182.10	195.40	191.90	187.30	189.70	217.95	181.58
2003-4	225.20	242.00	231.54	252.15	257.39								241.66

Source: Economic Research Service, U.S. Department of Agriculture (ERS-USDA)

Soybean Oil

Soybean oil is the natural oil extracted from whole soybeans. Typically, about 19% of a soybean's weight can be extracted as crude soybean oil. The oil content of U.S. soybeans correlates directly with the temperatures and amount of sunshine during the soybean pod-filling stages. Edible products produced with soybean oil include cooking and salad oils, shortening, and margarine. Soybean oil is the most widely used cooking oil in the US. It accounts for 80% of margarine production and for more than 75% of total US consumer vegetable fat and oil consumption. Soy oil is cholesterol-free and high in polyunsaturated fat. Soy oil is also used to produce inedible products such as paints, varnish, resins, and plastics. Of the edible vegetable oils, soy oil is the world's largest at about 32%, followed by palm oil and rapeseed oil. Soybean oil futures and options are traded on the Chicago Board of Trade (CBOT).

Prices – Soybean oil futures staged a sharp 33% rally during 2003, matching the 33% rally seen in 2002. Specifically, soybean oil on the weekly nearest futures chart rallied early in the year, faded through the summer, but then staged a strong rally into the year-end to post a new 5-1/2 year high of 29.00 cents per pound in early December. At 28 cents per pound, soybean futures closed the year only mildly below the 14-year high of 30.80 cents seen in Janu-

ary 1994 and the 20-year high of 33.70 cents seen in July 1988. Bullish factors in 2003 centered on aggressive Chinese buying, tight US and world supplies of both soybean oil and competing edible oils. Soy oil stocks in 2003 fell for the third consecutive year.

Supply – World production of soybeans in 2002/03 was a record-high 30.07 million metric tons, up 4.3% from the previous year's 28.82 million. The world's largest producers are the US with 8.521 million tons of production (28%), Brazil with 5.062 million tons (17%), and the European Union with 3.190 million tons (11%). US production of soybean oil in 2003/04 was forecast by the USDA at 16.660 billion pounds, down from 18.438 billion in 2002/3 and the record high of 18.898 billion in 2001/02.

Demand – World consumption of soybean oil was a record high 30.420 million metric tons in 2002-03, with the US accounting for 26% of world consumption at 2.768 million tons.

Trade – Global soybean oil exports in 2002/03 hit a record 10.160 million tons, up 11% from the previous year's 9.180 million tons. Argentina is the largest exporter with 4 million tons in 2002/03. Asia is the world's largest importer followed by the Middle East.

World Supply and Demand of Soybean Oil   In Thousands of Metric Tons

Year Beginning Oct. 1	Production Brazil	European Union	United States	Total	Exports Brazil	United States	Total	Imports India	Total	Consumption Brazil	European Union	India	United States	Total	Stocks[3] United States	Total
1994-5	3,796	2,708	7,082	20,161	1,486	1,217	6,287	60	5,986	2,466	2,040	555	5,857	19,209	516	2,026
1995-6	4,034	2,529	6,913	19,860	1,600	450	5,285	60	5,273	2,530	2,031	772	6,108	19,604	914	2,270
1996-7	3,723	2,582	7,145	20,318	1,268	922	6,004	49	5,904	2,600	1,784	706	6,471	20,544	690	1,944
1997-8	3,740	2,746	8,229	23,562	1,191	1,397	8,062	236	6,814	2,749	1,706	1,095	6,922	22,308	627	1,950
1998-9	3,931	2,753	8,202	24,650	1,381	1,076	8,170	833	7,850	2,850	1,694	1,805	7,101	24,500	689	2,170
1999-00	4,025	2,513	8,085	24,640	1,150	624	6,530	790	6,430	3,000	1,482	1,582	7,283	24,160	904	2,580
2000-1	4,319	2,982	8,355	26,750	1,530	636	7,250	1,400	6,900	3,075	1,929	2,020	7,401	26,250	1,255	2,720
2001-2	4,708	3,114	8,572	28,870	1,775	1,143	8,580	1,550	8,260	3,100	2,015	2,387	7,635	28,690	1,070	2,570
2002-3[1]	5,250	2,810	8,363	30,490	2,245	1,026	9,490	1,275	9,140	3,150	1,871	1,966	7,752	30,930	676	1,790
2003-4[2]	6,040	3,106	7,430	32,010	2,750	386	9,640	1,150	9,570	3,325	2,158	2,085	7,371	32,100	456	1,630

[1] Preliminary.   [2] Forecast.   [3] End of season.   *Source: Foreign Agricultural Service, U.S. Department of Agriculture (FAS-USDA)*

Supply and Distribution of Soybean Oil in the United States   In Millions of Pounds

Year Beginning Oct. 1	Production	Imports	Stocks Oct. 1	Exports	Total Domestic	Food Shortening	Margarine	Cooking & Salad Oils	Other Edible	Total Food	Non-Food Paint & Varnish	Resins & Plastics	Total Non-Food	Total Disappearance
1994-5	15,613	17	1,103	2,680	12,916	4,714	1,693	5,546	222	12,175	49	124	287	15,597
1995-6	15,240	95	1,137	992	13,465	4,702	1,699	5,317	159	11,877	48	119	297	14,457
1996-7	15,752	53	2,015	2,033	14,267	4,578	1,667	6,119	68	12,432	51	132	333	16,300
1997-8	18,143	60	1,520	3,079	15,262	4,688	1,623	6,188	78	12,576	49	128	490	18,341
1998-9	18,078	83	1,382	2,372	15,651	4,842	1,589	6,191	120	12,743	37	117	576	18,023
1999-00	17,825	83	1,520	1,376	16,057	7,153	1,481	7,075	132	15,841	65	96	586	17,433
2000-1	18,420	73	1,995	1,401	16,210	8,044	1,294	7,310	125	16,772	60	86	535	17,611
2001-2	18,898	46	2,767	2,519	16,833	8,572	1,242	7,880	125	17,818	60	85	519	19,352
2002-3[1]	18,438	46	2,359	2,261	17,091	8,393	1,179	7,912	119	17,604	64	88	520	19,352
2003-4[2]	16,380	235	1,491	850	16,250						65	75	607	17,100

[1] Preliminary .   [2] Forecast.   *Source: Economic Research Service, U.S. Department of Agriculture (ERS-USDA)*

243

SOYBEAN OIL

Stocks of Crude Soybean Oil in the United States, at End of Month   In Millions of Pounds

Crop Year	Oct.	Nov.	Dec.	Jan.	Feb.	Mar.	Apr.	May	June	July	Aug.	Sept.
1998-9	1,195.0	1,142.0	1,041.1	1,066.2	1,209.5	1,318.6	1,462.0	1,499.5	1,411.8	1,441.8	1,417.8	1,316.1
1999-00	1,378.3	1,422.9	1,516.5	1,742.4	1,829.7	1,847.2	1,847.5	1,760.3	1,802.9	1,903.7	1,831.3	1,773.4
2000-1	1,873.6	1,961.8	2,035.0	2,140.0	2,262.4	2,304.1	2,321.7	2,455.2	2,587.4	2,718.3	2,698.2	2,692.4
2001-2	2,553.4	2,606.0	2,658.1	2,815.7	2,686.6	2,741.9	2,661.2	2,757.5	2,529.3	2,350.9	2,338.2	2,176.7
2002-3	2,097.1	2,114.3	2,197.2	2,186.9	2,062.5	2,028.7	1,916.0	1,843.0	1,706.4	1,595.1	1,458.4	1,282.4
2003-4[1]	1,236.8	1,329.7	1,390.1	1,733.0								

[1] Preliminary.   *Source: Bureau of the Census, U.S. Department of Commerce*

Stocks of Refined Soybean Oil in the United States, at End of Month   In Millions of Pounds

Crop Year	Oct.	Nov.	Dec.	Jan.	Feb.	Mar.	Apr.	May	June	July	Aug.	Sept.
1998-9	221.7	264.4	246.5	246.7	296.1	289.0	254.2	267.8	235.6	229.4	213.0	203.4
1999-00	238.1	240.7	250.0	271.3	270.1	245.6	251.8	231.6	225.5	216.7	186.3	222.0
2000-1	187.2	205.7	263.1	239.3	211.5	199.9	184.1	200.9	189.3	177.2	171.7	184.8
2001-2	171.4	181.4	210.0	222.9	209.8	210.8	195.6	185.7	206.5	178.7	183.5	183.2
2002-3	197.1	212.0	202.3	209.8	209.5	215.9	204.1	210.8	222.1	199.1	196.0	208.3
2003-4[1]	175.0	200.8	189.9	208.3								

[1] Preliminary.   *Source: Bureau of the Census, U.S. Department of Commerce*

U.S. Exports of Soybean Oil[1], by Country of Destination   In Metric Tons

Year Beginning Oct. 1	Canada	Ecuador	Ethiopia	Haiti	India	Mexico	Morocco	Pakistan	Panama	Peru	Turkey	Venezuela	Total
1994-5	26,178	12,698	8,392	49,793	28,948	58,624	29,053	25,500	13,342	8,691	5,750	2,017	1,217,079
1995-6	43,912	1,155	4,426	15,041	20,841	46,644	0	0	9,512	35,999	1,960	1,877	449,876
1996-7	58,756	6,587	19,492	36,436	26,675	81,902	46,682	0	3,623	37,726	6,952	517	922,336
1997-8	26,711	10,897	4,175	14,191	38,610	102,950	30,493	0	13,591	49,426	2,452	654	1,396,755
1998-9	11,316	4,858	2,933	44,957	71,685	99,112	43,346	0	1,369	62,085	8,497	1,464	1,075,699
1999-00	22,715	0	13,627	25,214	23,413	118,079	14,091	0	299	66,686	15,680	414	623,651
2000-1	54,909	9,849	5,224	5,793	54,062	72,456	0	62,999	4,558	60,606	0	577	635,493
2001-2	87,047	0	2,225	9,452	88,529	161,760	39,439	59,999	12,616	37,677	85,199	635	1,142,755
2002-3[2]	123,907	0	11,997	1,973	42,727	196,031	18,112	38,215	2,241	20,349	26,500	311	1,025,528

[1] Crude & Refined oil combined as such.   [2] Preliminary.   *Source: Economic Research Service, U.S. Department of Agriculture (ERS-USDA)*

Production of Crude Soybean Oil in the United States   In Millions of Pounds

Year	Oct.	Nov.	Dec.	Jan.	Feb.	Mar.	Apr.	May	June	July	Aug.	Sept.	Total
1995-6	1,354	1,360	1,382	1,360	1,236	1,292	1,259	1,197	1,221	1,263	1,171	1,139	15,234
1996-7	1,401	1,430	1,473	1,474	1,348	1,413	1,254	1,216	1,196	1,176	1,141	1,231	15,752
1997-8	1,591	1,580	1,689	1,684	1,558	1,655	1,526	1,418	1,337	1,410	1,286	1,410	18,143
1998-9	1,598	1,598	1,611	1,528	1,439	1,587	1,453	1,450	1,383	1,451	1,452	1,528	18,078
1999-00	1,687	1,597	1,599	1,580	1,417	1,482	1,368	1,396	1,360	1,486	1,388	1,466	17,825
2000-1	1,673	1,591	1,579	1,642	1,436	1,602	1,485	1,479	1,449	1,526	1,506	1,453	18,420
2001-2	1,680	1,629	1,696	1,707	1,544	1,662	1,551	1,574	1,506	1,461	1,475	1,414	18,898
2002-3	1,693	1,632	1,696	1,613	1,474	1,633	1,448	1,492	1,391	1,482	1,440	1,445	18,438
2003-4[1]	1,631	1,611	1,605	1,619									19,395

[1] Preliminary.   *Source: Economic Research Service, U.S. Department of Agriculture (ERS-USDA)*

Production of Refined Soybean Oil in the United States   In Millions of Pounds

Year	Oct.	Nov.	Dec.	Jan.	Feb.	Mar.	Apr.	May	June	July	Aug.	Sept.	Total
1995-6	1,119.2	1,088.8	1,018.5	979.9	934.3	1,042.6	997.3	1,009.3	962.8	971.9	1,115.8	1,058.7	12,299
1996-7	1,111.7	1,064.1	1,025.7	969.8	931.5	1,057.1	1,023.7	1,026.2	984.8	1,019.1	1,094.3	1,072.5	12,381
1997-8	1,173.9	1,156.3	1,110.1	1,092.6	1,047.4	1,148.2	1,094.8	1,140.7	1,053.1	1,083.9	1,173.4	1,114.5	13,389
1998-9	1,200.6	1,108.8	1,042.2	1,016.7	976.7	1,138.2	1,073.2	1,087.7	1,060.7	1,058.6	1,122.6	1,116.2	13,002
1999-00	1,201.1	1,195.2	1,150.4	1,056.9	1,045.1	1,173.7	1,109.6	1,141.4	1,063.8	1,080.2	1,176.0	1,177.7	13,571
2000-1	1,260.3	1,159.7	1,093.4	1,107.5	1,166.8	1,211.3	1,170.0	1,234.1	1,204.6	1,222.8	1,317.4	1,201.2	14,349
2001-2	1,383.2	1,363.5	1,266.9	1,231.8	1,183.9	1,330.0	1,270.5	1,297.9	1,287.7	1,272.8	1,308.4	1,362.4	15,559
2002-3	1,451.2	1,367.2	1,262.2	1,224.5	1,181.0	1,308.2	1,238.6	1,378.8	1,316.1	1,293.8	1,290.5	1,334.8	15,647
2003-4[1]	1,393.0	1,350.9	1,226.6	1,205.6									15,528

[1] Preliminary.   *Source: Bureau of the Census, U.S. Department of Commerce*

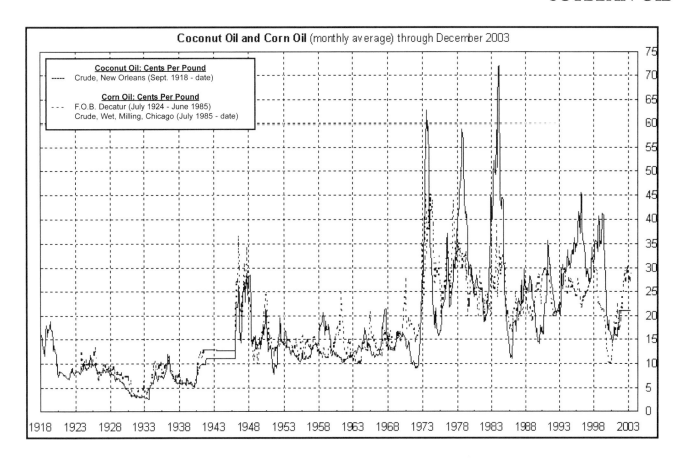

Coconut Oil and Corn Oil (monthly average) through December 2003

Coconut Oil: Cents Per Pound
----- Crude, New Orleans (Sept. 1918 - date)

Corn Oil: Cents Per Pound
- - - F.O.B. Decatur (July 1924 - June 1985)
Crude, Wet, Milling, Chicago (July 1985 - date)

Consumption of Soybean Oil in End Products in the United States   In Millions of Pounds

Year	Jan.	Feb.	Mar.	Apr.	May	June	July	Aug.	Sept.	Oct.	Nov.	Dec.	Total
1994	924.5	939.1	1,084.7	1,040.6	1,001.4	1,023.8	974.9	1,119.2	1,075.4	1,123.3	1,103.4	1,063.8	12,474
1995	991.1	950.0	1,093.8	1,006.2	1,077.3	1,020.8	948.7	1,046.1	1,042.3	1,092.0	1,067.7	1,002.6	12,339
1996	964.9	927.4	1,026.4	999.8	1,020.6	946.2	959.9	1,123.3	1,042.8	1,137.1	1,080.9	1,093.1	12,322
1997	1,086.0	979.7	1,104.9	1,060.4	1,034.1	995.2	991.4	1,126.1	1,067.8	1,128.5	1,100.0	1,087.8	12,762
1998	1,045.8	1,020.2	1,129.7	1,066.5	1,101.6	1,070.1	1,062.2	1,123.4	1,122.0	1,231.5	1,150.2	1,057.0	13,180
1999	1,031.5	979.0	1,156.1	1,087.7	1,091.9	1,079.5	1,082.9	1,185.0	1,185.7	1,183.0	1,199.3	1,135.6	13,397
2000	1,096.6	1,050.5	1,217.9	1,158.9	1,183.6	1,102.9	1,121.1	1,226.4	1,163.6	1,306.1	1,139.7	1,079.6	13,847
2001	1,065.9	1,151.7	1,308.8	1,202.4	1,224.2	1,261.6	1,307.6	1,557.5	1,411.0	1,687.3	1,624.0	1,485.8	16,288
2002	1,461.5	1,395.3	1,568.0	1,505.1	1,549.7	1,492.4	1,490.5	1,545.5	1,543.7	1,710.2	1,587.2	1,458.8	18,308
2003[1]	1,418.1	1,347.4	1,490.0	1,494.9	1,552.6	1,493.1	1,509.5	1,483.5	1,577.7	1,660.7	1,544.2	1,451.4	18,023

[1] Preliminary.   *Source: Bureau of the Census, U.S. Department of Commerce*

U.S. Exports of Soybean Oil (Crude and Refined)   In Millions of Pounds

Year	Jan.	Feb.	Mar.	Apr.	May	June	July	Aug.	Sept.	Oct.	Nov.	Dec.	Total
1994	120.4	144.6	94.4	46.1	111.6	36.1	57.7	184.6	254.0	154.8	303.2	305.9	1,813
1995	217.4	367.6	564.2	236.2	90.8	160.4	91.0	109.4	79.4	69.3	205.4	95.9	2,287
1996	189.1	97.0	68.0	75.3	63.9	16.1	27.1	28.0	56.7	121.0	303.8	213.3	1,259
1997	190.7	239.2	301.1	84.9	28.9	44.9	144.1	212.9	152.1	217.2	424.0	199.7	2,240
1998	449.4	387.6	268.6	191.1	148.1	204.7	161.8	316.0	108.9	189.6	343.5	376.7	3,146
1999	246.1	231.1	130.8	230.8	91.3	135.0	111.7	91.2	196.2	209.1	114.9	157.6	1,946
2000	103.0	146.1	161.3	91.5	48.3	109.8	105.8	57.0	69.0	43.9	115.2	261.6	1,313
2001	130.4	184.5	142.4	105.8	51.2	109.9	89.1	96.3	70.6	233.9	138.6	164.8	1,518
2002	249.7	446.8	233.2	233.8	87.0	345.8	180.7	95.4	109.8	113.6	194.9	210.2	2,501
2003[1]	295.1	299.8	276.8	226.8	109.8	96.7	234.5	96.8	105.9	152.5	111.2	135.3	2,141

[1] Preliminary.   *Source: Economic Research Service, U.S. Department of Agriculture (ERS-USDA)*

SOYBEAN OIL

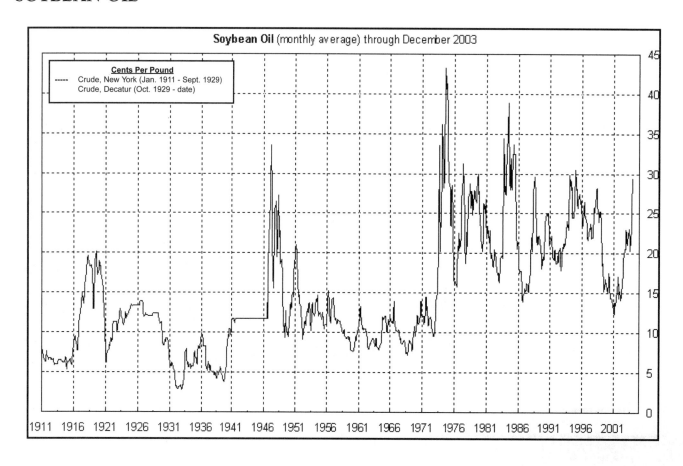

Stocks of Soybean Oil (Crude & Refined) at Factories and Warehouses in the U.S.　In Millions of Pounds

Year	Oct. 1	Nov. 1	Dec. 1	Jan. 1	Feb. 1	Mar. 1	Apr. 1	May 1	June 1	July 1	Aug. 1	Sept. 1
1994-5	1,103.1	1,055.5	1,026.9	1,055.2	1,116.8	1,128.8	1,059.5	1,089.6	1,130.4	1,111.6	1,142.0	1,100.0
1995-6	1,136.7	1,195.9	1,132.0	1,408.9	1,512.6	1,521.5	1,653.5	1,747.4	1,758.9	1,888.5	2,156.5	2,091.4
1996-7	2,015.4	1,992.9	1,898.4	2,027.1	2,172.3	2,203.2	2,171.3	2,163.8	2,143.2	2,137.9	1,978.1	1,699.9
1997-8	1,520.2	1,525.6	1,525.5	1,679.6	1,787.9	1,711.2	1,762.6	1,857.6	1,857.0	1,712.6	1,779.1	1,453.2
1998-9	1,382.4	1,416.8	1,406.5	1,312.9	1,505.6	1,607.6	1,716.2	1,640.5	1,767.3	1,647.4	1,671.2	1,630.8
1999-00	1,519.6	1,616.4	1,663.6	1,791.1	2,013.7	2,099.8	2,092.7	2,099.2	1,991.9	2,028.3	2,120.4	2,018.1
2000-1	1,995.3	2,060.8	2,167.5	2,298.0	2,379.7	2,474.0	2,504.0	2,505.8	2,656.1	2,776.7	2,895.5	2,869.9
2001-2	2,877.2	2,724.9	2,787.4	2,868.1	3,038.5	2,896.4	2,952.7	2,856.8	2,943.2	2,735.9	2,529.7	2,521.7
2002-3	2,358.6	2,280.1	2,326.1	2,398.0	2,395.7	2,271.9	2,244.6	2,120.2	2,053.9	1,928.5	1,794.2	1,654.4
2003-4[1]	1,490.6	1,411.8	1,530.4	1,579.9								

[1] Preliminary.　*Source: Economic Research Service, U.S. Department of Agriculture (ERS-USDA)*

Average Price of Crude Domestic Soybean Oil (in Tank Cars) F.O.B. Decatur　In Cents Per Pound

Year	Oct.	Nov.	Dec.	Jan.	Feb.	Mar.	Apr.	May	June	July	Aug.	Sept.	Average
1994-5	27.06	29.84	30.61	29.01	28.15	28.33	27.16	26.00	26.78	27.60	26.56	26.26	27.51
1995-6	26.56	25.41	24.76	23.69	23.65	23.60	25.82	26.50	24.95	24.10	23.99	23.92	24.70
1996-7	21.95	21.80	21.60	22.45	22.41	23.29	23.17	23.68	22.97	21.89	22.06	22.88	22.50
1997-8	24.31	25.73	25.08	25.09	26.51	27.09	28.10	28.28	25.83	24.88	23.99	25.13	25.84
1998-9	25.20	25.20	24.00	22.90	20.00	19.50	18.80	17.85	16.50	15.30	16.50	16.80	19.88
1999-00	16.08	15.63	15.30	15.63	15.09	16.21	17.52	16.75	15.65	14.70	14.34	14.24	15.60
2000-1	13.50	13.37	13.12	12.53	12.38	13.90	13.53	13.53	14.21	16.49	17.08	15.46	14.09
2001-2	14.38	15.23	15.10	14.82	14.15	14.75	15.31	15.98	17.69	19.12	20.61	20.32	16.46
2002-3	20.75	23.00	22.60	21.50	21.20	21.56	22.40	23.17	22.90	21.80	20.40	23.20	22.04
2003-4[1]	27.40	27.76	29.54	30.34	33.06								29.62

[1] Preliminary.　*Source: Economic Research Service, U.S. Department of Agriculture (ERS-USDA)*

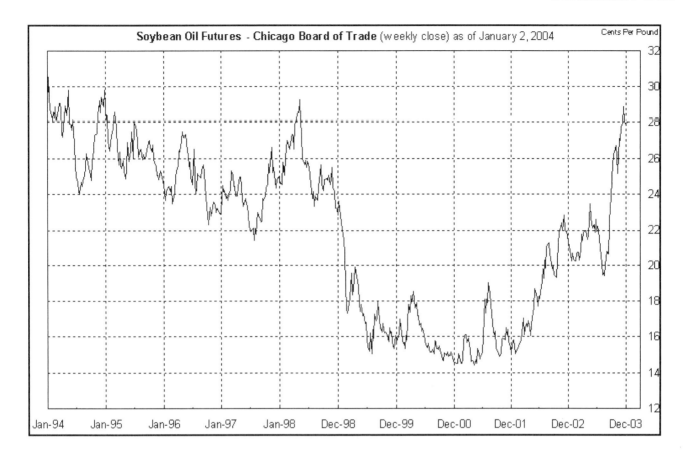

Average Open Interest of Soybean Oil Futures in Chicago   In Contracts

Year	Jan.	Feb.	Mar.	Apr.	May	June	July	Aug.	Sept.	Oct.	Nov.	Dec.
1994	97,198	99,640	100,334	98,659	97,595	83,165	93,994	88,196	81,735	86,901	108,327	114,928
1995	101,171	103,856	97,715	87,300	76,175	75,171	81,650	77,064	70,410	71,652	85,241	84,138
1996	87,214	85,611	87,859	95,954	95,422	86,366	81,440	80,090	83,211	98,514	97,496	86,119
1997	89,112	89,348	102,388	101,191	101,544	104,433	105,346	95,282	94,521	107,471	119,877	106,406
1998	105,798	121,657	142,100	160,004	159,248	139,934	117,487	112,177	115,879	115,260	110,386	104,738
1999	115,407	131,875	136,967	133,404	131,993	147,749	157,999	147,280	146,239	155,768	163,439	144,798
2000	131,948	135,196	143,699	155,114	134,093	140,582	134,392	135,506	136,590	135,584	142,712	134,873
2001	134,677	133,497	123,770	128,360	142,877	151,713	162,395	166,318	159,467	164,521	167,803	154,589
2002	149,103	158,157	149,913	136,198	128,707	129,480	135,762	143,144	146,759	139,626	169,978	155,871
2003	143,607	140,272	131,323	142,123	147,584	143,218	147,610	157,066	141,596	161,556	183,747	191,176

Source: Chicago Board of Trade (CBT)

Volume of Trading of Soybean Oil Futures in Chicago   In Contracts

Year	Jan.	Feb.	Mar.	Apr.	May	June	July	Aug.	Sept.	Oct.	Nov.	Dec.	Total[1]
1994	442,026	401,580	366,007	391,175	442,419	378,177	397,483	357,896	415,407	476,936	516,724	477,358	5,063.2
1995	424,387	363,695	464,413	355,884	457,682	418,182	377,355	330,507	303,893	317,201	431,711	366,426	4,611.3
1996	354,602	355,220	375,237	443,408	376,716	423,089	512,563	449,014	425,850	414,018	396,233	454,327	4,980.3
1997	473,290	381,921	503,998	445,848	389,741	439,626	442,846	375,122	417,970	413,722	489,541	511,369	5,285.0
1998	443,562	556,982	497,887	673,091	624,518	648,098	629,642	491,155	558,032	383,844	450,073	540,379	6,498.3
1999	367,303	555,097	520,622	463,236	350,850	489,184	516,205	552,198	523,376	395,243	497,090	433,491	5,663.9
2000	424,232	451,677	483,212	438,526	451,162	533,376	422,418	456,195	436,841	378,419	507,044	386,801	5,369.9
2001	327,570	458,445	416,718	443,454	403,110	541,194	751,299	612,349	447,390	550,995	579,460	502,341	6,034.3
2002	474,824	497,396	468,878	496,990	526,918	588,386	701,455	648,853	529,442	549,942	705,373	628,026	6,816.5
2003	522,939	540,645	473,694	618,483	520,043	740,549	761,460	594,687	636,469	733,405	656,464	618,502	7,417.3

[1] In thousands of contracts.   *Source: Chicago Board of Trade (CBT)*

Soybeans

Soybean is the common name for the annual leguminous plant and its seed. The soybean is a member of the oilseed family and is not considered a grain. The seeds are contained in pods and are nearly spherical in shape. The seeds are usually light yellow in color. The seeds contain 20% oil and 40% protein. Soybeans were an ancient food crop in China, Japan, and Korea and were only introduced to the US in the early 1800s. Today, soybeans are the third largest crop produced in the US behind corn and wheat. Soybean production in the US is concentrated in the Midwest and the lower Mississippi Valley. Soybean crops in the US are planted in May or June and are harvested in autumn. Soybean plants usually reach maturity 100-150 days after planting depending on growing conditions.

Soybeans are used to produce a wide variety of food products. The key value of soybeans lies in the relatively high protein content, which makes it an excellent source of protein without many of the negative factors of animal meat. Popular soy-based food products include whole soybeans (roasted for snacks or used in sauces, stews and soups), soy oil for cooking and baking, soy flour, protein concentrates, isolated soy protein (which contains up to 92% protein), soy milk and baby formula (as an alternative to dairy products), soy yogurt, soy cheese, soy nut butter, soy sprouts, tofu and tofu products (soybean curd), soy sauce (which is produced by a fermentation process), and meat alternatives (hamburgers, breakfast sausage, etc).

The primary market for soybean futures is at the Chicago Board of Trade. The CBOT's soybean contract calls for the delivery of 5,000 bushels of No. 2 yellow soybeans (at contract par), No. 1 yellow soybeans (at 6 cents per bushel above the contract price), or Nov. 3 yellow soybeans (at a 6 cents under the contract price). Soybean futures are also traded at exchanges in Brazil, Argentina, China, and Tokyo.

Prices – Soybean prices rallied sharply during 2003 by about 36% and closed the year at a 6-year high near $8 per bushel. Specifically, soybean prices on the weekly nearest futures chart traded in the $5.50-6.00 area in January-March and then rallied up to $6.50 in May. The market took a steep dive to $5.32 in August, but then entered into a sharp $3 rally that took the market to the 6-year high of $8.02 in late October. February 2004 soybeans closed the year at $7.92. A key bullish factor during the year was large purchases by China. The USDA in late 2003 raised its estimate of Chinese imports for the next year to a record of 808 million bushels. That is more soybeans than China imported from all sources last year and accounts for more than one-half of Chinese consumption. Looking ahead, the Brazilian soybean crop had a good start with plantings near 90%.

Supply – World soybean production during 2002/03 reached a new high of 196.66 million metric tons, up from 184.87 million in 2001/02 and the late 1990's average of less than 160 million tons. World production was forecasted to rise further to 199.46 million metric tons in 2003/04. The U.S. soybean crop year begins September 1. Soybeans now account for about 60% of the world's total oilseed production with cottonseed the closest competitor at a distant 33 million tons. The US is the world's largest producer of soybeans by far with its 78.669 million metric tons of production in the marketing year 2001/02 accounting for 43% of world production. The runners up are Brazil with 41.8 million metric tons (23% of world production), Argentina with 30.20 million metric tons (16%), and China with 15.45 million metric tons (8%). Of US soybean production of 2.452 billion bushels in 2003, the largest producing states were Illinois (15.6%), Iowa (14.6%), Minnesota (9.4%), Indiana (8.3%), Nebraska (7.2%), and Ohio (7.0%). U.S. farmers harvested a near record high 72.437 million acres of soybeans in 2002/3, down from 72.975 million in 2001/02. The average yield of 38.0 bushels per acre was slightly lower than the 39.6 bushels in 2001/02. US farmers produced 2.729 billion bushels of soybeans in 2002/3, down from 2.891 billion in 2001/02. The USDA is forecasting a further decline to 2.619 billion bushels in 2003/4. Ending stocks in the US were 4.61 million metric tons, down from 5.66 million in 2001/02 and are forecasted to fall further to 3.39 million on 2003/04.

Demand – The distribution tables for US soybeans for 2002/3 (preliminary) show that of 2.793 billion bushels of soybean consumption, 65% (1.615 billion bushels) went for crushing into soy meal and soy oil, 42% went to exports (1.045 billion bushels), and 5% went to seed, feed and residual (133 million bushels). For 2003/04, the USDA is forecasting a decline in crushings to 1.485 billion bushels (59%), a decline in exports to 890 million bushels (36%), and a slight reduction in seed/feed/residuals to 129 million bushels (5%).

Trade – World soybean trade in 2002/03 hit a record high 64 million metric tons (up from 54 million in 2001/2) and was forecast to rise to 67 million metric tons in 2003/4. Soybeans account for about 80% of total world oilseed trade. Of the total 63.17 million metric tons of soybeans exported worldwide in 2002/03, the world's largest exporter was the US with 28.44 million metric tons (45% of world total). The US was followed fairly closely by Brazil with 21.46 million metric tons (34%) and Argentina was a distant third with 8.71 million (14%). While US exports were little changed in the past few years, Brazil's exports increased sharply to 21.46 million metric tons in 2002/03 from 15.00 million in 2001/02 and are expected to increase further to 25.80 in 2003/04. Of the world's total imports in 2002/03 of 64.10 million metric tons, the world's largest importer was China with 21.42 million metric tons (33%), followed by the European Union with 17.05 million (27%), Latin America with 7.44 million (12%), and the Middle East and North Africa with 3.13 million (5%). China's imports in 2002/3 of 21.42 million metric tons dramatically increased from 10.39 in 2001/02 and 13.25 million in 2000/01.

World Production of Soybeans   In Thousands of Metric Tons

Crop Year[4]	Argen-tina	Bolivia	Brazil	Canada	China	India	Indo-nesia	Mexico	Para-guay	Thai-land	United States	Ex-USSR	World Total
1993-4	12,400	735	24,700	1,851	15,310	4,000	1,565	497	1,800	480	50,885	557	117,767
1994-5	12,500	810	25,900	2,251	16,000	3,236	1,680	523	2,200	450	68,444	451	137,696
1995-6	12,430	900	24,150	2,293	13,500	4,476	1,517	190	2,400	368	59,174	320	124,915
1996-7	11,000	862	27,327	2,170	13,234	4,028	1,517	56	2,670	359	64,781	303	131,910
1997-8	19,800	1,038	32,665	2,738	14,737	5,150	1,357	185	2,850	000	73,177	505	158,458
1998-9	20,800	1,071	31,377	2,737	15,153	5,300	1,306	150	3,053	321	74,599	344	160,587
1999-00	21,200	974	34,127	2,781	14,251	5,160	1,383	133	2,980	319	72,225	399	160,197
2000-1[1]	27,400	1,198	39,058	2,703	15,411	5,010	1,019	102	3,511	324	75,055	424	175,265
2001-2[2]	30,100	1,245	42,769	1,635	15,450	5,350	863	122	3,300	292	78,672	442	184,687
2002-3[3]	34,800	1,300	50,000	2,335	16,400	3,850	909	84	4,400	310	74,291	521	193,494

[1] Preliminary.   [2] Estimate.   [3] Forecast.   [4] Spilt year includes Northern Hemisphere crops harvested in the late months of the first year shown combined with Southern Hemisphere crops harvested in the early months of the following year.   Sources: Oil World; Foreign Agricultural Service, U.S. Department of Agriculture (FAS-USDA)

World Crushings and Ending Stocks of Soybeans   In Thousands of Metric Tons

Year	Argen-tina	Brazil	China	Germany	India	Japan	Mexico	Nether-lands	United States	World Total	Brazil	United States	World Total
				Crushings								Ending Stocks	
1993-4	8,718	18,736	7,605	2,781	3,600	3,700	2,640	3,582	34,716	102,071	651	5,691	9,045
1994-5	9,280	21,599	8,590	3,286	2,750	3,760	2,330	3,991	38,242	112,509	710	9,112	12,876
1995-6	9,927	20,154	7,470	3,242	4,046	3,700	2,436	3,940	37,273	110,733	825	4,993	8,506
1996-7	11,046	20,022	8,500	3,550	3,410	3,772	3,020	3,996	39,350	116,473	475	3,588	7,802
1997-8	12,886	19,946	10,210	3,816	4,460	3,682	3,430	4,108	43,792	127,004	6,800	5,440	25,070
1998-9	17,492	21,174	11,340	3,869	4,670	3,673	3,580	4,068	43,534	134,282	7,510	9,480	27,290
1999-00	17,074	21,084	15,870	3,589	4,440	3,769	3,810	4,153	42,794	137,908	8,640	7,900	28,020
2000-1[1]	17,300	22,742	19,250	4,124	4,270	3,763	4,185	4,148	44,606	147,546	8,380	6,740	30,920
2001-2[2]	20,859	24,692	20,580	4,199	4,620	3,973	4,360	4,023	46,099	160,250	11,150	5,670	32,190
2002-3[3]	24,600	28,100	24,400	4,030	3,300	4,150	4,560	3,600	44,250	168,970	9,890	4,760	29,350

[1] Preliminary.   [2] Estimate.   [3] Forecast.   Sources: Oil World; Foreign Agricultural Service, U.S. Department of Agriculture (FAS-USDA)

World Imports and Exports of Soybeans   In Thousands of Metric Tons

Year	China	Germany	Japan	Mexico	Nether-lands	Taiwan	World Total	Argen-tina	Brazil	Canada	Paraguay	United States	World Total
			Imports							Exports			
1993-4	125	2,785	4,855	2,200	4,137	2,500	29,077	2,957	5,395	489	1,200	16,006	27,982
1994-5	155	3,363	4,837	1,867	4,624	2,598	32,686	2,614	3,492	542	1,450	22,867	32,251
1995-6	795	3,249	4,776	2,401	4,300	2,646	32,904	2,014	3,633	599	1,600	23,108	31,969
1996-7	2,350	3,384	5,043	3,288	4,538	2,632	36,600	484	8,425	437	1,786	24,418	36,480
1997-8	2,944	3,472	4,870	3,489	4,799	2,387	39,334	2,842	8,759	738	2,271	23,828	39,392
1998-9	3,858	3,587	4,807	3,848	4,836	2,214	39,548	3,059	8,932	814	1,996	23,890	39,763
1999-00	10,106	2,543	4,907	4,107	5,214	2,318	46,276	4,126	11,100	901	1,934	26,621	45,891
2000-1[1]	13,246	3,420	4,767	4,309	5,495	2,331	53,125	7,156	15,469	752	2,553	26,505	53,184
2001-2[2]	10,386	3,474	5,023	4,480	5,351	2,578	53,825	5,950	15,004	430	2,226	29,204	53,745
2002-3[3]	18,000	3,470	5,180	4,720	4,760	2,540	61,410	9,100	20,400	530	2,720	27,650	61,470

[1] Preliminary.   [2] Estimate.   [3] Forecast.   Sources: Oil World; Foreign Agricultural Service, U.S. Department of Agriculture (FAS-USDA)

Supply and Distribution of Soybeans in the United States   In Millions of Bushels

Crop Year Beginning Sept. 1	Farms	Mills, Elevators[3]	Total	Pro-duction	Total Supply	Crushings	Exports	Seed, Feed & Residual	Total Distri-bution
		Supply					Distribution		
		Stocks, Sept. 1							
1994-5	59.1	150.0	209.1	2,514.9	2,729.5	1,405.0	840.0	149.0	2,394.0
1995-6	105.1	229.7	334.8	2,174.3	2,513.5	1,370.0	849.0	111.0	2,330.0
1996-7	59.5	123.9	183.5	2,380.3	2,572.6	1,436.0	886.0	118.0	2,440.0
1997-8	43.6	88.2	131.8	2,688.8	2,825.6	1,597.0	874.0	155.0	2,626.0
1998-9	84.3	115.5	199.8	2,741.0	2,945.0	1,590.0	805.0	202.0	2,597.0
1999-00	145.0	203.5	348.5	2,653.8	3,006.0	1,578.0	973.0	165.0	2,716.0
2000-1	112.5	177.7	290.2	2,757.8	3,052.0	1,640.0	996.0	168.0	2,804.0
2001-2	83.5	164.2	247.7	2,890.7	3,141.0	1,700.0	1,064.0	169.0	2,933.0
2002-3[1]	62.7	145.3	208.0	2,749.3	2,962.0	1,615.0	1,045.0	124.0	2,784.0
2003-4[2]	58.0	120.3	178.3	2,417.6	2,604.0	1,455.0	900.0	124.0	2,479.0

[1] Preliminary.   [2] Estimate.   [3] Also warehouses.   Source: Economic Research Service, U.S. Department of Agriculture (ERS-USDA)

SOYBEANS

Salient Statistics & Official Crop Production Reports of Soybeans in the U.S.　In Millions of Bushels

Year	Planted ---- 1,000 Acres ----	Acreage Har-vested	Yield Per Acre (Bu.)	Farm Price ($ / Bu.)	Farm Value (Million Dollars)	Yield of Oil	Yield of Meal	Aug. 1	Sept. 1	Oct. 1	Nov. 1	Dec. 1	Final
1994-5	61,670	60,859	41.4	5.48	13,781	11.08	47.33	2,282,367	2,316,077	2,458,087	2,522,527	----	2,516,694
1995-6	62,575	61,624	35.3	6.72	14,611	11.15	47.69	2,245,901	2,284,551	2,190,661	2,182,991	----	2,176,814
1996-7	64,205	63,409	37.6	7.35	17,495	10.91	47.36	2,299,675	2,269,505	2,346,220	2,402,610	----	2,380,274
1997-8	70,005	69,110	38.9	6.47	17,396	11.25	47.41	2,744,451	2,745,891	2,721,843	2,736,115	----	2,688,750
1998-9	72,025	70,441	38.9	4.93	13,513	11.30	47.25	2,824,744	2,908,604	2,768,919	2,762,609	----	2,741,014
1999-00	73,730	72,446	36.6	4.63	12,287	11.34	47.76	2,869,519	2,778,392	2,696,272	2,672,972	----	2,653,758
2000-1	74,266	72,408	38.1	4.54	12,548	11.24	48.06	2,988,669	2,899,571	2,822,821	2,777,036	----	2,757,810
2001-2	74,075	72,975	39.6	4.38	12,606	11.14	44.27	2,867,474	2,833,511	2,907,042	2,922,914	----	2,890,682
2002-3[1]	73,923	72,437	38.0	5.53	15,215	11.39	43.90	2,628,387	2,655,819	2,653,798	2,689,691	----	2,749,340
2003-4[2]	73,404	72,321	33.4	7.25	17,465			2,862,039	2,642,644	2,468,390	2,451,759	----	2,417,565

[1] Preliminary.　[2] Forecast.　Source: National Agricultural Statistics Service, U.S. Department of Agriculture (NASS-USDA)

Stocks of Soybeans in the United States　In Thousands of Bushels

Year	On Farms Mar. 1	Jun. 1	Sept. 1	Dec. 1	Off Farms[1] Mar. 1	Jun. 1	Sept. 1	Dec. 1	Total Stocks Mar. 1	Jun. 1	Sept. 1	Dec. 1
1994	425,700	195,000	59,080	985,800	595,917	360,260	150,037	1,116,156	1,021,617	555,260	209,117	2,101,956
1995	635,300	348,800	105,130	861,500	734,898	443,072	229,684	971,929	1,370,198	791,872	334,814	1,833,429
1996	512,000	234,100	59,523	935,100	678,356	388,701	123,935	889,984	1,190,356	622,801	183,458	1,825,084
1997	514,000	216,000	43,600	1,048,000	541,754	283,890	88,233	951,417	1,055,754	499,890	131,833	1,999,417
1998	637,000	318,000	84,300	1,187,000	565,922	275,654	115,499	999,440	1,202,922	593,654	199,799	2,186,440
1999	815,000	458,000	145,000	1,150,000	642,338	390,573	203,482	1,032,666	1,457,338	848,573	348,482	2,182,666
2000	730,000	370,000	112,500	1,217,000	665,986	404,425	177,662	1,022,791	1,395,986	774,425	290,162	2,239,791
2001	780,000	365,000	83,500	1,240,000	623,908	343,180	164,247	1,035,713	1,403,908	708,180	247,747	2,275,713
2002	687,000	301,200	62,700	1,170,000	648,987	383,721	145,320	943,641	1,335,987	684,921	208,020	2,113,641
2003	635,500	272,500	58,000	820,000	565,528	329,862	120,329	866,381	1,201,028	602,362	178,329	1,686,381

[1] Includes stocks at mills, elevators, warehouses, terminals and processors.　NA = Not avaliable.　Source: National Agricultural Statistics Service, U.S. Department of Agriculture (NASS-USDA)

Commercial Stocks of Soybeans in the United States, on First of Month　In Millions of Bushels

Year	Jan.	Feb.	Mar.	Apr.	May	June	July	Aug.	Sept.	Oct.	Nov.	Dec.
1994	62.6	65.3	54.4	46.3	40.7	34.7	29.9	24.3	19.8	11.5	68.1	83.4
1995	80.7	72.5	67.8	63.5	51.8	50.8	44.3	35.7	33.6	23.0	60.8	61.7
1996	57.2	57.2	59.2	54.7	56.2	44.9	36.9	32.7	12.0	5.3	55.2	50.6
1997	32.6	28.8	22.9	26.0	29.2	24.7	14.3	12.8	6.3	4.5	50.2	49.4
1998	35.3	31.2	22.9	18.4	14.5	14.2	10.2	9.7	8.7	18.6	43.5	40.6
1999	39.1	31.5	29.0	28.7	25.0	18.9	16.1	17.3	14.1	19.5	46.9	42.3
2000	34.1	28.3	30.0	23.9	23.8	20.6	17.0	12.3	8.6	15.5	38.2	37.9
2001	34.5	28.8	25.2	22.5	16.3	15.0	12.9	13.4	11.9	9.6	34.7	38.2
2002	29.6	27.0	22.2	21.0	18.4	15.4	14.4	10.2	4.6	8.4	26.9	28.4
2003	25.9	13.2	13.9	12.8	9.7	9.4	11.7	7.6	4.5	7.0	33.0	36.7

Source: Livestock Division, U.S. Department of Agriculture (LD-USDA)

Stocks of Soybeans at Mills in the United States, on First of Month　In Millions of Bushels

Year	Sept.	Oct.	Nov.	Dec.	Jan.	Feb.	Mar.	Apr.	May	June	July	Aug.
1993-4	42.0	28.0	108.6	114.9	120.9	126.1	118.5	119.7	98.7	97.8	90.0	63.5
1994-5	47.9	46.8	114.1	124.3	108.0	114.7	114.3	112.6	94.1	81.2	69.1	55.1
1995-6	52.8	54.2	125.6	129.1	120.0	123.3	121.9	110.6	104.2	92.5	70.4	57.4
1996-7	40.7	23.4	101.1	117.4	106.0	112.6	122.2	104.9	89.2	78.2	64.0	43.6
1997-8	28.3	37.0	126.4	124.3	110.3	98.7	93.4	72.0	56.9	41.0	42.5	44.1
1998-9	32.8	66.5	175.0	154.3	131.0	109.6	102.5	93.7	80.5	56.9	55.5	48.1
1999-00	41.7	70.8	162.9	144.7	144.2	140.3	137.8	129.6	98.7	78.7	78.4	52.1
2000-1	52.1	56.8	179.4	166.8	137.8	143.3	127.0	120.6	94.9	86.1	79.3	69.0
2001-2	69.0	41.3	152.8	137.1	121.4	129.6	128.2	112.9	104.2	88.2	67.9	65.4
2002-3[1]	46.4	36.3	114.5	113.5	106.0	109.2	103.5	91.5	91.6	76.1	64.9	55.6

[1] Preliminary.　Source: Economic Research Service, U.S. Department of Agriculture (ERS-USDA)

Production of Soybeans for Beans in the United States, by State In Millions of Bushels

Year	Arkansas	Illinois	Indiana	Iowa	Kentucky	Michigan	Minnesota	Mississippi	Missouri	Nebraska	Ohio	Tennessee	Total
1994	115.6	429.1	215.3	442.9	42.4	57.0	224.0	57.0	173.3	134.4	173.6	38.3	2,516.7
1995	88.4	378.3	196.7	407.4	41.4	59.6	234.9	37.8	132.8	101.0	153.1	34.6	2,176.8
1996	112.0	398.9	203.7	415.8	44.8	46.7	224.2	54.3	149.9	135.5	157.2	38.5	2,380.3
1997	109.8	427.9	230.6	478.4	42.1	71.6	255.5	64.2	174.6	143.8	191.0	40.8	2,688.8
1998	85.0	464.2	231.0	496.8	36.0	73.7	285.6	48.0	170.0	165.0	103.0	35.1	2,741.0
1999	92.4	443.1	210.5	478.4	24.4	77.6	289.8	44.7	147.1	180.6	162.0	22.8	2,653.8
2000	80.3	459.8	252.1	464.6	45.2	73.1	293.2	34.8	175.0	173.9	186.5	28.8	2,757.8
2001	91.2	477.9	273.9	480.5	48.8	63.9	266.4	37.0	186.2	223.0	187.8	35.4	2,890.7
2002	96.5	453.7	239.5	499.2	41.6	78.5	308.9	43.8	170.0	176.3	146.3	34.7	2,749.3
2003[1]	109.8	374.1	203.3	337.6	53.3	53.7	229.4	55.8	143.3	179.6	162.6	45.9	2,417.6

[1] Preliminary. *Source: Agricultural Statistics Board, U.S. Department of Agriculture (ASB-USDA)*

United States Exports of Soybeans In Millions of Bushels

Year	Sept.	Oct.	Nov.	Dec.	Jan.	Feb.	Mar.	Apr.	May	June	July	Aug.	Total
1993-4	30.1	73.6	72.4	73.9	71.0	67.8	53.6	34.8	27.5	26.7	17.1	40.7	589.1
1994-5	42.3	99.9	78.5	104.2	89.3	91.4	83.1	80.7	45.2	35.5	41.2	46.7	838.1
1995-6	70.7	77.4	65.5	89.6	106.2	82.9	93.5	52.9	42.1	51.8	46.0	52.6	851.2
1996-7	41.6	95.8	152.4	121.6	106.5	105.7	68.2	58.8	43.0	32.4	23.2	36.5	885.9
1997-8	42.6	174.3	150.4	121.2	91.1	94.8	56.9	36.7	27.3	24.7	27.9	26.6	874.3
1998-9	27.9	135.6	106.3	90.4	84.3	66.8	72.4	52.5	37.8	36.4	36.7	57.5	804.7
1999-00	69.4	122.8	104.5	109.1	104.0	103.1	109.7	50.6	45.6	46.0	50.3	58.4	973.4
2000-1	51.4	141.4	123.0	106.6	103.3	126.5	135.2	52.8	39.8	39.5	33.1	43.4	995.9
2001-2	31.7	158.9	158.0	133.2	157.2	132.0	63.8	46.0	45.6	43.2	56.0	38.0	1,063.7
2002-3[1]	30.9	136.7	152.8	114.7	157.0	154.0	91.5	66.4	38.6	30.8	39.0	32.7	1,045.0

[1] Preliminary. *Source: Economic Research Service, U.S. Department of Agriculture (ERS-USDA)*

Spread Between Value of Products and Soybean Price in the United States In Cents Per Bushel

Year	Sept.	Oct.	Nov.	Dec.	Jan.	Feb.	Mar.	Apr.	May	June	July	Aug.	Average
1993-4	95	108	105	92	93	99	88	85	89	88	94	118	96
1994-5	117	134	114	107	104	103	85	72	58	74	62	65	91
1995-6	68	82	58	64	53	48	53	67	44	50	52	47	57
1996-7	84	92	105	92	74	74	62	54	82	67	94	123	83
1997-8	177	96	108	87	57	51	35	33	33	29	53	43	67
1998-9	53	53	38	40	33	30	35	37	34	36	47	45	40
1999-00	48	61	64	58	75	61	70	70	80	81	69	62	66
2000-1	81	76	77	89	85	59	65	72	67	81	96	92	78
2001-2	102	108	106	83	86	65	65	65	57	63	64	89	79
2002-3	77	73	52	60	53	52	61	53	62	59	72	74	62

Source: Economic Research Service, U.S. Department of Agriculture (ERS-USDA)

Soybean Crushed (Factory Consumption) in the United States In Milions of Bushels

Year	Sept.	Oct.	Nov.	Dec.	Jan.	Feb.	Mar.	Apr.	May	June	July	Aug.	Total
1993-4	98.4	113.7	114.4	114.1	110.7	103.3	113.3	105.6	103.0	97.2	101.0	101.0	1,276
1994-5	105.9	119.3	122.5	128.5	127.3	116.5	128.1	119.4	114.2	105.6	108.4	109.5	1,405
1995-6	107.4	120.6	123.4	125.1	122.8	111.2	115.5	112.1	106.3	107.5	111.9	105.7	1,370
1996-7	100.9	127.0	133.1	138.1	137.3	125.1	130.1	114.8	110.7	108.9	106.1	103.8	1,436
1997-8	110.8	142.2	142.8	153.1	151.8	138.3	147.0	134.0	123.9	117.5	123.8	111.9	1,597
1998-9	123.9	142.4	143.0	144.6	136.4	127.6	140.0	128.4	128.0	121.2	127.3	126.9	1,590
1999-00	133.8	150.2	142.8	143.0	139.2	125.4	130.4	121.5	121.0	117.9	130.2	122.2	1,578
2000-1	128.9	149.1	143.1	142.3	146.7	128.9	141.8	131.1	132.7	128.0	133.6	133.5	1,640
2001-2	128.2	150.2	149.1	153.4	155.1	139.0	149.8	139.2	140.6	134.6	129.8	130.6	1,700
2002-3[1]	122.3	149.5	145.7	150.2	142.7	129.2	142.7	127.0	130.5	121.4	129.3	125.1	1,615

One Bushel = 60 Pounds. [1] Preliminary. *Source: Economic Research Service, U.S. Department of Agriculture (ERS-USDA)*

SOYBEANS

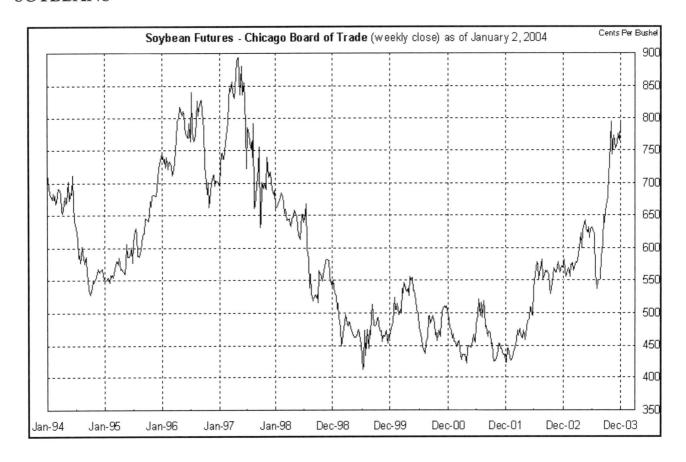

Average Open Interest of Soybean Futures in Chicago   In Contracts

Year	Jan.	Feb.	Mar.	Apr.	May	June	July	Aug.	Sept.	Oct.	Nov.	Dec.
1994	177,648	167,217	156,059	147,569	145,798	150,203	132,010	121,126	126,947	147,198	137,187	136,351
1995	138,345	138,794	137,843	138,624	133,533	143,119	143,671	135,584	144,409	167,200	174,775	194,021
1996	198,731	199,150	192,927	207,284	191,989	179,548	180,817	182,324	196,361	178,872	155,937	152,966
1997	157,728	176,242	189,352	188,617	186,792	159,720	141,658	133,732	150,606	172,098	148,760	150,201
1998	135,340	142,778	147,900	152,732	143,994	149,563	133,532	140,236	158,627	163,759	143,814	146,463
1999	152,757	166,003	162,690	166,565	164,777	163,663	157,433	134,105	146,087	174,583	164,306	153,693
2000	149,468	172,494	174,465	195,189	193,500	167,678	140,894	126,952	149,074	183,734	168,023	177,324
2001	160,730	164,017	148,190	156,781	137,227	153,190	181,194	165,630	167,677	195,366	175,522	173,116
2002	156,898	169,242	169,882	164,388	156,548	188,692	220,758	201,494	201,808	210,033	208,099	213,868
2003	201,536	217,680	226,421	251,314	230,325	222,185	190,206	190,533	232,030	265,088	241,320	252,874

Source: Chicago Board of Trade (CBT)

Volume of Trading of Soybean Futures in Chicago   In Thousands of Contracts

Year	Jan.	Feb.	Mar.	Apr.	May	June	July	Aug.	Sept.	Oct.	Nov.	Dec.	Total
1994	1,134.6	898.5	922.0	919.3	1,158.4	1,197.0	892.4	688.4	622.6	857.0	825.8	633.2	10,749
1995	614.0	572.0	799.6	698.3	949.4	1,050.8	1,196.7	817.0	800.2	1,127.8	840.4	1,145.4	10,612
1996	1,302.6	1,122.9	1,009.4	1,683.2	1,149.3	989.5	1,295.9	989.8	1,050.2	1,002.7	1,695.6	940.1	14,231
1997	1,119.8	1,254.2	1,405.9	1,585.5	1,391.1	1,355.6	1,217.4	835.0	852.3	1,505.8	1,010.7	1,006.6	14,540
1998	875.7	971.2	935.9	1,116.2	973.6	1,378.8	1,286.3	884.5	864.4	1,264.6	867.0	1,012.9	12,431
1999	871.1	1,025.3	1,440.1	963.5	823.6	1,149.5	1,502.5	1,669.8	903.0	1,158.6	839.4	872.3	12,482
2000	1,071.9	1,099.3	1,191.6	1,079.1	1,321.6	1,302.0	883.4	801.4	860.9	1,188.8	932.5	895.3	12,628
2001	935.0	947.4	843.1	916.3	909.5	1,155.6	1,508.1	1,122.0	648.7	1,356.1	964.7	844.1	12,150
2002	1,078.8	899.9	1,065.7	1,238.6	1,048.3	1,311.8	1,762.2	1,346.4	1,002.9	1,486.1	1,070.9	1,163.5	14,475
2003	1,267.3	1,222.9	997.1	1,588.9	1,368.2	1,723.4	1,385.7	1,193.5	1,308.5	2,416.3	1,535.4	1,538.5	17,546

Source: Chicago Board of Trade

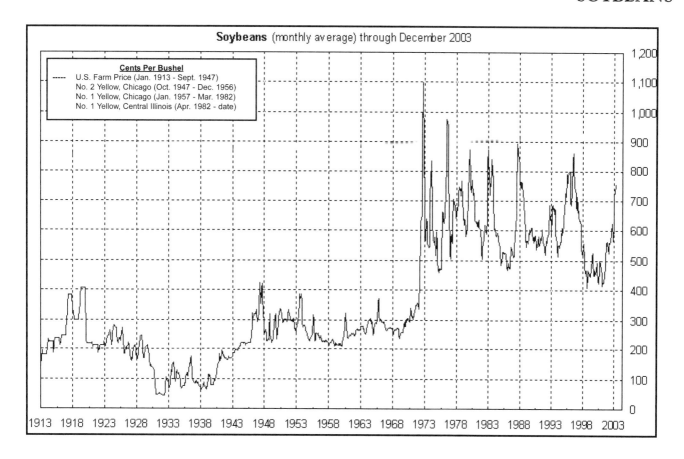

Average Cash Price of No. 1 Yellow Soybeans at Illinois Processor   In Cents Per Bushel

Year	Sept.	Oct.	Nov.	Dec.	Jan.	Feb.	Mar.	Apr.	May	June	July	Aug.	Average
1993-4	643	606	664	694	701	686	692	670	689	685	603	576	659
1994-5	557	531	566	567	558	560	574	578	580	577	623	602	573
1995-6	632	656	686	717	737	730	726	791	808	778	795	816	739
1996-7	820	711	704	708	737	769	833	854	878	837	769	741	780
1997-8	703	684	727	699	679	680	662	649	649	640	642	556	664
1998-9	533	536	572	558	532	490	475	480	468	462	425	465	500
1999-00	485	470	464	460	473	500	513	529	542	510	474	463	490
2000-1	484	468	483	506	477	457	451	441	457	474	517	510	477
2001-2	469	430	441	438	437	440	464	471	492	519	575	567	479
2002-3[1]	579	541	575	566	570	590	580	611	640	635	601	589	590

[1] Preliminary.   *Source: Economic Research Service, U.S. Department of Agriculture (ERS-USDA)*

Average Price Received by Farmers for Soybeans in the United States   In Dollars Per Bushel

Year	Sept.	Oct.	Nov.	Dec.	Jan.	Feb.	Mar.	Apr.	May	June	July	Aug.	Average
1994-5	5.47	5.30	5.36	5.41	5.47	5.40	5.51	5.55	5.56	5.68	5.90	5.83	5.48
1995-6	5.98	6.15	6.40	6.76	6.77	7.01	7.00	7.43	7.69	7.41	7.62	7.82	6.72
1996-7	7.79	6.94	6.90	6.91	7.13	7.38	7.97	8.23	8.40	8.16	7.52	7.25	7.35
1997-8	6.72	6.50	6.85	6.71	6.69	6.57	6.40	6.26	6.26	6.16	6.14	5.43	6.47
1998-9	5.25	5.18	5.40	5.37	5.32	4.80	4.61	4.63	4.51	4.44	4.20	4.39	4.93
1999-00	4.57	4.48	4.45	4.43	4.62	4.79	4.91	5.00	5.19	4.93	4.53	4.45	4.63
2000-1	4.59	4.45	4.55	4.78	4.68	4.46	4.39	4.22	4.33	4.46	4.79	4.85	4.54
2001-2	4.53	4.09	4.16	4.20	4.22	4.22	4.38	4.47	4.64	4.88	5.35	5.53	4.38
2002-3	5.39	5.20	5.46	5.46	5.51	5.55	5.60	5.82	6.07	6.09	5.83	5.68	5.64
2003-4[1]	6.06	6.61	7.05	7.17	7.34	7.99							7.04

[1] Preliminary.   *Source: Economic Research Service, U.S. Department of Agriculture (ERS-USDA)*

Stock Index Futures, U.S.

A stock index is simply a group of underlying stocks. Indexes can be either price-weighted or capitalization-weighted. In a price-weighted index, like the Dow Jones Industrials Average, the prices of each of the stocks are simply added up and divided by some divisor, meaning that stocks with higher prices have a higher weighting in the index value. In a capitalization-weighted index, such as the Standard and Poor's 500 index, the weighting of each stock corresponds to the size of the company as determined by its capitalization (i.e., the total dollar value of its stock). Stock indexes cover a variety of different sectors. For example, the DJIA contains 30 blue-chip stocks. The S&P 500 index includes 500 of the largest blue-chip US companies. The NYSE index includes all the stocks that trade at the New York Stock Exchange. The Nasdaq 100 includes the largest 100 companies that trade on the Nasdaq Exchange. The most popular US stock index futures contract is the S&P 500 at the Chicago Mercantile Exchange (CME).

Prices – The US stock market showed an impressive rally during 2003 and posted positive annual returns for the first time since 1999. The S&P 500 was up 26% on the year and posted a new 1-3/4 year high in December. The Dow Jones Industrials index rallied 25% during 2003 and also posted a new 1-3/4 year high in December. The Nasdaq Composite rallied 50% during the year and closed at a new 2-year high. The Russell 2000 index of small cap stocks rallied sharply by 46% in 2003, far out-pacing the gains in the large-cap stocks.

The US stock market rally in 2003 was driven by a sharp improvement in corporate earnings and by the fact that the US economy finally appeared to be emerging from its 2000-2003 slump. Stock market investors were also encouraged that the Federal Reserve at the end of 2003 was still talking about rates remaining low for a "considerable period," meaning that the Fed did not plan to slam on the brakes in response to the late year economic rebound. In addition, the Bush Administration on May 28 signed a tax bill into law that reduced taxes on dividends, thus making dividend-paying stocks more favorable investments.

Earnings for the S&P 500 companies were up +20% year-on-year in Q3-2003, much better than market expectations earlier in the year. That was the fifth consecutive quarter of year-on-year growth in S&P 500 earnings. Over 64% of companies in Q3 reported positive earnings surprises. Earnings growth was expected to remain very strong in Q4, near +19% year-on-year. Revenue growth in Q3 was up +1.4% year-on-year and +3.5% quarter-on-quarter. The boost in revenue was helpful, but the extent of the earnings surge shows that companies were squeezing out more profits through ongoing cost-cutting and productivity enhancements.

Despite the sharp rally during 2003, the stock market at the end of 2003 did not appear to be over-priced. The price/earnings (P/E) ratio for the S&P 500 fell to 27 at the end of 2003 from 32 at the beginning of the year. The lower P/E ratio was due to the fact that earnings soared during the year, outstripping even the rally in prices. Still, the P/E of 27 was higher than the post-war average of 16 and some market participants were therefore skeptical about whether stocks might be able to rally as much in 2004 as they did in 2003.

Dow Jones Industrial Average (30 Stocks)

Year	Jan.	Feb.	Mar.	Apr.	May	June	July	Aug.	Sept.	Oct.	Nov.	Dec.	Average
1994	3,868.4	3,905.6	3,817.0	3,661.5	3,708.0	3,737.6	3,718.3	3,797.5	3,880.6	3,868.1	3,792.5	3,770.3	3,793.8
1995	3,872.5	3,953.7	4,062.8	4,230.7	4,391.6	4,510.8	4,684.8	4,639.3	4,746.8	4,760.5	4,935.8	5,136.1	4,493.8
1996	5,179.4	5,518.7	5,612.2	5,579.9	5,616.7	5,671.5	5,496.3	5,685.5	5,804.0	5,995.1	6,318.4	6,435.9	5,742.8
1997	6,707.0	6,917.5	6,901.1	6,657.5	7,242.4	7,599.6	7,990.7	7,948.4	7,866.6	7,875.8	7,677.4	7,909.8	7,441.1
1998	7,808.4	8,323.6	8,709.5	9,037.4	9,080.1	8,873.0	9,097.1	8,478.5	7,909.8	8,164.3	9,005.8	9,018.7	8,625.5
1999	9,345.9	9,323.0	9,753.6	10,443.5	10,853.9	10,704.0	11,052.2	10,935.5	10,714.0	10,396.9	10,809.8	11,246.4	10,464.9
2000	11,281.3	10,541.9	10,483.4	10,944.4	10,580.3	10,582.9	10,663.0	11,014.5	10,967.9	10,441.0	10,666.1	10,652.4	10,734.9
2001	10,682.7	10,774.6	10,081.3	10,234.5	11,005.0	10,767.2	10,444.5	10,314.7	9,042.6	9,220.8	9,721.8	9,979.9	10,189.1
2002	9,923.8	9,891.1	10,501.0	10,165.2	10,080.5	9,492.4	8,616.5	8,685.5	8,160.2	8,048.1	8,625.7	8,526.7	9,226.4
2003	8,474.4	7,916.2	7,977.7	8,332.1	8,623.4	9,098.1	9,154.5	9,284.8	9,492.5	9,683.6	9,762.2	10,124.7	8,993.7

Average. *Source: New York Stock Exchange (NYSE)*

Dow Jones Transportation Average (20 Stocks)

Year	Jan.	Feb.	Mar.	Apr.	May	June	July	Aug.	Sept.	Oct.	Nov.	Dec.	Average
1994	1,812.1	1,810.4	1,719.9	1,614.7	1,602.2	1,619.2	1,596.2	1,602.8	1,553.7	1,485.8	1,473.7	1,415.3	1,608.8
1995	1,515.8	1,547.2	1,584.6	1,648.9	1,646.2	1,699.3	1,852.1	1,883.9	1,961.4	1,922.9	2,008.3	2,029.5	1,775.0
1996	1,932.7	2,030.0	2,136.0	2,180.0	2,229.1	2,213.4	2,053.1	2,060.4	2,050.8	2,100.1	2,224.3	2,273.9	2,123.7
1997	2,295.0	2,341.4	2,427.8	2,464.0	2,635.1	2,711.4	2,858.0	2,925.8	3,086.0	3,239.9	3,155.7	3,233.5	2,781.1
1998	3,275.8	3,456.8	3,521.5	3,586.5	3,401.9	3,373.2	3,459.3	3,021.1	2,763.0	2,647.8	2,953.4	3,027.6	3,207.3
1999	3,172.0	3,188.3	3,296.4	3,477.7	3,628.2	3,396.1	3,423.7	3,207.0	3,006.2	2,928.7	2,988.7	2,902.1	3,217.9
2000	2,812.2	2,483.4	2,534.5	2,823.9	2,813.2	2,717.2	2,822.3	2,835.6	2,641.5	2,491.0	2,792.3	2,822.9	2,715.8
2001	3,029.9	3,010.2	2,792.5	2,776.6	2,908.2	2,770.4	2,887.3	2,852.1	2,344.8	2,217.3	2,404.6	2,603.0	2,716.4
2002	2,735.3	2,719.1	2,942.9	2,776.0	2,734.8	2,702.2	2,432.1	2,318.5	2,216.0	2,216.6	2,321.6	2,331.7	2,537.2
2003	2,297.3	2,102.5	2,094.6	2,278.7	2,429.9	2,459.6	2,554.5	2,617.3	2,744.7	2,841.3	2,920.0	2,969.3	2,525.8

Average. *Source: New York Stock Exchange (NYSE)*

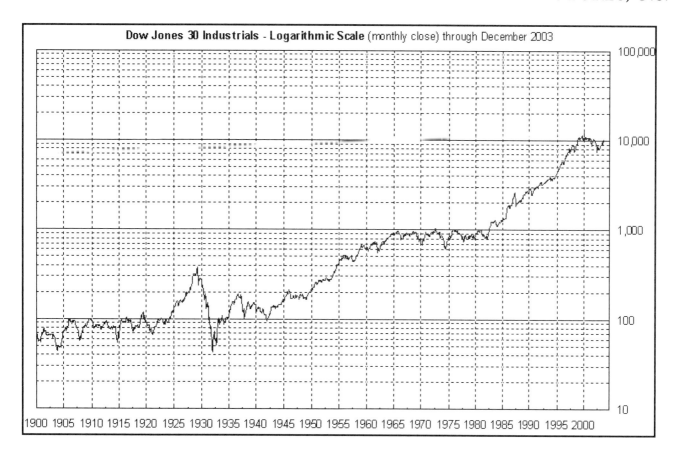

Dow Jones 30 Industrials - Logarithmic Scale (monthly close) through December 2003

Dow Jones Industrial Average (30 Stocks)

Year	Jan.	Feb.	Mar.	Apr.	May	June	July	Aug.	Sept.	Oct.	Nov.	Dec.	Average
1994	3,868.4	3,905.6	3,817.0	3,661.5	3,708.0	3,737.6	3,718.3	3,797.5	3,880.6	3,868.1	3,792.5	3,770.3	3,793.8
1995	3,872.5	3,953.7	4,062.8	4,230.7	4,391.6	4,510.8	4,684.8	4,639.3	4,746.8	4,760.5	4,935.8	5,136.1	4,493.8
1996	5,179.4	5,518.7	5,612.2	5,579.9	5,616.7	5,671.5	5,496.3	5,685.5	5,804.0	5,995.1	6,318.4	6,435.9	5,742.8
1997	6,707.0	6,917.5	6,901.1	6,657.5	7,242.4	7,599.6	7,990.7	7,948.4	7,866.6	7,875.8	7,677.4	7,909.8	7,441.1
1998	7,808.4	8,323.6	8,709.5	9,037.4	9,080.1	8,873.0	9,097.1	8,478.5	7,909.8	8,164.3	9,005.8	9,018.7	8,625.5
1999	9,345.9	9,323.0	9,753.6	10,443.5	10,853.9	10,704.0	11,052.2	10,935.5	10,714.0	10,396.9	10,809.8	11,246.4	10,464.9
2000	11,281.3	10,541.9	10,483.4	10,944.4	10,580.3	10,582.9	10,663.0	11,014.5	10,967.9	10,441.0	10,666.1	10,652.4	10,734.9
2001	10,682.7	10,774.6	10,081.3	10,234.5	11,005.0	10,767.2	10,444.5	10,314.7	9,042.6	9,220.8	9,721.8	9,979.9	10,189.1
2002	9,923.8	9,891.1	10,501.0	10,165.2	10,080.5	9,492.4	8,616.5	8,685.5	8,160.2	8,048.1	8,625.7	8,526.7	9,226.4
2003	8,474.4	7,916.2	7,977.7	8,332.1	8,623.4	9,098.1	9,154.5	9,284.8	9,492.5	9,683.6	9,762.2	10,124.7	8,993.7

Average.   Source: New York Stock Exchange (NYSE)

Standard & Poor's 500 Composite Price Index

Year	Jan.	Feb.	Mar.	Apr.	May	June	July	Aug.	Sept.	Oct.	Nov.	Dec.	Average
1994	473.0	471.6	463.8	447.2	451.0	454.8	451.4	464.2	467.0	463.8	461.0	455.2	460.3
1995	465.3	481.9	493.2	507.9	523.8	539.4	557.4	559.1	578.8	582.9	595.5	614.6	541.6
1996	614.4	649.5	647.1	547.2	661.2	668.5	644.1	662.7	674.9	701.5	735.7	743.3	662.5
1997	766.1	798.4	792.2	763.9	833.1	876.3	925.3	927.7	937.0	951.2	938.9	962.4	872.7
1998	963.4	1,023.7	1,076.8	1,112.2	1,108.4	1,108.4	1,156.6	1,074.6	1,020.7	1,032.5	1,144.5	1,190.0	1,084.3
1999	1,248.7	1,246.6	1,281.7	1,334.8	1,332.1	1,322.6	1,381.0	1,327.5	1,318.2	1,300.0	1,391.0	1,428.7	1,326.1
2000	1,425.6	1,388.9	1,442.2	1,461.4	1,418.5	1,462.0	1,473.0	1,485.5	1,468.0	1,390.1	1,375.0	1,330.9	1,426.8
2001	1,335.6	1,305.8	1,185.9	1,189.8	1,270.4	1,238.8	1,204.5	1,178.5	1,047.6	1,076.6	1,129.7	1,144.9	1,192.3
2002	1,140.2	1,100.7	1,153.8	1,112.0	1,079.3	1,014.1	903.6	912.6	867.8	854.6	909.9	899.2	995.6
2003	895.8	837.6	846.6	890.0	936.0	988.0	992.5	989.5	1,019.4	1,038.7	1,049.9	1,080.6	963.7

Average.   Source: Index and Option Market (IOM), division of the Chicago Mercantile Exchange (CME)

STOCK INDEX FUTURES, U.S.

Composite Index of Leading Indicators (1992 = 100)

Year	Jan.	Feb.	Mar.	Apr.	May	June	July	Aug.	Sept.	Oct.	Nov.	Dec.	Average
1994	101.2	101.0	101.5	101.4	101.4	101.4	101.2	101.5	101.4	101.5	101.6	101.6	101.4
1995	101.5	101.1	100.7	100.6	100.4	100.5	100.7	101.0	101.1	100.9	100.9	101.2	100.9
1996	100.5	101.4	101.6	101.8	102.1	102.3	102.3	102.4	102.5	102.5	102.5	102.6	102.0
1997	102.8	103.3	103.4	103.3	103.6	103.6	103.9	104.0	104.3	104.4	104.7	104.6	103.8
1998	104.8	105.2	105.4	105.4	105.4	105.2	105.6	105.6	105.6	105.7	106.2	106.4	105.5
1999	104.5	104.7	104.8	104.7	105.0	105.3	105.6	105.5	105.4	105.5	105.7	110.3	105.6
2000	110.7	110.3	110.5	110.5	110.5	110.4	109.8	109.9	109.9	109.5	109.2	108.8	110.0
2001	108.9	109.0	108.7	108.6	109.3	109.5	109.8	109.7	109.1	109.2	110.1	110.5	109.4
2002	111.0	111.0	111.0	110.8	111.4	111.2	111.0	110.9	110.4	110.4	111.0	111.1	110.9
2003[1]	111.0	110.6	110.4	110.5	111.6	112.0	112.8	113.2	113.3	113.9	114.1	114.3	112.3

[1] Preliminary.   *Source: The Conference Board (TCB) Copyrighted.*

Consumer Confidence, The Conference Board   (1985 = 100)

Year	Jan.	Feb.	Mar.	Apr.	May	June	July	Aug.	Sept.	Oct.	Nov.	Dec.	Average
1994	82.6	79.9	86.7	92.1	88.9	92.5	91.3	90.4	89.5	89.1	100.4	103.4	90.6
1995	101.4	99.4	100.2	104.6	102.0	94.6	101.4	102.4	97.3	96.3	101.6	99.2	100.0
1996	88.4	98.0	98.4	104.8	103.5	100.1	107.0	112.0	111.8	107.3	109.5	114.2	104.6
1997	118.7	118.9	118.5	118.5	127.9	129.9	126.3	127.6	130.2	123.4	128.1	136.2	125.4
1998	128.3	137.4	133.8	137.2	136.3	138.2	137.2	133.1	126.4	119.3	126.4	126.7	131.7
1999	128.9	133.1	134.0	135.5	137.7	139.0	136.2	136.0	134.2	130.5	137.0	141.7	135.3
2000	144.7	140.8	137.1	137.7	144.7	139.2	143.0	140.8	142.5	135.8	132.6	128.6	139.0
2001	115.7	109.3	116.9	109.9	116.1	118.9	116.3	114.0	97.0	85.3	84.9	94.6	106.6
2002	97.8	95.0	110.7	108.5	110.3	106.3	97.4	94.5	93.7	79.6	84.9	80.7	96.6
2003[1]	78.8	64.8	61.4	81.0	83.6	83.5	77.0	81.7	77.0	81.7	92.5	91.7	79.6

[1] Preliminary.   *Source: The Conference Board (TCB) Copyrighted.*

Capacity Utilization Rates (Total Industry)   In Percent

Year	Jan.	Feb.	Mar.	Apr.	May	June	July	Aug.	Sept.	Oct.	Nov.	Dec.	Average
1994	82.6	82.8	83.2	83.3	83.7	83.9	84.1	83.9	83.8	84.1	84.4	84.9	83.9
1995	84.9	84.5	84.3	83.9	83.7	83.6	83.4	83.8	83.9	83.3	83.2	83.0	83.4
1996	82.4	83.2	82.6	83.1	83.2	83.5	83.2	83.2	83.1	83.0	82.5	82.5	82.4
1997	82.4	82.6	82.5	82.6	82.4	82.3	82.6	82.8	82.7	83.4	83.4	83.4	82.9
1998	83.0	82.6	82.6	82.6	82.6	81.5	81.1	82.0	81.3	81.5	80.9	80.6	81.8
1999	80.4	80.4	80.5	80.4	80.5	80.5	80.7	80.7	80.6	81.0	81.5	81.7	81.4
2000	81.9	82.0	82.2	82.5	82.7	82.7	82.3	82.6	82.4	81.2	80.7	80.2	81.8
2001	79.3	78.9	78.5	77.8	77.5	76.7	76.7	76.4	75.5	75.0	75.1	74.6	77.4
2002	75.0	75.1	75.3	75.6	75.7	76.4	76.4	76.1	76.0	75.4	75.4	74.9	75.6
2003[1]	75.2	75.4	74.8	74.2	74.1	74.0	74.5	74.6	74.9	75.1	75.8	75.8	74.9

[1] Preliminary.   *Source: Bureau of Economic Analysis, U.S. Department of Commerce (BEA)*

Manufacturers New Orders, Durable Goods   In Billions of Constant Dollars

Year	Jan.	Feb.	Mar.	Apr.	May	June	July	Aug.	Sept.	Oct.	Nov.	Dec.	Average
1994	142.23	138.88	140.91	141.21	142.61	146.15	142.60	145.92	146.93	145.72	149.89	152.88	144.66
1995	153.42	151.82	151.72	146.32	149.74	148.21	147.45	152.12	156.78	154.37	154.09	158.89	154.10
1996	158.86	155.10	157.67	156.01	162.59	162.67	168.25	162.76	170.45	170.59	169.34	166.02	163.48
1997	171.73	174.80	170.02	173.13	177.05	176.93	175.82	181.08	181.15	181.33	189.71	181.44	177.03
1998	184.33	183.87	184.17	187.35	181.58	182.22	186.22	190.39	193.18	189.33	190.21	197.11	194.42
1999	211.18	203.31	209.39	204.68	206.78	207.27	216.02	218.02	214.83	212.77	215.34	229.47	209.76
2000	225.14	221.12	230.44	217.17	232.76	254.20	220.74	227.27	232.41	217.30	221.14	220.90	220.55
2001	197.36	205.41	209.56	198.11	201.86	196.99	196.53	194.41	174.92	199.09	187.14	188.34	195.44
2002	190.08	194.99	191.78	192.65	193.48	184.76	200.59	198.62	189.66	192.67	190.66	190.01	192.80
2003[1]	194.21	192.26	194.57	190.00	189.13	194.23	197.42	197.20	201.28	208.75	203.51		196.59

[1] Preliminary.   *Source: Bureau of Economic Analysis, U.S. Department of Commerce (BEA)*

Corporate Profits After Tax -- Quarterly   In Billions of Dollars

Year	First Quarter	Second Quarter	Third Quarter	Fourth Quarter	Average	Year	First Quarter	Second Quarter	Third Quarter	Fourth Quarter	Average
1992	314.2	320.9	281.9	316.8	308.5	1998	491.8	485.0	480.1	472.2	482.3
1993	325.6	340.8	343.5	370.1	345.0	1999	501.3	506.9	507.1	542.0	514.3
1994	349.4	379.8	401.0	416.6	386.7	2000	526.1	533.3	523.2	509.2	523.0
1995	440.1	456.6	464.8	468.5	457.5	2001	489.7	507.1	458.1	428.5	470.9
1996	493.5	501.0	500.9	515.4	502.7	2002	437.0	444.3	453.8	472.5	451.9
1997	530.7	549.4	573.8	566.9	555.2	2003[1]	490.2	465.9	515.4		490.5

[1] Preliminary.   *Source: Bureau of Economic Analysis, U.S. Department of Commerce (BEA)*

Change in Manufacturing and Trade Inventories   In Billions of Dollars

Year	Jan.	Feb.	Mar.	Apr.	May	June	July	Aug.	Sept.	Oct.	Nov.	Dec.	Average
1994	15.3	45.1	-8.1	42.1	114.2	56.3	60.8	98.6	60.3	71.8	65.3	64.5	57.2
1995	127.4	78.5	100.6	97.6	54.4	48.1	42.9	50.6	51.4	61.8	24.1	-39.7	58.5
1996	66.2	14.2	-27.7	61.5	-8.4	80.3	123.6	-272.1	90.6	143.4	86.1	72.0	19.9
1997	107.0	103.4	76.3	56.2	25.2	76.8	20.9	19.1	91.5	55.2	43.1	28.2	47.1
1998	27.8	86.1	85.7	38.5	5.5	11.4	-91.6	47.9	67.6	36.3	51.0		34.0
1999	10.4	36.8	66.7	31.2	44.4	61.6	67.2	42.5	58.0	50.4	121.1	70.9	50.6
2000	69.5	59.5	17.5	38.8	82.8	129.5	8 7	87.4	10.1	77.7	26.4	5.8	63.7
2001	1.7	-40.5	-73.0	-36.6	-38.9	-105.1	-68.2	-34.2	-75.3	-200.6	-139.2	-78.7	-65.2
2002	-0.9	-31.5	-47.8	-20.1	33.6	27.8	78.5	3.5	-106.8	18.5	33.0	-86.0	23.8
2003[1]	36.3	91.8	45.8	0.1	111.8	5.0	-26.4	-54.8	57.0	59.7	49.5		34.2

[1] Preliminary.   *Source: Bureau of Economic Analysis, U.S. Department of Commerce (BEA)*

Productivity: Index of Output per Hour, All Persons, Nonfarm Business -- Quarterly   (1992 = 100)

Year	First Quarter	Second Quarter	Third Quarter	Fourth Quarter	Average	Year	First Quarter	Second Quarter	Third Quarter	Fourth Quarter	Average
1992	99.3	99.9	99.7	101.1	100.0	1998	106.6	106.6	107.3	111.5	110.2
1993	100.1	99.7	100.1	100.8	100.2	1999	112.2	112.4	113.6	115.8	113.2
1994	100.2	100.5	101.0	101.2	100.7	2000	116.2	118.0	116.7	117.8	117.2
1995	100.5	100.9	101.3	101.1	100.7	2001	117.8	118.4	117.2	119.3	118.2
1996	101.5	101.7	102.0	102.4	103.7	2002	121.8	122.3	123.8	126.0	123.5
1997	103.4	104.0	105.6	105.9	107.2	2003[1]	126.7	128.9	131.8		129.1

[1] Preliminary.   *Source: Bureau of Economic Analysis, U.S. Department of Commerce (BEA)*

Civilian Unemployment Rate

Year	Jan.	Feb.	Mar.	Apr.	May	June	July	Aug.	Sept.	Oct.	Nov.	Dec.	Average
1994	6.7	6.6	6.5	6.4	6.0	6.1	6.1	6.1	5.9	5.8	5.6	5.4	6.1
1995	5.6	5.5	5.4	5.7	5.6	5.6	5.7	5.7	5.7	5.5	5.6	5.6	5.6
1996	5.7	5.5	5.5	5.5	5.5	5.3	5.4	5.2	5.2	5.2	5.3	5.3	5.4
1997	5.4	5.3	5.2	4.9	4.8	5.0	4.9	4.9	4.9	4.8	4.6	4.7	5.0
1998	4.6	4.6	4.7	4.3	4.4	4.5	4.5	4.5	4.5	4.5	4.4	4.3	4.5
1999	4.3	4.4	4.2	4.3	4.2	4.3	4.3	4.2	4.2	4.1	4.1	4.1	4.2
2000	4.0	4.1	4.1	3.9	4.1	4.0	4.0	4.1	3.9	3.9	4.0	4.0	4.0
2001	4.2	4.2	4.3	4.5	4.4	4.5	4.5	4.9	4.9	5.4	5.7	5.8	4.8
2002	5.6	5.5	5.7	6.0	5.8	5.9	5.9	5.7	5.6	5.7	6.0	6.0	5.8
2003[1]	5.7	5.8	5.8	6.0	6.1	6.4	6.2	6.1	6.1	6.0	5.9	5.7	6.0

[1] Preliminary.   *Source: Bureau of Economic Analysis, U.S. Department of Commerce (BEA)*

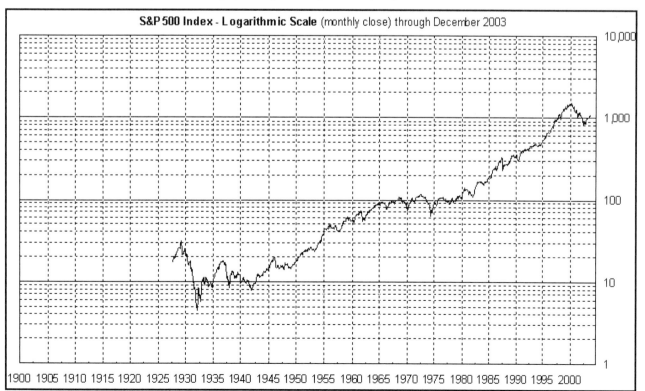

257

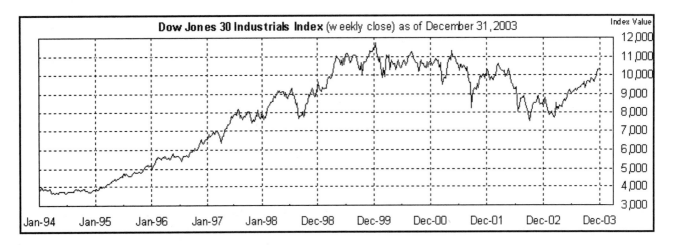

Dow Jones 30 Industrials Index (weekly close) as of December 31, 2003

S&P 500 Index (weekly close) as of December 31, 2003

NASDAQ 100 Index (weekly close) as of December 31, 2003

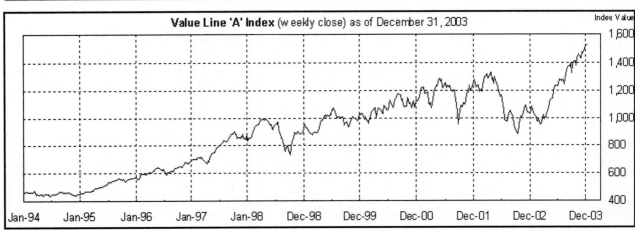

Value Line 'A' Index (weekly close) as of December 31, 2003

Volume of Trading of S&P 500 Stock Index Futures in Chicago   In Thousands of Contracts

Year	Jan.	Feb.	Mar.	Apr.	May	June	July	Aug.	Sept.	Oct.	Nov.	Dec.	Total
1994	2,130	2,605	4,173	2,781	2,808	3,805	2,187	2,789	3,837	3,364	3,517	3,749	37,745
1995	2,703	2,733	4,449	2,473	3,497	3,732	2,565	3,018	3,701	3,250	2,966	3,452	38,539
1996	3,520	3,872	4,011	2,722	3,456	3,530	3,215	2,577	3,739	3,298	2,916	3,751	40,607
1997	3,371	2,857	4,163	3,608	3,203	3,955	2,617	2,848	3,556	3,136	1,994	2,982	38,290
1998	2,270	1,878	3,018	2,237	2,253	3,524	2,139	3,019	3,802	2,598	1,831	2,835	31,404
1999	1,994	2,145	3,018	1,960	2,007	2,768	1,756	2,200	3,017	2,150	1,075	2,322	27,013
2000	1,011	1,917	2,956	1,651	1,685	2,226	1,079	1,358	2,149	1,681	1,636	2,212	22,461
2001	1,552	1,631	2,781	1,624	1,653	2,154	1,320	1,598	2,571	1,798	1,692	2,124	22,498
2002	1,459	1,677	2,251	1,473	1,585	2,721	2,206	1,615	2,943	1,931	1,374	2,465	23,700
2003	1,443	1,343	2,900	1,257	1,416	2,782	1,223	1,079	2,412	1,118	921	2,281	20,175

Source: Index and Option Market (IOM), division of the Chicago Mercantile Exchange (CME)

Average Open Interest of S&P 500 Stock Index Futures in Chicago   In Contracts

Year	Jan.	Feb.	Mar.	Apr.	May	June	July	Aug.	Sept.	Oct.	Nov.	Dec.
1994	376,450	391,648	420,130	401,636	438,218	599,134	434,056	455,742	475,868	461,188	487,162	502,740
1995	427,004	442,628	445,584	420,104	443,296	453,364	420,024	422,608	417,812	402,794	441,780	447,528
1996	406,400	428,058	419,688	368,620	399,070	407,914	369,248	382,266	413,944	374,726	416,102	448,382
1997	393,086	396,528	417,542	377,100	392,034	417,006	372,274	392,812	423,449	391,922	402,044	417,717
1998	394,410	408,851	417,721	365,746	371,732	412,739	370,410	385,820	434,838	405,395	421,928	435,907
1999	399,093	406,516	410,164	381,402	391,035	400,503	372,455	385,809	408,176	394,316	408,751	416,425
2000	369,295	374,365	400,089	379,651	383,677	409,448	380,118	391,867	416,600	413,912	447,245	498,049
2001	488,284	495,621	517,666	498,594	490,148	505,063	485,839	501,281	556,737	529,730	550,201	551,175
2002	495,352	519,023	542,358	513,048	542,839	592,888	594,727	621,558	644,806	607,848	631,224	647,022
2003	596,064	619,738	658,749	622,917	643,030	691,003	611,564	611,578	631,509	582,111	589,392	633,997

Source: Index and Option Market (IOM), division of the Chicago Mercantile Exchange (CME)

Volume of Trading of S&P 400 Midcap Stock Index Futures in Chicago   In Contracts

Year	Jan.	Feb.	Mar.	Apr.	May	June	July	Aug.	Sept.	Oct.	Nov.	Dec.	Total
1994	15,619	12,126	40,906	13,598	19,158	46,608	11,323	23,590	41,851	14,572	21,223	43,438	304,012
1995	12,097	13,983	36,531	8,674	11,263	31,526	10,076	15,921	42,147	18,905	20,464	46,907	268,494
1996	25,322	21,781	46,382	13,417	19,190	33,720	20,338	17,112	37,149	12,510	12,459	36,798	296,178
1997	13,698	14,968	33,860	16,993	15,463	33,287	12,162	14,923	39,164	18,063	10,776	43,242	266,599
1998	13,622	12,896	42,781	15,623	17,023	38,656	15,345	19,967	44,913	23,591	16,713	48,870	310,000
1999	18,752	20,938	43,395	27,664	16,574	42,709	17,790	18,188	39,723	18,341	19,974	42,073	326,121
2000	16,918	15,298	45,942	23,892	19,863	42,514	12,140	12,515	42,658	21,701	25,334	59,265	338,040
2001	21,527	19,884	58,286	18,061	19,258	50,331	22,029	23,805	50,706	23,741	19,591	51,641	378,860
2002	22,322	22,814	43,819	23,019	22,484	51,775	30,607	23,075	52,375	25,593	21,262	48,105	387,250
2003	18,827	18,392	44,454	15,841	15,194	40,597	15,153	12,082	43,112	15,253	13,109	50,797	302,811

Source: Index and Option Market (IOM), division of the Chicago Mercantile Exchange (CME)

Average Open Interest of S&P 400 Midcap Stock Index Futures in Chicago   In Contracts

Year	Jan.	Feb.	Mar.	Apr.	May	June	July	Aug.	Sept.	Oct.	Nov.	Dec.
1994	13,183	11,999	12,748	10,801	10,829	11,902	11,970	12,369	15,002	13,702	13,896	14,494
1995	13,787	13,355	11,130	9,275	9,329	9,929	11,198	11,708	13,107	11,702	12,341	12,863
1996	11,088	10,474	11,375	8,700	9,254	10,403	9,763	10,867	11,168	9,641	10,596	11,107
1997	11,215	11,825	11,258	9,721	10,807	10,877	11,292	12,346	13,505	11,595	11,874	13,329
1998	12,688	13,319	14,363	14,130	13,352	13,940	12,964	13,589	14,893	16,645	16,768	17,569
1999	16,191	16,309	14,573	12,154	12,705	14,422	14,263	13,496	13,182	12,699	13,933	14,902
2000	12,810	13,119	13,965	12,495	13,355	14,040	12,957	13,162	15,026	16,143	16,510	17,479
2001	15,246	15,461	17,235	16,953	15,623	16,606	16,334	16,132	16,718	15,109	15,307	15,337
2002	13,691	14,109	14,954	14,340	16,402	16,611	15,121	16,213	17,006	14,695	15,394	16,432
2003	13,793	13,498	14,530	13,120	13,353	13,986	13,123	13,029	13,726	14,014	15,465	17,446

Source: Index and Option Market (IOM), division of the Chicago Mercantile Exchange (CME)

STOCK INDEX FUTURES, U.S.

Volume of Trading of NASDAQ 100 Index Futures in Chicago   In Contracts

Year	Jan.	Feb.	Mar.	Apr.	May	June	July	Aug.	Sept.	Oct.	Nov.	Dec.	Total
1996	----	----	----	13,106	25,201	34,672	41,166	25,872	66,157	67,868	54,275	73,107	401,424
1997	49,939	57,417	82,118	81,402	72,027	90,522	63,757	62,095	61,425	72,595	48,929	79,626	821,852
1998	65,660	60,471	96,694	68,574	70,704	111,933	106,791	107,509	97,099	100,156	71,441	107,995	1,065,027
1999	111,120	132,436	169,368	181,776	172,840	226,193	164,822	176,429	242,149	209,007	218,672	317,418	2,322,230
2000	349,813	366,408	575,942	503,064	460,085	432,062	296,944	310,549	445,334	490,863	400,412	464,454	5,095,930
2001	422,811	416,445	650,488	498,026	487,334	542,305	369,731	369,845	474,133	516,469	391,042	434,690	5,573,319
2002	380,076	367,561	436,495	378,294	443,579	529,496	454,630	334,242	466,898	367,750	315,925	428,341	4,903,287
2003	360,307	301,454	487,716	301,395	330,640	519,597	350,514	251,058	488,363	322,898	259,960	447,119	4,421,021

Source: Index and Option Market (IOM), division of the Chicago Mercantile Exchange (CME)

Average Open Interest of NASDAQ 100 Index Futures in Chicago   In Contracts

Year	Jan.	Feb.	Mar.	Apr.	May	June	July	Aug.	Sept.	Oct.	Nov.	Dec.
1996	----	----	----	1,364	3,336	6,182	5,977	4,737	7,957	10,999	10,465	8,897
1997	6,610	7,064	8,073	7,627	7,587	8,270	6,346	8,255	8,444	6,235	8,831	8,210
1998	6,918	8,184	9,314	7,652	8,833	11,128	9,991	9,507	9,233	8,187	9,176	10,838
1999	10,669	14,766	19,786	21,286	23,028	26,938	21,646	22,765	21,808	19,946	23,429	27,876
2000	27,242	34,555	37,795	36,512	37,578	35,314	29,974	32,922	34,754	35,559	44,022	48,757
2001	46,582	49,495	59,916	56,328	49,337	54,394	50,854	55,234	61,665	51,977	61,196	67,769
2002	49,992	52,883	52,617	51,157	65,219	73,151	60,625	67,760	84,317	72,229	77,451	76,660
2003	71,219	79,905	87,252	71,636	77,717	88,914	80,002	83,940	91,685	75,191	85,651	86,480

Source: Index and Option Market (IOM), division of the Chicago Mercantile Exchange (CME)

Volume of Trading of Dow Jones Industrials Index Futures in Chicago   In Contracts

Year	Jan.	Feb.	Mar.	Apr.	May	June	July	Aug.	Sept.	Oct.	Nov.	Dec.	Total
1997	----	----	----	----	----	----	----	----	----	300,771	203,534	249,191	753,496
1998	260,628	244,907	293,651	284,515	259,720	358,647	298,254	366,874	381,320	344,732	224,397	246,441	3,564,086
1999	284,341	262,932	341,744	365,209	364,417	365,429	279,381	342,753	386,373	378,531	266,183	257,805	3,895,098
2000	322,046	340,377	472,179	321,026	284,005	270,374	215,234	211,612	277,620	319,636	267,051	268,010	3,569,170
2001	275,814	310,088	594,326	411,767	377,620	389,919	320,335	410,927	573,479	520,885	375,793	329,898	4,890,851
2002	409,009	472,893	538,804	467,571	456,210	616,754	811,518	539,507	639,154	699,005	427,235	407,665	6,485,325
2003	452,579	426,198	559,372	428,972	410,967	473,432	368,277	286,508	367,845	218,394	157,726	266,032	4,416,302

Source: Chicago Board of Trade (CBT)

Average Open Interest of Dow Jones Industrials Index Futures in Chicago   In Contracts

Year	Jan.	Feb.	Mar.	Apr.	May	June	July	Aug.	Sept.	Oct.	Nov.	Dec.
1997	----	----	----	----	----	----	----	----	----	5,249	11,542	15,952
1998	14,853	15,558	14,421	13,846	14,464	16,226	15,707	17,586	18,569	17,416	17,795	17,597
1999	16,794	19,401	19,807	20,492	25,890	22,198	21,556	25,333	23,977	24,847	22,342	17,299
2000	13,713	16,331	20,443	18,157	19,253	17,394	14,367	15,748	14,840	15,087	19,113	20,966
2001	21,830	23,423	28,340	32,497	33,767	29,357	26,792	33,015	35,451	31,997	30,598	27,018
2002	23,862	35,588	37,582	28,714	32,810	34,482	32,412	32,272	34,665	31,923	34,045	31,892
2003	27,032	30,429	34,371	31,160	34,936	36,352	36,773	43,974	41,747	34,066	37,835	39,727

Source: Chicago Board of Trade (CBT)

Volume of Trading of E-mini NASDAQ 100 Index Futures in Chicago   In Thousands of Contracts

Year	Jan.	Feb.	Mar.	Apr.	May	June	July	Aug.	Sept.	Oct.	Nov.	Dec.	Total
1999	----	----	----	----	----	29	62	83	90	105	113	193	675
2000	304	382	604	628	745	762	756	883	1,508	1,589	1,446	1,512	11,118
2001	1,845	1,942	2,603	2,873	2,908	2,969	2,529	2,568	2,387	3,935	3,151	2,595	32,304
2002	3,719	3,649	3,652	4,227	4,625	4,713	5,789	4,225	4,337	6,252	4,812	4,490	54,491
2003	5,200	4,620	5,749	5,132	5,075	6,323	6,369	4,816	7,095	6,601	5,254	5,655	67,889

Source: Index and Option Market (IOM), division of the Chicago Mercantile Exchange (CME)

Average Open Interest of E-mini NASDAQ 100 Index Futures in Chicago   In Contracts

Year	Jan.	Feb.	Mar.	Apr.	May	June	July	Aug.	Sept.	Oct.	Nov.	Dec.
1999	----	----	----	----	----	894	2,410	4,320	3,867	3,037	5,051	8,685
2000	8,582	9,250	11,117	15,625	23,465	26,095	23,863	31,506	30,956	33,123	58,709	54,420
2001	45,370	65,061	79,962	78,094	90,822	95,236	90,803	131,259	132,349	75,686	115,350	124,023
2002	78,070	94,150	98,159	100,849	153,348	176,394	130,337	171,043	162,133	110,952	154,104	155,987
2003	169,160	227,905	258,023	196,739	240,759	257,390	262,564	316,032	287,936	214,659	279,379	244,333

Source: Chicago Board of Trade (CBT)

Volume of Trading of E-mini S&P 500 Index Futures in Chicago   In Thousands of Contracts

Year	Jan.	Feb.	Mar.	Apr.	May	June	July	Aug.	Sept.	Oct.	Nov.	Dec.	Total
1997	----	----	----	----	----	----	----	----	190	282	194	220	886
1998	269	221	285	298	285	371	380	569	430	519	431	492	4,551
1999	576	636	775	602	843	868	887	1,065	1,144	1,237	1,072	964	10,669
2000	1,306	1,388	1,489	1,462	1,676	1,550	1,403	1,439	1,683	2,109	1,843	1,673	19,021
2001	2,226	2,231	3,191	3,067	2,931	2,905	2,925	3,478	3,601	5,255	4,021	3,289	39,119
2002	4,933	5,337	5,609	7,165	7,564	9,772	14,277	11,200	11,765	17,175	11,054	9,892	115,742
2003	13,584	10,601	15,820	13,520	12,846	15,040	14,854	10,860	15,354	14,558	11,002	11,108	161,177

Source: Index and Option Market (IOM), division of the Chicago Mercantile Exchange (CME)

Average Open Interest of E-mini S&P 500 Index Futures in Chicago   In Contracts

Year	Jan.	Feb.	Mar.	Apr.	May	June	July	Aug.	Sept.	Oct.	Nov.	Dec.
1997	----	----	----	----	----	----	----	----	6,122	10,749	16,652	15,594
1998	8,986	15,144	17,540	12,134	16,341	16,337	8,600	29,003	14,201	13,003	15,376	15,842
1999	16,215	24,969	20,971	44,037	20,790	22,077	16,960	25,551	24,960	25,056	30,013	26,544
2000	17,180	25,282	29,645	28,738	38,257	39,918	33,696	45,619	42,442	49,468	66,143	63,052
2001	55,514	68,516	79,934	91,866	110,788	91,638	97,093	126,197	152,253	134,662	224,754	178,681
2002	86,278	120,099	139,965	156,392	225,593	246,288	291,654	349,037	319,341	312,885	418,964	385,220
2003	265,170	356,616	490,037	567,591	741,790	718,511	399,502	492,470	513,398	460,938	467,668	525,310

Source: Index and Option Market (IOM), division of the Chicago Mercantile Exchange (CME)

Volume of Trading of NYSE Composite Stock Index Futures in New York   In Contracts

Year	Jan.	Feb.	Mar.	Apr.	May	June	July	Aug.	Sept.	Oct.	Nov.	Dec.	Total
1997	77,273	69,896	92,672	93,051	83,200	94,033	83,893	85,435	89,010	80,398	35,278	45,144	929,283
1998	39,823	33,856	46,307	36,316	35,765	47,905	61,862	93,694	73,646	50,314	27,106	50,457	597,051
1999	30,430	31,482	49,055	29,219	26,201	27,103	15,653	22,556	28,433	23,058	16,528	17,848	317,566
2000	15,324	16,603	21,235	14,394	10,637	11,210	4,307	5,574	5,085	6,145	5,170	9,974	125,658
2001	5,490	4,307	19,300	6,594	4,091	10,353	23,855	32,182	23,399	22,276	19,231	34,661	205,739
2002	20,273	21,056	26,949	27,801	24,166	22,325	21,873	14,561	13,193	10,821	5,897	7,564	216,479
2003	3,917	5,622	8,815	7,622	2,699	3,746	592	481	527	408	726	3,282	38,437

Source: New York Futures Exchange (NYFE)

Average Open Interest of NYSE Composite Stock Index Futures in New York   In Contracts

Year	Jan.	Feb.	Mar.	Apr.	May	June	July	Aug.	Sept.	Oct.	Nov.	Dec.
1997	3,126	3,232	3,194	2,801	3,154	2,744	2,316	2,823	2,780	2,384	3,005	4,354
1998	4,803	5,216	5,252	4,754	4,888	5,990	10,154	12,249	10,574	8,554	7,977	9,806
1999	8,299	8,661	5,457	4,050	4,169	3,849	3,419	3,882	3,730	3,958	4,447	4,260
2000	3,653	3,715	3,747	3,285	2,533	2,597	2,452	2,793	2,463	1,690	1,943	2,406
2001	2,387	2,648	3,510	3,694	2,929	2,408	5,271	5,802	5,451	6,448	6,884	6,617
2002	4,341	4,215	5,147	4,141	3,605	3,178	5,157	5,772	3,649	1,567	2,209	2,065
2003	1,255	1,496	1,781	1,494	1,194	933	593	665	640	533	604	752

Source: New York Futures Exchange (NYFE)

Volume of Trading of Mini-Value Line Stock Index Futures in Kansas City   In Contracts

Year	Jan.	Feb.	Mar.	Apr.	May	June	July	Aug.	Sept.	Oct.	Nov.	Dec.	Total
1997	12,598	10,997	14,706	17,397	12,881	12,138	12,159	15,974	14,037	13,415	6,191	11,987	154,480
1998	7,086	4,989	6,893	6,590	7,307	7,537	5,067	8,700	7,170	5,959	3,894	4,978	76,170
1999	2,938	3,241	4,800	3,958	1,915	3,546	1,792	1,739	2,184	1,908	1,225	1,547	30,793
2000	1,397	1,097	1,468	1,054	1,280	811	698	642	1,003	1,328	1,526	1,460	13,764
2001	1,248	1,470	2,441	1,650	902	1,325	1,183	1,071	1,982	1,591	1,104	1,387	17,354
2002	1,513	1,237	1,598	1,283	1,794	1,511	1,878	1,113	974	1,472	1,467	1,530	17,370
2003	376	181	721	264	90	88	46	153	80	94	94	204	2,391

Source: Kansas City Board of Trade (KCBT)

Average Open Interest of Mini-Value Line Stock Index Futures in Kansas City   In Contracts

Year	Jan.	Feb.	Mar.	Apr.	May	June	July	Aug.	Sept.	Oct.	Nov.	Dec.
1997	1,459	1,354	1,338	1,448	1,326	1,686	2,160	2,523	1,980	1,477	1,213	1,675
1998	1,739	1,442	1,433	1,498	1,549	1,390	697	839	667	696	914	780
1999	746	738	699	725	900	967	515	503	381	314	300	283
2000	273	284	246	135	155	148	155	216	179	182	181	185
2001	233	333	377	233	275	285	283	268	222	125	249	368
2002	299	348	367	372	359	229	142	161	100	127	300	417
2003	376	328	169	89	45	33	26	33	48	36	40	46

Source: Kansas City Board of Trade (KCBT)

Stock Index Futures, Worldwide

World stocks – World stock markets in 2003 put in a stellar performance, shaking off the bear market that plagued the markets since late 2000. The MSCI World Index, a benchmark for large companies based in 23 developed countries, rallied 33.2% in 2003, shaking off three consecutive years of declines (2002 –19.5%, 2001 –16.5%, 2000 –12.9%). That three-year decline in 2000-2002 was the longest string of losses in the MSCI World Index since the introduction of the index in 1970. Still, the rally in 2003 was only enough to retrace 50.5% of the 1,747-point plunge seen from the record high of 3772.659 posted in March 2000 to the 7-year low of 2025.606 posted in September 2002. In addition, the total return from the MSCI World Index at the end of 2003 was still negative at –0.47% on a 5-year horizon.

The world stock markets took off in 2003 after the war with Iraq concluded and business and consumer confidence began to recover. The 3-year slump in the world economy and stock markets finally came to a close in response to heavy doses of monetary stimulus in all major regions of the world and with fiscal stimulus from the US. The stocks that benefited the most in 2003 were IT stocks, commodity-based stocks, cyclical stocks, and the emerging markets. However, sectors such as cyclical stocks and the emerging markets could stall in 2004 if interest rates rise as expected and cause concern about slower world economic growth and higher financial risks for the emerging markets.

Small-Capitalization Stocks – World small-cap stocks did better than the large-cap stocks in 2003. The MSCI World Small-Cap Index, which tracks companies with market caps between $200 million and $1.5 billion, rallied +55.5% in 2003, performing much better than the MSCI World Index of +33.2%. Small-cap stocks typically perform better than large-caps in the early stages of a bull market because they typically get beaten down much more during bear markets when risks are higher and therefore have farther to rebound once economic conditions improve.

World Industry Groups – World stocks were led higher in 2003 by a sharp advance in technology stocks, which finally snapped back after their bubble burst back in 2000. The technology industry in 2000-2003 was plagued by severe overcapacity and a sharp drop in profits. The MSCI World Information Technology Index in 2003 rallied +47.6%, outperforming the World Index increase of +33.2% by more than 14 percentage points. The IT sector has a long way to go, however, before overcoming the losses in the 2000-2003 period (2002 –39%, 2001 –30%, 2000 –42%).

The second best performing industry group in 2003 was World Materials stocks, which benefited from the extremely sharp rally in basic commodity prices in the second half of 2003. The MSCI World Materials Index, which tracks the world's largest companies producing cement, chemicals, lumber, and metals, rallied +41.9% in 2003, more than overcoming the losses seen in the previous three years (2002 – 6.3%, 2001 –6.8%, 2000 –14.9%).

Emerging markets – Emerging stock markets did very well in 2003 as the prospects greatly improved for emerging economies with the sharp upward turn in world economic growth. In addition, many of the emerging market economies are dependent on commodity exports and that was a sector that soared in the second half of 2003 along with commodity prices. The MSCI Emerging Markets Free Index, which tracks companies based in 26 emerging countries, rallied +51.6% in 2003, doing much better than the stock markets in developed countries. Emerging market stock funds saw a heavy influx of investor capital in 2003 totaling more than $11 billion in 2003, according to EmergingPorfolio.com Fund Research, which was the highest inflow since the firm started keeping records in 1996.

North America – In North America, Mexico's stock market smartly beat both the US and Canadian stock markets. The Mexican Bolsa index closed 2003 up +43.55%, beating the S&P 500 gain in the US of +26.38%, and the gain in the Toronto Exchange Composite index of +24.29%.

Latin America – In Latin America, there were some very impressive gains. Venezuela did the best with a +177% gain, followed by Argentina at +104%, Brazil (+97%), Peru (+74%), Jamaica (+49%), Chile (+48%), and Columbia (+42%). The only losses in Latin America were in Ecuador and Costa Rico, which each saw 8% declines.

Europe – Europe put in a weaker performance than other world stock markets mainly because of the lagging improvement in the European economy in 2003 and the strength in the euro, which depressed export growth. The Dow Jones European Stoxx 50 index in 2003 showed a gain of only +10.50%. Within Europe, the German Dax index did well at +37%, followed by Italy's Ibex 35 index, which closed +28%. The French CAC40 index closed +16% and the UK FTSE 100 index lagged with a +14% gain.

While the strong euro hurt the profit of export-oriented European companies, it greatly helped dollar-based investors in European stocks. The Dow Jones European Stoxx 50 index rallied +10.5% in euro terms in 2003, but rallied nearly three times as much by +32.6% in dollar terms. That meant that a dollar-based investor did better in European stocks than in US stocks, after taking into account the sharp rally in the euro against the dollar.

Asia – Asia saw some sharp stock market gains like the rest of the world. The Japanese Nikkei index closed the year up +24.5% as it finally appeared that Japan was starting to come out of its decade-long slump. Japan was helped by banking system reforms, exports to China, and by the Bank of Japan's stepped-up monetary stimulus efforts. The Morgan Stanley Capital International China index closed +77% in 2003. Thailand's SET index led Asian stocks as a whole with a 117% rally, with India coming in second at +73%, and Pakistan third at +67%.

The MSCI Far East index rallied 34% as the Far East countries were all boosted by the sharp growth in China. China's imports from its nearby trading partners lifted all boats in the Far East. In addition, global investors poured capital into the Far East in a play on China. US mutual funds bought more than $12 billion of Asian stocks in 2003, a dramatically better performance than the net selling of $2.4 billion in 2002, according to figures from EmergingPorfolio.com. Asian stocks are expected to do well again in 2004 due to the ongoing dramatic growth in China and a recovery in Japan.

STOCK INDEX FUTURES, WORLDWIDE

Comparison of International Stock Price Indexes   (1990 = 100)

Year	Jan.	Feb.	Mar.	Apr.	May	June	July	Aug.	Sept.	Oct.	Nov.	Dec.	Average
United States
1997	236.3	237.7	227.6	240.9	255.0	266.1	286.8	270.4	284.7	274.9	287.2	291.7	263.3
1998	294.7	315.4	331.2	334.2	327.9	340.8	336.9	287.7	305.7	330.2	349.8	369.5	327.0
1999	384.6	372.2	386.7	401.3	391.3	412.6	399.4	396.9	385.6	409.7	417.5	441.6	400.0
2000	419.2	410.7	450.5	436.6	427.0	437.2	430.1	456.2	431.8	429.7	395.3	396.9	426.8
2001	410.6	372.7	348.8	375.6	377.5	368.0	364.1	340.7	313.0	310.0	342.5	345.1	356.4
2002	339.7	332.7	344.9	323.7	320.8	297.5	274.0	275.4	245.1	266.2	281.4	264.5	297.2
2003[1]	257.2	252.8	255.0	275.6	289.6	292.9	297.7	303.0	299.4	315.8	318.1	334.2	290.9
Canada
1997	178.6	180.0	171.0	174.7	186.6	188.2	201.0	193.3	205.8	200.0	190.4	195.8	188.8
1998	195.8	207.3	220.9	224.0	221.9	215.3	202.6	161.7	164.0	181.5	185.4	189.6	197.5
1999	196.7	184.5	192.9	205.0	200.0	204.9	207.0	203.8	203.4	212.1	219.9	245.9	206.3
2000	247.9	266.8	276.6	273.2	270.4	298.0	304.2	328.8	303.3	281.8	257.8	261.1	280.8
2001	272.5	236.1	222.4	232.3	238.6	226.1	224.8	216.3	199.9	201.3	217.1	224.7	226.0
2002	223.6	223.2	229.5	224.0	223.8	208.9	193.1	193.3	180.7	182.7	192.1	193.3	205.7
2003[1]	192.0	191.6	185.4	192.5	200.5	204.1	212.2	219.5	216.9	227.2	229.7	240.3	209.3
France
1997	138.5	143.5	146.2	145.2	142.2	157.3	169.2	152.4	165.5	150.7	157.3	165.0	152.8
1998	174.5	188.3	213.3	213.5	222.4	231.3	229.8	200.9	176.0	193.8	211.5	216.9	206.0
1999	233.9	225.2	231.0	242.4	239.4	249.6	241.1	252.5	252.6	269.0	293.9	327.8	254.9
2000	311.4	340.6	345.9	353.2	353.6	354.7	360.0	364.5	344.8	352.0	326.2	326.1	344.4
2001	330.0	295.3	285.0	310.3	300.1	287.5	279.8	258.0	224.4	238.9	246.3	254.5	275.8
2002	245.5	245.6	257.9	245.5	235.2	214.5	187.9	185.2	152.8	173.3	183.0	168.6	207.9
2003[1]	161.6	151.5	144.1	162.5	164.6	169.7	176.6	182.2	172.5	185.6	188.4	195.8	171.3
Germany[2]
1997	147.0	157.8	167.8	167.1	172.2	183.8	209.6	184.1	195.3	177.8	186.0	196.3	221.4
1998	204.9	217.5	234.9	302.0	329.3	348.7	347.3	285.8	264.6	276.2	297.0	295.8	299.1
1999	305.1	290.4	288.8	318.9	299.8	318.0	301.6	311.6	304.5	326.7	348.6	411.4	318.8
2000	404.2	452.0	449.3	438.4	420.4	407.9	425.1	426.7	401.9	418.5	376.8	380.4	416.8
2001	401.8	367.1	344.7	370.4	362.0	358.2	346.5	306.8	254.7	269.6	295.0	305.1	331.8
2002	302.0	297.9	319.1	298.1	284.9	259.1	218.8	219.5	163.7	186.4	196.3	171.0	243.1
2003[1]	162.5	150.6	143.3	173.9	176.4	190.4	206.2	206.0	192.6	216.2	221.5	234.4	189.5
Italy
1997	119.8	115.4	115.3	119.5	117.9	130.0	144.5	136.6	155.0	144.6	149.4	164.0	134.3
1998	184.0	194.3	239.3	220.9	236.1	222.1	240.5	208.1	184.6	194.1	223.7	231.5	214.9
1999	231.7	234.1	245.4	245.9	237.1	237.5	221.5	230.4	231.0	226.5	241.3	282.8	238.8
2000	276.8	330.7	308.7	303.1	307.1	309.0	308.5	320.5	307.2	318.8	316.3	298.3	308.8
2001	303.3	276.4	267.4	278.1	266.1	254.1	249.1	237.9	197.7	208.7	220.9	223.1	248.6
2002	223.6	220.8	233.9	227.6	214.5	196.7	182.7	183.2	157.1	170.0	185.9	170.0	197.2
2003[1]	162.6	166.3	157.2	173.3	180.5	181.1	181.6	184.4	181.5	189.0	196.3	195.6	179.1
Japan
1997	63.6	64.4	62.5	66.4	69.6	71.5	70.5	63.2	62.1	57.1	57.7	52.9	63.5
1998	57.7	58.4	57.3	54.3	54.4	54.9	56.8	48.9	46.5	47.1	51.6	48.0	53.0
1999	50.3	49.8	54.9	57.9	55.9	60.8	62.0	60.5	61.1	62.2	64.4	65.7	58.8
2000	67.8	69.2	70.6	62.4	56.7	60.4	54.6	58.5	54.6	50.4	50.8	47.8	58.7
2001	48.0	44.7	45.1	48.3	46.0	45.0	41.1	37.2	33.9	36.0	37.1	36.6	41.6
2002	34.7	36.7	38.2	39.9	40.8	36.8	34.3	33.4	32.6	30.0	32.0	29.8	34.9
2003[1]	28.9	29.0	27.7	27.2	29.2	31.5	33.2	35.9	35.5	35.5	35.0	37.0	32.1
United Kingdom
1997	192.8	194.7	194.0	197.3	203.3	201.8	212.0	210.3	226.8	211.9	211.4	222.7	206.6
1998	234.3	247.9	257.0	257.6	258.9	253.4	252.6	225.5	216.6	231.4	242.7	247.0	243.7
1999	249.0	261.0	267.4	279.8	266.9	272.2	270.2	271.5	261.1	268.3	285.2	299.5	271.0
2000	274.9	276.2	287.3	277.3	278.7	279.9	282.9	296.3	279.8	284.4	272.1	275.6	280.5
2001	279.9	264.9	250.5	265.0	259.7	252.0	246.1	239.3	216.2	222.9	232.2	233.1	246.8
2002	230.6	227.9	236.2	232.1	228.7	209.1	189.4	189.0	166.4	179.1	185.0	174.9	204.0
2003[1]	159.1	162.5	160.3	174.7	181.9	182.1	189.0	190.7	187.3	196.3	198.3	203.9	182.2

[1] Preliminary.   [2] Federal Republic of Germany.   Not Seasonally Adjusted.   *Source: Economic and Statistics Administration,*
U.S. Department of Commerce (ESA)

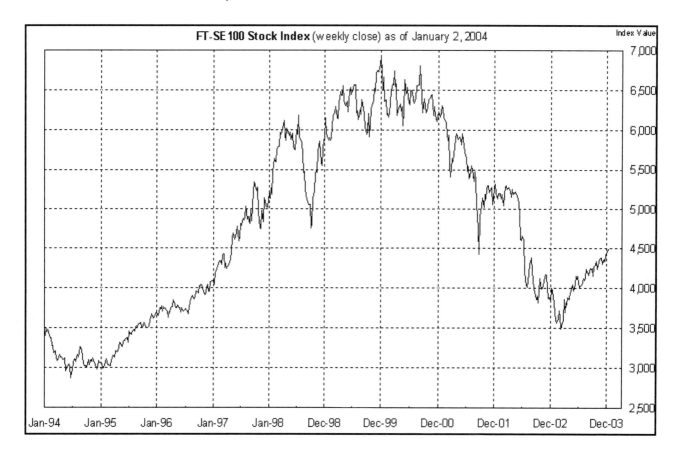

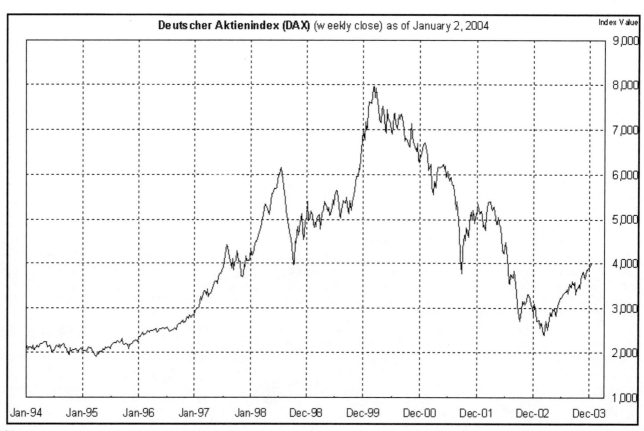

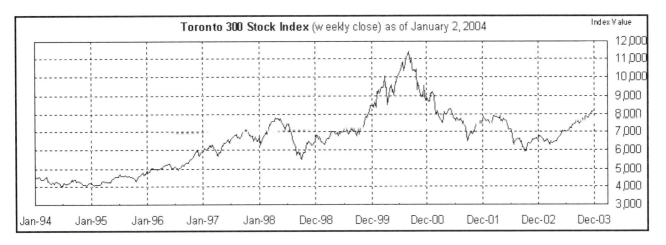

Toronto 300 Stock Index (weekly close) as of January 2, 2004

CAC-40 Stock Index (weekly close) as of January 2, 2004

Hang Seng Stock Index (weekly close) as of January 2, 2004

Nikkei 225 Stock Index (weekly close) as of December 30, 2003

Sugar

The white crystalline substance called sugar is the organic chemical compound sucrose, one of several related compounds all known as sugars. These include glucose, dextrose, fructose, and lactose. All sugars are members of the larger group of compounds called carbohydrates and are characterized by a sweet taste. Sucrose is termed a double sugar because it is composed of one molecule of glucose and one molecule of fructose. While sucrose is common in many plants, it occurs in the highest concentration in sugarcane (Saccharum officinarum) and sugar beets (Beta vulgaris). Sugarcane is about 7 to 18 percent sugar by weight while sugar beets are 8 to 22 percent.

Sugarcane is a member of the grass family and a perennial. It is thought to have originated in New Guinea several thousand years ago, migrating toward Asia and India to the west and into the islands of Polynesia to the east. Sugarcane is cultivated in tropical and subtropical regions around the world roughly between the Tropics of Cancer and Capricorn. It grows best in hot, wet climates where there is heavy rainfall followed by a dry season. On a commercial basis sugarcane is not grown from seeds but from cuttings or pieces of the stalk.

Sugar beets, which are produced in temperate or colder climates, are annuals grown from seeds.

Sugar beets do best with moderate temperatures and evenly distributed rainfall. The beets are planted in the spring and harvested in the fall. The sugar is contained in the root of the beet but the sugars from beets and cane are identical. Sugar beet production takes place mostly in Europe, the US, China, and Japan. Sugar beets are refined to yield white sugar and very little raw sugar is produced.

Sugar beets and sugar cane are produced in over 100 countries around the world. Of all the sugar produced, about 25 percent is processed from sugar beets and the remainder from sugar cane. The trend has been that production of sugar from cane is increasing relative to that produced from beets. The significance of this in that sugarcane is a perennial plant while the sugar beet is an annual, and due to the longer production cycle, sugarcane production and the sugar processed from that cane, may not be quite as responsive to changes in price.

Brazil is currently the largest producer and exporter of sugar in the world. U.S. production is about evenly divided between beet sugar and cane sugar production. The largest sugar beet producing states are Minnesota, Idaho, North Dakota, and Michigan and the largest cane producers are Florida, Louisiana, Texas, and Hawaii.

Sugar futures are traded on the Bolsa de Mercadorias & Futuros (BM&F), Kansai Commodities Exchange (KANEX), the Tokyo Grain Exchange (TGE), the London International Financial Futures and Options Exchange (LIFFE), and the CSCE Division of the New York Board of Trade (NYBOT). Options are traded on the BM&F, the TGE, the LIFFE and the NYBOT.

Raw sugar is traded on the CSCE Division of the New York Board of Trade while white sugar is traded on the London International Financial Futures Exchange (LIFFE). The most actively traded contract is the No. 11 (World) sugar contract at the CSCE. The No. 11 contract calls for the delivery of 112,000 pounds (50 long tons) of raw cane centrifugal sugar from any of 28 foreign countries of origin and the United States. The CSCE also trades the No. 14 sugar contract (Domestic), which calls for the delivery of raw centrifugal cane sugar in the United States. Futures on white sugar are traded on the London International Financial Futures Exchange and call for the delivery of 50 metric tons of white beet sugar, cane crystal sugar, or refined sugar of any origin from the crop current at the time of delivery.

Prices – World sugar prices on the CSCE No.11 sugar nearest-futures chart showed a downtrend during most of 2003 and remained in a generally depressed state not much above the 20-year lows. Specifically, world sugar prices in early 2003 rallied to a 2-1/2 year high of 9 cents/pound, but then entered a bear market that lasted the rest of the year. World sugar closed the year near 5.5 cents/pound, only one-half cent above the 3-1/2 year low near 5 cents posted in mid-2002 and only about 1 cent above the 20-year low of 4.4 cents posted in May 1999. The main bearish factor during 2003 was another very high production year in 2003/4 that was only slightly lower than the record posted in 2002/3. In addition, Brazilian exports hit a record high and Chinese imports dropped due to continued high domestic production.

Supply – World production of centrifugal (raw) sugar in 2003/4 was forecast by the USDA to drop to 144.635 million metric tons, down 1.8% from the record production level of 147.336 seen in 2002/3. Brazil was the world's largest producer of centrifugal sugar with 16% of world production in 2002/3, followed by India (14%), China (6%), and the US (5%). US centrifugal sugar production in 2003/4 was forecast at 8.070 million metric tons, up 6.2% from 7.6 million in 2002/3. Brazil's centrifugal sugar production in 2003/4 was forecast at a record 24.780 million metric tons, up 4.1% from 23.81 million in 2002/3. India's 2003/4 production was forecast at 19.88 million metric tons, down 10.0% from 22.10 million in 2002/3. Chinese production in 2003/4 was forecast to remain very high at 10.07 million, although down 5.3% from 10.637 million in 2002/3. World ending stocks of centrifugal sugar were forecast to drop to 34.499 million metric tons, down 6.9% from 37.045 million in 2002/3.

Demand – World consumption of centrifugal (raw) sugar was forecast by the USDA to rise slightly by 1.1% to 139.311 million metric tons in 2003/4 from 137.725 million in 2002/3. US consumption was forecast to drop to 8.778 million metric tons, down 4% from 9.135 million in 2002/3.

Exports – World exports of centrifugal sugar were forecast to fall slightly to 45.107 million metric tons from 45.724 million in 2002/3, although that is still a high level of exports on an historical basis. Brazil is the world's largest exporter of sugar with about 30% of world exports. Brazilian exports in 2003/4 were forecast to rise to a new record 14.250 million metric tons, up 1.8% from 14.000 million in 2002/3. The import of sugar into the US is restricted by tariff-rate quotas and US sugar imports in 2003/4 were forecast at 1.437 million metric tons, down 7.5% from 1.554 million in 2002/3.

World Production, Supply & Stocks/Consumption Ratio of Sugar   In 1000's of Metric Tons (Raw Value)

Marketing Year	Beginning Stocks	Production	Imports	Total Supply	Exports	Domestic Consumption	Ending Stocks	Stocks/ Consumption Percentage
1994-5	19,288	115,920	31,317	167,553	30,289	113,716	22,520	19.8
1995-6	22,756	122,212	32,457	179,250	34,282	116,574	26,569	22.8
1996-7	26,569	122,496	32,803	184,990	35,925	119,667	26,276	22.0
1997-8	26,276	124,997	32,494	186,659	35,386	122,918	26,001	21.9
1998-9	26,001	130,880	36,032	193,813	37,357	124,193	32,263	26.0
1999-00	32,372	136,531	36,073	204,976	41,448	127,395	36,133	28.4
2000-1	36,133	130,495	38,646	205,274	37,686	130,164	37,424	28.8
2001-2	37,424	134,888	37,695	210,007	41,228	134,790	33,989	25.2
2002-3[1]	33,989	147,336	39,169	220,494	45,724	137,725	37,045	26.9
2003-4[2]	37,045	144,635	37,237	218,917	45,107	139,311	34,499	24.8

[1] Preliminary.   [2] Forecast.   *Source: Foreign Agricultural Service, U.S. Department of Agriculture (FAS-USDA)*

World Production of Sugar (Centrifugal Sugar-Raw Value)   In Thousands of Metric Tons

Year	Australia	Brazil	China	Cuba	France	Germany	India	Indonesia	Mexico	Thailand	United States	Ukraine	World Total
1994-5	5,196	12,500	6,299	3,300	4,363	3,991	16,410	2,450	4,556	5,448	7,191	3,600	115,920
1995-6	5,049	13,700	6,686	4,400	4,564	4,159	18,225	2,090	4,660	6,223	6,686	3,800	122,212
1996-7	5,659	14,650	7,789	4,200	4,594	4,558	14,616	2,094	4,835	6,013	6,536	2,935	122,496
1997-8	5,567	15,700	8,631	3,200	NA	NA	14,592	2,190	5,490	4,245	7,276	2,032	124,997
1998-9	4,997	18,300	8,969	3,760	NA	NA	17,436	1,492	4,982	5,386	7,597	2,000	130,880
1999-00	5,448	20,100	7,525	4,060	NA	NA	20,219	1,690	4,979	5,721	8,203	1,720	136,531
2000-1	4,162	17,100	6,849	3,500	NA	NA	20,480	1,800	5,220	5,107	7,956	1,687	130,495
2001-2	4,662	20,400	8,305	3,700	NA	NA	20,475	1,725	5,169	6,397	7,174	1,790	134,888
2002-3[1]	5,371	23,810	10,637	2,000	NA	NA	22,100	1,755	5,229	7,303	7,600	1,550	147,336
2003-4[2]	5,114	24,780	10,070	2,000	NA	NA	19,880	1,900	5,464	7,690	8,070	1,400	144,635

[1] Preliminary.   [2] Forecast.   NA = Not available.   *Source: Foreign Agricultural Service, U.S. Department of Agriculture (FAS-USDA)*

World Stocks of Centrifugal Sugar at Beginning of Marketing Year   In Thousands of Metric Tons (Raw Value)

Year	Australia	Brazil	China	Cuba	France	Germany	India	Iran	Mexico	Philippines	United Kingdom	United States	World Total
1994-5	125	455	1,168	170	784	511	2,776	400	575	412	450	1,213	19,288
1995-6	152	710	3,215	647	437	271	5,990	270	601	100	453	1,126	22,756
1996-7	101	510	2,684	567	684	331	8,455	300	714	511	457	1,354	26,569
1997-8	228	860	2,784	484	NA	NA	6,979	330	634	345	NA	1,350	26,276
1998-9	253	560	2,515	568	NA	NA	5,850	350	991	183	NA	1,523	26,901
1999-00	183	1,010	2,548	488	NA	NA	7,374	350	941	454	NA	1,487	32,372
2000-1	518	710	1,851	438	NA	NA	10,710	398	1,063	330	NA	2,013	36,133
2001-2	634	860	1,004	238	NA	NA	11,985	368	1,548	322	NA	1,978	37,424
2002-3[1]	507	210	869	128	NA	NA	11,670	NA	1,172	239	NA	1,294	33,989
2003-4[2]	463	270	2,070	78	NA	NA	11,090	NA	1,193	277	NA	1,184	37,045

[1] Preliminary.   [2] Forecast.   NA = Not available..   *Source: Foreign Agricultural Service, U.S. Department of Agriculture (FAS-USDA)*

Centrifugal Sugar (Raw Value) Imported into Selected Countries   In Thousands of Metric Tons

Year	Algeria	Canada	China	France	Iran	Rep. of Korea	Malaysia	Morocco	Nigeria	Russia	United Kingdom	United States	World Total
1994-5	990	1,020	4,110	361	800	1,345	1,030	455	490	2,700	1,261	1,664	31,317
1995-6	1,000	1,174	1,775	523	940	1,411	1,120	477	542	3,200	1,361	2,536	32,457
1996-7	920	1,057	1,014	553	1,200	1,497	1,166	513	555	3,600	1,260	2,517	32,803
1997-8	925	1,061	420	NA	1,110	1,424	1,065	586	660	4,210	NA	1,962	32,494
1998-9	925	1,188	543	NA	1,075	1,403	1,188	470	700	5,400	NA	1,655	36,032
1999-00	930	1,207	687	NA	1,315	1,514	1,158	590	825	5,170	NA	1,484	36,073
2000-1	955	1,211	1,083	NA	1,200	1,520	1,257	497	714	5,650	NA	1,443	38,646
2001-2	950	1,239	1,375	NA	1,200	1,545	1,400	455	760	4,850	NA	1,393	37,695
2002-3[1]	NA	1,190	600	NA	NA	NA	NA	NA	NA	3,900	NA	1,554	39,169
2003-4[2]	NA	1,350	585	NA	NA	NA	NA	NA	NA	3,800	NA	1,437	37,237

[1] Preliminary.   [2] Forecast.   NA = Not available.   *Source: Foreign Agricultural Service, U.S. Department of Agriculture (FAS-USDA)*

SUGAR

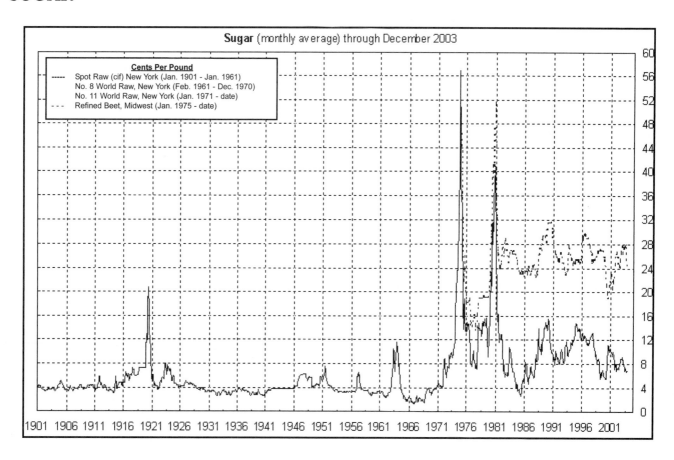

Centrifugal Sugar (Raw Value) Exported From Selected Countries   In Thousands of Metric Tons

Year	Aus-tralia	Brazil	Cuba	Dominican Republic	France	Ger-many	Mau-ritius	Mexico	South Africa	Swazi-land	Thai-land	United Kingdom	Total
1994-5	4,321	4,300	2,600	295	3,004	1,417	508	235	369	296	3,809	263	30,289
1995-6	4,242	5,800	3,830	325	2,735	1,180	560	587	399	307	4,537	327	34,282
1996-7	4,564	5,800	3,598	364	2,730	1,430	602	750	1,056	293	4,194	388	35,925
1997-8	4,554	7,200	2,426	270	NA	NA	613	1,224	1,160	272	2,839	NA	35,386
1998-9	4,076	8,750	3,120	191	NA	NA	626	524	1,355	271	3,352	NA	37,357
1999-00	4,123	11,300	3,400	185	NA	NA	346	318	1,410	304	4,147	NA	41,448
2000-1	3,056	7,700	2,980	185	NA	NA	554	155	1,580	251	3,394	NA	37,686
2001-2	3,594	11,600	3,100	185	NA	NA	635	413	1,235	267	4,157	NA	41,228
2002-3[1]	4,220	14,000	1,350	185	NA	NA	NA	46	1,565	NA	5,100	NA	45,724
2003-4[2]	3,893	14,250	1,250	185	NA	NA	NA	66	1,300	NA	5,800	NA	45,107

[1] Preliminary.   [2] Estimate.   [3] Forecast.   NA = Not available.   *Source: Foreign Agricultural Service, U.S. Department of Agriculture (FAS-USDA)*

Average Wholesale Price of Refined Beet Sugar[1]--Midwest Market   In Cents Per Pound

Year	Jan.	Feb.	Mar.	Apr.	May	June	July	Aug.	Sept.	Oct.	Nov.	Dec.	Average
1994	25.75	25.50	25.50	24.50	24.75	25.25	25.00	25.00	24.70	25.00	25.38	26.50	25.15
1995	25.50	25.50	25.50	25.50	25.13	25.10	24.75	24.75	25.50	25.75	28.13	28.85	25.83
1996	28.69	29.00	29.50	29.50	29.70	29.50	29.50	29.00	29.00	29.00	29.00	29.00	29.20
1997	29.00	29.00	28.13	28.00	28.00	27.50	27.00	26.65	26.38	24.90	25.00	25.50	27.09
1998	25.50	25.50	25.50	25.50	26.00	26.00	26.00	26.00	26.50	26.90	27.00	27.00	26.12
1999	27.20	27.13	27.00	27.00	27.00	27.00	27.00	27.00	27.00	26.00	26.00	25.20	26.71
2000	23.38	22.25	21.50	21.00	19.75	19.00	19.00	19.00	20.70	21.25	21.00	21.80	20.80
2001	23.13	22.75	22.00	20.50	21.38	21.90	22.50	22.50	24.63	25.75	26.20	26.50	23.31
2002	26.75	26.00	25.95	24.63	24.50	24.00	24.00	25.40	26.25	26.75	27.40	27.88	25.79
2003[2]	27.80	26.50	27.13	27.63	28.00	28.00	27.63	25.50	24.00	24.70	23.94	23.63	26.21

[1] These are f.o.b. basis prices in bulk, not delivered prices.   [2] Preliminary.   *Source: Economic Research Service, U.S. Department of Agriculture (ERS)*

Average Price of World Raw Sugar[1]   In Cents Per Pound

Year	Jan.	Feb.	Mar.	Apr.	May	June	July	Aug.	Sept.	Oct.	Nov.	Dec.	Average
1994	10.29	10.80	11.71	11.10	11.79	12.04	11.73	12.05	12.62	12.75	13.88	14.76	12.13
1995	14.87	14.43	14.58	13.63	13.49	13.99	13.46	13.75	12.72	11.94	11.96	12.40	13.44
1996	12.57	12.97	13.07	12.43	11.94	12.54	12.83	12.33	11.87	11.65	11.29	11.38	12.24
1997	11.13	11.06	11.17	11.50	11.54	12.02	12.13	12.54	12.65	12.86	13.19	12.90	12.06
1998	11.71	11.06	10.66	10.27	10.17	9.33	9.70	9.50	8.21	8.24	8.73	8.59	9.68
1999	8.40	7.05	6.11	5.44	5.83	6.67	6.11	6.39	6.98	6.00	6.54	6.00	6.54
2000	5.04	5.51	5.54	6.48	7.33	8.72	10.18	11.14	10.35	10.96	10.02	10.23	8.51
2001	10.63	10.26	9.64	9.27	9.96	9.80	9.48	8.77	8.60	7.15	7.80	8.02	9.12
2002	7.96	6.81	7.27	7.12	7.33	7.07	8.02	7.86	8.54	8.84	8.87	8.81	7.88
2003[2]	8.56	9.14	8.50	7.92	7.41	6.85	7.18	7.30	6.70	6.74	6.83	6.95	7.51

[1] Contract No. 11, f.o.b. stowed Caribbean port, including Brazil, bulk spot price.   [2] Preliminary.   *Source: Economic Research Service, U.S. Department of Agriculture (ERS-USDA)*

Average Price of Raw Sugar in New York (C.I.F., Duty/Free Paid, Contract #12/#14)   In Cents Per Pound

Year	Jan.	Feb.	Mar.	Apr.	May	June	July	Aug.	Sept.	Oct.	Nov.	Dec.	Average
1994	22.00	21.95	21.95	22.08	22.18	22.44	22.72	21.84	21.78	21.58	21.57	22.35	22.04
1995	22.65	22.69	22.46	22.76	23.10	23.09	24.47	23.18	23.21	22.67	22.60	22.63	22.96
1996	22.39	22.68	22.57	22.71	22.62	22.48	21.80	22.51	22.38	22.37	22.12	22.14	22.40
1997	21.88	22.07	21.81	21.79	21.70	21.62	22.04	22.21	22.30	22.27	21.90	21.93	21.96
1998	21.85	21.79	21.74	22.14	22.31	22.42	22.66	22.19	21.92	21.67	21.83	22.19	22.06
1999	22.41	22.38	22.55	22.57	22.65	22.61	22.61	21.24	20.10	19.50	17.45	17.87	21.16
2000	17.70	17.24	18.46	19.43	19.12	19.31	17.64	18.12	18.97	21.15	21.39	20.56	19.09
2001	20.81	21.18	21.40	21.51	21.19	21.04	20.64	21.10	20.87	20.90	21.19	21.43	21.11
2002	21.03	20.69	19.92	19.73	19.52	19.93	20.86	20.91	21.65	21.94	22.22	22.03	20.87
2003[1]	21.62	21.91	22.14	21.87	21.80	21.62	21.32	21.26	21.34	20.92	20.91	20.37	21.42

[1] Preliminary.   *Source: Economic Research Service, U.S. Department of Agriculture (ERS-USDA)*

Supply and Utilization of Sugar (Cane and Beet) in the United States   In 1,000's of Short Tons (Raw Value)

	Supply									Utilization			Domestic Disappearance	
	Production			Offshore Receipts							Net Changes in Invisible Stocks	Refining Loss Ad-justment	In Poly-hydric Alcohol[4]		
Year	Cane	Beet	Total	Foreign	Terri-tories	Total	Beginning Stocks	Total Supply	Total Use	Exports				Total	Per Capita
1995-6	3,454	3,916	7,370	2,777	0	2,777	1,241	11,388	9,896	385	-43	0	13	9,441	65.1
1996-7	3,191	4,013	7,205	2,774	0	2,774	1,492	11,471	9,983	211	30	0	21	9,564	65.8
1997-8	3,631	4,389	8,020	2,163	0	2,163	1,488	11,671	9,992	179	-2	0	20	9,672	65.6
1998-9	3,952	4,423	8,375	1,824	0	1,824	1,679	11,878	10,238	230	-58	0	25	9,872	66.5
1999-00	4,076	4,956	9,032	1,636	0	1,636	1,639	12,317	10,090	124	-144	0	32	9,993	66.0
2000-1	4,089	4,680	8,769	1,591	0	1,591	2,216	12,576	10,396	141	125	0	34	9,998	65.3
2001-2[1]	3,985	3,915	7,900	1,535	0	1,535	2,180	11,615	10,196	137	-24	0	33	9,894	NA
2002-3[2]	3,965	4,415	8,380	1,732	0	1,732	1,419	11,531	10,273	142	157	0	24	9,767	NA
2003-4[3]	4,106	4,824	8,930	1,584	0	1,584	1,259	11,773	9,835	160	0	0	25	9,465	NA

[1] Preliminary.   [2] Estimate.   [3] Forecast.   [4] Includes feed use.   Source: Economic Research Service, U.S. Department of Agriculture (ERS-USDA)

Sugar Cane for Sugar & Seed and Production of Cane Sugar and Molasses in the United States

	Acreage Harvested 1,000 Acres	Yield of Cane Per Harvested Acre Net Tons	Production for Sugar 1,000 Tons	Production for Seed 1,000 Tons	Production Total 1,000 Tons	Sugar Yield Per Acre Short Tons	Farm Price $ Per Ton	Farm Value of Cane Used for Sugar 1,000 Dollars	Farm Value of Cane Used for Sugar & Seed 1,000 Dollars	Sugar Production Raw Value Total 1,000 Tons	Sugar Production Raw Value Per Ton of Cane in Lbs.	Sugar Production Refined Basis 1,000 Tons	Molasses Made Edible 1,000 Gallons	Molasses Made Total[3] 1,000 Gallons
Year														
1995	932.3	33.0	29,155	1,641	30,796	3.90	29.5	859,604	906,956	3,489	----	----	----	195,429
1996	888.9	33.1	27,687	1,777	29,464	----	28.3	784,113	833,297	----	----	----	----	----
1997	914.0	34.7	30,003	1,706	31,709	----	28.1	842,840	890,257	----	----	----	----	----
1998	947.1	36.6	32,743	1,964	34,707	----	27.3	893,049	944,562	----	----	----	----	----
1999	993.3	35.5	33,577	1,722	35,299	----	25.6	859,175	901,900	----	----	----	----	----
2000	1,023.3	35.0	34,291	1,823	36,114	----	26.1	895,917	941,791	----	----	----	----	----
2001	1,027.8	33.7	32,775	1,812	34,587	----	29.0	951,813	1,003,046	----	----	----	----	----
2002[1]	1,023.2	34.7	33,903	1,650	35,553	----	28.4	961,896	1,007,142	----	----	----	----	----
2003[2]	997.8	34.6	32,506	1,997	34,503	----	----	----	----	----	----	----	----	----

[1] Preliminary.   [2] Estimate.   [3] Excludes edible molasses.   *Source: Economic Research Service, U.S. Department of Agriculture (ERS-USDA)*

SUGAR

U.S. Sugar Beets, Beet Sugar, Pulp & Molasses Produced from Beets and Raw Sugar Spot Prices

Year of Harvest	------- Acreage ------- Planted	Harvested	Yield Per Harvested Acre Ton	Pro- duction 1,000 Tons	Sugar Yield Per Acre Sh. Tons	Price[3] Dollars	- Sugar Production - Farm Value $1,000	Equiv- alent Raw Value[4]	Refined Basis	World[5] Refined #5	----- CSCE ----- #11 World	N.Y. Duty Paid	Wholesale List Price HFCS (42%) Midwest
	----- 1,000 Acres -----							-- 1,000 Short Tons --		------ In Cents Per Pound -----			
1994	1,476	1,443	22.1	31,853	3.17	38.80	1,234,470	4,578	4,090	15.66	12.13	22.04	20.17
1995	1,445	1,420	19.8	28,065	2.78	38.10	1,070,663	3,944	----	17.99	13.44	22.96	15.63
1996	1,368	1,323	20.2	26,680	3.06	45.40	1,211,001	3,900	----	16.64	12.24	22.40	14.46
1997	1,459	1,428	20.9	29,886	3.00	38.80	1,160,029	----	----	14.33	12.06	21.96	10.70
1998	1,498	1,451	22.4	32,499	----	36.40	1,181,494	----	----	11.59	9.68	22.06	10.58
1999	1,561	1,527	21.9	33,420	----	37.20	1,242,895	----	----	9.10	6.54	21.16	11.71
2000	1,564	1,373	23.7	32,541	----	34.20	1,113,030	----	----	9.97	8.51	19.09	11.32
2001	1,371	1,243	20.7	25,764	----	39.80	1,025,306	----	----	11.29	9.12	21.11	11.90
2002[1]	1,427	1,361	20.4	27,718	----	39.30	1,089,287	----	----	10.35	7.88	20.87	13.05
2003[2]	1,365	1,348	22.7	30,605	----	----	----	----	----	9.74	7.51	21.42	13.24

[1] Preliminary. [2] Estimate. [3] Includes support payments, but excludes Government sugar beet payments. [4] Refined sugar multiplied by factor of 1.07. [5] F.O.B. Europe. *Source: Economic Research Service, U.S. Department of Agriculture (ERS-USDA)*

Sugar Deliveries and Stocks in the United States   In Thousands of Short Tons (Raw Value)

Year	Quota Allocation	Actual Imports	Cane Sugar Refineries	Beet Sugar Factories	Importers of Direct Con- sumption Sugar	Mainland Cane Sugar Mills[3]	Total Deliveries	Total Domestic Con- sumption	Cane Sugar Re- fineries[4]	Beet Sugar Factories	CCC	Refiners' Raw	Mainland Cane Mills	Total
			----------- Deliveries by Primary Distributors -----------						---------------------------- Stocks , Jan. 1 ----------------------------					
1994	----	----	4,929	4,170	78	12	9,177	9,177	218	1,696	0	438	1,160	3,512
1995	2,413.1	2,308.0	4,808	4,486	44	15	9,337	9,337	185	1,594	6	448	906	3,139
1996	2,339.1	2,276.9	5,539	3,923	33	14	9,496	9,496	195	1,383	0	334	996	2,909
1997	1,791.3	1,733.3	5,553	3,997	27	----	9,578	9,578	196	1,520	0	323	1,156	3,195
1998	1,289.7	1,254.2	5,349	4,313	24	----	9,686	9,684	212	1,535	0	322	1,308	3,377
1999	----	----	5,419	4,536	41	----	9,996	9,996	255	1,499	0	332	1,335	3,421
2000	----	----	5,508	4,433	36	----	9,977	9,977	208	1,554	0	356	1,737	3,855
2001	----	----	5,172	4,680	58	----	9,911	9,917	262	1,500	767	274	1,533	4,337
2002[1]	----	----	5,407	4,291	109	----	9,808	9,836	288	1,472	634	351	1,781	4,525
2003[2]	----	----	5,229	4,260	56	----	9,545		298	1,300	246	299	1,289	3,432

[1] Preliminary. [2] Estimate. [3] Sugar for direct consumption only. [4] Refined. *Source: Economic Research Service, U.S. Department of Agriculture (ERS-USDA)*

Sugar, Refined--Deliveries to End User in the United States   In Thousands of Short Tons

Year	Bakery & Cereal Products	Beverages	Confec- tionery[2]	Hotels, Restaurant & Insti- tutions	Ice Cream & Dairy Products	Canned, Bottled & Frozen Foods	All Other Food Uses	Retail Grocers[3]	Whole- sale Grocers[4]	Non-food Uses	Non- industrial Uses	Industrial Uses	Total Deliveries
1994	1,952	156	1,313	93	453	322	704	1,269	2,039	77	3,598	4,977	8,575
1995	1,905	169	1,372	103	452	279	863	1,236	2,173	64	3,701	5,103	8,804
1996	1,993	196	1,335	80	445	318	849	1,263	2,241	66	3,759	5,202	8,962
1997	2,161	158	1,350	78	436	308	793	1,281	2,283	66	3,828	5,272	9,100
1998	2,301	165	1,336	79	438	331	907	1,230	2,223	76	3,761	5,556	9,317
1999	2,312	179	1,361	72	499	346	862	1,263	2,257	71	3,804	5,630	9,434
2000	2,264	168	1,328	71	499	330	817	1,242	2,241	85	3,893	5,491	9,383
2001	2,273	158	1,316	59	484	310	800	1,255	2,250	74	3,927	5,414	9,341
2002	2,069	189	1,221	53	530	297	736	1,322	2,374	99	4,114	5,141	9,255
2003[1]	2,043	209	1,086	51	534	298	614	1,266	2,551	99	4,224	4,884	9,108

[1] Preliminary. [2] And related products. [3] Chain stores, supermarkets. [4] Jobbers, sugar dealers. *Source: Economic Research Service, U.S. Department of Agriculture (ERS-USDA)*

Deliveries[1] of All Sugar by Primary Distributors in the U.S., by Quarters   In Thousands of Short Tons

Year	First Quarter	Second Quarter	Third Quarter	Fourth Quarter	Total	Year	First Quarter	Second Quarter	Third Quarter	Fourth Quarter	Total
1992	1,985	2,178	2,390	2,273	8,259	1998	2,233	2,428	2,565	2,458	9,213
1993	2,039	2,172	2,432	2,277	8,420	1999	2,208	2,553	2,655	2,580	9,434
1994	2,121	2,265	2,532	2,260	8,646	2000	2,318	2,484	2,611	2,564	9,383
1995	2,105	2,311	2,542	2,379	8,801	2001	2,225	2,353	2,419	2,344	9,341
1996	2,191	2,355	2,519	2,430	8,964	2002	2,116	2,299	2,602	2,241	9,258
1997	2,143	2,401	2,591	2,443	9,100	2003[2]	2,093	2,271	2,700		9,419

Raw Value. [1] Includes for domestic consumption and for export. [2] Preliminary. *Source: Economic Research Service, U.S. Department of Agriculture (ERS-USDA)*

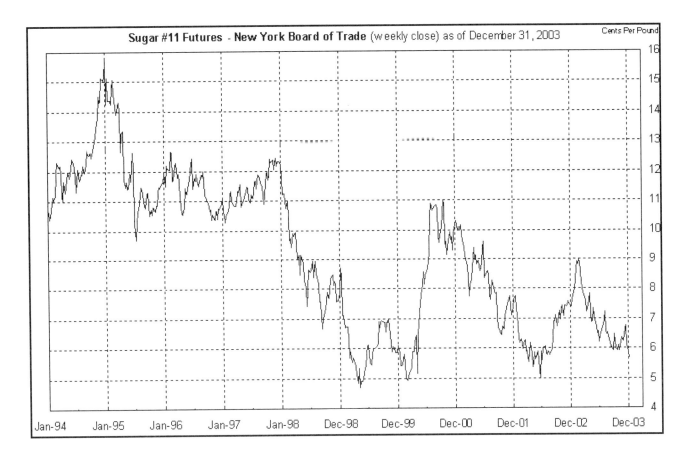

Average Open Interest of World Sugar No. 11 Futures in New York   In Contracts

Year	Jan.	Feb.	Mar.	Apr.	May	June	July	Aug.	Sept.	Oct.	Nov.	Dec.
1994	108,936	123,148	137,582	115,060	117,030	126,843	106,749	118,057	141,361	140,011	171,843	191,801
1995	186,893	167,451	149,027	152,600	127,978	121,877	114,027	119,787	114,069	119,561	140,008	157,779
1996	156,047	159,563	150,093	142,773	137,897	148,447	144,527	153,845	153,202	144,830	150,866	150,573
1997	155,156	147,198	143,623	166,143	150,480	175,139	165,884	197,331	187,477	158,065	200,486	201,922
1998	206,100	212,072	183,472	182,770	171,555	186,978	149,536	152,754	155,076	138,762	139,896	148,983
1999	165,717	176,465	168,624	188,324	196,864	177,266	142,416	151,621	189,606	161,760	167,549	175,125
2000	191,464	199,031	193,554	187,810	201,756	200,973	172,361	171,808	160,809	154,101	148,035	145,760
2001	157,478	158,192	158,448	167,555	131,640	126,426	112,483	128,181	139,915	146,058	163,358	170,710
2002	184,096	205,138	194,541	187,415	157,738	158,276	149,202	170,667	202,144	207,456	207,598	217,904
2003	244,036	265,758	220,971	192,497	170,867	184,257	180,898	196,857	195,200	185,917	200,605	207,768

Source: New York Board of Trade (NYBOT)

Volume of Trading of World Sugar No. 11 Futures in New York   In Contracts

Year	Jan.	Feb.	Mar.	Apr.	May	June	July	Aug.	Sept.	Oct.	Nov.	Dec.	Total
1994	289,593	486,222	360,787	472,388	407,343	443,002	252,012	349,079	471,899	316,330	484,943	387,620	4,719,218
1995	591,861	489,274	472,519	478,757	352,000	485,131	298,756	402,358	360,086	246,584	278,906	254,850	4,711,082
1996	550,780	544,514	341,940	526,255	384,302	496,745	279,707	290,732	562,082	264,290	203,921	306,584	4,751,852
1997	436,935	493,199	268,343	618,176	308,563	575,264	400,150	427,082	580,551	440,208	323,286	413,214	5,284,971
1998	601,378	688,036	431,818	551,628	364,203	686,997	294,354	370,179	527,270	303,951	358,096	346,201	5,524,111
1999	683,891	543,477	452,485	688,181	361,895	762,271	346,534	408,289	657,572	344,434	405,495	256,775	5,911,299
2000	422,527	609,793	501,115	617,633	523,939	717,700	376,769	420,611	622,350	507,562	371,824	242,027	5,933,850
2001	410,492	545,538	380,640	567,921	426,987	515,561	356,483	419,123	447,349	348,896	413,965	317,374	5,150,329
2002	568,789	629,533	417,314	693,589	412,150	610,338	529,509	381,027	756,038	402,811	432,100	340,558	6,173,756
2003	566,040	797,616	443,842	729,453	489,195	719,819	535,892	545,886	760,213	475,322	403,091	674,355	7,140,724

Source: New York Board of Trade (NYBOT)

Sulfur

Sulfur is an odorless, tasteless, light yellow, nonmetallic element. Its atomic symbol is S and its atomic number is 16. As early as 2000 BC, Egyptians used sulfur compounds to bleach fabric. The Chinese used sulfur as an essential component when they developed gunpowder in the 13th century.

Sulfur is widely found in both its free and combined states. Free sulfur is found mixed with gypsum and pumice stone in volcanic regions. Sulfur dioxide is an air pollutant released from the combustion of fossil fuels. The most important use of sulfur is the production of sulfur compounds. Sulfur is used in skin ointments, matches, dyes, gunpowder, and phosphoric acid.

Supply – World production of sulfur (all forms) in 2001, the latest reporting year, fell –1.4% to 57.300 million metric tons from the 12-year high of 58.100 million metric tons seen in 2000. The world's largest producers of sulfur are

Canada with 16.3% of world production in 2001, the US (16.1%), Russia (10.9%), and China (9.4%). US production of sulfur in 2001 fell by –10.2% to a 30-year low of 9.250 million metric tons.

Demand – US consumption of elemental sulfur in 2001 fell –16.2% to a 30-year low of 9.300 million metric tons. US consumption of sulfuric acid in 2001 fell –0.9% to 9.530 million metric tons. The main usage for sulfuric acid is for phosphate fertilizers, which accounted for 72% of total usage in 2001. Other usages include petroleum refining (6.2%), pulp mill and paper products (2.0%), inorganic chemicals (1.7%), and synthetic rubber and plastic (0.7%).

Trade – US exports of recovered sulfur in 2001 fell –9.1% to 48.800 million metric tons from the 6-year high of 53.700 million metric tons in 2000. US imports of sulfur in 2001 fell sharply by –25.8% to 1.730 million metric tons from 2.330 million metric tons in 2000.

World Production of Sulfur (All Forms) In Thousands of Metric Tons

Year	Canada	China	France	Germany	Iraq	Japan	Mexico	Poland	Russia	Saudi Arabia	Spain	United States	World Total
1995	8,953	7,030	1,170	1,110	475	3,110	1,241	2,591	3,840	2,400	786	11,800	54,000
1996	9,490	7,260	1,090	1,110	475	3,150	1,280	1,982	3,800	2,300	943	11,800	55,200
1997	9,480	7,670	1,060	1,160	450	3,391	1,340	1,985	3,750	1,750	967	12,000	56,900
1998	9,694	6,170	1,110	1,180	450	3,428	1,387	1,675	4,651	2,050	993	11,700	57,400
1999	10,116	5,770	1,100	1,190	----	3,462	1,334	1,524	5,265	1,940	955	11,500	57,400
2000	9,946	5,560	1,110	1,240	----	3,486	1,325	1,831	5,900	2,101	708	10,500	58,300
2001[1]	8,916	5,380	1,100	1,240	----	3,773	1,450	1,352	6,250	2,350	668	9,470	57,700
2002[2]	8,538	5,730	1,000	1,240	----	3,200	1,450	1,220	6,350	2,230	685	9,270	57,700

[1] Preliminary. [2] Estimate. *Source: U.S. Geological Survey (USGS)*

Salient Statistics of Sulfur in the United States In Thousands of Metric Tons (Sulfur Content)

Year	Native Sulfur[3] Frasch	Recovered Petroleum & Coke	Recovered Natural Gas	Total	By-product Sulfuric Acid	Other Sulfuric Acid Compounds	Production (All Forms)	Imports Sulfuric Acid[4]	Exports Sulfuric Acid[4]	Producer Stocks Dec. 31[5]	Apparent Consumption (All Forms)	Frasch	Recovered	Average $ Per Metric Ton
1995	3,150	5,040	2,210	7,250	1,400	----	11,800	1,920	170	583	14,300	W	W	44.46
1996	2,900	5,370	2,100	7,480	1,430	----	11,800	2,070	117	646	13,600	W	W	34.11
1997	2,820	5,230	2,420	7,650	1,550	----	12,000	2,010	118	761	13,900	W	W	36.06
1998	1,800	6,060	2,160	8,220	1,610	----	11,700	2,040	155	283	14,200	W	W	29.14
1999	1,780	6,210	2,010	8,220	1,320	----	11,500	1,370	155	451	13,800	W	W	37.81
2000	900	6,360	2,020	8,380	1,030	----	10,500	1,420	191	208	12,700	----	----	24.73
2001[1]	----	6,480	2,000	8,490	982	----	9,470	1,410	210	232	10,900	----	----	10.11
2002[2]	----	6,750	1,760	8,500	772	----	9,270	1,060	147	181	11,400	----	----	25.00

[1] Preliminary. [2] Estimate. [3] Or sulfur ore; Withheld included in natural gas. [4] Basis 100% H2SO4, sulfur equivalent. [5] Frasch & recovered.
[6] Data 1996 to date includes Frasch. W = Withheld proprietary data. *Source: U.S. Geological Survey (USGS)*

Sulfur Consumption & Foreign Trade of the United States In Thousands of Metric Tons (Sulfur Content)

Year	Native Sulfur Frasch	Recovered Sulfur	Total Elemental Form	Total Sulfuric Acid	Pulpmills & Paper Product	Inorganic Chemicals[3]	Synthetic Rubber & Plastic	Phosphatic Fertilizers	Petroleum Refining[4]	Exports Frasch	Exports Recovered	Exports Value 1,000 $	Imports Frasch	Imports Recovered	Imports Value 1,000 $
1995	W	12,300	12,300	11,500	319	170	245	8,200	479	----	906	66,200	----	2,510	143,000
1996	W	11,500	11,500	10,900	343	152	270	7,380	525	----	855	51,700	----	1,960	70,200
1997	W	11,800	11,800	10,700	334	232	85	7,000	610	----	703	36,000	----	2,060	64,900
1998	W	11,900	11,900	10,600	134	174	69	7,590	632	----	889	35,400	----	2,270	58,400
1999	W	11,700	11,700	10,400	138	174	68	7,770	508	----	685	35,800	----	2,580	51,600
2000	W	11,100	11,100	9,620	136	152	68	7,110	497	----	762	53,700	----	2,330	39,400
2001	W	9,520	9,520	9,530	194	158	68	6,840	591	----	675	48,800	----	1,730	22,100
2002[1]	W	10,400	10,400	8,760	122	27	66	7,160	90	----	687	40,000	----	2,560	26,800

[1] Preliminary. [2] Sulfur equivalent. [3] Including inorganic pigments, paints & allied products, and other inorganic chemicals & products.
[4] Including other petroleum and coal products. W = Withheld proprietary data. NA = Not available. *Source: U.S. Geological Survey (USGS)*

Sunflowerseed, Meal and Oil

Sunflowers are native to South and North America, but are now grown almost worldwide. Sunflowerseed oil accounts for approximately 14% of the world production of seed oils. Sunflower varieties that are commercially grown contain from 39% to 49% oil in the seed. Sunflower crops produce about 50 bushels of seed per acre on average, which yields approximately 50 gallons of oil.

Sunflowerseed oil accounts for around 80% of the value of the sunflower crop. Refined sunflowerseed oil is edible and used primarily as a salad and cooking oil and in margarine. Crude sunflowerseed oil is used industrially for making soaps, candles, varnishes, and detergents. Sunflowerseed oil contains 93% of the energy of US No. 2 diesel fuel and is being explored as a potential alternate fuel source in diesel engines. Sunflower meal is used in livestock feed and when fed to poultry, increases the yield of eggs. Sunflower seeds are also used for birdfeed and as a snack for humans.

Prices – The average price received by US farmers for sunflower seeds was $12.00 per hundred pounds in December 2003, which was slightly lower than the $12.16 average seen in the marketing year 2002/3 (Sep/Aug) but sharply higher than the trough of $7.39 seen in 2000/1.

Supply – World sunflowerseed production in 2003/4 was forecast to rise by 7.6% to 25.73 million metric tons from 23.92 million. Despite the higher production level, demand was strong and stocks in 2003/4 were forecast to drop 8% to 830,000 metric tons. The world's largest producer of sunflowerseeds is the former Soviet Union with 37% of the crop in 2003/4, followed by Argentina (13%), Eastern Europe (12%), and the European Union (10%). World production of sunflowerseed oil rose 8% to 9.03 million metric tons from 8.37 million in 2002/3. US production of sunflowerseeds in 2003/4 was forecast at 1.19 million metric tons, up 5.3% from 1.13 million 2002/3.

Demand – In 2003/4, a forecasted 87% of the sunflowerseed production went into crushing for oil and meal products, little changed from 2002/3. Consumption of sunflowerseed meal was up 9% to 8.97 million metric tons in 2003/4 while consumption of sunflowerseed oil was up 7% to 9.80 million metric tons.

Trade – World exports of sunflowerseeds in 2003/4 was forecast at 3.38 million metric tons, up sharply by 48% from 2.28 million in 2002/3. Exports account for 13% of world production. The world's largest exporters in 2002/3 were Argentina (with 21% of world exports), Hungary (15.2%), the former Soviet Union (15.1%), and the US (10%). The world's largest importers were the Netherlands (with 17.4% of world imports), Turkey (17.4%), Spain (10.2%), and Germany (9.5%).

World Production of Sunflowerseed   In Thousands of Metric Tons

Crop Year	Argentina	Bulgaria	China	France	Hungary	India	Romania	South Africa	Spain	Turkey	United States	Ex-USSR	World Total
1993-4	3,850	440	1,282	1,640	700	1,400	696	390	1,215	700	1,167	5,251	20,600
1994-5	5,900	595	1,370	2,050	665	1,204	767	450	979	600	2,193	4,356	23,342
1995-6	5,600	650	1,270	1,900	730	1,400	933	755	575	750	1,819	7,368	25,720
1996-7	5,450	527	1,333	1,996	905	1,250	1,096	560	1,178	670	1,614	5,316	24,410
1997-8	5,630	438	1,176	1,995	540	890	869	585	1,373	672	1,668	5,442	23,452
1998-9	7,180	524	1,465	1,713	718	944	1,073	1,109	1,097	850	2,392	5,762	27,405
1999-00	5,760	660	1,765	1,868	793	801	1,301	531	579	820	1,969	7,394	26,846
2000-1	2,970	423	1,954	1,833	484	730	721	638	848	630	1,608	7,820	23,140
2001-2[1]	3,750	405	1,750	1,581	632	870	824	929	871	530	1,551	5,444	21,649
2002-3[2]	3,750	523	1,900	1,496	779	1,320	880	708	757	820	1,133	7,234	23,891

[1] Preliminary.   [2] Forecast.   Source: Economic Research Service, U.S. Department of Agriculture (ERS-USDA)

World Imports and Exports of Sunflowerseed   In Thousands of Metric Tons

Crop Year	Imports France	Germany	Netherlands	Spain	Turkey	World Total	Exports Argentina	France	Hungary	Ex-USSR	United States	Uraguay	World Total
1993-4	194	331	427	170	100	2,615	580	516	250	755	99	----	2,545
1994-5	109	279	543	472	550	3,287	884	628	260	708	287	----	3,173
1995-6	300	366	617	681	500	3,972	550	480	249	1,750	224	----	3,647
1996-7	338	406	496	296	532	3,343	65	78	212	2,422	117	91	3,310
1997-8	208	278	439	312	554	3,049	504	64	104	1,744	265	60	3,049
1998-9	395	364	477	576	766	3,995	940	29	152	1,944	291	106	4,050
1999-00	130	261	650	443	466	3,128	265	27	236	1,414	168	28	3,048
2000-1	176	300	477	369	326	2,740	94	11	188	1,850	153	21	2,748
2001-2[1]	46	146	341	200	223	1,707	342	25	228	223	176	130	1,689
2002-3[2]	134	205	426	297	140	2,336	280	6	365	570	129	200	2,346

[1] Preliminary.   [2] Forecast.   Source: Economic Research Service, U.S. Department of Agriculture (ERS-USDA)

SUNFLOWERSEED, MEAL AND OIL

Sunflowerseed Statistics in the United States In Thousands of Metric Tons

Crop Year Beginning Sept. 1	Harvested Acres 1,000	Harvested Yield Per Cwt.	Farm Price $ Per Metric Ton	Value of Production Million $	Supply Stocks, Sept. 1	Supply Production	Supply Imports	Supply Total	Disappearance Crush	Disappearance Exports	Disappearance Non-oil Use & Seed	Disappearance Total
1996-7	2,479	14.36	258	416.4	205	1,614	18	1,837	844	149	648	1,641
1997-8	2,792	13.17	256	426.5	196	1,668	29	1,893	1,061	189	551	1,801
1998-9	3,492	15.10	225	559.0	92	2,392	34	2,518	1,178	260	849	2,287
1999-00	3,441	12.62	166	326.9	231	1,969	41	2,241	1,139	205	666	2,010
2000-1	2,647	13.39	152	244.2	231	1,608	66	1,905	923	201	625	1,749
2001-2	2,555	13.38	215	326.0	156	1,551	76	1,783	760	235	680	1,675
2002-3[1]	2,180	11.42	220-250	299.6	108	1,129	98	1,335	319	164	653	1,136
2003-4[2]	2,197	12.13		312.6	199	1,209	105	1,513	606	178	627	1,411

[1] Preliminary.   [2] Forecast.   Source: Economic Research Service, U.S. Department of Agriculture (ERS-USDA)

World Production of Sunflowerseed Oil and Meal In Thousands of Metric Tons

Year	Sunflowerseed Oil Argentina	France	Spain	Turkey	Ex-USSR	World Total	Sunflowerseed Meal Argentina	France	Spain	Turkey	United States	Ex-USSR	World Total
1995-6	2,000	593	470	482	1,920	9,016	2,100	720	485	430	458	1,805	10,155
1996-7	2,159	689	550	503	1,229	9,109	2,260	838	639	561	456	1,235	10,804
1997-8	2,166	543	617	544	1,258	8,440	2,300	697	717	607	507	1,306	10,056
1998-9	2,356	591	612	628	1,467	9,264	2,426	759	711	701	624	1,477	10,962
1999-00	2,143	614	527	520	2,221	9,539	2,111	749	613	583	555	2,207	10,970
2000-1	1,463	645	503	400	2,374	8,617	1,441	797	585	449	464	2,310	9,925
2001-2[1]	1,308	471	444	314	2,066	7,472	1,268	604	516	353	364	2,088	8,667
2002-3[2]	1,534	499	444	383	2,650	8,599	1,515	614	516	430	201	2,575	9,776

[1] Preliminary.   [2] Forecast.   Source: Economic Research Service, U.S. Department of Agriculture (ERS-USDA)

Sunflower Oil Statistics in the United States In Thousands of Metric Tons

Crop Year Beginning Oct. 1	Supply Stocks, Oct. 1	Supply Production	Supply Imports	Supply Total	Disappearance Exports	Disappearance Domestic	Disappearance Total	Minneapolis, Crude $ Per Metric Ton
1996-7	67	381	10	458	322	94	458	497
1997-8	42	435	3	480	370	83	480	608
1998-9	27	534	2	563	363	145	563	446
1999-00	55	474	2	531	286	174	531	364
2000-1	71	396	4	471	247	162	471	357
2001-2	62	305	16	383	205	168	383	529
2002-3[1]	10	156	28	194	52	130	194	496-562
2003-4[2]	12	263	14	289	91	180	289	

[1] Preliminary.   [2] Forecast.   Source: Economic Research Service, U.S. Department of Agriculture (ERS-USDA)

Sunflower Meal Statistics in the United States In Thousands of Metric Tons

Crop Year Beginning Oct. 1	Supply Stocks, Oct. 1	Supply Production	Supply Imports	Supply Total	Disappearance Exports	Disappearance Domestic	Disappearance Total	28% Protein $ Per Metric Ton
1996-7	5	440	----	445	21	419	445	122
1997-8	5	494	----	499	13	481	499	90
1998-9	5	617	----	622	41	576	622	72
1999-00	5	549	----	554	21	528	554	83
2000-1	5	458	----	463	8	450	463	100
2001-2	5	358	26	389	26	358	389	96
2002-3[1]	5	172	----	177	3	169	177	95
2003-4[2]	5	299	----	304	5	294	304	102-132

[1] Preliminary.   [2] Forecast.   Source: Economic Research Service, U.S. Department of Agriculture (ERS-USDA)

Average Price Received by Farmers for Sunflower[2] in the United States In Dollars Per Hundred Pounds

Year	Sept.	Oct.	Nov.	Dec.	Jan.	Feb.	Mar.	Apr.	May	June	July	Aug.	Average
1998-9	11.50	10.80	10.70	11.00	11.50	12.00	10.80	9.62	9.80	9.54	9.09	8.28	10.39
1999-00	8.76	6.99	6.87	7.52	7.34	8.72	8.53	7.93	9.63	8.09	8.16	7.82	8.03
2000-1	6.31	5.76	6.20	6.49	6.92	7.29	7.46	7.67	7.99	8.40	8.71	9.48	7.39
2001-2	8.64	8.19	9.10	9.71	9.52	10.00	10.20	10.50	10.50	11.80	13.80	12.90	10.41
2002-3	13.10	12.00	12.00	12.30	12.10	12.50	12.50	12.50	12.20	11.80	13.80	12.90	10.41
2003-4[1]	10.40	11.40	11.60	11.60	12.10	12.40							12.16
													11.58

[1] Preliminary.   [2] KS, MN, ND and SD average.   Source: Economic Research Service, U.S. Department of Agriculture (ERS-USDA)

Tall Oil

Tall oil is a product of the paper and pulping industry. Crude tall oil is the major byproduct of the kraft or sulfate processing of pinewood. Crude tall oil starts as tall oil soap which is separated from recovered black liquor in the kraft pulping process. The tall oil soap is acidified to yield crude tall oil. The resulting tall oil is then fractionated to produce fatty acids, rosin, and pitch. Crude tall oil contains 40-50 percent fatty acids such as oleic and linoleic acids; 5-10 percent sterols, alcohols, and other neutral components. The demand is for the tall oil rosin and fatty acids which are used to produce adhesives, coatings, and ink resins. The products find use in lubricants, soaps, linoleum, flotation and waterproofing agents, paints, varnishes, and drying oils.

Since tall oil and its production are derived from the paper and pulping industry, the amount of tall oil produced is related in part to the pulp industry and in part to the U.S. economy.

Consumption of Tall Oil in Inedible Products in the United States   In Millions of Pounds

Year	Jan.	Feb.	Mar.	Apr.	May	June	July	Aug.	Sept.	Oct.	Nov.	Dec.	Total
1995	99.8	93.6	96.9	95.8	87.3	96.5	93.1	102.3	89.4	91.6	100.5	88.9	1,136
1996	93.1	103.4	89.2	104.1	100.5	96.6	85.4	100.7	94.9	111.5	101.4	98.8	1,180
1997	111.5	89.0	91.0	99.5	97.0	105.8	103.7	94.4	84.7	87.2	87.3	88.4	1,139
1998	86.7	114.4	113.2	120.0	108.0	101.8	117.2	114.8	120.3	111.6	119.0	121.0	1,348
1999	99.4	115.1	111.0	114.0	99.9	109.2	119.1	113.0	103.9	108.4	106.4	102.2	1,302
2000	91.7	88.1	106.4	97.5	90.9	98.8	91.8	106.6	94.9	93.7	89.4	96.2	1,146
2001	97.7	96.4	104.4	101.6	105.1	100.7	99.9	98.3	102.4	81.4	87.7	74.4	1,150
2002	93.4	132.9	115.0	121.3	109.3	121.6	128.5	130.2	121.5	141.9	115.5	118.6	1,450
2003[1]	136.1	119.9	136.9	126.3	121.7	121.9	119.3	111.6	131.4	124.1	104.9	120.1	1,474

[1] Preliminary.   Source: Bureau of the Census, U.S. Department of Commerce

Production of Crude Tall Oil in the United States   In Millions of Pounds

Year	Oct.	Nov.	Dec.	Jan.	Feb.	Mar.	Apr.	May	June	July	Aug.	Sept.	Total
1995-6	109.8	105.2	105.2	115.5	123.3	126.9	108.9	120.3	120.3	120.5	124.9	112.9	1,281.0
1996-7	119.2	113.9	114.5	119.9	125.1	125.1	118.5	116.6	116.4	135.0	132.9	130.8	1,337.2
1997-8	122.7	115.4	135.4	137.7	126.6	127.5	132.3	131.2	131.1	132.0	120.2	121.1	1,540.6
1998-9	118.4	113.4	119.3	118.0	115.2	134.6	121.0	103.8	100.7	103.2	103.5	113.6	1,364.8
1999-00	93.8	101.6	107.8	101.3	104.6	115.2	95.4	91.8	99.5	94.5	97.0	86.5	1,202.6
2000-1	92.3	91.6	81.4	94.9	83.7	103.7	99.7	99.9	95.1	94.1	105.4	93.0	1,134.8
2001-2	99.1	100.7	86.5	101.8	93.7	105.5	104.2	96.0	88.5	94.7	103.6	91.4	1,165.6
2002-3	102.5	87.3	101.8	108.7	89.8	111.5	108.3	99.6	91.8	109.2	100.8	97.1	1,208.6
2003-4[1]	102.1	87.9	109.0	106.3									1,215.6

[1] Preliminary.   Source: Bureau of the Census, U.S. Department of Commerce

Stocks of Crude Tall Oil in the United States, on First of Month   In Millions of Pounds

Year	Oct.	Nov.	Dec.	Jan.	Feb.	Mar.	Apr.	May	June	July	Aug.	Sept.
1995-6	120.9	117.5	112.9	100.7	105.7	120.3	146.0	131.8	127.0	130.5	138.7	147.3
1996-7	172.3	192.1	167.4	182.4	173.0	196.0	200.8	220.6	187.3	237.5	248.5	242.2
1997-8	208.6	187.9	209.7	202.1	202.8	219.4	256.8	254.1	239.1	259.1	278.4	245.2
1998-9	268.7	219.8	200.3	197.5	164.8	156.9	163.3	177.5	183.0	180.7	183.6	152.7
1999-00	146.8	130.9	135.3	121.5	131.8	153.5	136.6	138.5	154.6	130.5	136.7	117.1
2000-1	110.5	102.4	105.4	117.0	118.9	118.2	134.4	139.6	171.7	132.0	160.5	145.4
2001-2	132.7	125.6	142.1	127.9	135.8	155.2	165.6	177.4	190.7	175.4	161.8	155.1
2002-3	160.2	154.1	155.7	160.5	176.0	167.4	156.3	173.4	163.7	180.3	199.3	209.5
2003-4[1]	210.7	207.3	203.0	210.2	209.6							

[1] Preliminary.   Source: Bureau of the Census, U.S. Department of Commerce

Stocks of Refined Tall Oil in the United States, on First of Month   In Millions of Pounds

Year	Oct.	Nov.	Dec.	Jan.	Feb.	Mar.	Apr.	May	June	July	Aug.	Sept.
1995-6	10.1	11.6	7.9	6.0	7.9	9.7	8.5	10.4	8.5	6.0	6.1	7.2
1996-7	8.3	7.0	7.5	8.9	6.5	26.5	17.4	31.7	20.9	32.0	13.2	16.6
1997-8	32.3	25.6	34.9	21.4	30.4	17.0	14.2	13.0	13.1	15.1	14.7	15.3
1998-9	15.1	14.9	17.0	12.5	14.8	9.9	7.2	7.6	7.2	7.3	6.3	7.0
1999-00	7.5	7.0	8.5	9.1	9.8	11.0	9.8	13.7	10.4	7.8	11.9	8.2
2000-1	9.6	9.0	9.9	10.2	10.7	12.5	11.8	13.9	12.6	19.5	13.4	21.6
2001-2	22.4	17.2	17.1	19.9	20.7	20.9	21.5	22.7	20.9	18.6	18.4	16.0
2002-3	13.3	16.5	18.7	20.1	20.1	18.6	20.4	19.7	15.8	14.5	13.5	13.9
2003-4[1]	13.1	20.1	19.6	19.9	19.2							

[1] Preliminary.   Source: Bureau of the Census, U.S. Department of Commerce

Tallow and Greases

Tallow and grease come from processing (rendering) the fat of cattle. Tallow is used to produce both edible and inedible products. Edible products include margarine, cooking oil, and baking products. Inedible tallow products include soap, candles, and lubricants. The months with the highest levels of edible tallow use are May through August. Per capita use of edible tallow has been increasing over the last several years. In 1991, per capita use of tallow was 3.9 pounds while in 2000 it was 5.8 pounds. Production of tallow and greases is directly related to the number of cattle produced. Those countries that are the leading cattle producers are also the largest producers of tallow. The American Fats and Oils Association provides specifications for a variety of different types of tallow and grease, including edible tallow, lard (edible), top white tallow, all beef packer tallow, extra fancy tallow, fancy tallow, bleachable fancy tallow, prime tallow, choice white grease, and yellow grease. The specifications include such things as the melting point, color, density, moisture content, insoluble impurities, and others.

Prices– Tallow prices (edible) rallied sharply in 2003, along with the price of cattle. Tallow prices rallied to 23.08 cents/pound in December 2003, producing an average price for the year of 18.30 cents/pound. That was the highest average yearly price seen since 1997. The price of inedible tallow and grease rallied to an average price of 18.3 cents in 2003, up from 13.5 cents in 2002.

Supply – World production of tallow and greases (edible and inedible) has averaged over 8 million metric tons since 1993. The U.S. is by far the world's largest producer of tallow and greases with about 43 percent of the world total. The next largest producer was Australia with about 6 percent of the world output. Brazil had about 6 percent of global tallow production. Other large producers include Canada, Argentina, France, and South Korea. U.S. production of edible tallow in 2001 was 1.84 billion pounds, virtually the same production level as in the year 2000. The general trend has been an increase in the production of edible tallow. The total supply of edible tallow in 2001 was estimated at 1.91 billion pounds. US production of inedible tallow and greases in 2003 was 6.333 billion pounds, down from the 7.156 billion in 2002. US exports of inedible tallow and grease in 2003 were 330 million pounds, down from 384 million pounds in 2002.

Demand – US usage of tallow in 2001 was estimated at 1.52 billion pounds, down 5 percent from 2000. Of total US production in 2001, exports were 365 million pounds, up 47 percent from 2000. Mexico is the largest importer of tallow.

World Production of Tallow and Greases (Edible and Inedible)   In Thousands of Metric Tons

Year	Argentina	Australia	Brazil	Canada	France	Germany	Rep. of Korea	Netherlands	New Zealand	Russia	United Kingdom	United States	World Total
1991	285	530	340	193	185	270	85	150	132	386	230	3,180	6,968
1992	268	472	336	212	275	197	121	150	134	352	225	3,309	7,077
1993	260	526	429	209	240	178	115	163	145	706	212	3,650	8,492
1994	250	446	435	213	206	167	120	159	135	437	215	3,851	8,258
1995	248	423	46	217	220	166	118	158	147	377	230	3,756	8,312
1996	240	397	467	242	220	168	198	161	155	400	165	3,581	8,184
1997	265	456	460	250	220	167	209	200	161	340	160	3,467	8,342
1998	220	560	467	265	220	166	235	190	150	340	170	3,694	8,374
1999[1]	235	565	480	285	220	165	230	168	135	330	180	3,855	8,584
2000[2]	230	540	505	290	220	165	230	192	142	310	195	3,562	8,312

[1] Preliminary.   [2] Forecast.   Source: Foreign Agricultural Service, U.S. Department of Agriculture (FAS-USDA)

Salient Statistics of Tallow and Greases (Inedible) in the United States   In Millions of Pounds

	Supply				Consumption			Wholesale Prices, Cents/Lb.	
Year	Production	Stocks, Jan. 1	Total	Exports	Soap	Feed	Total	Edible, (Loose) Chicago	Inedible, No. 1 Chicago
1994	6,364	320	6,684	3,039	301	2,183	3,246	18.4	17.4
1995	6,481	350	6,831	2,486	264	2,071	2,334	21.4	19.2
1996	6,242	373	6,615	1,807	245	2,389	2,634	22.0	20.1
1997	6,249	266	6,515	775	245	2,401	2,646	23.5	20.8
1998	6,644	339	6,983	1,041	228	2,533	2,761	19.1	17.5
1999	7,079	437	7,516	877	229	2,847	3,076	15.1	13.0
2000	7,035	405	7,440	791	146	2,727	2,849	11.6	10.0
2001	6,870	347	7,217	616	107	2,834	2,843	13.7	12.0
2002[1]	7,156	327	7,482	384	W	2,886	2,886	14.8	13.5
2003[2]	6,246	240	6,486	307	W	2,434	2,434	20.3	18.3

[1] Preliminary.   [2] Estimate.   Sources: Economic Research Service, U.S. Department of Agriculture (ERS-USDA); Bureau of the Census, U.S. Department of Commerce

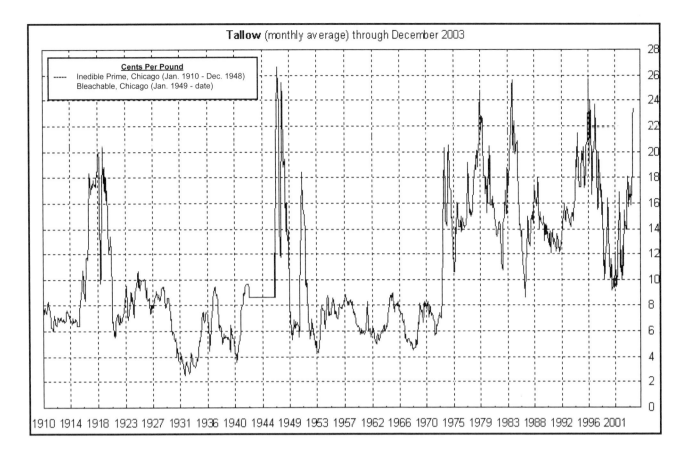

Tallow (monthly average) through December 2003

Cents Per Pound
----- Inedible Prime, Chicago (Jan. 1910 - Dec. 1948)
Bleachable, Chicago (Jan. 1949 - date)

Supply and Disappearance of Edible Tallow in the United States   In Millions of Pounds, Rendered Basis

Year	Supply Stocks Jan. 1	Production	Total	Disappearance Domestic	Exports	Total	Diret Use	Baking or Frying Fats	Per Capita (Lbs.)
1993	33	1,425	1,470	1,127	310	1,437	412	404	4.4
1994	33	1,510	1,606	1,275	295	1,570	639	405	4.9
1995	36	1,536	1,590	1,268	279	1,548	533	374	4.9
1996	43	1,520	1,568	1,317	218	1,535	602	320	5.0
1997	33	1,416	1,455	1,223	185	1,408	585	312	4.6
1998	47	1,537	1,586	1,301	246	1,547	868	259	4.8
1999	39	1,729	1,775	1,425	317	1,742	998	262	5.2
2000	33	1,840	1,881	1,593	248	1,841	1,137	283	5.8
2001[1]	40	1,844	1,915	1,511	364	1,875	978	NA	4.5
2002[2]	40	1,969	2,018	1,482	511	1,993	968	NA	4.5

[1] Preliminary.   [2] Forecast.   *Sources: Economic Research Service, U.S. Department of Agriculture (ERS-USDA); Bureau of the Census, U.S. Department of Commerce*

Wholesale Price of Tallow, Inedible, No. 1 Packers (Prime), Delivered, Chicago   In Cents Per Pound

Year	Jan.	Feb.	Mar.	Apr.	May	June	July	Aug.	Sept.	Oct.	Nov.	Dec.	Average
1994	15.00	15.00	15.22	15.19	15.25	15.63	16.67	18.64	19.50	19.78	20.38	22.48	17.40
1995	21.75	18.86	18.00	17.75	17.50	17.89	19.61	19.81	19.53	19.46	19.75	20.08	19.17
1996	19.45	17.00	17.03	17.54	19.37	19.50	20.98	22.40	25.98	21.05	19.65	21.63	20.13
1997	23.40	22.88	19.35	17.39	18.09	19.64	19.65	20.10	20.88	22.13	22.88	22.60	20.75
1998	18.20	16.88	17.58	17.70	20.35	19.63	17.31	17.57	16.69	16.98	16.90	16.70	17.71
1999	16.30	12.53	11.18	11.38	10.40	11.49	11.50	11.69	14.38	16.37	14.95	13.88	13.00
2000	11.89	10.14	10.67	10.21	11.60	10.74	9.19	9.48	10.07	10.05	9.35	11.23	10.39
2001	12.17	9.46	9.62	10.26	10.19	12.35	15.44	16.83	13.75	11.24	10.60	12.34	12.02
2002	10.00	10.54	12.64	11.06	11.59	15.47	14.80	14.00	14.23	13.98	15.91	18.08	13.53
2003[1]	17.13	15.65	16.60	16.54	16.48	17.30	16.08	15.85	18.70	22.78	23.37	23.08	18.30

[1] Preliminary.   *Sources: Economic Research Service, U.S. Department of Agriculture (ERS-USDA)*

Tea

Tea is the common name for a family of mostly woody flowering plants. The tea family contains about 600 species placed in 28 genera and they are distributed throughout the tropical and subtropical areas, with most species occurring in eastern Asia and South America. The tea plant is native to Southeast Asia. There are more than 3,000 varieties of tea, each with its own distinct character, and each generally named for the area in which it is grown. Tea has been consumed in China since perhaps the 28th century BC and certainly since the 10th century BC. In 2737 BC, the Chinese Emperor Shen Nung, according to Chinese mythology, was a scholar and herbalist. While his servant boiled drinking water, a leaf from the wild tea tree he was sitting under dropped into the water and Shen Nung decided to try the brew. Today, half the world's population drinks tea, and tea is the world's most popular beverage next to water.

Tea is a healthful drink and contains antioxidants, fluoride, niacin, folic acid, and as much vitamin C as a lemon. The average 5 oz. cup of brewed tea contains approximately 40 to 60 milligrams of caffeine (compared to 80 to 115 mg in brewed coffee). Decaffeinated tea has been available since the 1980s. Herbal tea contains no true tea leaves but is actually brewed from a collection of herbs and spices.

Tea grows mainly between the tropic of Cancer and the tropic of Capricorn, requiring 40 to 50 inches of rain per year and a temperature ideally between 50 to 86 degrees Fahrenheit. In order to rejuvenate the bush and keep it at a convenient height for the pickers to access, the bushes must be pruned every four to five years. A tea bush can produce tea for 50 to 70 years, but after 50 years, the yield is reduced.

The two key factors in determining different varieties of tea are the production process (the sorting, withering, rolling, fermentation, and drying methods) and the growing conditions (the geographical region, growing altitude, and soil type). Black tea, often referred to as fully fermented tea, is produced by allowing picked tea leaves to wither and ferment for up to 24 hours. After fermenting, the leaves are fired, which stops oxidation. Green tea, or unfermented tea, is produced by immediately and completely drying the leaves and omitting the oxidization process, thus allowing the tea to remain green in color.

Supply – World production of tea in 2001, the latest full reporting year, rose +1.5% to 2.991 million metric tons from 2.948 million metric tons in 2000. The world's largest producer of tea in 2001 was India with 25.0% of world production, followed closely by China with 24.1% of world production. Other key producers include Sri Lanka (9.5%), Kenya (8.0%), Turkey (6.0%), and Indonesia (5.6%).

Trade – US tea imports in 2002 fell to 171,829 metric tons in 2002 from 172,829 metric tons in 2001. The world's largest tea importers in 2000 were Russia with 12.6% of total world imports, the United Kingdom (12.4%), Pakistan (8.9%), and the US (7.0%). The world's largest exporters are Sri Lanka with 19.4% of world exports in 2000, China (15.6%), Kenya (14.7%), and India (13.6%).

World Tea Production, in Major Producing Countries   In Thousands of Metric Tons

Year	Argen-tina	Bang-ladesh	China	India	Indo-nesia	Iran	Japan	Kenya	Malawi	Sri Lanka	Turkey	Ex-USSR[2]	World Total
1996	47.0	48.0	617.0	780.0	166.0	62.0	89.0	257.0	37.0	258.0	115.0	42.0	2,710
1997	54.0	53.0	637.0	811.0	149.0	69.0	91.0	221.0	44.0	277.0	140.0	39.0	2,791
1998	57.0	51.0	688.0	870.0	166.0	60.0	83.0	294.0	40.0	280.0	178.0	52.0	3,040
1999	56.0	56.0	697.0	870.0	161.0	80.0	88.0	249.0	48.0	284.0	178.0	65.0	3,078
2000	53.0	46.0	704.0	835.0	162.0	50.0	85.0	236.0	45.0	306.0	139.0	27.0	2,947
2001	63.0	52.0	722.0	848.0	163.0	51.0	85.0	217.0	37.0	295.0	143.0	25.0	2,980
2002[1]	63.0	52.0	760.0	826.0	163.0	51.0	85.0	287.0	38.0	310.0	150.0	23.0	3,100

[1] Preliminary.   [2] Mostly Georgia and Azerbaijan.   *Sources: Foreign Agricultural Service, U.S. Department of Agriculture (FAS-USDA); Food and Agriculture Organization of the United Nations (FAO-UN)*

World Tea Exports from Producing Countries   In Metric Tons

Year	Argen-tina	Bang-ladesh	Brazil	China	India	Indo-nesia	Kenya	Malawi	P. New Guinea	Sri Lanka	Vietnam	Zimbabwe	World Total
1995	41,175	26,445	7,252	169,788	158,333	79,227	258,564	32,600	4,200	178,005	18,800	9,156	1,179,705
1996	35,042	20,981	3,891	173,145	138,360	101,532	260,819	36,700	9,300	218,714	20,800	11,540	1,234,708
1997	56,806	21,740	3,404	205,381	191,472	66,843	199,224	39,824	6,500	267,726	32,901	13,057	1,315,534
1998	58,987	25,049	3,208	219,325	201,798	67,219	263,685	40,518	6,600	270,938	33,000	11,076	1,415,223
1999	52,144	21,494	2,914	202,681	177,507	97,847	245,716	30,000	8,200	268,330	37,300	15,722	1,372,179
2000[1]	50,000	14,300	3,714	230,696	200,868	105,581	217,282	69,600	8,500	287,005	----	16,916	1,491,846
2001[2]	58,068	6,400	4,082	252,204	177,603	99,797	211,592	69,600	8,800	293,524	----	6,162	1,473,395

[1] Preliminary.   [2] Estimate.   *Source: Food and Agriculture Organization of the United Nations (FAO-UN)*

Imports of Tea in the United States   In Metric Tons

Year	Jan.	Feb.	Mar.	Apr.	May	June	July	Aug.	Sept.	Oct.	Nov.	Dec.	Total
1998	11,024	10,214	17,269	15,938	17,479	13,672	16,276	14,318	7,852	8,758	8,649	9,839	151,287
1999	11,017	9,796	14,737	15,041	17,271	17,007	14,794	15,743	9,468	11,935	10,628	10,604	158,040
2000	10,831	13,475	18,217	15,929	19,861	18,367	14,396	13,008	10,725	10,873	11,662	10,611	167,952
2001	14,596	11,917	15,237	16,772	15,802	16,426	16,041	14,415	11,917	14,072	14,548	11,150	172,893
2002	14,785	14,237	16,029	17,326	18,747	15,158	15,189	11,977	9,777	14,384	12,148	12,073	171,829
2003[1]	15,045	13,556	15,649	17,806	18,793	15,094	15,285	13,850	11,228	16,420	11,427	13,059	177,211

[1] Preliminary.   *Source: Foreign Agricultural Service, U.S. Department of Agriculture (FAS-USDA)*

Tin

Tin is a silvery-white, lustrous gray metallic element. Tin is soft, pliable and has a highly crystalline structure. When a tin bar is bent or broken, a crackling sound called a "tin cry" is produced due to the breaking of the tin crystals. People have been using tin for at least 5,500 years. Tin has been found in the tombs of ancient Egyptians, and tin and lead were considered different forms of the same metal. Tin was exported to Europe in large quantities from Cornwall, England, during the Roman period, approximately 2100 to 1500 BC. Cornwall was one of the world's leading sources of tin for much of its known history and into the late 19th century.

The principal ore of tin is the mineral cassiterite, which is found in Malaya, Bolivia, Indonesia, Thailand, and Nigeria. About 80% of the world's tin deposits occur as unconsolidated placer deposits in river beds and valleys or on the sea floor, with only about 20% occurring as primary hardrock lodes. Tin deposits are generally small and almost always found closely allied to the granite from which it originates. Tin is also recovered as a by-product of mining tungsten, tantalum, and lead. After extraction, tin ore is ground and washed to remove impurities, roasted to oxidize the sulfides of iron and copper, washed a second time, and is then reduced by carbon in a reverberatory furnace. Electrolysis may also be used to purify tin.

Pure tin, rarely used by itself, was used as currency in the form of tin blocks and was considered legal tender for taxes in Phuket, Thailand, until 1932. Tin is used in the manufacture of coatings for steel containers used to preserve food and beverages. Tin is also used in solder alloys, electroplating, ceramics, and in plastic. The world's major tin research and development laboratory, ITRI Ltd., is now over six years old as a private institution. The laboratory is funded by companies that produce and consume tin. The focus of the research efforts have been on possible new uses for tin that would take advantage of tin's relative non-toxicity to replace other metals in various products. Some of the replacements could be lead-free solders, antimony-free flame-retardant chemicals, and lead-free shotgun pellets. No tin is mined in the U.S. currently.

Tin futures and options trade on the London Metal Exchange (LME). Tin has traded on the LME since 1877 and the standard tin contract began in 1912. The futures contract calls for the delivery of 5 metric tons of tin ingots of at least 99.85% purity. The contract trades in terms of US dollars per metric ton.

Prices – The average price of tin (straights) in 2003 rose to $3.31 per pound from the 20-year year low of $2.83 per pound seen in 2002 (i.e., since 1973). The average price of ex-dock tin in New York rose to $2.32 per pound from the 21-year low of $1.99 per pound in 2001 (i.e., since 1972). Tin prices in 2003 recovered along with the rest of the basic metal complex.

Supply – World mine production of tin in 2002 fell sharply by 19% to a 3-year low of 249,000 from 308,000 as the marketplace reacted to lower prices. The world's largest mine producers of tin are China with 32% of world production in 2002, Peru (26%), and Indonesia (22%). Mine production in Peru has risen sharply in the last few years and recent production levels in the 65,000-70,000 metric ton range are more than double the levels seen in 1997.

World smelter production of tin fell –5.8% in 2002 to 278,000 metric tons from 295,000 in 2001. The world's largest producers of smelted tin are Malaysia with 16% of world production, China (14%), Indonesia (12%), and Brazil (10%). The US does not mine tin, and therefore supply consists only of scrap and imports. US tin recovery in 2002 fell to 7,750 metric tons from 7,800 in 2001.

Demand – US consumption of tin (pig) in 2003 was on track to fall to about 45,800 metric tons from 46,655 metric tons in 2002 and post a new 6-year low. The breakdown of US consumption of tin by finished products in 2002 shows that the largest consuming industry of tin is solder (with 35% of consumption), followed by chemicals (21%), tin plate (20%), and bronze and brass (8%).

Trade – The US relied on imports for 79% of its consumption in 2002. US imports of unwrought tin metal rose to 42,200 metric tons in 2002 from 37,500 in 2001. The largest sources of US imports in 2002 were China (with 7,600 metric tons of imports), Bolivia (6,150 metric tons), Brazil (4,840 metric tons), and Indonesia (3,340 metric tons). US exports of tin fell to 2,940 metric tons in 2002 from 4,350 metric tons in 2001.

World Mine Production of Tin   In Metric Tons (Contained Tin)

Year	Australia	Bolivia	Brazil	China	Indo-nesia	Malaysia	Nigeria	Peru	Portugal	Russia	Thailand	United Kingdom	World Total
1993	8,057	18,634	26,500	49,100	29,000	10,384	200	14,310	5,334	13,100	6,363	2,232	190,000
1994	7,495	16,169	16,619	54,100	30,610	6,458	278	20,275	4,332	10,460	3,926	1,922	178,000
1995	8,656	14,419	17,317	61,900	46,058	6,402	357	22,331	4,627	9,000	2,201	1,973	201,000
1996	8,828	14,802	19,617	69,600	52,304	5,174	139	27,004	4,637	8,000	1,300	2,103	220,000
1997	10,169	12,898	19,065	67,500	55,175	5,065	150	27,952	2,667	7,500	746	2,396	217,000
1998	10,204	11,308	14,238	70,100	53,959	5,754	200	49,574	3,100	4,500	1,656	376	231,000
1999	10,011	12,417	13,202	80,100	47,754	7,340	200	59,191	2,200	4,500	2,712	----	245,000
2000	9,146	12,464	14,200	99,400	51,629	6,307	300	70,501	1,200	5,000	2,166	----	278,000
2001[1]	9,602	12,298	12,500	95,000	90,000	4,972	200	69,696	1,200	4,500	2,522	----	308,000
2002[2]	6,268	15,242	13,000	80,000	54,000	4,215	200	65,400	1,000	2,900	1,104	----	249,000

[1] Preliminary.   [2] Estimate.   *Source: U.S. Geological Survey (USGS)*

TIN

World Smelter Production of Primary Tin   In Metric Tons

Year	Australia	Bolivia	Brazil	China	Indo-nesia	Japan	Malaysia	Mexico	Russia	South Africa	Spain	Thailand	World Total
1993	222	14,541	26,900	52,100	30,415	804	40,079	1,640	13,400	452	500	8,099	215,000
1994	315	15,285	20,400	67,800	31,100	706	37,990	768	11,500	43	500	7,759	216,000
1995	570	17,709	16,787	67,700	38,628	630	39,433	770	9,500	----	500	8,243	223,000
1996	460	16,733	18,361	71,500	39,000	524	38,051	1,234	9,000	----	150	10,981	211,000
1997	605	16,853	17,525	67,700	52,658	507	34,822	1,188	6,700	----	150	11,986	241,000
1998	655	11,102	14,900	79,300	53,401	500	27,201	1,078	3,000	----	100	15,353	247,000
1999	600	11,166	12,787	90,800	49,105	568	28,913	1,258	3,400	----	50	17,306	266,000
2000	775	9,353	13,773	112,000	46,432	593	26,228	1,107	3,700	----	----	17,076	288,000
2001	1,171	11,300	12,300	105,000	53,470	668	30,417	----	3,100	----	----	21,357	295,000
2002[1]	611	10,976	12,500	93,000	53,000	659	30,000	1,200	3,150	----	----	21,500	278,000

[1] Preliminary.   Source: U.S. Geological Survey (USGS)

United States Foreign Trade of Tin   In Metric Tons

		Concentrates[2] (Ore)			Imports for Consumption								
	Exports	Total			Total				Indo-		Singa-		United
Year	(Metal)	All Ore	Bolivia	Peru	All Metal	Bolivia	Brazil	China	nesia	Malaysia	pore	Thailand	Kingdom
1993	2,600	-----	-----	-----	33,682	8,027	11,366	4,202	5,678	846	220	-----	6
1994	2,560	-----	-----	-----	32,400	7,260	9,990	3,230	6,620	1,390	142	-----	666
1995	2,790	-----	-----	-----	33,200	6,630	8,070	5,610	7,230	3,810	40	-----	97
1996	3,670	-----	-----	-----	30,200	6,290	9,460	2,760	7,550	965	120	-----	243
1997	4,660	57	-----	-----	40,600	6,680	8,610	4,710	7,610	1,640	120	600	20
1998	5,020	-----	-----	-----	44,000	5,160	4,710	9,870	7,880	1,870	822	540	790
1999	6,770	-----	-----	-----	47,500	3,850	4,700	13,900	7,930	944	60	20	60
2000	6,640	-----	-----	-----	44,900	6,330	5,860	10,200	5,320	214	20	-----	514
2001	4,350	-----	-----	-----	37,500	6,040	5,510	6,360	3,880	674	145	-----	118
2002[1]	2,940	-----	-----	-----	42,200	6,150	4,840	7,600	3,340	122	-----	-----	2

[1] Preliminary.   [2] Tin content.   Source: U.S. Geological Survey (USGS)

Consumption (Total) of Tin (Pig) in the United States   In Metric Tons

Year	Jan.	Feb.	Mar.	Apr.	May	June	July	Aug.	Sept.	Oct.	Nov.	Dec.	Total
1994	3,500	3,700	3,700	3,600	3,600	3,700	3,500	3,400	2,500	3,600	3,600	3,400	42,700
1995	3,500	3,600	3,680	3,726	3,877	3,833	3,544	3,895	3,825	3,823	3,735	3,770	44,808
1996	3,862	3,938	3,940	3,878	3,894	3,976	3,926	3,996	3,687	3,779	3,908	3,730	48,800
1997	4,953	4,025	4,023	4,067	3,999	4,079	3,936	3,912	4,050	4,098	3,964	4,250	44,350
1998	4,410	4,493	4,445	4,508	4,388	4,483	4,273	4,300	4,404	4,402	4,348	4,268	52,720
1999	4,660	4,667	4,790	4,790	4,760	4,700	4,254	4,396	4,340	4,316	4,275	4,227	55,100
2000	4,362	4,466	4,430	4,377	4,466	4,470	4,398	4,476	4,397	4,460	4,244	4,157	47,040
2001	4,252	4,185	4,095	4,141	4,148	4,128	4,055	4,163	4,153	4,197	4,129	3,974	49,620
2002	3,965	3,866	3,868	3,819	4,087	3,887	3,887	3,842	3,835	3,966	3,822	3,811	46,655
2003[1]	3,814	3,808	3,851	3,891	3,701	3,814	3,841	3,850	3,803	3,816	3,764	3,887	45,840

[1] Preliminary.   Source: U.S. Geological Survey (USGS)

Tin Stocks (Pig-Industrial) in the United States, on First of Month   In Metric Tons

Year	Jan.	Feb.	Mar.	Apr.	May	June	July	Aug.	Sept.	Oct.	Nov.	Dec.
1994	3,651	4,635	3,775	3,967	3,471	3,470	3,825	3,027	2,891	2,980	2,844	2,908
1995	2,741	3,931	3,850	2,780	3,000	3,080	3,210	3,910	3,800	3,880	4,380	4,290
1996	4,580	6,000	5,200	4,390	4,880	5,590	5,760	5,640	4,790	4,580	4,810	6,810
1997	4,670	5,100	5,610	5,600	5,070	5,270	5,180	5,650	5,590	5,420	5,290	5,590
1998	6,100	5,570	5,390	5,840	6,170	5,940	5,830	5,580	6,660	6,270	5,880	5,710
1999	5,620	8,120	7,770	7,760	7,760	7,510	7,750	7,560	7,870	7,790	8,390	8,800
2000	8,300	8,330	7,960	7,580	7,810	7,930	8,090	8,240	7,820	8,210	7,200	7,970
2001	8,140	8,330	8,360	8,460	8,270	8,640	8,760	8,760	8,920	9,030	7,630	7,470
2002	7,700	7,320	7,020	6,990	6,870	6,600	6,540	6,590	6,670	7,130	6,880	6,950
2003[1]	7,280	6,980	6,690	6,640	6,390	6,400	6,380	6,420	6,250	6,180	6,190	6,340

[1] Preliminary.   Source: U.S. Geological Survey (USGS)

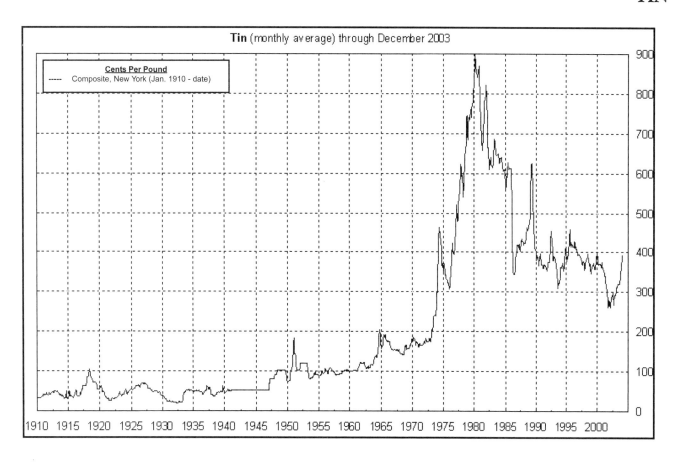

Average Price of Ex-Dock Tin in New York[1]   In Cents Per Pound

Year	Jan.	Feb.	Mar.	Apr.	May	June	July	Aug.	Sept.	Oct.	Nov.	Dec.	Average
1994	249.55	267.55	261.20	258.49	264.18	264.45	254.83	249.18	255.10	262.46	293.72	284.99	263.81
1995	374.77	260.25	266.45	288.00	283.62	314.33	316.06	331.64	304.12	297.77	304.47	300.28	303.48
1996	299.55	297.45	296.68	308.49	306.71	296.20	298.47	291.30	292.13	285.11	285.87	280.61	294.88
1997	281.91	281.34	281.51	274.36	274.23	267.31	261.03	259.85	262.56	266.77	268.33	262.61	270.15
1998	249.39	252.65	262.36	271.65	279.50	284.27	268.87	270.98	260.79	259.17	261.82	251.75	264.43
1999	244.46	251.04	255.13	256.97	269.42	253.64	251.09	251.32	256.38	260.70	278.24	274.51	258.73
2000	283.63	271.70	263.42	259.59	259.70	260.16	257.77	255.92	262.54	254.56	253.64	252.19	261.24
2001	249.32	246.91	243.14	238.33	238.53	231.14	210.17	188.42	179.53	181.38	194.77	195.90	216.46
2002	189.23	183.23	187.65	195.36	201.95	208.01	211.51	188.36	193.79	206.67	205.94	206.63	199.15
2003	201.53	217.98	219.58	217.90	225.40	223.69	225.81	229.58	233.59	248.22	252.93	285.40	231.80

Source: American Metal Market (AMM)

Average Price of Tin (Straights) in New York   In Cents Per Pound

Year	Jan.	Feb.	Mar.	Apr.	May	June	July	Aug.	Sept.	Oct.	Nov.	Dec.	Average
1994	334.38	362.81	361.86	363.65	371.63	372.59	360.45	353.85	362.48	371.82	411.63	401.31	369.04
1995	415.05	379.08	378.61	395.99	399.17	433.75	438.04	458.66	423.71	417.23	425.41	419.75	415.37
1996	418.68	415.65	414.71	429.34	427.24	413.65	416.63	409.12	407.79	400.25	400.65	394.46	412.35
1997	396.18	395.50	395.64	386.52	386.58	377.83	369.97	369.01	372.45	377.39	378.00	371.35	381.37
1998	356.97	359.76	370.96	381.99	392.16	397.36	377.72	380.02	368.89	366.87	370.49	357.69	373.41
1999	348.77	356.50	361.11	363.01	372.62	359.05	359.96	357.35	366.06	370.68	392.04	288.77	357.99
2000	400.90	384.13	372.50	368.42	370.13	370.81	366.49	364.65	375.25	363.54	362.94	360.68	371.70
2001	356.37	352.87	348.19	341.59	340.61	329.68	302.57	276.55	263.17	264.88	281.23	279.46	311.43
2002	271.59	263.91	270.54	280.98	288.74	296.02	299.39	269.30	277.60	293.79	292.40	292.95	283.10
2003	304.44	312.32	314.52	312.26	321.92	319.67	322.10	327.16	332.21	350.90	356.46	396.46	330.87

Source: U.S. Geological Survey (USGS)

TIN

Tin Plate Production & Tin Recovered in the United States   In Metric Tons

	Tin Content of Tinplate Produced				Tin Recovered from Scrap by Form of Recovery								
	Tinplate (All Forms)												
	Tinplate Waste		Tin Content	Tin Per Tonne of Plate	Tin	Bronze		Type		Anti-monial	Chemical Com-		Grand
Year	---- Gross Weight ----		(Tonne)	(Kilograms)	Metal	& Brass	Solder	Metal	Babbitt	Lead	pounds	Misc.[2]	Total
1993	196,874	1,625,132	9,945	6.0	112	10,670	W	43	51	796	W	W	11,672
1994	188,921	1,528,303	9,396	6.1	NA	NA	NA	NA	NA	NA	NA	NA	NA
1995	205,000	1,660,000	9,600	5.8	W	11,200	W	39	W	335	W	W	11,600
1996	181,100	1,551,000	9,617	6.2	W	11,400	W	37	34	171	W	W	11,600
1997	157,000	2,010,000	9,300	4.6	W	12,200	W	W	W	149	W	W	12,300
1998	W	1,700,000	8,900	5.2	NA	NA	NA	NA	NA	NA	NA	NA	NA
1999	W	1,750,000	9,080	5.2	NA	NA	NA	NA	NA	NA	NA	NA	NA
2000	119,000	1,320,000	8,800	6.7	NA	NA	NA	NA	NA	NA	NA	NA	NA
2001	97,800	2,000,000	7,800	3.9	NA	NA	NA	NA	NA	NA	NA	NA	NA
2002[1]	45,900	2,450,000	7,750	3.2	NA	NA	NA	NA	NA	NA	NA	NA	NA

[1] Preliminary.   [2] Includes foil, terne metal, cable lead, and items indicated by symbol W.   W = Withheld Proprietary data.
Source: U.S. Geological Survey (USGS)

Consumption of Primary and Secondary Tin in the United States   In Metric Tons

| | Net Import Reliance as a % of Apparent | Industry Stocks | Net Receipts | | | | Available | Stocks Dec. 31 (Total Available Less Total | Total | Consumed in Manu-facturing |
Year	Consumption	Jan. 1[2]	Primary	Secondary	Scrap	Total	Supply	Processed)	Processed	Products
1993	84	8,556	37,700	3,280	8,768	49,700	58,300	11,566	46,700	46,600
1994	83	9,540	35,400	4,210	4,940	44,500	54,100	11,600	42,500	42,200
1995	84	8,480	39,400	5,020	6,240	50,600	59,100	13,000	46,100	46,000
1996	83	9,300	39,200	2,750	6,140	48,100	57,300	12,500	44,900	44,700
1997	85	9,180	39,000	2,360	6,010	47,300	56,500	11,900	44,600	44,400
1998	85	9,280	39,900	2,490	6,240	48,600	57,900	12,000	45,800	45,700
1999	85	9,290	40,500	2,790	6,360	49,700	58,900	11,900	47,000	46,900
2000	86	8,910	41,400	2,990	6,050	50,400	59,300	12,200	47,100	47,000
2001	88	8,830	34,500	2,180	4,770	41,400	50,200	8,220	42,000	41,900
2002[1]	79	8,500	34,300	1,610	4,320	40,300	48,800	8,730	40,000	39,800

[1] Preliminary.   [2] Includes tin in transit in the U.S.   *Source: U.S. Geological Survey (USGS)*

Consumption of Tin in the United States, by Finished Products   In Metric Tons (Contained Tin)

Year	Tinplate[2]	Solder	Babbitt	Bronze & Brass	Tinning	Chem-icals[3]	Tin Powder	Bar Tin & Anodes	White Metal	Other	Total	Total Primary	Total Secondary
1993	9,650	19,000	823	3,093	1,249	6,446	608	946	789	3,927	46,600	34,600	11,900
1994	9,480	15,100	831	3,080	1,230	5,740	625	1,190	992	3,990	42,200	33,700	8,530
1995	9,670	17,700	871	2,830	1,110	7,060	W	1,200	965	4,550	46,000	35,200	10,800
1996	9,340	15,600	851	2,760	2,050	7,520	573	1,150	1,340	3,230	44,700	36,500	8,180
1997	9,350	15,900	909	3,160	1,210	8,170	W	684	754	3,980	44,400	36,200	8,250
1998	8,900	16,900	1,020	3,610	1,100	8,180	W	704	778	4,260	45,700	37,100	8,620
1999	9,150	18,700	1,610	3,410	905	8,220	W	721	943	3,220	46,900	38,000	8,890
2000	8,800	18,800	1,660	3,360	1,200	8,040	W	714	1,260	3,210	47,000	38,100	8,940
2001	7,800	17,000	770	3,430	1,070	7,590	W	570	1,390	2,230	41,900	34,200	7,630
2002[1]	7,750	13,800	1,310	3,040	679	8,400	W	617	1,320	2,920	39,800	34,000	5,830

[1] Preliminary.   [2] Includes small quantity of secondary pig tin and tin acquired in chemicals.   [3] Including tin oxide.   W = Withheld proprietary data.
Source: U.S. Geological Survey (USGS)

Titanium

Titanium is a silver-white, metallic element used primarily to make light, strong alloys. Its atomic symbol is Ti. It ranks ninth in abundance among the elements in the crust of the earth but is never found in the pure state. It occurs as an oxide in various minerals. It was first discovered in 1791 by Rev. William Gregor and was first isolated as a basic element in 1910. Titanium was named after the mythological Greek god Titan.

Pure titanium is soluble in concentrated acids but insoluble in water. Titanium is extremely brittle when cold, but is malleable and ductile at a low red heat, thus easily fabricated. Due to its strength, low weight, and resistance to corrosion, titanium is used in metallic alloys and as a substitute for aluminum. It is used extensively in the aerospace industry, in desalination plants, construction, medical implants, paints, pigments, and lacquers.

Prices – The price of the mineral ilmenite, a primary source of titanium, has generally risen over the past decade and hit new highs of $90-110 per metric ton in 2001. The price of titanium metal sponge in 2001 fell to $3.58 per pound from $3.95 in 2000. The price of titanium dioxide pigments (Anatase) was unchanged in 2001 at 92-94 cents per pound. The price of titanium dioxide pigments (Rutile) rose to $1.00-1.09 in 2001 from $0.99-1.02 in 2000.

Supply – World production of titanium ilmenite concentrates in 2001 rose +1.0% to a new record high of 5.060 million metric tons. The largest producer of titanium ilmenite concentrates is Australia with 40.5% of world production in 2001, followed by Norway with 14.8%, Ukraine with 11.9%, and India with 8.5%.

World production of titanium rutile concentrates in 2001 fell –2.3% to 378,000 metric tons from 387,000 metric tons in 2000. The world's largest producers are Australia with 55% of world production, followed by South Africa with 24% and the Ukraine with 16%.

Demand – US consumption of titanium dioxide pigment in 2001 fell -4.3% to 1.100 million metric tons from 1.150 million metric tons in 2000. US consumption of ilmenite in 2001 fell -5.6% to 1.180 million metric tons from 1.250 million metric tons in 2000. US consumption of rutile in 2001 fell sharply by -10.1% to 483,000 metric tons from 537,000 metric tons in 2000.

Trade – US imports of titanium dioxide pigment in 2001 fell –4.1% to 209,000 and accounted for 19% of US consumption. US imports of ilmenite in 2001 rose +15.5% to 1.060 million metric tons and accounted for 90% of US consumption. US imports of rutile in 2001 fell –25.8% to 325,000 and accounted for 67% of US consumption.

Average Prices of Titanium in the United States

Year	Ilmenite F.O.B. Australian Ports	Slag, 85% TiO2 F.O.B. Richards Bay, South Africa	Rutile Large Lots Bulk, F.O.B. U.S. East Coast	Rutile Bagged F.O.B. Australian Ports	Average Price of Grade A Titanium Sponge, F.O.B. Shipping Point	Titanium Metal Sponge	Titanium Dioxide Pigments, F.O.B. U.S. Plants	
	---- Dollars Per Metric Ton ----					---- Dollars Per Pound ----		
1993	61-64	330	NA	370-400	3.75	3.50-4.00	.99	.92-.95
1994	74-80	334	410-430	450-480	3.96	3.75-4.25	.94-.96	.92-.94
1995	81-85	349	550-650	650-800	4.06	4.25-4.50	.92-.96	.99-1.03
1996	82-92	353	525-600	700-800	----	4.25-4.50	1.06-1.08	1.08-1.10
1997	68-81	391	500-550	650-710	----	4.25-4.50	1.01-1.03	1.04-1.06
1998	72-77	386	470-530	570-620	----	4.25-4.50	.96-.98	.97-.99
1999	90-103	406	435-510	500-530	----	3.70-4.80	.92-.94	.99-1.02
2000	83-105	425	470-500	480-570	----	3.95	.92-.94	.99-1.02
2001[1]	90-110	419	450-500	475-565	----	3.58	.92-.94	1.00-1.09
2002[2]	85-100	445	430-470	400-540	----	3.64	.85-.95	.85-.95

[1] Preliminary. [2] Estimate. NA = Not available. *Source: U.S. Geological Survey (USGS)*

Salient Statistics of Titanium in the United States   In Metric Tons

Year	Titanium Dioxide Pigment — Production	Imports[3]	Apparent Consumption	Ilmenite — Imports[3]	Consumption	Titanium Slag — Imports[3]	Consumption	Rutile[4] — Imports[3]	Consumption	Exports — Ores & Concentrates	Scrap	Dioxide & Pigments	Ingots, Billets, Etc.
1993	1,161,561	171,939	1,028,311	301,000	693,940	476,000	545,809	371,481	464,825	15,202	3,893	261,000	1,511
1994	1,250,000	176,000	1,090,000	808,000	W	472,000	583,000	332,000	510,000	19,000	4,120	313,000	1,559
1995	1,250,000	183,000	1,130,000	861,000	1,410,000	388,000	582,000	318,000	480,000	32,300	3,420	306,000	2,560
1996	1,230,000	167,000	1,070,000	939,000	1,400,000	421,000	----	324,000	398,000	15,500	3,410	292,000	3,130
1997	1,340,000	194,000	1,130,000	952,000	1,520,000	----	----	336,000	489,000	23,800	5,500	362,000	3,860
1998	1,330,000	200,000	1,140,000	1,010,000	1,300,000	----	----	387,000	421,000	59,700	7,010	356,000	3,780
1999	1,350,000	225,000	1,160,000	1,070,000	1,280,000	----	----	344,000	494,000	9,380	8,130	344,000	3,390
2000	1,400,000	218,000	1,150,000	918,000	1,250,000	----	----	438,000	537,000	18,900	5,060	423,000	2,980
2001[1]	1,330,000	209,000	1,100,000	1,060,000	1,180,000	----	----	325,000	483,000	7,800	7,500	349,000	3,260
2002[2]	1,410,000	231,000	1,120,000	840,000	1,300,000	----	----	390,000	487,000	3,810	6,000	485,000	3,460

[1] Preliminary. [2] Estimate. [3] For consumption. [4] Natural and synthetic. [5] 1994 to date includes Slag. W = Withheld proprietary data.
Source: U.S. Geological Survey (USGS)

TITANIUM

World Production of Titanium Illmenite Concentrates   In Thousands of Metric Tons

Year	Aus-tralia[2]	Brazil	China	India	Malaysia	Norway	Sierra Leone	Sri Lanka	Thailand	Ukraine	World Total	Titaniferous Slag[4] Canada	South Africa
1993	1,804	90.6	155.0	320.0	279.0	713.0	62.9	76.9	20.82	450	3,990	653	892
1994	1,817	97.4	155.0	300.0	116.7	826.4	47.4	60.4	1.68	530	3,970	764	744
1995	2,011	102.1	160.0	290.0	151.7	833.2	----	49.7	.03	359	4,010	815	990
1996	2,061	98.0	165.0	330.0	244.6	746.6	----	62.8	----	250	4,010	825	1,000
1997	2,265	97.2	170.0	332.0	167.5	750.0	----	18.0	----	500	4,470	850	1,100
1998	2,409	103.0	175.0	378.0	124.7	590.0	----	34.1	----	507	4,530	950	1,100
1999	2,008	96.0	180.0	378.0	127.7	600.0	----	----	----	537	4,150	950	1,168
2000	2,173	123.0	185.0	380.0	124.8	750.0	----	----	----	577	5,010	950	1,057
2001	2,047	111.1	185.0	430.0	129.8	750.0	----	----	----	650	5,110	950	1,090
2002[1]	1,956	115.0	185.0	460.0	106.0	750.0	----	----	----	670	4,950	900	1,150

[1] Preliminary.   [2] Includes leucoxene.   [4] Approximately 10% of total production is ilmenite. Beginning in 1988, 25% of Norway's ilmenite production was used to produce slag containing 75% TiO2.   NA = Not available.   *Source: U.S. Geological Survey (USGS)*

World Production of Titanium Rutile Concentrates   In Metric Tons

Year	Australia	Brazil	India	Sierre Leone	South Africa	Sri Lanka	Thailand	Ukraine	World Total
1993	186,000	1,744	13,900	152,000	85,000	2,643	87	60,000	501,000
1994	233,000	1,911	14,000	137,000	78,000	2,410	49	80,000	545,000
1995	195,000	1,985	14,000	----	90,000	2,697	----	112,000	416,000
1996	180,000	2,018	15,000	----	115,000	3,532	----	50,000	366,000
1997	233,000	1,742	14,000	----	123,000	2,970	----	50,000	425,000
1998	238,000	1,800	16,000	----	130,000	1,930	----	50,000	438,000
1999	179,000	4,300	16,000	----	100,000	----	----	49,000	348,000
2000	208,000	3,162	17,000	----	100,000	----	----	58,600	387,000
2001	206,000	1,791	19,000	----	90,000	----	----	60,000	377,000
2002[1]	218,000	2,000	18,000	----	100,000	----	----	70,000	408,000

[1] Preliminary.   NA = Not available.   *Source: U.S. Geological Survey (USGS)*

World Production of Titanium Sponge Metal & U.S. Consumption of Titanium Concentrates

	Production of Titanium (In Metric Tons) Sponge Metal[2]					U.S. Consumption of Titanium Concentrates, by Products (In Metric Tons) Ilmenite (TiO$_2$ Content)				Rutile (TiO$_2$ Content) Welding Rod			
Year	China	Japan	Russia	United Kingdom	United States	Total	Pigments	Misc.	Total	Coatings	Pigments	Misc.	Total
1993	2,000	14,400	20,000	1,000	27,938	37,000	434,097	451	434,548	W	405,784	30,223	436,007
1994	2,000	14,400	12,000	----	29,510	33,000	W	637	W	W	460,000	18,500	478,500
1995	2,000	16,000	12,000	----	W	35,000	1,010,000	[3]	1,010,000	W	417,000	22,300	439,300
1996	2,000	21,100	18,000	----	W	51,000	1,010,000	[3]	1,010,000	W	341,000	24,200	365,000
1997	2,000	24,100	20,000	----	W	58,000	1,410,000	[3]	1,410,000	W	406,000	27,600	434,000
1998	----	----	----	----	----	----	1,290,000	14,000	1,300,000	W	384,000	37,300	421,000
1999	----	----	----	----	----	----	1,270,000	13,400	1,280,000	----	469,000	25,800	494,000
2000	----	----	----	----	----	----	1,240,000	13,900	1,250,000	----	513,000	24,100	537,000
2001	----	----	----	----	----	----	1,160,000	15,400	1,180,000	----	455,000	28,500	483,000
2002[1]	----	----	----	----	----	----	1,280,000	16,000	1,300,000	----	464,000	22,900	487,000

[1] Preliminary.   [2] Unconsolidated metal in various forms.   [3] Included in Pigments.   NA = Not available.   W = Withheld proprietary data.
Source: U.S. Geological Survey (USGS)

Tobacco

Tobacco is a member of the nightshade family. It is commercially grown for its leaves and stems, which are rolled into cigars, shredded for use in cigarettes and pipes, processed for chewing, or ground into snuff. Christopher Columbus introduced tobacco cultivation and use to Spain after observing natives from the Americas smoking loosely rolled tobacco-stuffed tobacco leaves.

Tobacco is cured, or dried, after harvesting and then aged to improve its flavor. The four common methods of curing are: air cured, fire cured, sun cured, and flue cured. Flue curing is the fasted method of curing and requires only about a week compared with up to 10 weeks for other methods. Cured tobacco is tied into small bundles of about 20 leaves and aged one to three years.

Virginia tobacco is by far the most popular type used in pipe tobacco. It is the mildest of all blending tobaccos. Approximately 60% of the US tobacco crop is Virginia. Burley tobacco is the next most popular tobacco and is an air-cured tobacco. It burns slowly and is a cool smoke. Other tobacco varieties include Perique, Kentucky, Oriental, and Latakia.

Prices – Tobacco prices (Types 11-37) half way through the 2003/4 marketing year (July-June) rallied to an average of $1.89 per pound from $1.84 in 2002/3. Average yearly tobacco prices have remained in the tight range of $1.83-$1.90 over the past four marketing years, up from the $1.78-$1.80 range seen in the previous three years.

Supply – World production of tobacco in 2001, the last full reporting year for the series, fell -3.6% to 6.582 million metric tons from 6.826 million metric tons. The world's largest producer of tobacco in 2001 by far was China with 39.3% of world production, followed at a distance by India (with 8.9% of world production), Brazil (8.2%), and the US (6.2%). US production in 2001 of 408,236 metric tons was down by nearly 50% from the 2-decade high of 810,154 metric tons in 1997.

US tobacco is primarily grown in the mid Atlantic states which account for more than 86% of US production. Specifically, the largest tobacco producing states in the US are North Carolina (with 39.9% of US production in 2002), Kentucky (25.6%), Tennessee (8.0%), South Carolina (6.6%), and Georgia (6.2%).

Flue-cured tobacco (type 11-14) is the most popular type grown in the US with production of 525.940 million pounds in 2002, down from 579.091 million pounds in 2001. The second most popular type is burley tobacco (type 31) that had a production of 303.895 million pounds in 2002, down from 334.066 million pounds in 2001.

US production of tobacco in 2002 fell to 886 million pounds, down 10.6% from 992 million pounds in 2001 and down 50% from the 2-decade high of 1.787 billion pounds posted in 1997. US farmers have sharply reduced the planting acreage for tobacco. In the last two years, farmers have planted about 430,000 acres of tobacco, much less than the 600,000+ acres planted in the 1988-99 period. Yields have been fairly constant and have averaged about 2,100 pounds per acre in the past 10 years, with a variation of plus or minus 10%. The farm value of the US tobacco crop fell to $1.726 billion in 2002 from $1.952 billion in 2001 and $2.002 billion in 2000.

US production of flue-cured tobacco (Types 11-14) in 2002/3 rose to 565.0 million pounds from 544.4 million pounds in 2001/2. US production of burley tobacco (Type 31) in 2002/3 fell to 300.0 million pounds from 343.7 million pounds in 2001/2, and was down by more than 50% since the 10-year high of 628.2 million pounds in 1997/8.

US production of cigarettes in 2002 was unchanged from 2001 at 580.0 billion, although that was down sharply by 19% from 10-years earlier (718.5 billion in 1992). US production of cigars fell slightly to 2.900 billion from 2.993 billion in 2001, but that was up by 67% from 10 years earlier (1.741 billion in 1992). US production of chewing tobacco in 2002 was unchanged from 2001 at 47.2 million pounds, which was down sharply by 31% from 10-years earlier.

Demand – US per capita consumption of tobacco products in 2001, the last full reporting year, fell to 4.14 pounds per person per year, down from 4.22 pounds in 2000 and 5.60 pounds 10 years earlier (1990). Per capita cigarette consumption in 2002 rose to 3.60 pounds from 3.40 pounds in 2001, but per capita consumption of cigars fell to .58 pounds from .65 pounds in 2001 and chewing tobacco per capita consumption fell to .40 pounds from .47 pounds in 2001. Per capita consumption of loose smoking tobacco was unchanged at 0.15 pounds.

Trade – US tobacco exports in 2002/3 fell sharply to 261.9 million pounds from 386.5 pounds in 2001/2. Meanwhile, US tobacco imports in 2002/3 were little changed from 2001/2 at 566.6 million pounds. The US exported 135.0 billion cigarettes and 270 million cigars in 2002/3.

World Production of Leaf Tobacco   In Metric Tons

Year	Brazil	Canada	China	Greece	India	Indo-nesia	Italy	Japan	Pakistan	Turkey	United States	Zim-babwe	World Total
1993	608,000	86,094	3,451,000	148,000	580,600	152,800	135,698	67,430	105,966	338,068	731,914	235,286	8,261,069
1994	442,000	71,500	2,238,000	135,400	528,000	160,000	131,010	79,503	100,351	187,733	717,990	177,816	6,391,977
1995	398,000	79,287	2,317,700	131,875	587,100	171,400	124,492	78,212	80,917	204,900	575,380	209,042	6,376,704
1996	439,000	65,320	3,076,000	131,000	562,750	177,000	130,590	66,031	80,760	229,400	688,258	207,767	6,962,473
1997	576,600	71,110	4,251,000	132,450	623,700	184,300	140,634	68,504	86,279	310,850	810,154	192,144	8,822,851
1998	447,000	69,300	2,365,000	132,200	633,200	148,980	132,030	63,959	92,728	260,750	802,014	223,977	6,788,827
1999	595,000	64,864	2,469,300	129,700	648,600	156,882	130,762	64,727	103,430	250,484	586,355	198,967	6,868,133
2000	589,000	64,864	2,552,000	126,700	661,600	185,121	129,937	60,803	104,096	250,495	453,600	245,214	6,855,093
2001[1]	542,400	64,864	2,349,627	126,000	585,600	172,200	130,487	60,565	82,854	207,261	449,745	200,096	6,774,308
2002[2]	674,000	64,864	2,328,978	126,200	635,500	170,150	130,400	60,000	93,400	160,476	418,439	200,096	6,754,505

[1] Preliminary.   [2] Estimate.   *Source: Foreign Agricultural Service, U.S. Department of Agriculture (FAS-USDA)*

TOBACCO

Production and Consumption of Tobacco Products in the United States

Year	Cigarettes (Billions)	Cigars[3] (Millions)	Chewing Tobacco — Plug	Twist	Loose-leaf	Total	Smoking Tobacco	Snuff[4]	Consumption[5] of Per Capita[6] — Cigarettes (Number)	Cigars[3] (Number)	Cigarettes (Pounds)	Cigars[3] (Pounds)	Smoking Tobacco (Pounds)	Chewing Tobacco (Pounds)	Total Products (Pounds)
1994	725.5	1,942	4.6	1.1	56.8	62.5	13.4	15.1	2,524	25.3	4.23	.41	.16	.67	4.90
1995	746.5	2,058	4.1	1.1	57.7	62.9	12.2	60.2	2,505	27.5	4.22	.45	.13	.67	4.67
1996	754.5	2,413	3.9	1.1	56.0	61.1	12.0	61.5	2,482	32.7	4.20	.54	.12	.64	4.70
1997	722.8	2,324	3.5	1.0	53.7	58.1	11.4	64.3	2,423	36.9	4.10	.61	.12	.64	4.55
1998	679.7	2,751	3.1	1.0	49.2	53.3	11.7	65.5	2,320	38.0	3.70	.62	.12	.64	4.49
1999	606.6	2,938	2.8	0.9	47.2	50.9	14.7	67.0	2,136	39.5	3.60	.65	.14	.52	4.32
2000	594.6	2,825	2.5	0.8	46.0	49.4	13.6	69.5	2,092	38.1	3.50	.63	.15	.49	4.14
2001	562.4	3,743	2.4	0.8	43.9	47.0	12.7	70.9	2,026	40.5	3.40	.66	.15	.47	4.11
2002[1]	532.0	3,816	2.2	0.8	42.7	45.7	15.5	72.7	1,979	40.1	3.50	.66	.15	.40	4.23
2003[2]	500.0		1.8	0.7	39.2	41.7	18.9	74.7	1,903	40.3	3.30	.66	.11		4.10

[1] Preliminary. [2] Estimate. [3] Large cigars and cigarillos. [4] Includes loose-leaf. [5] Consumption of tax-paid tobacco products. Unstemmed processing weight. [6] 18 years and older. *Source: Economic Research Service, U.S. Department of Agriculture (ERS)*

Production of Tobacco in the United States, by States   In Thousands of Pounds

Year	Florida	Georgia	Indiana	Kentucky	Maryland	North Carolina	Ohio	Pennsylvania	South Carolina	Tennessee	Virginia	Wisconsin	Total
1994	16,575	80,660	15,265	453,687	12,750	599,853	18,360	18,360	108,100	132,289	106,092	5,866	1,582,896
1995	17,676	84,000	13,601	328,581	11,475	484,599	15,015	15,685	105,000	92,907	81,269	6,220	1,268,538
1996	20,100	113,620	14,972	395,542	10,000	585,542	12,640	16,817	117,810	109,888	103,543	5,162	1,518,704
1997	19,053	89,225	18,690	497,928	12,000	731,199	22,230	17,020	126,360	114,292	117,576	5,690	1,787,399
1998	17,102	90,200	17,000	443,628	9,100	551,730	17,934	15,720	92,250	111,100	95,898	4,230	1,479,867
1999	15,312	64,020	11,700	408,492	9,100	448,980	17,052	11,170	78,000	122,601	88,855	2,818	1,292,692
2000	11,475	68,820	7,980	283,065	8,265	406,500	13,200	10,170	81,260	95,958	56,613	2,255	1,052,999
2001	11,700	64,206	9,450	254,653	3,300	386,920	11,956	6,166	78,400	86,893	63,415	3,619	991,223
2002	11,960	55,650	8,000	222,991	2,380	347,920	9,625	6,815	59,475	75,261	64,407	3,817	878,592
2003[1]	11,000	60,480	8,400	229,840	2,175	310,695	9,010	7,880	63,000	72,870	42,679	4,277	831,204

[1] Preliminary. *Source: Agricultural Statistics Board, U.S. Department of Agriculture (ASB-USDA)*

Salient Statistics of Tobacco in the United States

Year	Acres Harvested 1,000 Acres	Yield Per Acre Pounds	Production Million Pounds	Farm Price Cents/Lb.	Farm Value Million $	Tobacco (July-June) Exports[2]	Imports[3]	U.S. Exports of Cigarettes (Millions)	Cigars & Cheroots (Millions)	All Tobacco	Smoking Tobacco	Stocks of Tobacco[5] Various Types — All Tobacco	Fire Cured[6]	Cigar Filler[7]	Maryland
1994	671.1	2,359	1,583	177.4	2,779	442.1	537.5	220,200	74	434	77.0	2,588	69.7	24.1	8.4
1995	663.1	1,913	1,269	182.0	2,305	432.6	623.3	231,100	94	462	91.8	2,541	80.5	20.5	9.7
1996	733.1	2,072	1,519	188.2	2,854	533.1	717.2	243,900	67	486	110.4	2,225	80.2	17.9	11.7
1997	836.2	2,137	1,787	180.2	3,217	450.1	565.8	217,000	86	487	118.2	2,031	83.3	13.2	15.0
1998	717.7	2,061	1,480	182.8	2,701	461.9	529.6	201,300	93	467	142.5	2,250	84.8	13.0	18.7
1999	647.2	1,997	1,293	182.8	2,356	394.7	480.2	151,400	84	423	151.1	2,301	86.7	11.4	20.6
2000	472.4	2,229	1,053	191.0	2,002	351.4	457.8	148,300	113	397	136.1	2,388	87.8	9.5	16.0
2001	432.3	2,293	991	195.7	1,940	386.7	568.0	133,900	124	411	118.2	1,893	93.8	12.1	13.4
2002	428.7	2,049	879	193.8	1,703	325.6	549.3	127,200	236	338	144.0	1,738	99.5	12.3	14.4
2003[1]	416.2	1,997	831	196.7	1,635	274.8	691.7	119,600	97	326	132.3	1,584	100.5	12.3	15.4

[1] Preliminary. [2] Domestic. [3] For consumption. [4] In bulk. [5] Flue-cured and cigar wrapper, year beginning July 1; for all other types, October 1. [6] Kentucky-Tennessee types 22-23. [7] Types 41-46. *Source: Economic Research Service, U.S. Department of Agriculture (ERS-USDA)*

Tobacco Production in the United States, by Types   In Thousands of Pounds (Farm-Sale Weight)

Year	11-14	21	22	23	31	32	35-36	37	41	41-61	51	54	55	61
1994	869,920	2,403	31,723	14,205	612,398	19,770	11,797	124	11,340	20,680	1,808	4,180	1,686	1,666
1995	746,616	1,540	26,609	11,041	436,343	17,935	8,488	79	9,225	19,887	2,441	4,513	1,707	2,001
1996	908,345	1,738	29,461	13,029	520,483	16,545	8,550	112	10,272	20,441	2,901	3,610	1,552	2,106
1997	1,047,438	1,968	27,952	12,342	648,633	18,240	8,196	119	10,780	22,511	3,637	4,194	1,496	2,404
1998	812,797	2,340	25,922	11,573	582,336	15,370	9,663	122	9,450	19,744	3,633	3,270	960	2,431
1999	656,752	2,672	24,773	10,630	555,185	14,350	11,640	155	5,920	16,535	4,169	2,252	566	3,628
2000	598,915	2,548	34,167	14,920	362,788	13,395	15,896	165	5,040	10,205	1,070	1,825	430	1,840
2001	579,091	2,202	30,720	12,377	334,066	5,346	13,949	154	4,120	13,318	3,822	3,042	577	1,757
2002	517,035	1,471	23,292	10,145	297,711	4,785	10,570	116	4,410	13,467	4,021	3,151	666	1,219
2003[1]	468,830	845	23,600	9,720	298,105	4,775	10,950	84	5,280	14,295	3,216	3,500	777	1,522

[1] Preliminary. *Source: Agricultural Statistics Board, U.S. Department of Agriculture (ASB-USDA)*

U.S. Exports of Unmanufactured Tobacco   In Millions of Pounds (Declared Weight)

Year	Australia	Belgium-Luxem.	Denmark	France	Germany	Italy	Japan	Nether-lands	Sweden	Switzer-land	Thailand	United Kingdom	Total
1993	5.7	12.8	15.5	4.3	52.1	7.3	124.7	38.1	8.1	6.1	17.8	20.8	458.0
1994	6.4	12.3	14.9	3.1	54.1	11.3	126.2	30.9	7.3	6.0	19.0	14.7	433.9
1995	4.8	17.9	14.6	3.9	70.7	14.8	106.9	39.2	3.0	14.4	19.0	14.2	461.8
1996	5.6	39.7	15.1	3.2	60.1	17.3	88.7	40.4	3.7	14.9	15.9	34.4	485.5
1997	4.2	38.9	15.5	7.0	72.2	18.3	80.5	30.2	5.2	11.4	21.6	18.2	487.4
1998	5.0	25.2	14.8	6.6	84.6	13.6	85.3	43.9	2.6	10.3	14.2	15.6	466.3
1999	3.2	18.3	14.9	5.6	71.9	15.1	60.3	64.5	3.9	16.1	6.8	9.0	417.5
2000	3.6	23.2	15.7	5.5	86.1	15.8	63.6	19.7	3.5	9.5	7.3	7.3	402.4
2001	3.4	49.7	12.2	11.5	94.8	6.2	51.6	21.6	3.6	14.4	7.7	1.6	409.7
2002[1]	4.5	29.4	13.6	10.3	59.5	8.6	49.6	10.3	1.2	27.3	12.6	6.0	338.0

[1] Preliminary.   Source: Economic Research Service, U.S. Department of Agriculture (ERS-USDA)

U.S. Salient Statistics for Flue-Cured Tobacco (Types 11-14) in the United States   In Millions of Pounds

Crop Year	Acres Harvested 1,000	Yield Per Acre Pounds	Mar-ketings	Stocks July 1	Total Supply	Exports	Domestic Disap-pearance	Total Disap-pearance	Farm Price Cents/Lb.	Placed Under Gov't Loan Million Lb.	Price Support Level Cents/Lb.	Loan Stocks Nov. 30	Loan Stocks Uncom-mitted
1994-5	360.0	2,420	807	1,295	2,102	346	569	346	169.8	97.7	158.3	298.5	396.5
1995-6	386.2	1,933	854	1,187	2,041	345	531	345	179.4	12.0	159.7	157.6	62.3
1996-7	422.2	2,151	897	1,166	2,063	391	555	391	183.4	1.8	160.1	181.0	.0
1997-8	458.3	2,285	1,014	1,117	2,130	336	541	336	172.0	195.5	162.1	145.3	.0
1998-9	368.8	2,204	815	1,253	2,068	341	492	341	175.5	82.4	162.8	311.5	182.7
1999-00	303.8	2,162	654	2,162	2,816	262	437	262	173.7	136.4	163.2	318.3	144.9
2000-1	250.0	2,396	564	1,189	1,754	238	479	238	179.3	27.4	164.0	256.9	135.9
2001-2	238.1	2,432	544	1,036	1,581	276	389	276	185.7	15.0	166.0	93.2	65.0
2002-3[1]	245.6	2,105	565	916	1,481	220	423	220	182.5	24.8	165.6	17.8	12.8
2003-4[2]	234.4	2,000	508	838	1,345	190	410	190	185.2		166.3	70.6	68.7

[1] Preliminary.   [2] Estimate.   Source: Economic Research Service, U.S. Department of Agriculture (ERS-USDA)

Salient Statistics for Burley Tobacco (Type 31) in the United States   In Millions of Pounds

Crop Year	Acres Harvested 1,000	Yield Per Acre Pounds	Mar-ketings	Stocks Oct. 1	Total Supply	Exports	Domestic Disap-pearance	Total Disap-pearance	Farm Price Cents/Lb.	Gross Sales[3]	Price Support Level Cents/Lb.	Loan Stocks Nov. 30	Loan Stocks Uncom-mitted
1994-5	266.0	2,300	568	1,014	1,582	159	464	623	184.1	455.7	171.4	345.2	380.8
1995-6	234.2	1,863	483	959	1,441	165	386	551	185.5	341.6	172.5	212.5	50.8
1996-7	268.3	1,940	516	890	1,407	209	446	656	192.2	422.6	173.7	216.8	27.1
1997-8	335.3	1,934	628	751	1,379	168	379	548	188.5	337.9	176.0	105.6	38.5
1998-9	307.1	1,896	590	832	1,422	169	349	520	190.3	431.6	177.8	183.8	142.2
1999-00	303.6	1,829	551	901	1,453	139	273	413	182.9	356.6	178.9	226.6	186.7
2000-1	193.8	1,957	315	1,040	1,355	142	524	666	196.3	169.7	180.5	420.7	336.5
2001-2	167.6	2,033	344	689	1,033	140	245	385	197.3	258.5	182.6	119.3	74.8
2002-3[1]	158.6	1,877	300	648	948	149	221	370	197.9	217.7	183.5	124.2	46.1
2003-4[2]	156.2	1,908	290	578	868	135	206	341		197.3	184.9	91.7	26.5

[1] Preliminary.   [2] Estimate.   [3] Before Christmas holidays.   Source: Economic Research Service, U.S. Department of Agriculture (ERS-USDA)

Exports of Tobacco from the United States (Quantity and Value)   In Metric Tons

Year	Unmanufactured Flue-Cured	Value 1,000 USD	Burley	Value 1,000 USD	Total	Value 1,000 USD	Manu-factured	Value 1,000 USD
1993	111,636	752,646	51,892	389,964	207,747	1,306,067	49,669	4,253,286
1994	107,411	749,305	49,859	380,993	196,792	1,302,744	63,837	5,367,220
1995	123,040	866,208	47,129	365,206	209,481	1,399,863	77,135	5,221,487
1996	112,797	786,473	52,202	380,012	222,316	1,390,311	83,383	5,238,340
1997	116,457	832,381	56,803	454,849	221,510	1,553,314	85,734	4,956,392
1998	110,435	776,640	50,167	409,773	211,930	1,458,877	----	4,517,500
1999	86,838	611,054	49,398	404,564	191,975	1,311,643	----	3,232,862
2000	84,980	606,145	36,649	306,883	179,892	1,204,085	----	4,012,711
2001[1]	89,242	653,795	41,254	352,256	186,300	1,268,839	----	2,734,378
2002[2]	72,838	530,580	39,083	326,580	153,427	1,049,709	----	1,948,161

[1] Preliminary.   [2] Forecast.   NA = Not available.   Source: Foreign Agricultural Service, U.S. Department of Agriculture (FAS-USDA)

Tung Oil

Tung oil is a yellow drying oil produced from the seed of the tung tree. The seeds or nuts of the tung tree are harvested and pressed to yield the tung oil. Tung oil is mostly used as an industrial lubricant and drying agent, in fact it is the most powerful drying agent known. It is also used in paints and varnishes as well as in soaps, inks, and electrical insulators. Tung oil is poisonous, containing glycerol esters of unsaturated fats. The oil is also used as a substitute for linseed oil in paints, varnishes, and linoleum and as a waterproofing agent.

Prices – The price of tung oil in 2002 (through Oct) fell sharply by –29% to a 13-year low of 43.53 cents per pound from 61.63 cents in 2001.

Demand – US consumption of tung oil has fallen steadily and sharply over the past decade. In 2003 (through Oct), US consumption plunged 42% to 4.362 million pounds from 7.547 million pounds in 2002. The 2003 consumption level was down by 80% from the peak year of 21.645 million pounds in 1996.

Trade – US imports of tung oil in 2001 rose 25% to 4,429 metric tons. The US in 2001 was the largest importer of tung oil, accounting for 18% of world imports. Other major importers are South Korea (with 14% of world imports), the Netherlands (11%), and Japan (7%). The world's largest exporter of tung oil by far is China with 17,615 metric tons of exports in 2001, accounting for 79% of total world exports.

World Tung Oil Trade   In Metric Tons

| | Imports | | | | | | | | Exports | | | | |
Year	Germany	Hong Kong	Japan	Netherlands	South Korea	Taiwan	United States	World Total	Argentina	China	Hong Kong	Paraguay	World Total
1996	863	1,247	3,619	1,926	7,317	4,244	3,944	31,142	2,427	19,718	1,266	3,156	28,726
1997	733	1,404	6,807	1,702	6,345	5,931	6,264	38,013	3,976	30,012	991	4,260	41,851
1998	601	1,101	3,813	2,738	4,410	5,730	3,880	31,657	2,205	21,743	552	2,161	28,933
1999	1,002	470	2,455	2,488	3,560	6,699	5,822	31,771	1,425	24,172	560	2,303	31,240
2000	885	416	2,225	2,700	4,900	4,346	3,554	29,085	1,870	24,213	494	2,799	31,049
2001[1]	582	36	1,647	2,700	3,390	2,113	4,429	24,291	1,061	17,615	108	1,974	22,411
2002[2]	325	702	1,930	1,793	6,968	5,185	4,166	30,166	916	23,334	589	4,390	30,502

[1] Preliminary.   [2] Estimate.   *Source: The Oil World*

Consumption of Tung Oil in Inedible Products in the United States   In Thousands of Pounds

Year	Jan.	Feb.	Mar.	Apr.	May	June	July	Aug.	Sept.	Oct.	Nov.	Dec.	Total
1997	934	1,922	2,720	2,170	1,335	2,034	2,618	1,262	1,267	1,099	857	1,157	19,375
1998	935	1,146	1,342	1,103	1,536	1,255	1,248	1,172	1,214	1,216	1,037	1,112	14,316
1999	862	797	967	1,071	2,137	1,140	1,519	1,043	1,012	933	962	937	13,380
2000	1,065	1,083	1,064	1,193	1,159	1,176	1,107	1,224	733	711	700	648	11,863
2001	1,044	842	533	366	281	431	253	430	399	411	243	235	5,468
2002	427	476	583	410	471	454	428	877	695	978	862	886	7,547
2003[1]	685	276	508	317	322	233	270	349	406	269	376	228	4,239

[1] Preliminary.   *Source: Bureau of the Census, U.S. Department of Commerce*

Stocks of Tung Oil at Factories & Warehouses in the U.S., on First of Month   In Thousands of Pounds

Year	Jan.	Feb.	Mar.	Apr.	May	June	July	Aug.	Sept.	Oct.	Nov.	Dec.
1997	2,373	2,754	3,417	2,808	2,134	2,230	2,230	1,561	2,525	2,535	2,311	2,326
1998	2,484	3,116	4,548	3,949	3,357	3,300	2,435	2,409	3,578	2,523	2,501	2,272
1999	2,010	3,427	5,427	3,740	3,078	2,788	2,710	2,346	2,047	1,959	1,359	1,002
2000	691	910	611	2,555	2,254	1,982	1,658	1,381	1,262	1,217	1,011	827
2001	685	2,438	2,181	2,131	1,881	1,727	1,578	1,168	1,046	714	W	W
2002	W	W	W	W	1,341	1,206	885	516	483	551	560	478
2003[1]	490	W	858	763	722	790	398	W	W	W	W	W

[1] Preliminary.   W = Withheld proprietary data.   *Source: Bureau of the Census, U.S. Department of Commerce*

Average Price of Tung Oil (Imported, Drums) F.O.B. in New York   In Cents Per Pound

Year	Jan.	Feb.	Mar.	Apr.	May	June	July	Aug.	Sept.	Oct.	Nov.	Dec.	Average
1997	74.00	92.00	92.00	103.00	103.00	103.00	103.00	108.00	110.00	110.00	110.00	110.00	101.50
1998	110.00	110.00	110.00	110.00	100.00	100.00	100.00	100.00	100.00	100.00	100.00	100.00	103.33
1999	100.00	100.00	100.00	100.00	100.00	74.00	74.00	74.00	74.00	74.00	74.00	74.00	84.83
2000	59.00	59.00	59.00	59.00	59.00	59.00	59.00	59.00	59.00	59.00	59.00	59.00	59.00
2001	60.50	62.00	62.00	62.00	62.00	62.00	62.00	62.00	62.00	62.00	60.50	60.50	61.63
2002	60.50	44.50	44.50	42.00	40.00	40.00	40.00	40.00	40.00	43.75	45.00	45.00	43.77
2003[1]	45.00	45.00	52.80	84.75	85.00	85.00	85.00	85.00	85.00				72.51

[1] Preliminary.   *Source: Economic Research Service, U.S. Department of Agriculture (ERS-USDA)*

Tungsten

Tungsten is a grayish-white, lustrous, metallic element. The atomic symbol for tungsten is W because of its former name of Wolfram. The atomic number is 74. Tungsten has the highest melting point of any metal at about 3410 degrees Celsius and boils at about 5660 degrees Celsius. In 1781, the Swedish chemist Carl Wilhelm Scheele discovered tungsten.

Tungsten is never found in nature but occurs in wolframite, scheelite, huebnertite, and ferberite. Tungsten has excellent corrosion resistance qualities and is resistant to most mineral acids. Tungsten is used as filaments in incandescent lamps, electron and television tubes, alloys of steel, spark plugs, electrical contact points, cutting tools, and in the chemical and tanning industries.

Prices – The average price of tungsten at US ports in 2001, the latest reporting year, rose +36% to a 19-year high of $87.72 per ton from $64.67 in 2000.

Supply – World concentrate production of tungsten in 2002 rose by 31% from 2001 to a 12-year high of 59,100 metric tons. The world's largest producer of tungsten by far is China with 49,500 metric tons of production in 2002 representing 84% of total world production. The only other producer of consequence is Russia with 3,400 metric tons of production representing 6% of world production.

Trade – The US in 2002 relied on imports for 70% of its tungsten consumption, up from 59% in 2001. US imports for consumption in 2002 rose to 4,090 metric tons from 2,680 metric tons in 2001. US exports were negligible at 94 metric tons.

World Concentrate Production of Tungsten   In Metric Tons (Contained Tungsten[3])

Year	Australia	Austria	Bolivia	Brazil	Burma	China	Kazakhstan	Mongolia	Peru	Portugal	Rep. of Korea	Russia	World Total
1996	----	1,413	582	99	334	26,500	----	17	332	776	----	3,000	34,700
1997	----	1,400	513	40	272	25,000	----	26	280	1,036	----	3,000	33,200
1998	----	1,423	497	----	178	30,000	----	35	76	831	----	3,000	37,400
1999	----	1,610	334	13	87	31,100	----	27	----	434	----	3,500	37,900
2000	----	1,600	382	14	74	37,000	----	52	----	743	----	3,500	44,000
2001[1]	----	1,237	533	31	71	38,500	----	63	----	700	----	3,500	45,300
2002[2]	----	1,400	500	30	70	49,500	----	60	----	700	----	3,400	59,100

[1] Preliminary.   [2] Estimate.   [3] Conversion Factors: WO3 to W, multiply by 0.7931; 60% WO3 to W, multiply by 0.4758.
Source: U.S. Geological Survey (USGS)

Salient Statistics of Tungsten in the United States   In Metric Tons (Contained Tungsten)

Year	Net Import Reliance as a % of Apparent Consumption	Total Consumption	Tool	Steel Stainless & Heat Assisting	Alloy Steel[3]	Superalloys	Cutting & Wear Resistant Materials	Products Made from Metal Powder	Miscellaneous	Chemical and Ceramic	Exports	Imports for Consumption	Stocks at End of Year Concentrates Consumers	Stocks at End of Year Concentrates Producers
1996	89	5,260	434	107	177	371	5,960	687	0	97	18	4,190	569	44
1997	84	6,590	361	151	277	366	6,280	828	151	123	12	4,850	658	44
1998	78	3,210	[4]	532	219	333	6,640	1,270	532	97	10	4,750	603	W
1999	81	2,100	W	486	189	306	5,910	1,860	----	93	26	2,870	376	W
2000	68	W	W	408	W	498	5,960	W	----	89	70	2,370	W	W
2001[1]	59	W	W	389	W	599	5,650	W	----	80	220	2,680	W	W
2002[2]	70	W	W	313	W	426	4,820	W	----	133	94	4,090	W	W

[1] Preliminary.   [2] Estimate.   [3] Other than tool.   [4] Included with stainless & heat assisting.   W = Withheld proprietary data; included with Miscellaneous.   *Source: U.S. Geological Survey*

Average Price of Tungsten at European Market (London)   In Dollars Per Metric Ton

Year	Jan.	Feb.	Mar.	Apr.	May	June	July	Aug.	Sept.	Oct.	Nov.	Dec.	Average
1997	48.00	49.00	50.00	50.00	50.00	50.00	50.00	43.00	43.00	43.00	46.00	46.00	47.33
1998	46.00	46.00	46.00	46.00	46.00	46.00	45.00	43.00	43.00	43.00	43.00	43.00	40.00
1999	37.38	38.50	38.50	38.50	38.50	38.50	38.50	40.36	43.00	43.00	43.00	43.00	40.25
2000	43.00	43.00	43.50	44.00	44.00	44.00	42.75	41.43	44.00	45.63	51.06	52.50	44.93
2001	66.56	70.00	70.50	70.50	70.50	70.50	70.50	68.06	64.07	59.39	50.99	48.72	58.43

65% WO3 Basis, C.I.F., combined wolframite and scheelite quotations; data thru 1970 are for 60% WO3.   *Source: U.S. Geological Survey (USGS)*

Average Price of Tungsten at U.S. Ports (Including Duty)   In Dollars Per Short Ton

Year	Jan.	Feb.	Mar.	Apr.	May	June	July	Aug.	Sept.	Oct.	Nov.	Dec.	Average
1999	49.50	49.50	49.50	49.50	48.57	48.75	49.16	50.88	51.50	54.44	54.75	54.75	52.00
2000	53.75	53.75	53.75	53.29	50.50	50.50	51.88	53.50	69.00	74.00	76.00	78.92	64.67
2001	83.50	86.00	90.00	93.00	96.15	96.50	93.88	92.88	91.00	89.89	83.84	79.57	87.72
2002	----	70.00	70.00	70.00	70.00	68.13	57.88	59.88	60.25	60.25	60.25	60.25	64.26
2003	60.25	61.55	63.00	63.00	63.00	63.00	63.00	63.00	63.00	63.00	63.00	63.00	62.65

U.S. Spot Quotations, 65% WO3, Basis C.I.F.   *Source: U.S. Geological Survey (USGS)*

Turkeys

During the past three decades, the turkey industry has experienced tremendous growth in the US. Turkey production has more than tripled since 1970, with a current value of over $7 billion. Turkey was not a popular dish in Europe until a roast turkey was eaten on June 27, 1570, at the wedding feast of Charles XI of France and Elizabeth of Austria. The King was so impressed with the birds that the turkey subsequently became a popular dish at banquets held by French nobility.

The most popular turkey product continues to be the whole bird, with heavy demand at Thanksgiving and Christmas. The primary breeders maintain and develop the quality stock, concentrating on growth and conformation in males and fecundity in females, as well as characteristics important to general health and welfare. Turkey producers are divided into large companies that produce turkeys all year round, and relatively small companies and farmers who produce turkeys primarily for the seasonal market.

Prices – The average price received by farmers for turkeys in the US in 2003 fell –2.4% to 35.5 cents per pound from 36.4 cents in 2002 which was substantially lower than the 7-year high of 41.4 cents posted in 2000. The average retail price of turkeys (whole frozen) in the US in 2003 rose +3.0% to 108.4 cents per pound from 105.3 cents in 2002.

That was only slightly below the record yearly high of 109.7 cents posted in 2001. Turkey prices have more than doubled from the low 40-cent area seen in the early 1970s.

Supply – World production of turkeys in 2003 rose by +0.8% to a record high of 4.937 million metric tons from 4.896 million metric tons in 2002. World production of turkeys has grown by more than two and one-half times since 1980 when production was 2.090 million metric tons. The US is the largest producer of turkeys by far with 2.541 million metric tons of production in 2003, representing 44% of world production. The value of US turkey production in 2002 was $2.700 billion.

Demand – World consumption of turkeys in 2003 rose +0.9% to 4.718 million metric tons, which was just below the record high of 4.744 million metric tons posted in 2001. US turkey consumption of 2.319 million metric tons in 2003 accounted for 49% of world consumption.

US per capita consumption of turkeys in 2003 was unchanged from 2002 at 17.7 pounds per year. US per capital consumption of turkeys has been in the range of 17-18 pounds since 1990, which marks a substantial increase from the 1970 level of 8.1 pounds and the 1980 level of 10.3 pounds.

Production and Consumption of Turkey Meat, by Selected Countries   In Thousands of Metric Tons (RTC)

	Production							Consumption							
Year	Canada	France	Germany	Italy	United Kingdom	United States	World Total	Canada	France	Germany	Italy	United Kingdom	United States	World Total
1994	133	568	180	269	266	2,239	4,055	128	330	295	245	271	2,110	3,894
1995	141	650	206	294	289	2,299	4,292	126	353	327	262	287	2,133	4,121
1996	146	671	217	315	293	2,450	4,372	123	352	361	277	298	2,225	4,185
1997	142	708	243	338	293	2,455	4,503	126	332	386	295	277	2,141	4,155
1998	139	725	256	361	268	2,366	4,571	139	360	396	302	276	2,214	4,532
1999	139	682	271	343	264	2,372	4,734	136	369	410	310	255	2,223	4,707
2000	152	720	272	330	265	2,419	4,758	137	376	412	303	250	2,223	4,668
2001	149	735	272	350	268	2,490	4,847	135	394	412	317	250	2,269	4,744
2002[1]	147	----	----	----	----	2,533	4,896	143	----	----	----	----	2,288	4,678
2003[2]	152	----	----	----	----	2,541	4,937	146	----	----	----	----	2,319	4,718

[1] Preliminary.   [2] Forecast.   *Source: Foreign Agricultural Service, U.S. Department of Agriculture (FAS-USDA)*

Salient Statistics of Turkeys in the United States

			Liveweight		Value of Production		Ready-to-Cook Basis					Production Costs		Wholesale Ready-to-Cook	
								Beginning Stocks		Consumption					3-Region
	Poults Placed[3]	Number Raised[4]	Produced	Price		Production		Exports	Total	Per Capita	Feed	Total	Production Costs	Weighted Average Price[5]
Year	In Thousands		Mil. Lbs.	Cents/Lb.	Million $	In Millions of Pounds				Lbs.	Liveweight Basis			
1993	308,871	287,650	6,432.6	39.0	2,509.1	4,798	272	244	4,577	17.7	22.20	35.86	61.12	62.83
1994	317,468	286,585	6,540.3	40.4	2,643.1	4,937	249	280	4,652	17.8	24.00	37.70	63.40	65.90
1995	320,882	292,356	6,761.3	41.0	2,769.4	5,069	254	348	4,705	17.9	21.90	35.60	60.80	66.20
1996	325,375	302,713	7,222.8	43.3	3,124.5	5,466	271	438	4,907	18.5	31.60	45.30	72.90	66.80
1997	305,612	301,251	7,225.1	39.9	2,884.4	5,478	328	606	4,720	17.6	28.20	41.90	68.70	63.80
1998	297,798	285,204	7,050.9	38.0	2,679.3	5,281	415	446	4,880	18.0	22.96	36.66	62.12	62.15
1999	297,387	270,494	6,886.4	40.8	2,809.9	5,297	304	378	4,902	18.0	19.00	32.70	57.17	67.81
2000	298,094	269,969	6,942.8	40.7	2,822.7	5,402	254	445	4,902	17.0	19.98	33.68	58.40	68.06
2001[1]	301,721	272,059	7,154.8	39.0	2,790.3	5,524	241	494	4,975	17.5	20.55	34.25	59.11	63.63
2002[2]	296,877	272,429	7,406.1	36.5	2,700.3	5,600	252	495	5,009	17.7	20.85	34.55	59.48	61.09

[1] Preliminary.   [2] Estimate.   [3] Poults placed for slaughter by hatcheries.   [4] Turkeys place August 1-July 31.   [5] Regions include central, eastern and western. Central region receives twice the weight of the other regions in calculating the average.   *Source: Economic Research Service, U.S. Department of Agriculture (ERS-USDA)*

Turkey-Feed Price Ratio in the United States   In Pounds[1]

Year	Jan.	Feb.	Mar.	Apr.	May	June	July	Aug.	Sept.	Oct.	Nov.	Dec.	Average
1994	5.4	5.4	5.5	5.8	5.9	6.1	6.9	7.4	7.4	7.9	7.9	7.3	6.6
1995	6.8	6.4	6.5	6.4	6.3	6.3	6.0	6.3	6.4	6.4	6.5	5.7	6.3
1996	5.3	5.2	5.1	4.8	4.6	4.9	4.9	4.8	5.3	6.2	6.4	6.1	5.3
1997	5.4	5.1	5.0	5.1	5.3	5.6	6.0	5.9	6.1	6.2	6.2	5.8	5.7
1998	5.4	5.2	5.4	5.7	5.8	6.1	6.5	7.6	8.1	8.3	8.2	7.5	6.7
1999	6.5	7.1	7.5	7.8	8.2	8.7	9.7	9.5	9.6	10.0	9.9	9.2	8.6
2000	7.6	7.2	7.6	7.9	7.8	8.5	9.5	10.0	10.1	10.0	9.8	8.1	8.7
2001	7.3	7.5	7.7	8.0	8.1	8.3	7.9	7.8	8.3	9.6	9.6	8.1	8.2
2002	7.2	7.2	6.8	6.8	7.3	7.3	6.9	6.3	6.0	6.1	6.5	6.4	6.7
2003[2]	5.7	5.9	5.9	5.8	5.6	5.7	5.8	5.6	5.9	6.2	6.2	5.6	5.8

[1] Pounds of feed equal in value to one pound of turkey, liveweight.   [2] Preliminary.   [3] New data series due to NASS switching to basing ration costs on raw ingredient prices (corn and soybeans) rather than commercial feed prices.   *Source: Economic Research Service, U.S. Department of Agriculture (ERS-USDA)*

Average Price Received by Farmers for Turkeys in the United States (Liveweight)   In Cents Per Pound

Year	Jan.	Feb.	Mar.	Apr.	May	June	July	Aug.	Sept.	Oct.	Nov.	Dec.	Average
1994	37.0	37.3	38.4	39.2	39.9	40.3	40.6	42.1	43.1	44.5	44.3	42.2	40.7
1995	39.3	37.2	38.3	38.3	38.4	39.3	39.6	41.9	43.6	45.2	47.3	44.0	41.0
1996	40.9	42.4	41.8	42.2	43.2	44.4	45.0	44.3	44.2	45.1	45.5	43.2	43.5
1997	38.6	36.4	37.8	39.7	41.3	41.6	41.1	41.0	41.1	41.0	41.9	38.7	40.0
1998	35.5	34.0	34.6	35.7	35.5	35.9	37.5	38.6	40.2	42.7	43.8	40.3	37.9
1999	34.8	35.7	37.0	38.7	39.4	41.3	42.0	43.0	44.3	45.3	45.3	42.2	40.8
2000	36.4	35.7	38.2	40.0	40.8	41.8	42.2	43.2	44.8	46.1	47.1	40.5	41.4
2001	36.6	36.3	37.1	37.6	38.2	38.3	38.5	38.7	40.5	44.2	44.5	38.7	39.1
2002	34.1	34.1	32.9	32.9	35.8	37.2	38.6	38.2	37.2	37.2	39.8	38.7	36.4
2003[1]	34.6	34.5	35.1	35.1	34.4	34.4	33.1	32.2	35.7	38.6	40.7	37.7	35.5

[1] Preliminary.   *Source: Economic Research Service, U.S. Department of Agriculture (ERS-USDA)*

Average Wholesale Price of Turkeys[1] (Hens, 8-16 Lbs.) in New York   In Cents Per Pound

Year	Jan.	Feb.	Mar.	Apr.	May	June	July	Aug.	Sept.	Oct.	Nov.	Dec.	Average
1994	60.09	59.32	60.98	61.58	63.14	64.61	65.26	66.39	68.98	73.13	74.01	70.35	65.65
1995	60.71	58.54	60.04	60.05	60.57	62.76	64.78	68.52	72.92	76.73	80.31	70.35	66.36
1996	64.60	64.65	65.07	64.82	65.39	65.85	65.66	64.94	64.16	69.09	73.58	70.05	66.49
1997	59.71	57.84	59.30	62.93	66.64	68.60	68.59	68.20	67.89	67.33	70.07	62.18	64.94
1998	55.65	54.04	55.49	55.49	58.68	58.14	58.68	63.17	65.65	71.52	72.95	69.00	61.54
1999	57.67	58.84	61.69	63.02	65.55	68.89	71.62	73.57	76.28	79.30	78.99	72.39	68.98
2000	61.58	61.84	65.35	67.38	69.18	70.36	71.55	73.61	76.53	78.74	79.58	70.31	70.50
2001	61.50	61.18	62.38	63.45	65.65	66.00	66.10	66.38	68.81	72.86	73.48	67.71	66.29
2002	60.86	60.03	59.00	59.52	63.52	65.68	66.52	66.56	67.15	67.75	69.79	66.96	64.45
2003[2]	61.04	61.13	61.24	61.43	60.36	60.12	58.18	57.74	61.52	66.08	69.33	66.85	62.09

[1] Ready-to-cook.   [2] Preliminary.   *Source: Economic Research Service, U.S. Department of Agriculture (ERS-USDA)*

Certified Federally Inspected Turkey Slaughter in the U.S. (RTC Weights)   In Millions of Pounds

Year	Jan.	Feb.	Mar.	Apr.	May	June	July	Aug.	Sept.	Oct.	Nov.	Dec.	Total
1994	347.8	342.0	400.9	380.6	415.6	457.9	405.6	483.6	447.7	459.1	453.9	397.5	4,992
1995	386.3	368.9	433.1	369.6	441.4	478.4	409.1	447.3	419.5	480.2	463.0	394.4	5,091
1996	412.4	426.5	422.3	430.9	483.0	454.7	484.8	476.6	440.9	518.1	465.9	406.1	5,422
1997	439.7	389.5	399.6	448.8	465.8	481.4	488.8	453.0	457.6	510.0	450.6	457.9	5,443
1998	430.5	407.7	437.8	444.0	419.1	454.2	456.0	409.9	425.3	470.5	459.5	428.2	5,243
1999	408.9	361.0	428.8	435.8	438.6	452.4	434.7	464.3	451.3	468.7	487.6	425.4	5,257
2000	396.9	412.4	466.2	413.5	489.2	479.4	422.8	481.6	423.0	494.7	478.2	396.5	5,354
2001	458.3	405.9	458.7	425.1	485.1	460.7	465.1	481.7	409.2	536.2	477.7	413.2	5,477
2002	477.2	442.1	447.8	487.2	496.7	448.0	474.7	475.9	439.4	519.0	488.2	457.9	5,654
2003[1]	473.6	427.1	464.6	471.1	475.8	478.0	483.9	449.3	453.6	522.8	450.3	436.1	5,586

[1] Preliminary.   *Source: Economic Research Service, U.S. Department of Agriculture (ERS-USDA)*

TURKEYS

Per Capita Consumption of Turkeys in the United States   In Pounds

Year	First Quarter	Second Quarter	Third Quarter	Fourth Quarter	Total	Year	First Quarter	Second Quarter	Third Quarter	Fourth Quarter	Total
1993	3.5	3.7	3.9	6.5	17.7	1999	3.8	3.8	4.4	5.8	18.0
1994	3.6	3.9	4.4	6.2	17.8	2000	3.7	4.2	4.4	5.5	17.8
1995	3.6	3.9	4.2	6.2	17.9	2001	3.9	3.8	4.3	5.6	17.5
1996	3.7	3.9	4.6	6.2	18.5	2002	3.5	3.9	4.4	5.9	17.7
1997	3.5	4.0	4.2	6.0	17.6	2003[1]	3.6	3.9	4.6	5.3	17.4
1998	3.9	3.9	4.2	6.0	18.1	2004[2]	3.7	3.8	4.2	5.6	17.3

[1] Preliminary.   [2] Estimate.   *Source: Economic Research Service, U.S. Department of Agriculture (ERS-USDA)*

Storage Stocks of Turkeys (Frozen) in the United States on First of Month   In Millions of Pounds

Year	Jan.	Feb.	Mar.	Apr.	May	June	July	Aug.	Sept.	Oct.	Nov.	Dec.
1994	249.1	279.8	304.8	346.5	399.1	461.4	539.2	588.1	623.4	648.6	636.2	280.7
1995	254.4	312.9	359.5	432.1	466.2	536.3	598.8	651.1	678.2	686.0	644.2	270.1
1996	271.3	339.2	423.1	445.4	514.5	587.4	679.7	718.2	723.2	721.0	658.3	347.8
1997	328.0	401.0	446.4	496.5	543.3	611.8	667.9	714.3	742.0	770.7	736.6	438.6
1998	415.1	497.6	512.7	527.0	579.7	614.1	656.5	701.8	706.8	699.5	658.7	310.4
1999	304.3	363.8	375.6	374.9	455.4	494.3	556.1	599.0	580.3	596.4	494.5	252.3
2000	254.3	319.4	353.9	391.4	416.9	480.3	506.8	524.0	524.9	528.1	473.9	261.1
2001	241.3	291.4	333.5	355.8	392.6	456.0	506.7	534.2	545.3	542.0	497.9	260.0
2002	240.5	327.1	413.2	457.6	515.2	578.2	644.1	706.2	685.6	672.4	624.9	334.3
2003[1]	333.0	451.9	468.9	539.1	573.5	658.8	718.2	722.5	706.5	647.5	582.7	350.7

[1] Preliminary.   *Source: Economic Research Service, U.S. Department of Agriculture (ERS-USDA)*

Average Retail[2] Price of Turkeys (Whole frozen) in the United States   In Cents Per Pound

Year	Jan.	Feb.	Mar.	Apr.	May	June	July	Aug.	Sept.	Oct.	Nov.	Dec.	Average
1994	70.3	69.4	70.6	70.9	72.0	72.6	72.8	74.8	77.3	79.9	83.3	77.3	74.3
1995	69.5	67.1	68.5	68.6	70.1	72.5	74.2	77.8	81.6	84.9	86.5	77.5	74.9
1996	103.5	104.7	106.9	101.4	104.3	104.1	104.4	108.6	106.5	107.4	98.1	102.0	104.3
1997	106.3	106.7	104.7	103.2	104.5	107.8	107.4	109.2	108.9	106.2	97.6	98.2	105.1
1998	103.4	100.1	99.6	97.2	95.7	99.1	100.8	102.4	105.2	102.5	93.4	95.4	99.6
1999	96.9	100.1	98.4	93.6	97.5	100.5	103.1	101.5	101.8	102.5	96.4	97.6	99.2
2000	101.3	102.5	101.5	99.7	102.9	106.5	109.5	104.5	104.4	106.7	98.1	99.4	103.1
2001	108.8	112.5	112.7	109.7	109.4	110.9	111.0	113.5	116.2	114.6	98.0	99.5	109.7
2002	102.2	105.1	106.6	104.0	102.5	107.3	108.0	106.8	106.6	111.7	103.8	98.8	105.3
2003[1]	106.6	105.8	105.5	100.1	106.0	110.6	113.4	116.2	116.7	111.2	100.6	105.4	108.2

[1] Preliminary.   [2] Data prior to 1996 are prices to selected retailers.   *Source: Economic Research Service, U.S. Department of Agriculture (ERS-USDA)*

Average Retail-to-Consumer Price Spread of Turkeys (Whole) in the United States   In Cents Per Pound

Year	Jan.	Feb.	Mar.	Apr.	May	June	July	Aug.	Sept.	Oct.	Nov.	Dec.	Average
1994	27.5	29.7	28.1	25.1	27.1	28.8	28.7	27.6	27.1	25.5	13.9	20.3	25.8
1995	28.5	32.0	33.7	32.1	32.7	32.8	30.8	28.2	27.0	20.1	10.6	21.2	27.5
1996	30.4	30.7	33.6	28.0	29.3	28.0	27.9	32.1	30.3	28.9	18.0	26.6	28.7
1997	38.3	40.7	37.5	32.0	29.6	32.0	32.0	34.5	34.3	31.9	20.0	26.9	32.5
1998	38.8	37.2	35.2	31.2	29.4	30.7	29.6	29.0	29.3	21.3	10.3	19.0	28.4
1999	29.9	32.7	28.6	21.3	22.5	22.6	23.2	29.1	18.5	17.6	12.0	19.6	23.1
2000	32.1	33.9	29.1	25.9	27.6	29.5	30.9	23.7	21.1	21.7	13.4	23.1	26.0
2001	39.5	43.3	42.5	39.1	37.7	38.7	38.6	40.5	41.0	35.6	18.7	27.0	36.9
2002	34.2	37.9	40.7	38.3	32.9	35.9	35.9	34.9	35.4	40.2	29.8	24.6	35.1
2003[1]	38.4	37.6	36.8	31.2	38.1	42.9	47.1	50.0	47.2	37.8	25.1	33.2	38.8

[1] Preliminary.   *Source: Economic Research Service, U.S. Department of Agriculture (ERS-USDA)*

Uranium

Uranium is a chemically reactive radioactive, steel-gray, metallic element and is the main fuel used in nuclear reactors. Uranium is the heaviest of all the natural elements. Its atomic symbol is U and its atomic number is 92. Traces of uranium have been found in archeological artifacts dating back to 79 AD. Uranium was discovered in pitchblende by German chemist Martin Heinrich Klaproth, in 1789. Klaproth named it uranium after the recently discovered planet Uranus. French physicist Antoine Henri Becquerel discovered the radioactive properties of uranium in 1896 when he produced an image on a photographic plate covered with a light-absorbing substance. Following Becquerel's experiments, investigations of radioactivity led to the discovery of radium and to new concepts of atomic organization.

The principal use for uranium is fuel in nuclear power plants. Demand for uranium concentrates is directly linked to the level of electricity generated by nuclear power plants. Uranium ores are widely distributed throughout the world and are primarily found in Canada, DRC (formerly Zaire), and the US. Uranium is obtained from primary mine production and secondary sources. Two Canadian companies are the primary producers of uranium from deposits in the Athabasca Basin of northern Saskatchewan. Specifically, the companies Cameco accounted for 19% of global mine production in 2000 and Cogema Resources accounted for 15% of world production. Secondary sources of uranium include excess inventories from utilities and other fuel cycle participants, used reactor fuel, and dismantled Russian nuclear weapons.

Prices – The average price of delivered uranium in 2002 rose by +2.1% to $10.36 per pound from $10.15 in 2001. The 2001 price of $10.15 was a record low for the data series that goes back to 1981. The price of delivered uranium in 2002 of $10.36 was roughly one-third of the price of $30 per pound and above seen in the 1980s through 1986 when the price started falling.

Supply – World production of uranium oxide (U308) concentrate in 2001 rose +9.0% to a 10-year high of 47,395 short tons from 43,475 short tons in 2000. The world's two largest uranium producers are Canada with 16,270 short tons of production in 2001, representing 34% of world production, and Australia with 10,035 short tons of production in 2001, representing 21% of world production. Smaller producers include Niger (with 8.0% of world production), Namibia (6.1%), the US (2.8%), South Africa (2.4%), the Ukraine (2.2%), China (1.4%), the Czech Republic and Slovakia (1.3%), and France (0.4%).

US uranium production in 2001 fell 30% to a record low of 1,315 short tons from 1,890 short tons in 2000. US production reached a peak of 21,850 short tons in 1980 and production has fallen steadily since then to the record low in 2001.

Trade – US imports of uranium in 2001 rose +13% to a record high of 52.7 million pounds from 46.7 million pounds in 2000. The US is being forced to import more uranium as domestic production steadily declines. US exports of uranium rose +31% in 2001 to 15.4 million pounds from 11.7 million pounds in 2000.

World Production of Uranium Oxide (U_3O_8) Concentrate   In Short Tons (Uranium Content)

Year	Australia	Canada	China	Czech Rep. & Slovakia	France	Gabon	Germany	Namibia	Niger	South Africa	United States	Ex-USSR	World Total
1992	3,032	12,087	1,039	2,040	2,755	702	325	2,199	3,855	2,449	2,822	11,205	46,124
1993	2,949	11,990	1,300	911	2,220	769	195	2,168	3,786	2,261	2,587	10,491	43,027
1994	3,050	11,950	----	----	1,700	750	----	2,500	3,800	2,250	1,950	----	41,750
1995	4,900	13,600	----	----	1,250	800	----	2,600	3,750	1,850	3,050	----	43,050
1996	6,450	15,250	----	----	1,200	750	----	3,150	4,300	2,200	3,150	----	46,650
1997	7,150	15,650	----	----	940	600	----	3,770	4,500	1,065	2,900	----	46,550
1998	6,350	14,200	----	----	660	950	----	3,590	4,850	1,250	2,435	----	44,110
1999	7,875	10,680	----	----	450	380	----	3,495	3,790	1,195	2,325	----	39,640
2000[1]	9,830	13,875	655	795	525	----	45	2,430	3,270	1,305	1,890	655	43,475
2001[2]	10,035	16,270	650	595	195	----	----	2,910	3,795	1,135	1,315	1,050	47,395

[1] Preliminary.   [2] Estimate.   *Source: American Bureau of Metal Statistics, Inc. (ABMS)*

Commercial and U.S. Government Stocks of Uranium, End of Year   In Millions of Pounds U_3O_8 Equivalent

	Utility		Domestic Supplier		Total	DOE Owned & USEC Held	
Year	Natural Uranium	Enriched Uranium[1]	Natural Uranium	Enriched Uranium[1]	Commercial Stocks	Natural Uranium	Enriched Uranium[1]
1993	57.9	23.3	19.1	5.4	105.7	52.4	26.9
1994	42.4	23.0	17.4	4.1	86.9	57.2	28.0
1995	41.2	17.5	13.2	.5	72.5	82.0	28.8
1996	42.2	23.9	13.0	1.0	80.0	83.2	25.3
1997	47.1	18.8	10.3	30.1	106.2	53.2	----
1998	42.1	23.7	35.0	35.7	136.5	24.5	----
1999	44.8	13.5	29.5	39.4	127.1	53.1	----
2000	36.0	18.9	12.6	43.8	111.3	53.1	----
2001	34.4	21.2	9.2	39.0	103.8	53.1	----
2002	32.1	21.2	15.0	32.9	101.1	51.8	----

[1] Includes amount reported as UF_6 at enrichment suppliers.   DOE = Department of Energy   USEC = U.S. Energy Commission
Source: Energy Information Administration, U.S. Department of Energy (EIA-DOE)

URANIUM

Reported Average Price Settlements for Purchases by U.S. Utilities and Domestic Suppliers   In $/Pound

Year of Delivery	Contract Price	Market Price[1]	Price & Cost Floor	Total	Contract & Market	Year of Delivery	Contract Price	Market Price[1]	Price & Cost Floor	Total	Contract & Market
		Averages of Reported Prices						Averages of Reported Prices			
1993	14.96	9.57	14.87	11.03	13.14	1998	12.53	9.33	13.50	10.31	12.37
1994	10.68	9.76	20.03	10.57	10.63	1999	12.72	9.52	14.75	11.16	12.57
1995	10.58	10.19	17.86	12.05	10.79	2000	12.31	9.11	----	11.04	----
1996	13.40	13.66	16.13	14.91	13.72	2001	11.72	8.04	----	10.15	----
1997	13.33	11.20	14.52	12.11	13.13	2002	10.73	9.79	----	10.36	----

[1] No floor.   Note: Price excludes uranium delivered *under litigation settlements. Price is given in year-of-delivery dollars.*
Source: Energy Information Administration, U.S. Department of Energy (EIA-DOE)

Uranium Industry Statistics in the United States   In Millions of Pounds U$_3$O$_8$

Year	Production — Mine	Concentrate rate	Concentrate Shipments	Exploration	Mining	Milling	Processing	Total	Deliveries to U.S. Utilities[1]	Average Price Delivered Uranium $/Lb. U$_3O_8$	Imports	Avg. Price Delivered Uranium Imports $/Lb. U$_3O_8$	Exports
1993	2.0	3.063	3.374	36	133	65	145	871	15.5	13.14	41.9	10.53	3.0
1994	2.5	3.352	6.319	41	157	105	149	980	38.3	10.40	36.6	8.95	17.7
1995	3.5	6.000	5.500	27	226	121	161	1,107	43.4	11.25	41.3	10.20	9.8
1996	4.7	6.300	6.000	27	333	155	175	1,118	47.3	14.12	45.4	13.15	11.5
1997	4.7	5.600	5.800	30	413	175	175	1,097	42.0	12.88	43.0	11.81	17.0
1998	4.8	4.700	4.900	30	518	160	203	1,120	42.7	12.14	43.7	11.19	15.1
1999	4.5	4.600	5.500	7	310	201	132	848	47.9	11.63	47.6	10.55	8.5
2000	3.1	4.000	3.200	1	157	106	137	627	51.8	11.04	44.9	9.84	13.6
2001	2.6	2.600	2.200	0	81	42	122	423	55.4	10.15	46.7	9.51	11.7
2002	2.4	2.300	3.800	W	W	104	100	426	52.7	10.36	52.7	10.05	15.4

[1] From suppliers under domestic purchases.   *Source: Energy Information Administration, U.S. Department of Energy (EIA-DOE)*

Month-End Uranium (U$_3$O$_8$) Transaction Values[1]   In Dollars Per Pound

Year	Jan.	Feb.	Mar.	Apr.	May	June	July	Aug.	Sept.	Oct.	Nov.	Dec.	Average
1994	8.58	8.45	8.25	8.25	8.23	8.25	8.23	8.15	8.13	8.10	8.13	8.25	8.25
1995	8.30	8.45	8.65	8.78	9.18	9.48	9.50	9.83	9.83	9.83	9.95	10.05	9.32
1996	10.20	10.48	10.93	11.70	13.03	13.25	14.93	15.18	15.40	15.53	15.48	15.38	13.45
1997	15.33	15.08	14.85	14.75	14.43	10.95	10.68	10.45	10.55	10.48	10.43	10.53	12.37
1998	10.63	10.63	10.60	10.05	10.00	9.80	9.80	9.73	9.55	9.35	9.25	9.05	9.87
1999	9.03	9.08	9.20	9.20	9.53	9.48	9.48	9.40	9.35	9.23	9.18	9.13	9.27
2000	9.03	8.70	8.55	8.50	8.40	8.18	8.13	7.98	7.88	7.40	7.15	6.80	8.06
2001	6.78	6.83	6.83	7.25	7.38	7.45	7.83	7.95	9.00	9.47	9.44	9.50	7.97
2002	9.58	9.72	9.90	9.76	9.90	9.90	9.88	9.85	9.79	9.85	9.86	9.97	9.83
2003	10.20	10.10	10.10	10.16	10.84	10.90	10.90	11.13	11.47	12.32	13.18	13.98	11.27

[1] Transaction value is a weighed average price of recent natural uranium sales transactions, based on prices paid on transactions closed within the previous three-month period for which delivery is scheduled within one year of the transaction date; at least 10 transactions involving a sum total of at least 2 million pounds of U$_3$O$_8$ equivalent.   *Source: American Metal Market (AMM)*

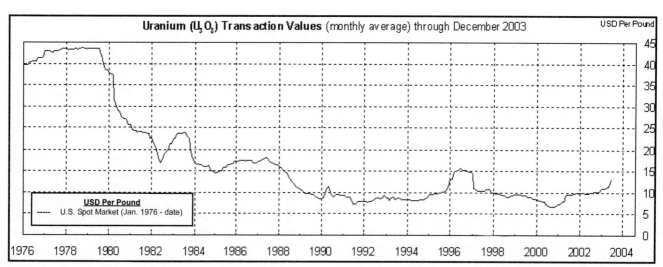

294

Vanadium

Vanadium is a silvery-white, soft, ductile, metallic element with the atomic symbol V and the atomic number 23. Discovered in 1801, but mistaken for chromium, vanadium was rediscovered in 1830, by Swedish chemist Nils Sefstrom, who named the element in honor of the Scandinavian goddess Vanadis.

Never found in the pure state, vanadium is found in about 65 different minerals such as carnotite, roscoelite, vanadinite, and patronite, as well as in phosphate rock, certain iron ores, some crude oils, and meteorites. Vanadium is one of the hardest of all metals. It melts at about 1890 degrees Celsius and boils at about 3380 degrees Celsius.

Vanadium has good structural strength and is used as an alloying agent with iron, steel, and titanium. It is used in aerospace applications, transmission gears, photography, as a reducing agent, and as a drying agent in various paints.

Prices – The price of vanadium in 2001 fell to the range of $3.60-4.50 per pound from $3.85-6.60 in 2000, and hit the lowest level in 5 years.

Supply – Nearly all (99.7%) vanadium is produced from ores, concentrates, and slag, with the remainder coming from petroleum residues, ash, and spent catalysts. World pro-duction of vanadium in 2002 rose +4.9% to a record high of 60,200 metric tons from 57,400 metric tons in 2001.

The world's largest producer of vanadium is China with 33,000 metric tons of production in 2002, representing 55% of world production. The two other major producers are South Africa with 30% of world production, followed by Russia with 13% of world production. Production in Russia and South Africa has been relatively stable in recent years, while China's production has grown very rapidly. China's production level of 33,000 metric tons in 2002 was more than double that in 1998 and more than 7 times the amount produced in 1991. Japan is the only significant producer of vanadium from petroleum residues, ash, and spent catalysts with 245 metric tons of production in each of the last 8 years.

Trade – The US exports very little vanadium. US imports of vanadium were mainly in the form of ore, slag and residues with 3,330 metric tons of imports in 2002, up 12% from 2,980 metric tons in 2001. Other key import categories of vanadium were ferro-vanadium (2,520 metric tons), vanadium pent-oxide, anhydride (406 metric tons), and oxides and hydroxides (42 metric tons).

World Production of Vanadium In Metric Tons (Contained Vanadium)

| | | | --- From Ores, Concentrates and Slag --- | | | | From Petroleum Residues, Ash, Spent Catalysts | | | |
| | | | ------ Republic of South Africa ------ | | | | | | | |
Year	China[3]	Russia	Content of Pentoxide & Vanadate Products	Content of Vanadiferous Slag Products	Total	Total[4]	Japan[3]	United States[6]	Total	World Total
1993	5,000	12,800	6,650	8,400	15,051	33,900	252	2,867	3,120	37,000
1994	5,400	11,900	6,050	9,600	16,350	34,700	252	2,740	2,990	37,700
1995	13,700	11,000	6,500	9,000	16,297	42,100	245	1,990	2,240	44,400
1996	14,000	11,000	----	----	14,770	40,900	245	3,730	3,980	45,800
1997	15,000	9,000	----	----	15,590	40,700	245	----	245	40,900
1998	15,500	9,000	----	----	18,868	44,500	245	----	245	44,700
1999	26,000	7,000	----	----	17,612	51,600	245	----	245	51,900
2000	30,000	7,000	----	----	18,021	56,000	245	----	245	56,300
2001[1]	30,000	8,000	----	----	18,184	57,200	245	----	245	57,400
2002[2]	33,000	8,000	----	----	18,000	60,000	245	----	245	60,200

[1] Preliminary. [2] Estimate. [3] In vanadiferous slag product. [4] Excludes U.S. production. [5] In vanadium pentoxide product.
[6] In vanadium pentoxide and ferrovanadium products. *Source: U.S. Geological Survey(USGS)*

Salient Statistics of Vanadium in the United States In Metric Tons (Contained Vanadium)

Year	Con-sumer & Producer Stocks, Dec. 31	Tool Steel	Cast Irons	High Strength, Low Alloy	Stainless & Heat Re-sisting	Super-alloys	Carbon	Full Alloy	Total	Average $ Per Lb. V₂O₅	Vanadium Pent-oxide Anhydride	Oxides & Hydr-oxides	Ferro-Vana-dium	Slag, Re-sidues	Ores, Vanadium Pent-oxide Anhydride	Oxides & Hydr-oxides	Ferro-Vana-dium
1993	900	373	21	981	33	13	1,413	789	3,973	1.45	126	895	219	1,454	70	19	1,630
1994	1,110	424	31	979	26	16	1,680	777	4,290	1.55	335	1,050	374	1,900	294	3	1,910
1995	1,100	443	40	1,070	32	20	1,870	833	4,640	4.63	229	1,010	340	2,530	547	36	1,950
1996	1,070	433	W	890	22	16	1,820	1,030	4,200	3.11	241	2,670	479	2,270	485	11	1,880
1997	1,000	481	W	944	20	24	1,800	908	4,730	7.40-11.00	614	385	446	2,950	711	126	1,840
1998	336	269	W	950	42	20	1,650	891	4,380	5.25-15.50	681	232	579	2,400	847	33	1,620
1999	348	344	W	865	W	14	1,050	861	3,620	4.35-6.25	747	70	213	1,650	208	----	1,930
2000	303	225	W	944	W	17	1,090	773	3,030	3.85-6.60	653	100	172	1,890	902	14	2,510
2001[1]	251	146	W	797	W	18	1,030	689	2,660	3.60-4.50	670	385	70	2,980	600	1,080	2,550
2002[2]	221	270	W	900	W	12	731	748	2,690		453	443	142	3,330	406	42	2,520

[1] Preliminary. [2] Estimate. W = Withheld proprietary data. *Source: U.S. Geological Survey (USGS)*

Vegetables

Vegetables are the edible products of herbaceous plants, which are plants with soft stems. Vegetables are grouped according to the edible part of each plant: leaves (lettuce), stalks (celery), roots (carrot), tubers (potato), bulbs (onion), fruits (tomato), seeds (pea), and flowers (broccoli). Each of these groups contributes to diet in its own way. Fleshy roots are high in energy value and good sources of the vitamin B group, seeds are relatively high in carbohydrates and proteins, while leaves, stalks, and fruits are excellent sources of minerals, vitamins, water, and roughage. Vegetables are an important food for the maintenance of health and prevention of disease. Higher intakes of vegetables have been shown to lower the risks of cancer and coronary heart disease.

Vegetables are best consumed fresh in their raw state in order to derive the maximum benefits from their nutrients. On the other hand, canned and frozen vegetables, often thought inferior to fresh vegetables, are sometimes nutritionally superior to fresh produce because they are usually processed immediately after harvest when nutri-ent content is at its peak. When cooking vegetables, aluminum utensils should not be used, because aluminum is a soft metal that is acted upon by both food acids and alkalis. Scientific evidence shows that tiny particles of aluminum from foods cooked in aluminum utensils enter the stomach and can injure the sensitive lining of the stomach.

Prices – The index of prices received by growers in the US rose moderately in 2003 to about 150 from 137.7 in 2002. Vegetable prices have been on the upswing since the 11-year low of 117.7 was established in 1999.

Demand – The leading vegetable in terms of US per capita consumption in 2003 was the potato with 135.8 pounds of consumption. Runner-up vegetables were tomatoes (87.9 pounds), sweet corn (27.1 pounds), lettuce (23.0 pounds), and onions (19.5 pounds). Total US per capita consumption of vegetables (excluding potatoes) in 2003 was 293.3 pounds, up from 289.2 pounds in 2002. Including potatoes, US total per capital vegetable consumption was 445.7 pounds.

Index of Prices Received by Growers for Commercial Vegetables[1] in the United States

Year	Jan.	Feb.	Mar.	Apr.	May	June	July	Aug.	Sept.	Oct.	Nov.	Dec.	Average
1998	122	116	125	156	129	110	121	114	114	133	113	117	123
1999	105	112	121	130	118	110	104	106	105	97	98	116	110
2000	98	86	107	135	131	117	119	129	143	125	144	115	121
2001	122	148	138	137	143	119	124	144	134	102	101	151	130
2002	158	190	270	121	120	111	117	120	118	106	116	154	142
2003[2]	115	112	121	136	141	153	118	140	145	145	184	162	139

Not seasonally adjusted. 1990-92=100. [1] Includes fresh and processing vegetables. [2] Preliminary. *Source: National Agricultural Statistics Service, U.S. Department of Agriculture (NASS-USDA)*

Index of Prices Received by Growers for Fresh Vegetables (0113-02) in the United States

Year	Jan.	Feb.	Mar.	Apr.	May	June	July	Aug.	Sept.	Oct.	Nov.	Dec.	Average
1998	133.1	136.6	148.2	162.9	123.2	106.5	153.7	114.9	135.0	161.9	131.2	148.1	137.9
1999	131.9	93.1	117.4	144.4	111.3	125.8	103.4	113.7	117.5	101.6	100.9	151.6	117.7
2000	111.3	100.5	122.3	126.8	152.0	128.1	127.2	136.7	155.9	165.0	173.9	120.3	135.0
2001	147.0	168.6	178.7	145.6	144.9	129.4	109.7	127.2	132.3	112.3	105.9	121.0	135.2
2002	146.1	188.7	242.5	101.7	107.2	123.2	127.1	125.4	116.7	126.9	127.4	119.0	137.7
2003[1]	147.8	127.5	153.0	167.7	165.0	138.8	133.3	136.6	173.9	156.9	148.2	185.4	152.8

Not seasonally adjusted. 1990-92=100. [1] Preliminary. *Source: National Agricultural Statistics Service, U.S. Department of Agriculture (NASS)*

Producer Price Index of Canned[1] Processed Vegetables (0244) in the United States   1982 = 100

Year	Jan.	Feb.	Mar.	Apr.	May	June	July	Aug.	Sept.	Oct.	Nov.	Dec.	Average
1998	121.2	121.9	121.8	121.8	121.9	121.9	122.0	122.0	120.0	119.6	120.0	120.0	121.2
1999	120.6	120.6	120.9	120.9	121.0	121.0	120.8	120.9	120.7	120.7	121.3	121.3	120.9
2000	121.3	120.8	121.2	120.9	121.2	121.5	121.1	120.9	121.1	121.6	121.7	121.3	121.2
2001	121.4	121.4	121.3	121.3	121.4	121.9	124.1	124.9	125.3	126.5	128.0	128.1	123.8
2002	128.3	128.2	128.0	128.2	128.3	128.0	127.7	129.4	128.7	129.5	129.1	129.1	128.5
2003[2]	128.8	129.0	128.9	129.3	129.4	129.3	129.4	129.1	129.2	130.9	131.0	131.4	129.6

Not seasonally adjusted. [1] Includes canned vegetables and juices, including hominy and mushrooms. [2] Preliminary. *Source: Bureau of Labor Statistics, U.S. Department of Labor (BLS)*

Producer Price Index of Frozen Processed Vegetables (0245) in the United States   1982 = 100

Year	Jan.	Feb.	Mar.	Apr.	May	June	July	Aug.	Sept.	Oct.	Nov.	Dec.	
1998	125.2	126.0	124.8	125.7	125.0	124.6	125.5	125.6	125.3	125.6	125.5	125.2	125.3
1999	125.8	126.6	125.6	126.7	125.9	126.0	126.8	126.1	126.0	126.4	125.5	125.3	126.1
2000	125.4	126.2	125.7	126.3	126.3	124.9	125.9	126.4	126.2	126.9	126.1	126.2	126.0
2001	127.6	128.5	127.7	128.7	128.4	127.7	128.9	128.8	128.8	130.0	129.2	129.1	128.6
2002	130.0	131.1	130.1	131.2	130.7	129.7	131.4	131.3	131.5	132.2	131.9	132.6	131.1
2003[1]	133.4	134.1	133.3	134.0	134.1	133.9	134.9	134.2	133.9	135.2	135.0	134.7	134.2

Not seasonally adjusted. [1] Preliminary. *Source: Bureau of Labor Statistics, U.S. Department of Labor (BLS)*

Per Capita Use of Selected Commercially Produced Fresh and Processing Vegetables in the U.S.
In Pounds, farm weight basis

Crop	1993	1994	1995	1996	1997	1998	1999	2000	2001	2002[10]	2003[11]
Asparagus, All	1.0	0.9	1.0	0.9	1.0	1.0	1.2	1.3	1.2	1.3	1.3
Fresh	0.6	0.6	0.6	0.6	0.7	0.7	0.9	1.0	0.9	1.0	1.0
Canning	0.3	0.2	0.3	0.2	0.2	0.2	0.2	0.2	0.2	0.2	0.2
Freezing	0.1	0.1	0.1	0.1	0.1	0.1	0.1	0.1	0.1	0.1	0.1
Snap beans, All	7.2	7.2	6.8	7.2	6.7	7.5	7.6	7.8	7.9	7.3	7.6
Fresh	1.5	1.5	1.6	1.5	1.3	1.7	1.9	2.0	2.2	2.1	2.1
Canning	4.0	3.8	3.5	3.8	3.6	3.8	3.7	4.0	3.8	3.5	3.7
Freezing	1.7	1.9	1.7	1.9	1.8	2.0	2.0	1.8	1.9	1.7	1.8
Broccoli, All[1]	5.6	6.7	6.9	7.0	7.3	7.2	8.6	8.4	7.6	7.1	7.6
Fresh	3.3	4.4	4.3	4.5	5.0	5.1	6.5	6.1	5.6	5.0	5.5
Freezing	2.3	2.3	2.6	2.5	2.3	2.1	2.1	2.3	2.0	2.1	2.1
Cabbage, All	10.7	10.3	9.5	9.3	10.4	9.9	8.8	10.4	10.4	9.7	9.9
Fresh	9.3	9.1	8.1	8.3	9.0	8.5	7.6	9.0	9.1	8.4	8.6
Canning (kraut)	1.4	1.2	1.4	1.0	1.4	1.4	1.2	1.4	1.3	1.3	1.3
Carrots, All[2]	14.6	16.9	15.4	16.9	18.2	16.9	14.7	14.3	14.0	12.5	12.7
Fresh	10.8	12.7	11.2	12.4	14.1	12.7	10.9	10.5	10.6	9.5	9.5
Canning	1.0	1.4	1.6	1.7	1.5	1.4	1.4	1.1	1.9	1.2	1.5
Freezing	2.8	2.8	2.6	2.8	2.6	2.8	2.4	2.7	1.5	1.8	1.7
Cauliflower, All[1]	2.8	2.6	2.2	2.2	2.2	2.3	2.4	2.6	2.1	1.8	2.1
Fresh	2.1	2.0	1.6	1.7	1.8	1.5	1.9	2.0	1.6	1.5	1.7
Freezing	0.7	0.6	0.6	0.5	0.4	0.8	0.5	0.6	0.5	0.3	0.4
Celery	7.3	7.2	6.9	7.0	6.5	6.5	6.6	6.4	6.6	6.5	6.5
Sweet Corn, All[3]	27.8	27.4	28.5	29.1	27.5	28.3	28.3	27.2	27.4	26.1	27.1
Fresh	7.0	8.2	7.8	8.3	8.3	9.3	9.1	9.2	9.4	8.9	9.4
Canning	11.1	10.1	10.4	10.4	9.1	9.2	9.1	9.0	8.7	7.8	8.0
Freezing	9.7	9.1	10.3	10.4	10.1	9.8	10.1	9.0	9.3	9.4	9.7
Cucumbers, All	9.5	10.2	10.6	10.0	11.6	10.5	11.0	11.3	10.1	11.5	11.2
Fresh	5.2	5.4	5.6	5.9	6.4	6.5	6.8	6.4	6.4	6.7	6.7
Pickling	4.3	4.8	5.0	4.1	5.2	4.0	4.2	4.9	3.7	4.8	4.5
Melons	24.5	25.4	26.1	28.9	28.2	27.3	29.4	26.9	28.3	27.4	28.0
Watermelon	14.2	15.0	15.2	16.6	15.5	14.3	15.4	13.9	15.1	13.9	14.8
Cantaloupe	8.6	8.4	9.0	10.3	10.5	10.7	11.5	10.8	11.2	11.3	11.0
Honeydew	1.7	2.0	1.9	2.0	2.2	2.3	2.5	2.2	2.0	2.2	2.2
Lettuce, All	29.4	30.7	28.1	27.4	30.5	28.3	31.6	32.0	31.8	30.7	31.0
Head lettuce	24.4	25.0	22.2	21.6	23.9	21.6	23.9	23.4	23.5	22.4	22.3
Romaine & Leaf	5.0	5.7	5.9	5.8	6.6	6.7	7.7	8.6	8.3	8.3	8.7
Onions, All	19.2	17.8	19.1	19.1	19.7	19.4	20.4	20.1	18.9	19.9	18.8
Fresh	17.2	16.9	17.8	18.3	18.8	18.3	18.1	18.3	17.8	18.7	17.4
Dehydrating	2.0	0.9	1.3	0.8	0.9	1.1	2.3	1.8	1.1	1.2	1.4
Green Peas, All[4]	3.5	3.5	3.7	3.4	3.5	3.3	3.4	3.6	3.4	2.9	3.2
Canning	1.6	1.4	1.6	1.5	1.5	1.4	1.4	1.5	1.4	1.2	1.3
Freezing	1.9	2.1	2.1	1.9	2.0	1.9	2.0	2.1	2.0	1.7	1.9
Peppers, All	11.3	10.7	9.9	11.7	10.9	11.1	11.4	12.0	11.7	12.1	12.2
Bell Peppers, All	6.1	6.4	6.2	7.1	6.4	6.4	6.7	7.0	6.7	7.0	7.1
Chile Peppers, All	5.2	4.3	3.7	4.6	4.5	4.7	4.7	5.0	5.0	5.1	5.1
Tomatoes, All	92.1	92.5	91.4	90.5	89.4	91.5	89.0	87.7	82.9	87.3	88.9
Fresh	16.3	16.2	16.8	17.4	16.8	17.5	17.8	17.6	17.4	18.3	18.6
Canning	75.8	76.3	74.6	73.1	72.6	74.0	71.2	70.1	65.5	69.0	70.3
Other, Fresh[5]	8.4	8.9	8.4	8.8	9.2	10.0	10.5	18.8	17.3	17.9	18.3
Other, Canning[6]	1.9	2.6	2.4	2.2	2.3	2.1	2.5	2.6	2.7	2.3	2.6
Other, Freezing[7]	2.7	2.9	2.8	3.1	3.0	2.9	3.2	3.2	3.1	3.7	3.5
Subtotal, All[8]	279.5	284.4	279.7	284.7	288.1	286.0	290.6	296.5	287.4	288.1	292.4
Fresh	149.0	155.6	151.1	158.1	163.0	160.3	166.3	173.2	171.7	169.6	171.4
Canning	106.6	106.1	104.5	102.6	101.9	102.2	99.6	99.8	94.2	96.4	98.5
Freezing	21.9	21.8	22.8	23.2	22.3	22.4	22.4	21.7	20.3	20.9	21.1
Potatoes, All	136.7	136.7	136.9	145.0	141.4	138.1	136.5	138.7	138.0	132.2	135.1
Fresh	50.1	49.6	49.2	49.9	48.5	47.0	48.0	47.3	46.4	44.5	45.2
Processing	86.6	87.1	87.7	95.1	92.9	91.1	88.5	91.4	91.6	87.7	89.9
Sweet Potatoes	3.7	4.5	4.2	4.3	4.3	3.8	3.7	4.2	4.4	3.8	4.0
Mushrooms	3.7	4.0	3.8	3.9	4.0	3.9	4.1	4.1	3.9	4.1	4.1
Dry Peas & Lentils[9]	0.2	0.6	0.7	0.5	0.5	1.5	1.4	1.2	0.6	0.9	1.0
Dry Edible Beans	7.3	7.7	7.6	7.3	7.4	7.3	7.5	7.5	7.2	7.4	7.3
Total, All Items	431.1	437.9	432.9	445.7	445.7	440.6	443.8	452.2	441.5	436.5	443.9

[1] All production for processing broccoli and cauliflower is for freezing. [2] Industry allocation suggests that 27 percent of processing carrot production is for canning and 73 percent is for freezing. [3] On-cob basis. [4] In-shell basis. [5] Includes artichokes, brussels sprouts, eggplant, endive/escarole, garlic, radishes, and spinach. [6] Includes beets, chile peppers (1980-94, all uses), and spinach. [7] Includes green lima beans, spinach, and miscellaneous freezing vegetables. [8] Fresh, canning, and freezing data do not add to the total because onions for dehydrating are included in the total. [9] Preliminary. [10] Forecast. Source: Economic Research Service, U.S. Department of Agriculture (ERS-USDA)

VEGETABLES

Average Price Received by Growers for Broccoli in the United States   In Dollars Per Cwt.

Year	Jan.	Feb.	Mar.	Apr.	May	June	July	Aug.	Sept.	Oct.	Nov.	Dec.	Season Average
1996	34.60	22.00	30.90	25.20	28.20	30.60	24.10	24.10	23.90	24.30	31.10	28.60	27.10
1997	36.80	27.80	25.90	24.20	23.10	30.30	27.50	23.30	31.20	40.70	27.00	30.20	29.10
1998	34.90	27.10	31.70	40.50	27.10	29.60	23.30	27.60	29.20	32.80	25.80	31.20	30.20
1999	27.70	20.10	23.20	20.20	18.60	23.10	18.70	27.40	29.30	23.00	21.60	39.20	24.10
2000	22.60	20.10	27.40	23.20	44.30	30.00	31.50	25.20	27.70	34.10	56.00	34.10	31.00
2001	22.70	32.30	24.70	26.90	25.50	27.00	23.60	27.10	22.90	24.20	22.20	20.00	26.50
2002	55.30	44.40	33.80	24.00	20.80	28.40	27.00	29.60	40.60	24.00	37.10	35.00	31.20
2003[1]	25.20	40.90	28.10	27.10	29.70	24.60	27.00	29.80	49.10	38.90	42.40	52.80	32.50

[1] Preliminary.   Source: National Agricultural Statistics Service, U.S. Department of Agriculture (NASS-USDA)

Average Price Received by Growers for Carrots in the United States   In Dollars Per Cwt.

Year	Jan.	Feb.	Mar.	Apr.	May	June	July	Aug.	Sept.	Oct.	Nov.	Dec.	Season Average
1996	12.60	13.80	15.90	15.70	12.00	11.00	10.50	14.50	12.60	12.00	16.00	17.20	13.40
1997	15.00	14.70	13.40	12.60	12.60	12.60	12.60	13.10	12.70	12.10	12.50	16.80	12.90
1998	14.00	13.00	13.00	12.60	12.00	11.90	10.60	10.80	10.60	10.90	11.60	11.00	12.00
1999	16.10	19.60	21.50	26.50	25.40	22.80	17.20	13.30	10.10	10.50	11.30	11.50	16.80
2000	9.49	11.60	11.80	12.30	13.80	14.70	15.70	14.50	14.00	14.20	14.30	15.50	13.10
2001	15.90	16.70	17.30	17.30	17.60	20.10	22.00	19.90	15.70	17.50	18.50	19.50	17.20
2002	19.30	19.70	21.10	21.20	21.30	21.60	20.60	20.10	18.10	17.90	18.70	19.50	19.00
2003[1]	19.30	19.10	18.70	19.40	19.90	19.90	19.90	20.40	20.10	19.40	21.40	24.30	19.10

[1] Preliminary.   Source: National Agricultural Statistics Service, U.S. Department of Agriculture (NASS-USDA)

Average Price Received by Growers for Cauliflower in the United States   In Dollars Per Cwt.

Year	Jan.	Feb.	Mar.	Apr.	May	June	July	Aug.	Sept.	Oct.	Nov.	Dec.	Season Average
1996	35.20	36.10	52.80	37.00	37.70	35.70	24.30	27.20	23.80	29.20	30.00	31.10	33.00
1997	30.40	34.70	32.90	27.90	20.70	31.20	38.90	23.40	34.60	47.10	27.60	36.20	32.30
1998	39.10	43.20	49.10	44.70	35.50	26.40	23.20	26.10	32.30	25.90	33.20	37.50	34.50
1999	29.40	31.10	42.80	46.40	23.40	25.50	19.60	25.40	21.70	22.30	35.10	55.50	30.00
2000	22.90	30.20	32.00	34.80	46.00	31.20	37.50	25.20	25.40	21.60	65.30	28.00	32.00
2001	25.70	37.00	23.50	46.50	26.30	37.40	25.60	25.50	24.80	21.70	20.10	20.00	29.20
2002	65.50	30.80	44.10	25.10	26.40	32.70	27.80	24.00	24.70	22.50	37.60	50.00	32.00
2003[1]	24.60	30.70	30.80	27.60	39.50	46.30	27.40	24.90	40.40	25.80	56.90	81.50	33.00

[1] Preliminary.   Source: National Agricultural Statistics Service, U.S. Department of Agriculture (NASS-USDA)

Average Price Received by Growers for Celery in the United States   In Dollars Per Cwt.

Year	Jan.	Feb.	Mar.	Apr.	May	June	July	Aug.	Sept.	Oct.	Nov.	Dec.	Season Average
1996	7.90	8.50	12.20	11.60	8.90	11.50	11.50	10.30	11.60	9.79	12.40	13.40	10.50
1997	16.20	16.20	12.30	10.50	15.40	9.89	19.30	17.00	14.30	13.40	18.40	19.10	14.70
1998	11.20	11.40	16.40	13.80	15.40	12.40	10.60	10.30	10.50	10.40	11.90	14.00	12.30
1999	9.51	8.47	8.35	10.20	12.80	18.30	14.00	10.30	10.60	9.14	12.80	17.20	12.00
2000	19.20	16.00	12.90	21.20	25.60	29.10	18.30	20.30	15.30	12.90	19.40	21.50	18.50
2001	14.60	15.00	15.80	19.10	24.00	33.70	13.50	9.33	9.43	8.22	9.01	13.00	14.40
2002	10.10	19.50	23.50	18.60	12.30	9.37	10.80	10.90	11.70	9.98	15.30	9.50	12.80
2003[1]	8.29	11.80	12.60	17.00	11.00	9.34	12.50	11.80	13.00	15.90	20.60	15.30	13.60

[1] Preliminary.   Source: National Agricultural Statistics Service, U.S. Department of Agriculture (NASS-USDA)

Average Price Received by Growers for Sweet Corn in the United States   In Dollars Per Cwt.

Year	Jan.	Feb.	Mar.	Apr.	May	June	July	Aug.	Sept.	Oct.	Nov.	Dec.	Season Average
1996	29.90	30.20	28.90	21.90	17.50	14.00	18.90	17.40	16.70	17.90	19.40	17.70	16.90
1997	29.00	25.80	33.90	26.10	21.20	17.10	18.60	18.00	16.60	15.20	18.90	19.90	17.70
1998	18.70	31.60	24.20	20.10	17.10	14.00	16.40	16.40	18.10	25.30	24.80	14.30	17.20
1999	19.60	23.30	21.80	18.90	18.50	15.00	17.30	16.60	17.30	16.50	28.40	40.70	17.20
2000	31.50	25.10	19.30	18.70	14.40	18.00	22.00	20.70	20.10	24.00	16.80	33.00	18.20
2001	32.70	34.00	26.10	18.10	24.60	18.60	19.80	19.20	19.00	23.80	24.80	22.60	19.50
2002	24.80	23.50	26.30	19.40	20.80	18.80	27.90	21.80	22.50	25.80	15.50	18.30	19.20
2003[1]	29.00	24.00	18.90	15.10	16.30	15.40	19.70	19.00	18.70	18.50	25.90	29.90	19.10

[1] Preliminary.   Source: National Agricultural Statistics Service, U.S. Department of Agriculture (NASS-USDA)

Average Price Received by Growers for Head Lettuce in the United States   In Dollars Per Cwt.

Year	Jan.	Feb.	Mar.	Apr.	May	June	July	Aug.	Sept.	Oct.	Nov.	Dec.	Season Average
1994	7.91	11.80	9.71	11.70	11.40	13.80	10.60	10.90	17.30	22.10	22.40	37.20	13.30
1995	13.40	9.32	27.00	48.20	47.00	15.60	12.60	15.20	25.60	13.30	11.50	16.10	23.50
1996	11.30	14.90	16.50	13.20	13.30	15.20	12.70	23.50	13.70	15.40	17.70	8.87	14.70
1997	14.90	9.58	13.50	15.70	10.40	14.90	17.10	22.80	22.30	34.80	22.20	25.10	17.50
1998	19.00	10.90	12.50	27.20	14.30	11.80	15.50	16.40	14.00	21.00	10.00	12.50	16.10
1999	10.30	15.50	16.30	20.20	14.00	11.40	12.70	12.00	13.10	13.10	10.70	16.20	13.30
2000	14.60	9.28	14.10	22.80	23.60	13.50	15.00	19.20	29.40	16.20	19.90	12.00	17.40
2001	13.60	22.80	15.10	21.60	18.80	12.10	16.40	26.90	26.20	11.50	10.90	10.00	17.90
2002	26.20	44.10	86.40	14.10	10.20	10.60	11.30	14.60	14.30	13.50	11.90	30.00	21.20
2003[1]	12.10	11.80	9.64	14.10	21.20	32.20	11.90	21.50	23.90	26.30	45.20	25.70	18.20

[1] Preliminary.   Source: National Agricultural Statistics Service, U.S. Department of Agriculture (NASS-USDA)

Average Price Received by Growers for Tomatoes in the United States   In Dollars Per Cwt.

Year	Jan.	Feb.	Mar.	Apr.	May	June	July	Aug.	Sept.	Oct.	Nov.	Dec.	Season Average
1994	41.50	19.30	24.50	16.50	20.60	31.30	26.90	30.60	22.70	28.50	31.20	37.40	27.40
1995	41.10	29.80	37.10	20.50	14.70	35.70	24.40	19.60	19.50	22.50	33.10	25.00	25.50
1996	18.40	40.00	81.70	50.50	24.40	24.20	26.00	22.10	23.40	28.30	29.70	30.40	28.10
1997	32.10	45.90	57.40	24.90	32.20	30.30	29.20	27.60	25.90	26.50	43.60	40.80	31.70
1998	26.40	44.00	34.00	37.20	36.50	29.00	40.90	25.10	28.40	43.00	42.10	42.20	35.20
1999	33.50	23.40	22.30	23.70	21.00	29.00	23.10	25.00	26.50	21.30	26.00	28.90	25.90
2000	21.40	21.10	33.00	34.80	23.10	21.80	24.60	33.90	29.50	42.60	47.80	37.60	30.80
2001	43.80	29.10	56.40	19.00	37.80	28.50	27.40	27.60	23.50	28.60	28.50	25.00	30.40
2002	40.50	26.60	38.50	34.30	29.60	33.00	28.50	25.80	23.70	27.60	40.10	38.00	32.30
2003[1]	47.20	31.70	53.30	30.10	22.60	45.30	37.70	49.50	34.70	31.20	34.60	33.70	37.00

[1] Preliminary.   Source: National Agricultural Statistics Service, U.S. Department of Agriculture (NASS-USDA)

Frozen Vegetables: January 1 and July 1 Cold Storage Holdings in the U.S.   In Thousands of Pounds

Crop	1999 July 1	2000 Jan. 1	July 1	2001 Jan. 1	July 1	2002 Jan. 1	July 1	2003 Jan. 1	July 1	2004[1] Jan. 1
Asparagus	15,712	12,076	15,494	11,359	14,705	10,686	10,954	6,988	10,977	7,368
Limas, Fordhook	4,924	15,302	4,670	14,353	6,742	14,304	7,323	13,068	4,646	5,984
Limas, Baby	33,466	56,691	24,550	32,577	17,169	50,358	30,017	45,544	20,570	46,383
Green Beans, Reg. Cut	61,831	150,310	48,483	147,391	49,355	140,311	48,312	167,669	55,559	126,175
Green Beans, Fr. Style	20,694	36,080	16,481	28,568	8,955	20,517	7,398	19,726	7,272	23,166
Broccoli, Spears	49,485	34,354	35,731	33,295	35,926	38,035	56,679	67,727	81,782	47,135
Broccoli, Chopped & Cut	139,675	123,021	99,478	74,665	89,062	76,491	66,486	67,727	81,782	47,135
Brussels sprouts	15,145	25,649	14,913	19,632	12,244	17,595	10,645	20,220	11,053	18,961
Carrots, Diced	46,993	94,465	46,718	110,335	60,047	89,361	47,110	99,188	36,340	98,398
Carrots, Other	115,576	212,732	133,499	185,041	101,103	186,831	91,705	143,368	90,741	154,404
Cauliflower	32,894	57,812	37,597	44,974	26,866	36,443	25,589	35,635	16,083	28,146
Corn, Cut	147,339	330,204	121,653	315,297	97,601	351,820	137,242	402,164	176,505	494,490
Corn, Cob	108,050	255,662	105,327	255,615	74,548	263,457	85,566	262,338	108,477	288,957
Mixed vegetables	46,699	51,537	47,855	46,312	47,647	51,453	45,248	41,396	42,360	43,537
Okra	51,951	39,837	53,942	47,217	42,863	35,939	35,964	46,616	35,847	37,596
Onion Rings	13,397	17,026	12,284	14,485	7,799	6,978	8,619	9,636	7,772	6,915
Onions, Other	35,605	41,236	53,534	40,420	38,277	29,893	32,143	29,844	28,757	31,717
Blackeye Peas	5,598	6,517	3,517	4,438	3,257	4,473	5,896	6,323	5,340	3,292
Green Peas	226,888	276,154	254,497	295,784	240,139	224,715	198,452	171,161	162,836	180,850
Peas and Carrots Mixed	10,062	11,314	7,512	7,770	8,571	8,847	6,746	6,597	7,897	6,581
Spinach	142,617	73,349	99,820	50,765	97,278	63,368	106,198	56,193	104,522	46,492
Squash, Summer/Zucchini	49,942	58,254	41,097	42,572	31,839	43,198	36,878	44,617	33,549	43,614
Southern greens	39,455	26,944	36,237	38,934	28,131	35,861	26,478	22,986	20,243	18,749
Other Vegetables	243,759	272,866	280,841	340,043	248,289	336,555	24,187	313,421	265,556	329,499
Total	1,657,757	2,279,392	1,595,730	2,201,842	1,388,413	2,137,489	1,369,523	2,081,751	1,388,373	2,118,594
Potatoes, French Fries	965,960	945,637	929,810	959,035	1,083,484	1,010,098	937,933	877,292	900,194	869,521
Potatoes, Other Frozen	268,166	219,752	256,500	230,628	271,650	229,659	285,605	253,920	281,594	250,897
Potatoes, Total	1,234,126	1,165,389	1,186,310	1,189,663	1,355,134	1,239,757	1,223,538	1,131,212	1,181,788	1,120,418
Grand Total	2,891,883	3,444,781	2,782,040	3,391,505	2,743,547	3,377,246	2,593,061	3,212,963	2,570,161	3,239,012

[1] Preliminary.   Source: National Agricultural Statistics Service, U.S. Department of Agriculture (NASS-USDA)

Wheat

Wheat is now a cereal grass but was originally a wild grass. It has been grown in temperate regions and cultivated for food since prehistoric times. Wheat is believed to have originated in southwestern Asia. Archeological research indicates that wheat was grown in the Nile Valley about 5,000 BC. Wheat is not native to the US and was first grown here in 1602 near the Massachusetts coast. The common types of wheat grown in the US are spring and winter wheat. Wheat planted in the spring for summer or fall harvest is mostly red wheat. Wheat planted in the fall or winter for spring harvest is mostly white wheat. Winter wheat accounts for nearly three-fourths of total US production. Wheat is used mainly as a human food and supplies about 20% of the food calories for the world's population. The primary use for wheat is flour, but it is also used in brewing and distilling, and to make oil, gluten, straw for livestock bedding, livestock feed, hay or silage, newsprint, and other products.

Wheat futures and options are traded on the Mercado a Termino de Buenos Aires (MAT), Sydney Futures Exchange (SFE), London International Financial Futures and Options Exchange (LIFFE), Marche a Terme International de France (MATIF), Budapest Commodity Exchange (BCE), the Chicago Board of Trade (CBOT), the Kansas City Board of Trade (KCBT), the Minneapolis Grain Exchange (MGE), the Mid America Commodity Exchange (MidAm) and the Winnipeg Commodity Exchange (WCE). The Chicago Board of Trade's wheat futures contact calls for the delivery of soft red wheat (No. 1 and 2), hard red winter wheat (No. 1 and 2), dark northern spring wheat (No. 1 and 2), No.1 northern spring at 3 cent/bushel premium, or No. 2 northern spring at par.

Prices – Wheat prices on the CBOT nearest futures chart showed weakness in early 2003 and dipped to a 1-1/2 year low of $2.73 per bushel in late April. However, wheat prices then showed strength through the remainder of the year and closed the year at $4.06, just below the 1-year high of $4.09 posted in early December. In the bigger picture, wheat prices in 2003 closed just 28 cents below the 6-1/2 year high of $4.34 posted in September 2002. Bullish factors for 2003 in the latter three quarters of the year centered on (1) a short-fall in production as consumption in 2003/4 is expected to exceed production for the sixth consecutive year, (2) very tight world inventories which are at their lowest since the 1980s, and (3) strong import demand for US wheat exports with the smaller 2003 crops in Europe and China. China became a net importer of wheat in the latter part of 2003 for the first time since 1999/2000 due to lower domestic production. US sales of wheat to China in 2003 posted a 7-year high.

Supply – World wheat production in 2003/4 was forecast to fall by 2.5% to 552.660 million metric tons from 566.843 million in 2002/3 and by 5.0% from 581.859 million in 2001/2. World ending stocks in 2003/4 are expected at 127.263 million metric tons, down sharply by 23% from 165.442 million in 2002/3 and by an overall 37% from 201.108 million in 2001/2. The world's largest wheat producers in 2002/3 were the European Union with 103.872 million metric tons of production (or 18% of world production), China with 90.290 million (16%), India with 71.810 million (13%), Russia with 50.550 million (9%), and the US coming in fifth with 44.062 million (8%).

US wheat production in 2003/4 was forecast at 63.590 million metric tons, up from the very low 2002/3 wheat production of 44.062 million in 2002/3 and 53.262 million in 2001/2. The US 2003/4 wheat crop (June/May) was forecast at 2.337 billion bushels, up sharply from 1.619 billion in 2002/3. US stocks for the 2003/4 marketing year (June 1) were forecasted at 491.4 million bushels, down sharply from 777.1 million in 2002/3. US farmers planted 61.7 million acres with wheat in 2003, up from 60.468 million in 2002. Yields were very strong in 2003 at 44.2 bushels per acre, up from a poor 35.3 bushels in 2002. The breakdown of US production in 2003 was 1.707 billion bushels of winter wheat (73% of total), 533 million bushels of other spring wheat (23%), and 97 million bushels of durum wheat (4%). The largest US wheat producing states in 2003 were Kansas (with 28% of US production), Oklahoma (11%), Washington (7%), and Texas (6%).

Demand – World wheat consumption in 2003/4 was forecast at 590.839 million metric tons, down from 602.509 in 2002/3 but above 586.482 million in 2001/2. The world's largest consumers of wheat in 2002/3 were China with 105.200 million metric tons of consumption (accounting for 17% of world consumption), the European Union with 97.100 million (16%), India with 74.644 million (12%), Russia with 39.320 million (7%), and the US coming in fifth with 30.695 million metric tons of production (5%). In the US, total disappearance (consumption) in 2003/4 was forecast at 2.320 billion bushels, with a breakdown of 910.0 million bushels for food (accounting for 39% of total disappearance), 85.0 million bushels for seed (4%), 225.0 million bushels for feed and residuals (10%), and 1.100 billion bushels for exports (47%).

Trade – World trade in wheat in 2003/4 is expected to decline to 99.450 million metric tons, down from 108.402 million in 2002/3 and 110.362 million in 2001/2. The largest exporters of wheat in 2002/3 were the US with 22.969 million metric tons of exports (accounting for 21% of world exports), the European Union with 16.315 million (15%), Russia with 12.621 million (12%), and Australia with 10.946 million (10%). US exports in 2003/4 are expected to grow to 31.000 million metric tons, up sharply by 35% from 22.969 million in 2002/3. Many countries are importers of wheat, with the largest in 2002/3 being the European Union with 12.000 million metric tons (accounting for 11% of world production), Brazil with 6.631 million (6.1%), Egypt with 6.300 million (5.8%), and Algeria with 6.000 million (5.5%). US wheat imports in 2003/4 are forecasted to rise slightly to 2.000 million metric tons from 1.960 million in 2002/3.

WHEAT

World Production of Wheat   In Thousands of Metric Tons

Year	Argentina	Australia	Canada	China	France	Germany	India	Pakistan	Russia	Turkey	United Kingdom	United States	World Total
1994-5	11,300	8,903	23,122	99,300	30,549	16,481	59,840	15,212	32,100	14,700	13,314	63,167	523,966
1995-6	8,600	16,504	25,037	102,215	30,862	17,763	65,470	17,002	30,100	15,500	14,310	59,404	538,410
1996-7	15,900	22,925	29,801	110,570	35,940	18,922	62,097	16,907	34,900	16,000	16,102	61,980	581,912
1997-8	14,800	19,224	24,280	123,289	33,764	19,827	69,350	16,650	44,200	16,000	15,018	67,534	609,185
1998-9	13,300	21,465	24,076	109,726	39,793	20,188	66,350	18,694	27,000	18,000	15,470	69,327	589,697
1999-00	16,400	24,757	26,941	113,880	37,000	19,620	70,780	17,854	31,000	16,500	14,870	62,569	585,348
2000-1	16,230	22,108	26,519	99,640	37,560	21,620	76,369	21,079	34,450	18,000	16,700	60,758	581,546
2001-2[1]	15,500	24,854	20,568	93,873	31,570	22,840	69,680	19,023	46,900	15,500	11,580	53,262	581,569
2002-3[2]	12,300	10,058	16,198	90,290	38,930	20,820	71,810	18,226	50,550	16,800	15,970	44,062	566,392
2003-4[3]	13,500	24,500	23,500	86,000	30,700	19,300	69,300	18,200	34,000	16,800	14,290	63,590	551,768

[1] Preliminary.   [2] Estimate.   [3] Forecast.   *Source: Foreign Agricultural Service, U.S. Department of Agriculture (FAS-USDA)*

World Supply and Demand of Wheat   In Millions of Metric Tons/Hectares

Crop Year	Area Harvested	Yield	Pro-duction	World Trade	Utilization Total	Ending Stocks	Stocks as a % of Utilization
1994-5	214.3	2.44	523.1	101.5	542.4	162.1	29.9
1995-6	218.8	2.46	538.0	99.2	544.8	155.3	28.5
1996-7	230.2	2.53	582.6	104.0	573.4	164.5	28.7
1997-8	228.4	2.67	610.0	104.4	578.3	196.1	33.9
1998-9	225.0	2.62	589.9	102.0	579.0	207.1	35.8
1999-00	215.4	2.72	585.3	112.7	584.5	207.9	35.6
2000-1	218.6	2.66	581.5	103.6	583.7	205.7	35.2
2001-2[1]	214.8	2.71	581.6	110.4	586.3	201.0	34.3
2002-3[2]	214.2	2.64	566.4	108.9	601.8	165.6	27.5
2003-4[3]	208.5	2.65	551.8	100.6	591.4	125.9	21.3

[1] Preliminary.   [2] Estimate.   [3] Forecast.   *Source: Foreign Agricultural Service, U.S. Department of Agriculture (FAS-USDA)*

Salient Statistics of Wheat in the United States

Crop Year	Planting Intentions	Winter	Spring	All	Average - All Yield Per Acre in Bushels	Value of Production $1,000	Domestic Exports[2]	Imports[3]	Flour	Cereal
	-- 1,000 Acres --						-- In Millions of Bushels --		-- In Pounds --	
1994-5	70,349	41,335	20,415	61,770	37.6	7,968,237	1,188.3	91.9	143.0	5.2
1995-6	69,132	40,972	19,973	60,945	35.8	9,787,213	1,241.1	67.9	140.0	5.4
1996-7	75,105	39,574	23,245	62,819	36.3	9,782,238	1,001.5	92.3	147.0	5.4
1997-8	70,412	41,340	21,500	62,840	39.5	8,286,741	1,040.4	94.9	147.0	5.4
1998-9	65,821	40,126	18,876	59,002	43.2	6,780,623	1,046.0	103.0	143.0	5.4
1999-00	62,714	35,486	18,337	53,823	42.7	5,593,989	1,086.5	94.5	144.0	5.3
2000-1	62,629	35,072	18,061	53,133	42.0	5,782,107	1,062.0	89.8	146.0	5.1
2001-2	59,597	31,295	17,338	48,633	40.2	5,440,217	962.3	107.6	----	----
2002-3	60,468	29,751	16,166	45,917	35.3	5,679,400	854.2	77.4	----	----
2003-4[1]	61,700	36,541	16,186	52,839	44.2	7,954,899	1,150.0	75.0	----	----

[1] Preliminary.   [2] Includes flour milled from imported wheat.   [3] Total wheat, flour & other products.   [4] Civilian only.   [5] Year beginning June.
Source: Economic Research Service, U.S. Department of Agriculture (ERS-USDA)

Supply and Distribution of Wheat in the United States   In Millions of Bushels

Crop Year Beginning June 1	On Farms	Mills, Elevators[3]	Totl Stocks	Production	Imports[4]	Total Supply	Food	Seed	Feed & Res-idual[5]	Total	Exports[4]	Total Disappear-ance
1994-5	175.3	393.2	568.5	2,321.0	91.9	2,981.4	853.0	89.0	344.5	1,286.6	1,188.3	2,474.8
1995-6	163.4	343.2	506.6	2,182.7	67.9	2,757.2	882.9	103.5	153.7	1,140.1	1,241.1	2,381.2
1996-7	74.6	301.4	376.0	2,277.4	92.3	2,745.7	890.7	102.3	307.6	1,300.6	1,001.5	2,302.1
1997-8	154.6	289.0	443.6	2,481.5	94.9	3,020.0	914.1	92.5	250.5	1,257.1	1,040.4	2,297.5
1998-9	224.2	498.3	722.5	2,547.3	103.0	3,372.8	909.7	80.5	391.3	1,380.9	1,046.0	2,426.9
1999-00	277.7	668.2	945.9	2,299.0	94.5	3,339.4	921.0	91.8	288.3	1,301.1	1,088.6	2,389.7
2000-1	226.8	723.0	949.7	2,232.5	89.8	3,272.0	949.6	79.8	304.4	1,333.8	1,062.0	2,395.9
2001-2	197.3	678.9	876.2	1,957.0	107.6	2,940.8	926.4	83.8	191.2	1,201.4	962.3	2,163.7
2002-3[1]	216.8	560.3	777.1	1,619.0	77.4	2,473.5	917.5	83.8	126.4	1,127.8	854.2	1,982.1
2003-4[2]	132.1	359.3	491.4	2,336.5	75.0	2,902.9	910.0	84.0	225.0	1,219.0	1,125.0	2,344.0

[1] Preliminary.   [2] Estimate.   [3] Also warehouses and all off-farm storage not otherwise designated, including flour mills.   [4] Imports & exports are for wheat, including flour & other products in terms of wheat.   [5] Mostly feed use.   *Source: Economic Research Service, U.S. Department of Agriculture*

WHEAT

Stocks, Production and Exports of Wheat in the United States, by Class   In Millions of Bushels

Year Beginning June 1	Hard Spring Stocks June 1	Hard Spring Pro-duction	Hard Spring Exports[3]	Durum[2] Stocks June 1	Durum[2] Pro-duction	Durum[2] Exports[3]	Hard Winter Stocks June 1	Hard Winter Pro-duction	Hard Winter Exports[3]	Soft Red Winter Stocks June 1	Soft Red Winter Pro-duction	Soft Red Winter Exports[3]	White Stocks June 1	White Pro-duction	White Exports[3]
1994-5	201	515	292	28	97	40	227	971	422	45	434	212	67	304	222
1995-6	193	475	230	26	102	39	194	825	384	37	456	250	57	325	238
1996-7	106	631	300	25	116	38	154	759	286	35	420	140	55	352	237
1997-8	166	491	240	31	88	57	143	1,098	358	45	472	180	59	332	205
1998-9	220	486	247	26	138	40	307	1,180	453	80	443	105	90	301	198
1999-00	233	448	230	55	99	44	435	1,051	486	136	454	170	87	247	160
2000-1	218	502	230	50	110	50	458	846	403	133	471	176	91	303	203
2001-2	210	476	216	45	84	50	411	767	349	135	400	199	75	232	147
2002-3	230	354	258	33	79	37	363	612	307	78	332	105	73	241	147
2003-4[1]	145	500	153	28	97	30	188	1,063	270	55	379	46	75	298	83

[1] Preliminary.   [2] Includes Red Durum.   [3] Includes four made from U.S. wheat & shipments to territories.   *Source: Economic Research Service, U.S. Department of Agriculture (ERS-USDA)*

Seeded Acreage, Yield and Production of all Wheat in the United States

Year	Seeded Acreage -- 1,000 Acres Winter	Other Spring	Durum	All	Yield Per Harvested Acre (Bushels) Winter	Other Spring	Durum	All	Production (1,000,000 Bushels) Winter	Other Spring	Durum	All
1994	49,197	18,329	2,823	70,349	40.2	31.8	35.6	37.6	1,661.9	562.3	96.7	2,321.0
1995	48,686	17,010	3,436	69,132	37.7	32.2	30.5	35.8	1,544.7	535.7	102.3	2,182.6
1996	51,445	20,030	3,630	75,105	37.1	35.1	32.6	36.3	1,469.6	691.7	116.1	2,277.4
1997	47,985	19,117	3,310	70,412	44.6	29.9	27.6	39.5	1,845.5	548.2	87.8	2,481.5
1998	46,449	15,567	3,805	65,821	46.9	34.9	37.0	43.2	1,880.7	528.5	138.1	2,547.3
1999	43,331	15,348	4,035	62,714	47.8	34.1	27.8	42.7	1,696.6	503.1	99.3	2,299.0
2000	43,393	15,299	3,937	62,629	44.7	38.4	30.7	42.0	1,562.7	556.6	109.8	2,232.5
2001	41,078	15,609	2,910	59,597	43.5	35.2	30.0	40.2	1,361.5	512.0	83.6	1,957.0
2002	41,845	15,714	2,909	60,468	38.5	29.3	29.4	35.3	1,145.6	393.9	79.5	1,619.0
2003[1]	44,945	13,840	2,915	61,700	46.7	39.7	33.7	44.2	1,707.1	532.8	96.6	2,336.5

[1] Preliminary.   *Source: Economic Research Service, U.S. Department of Agriculture (ERS-USDA)*

Production of Winter Wheat in the United States, by State   In Thousands of Bushels

Year	Colorado	Idaho	Illinois	Kansas	Missouri	Montana	Neb-raska	Ohio	Okla-homa	Oregon	Texas	Wash-ington	Total
1994	76,500	56,880	50,400	433,200	50,400	64,750	71,400	68,440	143,100	55,680	75,400	124,200	1,661,943
1995	102,600	58,520	68,110	286,000	47,970	54,800	86,100	73,810	109,200	57,750	75,600	133,300	1,544,653
1996	70,400	68,800	41,800	255,200	48,750	61,380	73,500	51,870	93,100	58,680	75,400	164,500	1,469,618
1997	86,400	68,800	66,490	501,400	58,320	55,100	70,300	68,670	169,600	53,790	118,900	141,900	1,845,528
1998	99,450	63,140	57,600	494,900	57,500	48,750	82,800	74,240	198,900	52,930	136,500	136,500	1,880,733
1999	103,200	53,960	60,600	432,400	44,160	36,860	81,600	72,100	150,500	29,610	122,400	96,860	1,696,580
2000	68,150	65,700	52,440	347,800	49,400	44,550	59,400	79,920	142,800	45,260	66,000	131,400	1,562,733
2001	66,000	51,830	43,920	328,000	41,040	19,140	59,200	60,300	122,100	28,000	108,800	106,750	1,361,479
2002	36,300	54,510	31,850	267,300	34,200	21,000	48,640	50,220	100,800	29,110	78,300	103,250	1,145,602
2003[1]	77,000	57,600	52,650	480,000	53,070	63,640	83,720	68,000	179,400	47,940	96,600	117,000	1,707,069

[1] Preliminary.   *Source: Crop Reporting Board, U.S. Department of Agriculture (CRB-USDA)*

Official Winter Wheat Crop Production Reports in the United States   In Thousands of Bushels

Crop Year	May 1	June 1	July 1	August 1	September 1	Current December	Final
1994-5	1,657,938	1,674,563	1,658,426	1,670,436	1,670,436	-----	1,661,043
1995-6	1,638,211	1,608,396	1,529,950	1,552,230	1,552,230	-----	1,544,653
1996-7	1,363,851	1,369,861	1,484,836	1,494,716	-----	-----	1,477,058
1997-8	1,561,470	1,603,580	1,780,554	1,855,474	-----	-----	1,845,528
1998-9	1,706,784	1,743,294	1,898,719	1,914,359	-----	-----	1,880,733
1999-00	1,614,799	1,611,559	1,673,222	1,688,582	-----	-----	1,696,580
2000-1	1,648,805	1,621,966	1,588,376	1,594,321	-----	-----	1,562,733
2001-2	1,341,381	1,321,126	1,366,192	1,385,048	-----	-----	1,361,479
2002-3	1,300,726	1,237,671	1,178,320	1,158,710	-----	-----	1,145,602
2003-4[1]	1,563,314	1,626,376	1,715,912	1,712,150	-----	-----	1,707,069

[1] Preliminary.   *Source: Crop Reporting Board, U.S. Department of Agriculture (CRB-USDA)*

Production of All Spring Wheat in the United States, by State   In Thousands of Bushels

| | Durum Wheat | | | | | | Other Spring Wheat | | | | | | | |
Year	Arizona	California	Mon-tana	North Dakota	South Dakota	Total Durum	Idaho	Minne-sota	Mon-tana	North Dakota	Oregon	South Dakota	Wash-ington	Total Other
1994	8,554	5,605	5,340	76,375	598	96,747	43,400	70,000	100,500	278,775	2,900	51,480	9,800	562,291
1995	8,514	6,800	7,950	77,760	896	102,280	44,800	70,400	133,000	221,400	5,928	33,600	20,470	535,658
1996	14,760	13,800	7,000	79,380	720	116,090	50,400	105,000	106,600	313,500	6,405	83,250	18,170	691,680
1997	8,010	13,680	7,540	57,860	513	87,783	45,030	75,200	118,900	210,000	6,600	63,000	23,220	548,155
1998	15,120	15,750	12,040	94,400	624	138,110	89,270	78,720	108,000	211,200	4,560	59,200	20,925	528,469
1999	7,275	8,925	9,450	72,000	1,512	99,322	50,560	78,000	108,000	168,000	5,049	59,850	27,280	503,108
2000	8,075	9,700	13,160	78,300	468	109,805	42,750	95,550	77,500	230,400	5,750	60,040	33,480	550,902
2001	7,917	8,505	11,880	54,600	576	83,556	33,320	79,200	65,550	234,600	4,650	64,350	25,830	512,008
2002	8,455	9,000	12,995	48,750	110	79,450	33,150	61,200	75,900	165,200	4,900	24,000	26,445	393,949
2003[1]	11,500	11,500	14,490	58,410	621	96,637	29,700	104,400	59,400	252,800	5,600	56,280	22,345	532,820

[1] Preliminary.   Source: Crop Reporting Board, U.S. Department of Agriculture (CRB-USDA)

Grindings of Wheat by Mills in the United States   In Millions of Bushels (60 Pounds Each)

Year	July	Aug.	Sept.	Oct.	Nov.	Dec.	Jan.	Feb.	Mar.	Apr.	May	June	Total
1994-5	68.9	78.7	76.3	77.9	75.9	71.1	69.0	65.2	76.9	66.6	74.7	71.9	873.1
1995-6	69.8	77.8	74.2	78.4	74.8	70.0	70.1	72.4	72.1	69.4	72.6	67.7	869.1
1996-7	73.6	77.4	75.1	82.7	73.7	71.3	69.6	66.9	70.3	73.2	72.5	72.2	878.6
1997-8	76.4	75.8	78.4	82.7	75.3	74.8	-----	215.5	-----	-----	216.6	-----	895.5
1998-9	-----	224.7	-----	-----	238.6	-----	-----	213.5	-----	-----	228.0	-----	904.9
1999-00	-----	234.0	-----	-----	242.2	-----	-----	225.6	-----	-----	226.8	-----	928.7
2000-1	-----	244.7	-----	-----	247.7	-----	-----	223.8	-----	-----	221.3	-----	937.5
2001-2	-----	230.2	-----	-----	238.7	-----	-----	217.0	-----	-----	217.6	-----	903.6
2002-3	-----	230.3	-----	-----	228.1	-----	-----	213.7	-----	-----	213.4	-----	885.6
2003-4[1]	-----	228.4	-----	-----	220.5	-----	-----	-----	-----	-----	-----	-----	897.9

[1] Preliminary.   Source: Bureau of the Census, U.S. Department of Commerce

Wheat Stocks in the United States   In Millions of Bushels

| | On Farms | | | | Off Farms | | | | Total Stocks | | | |
Year	Mar. 1	June 1	Sept. 1	Dec. 1	Mar. 1	June 1	Sept. 1	Dec. 1	Mar. 1	June 1	Sept. 1	Dec. 1
1994	363.2	175.3	859.8	575.6	664.8	393.2	1,209.7	920.6	1,028.0	568.5	2,069.5	1,491.1
1995	335.3	163.4	743.6	477.0	633.8	343.2	1,137.5	861.3	969.1	506.6	1,881.1	1,338.3
1996	220.6	74.6	824.5	584.2	602.9	301.4	899.7	634.7	823.5	376.0	1,724.2	1,218.8
1997	320.8	154.6	794.4	604.0	501.1	289.0	1,282.0	1,015.2	821.8	443.6	2,076.3	1,619.2
1998	399.9	224.2	885.7	680.2	766.6	498.3	1,499.6	1,215.5	1,166.6	722.5	2,385.3	1,895.7
1999	471.2	277.7	888.1	647.4	979.2	668.2	1,557.0	1,236.3	1,450.4	945.9	2,445.0	1,883.7
2000	424.7	226.8	808.4	623.4	991.8	723.0	1,544.3	1,182.7	1,416.5	949.7	2,352.7	1,806.1
2001	384.8	197.3	696.9	517.9	953.6	678.9	1,459.0	1,105.6	1,338.4	876.2	2,155.8	1,623.5
2002	338.5	216.8	580.2	384.8	871.3	560.3	1,170.8	935.1	1,209.8	777.1	1,751.0	1,319.9
2003[1]	236.3	132.1	687.3	491.9	670.3	359.3	1,351.7	1,029.2	906.6	491.4	2,039.0	1,521.1

[1] Preliminary.   Source: National Agricultural Statistics Service, U.S. Department of Agriculture (NASS-USDA)

Wheat Supply and Distribution in Canada, Australia and Argentina   In Millions of Metric Tons

| | Canada (Year Beginning Aug. 1) | | | | | Australia (Year Beginning Oct. 1) | | | | | Argentina (Year Beginning Dec. 1) | | | | |
| | Supply | | | Disappearance | | Supply | | | Disappearance | | Supply | | | Disappearance | |
Crop Year	Stocks Aug. 1	New Crop	Total Supply	Domestic	Exports[3]	Stocks Oct. 1	New Crop	Total Supply	Domestic	Exports[3]	Stocks Dec. 1	New Crop	Total Supply	Domestic	Exports[3]
1994-5	11.1	23.1	34.2	7.8	20.9	3.7	8.9	12.7	3.9	6.4	.4	11.3	11.7	4.3	7.3
1995-6	5.7	25.0	30.7	7.8	16.3	2.4	16.5	18.9	3.7	13.3	.2	8.6	8.8	4.2	4.5
1996-7	6.7	29.8	36.5	8.2	19.5	2.0	22.9	24.9	3.3	19.2	.2	15.9	16.1	4.9	10.2
1997-8	9.0	24.3	33.3	7.3	20.1	2.4	19.2	21.6	5.0	15.3	1.0	15.7	16.7	4.8	11.2
1998-9	6.0	24.1	30.1	8.1	14.7	1.3	21.5	22.8	4.5	16.5	.8	13.3	14.1	4.9	8.6
1999-00	7.4	26.9	34.4	8.1	19.2	1.9	24.8	26.6	5.2	17.8	.7	16.4	17.1	4.9	11.6
2000-1	7.3	26.5	33.8	7.0	17.3	3.6	22.1	25.7	5.3	15.9	.6	16.2	16.8	5.0	11.3
2001-2	9.7	20.6	30.2	7.6	16.3	4.5	24.9	29.4	5.4	16.4	.6	15.5	16.1	4.9	10.1
2002-3[1]	6.7	16.2	22.9	8.3	9.4	7.6	10.1	17.7	6.1	9.1	1.1	12.3	13.4	5.2	6.8
2003-4[2]	5.7	23.5	29.2	7.7	16.0	2.7	24.5	27.2	6.2	17.5	1.5	13.5	15.0	5.3	8.0

[1] Preliminary.   [2] Forecast.   [3] Including flour.   Source: Foreign Agricultural Service, U.S. Department of Agriculture (FAS-USDA)

WHEAT

Quarterly Supply and Disappearance of Wheat in the United States   In Millions of Bushels

Crop Year Beginning June 1	Supply				Disappearance						Ending Stocks		
					Domestic Use					Total			
	Beginning Stocks	Production	Imports[3]	Total Supply	Food	Seed	Feed & Residual[7]	Total	Exports[3]	Disap-pearance	Gov't Owned[4]	Privately Owned[5]	Total Stocks
1993-4	530.7	2,396.4	108.8	3,035.9	871.7	96.3	271.7	1,239.7	1,227.8	2,467.4	150.3	418.2	568.5
June-Aug.	530.7	2,396.4	14.6	2,941.7	211.3	1.3	295.8	508.4	300.7	809.1	149.9	1,982.7	2,132.6
Sept.-Nov.	2,132.6	-----	30.1	2,162.7	225.3	60.9	-38.5	247.7	329.2	577.0	150.3	1,435.4	1,585.7
Dec.-Feb.	1,585.7	-----	26.9	1,612.6	211.0	2.3	39.0	252.3	332.3	584.6	150.4	877.6	1,028.0
Mar.-May	1,028.0	-----	37.2	1,065.2	224.1	31.8	-24.7	231.2	265.5	496.7	150.3	418.2	568.5
1994-5	568.5	2,321.0	92.0	2,981.4	852.5	89.2	344.9	1,286.6	1,188.3	2,474.9	142.1	364.5	506.6
June-Aug.	568.5	2,321.0	30.7	2,920.2	213.2	1.6	376.3	591.1	259.6	850.7	146.4	1,923.1	2,069.5
Sept.-Nov.	2,069.5	-----	21.4	2,090.9	229.3	61.1	-28.8	261.6	338.2	599.8	142.8	1,348.3	1,491.1
Dec.-Feb.	1,491.1	-----	17.7	1,508.8	201.5	2.2	25.6	229.3	310.4	539.7	142.3	826.8	969.1
Mar.-May	969.1	-----	22.2	991.2	208.5	24.3	-28.2	204.6	280.1	484.7	142.1	364.5	506.6
1995-6	506.6	2,182.6	67.9	2,757.1	882.9	104.1	153.0	1,139.9	1,241.1	2,381.1	118.2	257.8	376.0
June-Aug.	506.6	2,182.6	22.7	2,711.9	215.3	8.0	305.0	528.3	302.5	830.8	141.5	1,739.6	1,881.1
Sept.-Nov.	1,881.1	-----	16.3	1,897.4	232.2	64.9	-98.7	198.3	360.8	559.1	141.2	1,197.1	1,338.3
Dec.-Feb.	1,338.3	-----	11.8	1,350.0	215.8	3.0	13.3	232.1	294.5	526.6	137.5	686.0	823.5
Mar.-May	823.5	-----	17.2	840.7	219.6	28.2	-66.5	181.3	283.4	464.6	118.2	257.8	376.0
1996-7	376.0	2,277.4	92.3	2,745.7	890.7	102.3	307.6	1,300.6	1,001.5	2,302.1	93.0	350.6	443.6
June-Aug.	376.0	2,277.4	14.9	2,668.3	223.7	8.7	377.5	610.0	334.1	944.1	109.5	1,614.7	1,724.2
Sept.-Nov.	1,724.2	-----	20.7	1,744.9	233.8	59.9	-76.0	217.8	308.3	526.1	96.1	1,122.7	1,218.8
Dec.-Feb.	1,218.8	-----	27.1	1,245.9	212.7	1.8	30.3	244.7	179.3	424.1	95.3	726.5	821.8
Mar.-May	821.8	-----	29.7	851.6	220.5	31.8	-24.2	228.1	179.8	407.9	93.0	350.6	443.6
1997-8	443.6	2,481.5	94.9	3,020.0	914.1	92.5	250.5	1,257.1	1,040.4	2,297.5	94.2	628.3	722.5
June-Aug.	443.6	2,481.5	22.7	2,947.8	227.9	3.1	352.2	583.2	288.2	871.4	93.2	1,983.1	2,076.3
Sept.-Nov.	2,076.3	-----	22.8	2,099.1	238.7	58.6	-113.4	183.9	296.0	479.9	93.1	1,526.1	1,619.2
Dec.-Feb.	1,619.2	-----	23.8	1,643.0	219.2	2.1	.3	221.6	254.9	476.4	93.0	1,073.6	1,166.6
Mar.-May	1,166.6	-----	25.7	1,192.2	228.3	28.7	11.4	268.4	201.3	469.8	94.2	628.3	722.5
1998-9	722.5	2,547.3	103.0	3,372.8	909.7	80.5	542.1	1,532.4	1,042.2	2,574.6	127.9	818.0	945.9
June-Aug.	722.5	2,547.3	24.4	3,294.2	225.7	1.0	424.9	651.6	257.3	908.9	99.8	2,285.5	2,385.3
Sept.-Nov.	2,385.3	-----	23.9	2,409.2	240.7	54.9	73.8	369.5	291.8	661.2	126.6	1,769.1	1,895.7
Dec.-Feb.	1,895.7	-----	27.7	1,923.4	213.2	1.4	11.6	226.2	246.8	473.0	124.2	1,326.2	1,450.4
Mar.-May	1,450.4	-----	27.0	1,477.4	230.1	23.2	31.8	285.1	246.3	531.5	127.9	818.0	945.9
1999-00	945.9	2,299.0	94.5	3,339.4	924.7	91.6	283.8	1,300.1	1,089.5	2,389.6	103.9	845.8	949.7
June-Aug.	945.9	2,299.0	30.6	3,275.5	230.5	6.4	270.0	506.9	323.6	830.5	132.2	2,312.8	2,445.0
Sept.-Nov.	2,445.0	-----	19.5	2,464.5	241.1	54.6	-8.0	287.7	291.3	579.0	115.0	1,770.6	1,885.6
Dec.-Feb.	1,885.6	-----	19.4	1,905.1	220.9	2.3	30.7	253.9	235.9	489.8	108.7	1,306.6	1,416.5
Mar.-May	1,415.3	-----	25.0	1,440.3	232.2	28.4	-8.8	251.8	238.8	490.6	103.9	845.8	949.7
2000-1	949.7	2,232.0	90.0	3,272.0	956.0	80.0	298.0	1,334.0	1,061.0	2,395.0	96.9	779.3	876.2
June-Aug.	949.7	2,232.0	20.0	3,203.0	239.0	1.0	324.0	564.0	286.0	850.0	108.9	2,243.8	2,352.7
Sept.-Nov.	2,353.0	-----	25.0	2,378.0	253.0	50.0	-24.0	279.0	293.0	572.0	102.9	1,703.2	1,806.1
Dec.-Feb.	1,805.0	-----	21.0	1,828.0	231.0	3.0	5.0	239.0	250.0	489.0	104.4	1,234.0	1,338.4
Mar.-May	1,340.0	-----	23.0	1,631.0	234.0	25.0	-7.0	252.0	233.0	485.0	96.9	779.3	876.2
2001-2	876.2	1,957.0	107.5	2,940.8	926.3	83.6	192.5	1,202.4	961.3	2,163.7	96.9	680.2	777.1
June-Aug.	876.2	1,957.0	25.7	2,858.9	233.8	3.5	247.5	484.8	218.3	703.1	97.7	2,058.1	2,155.8
Sept.-Nov.	2,155.8	-----	29.0	2,184.9	245.1	51.7	-23.2	273.6	287.8	561.4	96.9	1,526.5	1,623.4
Dec.-Feb.	1,623.5	-----	27.6	1,651.0	220.7	2.0	-7.2	215.5	225.7	441.2	96.9	1,112.9	1,209.8
Mar.-May	1,209.8	-----	25.2	1,235.0	226.7	26.4	-24.6	228.5	229.4	457.9	96.9	680.2	777.1
2002-3[1]	777.0	1,619.0	78.0	2,474.0	917.0	84.0	126.0	1,127.0	855.0	1,982.0			491.0
June-Aug.	777.0	1,619.0	27.0	2,423.0	233.0	3.0	196.0	432.0	240.0	672.0	91.4	1,659.6	1,751.0
Sept.-Nov.	1,751.0	-----	23.0	1,774.0	240.0	54.0	-75.0	219.0	235.0	454.0	80.9	1,239.0	1,320.0
Dec.-Feb.	1,320.0	-----	13.0	1,333.0	217.0	3.0	12.0	232.0	194.0	426.0			907.0
Mar.-May	905.0	-----	15.0	922.0	227.0	24.0	-7.0	244.0	186.0	430.0			491.0
2003-4[2]	491.0	2,337.0	78.0	2,906.0	934.0	110.0	498.0	1,542.0	1,146.0	2,688.0			559.0
June-Aug.	491.0	2,337.0	16.0	2,844.0	227.0	2.0	309.0	538.0	266.0	804.0			2,039.0
Sept.-Nov.	2,039.0	----	23.0	2,062.0	240.0	53.0	-60.0	233.0	307.0	540.0			1,521.0

[1] Preliminary.   [2] Forecast.   [3] Imports & exports include flour and other products expressed in wheat equivalent.   [4] Uncommitted, Government only.   [5] Includes total loans.   [6] Less than 50,000 bushels.   [7] Includes alcoholic beverages.   *Source: Economic Research Service, U.S. Department of Agriculture (ERS-USDA)*

304

Wheat Government Loan Program Data in the United States   Loan Rates (Cents Per Bushel)

Crop Year Beginning June 1	National Average	Target Rate	Corn Belt (Soft Red Winter)	Central & Southern Plains (Hard Winter)	Northern Plains (Spring & Durum)	Pacific Northwest (White)	Placed Under Loan	% of Production	Acquired by CCC Under Program	Total Stocks	Total CCC Stocks	CCC Loans	Farmer-Owned Reserve	"Free"
				Farm Loan Prices							Stocks Ending May 31 / Outstanding			
											In Millions of Bushels			
1995-6	258	400	254	258	258	276	114	5.2	0	376	118	13	0	245
1996-7	258	NA	253	257	258	271	194	8.1	0	444	93	72	0	279
1997-8	258	NA	253	257	258	271	248	----	0	723	94	134	0	494
1998-9	258	NA	253	257	258	271	----	----	0	946	128	140	0	678
1999-00	258	NA	253	257	258	271	----	----	0	950	104	62	0	784
2000-1	258	NA	253	257	258	271	----	----	0	876	97	42	0	737
2001-2[1]	258	NA	255	254	264	270	----	----	0	777	99	78	0	600
2002-3[2]	280	386	NA	NA	NA	NA	----	----	0	491	66	32	0	359

[1] Preliminary.   [2] Estimate.   [3] The national average loan rate at the farm as a percentage of the parity-priced wheat at the beginning of the marketing year.   [4] Beginning with the 1996-7 marketing year, target prices are no longer applicable.   NA = Not avaliable.   *Source: Agricultural Marketing Service, U.S. Department of Agriculture (AMS-USDA)*

Exports of Wheat (Only)[2] from the United States   In Thousands of Bushels

Year	June	July	Aug.	Sept.	Oct.	Nov.	Dec.	Jan.	Feb.	Mar.	Apr.	May	Total
1995-6	78,355	88,649	119,797	131,424	117,679	105,535	99,175	96,085	91,876	108,800	90,373	78,303	1,206,051
1996-7	73,715	108,437	145,840	125,910	98,302	75,245	50,979	63,431	59,039	55,936	69,821	47,640	974,295
1997-8	65,654	92,465	123,141	119,029	89,331	79,528	80,906	97,090	68,972	63,914	64,623	68,359	1,013,012
1998-9	67,372	86,605	96,664	90,507	109,168	81,913	96,486	73,017	63,794	65,522	86,066	85,057	1,002,171
1999-00	90,594	110,814	107,168	91,438	96,154	89,211	84,460	71,763	64,198	68,836	73,815	87,789	1,036,240
2000-1	88,581	82,739	104,944	113,785	82,716	86,034	94,705	60,743	85,797	71,502	83,157	68,908	1,023,611
2001-2	59,190	64,911	89,582	86,941	94,598	99,800	81,369	72,114	63,446	78,070	84,211	58,449	932,681
2002-3	63,219	78,013	92,345	73,606	78,866	75,678	69,485	62,769	48,618	65,990	55,764	59,438	823,791
2003-4[1]	54,665	88,042	115,869	125,312	101,168	76,222							1,122,556

[1] Preliminary.   [2] Grains.   *Source: Economic Research Service, U.S. Department of Agriculture (ERS-USDA)*

United States Wheat and Wheat Flour Imports and Exports   In Thousands of Bushels

Crop Year Beginning June 1	Wheat Suitable for Milling	Wheat Unfit for Human Consumption	Grain	Flour & Products[2]	Total	P.L. 480	Foreign Donations Sec. 416	Aid[3]	Total Concessional	CCC Export Credit	Export Exhancement Programs	Total U.S. Wheat Exports
	Imports					Exports						
			Wheat Equivalent			In Thousands of Metric Tons						
1994-5	70,561	----	70,562	21,386	91,946	1,491	0	NA	1,948	4,202	18,073	32,088
1995-6	47,753	----	47,753	20,180	67,933	1,530	0	NA	1,530	5,662	570	33,708
1996-7	71,727	----	71,727	20,605	92,333	1,009	0	NA	1,155	4,844	0	24,526
1997-8	73,245	----	73,245	21,556	94,801	1,453	0	NA	1,727	5,460	0	25,791
1998-9	79,766	----	79,766	23,220	102,987	556	4,682	NA	5,334	3,621	0	28,806
1999-00	72,408	----	72,408	22,103	94,510	674	2,635	NA	3,436	3,691	0	27,838
2000-1	66,313	----	66,313	23,512	89,825	1,294	1,638	NA	3,109	4,026	0	25,275
2001-2[1]	82,615	----	82,615	24,930	107,545	1,093	875	NA	2,035	4,441	0	25,353

[1] Preliminary.   [2] Includes macaroni, semolina & similar products.   [3] Shipment mostly under the Commodity Import Program, financed with foreign aid funds.   NA = Not available.   *Source: Economic Research Service, U.S. Department of Agriculture (ERS-USDA)*

Comparative Average Cash Wheat Prices   In Dollars Per Bushel

Crop Year Beginning June 1	Received by U.S. Farmers	No. 2 Soft Red Winter, Chicago	No. 1 Hard Red Ordinary Protein, Kansas City	No. 2 Soft Red Winter, St. Louis	No. 1 Dark Northern Spring 14%	No. 1 Hard Amber Durum	No. 1 Soft White, Portland, Oregon	No. 2 Western White Pacific Northwest	No. 2 Soft White, Toledo	Australian Standard Wheat	Canada Vancouver No. 1 CWRS 13 1/2%	Argentina F.O.B. B.A.	U.S. Gulf No. 2 Hard Winter	Rotterdam C.I.F. U.S. No. 2 Hard Winter
	Minneapolis									Export Prices[2] (U.S. $ Per Metric Ton)				
1996-7	4.30	3.92	4.88	4.10	4.97	5.59	4.54	4.26	3.71	229	230	218	207	239
1997-8	3.38	3.29	3.71	3.43	4.31	5.97	3.81	3.41	3.12	192	181	157	160	209
1998-9	2.65	2.46	3.08	2.40	3.83	4.06	3.02	2.64	2.27	154	163	120	126	181
1999-00	2.48	2.19	2.87	2.39	3.65	4.22	3.02	2.72	1.94	143	152	114	112	NA
2000-1	2.62	2.39	3.30	2.39	3.62	4.59	2.99	2.72	2.98	145	149	118	114	163
2001-2	2.78	2.69	3.25	2.80	3.61	4.99	3.48	3.67	2.67	157	149	121	125	161
2002-3	3.56	3.40	4.22	3.50	4.47	4.25	3.95	4.58	3.34	192	199	158	160	190
2003-4[1]	3.30-3.40	3.52	3.84	3.65	4.23	5.30	3.79	4.07	3.42				148	

[1] Preliminary.   [2] Calendar year.   NA = Not available.   *Source: Economic Research Service, U.S. Department of Agriculture (ERS-USDA)*

WHEAT

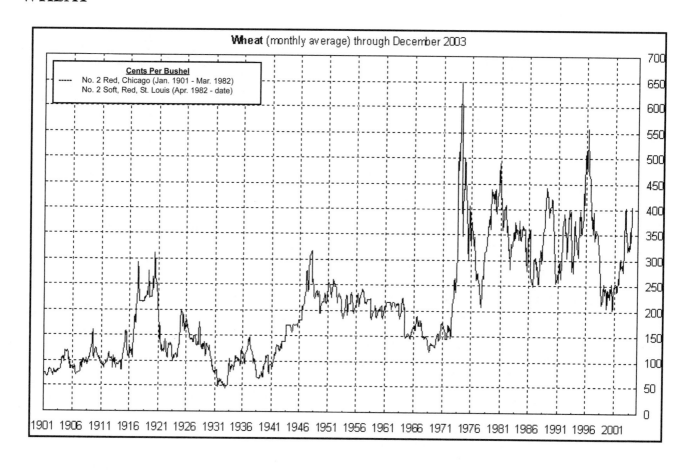

Wheat (monthly average) through December 2003

Cents Per Bushel
- - - - No. 2 Red, Chicago (Jan. 1901 - Mar. 1982)
No. 2 Soft, Red, St. Louis (Apr. 1982 - date)

Average Price of No. 2 Soft Red Winter (30 Days) Wheat in Chicago   In Dollars Per Bushel

Year	June	July	Aug.	Sept.	Oct.	Nov.	Dec.	Jan.	Feb.	Mar.	Apr.	May	Average
1994-5	3.21	3.14	3.37	3.75	3.83	3.63	3.76	3.68	3.55	3.39	3.40	3.56	3.52
1995-6	3.91	4.41	4.28	4.53	4.72	4.85	5.04	4.92	5.10	4.99	5.65	5.57	4.83
1996-7	4.94	4.64	4.49	4.33	3.96	3.57	3.54	3.47	3.29	3.49	3.77	3.57	3.92
1997-8	3.38	3.30	3.52	3.49	3.51	3.44	3.31	3.27	3.26	3.25	2.91	2.87	3.29
1998-9	2.72	2.51	2.39	2.32	2.56	2.58	2.49	2.46	2.28	2.63	2.31	2.24	2.46
1999-00	2.20	1.94	2.09	2.12	1.98	1.96	2.12	2.34	2.38	2.34	2.30	2.45	2.19
2000-1	2.41	2.14	2.08	2.13	2.36	2.42	2.47	2.57	2.49	2.56	2.52	2.51	2.39
2001-2	2.40	2.56	2.57	2.57	2.68	2.75	2.83	2.96	2.74	2.76	2.75	2.73	2.69
2002-3	2.81	3.19	3.42	3.92	3.89	3.85	3.53	3.32	3.44	3.14	3.08	3.25	3.40
2003-4[1]	3.11	3.23	3.63	3.46	3.42	3.87	3.92						3.52

[1] Preliminary.   *Source: Economic Research Service, U.S. Department of Agriculture (ERS-USDA)*

Average Price[1] Received by Farmers for Wheat in the United States   In Dollars Per Bushel

Year	June	July	Aug.	Sept.	Oct.	Nov.	Dec.	Jan.	Feb.	Mar.	Apr.	May	Average
1994-5	3.21	3.04	3.25	3.57	3.76	3.75	3.74	3.69	3.61	3.52	3.48	3.66	3.45
1995-6	3.84	4.10	4.26	4.53	4.72	4.81	4.88	4.83	4.98	5.07	5.32	5.73	4.55
1996-7	5.25	4.73	4.58	4.37	4.18	4.14	4.06	4.03	3.88	3.93	4.11	4.09	4.28
1997-8	3.52	3.23	3.56	3.67	3.55	3.50	3.45	3.33	3.27	3.32	3.15	3.06	3.38
1998-9	2.77	2.56	2.39	2.41	2.79	2.97	2.87	2.80	2.74	2.65	2.62	2.53	2.68
1999-00	2.50	2.22	2.53	2.58	2.57	2.66	2.52	2.51	2.54	2.59	2.57	2.59	2.53
2000-1	2.50	2.32	2.41	2.44	2.68	2.83	2.87	2.85	2.83	2.87	2.86	2.98	2.70
2001-2	2.74	2.70	2.73	2.85	2.87	2.87	2.88	2.87	2.83	2.87	2.83	2.81	2.82
2002-3	2.92	3.21	3.63	4.21	4.38	4.25	4.06	3.89	3.70	3.54	3.37	3.33	3.71
2003-4[2]	3.07	2.95	3.34	3.39	3.45	3.59	3.69	3.68	3.68				3.43

[1] Includes an allowance for unredeemed loans and purchases.   [2] Preliminary.   *Source: Economic Research Service, U.S. Department of Agriculture*

Average Price of No. 1 Hard Red Winter (Ordinary Protein) Wheat in Kansas City   In Dollars Per Bushel

Year	June	July	Aug.	Sept.	Oct.	Nov.	Dec.	Jan.	Feb.	Mar.	Apr.	May	Average
1994-5	3.60	3.48	3.70	4.05	4.31	4.24	4.27	4.06	3.98	3.87	3.86	4.22	3.97
1995-6	4.72	4.98	4.76	5.00	5.28	5.34	5.51	5.40	5.67	5.63	6.60	7.02	5.49
1996-7	6.12	5.34	5.01	4.70	4.76	4.78	4.70	4.61	4.52	4.58	4.78	4.61	4.88
1997-8	4.08	3.57	3.84	3.86	3.88	3.87	3.72	3.61	3.64	3.61	3.39	3.41	3.71
1998-9	3.16	3.02	2.74	2.81	3.30	3.42	3.31	3.27	3.05	3.02	2.94	2.89	3.08
1999-00	2.93	2.68	2.85	2.92	2.80	2.89	2.81	2.90	2.94	2.91	2.84	2.95	2.87
2000-1	3.07	2.97	2.89	3.13	3.41	3.45	3.47	3.54	3.35	3.45	3.41	3.49	3.30
2001-2	3.32	3.20	3.15	3.18	3.28	3.37	3.26	3.29	3.25	3.23	3.24	3.21	3.25
2002-3	3.55	3.92	4.29	5.04	5.10	4.76	4.40	4.06	4.08	3.80	3.79	3.87	4.22
2003-4[1]	3.63	3.34	3.87	3.74	3.79	4.21	4.31						3.84

[1] Preliminary.   Source: Economic Research Service, U.S. Department of Agriculture (ERS-USDA)

Average Price of No. 1 Dark Northern Spring (14% Protein) Wheat in Minneapolis   In Dollars Per Bushel

Year	June	July	Aug.	Sept.	Oct.	Nov.	Dec.	Jan.	Feb.	Mar.	Apr.	May	Average
1994-5	4.20	4.14	4.00	4.27	4.40	4.41	4.37	4.21	4.09	4.11	4.30	4.61	4.26
1995-6	4.89	5.52	5.06	5.27	5.52	5.63	5.80	5.62	5.82	5.81	6.53	7.14	5.72
1996-7	6.73	6.04	5.29	4.63	4.69	4.64	4.51	4.62	4.45	4.62	4.78	4.58	4.97
1997-8	4.44	4.36	4.49	4.36	4.35	4.42	4.27	4.12	4.15	4.26	4.29	4.24	4.31
1998-9	4.01	3.89	3.58	3.53	4.03	4.15	3.97	3.92	3.78	3.79	3.65	3.61	3.83
1999-00	3.73	3.68	3.58	3.55	3.70	3.78	3.64	3.37	3.59	3.65	3.69	3.80	3.65
2000-1	3.78	3.50	3.29	3.17	3.69	3.77	3.52	3.79	3.68	3.63	3.73	3.88	3.62
2001-2	3.81	3.72	3.54	3.52	3.71	3.69	3.59	3.55	3.51	3.51	3.55	3.59	3.61
2002-3	3.64	4.03	4.37	5.24	5.20	4.99	4.47	4.34	4.52	4.36	4.22	4.20	4.47
2003-4[1]	4.12	4.00	4.15	4.03	4.31	4.59	4.43						4.23

[1] Preliminary.   Source: Economic Research Service, U.S. Department of Agriculture (ERS-USDA)

Average Farm Prices of Winter Wheat in the United States   In Dollars Per Bushel

Year	June	July	Aug.	Sept.	Oct.	Nov.	Dec.	Jan.	Feb.	Mar.	Apr.	May	Average
1996-7	5.14	4.67	4.52	4.28	4.07	4.05	4.04	4.02	3.90	3.98	4.14	4.14	4.25
1997-8	3.42	3.16	3.39	3.47	3.42	3.31	3.25	3.16	3.16	3.15	2.94	2.90	3.23
1998-9	2.68	2.47	2.25	2.29	2.66	2.76	2.68	2.70	2.55	2.53	2.48	2.34	2.53
1999-00	2.32	2.12	2.35	2.46	2.47	2.42	2.27	2.32	2.37	2.37	2.32	2.44	2.35
2000-1	2.43	2.23	2.31	2.37	2.63	2.70	2.76	2.77	2.74	2.85	2.77	2.94	2.63
2001-2	2.68	2.67	2.71	2.81	2.82	2.82	2.78	2.81	2.75	2.81	2.75	2.73	2.76
2002-3	2.90	3.19	3.63	4.15	4.32	4.18	3.87	3.66	3.52	3.29	3.19	3.19	3.59
2003-4[1]	2.93	2.89	3.28	3.32	3.37	3.55	3.63	3.66	3.60				3.36

[1] Preliminary.   Source: National Agricultural Statistics Service, U.S. Department of Agriculture (NASS-USDA)

Average Farm Prices of Durum Wheat in the United States   In Dollars Per Bushel

Year	June	July	Aug.	Sept.	Oct.	Nov.	Dec.	Jan.	Feb.	Mar.	Apr.	May	Average
1996-7	5.58	5.13	5.03	4.69	4.78	4.56	4.59	4.47	4.31	4.32	4.40	4.50	4.70
1997-8	4.21	4.61	5.23	5.35	5.09	5.25	5.17	5.02	4.71	4.68	4.45	4.29	4.84
1998-9	3.98	3.39	3.23	3.03	3.04	3.08	3.05	3.20	2.84	2.82	2.80	2.84	3.11
1999-00	2.93	2.89	2.76	2.29	2.30	2.64	2.96	2.90	2.88	2.63	2.89	3.02	2.76
2000-1	2.71	2.90	2.33	2.32	2.42	2.97	3.03	2.94	2.60	2.40	2.52	2.53	2.64
2001-2	3.37	2.74	2.38	3.02	2.91	3.04	3.41	3.44	3.49	3.33	3.33	3.41	3.16
2002-3	3.41	3.44	3.54	4.18	4.43	4.52	4.26	4.23	4.28	4.14	3.98	3.99	4.03
2003-4[1]	3.99	3.85	3.78	3.94	3.90	3.91	3.96	3.97	4.03				3.93

[1] Preliminary.   Source: National Agricultural Statistics Service, U.S. Department of Agriculture (NASS-USDA)

Average Farm Prices of Other Spring Wheat in the United States   In Dollars Per Bushel

Year	June	July	Aug.	Sept.	Oct.	Nov.	Dec.	Jan.	Feb.	Mar.	Apr.	May	Average
1996-7	5.48	5.30	4.63	4.41	4.23	4.11	4.01	3.95	3.80	3.83	4.04	3.94	4.31
1997-8	3.74	3.66	3.75	3.64	3.49	3.55	3.51	3.45	3.34	3.42	3.41	3.31	3.52
1998-9	3.22	3.08	2.69	2.62	3.04	3.23	3.19	3.12	3.09	3.00	2.95	2.92	3.01
1999-00	3.01	2.93	2.86	2.86	2.79	2.94	2.87	2.82	2.82	2.85	2.89	2.92	2.88
2000-1	2.90	2.74	2.59	2.59	2.80	2.97	2.98	2.96	2.99	2.99	3.05	3.13	2.89
2001-2	3.03	2.78	2.84	2.87	2.96	2.91	2.96	2.88	2.86	2.90	2.91	2.91	2.90
2002-3	2.98	3.31	3.66	4.30	4.45	4.26	4.15	4.03	3.82	3.71	3.49	3.55	3.81
2003-4[1]	3.46	3.29	3.39	3.42	3.54	3.67	3.75	3.66	3.75				3.55

[1] Preliminary.   Source: National Agricultural Statistics Service, U.S. Department of Agriculture (NASS-USDA)

WHEAT

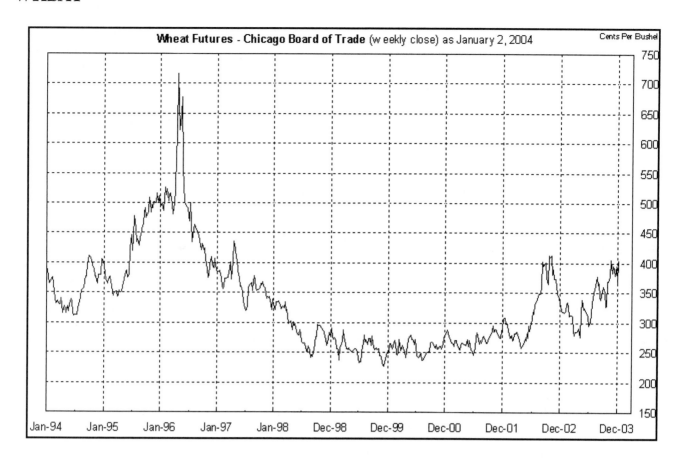

Wheat Futures - Chicago Board of Trade (weekly close) as January 2, 2004

Cents Per Bushel

Average Open Interest of Wheat Futures in Chicago   In Contracts

Year	Jan.	Feb.	Mar.	Apr.	May	June	July	Aug.	Sept.	Oct.	Nov.	Dec.
1994	53,912	48,013	45,110	47,430	44,552	54,622	57,151	65,388	73,200	78,419	70,815	67,150
1995	66,715	67,768	55,973	55,612	67,875	90,208	101,351	90,800	91,505	103,987	102,475	99,422
1996	102,718	104,807	91,378	98,260	93,378	81,211	69,222	66,128	65,561	65,639	60,810	58,533
1997	63,388	71,304	76,747	85,516	84,721	83,675	92,815	105,320	104,587	108,480	101,089	90,386
1998	96,870	99,103	97,585	114,193	115,199	116,008	121,794	127,240	125,747	131,322	130,186	116,249
1999	119,096	131,961	118,503	117,905	111,541	117,075	120,365	129,748	128,403	135,884	140,798	124,063
2000	127,419	135,316	123,980	128,462	130,938	133,527	139,194	144,953	141,803	150,592	153,287	134,997
2001	145,802	146,927	137,377	138,876	134,051	151,951	142,399	143,574	136,514	126,772	113,456	104,975
2002	118,192	118,484	112,469	112,870	96,050	98,047	118,041	131,303	129,913	114,544	101,354	82,934
2003	92,679	99,882	95,464	99,500	97,750	96,230	92,484	119,817	110,703	109,449	125,335	120,376

Source: Chicago Board of Trade (CBT)

Volume of Trading of Wheat Futures in Chicago   In Contracts

Year	Jan.	Feb.	Mar.	Apr.	May	June	July	Aug.	Sept.	Oct.	Nov.	Dec.	Total
1994	288,321	211,703	187,617	244,544	300,324	370,135	272,492	330,758	343,548	398,041	354,975	318,173	3,620,631
1995	353,603	302,950	316,330	279,099	345,455	598,762	507,876	527,716	436,145	472,794	454,352	359,985	4,955,067
1996	628,340	510,138	455,981	660,722	531,979	512,883	452,690	345,626	305,448	362,047	359,005	261,108	5,385,967
1997	312,680	373,411	368,547	567,099	422,935	469,158	470,992	493,225	401,277	405,978	432,621	340,722	5,058,645
1998	363,511	473,114	452,186	514,557	432,167	601,149	401,508	490,242	475,766	543,680	539,488	394,201	5,681,569
1999	426,524	597,448	710,375	559,211	444,696	674,580	523,516	665,897	536,014	437,689	613,633	380,442	6,570,025
2000	467,050	691,068	522,394	490,694	627,722	759,371	461,068	572,879	388,237	466,328	596,581	364,139	6,407,531
2001	551,756	595,312	536,141	579,992	537,836	720,350	695,339	600,341	385,930	629,479	614,734	354,331	6,801,541
2002	602,956	593,112	501,142	563,072	419,272	689,807	586,449	651,607	682,906	609,435	594,373	378,760	6,872,891
2003	438,021	526,001	411,017	496,770	638,590	661,840	585,073	689,593	536,452	778,863	739,791	465,405	6,967,416

Source: Chicago Board of Trade (CBT)

WHEAT

Commercial Stocks of Domestic Wheat[1] in the United States, on First of Month   In Millions of Bushels

Year	July	Aug.	Sept.	Oct.	Nov.	Dec.	Jan.	Feb.	Mar.	Apr.	May	June
1994-5	145.7	203.9	243.0	269.7	268.6	238.2	199.5	181.0	162.5	150.2	108.7	91.8
1995-6	92.3	161.7	201.1	234.3	228.3	200.2	178.7	170.8	156.6	137.7	107.6	87.2
1996-7	86.3	112.9	128.0	145.3	117.2	94.9	89.0	80.4	77.0	75.6	68.1	64.6
1997-8	80.1	186.3	235.2	268.1	258.1	231.4	196.8	178.1	170.6	158.0	146.4	145.7
1998-9	209.8	265.0	314.9	325.6	307.3	291.3	272.9	265.7	256.8	251.5	236.7	218.3
1999-00	248.6	294.9	335.8	354.0	334.6	301.5	277.4	273.7	267.8	266.3	247.6	240.3
2000-1	275.5	310.3	335.3	335.5	306.2	286.6	263.7	251.7	243.2	243.7	224.5	221.0
2001-2	271.0	296.6	318.7	321.9	291.9	251.8	224.5	224.6	217.2	195.6	177.3	176.0
2002-3	193.9	207.7	237.2	241.0	237.7	218.8	195.1	179.7	158.3	133.1	107.2	93.8
2003-4	133.3	171.9	212.0	226.3	220.7	198.1	145.0	126.3	113.1			

[1] Domestic wheat in storage in public and private elevators in 39 markets and wheat afloat in vessels or barges at lake and seaboard ports, the first Saturday of the month.   Source: Livestock Division, U.S. Department of Agriculture (LD-USDA)

Stocks of Wheat Flour Held by Mills in the United States   In Thousands of Sacks -- 100 Pounds

Year	Jan. 1	April 1	July 1	Oct. 1	Year	Jan. 1	April 1	July 1	Oct. 1
1992	5,660	5,210	5,841	5,864	1998	6,343	6,245	6,210	7,345
1993	5,487	4,863	6,197	5,882	1999	7,544	5,920	5,697	4,265
1994	5,611	5,904	5,834	6,020	2000	5,099	5,217	5,062	5,244
1995	7,060	6,496	6,312	6,582	2001	5,241	5,506	5,178	5,393
1996	6,869	6,927	6,400	6,350	2002	5,377	5,164	4,632	4,184
1997	6,671	6,040	5,820	6,330	2003[1]	4,265	4,233	4,308	4,028

[1] Preliminary.   Source: Bureau of the Census, U.S. Department of Commerce

Average Producer Price Index of Wheat Flour (Spring)   June 1983 = 100

Year	Jan.	Feb.	Mar.	Apr.	May	June	July	Aug.	Sept.	Oct.	Nov.	Dec.	Average
1994	111.8	110.5	108.9	107.9	109.4	106.4	100.8	101.2	109.1	112.0	110.9	111.4	108.4
1995	110.7	108.5	107.9	109.8	113.5	118.6	127.4	126.7	129.5	132.6	132.3	133.5	120.9
1996	130.4	138.0	136.6	137.6	160.1	146.8	138.0	127.0	121.5	125.7	121.7	121.4	133.7
1997	119.4	119.3	116.6	121.8	120.8	117.4	112.1	113.5	115.1	112.6	111.5	111.1	115.9
1998	106.8	108.1	111.5	110.1	109.9	106.4	105.5	101.8	100.9	106.6	107.8	104.8	106.7
1999	104.8	102.7	105.0	100.5	102.2	102.7	100.7	103.5	101.4	99.8	101.4	96.8	101.8
2000	99.9	99.9	100.2	99.4	100.1	101.7	100.2	100.4	101.2	105.2	103.6	104.4	101.4
2001	104.7	105.1	106.2	105.7	106.9	108.2	107.9	106.8	107.4	110.0	109.5	108.8	107.3
2002	109.6	109.6	110.6	106.5	108.2	108.8	112.6	115.5	120.9	123.0	119.3	116.6	113.4
2003[2]	119.4	121.6	120.2	120.3	122.6	121.6	119.2	122.2	120.0	116.3	122.5	124.8	120.9

[1] Standard patent.   [2] Preliminary.   Source: Bureau of Labor Statistics, U.S. Department of Commerce (BLS) (0212-0301)

World Wheat Flour Production (Monthly Average)   In Thousands of Metric Tons

Year	Australia	France	Germany	Hungary	India	Japan	Kazakhstan	Rep. of Korea	Mexico	Poland	Russia	Turkey	United Kingdom
1994	116.9	470.8	378.8	62.9	400.0	387.2	157.0	132.6	219.8	150.5	348.0	104.9	353.0
1995	112.6	473.1	382.3	84.0	400.0	389.3	131.0	139.9	210.7	156.9	274.6	119.7	358.0
1996	123.8	450.0	394.2	75.1	400.0	389.6	132.7	141.2	215.9	164.1	309.7	132.1	371.0
1997	129.7	NA	404.8	77.7	412.5	388.1	127.3	145.9	216.0	175.3	361.9	159.1	369.0
1998	146.8	NA	407.5	70.1	430.6	382.0	128.8	143.5	213.2	172.1	347.8	152.6	377.0
1999	154.8	NA	423.6	69.1	182.2	386.7	105.2	152.8	204.8	125.0	360.0	156.6	NA
2000	NA	NA	405.5	73.9	202.5	386.0	79.5	155.9	206.0	125.4	405.0	162.0	381.0
2001	NA	NA	403.1	84.4	197.2	407.9	78.2	142.8	221.1	126.8	450.9	145.2	372.5
2002[1]	NA	NA	415.3	79.2	211.6	382.0	128.6	151.2	218.1	135.2	136.2	140.4	NA
2003[2]	NA	NA	419.3	67.6	224.3	378.2	132.2	147.5	215.2	143.8	439.1	145.0	NA

[1] Preliminary.   [2] Estimate.   NA = Not available.   Source: United Nations (UN)

WHEAT

Production of Wheat Flour in the United States   In Millions of Sacks (100 Pounds Each)

Year	July	Aug.	Sept.	Oct.	Nov.	Dec.	Jan.	Feb.	Mar.	Apr.	May	June	Total
1995-6	31.0	34.5	33.0	35.1	33.4	31.2	31.6	32.3	32.2	31.2	33.2	30.6	389.3
1996-7	33.9	35.6	34.6	37.5	33.1	32.0	31.3	30.0	31.8	33.1	32.6	32.5	397.9
1997-8	34.0	34.3	35.1	37.2	33.8	33.5	-----	96.0	-----	-----	96.2	-----	400.1
1998-9	-----	100.2	-----	-----	106.5	-----	-----	96.1	-----	-----	103.5	-----	406.3
1999-00	-----	104.2	-----	-----	108.2	-----	-----	101.1	-----	-----	101.6	-----	415.2
2000-1	-----	108.8	-----	-----	109.7	-----	-----	99.4	-----	-----	97.2	-----	415.1
2001-2	-----	102.1	-----	-----	105.8	-----	-----	96.0	-----	-----	96.3	-----	400.2
2002-3	-----	102.1	-----	-----	100.3	-----	-----	95.1	-----	-----	96.0	-----	393.5
2003-4[1]	-----	102.4	-----	-----	100.8	-----	-----		-----	-----		-----	406.3

[1] Preliminary.   *Source: Bureau of the Census, U.S. Department of Commerce*

United States Wheat Flour Exports (Grain Equivalent[2])   In Thousands of Bushels

Year	June	July	Aug.	Sept.	Oct.	Nov.	Dec.	Jan.	Feb.	Mar.	Apr.	May	Total
1995-6	2,822	5,018	7,520	2,249	2,080	1,221	3,458	808	2,537	1,230	2,415	1,831	33,189
1996-7	2,006	2,008	1,669	3,133	2,496	2,748	2,240	1,347	1,920	2,521	1,259	2,125	25,472
1997-8	1,803	2,900	1,621	3,101	2,524	1,634	3,118	1,426	2,725	1,309	1,269	963	25,393
1998-9	1,971	1,740	2,027	2,914	3,812	2,354	6,838	2,551	3,341	4,126	3,105	1,948	36,728
1999-00	4,160	3,638	2,586	6,503	4,576	2,332	3,023	2,924	6,108	2,615	3,193	1,286	42,944
2000-1	3,620	3,805	1,623	3,174	4,165	2,332	2,741	2,236	2,365	2,200	3,868	2,163	34,292
2001-2	1,412	661	1,990	1,005	3,226	2,534	2,479	2,207	3,294	2,301	2,802	2,759	26,670
2002-3	1,474	1,547	753	1,373	2,437	2,854	4,645	1,049	884	1,146	1,083	541	19,786
2003-4[1]	824	1,074	3,444	1,087	765	1,295							16,978

[1] Preliminary.   [2] Includes meal, groats and durum.   *Source: Economic Research Service, U.S. Department of Agriculture (ERS-USDA)*

Supply and Distribution of Wheat Flour in the United States

Year	Wheat Ground - 1,000 Bu. -	Millfeed Production - 1,000 Tons -	Flour Production[2]	Flour & Product Imports	Total Supply	Exports Flour	Exports Products	Domestic Disappearance	Total Population July 1 - Millions -	Per Capita Disappearance - Pounds -
					In 1,000 Cwt.					
1994	884,707	7,186	392,519	8,425	400,944	23,801	811	376,332	263.2	143.0
1995	869,296	7,144	388,689	8,918	397,607	23,615	857	373,135	266.4	140.1
1996	878,070	7,042	397,776	8,574	406,350	10,651	881	394,818	269.5	146.5
1997	885,843	6,886	404,143	8,684	412,827	11,038	1,167	400,622	272.8	146.9
1998	902,532	7,301	403,880	9,830	413,625	12,574	1,353	394,817	276.0	145.9
1999	917,797	7,040	411,968	9,295	416,354	21,297	1,633	393,377	279.3	142.6
2000	944,868	7,374	421,270	9,666	403,936	16,005	1,693	413,238	282.4	146.3
2001	914,036	7,275	404,521	10,130	414,651	10,507	1,695	402,449	285.6	140.9
2002[1]	893,107	6,908	394,700	11,289	411,747	9,266	1,729	400,752	288.6	138.9

[1] Preliminary.   [2] Commercial production of wheat flour, whole wheat, industrial and durum flour and farina reported by Bureau of Census.
Source: Economic Research Service, U.S. Department of Agriculture (ERS-USDA)

Wheat and Flour -- Price Relationships at Milling Centers in the United States   In Dollars

	At Kansas City					At Minneapolis				
		Wholesale Price of		Total Products			Wholesale Price of		Total Products	
Crop Year (June-May)	Cost of Wheat to Produce 100 lb. Flour[1]	Bakery Flour 100 lb. Flour[2]	By-Products Obtained 100 lb. Flour[3]	Actual	Over Cost of Wheat	Cost of Wheat to Produce 100 lb. Flour[1]	Bakery Flour 100 lb. Flour[2]	By-Products Obtained 100 lb. Flour[3]	Actual	Over Cost of Wheat
1994-5	9.25	10.50	1.21	11.71	2.46	9.71	11.01	1.04	12.05	2.34
1995-6	12.97	13.35	1.93	15.28	2.31	13.04	13.03	1.68	14.71	1.67
1996-7	11.22	11.89	1.92	13.81	2.60	11.32	11.68	1.87	13.54	2.22
1997-8	9.03	9.99	1.43	11.41	2.38	9.83	10.62	1.34	11.96	2.12
1998-9	7.91	9.06	1.08	10.15	2.23	8.76	9.80	1.02	10.82	2.06
1999-00	7.74	8.86	.98	9.84	2.10	8.29	9.30	.95	10.24	1.95
2000-1	7.95	9.36	1.06	10.42	2.48	8.24	9.28	.97	10.24	2.01
2001-2	7.63	8.98	1.13	10.11	2.48	8.20	9.11	1.09	10.21	2.01
2002-3	9.94	11.21	1.22	12.42	2.48	9.82	11.08	1.21	12.29	2.47
June-Aug.	8.98	10.35	1.01	11.36	2.38	9.15	9.88	1.07	10.95	1.80
Sept.-Nov.	11.32	12.57	1.29	13.86	2.54	10.19	12.45	1.40	13.85	3.66
Dec.-Feb.	9.52	10.70	1.34	12.04	2.52	10.13	10.92	1.16	12.08	1.95

[1] Based on 73% extraction rate, cost of 2.28 bushels: At Kansas City, No. 1 hard winter 13% protein; and at Minneapolis, No. 1 dark northern spring,
14% protein.   [2] quoted as mid-month bakers' standard patent at Kansas City and spring standard patent at Minneapolis, bulk basis.   [3] Assumed 50-
50 millfeed distribution between bran and shorts or middlings, bulk basis.   *Source: Agricultural Marketing Service, U.S. Department of Agriculture
(AMS-USDA)*

Wool

Wool is light, warm, absorbs moisture, and is resistant to fire. Wool is also used for insulation in houses, for carpets and furnishing, and for bedding. Sheep are sheared once a year and produce about 4.3 kg of "greasy" wool per year.

Greasy wool is wool that has not been washed or cleaned. Wool fineness is determined by fiber diameter, which is measured in microns (one millionth of a meter). Fine wool is softer, lightweight, and produces fine clothing. Merino sheep produce the finest wool.

Wool futures and options are traded on the Sydney Futures Exchange (SFE), where there are futures and contracts on greasy wool, and futures on fine wool and broad wool. All three contracts call for the delivery of merino combing wool. Wool yarn futures are traded on the Chubu Commodity Exchange (CCE), the Osaka Mercantile Exchange (OME) and the Tokyo Commodity Exchange (TOCOM).

Prices – Average wool prices at US mills in 2003 rose sharply to $2.42 per pound from $1.90 in 2002, and were sharply higher than the 3-decade low of $1.09 posted in 2000. The value of US wool production was only $15 million in 2001.

Supply – World production of wool has been falling in the past decade due to the increased use of polyester fabrics. Wool production in 2000, the latest reporting year for the data series, of 1.343 million metric tons was only 1,000 tons above the record low of 1.342 metric tons posted in 1999. The world's largest produces of degreased wool in 2000 were Australia with 33% of world production, followed by New Zealand (14%), and China (11%).

US wool production of 12,000 metric tons in 2000 accounted for less than 1% of world production. US production of wool goods fell to a record low of 24.1 million yards, which represents an 87% drop from production of 184 million yards 10 years earlier in 1993. The US sheep herd fell to a record low of 5.700 million sheep in 2001, which is roughly half the herd seen 10 years ago.

Demand – US consumption of wool has dropped sharply, along with production, and fell to a record low of 37.3 million pounds in 2002. The breakdown of US mill consumption in 2001 showed that wool usage for carpets was 13.31 million pounds, which was on the lower end of the range seen in the past decade. However, the real plunge in wool usage is due to lower wool apparel consumption which fell to a record low of 52.969 million pounds in 2001, and that is sharply lower than the figure of 120 million seen 10 years earlier.

Trade – US exports of domestic wool totaled 6.200 million pounds in 2001, while imports were double that at 15.817 million pounds.

World Production of Wool   In Metric Tons--Degreased

Year	Argentina	Australia	China	Kazak-hstan	New Zealand	Pakistan	Romania	Russia	South Africa	United Kingdom	United States	Uruguay	Total
1994	48,000	570,000	130,000	55,000	214,000	31,000	17,000	73,000	40,000	47,000	16,000	50,000	1,693,000
1995	44,000	475,000	141,000	35,000	214,000	32,000	16,000	56,000	35,000	48,000	15,000	46,000	1,512,000
1996	39,000	457,000	152,000	25,000	199,000	32,000	16,000	46,000	37,000	46,000	13,000	43,000	1,459,000
1997	36,000	472,000	130,000	21,000	228,000	34,000	13,000	36,000	34,000	46,000	13,000	46,000	1,440,000
1998	34,000	452,000	141,000	15,000	219,000	23,000	12,000	29,000	32,000	48,000	12,000	42,000	1,388,000
1999	36,000	437,000	144,000	13,000	220,000	23,000	13,000	24,000	34,000	47,000	11,000	34,000	1,369,000
2000	32,000	452,000	146,000	14,000	202,000	23,000	11,000	20,000	32,000	45,000	11,000	32,000	1,356,000
2001[1]	32,000	416,000	149,000	14,000	199,000	24,000	10,000	20,000	32,000	39,000	10,000	32,000	1,310,000
2002[2]	31,000	395,000	152,000	14,000	199,000	24,000	12,000	20,000	32,000	42,000	10,000	27,000	1,292,000

[1] Preliminary.   [2] Estimate.   *Source: Food and Agriculture Organization of the United Nations (FAO-UN)*

Production of Wool Goods[1] in the United States   In Millions of Yards

Year	First Quarter	Second Quarter	Third Quarter	Fourth Quarter	Total	Year	First Quarter	Second Quarter	Third Quarter	Fourth Quarter	Total
1994	49.1	51.1	39.4	39.0	178.6	1999	25.0	20.9	17.4	14.6	77.9
1995	46.8	45.9	35.2	34.3	162.2	2000	17.9	18.0	13.4	17.4	66.7
1996	44.8	43.6	30.8	32.8	152.0	2001	20.8	12.4	11.0	9.0	53.2
1997	42.7	49.7	42.3	40.5	175.2	2002	7.4	8.6	6.2	5.5	27.7
1998	38.8	37.5	29.6	26.3	132.2	2003[2]	6.6	6.3	5.2	4.7	22.8

[1] Woolen and worsted woven goods, except woven felts.   [2] Preliminary.   *Source: Bureau of the Census, U.S. Department of Commerce*

Consumption of Apparel Wool in the United States   In Millions of Pounds--Clean Basis

Year	First Quarter	Second Quarter	Third Quarter	Fourth Quarter	Total	Year	First Quarter	Second Quarter	Third Quarter	Fourth Quarter	Total
1994	36.3	35.6	32.7	34.0	138.6	1999	17.3	16.8	15.8	13.6	63.5
1995	36.3	35.5	29.4	28.1	129.3	2000	17.4	16.1	14.6	13.9	62.0
1996	39.1	36.2	27.4	26.8	129.5	2001	17.0	13.5	11.6	10.9	53.0
1997	33.1	33.8	30.6	32.8	130.4	2002	11.0	10.5	6.5	W	37.3
1998	29.3	29.6	21.9	17.5	98.4	2003[2]	W	W	W	W	W

[1] Woolen and worsted woven goods, except woven felts.   [2] Preliminary.   *Source: Bureau of the Census, U.S. Department of Commerce*

WOOL

Salient Statistics of Wool in the United States

Year	Sheep & Lambs Shorn[4] -1,000's-	Weight Per Fleece -In Lbs.-	Shorn Wool Production 1,000 Lbs.	Price Per Lb.	Value of Production 1,000 $	Payment Support --Cents Per Lb.--	Payment Rate	Total Wool Production	Domestic Production	Exports Domestic Wool	Dutiable Imports for Consumption[3] 48's & Finer	Total New Supply[2]	Duty Free Imports (Not Finer than 46's)	Mill Consumption Apparel	Mill Consumption Carpet
								In Thousands of Pounds							
1994	8,877	7.73	68,577	78.0	52,377	209	131.0	68,577	36,209	2,863	64,889	122,880	24,645	138,563	14,739
1995	8,138	7.80	63,513	104.0	64,277	212	108.0	63,513	33,535	6,042	63,781	116,313	25,039	129,299	12,667
1996	7,279	7.79	56,669	70.0	39,659	----	----	56,159	29,921	5,715	54,063	99,575	20,971	129,525	12,311
1997	7,032	7.70	53,889	84.0	45,172	----	----	53,578	28,630	4,732	51,484	100,003	24,295	130,386	13,576
1998	6,428	7.70	49,255	60.0	29,415	----	----	49,255	30,321	1,700	45,760	94,814	23,121	98,373	16,331
1999	6,150	7.60	46,549	38.0	17,860	----	20.0	46,549	24,800	3,694	21,251	63,955	20,723	63,535	13,950
2000	6,100	7.60	46,400	33.0	15,377	----	40.0	46,446	24,500	6,629	23,874	62,785	20,003	62,041	15,205
2001	5,700	7.60	43,000	36.0	15,311	----	----	43,016	22,700	6,154	15,817	52,128	18,667	52,969	13,310
2002[1]	5,500	7.60	41,200	53.0		100	----		21,700	8,500	10,526		14,012	36,015	6,891

[1] Preliminary. [2] Production minus exports plus imports; stocks not taken into consideration. [3] Apparel wool includes all dutiable wool; carpet wool includes all duty-free wool. [4] Includes sheep shorn at commercial feeding yards. *Source: Economic Research Service, U.S. Department of Agriculture (ERS-USDA)*

Shorn Wool Prices

Year	U.S. Farm Price Shorn Wool Greasy Basis[1] -Cents/Lb.-	Australian Offering Price, Clean[2] — Grade 70's Type 61	Grade 64's Type 63	Grade 64/70's Type 62	Grade 60/62's Type 64A	Grade 58's-56's 433-34	Market Indicator[3] -Cents/Kg.-	Graded Territory Shorn Wool, Clean Basis[4] — 64's Staple 2 3/4" & up	60's Staple 3" & up	58's Staple 3 1/4" & up	56's Staple 3 1/4" & up	54's Staple 3 1/2" & up
		In Dollars Per Pound						In Dollars Per Pound				
1994	78.0	3.72	2.43	3.01	1.96	1.86	547	2.12	1.50	1.26	1.27	1.21
1995	104.0	3.22	2.81	3.01	2.49	2.33	888	2.49	1.93	1.77	1.63	1.53
1996	70.0	2.81	2.34	2.54	1.96	1.84	619	1.93	1.54	1.43	1.31	1.22
1997	84.0	3.56	2.57	2.90	2.06	1.95	615	2.38	1.78	1.64	1.43	1.14
1998	60.0	2.60	1.84	1.92	1.64	1.60	663	1.62	1.31	1.21	1.06	.94
1999	38.0	2.53	1.48	1.66	1.36	1.33	524	1.10	.85	.74	.66	.59
2000	33.0	2.80	1.50	1.69	1.37	1.30	625	1.08	.75	.65	.57	.53
2001	36.0	2.42	1.66	1.69	1.60	1.54	764	1.21	.91	.77	.66	.65
2002	53.0	2.87	2.68	2.70	2.63	2.55	841	1.90	1.41	1.40	1.19	1.02

[1] Annual weighted average. [2] F.O.B. Australian Wool Corporation South Carolina warehouse in bond. [3] Index of prices of all wool sold in Australia for the crop year July-June. [4] Wool principally produced in Texas and the Rocky Mountain States. *Source: Economic Research Service, U.S. Department of Agriculture (ERS-USDA)*

Average Wool Prices[1] --Australian-- 64's, Type 62, Duty Paid--U.S. Mills   In Cents Per Pound

Year	Jan.	Feb.	Mar.	Apr.	May	June	July	Aug.	Sept.	Oct.	Nov.	Dec.	Average
1994	204	216	205	223	249	258	243	248	259	256	273	297	244
1995	281	297	302	302	307	308	292	284	266	236	242	237	280
1996	240	237	238	234	242	245	236	234	228	220	225	232	234
1997	234	261	254	261	279	287	NA	270	262	250	245	240	258
1998	218	225	247	205	214	179	NA	144	144	140	156	147	184
1999	158	150	157	156	150	149	152	148	139	139	143	137	148
2000	154	146	144	156	156	154	155	151	149	146	140	148	150
2001	160	168	164	158	164	166	167	172	169	159	166	183	166
2002	218	243	250	251	249	259	255	254	268	312	322	328	267
2003	344	346	326	333	299	326	316	308	306	292	285	290	314

[1] Raw, clean basis. NA = Not available. *Source: Economic Research Service, U.S. Department of Agriculture (ERS-USDA)*

Average Wool Prices --Domestic[1]-- Graded Territory, 64's, Staple 2 3/4 & Up--U.S. Mills   In Cents Per Pound

Year	Jan.	Feb.	Mar.	Apr.	May	June	July	Aug.	Sept.	Oct.	Nov.	Dec.	Average
1994	140	150	170	201	226	230	230	235	250	238	238	252	213
1995	245	252	265	288	295	285	261	250	235	185	208	192	247
1996	188	192	197	197	195	192	192	192	192	192	190	190	192
1997	190	190	208	228	248	255	255	255	255	255	260	260	238
1998	236	195	195	188	177	170	170	150	115	115	115	115	162
1999	115	115	115	110	117	122	116	110	105	100	110	95	111
2000	95	95	101	110	125	125	125	120	107	105	105	97	109
2001	95	100	108	129	137	125	127	122	126	130	122	127	121
2002	134	150	170	181	189	200	200	200	198	204	223	233	190
2003	236	260	258	250	223	234	239	243	243	243	232	233	241

[1] Raw, shorn, clean basis. *Source: Economic Research Service, U.S. Department of Agriculture (ERS-USDA)*

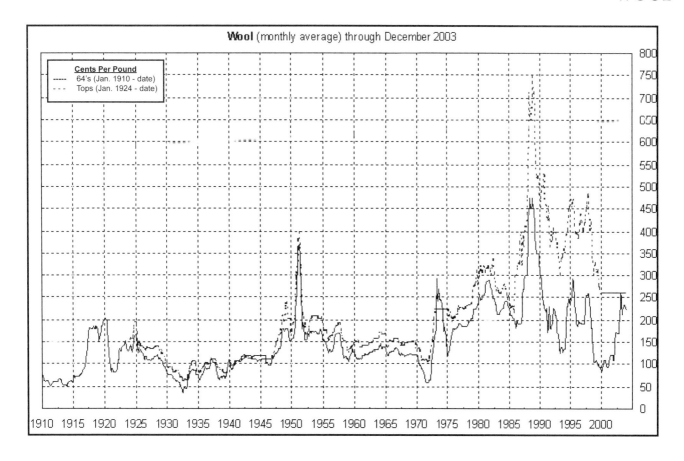

Wool: Mill Consumption, by Grades in the U.S., Scoured Basis   In Millions of Pounds

| | Apparel Class[1] | | | | | | | |
| | Woolen System | | | Worsted System | | | | |
Year	60's & Finer	Coarser Than 60's	Total	60's & Finer	Coarser Than 60's	Total	All Total	Carpet Wool[2]
1993	40,895	26,624	67,519	58,834	15,027	73,861	141,380	15,431
1994	35,960	26,038	61,998	59,599	16,966	76,565	138,563	14,739
1995	30,211	27,089	57,300	54,980	17,019	71,999	129,299	12,667
1996	42,141	27,575	69,716	46,057	13,752	59,809	129,525	12,311
1997	49,038	21,303	70,341	48,153	11,892	60,045	130,386	13,576
1998	31,258	15,079	46,337	42,243	9,793	52,036	98,373	16,331
1999	18,379	10,772	29,151	27,429	6,955	34,384	63,535	13,950
2000	18,503	13,432	31,935	NA	NA	30,106	62,041	15,205
2001[3]	16,062	9,849	25,911	NA	NA	27,058	52,969	13,310
2002[4]	9,627	8,482	18,109	NA	NA	17,906	36,015	6,891

[1] Domestic & duty-paid foreign.   [2] Duty-free foreign.   [3] Preliminary.   [4] Estimate.   *Source: Economic Research Service, U.S. Department of Agriculture (ERS-USDA)*

United States Imports[1] of Unmanufactured Wool (Clean Yield)   In Millions of Pounds

Year	Jan.	Feb.	Mar.	Apr.	May	June	July	Aug.	Sept.	Oct.	Nov.	Dec.	Total
1994	10.0	7.7	7.7	12.7	7.5	7.7	6.9	6.5	4.1	5.7	8.1	7.0	91.7
1995	10.4	7.7	10.8	6.0	11.5	5.2	7.3	7.3	4.9	7.9	7.7	4.1	90.6
1996	9.6	9.1	8.8	5.6	7.0	5.9	5.3	6.6	3.1	4.6	4.6	5.1	75.3
1997	5.1	5.8	5.8	6.6	5.8	4.2	4.9	4.2	4.8	8.5	7.3	8.6	71.5
1998	8.8	5.4	5.4	7.2	5.9	5.5	5.7	4.4	3.3	7.3	4.9	4.3	68.0
1999	6.2	3.6	3.9	7.9	3.5	3.0	3.7	3.1	2.6	3.8	2.8	2.5	46.3
2000	4.9	3.8	3.8	4.6	5.1	2.7	3.2	3.7	4.3	3.2	3.5	2.4	45.0
2001	4.9	4.3	4.3	1.5	2.9	2.8	4.0	1.9	2.0	2.8	1.3	1.3	34.1
2002	1.9	1.8	2.6	2.4	2.3	1.5	1.6	1.2	1.9	2.4	2.1	3.1	24.6
2003[2]	2.5	2.8	2.3	2.2	2.1	1.8	1.2	1.1	0.8	1.6	1.1	1.2	20.8

[1] For consumption.   [2] Preliminary.   *Source: Economic Research Service, U.S. Department of Agriculture (ERS-USDA)*

Zinc

Zinc is utilized as a protective coating for other metals, such as iron and steel, in a process known as galvanizing. Zinc finds use as an alloy with copper to make brass and also as an alloy with aluminum and magnesium. There are, however, a number of substitutes for zinc in chemicals, electronics, and pigments. For example, with aluminum, steel and plastics can substitute for galvanized sheets. Aluminum alloys can also replace brass.

Zinc futures and options are traded on the London Metals Exchange (LME). The LME zinc futures contract calls for the delivery of 25 metric tons of at least 99.995% purity zinc ingots (slabs and plates). The contract trades in terms of US dollars per metric ton. Zinc first started trading on the LME in 1915.

Prices – Zinc prices in 2003 rose to an average 40.36 cents per pound from the 23-year low of 39.64 cents in 2002. Zinc prices were depressed in 2002 due to the weak economy and were able to rally along with the other metals in 2003 due to the weak dollar and stronger economy. Still, the 40.36-cent-price of zinc in 2003 was well below the 51-56 cent area seen in 1998-2000 before the US economic slowdown began in 2000.

Supply – World smelter production of zinc in 2002 fell −4.7% to a 3-year low of 8.910 million metric tons from 9.350 million metric tons in 2001. The world's largest producer of zinc is Canada with 8.9% of world smelter production in 2002, followed by Japan with 7.5%, and Australia with 6.4%. US smelter production accounted for only 3.3% of world production in 2002. Australia's production has been rising rapidly in recent years and in 2002, production of 271,500 metric tons was up 75% from just four years earlier. Mexico's production has also been rising rapidly and 2002 production of 320,000 metric tons was up nearly 50% from three years earlier.

US mine production of recoverable zinc was on track to fall to 745,100 metric tons in 2003, down from 754,600 in 2002, but above the 10-year US production average of 698,000. US production of slab zinc on a primary basis fell to 182,000 metric tons in 2002 from 203,000 in 2001, while

secondary production rose to 113,000 metric tons in 2002 from 108,000 in 2001.

Demand – US consumption of slab zinc in 2002 rose slightly to 1.180 million metric tons from the 9-year low of 1.1140 million posted in 2001. US consumption of all classes of zinc in 2003 rose to 1.43 million metric tons from the 9-year low of 1.410 million metric tons in 2001. Consumption of slab zinc by fabricators in the US was on track to rise to 420,300 metric tons in 2003, up 16.7% from 403,600 metric tons in 2002. The 2002 production level was a record low going back to the beginning of the data series in 1979.

The breakdown of consumption by industries for 2002 showed that galvanizers accounted for 53% of slab zinc consumption, 21% by the zinc-base industry, 18% for brass products, and the rest for other miscellaneous industries. The consumption breakdown by grades showed that 59% was special high grade, 23% prime western, 12% high grade, and 6% re-melt and other. Within that grade breakdown, high grade has been rising while prime Western consumption has fallen by nearly half in the past 3 years.

Trade – The US relies on imports for 60% of its consumption of zinc, up sharply from the 35% average seen in the 1990s. US imports for consumption of slab zinc rose to 874,000 metric tons in 2002 from 813,000 metric tons in 2001, while imports of zinc ore rose to 122,000 metric tons from 84,000 metric tons in 2001. The dollar value of US zinc imports in 2002 fell to an 8-year low of $888 million from $937 million in 2001.

The breakdown of imports in 2002 versus 2001 shows gains in the imports of (1) ore, (2) blocks, pigs and slabs, (3) dross, ashes and fume, and (4) dust, powder and flakes. Declines were seen in the imports of (1) sheets, plates, and other, and (2) waste/scrap. Regarding zinc exports, US exports of zinc ore and concentrates rose to 822,000 metric tons in 2002 from 696,000 metric tons in 2001. US waste/scrap exports in 2002 rose to 47,700 from 44,000 metric tons, and zinc dust (blue powder) exports rose to 5,600 from 4,690 metric tons.

Salient Statistics of Zinc in the United States   In Metric Tons

Year	Slab Zinc Production Primary	Secondary	Mine Production (Recovered)	Imports for Consumption Slab Zinc	Ore (Zinc Content)	Exports Slab Zinc	Ore (Zinc Content)	Consumption Slab Zinc	Consumed as Ore	All Classes[3]	Net Import Reliance as a % of Consumption	High-Grade, Price -Cents/Lb.-
1993	240,000	141,000	488,374	723,563	33,093	1,410	311,278	1,120,000	2,200	1,340,000	36	46.15
1994	216,600	139,000	570,000	793,000	27,374	6,310	389,000	1,180,000	2,400	1,400,000	35	49.26
1995	232,000	131,000	603,000	856,000	10,300	3,080	424,000	1,230,000	2,400	1,460,000	35	55.83
1996	226,000	140,000	586,000	827,000	15,100	1,970	425,000	1,210,000	1,400	1,450,000	33	51.11
1997	226,000	141,000	605,000	876,000	49,600	3,630	461,000	1,260,000	----	1,500,000	35	64.56
1998	234,000	134,000	722,000	879,000	46,300	2,330	552,000	1,290,000	----	1,590,000	35	51.43
1999	241,000	131,000	808,000	1,060,000	74,600	1,880	531,000	1,430,000	----	1,700,000	30	53.48
2000	228,000	143,000	805,000	915,000	52,800	2,770	523,000	1,330,000	----	1,630,000	60	55.61
2001[1]	203,000	108,000	799,000	813,000	84,000	1,180	696,000	1,140,000	----	1,410,000	60	43.96
2002[2]	182,000	113,000	754,000	874,000	122,000	1,160	822,000	1,180,000	----	1,430,000	60	38.64

[1] Preliminary.   [2] Estimate.   [3] Based on apparent consumption of slab zinc plus zinc content of ores and concentrates and secondary materials used to make zinc dust and chemicals.   Source: U.S. Geological Survey (USGS)

World Smelter Production of Zinc[3]   In Thousands of Metric Tons

Year	Australia	Belgium	Canada	France	Germany	Italy	Japan	Kazakhstan	Mexico	Poland	Spain	United States	World Total
1993	321.0	299.6	659.9	310.0	380.9	182.0	744.6	263.0	209.9	149.1	341.6	382.0	7,360
1994	328.0	306.2	691.0	306.0	359.9	203.6	713.0	172.4	209.2	154.4	294.7	356.0	7,330
1995	325.0	301.1	720.3	300.0	322.5	180.4	711.1	169.2	222.7	162.7	358.0	363.0	7,370
1996	331.0	234.4	715.6	324.3	327.0	269.0	642.3	190.0	221.7	163.1	360.8	366.0	7,610
1997	317.0	243.6	703.8	346.1	251.7	227.7	650.2	189.0	231.4	171.0	364.2	367.0	7,920
1998	322.0	205.0	745.1	321.0	334.0	231.6	652.7	240.7	230.3	175.0	360.0	368.0	8,170
1999	348.5	232.4	776.9	333.1	333.0	152.8	683.6	249.3	218.9	178.9	393.0	371.0	8,550
2000	494.5	251.7	779.9	350.0	350.0	170.3	698.8	262.2	303.8	173.0	386.3	371.0	9,190
2001[1]	558.5	259.3	661.2	347.0	347.0	177.8	684.1	277.1	320.0	174.7	418.0	311.0	9,350
2002[2]	571.5	260.0	793.5	350.0	350.0	176.0	670.6	286.3	320.0	175.0	488.0	294.0	8,910

[1] Preliminary.   [2] Estimate.   [3] Secondary metal included.   *Source: U.S. Geological Survey (USGS)*

Consumption (Reported) of Slab Zinc in the United States, by Industries and Grades   In Metric Tons

Year	Total	By Industries					By Grades			
		Galvanizers	Brass Products	Zinc-Base Alloy[3]	Zinc Oxide	Other	Special High Grade	High Grade	Remelt and Other	Prime Western
1993	1,035,000	532,400	139,500	222,000	63,448	141,100	403,696	116,500	71,202	182,309
1994	859,000	395,000	107,000	196,000	68,300	92,400	486,000	112,000	68,400	192,000
1995	1,240,000	390,000	91,500	194,000	70,900	90,800	135,000	98,200	54,400	251,000
1996	788,000	398,000	87,400	142,000	[4]	161,000	385,000	111,000	54,000	238,000
1997	672,000	347,000	76,800	107,000	[4]	141,000	319,000	88,700	57,200	207,000
1998	647,000	320,000	60,300	122,000	[4]	145,000	331,000	72,800	51,700	192,000
1999	614,000	308,000	78,200	105,000	[4]	124,000	317,000	58,400	55,400	184,000
2000	640,000	293,000	82,800	123,000	[4]	NA	332,000	60,600	41,500	206,000
2001[1]	543,000	281,000	74,400	91,200	[4]	NA	294,000	54,000	30,300	165,000
2002[2]	496,000	265,000	86,800	103,000	[4]	NA	294,000	61,400	28,000	113,000

[1] Preliminary.   [2] Estimated.   [3] Die casters.   [4] Included in other.   *Source: U.S. Geological Survey (USGS)*

United States Foreign Trade of Zinc   In Metric Tons

Year	Ores[1]	Imports for Consumption						Zinc Ore & Manufactures Exported						
		Blocks, Pigs, Slabs	Sheets, Plates, Other	Waste & Scrap	Dross, Ashes, Fume	Dust, Powder & Flakes	Total Value $1,000	Blocks, Pigs, Anodes, etc. — Unwrought	Unwrought Alloys	Wrought & Alloys — Sheets, Plates & Strips	Angles, Bars, Rods, etc.	Waste & Scrap	Dust (Blue Powder)	Zinc Ore & Concentrates
1993	33,093	723,563	135	38,079	11,862	16,218	799,999	8,765	----	----	----	46,385	6,727	311,278
1994	27,374	793,482	475	51,676	12,152	11,954	878,100	13,220	----	----	----	58,297	6,603	389,488
1995	10,300	856,000	332	42,300	10,900	11,700	1,018,620	----	----	----	----	55,900	8,840	424,000
1996	15,100	827,000	16,900	31,900	14,500	10,300	1,001,800	----	----	----	----	45,500	11,100	425,000
1997	49,600	876,000	19,200	29,600	----	11,700	1,340,390	----	----	----	----	46,100	9,980	461,000
1998	46,300	879,000	16,900	29,200	----	17,600	1,098,690	----	----	----	----	35,000	5,530	552,000
1999	74,600	966,000	22,600	26,600	20,000	21,300	1,133,890	----	----	----	----	28,200	5,050	531,000
2000	52,800	915,000	9,380	36,500	15,500	26,700	1,272,750	----	----	----	----	36,100	4,830	523,000
2001[2]	84,000	813,000	7,240	39,300	12,000	26,700	937,110	----	----	----	----	44,000	4,690	696,000
2002[3]	122,000	874,000	1,640	31,200	15,500	30,900	887,785	----	----	----	----	47,700	5,660	822,000

[1] Zinc content.   [2] Preliminary.   [3] Estimate.   NA = Not available.   *Source: U.S. Geological Survey (USGS)*

Mine Production of Recoverable Zinc in the United States   In Thousands of Metric Tons

Year	Jan.	Feb.	Mar.	Apr.	May	June	July	Aug.	Sept.	Oct.	Nov.	Dec.	Total
1994	43.2	40.2	48.4	44.0	47.9	47.1	52.5	47.1	50.1	41.6	46.0	48.0	557.0
1995	49.8	48.1	52.8	45.6	54.5	50.0	50.2	55.0	48.1	52.0	47.8	48.1	601.0
1996	52.4	48.9	49.7	45.5	50.7	49.9	53.7	48.1	46.8	43.4	43.1	42.6	600.0
1997	46.2	45.7	45.8	47.9	49.7	45.3	45.9	49.8	53.0	47.6	44.2	48.4	574.0
1998	50.1	48.3	56.5	56.2	56.7	55.0	59.5	57.2	60.1	55.7	62.0	61.9	722.0
1999	61.4	57.6	63.0	67.0	61.7	62.8	68.2	72.1	60.8	67.8	61.2	65.9	808.0
2000	64.4	56.6	68.5	64.5	70.2	65.3	68.1	71.4	59.6	62.3	63.5	67.2	814.0
2001	68.4	60.5	62.2	65.2	66.9	66.1	66.7	67.6	60.9	67.1	54.0	55.4	799.0
2002	61.3	60.4	67.8	55.2	63.4	63.8	66.0	67.2	54.4	68.3	61.3	65.5	754.6
2003[1]	65.2	60.2	62.7	54.0	65.2	64.0	64.5	59.6	63.3	58.6	61.0	60.5	738.8

[1] Preliminary.   *Source: U.S. Geological Survey (USGS)*

ZINC

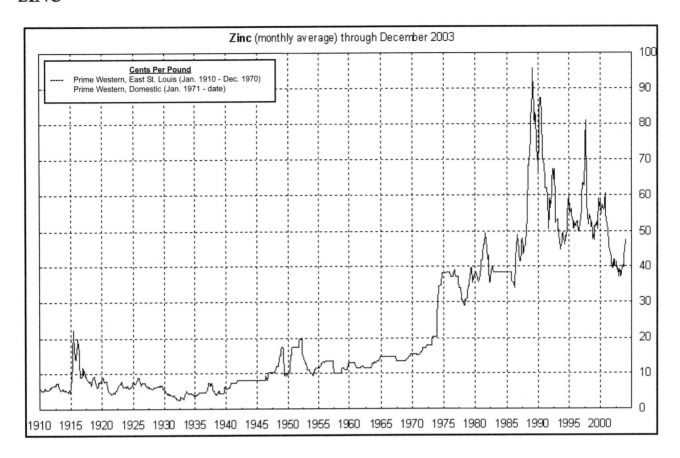

Zinc (monthly average) through December 2003

Cents Per Pound
----- Prime Western, East St. Louis (Jan. 1910 - Dec. 1970)
Prime Western, Domestic (Jan. 1971 - date)

Consumption of Slab Zinc by Fabricators in the United States   In Thousands of Metric Tons

Year	Jan.	Feb.	Mar.	Apr.	May	June	July	Aug.	Sept.	Oct.	Nov.	Dec.	Average
1994	50.8	53.7	55.7	58.5	58.7	52.7	48.0	53.2	53.6	53.9	52.5	45.0	623.0
1995	51.3	57.8	56.3	57.9	53.4	58.0	44.0	44.0	58.8	57.0	56.0	54.5	838.0
1996	56.3	55.6	59.3	55.7	56.3	55.9	48.9	48.1	54.4	56.4	54.2	53.1	788.0
1997	47.2	43.1	48.6	50.1	48.1	45.3	45.1	45.5	50.9	49.6	44.3	46.2	588.0
1998	46.3	45.2	47.4	44.8	45.4	49.0	46.0	45.0	45.9	45.9	40.5	43.9	647.0
1999	40.5	45.4	43.8	40.3	42.5	47.1	37.8	40.1	42.0	42.8	41.1	39.7	614.0
2000	41.8	44.6	47.7	45.6	44.4	49.1	42.0	43.3	42.6	47.5	43.8	40.2	640.0
2001	45.4	43.5	44.1	42.7	43.6	38.2	30.6	39.2	37.7	35.7	32.1	27.3	543.0
2002	31.2	31.3	30.4	33.1	34.9	34.4	34.3	35.8	36.1	36.1	32.7	33.3	403.6
2003[1]	33.1	33.1	34.4	35.2	34.7	38.2	34.2	35.5	36.8	36.8	35.3	36.1	423.4

[1] Preliminary.   Source: U.S. Geological Survey (USGS)

Average Price of Zinc, Prime Western Slab (Delivered U.S. Basis)   In Cents Per Pound

Year	Jan.	Feb.	Mar.	Apr.	May	June	July	Aug.	Sept.	Oct.	Nov.	Dec.	Total
1994	49.64	48.29	46.70	46.16	47.66	48.42	48.81	48.26	50.55	53.81	58.64	57.41	50.36
1995	60.11	55.44	54.84	56.08	54.61	53.08	53.75	52.00	50.77	50.42	52.52	51.60	53.77
1996	51.38	51.86	52.66	51.03	50.76	49.75	49.86	50.86	51.22	51.76	53.81	53.39	51.53
1997	55.64	59.82	63.28	62.62	65.65	67.78	75.29	80.89	78.96	62.55	57.83	54.45	65.40
1998	55.43	51.86	51.98	54.31	52.77	50.78	52.23	51.64	50.29	47.63	48.74	48.44	51.23
1999	47.29	51.11	51.68	51.07	52.20	50.35	53.73	56.28	59.12	57.07	56.91	58.75	53.84
2000	58.44	54.67	55.60	56.14	57.44	55.67	56.52	58.04	60.53	54.67	53.07	53.00	56.15
2001	51.82	51.29	50.55	48.95	47.54	45.56	43.62	42.53	41.14	39.53	39.99	39.25	45.15
2002	40.98	39.97	42.15	41.66	39.97	39.70	41.01	38.91	39.26	39.08	36.99	38.52	39.64
2003	38.88	38.46	38.48	36.99	37.86	38.57	40.30	39.77	39.84	43.44	44.11	47.60	40.36

Source: American Metal Market (AMM)

CRB Yearbooks CD

Table of Contents

QuickSearch is a trademark of dataDisc, Inc.
Segments of this manual reprinted with permission by dataDisc, Inc.

Factual information contained in the CRB Yearbooks CD has been obtained from sources believed to be reliable but are not necessarily inclusive and are not guaranteed in any way and should not be construed as a representation by us.

Chapter 1: Installation

Installing QuickSearch

To run QuickSearch, you will need:
- 386/25 processor or faster
- Windows 3.1, Windows NT or Windows 95/98/00
- 5 MB of memory
- 5 MB of hard disk space
- CD-ROM drive
- Mouse or compatible pointer

To Install:
1) Place the disc in the CD-ROM drive. If installation does not start automatically proceed to step 2.
2) Click Start; Select Run
3) Type D:\Autoplay, where D is the letter representing your CD-ROM drive. Press the enter key and follow the instructions.

Chapter 2: Searching and Browsing

Selecting Text to Search

Searches can be conducted across all the text in a *QuickSearch* document (full-text), restricted to a specific field (fielded search), or restricted to a selected table of contents section.

Everywhere in text - searches the full text of the *QuickSearch* document (except for user-defined notes and bookmarks). Choose **Everywhere in text** in the Search dialog box to specify a full-text search.

Fielded Search - searches a specific field and ignores all text outside of that field. To specify a fielded search:

1) Click **Selected field** under **Select where to search.**
2) Select a field from the list of available fields.

Current Table of Contents section - restricts a research only to a Table of Contents (TOC) section.

1) Click the TOC section in the TOC window.
2) Click the Search button on the toolbar <u>OR</u> select Search/Search from the main menu.
3) Click *Current Table of Contents section* under *Select where to search.*

Note: Search results will represent the selected TOC Section and its sublevels.

Types of Searches

Search for Phrase
Type an exact phrase you wish to find, e.g. "Business is the key." Use quotation marks around the search text to distinguish a *phrase search* from a *word search* or choose *Search for phrase* in the **Search/More>>** dialog box. The QuickSearch default setting is a phrase search.

Search for Words
Two types of word searches may be conducted - single words or words in proximity as determined by **Search Operators**. To conduct a word search, choose *Search for word(s)* in the **Search/More>>** dialog box.

1) **Single Word** - Enter any single word, e.g. BUSI-NESS, to find all occurrences in the document.

2) **Words in Proximity** - Enter any series of words that you wish to find near each other (e.g. BUSINESS INCREASE). Before conducting a *proximity search*, define a search range/proximity in the **Search/ More>>** dialog box. The default setting is 4 words. A typical sentence has 10 words, a typical paragraph has 25 words, and a typical page has 500 words.

Refine Last Search

The **Refine last search** feature can be used to modify your most recent search. (See the Advanced Searching section of this chapter.)

Search Operators

Boolean, wildcard and phrase search operators are available by selecting **MORE>>** in the **Search** dialog box. Double-click on any operator to add it to the Search command line *or* type the operator in the **Type the text to find** box.

To see example of each operator:
- Click the **Search** button and then the **More>>** button.
  OR
- Select **Search/Search** from the main menu and **More>>**.
- Click once on the operator you wish to view.

The following operators are available for a word search:

AND (&) - BUSINESS AND INCREASE - Returns all occurrences of BUSINESS and INCREASE in the specified search range that are near each other. "Near" is defined using the Word Proximity setting in the **Search/ More>>** dialog box.

OR (|) - BUSINESS OR INCREASE - Returns all occurrences of the words in the specified search range without regard to proximity.

NOT (~) - BUSINESS NOT INCREASE - Returns all occurrences of the word BUSINESS that are not near the word INCREASE in the specified search range. "Near" is defined using the Word Proximity setting in the **Search/ More>>** dialog box.

Wildcard (*) - Use the asterisk (*) at the end of any part of a word to represent any character or combination of characters. For example, BUSI* may return hits such as *business, businesses, busing,* and *Businowski*. The wildcard operator cannot be used in a phrase search.

Conducting a Search

Basic Searching

1) Click the Search button on the Reader toolbar OR select Search/Search from the main menu.

2) In the **Search** dialog box, select where to search choosing one of the following:
- Everywhere in text
- Selected field*
- Current Table of Contents

*Note: Click a field or a TOC entry before choosing Selected field or Current Table of Contents section.

3) Type the search text (word, words within proximity or phrase) in the *Type the text to find* box or double click on any entry in the **Word Wheel** to select it as search text.

4) Click **Search** in the dialog box. "Hits" will be highlighted in the text and displayed in context in a separate **Hit List** window. The number of hits also will be displayed on the status bar at the bottom of the screen.

Advanced Searching

Search for Words

1) Begin a search by completing steps 1-3 of a Basic Search.

2) Select **More>>** to expand the Search dialog box and change to a *Search for Word(s)* and/or select other **Search Operators** which alter the nature of the search to be conducted. A *Search for Phrase* is conducted unless you select another type of search.

3) Specify the **Word Proximity** in the **Search/ More>>** dialog box, if you are conducting an AND or NOT search. The default proximity is 4 words.

4) Click **Search** in the dialog box. "Hits" will be highlighted in the text and displayed in context in a separate **Hit List** window. The number of hits also will be displayed on the status bar at the bottom of the screen.

Refine Last Search

To refine the last research:

1) Begin a search by completing steps 1-3 of a Basic Search. Click the **More>>** button on the **Search** dialog box to access all search parameters.

2) Click the **Refine last search** box in the lower left corner of the **Search** dialog box.

3) Select the **Boolean** operator to be applied to the refined search (just to the right of the *Refine last search* check box).

4) Preview the format for the refined search in the *Refined Search box* at the bottom of the **Search** dialog box.

5) Type the **[New text to Find]** word(s) in the *Type the text to find* box at the top of the **Search** dialog box.

6) Click **Search**.

Example:

Your first search in the Constitution was for the word "House." If you want to narrow the search results to include only hits of "House" which are not near "senate," you can return to the **Search** dialog box, select **Refine last search**, select the *NOT* operator, specify the word proximity, type "Senate" in the *Type the text t*o find box at the top of the **Search** dialog box and click the **Search** button. The **Hit List** will display only hits of "House" which were not located near "Senate" ("near" depends on the proximity that you specified). The final search command would look as follows:

(House) ~ (Senate)

This search could be further refined by selecting **Refine last search** and repeating the steps above.

Example:

If you want to find only occurrences of "House *NOT* Senate" which are near "Representative," return to the Search dialog box, select **Refine last search**, select the *AND* operator, specify the word proximity, type "Representatives" in the *Type the text to find* box at the top of the **Search** dialog box and click on the **Search** button. The **Hit List** would display only hits of "House" which were near "Representatives" but not located near "Senate" ("near" depends on the proximity that you specified). The final search command would look as follows:

[(House) ~ (Senate)] & (Representatives)

Search Results

Browsing Search Results

Hit List

After conducting a search, each occurrence of the e search text in the document will be displayed in context in a separate **Hit List** window. Double click on any entry in the **Hit List** to move to the corresponding section of text.

Highlighted Hits in the Text

After conducting a search, each occurrence of the search text is highlighted in the text of the document.

1) Click the **First/Previous/Next/Last (Hit)** buttons to move between highlighted hits in the text.
2) The number of the current hit being viewed and the total number of hits are displayed in the Status bar at the bottom of the screen.

Removing the Hit List

1) Click the **Clear** button on the toolbar **OR** select **Search/Clear Search** from the main menu to remove the current **Hit List** window and the highlighting from the hits in the text.
2) Turn off the **Hit List** for future searches by selecting **Edit/Preferences** to open the **Document Preferences** dialog box. Click the **Reader** tab to open **Reader Preferences.** Deselect *Show Hit List?.*

Reader Preferences

Select **Edit/Preferences** from the main menu to open the **Document Preference** dialog box. The box includes three tabs: **Reader, Author,** and **Stopper Word List.**

Reader Preferences include:

CD-ROM Drive Letter

Every CD-ROM player is assigned a drive letter. (It is usually the last drive letter after your other drives.)

Default Word Search Proximity

Set the default proximity (the number of words between selected words) to be applied in multiple word (non-phrase) searches.

Show Hit List?

Click **Show Hit List***?* to open a **Hit List** automatically after conducting a Search. The Hit List shows "hits" - items found - when you do a search. Browse hits by clicking the **Next/Previous Hit** buttons on the toolbar or selecting **Search/Search** from the main menu. All hits will be highlighted in the text even if a **Hit List** is not activated.

TOC Window Color

Click the **TOC Window Color** button to open a dialog box containing table of Contest background color options. Select from a present color chart, or create a custom color and select it. Click **OK.**

SAVE YOUR DOCUMENT after you select preferences!

Table of Contents Browsing

Hyperlinks

The Table of Contents (TOC) provides a convenient method for accessing any section of the *QuickSearch* document. Each TOC entry is hyper-linked to the corresponding section of text; just click on an entry and *QuickSearch* automatically will move the corresponding section to the text window.

Multiple Levels

QuickSearch TOC's may include up to 32 levels. If there are sublevels in a TOC section, a "+" will appear in front of the TOC entry. To open the next level, click on the "+".

Automatic Tracing

As you move through a *QuickSearch* document (scroll, Next Hit, Previous Hit, etc.) the Table of Contents will "track" your location in the document automatically. A box outline indicates the current TOC section.

Chapter 3: Viewing Images

A *QuickSearch* document may contain **hyperlinked** or **embedded** images. Different methods are used for finding and viewing each type of image

Finding Images

Finding Hyperlinked Images
You can find hyperlinked images in a **QuickSearch** document by using any of the following options:
- **List** of images
- **Next/Previous Image** buttons or menu selections
- **Search** feature
- **Special formatting**/camera icon

Image List - Open a comprehensive list of hyperlinked images in the document.
1) Click the **Image List** button on the Toolbar *OR* select **Search/Image List** from the main menu.
2) Double click on an image title in the **Image List** to open the image.

Browsing Images - You can browse through images using the **Next/Previous Image** buttons or menu selections.
1) Select Nest/Previous Image buttons OR Search/First (Nest, Previous, Last) Image from the main menu.
2) The **Next and Previous Image** buttons or menu selections move the reader sequentially through images in the document.
3) The **First** and **Last Image** menu selections move only to the first or last image in the document.

Searching for Words in Hyperlinked Image Titles - As each hyper-linked image file is added to a **QuickSearch** document, it is given an *Image Title.* The Image Title appears with an optional camera icon at the point you have chosen in the text window. The Image Title is indexed with other text and may be found using a word or phrase search (see Chapter 1 - *Searching & Browsing*).

Look for Special Formatting/Camera Icon – Hyperlinked images can be found by looking for words that have special formatting (the default is double-underlined text). Double click on the specially formatted text to open the image. A camera icon may precede the specially formatted image title. The image can also be opened by clicking on the camera icon.

Finding Embedded Images

Embedded images appear in the text at the point you have chosen. They may be found by:
- Scrolling through text
- Conducting a search for words/phrases that appear near the image.

Scrolling for an Embedded Image
Use the vertical scroll bar to scan text and locate embedded images.

Searching for an Embedded Image*
Search for text that has been placed near an image and marked as hidden.

*Note: **Titles of embedded images will** NOT **appear on an Image List.** The Image List feature is only for hyperlinked images.

Zooming Hyper-linked Images

Marquee Image Zooming*

Marquee Image Zooming allows you to select a portion of a **hyper-linked image** and enlarge it to the size of the image window. **QuickSearch** allows you to zoom to a single pixel.
*Note: Marquee Image Zooming **is available ONLY for hyper-linked images.**

1) Click a **hyperlinked image title** or camera icon to open the image window.
2) Click on and hold the **left mouse** button and drag a box around the image area you want to enlarge.
3) When the area is defined, release the mouse button. The area selected will fill the **Image Window**.
4) Steps 2 and 3 may be repeated to continuing zooming.
5) To return the image to its original size, click once on the image with the **left mouse** button.

Image Panning

Image Panning allows you to use the horizontal/vertical scroll bars* to move around a **hyperlinked** image that has been enlarged by Marquee zooming.
Click an arrow on the scroll bar *OR* click and drag the horizontal or vertical scroll bar button to move the image across the screen.
*Note: **Scroll bars do not appear on-screen until an image has been zoomed.**

Scale to Gray

Some 1 bit (black & white) hyperlinked images can be sharpened by using the **Scale to Gray** feature. **Scale to Gray** will fill in missing pixels to improve the quality of an image. This feature is particularly useful for viewing scanned document images.

To use Scale to Gray:
1) Open a hyperlinked image
2) Select **View/Scale to Gray** from the main menu
3) **Scale to Gray** will remain active until it is deselected.

Chapter 4: Printing

The **Print** feature will print **text** and **images** in the following forms:
- Highlighted lines or blocks of text
- Selected Tables of Contents section(s)
- Search results ("hit" lists)
- Embedded images
- Hyper-linked images
- Zoomed portions of Hyper-linked images

Print Hints

Highlighted text, images and TOC sections will print in order as they are found in the document.

The printed size of Zoomed and Hyper-linked images may vary between portrait and landscape page orientation settings (found via **File/Print Setup**).

You can print *multiple* TOC sections by:
- Using the **Shift** key to select a series of *adjacent* TOCs.
- Using the **CTRL** key to individually select *specific* TOCs.
- Using the **Shift** and **CTRL** keys alternately to select specific TOC groupings.

Printing specifications can be set from the Windows Print Manager utility.
Make **Print Setup** modifications *before* you **Print.**

Printing Text or Images

To Print portions of a document:
1) Highlight lines and/or block(s) of text.
2) Click the **Print** button on the toolbar.
OR
Select the **File/Print** from the main menu.
OR
Press **CTRL+P**.

To Print a Single TOC section:
1) Click the TOC heading in the **Table of Contents** window.
2) Click the **Print** button on the toolbar.
OR
Select the **File/Print TOC selection(s)** from the main menu.
OR
Click the **right mouse** button and select **Print TOC selection(s).**
OR
Press **CTRL+P**.
*Note: All the sublevels in the TOC section will be printed.

To Print Multiple TOC sections:
1) Click the first TOC section you want to print from the **Table of Contents** window.
2) Press and hold the **CTRL** key while you click the order TOC sections you want to print. They do not have to be adjacent.
3) When you have finished selecting TOCs, click the **Print** button on the toolbar.
OR
Select **File/Print TOC selection(s)** from the main menu.
OR
Click the **right mouse** button and select **Print TOC selection(s).**
OR
Press **CTRL+P**.

To Print adjacent TOC sections:
1) Click the *first* TOC section you want to print from the **Table of Contents** window.
2) Press and hold the **Shift** key, and click the last TOC section in the series (all TOC sections between the first and last will be selected automatically).
3) Click the **Print** button on the toolbar.
OR
Select **File/Print TOC selection** from the main menu.
OR
Click the **right mouse** button and select **Print TOC selection(s).**
OR
Press **CTRL+P**.

*Note: **Multiple TOC Selection functions (highlighting using the** Shift **and/or** CTRL **keys) can be used in combination to select specific TOC groupings.**

To Print Embedded Images:
1) Highlight (double click) the embedded image(s) you want ant to print.
2) Click the **Print** button on the Toolbar.
OR
Select **File/Print** from the main menu.
OR
Press **CTRL+P**.

To Print a Hyperlinked Image:
You can print a **Hyperlinked Image** or a zoomed portion of a Hyperlinked Image.
1) Open the image by double clicking the **Image title** and/or the **camera icon.**
OR
Click the **Image List** button on the toolbar and double click the **Image title** from the list.
2) Click the **Print** button on the Toolbar.
OR
Select **File/Print** from the main menu.
OR
Press **CTRL+P**.

Print Setup

The Print Setup option allows you to select printer type, page orientation, paper size, paper source, and printer properties (paper, graphics, fonts, device options). Make these selections **before** you print.

To change the Print Setup:
1) Select **File/Print Setup** from the main menu.
2) In the **Print Setup** dialog box, click the down arrow in the **Name** pull down menu, select a printer type and enter it in the **Name** window (or click **Network** to access Network printer options).
3) To select new printer properties select **Properties** and make modifications.
4) Select **Landscape** or **Portrait.**
5) Select **OK** to exit.

Page Layout
You can adjust the top, bottom, left, and right margins of a printed page as follows:
1) Select **File/Page Layout** from the main menu.
2) In the **Page Parameters** dialog box, set margins (in inches) and click **OK.**

Chapter 5: User Annotations

The reader may customize a *QuickSearch* document by adding "margin" Bookmarks and Notes.

Annotate functions enable the reader to make customized **Bookmarks** in the text and make private, unsearchable comments about a document with **Notes.** The **Bookmark** feature enables the reader to "save his place," while the **Notes** feature allows the reader to "write in the margins" of the text.

Using Bookmarks

To add a Bookmark to a document:
1) Highlight a portion of text or place the cursor where you would like to add the Bookmark.
2) Click on the **Bookmark** icon on the Reader toolbar *OR* select **Annotate/Bookmark** from the main menu or select **Insert Bookmark** from the **right mouse** button menu. If text has been highlighted, it is shown in the **Edit Bookmark/Name** text box. If not, enter a name for the bookmark in the text box.
3) Click **Add** to place the selected text in the **Current Bookmarks** list.
4) Click **Go to** to scroll text to the point where the bookmark appears.
5) Click **Close** to close the Bookmark dialog box.

To go to a Bookmark:
1) Click on the **Bookmark** button on the toolbar *OR* select **Insert Bookmark** from the **right mouse** button menu to open the list of Current Bookmarks.
2) Highlight the bookmark you want to move to in the text.
3) Click **Go to.** The selected text will move to the top of the text window.

To edit a Bookmark:
1) Click on the **Bookmark** icon on the toolbar *OR* select **Annotate/Bookmark** from the main menu *OR* select **Insert Bookmark** from the **right mouse** button menu to open the dialog box containing current bookmarks.
2) In the **Current Bookmarks** list, click on the bookmark you wish to edit. It will appear in the **Edit Bookmark/Name** window.
3) Make changes and click **Add.**

To remove a Bookmark:
1) Click the **Bookmark** icon on the Reader toolbar or select **Insert Bookmark** from the **right mouse** button menu to open the dialog box containing current bookmarks.
2) In the **Current Bookmarks** list, click on the bookmark you wish to remove. It will appear in the **Edit Bookmark/Name** text box.
3) Click **Remove.**

Using Notes

To add a Note to a document:
1) Place the cursor in the text window where you want the note to appear.
2) Click on the **Notepad** button *OR* select **Annotate/Notes/Insert** from the main menu *OR* select **Insert Note** from the **right mouse** button menu to open the **Notepad** dialog box.
3) Type in the note and click **Save;** a Notepad icon appears in the left margin next to the specified line of text.

To View a Note:
1) Double click the **Notepad** icon in the left margin.
2) The **Notepad** dialog box displays the note.

To Edit a Note:
1) Double click the icon of the note you want to edit.
2) Make changes to text.
3) Click **Save.**

To Remove a Note:
1) Place the cursor on the **Notepad** icon and select **Annotate/Note/Delete** from the main menu *OR* select **Delete Note** from the **right mouse** button menu.
2) A dialog box will ask you to confirm the note deletion.
3) Click **Yes.** The icon will disappear after scrolling in the document.